DISCOVER SOCIOLOGY

Second Edition

With love and gratitude, I dedicate this book to Anna, Niklavs, and Joe.
You are my favorite social group!

This book is also fondly dedicated to the memory of my coauthor,
colleague, and friend, Bill Chambliss.

—DSE

SOCIOLOGY

Second Edition

William J. Chambliss
Daina S. Eglitis
George Washington University

Los Angeles | London | New Delhi
Singapore | Washington DC | Boston

Los Angeles | London | New Delhi
Singapore | Washington DC | Boston

FOR INFORMATION:

SAGE Publications, Inc.
2455 Teller Road
Thousand Oaks, California 91320
E-mail: order@sagepub.com

SAGE Publications Ltd.
1 Oliver's Yard
55 City Road
London EC1Y 1SP
United Kingdom

SAGE Publications India Pvt. Ltd.
B 1/I 1 Mohan Cooperative Industrial Area
Mathura Road, New Delhi 110 044
India

SAGE Publications Asia-Pacific Pte. Ltd.
3 Church Street
#10-04 Samsung Hub
Singapore 049483

Printed in the United States of America

Library of Congress Cataloging-in-Publication Data

Chambliss, William J.

Discover sociology / William J. Chambliss, Daina S. Eglitis, The George Washington University. — Second Edition.

pages cm
Includes index.

ISBN 978-1-4833-6520-6 (pbk. : alk. paper)

1. Sociology. I. Eglitis, Daina Stukuls. II. Title.

HM585.C4473 2015

301—dc23 2014047563

This book is printed on acid-free paper.

Acquisitions Editor: Jeff Lasser
Development Editor: Nathan Davidson
Digital Content Editor: Gabrielle Piccininni
Editorial Assistant: Alexandra Croell
Production Editor: Libby Larson
Copy Editor: Judy Selhorst
Typesetter: C&M Digitals (P) Ltd.
Proofreader: Wendy Jo Dymond
Indexer: Michael Ferreira
Cover Designer: Scott Van Atta
Marketing Manager: Erica DeLuca

15 16 17 18 19 10 9 8 7 6 5 4

ABOUT THE AUTHORS

William J. Chambliss (PhD, Indiana University) was a professor of sociology at The George Washington University from 1986 to 2014. During his long and distinguished career, he wrote and edited close to two dozen books and produced numerous articles for professional journals in sociology, criminology, and law. The integration of the study of crime with the creation and implementation of criminal law was a central theme in his writings and research. His articles on the historical development of vagrancy laws, the legal process as it affects different social classes and racial groups, and his efforts to introduce the study of state-organized crimes into the mainstream of social science research are among the most recognized achievements of his career. Dr. Chambliss was the recipient of numerous awards and honors, including a doctorate of laws *honoris causa,* University of Guelph, Guelph, Ontario, Canada, 1999; the 2009 Lifetime Achievement Award, Sociology of Law, American Sociological Association; the 2009 Lifetime Achievement Award, Law and Society, Society for the Study of Social Problems; the 2001 Edwin H. Sutherland Award, American Society of Criminology; the 1995 Major Achievement Award, American Society of Criminology; the 1986 Distinguished Leadership in Criminal Justice, Bruce Smith Sr. Award, Academy of Criminal Justice Sciences; and the 1985 Lifetime Achievement Award, Criminology, American Sociological Association. Professor Chambliss also served as president of the American Society of Criminology and the Society for the Study of Social Problems.

Daina S. Eglitis (PhD, University of Michigan–Ann Arbor) is an associate professor of sociology and international affairs and the director of undergraduate studies in the Department of Sociology at The George Washington University. Her scholarly interests include class and social stratification, historical sociology, contemporary theory, gender, and culture. She is the author of *Imagining the Nation: History, Modernity, and Revolution in Latvia* (Penn State Press, 2002), as well as numerous articles on social life and social change in postcommunist Latvia. She has held two Fulbright awards in Latvia and is a past recipient of research awards from the American Council of Learned Societies, the National Council for Eurasian and East European Research, the International Research and Exchanges Board, and the Woodrow Wilson International Center for Scholars. Dr. Eglitis is the author of "The Uses of Global Poverty: How Economic Inequality Benefits the West," an article widely used by undergraduate students. At GWU, she particularly enjoys teaching courses in contemporary sociological theory, class and inequality, and introduction to sociology. She frequently presents and writes on the topic of teaching and learning and is the author of the *Teaching Sociology* article "Performing Theory: Dramatic Learning in the Theory Classroom" (October 2010). Outside the classroom, Dr. Eglitis loves to travel to new places and enjoys the company of her fantastic husband, Joe, and wonderful children, Niklavs and Anna.

BRIEF CONTENTS

DETAILED CONTENTS

Chapter 3: Culture and Mass Media 52

RICHARD NOWITZ/National Geographic Creative

Chapter 4: Socialization and Social Interaction 78

Will & Deni McIntyre/Photo Researchers, Inc

Chapter 5: Groups, Organizations, and Bureaucracies 104

AP Photo/Emilio Morenati

Chapter 6: Deviance and Social Control 128

REUTERS/Tomas Bravo

Chapter 7: Social Class and Inequality in the United States 154

© Lisa Wiltse/Corbis

Chapter 8: Global Inequality and Poverty 180

Reuters/Carlos Jasso

Chapter 9: Race and Ethnicity 202

AARON HUEY/National Geographic Creative

Chapter 10: Gender and Society 232

REUTERS/Mark Blinch

Chapter 11: Families and Society 264

The India Today Group/Contributor/Getty Images

Chapter 12: Education and Society 294

The Washington Post/Contributor/Getty Images

Chapter 13: Religion and Society 320

© Gideon Mendel/Corbi

Chapter 14: The State, War, and Terror 348

REUTERS/Nayer Haslamoun

Chapter 15: Work, Consumption, and the Economy 380

REUTERS/Vivek Prakash

Chapter 16: Health and Medicine 406

© Richard T. Nowitz/CORBIS

Chapter 17: Population, Urbanization, and the Environment 430

© Randy Olson/National Geographic Society/Corbis

Chapter 18: Social Movements and Social Change 460

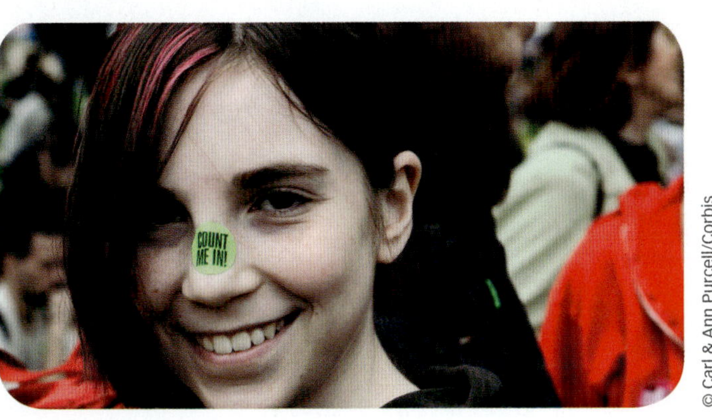

© Carl & Ann Purcell/Corbis

PREFACE

Years ago a sociologist wrote that if you are the kind of person who walks down a dark street and wonders what is going on inside the houses where lights shine through the windows, then you are a sociologist by nature. *Curiosity* is the bedrock of all scientific inquiry, because curiosity underlies the motivation and passion to seek answers to hard questions. But curiosity is not enough. To be a component of good sociology, curiosity must be disciplined: Answers must be sought within the scientific tradition of gathering data through systematic observations and explaining the findings with carefully constructed explanations or theories. In this text, our goal is to pique students' curiosity about the social world—and then to give them the academic tools to understand that world, analyze it, and maybe even change it.

There are many sociology textbooks, some of which are very good. We believe that our contribution to the marketplace of sociological texts and ideas is a book that engages the sociology student's curious mind—and then offers him or her the theoretical, conceptual, and empirical tools to analyze and understand the issues that affect our world, both local and global. We have written this book in a way that we hope will encourage students to keep reading, not only because of assigned pages but also because, with the encouragement of the instructor and the text, they have a desire to know more! We also endeavor to show the value of the discipline of sociology as a source of critical skills that students take with them as they prepare to pursue careers and begin job searches or undertake graduate education. We are delighted that the first edition of *Discover Sociology* was well received, and it is our goal in this new edition to keep the best of that work while integrating new ideas, research, and events to keep the book fresh and interesting. In the following we review some of the key features in this second edition.

CHAPTER OPENERS THAT SPEAK TO STUDENTS

In this book, you will find chapters that begin with openers drawn from the real world and that endeavor to speak to students and to the kinds of experiences or concerns they have as students, as well as in other roles in the family or at work. From the question of whether the use of "study drugs" should be considered cheating to an examination of research showing a correlation between rising student debt and declining rates of marriage, the book's openers offer instructors a terrific way to begin discussions to which students will eagerly contribute. The beginning of each chapter also features three "What do you think?" questions to engage students' curiosity and give a small preview of interesting issues that will be covered in the chapter.

SOCIOLOGY IS A SCIENTIFIC DISCIPLINE

Every chapter in the book integrates empirical research from sociology, highlighting the point that sociology is about the *scientific understanding* of the social world—rigorous research can illuminate the social roots of diverse phenomena and institutions, ranging from poverty and deviance to capitalism and the nuclear family. Research may also result in conflicting or ambiguous conclusions. Students learn that social life is complex and that sociological research is an ongoing effort to explain why things are as they are—and how they might change.

KEY THEMES AND BOXED FEATURES

Each chapter has a mix of boxed features that highlight key themes in this book.

- The **sociological imagination**, of course, is a foundational concept in the discipline. It is important throughout the book, and we also feature **Private Lives, Public Issues** boxes that illustrate the relationship between our individual lives and the social forces that shape them.

- Second, **power** is a key theme in sociology—and in this text. Sociologists want to know how power is distributed, how it is reproduced, and how it is exercised in social relationships and institutions. The unequal distribution of power is one important topic of sociological inquiry, and this text offers **Inequality Matters** boxes that probe manifestations of and explanations for power and resource disparities.

- Third, we emphasize **the importance of being a critical consumer of information.** We are surrounded by sources of data that stream into our lives from the Internet, newspapers, peers and colleagues, friends and family, and academic studies. Sociology asks us to look carefully at information and to understand its sources and assumptions in order to ascertain what it illuminates and what it obscures. To this end, we include **Behind the Numbers** boxes to give students the opportunity to look critically and carefully at statistical information on social problems such as unemployment and poverty, among others.

- Fourth, we live in a world of unprecedented **technological transformation**, and new technologies are rapidly changing our world in ways that are both thrilling and worrisome. The book's **Technology and Society** boxes provide a sociological perspective on some of these important developments.

- Finally, the book highlights **globalization** and **global perspectives** in an effort to help students develop a fuller understanding of the place of their lives, their communities, and their country in an interconnected, interdependent, and multicultural international environment—and to enable them to see how other countries around the world are experiencing societal changes and challenges. The book's **Global Society** boxes are part of this effort.

All of the boxed features include questions for students to help them reflect on the material and link it back to the chapter's larger themes.

NEW IN THIS EDITION

We have been very pleased by the warm and enthusiastic reception of the first edition of *Discover Sociology* among faculty and students. In this second edition, we have sought to keep the best parts of the first while responding to the ideas and requests of reviewers and faculty for new or expanded coverage of such topics as global inequality, mass media, and sports and society. This edition features updated social indicators, bringing in the latest data available from the U.S. Census Bureau, the Bureau of Labor Statistics, the Centers for Disease Control and Prevention, and the Pew Research Center, among others, as well as a variety of new openers and essay boxes that show the sociological significance of interesting current events.

NEW CHAPTER: GLOBAL INEQUALITY AND POVERTY

This edition of *Discover Sociology* includes a new chapter—"Global Inequality and Poverty" (Chapter 8). The analysis and theorization of inequality are among the centerpieces of both classical and contemporary sociology, and today, as our world becomes more connected and complex, our need to understand inequality through a global lens is growing. While many sociological forces are widening the gap between rich and poor, other forces—including mobile technology—may have the power to shrink the gap. Sociology offers significant ways of understanding the global picture that can benefit students who will inhabit a world in which borders will decline in significance as economic, social, technological, and cultural connections grow.

EXPANDED CHAPTER ON CLASS AND INEQUALITY IN THE UNITED STATES

Our previous chapter on class and inequality was well received, and we are pleased that reviewers, instructors, and students appreciated the broad coverage of important contemporary issues, including the expanding income and wealth gaps, the debate over the minimum wage, and the discussion of household poverty. In this edition, we have expanded our coverage of class and inequality in Chapter 7 to include a consideration of *neighborhood poverty,* a growing phenomenon, the effects of which are felt across communities, in poor and nonpoor households alike. We distinguish between household poverty and neighborhood poverty and discuss the newest research on neighborhood poverty.

MORE COVERAGE OF MEDIA ISSUES

In response to reviewer and instructor suggestions, we have expanded Chapter 3 to offer more coverage of culture and media. Many students today are deeply immersed and interested in mass media. Chapter 3 uses numerous examples from the mass media (including zombies!) to illuminate key sociological concepts and explores some of the important theoretical insights sociologists have offered on the social significance of mass media, which is a dynamic and powerful part of contemporary culture.

A NEW APPROACH TO STATE AND POLITICS

This edition of *Discover Sociology* features a new approach to the discussion of state and politics. In Chapter 14, we pay particular attention to the state as a sociological phenomenon and, notably, as an important actor in the historical and global phenomena of war making and war fighting, discussing specifically the functions, beneficiaries, and losers in modern war. The chapter also takes a sociological perspective on the complex and contemporary topics of terror and terrorists, problems that states and societies across the globe are confronting today.

UPDATED OPENERS AND BOXES

This edition features a variety of new chapter openers and essay boxes that draw from events of contemporary interest and concern. Among the updated openers are sociologically relevant stories on the zombie phenomenon in the United States (Chapter 3), the births and deaths of states (Chapter 14), and the nascent low-wage workers' movement (Chapter 18). New boxes draw readers' attention to the debate over social media activism (or, as some observers have called it, "slacktivism"), the role of sports in social change, and the function of social media for terror groups—among many others.

CONNECTING SOCIOLOGY AND CAREER SUCCESS

As an instructor of introductory sociology, you are probably frequently asked by students, "What can I do with a sociology degree?" This is an important question for students (and, often, their parents) and instructors. This book offers instructors and students a unique feature that speaks directly, clearly, and specifically to this question. Each chapter provides an essay that accomplishes two major tasks. First, early essays guide students through key steps in the *career development process* that can begin as early as freshman year. Second, later essays *highlight specific skills students learn as sociology majors, describe those skills, and then connect those skills to particular occupational fields and jobs where employers seek those skills.* This feature gives students critical information for charting paths to careers and offers instructors information from the perspective of career development professionals that can help them show students the linkage between sociological skills and future careers in a wide array of jobs and occupational fields.

It is important to note that this feature is not only for sociology majors! Sociology is often among the general education courses completed by students across a variety of disciplines, and it can help all students develop important skills, such as critical thinking, data literacy, and communication, that they will need in the workplace. A recent *Washington Post* report on technology jobs, for instance, notes:

> As tech jobs evolve at the pace of light through fiber-optic cable, . . . leaders of tech firms such as Mozilla, Reddit and Tumblr say students should consider schools that not only will teach them traditional skills like coding, but also the softer skills that aren't listed in the course guide but are essential to the 21st-century workplace: working with others, problem-solving, the ability to pick up enough from disciplines other than their own to create products users believe are indispensable to their lives. (Lednicer, 2014)

Clearly, for students across disciplines, there is value in understanding and naming the skills that they gain when they study sociology. We encourage all students to take advantage of this valuable feature.

PHOTOS AND GRAPHICS

The photographs in this edition have been carefully selected to help students put images together with ideas, events, and phenomena. A good photo can engage a student's curiosity and give him or her a visual vehicle for remembering the material under discussion. This has been our goal in choosing the photos included here. We have also carefully prepared visually appealing graphics, including tables, figures, and maps, to attract students' attention and enhance learning.

GLOSSARIES FOR LEARNING

This book features marginal glossaries, offering students easy access to definitions of key concepts, phenomena, and institutions. Additionally, key terms are bolded in the text, and a comprehensive glossary is available at the end of the book.

CHAPTER REVIEW

Every chapter ends with a summary of key learning points and a set of discussion questions to review what students have learned and to foster critical thinking about the materials.

ANCILLARIES

Discover Sociology includes a comprehensive ancillary package that utilizes new media and a wide range of instructional technologies designed to support instructor course preparation and student learning.

STUDENT STUDY SITE

An open-access student study site, available at edge.sagepub.com/chambliss2e, provides a variety of additional resources to build students' understanding of the book content and extend their learning beyond the classroom. Students will have access to the following features for each chapter:

- An online Action Plan includes tips and feedback on progress through the course and materials, which allows students to individualize their learning.
- **SAGE Journal Articles:** *Exclusive!* Certain full-text journal articles have been carefully selected for each chapter. Each article supports and expands on the concepts presented in the chapter. This feature also provides questions to focus and guide student interpretation. Combine cutting-edge academic journal scholarship with the topics in your course for a robust classroom experience.
- **Reference, CQ Researcher, and Pacific Standard magazine links:** Each chapter includes links to relevant articles from SAGE handbooks and encyclopedias, as well as links to articles from *CQ Researcher* and *Pacific Standard* magazine.
- **Video, Audio, and Web Links:** These carefully selected, Web-based resources feature relevant interviews, lectures, personal stories, inquiries, and other content for use in independent or classroom-based explorations of key topics.
- **eFlashcards and Web Quizzes:** These mobile-friendly resources reinforce understanding of key terms and concepts that have been outlined in the chapters.
- And much more!

INSTRUCTOR TEACHING SITE

A password-protected instructor teaching site, available at edge.sagepub.com/chambliss2e, provides integrated sources for all instructor materials, including the following key components for each chapter:

- The **Microsoft Word test bank** contains multiple-choice, true/false, short-answer, and essay questions for each chapter. The test bank provides you with a diverse range of prewritten options as well as the opportunity to edit any question and/or insert your own personalized questions to assess students' progress and understanding effectively.
- The **Diploma electronic test bank** can be used on PCs and Macs. Containing multiple-choice, true/false, short-answer, and essay questions per chapter, the test bank provides you with a diverse range of prewritten options as well as the opportunity to edit any questions and/or insert your own personalized questions to assess students' progress and understanding effectively. Diploma is also compatible with many popular learning management systems, so you can easily get your test questions into your online course.
- Editable, chapter-specific Microsoft **PowerPoint slides** offer you complete flexibility in easily creating a multimedia presentation for your course. Highlight essential content, features, and artwork from the book.
- **Lecture notes** summarize key concepts on a chapter-by-chapter basis to help with preparation for lectures and class discussions.
- **Sample course syllabi** for semester and quarter courses provide suggested models for use in the creation of syllabi for your courses.

- **Chapter-specific discussion questions** can help you launch classroom interaction by prompting students to engage with the material and by reinforcing important content.
- Lively and stimulating **ideas for class activities** can be used in class to reinforce active learning. The activities apply to individual or group projects.
- And much more!

INTERACTIVE E-BOOK

Discover Sociology is also available as an interactive e-book, which can be packaged free with the book or purchased separately. This interactive e-book offers links to Web, audio, and video resources, as well as original author video.

ACKNOWLEDGMENTS

We are grateful to the terrific editors and staff at SAGE, including Nathan Davidson, Jeff Lasser, Erica DeLuca, Nick Pachelli, Libby Larson, and Scott Van Atta. It has been a privilege to work with such a creative, encouraging, and supportive group. We are also indebted to colleagues and graduate students who helped with the materials that went into the book. Among those who contributed ideas and assistance are the Department of Sociology at GWU's Michelle Kelso, Steven Tuch, Greg Squires, Ivy Ken, and Fran Buntman. In addition, we owe a debt of gratitude to Ann Scammon of the GWU Career Center, whose contributions to the material on career development have been incredibly valuable. We would like to extend special thanks to the excellent research assistants who have supported this book: for the second edition, Ann Horwitz and Chris Moloney; for the first edition, Chris Moloney, Jee Jee Kim, Claire Cook, Scott Grether, Ken Leon, Ceylan Engin, and Adam Bethke. Finally, for their patience and support, we also thank the Sociology Department office staff, Maureen Kentoff and Octavia Kelsey. This project could not have been brought to completion without the valuable help and skills of all of the people named.

We are also grateful to our families for their support. Daina would like to acknowledge in particular the valuable patience, support, ideas, and distraction of her wonderful children, Niklavs and Anna, and amazing husband, Joseph Burke. Daina is also grateful to her mother, Silvia Stukuls, who has always been willing to help. There is really no way to thank them all enough.

Finally, we wish to thank all of the reviewers listed below, who contributed greatly to the textbook through excellent suggestions, creative insights, and helpful critiques.

REVIEWERS FOR THE SECOND EDITION

Dianne Berger-Hill, *Old Dominion University*; Alison J. Bianchi, *University of Iowa*; Michael Bourgoin, *Queens College, The City University of New York*; Paul E. Calarco Jr., *Hudson Valley Community College*; Nicolette Caperello, *Sierra College*; Susan E. Claxton, *Georgia Highlands College*; Sonya R. De Lisle, *Tacoma Community College*; Heather A. Downs, *Jacksonville University*; Leslie Elrod, *University of Cincinnati*; S. Michael Gaddis, *University of Michigan*; Cherly Gary-Furdge, *North Central Texas College*; Louis Gesualdi, *St. John's University*; Todd Goodsell, *University of Utah*; Matthew Green, *College of DuPage*; Ashley N. Hadden, *Western Kentucky University*; Othello Harris, *Miami University*; Michael M. Harrod, *Central Washington University*; Sarah Jacobson, *Harrisburg Area Community College*; Kimberly Lancaster, *Coastal Carolina Community College*; Katherine Lawson, *Chaffey Community College*; Jason J. Leiker, *Utah State University*; Kim MacInnis, *Bridgewater State University*; Barret Michalec, *University of Delaware*; Amanda Miller, *University of Indianapolis*; Christine Mowery, *Virginia Commonwealth University*; Scott M. Myers, *Montana State University*; Frank A. Salamone, *Iona College*; Bonita A. Sessing-Matcha, *Hudson Valley Community College*; Richard States, *Allegany College of Maryland*; Myron T. Strong, *Community College of Baltimore County*; Heather Laine Talley, *Western Carolina University*; PJ Verrecchia, *York College of Pennsylvania*; Jerrol David Weatherly, *Coastal Carolina Community College*; Debra L. Welkley, *California State University, Sacramento*; and Luis Zanartu, *Sacramento City College.*

REVIEWERS FOR THE FIRST EDITION

Kristian P. Alexander, *Zayed University*; Lori J. Anderson, *Tarleton State University*; Shannon Kay Andrews, *University of Tennessee at Chattanooga*; Joyce Apsel, *New York University*; Gabriel Aquino, *Westfield State College*; Janet Armitage, *St. Mary's University*; Dionne Mathis Banks, *University of Florida*; Michael S. Barton, *University at Albany*; Jeffrey W. Basham, *College of the Sequoias*; Paul J. Becker, *University of Dayton*; Alison J. Bianchi, *University of Iowa*; Kimberly Boyd, *Piedmont Virginia Community College*; Mariana Branda, *College of the Canyons*; Jennifer Brennom, *Kirkwood Community College*; Denise Bump, *Keystone College*; Nicolette Caperello, *Sierra College*; Michael J. Carter, *California State University, Northridge*; Vivian L. Carter, *Tuskegee University*; Shaheen A. Chowdhury, *College of DuPage*; Jacqueline Clark, *Ripon College*; Susan Eidson Claxton, *Georgia Highlands College*; Debbie Coats, *Maryville University*; Angela M. Collins, *Ozarks Technical Community College*; Scott N. Contor, *Idaho State University*; Denise A. Copelton, *The College at Brockport, State University of New York*; Carol J. Corkern, *Franklin University*; Jennifer Crew Solomon, *Winthrop University*; William F. Daddio, *Georgetown University*; Jeffrey S. Debies-Carl, *University of New Haven*; Melanie Deffendall, *Delgado Community College*; Marc Jung-Whan de Jong, *State University of New York, Fashion Institute of Technology*; David R. Dickens, *University of Nevada, Las Vegas*; Keri Diggins, *Scottsdale Community College*; Amy M. Donley, *University of Central Florida*; Amanda Donovan, *Bristol Community College*; Heather A. Downs, *Jacksonville University*; Daniel D. Doyle, *Bay College*; Dorothy E. Everts, *University of Arkansas–Monticello*;

Gary Feinberg, *St. Thomas University*; Bernie Fitzpatrick, *Western Connecticut State University*; Tonya K. Frevert, *University of North Carolina at Charlotte*; Cherly Furdge, *North Central Texas College*; S. Michael Gaddis, *University of North Carolina at Chapel Hill*; Robert Garot, *John Jay College of Criminal Justice*; Todd A. Garrard, *University of Texas at San Antonio*; Cherly Gary-Furdge, *North Central Texas College*; Marci Gerulis-Darcy, *Metropolitan State University*; Louis Gesualdi, *St. John's University*; Jennifer E. Givens, *University of Utah*; John Glass, *Collin College*; Malcolm Gold, *Malone University*; Thomas B. Gold, *University of California, Berkeley*; Matthew Green, *College of DuPage*; Johnnie M. Griffin, *Jackson State University*; Randolph M. Grinc, *Caldwell College*; Greg Haase, *Western State College of Colorado*; Dean H. Harper, *University of Rochester*; Anne S. Hastings, *University of North Carolina at Chapel Hill*; Anthony L. Haynor, *Seton Hall University*; Roneiko Henderson-Beasley, *Tidewater Community College*; Marta T. Henriksen, *Central New Mexico Community College*; Klaus Heyer, *Nunez Community College*; Jeremy D. Hickman, *University of Kentucky*; Bonniejean Alford Hinde, *College of DuPage*; Joy Crissey Honea, *Montana State University Billings*; Caazena P. Hunter, *University of North Texas*; John Iceland, *Pennsylvania State University*; Robert B. Jenkot, *Coastal Carolina University*; Wesley G. Jennings, *University of South Florida*; Audra Kallimanis, *Wake Technical Community College*; Ali Kamali, *Missouri Western State University*; Leona Kanter, *Mercer University*; Earl A. Kennedy, *North Carolina State University*; Lloyd Klein, *York College, The City University of New York*; Julie A. Kmec, *Washington State University*; Todd M. Krohn, *University of Georgia*; Veena S. Kulkarni, *Arkansas State University*; Karen F. Lahm, *Wright State University*; Amy G. Langenkamp, *Georgia State University*; Barbara LaPilusa, *Montgomery College*; Jason LaTouche, *Tarleton State University*; Ke Liang, *Baruch College, The City University of New York*; Carol S. Lindquist, *Bemidji State University*; Travis Linnemann, *Kansas State University*; Stephen Lippmann, *Miami University*; David G. LoConto, *Jacksonville State University*; Rebecca M. Loew, *Middlesex Community College*; Jeanne M. Lorentzen, *Northern Michigan University*; Betsy Lucal, *Indiana University South Bend*; George N. Lundskow, *Grand Valley State University*; Crystal V. Lupo, *Auburn University*; Brian M. Lynch, *Quinebaug Valley Community College*; Kim A. MacInnis, *Bridgewater State University*; Mahgoub El-Tigani Mahmoud, *Tennessee State University*; Lori Maida, *The State University of New York*; Hosik Min, *Norwich University*; Madeline H. Moran, *Lehman College, The City University of New York*; Amanda Moras, *Sacred Heart University*; Rebecca Nees, *Middle Georgia College*; Christopher Oliver, *University of Kentucky*; Sophia M. Ortiz, *San Antonio College*; Kathleen N. Overmiller, *Marshall University*; Josh Packard, *Midwestern State University*; Marla A. Perry, *Nashville State Community College*; Daniel Poole, *Salt Lake Community College*; Shana L. Porteen, *Finlandia University*; Eric Primm, *University of Pikeville*; Jeffrey Ratcliffe, *Drexel University*; Jo Reger, *Oakland University*; Daniel Roddick, *Rio Hondo College*; David Rohall, *Western Illinois University*; Olga I. Rowe, *Oregon State University*; Josephine A. Ruggiero, *Providence College*; Frank A. Salamone, *Iona College*; Stephen J. Scanlan, *Ohio University*; Michael D. Schulman, *North Carolina State University*; Maren T. Scull, *University of Colorado Denver*; Shane Sharp, *Northern Illinois University*; Mark Sherry, *The University of Toledo*; Amber M. Shimel, *Liberty University*; Vicki Smith, *University of California, Davis*; Dan Steward, *University of Illinois at Urbana-Champaign*; Myron T. Strong, *Community College of Baltimore County*; Richard Sullivan, *Illinois State University*; Sara C. Sutler-Cohen, *Bellevue College*; Joyce Tang, *Queens College, The City University of New York*; Debra K. Taylor, *Metropolitan Community College–Maple Woods*; Richard Tewksbury, *University of Louisville*; Kevin A. Tholin, *Indiana University–South Bend*; Brian Thomas, *Saginaw Valley State University*; Lorna Timmerman, *Indiana University East*; Cynthia Tooley-Heddlesten, *Metropolitan Community Colleges–Blue River*; Okori Uneke, *Winston-Salem State University*; Paula Barfield Unger, *McLennan Community College*; PJ Verrecchia, *York College of Pennsylvania*; Joseph M. Verschaeve, *Grand Valley State University*; Edward Walker, *University of California, Los Angeles*; Tom Ward, *New Mexico Highlands University*; Lisa Munson Weinberg, *Florida State University*; Casey Welch, *Flagler College*; Shonda Whetstone, *Blinn College*; S. Rowan Wolf, *Portland Community College*; Loreen Wolfer, *University of Scranton*; Jason Wollschleger, *Whitworth University*; and Kassia R. Wosick, *New Mexico State University.*

DISCOVER SOCIOLOGY

IN THIS CHAPTER

© Bob Sacha/Corbi

WHAT DO YOU THINK?

1. Can societies be studied scientifically? What does the scientific study of societies entail?
2. What is a theory? What is the role of theories in sociology?
3. In your opinion, what social issues or problems are most interesting or important today? What questions about them would you like to study?

MAURICIO HANDLER/National Geographic Creative

A CURIOUS MIND

A goal of this book is to take you on a sociological journey. But let's begin with a basic question: **What is sociology?** First of all, sociology is a discipline of and for curious minds! Sociologists are deeply committed to answering the question, "Why?" Why are some people desperately poor and others fabulously wealthy? Why does racial segregation in housing and public education exist, and why does it persist half a century after civil rights laws were enacted? What accounts for the declining marriage rate among the working class and the poor in the United States? How can we explain the fact that low-income people are more likely to be overweight or obese than their middle-class counterparts? Why is the proportion of women entering and completing college rising while the proportion of men has fallen? Why, in spite of this, do men as a group still earn higher incomes than women as a group do? And how is it that social media are being simultaneously praised as instruments of transformational activism and criticized as causes of social alienation and civic disengagement? Take a moment now to think about some *why* questions you have about society and social life: As you look around you, hear the news, and interact with other people, what strikes you as fascinating—but perhaps difficult to understand? What are you curious about?

Sociology is an academic discipline that takes a scientific approach to answering the kinds of questions our curious minds imagine. When we say that sociology is **scientific**, we mean that it is *a way of learning about the world that combines logically constructed theory and systematic observation.* The goal of sociological study and research is to base answers to questions like those above on a careful examination of the roots of social phenomena such as poverty, segregation, and the wage gap. Sociologists do this with *research methods*—surveys, interviews, observations, and archival research, among others—which yield data that can be tested, challenged, and revised. In this text, you will see how sociology is done—and you will learn how to do sociology yourself.

Concisely stated, **sociology** is *the scientific study of human social relationships, groups, and societies.* Unlike *natural sciences* such as physics, chemistry, and biology, sociology is one of several *social sciences* engaged in the scientific study of human beings and the social worlds they consciously create and inhabit. The purpose of sociology is to understand and generate new knowledge about human behavior, social relations, and social institutions on a larger scale. The sociologist adheres to the principle of **social embeddedness**: the idea that *economic, political, and other forms of human behavior are fundamentally shaped by social relations.* Thus, sociologists pursue studies on a wide range of issues occurring within, between, and among families, communities, states, nations, and the world. Other social sciences, some of which you may be studying, include anthropology, economics, political science, and psychology.

Sociology is a field in which students have the opportunity to build a broad spectrum of important skills, ranging from gathering and analyzing information to identifying and solving problems to effective written and oral communication. Throughout this book, we draw your attention to important skills you can gain through the study of sociology and the kinds of skills employers in different occupational fields are seeking in potential employees. Sociology opens the door to both greater understanding of the social world and a range of career and graduate study possibilities.

Doing sociology requires that you build a foundation on which the knowledge you gain will rest. Some of the key foundations of sociology are the *sociological imagination* and *critical thinking.* We turn to these below. ■

Scientific: A way of learning about the world that combines logically constructed theory and systematic observation.

Sociology: The scientific study of human social relations, groups, and societies.

Social embeddedness: The idea that economic, political, and other forms of human behavior are fundamentally shaped by social relations.

Sociological imagination: The ability to grasp the relationship between individual lives and the larger social forces that help to shape them.

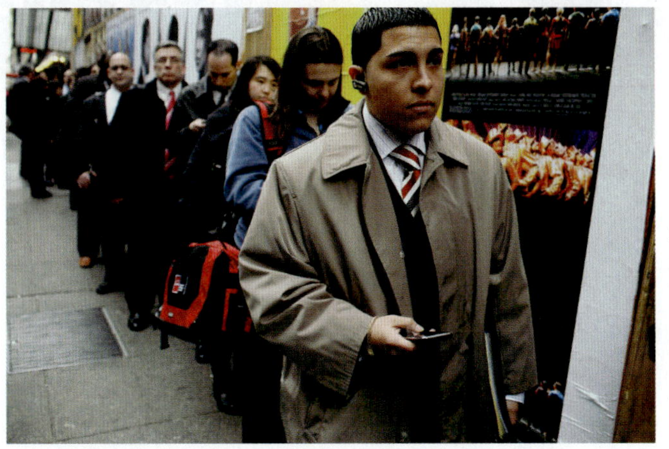

© Andrew Lichtenstein/Corbis

Unemployment is not equally distributed among U.S. demographic groups; those without a high school diploma or college degree have been hit hard by the loss of well-paying jobs in manufacturing since the late1970s. The cost of not getting an education increasingly includes not just higher rates of unemployment but also diminished earning power. ■

THE SOCIOLOGICAL IMAGINATION

As we go about our daily routines, we may forget that large-scale economic, political, and cultural forces shape even the most personal aspects of our lives. When parents divorce, for example, we tend to focus on individual explanations: A father was devoted more to his work than to his family; a mother may have felt trapped in an unhappy marriage but stuck with it for the sake of young children. Yet while personal issues are inevitable parts of a breakup, they can't tell the whole story. When so many U.S. marriages end in divorce, forces larger than incompatible personalities or marital discord are at play. But what are those greater social forces, exactly?

As sociologist C. Wright Mills (1959/2000b) suggested half a century ago, uncovering the relationship between what he called *personal troubles* and *public issues* calls for a **sociological imagination**. The sociological imagination is *the ability to grasp the relationship between individual lives and the larger social forces that shape them*—that is, to see where biography and history intersect.

In a country like the United States, where individualism is part of the national heritage, people tend to believe that each person creates his or her life's path and to largely disregard the social context in which this happens. When we cannot get a job, fail to earn enough to support a family, or experience marital separation, for example, we tend to see it as a personal trouble. We do not necessarily see it as a public issue. The sociological imagination, however, invites us to make the connection and to step away from the vantage point of a single life experience to see how powerful social forces—for instance, changes in social norms, ethnic or sex discrimination, large shifts in the economy,

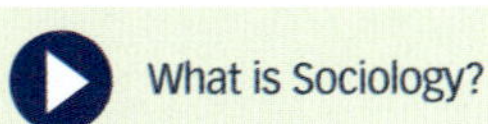

Mill's Sociological Imagination   What is Sociology?

PRIVATE LIVES, PUBLIC ISSUES

WHY ARE DIVORCE RATES SO HIGH?

In the United States, the probability of a first marriage ending in separation or divorce within 5 years is 22%; after 10 years, it rises to 36%. Over the longer term, the rate of marital dissolution is closer to 50% (Goodwin, Mosher, & Chandra, 2010). Just half a century ago, most marriages were "'til death do us part." What accounts for the change?

The sociological imagination shows us that marriage and divorce, seemingly the most private of matters, are as much public issues as personal ones. Consider the fact that when wages for working people lagged from the mid-1970s to the late 1990s, growing numbers of women went to work to help their families make ends meet. Many middle-class women also went to college and pursued careers as a means of personal fulfillment. In fact, today more women than men finish undergraduate degrees. As a result of trends like these, women today enjoy a higher measure of economic independence than ever before. The combination of educational attainment and satisfying careers reinforces women's independence, making it easier for those who are in unhappy marriages to leave them. Greater social acceptance of divorce has also removed much of the stigma once associated with failed marriages.

Social trends like those described have made it more likely that an unhappy couple will divorce rather than stay in a failing marriage. Thus, this *private trouble* is in many respects strongly influenced by *public issues* such as women's rising economic independence and the dynamism of cultural norms related to marriage and divorce.

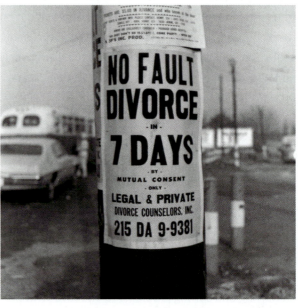

Marriage is one of the most private and personal forms of a relationship between two people. How can marriage—and divorce—be viewed through a sociological lens?

THINK IT THROUGH

▶ What other "private troubles" could sociologists identify as "public issues"?

or the beginning or end of a military conflict—shape the obstacles and opportunities that contribute to the unfolding of our own life's story. Among Mills's (1959/2000b) most often cited examples is the following:

> When, in a city of 100,000, only one man is unemployed, that is his personal trouble, and for its relief we properly look to the character of the man, his skills, and his immediate opportunities. But when in a nation of 50 million employees, 15 million men are unemployed, that is an issue, and we may not hope to find its solution within the range of opportunities open to any one individual. The very structure of opportunities has collapsed. Both the correct statement of the problem and the range of possible solutions require us to consider the economic and political institutions of the society, and not merely the personal situation and character of a scatter of individuals. (p. 9)

To apply the idea to contemporary economic conditions, we might look at recent college graduates. If many of the young people who graduated from college in the middle years of the

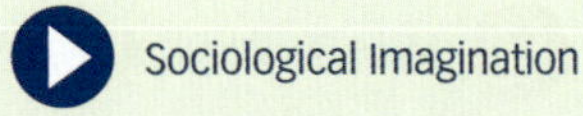

AP Photo/Patrick Semansky

C. Wright Mills highlighted the use of the sociological imagination in studying social issues. When 16% of urban residents are poor by the government's official measure, we cannot assume the sole cause is personal failings but must ask how large-scale social and economic forces are implicated in widespread socioeconomic disadvantage experienced in many communities.

2000s found the jobs they wanted, they may have accounted for their success by citing personal effort or solid academic qualifications. These are, of course, very important, but the sociological imagination suggests that there are also larger social forces at work—a booming economy in this period contributed to a low rate of unemployment among the college educated. Consider, for instance, that while unemployment among young male college graduates was just under 7% in 2007 (just before an economic crisis hit in the United States), by 2010 it had peaked at more than 12%. For young female college graduates, it grew from less than 5% in 2007 to a peak of more than 9% in 2011. In 2013, it took a downward turn for both groups before rising slightly in 2014 (Figure 1.1). If your friends or relatives who graduated into the labor market during the economic crisis or even the first years following that period encountered difficulties securing solid first jobs, this suggests that personal effort and qualifications are only part of the explanation for the success of one graduating class and the frustration of another.

Understanding this relationship is particularly critical for people in the United States, who often regard individuals as fully responsible for their own successes and failures. For instance, it is easy to fault the poor for their poverty, assuming they only need to "pull themselves up by their bootstraps." We may neglect the powerful role of social forces like racial or ethnic discrimination, the outsourcing or automation of manufacturing jobs that used to employ those with less education, or the poor state of education in many economically distressed rural and urban areas. The sociological imagination implores us to seek the intersection between private troubles, such as a family's poverty, and public issues, such as lack of access to good schooling or jobs, to develop a more informed and comprehensive understanding of the social world and social issues.

It is useful, when we talk about the sociological imagination, to bring in the concepts of agency and structure. Sociologists often talk about social actions—individual and group behavior—in these terms. **Agency** can be understood as *the ability of individuals and groups to exercise free will and to make social changes* on a small or large scale. **Structure** is a complex term but may be defined as *patterned social arrangements that have effects on agency*—structure may enable or constrain social action. For example, sociologists talk about the *class structure,* which is composed of social groups who hold varying amounts of resources such as money, political voice, and social status. They also identify *normative structures*—for instance, they might analyze patterns of social norms regarding "appropriate" gender behaviors in different cultural contexts.

Sociologists take a strong interest in the relationship between structure and agency. Consider that, on one hand, we all have the ability to make choices—so we have free will and we can opt for one path over another. On the other hand, the structures that surround us impose obstacles on us or afford us opportunities: We can make choices, but they may be enabled or constrained by structure. For instance, in the early 1900s, we would surely have found bright young women in the U.S. middle class who wanted to study to be doctors or lawyers. The social norms of the time, however, suggested that young women

Agency: The ability of individuals and groups to exercise free will and to make social changes on a small or large scale.

Structure: Patterned social arrangements that have effects on agency.

FIGURE 1.1 Unemployment Rates Among Young College Graduates in the United States, 1989–2014

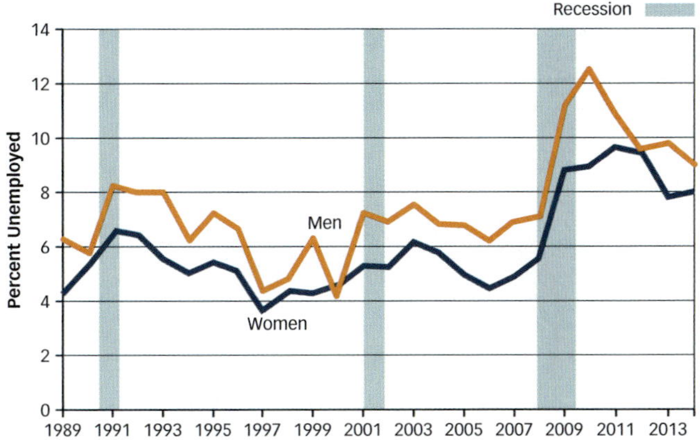

SOURCE: Shierholz, Heidi, Natalie Sabadish, and Hilary Wething. (2012). "The Class of 2012: Labor market for young graduates remains grim." Briefing paper 340. Figure G. Washington, DC: Economic Policy Institute. Reprinted with permission.

of this status were better off marrying and starting families. There were also legal constraints to women's entry into higher education and the paid labor force. So while the women in our example might have individually argued and pushed to go to college and have professional careers, the dreams of this group were constrained by powerful normative and legal structures that identified women's place as being in the home.

Consider the relationship between the class structure and individual agency as another way of thinking about social mobility in U.S. society. If, for instance, a young man today whose parents are well educated and whose family is economically prosperous wishes to go to college and become a doctor, his position in the class structure (or the position of his family) is *enabling*—that is, it makes it likely that he will be able to make this choice and to realize it. If, however, a young man from a poor family with no college background dreams of being an engineer and wants to study in college, his position in the class structure is likely to be *constraining*: Not only does his family have insufficient economic means to pay for college, but he may also be studying in an underfunded or underperforming high school that cannot provide the advanced courses he needs to prepare for college. His lack of college role models may also be a factor. This does not mean that inevitably the first young man will go to college and the second will not; it does, however, suggest that probabilities favor the first college aspirant over the second.

Put succinctly, in order to understand why some students go to college and others do not, sociologists would say that we cannot rely on individual choice or will (agency) alone—structures, whether subtly or quite obviously, exercise an influence on social behavior and outcomes. At the same time, we should not see structures as telling the whole story of social behavior, because history shows the power of human agency in making change even in the face of obstacles. Agency itself can transform structures (for example, think about the ways women's historical activism has helped to transform limiting gender norms for women today). Sociologists weight both agency and structure and continue to seek to understand how the two interact and connect in affecting social behavior. For the most part, sociologists understand the relationship as reciprocal—that is, it goes in both directions, as structure affects agency and agency, in turn, can change the dimensions of a structure (Figure 1.2).

FIGURE 1.2 Structure and Agency

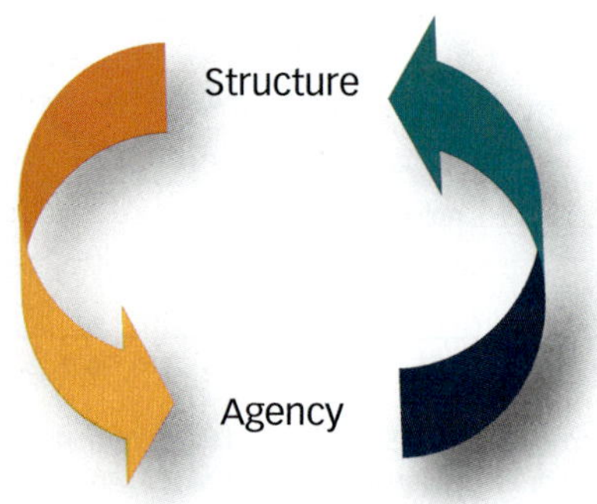

CRITICAL THINKING

Applying the sociological perspective requires more than an ability to use the sociological imagination. It also demands **critical thinking**, *the ability to evaluate claims about truth by using reason and evidence.* In everyday life, we frequently accept things as "true" because they are familiar, feel right, or are consistent with our beliefs. Critical thinking takes a different approach—recognizing poor arguments, rejecting statements not supported by evidence, and questioning our assumptions. One of the founders of modern sociology, Max Weber, captured the spirit of critical thinking in two words when he said that a key task of sociological inquiry is to openly acknowledge "inconvenient facts."

Critical thinking requires us to be open-minded, but it does not mean that we must accept all arguments as equally valid. Those supported by logic and backed by evidence are clearly preferable to those that are not. For instance, we may passionately agree with Thomas Jefferson's famous statement "that government is best that governs least." However, as sociologists we must also ask, "What evidence backs up the claim that less government is better under all circumstances?"

To think critically, it is useful to follow six simple rules (adapted from Wade & Tavris, 1997):

1. **Be willing to ask any question, no matter how difficult.** The belief in small government is a cherished U.S. ideal. But sociologists who study the role of government in modern society must be willing to ask whether there are circumstances under which more—not less—government is better. Government's role in areas such as homeland security, education, and health care has grown in the past several years—what are the positive and negative aspects of this growth?

2. **Think logically and be clear.** Logic and clarity require us to define concepts in a way that allows us to study them. "Big government" is a vague concept that must be made more precise and measurable before it provides for useful research. Are we speaking of federal, state, or local government, or all of these? Is "big" measured by the cost of government services, the number of agencies or offices within the government, the number of people working for it, or something else? What did Jefferson mean by "best," and what would that "best" government look like? Who would have the power to define this notion in any case?

Critical thinking: The ability to evaluate claims about truth by using reason and evidence.

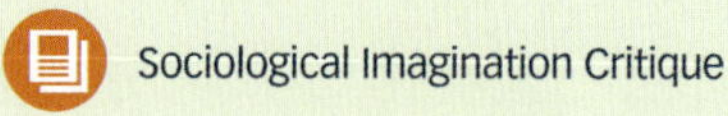

REUTERS/Charles Platia

Major metropolitan areas like New York City, Paris, and London are heavily monitored by security cameras, especially since the September 11, 2001, terrorist attacks. Defining the appropriate balance between privacy and increased security is a contemporary challenge for governments and societies.

3. **Back up your arguments with evidence.** Founding Father Thomas Jefferson is a formidable person to quote, but quoting him does not prove that smaller government is better in the 21st century. To find evidence, we need to seek out studies of contemporary societies to see whether there is a relationship between a population's well-being and the size of government or the breadth of services it provides. Because studies may offer contradictory evidence, we also need to be able to assess the strengths and weaknesses of arguments on different sides of the issue.

4. **Think about the assumptions and biases—including your own—that underlie all studies.** You may insist that government has a key role to play in modern society. On the other hand, you may believe with equal passion that big government is one root of the problems in the United States. Critical thinking, however, requires that we recognize our beliefs and biases. Otherwise we might unconsciously seek out only evidence that supports our argument, ignoring evidence to the contrary. Passion has a role to play in research: It can motivate us to devote long hours to studying an issue. But passion should not play a role when we are weighing evidence and drawing conclusions.

5. **Avoid anecdotal evidence.** It is tempting to draw a general conclusion from a single experience or anecdote, but that experience may illustrate the exception rather than the rule. For example, you may know someone who just yesterday received a letter mailed 2 years ago, but that is not evidence that the U.S. Postal Service is inefficient or does not fulfill its mandates. To determine whether this government agency is working well, you would have to study its entire mail delivery system and its record of work over time.

6. **Be willing to admit when you are wrong or uncertain about your results.** Sometimes we expect to find support for an argument only to find that things are not so clear. For example, consider the position of a sociologist who advocates small government and learns that Japan and Singapore initially became economic powerhouses because their governments played leading roles in promoting growth of a sociologist who champions an expanded role for government but learns from the downturn of the 1990s in the Asian economies that some things can be better achieved by private enterprise. The answers we get are sometimes contradictory, and we learn from recognizing the error of our assumptions and beliefs as well.

Critical thinking also means becoming "critical consumers" of the information—news, blogs, surveys, texts, magazines, and scientific studies—that surrounds us. To be a good sociologist, it is important to look beyond the commonsense understanding of social life and develop a critical perspective. Being critical consumers of information entails paying attention to the sources of information we encounter and asking questions about how data were gathered.

THE DEVELOPMENT OF SOCIOLOGICAL THINKING

Humans have been asking questions about the nature of social life as long as people have lived in societies. Aristotle and Plato wrote extensively about social relationships more than 2,000 years ago. Ibn Khaldun, an Arab scholar writing in the 14th century, advanced a number of sociological concepts we recognize today, including ideas about social conflict and cohesion. Yet modern sociological concepts and research methods did not emerge until the 19th century, after the Industrial Revolution, and then largely in those European nations undergoing dramatic societal changes like industrialization and urbanization.

THE BIRTH OF SOCIOLOGY: SCIENCE, PROGRESS, INDUSTRIALIZATION, AND URBANIZATION

We can trace sociology's roots to four interrelated historical developments that gave birth to the modern world: the *scientific revolution,* the *Enlightenment, industrialization,* and *urbanization.* Since these developments initially occurred in Europe, it is not surprising that sociological perspectives and ideas evolved there during the 19th century. By the end of the 19th century, sociology had taken root in North America as well; somewhat later, it gained a foothold in Central and South America, Africa, and Asia. Sociology throughout the world initially bore the stamp of its European and North American origins, though recent decades have brought a greater diversity of perspectives to the discipline.

THE SCIENTIFIC REVOLUTION The rise of modern natural and physical sciences, beginning in Europe in the 16th century, offered scholars a more advanced understanding of the physical world. The success of natural science contributed to the belief that science could also be fruitfully applied to human affairs, thereby enabling people to improve society or even perfect it. Auguste Comte (1798–1857) coined the term *sociology* to characterize what he believed would be a new "social physics"—that is, the scientific study of society.

THE ENLIGHTENMENT Inspired in part by the success of the physical sciences, French philosophers in the 18th century such as Voltaire (1694–1778), Montesquieu (1689–1755), Diderot (1719–1784), and Rousseau (1712–1778) promised that humankind could attain lofty heights by applying scientific understanding to human affairs. Enlightenment ideals such as equality, liberty, and fundamental human rights found a home in the emerging social sciences, particularly sociology. Émile Durkheim (1858–1917), considered by many to be the first modern sociologist, argued that sociological understanding would create a more egalitarian, peaceful society, in which individuals would be free to realize their full potential. Many of sociology's founders shared the hope that a fairer and more just society would be achieved through the scientific understanding of society.

THE INDUSTRIAL REVOLUTION The Industrial Revolution, which began in England in the mid- to late 18th century and soon spread to other countries, dramatically changed European societies. Traditional agricultural economies and the small-scale production of handicrafts in the home gave way to more efficient, profit-driven manufacturing based in factories. For instance, in 1801 in the English city of Leeds, there were about 20 factories manufacturing a variety of goods. By 1838, Leeds was home to 106 woolen mills alone, employing 10,000 people.

Small towns, including Leeds, were transformed into bustling cities, showcasing extremes of wealth and poverty as well as opportunity and struggle. In the face of rapid social change and growing inequality, sociologists sought to gain a social scientific perspective on what was happening and how it had come about. For example, German theorist and revolutionary Karl Marx (1818–1883), who had an important impact on later sociological theorizing about modern societies and economies, predicted that industrialization would make life increasingly intolerable for the masses. He believed that private property ownership by the wealthy allowed for the exploitation of working people and that its elimination, and revolution, would bring about a utopia of equality and genuine freedom for all.

URBANIZATION: THE POPULATION SHIFT TOWARD CITIES Industrialization fostered the growth of cities, as people streamed from rural fields to urban factories in search of work. By the end of the 19th century, more than 20 million people lived in English cities. The population of London alone exceeded 7 million by 1910.

PRISMA ARCHIVO/Alamy

The harnessing of waterpower and the development of the steam engine helped give rise to the industrial era and to factories, immortalized by writers such as Charles Dickens, in which men, women, and even children toiled for hours in wretched working conditions. Poet William Blake called these workplaces the "dark satanic mills."

Early industrial cities were often fetid places, characterized by pollution and dirt, crime, and crowded housing tenements. In Europe, early sociologists lamented the passing of communal village life and its replacement by a savage and alienating urban existence. Durkheim, for example, worried about the potential breakdown of stabilizing beliefs and values in modern urban society. He argued that whereas traditional communities were held together by shared culture and **norms**, or *accepted social behaviors and beliefs,* modern industrial communities were threatened by **anomie**, or *a state of normlessness that occurs when people lose sight of the shared rules and values that give order and meaning to their lives.* In a state of anomie, individuals often feel confused and anxious because they do not know how to interact with each other and their environment. Durkheim raised the question of what would hold societies and communities together as they shifted from homogeneity and shared cultures and values to heterogeneous masses of diverse occupations, cultures, and norms.

19TH-CENTURY FOUNDERS

Despite its largely European origins, early sociology sought to develop universal understandings that would apply to other peoples, times, and places. The discipline's principal acknowledged founders—Auguste Comte, Harriet Martineau, Émile Durkheim, Karl Marx, and Max Weber—left their marks on sociology in different ways.

Norms: Accepted social behaviors and beliefs.

Anomie: A social condition of normlessness; a state of normative uncertainty that occurs when people lose touch with the shared rules and values that give order and meaning to their lives.

As a founding figure in the social sciences, Auguste Comte is associated with positivism, or the belief that the study of society must be anchored in facts and the scientific method.

AUGUSTE COMTE Auguste Comte (1798–1857), a French social theorist, is credited with founding modern sociology, naming it, and establishing it as the scientific study of social relationships. The twin pillars of Comte's sociology were the study of **social statics**, *the way society is held together,* and the analysis of **social dynamics**, *the laws that govern social change.* Comte believed social science could be used effectively to manage the social change resulting from modern industrial society, but always with a strong respect for traditions and history.

Comte proclaimed that his new science of society was **positivist**. This meant that it was to be *based on facts alone,* which should be determined scientifically and allowed to speak for themselves. Comte argued that this purely factual approach was the proper method for sociology. He argued that all sciences—and all societies—go through three stages. The first stage is a *theological* one, in which key ways of understanding the world are framed in terms of superstition, imagination, and religion. The second stage is a *metaphysical* one, characterized by abstract speculation but framed by the basic belief that society is the product of natural rather than supernatural forces. The third and last stage is one in which knowledge is based on *scientific reasoning* "from the facts." Comte saw himself as leading sociology toward its final positivist stage.

Comte left a lasting mark on modern sociology. The scientific study of social life continues to be the goal of sociological research. His belief that social institutions have a strong impact on individual behavior—that is, that our actions are the products of personal choices *and* the surrounding social context—remains at the heart of sociology.

Social statics: The way society is held together.

Social dynamics: The laws that govern social change.

Positivist: Science that is based on facts alone.

HARRIET MARTINEAU Harriet Martineau (1802–1876) was an English sociologist who, despite deafness and other physical challenges, became a prominent social and historical writer. Her greatest handicap was being a woman in male-dominated intellectual circles that failed to value female voices. Today she is frequently recognized as the first major woman sociologist.

Deeply influenced by Comte's work, Martineau translated his six-volume treatise on politics into English. Her editing helped make Comte's esoteric prose accessible to the English-speaking

Interestingly, Harriet Martineau translated into English the work of Auguste Comte, who dismissed women's intellect, saying, "Biological philosophy teaches us that . . . radical differences, physical and moral, distinguish the sexes . . . biological analysis presents the female sex . . . as constitutionally in a state of perpetual infancy, in comparison with the other" (Kandal, 1988, p. 75).

world, ensuring his standing as a leading figure in sociology. Martineau was also a distinguished scholar in her own right. She wrote dozens of books, more than a thousand newspaper columns, and 25 novels, including a three-volume study, *Society in America* (1837), based on observations of the United States that she made during a tour of the country.

Martineau, like Comte, sought to identify basic laws that govern society. She derived three of her four "laws" from other theorists. The fourth law, however, was her own and reflected her progressive (today we might say feminist) principles: For a society to evolve, it must ensure social justice for women and other oppressed groups. In her study of U.S. society, Martineau treated slavery and women's experience of dependence in marriage as indicators of the limits of the moral development of the United States. In her view, the United States was unable to achieve its full social potential while it was morally stunted by persistent injustices like slavery and women's inequality. The question of whether the provision of social justice is critical to societal development remains a relevant and compelling one today.

ÉMILE DURKHEIM Auguste Comte founded and named the discipline of sociology, but French scholar Émile Durkheim (1858–1917) set the field on its present course. Durkheim established the early subject matter of sociology, laid out rules for conducting research, and developed an important theory of social change.

For Durkheim, sociology's subject matter was **social facts**, *qualities of groups that are external to individual members yet constrain their thinking and behavior.* Durkheim argued that such social facts as religious beliefs and social duties are external—that is, they are part of the social context and are larger than our individual lives. They also have the power to shape our behavior. You may feel compelled to act in certain ways in different contexts—in the classroom, on a date, at a religious ceremony—even if you are not always aware of such social pressures.

Durkheim also argued that *only social facts can explain other social facts.* For example, there is no scientific evidence that men have an innate knack for business compared with women—but in 2012, women headed just 18 of the *Fortune* 500 companies. A Durkheimian approach would highlight women's experience in society—where historically they have been socialized into more domestic values or restricted to certain noncommercial professions—and the fact that the social networks that foster mobility in the corporate world today are still primarily male to help explain why men dominate the upper ranks of the business world.

Durkheim's principal concern was explaining the impact of modern society on **social solidarity**, *the bonds that unite the members of a social group.* In his view, in traditional society these bonds are based on similarity—people speak the same language, share the same customs and beliefs, and do similar work tasks. He called this *mechanical solidarity.* In modern industrial society, however, bonds based on similarity break down.

Pictorial Press Ltd/Alamy

Émile Durkheim pioneered some of sociology's early research on such topics as social solidarity and suicide. His work continues to inform sociological study and understanding of social bonds and the consequences of their unraveling.

Everyone has a different job to perform in the industrial division of labor, and modern societies are more likely to be socially diverse. However, workers in different occupational positions are dependent on one another for things like safety, education, and the provision of food and other goods essential to survival. The people filling these positions may not be alike in culture, beliefs, or language, but their dependence on one another contributes to social cohesion. Borrowing from biology, Durkheim called this *organic solidarity,* suggesting that modern society functions as an interdependent organic whole, like a human body.

Yet organic solidarity, Durkheim argued, is not as strong as mechanical solidarity. People no longer necessarily share the same norms and values. The consequence, according

Social facts: Qualities of groups that are external to individual members yet constrain their thinking and behavior.

Social solidarity: The bonds that unite the members of a social group.

to Durkheim, is anomie. In this weakened condition, the social order disintegrates and pathological behavior increases (Durkheim, 1922/1973a).

Consider whether the United States, a modern and diverse society, is held together primarily by organic solidarity, or whether the hallmark of mechanical solidarity, a **collective conscience**—*the common beliefs and values that bind a society together*—is in evidence. Do public demonstrations of patriotism on nationally significant anniversaries such as September 11 and July 4 indicate mechanical solidarity built on a collective sense of shared values, norms, and practices? Or do the deeply divisive politics of recent years suggest social bonds based more fully on practical interdependence?

KARL MARX The extensive writings of Karl Marx (1818–1883) influenced the development of economics and political science as well as sociology. They also shaped world politics and inspired communist revolutions in Russia (later the Soviet Union), China, and Cuba, among others.

Marx's central idea was deceptively simple: Virtually all societies throughout history have been divided into economic classes, with one class prospering at the expense of others. All human history, Marx believed, should be understood as the product of **class conflict**, *competition between social classes over the distribution of wealth, power, and other valued resources in society* (Marx & Engels, 1848/1998).

In the period of early industrialization in which he lived, Marx condemned capitalism's exploitation of *working people,* the **proletariat**, by the *ownership class,* the **bourgeoisie**. As we will see in later chapters, Marx's views on conflict and inequality are still influential in contemporary sociological thinking, even among sociologists who do not share his views on society.

Marx focused his attention on the emerging capitalist industrial society (Marx, 1867/1992a, 1885/1992b, 1894/1992c). Unlike his contemporaries in sociology, however, Marx saw capitalism as a transitional stage to a final period in human history in which economic classes and the unequal distribution of rewards and opportunities linked to class inequality would disappear and be replaced by a utopia of equality.

Although many of Marx's predictions have not proven to be correct, his critical analysis of the dynamics of capitalism proved insightful. Among other things, Marx argued that capitalism would lead to accelerating technological change, the replacement of workers by machines, and the growth of monopoly capitalism.

Karl Marx was a scholar and critic of early capitalism. His work has been thoroughly studied and critiqued around the world.

Marx also presciently predicted that ownership of the **means of production**, *the sites and technology that produce the goods (and sometimes services) we need and use,* would come to be concentrated in fewer and fewer hands. As a result, he believed, a growing wave of people would be thrust down into the proletariat, which owns only its own labor power. In modern society, large corporations have progressively swallowed up or pushed out smaller businesses; where small lumberyards and pharmacies used to serve many communities, corporate giants such as Home Depot, CVS, and Best Buy have moved in, putting locally owned establishments out of business.

In many U.S. towns, small business owners have joined forces to protest the construction of "big box" stores like Walmart (now the largest private employer in the United States), arguing that these enormous establishments, while they offer cheap goods, wreak havoc on local retailers and bring only the meager economic benefit of masses of entry-level, low-wage jobs. From a Marxist perspective, we might say that the local retailers, in resisting the incursion of the capitalist behemoth Walmart, are fighting their own "proletarianization." Even physicians, many

Collective conscience: The common beliefs and values that bind a society together.

Class conflict: Competition between social classes over the distribution of wealth, power, and other valued resources in society.

Proletariat: The working class; wage workers.

Bourgeoisie: The capitalist (or property-owning) class.

Means of production: The sites and technology that produce the goods we need and use.

of whom used to own their own means of production in the form of private medical practices, have increasingly been driven by economic necessity into working for large health maintenance organizations (HMOs), where they are salaried employees.

Unlike Comte and Durkheim, Marx thought social change would be revolutionary, not evolutionary, and would be the product of oppressed workers rising up against a capitalist system that exploits the many to benefit the few.

MAX WEBER Max Weber (1864–1920), a German sociologist who wrote at the beginning of the 20th century, left a substantial academic legacy. Among his contributions are an analysis of how Protestantism fostered the rise of capitalism in Europe (Weber, 1904–1905/2002) and insights into the emergence of modern bureaucracy (Weber, 1919/1946). Weber, like other founders of sociology, took up various political causes, condemning injustice wherever he found it. Although pessimistic about capitalism, he did not believe, as did Marx, that some alternative utopian form of society would arise. Nor did he see sociologists enjoying privileged insights into the social world that would qualify them to wisely counsel rulers and industrialists, as Comte (and, to some extent, Durkheim) had envisioned.

Weber believed that an adequate explanation of the social world begins with the individual and takes into account the *meaning* of what people say and do. While he argued that research should be scientific and value-free, Weber also believed that to explain what people do, we must use a method he termed ***Verstehen***, the German word for *interpretive understanding*. This methodology, rarely used by sociologists today, sought to explain social relationships by having the sociologist/observer imagine how the subjects being studied might have perceived and interpreted the situation. Studying social life, Weber felt, is not like studying plants or chemical reactions, because human beings act on the basis of meanings and motives.

Weber's theories of social and economic organization have also been highly influential (Weber, 1921/2012). Weber argued that the modern Western world showed an ever-increasing reliance on logic, efficiency, rules, and reason. According to him, modern societies are characterized by the development and growing influence of **formal rationality**, *a context in which people's pursuit of goals is increasingly shaped by rules, regulations, and larger social structures.* One of Weber's most widely known illustrations of formal rationality comes from his study of **bureaucracies**, *formal organizations characterized by written rules, hierarchical authority, and paid staff, intended to promote organizational efficiency.* Bureaucracies, for Weber, epitomized formally rational systems: On one hand, they offer clear, knowable rules and regulations for the efficient pursuit of particular ends, like obtaining a passport or getting financial aid for higher education. On the other hand, he feared, the bureaucratization of modern society would also progressively strip people of their humanity and creativity and result in an *iron cage* of rationalized structures with irrational consequences.

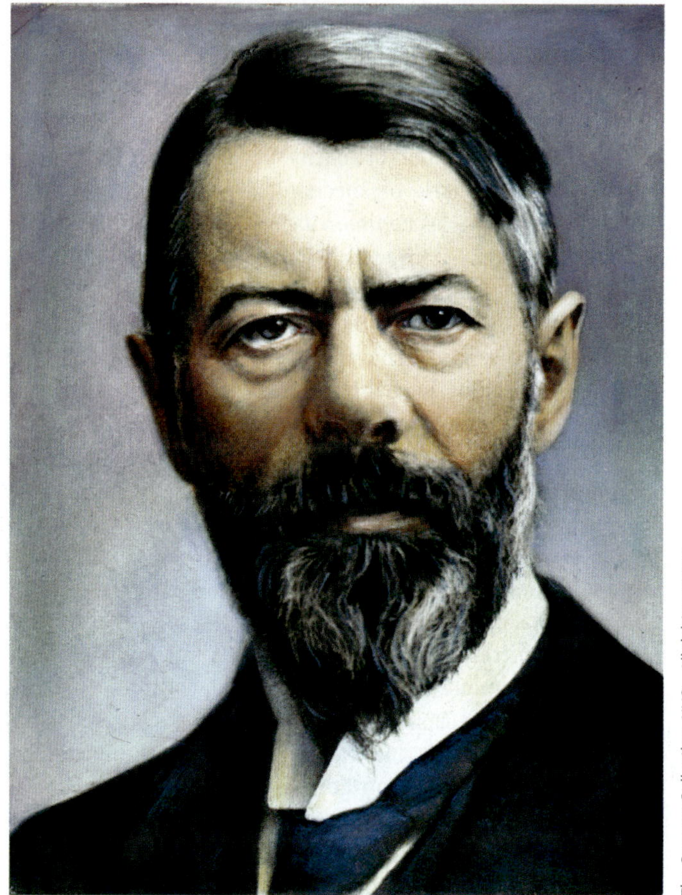

Max Weber made significant contributions to the understanding of how capitalism developed in Western countries and its relationship to religious beliefs. His work on formal rationality and bureaucracy continues to influence sociologists' study of modern society.

Weber's ideas about bureaucracy were remarkably prescient in their characterization of our bureaucratic (and formally rationalized) modern world. Today we are also confronted regularly with both the incredible efficiency and the baffling irrationality of modern bureaucratic structures. Within moments of entering into an efficiently concluded contract with a wireless phone service provider, we can become consumers of a cornucopia of technological opportunities, with the ability to chat on the phone or receive text messages from virtually anywhere, post photographs or videos online, and pass the time playing downloaded games. Should we later be confused by a bill and

Verstehen: The German word for interpretive understanding; Weber's proposed methodology for explaining social relationships by having the sociologist imagine how subjects might perceive a situation.

Formal rationality: A context in which people's pursuit of goals is shaped by rules, regulations, and larger social structures.

Bureaucracies: Formal organizations characterized by written rules, hierarchical authority, and paid staff, intended to promote organizational efficiency.

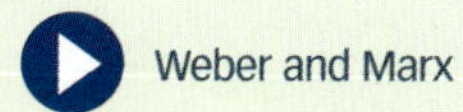

Weber and Marx

need to speak to a company representative, however, we may be shuttled through endless repetitions of an automated response system that never seems to offer us the option of speaking with another human being. Today, Weber's presciently predicted irrationality of rationality is alive and well.

EARLY 20TH-CENTURY U.S. SOCIOLOGY

Sociology was born in Europe, but it took firm root in U.S. soil, where it was heavily influenced by turn-of-the-century industrialization and urbanization, as well as by racial strife and discrimination. Strikes by organized labor, corruption in government, an explosion of European immigration, racial segregation, and the growth of city slums all helped mold early sociological thought in the United States. By the late 1800s, a number of universities in the United States were offering sociology courses. The first faculties of sociology were established at the University of Kansas (1889), the University of Chicago (1892), and Atlanta University (1897).

ROBERT EZRA PARK The sociology department at the University of Chicago, which gave us what is often known as the "Chicago School" of sociology, dominated the new discipline in the United States at the start of the 20th century. Chicago sociologist Robert Ezra Park (1864–1944) pioneered the study of urban sociology and race relations. Once a muckraking journalist, Park was an equally colorful academic, reportedly coming to class in disheveled clothes and with shaving soap still in his ears. But his students were devoted to him, and his work was widely recognized. His 1921 textbook *An Introduction to the Science of Sociology,* coauthored with his Chicago colleague Ernest Burgess, helped shape the discipline. The Chicago School studied a broad spectrum of social phenomena, from hoboes and flophouses (inexpensive dormitory-style housing) to movie houses, dance halls, and slums, and from youth gangs and mobs to residents of Chicago's ritzy Gold Coast.

Park was a champion of racial integration, having once served as personal secretary to the African American educator Booker T. Washington. Yet racial discrimination was evident in the treatment of Black sociologists, including W. E. B. Du Bois, a contemporary of many of the sociologists working in the Chicago School.

W. E. B. DU BOIS A prominent Black sociologist and civil rights leader at the African American Atlanta University, W. E. B. Du Bois (1868–1963) developed ideas that were considered too radical to find broad acceptance in the sociological community. At a time when the U.S. Supreme Court had ruled that segregated "separate but equal" facilities for Blacks and Whites were constitutional and when lynching of Black Americans had reached an all-time high, Du Bois condemned the deep-seated racism of White society. Today, his writings on race relations and the lives of U.S. Blacks are classics in the field.

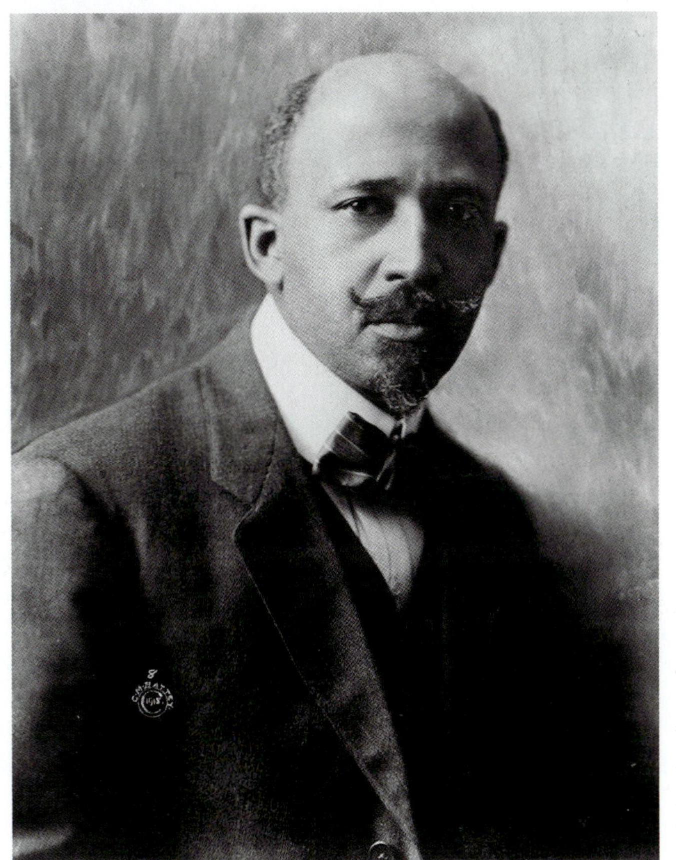

Public domain—Library of Congress

W. E. B. Du Bois, the first African American to receive a PhD from Harvard, wrote 20 books and more than 100 scholarly articles on race and race relations. Today many of his works are classics in the study of African American lives and race relations in the United States.

Du Bois sought to show that racism was widespread in U.S. society. He was also critical of Blacks who had "made it" and then turned their backs on those who had not. One of his most enduring ideas is that in U.S. society, African Americans are never able to escape a fundamental awareness of race. They experience a **double consciousness**, as he called it—*an awareness of themselves both as Americans and as Blacks, never free of racial stigma.* He wrote, "The Negro is sort of a seventh son . . . gifted with second-sight . . . this sense of always looking at one's self through the eyes of others" (Du Bois, 1903/2008, p. 12). Today as in Du Bois's time, physical traits such as skin color may shape people's perceptions and interactions in significant and complex ways.

Double consciousness: Among African Americans, an awareness of being both American and Black, never free of racial stigma.

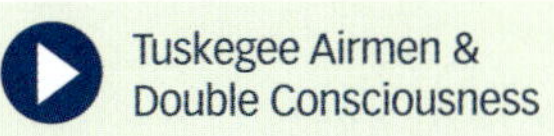
Tuskegee Airmen & Double Consciousness

THE MID-20TH CENTURY IN U.S. SOCIOLOGY

After World War II, sociology began to apply sophisticated quantitative models to the study of social processes. There was also a

Fritz Goro/Contributor/Getty Images

The "sociological imagination" involves viewing seemingly personal issues through a sociological lens. C. Wright Mills is best known for coining this catchy and popular term.

growing interest in the grand theories of the European founders. At Columbia University, Robert K. Merton (1910–2003) undertook wide-ranging studies that helped further establish sociology as a scientific discipline. Merton is best known for his theory of deviance (Merton, 1938), his work on the sociology of science (Merton, 1996), and his iteration of the distinction between *manifest* and *latent* functions (Merton, 1968). He emphasized the development of theories in what he called the "middle range"—midway between the grand theories of Weber, Marx, and Durkheim and quantitative studies of specific social problems.

Another Columbia University sociologist, C. Wright Mills (1916–1962), renewed interest in Max Weber by translating many of his works into English and applying his ideas to the contemporary United States. But Mills, who also drew on Marx, identified himself as a "plain Marxist." His concept of the sociological imagination can be traced in part to Marx's famous statement that "man makes history, but not under circumstances of his own choosing," meaning that while we are agents of free will, the social context has a profound impact on the obstacles or opportunities in our lives.

Mills synthesized Weberian and Marxian traditions, applying sociological thinking to the most pressing problems of the day, particularly inequality. He advocated an activist sociology with a sense of social responsibility. Like many sociologists, he was willing to turn a critical eye on "common knowledge," including the belief that the United States is a democracy that represents the interests of all the people. In a provocative study, he examined the workings of the "power elite," a small group of wealthy businessmen, military leaders, and politicians who Mills believed ran the country largely in their own interests (Mills, 1956/2000a).

WHY SO FEW FOUNDING MOTHERS?

Why did so few women social scientists find a place among sociology's founders? After all, the American (1776) and French (1789) revolutions elevated such lofty ideals as freedom, liberty, and equality. Yet long after these historical events, women and minorities were still excluded from public life in Europe and North America. Democracy—which gives people the right to participate in their governance—was firmly established as a principle for nearly a century and a half in the United States before women achieved the right to vote in 1920. In France, it took even longer—until 1945.

Sociology as a discipline emerged during the first modern flourishing of feminism in the 19th century. Yet women and people of non-European heritage were systematically excluded from influential positions in the European universities where sociology and other modern social sciences originated. When women did pursue lives as scholars, the men who dominated the social sciences largely ignored their writings. Feminist scholar Julie Daubié won a prize from the Lyon Academy for her essay "Poor Women in the Nineteenth Century," yet France's public education minister denied her a diploma on the grounds that he would be "forever holding up his ministry to ridicule" (Kandal, 1988, pp. 57–58). Between 1840 and 1960, almost no women held senior academic positions in the sociology departments of any European or U.S. universities, with the exception of exclusively women's colleges.

A number of woman scholars managed to overcome the obstacles to make significant contributions to sociological inquiry. For example, in 1792 the British scholar Mary Wollstonecraft published *A Vindication of the Rights of Women,* arguing that scientific progress could not occur unless women were allowed to become men's equals by means of universal education. In France in 1843, Flora Tristan called for equal rights for women workers, "the last remaining slaves in France." Also in France, Aline Valette published *Socialism and Sexualism* in 1893, nearly three-quarters of a century before the term *sexism* found its way into spoken English (Kandal, 1988).

One of sociology's most prominent early figures, Jane Addams (1860–1935), never won a full-time position at the University of Chicago in spite of the school's "progressive" leanings. The University of Chicago even denied her an honorary degree—though she wrote 11 books and hundreds of articles and was awarded the Nobel Peace Prize in 1931 for her dedication to social reform.

Addams is best known as the founder of Hull House, a settlement house for the poor, sick, and aged that became a center for political activists and social reformers. Less well known is the

Underappreciated during her time, Jane Addams was a prominent scholar and early contributor to sociology. She is also known for her political activism and commitment to social reform.

fact that under Addams's guidance, the residents of Hull House engaged in important research on social problems in Chicago. *Hull House Maps and Papers,* published in 1895, pioneered the study of Chicago neighborhoods, helping to shape the research direction of the Chicago School of sociology. Following Addams's lead, Chicago sociologists mapped the city's neighborhoods, studied their residents, and helped create the field of community studies.

As sociologists like Harriet Martineau, Jane Addams, Julie Daubié, and others experienced, early female sociologists were not accorded the same status as their male counterparts. Only recently have many of their writings been "rediscovered" and their contributions acknowledged in sociology.

Sociological theories: Logical, rigorous frameworks for the interpretation of social life that make particular assumptions and ask particular questions about the social world.

Macro-level paradigms: Theories of the social world that are concerned with large-scale patterns and institutions.

Micro-level paradigm: A theory of the social world that is concerned with small-group social relations and interactions.

Structural functionalism: A theory that seeks to explain social organization and change in terms of the roles performed by different social structures, phenomena, and institutions; also known as *functionalism.*

SOCIOLOGY: ONE WAY OF LOOKING AT THE WORLD—OR MANY?

Often, multiple sociologists look at the same events, phenomena, or institutions and draw different conclusions. How can this be? One reason is that they may approach their analyses from different theoretical perspectives. In this section, we explore the key theoretical paradigms in sociology and look at how they are used as tools for the analysis of society.

Sociological theories are *logical, rigorous frameworks for the interpretation of social life that make particular assumptions and ask particular questions about the social world.* The word *theory* is rooted in the Greek word *theoria,* which means "a viewing." An apt metaphor for a theory is a pair of glasses. You can view a social phenomenon such as socioeconomic inequality or poverty, deviance, or consumer culture, or an institution like capitalism or the family, using different theories as lenses.

As you will see in the next section, in the discipline of sociology there are several major categories of theories that seek to examine and explain social phenomena and institutions. Imagine the various sociological theories as different pairs of glasses, each with colored lenses that change the way you see an image: You may look at the same institution or phenomenon as you put on each pair, but it will appear different depending on the glasses you are wearing. Keep in mind that sociological theories are not "truths" about the social world. They are logical, rigorous analytical tools that we can use to inquire about, interpret, and make educated predictions about the world around us. From the vantage point of any sociological theory, some aspects of a phenomenon or an institution are illuminated while others are obscured. In the end, theories are more or less useful depending on how well *empirical data*—that is, knowledge gathered by researchers through scientific methods—support their analytical conclusions. Below, we outline the basic theoretical perspectives that we will be using in this text.

The three dominant theoretical perspectives in sociology are *structural functionalism, social conflict theory,* and *symbolic interactionism.* We outline their basic characteristics below and will revisit them again throughout the book. Symbolic interactionism shares with the functionalist and social conflict paradigms an interest in interpreting and understanding social life. However, the first two are **macro-level paradigms**, *concerned with large-scale patterns and institutions.* Symbolic interactionism is a **micro-level paradigm**—that is, it is *concerned with small-group social relations and interactions.*

Structural functionalism, social conflict theory, and symbolic interactionism form the basic foundation of contemporary sociological theorizing (Table 1.1). Throughout this book we will introduce variations on these theories, as well as new and evolving theoretical ideas in sociology.

THE FUNCTIONALIST PARADIGM

Structural functionalism (or functionalism—the term we use in this book) *seeks to explain social organization and change in*

TABLE 1.1 The Three Principal Sociological Paradigms

Theoretical Perspective and Founding Theorist(s)	Structural Functionalism *Émile Durkheim*	Social Conflict *Karl Marx*	Symbolic Interactionism *Max Weber, George Herbert Mead*
Assumptions about self and society	Society is a system of interdependent, interrelated parts, like an organism, with groups and institutions contributing to the stability and equilibrium of the whole social system.	Society consists of conflicting interests, but only some groups have the power and resources to realize their interests. Some groups benefit from the social order at the expense of other groups.	The self is a social creation; social interaction occurs by means of symbols such as words, gestures, and adornments; shared meanings are important to successful social interactions.
Key focus and questions	Macrosociology: What keeps society operating smoothly? What functions do different societal institutions and phenomena serve for society as a whole?	Macrosociology: What are the sources of conflict in society? Who benefits and who loses from the existing social order? How can inequalities be overcome?	Microsociology: How do individuals experience themselves, one another, and society as a whole? How do they interpret the meanings of particular social interactions?

terms of the roles performed by different social structures, phenomena, and institutions. Functionalism characterizes society as made up of many interdependent parts—an analogy often cited is the human body. Each part serves a different function, but all parts work together to ensure the equilibrium and health of the entity as a whole. Society too is composed of a spectrum of different parts with a variety of different functions, such as the government, the family, religious and educational institutions, and the media. According to the theory, together these parts contribute to the smooth functioning and equilibrium of society.

The key question posed by the functionalist perspective is, "What function does a particular institution, phenomenon, or social group serve for the maintenance of society?" That is, what contribution does a given institution, phenomenon, or social group make to the equilibrium, stability, and functioning of the whole? Note the underlying assumption of functionalism: Any existing institution or phenomenon does serve a function; if it served no function, it would evolve out of existence. Consequently, the central task of the functionalist sociologist is to discover what function an institution or a phenomenon—for instance, the traditional family, capitalism, social stratification, or deviance—serves in the maintenance of the social order.

Émile Durkheim is credited with developing the early foundations of functionalism. Among other ideas, Durkheim observed that all known societies have some degree of deviant behavior, such as crime. The notion that deviance is functional for societies may seem counterintuitive: Ordinarily, we do not think of deviance as beneficial or necessary to society. Durkheim, however, reasoned that since deviance is universal, it must serve a social function—if it did not serve a function, it would cease to exist. Durkheim concluded that one function of deviance—specifically, of society's labeling of some acts as deviant—is to remind members of society what is "normal" or "moral"; when a society punishes deviant behavior, it reaffirms people's beliefs in what is right and good.

Talcott Parsons (1902–1979) expanded functionalist analysis by looking at whole social systems such as government, the economy, and the family and how they contribute to the functioning of the whole social system (Parsons, 1964/2007, 1967). For example, he wrote that traditional sex roles for men and women contribute to stability on both the micro familial level and the macro societal level. Parsons argued that traditional socialization produces *instrumental* or rational and work-oriented males, and *expressive* or sensitive, nurturing, and emotional females. Instrumental males, he reasoned, are well suited for the competitive world of work, while their expressive female counterparts are appropriately prepared to care for the family. According to Parsons, these roles are complementary and positively functional, leading men and women to inhabit different spheres of the social world. Complementary rather than competing roles contribute to solidarity in a marriage by reducing competition between husband and wife. Critics have rejected this idea as a justification of inequality.

As this example suggests, functionalism is conservative in that it tends to accept rather than question the status quo; it holds that any given institution or phenomenon exists because it is functional for society, rather than asking whether it might benefit one group to the detriment of others, as critics say Parsons's position on gender roles does. One of functionalism's long-standing weaknesses is a failure to recognize inequalities in the distribution of power and resources and how those affect social relationships.

Robert Merton attempted to refine the functionalist paradigm by demonstrating that not all social structures work to maintain or strengthen the social organism, as Durkheim and other early functionalists seemed to suggest. According to Merton, a social institution or phenomenon can have both positive functions and problematic dysfunctions. Merton broadened the functionalist idea by suggesting that **manifest functions**

Manifest functions: Functions of an object, an institution, or a phenomenon that are obvious and intended.

REUTERS/Alessandro Bianchi

The manifest function of a vehicle is to transport a person efficiently from point A to point B. One latent function is to say something about the status of the driver.

are *the obvious and intended functions of a given phenomenon or institution.* **Latent functions**, by contrast, are *functions that are not recognized or expected.* A manifest function of war, for instance, is usually to vanquish an enemy, perhaps to defend a territory or to claim it. Latent functions of war—those that are not the overt purpose but may still have powerful effects—may include increased patriotism in countries engaged in the war, a rise in the profits of companies manufacturing military equipment or contracting workers to the military, and changes in national budgetary priorities.

THE SOCIAL CONFLICT PARADIGM

In contrast to functionalism, the **social conflict paradigm** (which we refer to in this book as conflict theory) *seeks to explain social organization and change in terms of the conflict built into social relationships.* Conflict theory is rooted in the ideas about class and power put forth by Karl Marx. While Durkheim's structural functionalist lens asked how different parts of society contribute to stability, Marx asked about the roots of conflict. Conflict theorists pose the questions "Who benefits from the way social institutions and relationships are structured?" and "Who loses?" The social conflict paradigm focuses on what divides people rather than on what unites them. It presumes that group interests (such as social class interests) drive relationships, and that various groups in society (for instance, social classes or genders or ethnic or racial groups) will act in their own interests. Conflict theory thus assumes not that interests are shared but rather that they may be irreconcilable and, importantly, that only some groups have the power and resources to realize their interests. Because of this, conflict is—sooner or later—inevitable.

From Marx's perspective, the bourgeoisie benefits directly from the capitalist social order. If, as Marx suggests, the capitalist class has an interest in maximizing productivity and profit and minimizing costs (like the cost of labor in the form of workers' wages), and the working class has an interest in earning more and working less, then the interests of the two classes are difficult to reconcile. The more powerful group in society generally has the upper hand in furthering its interests.

After Marx, the body of conflict theory expanded tremendously. In the 20th century and today, theorists have extended the reach of the perspective to consider, for instance, how control of culture and the rise of technology (rather than just control of

Latent functions: Functions of an object, an institution, or a phenomenon that are not recognized or expected.

Social conflict paradigm: A theory that seeks to explain social organization and change in terms of the conflict that is built into social relations; also known as *conflict theory.*

INEQUALITY MATTERS

WHY ARE SOME PEOPLE POOR AND OTHERS RICH?

The concentration of wealth in the hands of a small elite and the widespread struggle of millions to make do with scant resources are critical issues on both the domestic and global levels. One common explanation of the wealth disparity in the United States is that it results from individual differences in talent and ambition. While such factors play a role, the fact that more than 15% of the population lives below the poverty line, including disproportionate numbers of Blacks, Latinos, and women (DeNavas-Walt, Proctor, & Smith, 2012), should lead our sociological imaginations to recognize that social and economic forces also underlie inequality.

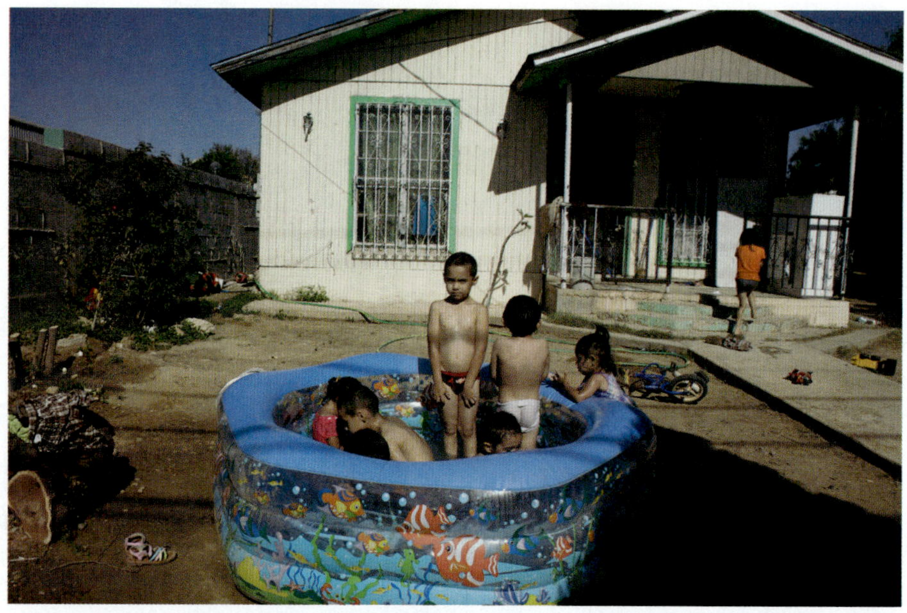

© Lisa Wiltse/Corbis

Why are children of poor parents more likely to be poor as adults? This is a question of fundamental interest to sociologists.

Discrimination can place entire groups of people at an economic disadvantage. Women as a group continue to earn less than men as a group—as do Blacks and Latinos relative to White Americans. Importantly as well, educational opportunity is not equally distributed, because in most U.S. states schools are still funded primarily by local property taxes; consequently, high-value areas have more funds than low-value areas to spend on teachers, textbooks, and technology. Without a strong educational foundation that prepares them for a competitive economy, already poor children are likely to remain poor as adults.

Economic changes have also spurred the growth of inequality. Automation and the movement abroad of factory work have significantly reduced employment opportunities for less educated workers. Service jobs, including restaurant and retail work, have expanded as the manufacturing sector has contracted, but these positions are far less likely to pay a living wage or give workers a lift into the middle class. Education is thus more critical than ever, but poor children are the least likely to get the solid skills they need to succeed.

THINK IT THROUGH

▶ In his inaugural address of 2013, President Obama stated that one of his goals in his second term as president was to see that a young girl born into poverty would know that she had every opportunity to realize her hopes. How are such opportunities created and expanded? What do you think?

the means of production) underpins class domination (Adorno, 1975; Horkheimer, 1947), as well as how the expanded middle class can be accommodated in a Marxist perspective (Wright, 1998). Some of feminist theory's key ideas also reflect a conflict-oriented perspective, though the focus shifts from social class to gender power and conflict (Connell, 2005), as well as ways in which race is implicated in relations of power (Collins, 1990).

Recall Durkheim's functionalist analysis of crime and deviance. According to this perspective, society defines crime to reaffirm people's beliefs about what is right and dissuade them from deviating. A conflict theorist might argue that dominant groups in society define the behaviors labeled criminal or deviant *because they have the power to do so.* For example, street crimes such as mugging someone to get his wallet and carjacking are clearly defined and punished as criminal behavior. They are also amply represented in reality television programs, movies, and other cultural products as images of criminal deviance. On the other hand, corporate or white-collar crime, which may cause the loss of money or even of lives, is less likely to be clearly defined, represented, and punished as criminal. From a conflict perspective, white-collar crime is more likely to be committed by members of the upper class (for instance, business or political leaders or financiers) and is less likely to be punished harshly than street crime, which is associated with the lower-income classes, though white-collar crime may have even greater economic and health consequences. A social conflict theorist would draw our attention to the fact that the decision makers who pass our laws are mostly members of the upper class and govern in the interests of capitalism and their own socioeconomic peers.

A key weakness of the social conflict paradigm is that it overlooks the forces of stability, equilibrium, and consensus in society. The assumption that groups have conflicting, even irreconcilable, interests and that those interests are realized by those with power at the expense of those with less power fails to account for forces of cohesion and stability in societies.

SYMBOLIC INTERACTIONISM

Symbolic interactionism argues that *both the individual self and society as a whole are the products of social interactions based on language and other symbols.* The term *symbolic interactionism* was coined by U.S. sociologist Herbert Blumer (1900–1987) in 1937, but the approach originated in the lectures of George Herbert Mead (1863–1931), a University of Chicago philosopher allied with the Chicago School of sociology. The symbolic interactionist paradigm argues that people acquire their sense of who they are only through interaction with others. They do this by means of **symbols**, *representations of things that are not immediately present to our senses.* Symbols include such things as words, gestures, emoticons, and tattoos, among others.

Recall our earlier discussions of the theoretical interpretations of deviance and crime. A symbolic interactionist might focus on the ways in which people label one another as deviant (a symbolic act that uses language), the factors that make such a label stick, and the meanings underlying such a label. If you are accused of committing a crime you did not commit, how will the label of "criminal" affect the way others see you? How will it affect the way you see yourself, and will you begin to act differently as a result? Can being labeled "deviant" be a self-fulfilling prophecy? For the symbolic interactionist, sociological inquiry is the study of how people interact and how they create and interpret symbols in the social world.

While symbolic interactionist perspectives draw our attention to important micro-level processes in society, they may miss the larger structural context of those processes, such as discovering who has the power to make laws defining what or who is deviant. For this reason, many sociologists seek to utilize both macro- and micro-level perspectives when analyzing social phenomena such as deviance.

The three paradigms described above lead to diverse images of society, research questions, and conclusions about the patterns and nature of social life. Each "pair of glasses" can provide a different perspective on the social world. Throughout this text, the three major theoretical paradigms—and some new ones we will encounter in later chapters—will help us understand key issues and themes of sociology.

PRINCIPAL THEMES IN THIS TEXT

We began this chapter with a list of *why* questions with which sociologists are concerned—and about which any one of us might be curious. Behind these questions, we find several major themes, which are also some of the main themes in this book. Three important themes for sociology—and for us—are (1) *power and inequality* and the ways in which the unequal distribution of social, economic, and political power and resources shapes opportunities, obstacles, and relationships; (2) the societal changes occurring as a result of *globalization* and the rising *social diversity* of modern societies; and (3) the powerful impact of *technological change* on modern lives, institutions, and states.

POWER AND INEQUALITY

As we consider broad social topics such as gender, race, social class, and sexual orientation and their effects on social relationships and resources, we will be asking who has **power**—*the ability to mobilize resources and achieve goals despite the resistance of others*—and who does not. We will also ask about variables that influence the uneven distribution of power, and how some groups use power to create advantages for themselves (and disadvantages for others) and how disadvantaged groups mobilize to challenge the powerful.

Power is often distributed unequally and can be used by those who possess it to marginalize other social groups. **Inequality** refers to *differences in wealth, power, opportunity, and other valued resources.* The existence of inequality not only raises moral and ethical questions about fairness; it can tear at the very fabric of societies, fostering social alienation and instability. It may also have negative effects on local and national economies. Notably, economic inequality is increasing both within and between many countries around the globe, a fact that makes understanding the

Symbolic interactionism: A microsociological perspective that posits that both the individual self and society as a whole are the products of social interactions based on language and other symbols.

Symbols: Representations of things that are not immediately present to our senses.

Power: The ability to mobilize resources and achieve goals despite the resistance of others.

Inequality: Differences in wealth, power, and other valued resources.

roots and consequences of this phenomenon—that is, asking the *why* questions—ever more important.

GLOBALIZATION AND DIVERSITY

Globalization is *the process by which people all over the planet become increasingly interconnected economically, politically, culturally, and environmentally.* Globalization is not new. It began nearly 200,000 years ago when humans first spread from their African cradle into Europe and Asia. For thousands of years, humans have traveled, traded goods, and exchanged ideas over much of the globe, using seaways or land routes such as the famed Silk Road, a stretch of land that links China and Europe. But the rate of globalization took a giant leap forward with the Industrial Revolution, which accelerated the growth of global trade. It made another dramatic jump with the advent of the information age, drawing together individuals, cultures, and countries into a common global web of information exchange. In this book, we consider the variable manifestations, functions, and consequences of globalization in areas like the economy, culture, and the environment.

Growing contacts between people and cultures have made us increasingly aware of social diversity as a feature of modern societies. **Social diversity** is *the social and cultural mixture of different groups in society and the societal recognition of difference as significant.* The spread of culture through the globalization of media and the rise of migration has created a world in which virtually no place is isolated. As a result, many nations today, including the United States, are characterized by a high degree of social diversity.

Social diversity brings a unique set of sociological challenges. People everywhere have a tendency toward **ethnocentrism**, *a worldview whereby they judge other cultures by the standards of their own culture* and regard their own way of life as "normal" and better than others. From a sociological perspective, no group can be said to be more human than any other. Yet history abounds with examples of people lashing out at others whose religions, languages, customs, races, or sexual orientations differed from their own.

TECHNOLOGY AND SOCIETY

Technology is *the practical application of knowledge to transform natural resources for human use.* The first human technology was probably the use of rocks and other blunt instruments as weapons, enabling humans to hunt large animals for food. Agriculture—planting crops such as rice or corn in hopes of reaping a yearly harvest—represents another technological advance, one superior to simple foraging in the wild for nuts and berries. The use of modern machinery, which ushered in the Industrial Revolution, represents still another technological leap, multiplying the productivity of human efforts.

Today we are in the midst of another revolutionary period of technological change: the information revolution. Thanks to the microchip, the Internet, and mobile technology, an increasing number of people around the world now have instant access to a mass of information that was unimaginable just 10 or 20 years ago. The information revolution is creating postindustrial economies based far more heavily on the production of knowledge than on the production of goods, as well as new ways of communicating that have the potential to draw people around the world together—or tear them apart.

WHY STUDY SOCIOLOGY?

A sociological perspective highlights the many ways that we both influence and are powerfully influenced by the social world around us: Society shapes us, and we, in turn, shape society. A sociological perspective also helps us to see the social world through a variety of different lenses (recall the glasses metaphor we used when talking about theory): Sociologists might explain class differences and why they persist, for instance, in many different ways. Each one may illuminate particular aspects of the phenomenon, enabling us to assemble a fuller, more rigorous perspective on social life. In this sense, "the" sociological perspective is really a collection of sociological perspectives we can use as analytical tools.

Why are the issues and questions posed by sociology incredibly compelling for all of us to understand? One reason is that, as we will see throughout this book, many of the social issues sociologists study—marriage, fertility, poverty, unemployment, consumption, discrimination, and many others—are related to one another in ways we may not immediately see. *The sociological perspective helps us to make connections between diverse social phenomena.* When we understand these connections, we are better able to address social problems and to make (or vote for) policy choices that benefit society.

For example, a phenomenon like the *decline of marriage among the working class,* which we mentioned at the start of the chapter, is related to growing globalization, declining employment in the manufacturing sector, and the persistently high rate of poverty among single mothers. Consider these social phenomena as pieces of a puzzle. One of the defining characteristics of economic globalization is the movement of manufacturing industries away from the United States to lower-wage countries. As a result, jobs in U.S. manufacturing, an economic sector dominated by men, have been declining since the 1970s. The decreasing number of less educated men able to earn a good enough wage to support a family in turn is related to a decline in marriage among the working class.

Globalization: The process by which people all over the planet become increasingly interconnected economically, politically, culturally, and environmentally.

Social diversity: The social and cultural mixture of different groups in society and the societal recognition of difference as significant.

Ethnocentrism: A worldview whereby one judges other cultures by the standards of one's own culture and regards one's own way of life as "normal" and better than others.

Technology: The practical application of knowledge to transform natural resources for human use.

GLOBAL ISSUES

YOU, THE GLOBAL CONSUMER

Try a simple experiment. Walk through your dorm room, apartment, or house and make a list of the places of manufacture of some of the products you find. Be sure to examine electronic equipment such as your television, laptop, or smartphone. Go through your closets and drawers, checking the labels on your clothing and footwear. What about your bicycle or your car? If you are a good detective, you will find that people who live outside the United States made many of the necessities of your everyday life. Even your U.S.-manufactured car is likely to have parts that have passed through the hands of workers abroad.

According to a recent story in the *New York Times,* fully 90% of footwear sold in the United States is manufactured elsewhere (Manning, 2009). So much of our apparel is made abroad that some student groups have campaigned to ensure that the college apparel marketed by their schools is not made in sweatshops. United Students Against Sweatshops (www.usas.org) now has chapters across the United States.

AP Photo/Richard Vogel

The expensive sneakers that many Americans enjoy wearing in and outside the gym are often made by poorly compensated female labor abroad. Do labor conditions matter to U.S. consumers? Should they matter? ■

While global production based on the use of low-wage labor around the world has reduced the prices of many things we consume, it has also contributed to declining wages and lost jobs for manufacturing workers in the United States, as well as the employment of millions of people around the world in factories that are poorly regulated and operate largely outside the view of the consumers who buy their products. On one hand, these new industrial workers potentially benefit from expanded job opportunities. On the other hand, the world's workers, many of whom are women, are vulnerable to exploitation and their wages are often very low, their hours long, and their work sites unpleasant or even hazardous. The conditions under which some workers toil today recall the 19th-century English factories that inspired Karl Marx to advance his powerful critique of capitalism's darker side.

THINK IT THROUGH

▶ Many questions remain for sociological investigation: Who benefits and who loses as a result of the explosive growth in global production? Will globalization bring a better world to all or to only a select few? What is our role as consumers in the global chain of production, and how do our consumption choices affect industries and economies at home and abroad?

While marriage rates fall, however, many women still desire to have families, so the proportion of nonmarital births rises. Single mothers with children are among the demographic groups in the United States most likely to be poor, and their poverty rate has remained relatively high even in periods of economic prosperity.

While the relationships between sociological factors are complex and sometimes indirect, when sociology helps us fit them together, we gain a better picture of the issues confronting all of us—as well as U.S. society and the larger world. Let's begin our journey.

TECHNOLOGY & SOCIETY

THE EXPLOSIVE GROWTH OF THE INTERNET

The Internet, which has revolutionized the way the world shares information, is barely four decades old. The first Internet message was sent from the University of California, Los Angeles, to Stanford University in 1969 on a small, experimental Department of Defense network. The initial effort experienced a glitch—the system reportedly crashed as the letter *G* of the word *LOGIN* was typed! Not until the mid-1980s was Internet technology sufficiently developed to make it possible for anyone with a computer to plug into the network. Since it was initially difficult to send anything more than simple text-based messages, the early Internet was used mainly by a handful of researchers and scholars.

©iStockphoto.com/Lance

Today's digital age has given us Internet access virtually everywhere, whether we are 35,000 feet in the sky, traveling on a bus, or waiting for class to begin. ■

Part-time University of Illinois programmer Marc Andreessen developed the easy-to-use World Wide Web, with its graphical interface and ability to send sound and images, in 1992. Andreessen called his new program Mosaic and gave it away free on the Internet. Within a year and a half, the number of Internet users had tripled to 20 million, and Mosaic had morphed into the Netscape browser. In 1998, Netscape spun off Mozilla, a company that today maintains the Firefox browser. In the summer of 2000, there were 93 million Internet hosts worldwide. By the summer of 2012 there were 908 million and counting, along with about 200 million active websites. In 2014 it was projected that 44% of households worldwide would have Internet access by the end of that year, and there would be almost 3 billion Internet users. The rate of growth shows no signs of slowing (International Telecommunication Union, 2011, 2014; Internet Systems Consortium, 2012; Netcraft, 2012).

A recent study by the Pew Research Center's Internet and American Life Project estimated that 90% of U.S. adults own some type of portable electronic device (Gahran, 2012). As you pass through a public space such as an airport or a mall or ride on public transportation in a metropolitan area, you see people engaging in a multitude of behaviors and activities facilitated by the growth of high-tech gadgetry. Social media platforms like YouTube, Facebook, Twitter, SnapChat, and Tumblr allow individuals across the globe to post videos and other media to share within the Internet community of millions.

THINK IT THROUGH

▶ Will such widely accessible and vastly powerful technology enable people to play a greater role in shaping their own destinies? Will digital technology be emancipating, or will it come to threaten our privacy and security in ways we cannot yet grasp?

WHAT CAN I DO WITH A SOCIOLOGY DEGREE?

CAREER DEVELOPMENT AND SKILLS AND CAREERS: AN INTRODUCTION

A short feature will appear near the end of each chapter of *Discover Sociology* that links your study of sociology to potential careers. It is intended to help you answer the question "What can I do with a sociology degree?" An important goal of these features is to highlight the core knowledge and professional skills that you will develop through your education as a sociology major. This set of competencies and skills, which range from critical thinking and writing skills to aptitude in qualitative and quantitative research to the understanding of diversity and conflict dynamics, prepares you for the workforce, as well as for graduate and professional school. Many of the chapters ahead will highlight information about the *occupational fields, job titles, and work activities* that can be linked to the knowledge and skills you will learn as a sociology major. The *Skills and Careers* essays (Chapters 5–11 and 14–17) will describe professional skills, discuss their development through the study of sociology, and link them with specific occupational fields and jobs in which employers seek employees who have the skills discussed.

A second goal of the feature is to help you more fully identify and articulate your current and developing job-related skills, interests, and values, as well as to show you how to begin to explore careers, how to perform an effective internship or job search, and how to create a personal career action plan (see the career development wheel). These *Career Development* features are intended to benefit both sociology majors and students majoring in other disciplines—career planning is important no matter your chosen field. The first chapter essays (Chapters 2–4) discuss the basics of career development. Two later chapters (Chapters 12 and 13) offer discussions of how graduate or professional school may fit into your career development plans. We hope that you find these features useful!

THINK ABOUT CAREERS

- What are your potential career interests? Did you come to college with a specific interest, or have you developed new interests during your studies?
- Have you spoken with anyone—family members, career counselors, professors, practitioners, or others—about your career interests? With whom might you speak to learn more about your field of interest?

Anne V. Scammon, Managing Director, Curricular and Strategic Initiatives, Center for Career Services at the George Washington University in Washington, DC, contributed to the skills and careers feature ("What Can I Do with a Sociology Degree?") in this text and accompanying online supplements. With Anne Scammon's support, key skills developed through the study of sociology were identified and linked to specific job titles and occupations. She also developed information related to career self-assessment, exploration, obtaining experience, job search strategies, and graduate school options for students.

SUMMARY

- **Sociology** is the scientific study of human social relationships, groups, and societies. Its central task is to ask what the dimensions of the social world are, how they influence our behavior, and how we in turn shape and change them.
- Sociology adheres to the principle of **social embeddedness**, the idea that economic, political, and other forms of human behavior are fundamentally shaped by social relationships. Sociologists seek to study through scientific means the social worlds that human beings consciously create.
- The **sociological imagination** is the ability to grasp the relationship between our individual lives and the larger social forces that help to shape them. It helps us see the connections between our private lives and public issues.
- **Critical thinking** is the ability to evaluate claims about truth by using reason and evidence. Often we accept things as true because they are familiar, seem to mesh with our own experiences, and sound right. Critical thinking instead asks us to recognize poor arguments, reject statements not supported by evidence, and even question our own assumptions.
- Sociology's roots can be traced to the scientific revolution, the Enlightenment, industrialization and the birth of modern capitalism, and the urbanization of populations. Sociology emerged in part as a tool to enable people to understand dramatic changes taking place in modern societies.
- Sociology generally traces its classical roots to Auguste Comte, Émile Durkheim, Max Weber, and Karl Marx. Early work in sociology reflected the concerns of the men who founded the discipline.
- In the United States, scholars at the University of Chicago focused on reforming social problems stemming from industrialization and urbanization. Women and people of color worked on the margins of the discipline because of persistent discrimination.
- Sociologists base their study of the social world on different theoretical perspectives that shape theory and guide research, often resulting in different conclusions. The major sociological paradigms are **structural functionalism**, the **social conflict paradigm**, and **symbolic interactionism**.
- Major themes in sociology include the distribution of **power** and growing inequality, **globalization** and its accompanying social changes, the growth of **social diversity**, and the way advances in **technology** have changed communication, commerce, and communities.
- The early founders of sociology believed that scientific knowledge could lead to shared social progress. Some modern sociologists question whether such shared scientific understanding is indeed possible.

KEY TERMS

scientific, 4
sociology, 5
social embeddedness, 5
sociological imagination, 5
agency, 7
structure, 7
critical thinking, 8
norms, 10
anomie, 10
social statics, 11
social dynamics, 11
positivist, 11
social facts, 12
social solidarity, 12
collective conscience, 13
class conflict, 13
proletariat, 13
bourgeoisie, 13
means of production, 13
Verstehen, 14
formal rationality, 14
bureaucracies, 14
double consciousness, 15
sociological theories, 17
macro-level paradigms, 17
micro-level paradigm, 17
structural functionalism, 17
manifest functions, 18
latent functions, 19
social conflict paradigm, 19
symbolic interactionism, 21
symbols, 21
power, 21
inequality, 21
globalization, 22
social diversity, 22
ethnocentrism, 22
technology, 22

DISCUSSION QUESTIONS

1. Think about Mills's concept of the sociological imagination and its ambition to draw together what Mills called *private troubles* and *public issues.* Think of a private trouble that sociologists might classify as also being a public issue. Share your example with your classmates.

2. What is critical thinking? What does it mean to be a critical thinker in our approach to understanding society and social issues or problems?

3. In the chapter, we asked why there were so few "founding mothers" in sociology. What factors explain the dearth of women's voices? What about the lack of minority voices? What effects do you think these factors may have had on the development of the discipline?

4. What is theory? What is its function in the discipline of sociology?

5. Recall the three key theoretical paradigms discussed in this chapter—structural functionalism, conflict theory, and symbolic interactionism. Discuss the ways these diverse "glasses" analyze deviance, its labeling, and its punishment in society. Try applying a similar analysis to another social phenomenon, such as class inequality or traditional gender roles.

SAGE edge™

Sharpen your skills with SAGE edge at **edge.sagepub.com/chambliss2e**

A personalized approach to help you accomplish your course work goals in an easy-to-use learning environment.

DISCOVER SOCIOLOGICAL RESEARCH

IN THIS CHAPTER

WHAT DO YOU THINK?

1. What kinds of research questions could one pose in order to gain a better understanding of sociological issues like bullying, long-term poverty, gang violence, or the high dropout rate in some high schools? What kinds of research methods would be appropriate for studying these issues?
2. What factors do you think affect the honesty of people's responses to survey questions?
3. What makes a sociological research project ethical or unethical?

REUTERS/Lucy Nicholson

RESEARCHING THE CONSEQUENCES OF THE U.S. PRISON BOOM

The United States imprisons more of its people than any other modern country on the planet. About 3% of U.S. adults are in the correctional system: "2.2 million people in prisons and jails, and an additional 4.8 million on probation or parole" (Goffman, 2014, p. xi). Data show that the climb in the prison population began in the 1970s and rose steeply in the 1980s, with significant numbers of poor men and women of color pulled into the criminal justice system, many for minor drug crimes and other nonviolent offenses. The effects of this "prison boom" are not only individual; mass incarceration has also had consequences for already struggling neighborhoods in urban America (see Figures 2.1a and 2.1b).

In *On the Run: Fugitive Life in an American City* (2014), sociologist Alice Goffman writes that her work is an on-the-ground account of the U.S. prison boom: a close-up look at young men and women living in one poor and segregated Black community transformed by unprecedented levels of imprisonment and by the more hidden systems of policing and supervision that have accompanied them. Because the fear of capture and confinement has seeped into community members' basic activities of daily living—work, family, romance, friendship, and even much-needed medical care—it is an account of a community *on the run* (p. xii).

Goffman explores the norms and practices that govern life in a neighborhood ravaged by economic and social marginality and the pervasive effects of the reality and threat of imprisonment. For example, in the absence of opportunities for legitimate employment, she notes the birth of a shadow economy that caters to the "fugitive life" she describes: Some wily entrepreneurs peddle "clean" urine to neighbors who are on parole and subject to drug testing. Goffman's work is significant because it carefully examines the effects of the mass incarceration phenomenon on personal lives and relationships and the daily life of a community.

Goffman conducted research in the city of Philadelphia for six years, combining interviews with individuals working in the criminal justice system, including police and prison guards, and regular interactions with residents of her adopted neighborhood. She utilized participant and nonparticipant

FIGURE 2.1A Imprisonment Rates in Selected Philadelphia Neighborhoods, 2008

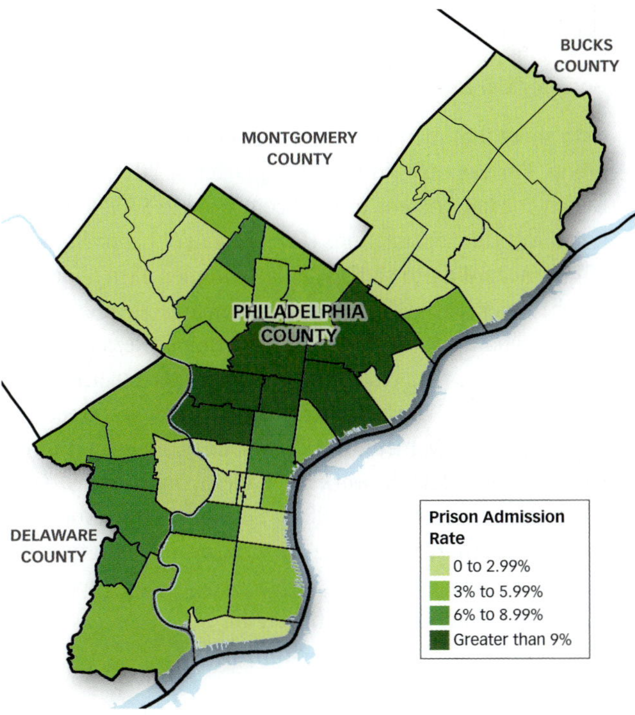

FIGURE 2.1B Percentage of Non-Whites in Selected Philadelphia Neighborhoods, 2008

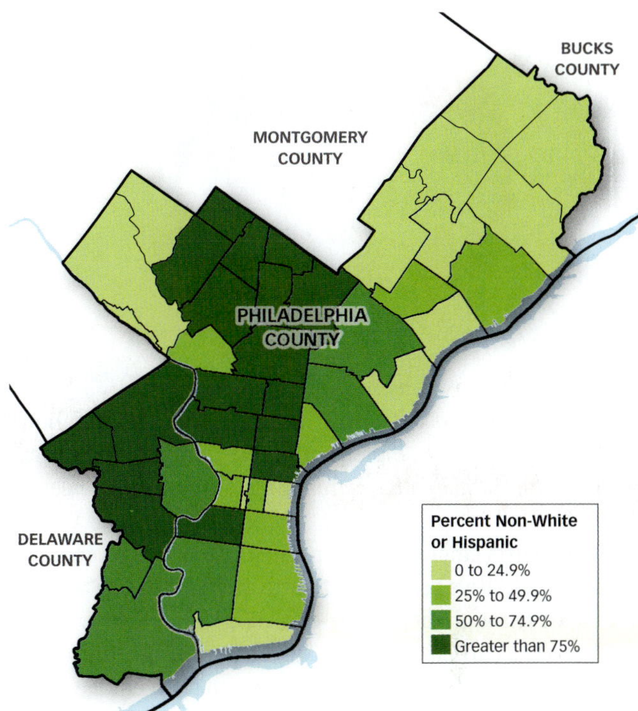

SOURCE: Based on data from the The Justice Mapping Center.

observation in gathering information about the social environment. Goffman's work is a good example of qualitative sociological research, and she recognizes its potential significance to academic and policy debates. Utilizing a scientific approach and rigorous field research, Goffman is able to cast light on how neighborhoods and their residents, whether or not they are involved in criminal activity, understand and experience the powerful consequences of mass imprisonment.

Scientific method: A way of learning about the world that combines logically constructed theory and systematic observation to provide explanations of how things work.

Deductive reasoning: The process of taking an existing theory and logically deducing that if the theory is accurate, we should discover other patterns of behavior consistent with it.

Hypotheses: Ideas about the world, derived from theories, that can be disproved when tested against observations.

Inductive reasoning: The process of generalizing to an entire category of phenomena from a particular set of observations.

In this chapter, we examine the ways sociologists like Alice Goffman study the social world. First, we distinguish between sociological understanding and common sense. Then we discuss the key steps in the research process itself. We examine how sociologists test their theories using a variety of research methods, and, finally, we consider the ethical implications of doing research on human subjects.

SOCIOLOGY AND COMMON SENSE

Science is a unique way of seeing and investigating the world around us. The essence of the **scientific method** is straightforward: It is *a process of gathering empirical (scientific and specific) data, creating theories, and rigorously testing theories.* In sociological research, theories and empirical data exist in a dynamic relationship (Figure 2.2). Some research begins from general theories, which offer "big picture" ideas about social life: **Deductive reasoning** *starts from broad theories but proceeds to break them down into more specific and testable hypotheses.* Sociological **hypotheses** are *ideas about the world that describe possible relationships between social phenomena.* Some research begins from the ground up: **Inductive reasoning**

■ **FIGURE 2.2 The Relationship Between Theory and Research**

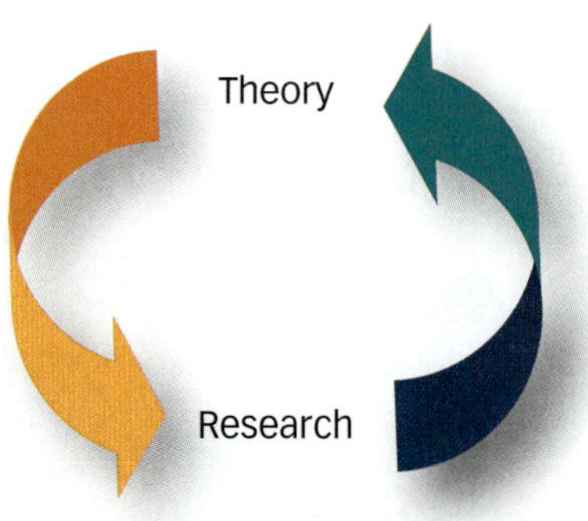

starts from specific data, such as interviews or field notes, which may focus on a single community or event, and endeavors to identify larger patterns from which to derive more general theories.

Sociologists employ the scientific method in both quantitative and qualitative research. **Quantitative research**, which is often done through methods such as large-scale surveys, *gathers data that can be quantified and offers insight into broad patterns of social behavior* (for example, the percentage of U.S. adults who use corporal punishment with their children) *and social attitudes* (for example, the percentage of U.S. adults who approve of corporal punishment) without necessarily delving into the meaning of or reasons for the identified phenomena. **Qualitative research**, such as that conducted by Alice Goffman, is *characterized by data that cannot be quantified (or converted into numbers), focusing instead on generating in-depth knowledge of social life, institutions, and processes* (for example, why parents in particular social groups are more or less likely to use spanking as a method of punishment). It relies on the gathering of data through methods such as focus groups, participant and nonparticipant observation, interviews, and archival research. Generally, population samples in qualitative research are small because they focus on in-depth understanding.

Personal experience and common sense about the world are often fine starting points for sociological research. They can, however, mislead us. In the 14th century, common sense suggested to people that the earth was flat; after all, it *looks* flat. Today, influenced by stereotypes and media portrayals of criminal behaviors, many people believe Black high school and college students are more likely than their White counterparts to use illegal drugs such as marijuana, cocaine, crack, and heroin. But common sense misleads on both counts. The earth is not flat (as you know!), and Black high school and college students are slightly *less* likely than White students to use illegal drugs (Table 2.1).

Consider the following ideas, which many believe to be true, though all are false:

Common Wisdom:

I know women who earn more than their husbands or boyfriends. The gender wage gap is no longer an issue in the United States.

Sociological Research:

Data show that men as a group earn more than women as a group. For example, in the first quarter of 2014, men had a weekly median income of $872 compared to $722 for women for all full-time occupations (U.S. Bureau of Labor Statistics, 2014f). According to statistical data, women earn about 82% of what men earn. This statistic compares all men and all women who work full-time and year-round. Reasons for the gap include worker characteristics (such as experience and education), job characteristics (such as hours required), devaluation of "women's work" by society, and pay discrimination against female workers (Cabeza, Johnson, & Tyner, 2011; Reskin & Padavic, 2002). So while some women, of course, earn more than some men, the overall pattern of men outearning women remains in place today. This topic is discussed in greater detail in Chapter 10.

Common Wisdom:

Homeless people are poor and lack adequate shelter because they do not work.

Sociological Research:

Some of the homeless cannot find work or are too disabled by mental or physical problems to work. Many, however, do

■ **TABLE 2.1 Annual Prevalence Rate of Drug Use by 12th Graders, 2013.**

	Marijuana	Cocaine	Crack	LSD	Ecstasy
White	35.6	0.7	1.0	2.5	4.0
Black	35.0	0.6	0.9	0.8	1.1
Hispanic	39.2	1.5	1.7	1.7	4.5

Johnston, L. D., O'Malley, P. M., Bachman, J. G., Schulenberg, J. E. & Miech, R.A. (2014). Demographic subgroup trends among adolescents in the use of various licit and illicit drugs, 1975–2013. *Monitoring the Future Occasional Paper No. 81*. Ann Arbor, MI: Institute for Social Research.

Quantitative research: Research that gathers data that can be quantified and offers insight into broad patterns of social behavior and social attitudes.

Qualitative research: Research that is characterized by data that cannot be quantified (or converted into numbers), focusing instead on generating in-depth knowledge of social life, institutions, and processes.

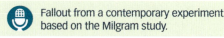

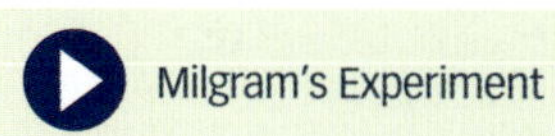

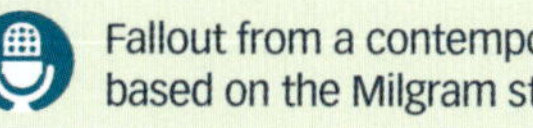

Fallout from a contemporary experiment based on the Milgram study.

© Bettmann/CORBIS

The Metropolitan Washington Council of Governments distinguishes between the "permanently supported homeless," who have housing but are at risk due to extreme poverty and/or disability, and the "chronically homeless," who are continually homeless for a year or more or at least four times in three years. Do you think that these categories fully encompass the homeless population?

work. Research suggests that about 44% of homeless adults work for pay (National Coalition for the Homeless, 2009b), and the U.S. Conference of Mayors (2011) reports that 15% of the homeless are regularly employed full- or part-time. However, low wages and poor benefits in the service industry, where many less educated people work, as well as a shortage of adequate housing options for low-income families, can make finding permanent shelter a challenge even for those who work for pay. To understand how declining wages magnify the strain on low-income families, consider this: In many U.S. cities, to make ends meet, a household needs more than one full-time minimum-wage employee to afford the fair market rent price for a two-bedroom apartment (National Low Income Housing Coalition, 2009). The contemporary reality is that wages are not keeping up with the rate of inflation, which further adds to the economic hardships that low-income families endure. These topics are discussed in fuller detail in Chapter 7.

Common Wisdom:

Education is the great equalizer. All children in the United States have the opportunity to get a good education. Low academic achievement is a personal failure.

Sociological Research:

Public education is free and open to all in the United States, but the quality of education can vary dramatically. Consider the fact that in many U.S. states and localities, a major source of public school funding is local property taxes, which constitute an average of about 44% of funding (state and federal allocations make up the rest). As such, communities with high property values have richer sources of funding from which to draw educational resources, while poor communities—even those with high tax rates—have more limited pools. As well, high levels of racial segregation persist in U.S. schools. In fact, Latino and Black students are more likely to be in segregated schools today than were their counterparts in earlier decades. Research shows a relationship between academic performance and class and racial segregation: Students who are not isolated in poor, racially segregated schools perform better on a variety of academic measures than those who are (Condron, 2009; Logan, Minca, & Adar, 2012). The problem of low academic achievement is complex, and no single variable can explain it. At the same time, the magnitude and persistence of this problem suggests that we are looking at a phenomenon that is a public issue rather than just a personal trouble. We discuss issues of class, race, and educational attainment further in Chapter 12.

Even deeply held and widely shared beliefs about society and social groups may be inaccurate—or more nuanced and complex than they appear on the surface. Until it is tested, common sense is merely conjecture. Careful research allows us to test our beliefs to gauge whether they are valid or merely anecdotal. From a sociological standpoint, empirical evidence is granted greater weight than common sense. By basing their decisions on scientific evidence rather than personal beliefs or common wisdom, researchers and students can draw informed conclusions and policy makers can ensure that policies and programs are data driven and maximally effective.

RESEARCH AND THE SCIENTIFIC METHOD

Scientific theories *answer questions about how and why scientific observations are as they are.* A good scientific theory has the following characteristics:

- *It is logically consistent.* One part of the theory does not contradict another part.
- *It can be disproved.* If the findings contradict the theory, then we can deduce that the theory is wrong. While we can say that testing has failed to disprove the theory, however, we cannot assume the theory is "true" if testing confirms it. Theories are always subject to further testing, which may point to needed revisions, highlight limitations, or strengthen conclusions.

Scientific theories: Explanations of how and why scientific observations are as they are.

CQR Sentencing Reform for Drugs

Qualitative v. Quantitative Research Methods

Theories are made up of **concepts**, ideas that summarize a set of phenomena. Concepts are the building blocks of research and prepare a solid foundation for sociological work. Some of the key concepts in sociology are social stratification, social class, power, inequality, and diversity, which we introduced in the opening chapter.

In order to gather data and create viable theories, we need to define concepts in ways that are precise and measurable. A study of social class, for example, would need to begin with a working definition of that term. An **operational definition** of a concept *describes the concept in such a way that we can observe and measure it.* Many sociologists define social class in terms of dimensions such as income, wealth, education, occupation, and consumption patterns. Each of these aspects of class has the potential to be measurable. We may construct operational definitions in terms of *qualities* or *quantities* (Babbie, 1998; Neuman, 2000). In terms of qualities, we might say, for instance, that the "upper-middle class" is composed of those who have completed graduate or professional degrees, even though there may be a broad income spread between those with master's degrees in English and those with master's degrees in business administration. This definition is based on an assumption of class as a social position that derives from educational attainment. Alternatively, using quantity as a key measure, we might operationally define "upper class" as households with annual income greater than $150,000 and "lower class" as households with annual income of less than $20,000. This definition takes income as the preeminent determinant of class position, irrespective of education.

Consider a social issue of contemporary interest—bullying. Imagine that you want to conduct a research study of bullying to determine how many female middle schoolers have experienced bullying in the past academic year. You would need to begin with a clear definition of bullying that operationalizes the term. That is, in order to measure how many girls have experienced bullying, you would need to articulate *what constitutes bullying.* Would you include physical bullying? If so, how many instances of being pushed or punched would constitute bullying? Would you include cyberbullying? What kinds of behaviors would be included in that category? To study a phenomenon like bullying, it is not enough to assume that "we know it when we see it." Empirical research relies on the careful and specific definition of terms and the recognition of how definitions and methods affect research outcomes.

RELATIONSHIPS BETWEEN VARIABLES

In studying social relationships, sociologists also need *variables.* A **variable** is *a concept that can take on two or more possible values.* For instance, sex can be male or female, work status can be employed or unemployed, and geographic location can be inner-city, suburbs, or rural area. We can measure variables both *quantitatively* and *qualitatively.* **Quantitative variables** include *factors we can count,* such as crime rates, unemployment rates, and drug use frequency. **Qualitative variables** are *variables that express qualities and do not have numerical values.* Qualitative variables might include physical characteristics, such as gender or eye color, or attitudinal characteristics, such as a parent's preference for a private or public school or a commuter's preference for riding public transportation or driving to work.

© Martin Ruetschi/Keystone/Corbis

Some research on bullying relies on self-reports, while other data come from peer reports. Recent research (Branson & Cornell, 2009) suggests that more than twice as many students (11%) were labeled bullies in peer reports than in self-reports (5%), highlighting the fact that any method of data collection has limitations.

Sociological research often tries to establish a relationship between two or more variables. Suppose you want to find out whether more education is associated with higher earnings. After asking people about their years of schooling and their annual incomes, both of which are quantitative variables, you could estimate the degree of *correlation* between the two. **Correlation**—literally, "co-relationship"—is *the degree to which two or more variables are associated with one another.* Correlating the two variables "years of education" and "annual income" demonstrates that the greater the education, the higher the income (Figure 2.3). (Do you see the exception to that relationship? How might you explain it?)

Concepts: Ideas that describe a number of things that have something in common.

Operational definition: A definition of a concept that allows the concept to be observed and measured.

Variable: A concept or its empirical measure that can take on multiple values.

Quantitative variables: Factors that can be counted.

Qualitative variables: Variables that express qualities and do not have numerical values.

Correlation: The degree to which two or more variables are associated with one another.

When two variables are correlated, we are often tempted to infer a **causal relationship**, *a relationship between two variables in which one is the cause of the other.* However, just because two variables are correlated, we cannot assume that one causes the other. For example, ice cream sales rise significantly during the summer, as does the homicide rate. These two events are correlated in the sense that both increase during the hottest months. However, because the sharp rise in ice cream sales does not *cause* rates of homicide to increase (nor, clearly, does the rise in homicide rates cause a spike in ice cream consumption), these two phenomena do not have a causal relationship. *Correlation does not equal causation.*

Sometimes an observed correlation between two variables is the result of a **spurious relationship**—that is, a *correlation between two or more variables caused by another factor that is not being measured.* In the example above, the common factor missed in the relationship is, in fact, the temperature. When it's hot, more people want to eat ice cream. Studies also show that rising temperatures are linked to an increase in violent crimes—though after a certain temperature threshold (about 90 degrees), crimes wane again (Gamble & Hess, 2012). Among the reasons more violent crimes are committed in hot weather is the fact that people spend more time outdoors in social interactions when it is hot, which can lead to confrontations.

FIGURE 2.3 Correlation Between Education and Median Weekly Earnings in the United States, 2013

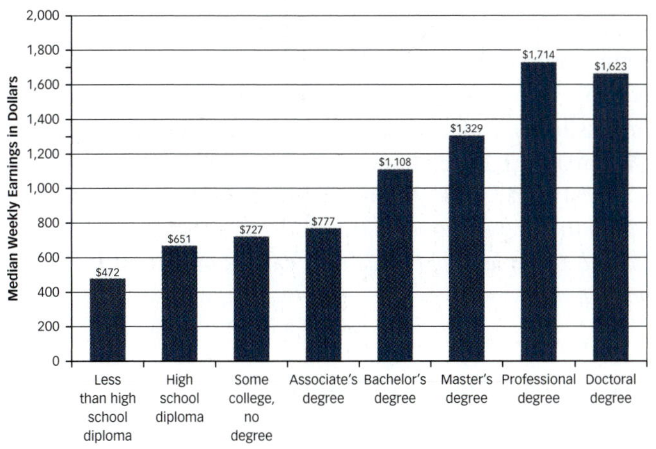

SOURCE: Bureau of Labor Statistics. (2013). Education pays. *Employment projections.* Washington, DC: U.S. Government Printing Office.

Causal relationship: A relationship between two variables in which one variable is the cause of the other.

Spurious relationship: A correlation between two or more variables that is actually the result of something else that is not being measured, rather than a causal link between the variables themselves.

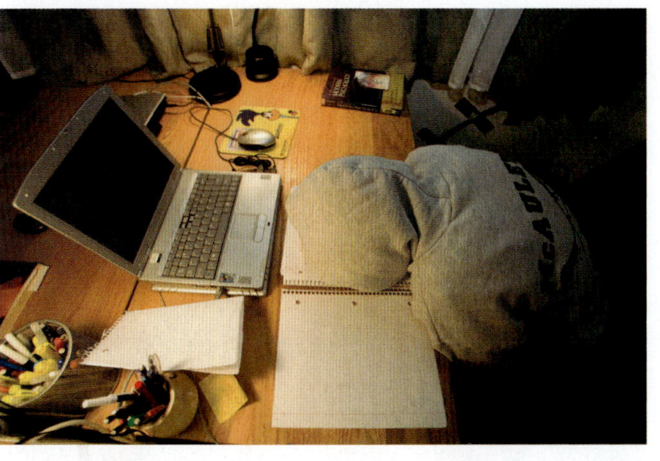

Getting enough sleep is one factor that can help students maintain good grades in college. How would you design a research study to examine the question of which factors correlate most strongly with solid grades?

Let's take another example that is close to home: Imagine that your school newspaper publishes a study concluding that coffee drinking causes poor test grades. The story is based on a survey of students that found those who reported drinking a lot of coffee the night before an exam scored lower than did their peers who had consumed little or no coffee. Having studied sociology, you wonder whether this relationship might be spurious. What is the "something else" that is not being measured here? Could it be that students who did not study in the days and weeks prior to the test and stayed up late the night before cramming—probably consuming a lot of coffee as they fought sleep—received lower test grades than did peers who studied earlier and got adequate sleep the night before the test? The overlooked variable, then, is the amount of studying students did in the weeks preceding the exam, and we are likely to find a positive correlation and evidence of causation in looking at time spent studying and grade outcomes.

Sociologists attempt to develop theories systematically by offering clear operational definitions, collecting unbiased data, and identifying evidence-based relationships between variables. Sociological research methods usually yield credible and useful data, but we must always critically analyze the results to ensure their validity and reliability and to check that hypothesized relationships are not spurious.

TESTING THEORIES AND HYPOTHESES

Once we have defined concepts and variables with which to work, we can endeavor to test a theory by positing a hypothesis. Hypotheses enable scientists to check the accuracy of their theories. For example, consider state-level data on obesity and poverty (Figures 2.4 and 2.5). Data from the U.S. Census Bureau for 2012 show that some positive correlation exists

FIGURE 2.4 **Self-Reported Obesity Rates by State, 2012**

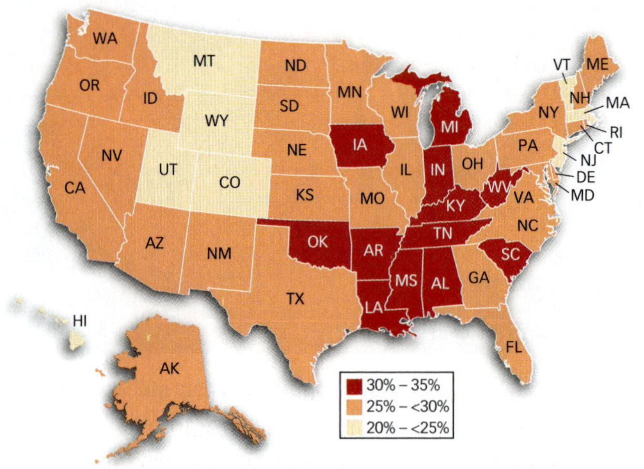

SOURCE: Centers for Disease Control. (2011). Prevalence of self-reported obesity among U.S. adults. *Behavior risk factor surveillance system.* Washington, DC.

FIGURE 2.5 **Poverty Rates by State, 2012**

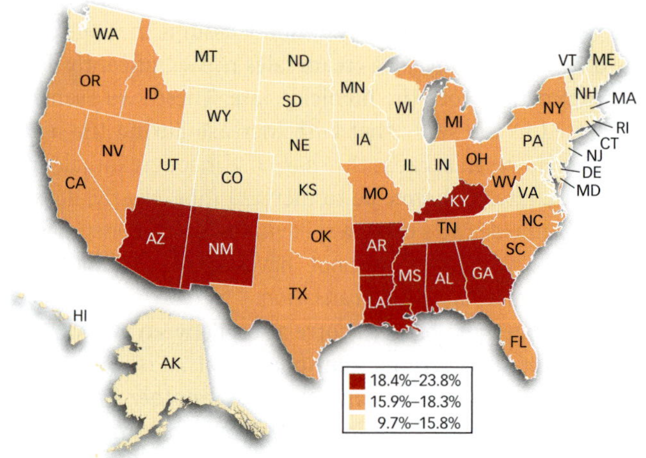

SOURCE: U.S. Census Bureau, "American FactFinder," 2010 American Community Survey.

between obesity and poverty rates at the state level. A positive correlation is *a relationship showing that as one variable rises or falls, the other does as well.* The variables' common trajectory suggests a possible relationship between poverty and obesity (Table 2.2), although, as we noted above, sociologists are quick to point out that correlation does not equal causation. Researchers are interested in creating and testing hypotheses to explain cases of positive correlation—they are also interested in explaining exceptions to the pattern of correlation between two (or more) variables.

In fact, researchers have explored and hypothesized the relationship between poverty and obesity. Among the conclusions they have drawn is that living in poverty—and particularly living in poor neighborhoods—puts people at higher risk of obesity, though the risk is greater for women than for men (Centers for Disease Control and Prevention, 2012d; Hedwig, 2011; Smith, 2009). Among the factors that researchers have identified as contributing to a causal path between poverty and obesity are the lack of access to healthy food choices, the lack of access to safe and nearby spaces for physical exercise, and a deficit of time to cook healthy foods and exercise. They have also cited the stress induced by poverty. While the data cannot lead us to conclude decisively that poverty is a cause of obesity, research can help us to gather evidence that supports or refutes a hypothesis about the relationship between these two variables. We look at this issue in greater depth in Chapter 16.

In the case of a **negative correlation**, *one variable increases as the other decreases.* As we discuss later in Chapter 11, which focuses on the family and society, researchers have found a negative correlation between male unemployment and rates of marriage. That is, as rates of male unemployment in a community rise, rates of marriage in the community fall. Observing this relationship, sociologists have conducted research to test explanations for it (Edin & Kefalas, 2005; Wilson, 2010).

Keep in mind that we can never prove theories to be decisively right—we can only prove them wrong. Proving a theory right would require the scientific testing of absolutely every possible hypothesis based on that theory—a fundamental impossibility. In fact, good theories are constructed in a way that makes it logically possible to prove them wrong. This is Karl Popper's (1959) famous **principle of falsification**, or **falsifiability**, which holds that *to be scientific, a theory must lead to testable hypotheses that can be disproved if they are wrong.*

VALIDITY AND RELIABILITY

For theories and hypotheses to be testable, both the concepts used to construct them and the measurements used to test

Negative correlation: A relation between two variables in which one increases as the other decreases.

Principle of falsification: The principle, advanced by philosopher Karl Popper, that a scientific theory must lead to testable hypotheses that can be disproved if they are wrong.

Falsifiability: The ability for a theory to be disproved; the logical possibility for a theory to be tested and proved false.

TABLE 2.2 Top 10 States: Obesity and Poverty, 2012

State	Percentage Obese	State	Percentage in Poverty
Louisiana	34.7	Mississippi	24.2
Mississippi	34.6	New Mexico	20.8
Arkansas	34.5	Louisiana	19.9
West Virginia	33.8	Arkansas	19.8
Alabama	33.0	Kentucky	19.4
Oklahoma	32.2	Georgia	19.2
South Carolina	31.6	Alabama	19.0
Indiana	31.4	Arizona	18.7
Kentucky	31.3	South Carolina	18.3
Michigan and Tennessee (tie)	31.1	North Carolina	18.0

SOURCES: U.S. Census Bureau. (2013). *Poverty: 2000 to 2012, American Community Survey Briefs; Centers for Disease Control and Prevention.* (2014). Prevalence of self-reported obesity among U.S. adults, 2012.

them must be accurate. When our observations adequately reflect the real world, our findings have **validity**—that is, *the concepts and measurements accurately represent what they claim to represent.* For example, suppose you want to know whether the crime rate in the United States has gone up or down. For years sociologists depended on police reports to measure crime. However, researchers could assess the validity of these tallies only if subsequent surveys were administered nationally to victims of crime. If the victim tallies matched those of the police reports, then researchers could say the police reports were a valid measure of crime in the United States. The National Crime Victimization Survey (NCVS) enables researchers to assess validity because it offers data on victimization, even for crimes that have not been reported to authorities.

Validity: The degree to which concepts and their measurements accurately represent what they claim to represent.

Reliability: The extent to which researchers' findings are consistent with the findings of different studies of the same thing, or with the findings of the same study over time.

Bias: A characteristic of results that systematically misrepresent the true nature of what is being studied.

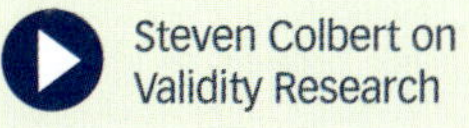
Steven Colbert on Validity Research

Sociologists are also concerned with the reliability of their findings. **Reliability** is *the extent to which the findings are consistent with the findings of different studies of the same phenomenon, or with the findings of the same study over time.* Sociological research may suffer from problems of validity and reliability because of **bias**, *a characteristic of results that systematically misrepresent the full dimensions of what is being studied.* Bias can creep into research due to the use of inappropriate measurement instruments. For example, suppose the administrator of a city wants to know whether homelessness has risen in recent years. She operationally defines "the homeless" as those who sleep in the street or in shelters and dispatches her team of researchers to city shelters to count the number of people occupying shelter beds or sleeping on street corners or park benches. A sociologist reviewing the research team's results might question the administrator's operational definition of what it means to be homeless and, by extension, her findings. Are the homeless solely those spending nights in shelters or on the streets? What about those who stay with friends after eviction or camp out in their cars? In this instance, a sociologist might suggest that the city's measure is biased because it misrepresents (and undercounts) the homeless population by failing to define the concept in a way that captures the broad manifestations of homelessness.

Bias can also occur in research when respondents do not tell the truth (see Table 2.3). A good example of this is a study in which respondents were asked whether they used illegal drugs or had driven while impaired. All were asked the same questions, but some were wired to a machine they were told was a lie detector. The subjects who thought their truthfulness was being monitored by a lie detector reported higher rates of illegal drug use than did subjects who did not. Based on the assumption that actual drug use would be about the same for both groups, the researchers concluded that the subjects who were not connected to the device were underreporting their actual illegal drug use and that simply asking people about drug use would lead to biased findings because respondents would not tell the truth. Do you think truthfulness of respondents is a general problem, or is it one researchers are likely to encounter only where sensitive issues such as drug use or racism are at issue?

OBJECTIVITY IN SCIENTIFIC RESEARCH

Even if sociologists develop theories based on good operational definitions and collect valid and reliable data, like all human beings they have passions and biases that may color their research. For example, criminologists long ignored the criminality of women because they assumed that women were not disposed toward criminal behavior. Researchers therefore did not have an accurate picture of women and crime until this bias was recognized and rectified.

INEQUALITY MATTERS

HOW MANY PEOPLE SUFFER FROM HOMELESSNESS?

Homelessness is a social problem in the United States. But how extensive is it? The National Law Center on Homelessness and Poverty (2012) estimates that more than 3 million people experience homelessness over the course of a year across the United States. Of these, 1.3 million are children; more than one-third of the entire homeless population is made up of families. While the majority of the homeless have access to transitional housing or emergency shelters, approximately 4 out of 10 are unsheltered, living in improvised conditions that are not suited for human habitation. Despite a decrease in the homeless population nationally, the rates for 24 individual states and the District of Columbia increased between 2009 and 2011 (National Alliance to End Homelessness, 2012).

Statistics vary, however, depending on the definitions and counting methodologies employed. In the early 1980s, the U.S. government was under pressure to provide services and assistance to a population of homeless that some claimed was large and growing. In response, the U.S. Department of Housing and Urban Development (HUD) conducted a study to determine the number of homeless people in cities and towns across the country. After analyzing all existing studies, government researchers called providers of services to the homeless and other experts in 60 cities and asked them to estimate the numbers of homeless people in their communities. Based on this research, the government concluded there were 250,000 to 350,000 homeless people in the United States. This figure was considerably lower than the estimate of 2 million that came from other sources outside the government (Burt, 1992).

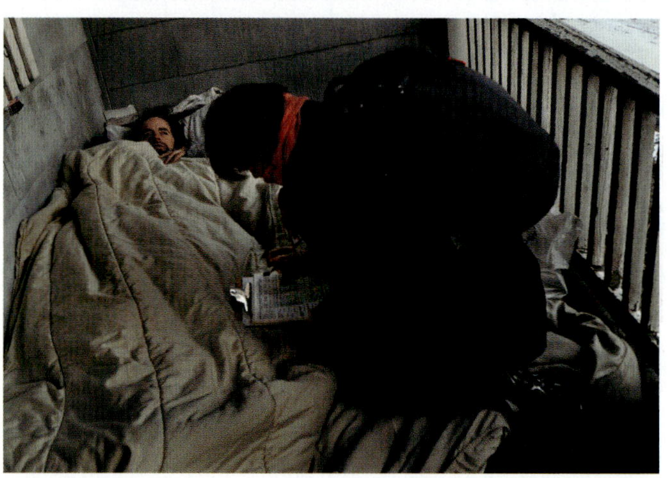
The Washington Post/Contributor/Getty Images

Understanding of research methods will help you recognize the challenges in gathering reliable statistics on populations that are outside the mainstream. In this photo, a volunteer conducts an interview with a homeless man, which helps local authorities assess how many homeless people are in the city and why they lack shelter.

Politicians used the HUD figures extensively, although some sociologists were skeptical (Appelbaum, 1986; Appelbaum, Dolny, Dreier, & Gilderbloom, 1991). First, HUD's *operational definition* of homelessness included only people sleeping on the streets and in shelters; it effectively excluded homeless people living in cars or abandoned buildings or taking temporary shelter with friends. Second, HUD based its figures on the estimates of shelter providers, police officers, and other local experts who admitted they were often only guessing. Finally, the HUD figures were based almost entirely on estimates of the homeless in the downtown areas of big cities, a methodological bias that excluded the numerous homeless people who lived in surrounding towns and suburbs. As a result of these problems, HUD's estimate of the national homeless population lacked validity.

THINK IT THROUGH

▶ Subsequent research has confirmed that by the early 1990s there were as many as 1 million homeless in the United States—three to four times the estimate produced by the government study. An axiom of sociological research is that it is not what you think you know that matters, but how you came to know it. The homeless represent a transient population that is challenging to count. The homeless have no fixed addresses, no consistent billing statements, and no easy way for researchers to locate them. What methods might you employ to attempt to systematically count the homeless people in your community? What kinds of resources do you think you would need?

TABLE 2.3 How Truthful Are Survey Respondents? (in percentages)

Survey Question	Threat of Validation		No Threat of Validation	
	Anonymous	Named	Anonymous	Named
Ever smoked?	63.5	72.9	60.5	67.8
Smoked in the last month?	34.5	39.5	25.9	21.8
Smoked in the last week?	26.0	25.5	14.4	17.6

SOURCE: Adams, J., Parkinson, L., Sanson-Fisher, R. W., & Walsh, R. A. (2008). Enhancing self-report of adolescent smoking: The effects of bogus pipeline and anonymity. *Addictive Behaviors, 33*(10), 1291–1296.

Personal values and beliefs may affect a researcher's **objectivity**, or *ability to represent the object of study accurately*. In the 19th century, sociologist Max Weber argued that in order for scientific research to be objective it has to have **value neutrality**—that is, *the course of the research must be free of the influence of personal beliefs and opinions*. The sociologist should acknowledge personal biases and assumptions, make them explicit, and prevent them from getting in the way of observation and reporting.

How can we best achieve objectivity? First, recall Karl Popper's principle of falsification, which proposes that the goal of research is not to prove our ideas correct but to find out whether they are wrong. To accomplish this, researchers must be willing to accept that the data they collect might contradict their most passionate convictions. Research should deepen human understanding, not prove a particular point of view.

Objectivity: The ability to represent the object of study accurately.

Value neutrality: The characteristic of being free of personal beliefs and opinions that would influence the course of research.

Replication: The repetition of a previous study using a different sample or population to verify or refute the original findings.

Research methods: Specific techniques for systematically gathering data.

Validity and Reliability homicide studies

A second way we can ensure objectivity is to invite others to draw their own conclusions about the validity of our data through **replication**, *the repetition of a previous study using a different sample or population to verify or refute the original findings*. For research to be replicated, the original study must spell out in detail the research methods employed. If potential replicators cannot conduct their studies exactly as the original study was performed, they might accidentally introduce unwanted variables. To ensure the most accurate replication of their work, researchers should archive original materials such as questionnaires and field notes and allow replicators access to them.

Popper (1959) described scientific discovery as an ongoing process of "confrontation and refutation." Sociologists usually subject their work to this process by publishing their results in scholarly journals. Submitted research undergoes a rigorous process of peer review, in which other experts in the field of study examine the work before the results are finalized and published. Once research has been published in a reputable journal such as the *American Sociological Review* or the *Journal of Health and Social Behavior*, other scholars read it with a critical eye. The study may then be replicated in different settings.

DOING SOCIOLOGICAL RESEARCH

Sociological research requires careful preparation and a clear plan that guides the work. The purpose of a sociological research project may be to obtain preliminary knowledge that will help formulate a theory or to evaluate an existing theory about society and social life. As part of the strategy, the researcher selects from a variety of **research methods**—*specific techniques for systematically gathering data*. In the following sections, we look at a range of research methods and examine their advantages and disadvantages. We also discuss how you might prepare a sociological research project of your own.

SOCIOLOGICAL RESEARCH METHODS

Sociologists employ a variety of methods to learn about the social world (Table 2.4). Since each has strengths and weaknesses, a good research strategy may be to use several different methods. If they all yield similar findings, the researcher is more likely to have confidence in the results. The principal methods are the survey, fieldwork (either participant observation or detached observation), experimentation, working with existing information, and participatory research.

TABLE 2.4 Key Sociological Research Methods

Method	Appropriate Circumstances
Survey research	When basic information about a large population is desired. Sociologists usually conduct survey research by selecting samples that are representative of the entire populations of interest.
Fieldwork	When detailed information is sought, and when surveys are impractical for getting the information desired (for example, in studying youth gangs). Fieldwork usually relies on relatively small samples, especially compared to surveys.
Detached observation	When researchers desire to stay removed from the people being studied and must gather data in a way that minimizes impact on the subjects. Detached observations are often supplemented with face-to-face interviews.
Participant observation	When firsthand knowledge of the subjects' direct experience is desired, including a deeper understanding of their lives.
Experimentation	When it is possible to create experimental and control groups that are matched on relevant variables but provided with different experiences in the experiment.
Use of existing information	When direct acquisition of data is either not feasible or not desirable because the event studied occurred in the past or because gathering the data would be too costly or too difficult.
Participatory research	When a primary goal is training people to gain political or economic power and acquire the necessary skills to do the research themselves.

SURVEY RESEARCH

A **survey** relies on a *questionnaire or interviews with a group of people in person or by telephone or e-mail to determine their characteristics, opinions, and behaviors.* Surveys are versatile, and sociologists often use them to test theories or simply to gather data. Some survey instruments, such as National Opinion Research Center questionnaires, consist of *closed-ended questions* that respondents answer by choosing from among the responses presented. Others, such as the University of Chicago's Social Opportunity Survey, consist of *open-ended questions* that permit respondents to answer in their own words.

An example of survey research conducted for data collection is the largest survey in the nation, the U.S. Census, which is conducted every 10 years. The census is not designed to test any particular theory. Rather, it gathers voluminous data about U.S. residents that researchers, including sociologists, use to test and develop a variety of theories.

Usually, a survey is conducted on *a relatively small number of people,* a **sample**, selected to represent a **population**, *the whole group of people to be studied.* The first step in designing a survey is to identify the population of interest. Imagine that you are doing a study of behavioral factors that affect grades in college. Who would you survey? Members of a certain age group only? People in the airline industry? Pet owners? To conduct a study well, we need to identify clearly the survey population that will most effectively help us answer the research question. In your study you would most likely choose to survey students now in college, because they offer the best opportunity to correlate grades with particular behaviors.

Once we have identified a population of interest, we will usually select a sample, as we seldom have the time or money to talk to all the members of a given population, especially if it is a large one. Other things being equal, larger samples better represent the population than smaller ones. However, with proper sampling techniques, sociologists can use relatively small (and therefore inexpensive) samples to represent large populations. For instance, a well-chosen sample of 1,000 U.S. voters can be used to represent 100,000 U.S. voters with a fair degree of accuracy, enabling surveys to make election predictions with reasonable confidence. Sampling is also used for looking at social phenomena such as drug or alcohol use in a population: CNN reported recently that 17% of high schoolers drink, smoke, or use drugs during the school day, based on a 1,000-student sample polled by the National Center on Addiction and Substance Abuse at Columbia University (Azuz, 2012).

Survey: A research method that uses a questionnaire or interviews administered to a group of people in person or by telephone or e-mail to determine their characteristics, opinions, and behaviors.

Sample: A portion of the larger population selected to represent the whole.

Population: The whole group of people studied in sociological research.

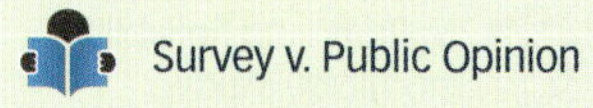

© James Marshall/Corbis

Since it is often impossible to sample every person in a target population, being well versed in research methodology enables a researcher to produce empirically rigorous data with a representative population sample.

Ideally, a sample should reflect the composition of the population we are studying. For instance, if you want to be able to use your research data about college students to generalize about the entire college student population of the United States, you would need to collect proportional samples from 2-year colleges, 4-year colleges, large universities, community colleges, online schools, and so on. It would not be adequate to survey only students at online colleges or only female students at private 4-year schools.

To avoid bias in surveys, sociologists may use **random sampling**, whereby *everyone in the population of interest has an equal chance of being chosen for the study.* Typically, they make or obtain a list of everyone in the population of interest. Then they draw names or phone numbers, for instance, by chance until the desired sample size is reached (today, most such work is done by computers). Large-scale random sample surveys permit researchers to draw conclusions about large numbers of people on the basis of relatively small numbers of respondents. This is an advantage in terms of time and money.

In constructing surveys, sociologists must take care to ensure that the questions and their possible responses will capture the respondents' points of view. The wording of questions is an important factor; poor wording can produce misleading results, as the following example illustrates. In 1993, an American Jewish Committee/Roper poll was taken to examine public attitudes and beliefs about the Holocaust. To the astonishment of many, results indicated that fully 22% of survey respondents expressed a belief the Holocaust had never happened. Not immediately noticed was the fact that the survey contained some very awkward wording, including the question "Does it seem possible or does it seem impossible to you that the Nazi extermination of the Jews never happened?" Can you see why such a question might produce a questionable result? The question's compound structure and double-negative wording almost certainly confused many respondents.

The American Jewish Committee released a second survey with different wording: "Does it seem possible to you that the Nazi extermination of the Jews never happened, or do you feel certain that it happened?" The results of the second poll were quite different. Only about 1% of respondents thought it was possible the Holocaust never happened, while 8% were unsure (Kagay, 1994). Despite the follow-up poll that corrected the mistaken perception of the previous poll's results, the new poll was not as methodologically rigorous as it could have been; a single survey question should ask for only one type of response. The American Jewish Committee's second survey contained a question that attempted to gauge two different responses simultaneously.

A weakness of surveys is that they may reveal what people say rather than what they do. Responses are sometimes self-serving, intended to make the interviewee look good in the eyes of the researcher. As we saw in an earlier example, a respondent may not wish to reveal his or her drinking or drug habits. A well-constructed survey, however, can overcome these problems. Assuring the respondent of anonymity, assigning interviewers with whom respondents feel comfortable, and building in questions that ask for the same information in different ways can reduce self-serving bias in survey research.

FIELDWORK

Fieldwork is *a method of research that uses in-depth and often extended study to describe and analyze a group or community.* Sometimes called *ethnography,* it takes the researcher into the "field," where he or she directly observes—and sometimes interacts with—subjects in their social environment. Social scientists, including sociologists and anthropologists, have employed fieldwork to study everything from hoboes and working-class gangs in the 1930s (Anderson, 1940; Whyte, 1943) to prostitution and drug use among inner-city women (Maher, 1997) and Vietnam veterans motorcycling across the country to the Vietnam Veterans Memorial in Washington, D.C. (Michalowski & Dubisch, 2001). Alice Goffman's (2014) work on the underground economy is another example of the use of fieldwork in sociological research.

Random sampling: Sampling in which everyone in the population of interest has an equal chance of being chosen for the study.

Fieldwork: A research method that relies on in-depth and often extended study of a group or community.

Field Work Methods

Most fieldwork combines several different methods of gathering information. These include interviews, detached observation, and participant observation.

An **interview** is *a detailed conversation designed to obtain in-depth information about a person and his or her activities.* When used in surveys, interview questions may be either open-ended or closed-ended. They may also be formal or informal. In fieldwork, the questions are usually open-ended to allow respondents to answer in their own words. Sometimes the interviewer prepares a detailed set of questions; at other times, the best approach is simply to have a list of relevant topics to cover.

Good researchers guard against influencing respondents' answers. In particular, they avoid the use of **leading questions**—that is, *questions that tend to elicit particular responses.* Imagine a question on attitudes toward the marine environment that reads "Do you believe tuna fishing with broad nets, which leads to the violent deaths of dolphins, should be regulated?" The bias in this question is obvious—the stated association of broad nets with violent dolphin deaths creates a bias in favor of a yes answer. Accurate data depend on good questions that do not lead respondents to answer in particular ways.

Sometimes a study requires that researchers in the field keep a distance from the people they are studying and simply observe without getting involved. The people being observed may or may not know they are being observed. This approach is called *detached observation.* In his study of two delinquent gangs (the "Saints" and the "Roughnecks"), William J. Chambliss, coauthor of this text, spent many hours observing gang members without actually being involved in what they were doing. With the gang members' permission, he sat in his car with the window rolled down so he could hear them talk and watch their behavior while they hung out on a street corner. At other times, he would observe them playing pool while he played at a nearby table. Chambliss sometimes followed gang members in his car as they drove around in theirs and sat near enough to them in bars and cafés to hear their conversations. Through his observations at a distance, he was able to gather detailed information on the kinds of delinquencies the gang members engaged in. He was also able to unravel some of the social processes that led to their behavior and observe other people's reactions to it.

Detached observation is particularly useful when the researcher has reason to believe other forms of fieldwork might influence the behavior of the people to be observed. It is also helpful for checking the validity of what the researcher has been told in interviews. A great deal of sociological information about illegal behavior has been gathered through detached observation.

One problem with detached observation is that the information gathered is likely to be incomplete. Without actually talking to people, we are unable to check our impressions against their experiences. For this reason, detached observation is usually supplemented by in-depth interviews. In his study of the delinquent gang members, Chambliss (1973, 2001) periodically interviewed them to complement his findings and check the accuracy of his detached observations.

Another type of fieldwork is *participant observation,* a mixture of active participation and detached observation. Participant observation can sometimes be dangerous. Chambliss's (1988b) research on organized crime and police corruption in Seattle, Washington, exposed him to threats from the police and organized crime network members who feared he would reveal their criminal activities. Goffman's (2014) work also included participant observation; she spent significant amounts of time with the residents of the Philadelphia neighborhood she studied, seeking to carefully document their voices and experiences.

EXPERIMENTATION

Experiments are *research techniques for investigating cause and effect under controlled conditions.* We construct experiments to measure the effects of **independent or experimental variables**, *variables we change intentionally,* on **dependent variables**, which *change as a result of our alterations to the independent variables.* To put it another way, researchers modify one controllable variable (such as diet or exposure to violent movie scenes) to see what happens to another variable (such as willingness to socialize or the display of aggression). Some variables, such as sex, ethnicity, and height, do not change in response to stimuli and thus do not make useful dependent variables.

In a typical experiment, researchers select participants who share characteristics such as age, education, social class, or experiences that are relevant to the experiment. The participants are then randomly assigned to two groups. The first, called the *experimental group,* is exposed to the independent variable—the variable the researchers hypothesize will affect the subjects' behavior. The second group is assigned to the *control group.* These subjects are not exposed to the independent variable—they receive no special attention. The researchers then measure both groups for the dependent variable. For example, if a neuroscientist wanted to conduct an experiment

Interview: A detailed conversation designed to obtain in-depth information about a person and his or her activities.

Leading questions: Questions that tend to elicit particular responses.

Experiments: Research techniques for investigating cause and effect under controlled conditions.

Independent or experimental variables: Variables that cause changes in other variables.

Dependent variables: Variables that change as a result of changes in other variables.

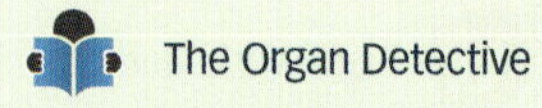

Daniel Hurst/Stock Connection Worldwide/Newscom

When looking at the relationship between violent video games and violent behaviors, researchers must account for many variables. What variables would you choose to test?

on whether listening to classical music affects performance on a math exam, he or she might have an experimental group listen to Mozart, Bach, or Chopin for an hour before taking a test. The control group would take the same test but would not listen to any music beforehand. In this example, exposure to classical music is the independent variable, and the quantifiable results of the math test are the dependent variable.

To study the relationship between violent video game play and aggression, researchers took a longitudinal approach by examining the sustained violent video game play and aggressive behavior of 1,492 adolescents in grades 9 through 12 (Willoughby, Adachi, & Good, 2012). Their results showed a strong correlation between playing violent video games and being more likely to engage in, or approve of, violence. This body of literature represents another example of the importance of research methodology; the same researchers, in a separate study, found that the level of competitiveness in a video game, and not the violence itself, had the greatest influence on aggressive behavior (Adachi & Willoughby, 2011). More research on this topic may help differentiate between the effects of variables and avoid conclusions based on spurious relationships.

WORKING WITH EXISTING INFORMATION

Sociologists frequently work with existing information and data gathered by other researchers. Why would researchers choose to reinterpret existing data? Perhaps they want to do a secondary analysis of statistical data collected by an agency such as the U.S. Census Bureau, which makes its materials available to researchers studying issues ranging broadly from education to poverty to racial residential segregation. Or they may want to work with archival data to examine the cultural products—posters, films, pamphlets, and such—used by an authoritarian regime in a given period to legitimate its power or disseminated by a social movement like the civil rights movement to spread its message to the masses.

Statistical data include *quantitative information obtained from government agencies, businesses, research studies, and other entities that collect data for their own or others' use.* The U.S. Bureau of Justice Statistics, for example, maintains a rich storehouse of information on a number of criminal justice social indicators, such as prison populations, incidents of crime, and criminal justice expenditures. Many other government agencies routinely conduct surveys of commerce, manufacturing, agriculture, labor, and housing. International organizations such as the United Nations and the World Bank collect annual data on the health, education, population, and economies of nearly all countries in the world. Many businesses publish annual reports that yield basic statistical information about their financial performance.

Document analysis is *the examination of written materials or cultural products: previous studies, newspaper reports, court records, campaign posters, digital reports, films, pamphlets, and other forms of text or images produced by individuals, government agencies, private organizations, and others.* However, because such documents are not always compiled with accuracy in mind, good researchers exercise caution in using them. People who keep records are often aware that others will see the records and take pains to avoid including anything unflattering. The diaries and memoirs of politicians are good examples of documents that are invaluable sources of data but that must be interpreted with great caution. The expert researcher looks at such materials with a critical eye, double-checking with other sources for accuracy where possible.

This type of research may include *historical research,* which entails the analysis of historical documents. Often such research is comparative, examining historical events in several different countries for similarities and differences. Unlike historians, sociologists usually identify patterns common to different times and places; historians tend to focus on particular times and places and are less likely to draw broad generalizations from their research. An early master of the sociological approach to historical research was Max Weber (1919/1946, 1921/1979), who contributed to our understanding of—among many other things—the differences between religious traditions in the West and those in East Asia.

Content analysis is the systematic examination of forms of documented communication. A researcher can take a content analysis approach by coding and analyzing patterns in cultural products like music, laws, tweets, blogs, and works of art. An

Statistical data: Quantitative information obtained from government agencies, businesses, research studies, and other entities that collect data for their own or others' use.

Document analysis: The examination of written materials or cultural products: previous studies, newspaper reports, court records, campaign posters, digital reports, films, pamphlets, and other forms of text or images produced by individuals, government agencies, or private organizations.

TECHNOLOGY & SOCIETY

DOES TECHNOLOGY AFFECT STUDYING?

In 2011, as it has every year since 2000, the National Survey of Student Engagement (NSSE) surveyed about 416,000 U.S. students at 673 institutions of higher education, asking about student relationships with faculty, note taking and study habits, and hours spent studying. One of the 2011 findings, consistent with the results of other recent surveys, was that students were spending far fewer hours studying than did their counterparts in previous decades. If in 1961 the average student reported studying about 24 hours per week, by 2011 the average student reported about 14 hours of study time (Babcock & Marks, 2010; NSSE, 2012). Within this figure are variations by major, ranging from about 24 hours per week for architecture majors to 10 for speech majors. Sociology majors reported studying an average of 13.8 hours per week (de Vise, 2012).

This study presents a number of interesting research questions, few of which are answered by the NSSE, which collected quantitative data but did not analyze the results. What factors might be behind the precipitous decline in self-reported hours spent studying?

Some existing hypotheses implicate modern technology for at least two reasons. First, it has been suggested that students study less because they are spending substantial time using social media such as Facebook. One pilot study at Ohio State University concluded that students who used Facebook had poorer grades than those who did not (Karpinski & Duberstein, 2009). These data suggest that another study could profitably look for correlations between social media use and study time.

© Sam Bloomberg-Rissman/Blend Images/Corbis

Has technology helped or hindered your studying in college? Does it mostly offer research help—or additional distractions?

Second, students may be reporting less study time because technology has cut the hours of work needed for some tasks. While preparing a research paper in the past may have demanded hours in the library stacks or in pursuit of an expert to interview, today an online search engine can bring up a wealth of data earlier generations could not have imagined. Far fewer students consult research librarians or use library databases today. Notably, however, a recent study suggests that the quality of data students have the skills to find in their searches is mixed and often low (Kolowich, 2011).

Technology is only one possible factor in the decline in the time U.S. students spend studying. Two economists, for instance, suggest that studying time has decreased as achievement standards have fallen (Babcock & Marks, 2010). But there is no denying that one of the most dramatic differences between the 1960s and today is the proliferation of technology, which suggests that an explanatory relationship may exist.

THINK IT THROUGH

▶ Imagine that your final paper for this semester involves answering the research question, "What is the impact of technology on studying and learning?" How would you go about answering this question? How would you collect data for your project?

exciting aspect of social science research is that your object of curiosity can become a research question. In 2009, sociologists conducted a content analysis of 403 gangsta rap songs to assess whether rap's reputation of being misogynistic (hostile to women) was justified (Weitzer & Kubrin, 2009). The analysis found that the songs did contain significant misogynistic undertones, reflecting larger stereotypical views of male and female characteristics.

PARTICIPATORY RESEARCH

While sociologists usually try to avoid having an impact on the people they study, one research method is employed specifically to foster change. *Participatory research* supports an organization or community trying to improve its situation when it lacks the necessary economic or political power to do so by itself. The researcher fully participates by training the members to conduct research on their own while working with them to enhance their power (Freire, 1972; Park, 1993; Whyte, 1991). Such research might be part of, for instance, empowering a community to act against the threat of HIV/AIDS, as has been done in places like San Francisco and Nairobi, Kenya. Participatory research is an effective way of conducting an empirical study while also furthering a community or organizational goal that will benefit from the results of the study.

FIGURE 2.6 Sociological Research Formula

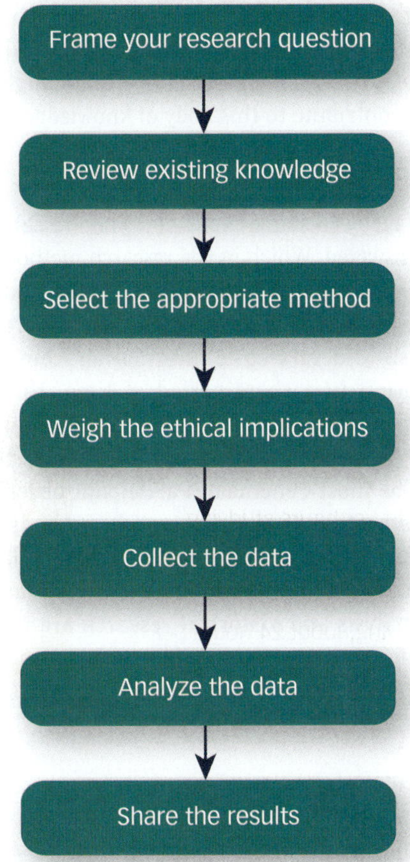

DOING SOCIOLOGY: A STUDENT'S GUIDE TO RESEARCH

Sociological research seldom follows a formula that indicates exactly how to proceed. Sociologists often have to feel their way as they go, responding to the challenges that arise during research and adapting new methods to fit the circumstances. Thus, the stages of research can vary even when sociologists agree about the basic sequence. At the same time, for student sociologists, it is useful to understand the key building blocks of good sociological research. As you read through the following descriptions of the stages, think about a topic of interest to you and how you might use that as the basis for an original research project.

FRAME YOUR RESEARCH QUESTION

"Good research," Thomas Dewey observed, "scratches where it itches." Sociological research begins with the formulation of a question or questions to be answered. Society offers an endless spectrum of compelling issues to study: Does exposure to violent video games affect the probability of aggressive behavior in adolescents? Does religious faith affect voting behavior? Is family income a good predictor of performance on standardized college entrance tests such as the SAT? Beyond the descriptive aspects of social phenomena, sociologists are also interested in *how* they can explain relationships between the variables they examine.

Formulating a research question precisely and carefully is one of the most important steps toward ensuring a successful research project. Research questions come from many sources. Some arise from problems that form the foundation of sociology, including an interest in socioeconomic inequalities and their causes and effects, or the desire to understand how power is exercised in social relationships. Sociologists are also mindful that solid empirical data are important to public policies on issues of concern such as poverty, occupational mobility, and domestic violence.

Keep in mind that you also need to define your terms. Recall our discussion of operationalizing concepts. For example, if you are studying middle school bullying, you need to make explicit your definition of bullying and how that will be measured. The same holds true if you are studying a topic such as illiteracy or aggressive behavior.

REVIEW EXISTING KNOWLEDGE

Once you identify the question you want to ask, you need to conduct a review of the existing literature on your topic. The literature may include published studies, unpublished papers, books, dissertations, government documents, newspapers and other periodicals, and, increasingly, data disseminated on the Internet. The key focus of the literature review, however,

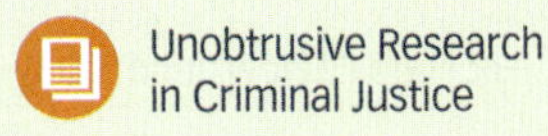
Unobtrusive Research in Criminal Justice

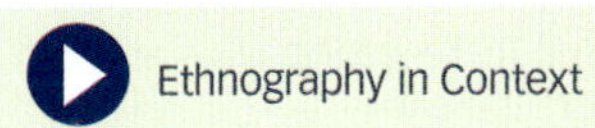
Ethnography in Context

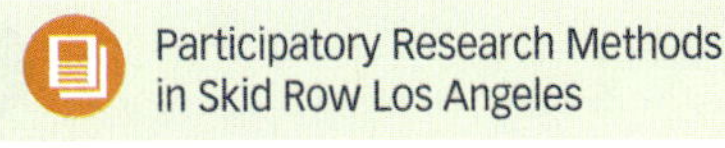
Participatory Research Methods in Skid Row Los Angeles

is usually published and peer-reviewed research studies. Your purpose in conducting the literature review is to learn about studies that have already been done on your topic of interest so that you can set your research in the context of existing studies. You will also use the literature review to highlight how your research will contribute to this body of knowledge.

SELECT THE APPROPRIATE METHOD

Now you are ready to think about how your research question can best be answered. Which of the research methods described earlier (1) will give the best results for the project and (2) is most feasible for your research circumstances, experience, and budget?

If you wish to obtain basic information from a relatively large population in a short period of time, then a survey is the best method to use. If you want to obtain detailed information about a smaller group of people, then interviews might be most beneficial. Participant observation and detached observation are ideal research methods for verifying data obtained through interviews, or, for the latter, when the presence of a researcher might alter the research results. Document analysis and historical research are good choices for projects focused on inaccessible subjects and historical sociology. Remember, sociological researchers often use multiple methods.

WEIGH THE ETHICAL IMPLICATIONS

Research conducted on other human beings—as much of sociological research is—poses certain ethical problems. An outpouring of outrage after the discovery of gruesome experiments conducted by the Nazis during World War II prompted the adoption of the Nuremberg Code, a collection of ethical research guidelines developed to help prevent such atrocities from ever happening again (Table 2.5). In addition to these basic guidelines, scientific societies throughout the world have adopted their own codes of ethics to safeguard against the misuse and abuse of human subjects.

Before you begin your research, it is important that you familiarize yourself with the American Sociological Association's Code of Ethics (www.asanet.org/about/ethics.cfm), as well as the standards of your school, and carefully follow both. Ask yourself whether your research will cause the subjects any emotional or physical harm. How will you guarantee their anonymity? Does the research violate any of your own ethical principles?

Most universities and research institutes require researchers to complete particular forms before undertaking experiments using human subjects, describing the research methods to be used and the groups of subjects who will take part. Depending on the type of research, a researcher may need to obtain written agreement from the subjects for their participation. Today, a study like that conducted by Philip Zimbardo in the 1970s at Stanford University (described in the *Private Lives, Public Issues* box) would be unlikely to be approved because of the stress put on the experiment's subjects in the course of the research. Approval of research involving human subjects is granted with an eye to both fostering good research and protecting the interests of those partaking in the study.

TABLE 2.5 The Nuremberg Code

	Directives for Human Experimentation
1.	The voluntary consent of the human subject is absolutely essential.
2.	The experiment should be such as to yield fruitful results for the good of society.
3.	The experiment should be so designed and based on the results of animal experimentation and a knowledge of the natural history of the disease.
4.	The experiment should be so conducted as to avoid all unnecessary physical and mental suffering and injury.
5.	No experiment should be conducted where there is an a priori reason to believe that death or disabling injury will occur.
6.	The degree of risk to be taken should never exceed that determined by the humanitarian importance of the problem to be solved by the experiment.
7.	Proper preparations should be made and adequate facilities provided to protect the experimental subject against even remote possibilities of injury, disability, or death.
8.	The experiment should be conducted only by scientifically qualified persons.
9.	During the course of the experiment the human subject should be at liberty to bring the experiment to an end.
10.	During the course of the experiment the scientist in charge must be prepared to terminate the experiment at any stage, if he has probable cause to believe, in the exercise of the good faith, superior skill, and careful judgment required of him that a continuation of the experiment is likely to result in injury, disability, or death to the experimental subject.

SOURCE: U.S. Department of Health and Human Services.

COLLECT AND ANALYZE THE DATA

Collecting data is the heart of research. It is time-consuming but exciting. During this phase, you will gather the information that will allow you to make a contribution to the sociological understanding of your topic. If your data set is qualitative—for example, open-ended responses to interview questions or observations of people—you will proceed by carefully reviewing and organizing your field notes, documents, and other sources of information. If your data set is quantitative—for example, completed closed-ended surveys—you will proceed by entering

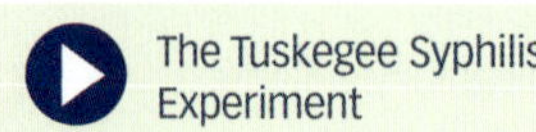
The Tuskegee Syphilis Experiment

Facebook's Newsfeed Study

Galerie Bilderwelt/Contributor/Getty Images

During the Nuremberg Trials, which brought key figures of the Nazi Party of Germany to justice, the practices of some Nazi medical personnel were found to be unethical and even criminal. The Nuremberg Code, which emerged from these trials, established principles for any type of human experimentation.

data into spreadsheets, comparing results, and analyzing your findings using statistical software.

Your analysis should offer answers to the research questions with which you began the study. Be mindful in interpreting your data and avoid conclusions that are speculative or not warranted by the actual research results. Do your data support or contradict your initial hypothesis? Or are they simply inconclusive? Report *all* of your results. Do your findings have implications for larger theories in the discipline? Do they suggest the need for further study of another dimension of the issue at hand? Good research need not have results that unequivocally support your hypothesis. A finding that refutes the hypothesis can be instructive as well.

SHARE THE RESULTS

However fascinating your research may be to you, its benefits are amplified when you take advantage of opportunities to share it with others. You can share your findings with the sociological community by publishing the results in academic journals. Before submitting research for publication, you must learn which journals cover your topic areas and review those journals' standards for publication. Some colleges and universities sponsor undergraduate journals that offer opportunities for students to publish original research.

Other outlets for publication include books, popular magazines, newspapers, video documentaries, and websites. Another way to communicate your findings is to give a presentation at a professional meeting. Many professional meetings are held each year; at least one will offer a panel suited to your topic. In some cases, high-quality undergraduate papers are selected for presentation. If your paper is one, relevant experts at the meeting will likely help you interpret your findings further.

SOCIOLOGY AND YOU: WHY LEARN TO DO SOCIOLOGICAL RESEARCH?

The news media provide us with an immense amount of round-the-clock information. Some of it is very good; some of it is misleading. Reported "facts" may come from sources that have agendas or are motivated by self-interest, such as political interest groups, lobbying groups, media outlets, and even government agencies. Perhaps the most problematic are "scientific" findings that are agenda driven, not scientifically unbiased. In particular because we live in a time of information saturation, it is important that we learn to be critical consumers of information and to ask questions about the quality of the data presented to us. Carefully gathered and precise data are important not only as sources of information but also as the basis of informed decision making on the part of elected officials and others in positions of power.

Because you now understand how valid and reliable data are gathered, you can better question the veracity and reliability of others' claims. For example, when a pollster announces that 80% of the "American people" favor Joe Conman for Congress, you can ask, "What was the size of the sample? How representative is it of the population? How was the survey questionnaire prepared? Exactly what questions were asked?" If it turns out that the data are based on the responses of 25 residents of a gated Colorado community or that a random sample was used but the survey included leading questions, you know the results do not give an accurate picture.

Similarly, your grasp of the research process allows you to have greater confidence in research that was conducted properly. You should put more stock in the results of a nationwide Centers for Disease Control and Prevention survey of college students' drug use or safe-sex choices that used carefully prepared questionnaires tested for their validity and reliability and less stock in data gathered by a reporter untrained in scientific methods who interviewed a small, nonrandom sample of students on a single college campus.

You have also taken the first step in learning how to gather and evaluate data yourself. Realizing the value of theories that can be tested and proven false if they are wrong is the first step in developing your own theories and hypotheses. By using the concepts, processes, and definitions introduced in this chapter, you can conduct research that is valid, appropriate, and even publishable.

In short, these research tools will help you be a more critical consumer of information and enhance your understanding of the social world around you. Other benefits of learning sociology will become apparent throughout the following chapters as you discover how the research process is applied to cultures, societies, and the institutions that shape your life.

PRIVATE LIVES, PUBLIC ISSUES

ZIMBARDO'S EXPERIMENT: THE INDIVIDUAL AND THE SOCIAL ROLE

Social psychologist Philip Zimbardo (1974; Haney, Banks, & Zimbardo, 1973) wanted to investigate how role expectations shape behavior. He was intrigued by the possibility that the frequently observed cruelty of prison guards was a consequence of the institutional setting and role, not the guards' personalities.

In an experiment that has since become well known, Zimbardo converted the basement of a Stanford University building into a makeshift prison. A newspaper ad seeking young men to take part in the experiment for pay drew 70 subject candidates, who were given a battery of physical and psychological tests to assess their emotional stability and maturity. The most mature 24 were selected for the experiment and randomly assigned to roles as "guards" or "prisoners." Those assigned to be prisoners were "arrested," handcuffed, and taken to the makeshift prison by the Palo Alto police. The behavior of the guards and the prisoners was filmed. Within a week, the prison setting took on many of the characteristics of actual prisons. The guards were often aggressive and seemed to take pleasure in being cruel. The prisoners began planning escapes and expressed hostility and bitterness toward the guards.

The subjects in the experiment so identified with their respective roles that many of them displayed signs of depression and anxiety. As a result, some were released early, and the experiment was canceled before the first week was over. Since the participants had all been screened for psychological and physical problems, Zimbardo concluded that the results could not be attributed to their personalities. Instead, the prison setting itself (the *independent variable*) appeared to be at the root of the guards' brutal behavior and the prisoners' hostility and rebelliousness (the *dependent variable*). Zimbardo's research shows how profoundly private lives are shaped by the behavioral expectations of the roles we occupy in social institutions.

Stanford University archives

Despite questions about the ethics of Philip Zimbardo's experiment, sociologists still study his work. Is it wrong to use research data gathered by means we now consider unethical? Do the results of research ever justify subjecting human beings to physical or psychological discomfort, invasion of privacy, or deception?

THINK IT THROUGH

▶ Zimbardo's experiment could not be repeated today, as it would violate guidelines for ethical research with human subjects. How might a researcher design an ethical experiment to test the question of the circumstances under which apparently "normal" individuals will engage in violent or cruel acts?

WHAT CAN I DO WITH A SOCIOLOGY DEGREE?

CAREER DEVELOPMENT: GETTING STARTED AND ASSESSING YOUR INTERESTS, VALUES, AND SKILLS

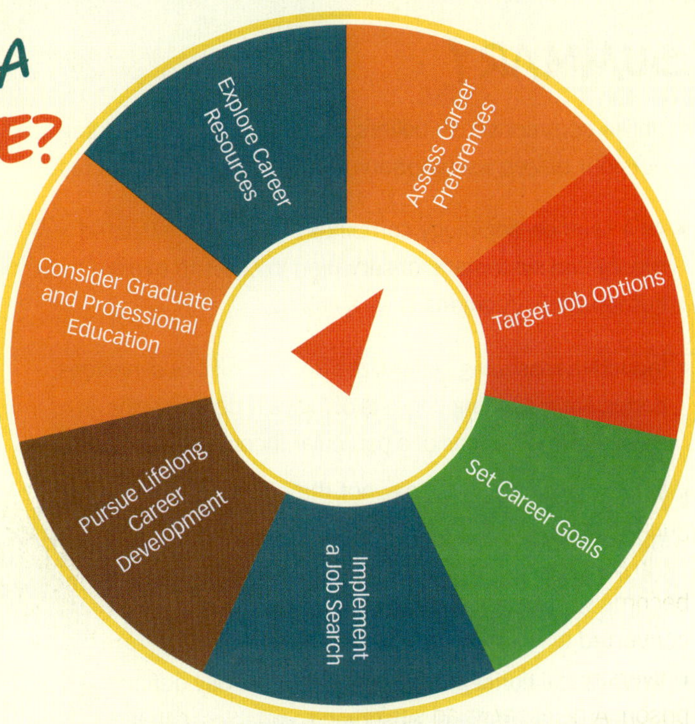

The skills and knowledge of career development and your job search are learned, practiced, and mastered over time. You will learn about yourself, make career decisions, manage workplace expectations, and pursue new opportunities throughout your professional life. Your career success starts with *self-reflection, exploration, the effective implementation of career and job search action plans, and a personal and professional commitment to your career.* The basic activities linked to these processes are shown in the career development wheel.

In this chapter, we focus on your assessment of career interests and preferences and your exploration of career and job options.

Assessment of Individual Career Interests and Preferences

Self-knowledge is an important element of career assessment and development. Learning about your career identity—*the values, aspirations, interests, talents, skills, and preferences related to careers*—is fundamental to your career success.

Careful self-assessment will help you determine what you do well and enjoy, what skills and talents you possess, how you prefer to work, what interests you actively pursue, what values drive your choices, and where your strengths and weaknesses lie. By matching your characteristics to careers and occupations, you will establish a basis for identifying your career options and a guide to further research and exploration.

Assessments may be completed individually, online, in a group setting, and/or with a career professional. Assessments often include information linking your career interests to potential academic majors. You may want to access the following *online assessment resources* to research your career identity:

- www.jobhuntersbible.com (*What Color Is Your Parachute?*)
- www.focuscareer.com (*Focus 2* Online Career Planning System)
- www.humanesources.com/products/program/do-what-you-are (Do What You Are)
- www.careerinfonet.org/occupations (CareerOneStop)

THINK ABOUT CAREERS

▶ Consider the components of a career identity noted above. What characteristics of your career identity can you identify at this point? How will you begin to establish the key aspects of your career identity?

SUMMARY

- Unlike commonsense beliefs, sociological understanding puts our biases, assumptions, and conclusions to the test.
- As a science, sociology combines logically constructed theory and systematic observation in order to explain human social relations.
- **Inductive reasoning** generalizes from specific observations; **deductive reasoning** consists of logically deducing the empirical implications of a particular theory or set of ideas.
- A good theory is logically consistent, testable, and valid. The **principle of falsification** holds that if theories are to be scientific, they must be formulated in such a way that they can be disproved if wrong.
- Sociological **concepts** must be operationally defined to yield measurable or observable variables. Often, sociologists operationally define variables so they can measure these in quantifiable values and assess **validity** and **reliability**, to eliminate **bias** in their research.
- Quantitative analysis permits us to measure correlations between variables and identify **causal relationships**. Researchers must be careful not to infer causation from correlation.
- Qualitative analysis is often better suited than **quantitative research** to producing a deep understanding of how the people being studied view the social world. On the other hand, it is sometimes difficult to measure the reliability and validity of **qualitative research**.
- Sociologists seek **objectivity** when conducting their research. One way to help ensure objectivity is through the **replication** of research.
- Research strategies are carefully thought-out plans that guide the gathering of information about the social world. They also suggest the choice of appropriate **research methods**.
- Research methods in sociology include **survey** research (which often relies on random sampling), **fieldwork** (including participant observation and detached observation), **experiments**, working with existing information, and participatory research.
- Sociological research typically follows seven steps: framing the research question, reviewing the existing knowledge, selecting appropriate methods, weighing the ethical implications of the research, collecting data, analyzing data, and sharing the results.
- To be ethical, researchers must be sure their research protects the privacy of subjects and does not cause them unwarranted stress. Scientific societies throughout the world have adopted codes of ethics to safeguard against the misuse and abuse of human subjects.

KEY TERMS

DISCUSSION QUESTIONS

1. Think about a topic of contemporary relevance in which you may be interested (for example, poverty, juvenile delinquency, teen births, or racial neighborhood segregation). Using what you learned in this chapter, create a simple research question about the topic. Match your research question to an appropriate research method. Share your ideas with classmates.

2. What is the difference between quantitative and qualitative research? Give an example of each from the chapter. In what kinds of cases might one choose one or the other research method in order to effectively address an issue of interest?

3. Sociologists often use interviews and surveys as methods for collecting data. What are potential problems with these methods of which researchers need to be aware? What steps can researchers take to ensure that the data they are collecting are of good quality?

4. Imagine that your school has recently documented a dramatic rise in plagiarism reported by teachers. Your sociology class has been invited to study this issue. Consider what you learned in this chapter about survey research and design a project to assess the problem.

5. In this chapter, you learned about the issue of ethics in research and read about the Zimbardo prison experiment. How should knowledge collected under unethical conditions (whether it is sociological, medical, psychological, or other scientific knowledge) be treated? Should it be used just like data collected under ethically rigorous conditions?

SAGE edge™

Sharpen your skills with SAGE edge at **edge.sagepub.com/chambliss2e**

A personalized approach to help you accomplish your coursework goals in an easy-to-use learning environment.

CULTURE AND MASS MEDIA

IN THIS CHAPTER

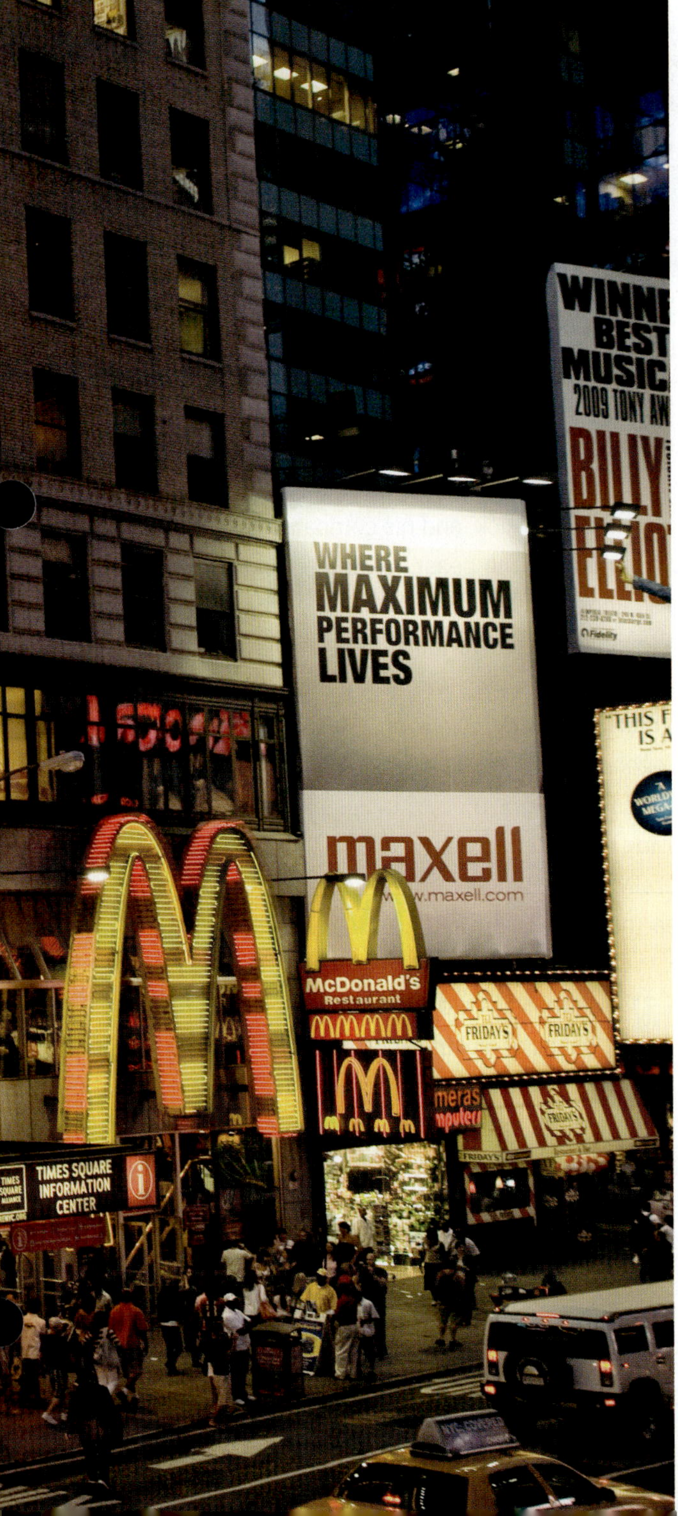

RICHARD NOWITZ/National Geographic Creative

WHAT DO YOU THINK?

1. Is the decision to cheat—whether in school, in a relationship, or otherwise—solely an individual choice, or should it be understood in the context of the culture in which a person lives?
2. What is the relationship between popular culture and violence? Do cultural representations of violence in films, television, music, and video games have an effect on attitudes and behaviors?
3. Does a shared "global culture" exist? If so, what are its components? How is it spread?

Peter Macdiarmid/Staff/Getty Images

ZOMBIE APOCALYPSE

In October 2013, more than 16 million viewers tuned in to watch the first episode of season 4 of the television program *The Walking Dead.* The program follows a small band of human survivors trying to evade flesh-eating zombies who have taken over. The main character, Rick, and his compatriots fight for survival against the fearsome "walkers," who relentlessly hunt human and beast. The undead have not only overrun the planet on this TV show, however; they also appear to have made some headway in taking over U.S. popular culture in recent years. Along with following the adventures of *The Walking Dead,* consumers of horror can read zombie books (such as *World War Z,* which was also made into a movie, and *The Zombie Survival Guide*), play zombie video games (for instance, *Resident Evil* and *House of the Dead*), and watch zombie films (like the popular *I Am Legend* and *28 Days Later*). In 2014, the Centers for Disease Control and Prevention even used the public interest in zombies to launch a disaster preparedness campaign, offering the U.S. public tips for surviving an onslaught of the undead. According to Dr. Ali Khan, the architect of the campaign "If you are generally well equipped to deal with a zombie apocalypse you will be prepared for a hurricane, pandemic, earthquake, or terrorist attack" (www.cdc.gov/phpr/zombies.htm).

Why have zombies become a cultural phenomenon in the 21st-century United States? Some writers suggest that films, television, and other cultural forms are a mirror of social anxieties: As sociologist Robert Wuthnow (1989) has written, "If cultural products do not articulate closely enough with their social settings, they are likely to be regarded . . . as irrelevant, unrealistic, artificial, and overly abstract" (p. 3). In the post–World War II period of the 1940s and 1950s, Americans were dogged by fears of technology run amok (particularly nuclear fears after the first use of an atomic weapon) and the threat of communist infiltration or invasion (Booker, 2001). Popular science fiction films like *The Day the Earth Stood Still* (1951) and *Invasion of the Body Snatchers* (1956) captured paranoia about alien beings who possessed powerful weapons and could arrive at any moment to destroy society and the state. The fear of communism and the concern about proliferation of destructive technology were embodied in otherworldly creatures who could enter a community undetected and crush resistance with deadly force.

Today, some writers suggest that the cultural proliferation of zombies is a window into contemporary fears. Kyle W. Bishop (2010) argues that the rise of zombie popularity after traumatic societal events like the terrorist attacks on New York City and Washington, D.C., on September 11, 2001, the disease fears generated by deadly outbreaks of viruses like SARS, and even Hurricane Katrina is not a coincidence. Rather, zombie stories resonate with a public that is anxious about the threat of societal calamity, whether natural or human-made. Zombies evoke, Bishop (2009) suggests, a fear response, though the object of fear is not necessarily the zombie itself: "Because the aftereffects of war, terrorism, and natural disasters so closely resemble the scenarios of zombie cinema . . . [these films have] all the more power to shock and terrify a population that has become otherwise jaded by more traditional horror films" (p. 18).

In a recent entertainment publication article on *The Walking Dead,* the highest-rated cable program on television, a journalist observes: "There's a fascinating question critics should be answering: What is it about a show that is so relentlessly bleak that allows it to still resonate at such unexpected scale? What does it say about America? . . . it's the polar opposite of the escapist fare that typically serves as popular entertainment, a dystopian nightmare if there ever was one" (Wallenstein, 2014). If critics don't have an answer, then sociologists might: Cultural products are more than just entertainment—they are a mirror of society. Popular culture in the form of films or television may capture our utopian dreams, but it is also a net that catches and reflects pervasive societal fears and anxieties. ■

Culture: The beliefs, norms, behaviors, and products common to the members of a particular group.

Material culture: The physical objects that are created, embraced, or consumed by society that help shape people's lives.

The ramifications of a vast material culture on the lives of ordinary Americans.

In this chapter, we will consider the multitude of functions of both culture and media, which constitute a key vehicle of culture, and we will seek to understand how culture both constructs and reflects society in the United States and around the globe. We begin our discussion with an examination of the basic concept of culture, taking a look at material and non-material culture as well as ideal and real culture in the United States. We then explore contemporary issues of language and its social functions in a changing world. The chapter also addresses issues of culture and media, asking how media messages may reflect and affect behaviors and attitudes. We then turn to the topic of culture and class and the sociological question of whether culture and taste are linked to class identity and social reproduction. Finally, we examine the evolving relationship between global and local cultures, in particular the influence of U.S. mass media on the world.

CULTURE: CONCEPTS AND APPLICATIONS

What is culture? The word *culture* might evoke images of song, dance, and literature—the beat of Latin salsa, Polish folk dances performed by girls with red ribbons braided into their hair, or the latest in a popular series of fantasy novels. It might remind you of a dish from the Old Country made by a beloved grandmother, or a spicy Indian meal you ate with friends from New Delhi.

Culture, from a sociological perspective, is composed of *the beliefs, norms, behaviors, and products common to the members of a particular group.* Culture is integral to our social experience of the world. It offers diversion and entertainment, but it also helps form our identities and gives meaning to the artifacts and experiences of our lives. Culture shapes and permeates material objects like folk costumes, rituals like nuptial and burial ceremonies, and language as expressed in conversation, poetry, stories, and music. As social beings we make culture, but culture also makes us, in ways that are both apparent and subtle.

MATERIAL AND NONMATERIAL CULTURE

Every culture has both material and nonmaterial aspects. We can broadly define **material culture** as the *physical objects created, embraced, or consumed by society that help shape people's lives.* Material culture includes television programs, computer games, software, and other artifacts of human creation. It also emerges from the physical environment inhabited by the community. For example, in the countries surrounding the Baltic Sea, including Poland, Latvia, and Lithuania, amber—a substance created when the resin of fallen seaside pines is hardened and smoothed by decades or centuries in the salty waters—is an important part of local cultures. It is valued

New York Daily News Archive/Contributor/Getty Images

Many people find flag burning offensive because the flag, an object of material culture, is a symbol of the country and its ideals. The Supreme Court, however, has held in a series of cases that symbolic expression is protected by the First Amendment, which explicitly protects free speech.

both for its decorative properties in jewelry and for its therapeutic properties; it is said to relieve pain. Amber has become a part of the material culture in these countries rather than elsewhere because it is a product of the physical environment in which these communities dwell.

Material culture also includes the types of shelters that characterize a community. For instance, in seaside communities, homes are often built on stilts to protect against flooding. The materials used to construct homes have historically been those available in the immediate environment—wood, thatch, or mud, for instance—although the global trade in timber, marble and granite, and other components of modern housing has transformed the relationship between place and shelter in many countries.

Nonmaterial culture is composed of the *abstract creations of human cultures, including ideas about behavior and living.* Nonmaterial culture encompasses aspects of the social experience, such as behavioral norms, values, language, family forms, and institutions. It also reflects the natural environment in which a culture has evolved.

While material culture is concrete and nonmaterial culture is abstract, the two are intertwined: Nonmaterial culture may attach particular meanings to the objects of material culture. For example, people will go to great lengths to protect an object of material culture such as a national flag, not because of what it is—imprinted cloth—but because of the nonmaterial culture it represents, including ideals about freedom and patriotic pride. In order to grasp the full extent of nonmaterial culture, you must first understand three of the sociological concepts that shape it: *beliefs, norms,* and *values* (Table 3.1).

BELIEFS We broadly define **beliefs** as *particular ideas that people accept as true.* We can believe based on faith, superstition, science, tradition, or experience. To paraphrase the words of sociologists W. I. Thomas and D. S. Thomas (1928), beliefs may be understood as real when they are real in their consequences. They need not be objectively true. For example, during the witch hunts in early colonial America, rituals of accusation, persecution, and execution could be sustained in communities such as Salem, Massachusetts, because there was a shared belief in the existence of witches and diabolical power. From 1692 through 1693, more than 200 people were accused of practicing witchcraft; of these, 20 were executed, 19 by hanging and 1 by being pressed to death between heavy stones. Beliefs, like other aspects of culture, are dynamic rather than static: When belief in the existence of witchcraft waned, so did the witch hunts. In 1711, a bill was passed that restored "the rights and good names" of those who had been accused, and in 1957, the state of Massachusetts issued a formal apology for the events of the past (Blumberg, 2007).

NORMS In any culture, there exists a set of ideas about what is right, just, and good, as well as what is wrong and unjust. Norms, as we noted in Chapter 1, are *accepted social behaviors and beliefs,* or the common rules of a culture that govern the behavior of people belonging to that culture.

Sociologist Robert Nisbet (1970) writes, "The moral order of society is a kind of tissue of 'oughts': negative ones which forbid certain actions and positive ones which [require certain] actions" (p. 226). We can think of norms as representing a set of "oughts" and "ought nots" that guide behavioral choices such as where to stand relative to others in an elevator, how long to

TABLE 3.1 Values, Norms, Folkways, Mores, Taboos, Laws, and Beliefs

Concept	Characteristics
Values	General ideas about what is good, right, or just in a culture
Norms	Culturally shared rules governing social behavior ("oughts" and "shoulds")
Folkways	Conventions (or weak norms), the violation of which is not very serious
Mores	Strongly held norms, the violation of which is very offensive
Taboos	Very strongly held norms, the violation of which is highly offensive and even unthinkable
Laws	Norms that have been codified
Beliefs	Particular ideas that people accept as true

Nonmaterial culture: The abstract creations of human cultures, including language and social practices.

Beliefs: Particular ideas that people accept as true.

hold someone's gaze in conversation, how to conduct the rites of passage that mark different stages of life, and how to resolve disagreements or conflicts. Some norms are enshrined in legal statutes; others are inscribed in our psyches and consciences. Weddings bring together elements of both.

The wedding ceremony is a central ritual of adult life with powerful social, legal, and cultural implications. It is also significant economically: The term *wedding industrial complex* (Ingraham, 1999) has been used to describe a massive industry that in 2011, for instance, generated more than $53 billion in revenues. This comes as little surprise when we consider that in 2011, the estimated average amount spent on a wedding was just over $25,000 (Wedding Report, 2012). The wedding as a key cultural image and icon is cultivated in families, religions, and the media. Wedding images are used to sell products ranging from cosmetics to furniture, and weddings constitute an important theme in popular movies, including *My Big Fat Greek Wedding* (2002), *Wedding Crashers* (2005), *Bridesmaids* (2011), and *The Big Wedding* (2013). Popular television series such as *The Office* and *Sex and the City* have used weddings as narratives for highly anticipated season finales. Today, the reality program *Say Yes to the Dress* enthralls viewers with the drama of choosing a wedding gown and *Four Weddings* pits four brides against one another to pull off the "perfect wedding," while *Bridezillas* follows the adventures of brides behaving badly. Clearly, the wedding ritual is a powerful artifact of our culture. In light of this, a sociologist might ask, "What are the cultural components of the ritual of entering matrimony, the wedding ceremony?"

Sociologist William Graham Sumner (1906/1959) distinguished among several different kinds of norms, each of which can be applied to weddings. **Folkways** are *fairly weak norms that are passed down from the past, the violation of which is generally not considered serious within a particular culture.* A folkway that has become part of many U.S. wedding rituals is the "giving away" of the bride: The father of the bride symbolically gives his daughter to the groom, signaling a change in the woman's identity from daughter to wife. Some couples today reject this ritual as patriarchal because it recalls earlier historical periods when a woman was treated as chattel given—literally—to her new husband by her previous keeper, her father.

Folkways: Fairly weak norms that are passed down from the past, the violation of which is generally not considered serious within a particular culture.

Mores: Strongly held norms, the violation of which seriously offends the standards of acceptable conduct of most people within a particular culture.

Taboos: Powerful mores, the violation of which is considered serious and even unthinkable within a particular culture.

Laws: Codified norms or rules of behavior.

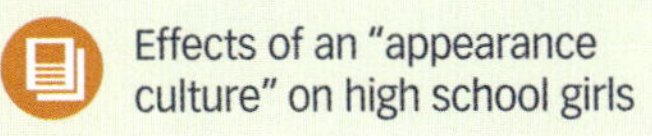

Effects of an "appearance culture" on high school girls

One folkway of the traditional U.S. wedding dates to the reign of Queen Victoria (1819–1901). In her 1840 wedding to the handsome Prince Albert, the "plain" Victoria wore a beautiful white gown. By the end of her life, the tradition was firmly in place, and the white gown had acquired new symbolism, representing purity and virginity (Ingraham, 1999).

Some modern couples are choosing to walk down the aisle together to signal an equality of roles and positions. While the sight of a couple going to the altar together might raise a few eyebrows among more traditional guests, this violation of the "normal" way of doing things does not constitute a serious cultural transgression and, because culture is dynamic, may in time become a folkway itself.

Mores (pronounced MOR-ays) are *strongly held norms, the violation of which seriously offends the standards of acceptable conduct of most people within a particular culture.* In a typical American wedding, the person conducting the ceremony plays an important role in directing the events, and the parties enacting the ritual are expected to respond in conventional ways. For instance, when the officiant asks the guests whether anyone objects to the union, the convention is for no one to object. When an objector surfaces (more often in television programs and films than in real life), the response of the guests is shock and dismay: The ritual has been disrupted and the scene violated.

Taboos are *powerful mores, the violation of which is considered serious and even unthinkable within a particular culture.* The label of taboo is commonly reserved for behavior that is extremely offensive: Incest, for example, is a nearly universal taboo. There may not be any taboos associated with the wedding ritual itself in the United States, but there are some relating to marital relationships. For instance, while in some U.S. states it is not illegal to marry a first cousin, in most modern communities doing so violates a basic taboo against intermarriage in families.

Laws are *codified norms or rules of behavior.* Laws formalize and institutionalize society's norms. There are laws that govern marriage in general: For instance, in some U.S. states, marriage

Do you think that being alone is stigmatized in our connected and busy world? Could it be considered a violation of U.S. cultural norms?

is legally open only to heterosexual adults who are not already married to other people. As of March 2014, 17 states (Hawaii, Washington, California, New Mexico, Minnesota, Iowa, Illinois, Maryland, Delaware, New Jersey, New York, Connecticut, Rhode Island, Massachusetts, Vermont, New Hampshire, and Maine) and the District of Columbia were permitting same-sex marriage, 10 states recognized some type of civil union or domestic partnership, and 33 states explicitly limited marriage to opposite-sex couples (Ahuja, Barnes, Chow, & Rivero, 2014).

Marriage equality groups and their supporters continue to fight prohibitions against same-sex marriage. A poll conducted in 2011 by the Pew Research Center (2012a) found that 47% of U.S. adults agreed same-sex marriage should be recognized as legally valid—43% disagreed. Just 3 years earlier, in a similar poll, 39% of adults agreed while 51% disagreed. This shift in poll results suggests that norms codified in laws are dynamic, too, and are not necessarily shared by all.

VALUES Like norms, values are components of nonmaterial culture in every society. **Values** are *the abstract and general standards in society that define ideal principles, like those governing notions of right and wrong.* Sets of values attach to the institutions of society at multiple levels. You may have heard about national or patriotic values, community values, and family values. These can all coexist harmoniously within a single society. Because we use values to legitimate and justify our behavior as members of a country or community, or as individuals, we tend to staunchly defend the values we embrace (Kluckhohn & Strodtbeck, 1961).

Is there a specific set of values we can define as "American"? According to a classic study by Robin M. Williams Jr. (1970), "American values" include personal achievement, hard work, material comfort, and individuality. U.S. adults value science and technology, efficiency and practicality, morality and humanitarianism, equality, and "the American way of life." A joint 1998 study on American values by Harvard University, the *Washington Post,* and the Kaiser Family Foundation identified similar points—hard work, self-reliance, tolerance, and the embrace of equal rights—though respondents also voiced important disagreements about such issues as the ideal size of the U.S. government and the degree to which the government should promote economic equality (Kaiser Family Foundation, 1998).

A 2010 study found an interesting split between those who agreed they would like to see "the federal government provide more services, even if it costs more in taxes" (49%) and those who agreed they would like to see "the federal government cost less in taxes," even if it meant the provision of fewer services (47%). In 2010, the proportion of survey respondents in favor of more services (even with higher taxes) rose by 10 percentage points (Kaiser Family Foundation, 2010b). What we value, then, varies across time and communities and may even be contradictory. Do these differences matter? Can we still speak of a unified body of "American values"? What do you think?

Structural functionalists including Talcott Parsons (1951) have proposed that values play a critical role in the social integration of a society. However, values do not play this role by themselves. They are abstract—vessels into which any generation or era pours its meanings in a process that can be both dynamic and contentious. For instance, equality is a value that has been strongly supported in the United States since

Values: The general standards in society that define ideal principles, like those governing notions of right and wrong.

the country's founding. The pursuit of equality was a powerful force in the American Revolution, and the Declaration of Independence declares that "all men are created equal" (Wood, 1993). However, equality has been defined quite differently across various eras of U.S. history. In the first half of the country's existence, "equality" did not include women or African Americans, who were by law excluded from its benefits. Over the course of the 20th century, equality became *more* equal, as the rights of all citizens of the United States, regardless of race, gender, or class status, were formally recognized as equal before the law.

IDEAL AND REAL CULTURE IN U.S. SOCIETY

Beauty is only skin deep. Don't judge a book by its cover. All that glitters is not gold. These bits of common wisdom are part of U.S. culture. We rarely recall where we first heard them; we simply know them, because they are part of the cultural framework of our lives. These three statements represent a commitment of sorts that society will value our inner qualities more than our outward appearances. They are also examples of **ideal culture**, *the values, norms, and behaviors that people in a given society profess to embrace,* even though the actions of the society may often contradict them.

Real culture consists of *the values, norms, and behaviors that people in a given society actually embrace and exhibit.* In the United States, for instance, empirical research shows that conventional attractiveness offers consistent advantages (Hamermesh, 2011). From childhood onward, the stories our parents, teachers, and the media tell us seem to sell the importance of beauty. Stories such as *Snow White, Cinderella,* and *Sleeping Beauty* connect beauty with morality and goodness, and unattractiveness with malice, jealousy, and other negative traits. The link between unattractive (or unconventional) appearance and unattractive behavior is unmistakable, especially in female figures. Think of other characters many American children are exposed to early in life, such as nasty Cruella de Vil in *101 Dalmatians,* the dastardly Queen of Hearts of *Alice in Wonderland,* and the angry octopod Ursula in *The Little Mermaid.*

On television, another medium that disseminates important cultural stories, physical beauty and social status are powerfully linked. Overweight or average-looking characters populate shows featuring working- or lower-middle-class people, for example *Family Guy, The Office,* and *New Girl.* Programs such as *Modern Family* and *Mike & Molly* offer leading characters who are pleasant and attractive—and often overweight. In the latter, for instance, Mike is a police officer and Molly, for the first three seasons, is an elementary school teacher (she later becomes an author). They have not broken the glass ceiling of high-status jobs that remain largely reserved for their thinner prime-time peers. Characters such as those we encounter on *Scandal, Mad Men, House of Cards,* and *Sex and the City* are almost invariably svelte and stylish—and occupy higher rungs on the status hierarchy.

Ideal culture: The values, norms, and behaviors that people in a given society profess to embrace.

Real culture: The values, norms, and behaviors that people in a given society actually embrace and exhibit.

Cultural inconsistency: A contradiction between the goals of ideal culture and the practices of real culture.

© AF archive/Alamy

Ursula, a character from the Disney film *The Little Mermaid,* is one of many children's story characters who combine an unattractive appearance with a flawed personality. How do we reconcile the idea that "beauty is only skin deep" with messages of popular culture?

There is a clear **cultural inconsistency**, *a contradiction between the goals of ideal culture and the practices of real culture,* in our society's treatment of conventional attractiveness. Do we "judge a book by its cover"? Studies suggest this is precisely what many of us do in a variety of social settings:

- In the workplace, conventionally attractive job applicants appear to have an advantage in securing jobs (Hamermesh, 2011; Marlowe, Schneider, & Nelson, 1996; Shahani-Denning, 2003; Tews, Stafford, & Zhu, 2009). A significant earnings penalty has been associated with shortness and unattractiveness (Harper, 2000).
- Women in one study who were an average of 65 pounds heavier than the norm of the study group earned about 7% less than their slimmer counterparts did, an effect equivalent to losing about one year of education or two years of experience. The link between obesity and a "pay penalty" has been confirmed by other studies (Harper, 2000; Lempert, 2007). Interestingly, some research has not found strong evidence that weight affects the wages of African American or Hispanic female workers (Cawley, 2001; DeBeaumont, 2009).
- In the courtroom, some defendants who do not meet conventional standards of attractiveness are disadvantaged (DeSantis & Kayson, 1997; Gunnell & Ceci, 2010; Taylor & Butcher, 2007). Mazzella and Feingold (1994)

CBS Photo Archive/Contributor/Getty Images

ABC Photo Archives/Contributor/Getty Images

The Granger Collection, NYC—All rights reserved.

Mike and Molly, Roseanne, and *The Honeymooners* are examples of sitcoms that feature main characters who are working-class people who also happen to be overweight. The next time you're flipping through the channels or watching a movie, take note of the relationship between socioeconomic status and appearance.

note that defendants charged with certain crimes, such as rape and robbery, benefit from being attractive. This is consistent with the "beautiful is good" hypothesis (Dion, Berscheid, & Walster, 1972), which attributes a tendency toward leniency to the belief that attractive people have more socially desirable characteristics. Ahola, Christianson, and Hellstrom (2009) suggest that female defendants in particular are advantaged by attractive appearance.

- Studies of college students have found that they are likely to perceive attractive people as more intelligent than unattractive people (Chia, Allred, Grossnickle, & Lee, 1998; Poteet, 2007). This bias has also been detected in students' evaluations of their instructors: A pair of economists recently found that the independent influence of attractiveness gives some instructors an advantage on undergraduate teaching evaluations (Hamermesh & Parker, 2005).

Another example of cultural inconsistency can be seen in our purported commitment to the ideal that "honesty is the best policy." We find an unambiguous embrace of honesty in the stories of our childhood. Think of *Pinocchio*: Were you warned as a child not to lie because it might cause your nose to grow? Did you ever promise a friend that you would not reveal his or her secret with a pinky swear and the words "Cross my heart and hope to die; stick a needle in my eye"? Yet most people do lie.

Why is this so? We may lie to protect or project a certain image of ourselves. Sociologist Erving Goffman (1959), a symbolic interactionist, called this *misrepresentation*. Goffman argued that all of us, as social actors, engage in this practice because we are concerned with "defining a situation"—whether it be a date or a job interview or a meeting with a professor or boss—in a manner favorable to ourselves. It is not uncommon for job seekers to pad their résumés, for instance, in order to leave the impression on potential employers that they are qualified or worthy. According to an overview of this issue posted on the website of the Society for Human Resource Management (SHRM; 2008), almost half of 3,100 hiring managers surveyed by CareerBuilder indicated that they had detected lying on a job candidate's résumé. Common lies included misrepresentations of educational credentials, salary levels, and even criminal records. About 43% of hiring managers also said they spent less than a minute looking at a single résumé during the initial screening process, suggesting that some dishonesty probably goes unnoticed.

Studies also suggest that cheating and plagiarism are common among high school students (Table 3.2). In one study of 23,000 high school students, about half reported that they had cheated on a test in the past year. Just under a third also responded that they had used the Internet to plagiarize assigned work (Josephson Institute Center for Youth Ethics, 2012). Interestingly, a 2009 study suggests that about half of teens age 17 and younger believe cheating is necessary for success (Josephson Institute of Ethics, 2009).

MEDIA, MARKETS, AND THE CULTURE OF THINNESS IN AMERICA

Whether you are male or female, you may sometimes experience feelings of inadequacy as you leaf through magazines like *Cosmopolitan*, *GQ*, *Vogue*, and *Maxim*. You may get a sense that, in this media-constructed universe, your face, hair, body, and clothing do not fit the masculine or feminine ideal. You may wish that you had the "right look" or that you were thinner. You would not be alone.

One survey of college-age women found that 83% desired to lose weight. Among these, 44% of women of normal weight intentionally ate less than they wanted, and most of the women did not have healthy dieting habits (Malinauskas, Raedeke, Aeby, Smith, & Dallas, 2006). According to a Canadian study, chronic dieters' sense of identity is often frail and reflects others' perceptions of them (Polivy & Herman, 2007). Indeed, a recent study examining body weight perceptions among college students found that women with exaggerated body weight perceptions were more likely to engage in unhealthy weight management strategies and were more depressed than those women with accurate perceptions of their weight (Harring, Montgomery, & Hardin, 2011).

Using our sociological imagination, we can deduce that the weight concerns many people experience as personal troubles are in fact linked to public issues: Worrying about (and even obsessing over) weight is a widely shared phenomenon. Millions of women diet regularly, and some manifest extreme attention to weight in the form of eating disorders. By one estimate, fully 9 million people in the United States are afflicted with eating disorders over the courses of their lives (Hudson, Hiripi, Pope, & Kessler, 2007), most of them women. The National Institute of Mental Health (2010) has reported that "women are three times as likely to experience anorexia (0.9 percent of women vs. 0.3 percent of men) and bulimia (1.5 percent of women vs. 0.5 percent of men) during their life. They are also 75 percent more likely to have a binge eating disorder (3.5 percent of women vs. 2.0 percent of men)."

REUTERS/Fred Prouser

This billboard in Hollywood, California, features excessively thin models. The models are selling clothing, but they are also sending a message to viewers about thinness and glamour. How significant is this message in U.S. culture? What are might be its consequences?

The diet industry in the United States is extremely profitable—by some estimates worth $60.9 billion a year (LaRosa, 2011). The fashion industry (among others) primarily employs models who are abnormally thin and whose images are airbrushed or digitally altered to "perfection." Psychologist Sarah Grogan (2008) asserts that the dieting, fashion, cosmetic surgery, and advertising industries are fueled by the successful manipulation and oppression of women. That is, manufacturers and marketers create a beauty culture based on total but artificial perfection and then sell products to "help" women achieve a look that is unachievable.

As individuals, we experience the consequences of this artificially created ideal as a personal trouble—unhappiness about our appearance—but the deliberate construction and dissemination of an unattainable ideal for the purpose of generating profits is surely a public issue. Reflecting a conflict perspective, psychologist Sharlene Hesse-Biber (1997) has suggested that to understand the eating disorders and disordered eating so common among U.S. women, we ought to ask not "'What can women do to meet the ideal?' but 'Who benefits from women's excessive concern with thinness?'" (p. 32). This is the sociological imagination at work.

THINK IT THROUGH

▶ How would you summarize the key factors that explain the broad gap between ideal culture, which entreats us not to judge a book by its cover, and real culture, which pushes women and men to pursue unattainable physical perfection?

TABLE 3.2 Ethical and Unethical Behavior Among High School Students in 2012 (in percentages)

	Never	Once	Two or More Times
Copied an Internet document for a class assignment	45	26	29
Cheated on a test	49	24	28
Lied to a teacher about something significant	45	26	29

SOURCE: Josephson Institute Center for Youth Ethics. (2012). *2012 Report Card on the Ethics of American Youth.*

Why do you think there is such a big gap between what we say and what we do? Do you think most people are culturally inconsistent? What about you?

ETHNOCENTRISM

Much of the time, a community's or society's cultural norms, values, and practices are internalized to the point where they become part of the natural order. Sociologist Pierre Bourdieu (1977) describes these internalized beliefs as **doxic**: *To a member of a given community or cultural group, common norms and practices appear as a part of the social order—just the way things are.* But the social organization of our lives is not natural, though it comes to appear that way. Instead, norms, values, and practices are *socially constructed.* That is, they are the products of decisions and directions chosen by groups and individuals (often, a conflict theorist would argue, those with the most power). And though all human societies share certain similarities, different societies construct different norms, values, and practices and then embrace them as "just the way things are."

Because we tend to perceive our own culture as "natural" and "normal," it emerges as the standard by which we tend to judge everything else. This is indicative of ethnocentrism, which, as noted in Chapter 1, is *a worldview whereby we judge other cultures by the standards of our own.* That which deviates from our own "normal" social order can appear exotic, even shocking. Other societies' rituals of death, for example, can look astonishingly different from those to which we are accustomed. This description of an ancient burial practice from the North Caucasus provides an illustration:

> Scythian-Sarmatian burials were horrible but spectacular. A royal would be buried in a *kurgan* [burial mound] alongside piles of gold, weapons, horses, and, Herodotus writes, "various members of his household: one of his concubines, his butler, his cook, his groom, his steward, and his chamberlain—all of them strangled." A year later, 50 fine horses and 50 young men would be strangled, gutted, stuffed with chaff, sewn up, then impaled and stuck around the *kurgan* to mount a ghoulish guard for their departed king. (Smith, 2001, pp. 33–34)

Let us interpret this historical fragment using two different cultural perspectives. From an **etic perspective**—that is, *the perspective of the outside observer*—the burial ritual looks bizarre and shockingly cruel. However, in order to understand it fully and avoid a potentially ethnocentric perspective, we need to call upon an **emic perspective**, *the perspective of the insider,* and ask, "What did people in this period believe about the royals? What did they believe about the departed and the experience of death itself? What did they believe about the utility of material riches in the afterlife and the rewards the afterlife would confer on the royals and those loyal to them?" Are there death rituals in the U.S. cultural repertoire that might appear exotic or strange to outsiders even though we see them as "normal"?

Putting aside the ethnocentric perspective allows us to embrace **cultural relativism**, *a worldview whereby we understand the practices of another society sociologically, in terms of that society's own norms and values and not our own.* In this way we can come closer to an understanding of cultural beliefs and practices such as those that surround the end of life. Whether the body of the departed is viewed or hidden, buried or burned, feasted with or feasted for, danced around or sung about, a culturally relativist perspective allows the sociologist to conduct his or her examination of the roots of these practices most rigorously.

We may also call on cultural relativism to help us understand the rituals of another people, the Nacirema, described here by anthropologist Herbert Miner (1956):

> Nacirema culture is characterized by a highly developed market economy which has evolved in a rich natural habitat. While much of the people's time is devoted to economic pursuits, a large part of the fruits of these labors and a considerable portion of the day are spent in ritual activity. The focus of this activity

Doxic: Taken for granted as "natural" or "normal" in society.

Etic perspective: The perspective of the outside observer.

Emic perspective: The perspective of the insider, the one belonging to the cultural group in question.

Cultural relativism: A worldview whereby the practices of a society are understood sociologically in terms of that society's norms and values, and not the norms and values of another society.

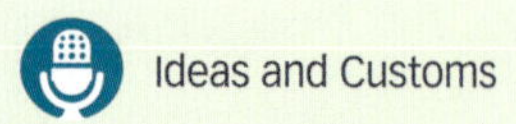

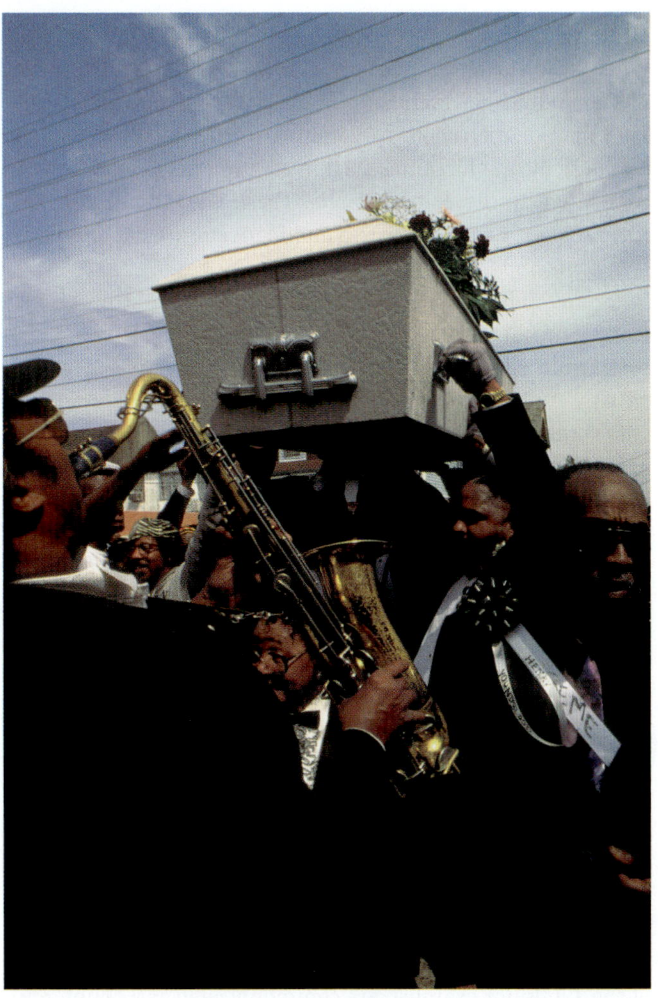

In the Tibetan sky burial, the body is left on a mountaintop exposed to the elements. This once-common practice of "giving alms to the birds" represented belief in rebirth and the idea that the body is just an unneeded empty shell. In Indonesia, mass cremations take place where bodies are placed in sarcophagi of various sizes with animal representations. In New Orleans, a casket is paraded through the street. Death and burial rituals are components of culture.

> is the human body, the appearance and health of which loom as a dominant concern in the ethos of the people. . . .
>
> The fundamental belief underlying the whole system appears to be that the human body is ugly and that its tendency is to debility and disease. Incarcerated in such a body, man's only hope is to avert these characteristics through the use of powerful influences of ritual and ceremony. Every household has one or more shrines devoted to this purpose. The more powerful individuals in this society have several shrines in their houses. . . .
>
> The focal point of the shrine is a box or chest which is built into the wall. In this chest are kept many charms and magical potions without which no native believes he could live. These preparations are secured from a variety of specialized practitioners. . . . However, the medicine men do not provide the curative potions for their clients, but decide what the ingredients should be and then write them down in an ancient and secret language. This writing is understood only by the medicine men and by the herbalists who, for another gift, provide the required charm. (pp. 503–504)

What looks strange here, and why? Did you already figure out that *Nacirema* is *American* spelled backward? Miner invites his readers to see American rituals linked to the body and health not as natural but as *part of a culture.* Can you think of other norms or practices in the United States that we could view from this perspective? What about the all-American game of baseball, the high school graduation ceremony, the youth language of texting, or the cultural obsession with celebrities or automobiles?

SUBCULTURES

When sociologists study culture, they do not presume that in any given country—or even community—there is a single culture. They may identify a dominant culture within any group, but significant cultural identities exist in addition to, or sometimes in opposition to, the dominant one. These are **subcultures**, *cultures that exist together with a dominant culture but differ from it in some important respects.*

Some subcultures, including ethnic subcultures, may embrace most of the values and norms of the dominant culture while simultaneously choosing to preserve the values, rituals, and languages of their (or their parents' or grandparents') cultures of origin. Members of ethnic subcultures such as Armenian Americans and Cuban Americans may follow political events in their heritage countries or prefer their children to marry within their groups. It is comfort in the subculture rather than rejection of the dominant culture that supports the vitality of many ethnic subcultures.

In a few cases, however, ethnic and other subcultures do reject the dominant culture surrounding them. The Amish choose to elevate tradition over modernity in areas such as transportation (many still use horse-drawn buggies), occupations (they rely on simple farming), and family life (women are seen as subordinate to men), and they lead a *retreatist* lifestyle in which their community is intentionally separated from the dominant culture.

Sociologists sometimes also use the term *counterculture* to designate subcultural groups whose norms, values, and practices deviate from those of the dominant culture. The hippies of the 1960s, for example, are commonly cited as a counterculture to mainstream "middle America," though many of those who participated in hippie culture aged into fairly conventional middle-class lives.

Though there are exceptions, the vast majority of subcultures in the United States are permeated by the dominant culture, and the influence runs both ways. What, for example, is an "all-American" meal? Your answer may be a hamburger and fries. But what about other U.S. staples, such as Chinese takeout and Mexican burritos? Mainstream culture has also absorbed the influence of the United States' multicultural heritage: Salsa music, created by Cuban and Puerto Rican American musicians in 1960s New York, is widely popular, and world music, a genre that reflects a range of influences from the African continent to Brazil, has a broad U.S. following. Some contemporary pop music, as performed by artists such as Lady Gaga, incorporates elements of British glam, U.S. hip-hop, and central European dance. The influence is apparent in sports as well: Soccer, now often the youth game of choice in U.S. suburbs, was popularized by players and fans from South America and Europe. Mixed martial arts, a combat sport popularized by the U.S. organization Ultimate Fighting Championship, incorporates elements of Greco-Roman wrestling, Japanese karate, Brazilian jujitsu, and muay Thai (from Thailand).

CULTURE AND LANGUAGE

Well over a billion people on our planet speak a dialect of Chinese as their first language. English and Spanish are the first languages of another 300 million people each. More than 182 million people speak Hindi, the primary official language of India, as a first language. In contrast, the world's 3,500 least widely spoken languages share just 8.25 million speakers. Aka, another language of India, has between 1,000 and 2,000 native speakers. The Mexican language of Seri has between 650 and 1,000. Euchee, a Native American language, has four fluent speakers left. According to a recent article in *National Geographic,* "one language dies every 14 days," and we can expect to lose about half the 7,000 languages spoken around the world by the end of the 21st century (Rymer, 2012). What is the significance of language loss for human culture?

Symbols, like the names we assign to the objects around us, are *cultural representations of social realities,* or, as we put it in Chapter 1, representations of things that are not immediately present to our senses. They may take the form of letters or words, images, rituals, or actions. When we use language, we imbue these symbols with meaning. **Language** is *a particular kind of symbolic system, composed of verbal, nonverbal, and sometimes written representations that are vehicles for conveying meaning.* Language is thus a key vehicle of culture.

In the 1930s, Edward Sapir and Benjamin Whorf developed the *Sapir-Whorf hypothesis,* which posits that our understandings and actions emerge from language—that is, the words and concepts of our own languages structure our perceptions of the social world. Language is also closely tied to cultural objects and practices. Consider that the Aka language has more than 26 words to describe beads, a rich vocabulary suited for a culture in which beads not only are decorative objects but also convey status and facilitate market transactions. In the Seri language, to inquire where someone is from you ask, "Where is your placenta buried?" This question references a historical cultural practice of burying a newborn's afterbirth by covering it with sand, rocks, and ashes (Rymer, 2012).

As languages like Aka and Seri die out, usually replaced by dominant tongues like Spanish, English, Chinese, Arabic, and Russian, we lose the opportunity to more fully understand the historical and contemporary human experience and the natural world. For instance, the fact that some small languages have no words linked to specific numbers and instead use only relative designations like "few" or "many" opens the possibility

Subcultures: Cultures that exist together with a dominant culture but differ in some important respects from that dominant culture.

Language: A system of symbolic verbal, nonverbal, and written representations rooted within a particular culture.

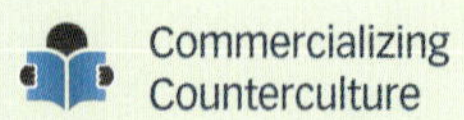
Commercializing Counterculture

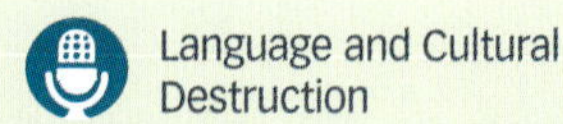
Language and Cultural Destruction

FIGURE 3.1 Endangered Languages Worldwide

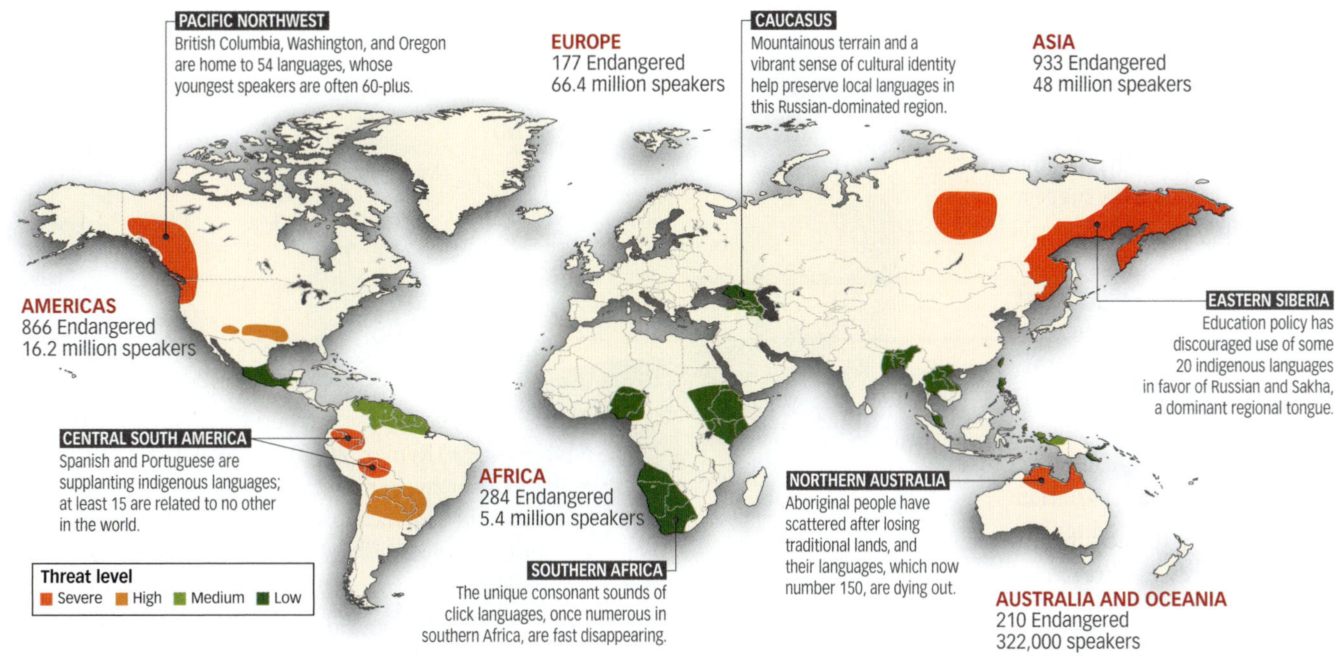

PACIFIC NORTHWEST
British Columbia, Washington, and Oregon are home to 54 languages, whose youngest speakers are often 60-plus.
EUROPE
177 Endangered
66.4 million speakers
CAUCASUS
Mountainous terrain and a vibrant sense of cultural identity help preserve local languages in this Russian-dominated region.
ASIA
933 Endangered
48 million speakers
AMERICAS
866 Endangered
16.2 million speakers
EASTERN SIBERIA
Education policy has discouraged use of some 20 indigenous languages in favor of Russian and Sakha, a dominant regional tongue.
CENTRAL SOUTH AMERICA
Spanish and Portuguese are supplanting indigenous languages; at least 15 are related to no other in the world.
AFRICA
284 Endangered
5.4 million speakers
NORTHERN AUSTRALIA
Aboriginal people have scattered after losing traditional lands, and their languages, which now number 150, are dying out.
Threat level
Severe
High
Medium
Low
SOUTHERN AFRICA
The unique consonant sounds of click languages, once numerous in southern Africa, are fast disappearing.
AUSTRALIA AND OCEANIA
210 Endangered
322,000 speakers

SOURCE: Mason, Virginia W. National Geographic Stock. Reprinted with permission.

that our number system may be a product of culture rather than of innate cognition as many believe. Or consider that the Seri culture, based in the Sonoran Desert, has names for animal species that describe behaviors that natural scientists are only beginning to document (Rymer, 2012). Language is a cultural vehicle that enables communication, illuminates beliefs and practices, roots a community in its environment, and contributes to the cultural richness of our world. Each language lost represents the erasure of cultural history, knowledge, and human diversity (Living Tongues Institute for Endangered Languages, n.d.).

LANGUAGE AND SOCIAL INTEGRATION

Conflict theorists focus on disintegrative forces in society, while functionalists study integrative forces. Where social conflict theorists see culture as serving the interests of the elite, functionalists argue that shared values and norms maintain social bonds both between individuals and between people and society (Parsons & Smelser, 1956). By serving as a vehicle for the dissemination of these values and norms, culture functions to keep society stable and harmonious and gives people a sense of belonging in a complex, even alienating, social world (Smelser, 1962). To illustrate, consider the issue of language use in the United States.

In part as a response to the increased use of Spanish and other languages spoken by members of the nation's large immigrant population, an English-only movement has arisen that supports the passage of legislation to make English the only official language of the United States and its government. Proponents argue that they want to "restore the great American melting pot," though the movement has roots in the early 20th century, when President Theodore Roosevelt wrote, "We have room for but one language in this country, and that is the English language, for we intend to see that the crucible turns our people out as Americans . . . and not as dwellers in a polyglot boarding house." Like today, Roosevelt's era was characterized by high rates of immigration to the United States.

How would a functionalist analyze the English-only movement? He or she might highlight language as a vehicle of social integration and a form of social glue. Indeed, the English-only movement focuses on the function of language as an integrative mechanism. For example, the organization ProEnglish states on its website (www.proenglish.org), "We work through the courts and in the court of public opinion to defend English's historic role as America's common, unifying language, and to persuade lawmakers to adopt English as the official language at all levels of government." The organization points out that 31 U.S. states have legislation declaring English the official language. From this perspective, the use of different primary languages in a single country is dysfunctional to the extent that it undermines the common socialization that comes from a shared language and culture.

A substantial proportion of U.S. residents support legislation making English the official language: a 2014 Huffington

Post/YouGov survey found that 70% of respondents agreed with this position (Swanson, 2014). At the same time, most homes and residents are already active users of English, even if one-fifth also use another home language. Census data suggest that about 80% of U.S. residents 5 years of age and older use only English at home. Just under 20% use a language other than English. Of this 20%, the majority of respondents (about 56%) indicate that they speak English "very well," though there is variation by age and primary language (Shin & Kominski, 2010).

FIGURE 3.2 Percentage of U.S. Population Speaking a Language Other Than English at Home, 2010

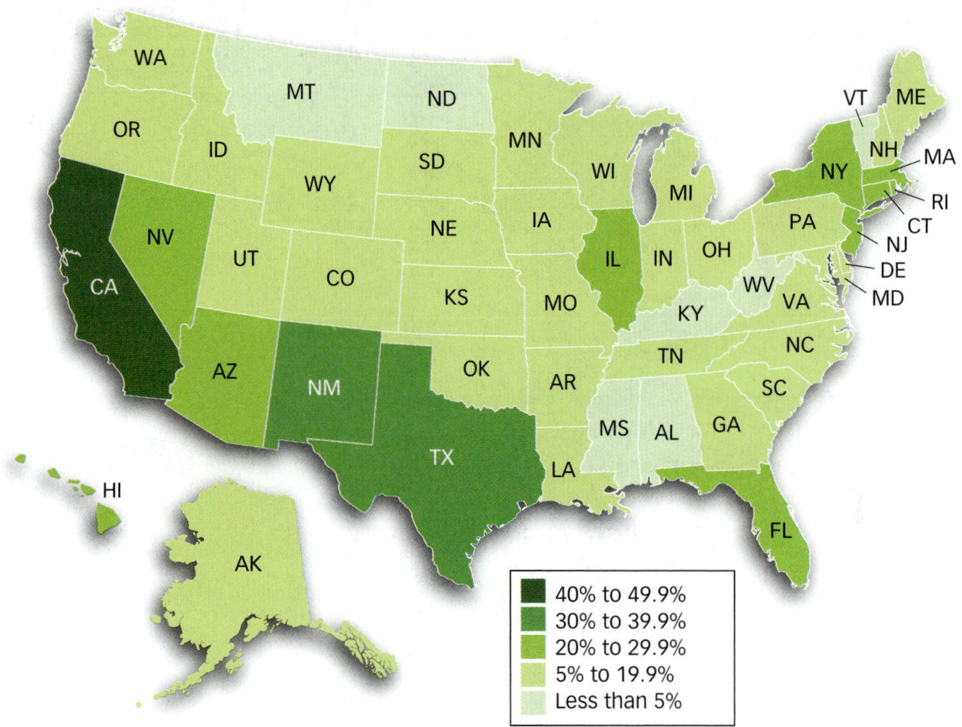

SOURCE: U.S. Census Bureau. (2010). "Population 5 Years and Older Who Spoke a Language Other Than English at Home by Hispanic Origin and Race: 2009." *American Community Survey Briefs.*

Many people embrace cultural diversity and emphasize the value of **multiculturalism**, *a commitment to respecting cultural differences rather than submerging them into a larger, dominant culture.* Multiculturalism recognizes that the country is as likely to be enriched by its differences as it is to be divided by them. In a globalizing world, knowledge of other cultures and proficiency in languages other than English is important. In fact, a functionalist might also regard the U.S. Census data cited above as indicative of *both* the common language that proponents of official English see as crucial to national unity and the cultural diversity that enriches the country and allows it to incorporate a variety of languages in its national and global political, cultural, and economic dealings—which is also positively functional for the country (Figure 3.2).

CULTURE AND MASS MEDIA

From the sociological perspective, we are all *cultured* because we all participate in and identify with a culture or cultures. In one conventional use of the term, however, some classes of people are considered *more cultured* than others. We refer to people who attend the symphony, are knowledgeable about classic literature and fine wines, and possess a set of distinctive manners as cultured, and we often assume a value judgment in believing that being cultured is better than being uncultured.

We commonly distinguish between high culture and popular culture. **High culture** consists of *music, theater, literature, and other cultural products that are held in particularly high esteem in society.* It can also encompass a particular body of literature or a set of distinctive tastes. High culture is usually associated with the wealthier, more educated classes in society, but this association can shift over time. William Shakespeare's plays were popular with the English masses when they were staged in open public theaters during his lifetime. Lobster was a meal of the poor in colonial America. This suggests that high culture's association with educated and upper-income elites may be more a function of accessibility—the prohibitive cost of theater tickets and lobster meat today, for instance—than with "good taste" as such.

Popular culture encompasses *the entertainment, culinary, and athletic tastes shared by the masses.* It is more accessible than high culture because it is widely available and less costly

Multiculturalism: A commitment to respecting cultural differences rather than trying to submerge them into a larger, dominant culture.

High culture: The music, theater, literature, and other cultural products that are held in particularly high esteem in society.

Popular culture: The entertainment, culinary, and athletic tastes shared by the masses.

LANGUAGE, RESISTANCE, AND POWER IN NORTHERN IRELAND

This chapter raises the problem of language loss—that is, the persistent and expanding extinction of small languages across our planet. In a few places, however, little-used languages are being revived for reasons that range from cultural to economic to political. In some instances, as in the case of Northern Ireland, language revival fits into all three categories.

The dominant language in the country of Northern Ireland has long been English, but there is a growing campaign to revive the Irish language, a tongue with little in common with English (consider the Irish word for independence: *neamhspleáchas*). The Irish language (also known as Irish Gaelic or *Gaeilge*) is a minority language in Northern Ireland. As of the country's 2001 census, 167,487 people (10.4% of the population) had "some knowledge of Irish" (Zenker, 2010). The use of Irish in Northern Ireland had nearly died out by the middle of the 20th century, but today efforts are under way to bring the language back to education, commerce, and political life ("In the Trenches," 2013).

Northern Ireland has a history of violent conflict with its British neighbor. Early in the 20th century, Ireland was shaken by conflict between the Irish Catholic majority and the Protestant minority, who supported British rule and feared the rule of the Catholic majority. In 1920, the British Parliament passed the Government of Ireland Act, which sought to pacify the parties with the separation of Ireland into a free state of southern counties. In 1922, the larger part of Ireland seceded from the United Kingdom to become the independent Irish Free State (after 1937, this became the current state of Ireland). The six northeastern counties, together known as Northern Ireland, remained within the United Kingdom. Northern Ireland has since been the site of sporadic conflict between (mainly Catholic) nationalists and (mainly Protestant) unionists (Kennedy-Pipe, 1997).

JIM RICHARDSON/National Geographic Creativ

The area remained largely peaceful until the late 1960s, when violence broke out in Londonderry and Belfast, foreshadowing three decades of armed conflict between British troops stationed in Northern Ireland and the rebellious Irish Republican Army (IRA), which represented primarily the interests of the Irish Catholic population. The violent conflicts over home versus British rule, which included terrorism committed by the IRA against British interests and populations, resulted in more than 3,000 deaths in this period (BBC, 2014b). A U.S.-brokered agreement helped to quell the violence in 1998, though sporadic problems remained. Nearly a decade later, in 2007, key parties to the conflict, including leaders of the Catholic and Protestant factions, took the reins of the country in a power-sharing agreement.

The interest in revival of the language dates back to the period of conflict, known locally as "the Troubles." In the 1960s, a small number of language enthusiasts set up a tiny Irish-speaking community in a Belfast neighborhood. By the 1970s, with the conflict in progress, Irish nationalist prisoners being held by the British in Maze Prison also began learning Irish, calling out words between cells and scrawling their words on the prison walls (Feldman, 1991). The effort spread to neighborhoods where families of the prisoners resided and, according to author Feargal Mac Ionnrachtaigh (2013), it became part of an "anti-colonial struggle."

Today, Irish nationalists, some of them veterans of the war against British rule, have taken up the mantle of Irish language revival, and the language is now the medium of instruction for about 5,000 schoolchildren in the country. While this is just a tiny fraction of the total school population, supporters of language revival occupy some key governmental positions in Northern Ireland, and there has been an effort to enact the Irish Language Act, which would establish new rights to the use of the language in official business, thus creating new job opportunities for fluent speakers ("In the Trenches," 2013).

Today Northern Ireland is peaceful. The Irish language, a part of the local heritage, is being revived. It remains to be seen, however, whether this will serve to draw together two communities with a long history of conflict (the country is about evenly split between the Catholic and Protestant communities) or will deepen the divide as the nationalist Catholic population embraces Irish while the pro-British Protestants resist.

THINK IT THROUGH

▶ Why does language matter to communities large and small? What does the Irish language revival movement share with movements like the official English movement in the United States, which supports a powerful and widespread language? How is it different?

to consume. Popular culture can include music that gets broad airplay on the radio, television shows and characters that draw masses of viewers (for example, *The Walking Dead, Game of Thrones, Dance Moms, Orange Is the New Black*), blockbuster films such as the *Hunger Games* or *X-Men* series, Oprah's Book Club, and spectator sports such as professional wrestling and baseball. Because it is an object of mass consumption, popular culture plays a key role in shaping values, attitudes, and consumption in society. It is an optimal topic of sociological study because, as we noted in our opening story about zombies, it not only *shapes* but *is shaped by* society.

Mass media are *media of public communication intended to reach and influence a mass audience.* The mass media constitute a vehicle that brings us culture, in particular—though certainly not exclusively—popular culture. While mass media permeate our lives today, their rise is more recent than we may realize. Theorist Jürgen Habermas (1962/1989) points out that the *public sphere* as a fundamental part of social life emerged only with the rise of industrial society; that is, prior to the development of printing presses and the spread of literacy, most communication was oral and local. The appearance of mass-circulation newspapers in the 1700s and the growth of literate populations spurred the growth of a public sphere in which information could be widely circulated and, as Habermas points out, public attitudes shaped. In the 20th century, mass media gained influence through the adoption of electronic means of communication ranging from the radio to television to the Internet.

Marshall McLuhan (1964) sought to understand the influence of mass media on society, suggesting that "the medium is the message"—that is, the medium itself has an influence on how the message is received and perceived. Television, for instance, is fundamentally different from print in how it communicates information. In looking at only a particular message, in other words, we may miss the power of the messenger itself and how that transforms social life. McLuhan also asserted that electronic media like television were constructing a *global village* in which people around the world, who did not and never would know one another, could be engaged with the same news event. For example, it was reported in the summer of 2010 that more than 3 billion people (nearly half of the world's population) watched some part of the World Cup soccer tournament in South Africa (Lipka, 2014).

From a sociological perspective, the function of the mass media can be paradoxical. On one hand, mass media are powerful and effective means for conveying information and contributing to the development of an informed citizenry: Mass-circulation newspapers, television networks like CNN and BBC, and radio news programs inform us about and help us to understand important issues. On the other hand, some sociologists argue that such media promote not active engagement in society but rather disengagement and distraction. Habermas (1962/1989), for instance, writes of the salons and coffeehouses of major European cities, where the exchange of informed opinions formed a foundation for later public political debates. However, he suggests, the potential for the development of an active public sphere has been largely quashed by the rise of media that have substituted mass entertainment for meaningful debate, elevating sound bites over sound arguments. (See the *Technology and Society* box for discussion of the ideas of other sociologists on this topic.) Do the mass media contribute to or diminish active engagement in the public sphere? Do they help to construct *citizens*, or do they create *consumers*? What do you think?

The mass media bring us the key forms of modern entertainment that constitute popular culture. While some researchers theorize the effects of mass media on the public sphere, others

Mass media: Media of public communication intended to reach and influence a mass audience.

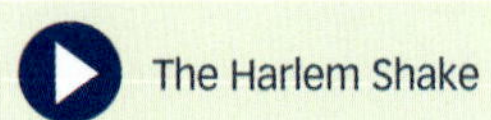
The Harlem Shake

TECHNOLOGY & SOCIETY

POWER, TECHNOLOGY, AND TELEVISION

Most conflict theorists, following the lead of Karl Marx, maintain that capitalism is a system characterized by oppression and rife with inequality. If this is so, why do working people, victimized by an economic order that enriches the upper socioeconomic classes at their expense, not rise up in protest? Sociologists Herbert Marcuse and Douglas Kellner have offered a few ideas.

Marcuse, writing in 1964, described technology in modern capitalist society as paving the road to a "comfortable, smooth, reasonable, democratic unfreedom" (p. 1). He believed that modern technology, employed in the service of capitalist interests, would lead to ever more effective—and even pleasant—methods of exerting external control over individuals. After all, spending the evening immersed in a reality TV program or an action film is much easier than rising up in protest or revolution. And we may not like the conditions of our work, but we are willing to work hard so we can get our hands on the newest iPhone. From this perspective, mass media (for instance, television) serve to socialize and pacify populations and are thus instruments of domination. Marcuse (1964) argued that the freedom of individuals had been "invaded and whittled down" by modern technology, and that the result was a "one-dimensional" society in which the ability to think negatively and critically about the social order was progressively crushed (p. 10).

GREG DALE/National Geographic Creative

Kellner (1990) expanded the argument that modern technology and media—and television in particular—constitute a threat to human freedom of thought and action in the realm of social change. Kellner suggested that the television industry "has the crucial ideological functions of legitimating the capitalist mode of production and delegitimating its opponents" (p. 9). That is, mainstream television appears to offer a broad spectrum of opinions, but in fact it systematically excludes opinions that seem to question the fundamental values of capitalism (for example, the right to accumulate unlimited wealth and power) or to critique not individual politicians, parties, and policies but the system within which they operate. Because television is such a pervasive force in our lives, the boundaries it draws around debates on capitalism, social change, and genuine democracy are significant.

THINK IT THROUGH

▶ Karl Marx wrote that the ruling ideas of any society are those of the ruling class. Arguably, many of those ideas are conveyed through the vehicle of TV. Does television, which delivers images and messages to our homes as we watch for an average of 7 hours a day, foster passivity and make us vulnerable to manipulation? What about the Internet? How does it expand human action, creativity, and freedom? How does it limit them?

look at how these media shape attitudes and practices—sometimes in negative ways. In the section that follows, we turn our attention to another dimension of culture: the controversial relationships among culture, mass media, and the negative but pervasive phenomenon of sexual violence against women.

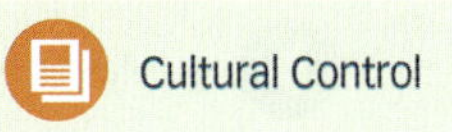

Cultural Control

CULTURE, MEDIA, AND VIOLENCE

Recent statistics suggest that rape and sexual assault devastate the lives of thousands of U.S. women every year. According to the National Crime Victimization Survey (NCVS), in 2012 there were 346,830 rapes, attempted rapes, or sexual assaults in the United States (Truman, Langton, & Planty, 2013). Men and boys also fall prey to these crimes, but women are the most commonly victimized.

One explanation for this number might be that sexual assaults are perpetrated by thousands of deviant individuals and are the outcomes of particular and individual circumstances. Applying the sociological imagination, however, means recognizing the magnitude of the problem and considering the idea that examination of individual cases alone is inadequate for fully understanding the phenomenon of rape and sexual assault in the United States. To paraphrase C. Wright Mills, it is clearly a personal trouble *and* a public issue.

Some researchers have posited the existence of a **rape culture**, *a social culture that provides an environment conducive to rape* (Boswell & Spade, 1996; Buchwald, Fletcher, & Roth, 2005; Sanday, 1990). According to some scholars, rape culture has been pervasive in the U.S. legal system. Feminist theorist and legal scholar Catharine MacKinnon (1989) argues that legislative and judicial processes regarding rape utilize a male viewpoint. Consider, for instance, that until the late 1970s most states did not treat spousal rape as a crime. This conclusion was based, at least in part, on the notion that a woman could not be raped by her husband because sexual consent was taken as implied in the marital contract.

Some researchers argue that the legal culture takes rape less seriously than other crimes of violence (Taslitz, 1999). Legal scholar Stephen J. Schulhofer (2000) has written that the law

> punishes takings by force (robbery), by coercive threats (extortion), by stealth (larceny), by breach of trust (embezzlement), and by deception (fraud and false pretenses). . . . Yet sexual autonomy, almost alone among our important personal rights, is not fully protected. The law of rape, as if it were only a law against the "robbery" of sex, remains focused almost exclusively on preventing interference by force. (pp. 100–101)

Schulhofer notes that this problem is linked to a culture that treats male sexual aggression as "natural." Taslitz (1999) asserts that the cultural stories brought into courtrooms render proceedings around rape problematic by situating them in myths, such as the idea that a female victim was "asking for it."

Some research in the fields of sociology and communications suggests that popular culture promotes rape culture by *normalizing violence*. This is not to argue that culture is a direct cause of sexual violence, but rather to suggest that popular culture renders violence part of the social scenery by making its appearance so common in films, video games, and music videos that it evolves from being shocking to being utterly ordinary (Katz & Jhally, 2000a, 2000b). How does this process occur?

Some scholars argue that popular media embrace *violent masculinity*, a form of masculinity that associates "being a man" with being aggressive and merciless. As well, the messages of popular culture may serve to normalize violence against women in particular. Tyler, The Creator, winner of the 2011 MTV Video Music Award for Best New Artist, has come under fire from parents, media outlets, and fellow musicians for his violently misogynistic and homophobic lyrics. Hip-hop has long been associated with the use of misogynistic lyrics (Morgan, 1999; Pough, 2004; Weitzer & Kubrin, 2009). Many commercial films and music videos also feature rough—even very violent—treatment of women, offered as entertainment. The most gratuitous violence in films such as *The Girl With the Dragon Tattoo* (2011), *The Killer Inside Me* (2010), *The Last Exorcism* (2010), and *Final Destination 5* (2011) is reserved for female victims. In early 2010, citizens in Japan and around the world expressed dismay and disgust when reports emerged about the popular dissemination of the video game *RapeLay*, in which a player stalks a young woman, her mother, and her sister on a train. In the game, the player uses the mouse to grope—and eventually rape—his victims.

Popular culture's most predictable normalization of violence against women occurs in pornography, a multibillion-dollar-a-year industry in the United States. Fictionalized portrayals of sexual activity range from coercion of a compliant and always willing female to violent rape simulations in which consent is clearly refused.

While researchers do not propose that lyrics or images disseminated by mass media cause sexual violence *directly*, some suggest that popular culture's persistent use of sex-starved, compliant, and easily victimized female characters sends messages that forced sex is no big deal, that women really want to be raped, and that some invite rape by their appearance. In a study of 400 male and female high school students, Cassidy and Hurrell (1995, cited in Workman & Freeburg, 1999) determined that respondents who heard a vignette about a rape scenario and then viewed a picture of the "victim" (in reality a model for the research) dressed in provocative clothing were more likely than those who saw her dressed in conservative clothing, or who saw no picture at all, to judge her responsible for her assailant's behavior, and to say his behavior was justified and not really rape. More recent studies have reproduced findings that rape myths are widely used to explain and even justify sexual violence (Hammond, Berry, & Rodriguez, 2011).

A 2003 study found that victims' attire is not a significant factor in sexual assault. Instead, rapists look for signs of passivity and submissiveness (Beiner, 2007). Why, with evidence to the contrary, do such rape myths, common but rarely true beliefs about rapists and rape victims, exist? Recent studies link regular exposure to popular print, television, film, and Internet media with acceptance of rape myths among college-age men and women (Kahlor & Morrison, 2007; Katz, 2006, cited in Lonsway et al., 2009; Reinders, 2006). Is this indicative of the

Rape culture: A social culture that provides an environment conducive to rape.

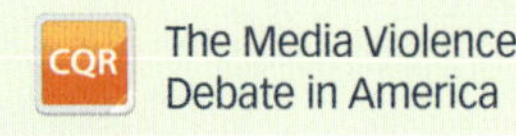

In *Captain America: The Winter Soldier,* a young man deemed unfit for the military is prepared instead for a top secret role as Captain America, a character who, according to the film, is "a superhero dedicated to defending American ideals." In this film, as in many others, the hero achieves key goals with violence.

existence of a rape culture? Is culture, particularly culture that includes vehicles like music and movies that give a platform to expressions of violence against women, a sociological antecedent of real sexual violence? What do you think?

CULTURE, CLASS, AND INEQUALITY

In their studies of culture and class, sociologists consider whether the musical and artistic tastes of different socioeconomic classes vary and, if so, why. While the answer may be interesting in itself, researchers are also likely to go a step farther and examine the links among culture, power, and class inequality. Particularly when using a social conflict lens, sociologists have long sought to show how elites use culture to gain or maintain power over other groups.

Sociologist Pierre Bourdieu has used culture to help explain the phenomenon of **social class reproduction**, *the way in which class status is reproduced from generation to generation.* Bourdieu (1984) discusses the concept of **cultural capital**, *wealth in the form of knowledge, ideas, verbal skills, and ways of thinking and behaving.* Karl Marx argued that the key to power in a capitalist system is *economic capital,* particularly possession of the means of production. Bourdieu extends this idea by suggesting that cultural capital can also be a source of power. Children from privileged backgrounds have access to markedly different stores of cultural capital than do children from working-class backgrounds.

Children of the upper and middle classes come into the education system—the key path to success in modern industrial societies—with a set of language and academic skills, beliefs, and models of success and failure that fit into and are validated by mainstream schools. Children from less privileged backgrounds enter with a smaller amount of validated cultural capital; their skills, knowledge base, and styles of speaking are not those that schools conventionally recognize and reward. For example, while a child from a working-class immigrant family may know how to care for her younger siblings, prepare a good meal, and translate for non-English-fluent parents, her parents (like many first-generation immigrants) may have worked multiple jobs and may not have had the skills to read to her or the time or money to expose her to enriching activities. By contrast, her middle-class peers are more likely to have grown up with parents who regularly read to them, took them to shows and museums, and quizzed them on multiplication problems. While both children come to school with *knowledge and skills,* the cultural capital of the middle-class child can be more readily "traded" for academic success—and eventual economic gains.

In short, schools serve as locations where the cultural capital of the better-off classes is exchanged for educational success and credentials. This difference in scholastic achievement then translates into economic capital, as high achievers assume prestigious, well-paid positions in the workplace. Those who do not have the cultural capital to trade for academic success are

Social class reproduction: The way in which class status is reproduced from generation to generation, with parents "passing on" a class position to their offspring.

Cultural capital: Wealth in the form of knowledge, ideas, verbal skills, and ways of thinking and acting.

Cultural Transmission

often tracked into jobs in society's lower tiers. Class is reproduced as cultural capital begets academic achievement, which begets economic capital, which again begets cultural capital for the next generation.

Clearly, however, the structure of institutional opportunities, while unequal, cannot alone account for broad reproduction of social class across generations. Individuals, after all, make choices about education, occupations, and the like. They have free will—or, as sociologists put it, *agency,* which is understood as the capacity of individuals to make choices and to act independently. Bourdieu (1977) argues that agency must be understood in the context of structure. To this end, he introduces the concept of **habitus**, *the internalization of objective probabilities and the expression of those probabilities as choice.* Put another way, people come to want that which their own experiences and those of the people who surround them suggest they can realistically have—and they act accordingly.

Consider the following hypothetical example of habitus in action. In a poor rural community where few people go to college, fewer can afford it, and the payoff of higher education is not obvious because there are no immediate role models with such experience, Bourdieu would argue that an individual's "choice" not to prioritize getting into college reflects both agency *and* structure. That is, she makes the choice not to prepare herself for college or to apply to college, but going to college would likely not have been possible for her anyway due to her economic circumstances and perhaps due to an inadequate education in an underfunded school. By contrast, the habitus of a young upper-middle-class person makes the choice of going to college almost unquestionable. Nearly everyone around her has gone or is going to college, the benefits of a college education are broadly discussed, and she is socialized from her early years to understand that college will follow high school—alternatives are rarely considered. Further, a college education is accessible—she is prepared for college work in a well-funded public school or a private school, and family income, loans, or scholarships will contribute to making higher education a reality. Bourdieu thus suggests that social class reproduction appears on its face to be grounded in individual choices and merit, but fundamental structural inequalities that underlie class reproduction often go unrecognized (or, as Bourdieu puts it, "misrecognized"), a fact that benefits the well-off.

CULTURE AND GLOBALIZATION

There is a pervasive sense around the world that globalization is creating a homogenized culture—a landscape dotted in every corner of the globe with the Golden Arches and the face of Colonel Sanders beckoning the masses to consume hamburgers and fried chicken. The familiar songs of Lady Gaga, Justin Bieber, and Beyoncé are broadcast on radio stations from Bangladesh to Bulgaria to Belize, while rebroadcasts of such popular U.S. soap operas as *The Bold and the Beautiful* provide a picture of ostensibly "average" U.S. lives on the world's television screens.

Frank Micelotta/Invision/AP

The worldwide success of North American pop artists such as Beyoncé (shown here) fosters imitation abroad. The threat of a homogenized global culture does not just mean the music of these artists is played everywhere—it means locally produced music often sounds nearly identical as well.

We see the effects of globalization—and of Americanization in particular—in cultural representations like McDonald's restaurants, U.S. pop music and videos, and bottles of Coca-Cola spreading around the world. According to press reports, even in the Taliban era in Afghanistan, a time when a deeply conservative Islamist ideology was enforced throughout society, the culture of global Hollywood seeped in through the cracks of fundamentalism's wall. In January 2001, the Taliban rounded up dozens of barbers in the capital city of Kabul because they had been cutting men's hair in a style known locally as the "Titanic": "At the time, Kabul's cooler young men wanted that Leonardo DiCaprio look, the one he sported in the movie. It was an interesting moment because under the Taliban's moral regime, movies were illegal. . . . Yet thanks to enterprising video smugglers who dragged cassettes over mountain trails by mule, urban Afghans knew perfectly well who DiCaprio was and what he looked like" (Freund, 2002, p. 24).

How should a sociologist evaluate the spread of a globalized culture? Is globalization, on balance, positive or negative for countries, communities, and corporate entities? Is it just business, or does it also have political implications? The conflict and functionalist perspectives offer us different ways of seeing contemporary **global culture**, a culture that *draws heavily, though by no means exclusively, on U.S. trends and tastes.*

Habitus: The internalization of objective probabilities and subsequent expression of those probabilities as choice.

Global culture: A type of culture—some would say U.S. culture—that has spread across the world in the form of Hollywood films, fast-food restaurants, and popular music heard in virtually every country.

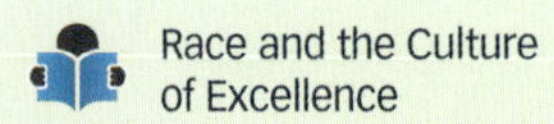

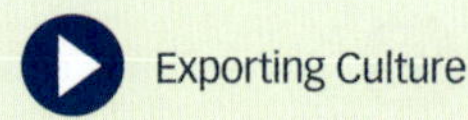

A functionalist examining the development and spread of a broad global culture might begin by asking, "What is its function?" He or she could deduce that globalization spreads not only material culture in the form of food and music but also nonmaterial culture in the form of values and norms. Globalized norms and values can strengthen social solidarity and consequently serve to reduce conflict between states and societies. Therefore, globalization serves the integrative function of creating some semblance of a common culture that can foster mutual understanding and a foundation for dialogue.

Recall from Chapter 1 that functionalism assumes the social world's many parts are interdependent. Indeed, globalization highlights both the cultural and the economic interdependence of countries and communities. The book *Global Hollywood* (Miller, Govil, McMurria, & Maxwell, 2002) describes what its authors call a *new international division of cultural labor,* a system of cultural production that crosses the globe, making the creation of culture an international rather than a national phenomenon (though profits still flow primarily into the core of the filmmaking industry in Hollywood).

The blockbuster film *Slumdog Millionaire* (2008) offers an example of the international division of cultural labor. The film was directed by Englishman Danny Boyle and codirected by New Delhi native Loveleen Tandan from a screenplay by Boyle's countryman Simon Beaufoy that was based on the 2005 novel *Q & A* by Indian writer Vikas Swarup. In 2009, the film, distributed in the United States by Warner Independent Pictures but shown internationally, received nine Academy Awards, including Best Picture. The Indian cast of *Slumdog Millionaire* includes both established local actors and young Mumbai slum dwellers, some of whom were later found to have earned very little from their efforts. Boyle has argued, however, that the filmmakers worked to ensure future educational opportunities and shelter for the young actors. The film's global appeal was huge, and it generated almost $378 million in box office returns, leading the *Wall Street Journal* to label it "the film world's first globalized masterpiece" (Morgenstern, 2008).

From the social conflict perspective, we can view the globalization of culture as a force with the potential to perpetuate economic inequality—particularly because globalization is a product of the developed world. While a functionalist would highlight the creative global collaboration and productive interdependence of a film like *Slumdog Millionaire,* a conflict theorist would ask, "Who benefits from such a production?" While Western film companies, producers, and directors walk away with huge profits, the slum dwellers used as actors or extras garner far less sustained global interest or financial gain.

A conflict theorist might also describe how the globalization of cheap fast food can cripple small independent eateries that serve indigenous (and arguably healthier) cuisine. An influx of global corporations inhibits some local people from owning their own means of production and providing employment to others. The demise of local restaurants, cafés, and food stalls represents a loss of the cuisines and thus the unique cultures of indigenous peoples. It also forces working people to depend on large corporations for their livelihoods, depriving them of economic independence.

Everett Collection

Did all of the actors who were part of *Slumdog Millionaire*, a blockbuster film, benefit from its success? The local extras—as well as some of the central characters—took away little financial gain from the film.

While functionalism and conflict theory offer different interpretations of globalization, both offer valuable insights. Globalization may bring people together through common entertainment, eating experiences, and communication technologies, and, at the same time, it may represent a threat—real or perceived—to local cultures and economies as indigenous producers are marginalized and the sounds and styles of different cultures are replaced by a single mold set by Western entertainment marketers.

Journalist Thomas Friedman has suggested that while most countries cannot resist the forces of globalization, it is not inevitably homogenizing. In *The Lexus and the Olive Tree: Understanding Globalization,* Friedman (2000) writes that "the most important filter is the ability to 'glocalize.' I define healthy glocalization as the ability of a culture, when it encounters other strong cultures, to absorb influences that naturally fit into and can enrich that culture, to resist those things that are truly alien and to compartmentalize those things that, while different, can nevertheless be enjoyed and celebrated as different" (p. 295). The concept of *glocalization* highlights the idea of cultural hybrids born of a pastiche of both local and global influences.

In *The Globalization of Nothing* (2007), sociologist George Ritzer proposes a view of globalization that integrates what he calls "grobalization," the product of "the imperialistic ambitions of nations, corporations, organizations, and the like and their desire . . . to impose themselves on various geographic areas" (p. 15). Ritzer adds that the

© Joachim Ladefoged/VII/Corbis

In its more than half-century of operation, McDonald's has become one of the most recognized icons of U.S. life and culture; Ronald McDonald is said to be the most recognized figure in the world after Santa Claus. McDonald's serves 47 million customers every day in an estimated 31,000 restaurants in 119 countries around the globe.

"main interest of the entities involved in grobalization is in seeing their power, influence, and in many cases profits grow (hence the term *grobalization*) throughout the world" (p. 16). The concept of *grobalization* draws from classical sociological theorists like Karl Marx and Max Weber. For instance, where Marx theorized capitalism's imperative of economic imperialism, Ritzer offers contemporary examples of grobalization's economic and cultural imperialism, exporting not only brand-name products but also the values of consumerism and the practical vehicles of mass consumption, such as credit cards.

How will the world's cultures shift in the decades to come? Will they globalize or remain localized? Will they glocalize or grobalize? Clearly, the material culture of the West, particularly of the United States, is powerful: It is pushed into other parts of the world by markets and merchants, but it is also pulled in by people eager to hitch their stars to the modern Western world. Local identities and cultures continue to shape people's views and actions, but there is little reason to believe that McDonald's, KFC, and Coca-Cola will drop out of the global marketplace. The dominance of U.S. films, music, and other cultural products is also likely to remain a feature of the world cultural stage.

WHY STUDY CULTURE AND MEDIA THROUGH A SOCIOLOGICAL LENS?

Culture is a vital component of a community's identity—through language, objects, and practices, culture embodies a community and its environment. Culture is powerful and complex. As we have seen in this chapter, cultural products, including those disseminated by the mass media, both reflect and shape our societal hopes and fears, norms and beliefs, and rituals and practices. From flesh-eating zombies and classical music to folk dances and folkways, culture is at the core of the human experience. We are all profoundly "cultured."

Culture can be a source of integration and harmony, as functionalists assert, or it can be a vehicle of manipulation and oppression, as conflict theorists often see it. There is compelling evidence for both perspectives, and context is critical for recognizing which perspective better captures the character of a given cultural scenario.

The study of culture is much more than just an intellectual exercise. In this chapter, you encountered several key cultural questions that are important objects of public discussion today. Do the mass media foster viewer engagement in public life, or do they distract and disengage us from the pressing problems of our times? Is violence in the media just entertainment, or does it contribute, even indirectly, to violence in relationships and society? Will the evolution of a more global culture play an integrative role between societies, or will smaller cultures resist homogenization and assert their own power, bringing about conflict rather than harmony? These are questions of profound importance in a media-saturated and multicultural world—a sociological perspective can help us to make sense of them.

WHAT CAN I DO WITH A SOCIOLOGY DEGREE?

CAREER DEVELOPMENT: EXPLORING CAREERS AND SETTING GOALS

Explore and Target Careers and Job Options

When you have completed an initial career identity assessment, reflect on your career options. Enlist the support of friends, family, and career professionals as you review career options. You can start by using online tools and library resources. Review general information about occupational fields and industries to identify a wide spectrum of career options. Examine specific aspects of careers and occupations, including *types of employers, job skills and titles, responsibilities, entry-level educational requirements, advancement potential, work environments, salaries and benefits,* and *employment trends.*

Use your research results to identify potential employers and link to their websites. Compare results for a variety of employers. Your career and occupational exploration and your employer research are the best ways to support and validate your career aspirations. *Online career exploration and employer resources* include the following:

- www.careerinfonet.org/Occupations/select_occupation.aspx (CareerOneStop)
- www.vault.com (Vault Career Intelligence)
- www.bls.gov/ooh/home.htm (U.S. Bureau of Labor Statistics, Occupational Outlook Handbook)
- www.onetonline.org (O*Net OnLine)

In addition to researching career trends and data, learn about career options firsthand through *informational interviews.* An informational interview is similar to any interview, except that you interview the individual working in your career field of interest to learn about his or her profession, career skills, education, current position, and/or employer. To request informational interviews, make contact through family members, friends, or school faculty and alumni and their networks.

Other options for exploring careers include internships, field studies, and part-time jobs. Internships offer opportunities for you to learn about career options in real-world settings, to test your career skills and interests, and to meet professionals in your field.

Make Career Decisions and Set Career Goals

Making *career decisions* is a key aspect of the career development process. Evaluate your alternatives and identify the advantages and disadvantages of each career. From here, you can begin to make a career choice, which will influence your career goals.

Career goals are important milestones that provide a structure enabling you to evaluate progress on your career path. Goals are not absolute, and you may update and change them as you continue to move ahead. Long-term goals are generally accomplished in 1, 5, or 10 years and incorporate your dreams and aspirations. Short-term goals (or objectives) are completed on a daily, weekly, monthly, or annual basis and identify specific tasks associated with your career plan.

THINK ABOUT CAREERS

▶ Explore some sample employer websites to gather information. What are the career and employment options in each organization? What information is highlighted and what do you learn about the employer? What can you conclude about the industry?

▶ Create three goals that you hope to accomplish in the next 5 years, then add short-term goals that support the completion of the long-term goal.

SUMMARY

- **Culture** consists of the beliefs, norms, behaviors, and products common to members of a particular social group. **Language** is an important component of cultures. The Sapir-Whorf hypothesis points to language's role in structuring perceptions and actions. Culture is a key topic of sociological study because as human beings we have the capacity to develop it through the creation of artifacts such as songs, foods, and values. Culture also influences our social development: We are products of our cultural beliefs, behaviors, and biases.

- Sociologists and others who study culture generally distinguish between material and nonmaterial culture. **Material culture** encompasses physical artifacts—the objects created, embraced, and consumed by a given society. **Nonmaterial culture** is generally abstract and includes culturally accepted ideas about living and behaving. The two are intertwined, because nonmaterial culture often gives particular meanings to the objects of material culture.

- Norms are the common rules of a culture that govern people's actions. **Folkways** are fairly weak norms, the violation of which is tolerable. **Mores** are strongly held norms; violating them is subject to social or legal sanction. **Taboos** are the most closely held mores; violating them is socially unthinkable. **Laws** codify some, though not all, of society's norms.

- **Beliefs** are particular ideas that people accept as true, though they need not be objectively true. Beliefs can be based on faith, superstition, science, tradition, or experience.

- **Values** are the general, abstract standards of a society and define basic, often idealized principles. We identify national values, community values, institutional values, and individual values. Values may be sources of cohesion or of conflict.

- **Ideal culture** consists of the norms and values that the people of a society profess to embrace. **Real culture** consists of the real values, norms, and practices of people in a society.

- Ethnocentrism is the habit of judging other cultures by the standards of one's own.

- Sociologists entreat us to embrace **cultural relativism**, a perspective that allows us to understand the practices of other societies in terms of those societies' norms and values rather than our own.

- Multiple cultures may exist and thrive within any country or community. Some of these are **subcultures**, which exist together with the dominant culture but differ in some important respects from it.

- **High culture** is an exclusive culture often limited in its accessibility and audience. High culture is widely associated with the upper class, which both defines and embraces its content. **Popular culture** encompasses entertainment, culinary, and athletic tastes that are broadly shared. As "mass culture," popular culture is more fully associated with the middle and working classes.

- **Rape culture** is a social culture that provides an environment conducive to rape. Some sociologists argue that we can best understand the high number of rapes and attempted rapes in the United States by considering both individual circumstances and the larger social context, which contains messages that marginalize and normalize the problem of sexual assault.

- **Global culture**—some would say U.S. culture—has spread across the world in the form of Hollywood films, fast-food restaurants, and popular music heard in virtually every country.

KEY TERMS

doxic, 62

etic perspective, 62

emic perspective, 62

cultural relativism, 62

subcultures,64

language, 64

multiculturalism,66

high culture, 66

popular culture, 66

mass media, 68

rape culture, 70

social class reproduction, 71

cultural capital, 71

habitus, 72

global culture, 72

DISCUSSION QUESTIONS

1. This chapter discusses tensions between ideal and real culture in attitudes and practices linked to conventional attractiveness and honesty. Can you think of other cases where ideal and real cultures appear to collide?

2. The chapter suggests that mass media may play a paradoxical role in society, offering both the information needed to bring about an informed citizenry and disseminating mass entertainment that distracts and disengages individuals from debates of importance. Which of these functions do you think is more powerful?

3. What is cultural capital? What, according to Bourdieu, is its significance in society? How is it accrued and how is it linked to the reproduction of social class?

4. The chapter presents an argument on the relationships among culture, mass media, and sexual violence with a discussion of the concept of a rape culture. Describe the argument. Do you agree or disagree with the argument? Explain your position.

5. Sociologist George Ritzer sees within globalization two processes—"glocalization" and "grobalization." What is the difference between the two? Which is, in your opinion, the more powerful process, and why do you believe this? Support your point with evidence.

SAGE edge™

Sharpen your skills with SAGE edge at **edge.sagepub.com/chambliss2e**

A personalized approach to help you accomplish your coursework goals in an easy-to-use learning environment.

SOCIALIZATION AND SOCIAL INTERACTION

IN THIS CHAPTER

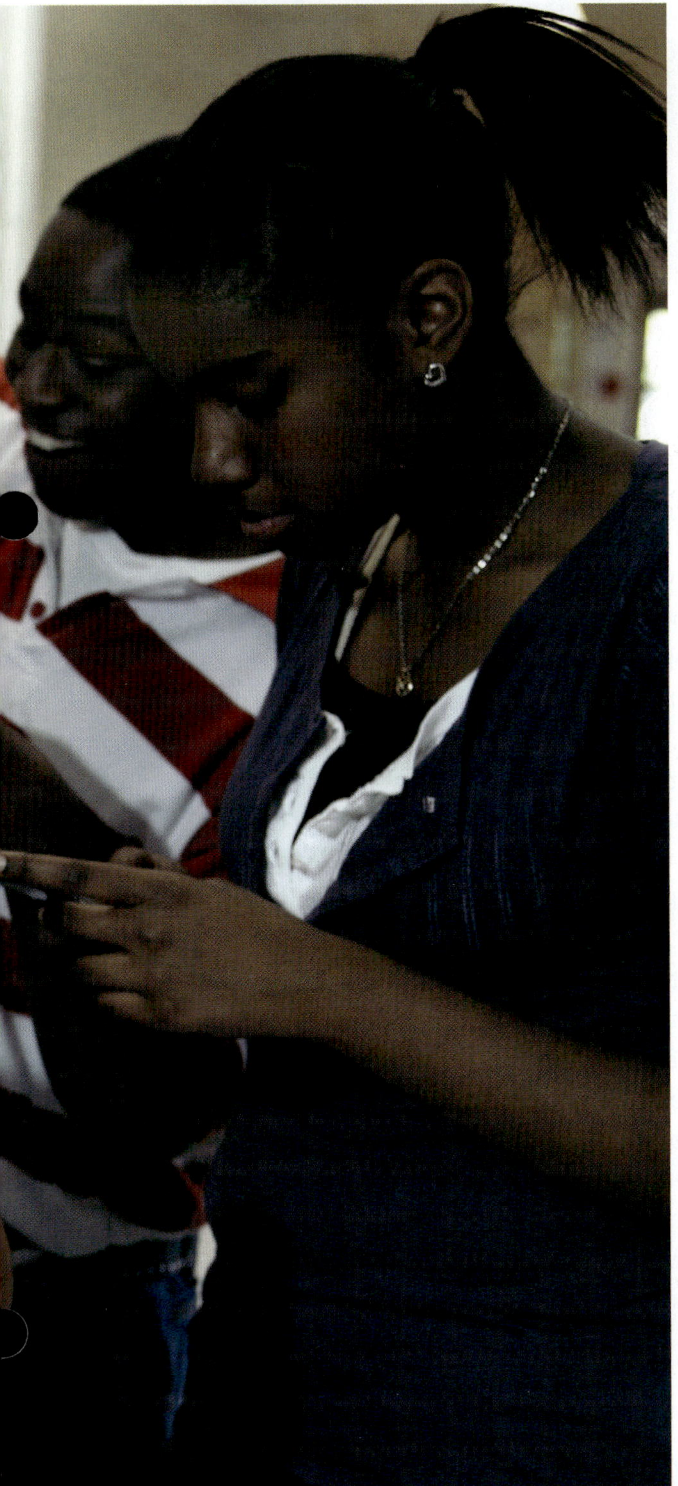

Will & Deni McIntyre/Photo Researchers, Inc.

WHAT DO YOU THINK?

1. Is the personality of an individual determined at birth?
2. Are the media today as important in a child's socialization as the child's family? Might the media be more important?
3. Do people adjust the presentation of their personalities in interactions in order to leave particular impressions? Might we say that we have different "social selves" that we present in different settings?

REUTERS/Aly Song

GIRLS, BOYS, AND TOYS

We can find a box (or several boxes) of toys in most U.S. homes with children. Many of us can look back on our childhoods—whether they are a recent or distant memory—and recall a favorite toy. It might have been a smiling doll, a stuffed animal, a hardy truck or tank, or a set of colorful blocks. If we were lucky, we had an array of toys from which to choose our fun. In this chapter, we talk about agents of socialization, that is, the entities (like families, peers, and schools) that teach us the norms, rules, and roles of society. From a sociological perspective, toys are not just toys—rather, they too are agents of socialization, contributing to children's early ideas of who they are and who they can be in society.

Like other key agents of socialization—families, peers, the media, school, and organized sports, among others—toys may contribute to a child's sense of socially accepted roles, aspirations for the future, and perceptions of opportunities and limitations. If we as social beings are made not born, as sociologists argue, then toys contribute to the construction of boys and girls in ways that can be both predictable and surprising.

In 2014, two researchers at Oregon State University published a study with some attention-getting results. In this research, 37 girls ages 4 to 7 were each given one of three toys with which to play: a Mrs. Potato Head, a glamorous Barbie doll, or a doctor Barbie doll. After a short period of play, each subject was shown pictures depicting 10 female- and male-dominated professions, like librarian, teacher, and flight attendant ("female" jobs) and pilot, doctor, and firefighter ("male" jobs). With each picture, the subject was asked, "Could you do this job when you grow up?" and "Could a boy do this job when he grows up?" (see Figure 4.1). Notably, girls who played with either of the Barbie dolls identified fewer jobs that they could do than did the girls who played with Mrs. Potato Head—and all of the girls in the study thought that a boy would be able to do a greater number of both the male- and

FIGURE 4.1 Number of Jobs Girls Think They Can Do Better or Worse Than Boys Based on Occupation Type

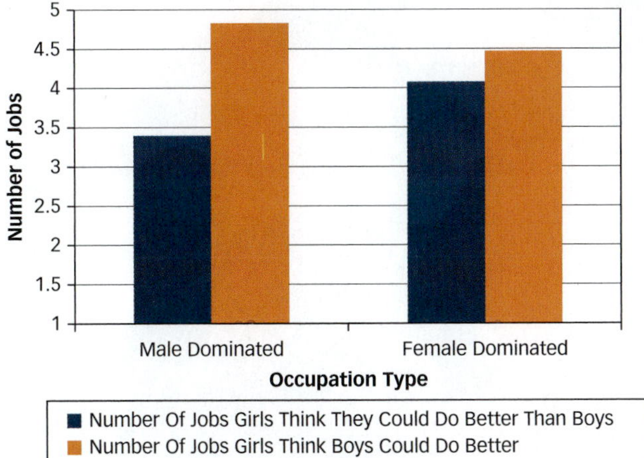

SOURCE: Sherman, A.M. and Zurbriggen, E.L. (2014). "'Boys Can Be Anything': Effect of Barbie Play on Girls' Career Cognitions." *Sex Roles,* online publication, March 5. Copyright © 2014 Springer Science + Business Media New York. Reprinted with permission.

female-dominated jobs (Sherman & Zurbriggen, 2014). Other research has shown that young girls exposed to Barbies express a stronger desire to be thin and have lower body self-esteem than do girls exposed to dolls with more realistic body proportions (Dittmar, Halliwell, & Ive, 2006).

These findings are provocative and raise some interesting questions: What is the power of toys? Do toys affect children's aspirations and perceptions? And why did *all* of the girls in the 2014 study judge themselves less capable than boys of doing a variety of jobs? Efforts have been made to expose young girls to more career options through toys; for instance, the popular Lego brand has introduced female Lego scientist figures, including an astronomer, a paleontologist, and a chemist, complete with a beaker (Gambino, 2014). Might such changes encourage greater future interest among girls in the STEM (science, technology, engineering, and mathematics) fields, where women are underrepresented? Do "boyish" toys already do that for boys? What do you think?

Socialization: The process by which people learn the culture of their society.

In this chapter, we examine the process of socialization and the array of agents that help shape our social selves and our behavioral choices. We begin by looking into the "nature versus nurture" debate and what sociology says about that debate. We then discuss the key agents of socialization, as well as the ways in which socialization may differ in total institutions and across the life course. We then examine theoretical perspectives on socialization. Finally, we look at social interaction and ways in which sociologists conceptualize our presentation of self and our group interactions.

THE BIRTH OF THE SOCIAL SELF

Socialization is *the process by which people learn the culture of their society.* It is a lifelong and active process in which individuals construct their sense of who they are, how to think, and how to act as members of their culture. Socialization is our primary way of reproducing culture, including norms and values and the belief that our culture represents "normal" social practices and perceptions.

TOSHIFUMI KITAMURA/Staff/Getty Images

A young girl prays for blessings in the New Year on the shoulders of her father at the Meiji shrine in Tokyo. Many components of one's culture are seamlessly passed down through habit, observational learning, and family practices.

The principal agents of socialization—including parents, teachers, religious institutions, friends, television, and the Internet—exert enormous influence on us. Much socialization takes place every day, usually without our thinking about it: when we speak, when others react to us, when we observe others' behavior—even if only in the movies or on television—and in virtually every other human interaction.

Debate has raged in the social sciences over the relative influence of genetic inheritance ("nature") and cultural and social experiences ("nurture") in shaping people's lives (Coleman & Hong, 2008; Ridgeway & Correll, 2004). If inborn biological predispositions explain differences in behaviors and interests between, say, sixth-grade boys and girls, or between a professional thief and the police officer who apprehends him, then understanding socialization will do little to help us understand those differences. On the other hand, if biology cannot adequately explain differences in attitudes, characters, and behaviors, then it becomes imperative that we examine the effects of socialization.

Almost no one today argues that behavior is entirely determined by either socialization or biology. There is doubtless an interaction between the two. What social scientists disagree about, however, is which is more important in shaping a person's personality, life chances, philosophy of life, and behavior. In this text we lean toward socialization because we think the evidence points in that direction.

Social scientists have found little evidence to support the idea that personalities and behaviors are rooted exclusively in "human nature." Indeed, very little human behavior is actually "natural." For example, humans have a biological capacity for language, but language is learned and develops only through interaction. The weight of socialization in the development of language, reasoning, and social skills is dramatically illustrated in cases of children raised in isolation. If a biologically inherited mechanism alone triggered language, it would do so even in people who grow up deprived of contact with other human beings. If socialization plays a key role, however, then such people would not only have difficulty learning to speak like human beings, but they would also lack the capacity to play the social roles to which most of us are so accustomed.

One of the most fully documented cases of social isolation occurred more than 200 years ago. In 1800, a "wild boy," later named Victor, was seen by hunters in the forests of Aveyron, a rural area of France (Shattuck, 1980). Victor had been living alone in the woods for most of his 12 or so years and could not speak, and although he stood erect, he ran using both arms and legs like an animal. Victor was taken into the home of Jean-Marc-Gaspard Itard, a young medical doctor who, for the next 10 years, tried to teach him the social and intellectual skills expected of a child his age. According to Itard's careful records, Victor managed to learn a few words, but he never spoke in complete sentences. Although he eventually learned to use the toilet, he continued to evidence "wild" behavior, including public masturbation. Despite the efforts of Itard and others, Victor was incapable of learning more than the most rudimentary social and intellectual skills; he died in Paris in 1828.

Nina Leen/Contributor/Getty Images

Given the choice in an experiment between a wire mother surrogate and a surrogate covered with cloth, the infant monkey almost invariably chose the cloth figure. How are human needs similar to and different from those we find in the animal kingdom?

Other studies of the effects of isolation have centered on children raised by their parents, but in nearly total isolation. For 12 years, from the time she was 1½ years old, "Genie" (a pseudonym) saw only her father, mother, and brother, and only when one of them came to feed her. Genie's father did not allow his wife or Genie to leave the house or have any visitors. Genie was either strapped to a child's potty-chair or placed in a sleeping bag that limited her movements. Genie rarely heard any conversation. If she made noises, her father beat her (Curtiss, 1977; Rymer, 1993).

When Genie was 13, her mother took her and fled the house. Genie was unable to cry, control her bowels, eat solid food, or talk. Because of her tight confinement, she had not even learned to focus her eyes beyond 12 feet. She was

Wild Child: The Story Of Feral Children

constantly salivating and spitting, and she had little controlled use of her arms or legs (Rymer, 1993).

Gradually Genie learned some of the social behavior expected of a child. For example, she became toilet trained and learned to wear clothes. However, although intelligence tests did not indicate reasoning disability, even after 5 years of concentrated effort on the part of a foster mother, social workers, and medical doctors, Genie never learned to speak beyond the level of a 4-year-old, and she never spoke with other people. Although she responded positively to those who treated her with sympathy, Genie's social behavior remained severely underdeveloped for the rest of her life (Rymer, 1993).

Genie's and Victor's experiences underscore the significance of socialization, especially during childhood. Their cases show that however rooted in biology certain capacities may be, they do not develop into recognizable human ways of acting and thinking unless the individual interacts with other humans in a social environment. Children raised in isolation fail to develop complex language, abstract thinking, notions of cooperation and sharing, or even a sense of themselves as people. In other words, they do not develop the hallmarks of what we know as humanity (Ridley, 1998).

Sociologists and other social scientists have developed a number of theories to explain the role of socialization in the development of social selves. What these theories recognize is that whatever the contribution of biology, ultimately people as social beings are made, not born. Below, we explore four approaches to understanding socialization: behaviorism, symbolic interactionism, developmental stage theories, and psychoanalytic theories.

BEHAVIORISM AND SOCIAL LEARNING THEORY

Behaviorism is *a psychological perspective that emphasizes the effect of rewards and punishments on human behavior.* It arose during the late 19th century to challenge the then-popular belief that human behavior results primarily from biological instincts and drives (Baldwin & Baldwin, 1986, 1988; Dishion, McCord, & Poulin, 1999). Early behaviorist researchers such as Ivan Pavlov (1849–1936) and John Watson (1878–1958), and later B. F. Skinner (1904–1990), demonstrated that even behavior thought to be purely instinctual (such as a dog salivating when it sees food) can be produced or extinguished through the application of rewards and punishments. Thus, a pigeon will learn to press a bar if that triggers the release of food (Skinner, 1938, 1953; Watson, 1924). Behaviorists concluded that both animal and human behavior can be learned, and neither is just instinctive.

When they turned to human beings, behaviorists focused on **social learning**, *the way people adapt their behavior in response to social rewards and punishments* (Baldwin & Baldwin, 1986; Bandura, 1977; Bandura & Walters, 1963). Of particular interest was the satisfaction people get from imitating others. Social learning theory thus combines the reward-and-punishment effects identified by behaviorists with the idea that we model the behavior of others; that is, we observe the way people respond to others' behavior.

Social learning theory would predict, for example, that if a boy gets high fives from his friends for talking back to his teacher—a form of encouragement rather than punishment—he is likely to repeat this behavior. What's more, other boys may imitate it. Social learning researchers have developed formulas for predicting how rewards and punishments affect behavior. For example, rewards given repeatedly may become less effective when the individual becomes satiated. If you have just eaten a huge piece of cake, you are less likely to feel rewarded by the prospect of another.

Social behaviorism is not widely embraced today as a rigorous perspective on human behavior. One reason is that only in carefully controlled laboratory environments is it easy to demonstrate the power of rewards and punishments. In real social situations the theory is of limited value as a predictor. For example, whether a girl who is teased ("punished") for playing football will lose interest in the sport depends on many other experiences, such as the support of family and friends and her own enjoyment of the activity. The simple application of rewards and punishments is hardly sufficient to explain why people repeat some behaviors and not others.

In addition, behaviorist theories violate Popper's principle of falsification (discussed in Chapter 2). Since what was previously rewarding may lose effectiveness if the person is satiated, if a reward does not work, we can always attribute its failure to satiation. Therefore, no matter the outcome of the experiment, the theory has to be true; it cannot be proven false. For these reasons sociologists find behaviorism an inadequate theory of socialization. To explain how people become socialized, they highlight theories that emphasize *symbolic interaction.*

SOCIALIZATION AS SYMBOLIC INTERACTION

Recall from the introductory chapter that *symbolic interactionism* views the self and society as resulting from social interaction based on language and other symbols. Symbolic interactionism has proven especially fruitful in explaining how individuals develop a social identity and a capacity for social interaction (Blumer, 1969, 1970; Hutcheon, 1999; Mead, 1934, 1938).

An early contribution to symbolic interactionism was Charles Horton Cooley's (1864–1929) concept of the **looking-glass self**, the *self-image that results from our interpretation*

Behaviorism: A psychological perspective that emphasizes the effect of rewards and punishments on human behavior.

Social learning: The way people adapt their behavior in response to social rewards and punishments.

Looking-glass self: The concept developed by Charles Horton Cooley that our self-image results from how we interpret other people's views of us.

CQR Deprivation of Social Interaction

of other people's views of us. For example, children who are frequently told they are smart or talented will tend to see themselves as such and act accordingly. On the other hand, children who are repeatedly told they lack intelligence or are "slow" will lose pride in themselves and act the part. According to Cooley (1902/1964), we are constantly forming ideas about how others perceive and judge us, and the resulting self-image—the way we view ourselves—is in turn the basis of our social interaction with others.

Cooley recognized that not everyone we encounter is equally important in shaping our self-image. **Primary groups** are *small groups characterized by intense emotional ties, face-to-face interaction, intimacy, and a strong, enduring sense of commitment.* Families, close friends, and lovers are all examples of primary groups likely to shape our self-image. **Secondary groups**, on the other hand, are *large and impersonal, characterized by fleeting relationships.* We spend much of our adult lives in secondary groups, such as college classrooms and workplaces, but secondary groups typically have less influence in forming our self-image than do primary groups. Both kinds of groups act on us throughout our lives; the self-image is not set in concrete at some early stage but continues to develop throughout adulthood (Barber, 1992; Berns, 1989).

Both primary and secondary groups also serve as **reference groups**, or *groups that provide standards for judging our attitudes or behaviors.* When you consider your friends' reactions to your dress or hairstyle or the brand of mobile phone you plan to buy, you are using your peers as a reference in shaping your decisions.

George Herbert Mead (1863–1931), widely regarded as the founder of symbolic interactionism, explored the ways in which self and society shape one another. Mead proposed that the self comprises two parts: the "I" and the "me." The **I** is *the impulse to act; it is creative, innovative, unthinking, and largely unpredictable.* The **me** is *the part of the self through which we see ourselves as others see us.* (Note the similarity between Mead's "me" and Cooley's "looking-glass self.") The I represents innovation; the me, social convention and conformity. In the tension between them, the me is often capable of controlling the I. When the I initiates a spontaneous act, the me raises society's response: *How will others regard me if I act this way?*

Mead further argued that people develop a sense of self through **role-taking**, *the ability to take the roles of others in interaction.* For example, a young girl playing soccer may pretend to be a coach; in the process, she learns to see herself (as well as other players) from a coach's perspective. Mead proposed that childhood socialization relies on an ever-increasing ability to take on such roles, moving from the extreme self-centeredness of the infant to an adult ability to take the standpoint of society as a whole. He outlined four principal stages in socialization that reflect this progression: the preparatory, play, game, and adult stages. The completion of each stage results in an increasingly mature social self.

CHRIS WALKER/KRT/Newscom

As a reference group, high school peers may provide the normative standards for a young person to judge his or her fashion sense, musical tastes, behavioral choices, and academic commitment. Does the power of peers as a reference group change in the college years?

1. During the *preparatory stage,* children younger than 3 years old relate to the world as though they are the center of the universe. They do not engage in true role-taking but respond primarily to things in their immediate environments, such as their mothers' breasts, the colors of toys, or the sounds of voices.

2. Children 3 or 4 years of age enter the *play stage,* during which they learn to take the attitudes and roles of the people with whom they interact. **Significant others** are *the specific people important in children's lives and whose views have the greatest impact on the children's self-evaluations.* By role-playing at being mothers or fathers, for example, children come to see themselves as their parents see them. However, according

Primary groups: Small groups characterized by intense emotional ties, face-to-face interaction, intimacy, and a strong, enduring sense of commitment.

Secondary groups: Groups that are large and impersonal and characterized by fleeting relationships.

Reference groups: Groups that provide standards for judging our attitudes or behaviors.

I: According to George Herbert Mead, the part of the self that is the impulse to act; it is creative, innovative, unthinking, and largely unpredictable.

Me: According to George Herbert Mead, the part of the self through which we see ourselves as others see us.

Role-taking: The ability to take the roles of others in interaction.

Significant others: According to George Herbert Mead, the specific people who are important in children's lives and whose views have the greatest impact on the children's self-evaluations.

Socialization and Men

© Jim West / Alam

Game playing is an activity found in some form in every culture. Some games, including basketball and soccer, require teamwork, while others, including checkers and mancala, are played by one person against another. Team sports games provide many socialization benefits, as young children learn how to interact with one another and develop their motor skills.

to Mead, they have not yet acquired the complex sense of self that lets them see themselves through the eyes of *many* different people—or society.

3. The *game* stage begins when children are about 5 and learn to take the roles of multiple others. The game is an effective analogy for this stage. For example, to be an effective basketball player, an individual must have the ability to see him- or herself from the perspective of teammates, the other team, and the coach, and must play accordingly. He or she must know the rules of the game. Successful negotiation of the social world also requires that people gain the ability to see themselves as others see them, to understand societal "rules," and to act accordingly. This stage signals the development of a self that is aware of societal positions and perspectives.

4. Game playing takes the child to the final, *adult stage,* which can appear as early as the first and second grades. Children at this stage have internalized the **generalized other**, *the sense of society's norms values by which people evaluate themselves.* They take into account a set of general principles that may or may not serve their self-interest—for example, voluntarily joining the army to fight in a war that might injure or kill them because patriotic young people are expected to defend their country. By the adult stage, a person is capable of understanding abstract and complex cultural symbols, such as love and hate, success and failure, friendship, and morality.

Mead also had a vision that in the future people would be able to assimilate a multitude of generalized others, adapting their behavior in terms of their own but also other people's cultures. Mead's "dream of a highly multicultural world" may someday be a reality as globalization makes ever more people aware of the value of other cultures.

STAGES OF DEVELOPMENT: PIAGET AND KOHLBERG

Like Mead and Cooley, the Swiss social psychologist Jean Piaget (1896–1980) believed humans are socialized in stages. Piaget devoted a lifetime to researching how young children develop the ability to think abstractly and make moral judgments (Piaget, 1926, 1928, 1930, 1932). His theory of **cognitive development**, based largely on studies of Swiss children at play (including his own), argues that *an individual's ability to make logical decisions increases as the person grows older.* Piaget noted that infants are highly **egocentric**, *experiencing the world as if it were centered entirely on them.* In stages over time, socialization lets children learn to use language and symbols, to think abstractly and logically, and to see things from different perspectives.

Piaget also developed a theory of moral development, which holds that as they grow, people learn to act according to abstract ideas about justice or fairness. This theory parallels his idea of cognitive development, since both describe overcoming egocentrism and acquiring the ability to take other points of view. Eventually children come to develop abstract notions of fairness, learning that rules should be judged relative to the circumstances. For example, even if the rules say "three strikes and you're out," an exception might be made for a child who has never played the game or who is physically challenged.

Lawrence Kohlberg (1927–1987) extended Piaget's ideas about moral development. In his best-known study, subjects were told the story of the fictitious "Heinz," who was unable to afford a drug that might prevent his wife from dying of cancer. As the story unfolds, Heinz breaks into the druggist's shop and steals the medication. Kohlberg asked his subjects what they would have done, emphasizing that there is no "right" or "wrong" answer. Using experiments such as this, Kohlberg (1969, 1983, 1984) proposed three principal stages (and several substages) of moral development:

1. The *preconventional stage,* during which people seek simply to achieve personal gain or avoid punishment. A person might support Heinz's decision to steal on the grounds that it would be too difficult to get the medicine by other means, or oppose it on the grounds that Heinz might get caught and go to jail. Children are typically socialized into this rudimentary form of morality between ages 7 and 10.

Generalized other: The abstract sense of society's norms and values by which people evaluate themselves.

Cognitive development: The theory, developed by Jean Piaget, that an individual's ability to make logical decisions increases as the person grows older.

Egocentric: Experiencing the world as if it were centered entirely on oneself.

2. The *conventional stage,* during which the individual is socialized into society's norms and values and would feel shame or guilt about violating them. The person might support Heinz's decision to steal on the grounds that society would judge him callous if he let his wife die, or oppose it because people would call Heinz a thief if he were caught. Children are socialized into this more developed form of morality at about age 10, and most people remain in this stage throughout their adult lives.

3. The *postconventional stage,* during which the individual invokes general, abstract notions of right and wrong. Even though Heinz has broken the law, his transgression has to be weighed against the moral cost of sacrificing his wife's life. People at the highest levels of postconventional morality will go beyond social convention entirely, appealing to a higher set of abstract principles.

Some scholars have argued that Kohlberg's theory reflects a strong male bias because it derives from male rather than female experience. Foremost among Kohlberg's critics is Carol Gilligan (1982; Gilligan, Ward, & Taylor, 1989), who argues that men may be socialized to base moral judgment on abstract principles of fairness and justice, but women are socialized to base theirs on compassion and caring. She showed that women scored lower on Kohlberg's measure of moral development because they valued how other family members were affected by Heinz's decision more than abstract considerations of justice. Because it assumes that abstract thinking represents a "higher stage" of development, Gilligan suggests, Kohlberg's measure is necessarily biased in favor of male socialization.

Research testing Gilligan's ideas has found that men and women alike adhere to *both* care-based and justice-based forms of moral reasoning (Gump, Baker, & Roll, 2000; Jaffee & Hyde, 2000). Differences between the sexes in these kinds of reasoning are in fact small or nonexistent. Studies of federal employees (Peek, 1999), a sample of men and women using the Internet (Anderson, 2000), and a sample of Mexican American and Anglo-American students (Gump et al., 2000) have all found no significant difference between men and women in the degree to which they employ care-based and justice-based styles of moral reasoning. In her effort to correct Kohlberg's research, which looked only at men, might Gilligan have also contributed to gender stereotypes?

BIOLOGICAL NEEDS VERSUS SOCIAL CONSTRAINTS: FREUD

Sigmund Freud (1856–1939), an Austrian psychiatrist, had a major impact on the study of socialization as well as the disciplines of psychology and psychiatry. Freud (1905, 1929, 1933) founded the field of **psychoanalysis**, *a psychological perspective that emphasizes the complex reasoning processes of the conscious and unconscious mind.* He stressed

FIGURE 4.2 The Id, Ego, and Superego, as Conceived by Freud

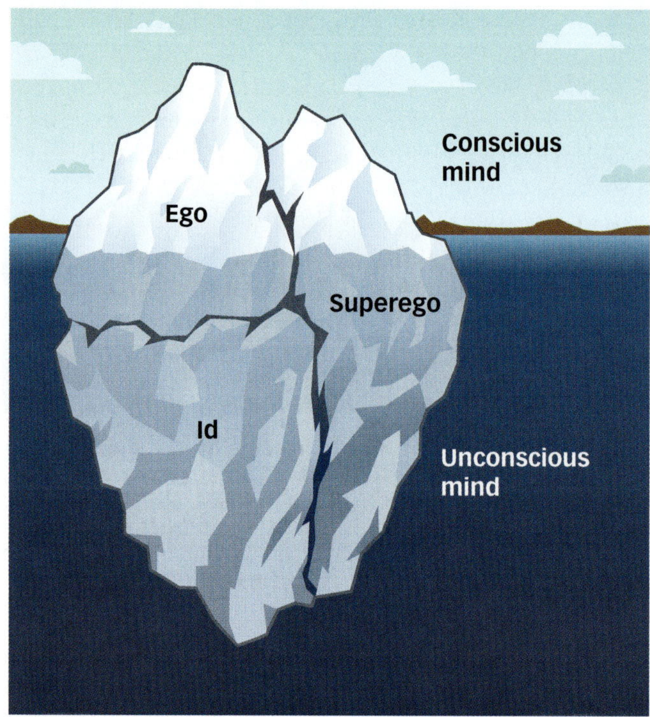

the role of the unconscious mind in shaping human behavior and theorized that early childhood socialization is essential in molding the adult personality by age 5 or 6. In addition, Freud sought to demonstrate that in order to to thrive, a society must socialize its members to curb their instinctive needs and desires.

According to Freud, the human mind has three components: the id, the ego, and the superego (Figure 4.2). The **id** is *the repository of basic biological drives and needs,* which Freud believed to be primarily bound up in sexual energy. (*Id* is Latin for "it," reflecting Freud's belief that this aspect of the human personality is not even truly human.) The **ego** (Latin for "I") is *the "self," the core of what we regard as a person's unique personality.* The **superego** consists of *the values and norms of society, insofar as they are internalized, or taken in,*

Psychoanalysis: A psychological perspective that emphasizes the complex reasoning processes of the conscious and unconscious mind.

Id: According to Sigmund Freud, the part of the mind that is the repository of basic biological drives and needs.

Ego: According to Sigmund Freud, the part of the mind that is the "self," the core of what is regarded as a person's unique personality.

Superego: According to Sigmund Freud, the part of the mind that consists of the values and norms of society, insofar as they are internalized, or taken in, by the individual.

by the individual. The concept of the superego is similar to the notion of a conscience.

Freud believed that babies are all id. Left to their own devices, they will seek instant gratification of their biological needs for food, physical contact, and nurturing. Therefore, according to Freud, to be socialized they must eventually learn to suppress such gratification. The child's superego, consisting of cultural "shoulds" and "should nots," struggles constantly with the biological impulses of the id. Serving as mediator between id and superego is the child's emerging ego. In Freud's view, the child will grow up to be a well-socialized adult to the extent that the ego succeeds in bending the biological desires of the id to meet the social demands of the superego.

Since Freud claimed that personality is set early in life, he viewed change as difficult for adults, especially if psychological troubles originate in experiences too painful to face or remember. Individuals must become fully aware of their repressed or unconscious memories and unacceptable impulses if they ever hope to change (Freud, 1933). Freud's psychoanalytic therapy focused on accessing deeply buried feelings in order to help patients alter current behaviors and feelings. Whereas Mead saw socialization as a lifelong process relying on many socialization agents, for Freud it stopped at a young age. Table 4.1 compares Mead's and Freud's views point by point.

TABLE 4.1 Comparison of Mead's and Freud's Theories of Socialization

Mead's Stages	Freud's Psychoanalytic Theory
Preparatory: Highly limited role-taking in which the individual views the world through his or her own eyes.	**Id:** The repository of basic biological drives and needs, which seeks instant gratification.
Play: The individual takes on the roles of significant others, one at a time.	**Ego:** The "self" that, once developed, balances the forces of the id and superego. The ego is necessary in the socialization process for the individual to become a well-adjusted adult.
Game: The individual is able to view the world through the eyes of multiple others, simultaneously.	**Superego:** The values and norms of society. May conflict with the id.
Maturity: The individual is able to take the attitude of the generalized other and can view the world through the eyes of society as a whole.	

SOURCE: Adapted from Mead, G. H. (1934). *Mind, self, and society.* Chicago: University of Chicago Press.

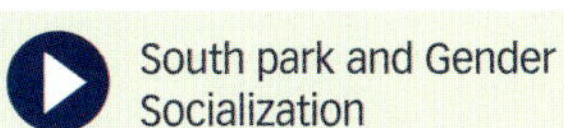
South park and Gender Socialization

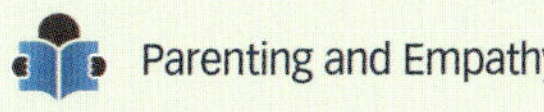
Parenting and Empathy

FIGURE 4.3 Agents of Socialization

AGENTS OF SOCIALIZATION

Among primary groups, the family is for most people the single most critical agent of socialization. Other significant agents are school, peer groups, work, religion, and technology and mass media, including the Internet and social media (Figure 4.3).

THE FAMILY

The family is a primary group in which children, especially during the earliest years of their lives, are physically and emotionally dependent on adult members. It plays a key role in transmitting norms, values, and culture across generations, and as a result it is the first and usually the foremost source of socialization in all societies.

Children usually first encounter their society in the family, learning socially defined roles like father, mother, sister, brother, uncle, aunt, and grandparent, and the expected behaviors attached to them. Parents often hold stereotypical notions of how boys and girls should be, and they reinforce gender behaviors in countless subtle and not-so-subtle ways. A father may be responsible for grilling and yard work, while a mother cooks dinner and cleans the house. On the other hand, some families embrace egalitarian or nonconventional gender roles. Although same-sex couple families are more likely than families headed by opposite-sex couples to challenge gender-normative roles and behaviors, they sometimes still enforce or support typical gender roles for their children (Ackbar, 2011; Bos & Sandfort, 2010).

The way parents relate to their child affects virtually every aspect of the child's behavior, including the ability to resolve conflicts through the use of reason instead of violence and the

PRIVATE LIVES, PUBLIC ISSUES

SPANKING AND AGGRESSIVE BEHAVIOR

While many people still believe in the adage "Spare the rod and spoil the child," the use of physical punishment in socializing children varies largely by social class. At a rate that has largely held steady in the past decades, about 65% of U.S. adults approve of spanking under certain circumstances. Interestingly, these adults are most likely to be members of the working class, rather than the middle or upper class (Berlin et al., 2009; Borgeson, 2001; Rosellini & Mulrine, 1998). Remember Kohn's (1989) research, which concluded that the experience of people in working-class employment is reflected in their child-rearing practices: Working-class parents are more likely to emphasize obedience than are middle-class parents, who tend to stress independent thinking. The use of corporal punishment, however, is not only a matter of social class or a private decision made by parents in the home. It is also a public issue with social consequences.

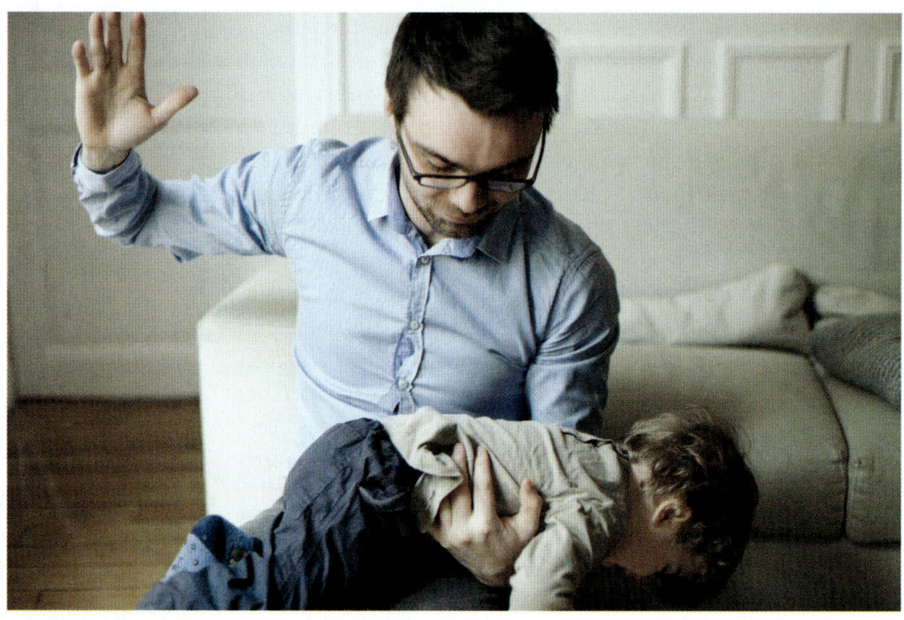

Spencer Grant/Photo Researchers, Inc.

Should parents spank their children? Ask some friends or classmates what they think. You may find a wide range of opinions on this practice.

Murray Straus, a prominent sociologist at the University of New Hampshire, found that when boys and girls 6 to 9 years old were spanked, they became more antisocial—more likely to cheat, tell lies, act cruelly to others, break things deliberately, and get into trouble at school (Straus, Sugarman, & Giles-Sims, 1997; also see McKee et al., 2007). Straus and his colleagues concluded that reducing corporal punishment would not only benefit children but also possibly reduce antisocial behavior.

Other research evidence supports Straus's conclusions (Borgeson, 2001; de Paul & Domenech, 2000). For example, one study concluded that corporal punishment, and even some lesser forms of parental punishment, could have a strong effect on a child's ability to cope later in life (Welsh, 1998). Similarly, the authors of a study of Israeli high school students found that adolescents whose parents routinely resorted to physical punishment were more likely than others to have psychiatric symptoms and lower levels of well-being in general (Bachar, Canetti, Bonne, DeNour, & Shalev, 1997). On the other hand, research by psychologist Marjorie Lindner Gunnoe (1997), which tracked more than 1,100 children over a 5-year period, found that while some 8- to 11-year-old boys, but not girls, who had been spanked regularly got into more fights at school, children of both sexes ages 4 to 7 who had been spanked regularly got into fewer fights than children who were not spanked. Most research, however, confirms the negative effects of spanking.

Although not all the research findings on the effects of physical punishment are in agreement, the evidence does suggest that spanking—an aggressive form of punishment—may result in aggressive behavior on the part of children. The parents' "private" decision to use corporal punishment becomes a "public issue," since children who are physically punished at home are more likely to become physically aggressive outside the home.

THINK IT THROUGH

▶ Using the knowledge you have gained through the study of socialization, and knowing the results of research on the effects of physical punishment on children's behavior, could you design a social policy or program to reduce the use of physical punishment in the home?

propensity for emotional stability or distress. The likelihood that young people will be victims of homicide, commit suicide, engage in acts of aggression against other people, use drugs, complete their secondary education, or have an unwanted pregnancy also is greatly influenced by childhood experiences in the family (Campbell & Muncer, 1998; McLoyd & Smith, 2002; Muncer & Campbell, 2000). For example, children who are regularly spanked or otherwise physically punished internalize the idea that violence is an acceptable means of achieving goals and are more likely than peers who are not spanked to engage in aggressive delinquent behavior. They are also more likely to have low self-esteem, suffer depression, and do poorly in school (Borgeson, 2001; Straus et al., 1997). (See the *Private Lives, Public Issues* box on page 88.)

Child-rearing practices within families can vary by ethnicity or religious affiliation. Because U.S. culture is ethnically diverse, it is difficult to describe a "typical" American family (Glazer, 1997; Stokes & Chevan, 1996). Among Latinos, for example, the family often includes grandparents, aunts, uncles, cousins, and in-laws, who share child-rearing responsibilities. Among African Americans as well, child rearing may be shared among a broader range of family members than in White families (Lubeck, 1985). Extended family patterns also occur among Afro-Caribbean immigrants and the Amish religious community of Pennsylvania (Forsythe-Brown, 2007; Ho, 1993; Stokes & Chevan, 1996).

Child-rearing practices may vary by social class as well. Parents whose jobs require them to be subservient to authority and to follow orders without raising questions typically stress obedience and respect for authority at home, while parents whose work gives them freedom to make their own decisions and be creative are likely to socialize their children into norms of creativity and spontaneity. Since many working-class jobs demand conformity while middle- and upper-middle-class jobs are more likely to offer independence, social class may be a key factor in explaining differences in child rearing (Kohn, 1989; Lareau, 2002).

Family patterns are changing rapidly in the United States, partly because of declining marriage rates and high rates of divorce. Such changes affect socialization. For example, children raised by a single parent may lack role models for the parent who is missing or experience economic hardship that in turn determines where they go to school or with whom they socialize. Children raised in blended families (the result of remarriage) may have stepparents and stepsiblings whose norms, values, and behavior are unfamiliar. Same-sex couple families may both challenge and, as noted earlier, reinforce conventional modes of socialization, particularly with respect to gender socialization. Although families are changing, the influence of agents of socialization remains powerful.

Hidden curriculum: The unspoken classroom socialization into the norms, values, and roles of a society that schools provide along with the "official" curriculum.

CQR Socialization and Education

Teen Shaming

Spencer Grant/Photo Researchers, Inc.

Schools are an important agent of socialization. Students learn academic skills and knowledge, but they also gain social skills, acquire dominant values of citizenship, and practice obedience to authority.

TEACHERS AND SCHOOL

Children in the United States often begin "schooling" when they enter day care or preschool as infants or toddlers, and they spend more hours each day and more days each year in school than was the case a hundred years ago (although they spend less time in school than their peers in Europe and Asia). Indeed, education has taken on a large role in helping young people prepare for adult society. In addition to reading, writing, math, and other academic subjects, schools are expected to teach values and norms like patriotism, competitiveness, morality, and respect for authority, as well as basic social skills. Some sociologists call this the **hidden curriculum**, that is, *the unspoken classroom socialization into the norms, values, and roles of a society that schools provide along with the "official" curriculum.* The hidden curriculum may include "lessons" in gender roles taught through teachers' differing expectations of boys and girls, with, for instance, boys pushed to pursue higher math while girls are encouraged to embrace language and literature (Sadker, Zittleman, & Sadker, 2003). It may also entail "lessons" that reinforce class status, with middle- and upper-class children having access to classes and schools with advanced subjects and high technology and poor children provided a smaller selection of less academically challenging or vocational classes and limited access to advanced teaching technologies (Bowles & Gintis, 1976; Kozol, 2005).

PEERS

Peers are people of the same age and, often, the same social standing. Peer socialization begins when a child starts to play with other children outside the family, usually during the first year of life, and grows more intense in school. Conformity to the norms and values of friends is especially compelling during adolescence and continues into adulthood (Harris, 2009; Ponton, 2000; Sebald, 2000). In U.S. society, most adolescents spend more time with their peers than with their families due to school, athletic activities, and other social and academic commitments. Sociological theories thus often focus on young people's peer groups to account for a wide variety of adult behavioral patterns, including the development of self-esteem and self-image, career choices, ambition, and deviant behavior (Cohen, 1955; Hine, 2000; Sebald, 2000).

Judith Rich Harris (2009) argues that after the first few years of life, a child's friends' opinions outweigh the opinions of parents. To manage these predominant peer group influences, she suggests, parents must try to ensure that their children have the "right" friends. But this is an increasingly complex problem when "friends" may be Internet acquaintances who are difficult to monitor and of whom parents may be unaware.

The adolescent subculture plays an extremely important part in the socialization of adolescents in the modern world. Researchers have described the following characteristics of this subculture (Hine, 2000; Sebald, 2000):

1. A set of norms not shared with the adult or childhood cultures and governing interaction, statuses, and roles.

2. An *argot* (the special vocabulary of a particular group) that is not shared with nonadolescents and is often frowned upon by adults and school officials. Think about the jargon used by young people who text—many adults can read it only with difficulty!

3. Various underground media and preferred media programs, music, and Internet sites.

4. Unique fads and fashions in dress and hairstyles that often lead to conflict with parents and other adult authorities over their "appropriateness."

5. A set of "heroes, villains, and fools." Sometimes adults are the "villains and fools," while the adults' "villains and fools" are heroes in the adolescent subculture.

6. A more open attitude than that found in the general culture toward experimentation with drugs and at times violence (fighting, for example).

Teenagers differ in the degree to which they are caught up in, and therefore socialized by, the adolescent subculture. Harris's (2009) claim that parents are largely irrelevant is no doubt an overstatement, yet in Western cultures peer socialization does play a crucial part in shaping many of the ideas, self-images, and attitudes that will persist throughout individuals' lives.

Sociologists use the term **anticipatory socialization** to describe the process of *adopting the behaviors or standards of a group one emulates or hope to join.* For example, teens who seek membership into a tough, streetwise gang will abandon mainstream norms for the dress and talk of the tougher youth they seek to emulate. Similarly, young people who aspire

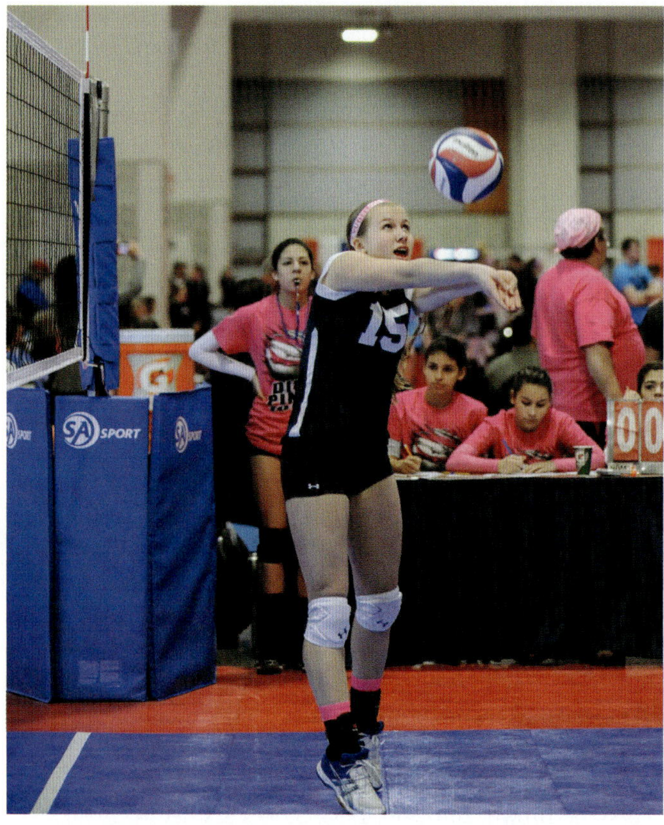

Author

Since the passage of Title IX in 1972, millions of girls have had the opportunity to participate in organized sports. Do social messages conveyed by male-dominated sports differ from those in female-dominated sports?

to be part of a respected group of athletes may adopt forms of dress and training practices that may lead to acceptance by the group. Anticipatory socialization looks to future expectations rather than just present experience.

ORGANIZED SPORTS

Organized sports are a fundamental part of the lives of millions of children in the United States: By one estimate, 21.5 million children and teens ages 6 to 17 participate in at least one organized sport (Kelley & Carchia, 2013). If it is the case, as psychologist Erik Erikson (1950) posited, that in middle childhood children develop a sense of "industry or inferiority," then it is surely the case that in a sports-obsessed country like the United States, one avenue for generating this sense of self is through participation in sports.

Being part of a sports team and mastering skills associated with sports are activities that are widely recognized in U.S. society as valuable; they are presumed to "build character" and to contribute to hard work, competitiveness, and the

Anticipatory socialization: Adoption of the behaviors or standards of a group one emulates or hopes to join.

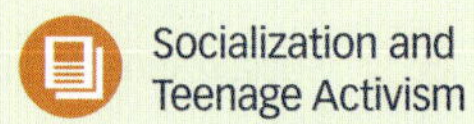
Socialization and Teenage Activism

Silver Screen Collection/Contributor/Getty Images

Getty Images/Staff/Getty Images

© AF archive/Alamy

Television offers a variety of female images ranging from independent working women to "fashionistas." From the *Mary Tyler Moore Show* (1970–1977) to *Sex and the City* (1998-2004) to *Pretty Little Liars* (2010–Present), images can both reflect and construct ideas about femininity.

ability to perform in stressful situations and under the gaze of others (Friedman, 2013), all of which are positively evaluated. In fact, research suggests that there are particular benefits of sports for girls, including lower rates of teen sexual activity and pregnancy (Sabo, Miller, Farrell, Melnick, & Barnes, 1999) and higher rates of college attendance, labor force participation, and entry into male-dominated occupations (Stevenson, 2010). Some studies have also found improved academic performance relative to nonparticipants for all athletes, though they have shown some variation in this effect by race and gender (Eccles & Barber, 1999; Miller, Melnick, Barnes, Farrell, & Sabo, 2005).

At the same time, sports participation has been associated in some research literature with socialization into negative attitudes, including homophobia. In a study of more than 1,400 teenagers, Osborne and Wagner (2007) found that boys who participated in "core" sports (football, basketball, baseball, and/or soccer) were three times more likely than their nonparticipant peers to express homophobic attitudes. In a country in which sports and sports figures are widely venerated and participation, particularly for boys, is labeled as "masculine," there may also be negative effects for boys who are not athletic or who do not enjoy sports.

RELIGION

Religion is a central part of the lives of many people around the world. While the United States has a notable proportion of inhabitants who identify as atheists, about 80% of U.S. adults indicate they are members of a religion, and nearly 40% attend religious services once a week. Even among the one-fifth of the population who declare themselves unaffiliated with any particular religion, 68% believe in God, and more than 20% say that they pray every day (Pew Forum on Religion and Public Life, 2012b). Beginning with Émile Durkheim, sociologists have noted the role of religion in fostering social solidarity. Talcott Parsons (1970) pointed out that religion also acts as an agent of socialization, teaching fundamental values and beliefs that contribute to a shared normative culture.

Different religions function in similar ways, giving their followers a sense of what is right and wrong, how to conduct themselves in society, and how to organize their lives. Some socialize their followers with abstract teachings about morality, service, or self-discipline, directing believers to, for example, serve their fellow human beings or to avoid the sin of vanity. Others contain abstract teachings but specific rules about dress and hairstyles. The Amish faith entreats young men to remain clean-shaven prior to marriage, but married men must grow beards. Sikh men of India wear turbans that cover their hair, which they do not cut.

Like other agents of socialization and social control, religion directs its followers to choose certain paths and behaviors and not others. This is not to say that we are compelled to behave a certain way but rather that socialization often leads us to control our own behavior because we fear social ostracism or other negative consequences.

MASS MEDIA, THE INTERNET, AND SOCIAL MEDIA

Among the most influential agents of socialization in modern societies are technology and the mass media. Newspapers, magazines, movies, radio, and television are all forms of mass media. Television may be a particularly influential agent of socialization: In the United States, the average child aged 2 to 11

FIGURE 4.4 Average Weekly Television Viewing by Age Group in the United States, 2011

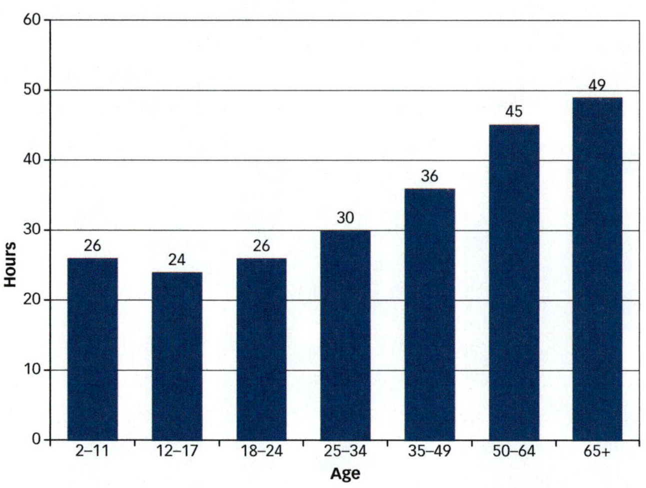

SOURCE: Data from Nielsen (2011) *State of the Media: The Cross Platform Report.* New York City: Nielsen Media Research.

spends more than 26 hours a week in front of the TV (Nielsen, 2011; see also Figure 4.4), and by age 5 to 8, nearly half have televisions in their bedrooms (Lewin, 2011b). By the time the typical American child reaches 18, he or she will have viewed nearly 18,000 hours of television. While television remains a staple in the daily lives of most children and young people, an increasing proportion of screen time is spent surfing Internet sites, watching online videos, texting, or interacting through sites like Facebook, all of which also contribute to socialization.

Child psychologists, sociologists, and parents' groups pay special attention to the impact of TV and other media violence on children and young adults. Media studies during the past 20 years have largely come to a common conclusion: Media violence has the clear potential to socialize children, teenagers, and even adults into a greater acceptance of real-life violence. This is true for males and females, Whites and non-Whites. Much media violence is directed against women, and a large body of research supports the conclusion that media violence promotes tolerance among men for sexual violence, including rape (Anderson et al., 2003; Greene & Krcmar, 2005). The argument is not that viewing violent shows is a direct cause of violence; rather, viewers may become immunized to the sight of violence. Still, given that most people who are exposed to violence in the media do not become violent, the part played by the media as an agent of socialization is probably less important than the contribution made by other agents, such as family and peers.

The media play a role in socialization by creating fads and fashions for how people should look, what they should wear, and what kinds of friendships they should have. These influences, and accompanying gender stereotypes, are particularly strong during adolescence. Children's cartoons, prime-time television, TV advertisements, and popular networks like MTV, TLC, and VH-1 often depict males and females, as well as people of particular races and ethnicities, in stereotyped ways. Teenage girls, for example, are likely to be depicted as boy-crazy and obsessed with their looks; teenage boys are shown as active, independent, and sexually and physically aggressive (Kahlenberg & Hein, 2010; Maher, Herbst, Childs, & Finn, 2008). Females' roles also portray mostly familial or romantic ideals, whereas males fulfill work-related roles (Lauzen, Dozier, & Horan, 2008). These stereotypes have been found to influence children's gender perceptions (Aubrey & Harrison, 2004; Gerding & Signorielli, 2014). Additionally, gender stereotypes influence beliefs across the spectrum of sexual orientation, with gay teens embracing stereotypes in ways comparable to their heterosexual peers (Bishop, Kiss, Morrison, Rushe, & Specht, 2014).

By some estimates, people in the United States now spend more than a billion hours per month using social networking sites, 407 million hours participating in online gaming, and 329 million hours e-mailing (Nielsen, 2010, 2011). While the long-term impacts of this massive level of use have yet to be determined, one clear way the Internet affects socialization is by changing social interaction. To name just one effect that was impossible 20 years ago, large groups of semianonymous individuals, often separated by great distances, can interact with one another in virtual communities, even forming close ties and friendships.

On the positive side, especially when online interactions are mixed with off-line face-to-face interactions, Internet use can foster new personal relationships and build stronger communities (Rule, 1999; Valentine, 2006; Wellman & Hampton, 1999). The types of friendships adolescents create and maintain through social media reflect the friendships they have off-line (Mazur & Richards, 2011). Since online interaction is often anonymous and occurs from the safety of familiar places, people with characteristics society tends to stigmatize, such as obesity or a stutter, can enter virtual communities where differences are not perceived or punished (McKenna & Bargh, 1998) and interests such as chess or movies can be shared. Finally, the moderate use of e-mail and the Internet can help children and teens maintain and strengthen interpersonal relationships (Subrahmanyam & Lin, 2007).

The Internet can have negative social consequences, too. Researchers have linked high levels of use with declines in communication within households, shrinking social circles, and increased depression and loneliness (Dokoupil, 2012a, 2012b; Kraut et al., 1998; Yen, Yen, & Ko, 2010). Extreme cases can develop into Internet addiction, a relatively recent phenomenon characterized by a search for social stimulation and escape from real-life problems (Armstrong, Phillips, & Saling, 2000; Block, 2008). Although the Internet can be a valuable learning tool for children, it can also damage their development by decreasing the time they spend in face-to-face interactions and exposing them to inappropriate information and images (Bremer & Rauch, 1998; Lewin, 2011b; Livingstone & Brake, 2010).

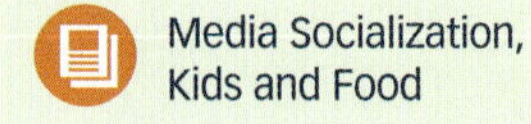
Media Socialization, Kids and Food

Another form of negative socialization is *cyberbullying*—taunting, teasing, or verbal attacks through e-mail, text, or social networking sites with the intent to hurt the victim (Van DeBosch & Van Cleemput, 2008). Cyberbullying is a growing problem of acute concern to social workers, child psychologists, and school administrators (Slovak & Singer, 2011). Children and adolescents who are bullied in real life are sometimes both cyberbullies and victims of cyberbullying (Dilmac, 2009; Smith et al., 2008; Tyman, Saylor, Taylor, & Comeaux, 2010). Victims take to the Internet to get revenge, often through anonymous attacks, but this perpetuates the bullying cycle online and in real life. One study found that hurtful cyberteasing between adolescents in romantic relationships can escalate into real-life shouting, throwing of objects, or hitting (Madlock & Westerman, 2011).

Modern technology may foster positive socialization, but it also has the potential to be detrimental on both the micro level of individual and small-group interactions and the macro level of communities and countries. Consider the role played today by social media in turning interest groups, and even ethnic groups, against one another. The Internet can be a powerful source of information, but it can also be a source of profound disinformation and hatred, as we discuss in the *Global Issues* box on page 95.

WORK

For most adults in the United States, postadolescent socialization begins with entry into the workforce. While workplace norms calling for conformity or individuality are frequently taught by parents in the home, expectations at work can differ from those we experience in primary groups such as the family and peer groups.

Arguably, workplace socialization has had a particular influence on women, dramatically changing gender roles in many countries, including the United States. Beginning in the 1960s, paid work afforded women increased financial independence, allowing them to marry later—or not at all—and bringing them new opportunities for social interaction and new social roles.

Employment also often socializes us into both the job role and our broader role as a "member" of a collective sharing the same employer. Becoming a teacher, chef, factory worker, lawyer, or retail salesperson, for instance, requires learning specific skills and the norms, values, and practices associated with that position. In that role, the employee may also internalize the values and norms of the employer and may even come to identify with the employer: Notice that employees who are speaking about their workplaces will often refer to them rather intimately, saying, for instance, not that "Company X is hiring a new sales manager" but rather that "*we* are hiring a new sales manager."

Even "occupations" outside the bounds of legality are governed by rules and roles learned through socialization. Harry King, a professional thief studied by one of the authors, learned not only how to break into buildings and open safes but also how to conform to the culture of the professional thief. A professional thief never "rats" on a partner, for example, or steals from mom-and-pop stores. In addition, King acquired a unique language that enabled him to talk to other thieves while in the company of nonthieves ("Square Johns"), police officers, and prison guards (King & Chambliss, 1984).

Careers & Self-Identity

SOCIALIZATION AND AGING

Most theories of socialization focus on infancy, childhood, and adolescence, but people do not stop changing once they become adults. Work, relationships, and the media, for example, shape socialization over the life course.

As people near the end of their working lives, anticipatory socialization again kicks in to help them envision their futures. Seniors may pay more attention to how friends react to retirement, whether they are treated differently as they age, and how the elderly are portrayed in the media. In U.S. media programming and advertisements, seniors are seriously underrepresented relative to their numbers in the nation's population. Older characters that are present are often gender stereotyped and wealthier than in the real world, but portrayals are usually positive, perhaps reflecting an attempt to appeal to this growing group (Kessler, Racoczy, & Staudinger, 2004; Lee, Carpenter, & Meyers, 2007).

There is a perception that seniors are more likely than younger adults to disengage from society, moving away from relationships, activities, and institutions that previously played key roles in their lives. While this is the case for some seniors, research suggests that most remain active as long as they are

Everett Collection

Meyrowitz (1985) writes that "old people are respected [in media portrayals] to the extent that they can behave like young people." Betty White is a highly recognized actress, whose roles are often humorous and appealing to younger crowds. Think about portrayals of the elderly you have seen recently in movies or on television. Do you agree with this assessment?

healthy (Rubin, 2006). In fact, the notion that seniors are disengaged is belied by the fact that many seniors are politically active (they have the highest rates of voting of any age group). As well, recent data published by the Pew Research Center's Internet and American Life Project shows that the strongest growth in Facebook use in 2013 was among users 65 years of age or older. About 45% of seniors who use the Internet are, the study shows, Facebook users (Pew Research Center, 2014b).

As people age, health and dying also become increasingly important and influential in structuring their perceptions and interactions. Married couples face the prospect of losing a spouse, and all seniors may begin to lose close friends. The question of what it might be like to live alone is more urgent for women than for men, since men, on average, die several years younger than women do. Very old people in particular are likely to spend time in the hospital, which requires being socialized into a total institution (discussed below). Growing older is thus influenced by socialization as significant and challenging as in earlier life stages.

Clearly, socialization is a lifelong process. Our early primary socialization lays a foundation for our social selves, which continue to develop through processes of secondary socialization, including our interactions with technology, media, education, and work. But can we be "resocialized"? That is, can our social selves be torn down and reconstituted in new forms that conform to the norms, roles, and rules of entirely different social settings? We explore this question in the following section.

TOTAL INSTITUTIONS AND RESOCIALIZATION

Although individuals typically play an active role in their own socialization, in one setting—the total institution—they experience little choice. **Total institutions** are *institutions that isolate individuals from the rest of society in order to achieve administrative control over most aspects of their lives.* Examples include prisons, the military, hospitals—especially mental hospitals—and live-in drug and alcohol treatment centers. Administrative control is achieved through rules that govern all aspects of daily life, from dress to schedules to interpersonal interactions. The residents of total institutions are subject to inflexible routines rigidly enforced by staff supervision (Goffman, 1961; Malacrida, 2005).

A major purpose of total institutions is **resocialization**, *the process of altering an individual's behavior through total control of his or her environment.* The first step is to break down the sense of self. In a total institution, every aspect of life is managed and monitored. The individual is stripped of identification with the outside world. Institutional haircuts, uniforms, round-the-clock inspections, and abuse, such as the harassment of new recruits to a military school, contribute to breaking down the individual's sense of self. In extreme situations, such as in concentration camps, psychological and even physical torture may also be used.

Once the institutionalized person is "broken," the institution begins rebuilding the personality. Desirable behaviors are rewarded with small privileges, such as choice of work duty in prisons. Undesirable behaviors are severely punished, as by the assignment of humiliating or painful work chores. Since the goal of the total institution is to change attitudes as well as behaviors, even a hint that the resident continues to harbor undesirable ideas may provoke disciplinary action.

How effective are total institutions in resocializing individuals? The answer depends partly on the methods used, partly on the individual, and partly on peer pressure. In the most extreme total institutions imaginable, Nazi concentration camps, some inmates came to identify with their guards and torturers, even helping them keep other prisoners under control. Most, however, resisted resocialization until their death or release (Bettelheim, 1979).

Prisons often fail at resocialization because inmates identify more with their fellow prisoners than with the administration's agenda. Inmates in U.S. prisons may well be resocialized, but it is not likely to be to the norms of prison officials or the wider society. Rather, prisoners learn the norms of other prisoners, and, as a result, many come out of prison more hardened in their criminal behavior than before.

Even when an institution is initially successful at resocialization, individuals who return to their original social environments often revert to earlier behavior. This reversal confirms that socialization is an ongoing process, continuing throughout a person's lifetime as a result of changing patterns of social interaction.

SOCIAL INTERACTION

Socialization at every stage of life occurs primarily through *social interaction*—interaction guided by the ordinary, taken-for-granted rules that enable people to live, work, and socialize together (Ridgeway & Smith-Lovin, 1999). Spoken words, gestures, body language, and other symbols and cues come together in complex ways to enable human communication. The sociologist must look behind the everyday aspects of social interaction to identify how it unfolds and how social norms and language make it possible.

Total institutions: Institutions that isolate individuals from the rest of society in order to achieve administrative control over most aspects of their lives.

Resocialization: The process of altering an individual's behavior through control of his or her environment, for example, within a total institution.

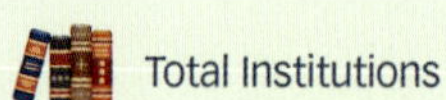
Total Institutions

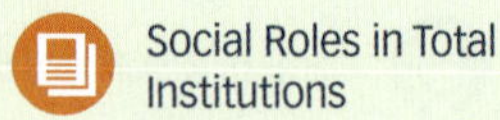
Social Roles in Total Institutions

GLOBAL ISSUES

SOCIALIZING HATRED IN A REGION OF CONFLICT

Throughout history, human beings everywhere have engaged in conflicts pitting one ethnic group against another. In the South Caucasus, conflict between ethnic groups has a long and bloody history. Nagorno-Karabakh, for example, is a sliver of land to which both Armenia and Azerbaijan lay historical claim. From 1988 to 1994, the two countries fought a deeply destructive war over the territory that killed 30,000 people and displaced more than a million others. While armed conflict is now limited to border skirmishes, formal and informal media in both countries exacerbate tensions—and perhaps increase the risk of future conflict—by socializing Armenians and Azeris to hate one another.

A woman walks past a wall decorated with the national colors in a street of Stepanakert, the capital of the self-proclaimed Republic of Nagorno-Karabakh, a mostly Armenian-populated enclave claimed by Azerbaijan. The final status of the republic has yet to be resolved, and it is recognized only by Armenia.

In 2011, the London-based nongovernmental organization International Alert (www.international-alert.org) used document analysis to study the way Armenians and Azeris perceive one another. Examining sources from school texts to online news sites and blogs to political speeches, the researchers hoped "to identify key words, narratives, and other innuendos that reference the concept of 'us vs. them' or 'friend vs. enemy'" (Geybullayeva, 2012). They found some alarming trends, particularly in the blogosphere.

Armenians and Armenia were common topics in the Azeri blogosphere, and many posts offered deeply negative and dehumanizing characterizations. Geybullayeva (2012) writes that in one post, "the author compared Armenia to a disease that should be eradicated." Other posts celebrated the killing of a civilian Armenian shepherd living near the border, lauding his death as "happy news" because there was one fewer Armenian. Geybullayeva suggests that youth, who are the most active users of the Internet, are the most likely to be affected by such messages, which both reflect and reproduce hatred for their ethnic neighbors.

Azeris are hardly alone in the blogosphere of hate. The Internet can bring people together through social networking and other means, but it can also tear them apart, functioning as a platform for socializing groups, and even generations, into hostility and hatred.

THINK IT THROUGH

▶ Should national laws or international agreements seek to restrict the use of the Internet as a platform for expressing or disseminating hatred of social groups? Would such laws violate the democratic value of "free speech"?

Social interaction usually requires conformity to social conventions. According to Scheff (1966), violation of the norms of interaction is generally interpreted as a sign that the person is "abnormal," perhaps even dangerous. A person in a crowded elevator who persists in engaging strangers in loud conversations, for example, and disheveled homeless people who shuffle down the street muttering to themselves evoke anxiety if not repugnance.

Norms govern a wide range of interactive behaviors. For example, making eye contact when speaking to someone is valued in mainstream U.S. culture; people who don't make eye contact are considered dishonest and shifty. By contrast, among the Navajo and the Australian Aborigines, as well as in many East Asian cultures, direct eye contact is considered disrespectful, especially with a person of greater authority. Norms also govern how close we stand to friends and strangers in making conversation. In North American and Northern European cultures, people avoid standing closer than a couple of feet from one another unless they are on intimate terms (Hall, 1973). Men in the United States are socialized to avoid displays of intimacy with other men, such as walking arm in arm. In Nigeria, however, men who are close friends or relatives hold hands when walking together, while in Italy, Spain, Greece, and some Middle Eastern countries, men commonly throw their arms around each other's shoulders, hug, and even kiss.

Two different approaches to studying social interaction are Erving Goffman's metaphor of interaction as theater and conversation analysts' efforts to study the way people manage routine talk. We discuss these approaches later, but first we look briefly at some sociologists' studies of social interaction.

STUDIES OF SOCIAL INTERACTION

Studies of social interaction have frequently drawn on the symbolic interactionist perspective. They illuminate nearly every form and aspect of social interaction. For example, research on battered women shows how victims of domestic violence redefine their situations to come to grips with abusive relationships (Hattery, 2001). One strategy is to deny the partner's violent behavior altogether, whereas another is to minimize the partner's responsibility, attributing it to external factors like unemployment, alcoholism, or mental illness. Or the victim will define her own role as caretaker and assume responsibility for "saving" the abusive partner. A woman who eventually decides to leave an abusive relationship must, some research suggests, redefine her situation so as to change her self-image. She must come to see herself as a victim of abuse who is capable of ending the abusive relationship, rather than as someone responsible for "solving" her mate's "problem" (Johnson & Ferraro, 1984).

Recent studies of social interaction have covered many topics, including the following:

- The way online gamers coordinate their individual actions with one another and through the user interface in order to succeed at games such as *World of Warcraft* (Williams & Kirschner, 2012)
- The strategies homeless youth use to manage and alleviate stigma, including creating friendships or attempting to pass as nonhomeless, as well as acting aggressive and fighting back (Roschelle & Kaufman, 2004)
- The ways in which a sense of "corporate social responsibility" is promoted and learned by corporate executives in the work environment (Shamir, 2011)

THE DRAMATURGICAL APPROACH: ERVING GOFFMAN

Erving Goffman (1959, 1961, 1963a, 1967, 1972), a major figure in the study of social interaction, developed a set of theoretical ideas that make it possible to observe and describe social interaction. Goffman used what he termed the **dramaturgical approach**, *the study of social interaction as if it were governed by the practices of theatrical performance.*

According to Goffman, people in their everyday lives are concerned, much like actors on a stage, with the **presentation of self**, that is, *the creation of impressions in the minds of others in order to define and control social situations.* For instance, to serve many customers simultaneously, a waiter must take charge with a "presentation of self" that is polite but firm and does not allow customers to usurp control by taking too much time ordering. After only a short time, the waiter asserts control by saying, "I'll give you a few minutes to decide what you want" and walks away.

As people interact, they monitor themselves and each other, looking for clues that reveal the impressions they are making on others. This ongoing effort at *impression management* results in a continual realignment of the individuals' "performances," as the "actors" refit their roles using dress, objects, voice, and gestures in a joint enterprise.

Continuing the metaphor of a theatrical performance, Goffman divides spheres of interaction into two stages. In the *front stage,* we are social actors engaged in a process of impression management through the use of props, costumes, gestures, and language. A professor lecturing to her class, a young couple on their first date, and a job applicant in an interview all are governed by existing social norms, so the professor will not arrive in her nightgown, nor will the prospective employee greet his interviewer with a high-five rather than a handshake. Just as actors in a play must stick to their scripts, so too, suggests Goffman, do we as social actors risk

Dramaturgical approach: Developed by Erving Goffman, the study of social interaction as if it were governed by the practices of theatrical performance.

Presentation of self: The creation of impressions in the minds of others in order to define and control social situations.

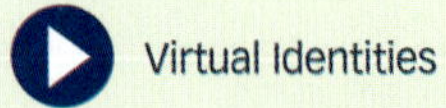
Virtual Identities

consequences (like failed interactions) if we diverge from the normative script.

Goffman offers insights into the techniques we as social actors have in our repertoire. Among them are the following:

- *Dramatic realization* is the actor's effort to mobilize his or her behavior to draw attention to a particular characteristic of the role he or she is assuming. What impression does a baseball umpire strive to leave on his audience (the teams and fans)? Arguably, he would like to embody authority, so he makes his calls loudly and with bold gestures.
- *Idealization* is an actor's effort to embody in his or her behaviors the officially accredited norms and values of a community or society. Those with fewer economic resources might purchase faux designer bags or watches in order to conform to perceived societal expectations of material wealth.
- *Misrepresentation* is part of every actor's repertoire, ranging from kind deception (telling a friend she looks great when she doesn't) to self-interested untruth (telling a professor a paper was lost in a computer crash when it was never written) to bald-faced prevarication (lying to conceal an affair). The actor wants to maintain a desired impression in the eyes of the audience: The friend would like to be perceived as kind and supportive, the student as conscientious and hardworking, and the spouse as loyal and loving.
- *Mystification* is largely reserved for those with status and power and serves to maintain distance from the audience in order to keep people in awe. Corporate leaders keep their offices on a separate floor and don't mix with employees, while celebrities may avoid interviews and allow their on-screen roles to define them as savvy and smart.

We may also engage in impression management as a team. A team consists of two or more actors cooperating to create a definition of the situation favorable to them. For example, members of a sports team work together, though some may be more skilled than others, to convey a definition of themselves as a highly competent and competitive group. Or the members of a family may work together to convey to their dinner guests that they are content and happy by acting cooperatively and smiling at one another during the group interaction.

The example of the family gives us an opportunity to explore Goffman's concept of the *back stage,* where actors let

Ethnomethodology: A sociological method used to study the body of commonsense knowledge and procedures by which ordinary members of a society make sense of their social circumstances and interaction.

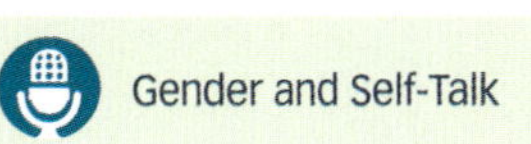
Gender and Self-Talk

Everett Collection

The film *The Wizard of Oz* offers a good example of mystification. Though the wizard is really, in his own words, "just a man," he maintains his status in Oz by hiding behind a curtain and using a booming voice and fiery mask to convey the impression of awesome power.

down their masks and relax or even practice their impression management. Before the dinner party, the home is a back stage. One parent is angry at the other for getting cheap rather than expensive wine, one sibling refuses to speak to the parent who grounded her, and the other won't stop texting long enough to set the table. Then the doorbell rings. Like magic, the home becomes the front stage as the adults smilingly welcome their guests and the kids begin to carry out trays of snacks and drinks. The guests may or may not sense some tension in the home, but they play along with the scenario so as not to create discomfort. When the party ends, the home reverts to the back stage, and each actor can relax his or her performance.

Goffman's work, like Mead's and the work of other sociologists focusing on socialization, sees the social self as an outcome of society and social interactions. Goffman, however, characterizes the social self not as a *possession*—a dynamic but still essentially real self—but rather as a *product* of a given social interaction, which can change as we seek to manage impressions for different audiences. Would you say that Mead or Goffman offers a better characterization of us as social actors?

ETHNOMETHODOLOGY AND CONVERSATION ANALYSIS

Routine, day-to-day social interactions are the building blocks of social institutions and ultimately of society itself. **Ethnomethodology** is used to study *the body of commonsense knowledge and procedures by which ordinary members of a society make sense of their social circumstances and interactions. Ethno* refers to "folk," or ordinary people; *methodology* refers to the methods they use to govern interaction—which are

INEQUALITY MATTERS

GENDER AND CONVERSATION

Men often claim they "cannot get a word in edgewise" when talking to women. However, conversation analysis research challenges this claim: In hundreds of recorded conversations between men and women, researchers found that men more frequently interrupted women than women interrupted men and that men used the interruptions to dominate the conversation. Men tended to speak more loudly and to be less polite than women, using loudness and rudeness (such as sarcastic remarks about what a woman had said) to control the conversation (Campbell, Klein, & Olson, 1992; Fishman, 1978; West, 1979; West & Zimmerman, 1977, 1983; Zimmerman & West, 1975, 1980). While men set the agenda and otherwise dominated the conversation, women often did the "work" of maintaining conversations by nodding their heads, saying "a-hah," and asking questions (DeFrancisco, 1991; Fishman, 1978; Leaper & Robnett, 2011; Tannen, 2001; West & Zimmerman, 1977, 1983).

This research shows that the rules and conventions governing ordinary talk are grounded in the larger society—society's gender roles, in which men generally assume a dominant position in interaction with women without even realizing it. In fact, not only do men not realize they are dominating the conversation; they think women dominate and "talk too much."

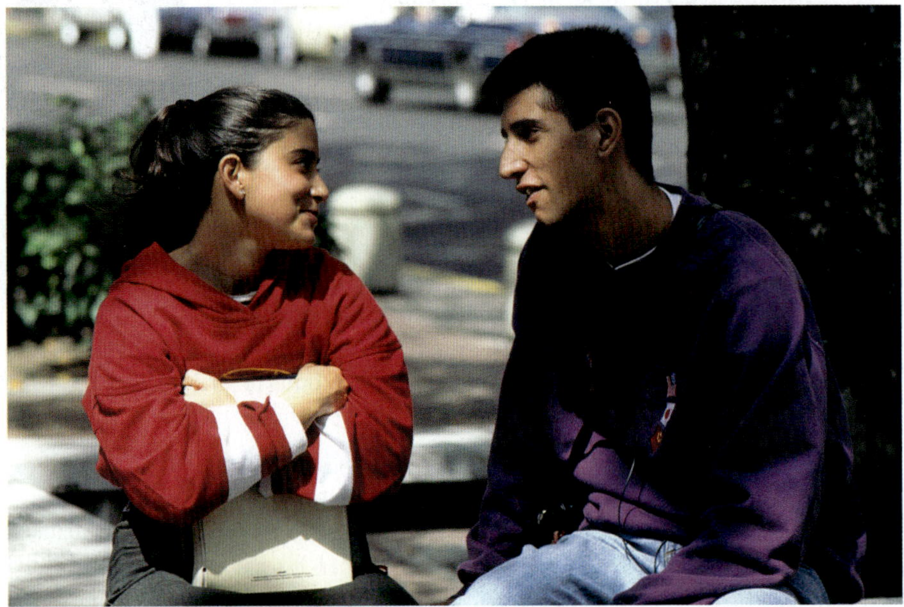

David R. Frazier / Photo Researchers, Inc.

Do you think that men and women communicate differently? How would you articulate differences you observe? Would you attribute them to nature or nurture?

The apparently private conversations between men and women thus reflect a fundamental issue in contemporary society: inequality between the sexes, including how inequality gets reproduced in subtle ways. The cultural stereotype of women as talkative and emotional and men as quiet and rational affects women even though its basis in reality is weak. No matter that men talk more and dominate conversations—women are made to feel unequal by the reproduction of the stereotype, and inequality between the sexes is reinforced. The private lives of people in conversations thus cannot be divorced from the way the larger social norms and stereotypes shape relationships between men and women.

THINK IT THROUGH

▶ The above discussion demonstrates how sociological research can shed light on "commonsense" assumptions—such as the assumption that women dominate conversations more than do men—by empirically testing them. Can you identify other stereotypical ideas about social interactions between different groups or individuals? How could you go about testing these ideas empirically?

as distinct as the methods used by sociologists to study them. Ethnomethodology was created through Harold Garfinkel's work in the early 1960s. Garfinkel (1963, 1985) sought to understand exactly what goes on in social interactions after observing that our interpretation of social interaction depends on the context. For example, if a child on a playground grabs another child's ball and runs with it, the teacher may see this as a sign of the child's aggressiveness, while fellow students see it as a display of courage. Social interaction and communication are not possible unless most people have learned to assign similar meanings to the same interactions. By studying the specific contexts of concrete social interactions, Garfinkel sought to understand how people come to share the same interpretations of social interactions.

Garfinkel also believed that in all cultures people expect others to talk in a way that is coherent and understandable and become anxious and upset when this does not happen. Making sense of one another's conversations is even more fundamental to social life than cultural norms, Garfinkel argued, since without ways of arriving at meaningful understandings, communication, and hence culture, is not possible. Because the procedures that determine how we make sense of conversations are so important to social interaction, another field developed from ethnomethodology that focuses on talk itself: conversation analysis.

Conversation analysis investigates *the way participants in social interaction recognize and produce coherent conversation* (Schegloff, 1990, 1991). In this context, *conversation* includes virtually any form of verbal communication, from routine small talk to emergency phone calls to congressional hearings and court proceedings (Heritage & Greatbatch, 1991; Hopper, 1991, Whalen & Zimmerman, 1987, 1990; Zimmerman, 1984, 1992).

Conversation analysis research suggests that social interaction is not simply a random succession of events. Rather, people construct conversations through a reciprocal process that makes the interaction coherent. One way in which we sequentially organize conversations is *turn taking,* a strategy that allows us to understand an utterance as a response to an earlier one and a cue to take our turn in the conversation. A person's turn ends once the other conversants indicate they have understood the message. For example, by answering "Fine" to the question "How are you?" you show that you have understood the question and are ready to move ahead.

On the other hand, answering "What do you mean?" or "Green" to the question "How are you?" is likely to lead to conversational breakdown. Conversational analysts have identified a number of techniques commonly used to repair such breakdowns. For example, if you begin speaking but realize midsentence that the other person is already speaking, you can "repair" this awkward situation by pausing until the original speaker finishes his or her turn and then restarting your turn.

Later research emphasized the impact of the larger social structure on conversations (Wilson, 1991). Sociologists looked at the use of power in conversations, including the power of the dispatcher over the caller in emergency phone calls (Whalen, Zimmerman, & Whalen, 1990; Zimmerman, 1984, 1992), of the questioner over the testifier in governmental hearings (Molotch & Boden, 1985), and of men over women in male–female interactions (Campbell et al., 1992; Fishman, 1978; West, 1979; West & Zimmerman, 1977, 1983; Zimmerman & West, 1975, 1980). The last instance, in particular, illustrates how the larger social structure—in this case, gender structure—affects conversation. Even at the most basic and personal level—a private conversation between two people—social structures exercise a potentially powerful influence.

Conversation analysis: The study of how participants in social interaction recognize and produce coherent conversation.

WHY STUDY SOCIALIZATION AND SOCIAL INTERACTION?

Have you ever wondered why you and some of your classmates or neighbors differ in worldviews, coping strategies for stress, or values concerning right and wrong? Understanding socialization and social interaction sheds light on such differences and what they mean to us in everyday life. For example, if you travel abroad, you will have a sense of how cultural differences come to be and appreciate that no culture is more "normal" than another—each has its own norms, values, and roles taught from earliest childhood.

By studying socialization, you also come to understand the critical socializing roles that peers, schools, and work environments play in the lives of children, adolescents, and young adults. The growing influence of the mass media, including the Internet and other technological innovations in communication, means we must pay close attention to these sources of socialization and social interaction as well. As people spend more time on the Internet talking to friends and strangers, experimenting with new identities, and seeking new forms of and forums for social interaction, sociologists may need to rethink some of their ideas about the influence of agents like parents and schools; perhaps these may recede in importance—or grow. Sociologists also ask how our presentation of self is transformed when we create social selves in the anonymous space of social media. What kinds of research could you imagine conducting to learn more about the digital world as an agent of socialization and a site of modern social interaction?

WHAT CAN I DO WITH A SOCIOLOGY DEGREE?

CAREER DEVELOPMENT: CREATING A JOB SEARCH PLAN AND PUTTING IT INTO ACTION

Your *job search action plan* should build on your career goals and focus on short- and medium-term activities. Break your goals into specific and manageable tasks to create action items. Strive to be as specific as possible with your action items by including details about who and what is involved in completing each task, identifying measurable outcomes, and noting time-based deadlines for when activities will be completed. Include in your job search action plan job search strategies that are likely to produce results.

We briefly discuss each of these strategies below. Additional resources for each can be found on the book's student study site, www.sagepub.com/chamblissintro.

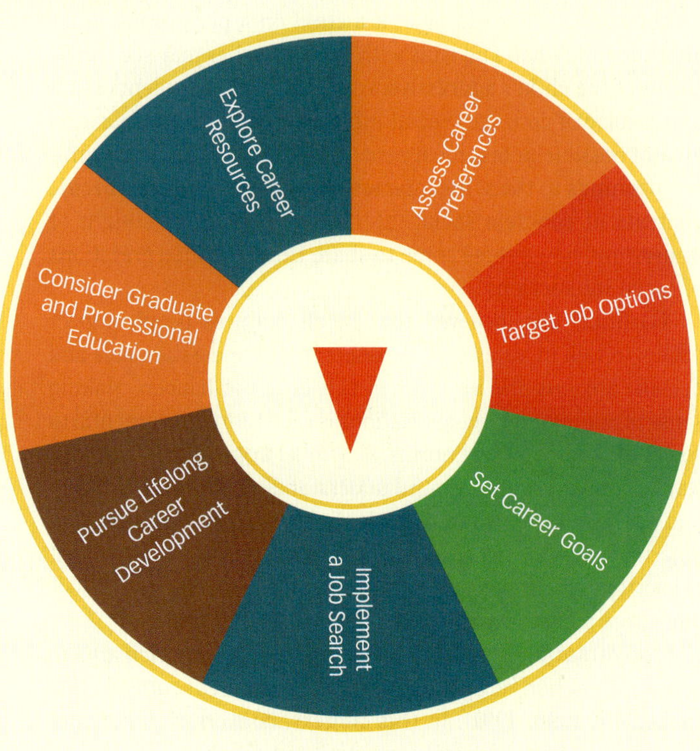

Target Employers

Based on your research, develop a list of 10 to 15 potential employers that align with your career and job search goals. Track the employers regularly to update your organizational knowledge and learn about new opportunities. Utilize LinkedIn and other social media sites to identify individuals and groups with whom you might connect in the organizations for information, introductions, and leads.

Network

Networking is about building relationships for the purpose of making connections to enhance your career and/or job search. People build their networks online, at their places of employment, through internships, and in their communities, as well as through professors, friends, friends of friends, family members, former employers, and fellow alumni. Consider conducting informational interviews such as those you previously used for career exploration to network and to learn about particular employers, industries, and individuals.

Market Yourself: Résumés

A résumé reviews your education, academic awards, employment and volunteer experiences, college and leadership activities, and language and technical skills. Start your experience descriptions with action verbs and omit all personal pronouns. Use qualifiers and quantifiers to describe the breadth and depth of your involvement in activities. Your résumé should be a single page in a standard 10- to 12-point font, printed on bond paper, and error-free.

Market Yourself: Cover Letters

Cover letters are a form of business writing and should follow a business letter format. The first paragraph of your cover letter should start with information about the reason for writing, identify how you learned of the position, and succinctly state how your skills, degree, and experience match the requirements of the position. The second paragraph should expand on information about your fit for the position, discuss your accomplishments, and use specific examples that parallel the experience and skills that the employer seeks. The third paragraph should identify career-related characteristics that will support your success in the position, such as resourcefulness, time management, and persistence. The final paragraph should restate your interest in the position, your availability to discuss the opportunity, and a reference to your contact information.

Market Yourself: Utilizing the Online Advantage

Utilize resources online to brand and market yourself, connect with individuals and groups, access job listings, link to employer and job listing sites, research employer information and occupational trends, and/or create a website or blog to highlight your career and professional activities and accomplishments. Expand your network by connecting with individuals and groups via social media and job listing sites.

Interview Strategies

An interview is your opportunity to articulate to the employer your skills, abilities, and accomplishments that best match the attributes that he or she is seeking in an ideal candidate. Be sure that you have researched the employer so that you can ask informed questions. Plan ahead so that you are able to arrive early for the interview. When you greet the interviewer, make eye contact, smile, and shake his or her hand firmly. As the interview begins, be professional, but be yourself. Listen to the interviewer's questions without interruption and allow yourself time to form responses before answering questions. Speak clearly and enthusiastically about your experiences and skills and offer detailed responses to questions that emphasize your experience, skills, and knowledge.

Within 24 hours after an interview, e-mail or mail a thank-you letter to each person with whom you met. Learn more about interviewing strategies, as well as questions frequently asked by employers and interviewees, on the book's online student site.

Evaluate and Negotiate Offers

When you receive a job offer, consider it carefully by reviewing the entire compensation package, which includes both salary and benefits. In addition to the compensation package, review the related pros or cons of accepting the position. To negotiate a change in the package, start with the salary by stating your preferred salary range. Restate your selling points, including why you believe that your skills, knowledge, and experience are the best fit for the position and how you will add value to the organization. Always frame your argument in relation to the employer's hiring needs and the goals of the organization rather than your preferences.

Reflect and Pursue Lifelong Career Development

Even when you have completed a specific job search, your career development is continuous. Practice lifelong learning and actively engage in professional development. Build your network, develop connections to colleagues, and demonstrate ethical behaviors in your professional activities. Continue to explore new opportunities and review and update your career goals. Seek to know and remain true to your career identity—the values, aspirations, interests, talents, skills, and preferences related to careers that are fundamental to your career satisfaction and success.

SUMMARY

- **Socialization** is a lifelong, active process by which people learn the cultures of their societies and construct a sense of who they are.
- What we often think of as "human nature" is in fact learned through socialization. Sociologists argue that human behavior is not determined biologically, though biology plays some role; rather, human behavior develops primarily through social interaction.
- Although some theories emphasize the early years, sociologists generally argue that socialization takes place throughout the life course. The theories of Sigmund Freud and Jean Piaget emphasize the early years, while those of George Herbert Mead (although his **role-taking** theory focuses on the earlier stages of the life course), Lawrence Kohlberg, and Judith Harris give more consideration to the whole life course. According to Mead, children acquire a sense of self through symbolic interaction, including the role-taking that eventually enables the adult to take the standpoint of society as a whole.
- Kohlberg built on Piaget's ideas to argue that a person's sense of morality develops through different stages, from that in which people strictly seek personal gain or seek to avoid punishment to the stage in which they base moral decisions on abstract principles.
- The immediate family provides the earliest and typically foremost source of socialization, but school, work, peers, religion, sports, and mass media, including the Internet, all play a significant role.
- Socialization may differ by social class. Middle-class families place a somewhat greater emphasis on creativity and independence, while working-class families often stress obedience to authority. These differences, in turn, reflect the corresponding workplace differences associated with social class.
- In **total institutions**, such as prisons, the military, and hospitals, individuals are isolated so that society can achieve administrative control over their lives. By enforcing rules that govern all aspects of daily life, from dress to schedules to interpersonal interactions, total institutions can open the way to **resocialization**, which is the breaking down of the person's sense of self and the rebuilding of the personality.
- According to Erving Goffman's **dramaturgical approach**, we are all actors concerned with the **presentation of self** in social interaction. People perform their social roles on the "front stage" and are able to avoid performing on the "back stage."
- **Ethnomethodology** is a method of analysis that examines the body of commonsense knowledge and procedures by which ordinary members of a society make sense of their social circumstances and interaction.
- **Conversation analysis**, which builds on ethnomethodology, is the study of the way participants in social interaction recognize and produce coherent conversation.

KEY TERMS

socialization, 81
behaviorism, 83
social learning, 83
looking-glass self, 83
primary groups, 84
secondary groups, 84
reference groups, 84
I, 84
me, 84
role-taking, 84
significant others, 84
generalized other, 85
cognitive development, 85
egocentric, 85
psychoanalysis, 86
id, 86
ego, 86
superego, 86
hidden curriculum, 89
anticipatory socialization, 90
total institutions, 94
resocialization, 94
dramaturgical approach, 96
presentation of self, 96
ethnomethodology, 97
conversation analysis, 99

DISCUSSION QUESTIONS

1. What are agents of socialization? What agents of socialization do sociologists identify as particularly important? Which of these would you say have the most profound effects on the construction of our social selves? Make a case to support your choices.

2. The United States is a country where sports are an important part of many people's lives—many Americans enjoy playing sports, while others follow their favorite sports teams closely in the media. How are sports an agent of socialization? What roles, norms, or values are conveyed through this agent of socialization?

3. What role does the way people react to you play in the development of your personality and your self-image? How can the reactions of others influence whether or not you develop skills as an athlete or a student or a musician, for example?

4. Recall Goffman's ideas about social interaction and the presentation of self. How have social media sites such as Facebook, Twitter, and Instagram affected the presentation of self? Have there been changes to what Goffman saw as our front and back stages?

5. What are the characteristics of total institutions such as prisons and mental institutions? How does socialization in a total institution differ from "ordinary" socialization?

Sharpen your skills with SAGE edge at **edge.sagepub.com/chambliss2e**

A personalized approach to help you accomplish your coursework goals in an easy-to-use learning environment.

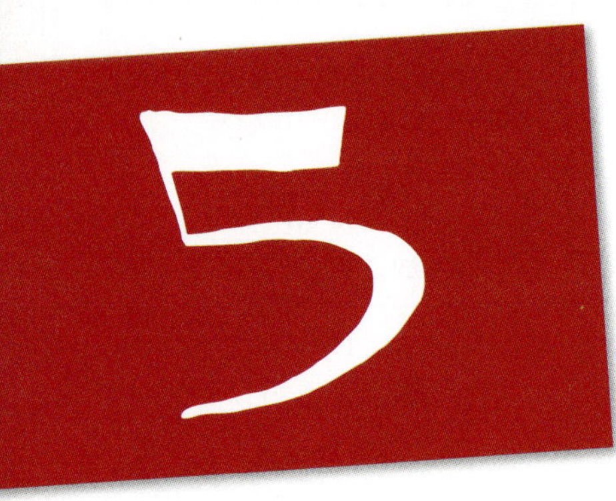

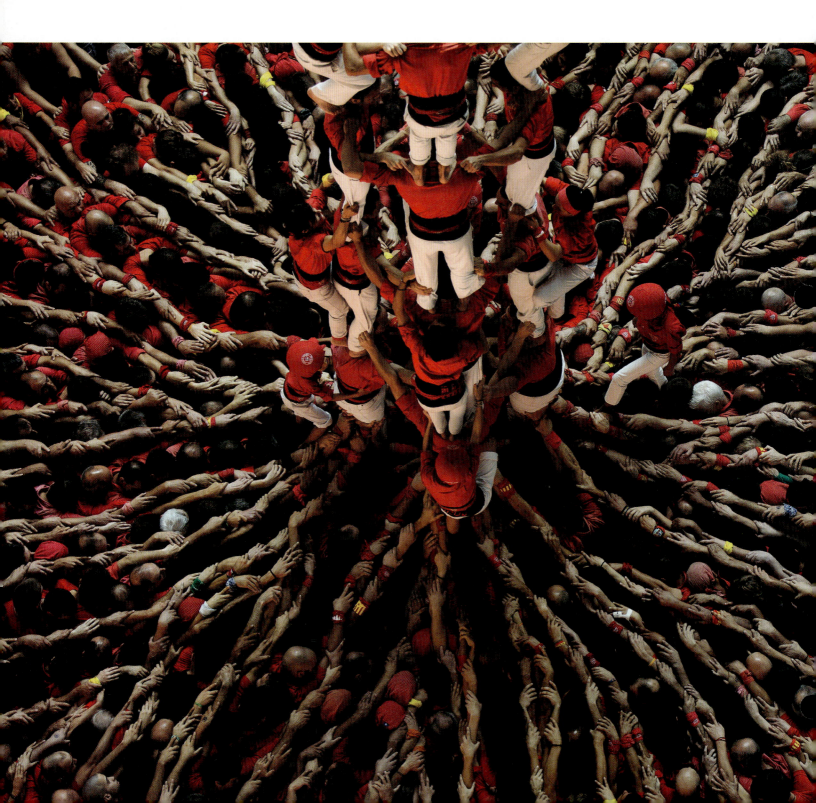

GROUPS, ORGANIZATIONS, AND BUREAUCRACIES

IN THIS CHAPTER

AP Photo/Emilio Morenatti

WHAT DO YOU THINK?

1. Do most people conform to the expectations of the groups to which they belong? What explains conformity? What explains dissent?
2. Why do many people think of bureaucracies as inefficient and annoying? What would be the alternative?
3. Could a group of college students working together on a societal issue such as rising student debt, child hunger, or veteran homelessness bring about significant social change?

Patrick Smith/Stringer/Getty Images

WHEN GROUPS THINK . . . GROUPTHINK

In June 2012, former Pennsylvania State University football assistant coach Jerry Sandusky was convicted by a Pennsylvania court of sexually abusing children who were under his care and supervision. Sandusky had contact with many boys through his respected position at Penn State and his Second Mile charity, a service organization with a mission to help disadvantaged young people through sports. The charges, witness testimony, and some of Sandusky's own admissions about, for instance, showering with boys in the Penn State locker room were shocking to most who heard them.

But they may not have been a shock to a number of Sandusky's colleagues at Penn State. According to an investigative report prepared by former FBI director Louis Freeh at the behest of the Penn State Board of Regents, many people were already aware of Sandusky's abusive activities. Some, like head football coach Joe Paterno and university president Graham Spanier, had been aware of allegations against Sandusky for years. So why did no one act to halt the abuse? Why were allegations and evidence of Sandusky's actions covered up by colleagues in the football program and the university administration?

The case is complex, and a spectrum of answers to these questions may be offered. One possibility, however, is that *groupthink* played a role. Groupthink is a phenomenon characterized by the members of a group choosing to elevate consensus and conformity—and preservation of the group—above other values. In an opinion piece published by *Time* magazine on groupthink at Penn State, two authors, a psychologist and a physician, argue that Penn State's athletic and administrative leaders chose to protect Sandusky, who was one of their elite group, rather than the victimized children, nearly all of whom were poor. They wanted to shield Sandusky—and the Penn State image and program—from damaging scrutiny. Their logic, deduced from e-mail traffic uncovered by Freeh, is characterized by the article's authors as follows: "This particular insider group managed to twist logic to the point where they thought it was more 'humane' to cover up the repeated allegations of Sandusky's abuse than to report them to police" (Cohen & DeBenedet, 2012).

When decisions are based primarily on how group members will react, rather than on ethical, professional, or legal considerations, groupthink can, as this case shows, lead to devastating outcomes. The influence of the group can foster deviance—but at the same time, group bonds are fundamental to our lives and a key part of socialization and social integration. The roles that groups play in society are clearly complex, and they are a key focus of sociological study.

We begin this chapter with an overview of the nature of social groups, looking at primary and secondary groups and their effects on our lives. We also examine the power of groups in fostering integration and enforcing conformity, among other key functions. We then turn to a discussion of the importance of capital in social group formation and action, followed by an exploration of the place of organizations in society. Next we address a topic about which Max Weber wrote extensively and with which we all have some experience—bureaucracies. We end the chapter with a consideration of the modern roles of governmental and nongovernmental organizations in the pursuit of social change.

© Jim Mahoney/Dallas Morning News/Corbis

Secondary groups may evolve into primary groups for some members. For example, when students taking the same course begin to socialize outside of class, they may create bonds of friendship that come to constitute a primary group.

THE NATURE OF GROUPS

The male elephant is a solitary creature, spending much of its life wandering alone, interacting with other elephants only when it is time to mate or if another male intrudes on its territory. Female elephants, by contrast, live their lives in groups. Both male and female human beings are like the female elephant: We are social animals who live our entire lives in the company of others. Our lives are social, and we can better understand them by looking at the types of groups with which we are associated. Each of us is born into an emotionally and biologically connected group we know as "the family." As we mature, we become increasingly interconnected with other people, some our own age and others not, at school, on sports teams, and through various other social interactions and increasingly via the Internet and social media. We consolidate and accumulate friends, teammates, and classmates—different groups with whom we interact on a regular basis. Eventually we get jobs and engage with coworkers and other people we encounter in the course of our work. Along the way we may form and maintain friendship groups, either in person or virtually, that share our interests in particular activities or lifestyles, such as poker, model airplanes, or music. Sometimes we are part of groups that gather for special events, like watching a college football game or attending a presidential inauguration or political demonstration.

A moment's reflection on these types of groups reveals that they differ in many important ways, particularly in the degree of intimacy and social support their members experience. Sociologists find this difference so fundamental that they use it to distinguish between *primary* and *secondary* groups. Primary groups are characterized by *intense emotional ties, intimacy, and identification with membership in the group.* Secondary groups are *large, impersonal groups with minimal emotional and intimate ties* (Cooley, 1909). Today, social networking sites and virtual, online groups that people are part of can include primary or secondary groups. Moreover, the Internet is increasingly blurring the boundary distinctions between primary and secondary groups—very large, ostensibly impersonal groups can take on a very intimate feeling thanks to the power of virtual communication and information sharing. As we will discuss later in this chapter, technology and the Internet have changed quite a lot about how we think of social relations and social groups.

Primary groups are of great significance because they exert a long-lasting influence on the development of our social selves (Cooley, 1902/1964). Charles Horton Cooley (1864–1929), who first introduced the distinction between primary and secondary groups, argued that people belong to primary groups mainly because these groups satisfy personal needs of belonging and fulfillment. People join secondary groups such as business organizations, schools, work groups, athletic clubs, and governmental bodies to achieve specific goals: to earn a living, to get a college degree, to compete in sports, and so on. (For a summary of the characteristics of primary and secondary groups, see Table 5.1.)

TABLE 5.1 The Characteristics of Primary and Secondary Groups

Characteristic	Primary Group	Secondary Group
Social distance of relationships	Low: face-to-face	High: indirect, remote
Intimacy	High: "fusion of personalities"	Low: relatively impersonal
Importance in forming the "social self"	Fundamental: earliest complete experience of social unity	Secondary: occurs later in life, no all-embracing experience of social unity
Degree of mutual identification with others	High: "we"	Low: "they"
Degree of permanence	High: change but slowly over time	Low: likely to change over time
Examples	Family; children's playgroups; neighborhood and community groups; clubs, fraternities, and sororities	Secondary schools, colleges, and universities; businesses and other workplaces; government agencies; bureaucracies of all sorts

THE POWER OF GROUPS

As you learned in Chapter 4, we often judge ourselves by how we think we appear to others, which Cooley termed the "looking-glass self." Groups as well as individuals provide the standards by which we make these self-evaluations. Robert K. Merton (1968), following Herbert Hyman (1942), elaborated on the concept of the reference group as a measure by which we evaluate ourselves. Importantly, a reference group provides a standard for judging our own attitudes or behaviors.

For most of us, the family is the reference group with the greatest impact in shaping our early view of ourselves. As we mature, and particularly during adolescence, peers replace or at least compete with the family as the reference group through which we define ourselves. Today, thanks to the growth of social media, many people establish "virtual" reference groups and intimate primary groups with people they have never seen face-to-face.

Reference groups may be primary, such as the family, or secondary, such as a group of soldiers in the same branch of service in the military. They may even be fictional. One of the chief functions of advertising, for example, is to create sets of imaginary reference groups that will influence consumers' buying habits. We are invited to purchase a particular vehicle or fragrance, for instance, in order to join an ostensibly exclusive group of sophisticated, sexy owners of that item. Reference groups can have powerful effects on our consumer choices, as well as on our other social actions.

THE EFFECTS OF SIZE

Another significant way in which groups differ has to do with their size. The German sociologist Georg Simmel (1858–1918) was one of the first to call attention to the influence of group size on people's behavior. Since Simmel's time, small-group researchers have conducted a number of laboratory experiments to discover how group size affects both the quality of interaction in the group and the group's effectiveness in accomplishing certain tasks (Levine & Crowther, 2008; Lucas & Lovaglia, 1998).

The simplest group, which Simmel (1955) called a **dyad**, *consists of two persons.* Simmel reasoned that dyads, which offer both intimacy and conflict, are likely to be simultaneously intense and unstable. To survive, they require the full attention and cooperation of both parties. Dyads are typically the sources of our most elementary social bonds, often constituting the groups in which we are most likely to share our deepest secrets. The commitment two people make through marriage is one way to form a dyadic group. But dyads can also be very fragile. If one person withdraws from the dyad, it vanishes. That is why, as Simmel believed, a variety of cultural and legal norms arise to support dyadic groups, including marriage, in societies where such groups are regarded as an important source of social stability.

Adding one other person to a dyad changes the group relationship considerably, making what Simmel termed a **triad**. Triads are apt to be more stable than dyads, since the presence of a third person relieves some of the pressure on the other two members to always get along and maintain the energy of the relationship. One person can temporarily withdraw his or her attention from the relationship without necessarily threatening it. In addition, if two members have a disagreement, the third can play the role of mediator, as when you try to patch up a falling-out between two friends or coworkers (see Figure 5.1).

On the other hand, however, an **alliance (or coalition)** may form between two members of a triad, enabling them to "gang up" on the third member, thereby destabilizing the group. Alliances are most likely to form when no member is clearly

Dyad: A group consisting of two persons.

Triad: A group consisting of three persons.

Alliance (or coalition): A subgroup that forms between group members, enabling them to dominate the group in their own interest.

Types of Indigenous Groups

TECHNOLOGY & SOCIETY

SOCIAL INTERACTIONS IN A NEW AGE OF COMMUNICATION

The technologies of social media can strengthen ties among members of primary and secondary groups, aid social change, and disseminate unfiltered news immediately as events unfold. At the same time, they allow anyone to disseminate information about anyone else with relative anonymity and no fact-checking, provide an avenue through which those with dangerous causes or desires may unite, and present opportunities for new forms of exploitation, bullying, and harassment. Whether human social interaction today is better or worse than in the past is irrelevant; it is simply significantly different.

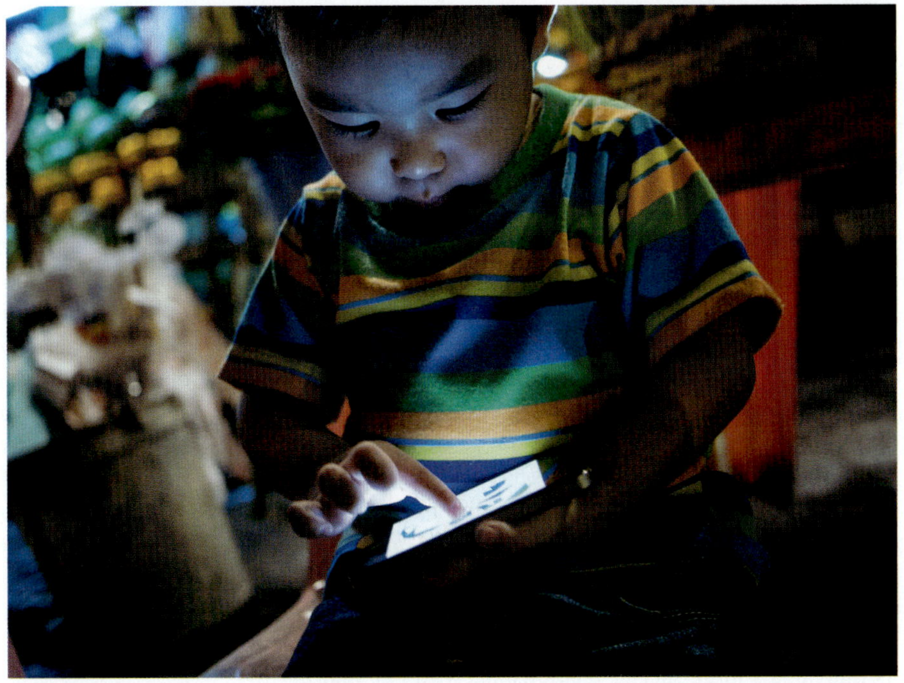

© Jon Hicks/Corbis

The dissemination of technology has resulted in nearly one third of the global population having access to the Internet. Many children today are growing up in a truly digital society, where technology is deeply entwined with their upbringing and socialization.

Estimates place the number of individuals with access to the Internet around the world at roughly 2.3 billion and climbing—so the Internet is already accessible to some degree to about 33% of the world's population (Internet World Stats, 2012). Facebook, the world's dominant social networking site, has 552 million daily users and more than 1 billion monthly users, the majority of them outside the United States (Facebook, 2012). Even so, recent data show that 3.3 million teens have left Facebook since 2011, along with 3.4 million 18- to 24-year-olds (Neal, 2014). They may be migrating toward social networks like Twitter and Instagram, which are popular among younger adults (Duggan & Smith, 2014). Additionally, the app Snapchat attracts 26% of cell phone users ages 18 to 29 (MarketingCharts, 2013). Nearly one in five people in the United States has gone out with someone he or she met online. Since its creation in 2003, LinkedIn has drawn more than 150 million members in more than 200 countries (LinkedIn, 2012). Pinterest allows users to create virtual pinboards to save and share links, recipes, photos, fashions, and countless other preferences (Pinterest, 2012). Increasingly, digital communications are becoming integrated and "intelligent," letting users link their Pinterest boards to their Facebook accounts and access them from their smartphones.

Not only does technology provide a means of increasing social interactions among individuals and groups, but it also presents opportunities for interactions that might otherwise never have taken place. The wife of a Washington State corrections officer received a "People You May Know" update on her Facebook page suggesting she might want to be friends with another woman. When she clicked on the other woman's profile, she found wedding photos of her husband and the other woman. Not only had her husband never told her he had been married before, but he was still married to the woman in the pictures. He was subsequently arrested and charged with bigamy (Rabiner, 2012).

There is a very good chance that the theorizing sociologists did about social groups and interactions in the 20th century will look quite different in the 21st century as our means of forming groups, feeling integrated, and interacting with others change.

THINK IT THROUGH

▶ How do virtual groups differ from in-person primary and secondary groups? What qualities do virtual and in-person groups share?

CQR Social Media Explosion

■ **FIGURE 5.1** **A Dyad and a Triad**

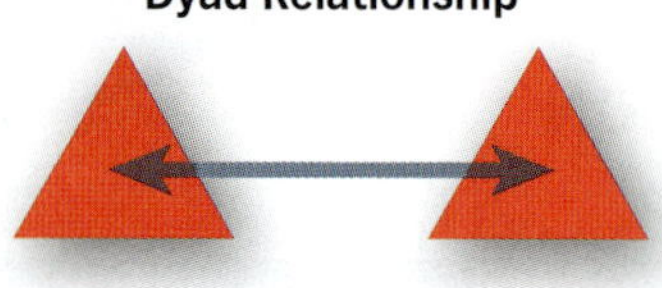

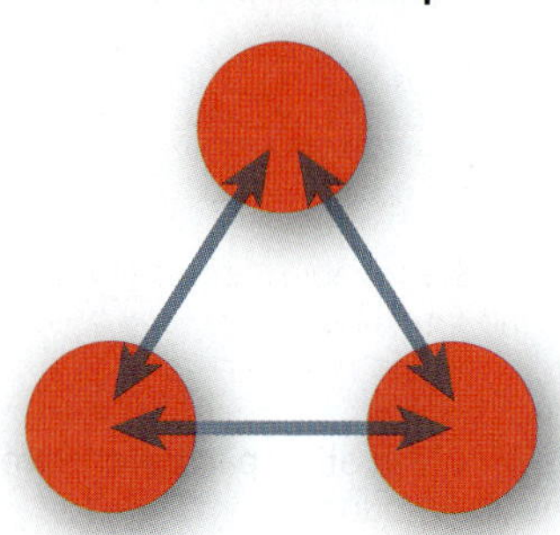

dominant and all three are competing for the same thing—for example, when three friends are given a pair of tickets to a concert and have to decide which two will go. Larger groups share some of the characteristics of triads. For instance, on the TV series *Survivor*, alliances form within the group of castaways as individuals forge special relationships with one another to avoid being eliminated by a group vote.

Theoretically, in forming an alliance a triad member is most likely to choose the weaker of the two other members, if there is one. But why would this be the case if picking a stronger member would strengthen the alliance? Choosing a weaker member enables the member seeking to form the alliance to exercise more power and control within the alliance. However, in some "revolutionary" coalitions, the two weaker members form an alliance to overthrow the stronger one (Goldstone, 2001; Grusky, Bonacich, & Webster, 1995).

Going from a dyad to a triad illustrates an important sociological principle first identified by Simmel: *As group size increases, the intensity of relationships within the group decreases while overall group stability increases.* There are exceptions to every principle, however. Intensity of interaction among individuals within a group decreases as the size of the group increases because, for instance, a larger number of outlets or alternative arenas for interaction exist for individuals who are not getting along (Figure 5.2). In a dyad, only a single relationship is possible; however, in a triad, three different two-person relationships can occur. Adding a fourth person leads to six possible two-person relationships, not counting subgroups that may form. In a 10-person group, the number of possible two-person relationships increases to 45! When one relationship doesn't work out to your liking, you can easily move on to another, as you sometimes may do at large parties.

Larger groups tend to be more stable than smaller ones because the withdrawal of some members does not threaten the survival of the entire group. For example, sports teams do not cease to exist simply because of the loss of one player, even though that player might have been important to the team's overall success. Beyond a certain size, perhaps a dozen people, groups may also develop a formal structure. Formal leadership roles may arise, such as president or secretary, and official rules may develop to govern what the group does. We discuss formal organizations later in this chapter.

Larger groups can sometimes be exclusive, since it is easier for their members to limit their social relationships to the group itself, avoiding relationships with nonmembers. This sense of being part of an in-group or clique is often what unites the members of fraternities, sororities, and other campus organizations. Cliquishness is especially likely to occur when a group consists of members who are similar to one another in such social characteristics as age, gender, class, race, or ethnicity. Members of rich families, for example, may sometimes be reluctant to fraternize with people from the working class, men may prefer to play basketball only with other men, and students who belong to a particular ethnic group may seek out each other's company in the dormitory or cafeteria. The concept of **social closure**, originally developed by Max Weber, is especially relevant here, insofar as it speaks to the *ability of*

■ **FIGURE 5.2** **A Complex Network of Relationships**

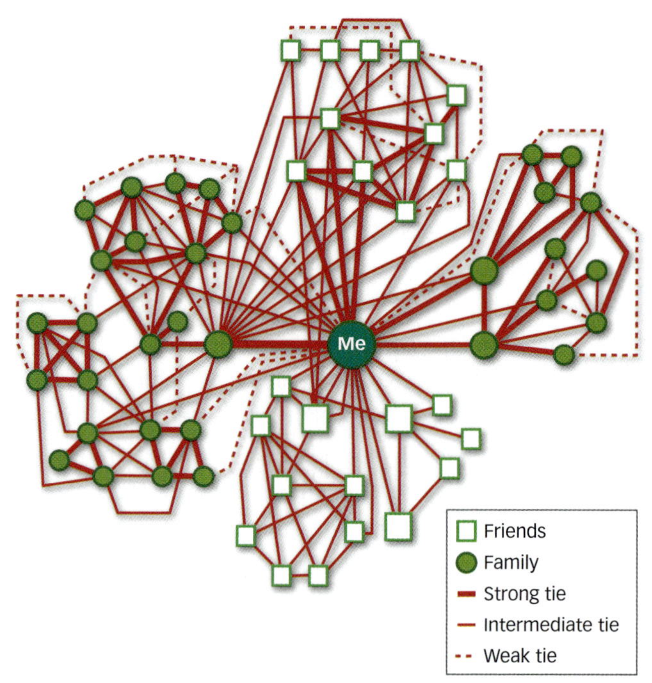

Social closure: The ability of a group to strategically and consciously exclude outsiders or those deemed "undesirable" from participating in the group or enjoying the group's resources.

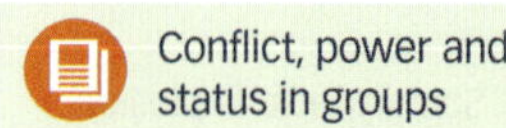

a group to strategically and consciously exclude outsiders or those deemed "undesirable" from participating in the group or enjoying the group's resources (Murphy, 1988; Parkin, 1979).

Groups don't always exclude outsiders, however (Blau, 1977; Stolle, 1998). For example, if your social group or club is made up of members from different social classes or ethnic groups, you are more likely to appreciate diversity thanks to your first-hand experience. This experience with difference may perhaps lead you to be more inclusive of others not like yourself in other aspects of your life, for example, in bringing together a group to work on a project. This, of course, is an optimistic outlook and one that we embrace and hope holds true in practice.

At the same time, researchers have found that exposure to differences of race, ethnicity, religion, social class, and other characteristics may in fact lead to negative consequences and exclusion—thus highlighting that there are two sides to every coin. The idea here is that exposure to "different" people or things may heighten the "threat" level that people feel and associate with differences, causing them to want to exclude those people or things from their lives (Blalock, 1967; Markert, 2010).

Nelson Mandela played an influential role in leading South Africa out of apartheid in the late 1980s and early 1990s. Prior to assuming the presidency of the post-apartheid South African government, Mandela, writing from a prison cell, inspired many South Africans, as well as people in other parts of the world, to form anti-apartheid coalitions and groups.

TYPES OF GROUP LEADERSHIP

A leader is a person able to influence the behavior of other members of a group. All groups tend to have leaders, even if the leaders do not have formal titles. Leaders come in a variety of forms: autocratic, charismatic, democratic, laissez-faire, bureaucratic, and so on. Some leaders are especially effective in motivating members of their groups or organizations, inspiring them to achievements they might not ordinarily accomplish. Such a **transformational leader** goes beyond the merely routine, *instilling in group members a sense of mission or higher purpose and thereby changing (transforming) the nature of the group itself* (Burns, 1978; Kanter, 1983; Mehra, Dixon, Brass, & Robertson, 2006).

Transformational leaders leave their marks on their organizations and can also be vital inspirations for social change in the world. Nelson Mandela, the first Black African president of postapartheid South Africa, had spent 27 years in prison, having been convicted of treason against the White-dominated government. Nonetheless, his moral and political position was so strong that upon his release he immediately assumed leadership of the African National Congress (ANC), leading that political group to the pinnacle of power in South Africa and then assuming the office of president of the entire nation.

Most leaders are not as visionary as Mandela, however. A leader who simply "gets the job done" is a **transactional leader**, concerned with accomplishing the group's tasks, getting group members to do their jobs, and making certain the group achieves its goals. Transactional leadership is routine leadership. For example, the teacher who effectively gets through the lesson plan each day but does not necessarily transform the classroom into a place where students explore new ways of thinking and behaving that change their educational lives is exercising transactional leadership.

For leaders to be effective, they must somehow get others to follow them. How do they do that? At one end of the spectrum, a leader might coerce people into compliance and subordination; at the other end, people may willingly comply with and subordinate themselves to a leader. The basic sociological notion of *power,* the ability to mobilize resources and achieve a goal despite the resistance of others, captures the first point (Emerson, 1962; Hall, 2003; Weber, 1921/2012). The related notion of **legitimate authority**, *power exercised over those who recognize it as deserved or earned,* captures the second (Blau, 1964). For example, prison guards often rely on the use of force to ensure compliance with their orders, whereas professors must depend on their legitimate authority if they hope to keep their students attentive and orderly.

Sociologists have typically found authority to be more interesting than the exercise of raw force. After all, it is not surprising that people will follow orders when someone holds a gun to their heads. But why do they go along with authority when they are *not* overtly compelled to do so?

Transformational leader: A leader who is able to instill in the members of a group a sense of mission or higher purpose, thereby changing the nature of the group itself.

Transactional leader: A leader who is concerned with accomplishing the group's tasks, getting group members to do their jobs, and making certain that the group achieves its goals.

Legitimate authority: A type of power that is recognized as rightful by those over whom it is exercised.

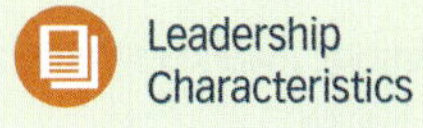
Leadership Characteristics

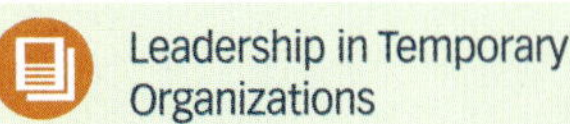
Leadership in Temporary Organizations

Part of the answer is that people often regard authority as legitimate when it seems to accompany the leadership position. A teacher, for example, would appear to possess the right to expect students to listen attentively and behave respectfully. Power stemming from an official leadership position is termed **positional power**; *it depends on the leader's role in the group* (Chiang, 2009; Hersey, Blanchard, & Natemeyer, 1987; Raven & Kruglianski, 1975). At the same time, some leaders derive their power from their unique ability to inspire others. Power that derives from the leader's personality is termed **personal power**; *it depends on the ability to persuade rather than the ability to command* (van Dijke & Poppe, 2006).

In most situations, the effective exercise of personal power, rather than positional power, is more likely to result in highly motivated and satisfied group members. When group members are confused or ill prepared to undertake a particular task, however, they seem to prefer the more command-oriented style associated with positional leadership (Hersey et al., 1987; Mizruchi & Potts, 1998; Patterson, 1989; Podsakoff & Schriesheim, 1985; Schaefer, 2011).

CONFORMITY TO GROUPS

Following group norms such as getting tattoos or piercings, or wearing the trendiest brand of jeans, seems relatively harmless. At the same time, conformity to group pressure can lead to destructive behavior such as drug abuse or serious crimes against others. For this reason, sociologists and social psychologists have long sought to understand why most people tend to go along with others—and under what circumstances they do not.

Some of the earliest studies of conformity to group pressures were conducted by psychologist Solomon Asch more than 60 years ago. In one of his classic experiments, Asch (1952) asked subjects to decide which of three lines of different length most closely matched a fourth (Figure 5.3). The differences between the line lengths were obvious; subjects had no difficulty making the correct match. Asch then arranged a version of the experiment in which the lines to be matched were presented in a group setting, with each person calling out the answer one at a time.

In this second version of the experiment, all but one of the subjects were secret accomplices of Asch's, who intentionally attempted to deceive the outsider in the group by saying that two lines that were *clearly* unequal in length were identical. The unwitting subject, always one of the last to call out an answer, was placed under group pressure to conform, even though the other answers given were wrong. Amazingly, in the experimental groups one third of the subjects gave the same wrong answer as that put forth by Asch's accomplices. In the experiments where no intentionally misleading answers were given, the subjects offered incorrect responses less than 1% of the time. Although the duped subjects sometimes stammered

FIGURE 5.3 The Asch Experiments: A Study in Conformity

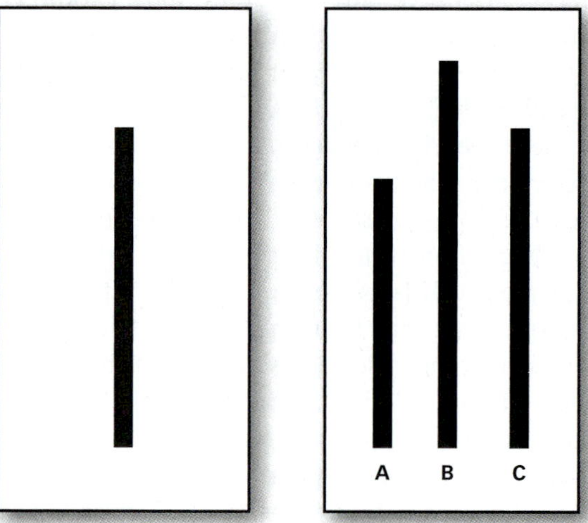

and fidgeted, they still yielded to the unspoken pressure to conform to the group's decision. Asch's experiments demonstrated that many people are willing to discount their own perceptions rather than contradict group consensus. How do you think you would respond if you were the subject in such an experiment (and had not read this account first)? Would you conform or dissent?

OBEDIENCE TO AUTHORITY Another classic study of conformity was conducted by Stanley Milgram (1963). One of his specific research questions concerned what allowed ordinary German citizens to go along with and even participate in the mass killing of Jews, Romani (also known as Gypsies), homosexuals, the disabled, and others who were judged socially undesirable by the Nazis during World War II. Obedience is a kind of conformity. Milgram thus desired to find the boundaries of obedience, to identify how far a person would be willing to go if an authority figure encouraged him or her to complete a given task. His study produced some chilling answers.

In Milgram's experiment male volunteers were told by an actor dressed in a white lab coat (an authoritative prop) to read aloud pairs of words from a list someone in another room was to memorize and repeat. Whenever the "learner" (an accomplice in the research) made a mistake, the subject was instructed to give the learner an electric shock by flipping a switch on an official-looking machine (which was actually fake). With each mistake, the voltage (intensity) of the purported shock was to be increased, until it eventually reached

Positional power: Power that stems officially from the leadership position itself.

Personal power: Power that derives from a leader's personality.

 Groupthink Among Rwanda's Youth

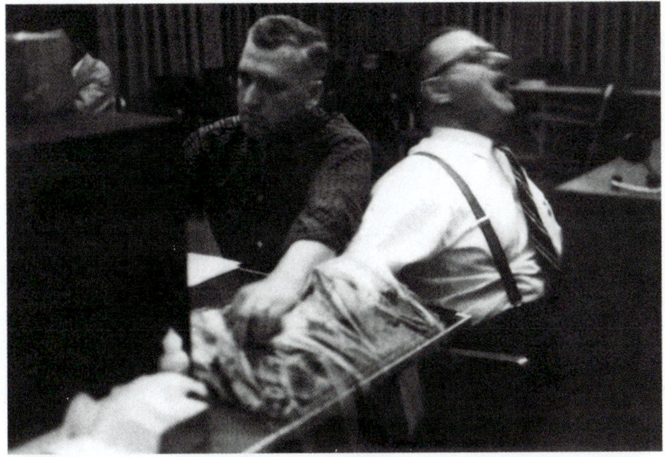

Alexandra Milgram

Most people would say that they are not capable of committing horrendous acts, yet Stanley Milgram's famous experiment illustrated how obedience to authority can lead people to commit actions that result in harm to others.

the highest levels, visibly labeled on the machine "450 volts—danger, severe shock."

In reality the learner never received any electric shocks, but he reacted audibly and physically as if he had, emitting cries that grew louder and more pained, pounding on the table, and moving about in his chair (the cries were prerecorded and played back). Meanwhile, the "scientist" ordered the subject to proceed with the experiment and continue administering shocks, saying things like "The experiment requires that you continue" even when the learner expressed concern about his "bad heart."

More than half the participants in the study obeyed the commands to keep going, administering what they believed to be electric shocks up to the maximum voltage until nothing but an eerie silence came from the other room. What happened here? How could ordinary, basically good people so easily conform to orders that turned them into potential accomplices to injury or death?

The answer, Milgram found, was deceptively simple: Ordinary people will conform to orders given by someone in a position of power or authority. They will do so even when those orders result in harm to other human beings. Many ordinary Germans who participated in the mass execution of Jews in Nazi concentration camps allegedly did so on the ground that they were "just following orders." Milgram's research, though ethically questionable, produced sobering findings for those who believe that only "other people" would bow to authority.

The 2012 film *Compliance,* which is based on real-life incidents, depicts the events that unfold when a prank phone caller, an unidentified male, calls a fast-food establishment and, pretending to be a police officer, enlists the aid of the store manager to help him crack an ostensibly important case. Once the manager agrees to help the "officer," the prankster tells the manager to perform increasingly invasive acts against a female employee. Obeying a figure believed to be a legitimate (though unseen) authority, in several of the incidents on which the movie is based, restaurant managers actually strip-searched female employees (Kavner, 2012; Wolfson, 2005).

Another example of obedience to authority even in the face of dangerous consequences took place at the Edgewood Arsenal in Maryland, the site of top-secret military experiments involving more than 7,000 U.S. soldiers from the 1950s through the 1970s. Many soldiers volunteered for duty at Edgewood unaware of, or even deceived about, exactly what would be asked of them. Once at Edgewood, they were informed that if they refused to participate in any "required" duties they could face jail time for insubordination or receive an unsatisfactory review in their personnel files, and during the Vietnam era some were reportedly threatened with being sent to war. The soldiers were experimented on repeatedly, often exposed to a variety of dangerous chemical and biological toxins, including sarin gas, VX gas, LSD, tranquilizers, and barbiturates, some of which produced extended and untreated hallucinations (Martin, 2012; Young & Martin, 2012). The Edgewood Arsenal experiments highlight the point that individuals are likely to comply with any demands made by persons in positions of authority out of fear of the repercussions associated with failure to comply, even if what they are asked to do seems dangerous or even potentially lethal to others—or to themselves.

GROUPTHINK Common sense tells us that "two minds are better than one." But, as our opening story on the sex abuse scandal at Pennsylvania State University suggests, pressures to go along with the crowd sometimes result in poor decisions rather than creative new solutions to problems. You have probably had the experience of feeling uneasy about voicing your opinion while in a group struggling with a difficult decision. Irving L. Janis (1972, 1989; Janis & Mann, 1977) coined the term **groupthink** to describe *what happens when members of a group ignore information that goes against the group consensus.* Not only does groupthink frequently embarrass potential dissenters into conforming, but it can also produce a shift in perceptions so that group members rule out alternative possibilities without seriously considering them. Groupthink may facilitate a group's reaching a quick consensus, but the consensus may also be ill chosen.

Janis undertook historical research to see whether groupthink had characterized U.S. foreign policy decisions, including the infamous Bay of Pigs invasion of Cuba in 1961. Newly elected president John F. Kennedy inherited from the preceding administration a plan to provide U.S. supplies and air cover while an invasion force of exiled Cubans parachuted into Cuba's

Groupthink: A process by which the members of a group ignore ways of thinking and plans of action that go against the group consensus.

Stanley Milgram's Work

Authority & Conformity

Bay of Pigs to liberate the country from Fidel Castro's communist government. A number of Kennedy's top advisers were certain the plan was fatally flawed but refrained from countering the emerging consensus. As it happened, the invasion was a disaster. The ill-prepared exiles were immediately defeated, Kennedy suffered public embarrassment, and the Cold War standoff between the Soviet Union and the United States deepened.

How could Kennedy's advisers, people of strong will and independent judgment educated at elite universities, have failed to voice their concerns adequately? Janis identified a number of possible reasons. For one, they were hesitant to disagree with the president lest they lose his favor. Nor did they want to diminish group harmony in a crisis situation where teamwork was all important. In addition, there was little time for them to consult outside experts who might have offered radically different perspectives. All these circumstances contributed to a single-minded pursuit of the president's initial ideas rather than an effort to generate effective alternatives.

Think about your own experiences working with groups, whether at work, on a class project, or in a campus organization. Have you ever "gone along to get along" or felt pressured to choose a particular path of action in spite of your own reservations? Or, conversely, have you ever chosen to refuse to conform in spite of the pressure? What factors affected your decision in either case?

ECONOMIC, CULTURAL, AND SOCIAL CAPITAL

One of the most important additions to the sociological study of groups is the contribution of the French school of thought known as **structuralism**, or *the idea that an overarching structure exists within which culture and other aspects of society must be understood.* A leading proponent, the French sociologist Pierre Bourdieu, provides an analytical framework that extends our understanding of the way group relationships and membership shape our lives. Bourdieu argues that several forms of *capital*—that is, social currency—stem from our association with different groups. These forms of capital are of importance in the reproduction of socioeconomic status in society.

Economic capital, the most basic form, consists of *money and material that can be used to access valued goods and services.* Depending on the social class you are born into and the progress of your education and career, you will have more or less access to economic capital and ability to take advantage of this form of capital. Another form is *cultural capital,* or your interpersonal skills, habits, manners, linguistic styles, tastes, and lifestyles. For instance, in some social circles, having refined table manners and speaking with a distinctive accent place a person in a social class that enhances his or her access to jobs, social activities, and friendship groups.

We often hear the phrase "It's not what you know; it's who you know." Indeed, history shows that social networks are important. The Kennedy family is one group that has had a disproportionate impact on American political life. Members of the Kennedy family have been elected to the presidency and Congress and have held other prestigious appointments in the federal government and private sector.

Friendship groups and other social contacts also provide **social capital**, *the personal connections and networks that enable people to accomplish their goals and extend their influence* (Bourdieu, 1984; Coleman, 1990; Putnam, 2000). College students who join fraternities and sororities expect that their "brothers" or "sisters" will help them get through the often challenging social and academic experiences of college. Other political, cultural, or social groups on campus offer comparable connections and opportunities. Many new—as well as more seasoned—employees (and prospective employees) join LinkedIn, a social media site that offers possibilities for people to expand their professional social networks, a key part of nurturing social capital.

While social capital is strongly influenced by socioeconomic class status, it may also be related to gender, to race, and intersectionally to both gender and race (McDonald & Day, 2010; McDonald, Lin, & Ao, 2009). In a study of social networks and their relationship to people's information about job leads, sociologists Matt Huffman and Lisa Torres (2002) found that women benefited from being part of networks that included

Structuralism: The idea that an overarching structure exists within which culture and other aspects of society must be understood.

Economic capital: Money and material that can be used to access valued goods and services.

Social capital: The social knowledge and connections that enable people to accomplish their goals and extend their influence.

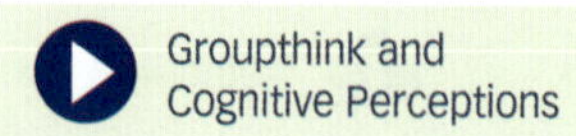
Groupthink and Cognitive Perceptions

Social Capital

more men than women; those who had more women in their social networks had a diminished probability of hearing about good job leads. Interestingly, the predominance of men or women in a man's social network made no discernible difference. The researchers suggested that perhaps the women were less likely to learn about job leads, and, notably, when they knew of leads, they were more likely to pass them along to men than to other women. Similarly, McDonald and Mair (2010) and Trimble and Kmec (2011) explored issues of networking in relation to women's career opportunities over their lifetimes and also the extent to which networks aid women in attaining jobs. Both teams of researchers found that social capital in the form of networks of relations has very distinct and important effects for women. The advent of professional networking sites online offers sociologists the opportunity to expand this research to see if and how gender affects social networks and their professional benefits, as research from the field of psychology suggests that job networking sites, including LinkedIn, play an important role in the job acquisition process (Bohnert & Ross, 2010).

Economic, cultural, and social capital confer benefits on individuals at least in part through membership in particular social groups. Characteristics such as class, race, ethnicity, and gender, among others, can have effects on the capital one has. Membership in organizations such as fraternities, exclusive golf clubs, or college alumni associations can offer important network access. These are some examples of the kinds of organizations that shape our lives and society, sometimes to our benefit, sometimes to our disadvantage. Below we look at organizations and their societal functions through the sociological lens.

ORGANIZATIONS

People frequently band together to pursue activities they could not readily accomplish by themselves. A principal means for accomplishing such cooperative actions is the **organization**, *a group with an identifiable membership that engages in concerted collective actions to achieve a common purpose* (Aldrich & Marsden, 1988). An organization can be a small primary group, but it is more likely to be a larger, secondary one: Universities, churches, armies, and business corporations are all examples of organizations. Organizations are a central feature of all societies, and their study is a core concern of sociology today.

Organizations tend to be highly formal in modern industrial and postindustrial societies. A **formal organization** is *rationally designed to achieve particular objectives, often by means of explicit rules, regulations, and procedures.* Examples include a state or county's department of motor vehicles or the federal Internal Revenue Service. As Max Weber (1919/1946) first recognized almost 100 years ago, modern societies are increasingly dependent on formal organizations. One reason is that formality is often a requirement for legal standing. For a college or university to be legally accredited, for example, it must satisfy explicit written standards governing everything from faculty hiring to fire safety. Today, formal organizations are the dominant form of organization across the globe.

TYPES OF FORMAL ORGANIZATIONS

Thousands of different kinds of formal organizations serve every imaginable purpose. Sociology seeks to simplify this diversity by identifying the principal types. Amitai Etzioni (1975) grouped organizations into three main types based on the reasons people join them: utilitarian, coercive, and normative. In practice, of course, many organizations, especially utilitarian and normative organizations, include elements of more than one type.

Utilitarian organizations are *those that people join primarily because of some material benefit they expect to receive in return for membership.* For example, you probably enrolled in college not only because you want to expand your knowledge and skills but also because you know that a college degree will help you get a better job and earn more money later in life. In exchange, you have paid tuition and fees, devoted countless hours to studying, and agreed to submit to the rules that govern your school, your major, and your courses. Many of the organizations people join are utilitarian, particularly those in which they earn a living, such as corporations, factories, and banks.

Coercive organizations are *those in which members are forced to give unquestioned obedience to authority.* People are often forced to join coercive organizations because they have been either sentenced to punishment (prisons) or remanded for mandatory treatment (mental hospitals or drug treatment centers). Coercive organizations may use force or the threat of force, and sometimes confinement, to ensure compliance with rules and regulations. Guards, locked doors, barred windows, and monitoring are all features of jails, prisons, and mental hospitals. Sometimes people join coercive organizations voluntarily, but once they are members they may not have the option of leaving as they desire. An example of such an organization is the military: While enlisting is voluntary in the United States,

Organization: A group with an identifiable membership that engages in concerted collective actions to achieve a common purpose.

Formal organization: An organization that is rationally designed to achieve its objectives, often by means of explicit rules, regulations, and procedures.

Utilitarian organizations: Organizations that people join primarily because of some material benefit they expect to receive in return for membership.

Coercive organizations: Organizations in which people are forced to give unquestioned obedience to authority.

PRIVATE LIVES, PUBLIC ISSUES

INDIVIDUALS, GROUPS, AND ACADEMIC ACHIEVEMENT

How did you do on your last exam or assignment in school? Certainly, all of us want to perform well and earn good grades. If your grade was outstanding, you probably credited the time you devoted to studying and preparing for class. If your grade was mediocre or poor, perhaps you attributed that to a lack of adequate time or effort on your part. Clearly, our own educational decisions and actions are of consequence in explaining our academic performance. Some research suggests, however, that *academic ability grouping*—that is, inclusion in a stronger, intermediate, or weaker group of learners—has a discernible effect on academic achievement. Consider the study described below, which was performed at the U.S. Air Force Academy (Carrell, Sacerdote, & West, 2011).

In an effort to improve academic performance and address the problem of dropouts, U.S. Air Force Academy leaders made a conscious effort to group cadets with weaker records together with those who had grade point averages above the mean. Their hypothesis was that the more academically able cadets would exercise a positive influence on their weaker peers, who were at greater risk of dropping out of the challenging program. In some instances, however, only stronger and weaker students were grouped, while in other experimental squadrons, stronger and weaker students were also mixed with those whose work was categorized as being in the middle. How would you hypothesize the effect of the conscious integration of academically weaker cadets with stronger students?

Perhaps predictably, the study found that weaker students did perform better in squadrons with stronger peers. Other research has also documented a positive effect for weaker learners in an environment with stronger students (Schofield, 2010). However, in the Air Force Academy study, that effect was present only when the weaker students were grouped with high performers *and* middle-level students. When the middle-level students were removed, leaving the strongest and weakest students in a group, the low-performing students did *worse* than their prior results would have predicted. Why would this be the case?

The researchers suggest that when only the strongest and weakest students were grouped together, they splintered into academically homogeneous groups—that is, the stronger students hung together and the weaker students hung together, muting the effect of mixing the cadets. When middle-level students were also part of a group, they functioned as a "glue," binding the group together, hindering the splitting of the ability groups, and thus bringing up the performance of the weakest students.

Notably, the researchers also found that the middle-level performers did best when they had their own group. The presence of the stronger and weaker students appeared, then, to lead to lower test scores than the middle-level students achieved when working in a homogeneous group.

Clearly, groups matter: Academic achievement is the outcome of individual effort and, as the research suggests, is subject to group effects. The findings of this research present a challenge that may not be easy for academic leaders to resolve: What can they do when some students benefit from being in groups with mixed levels of ability while others see greater results in single-level groups? What do you think?

THINK IT THROUGH

▶ What are we to conclude from this research? Who benefits and who loses from academic ability grouping? If the better performance of one group comes at a cost to the performance of another group, how should school leaders proceed in grouping by ability?

Scott Olson/Getty Images

The individuals here are part of a total institution, in which they are subject to regimentation and control of their daily activities by an authoritative body. They are expected to exhibit obedience to authority and to elevate the collective over the individual good.

once a person joins he or she is subject to close discipline and the demand for submission to authority in a rigidly hierarchical structure. Coercive organizations are examples of *total institutions,* which you read about in Chapter 4. By encompassing all aspects of people's lives, total institutions can radically alter people's thinking and behavior.

Normative organizations, or voluntary associations, are those that people join of their own will to pursue morally worthwhile goals without expectation of material reward. Belonging to such organizations may offer social prestige or moral or personal satisfaction. (Of course, such organizations may also serve utilitarian purposes, such as a charitable group you join partly to hand out your business card and boost your chances for monetary gain.)

The United States is a nation of normative organization joiners. Individuals affiliate with volunteer faith-related groups such as the YMCA, Hillel, and the Women's Missionary Society of the African Methodist Episcopal Church; charitable organizations such as the Red Cross; social clubs and professional organizations; politically oriented groups such as the National Association for the Advancement of Colored People (NAACP); and self-help groups such as Alcoholics Anonymous and Overeaters Anonymous. According to the National Center for Charitable Statistics (2009), there are more than 110,000 civic leagues and social welfare organizations, 77,000 fraternal societies, and 57,000 social and recreational clubs nationwide. They provide their members with a sense of connectedness while enabling them to accomplish personal and moral goals.

Normative organizations: Organizations that people join of their own will to pursue morally worthwhile goals without expectation of material reward; sometimes called *voluntary associations.*

Bureaucracy

Normative organizations may also erect barriers based on social class, race, ethnicity, and gender. Those traditionally excluded from such organizations, including women, Latinos, Native Americans, African Americans, and other people of color, have, in response, formed their own voluntary associations. Although it may seem that these, too, are exclusionary, such groups have a different basis for their creation—the effort to remedy social inequality. Social justice, as a result, is often their primary concern.

Below we shift our gaze from voluntary and coercive organizations to a phenomenon that is familiar to most of us—the bureaucracy. While we have some control over our membership in many organizations, we are all—as U.S. residents, taxpayers, students, or recipients of mortgage or college loans, among others—subject to the reach of modern bureaucracy.

BUREAUCRACIES

The authority structure of most large organizations today is bureaucratic. In this section we will look at the modern bureaucracy—the way it operates and some of its shortcomings. We will also see how bureaucratic structures have been modified or reformed to offer an alternative type of organization.

Max Weber (1919/1946) was the first sociologist to examine the characteristics of bureaucracy in detail. As noted in Chapter 1, Weber defined a bureaucracy as *a type of formal organization based on written procedural rules, arranged into a clear hierarchy of authority, and staffed by full-time paid officials.* Although Weber showed that bureaucracies could be found in many different societies throughout history, he argued that they became a dominant form of social organization only in modern society, where they came to touch key aspects of our daily lives. In particular, Weber suggested that bureaucracies are a highly rational form of organization because they were devised to achieve organizational goals with the greatest degree of efficiency—that is, to optimize the achievement of a task.

Note that when Weber characterized bureaucracies as rational he did not assume that they would always be *reasonable.* By *rational,* he meant that they were organized *based on knowable rules and regulations that laid out a particular path to a goal rather than on general or abstract principles or ideologies.* As we know from our own contacts with bureaucratic structures—whether they involve long waits on the phone to speak to a human being rather than a computer or the confusing pursuit of the correct person to whom one must turn in a critical student loan application—they are not, in fact, always reasonable.

To better understand the modern bureaucracy, Weber (1919/1946) identified what he referred to as the *ideal type* of this form of organization, describing the characteristics that would be found if the quintessential bureaucracy existed (Figure 5.4). While Weber recognized that no actual

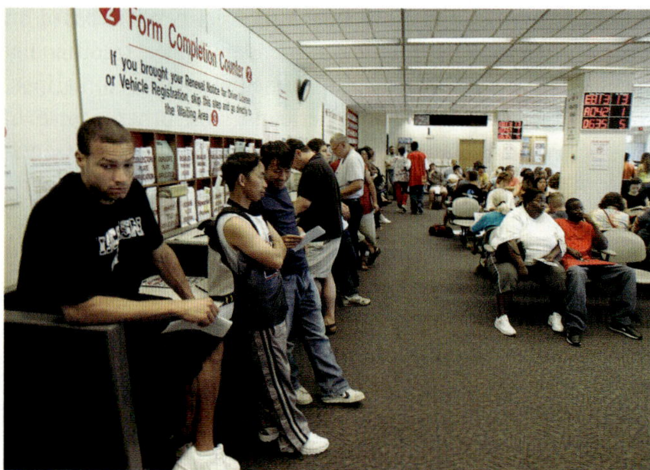
Form Completion Counter

AP Photo/ANDY MANIS

Today, a great deal of bureaucratic paperwork is done online. If we wish to apply for a passport, open a bank account, or renew a license, many of these tasks can be accomplished in front of a computer screen. What are some of the positive functions of this development? What are some dysfunctions?

bureaucracy necessarily possesses all of the characteristics he identifies, he argued that, by clearly articulating them, he was describing a standard against which actual bureaucracies could be judged and understood.

WRITTEN RULES AND REGULATIONS

The routine operation of the bureaucracy is governed by written rules and regulations, the purpose of which is to ensure that universal standards govern all aspects of bureaucratic behavior. Typically, rules govern everything from the hiring of employees to the reporting of an absence due to illness. They are usually spelled out in an organizational manual or handbook, now often available to employees on a human resources website, that describes in detail the requirements of each organizational position. While these rules and regulations can be lengthy and complex, they are, in theory, knowable, and the expectation is that those who work in and seek the services of a given organization will adhere to them—sometimes even if they don't seem to make sense!

- **Specialized offices:** Positions in a bureaucracy are organized into "offices" that create a division of labor within the organization. The duties of each office, such as bookkeeping or paying invoices, are described in the organizational manual. Each office specializes in one particular bureaucratic function to the exclusion of all others. Such specialization is one of the reasons that bureaucratic organization is said to be efficient; bureaucratic officials are supposed to become experts at their particular tasks, efficient cogs in a vast machine. The efficiency is, ideally, beneficial for the organization and its clients. If you are seeking to clear up a problem with your tuition bill, you will not visit the admissions office because you know the expert advice you seek is to be found in the student accounts office.
- **Hierarchy:** A bureaucracy is organized according to the vertical principle of hierarchy, so that each office has authority over one or more lower-level offices, and each in turn is responsible to a higher-level office. At the top, the leader of the organization stands alone; in the well-known words of then U.S. president Harry S. Truman, "The buck stops here." The organizational chart of a bureaucracy therefore generally looks like a pyramid. Again, efficiency is achieved through the knowable hierarchy of power that governs the organization.
- **Impersonality in record keeping:** Within a bureaucracy, communications are likely to be formal and impersonal. Written forms—"paperwork" or the electronic equivalent—substitute for more personalized human contact, because bureaucracies must maintain written records or databases of all important actions. Modern computer technology has vastly increased the ability of organizations to maintain and access records. In some ways, this is an advantage—for example, when it allows you to register for classes via smartphone instead of standing in line for hours waiting to fill out forms. On the other hand, you may regret the loss of human contact and the inflexibility of the process, however efficient it may be. This "impersonality" also, ideally, has the effect of ensuring that all clients are treated equally and efficiently rather than capriciously; in reality, however, people with substantial

FIGURE 5.4 **The Ideal Typical Bureaucracy**

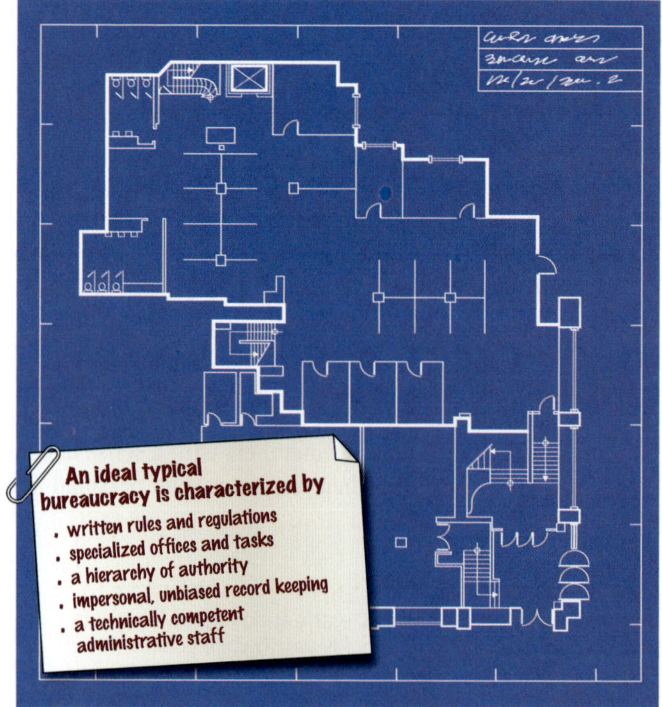
An ideal typical bureaucracy is characterized by
• written rules and regulations
• specialized offices and tasks
• a hierarchy of authority
• impersonal, unbiased record keeping
• a technically competent administrative staff

economic, social, or cultural capital often have the easiest time navigating bureaucracies.

- **Technically competent administrative staff:** A bureaucracy generally seeks to employ a qualified professional staff. Anyone who by training and expertise is able to perform the duties of a particular position in an office of the organization is deemed eligible to fill the position. Work in the bureaucracy is a full-time job, ideally providing a career path for the bureaucrat, who must demonstrate the training and expertise necessary to fill each successive position. In its "ideal" form, the system is a meritocracy—that is, positions are filled on the basis of merit or qualifications, typically demonstrated by performance on competitive exams, rather than based on applicants' knowing the "right" people. In practice, however—as is true of the other characteristics listed above—an actual bureaucracy is unlikely to meet this standard fully. In fact, getting hired into the organization and advancing in it are likely to be influenced not strictly by objective criteria such as education and experience but also by such social variables as age, gender, race, and social connections.

BUREAUCRACIES: A CRITICAL EVALUATION

Bureaucracies popularly evoke images of "paper pushers" and annoying red tape. In their studies of bureaucracy, sociologists, too, have had much to say about this form of organization, with mixed conclusions. Max Weber recognized that bureaucracies can, indeed, provide organizational efficiency in getting the job done. In contrast to earlier organizational forms, many of which filled positions through nepotism, bribes, or other non-merit-based forms of promotion and were founded to serve the needs of their leaders or small elite groups, modern bureaucracies have many redeeming qualities in spite of the frustrations they cause.

At the same time, Weber argued that a bureaucracy may create what he termed an *iron cage*—a prison of rules and regulations from which there is little escape (DiMaggio & Powell, 1983; Weber, 1904–1905/2002). The iron cage, which Weber memorably described as having the potential to be a "polar night of icy darkness," is a metaphor. We become "caged" in bureaucratic structures when we build them to serve us (as rules and regulations would ideally do) but they ultimately come to trap us by denying our humanity, creativity, and autonomy.

As you think about this metaphor of the iron cage, consider encounters with bureaucratic structures that you have had: If you've ever had the feeling that solving a personal or family problem with something like tuition, taxes, or immigration would require speaking to a human being with the power to make a decision or to see that your case is an exception in some way—but no such human was available!—then you can see what Weber meant. We make rules and regulations to keep order and to have a set of knowable guidelines for action and decisions, but what happens when the rules and regulations and their enforcement become the *ends* of an organization rather than *a means to an end*? Then we are in the iron cage.

Sociologists have identified a number of specific problems that plague bureaucracies, many of which may be familiar and could be thought of as representing *irrationalities of rationality*:

- **Waste and incompetence:** As long as administrators appear to be doing their jobs—filing forms, keeping records, responding to memos, and otherwise keeping busy—nobody really wants to question whether the organization as a whole is performing effectively or efficiently. Secure in their positions, bureaucrats may become inefficient, incompetent, and often indifferent to the clients they are supposed to serve.
- **Trained incapacity:** We have all seen bureaucrats who "go by the book" even when a situation clearly calls for fresh thinking. Thorstein Veblen (1899), a U.S. sociologist and contemporary of Weber's, termed this tendency *trained incapacity,* a learned inability to exercise independent thought. However intelligent they may otherwise be, such bureaucrats make poor judgments when it comes to decisions not covered by the rule book. They become so obsessed with following the rules and regulations that they lose the ability and flexibility to respond to new situations.
- **Goal displacement:** Bureaucracies may lose sight of the original goals they were created to accomplish. Large corporations such as General Motors and Hewlett-Packard and government organizations such as the Department of Homeland Security employ thousands of "middle managers" whose job it is to handle the paperwork required in manufacturing automobiles or computers, or in protecting the country. Perhaps understandably, such people may over time become preoccupied with getting their own jobs done and, driven by the need to ensure the continuation of particular practices or programs linked to their positions, eventually lose touch with the larger goals of the organization. The organization then becomes a sanctuary for bureaucrats who know and care little about making high-quality cars or computers or about keeping the country secure. This process adds to costs, lowers efficiency, and may prove detrimental to corporations that compete in a global economy and governments seeking to accomplish goals and stay within tight budgets.

Although Weber presented a sometimes chilling picture of bureaucracies operating as vast, inhuman machines, we all recognize that, in practice, there is often a human face behind the counter. In fact, much important work done in bureaucratic organizations is achieved through informal channels and personal ties and connections rather than through official channels, as sociologist Peter Blau showed in his research

(Blau & Meyer, 1987). For example, a student who wishes to register late for a class may avoid having to get half a dozen signatures if he or she knows the professor or a staff person in the registrar's office. However, because of the shortcomings of bureaucratic forms of organization, some theorists have argued for the development of alternative organizational forms. We discuss some of these after looking at the relationship between bureaucracy and democracy.

BUREAUCRACY AND DEMOCRACY

Max Weber argued that bureaucracies were an inevitable outgrowth of modern society, with its large-scale organizations, complex institutional structure, and concern with rationality and efficiency. Yet many observers have viewed bureaucracy as a stifling, irrational force that dominates our lives and threatens representative government. In *Les Employés* (1841/1985), French novelist Honoré de Balzac, who popularized the term *bureaucracy,* called it "the giant power wielded by pigmies" and a "fussy and meddlesome" government. Do bureaucracies inevitably lead to a loss of freedom and erosion of democracy? Are there more humanistic alternatives to bureaucracies that allow freer, more fulfilling participation in the organization? Let's look briefly at the views of sociologist Robert Michels on the incompatibility between democracy and bureaucracy, then see what some people have done to try to reform this organizational structure.

Michels (1876–1936), another contemporary of Weber's, argued that bureaucracy and democracy are fundamentally at odds. He observed that the Socialist Party in Germany, originally created to democratically represent the interests of workers, had become an oligarchy, a form of organization in which a small number of people exert great power. For him this was an example of what he termed the **iron law of oligarchy**, an *inevitable tendency for a large-scale bureaucratic organization to become ruled undemocratically by a handful of people.* (*Oligarchy* means the rule of a small group over many people.)

Following Weber, Michels argued that in a large-scale bureaucratic organization, the closer you are to the top, the greater the concentration of power. People typically get to the top because they are ambitious, hard-driving, and effective in managing the people below, or because they have economic and social capital to trade for proximity to power. Once there, leaders increase their social capital through specialized access to information, resources, and influential people, access that reinforces their power. They also often appoint subordinates who are loyal supporters and thus further enhance their position. Such leaders may come to regard the bureaucracy as a means to meet their own needs or those of their social group. The democratic purposes of an organization may become subordinate to the needs of the dominating group.

Since all modern societies require large-scale organizations to survive, Michels believed that democracies—or, in some cases, organizations—may sow the seeds of their own destruction by breeding bureaucracies that eventually grow into undemocratic oligarchies. While there are few signs that, for instance, the United States, which has many large-scale bureaucracies, is drifting from democracy, one could make a case that institutions like the U.S. Congress show some tendencies to act in the interests of political parties or powerful members rather than the interests of constituents. For example, a bill on disaster relief or unemployment insurance may be held up when a party leader feels that stalling the bill might confer political advantage on his or her party.

In response to what they feel is the stifling effect of bureaucratic organizations, some people have sought alternative forms of organizations designed to allow greater freedom and more fulfilling participation. For example, as part of the sweeping countercultural spirit of the late 1960s and early 1970s, many youthful activists joined collectives, small organizations that operate by cooperation and consensus. Food cooperatives, employee-run newspapers and health clinics, and "free schools" sprang up as organizations that sought to operate by consensus rather than by bureaucracy. Members of these organizations shunned hierarchy, avoided a division of labor based on expertise, and happily sacrificed efficiency in favor of more humanistic relationships.

The founders of these organizations believed they were reviving more personal organizational arrangements that could better enable society to reach certain goals. Although these organizations initially met with some success and left a legacy, they also confronted a larger society in which more conventional forms of organization effectively shut them out.

Members of such organizations as the food cooperatives and employee-run newspapers and health clinics of the 1960s and 1970s favored the values of cooperation and service over the more competitive and materialistic values of the larger society. In the exuberance of that period, members of collectives believed they were forging a radically new kind of antibureaucratic organization.

In her examination of early collectives, sociologist Joyce Rothschild-Whitt (1979) studied several that self-consciously rejected bureaucracy in favor of more cooperative forms. In one health clinic, for example, all jobs were shared (to the extent legally possible) by all members: Doctors would periodically answer telephones and clean the facility, while nurses and paramedical staff would conduct examinations and interview patients. While the doctors were paid somewhat more than the other staff members, the differences were not large and were the subject of negotiation by everyone who worked at the clinic.

As long as the collectives remained small, they were able to maintain their founders' values. On the other hand, vastly reduced pay differentials between professional and

Iron law of oligarchy: Robert Michels's theory that there is an inevitable tendency for a large-scale bureaucratic organization to become ruled undemocratically by a handful of people.

sional staff, job sharing, and collective decision making often made it difficult for the collectives to compete for employees with organizations that shared none of these values (Rothschild-Whitt, 1979). Doctors, for example, could make much more money in conventional medical practice, without being expected to answer telephones or sweep the floor. Over time the original cooperative values tended to erode, and many of the new organizations came to resemble conventional organizations in the larger society. Still, more than three decades after Rothschild-Whitt studied them, a number of these original groups still exist. Although they may have lost some of their collective zeal, they still operate more cooperatively than most traditional organizations.

A more recent foray away from hierarchically and bureaucratically organized entities has been made by the online retailer Zappos. In early 2014, the company announced that it planned to introduce a "holacracy," replacing traditional management structures with "self-governing 'circles.'" The goal of holacracy, according to a media account of the practice, is to "organize a company around the work that needs to be done instead of around the people who do it." Hence, a holacracy is devoid of job titles; instead, employees are integrated into multiple circles of cooperative workers. A few other companies are experimenting with holacracy as well (McGregor, 2014). Do workers perform well in contexts of dispersed or ambiguous authority? Can these self-governing circles exceed the productivity—and perhaps work satisfaction—of more traditionally organized companies? These questions remain to be answered.

THE GLOBAL ORGANIZATION

Organizations from multinational corporations to charitable foundations span the globe and increasingly contribute to what some sociologists believe is a "homogenization" of the world's countries (McNeely, 1995; Neyazi, 2010; Scott & Meyer, 1994; Thomas, Meyer, Ramirez, & Boli, 1987). You can listen to the same music, employ the same Internet search engine, see the same films, and eat the same meals (if you wish) in Bangalore and Baku as you do in Berlin and Boston.

Global organizations are not new. The Hanseatic League, a business alliance between German merchants and cities, dominated trade in the North and Baltic Seas from the mid-12th to the mid-18th centuries. The British East India Company virtually owned India and controlled the vast bulk of trade throughout the Far East for several centuries. In 1919, following World War I, the League of Nations was formed, uniting the most economically and militarily powerful nations of the world in an effort to ensure peace and put an end to war. When Germany withdrew and began expanding its borders throughout Europe, however, the League dissolved.

After World War II, a new effort at international governance was made in the form of the United Nations, begun in 1945. The United Nations is still important and active today: Its power is limited, but its influence has grown. It not only mediates disputes between nations, but it is also ever present in international activities ranging from fighting hunger and HIV/AIDS to mobilizing peacekeeping troops and intervening to address conflicts and their consequences.

International organizations exist in two major forms: those established by national governments and those established by private organizations. We consider each separately below.

INTERNATIONAL GOVERNMENTAL ORGANIZATIONS

The first type of global organization is the **international governmental organization (IGO)** established by treaties between governments. Most IGOs exist *to facilitate and regulate trade between the member countries, promote national security* (both the League of Nations and the United Nations were created after highly destructive world wars), *protect social welfare or human rights, or, increasingly, ensure environmental protection.*

Some of the most powerful IGOs today were created to unify national economies into large trading blocs. One of the most complex IGOs is the European Union, whose rules now govern 28 countries in Europe; 5 additional countries have applied for EU entry. The European Union was formed to create a single European economy in which businesses could operate freely across borders in search of markets and labor and workers could move freely in search of jobs without having to go through customs or show passports at border crossings. EU member states have common economic policies, and 18 of them share a single currency (the euro). Not all Europeans welcome economic unity, however, since it means their countries must surrender some of their economic power to the EU as a whole. Being economically united by a single currency also means the economic problems felt by one country are distributed among all the other countries to some degree. Thus, when economic crisis hit Europe in 2008, the severe economic woes of Greece, Portugal, and Spain, among others, caused serious problems for stronger EU economies, like that of Germany.

IGOs can also wield considerable military power, provided their member countries are willing to do so. The North Atlantic Treaty Organization (NATO) and the United Nations, for example, have sent troops from some of their participating nations into war zones in Iraq and Afghanistan in recent years. Yet because nations ultimately control the use of their own military forces, there are limits to the authority of even the most powerful military IGOs, whose strength derives from the voluntary participation of their member nations.

International governmental organization (IGO): An international organization established by treaties between governments for purposes of commerce, security, promotion of social welfare and human rights, or environmental protection.

IGOs often reflect inequalities in power among their members. For example, the UN Security Council is responsible for maintaining international peace and security and is therefore the most powerful organization within the United Nations. Its five permanent members include the United Kingdom, the United States, China, France, and Russia, which gives these countries significant clout over the Security Council's actions. The remaining 10 Security Council member countries are elected by the UN General Assembly for 2-year terms and therefore have less lasting power than the permanent members.

At the beginning of the 20th century, there were only about three dozen IGOs in the world, although data for that time are incomplete. By 1981, when consistent reporting criteria were adopted, there were 1,039; by 2011, the most recent year for which data are available, there were 7,608 (Union of International Associations, 2011; see also Figures 5.5 and 5.6).

FIGURE 5.5 Increase in Number of IGOs, 1909–2011

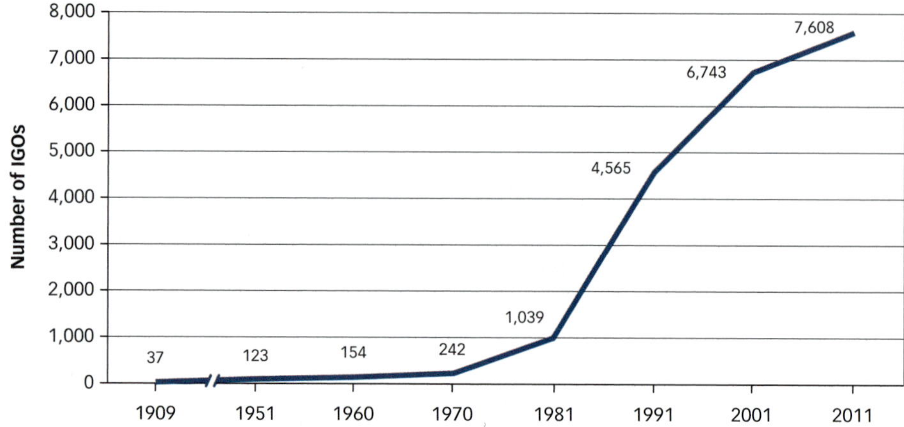

SOURCE: Union of International Associations. (2011). Historical overview of number of international organizations by type, 1909–2011. In *Yearbook of international organizations, 2011/2012 edition.* Herndon, VA: Brill.

FIGURE 5.6 Increase in Number of INGOs, 1909–2011

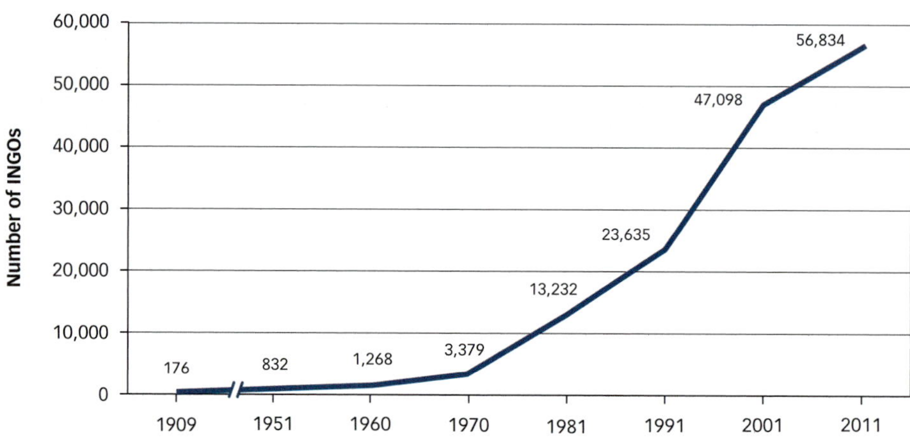

SOURCE: Union of International Associations. (2011). Historical overview of number of international organizations by type, 1909–2011. In *Yearbook of international organizations, 2011/2012 edition.* Herndon, VA: Brill.

INTERNATIONAL NONGOVERNMENTAL ORGANIZATIONS

The second type of global organization is the **international nongovernmental organization (INGO)**, *established by agreements between the individuals or private organizations making up the membership and existing to fulfill an explicit mission.* Examples include the International Planned Parenthood Federation, the International Sociological Association, the International Council of Women, and the environmental group Greenpeace. Global business organizations (GBOs) represent a subtype within the broader category of INGOs. The concept of the GBO captures the fluid and highly interconnected nature of our modern, globalized labor market in which employees often interact and communicate with people from other nations and cultures, facilitated by technology and online networks. Like the number of IGOs, the number of INGOs, including GBOs, has increased exponentially in recent years—from fewer than 200 near the beginning of the 20th century to more than 20,000 by 1985 and up to 56,834 in 2011 (Union of International Associations, 2011).

INGOs are primarily concerned with promoting the global interests of their members, largely through influencing the United Nations, other IGOs, or individual governments. They also engage in research, education, and the spread of information by means of international conferences, meetings, and journals. INGOs have succeeded in shaping the policies of powerful nations. One prominent (and highly successful) INGO is the International Campaign to Ban Landmines (ICBL). The organization, along with its founder, Jody Williams, was awarded the Nobel Peace Prize in 1997 for its success in getting a majority of the world's countries to agree to a treaty banning the devastating use of land mines. The Nobel Committee commended the ICBL for changing "a vision to a feasible reality," adding that "this work has grown into a convincing example of an effective policy for peace that could prove decisive in the international effort for disarmament" (quoted in ICBL, 2012).

International nongovernmental organization (INGO): An international organization established by agreements between the individuals or private organizations making up its membership and existing to fulfill an explicit mission.

GLOBAL ISSUES

AMNESTY INTERNATIONAL AND THE GLOBAL CAMPAIGN FOR HUMAN RIGHTS

In 2011, Jalila al-Salman, vice president of the Bahrain Teachers' Association (BTA), was arrested, held in solitary confinement for a week, and beaten. Both she and Mahdi Abu Dheeb, president of the BTA, were charged with using their positions "to call for a strike by teachers, halting the educational process, 'inciting hatred of the regime' and 'attempting to overthrow the ruling system by force'" (Amnesty International, 2012). Although al-Salman was released on bail, Abu Dheeb has been sentenced to 10 years in prison. In April 2012, he testified that he was being tortured, but his request to be released on bail was denied. Amnesty International (2012), a *normative organization* pursuing global human rights, believes al-Salman and Abu Dheeb are *prisoners of conscience,* arrested for no crime greater than being leaders of the BTA and "peacefully exercising their rights to freedom of expression and assembly." The organization also believes their status as civilians makes their prosecution in a military court inappropriate and illegal.

AP XHJ102

Arrested in Bahrain for organizing peaceful protests against conditions for teachers and public school children, the woman pictured here, Jalila al-Salman, was arrested for "inciting hatred of the regime." Amnesty International engaged in a human rights campaign to help al-Salman escape injustice.

According to Amnesty International (2012), governments in more than 20 countries executed 676 prisoners in 2011—but the actual total is likely much higher. A record number of protests occurred worldwide that year, leading to widespread brutality, arrests, and torture perpetrated by governments, since 91 countries uphold laws that restrict freedom of expression. Amnesty International also reports that tens of thousands of people throughout the world are imprisoned without having been charged with any crime.

Amnesty International has more than 5,000 affiliated local groups and 2.8 million members across more than 150 countries and territories, including 250,000 in the United States. One of its goals is to help secure the freedom of people imprisoned because of their political beliefs or actions, especially those in immediate danger of torture or execution. Amnesty International has helped thousands of individual prisoners since it was founded in Britain in 1961. It functions as a global pressure group made up of ordinary citizens. Anyone can join, pay nominal annual dues, and become part of a global "urgent action network" that is regularly mobilized to send government officials faxes, express mail, and e-mail requests on behalf of prisoners. Amnesty International also sends delegations to countries where government abuses are rampant. The reports these delegations write draw worldwide media attention to the world's prisons and political prisoners.

THINK IT THROUGH

▶ In cases of groups like Amnesty International, does size matter? Is a larger group more effective than a smaller collective of activists? Does the use of Internet platforms like Facebook, Twitter, and YouTube in social action campaigns make the size of the group of supporters more or less important?

Protests

The ICBL is affiliated with more than a thousand other INGOs in some 60 countries. Together they have focused public attention on the dangers posed to civilians of the more than 100 million antipersonnel mines that are a deadly legacy of past wars fought in Europe, Asia, and Africa. These mines are unlike other weapons. They can remain active for decades after a war, terrorizing and trapping whole populations. In Cambodia, for example, fertile croplands have been mined, threatening starvation to farmers who are not willing to risk a misstep that would reduce them or their family to a shower of scraps. The campaign's efforts resulted in a treaty banning the use, production, stockpiling, and transfer of antipersonnel land mines. The treaty, which became international law in March 2012, has been signed and ratified by 160 countries (ICBL, 2012).

Although they are far more numerous than IGOs and have achieved some successes, INGOs have far less power over state actions and policies, since legal power (including enforcement) ultimately lies with governmental organizations and treaties. In the effort to ban land mines, for instance, although most of the major powers in the world have signed the treaty, the United States, citing security concerns in Korea, has refused, as has Russia. Some INGOs, such as Amnesty International and Greenpeace, nonetheless wield considerable influence.

WHY STUDY GROUPS AND ORGANIZATIONS?

You now have a good idea of how the groups and organizations to which you belong exert influence over your life. They help to determine who you know and, in many ways, who you are. The primary groups of your earliest years were crucial in shaping your sense of self—a sense that will change only very slowly over the rest of your life. Throughout your life, groups are the wellspring of the norms and values that enable and enrich your social life. At the same time, they are the source of nonconforming behavior; the rebel is shaped by group membership as much as the more mainstream and conventional citizen.

Although groups remain central in our lives, group affiliation in the United States is rapidly changing. To some degree, long-standing conventional groups appear to be losing ground. For example, today's typical college students are less likely to join civic groups and organizations—or even to vote—than were their parents. At the same time, many are active "netizens," joining and creating groups for both amusement and civic or political causes through such vehicles as Facebook and Twitter.

The global economy and information technology are also redefining group life in ways we can already perceive. For instance, workers in earlier generations spent much of their careers in a relatively small number of long-lasting, bureaucratic organizations; younger workers today are much more likely to be part of a succession of networked, "flexible," and even virtual organizations.

How will these trends affect the quality of our social relationships? Will the blurring between primary and secondary groups continue and expand? Will our growing reliance on social media as a key forum for interaction foster integration or alienation? In our changing social environment, these questions pose important frontiers for sociological analysis.

WHAT CAN I DO WITH A SOCIOLOGY DEGREE?

SKILLS AND CAREERS: UNDERSTANDING AND FOSTERING SOCIAL CHANGE

Social change comes about as a result of shifts in the social order of society. While the changes may be evolutionary or revolutionary in pace, change is inevitable. *Understanding social change* and the factors that underlie its dynamics is key to bringing about positive change, whether at the micro or the macro level. Sociologists study factors that bring about large-scale social change—for instance, shifts in population growth or health, technological progress, economic changes, the mobilization of civil society, or the rise of a charismatic leader—and seek to understand barriers to normative or structural change. They are also interested in factors that affect change or resistance to change in smaller groups and communities. Skills in the areas of leadership, communications, strategic thinking, motivation and mobilization, and advocacy can evolve from knowledge gained in the study of social change. Students interested in social change may also take advantage of internships or practicums in community or political organizations involved in fostering positive change. Supervised practice and the opportunity for reflection on your work nurture skills in the area of social change.

In Chapter 5, we examined the phenomenon of *groupthink*—a form of decision making that elevates consensus and conformity over a critical, multidimensional approach to a problem. Groupthink may be a powerful obstacle to social action and social change. Consider the chapter's opening story, which focused on the decision of a small group of administrators and coaches at Pennsylvania State University to keep silent about the pedophilia of a colleague in order to maintain his and the athletic program's respectability. Could a trained leader have overcome the obstacles to action and challenged the consensus of resistance to altering the status quo? Could a skilled advocate have spoken out in favor of interests—such as those of the victimized children—that diverged from the perceived interests of the Penn State leaders? Sociologists are deeply interested in social change, which comes in many forms—it can range from normative changes in a small group to massive national political revolutions. Sociology is a discipline dedicated to understanding how change comes about, knowledge that is at the foundation of transformation.

Careers in social change may focus on specific areas, including the environment, labor, human rights, free speech, legal reform, social justice, conflict resolution, poverty, health care, gender equity, economic justice, and corporate ethics. They may be careers in public service (such as in federal, state, or local government) or in the private sector (with advocacy organizations or in research-focused organizations, for instance). An understanding of social change and the development of skills associated with fostering positive social change are important in *occupational fields* that include government, social services, nonprofit management and advocacy, education, health care, entrepreneurship, politics and lobbying, community service and volunteerism, and the law, among others. Some specific *job titles* associated with these fields are community outreach and education specialist, policy analyst, advocacy and public policy coordinator, community organizer, labor union organizer, human rights advocate, social worker, lobbyist, social policy analyst, program evaluator, and researcher.

THINK ABOUT CAREERS

- What kinds of social, political, economic, ecological, or other issues are of interest to you?
- What kinds of career paths might you envision emerging from your interests?

SUMMARY

- The importance of social groups in our lives is one of the salient features of the modern world. Social groups are collections of people who share a sense of common identity and regularly interact with one another based on shared expectations. There are many conceptual ways to distinguish social groups sociologically in order to better understand them.

- Among the most important characteristics of a group is whether or not it serves as a reference group—that is, a group that provides standards by which we judge ourselves in terms of how we think we appear to others, what sociologist Charles Horton Cooley termed the "looking-glass self."

- Group size is another variable that is an important factor in group dynamics. Although their intensity may diminish, larger groups tend to be more stable than smaller groups of two (**dyads**) or three (**triads**) people. While even small groups can develop a formal group structure, larger groups develop a formal structure.

- Formal structures include some people in leadership roles—that is, those group members who are able to influence the behavior of the other members. The most common form of leadership is **transactional**—that is, routine leadership concerned with getting the job done. Less common is **transformational leadership**, which is concerned with changing the very nature of the group itself.

- Leadership roles imply that the role occupant is accorded some power, the ability to mobilize resources and get things done despite resistance. Power derives from two principal sources: the personality of the leader (**personal power**) and the position that the leader occupies (**positional power**). Max Webe r highlighted the importance of charisma as a source of leadership as well as leadership deriving from traditional authority (a queen inherits a throne, for example).

- In general people are highly susceptible to group pressure. Many people will conform to group norms or obey orders from an authority figure, even when there are potentially negative consequences for others or even for themselves.

- Important aspects of groups are the networks that are formed between groups and among the people in them. Networks constitute broad sources of relationships, direct and indirect, including connections that may be extremely important in business and politics. Women, people of color, and lower-income people typically have less access to the most influential economic and political networks than do upper-class White males in U.S. society.

- As a consequence of unequal access to powerful social networks, there is an unequal division of social capital in society. **Social capital** is the knowledge and connections that enable people to cooperate with one another for mutual benefit and to extend their influence. Some social scientists have argued that social capital has declined in the United States during the last quarter century—a process they worry indicates a decline in Americans' commitment to civic engagement.

- **Formal organizations** are organizations that are rationally designed to achieve their objectives by means of rules, regulations, and procedures. They may be **utilitarian**, **coercive**, or **normative**, depending on the reasons for joining. One of the most common types of formal organizations in modern society is the bureaucracy. Bureaucracies are characterized by written rules and regulations, specialized offices, a hierarchical structure, impersonality in record keeping, and professional administrative staff.

- The **iron law of oligarchy** holds that large-scale organizations tend to concentrate power in the hands of a few people. As a result, even supposedly democratic organizations tend to become undemocratic when they become large.

- A number of organizational alternatives to bureaucracies exist. These include collectives, which emphasize cooperation, consensus, and humanistic relations. Networked organizations, which increase flexibility by reducing hierarchy, are like collectives in their organization.

- Two important forms of global organizations are **international governmental organizations (IGOs)** and **international nongovernmental organizations (INGOs)**. Both kinds of organizations play increasingly important roles in the world today, and IGOs—particularly the United Nations—may become key organizational actors as the pace of globalization increases.

KEY TERMS

dyad, 108
triad, 108
alliance (or coalition), 108
social closure, 110
transformational leader, 111
transactional leader, 111
legitimate authority, 111
positional power, 112
personal power, 112
groupthink, 113
structuralism, 114
economic capital, 114
social capital, 114
organization, 115
formal organization, 115
utilitarian organizations, 115
coercive organizations, 115
normative organizations, 117
iron law of oligarchy, 120
international governmental organization (IGO), 121
international nongovernmental organization (INGO), 122

DISCUSSION QUESTIONS

1. This chapter began with a look at the Penn State child sex abuse scandal through the conceptual lens of *groupthink.* Can you think of a time when a group to which you belonged was making a decision you thought was wrong—ethically, legally, or otherwise—but you went along anyway? How do your experiences confirm or refute Janis's characterization of groupthink and its effects?

2. List the primary and secondary groups of which you are a member, then make another list of the primary and secondary groups to which you belonged 5 years ago. Which groups in these two periods were most important for shaping (a) your view of yourself, (b) your political beliefs, (c) your goals in life, and (d) your friendships?

3. Think of a time when you chose to "go along to get along" with a group decision even when you were inclined to think or behave differently. Think of a time when you opted to dissent, choosing a path different from that pursued by your group or organization. How would you account for the different decisions? How might sociologists explain them?

4. What did Stanley Milgram seek to test in his human experiments at Yale University? What did he find? Do you think that a similar study today would find the same results? Why or why not?

5. Max Weber suggested that bureaucracy, while intended to maximize efficiency in tasks and organizations, could also be highly irrational. He coined the term *the iron cage* to talk about the web of rules and regulations he feared would ensnare modern societies and individuals. On one hand, societies create organizations that impose rules and regulations to maintain social order and foster the smooth working of institutions such as the state and the economy. On the other hand, members of society may often feel trapped and dehumanized by these organizations. Explain this paradox using an example of your own encounters with the "iron cage" of bureaucracy.

6 DEVIANCE AND SOCIAL CONTROL

IN THIS CHAPTER

REUTERS/Tomas Bravo

WHAT DO YOU THINK?

1. Is everyone deviant at least some of the time? Does this make deviance normal?
2. Why did the rate of imprisonment rise dramatically in the United States beginning in the 1980s? Why is the rate of imprisonment in the United States much higher than the rates in nearly all other modern states?
3. What methods of controlling deviance are available to countries and communities? What methods could be more or less effective?

© Loulou d'Aki/Demotix/Corbis

SNAKE SALVATION

In Appalachia—a region of the United States stretching from southwestern New York to northern Alabama—a Pentecostal religious ritual that would make many people cringe thrives: serpent handling.

Several deaths in recent years have drawn public, media, and law enforcement attention to the practice of serpent handling and to the Pentecostal religious communities where it takes place. On May 27, 2012, Pastor Randy "Mack" Wolford died after a rattlesnake bit him during a service at the House of the Lord Jesus Church in West Virginia (Duin, 2012; Pond, 2012). Pastor Wolford's father died of snakebite in 1983, highlighting the fact that serpent handling is a practice passed down through generations of Pentecostal families. Photojournalist Lauren Pond (2012) was on assignment for the *Washington Post* and photographed Mack Wolford's last hours, during which he refused any life saving medical treatments.

In January 2014, Jamie Coots, a third-generation snake handler and pastor of the Full Gospel Tabernacle in Jesus Name Church in Kentucky, was also killed by a rattlesnake bite he received during a religious service. Prior to his death, Coots and his family were featured on a reality show on the National Geographic channel called *Snake Salvation* that focused on their belief in the spiritual power and importance of snake handling (Fantz, 2014). Cody, Pastor Coots's son and himself a snake handler, was stunned by his father's death, telling a news reporter afterward that he believed "we're going to go home, he's going to lay on the couch, he's going to hurt, he's going to pray for a while and he's going to get better" (Johnson, 2014). One reason his father's death stunned Cody was that he had long accepted the Pentecostal belief, derived from Mark 16:17–18, that those individuals "anointed by God" will not be harmed by the bites of poisonous snakes (Fantz, 2014).

Mainstream society characterizes serpent handling as a deviant activity. By extension, the veil of deviance has also been cast over the Pentecostal religious congregations practicing it. In an episode of the FX television network series *Justified* that first aired in 2013, a snake-handling preacher visits the town of Harlan, Kentucky, and begins attempting to convert members of the town's population to his faith. The pastor is depicted in the program as deranged, and his intentions are portrayed as suspicious. The pastor is eventually killed during a confrontation with one of the show's main protagonists after being challenged to prove his faith and anointment by God by handling a poisonous rattlesnake.

The state of Tennessee criminalized snake handling in the 1940s in order to reduce the prevalence of what were considered "radical" Pentecostal churches. Kentucky continues to impose criminal misdemeanor fines on anyone caught using snakes for religious practices at public gatherings (Pond, 2012).

The phenomenon of serpent handling illuminates a key sociological point. The fact that serpent handling is condemned by some and embraced by others highlights the argument that many forms of societal deviance are not defined through consensus but instead are defined in relation to who has the power to label acts as deviant. The practices of less powerful societal groups, like serpent-handling Pentecostals, are more likely to be labeled deviant than the practices of dominant groups. The labeling of deviance almost always relies on a judgment by one individual or a group about the behavior or condition of another.

For the Pentecostal faithful, coming face-to-face with venomous snakes is far from deviant; rather, it is a sign of faith and therefore acceptable and meaningful. Meanwhile, to outsiders the practice may seem foolish, dangerous, and even criminal. Should it be criminalized and controlled, or should it be tolerated as a form of religious expression? More generally, should people be legally restricted from engaging in risky behaviors, like serpent handling or recreational drug use, if they know the consequences and accept them?

Deviance: Any attitude, behavior, or condition that violates cultural norms or societal laws and results in disapproval, hostility, or sanction if it becomes known.

Crime: Any act defined in the law as punishable by fines, imprisonment, or both.

Deviance comes in many forms and raises many interesting questions, but you should be forewarned: Many of these questions do not have clear-cut answers. As this chapter shows, deviance is a broad concept, encompassing a diverse array of attitudes, behaviors, and conditions, of which only a small part fall under the category of "crime." Explanations of deviance are no less expansive and diverse.

We begin this chapter by looking at how deviant behavior is defined. This is followed by an examination of different perspectives that sociologists take to understand and explain such behavior. We then briefly consider the distinction between deviance and crime and conclude with a look at how societies exercise control over those people and behaviors they define as deviant.

WHAT IS DEVIANT BEHAVIOR?

Deviance is *any attitude, behavior, or condition that violates cultural norms or societal laws and results in disapproval, hostility, or sanction if it becomes known.* By contrast, a **crime** is *an act, usually considered deviant, that is punishable by fines, imprisonment, or both.*

Several important aspects of our definition of deviance deserve greater elaboration. First, *deviance* is a broad term that may encompass crimes but often refers to noncriminal attitudes, behaviors, and conditions. Second, deviance is not restricted to specific groups, genders, or age ranges; both adults and youth can engage in deviance. Third, what is considered deviant can include things that are not consciously chosen, such as medical conditions, mental or physical illnesses, and physical defects and abnormalities. Fourth, deviance is a relative, subjective concept. Definitions of deviance vary from place to place, across time, and among groups within society. Finally, our definition of deviance suggests that it is primarily a reaction against something. Therefore, deviance is best seen as a label applied by people or groups within society to the attitudes, behaviors, or conditions of other people or groups. As such, moral, social, and legal judgments play a role in decisions regarding what is or is not deviant.

You may be wondering, Is all deviance criminal? In fact, most of the attitudes, behaviors, and conditions considered "deviant" by society are not criminal. For example, while having extensive tattoos or piercings may be considered deviant, it is not criminal. The follow-up question—Are all crimes deviant?—has a more complicated answer.

While the label *crime* applies to acts that are widely agreed to be deviant in nature (for example, murder, robbery, rape, the sexual exploitation of children, arson), such consensus is lacking regarding other kinds of crimes. Use of illicit drugs,

Sociologists suggest that what is labeled deviant depends on cultural norms and is subject to change. Tattoos, once limited to a few subcultures, are widely accepted in U.S. society, though individuals who change their appearance very dramatically are still subject to this label.

gambling, vagrancy, and adult prostitution are just a few examples of crimes that lack societal consensus about their deviance, but these are defined as crimes nonetheless. Once an act is labeled criminal, formal sanctions can be applied in order to control it and the people who engage in it. One should be extremely cautious not to make the erroneous assumption that every crime is considered deviant by all of society's members, or that every form of deviance is, or should be, criminalized.

The diversity of opinion surrounding the concepts of deviance and criminality stems from the fact that most societies in the modern world are pluralistic. **Pluralistic societies** are *made up of many different groups with different norms and values,* which may or may not change over time. In a pluralistic society, what is deviant for one group may be acceptable or normal in another, and even long-held beliefs and practices are sometimes subject to radical transformation over time. For example, in the 1800s, members of the Church of Jesus Christ of Latter-day Saints (Mormons) practiced polygamy—specifically, men could have multiple wives—but by the end of the 19th century the church officially condemned that practice. Similarly, in 2005, after centuries of supporting the execution of juveniles for **capital offenses**, *crimes considered so heinous they are punishable by death,* the U.S. Supreme Court ruled that it is unconstitutional to execute anyone for a crime he or she committed before the age of 18. Prior to this ruling, 22 individuals had been executed for crimes they committed while under the age of 18 (Death Penalty Information Center, 2010). In each case, norms pertaining to practices or punishment shifted over time, creating a "new normal." And, of course, the shifting legal status of marijuana, which is now legal to purchase and consume for medical purposes in a number of states and is legal for recreational use in Colorado and Washington State, is illustrative of shifting definitions of deviance.

Because there is so much disagreement about what constitutes deviant behavior, we should not be surprised to find that most people deviate from some of society's established norms a

Pluralistic societies: Societies made up of many diverse groups with different norms and values.

Capital offenses: Crimes considered so heinous they are punishable by death.

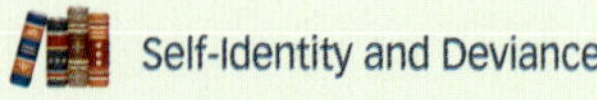

Topical Press Agency / Stringer/Getty Images

When was the last time a law enforcement officer arrested you because of what you were wearing to the pool or beach? In this old photo, a woman in Chicago is arrested for wearing a one-piece bathing suit without the "required" leg coverings. What are other examples of how definitions of deviance have evolved over time?

good deal of the time. As the data in Table 6.1 show, deviance is not limited solely to violating norms like not spitting on the sidewalk—even behaviors defined as criminal are committed much more often than most people might think.

HOW DO SOCIOLOGISTS EXPLAIN DEVIANCE?

What explains deviance? Below we look at a spectrum of theoretical perspectives that seek to explain why people engage in deviance. We can divide these theories broadly into explanatory and interactionist categories. Theories that try to explain why deviance does (or does not) occur, including biological, functional, and conflict perspectives, differ from interactionist theories, which seek to understand how deviance is defined, constructed, and enacted through social processes like labeling.

BIOLOGICAL PERSPECTIVES

Early social scientists were convinced that deviance—from alcoholism to theft to murder—was caused by biological or anatomical abnormalities (Hooton, 1939). For example, some early researchers claimed that *skull configurations of deviant individuals differed from those of nondeviants,* a theory known as **phrenology**. Other theorists claimed that deviants were **atavisms**, or *throwbacks to primitive early humans* (Lombroso, 1896), and that they also had body types that differed from those of noncriminals (Sheldon, 1949). These early biological theories have been disproven, but the search for biological causes of deviance continues, with some success in individual cases (Wright, Tibbetts, & Daigle, 2008). Advances in medical technology, especially increased use of magnetic resonance imaging (MRI and fMRI, or functional MRI), are proving fruitful in enabling researchers to uncover patterns of brain function, physiology, and response unique to some deviant or criminal individuals (Giedd, 2004). However, most modern biological theories do not attribute deviance to biology alone. Instead, they argue that deviance may be the product of an interaction between biological and environmental factors (Denno, 1990; Kanazawa & Still, 2000; Mednick, Moffitt, & Stack, 1987).

Phrenology: A theory that the skull shapes of deviant individuals differ from those of nondeviants.

Atavisms: Throwbacks to primitive early humans.

One method for testing biological theories is to compare children with their parents to see whether children of parents with deviant lifestyles are more likely to re-create those lifestyles than are children whose parents are not deviant. Research has found that people who suffer from alcoholism and some forms of mental illness (particularly schizophrenia, chronic depression, and bipolar personality disorder) are indeed more likely to have parents with similar problems than are people who do not have these conditions (Dunner, Gershon, & Barrett, 1988; Scheff, 1988).

However, studies comparing the frequency of deviance between generations do not always control for the possibility that children of alcoholic, schizophrenic, depressed, or bipolar parents may have learned coping strategies that show up as symptoms of these problems, rather than having inherited a biological predisposition. Children of farmers are more likely to be farmers than are children of urban office workers, but we would not therefore argue that farming is a biologically

TABLE 6.1 Self-Reported Deviant Behavior Among High School Seniors in the United States, 2012–2013

Deviant Act	Percentage
Robbery	5
Auto theft	7
Been arrested	9
Other drug use (besides marijuana)	11
Hurt someone who then needed medical help	13
Marijuana use	26
Shoplifting	27
Traffic ticket/warning	30

SOURCES: Johnston, L. D., Bachman, J. G., O'Malley, P. M., & Schulenberg, J. E. (2012). *Monitoring the Future: A continuing study of 12th grade youth.* Ann Arbor: Institute for Social Research, University of Michigan. Johnston, L. D., O'Malley, P. M., Miech, R. A., Bachman, J. G., & Schulenberg, J. E. (2014). *Monitoring the Future national results on drug use: 1975–2013: Overview, key findings on adolescent drug use.* Ann Arbor: Institute for Social Research, University of Michigan.

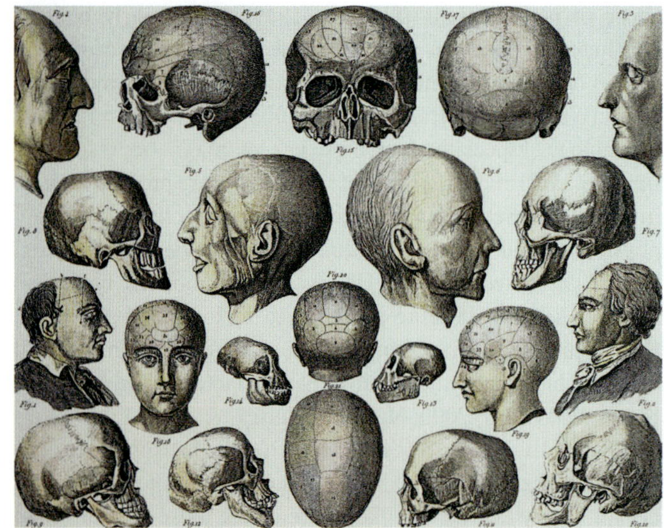
SPL / Science Source

Cesare Lombroso, an early criminologist, theorized that criminals were throwbacks to primitive humans. Although his theory has been disproved by research, the search for biological causes of criminality continues.

determined trait. Furthermore, many children of parents who are deviant are not deviant themselves, and many people with deviant lifestyles come from mainstream families (Chambliss & Hass, 2011; Katz & Chambliss, 1995; Scheff, 1988).

Studies that have found similarities in patterns of deviant behavior between twins are often cited as evidence in support of biological theories of deviance and crime. The Danish sociologist Karl Christiansen (1977) examined the life histories of 7,172 twins. Among these, 926 had been convicted of a crime. Christiansen found that 35% of the identical male twins who had been convicted of a crime had twin brothers who had also been convicted of a crime. Among male fraternal twins, 21% who had committed a crime had brothers who also had committed a crime (Christiansen, 1977; Mednick, Gabrielli, & Hutchings, 1987). Biological theorists interpret these findings as support for the theory that biological factors contribute to deviant and criminal behavior (Mednick, Gabrielli, & Hutchings, 1987).

Interestingly, critics of biological theories see this evidence as *disproving* the influence of biology. Among both men and women, in the vast majority of cases where one twin has committed a crime, the other twin has not. Moreover, if criminal behavior were genetically determined, we should expect that nearly all twin brothers or sisters of identical twins who are criminals should also be criminals (Katz & Chambliss, 1995). To the extent that identical twins do show similar patterns of deviance as adults, we can attribute these patterns to their common socialization: Identical twins are more likely than other siblings to be treated the same, dressed alike, and sometimes even confused with one another by acquaintances, teachers, and friends.

A more nuanced approach to biological explanations of deviance attempts to incorporate *both* sets of factors. The nature *versus* nurture paradigm is essentially converted to nature *and* nurture. Criminologist Kevin Beaver and a team of researchers took a more critical approach to this question by examining a general theory of crime posited by Gottfredson and Hirschi. A major tenet of this theory is that low self-control is largely a result of parental management influences and not biogenetic factors. Beaver's study, which analyzed twin data drawn from the National Longitudinal Study of Adolescent Health, estimated that genetic factors accounted for 52% to 64% of the variance in low self-control, with twins' nonshared environments accounting for the remaining variance (Beaver, Wright, DeLisi, & Vaughn, 2008). As rigorous and valid genetic and biological data become increasingly accessible, a school of thought within criminology is pursuing the question of how biological factors may play a part in crime and deviance.

FUNCTIONALIST PERSPECTIVES

Functionalist theories embrace the assumption that we must examine culture, especially shared norms and values, to understand why people behave the way they do. Recall that functionalist theory assumes society is characterized by a high degree of consensus on norms and values. It regards deviance as an abnormality that society seeks to eliminate, much as an organism seeks to rid itself of a parasite. At the same time, functionalist theory sees a certain amount of deviant behavior as useful—or functional—for society. It suggests that deviance—or the labeling of some behaviors as deviant—contributes to social solidarity by enhancing members' sense of the boundary between right and wrong (Durkheim, 1893/1997).

DEVIANCE AND SOCIAL SOLIDARITY Émile Durkheim (1858–1917), the father of functionalist theories of deviance, hypothesized that deviant behavior serves a useful purpose (a function) in society by drawing "moral boundaries," delineating what behavior is acceptable and what is not within a community. Durkheim argued that we can describe a society lacking consensus on what is right and wrong as being in a condition of *anomie,* a state of confusion that occurs when people lose sight of the shared rules and values that give order and meaning to their lives. In one of his most famous studies, Durkheim sought to show that anomie is a principal cause of suicide, itself a deviant act.

Durkheim (1897/1951) gathered extensive data on suicide in France and Italy and found that these data supported the theory that societies characterized by high levels of anomie also have high levels of suicide. Moreover, he argued that his research demonstrated that suicide rates vary depending on the level of *social solidarity,* or the social bonds that unite members of a group. Durkheim discovered, for example, that single men had higher rates of suicide than married men, Protestants a higher rate than Catholics, and men higher rates than women. Durkheim suggested that the higher rates were correlated with

AP Photo/The Daily Sentinel, Andrew D. Brosig

If you were to hypothesize that higher levels of social solidarity, or meaningful connections to others, are associated with lower levels of suicide, Émile Durkheim would agree. Volunteering for a cause that is meaningful to you is one of many channels that can strengthen social bonds.

lower levels of social solidarity in the groups to which people were attached.

Durkheim's research methods—the statistics as well as the sampling procedures—were primitive compared to modern-day methods. Since he first published his research, however, hundreds of studies have looked at suicide differences between men and women, between industrialized and developing countries, and even among the homeless. Most of these empirical studies have found considerable support for Durkheim's anomie theory (Cutright & Fernquist, 2000; Diaz, 1999; Kubrin, 2005; Lester, 2000; Simpson & Conklin, 1989; Wasserman, 1999). Durkheim's theory has spawned some of the most influential contemporary theories of deviance, including those of Robert Merton, Richard Cloward, and Lloyd Ohlin, which we discuss below.

STRUCTURAL STRAIN THEORY In the 1930s, American sociologist Robert K. Merton (1968) adapted Durkheim's concept of anomie into a general theory of deviance. According to Merton's theory, **structural strain** is *a form of anomie that occurs when a gap exists between the culturally defined goals of a society and the means available in society to achieve those goals.*

Structural strain: In Merton's reformulation of Durkheim's functionalist theory, a form of anomie that occurs when a gap exists between society's culturally defined goals and the means society makes available to achieve those goals.

Strain theory: The theory that when there is a discrepancy between the cultural goals for success and the means available to achieve those goals, rates of deviance will be high.

Opportunity theory: The theory that people differ not only in their motivations to engage in deviant acts but also in their *opportunities* to do so.

Merton argued that most people in a given society share a common understanding of the goals they should pursue as well as the legitimate means for achieving those goals. For example, success, as measured in terms of wealth, consumption, and prestige, is widely regarded as an important goal in U.S. society. Moreover, there appears to be widespread consensus on the legitimate means for achieving success—education, an enterprising spirit, and hard work, among others.

Most people pursue the goal of "success" by following established social norms. Merton referred to such behavior as *conformity.* However, success is not always attainable through conventional means, or conformity. When this occurs, Merton argued, the resulting contradiction between societal goals and the means of achieving them creates *strain,* which may result in four different types of deviant behavior. His **strain theory** suggests that *when there is a discrepancy between the cultural goals for success and the means available to achieve those goals, rates of deviance will be high.* Reactions to the discrepancy will lead to the types of deviance depicted in the first column in Table 6.2. It is important to note that since Merton's original formulation of strain theory, other researchers have expanded on his work. For example, Kaufman (2009) explored the relation between general strains and gender, finding that serious strains may affect men and women differently and influence their inclination to engage in deviance. Women, Kaufman found, are especially likely to engage in deviance in response to depression.

OPPORTUNITY THEORY Although Merton's theory helps us understand the structural conditions leading to high rates of deviance, it neglects the fact that not everyone has the same access to deviant solutions. This is the point made by Richard Cloward and Lloyd Ohlin (1960), who developed **opportunity theory** as an extension of Merton's strain theory. According to Cloward and Ohlin, *people differ not only in their motivations to engage in deviant acts but also in their opportunities to do so.* For instance, only the presence of a demand for illicit drugs, plus access to supplies of those drugs through producers, offers opportunities for individuals to be dealers. Similarly,

TABLE 6.2 Merton's Typology of Deviance

Type of Response	Cultural Goals	Legitimacy of Means
Conformity	Accept	Accept
Innovation	Accept	Reject
Ritualism	Reject	Accept
Retreatism	Reject	Reject
Rebellion	Reject/substitute	Reject/substitute

SOURCE: Data from Merton, Robert K. (1968, orig. 1938). *Social theory and social structure.* NY: Free Press. pp. 230–246

TECHNOLOGY & SOCIETY

DEVIANCE, CRIME, AND SOCIAL CONTROL IN AN AGE OF HIGH TECHNOLOGY

If a gun is fired in Washington, D.C., 300 "shot-spotter" microphones stand ready to pinpoint the gunshot's exact location and to alert police (Pethos, Fallis, & Keating, 2013). More than 120 cameras and a mobile surveillance platform nicknamed "Sky Patrol" watch over the city of Camden, New Jersey, where police cruisers are also outfitted with digital license plate scanners (Taibbi, 2013). These are just two examples of how technology is affecting the social control of deviance and crime. However, technology has also altered the types of crime and deviance occurring in society.

According to the United Nations Office on Drugs and Crime (2013), one third of the world's population has Internet access; by 2017, nearly 70% of people worldwide will have mobile broadband of the sort used by Internet-enabled smartphones. The Internet, smartphones, and new social media have given rise to new forms of crime and deviance while also enabling new manifestations of long-existing forms.

Cyberbullying is a new manifestation of an old problem. Cyberbullying expands "traditional" bullying beyond the boundaries of face-to-face interaction. The recent Miami Dolphins bullying scandal that involved player Richie Incognito sending demeaning and threatening text messages to teammate Jonathan Martin is an example of how technology has shifted the context within which bullying can take place (Wells, Karp, Birenboim, & Brown, 2014). The problems of child pornography and related forms of exploitation of unwilling subjects have also expanded as they have moved onto new technologically enabled platforms of distribution.

At the same time, Internet-based technologies have led to new forms of crime and deviance. One example is the "419" scam, a form of "advance fee fraud." This and similar scams target unsuspecting Internet users, promising them financial rewards, real estate deals, or other goods and services in exchange for wiring small advance fees or providing their personal banking information to initiate electronic funds transfers, ostensibly so they can receive payments. In reality, once a victim has wired the money or provided the information, he or she is left with nothing; the scammers disappear with the wired funds or use the banking information to take money *from* the target. Another example of a new form of crime and deviance enabled by the advent of the Internet is the creation of online illegal marketplaces that model themselves on legitimate online commerce sites such as Craigslist, eBay, and Amazon. Those sites, like Silk Road, whose founder was arrested by the FBI in October 2013, allow people to purchase illegal drugs, weapons, fake identity documents, and computer hacking tools, and even hire assassins; typically, they are accessible only through special Internet routers (Barratt, Ferris, & Winstock, 2014; Kushner, 2014).

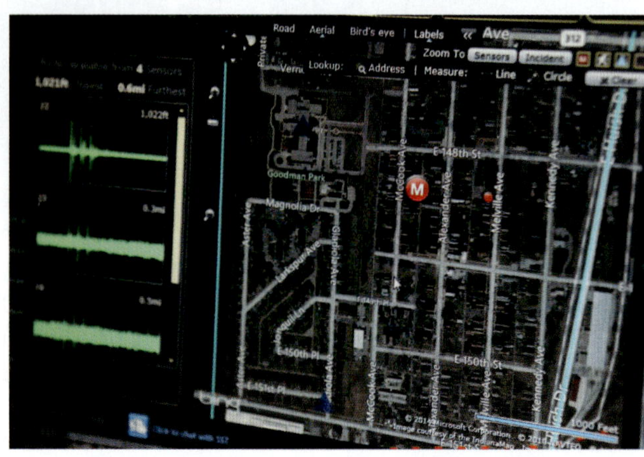

AP Photo/Jonathan Miano

Shot-spotter technology enables law enforcement authorities to identify gunfire and to rapidly locate the site of the gunfire.

The rise of cyberspace and related technologies has enabled greater communication and collaboration among individuals and groups, including members of deviant and criminal subcultures. Pedophiles who manufacture and trade child pornography are one extreme example of a deviant subculture whose existence has been strengthened by the Internet. New technologies, however, also have improved law enforcement agencies' surveillance of criminal activities globally and have enabled authorities to track down perpetrators by following their digital footprints. These cases reveal an interesting paradox of our contemporary digital age: Technological advances—often the very same ones—contribute to and sustain a multitude of deviant and criminal behaviors while also contributing to efforts to control and counteract those behaviors.

THINK IT THROUGH

▶ How do technologies like the Internet and smartphones enable authorities to exercise greater control over deviance and crime? How do they simultaneously have the potential to undermine authority and social control?

 Deviance in Technology  Man Up!

unless you have access to funds you can secretly convert to your own use, you are unlikely ever to consider embezzlement as an option, much less carry it out. Deviance is widespread in a community only when the opportunities for it exist.

CONTROL THEORY Agreeing with the functionalist claim that a society's norms and values are the starting point for understanding deviance, Gottfredson and Hirschi's (1990/2004) **control theory** *explains that the cause of delinquency or deviance* among children and teenagers *lies in the arena of social control.* Gottfredson and Hirschi differ from Durkheim and Merton, however, regarding the importance of a general state of anomie in creating deviance, arguing instead that a person's acceptance or rejection of societal norms depends on that individual's life experiences.

Gottfredson and Hirschi (1990/2004; also Hirschi, 2004) assert that deviance arises from **social bonds**, or *individuals' connections to others,* especially institutions, rather than from anomie. Forming strong social bonds with people and institutions that disapprove of deviance, they argue, keeps people from engaging in deviant behaviors. Conversely, people who do not form strong social bonds will engage in deviant acts because they have nothing to lose by acting on their impulses and do not fear the consequences of their actions.

Furthermore, control theorists argue that most deviant acts are spontaneous. For example, a group of teenagers see a drunken homeless man walking down the street and decide to rob him, or a man learns of a house whose owners are on vacation and decides to burglarize it. Some people will succumb to such temptations. Those who do not, according to Gottfredson and Hirschi, have a greater willingness to conform. This willingness, in turn, comes from associating with people who are committed to conventional roles and morality.

Some evidence supports control theory. For example, delinquency is somewhat less common among youth who have strong family attachments, perform well in school, and feel they have something to lose by appearing deviant in the eyes of others (Gottfredson & Hirschi, 1990/2004; Hirschi, 1969). On the other hand, we could scarcely argue that white-collar criminals such as Bernie Madoff, who pleaded guilty to massive financial fraud in 2009, do not have strong social bonds to society. The success of many white-collar criminals in business suggests that they have spent their lives conforming to societal norms, yet they also commit criminal acts that cost U.S. taxpayers, investors, and pension holders billions of dollars (McLean & Elkind, 2003). Thus, while control theory explanations of deviance and crime may prove useful in certain instances, they have limitations.

CONFLICT PERSPECTIVES

Recall that the conflict perspective makes the assumption that groups in society have different interests and differential access to resources with which to realize those interests. In contrast to the functionalist perspective, the conflict perspective does not assume shared norms and values. Rather, it presumes that groups with power will use that power to maintain control in society and keep other groups at a disadvantage. As we will see below, conflict theory can be fruitfully used in the study of deviance.

SUBCULTURES AND DEVIANCE More than three quarters of a century ago, Thorsten Sellin (1938) pointed out that the cultural diversity of modern societies results in conflicts between social groups over what kinds of behavior are right and wrong. Sellin argued that deviance is best explained through **subcultural theories**, which *identify the conflicting interests of certain segments of the population,* whether it be over culture (as in Sellin's case) or more generally over certain rituals or behaviors. For example, immigrants to the United States bring norms and values with them from their original cultures and, to the extent that these conflict with the norms and values of the adopted country, they may be perceived as deviant by the dominant culture.

Such deviance might create only minor breaches of U.S. conventions. For instance, an Indian woman wears a traditional sari, or a Middle Eastern man wears a head scarf. Other customary practices, however, might be serious violations of criminal laws. The practice of female circumcision by some immigrants to France from North Africa is a violation of French law. Domestic violence may be customary in some countries, but immigrants to the United States who practice domestic violence are in violation of U.S. law.

It is not only cultural differences between immigrants and the host country that create subcultures of deviance. Sociologists also analyze juvenile gangs, professional thieves, White racist groups, and a host of other deviant groups as subcultures in which criminality is the norm, despite the fact that these values contradict the norms of the wider society (Chambliss & King, 1984; Cohen, 1955; Etter, 1998; Hamm, 2002).

CLASS-DOMINANT THEORY **Class-dominant theories** *propose that what is labeled deviant or criminal—and therefore*

Control theory: The theory that the cause of deviance lies in the arena of social control and, specifically, the life experiences and relationships that people form.

Social bonds: Individuals' connections to others (see also *control theory*).

Subcultural theories: Theories that explain deviance in terms of the conflicting interests of more and less powerful segments of a population.

Class-dominant theories: Theories that propose that what is labeled deviant or criminal—and therefore who gets punished—is determined by the interests of the dominant class in a particular culture or society.

Jerome Sessini/Magnum Photos

Girls sometimes form gangs in neighborhoods where male street gangs are prevalent. These girl gangs are often "auxiliaries" of male gangs engaged in selling drugs and committing petty crimes. Joining a gang may require an initiation ritual that includes violence and even rape.

who gets punished—is determined by the interests of the dominant class (Quinney, 1970). For example, since labor is central to the functioning of capitalism, those who do not work will be labeled deviant in capitalist societies (Spitzer, 1975). In a similar vein, since private property is a key foundation of capitalism, those who engage in acts against property, such as stealing or vandalism, will be defined as deviant and likely as criminal. And, because profits are realized through buying and selling things in the capitalist marketplace, uncontrolled market activities (like selling drugs on the street or making alcohol without a license) will also be defined as deviant and criminal.

Critics of class-dominant theory point out that laws against the interests of the ruling class do get passed. Laws prohibiting insider trading on the stock market, governing the labor practices of corporations, and giving workers the right to strike and form trade unions were all signed over the strident opposition of capitalists (Chambliss, 2001). To incorporate these facts, William J. Chambliss (1988a) proposed a structural contradiction theory that takes into account the limitations, as well as the ultimate power, of capitalists in a capitalist society.

STRUCTURAL CONTRADICTION THEORY Rather than seeing the ruling class as all-powerful in determining what is deviant or criminal, **structural contradiction theory** argues that *conflicts generated by fundamental contradictions in the structure of society produce laws defining certain acts as deviant or criminal* (Chambliss, 1988a; Chambliss & Hass, 2011; Chambliss & Zatz, 1994). For instance, there is a fundamental structural contradiction in capitalist economies between the need to maximize profits (which keeps wages down) and the need to maximize consumption (which requires high wages). Consider a U.S. business that, to maximize profits, keeps wages and salaries down, perhaps by moving its factories to a part of the world where labor is cheap. As jobs are transferred to low-wage countries, the availability of jobs to unskilled and semiskilled workers in the United States declines. The loss of jobs produces downward pressure on wages and a loss of purchasing power. Yet capitalism depends on people buying the things that are produced—corporations cannot profit unless they sell their products.

Trapped in the contradiction between norms valuing consumerism and an economic system that can make consumption of desired material goods and services difficult or even impossible for many, some, but not all, people will resolve the conflict by resorting to deviant and criminal acts such as cheating on income taxes, writing bad checks, or profiting from illegal markets, such as by selling drugs or committing theft. Of course, it is not just lower-income people who deviate in order to increase their consumption of material goods. Everyone who wants to enjoy a higher standard of living is a candidate for deviant or criminal behavior, according to structural contradiction theory. The head of a giant corporation may be as tempted to violate criminal laws in order to increase company profits (and personal income) as is the 13-year-old from a poor family who snatches a pair of sunglasses from the drugstore.

Structural contradiction theory holds that societies with the greatest gaps between what people earn and what they are normatively enticed to buy will have the highest levels of deviance. Since industrial societies differ substantially in this regard, we can compare them to test this theory. Societies such as Finland, Denmark, Sweden, and Norway, for instance, provide a "social safety net" that guarantees all citizens a decent standard of living. Therefore, the lower classes in Scandinavian countries are able to come much closer to what their societies have established as a "normal" level of consumption. The fact that rates of assault, robbery, and homicide are anywhere from 3 to 35 times higher in the United States than in these countries (depending on which country is compared) is exactly what structural contradiction theory would predict (Archer & Gartner, 1984).

Globalization is another example of the way structural contradictions lead to changes in deviant behavior. The ability to trade worldwide increases the wealth of the nations that are able to take advantage of global markets. However, it also increases opportunities for criminal activities such as money laundering, stealing patents and copyrights, and smuggling people, arms, and drugs.

FEMINIST THEORY The sociological study of deviance—like most areas of academic study—has for centuries been dominated by men. As a result, most theories and research have

Structural contradiction theory: The theory that conflicts generated by fundamental contradictions in the structure of society produce laws defining certain acts as deviant or criminal.

GLOBAL ISSUES

GLOBALIZATION AND CRIMINAL OPPORTUNITIES

Globalization vastly increases the potential for crime networks to gain wealth and political power (Block & Weaver, 2004; Naylor, 2002). At the top of the list of crimes facilitated by processes linked to globalization are (1) money laundering; (2) smuggling, including the smuggling of human beings, military equipment, drugs, and stolen merchandise; and (3) terrorism.

Nearly every major bank in Europe and the United States has been found guilty of laundering money at one time or another. In December 2012, the British bank HSBC was fined $1.9 billion for laundering billions of dollars in drug profits and for allowing terrorist groups to launder money through its Mexican affiliate (Douglas, 2013). In 2011 and 2014, the Swiss bank UBS, the British bank Barclays, and the Royal Bank of Scotland were found guilty of international rigging of interest rates by fraudulently setting the rates established through the London Interbank Offered Rate (LIBOR), a benchmark for interest rates covering everything from home mortgages to student loans (BBC, 2014a; Douglas, 2013). There are no reliable data on how many of these crimes occur annually, in part because sociological and political awareness of such activities is only now coming to the fore. It is clear, however, that hundreds of billions of dollars are illegally laundered annually (Block & Weaver, 2004; Naylor, 2002).

The economies of entire nations depend at least in part on their supporting criminal enterprises through money laundering: Switzerland and Lichtenstein's bank secrecy laws as well as banking policies in numerous Caribbean nations enable money launderers from international criminal syndicates and terrorist organizations, as well as individuals evading taxes, to enjoy massive profits through criminal enterprises (Block & Weaver, 2004; Naylor, 2002).

© Oliver Burston/Ikon Images/Corbis

The international drug trade in cocaine, opium, heroin, methamphetamines, and marijuana is estimated to be between $300 billion and $400 billion a year—a sum larger than the wealth of most nations (Glenny, 2009; Woodiwiss, 2005). The production of opium, coca, methamphetamines, and marijuana is a major contributor to the economies of Afghanistan, Malaysia, Laos, Thailand, Pakistan, Turkey, Colombia, Peru, Bolivia, and Mexico (Global Commission on Drug Policy, 2011; Woodiwiss, 2005). Some of these countries—Afghanistan and Bolivia, for example—have a disproportionately high value of illicit drug revenue as a percentage of their gross domestic product (Naylor, 2002).

Trafficking in exotic and endangered plants and animals has always been a lucrative business, but in recent years smuggling of these products has increased in part due to the emergence of consumer markets for plant and animal products in rising economies such as China and Vietnam (Bremer, 2012). Goods ranging from traditional Asian medicines to carved ivory to high-priced furs to exotic pets are smuggled from their places of origin and sold clandestinely in backroom operations or on Internet websites and messaging boards. The stunning value of the trade explains its growth and persistence: It is estimated to generate more than $10 billion per year (U.S. Fish and Wildlife Service, Office of Law Enforcement Intelligence Unit, 2003).

The smuggling of people has also become a major international criminal enterprise. People pay large sums of money to be smuggled from poorer countries into wealthier ones where they imagine an opportunity for a better life. Women and girls are smuggled across borders for prostitution, sometimes under false pretenses, such as promises of jobs as waitresses or as nannies. The extent of trafficking in women and girls for prostitution can only be estimated, but law enforcement and international task forces point to an alarming increase in the smuggling of human beings (Polaris Project, 2013).

Globalization has brought many benefits to countries and communities, but it has also, as we have seen, contributed to the expansion of criminal enterprises.

THINK IT THROUGH

▶ Who is responsible for addressing the problem of globalized crime in the contemporary world? What sociological factors make the prevention and prosecution of globalized crime particularly challenging?

reflected a male point of view. Recent years, however, have witnessed a sea change in the sociological perspective, as women have become better represented in sociology.

In the 1980s, a **feminist perspective on deviance** emerged within the sociological tradition (Campbell, 1984; Chesney-Lind, 1989, 2004; Messerschmidt, 1986). The starting point of feminist explanations of deviance is the observation that *studies of deviance have been biased because almost all the research has been done by, and about, males, largely ignoring female perspectives on deviant behavior as well as analyses of differences in the types and causes of female deviance* (Messerschmidt, 1993). By ignoring the female population, deviance theory has avoided one of the most challenging issues in the field: Why do rates of deviance—and especially criminal deviance—vary by gender?

Early feminist theory argued that gender-specific cultural norms partly account for the different rates of deviance between men and women (Adler, 1975; Steffensmeier & Allen, 1998). For example, women traditionally have been socialized into the roles of wife and mother, where behavior is more tightly prescribed than it is for men. Moreover, women's deviant behavior is more likely to be subject to **stigmatization**—that is, to be *branded as highly disgraceful*—than is comparable male behavior. For example, a woman who has multiple sexual partners is shamed as a "slut," while a sexually promiscuous man is not disdained and might even be praised for being a "stud."

Feminists have argued that an adequate theory of deviance must take into account the particular ways in which women are victimized by virtue of their gender (Chesney-Lind, 2004; Mann & Zatz, 1998; Sokoloff & Raffel, 1995). For example, studies show that before becoming involved in the juvenile justice system, many girls labeled delinquent were runaways escaping sexual and physical abuse. In a study of girls in the Wisconsin juvenile justice system, Phelps et al. (1982) found that 79% had been victims of physical abuse, while fully half had been subjected to sexual abuse, a third of them at the hands of parents or relatives. This research supports the hypothesis that many girls labeled delinquent have been driven out of their homes by abusive parents or relatives. Their behavior in their lives on the streets, marked by petty crime, results from their efforts to survive.

Women also continue to be disproportionately represented in cases of inmate sexual assault and victimization. While women constitute only 7% of the total inmate population in the United States, they make up one third of all prisoner sexual victimization cases (Guerino & Beck, 2011).

INTERACTIONIST PERSPECTIVES

Interactionist perspectives provide a language and framework for looking at how deviance is constructed, including how individuals are connected to the social structure. Interactionist approaches also explain why some people are labeled deviant and behave in deviant ways while others do not. A central tenet of many interactionist approaches is that we see ourselves through the eyes of others, and our resulting sense of ourselves conditions how we behave. This idea has been applied to the study of deviant behavior in the development of both labeling theory and differential association theory.

LABELING THEORY **Labeling theory** holds that *deviant behavior is a product of the labels people attach to certain types of behavior* (Asencio & Burke, 2011; Lemert, 1951; Tannenbaum, 1938). From this perspective, deviance is seen as socially constructed. That is, labeling theory holds that deviance is the product of interactions wherein the response of some people to certain types of behaviors produces a label of *deviant* or *not deviant*. In turn, these labels, which also end up being applied to people engaging in certain types of behavior, can influence

Stigmatization: The branding of behavior as highly disgraceful (see also *labeling theory*).

Labeling theory: A symbolic interactionist approach holding that deviance is a product of the labels people attach to certain types of behavior.

Feminist perspective on deviance: A perspective that suggests that studies of deviance have been subject to gender bias and that both gender-specific cultural norms and the particular ways in which women are victimized by virtue of their gender help to account for deviance among women.

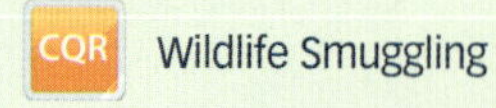

Wildlife Smuggling

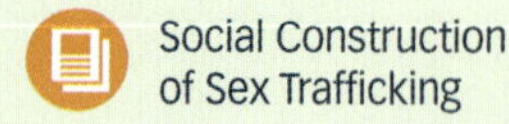
Social Construction of Sex Trafficking

how people conduct themselves. Thus, labeling theory is sometimes referred to as *societal reaction theory.*

One of the founders of labeling theory, Edwin Lemert (1951), argued that the labeling process has two steps: primary deviance and secondary deviance. **Primary deviance** occurs *at the moment an activity is labeled as deviant by others.* **Secondary deviance** occurs *when a person labeled deviant accepts the label as part of his or her identity and, as a result, begins to act in conformity with the label.* To illustrate his theory, Lemert reported on a group of people in the U.S. Northwest with an unusually high incidence of stuttering. Observing the interactions among people in this group, he concluded that stuttering was common in the group partly because the members were stigmatized and labeled as "stutterers" (primary deviance). These "stutterers" then began to view themselves through this label and increasingly acted in accordance with it—which included a greater amount of stuttering than otherwise would have been the case (secondary deviance).

Chambliss's (2001) observations of the Saints and the Roughnecks, discussed in the *Inequality Matters* box on page 142, also support labeling theory. The working-class boys he studied were labeled deviant while the middle-class boys he observed were not, despite the fact that both groups of boys engaged in delinquent behavior. Eventually, the adult careers of the two groups of boys evolved to be largely consistent with the labels attached to them and their behaviors during adolescence.

DIFFERENTIAL ASSOCIATION THEORY Another interactionist approach to the study of deviance looks at how deviance is transmitted culturally and argues that we learn deviant behaviors through our social interactions. **Differential association theory** holds that *deviant and criminal behavior results from regular exposure to attitudes favorable to acting in ways that are deviant or criminal* (Burgess & Akers, 1966; Church, Jaggers, & Taylor, 2012; Sutherland, 1929). For example, the corporate executive who embezzles company funds may have learned the norms and values appropriate to this type of criminal activity by associating with others already engaged in it. Similarly, kids and teenagers living in areas where selling and using drugs are common practices will be more likely than

In the Netherlands (pictured), where marijuana can legally be sold in licensed cafés, the incidence of lifetime use is lower than in the United States, where criminal penalties for possession and use are still common in most states. How would you explain this unexpected difference?

their peers not exposed to that subculture to develop attitudes favorable toward using and selling drugs. Conversely, populations with different subcultures or attitudes toward particular forms of deviance (such as illicit drug usage) may not experience the same rates of crime.

According to Sutherland's (1929) differential association theory, the more we associate with people whose behavior is deviant, the greater the likelihood that our behavior will also be deviant. Sutherland, therefore, linked deviance with such factors as the frequency and intensity of our associations with other people, how long they last, and how early in our lives they occur. Much has changed since Sutherland developed his theory, and today many of our interactions take place through technologies such as the Internet and smartphones. A modern adaptation of Sutherland's theory would certainly have to take into account the importance of the unique methods of interacting today in promoting both deviant and conforming behavior.

Symbolic interactionist theories, like functionalist and conflict theories, provide us with considerable insight into the social processes that lead to deviance and crime in society. We might come to the conclusion that each of the competing theories "makes sense" and has some empirical support yet also fails to explain all the behaviors we classify as deviant or criminal. This debate and interaction between theories is essential to the development of scientific knowledge (Popper, 1959). Thus, while there are many unique ways to examine the same topic without necessarily reaching one perfect answer with any of them, we should be reassured that each theoretical orientation presented in this chapter can be useful in explaining certain facets of deviance and crime. It is up to the researcher to decide which theory to use and why, and for others to determine whether the use of the theory was a success or failure.

Primary deviance: A term developed by Edwin Lemert; the first step in the labeling of deviance, it occurs at the moment an activity is labeled deviant (see also *secondary deviance*).

Secondary deviance: A term developed by Edwin Lemert; the second step in the labeling of deviance, it occurs when a person labeled deviant accepts the label as part of his or her identity and, as a result, begins to act in conformity with the label (see also *primary deviance*).

Differential association theory: The theory that deviant and criminal behavior results from regular exposure to attitudes favorable to acting in ways that are deviant or criminal.

INEQUALITY MATTERS

THE SAINTS AND THE ROUGHNECKS

Using detached observation and interviewing as his research methods, William Chambliss (2001) studied two gangs of teenage boys for 2 years. With the permission and cooperation of the boys, Chambliss was able to follow them, talk to them, and watch them during and after school hours. He named the two gangs "the Saints" and "the Roughnecks."

> Eight young men—children of good, stable, white upper-middle-class families, active in school affairs and destined for college—were some of the most delinquent boys at Hannibal High School. The Saints were frequently truant from school and drunk on the weekends. They drove their cars wildly and committed numerous acts of petty theft . . . and vandalism. Yet in school, among parents, and in the rest of the community they had the reputation of being "good kids, headed in the right direction." Not one was arrested for any misdeed during the two years of observation. . . .
>
> Six working-class white boys [Chambliss] called the Roughnecks hung out at the local drug store, where their harassment of passersby, public drinking, boisterous antics and fighting often got them into trouble with the community and with the police. To the school, the police, and the rest of the community the upper-middle-class boys were good, upstanding youths with bright futures. They were like Saints. But this same community treated the Roughnecks, whose delinquencies were comparable to those of the Saints, as though they were tough young criminals headed for even more serious trouble.
>
> Years later, Chambliss followed the after-high-school careers of the members of the two gangs. . . . All but one of the Saints had gone on to college and graduated, while several of the Roughnecks had become involved in criminal activities as adults: one was sentenced to prison for murder, another for manslaughter, and one became a member of an organized crime network.

Why did the Roughnecks and the Saints have such different careers after high school—careers that, by and large, lived up to the community's expectations?

First, the delinquencies of the Roughnecks were far more visible than those of the Saints. With their access to automobiles, the Saints were able to remove themselves from the sight of the community. But the Roughnecks congregated in a crowded area that everyone in the community passed frequently, including teachers and law enforcement officers. Second, the demeanors of the two sets of gang members differed. While the Saints showed remorse and respect, the Roughnecks offered a barely veiled contempt for authority. This resulted in different responses to their misdeeds. Third, adults in the community showed bias in favor of the Saints, who were presumed to be "good boys sowing wild oats" rather than "bad boys."

Labels matter. Those who were labeled as "bad" did, in fact, largely live up (or down) to this standard. Those whose youthful transgressions were not transformed into labels lived up to more positive expectations and became successful adults. These self-fulfilling prophecies suggest that the ways in which we opt to label individuals and groups can have important effects on actions and outcomes.

THINK IT THROUGH

▶ W. I. Thomas observed that if people define a situation as real, it is real in its consequences even if objectively it may not be true. Using Thomas's theory, how would you explain the different responses of the teachers, the police, and the community to the Saints and the Roughnecks?

TYPES OF DEVIANCE

As noted in the opening to this chapter, deviance comes in many varieties, from the relatively benign to the extremely harmful. In this section, we explore some of the ways in which deviance can manifest in society.

EVERYDAY DEVIANCE

A broad spectrum of acts could fall under the label of "everyday deviance," from plagiarism among high school or college students to shoplifting, underage alcohol consumption, spitting, using pornography, smoking, binge eating, eating meat, or calling in sick to work or school when you actually feel fine. All of these are considered deviant behaviors, actions, or conditions by some individuals and/or groups. Many of you reading this text engage in at least some types of deviance on a fairly regular basis.

In the commission of everyday deviance, we clearly recognize the pluralistic nature of U.S. society. Taking a subcultural perspective, we see that smoking is more acceptable among some specific societal subgroups (for instance, truck drivers) than it is among others (such as fitness instructors). So too with eating meat: The owner of a barbecue restaurant and a vegan are likely to hold starkly different views regarding the deviance of eating meat or subsisting on a vegan diet. In turn, these views are representative of the broader societal subcultures and groups to which these individuals belong.

Everyday deviance can be explained in a multitude of ways. For instance, we might utilize labeling theory. Pornography represents an interesting example in which both the behavior (using pornography) and the physical object (the pornographic movie or magazine) have been labeled as deviant. We could therefore easily make the argument that pornography is deviant simply because people have chosen to label it as such. Yet this explanation, as you might have sensed, is pretty basic. We could strengthen our understanding of what makes pornography deviant by including a conflict perspective. Thus, we could look at who in society has had the power to define pornography as deviant and what goals such a definition might have served for that particular group. The point is that deviance in its various forms has many potential explanations, which can be strengthened through the combination of different theoretical perspectives.

SEXUAL DEVIANCE

Sex, sexual orientations, and sexual practices are diverse, as are the responses to them. We are currently witnessing a process of redefinition of what deviance means within the context of intimate relationships. Look no further than the wildly popular novel *Fifty Shades of Grey,* which made headlines for its depiction of kinky sex and for being on the nightstands of many "ordinary" men and women. As the success of the book and its sequels indicates, we might even argue that some *traditional* notions regarding sex, sexual orientations, and sexual activities are themselves increasingly becoming viewed as deviant, because they simply do not reflect the realities of modern social life.

Definitions of sexual deviance can include many things—from the choices we make in terms of those with whom we begin intimate relationships to how and where those relationships are carried out. While we could utilize many explanations to examine sexual deviance, looking at the current debate over same-sex marriage from a conflict perspective, we see an ongoing struggle between those groups that have long determined what passes for acceptable sexual behavior (for instance, religious groups) and those that seek to redefine sexual behavior to include things other than heterosexual sex and marriage.

DEVIANCE OF THE POWERFUL

The crimes of the powerful are ubiquitous and wide-ranging, from the fraudulent reporting of corporate profits to the misleading of investors to bribery, corruption, misuse of public trust, and violence against ordinary citizens. The most powerful people in public life engage in many of the same types of deviance as ordinary men and women (McLean & Elkind, 2003; McLean & Nocera, 2010; Reiman & Leighton, 2012).

The mass media have a heyday when deviance committed by political leaders, celebrities, or athletes becomes public. When it was revealed that golfer Tiger Woods was having sexual relations with a multitude of women while he was married, the press spent weeks following the story in detail. Recently, the champion cyclist Lance Armstrong was stripped of his multiple Tour de France wins and banned from competitive cycling for life for his use of performance-enhancing drugs. Famed Major League Baseball player Alex Rodriguez of the New York Yankees was suspended for the entire 2014 season for using banned

Photo/Naples Daily News, Scott McIntyre

Deviance is not restricted to any particular class or social group. The powerful and elite commit deviance as well. In 2013, Congressman Trey Radel pleaded guilty to a charge of possessing cocaine. He resigned his office and was sentenced to a year of probation.

substances and then lying about it. Sociologically, what must be taken into account is that deviance knows no class bounds.

The response of the public to the deviance of political leaders is often particularly pointed given the immense trust, responsibility, and power vested in those individuals. For example, in 2012, the head of the Central Intelligence Agency, David Petraeus, previously the commanding general of coalition forces in Afghanistan, was engaged in an affair with his biographer while both were married. As a result of the affair becoming public, Petraeus had to resign as CIA director. The public response to deviance committed by powerful individuals often reflects not only dismay at the fact of deviance but also disdain for the hypocrisy, such as in the case of lawyer and former New York governor Eliot Spitzer, who prosecuted prostitution in New York with a vengeance only to be caught hiring a high-priced call girl to accompany him on a trip from New York to Washington, D.C. Late in 2013, New Jersey governor Chris Christie was caught up in a scandal when it was alleged that members of his staff had several lanes of the highway leading into New York City from the town of Fort Lee, New Jersey, shut down for "repairs" as retribution against Fort Lee's mayor for not supporting Christie's reelection.

On one hand, empirical data show that the powerful are more likely than those without power to escape punishment for deviance. On the other hand, those powerful figures who are caught in acts of deviance are often subject to acute media attention and public disdain. Should public figures be subject to particular scrutiny for their behavior, or should they be treated like everyone else?

CRIME

Our discussion thus far has been concerned primarily with deviance in a general sense—those attitudes, behaviors, and conditions that are widespread but generally not condemned by all or seen as especially serious. In this section, we discuss crime—acts that are sometimes considered deviant and are defined under the law as punishable by fines, imprisonment, or both. Law enforcement agencies across the United States take rigorous steps to record formally how much crime occurs, to prosecute criminal offenders, and to control and prevent crime.

VIOLENT AND PROPERTY CRIMES A great deal of effort is expended on the measurement of crime in U.S. society. This is accomplished through official, limited records like the FBI's Uniform Crime Reports (UCR) and the collection of survey data from individuals and households across the country via the National Crime Victimization Survey (NCVS). These measures of crime, especially the UCR, focus predominantly on violent and property crimes, serious forms of deviance that nearly every person in society agrees should be made illegal.

Violent crimes *include robbery (taking something from someone by physical force), murder, assault, and rape.* **Property crimes** *include burglary (taking something from a person's home), arson, larceny/theft, and motor vehicle theft.* Property crimes are much more common in the United States than violent crimes, although their number, like the number

FIGURE 6.1 Violent Crime Rate in the United States, 1993–2013

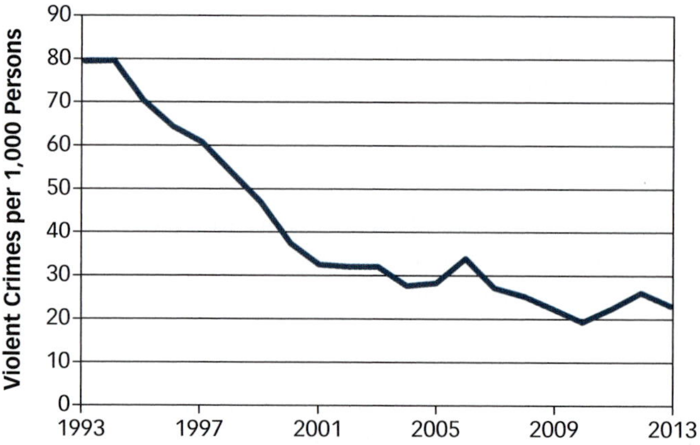

SOURCES: Office of Justice Programs Bureau of Justice Statistics. (2010). "National Crime Victimization Survey Violent Crime Trends, 1973–2008." *Key Facts at a Glance;* FBI UCR. 2012a. "Table 1: Crime in the United States by Volume and Rate". U.S. Department of Justice, Federal Bureau of Investigation, Criminal Justice Information Services Division.

FIGURE 6.2 Property Crime Rate in the United States, 1993–2013

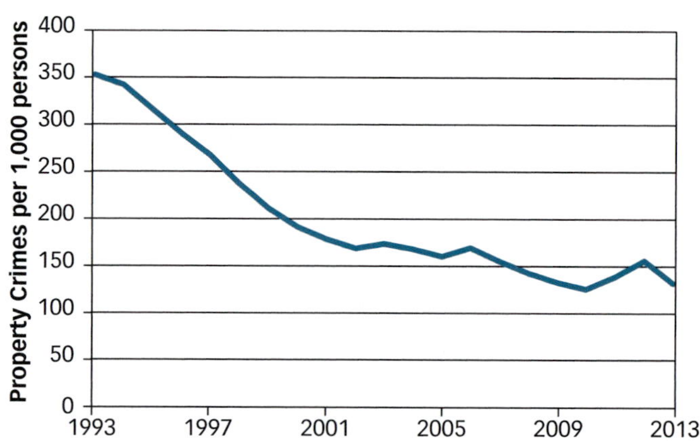

SOURCES: Office of Justice Programs Bureau of Justice Statistics. (2010). "National Crime Victimization Survey Violent Crime Trends, 1973–2008." *Key Facts at a Glance;* FBI UCR. 2012a. "Table 1: Crime in the United States by Volume and Rate". U.S. Department of Justice, Federal Bureau of Investigation, Criminal Justice Information Services Division.

Violent crimes: Crimes that involve force or threat of force, including robbery, murder, assault, and rape.

Property crimes: Crimes that involve the violation of individuals' ownership rights, including burglary, larceny/theft, arson, and motor vehicle theft.

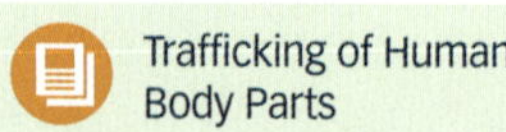

of violent crimes (Figure 6.1), has been steadily declining (see Figure 6.2). Variations of serious deviance, including violent and property crimes, can be analyzed from a variety of perspectives. For instance, violent crimes might be viewed from an opportunity theory perspective and property crimes in terms of societal strain. How might such analyses look?

ORGANIZED CRIME Sociologists define **organized crime** as *crime committed by criminal groups that provide illegal goods and services.* Gambling, prostitution, selling and trafficking in illegal drugs, black marketeering, loan sharking, and money laundering are some of the most prominent activities of organized crime (Block & Chambliss, 1981; Glenny, 2009; McCoy, 1991; Paoli, 2003).

To meet the demand for illegal goods and services, criminal organizations have flourished in U.S. urban areas since the 1800s (Woodiwiss, 2000). Over the years, they have recruited members and leadership from more impoverished groups in society, such as new immigrants in big cities, who may have great aspirations but limited means of achieving them (Block & Weaver, 2004). Consequently, organized crime has been dominated by the most recent arrivals to urban areas: Irish, Jewish, and Italian "mobs" in the past, and Asian, African, South American, and Russian "mobs" today (Albanese, 1989; Finckenauer & Waring, 1996; Hess, 1973).

Depictions of organized crime in movies and television shows such as *The Sopranos, The Godfather, Scarface,* and *Goodfellas* have popularized the erroneous impression that there is an international organization of criminals (the "Mafia") dominated by Italian Americans. The reality is that organized crime consists of thousands of different groups throughout the United States and the world. No single ethnic group or organization has control over most or even a major share of these activities, which include human trafficking and weapons and drug smuggling (Block & Weaver, 2004; Chambliss, 1988a).

CRIMES OF THE POWERFUL When most people think of crime, they think of the violent and property crimes discussed above—and they think of crimes committed by those in lower socioeconomic groups. But the forms of crime perpetrated by individuals and groups who possess great power, authority, and influence are also often deeply harmful to society.

White-collar crime is *crime committed by people of high social status in connection with their work* (Sutherland, 1949/1983). There are two principal types: crimes committed for the benefit of the individual who commits them, and crimes committed for the benefit of the organization for which the individual works.

White-collar crime: Crime committed by people of high social status in connection with their work.

Organized crime: Crime committed by criminal groups that provide illegal goods and services.

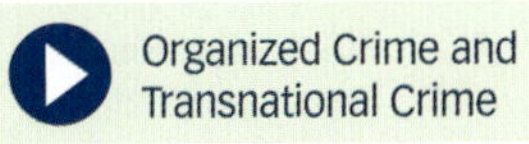
Organized Crime and Transnational Crime

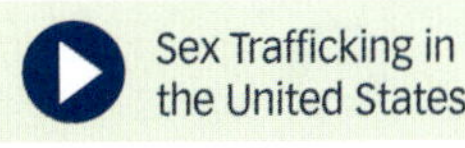
Sex Trafficking in the United States

White Collar Crime

Jonathan Ernst/Reuters/Newscom

In June of 2014, executives from General Motors Company were called in front of Congress to testify on the delayed ignition switch recall. Critics accuse the company of failing to recall cars with a serious defect that led to numerous deaths and injuries on the road.

Among the many white-collar crimes that benefit the individual are the theft of money by accountants who alter their employers' or clients' books and the overcharging of clients by lawyers. More costly types of white-collar crime occur when corporations and their employees engage in criminal conduct either through *commission,* that is, by doing something criminal, or *omission,* by failing to prevent something criminal or harmful from occurring.

White-collar crimes of all sorts receive considerable media attention. The following constitute just a small sample of white-collar criminal cases publicized over the past few years:

- In 2008, at the height of the U.S. recession, Bernard "Bernie" Madoff, a former Wall Street executive, was arrested and charged with managing an intricate criminal scheme that stole at least $50 billion from corporate and individual investors. Madoff pled guilty to 11 criminal counts in Manhattan's federal district courthouse and was sentenced to 150 years in prison (Rosoff, Pontell, & Tillman, 2010).
- In 2010, financial giant JPMorgan Chase was fined $48.6 million by British financial regulators for "failing to keep clients' funds separate from those of the firm." The error went undetected for more than 7 years and placed billions of dollars of client funds at risk of being lost (Werdigier, 2010).
- In 2012, Barclays and UBS (United Bank of Switzerland) were collectively fined more than $1.9 billion for intentionally manipulating interest rates (BBC, 2014a).
- General Motors Corporation, which received close to $50 billion in "bailout" funds from American taxpayers in order to stay financially solvent, was implicated in a scandal in early 2014 for failing to fix a defective ignition switch in

its Chevrolet Cobalt line of vehicles (Isidore, 2012; Wald, 2014). The company allegedly chose not to make the fix, which caused vehicles to lose power while running and may have resulted in more than a dozen deaths, because doing so would have added to the cost of each car (Lienert & Thompson, 2014). The National Highway Transportation Safety Administration, which is charged with regulating and investigating complaints about motor vehicle safety, knew of the deaths linked to the vehicles with defective switches as early as 2007 but did not act (Wald, 2014).

- In 2014, JPMorgan was fined again, this time more than $461 million, by the Financial Crimes Enforcement Network (FinCEN) of the U.S. Department of the Treasury for violating the Bank Secrecy Act by failing to report the suspicious activities of Bernie Madoff (FinCEN, 2014).

POLICE CORRUPTION AND POLICE BRUTALITY Policing is a job vested with trust, responsibility, and authority. Police officers are the frontline enforcers of laws that are expected to limit the amount of crime that occurs in society. When violent or property crimes are committed, we rely on the police for protection and investigation. Thus, when instances of corruption—whether it be accepting bribes or engaging in criminal activities—and other forms of deviance on the part of police come to light, the public is often shocked and outraged.

Such was the case in 2010 when a video surfaced that showed a University of Maryland student being beaten by several Prince George's County, Maryland, police officers following a collegiate basketball game. Prior to publication of a video corroborating the student's story that he did nothing wrong, the officers claimed he had assaulted them and resisted arrest. In 2013, 18 deputies of the Los Angeles County Sheriff's Department were charged in an FBI indictment alleging they engaged in corruption and violations of civil rights—including the beating of inmates at the L.A. County Jail (Wilson & Duke, 2013).

Police brutality has a long history in the United States. The responses of southern police officers and sheriffs, such as Bull Connor in Birmingham, Alabama, to the 1960s civil rights marches provide well-documented examples. Police brutality continues to occur, though it often escapes detection and sanction. The videotaped beating of Rodney King in the 1990s by four White members of the Los Angeles Police Department served as one vivid example of the treatment many minority city residents suffered at the hands, and batons, of the police. More recently, a drunken off-duty Chicago policeman named Anthony Abbate was caught on tape viciously beating and stomping a female bartender after she refused to serve him any more drinks (Walberg, 2009). Had the video not surfaced, it is possible the 250-pound Abbate's claim that he acted in self-defense in pummeling the 125-pound bartender would have been accepted.

Police corruption is no less serious than police brutality, and in fact it may be more so if we consider that entrenched corruption may significantly undermine the ability of the police to enforce laws effectively and can also lead to acts of targeted violence in some cases. Both corruption and brutality represent important forms of criminal deviance committed by official representatives of state authority. But how can we make sense of these forms of deviance?

In the case of both police corruption and the use of excessive force by law enforcement officers, Sutherland's differential association theory may provide valuable insights. Some studies and first-person accounts demonstrate that police officers are often exposed to various forms of deviance once they become members of the force (Kappeler, Sluder, & Alpert, 1998; Maas, 1997). Exposure to attitudes favorable to the commission of deviance and crime, especially in light of the intensity and duration of the relationships police officers form with one another, may lead some to engage in those same types of deviant or criminal behaviors. We can also view the police as having a distinct culture, and thus see police brutality and corruption in terms of the subcultural expectations that accompany police work. Members of the police subculture may see certain behaviors, actions, and perspectives, especially regarding the use of force and engaging in corrupt practices, as both necessary and normal parts of accomplishing the demands of police work.

STATE CRIMES Finally, we turn to perhaps the most harmful form of crime among the powerful: state crime. While police brutality and corruption are especially egregious examples of crimes occurring among those with power, state crimes rank above even them in terms of the seriousness and potential harm that may result from their commission.

State crimes *consist of criminal or other harmful acts of commission or omission perpetrated by state officials in the pursuit of their jobs as representatives of the government.* Needless to say, governments do not normally keep statistics on their own criminal behavior. Nonetheless, we do know from various contemporary and historical examples that such crimes are not uncommon (Chambliss, Michalowski, & Kramer, 2010; Green & Ward, 2004; Moloney & Chambliss, 2014; Rothe, 2009). Contemporary examples of state crime involving the U.S. government include the torture of detainees at the U.S. military prison in Guantánamo Bay, Cuba; the secret transportation and torture of battlefield detainees in foreign prisons; and even the violation of international laws leading up to the 2004 invasion of Iraq (Grey, 2006; Kramer & Michalowksi, 2005; Paglen & Thompson, 2006; Ratner & Ray, 2004). Globally, many studies have drawn attention to state crimes, including the Chinese government's role in the trafficking of human body parts. In the latter study, the author found that the organs of executed prisoners were harvested by government-approved doctors and were sold to corporations and other entities for use in organ transplantation and cosmetic surgery, often at substantial profits, without the consent of the prisoners' families (Lenning, 2007).

State crimes: Criminal or other harmful acts committed by state officials in the pursuit of their jobs as representatives of the government.

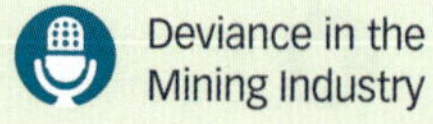
Deviance in the Mining Industry

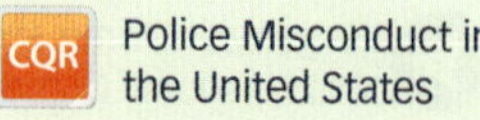
Police Misconduct in the United States

SOCIAL CONTROL OF DEVIANCE

The persistence of deviant behavior in society leads inevitably to a variety of measures designed to control it. **Social control** is defined as the *attempts by certain people or groups in society to control the behaviors of other individuals and groups in order to increase the likelihood that they will conform to established norms or laws.* Thus, deviance, the definition of which tends to require some sort of moral judgment, also attracts attempts at social control, usually exercised by those people or groups who possess **social power**, or *the ability to exercise social control.*

INFORMAL SOCIAL CONTROL

Informal social control is *the unofficial means through which deviance is discouraged in everyday interactions.* It ranges from frowning at someone's sexist assertion to threatening to take away a child's cell phone in order to coerce conformity to the parent's wishes. Informal social control mechanisms explain why people don't spit on the floor in a restaurant, do choose to pay back a friend who lent them $5, or say "thank you" in response to a favor. These behaviors and responses are governed not by formal laws but by informal expectations of which we are all aware and that lead us to make certain choices. Much of the time these informal social controls lead us into conformity with societal or group norms and away from deviance. Informal controls are thus responsible for keeping most forms of noncriminal deviance in check.

Socialization, which we have discussed in earlier chapters, thus plays a significant role in the success of informal social control. When parents seek to get their children to conform to the values and norms of their society, they teach them to do one thing and not another. Peer groups of workers, students, and friends also implement informal social control through means, such as embarrassment and criticism, that work to control behavior and thus deviance. Bonds to institutions and people enact various informal social controls on our behavior. Such bonds have been shown to be crucial in explaining why some people engage in deviance and others do not (Laub & Sampson, 2003; Sampson & Laub, 1990).

FORMAL SOCIAL CONTROL AND CRIMINAL DEVIANCE

The street-corner drug dealer who gets chased by the police, cornered, and forced violently to the ground is then handcuffed, packed into the back of a squad car, and hauled to jail. This is the experience of **formal social control**, *official attempts to discourage certain behaviors and visibly punish others.* In the modern world, formal social control is most often exercised by societal institutions associated with the state, including the police, prosecutors, courts, and prisons. The goal of all these institutions is to suppress, reduce, and punish those individuals or groups who engage in criminal forms of deviance. Theft, assault, vandalism, cheating on income taxes, fraudulent reporting of corporate earnings, and insider trading on the stock market—all have been deemed crimes and represent forms of criminal deviance. As such, they are subject to formal social control.

For an act to be criminal, several elements must be present. First, a specific law must prohibit the act, and a punishment of either prison or a fine, or both, must be specified for violation of the law. Most important, the act must be *intended, and the person committing the act must be capable of having the necessary intent.* Someone judged to be mentally ill, which U.S. criminal law defines as the person "not knowing right from wrong" at the time of the act, cannot have the required legal intent and therefore cannot be held criminally liable for committing an illegal act. However, the insanity defense is not accepted in all states: Idaho, Montana, Kansas, and Utah do not recognize insanity as a defense. In other state courts and federal courts, the burden of proof regarding a defendant's mental state is on the defendant. The U.S. Supreme Court refused to hear a case from Idaho in which a defendant claimed he had a constitutional right to claim insanity as a defense (Barnes, 2012).

RISING PRISON POPULATIONS Controlling serious, criminal forms of deviance typically includes the arrest and prosecution of individuals who have committed violent crimes or property crimes and, to a lesser extent, individuals engaged in police brutality or corruption, white-collar crime, organized crime, or state crime. Common sense would seem to indicate that most of the people subject to various formal social controls would be those implicated in some type of violent criminal deviance, such as rape, robbery, or murder. Interestingly, however, of the roughly 12 million arrests in the United States in 2012, fewer than 1 in 20 were for violent crimes; most arrests resulted from suspected violations of various drug laws (Federal Bureau of Investigation, 2012b).

Another indication of the importance of formal social control in the modern world is the unprecedented increase in the number of people imprisoned (Figures 6.3 and 6.4). The 2012 imprisonment rate in the United States was 480 per 100,000 residents (Carson & Golinelli, 2013). Indeed, while the U.S. prison population has declined slightly in recent years, the United States still imprisons a vastly higher percentage of its population than does any other industrial society. In total, about 1 in 35 U.S. adults today is under some form of correctional system supervision, either in prison or jail, on probation, or on parole (Glaze & Herberman, 2013).

The large and sudden increase in the number of people in prison or under some form of correctional supervision is particularly intriguing to sociologists, since it occurred during a period when both violent and property crime rates had been declining.

Social control: The attempts by certain people or groups in society to control the behaviors of other individuals and groups in order to increase the likelihood that they will conform to established norms or laws.

Social power: The ability to exercise social control.

Informal social control: The unofficial mechanism through which deviance and deviant behaviors are discouraged in society; most often occurs among ordinary people during the course of their interactions.

Formal social control: Official attempts to discourage certain behaviors and visibly punish others; most often exercised by the state.

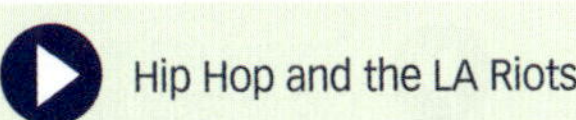

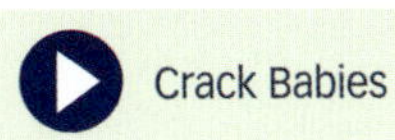

What then accounts for the unprecedented rise in imprisonment in the United States? The following are three key explanations:

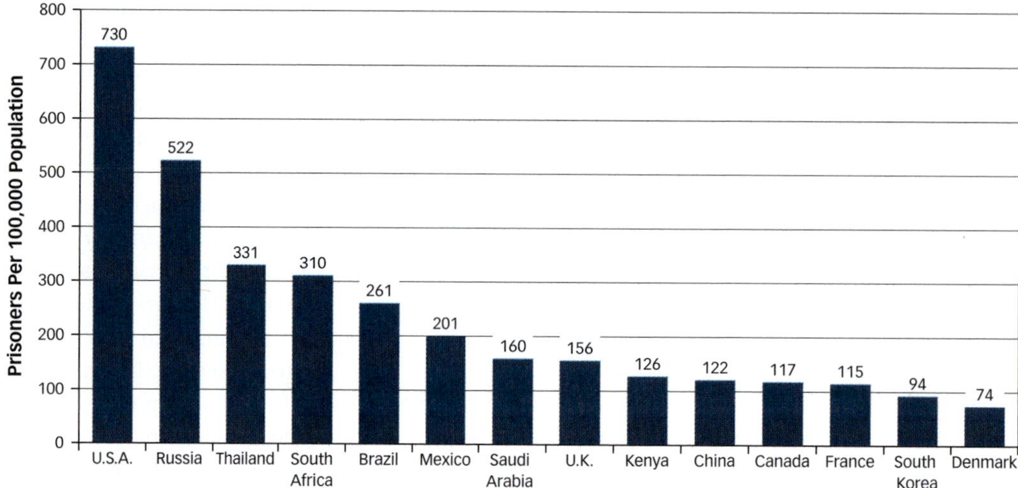

FIGURE 6.3 Incarceration Rates in Selected Countries, 2011

SOURCE: Adapted from Chambliss, William J. and Aida Hass (2011). *Criminology: Theory, Research and Practice,* New York: McGraw-Hill.

1. **Mandatory minimum sentences:** Federal and state legislators in the 1980s passed legislation stipulating that a person found guilty of a particular crime had to be sentenced to a minimum number of years in prison. This reduced judges' ability to use their discretion in sentencing and led to a substantial increase in the average prison term.

2. **"Three strikes" laws:** Many U.S. states and the federal government have passed laws that automatically impose a sentence of life in prison on anyone who is found guilty of committing three *felonies,* or serious crimes punishable by a minimum of one year in jail. (In November 2012, California passed a ballot initiative that slightly reduced the impact of the application of the state's three-strikes law.)

3. **The "war on drugs":** Efforts to reduce the trafficking of illegal drugs are responsible for a significant increase in the number of people in prison. For example, in 2012 there were just over 12 million arrests in the United States, of which 1.5 million were for minor drug law violations—not for serious trafficking or distribution offenses (Federal Bureau of Investigation, 2012b). As a result of increased arrest rates and longer sentences for minor drug-related offenses, about 60% of federal prison inmates and more than 30% of state prison inmates are serving time for the sale or possession of illegal drugs (Boncar & Beck, 1997).

FIGURE 6.4 U.S. State and Federal Prison Population, 1925–2012

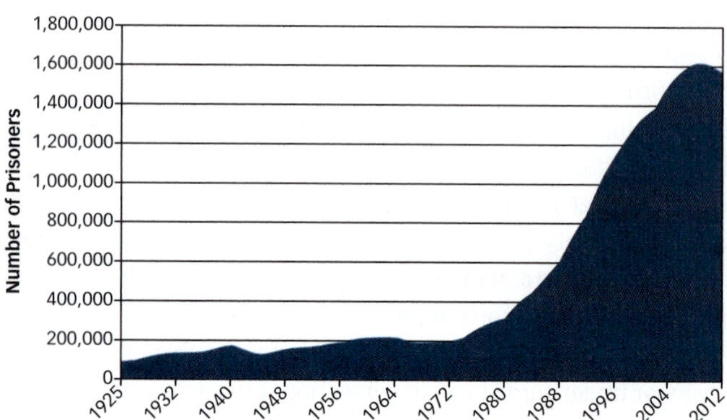

SOURCE: Reprinted with permission from The Sentencing Project.

Over the past several decades, changes in criminal laws and criminal sentencing have resulted in much stricter forms of social control in relationship to certain types of crime. In turn, this has led to a huge increase in the U.S. prison population. At the same time, these formal mechanisms of social control have not been applied equally, or proportionally, to all groups in society.

RACE, ETHNICITY, GENDER, AND CRIMINAL DEVIANCE

Three-strikes laws, mandatory minimum sentences, and the "war on drugs" have all contributed to increases in U.S. prison populations. However, those most likely to be imprisoned and punished for engaging in criminal deviance are disproportionately people of color. Blacks and Hispanics are arrested and imprisoned at much higher rates than Whites, despite the fact that Whites make up a much larger proportion of the total U.S. population (Chambliss, 2001; Glaze & Herberman, 2013).

Statistics show that 1 in 3 Black men will enter state or federal prison during his lifetime, compared to 1 in 6 Hispanic males and 1 in 17 White males (Sentencing Project, 2012). Black men are currently incarcerated at a rate of more than 2,800 per 100,000; for Hispanic men the rate is more than 1,100 per 100,000. White men, by contrast, have an incarceration rate of 463 per 100,000 (Carson & Golinelli, 2013). If current trends continue, Black males between the ages of 19 and 34 will experience an even

Mandatory minimum sentences: Legal requirements that persons found guilty of particular crimes must be sentenced to set minimum numbers of years in prison.

"Three strikes" laws: Laws that require sentences of life in prison for those who are found guilty of committing three felonies, or serious crimes.

"War on drugs": Actions taken by U.S. state and federal governments that are intended to curb the illegal drug trade and reduce drug use.

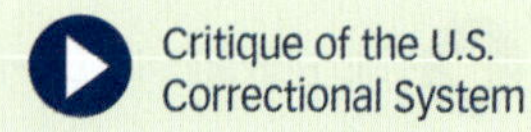

AP Photo/Paul Schirald

The television series *Orange is the New Black* tells the story of Piper Kerman, a young woman imprisoned for 15 months for a decade-old drug crime. The popular program is based on Kerman's best-selling book of the same name and shows both the extraordinary and banal experiences of life in a women's prison.

greater overrepresentation in the prison population (Figure 6.5). Incarceration rates for women, while lower overall than those for men, exhibit a similar disproportionate racial trend, with Black women twice as likely as Hispanic women and three times more likely than White women to end up in jail or prison (Carson & Golinelli, 2013; Sipes, 2012).

People of color are more likely than Whites to be arrested and imprisoned for a number of reasons, all of which relate to the extension of formal social control over criminal deviance (Mann & Zatz, 1998). First, impoverished inner-city residents are disproportionately non-White, and the inner city is where the "war on drugs" has been most avidly waged (Anderson, 1999; Chambliss, 2001). As a consequence, drug-related arrests disproportionately affect people of color, who, despite constituting only 13% of the total U.S. population, represent more than 30% of people arrested for drug violations.

FIGURE 6.5 Incarceration Rates by Race and Gender in the United States, 2012

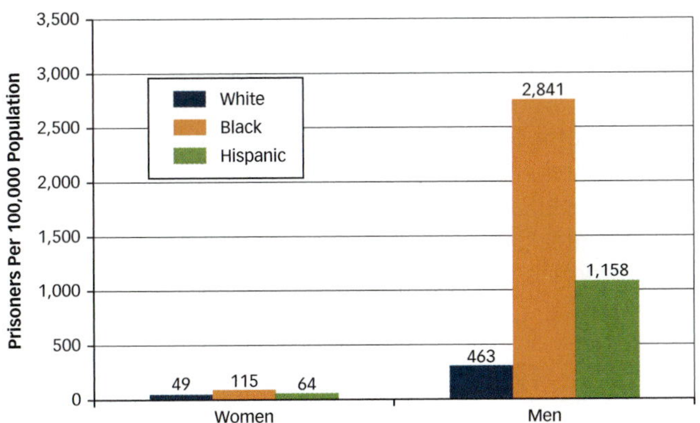

SOURCE: Carson, E. A., & Golinelli, D. (2013). *Prisoners in 2012: Trends in admissions and releases, 1991–2012*. Washington, DC: U.S. Department of Justice, Bureau of Justice Statistics.

Second, the work of policing generally focuses on poor neighborhoods, where crowded living conditions force many activities onto the streets. Illegal activities are therefore much more likely to attract police attention in poor neighborhoods than in dispersed suburban neighborhoods.

Finally, racism in practices of prosecution and sentencing may also account for greater arrest and imprisonment rates of people of color. Even though many more Whites than non-Whites are arrested for crimes, people of color are more likely to be imprisoned for their offenses (Austin, Dimas, & Steinhart, 1992).

WHY STUDY DEVIANCE?

The sociological perspective focuses the lens through which we view deviant behavior. It highlights the fact that the line between "deviant" and "normal" behavior is often arbitrary: What is deviant to one group is normal and even expected behavior to another.

Mainstream media and "official" depictions of deviance often overlook or ignore some of the more serious manifestations of deviance in the culture. So toso do local communities. For example, in his research on "the Saints" and "the Roughnecks," Chambliss (2001) found that middle-class boys were much more likely to have their deviant behavior written off as simply "sowing their wild oats," even though the behavior was dangerous and costly to society. On the other hand, the community was quick to judge, and apply deviant labels to, a lower-income group of boys. Such findings suggests a need for sociologists to delve more deeply into stereotypes of "gangs" and "delinquency" as phenomena associated almost exclusively with poor urban youth.

Similarly, sociological research and theory remind us that focusing on the deviance of the poor and minorities blinds us to an understanding of deviance among the rich and powerful. Criminal deviance, as discussed earlier in this chapter, is widespread throughout modern societies. Some of the most dangerous and costly patterns of deviant behavior are systematically practiced by corporate executives, politicians, and government officials. The sociological perspective demands that in such cases we ask questions about power and who has the power to define deviance and to enforce their definitions.

The findings of sociologists who study deviant behavior generally and criminal deviance in particular suggest that social control policies such as imprisonment have limited effects. Instead, these findings point to the need to change the social conditions that lead to criminality in the first place. The implications of most sociological studies of deviance are that street crime and gang activity in poor urban neighborhoods can best be controlled through the creation of jobs and other opportunities for those who otherwise cannot hope to succeed. In the case of white-collar, political, and governmental crimes, the organizational structures that make it rewarding to violate laws and social norms will have to change for there to be any hope of reducing deviance among the elite.

WHAT CAN I DO WITH A SOCIOLOGY DEGREE?

SKILLS AND CAREERS: PROBLEM SOLVING

Problem solving is a fundamental skill in social scientific disciplines such as sociology—and in a wide variety of contemporary occupational fields. Managing and addressing complex problems by identifying their dimensions, researching their roots, and using the knowledge gained rigorously and thoughtfully to craft well-reasoned responses is a skill set that is developed through careful study, research training, and practice. Problem solving is, in many respects, composed of other key skills we will discuss in the *Skills and Careers* features in this book, including data and information literacy, critical thinking, quantitative and qualitative research competency, understanding of conflict dynamics, understanding of diversity and global perspectives, and written communication. At the same time, it is a skill that has its own characteristics as a product of sociological training. Sociological research data, which form the centerpiece of much of what sociologists do and teach, cannot solve problems; rather, research data contribute to the informed understanding of the dimensions of a problem. Data are also used to hypothesize the roots of a problem. Once the roots of a problem are identified, they can be addressed through, for instance, policy or community interventions. Research can be used to follow up on whether and how solutions worked and to rework hypotheses based on new information.

In Chapter 6, we learned about a variety of theories that seek to explain deviant or criminal activities. Consider the problem of illegal drugs as a community concern. Drugs can be a problem for a community when, for instance, illicit drug markets contribute to a rise in neighborhood violence. How might a sociologist approach this problem? First, it is important to ascertain the dimensions of the problem. How will the problem at issue be defined, operationalized, and measured? Second, having established the dimensions of the problem, the sociologist must look for the roots of the problem. The sociologist may choose to study a particular neighborhood closely and to draw conclusions and perhaps make generalizations from data gathered through interviews, observations, examination of police records, or surveys, for instance. Or the sociologist might begin from an existing theory of deviance, such as opportunity theory or structural contradiction theory, and opt to test the theory through the collection of empirical evidence. Researching the roots of a problem can involve a spectrum of different approaches, and a sociologist often needs to try more than one to generate a comprehensive picture of the problem. Third, the sociologist can use the knowledge developed through research to craft possible approaches to the problem that get at the roots of the issue, and then use further research to test the effects of these approaches and to refine the analysis of the community drug problem. Social life is complex, and most serious social problems are not amenable to simple solutions. At the same time, the probability of successfully addressing a problem is appreciably greater when one has used careful research to understand its causes.

The problems encountered in different occupational fields vary, but the need for people who are skilled in breaking down a problem, defining it, analyzing it, crafting solutions based on good data, and effectively communicating identified paths of action is common across many areas. Among the *occupational fields* where problem-solving skills are very important are business and management, nonprofit and volunteer management, nongovernmental organization management, education and training, criminal justice, politics, law, mediation and negotiation, health administration, marketing, public relations, and research. Among the *job titles* that are associated with these fields are the following: social worker or youth counselor, caseworker, psychologist, educator or education administrator, policy director or analyst, researcher, business manager or executive, social media manager, advertising manager or executive, Peace Corps volunteer, labor relations manager, criminologist, detective, corporate trainer, and organizational development consultant.

THINK ABOUT CAREERS

▶ Think about career fields that might be of interest to you. What kinds of problems do people who work in this career field confront and address?

SUMMARY

- Notions of what constitutes **deviance** vary considerably and are relative to the norms and values of particular cultures as well as the labels applied by certain groups or individuals to specific behaviors, actions, practices, and conditions. Even **crimes**, which are particular forms of especially serious deviance, are defined differently from place to place and over time, and they depend on social and political processes.
- In **pluralistic societies** such as the United States, it is difficult to establish universally accepted notions of deviance.
- Most sociologists do not believe there is a direct causal link between biology and deviance. Whatever the role of biology, deviant behaviors are culturally defined and socially learned.
- Functionalist theorists explain deviance in terms of the functions it performs for society. Émile Durkheim argued that some degree of deviance serves to reaffirm society's normative boundaries. Robert K. Merton argued that deviance reflects structural strain between the culturally defined goals of a society and the means society provides for achieving those goals. **Opportunity theory** emphasizes access to deviance as a major source of deviance. **Control theory** focuses on the presence of interpersonal bonds as a means of keeping deviance in check.
- Conflict theories explain deviance in terms of the conflicts between different groups, classes, or subcultures in society. **Class-dominant theories** of deviance emphasize how wealthy and powerful groups are able to define as deviant any behavior that runs counter to their interests. **Structural contradiction theory** argues that conflicts are inherent in social structure; it sees the sorts of structural strains identified by Merton as being built into society itself. The **feminist perspective on deviance** reminds us that, until relatively recently, research on deviance was conducted almost exclusively on males. Recent feminist theories argue that many women labeled as deviant are themselves victims of deviant behavior, such as "delinquent" girls who are, in fact, runaways escaping sexual and physical abuse.
- Symbolic interactionist theorists argue that deviance, like all forms of human behavior, results from the ways in which we come to see ourselves through the eyes of others. One version of symbolic interactionism is **labeling theory**, which argues that deviance results mainly from the labels others attach to our behavior.
- Although crime is often depicted as concentrated among poor racial minorities, crimes are committed by people from all walks of life. **White-collar crime** and **state crime** are two examples of crime committed by people in positions of wealth and power. They exact enormous financial and personal costs from society.
- Deviance and **criminal deviance** are both controlled socially through mechanisms of **informal social control**, such as socialization, and **formal social control**, such as arrests and imprisonment.
- Criminal deviance is controlled formally, and in modern societies, including the United States, this most often means incapacitating criminals by imprisoning them. Among industrialized nations, the United States currently has the highest proportion of its population in prison, a situation that has given rise to a large and powerful crime control industry.
- Although there is a public perception in the United States that crime is increasing, crime has steadily decreased over the 35 years the federal government has been collecting systematic data on it. **Violent crimes** are the most heavily publicized, but the most common are **property crimes** and victimless crimes.
- A disproportionate number of people of color are arrested and incarcerated in the United States. In addition, the **"war on drugs"** is focused on urban areas, where poor people of color are concentrated.

KEY TERMS

opportunity theory,135

control theory, 137

social bonds, 137

subcultural theories, 137

class-dominant theories, 137

structural contradiction theory, 138

stigmatization, 140

labeling theory, 140

feminist perspective on deviance, 140

primary deviance, 141

secondary deviance, 141

differential association theory, 141

violent crimes, 144

property crimes, 144

organized crime, 145

white-collar crime, 145

state crimes, 146

social control, 147

social power, 147

informal social control, 147

formal social control, 147

mandatory minimum sentences, 148

"three strikes" laws, 148

"war on drugs," 148

DISCUSSION QUESTIONS

1. Measuring crime, including property crimes and violent crimes, can be challenging. Often, a single source is not enough to provide a comprehensive picture. What kinds of factors could affect the accuracy of statistics on the incidence of crime? How can a researcher overcome such problems to gain an accurate picture?
2. Labeling theories in the area of criminology suggest that labeling particular groups as deviant can set in motion a self-fulfilling prophecy. That is, people may become that which is expected of them—including becoming deviant or even criminally deviant. Can you think of other social settings where labeling theory might be applied?
3. Think about some theoretical explanations for why people commit crime—differential association, social control, labeling, and so on. You might conclude that they all make sense on an intuitive level. Yet there is contradictory evidence for each of these theories; that is, some data support each theory, and some data contradict it. What is the difference between seeing intuitive sense in a theory and testing it empirically?
4. Why, according to the chapter, has the rate of imprisonment risen in the United States since the 1980s? Why are a disproportionate number of prison inmates people of color?
5. Why, according to sociologists, are the "crimes of the powerful" (politicians, businesspeople, and other elites) less likely to be severely punished than those of the poor, even when those crimes have mortal consequences?

SAGE edge™

Sharpen your skills with SAGE edge at **edge.sagepub.com/chambliss2e**

A personalized approach to help you accomplish your coursework goals in an easy-to-use learning environment.

REUTERS/Tomas Bravo

7 SOCIAL CLASS AND INEQUALITY IN THE UNITED STATES

IN THIS CHAPTER

© Lisa Wiltse/Corbis

WHAT DO YOU THINK?

1. How equal or unequal is the distribution of income in the United States? What factors help explain income inequality?
2. What explains the existence and persistence of widespread poverty in the United States, one of the richest countries on earth?
3. Should the minimum wage be raised? What would be the costs of such an increase? What would be the benefits?

Melanie Stetson Freeman / Contributor/Getty Images

POVERTY AND PROSPERITY IN THE UNITED STATES

An article in a recent issue of *Bloomberg Markets* that reported on a growing demand among investors for trailer park properties in the United States profiled one such investor:

> When Dan Weissman worked at Goldman Sachs Group Inc. and, later, at a hedge fund, he didn't have to worry about methamphetamine addicts chasing his employees with metal pipes. Or SWAT teams barging into his workplace looking for arsonists.
>
> Both things have happened since he left Wall Street and bought five mobile home parks: four in Texas and one in Indiana. Yet he says he's never been so relaxed in his life. . . .
>
> [He] attributes his newfound calm to the supply-demand equation in the trailer park industry. With more of the U.S. middle class sliding into poverty and many towns banning new trailer parks, enterprising owners are getting rich renting the concrete pads and surrounding dirt on which residents park their homes.
>
> "The greatest part of the business is that we go to sleep at night not ever worrying about demand for our product. . . . It's the best decision I've ever made." (Effinger & Burton, 2014)

The decline of the U.S. middle class has wrought substantial consequences for millions of families. It has also, as the *Bloomberg* article suggests, opened new opportunities for others, including members of the upper class. The economic position of the middle class, particularly its less educated fraction, has been slowly declining since the 1970s, a process accelerated by the economic recession of 2007–2010, the effects of which are still felt in many families and communities. At the top of the economic ladder, however, incomes have risen and fortunes expanded. These important changes in the U.S. class structure are of great interest to sociologists. Helping you to understand them is a key goal of this chapter.

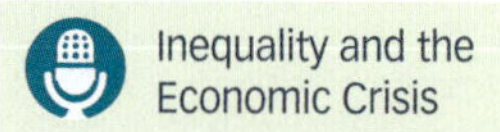

Inequality and the Economic Crisis

We begin this chapter with an examination of forms of stratification in traditional and modern societies, followed by a discussion of the characteristics of caste, social class, and stratification. Next, we look at important quantitative and qualitative dimensions of inequality and both household and neighborhood poverty in the United States. Finally, we discuss theoretical perspectives that consider the analytical question of why these economic phenomena exist and persist.

STRATIFICATION IN TRADITIONAL AND MODERN SOCIETIES

In the United States today, there is substantial **social inequality**—*a high degree of disparity in income, wealth, power, prestige, and other resources.* Sociologists capture the disparities between social groups conceptually with an image from geology: They suggest that society, like the earth's surface, is made up of different layers. **Social stratification** is thus *the systematic ranking of different groups of people in a hierarchy of inequality.* Sociologists seek to outline the quantitative dimensions and the qualitative manifestations of social stratification in the United States and around the globe, but—even more important—they endeavor to identify the social roots of stratification.

Stratification systems are considered "closed" or "open," depending on how much mobility between layers is available to groups and individuals within a society. Caste societies (closed) and class societies (open) represent two important examples of systems of stratification.

CASTE SOCIETIES

In a **caste society** *the social levels are closed, so that all individuals remain at the social level of their birth throughout life.* Social status is based on personal characteristics—such as race or ethnicity, parental religion, or parental caste—that are present at birth, and social mobility is virtually impossible. Social status, then, is the outcome of ascribed rather than achieved characteristics.

Historically, castes have been present in some agricultural societies, such as rural India and South Africa prior to the end of White rule in 1992. In the United States before the end of the Civil War in 1865, slavery imposed a racial caste system because enslavement was usually a permanent condition (except for those slaves who escaped or were freed by their owners). In the eyes of the law, the slave was a form of property without personal rights. Some argue that institutionalized racial inequality and limits on social mobility for African Americans remained fixtures of the U.S. landscape even after the end of slavery (Alexander, 2010; Dollard, 1957; Immerwahr, 2007). Indeed, enforced separation of Blacks and Whites was supported by federal, state, and local laws on education, family formation, public spaces, and housing as late as the 1960s.

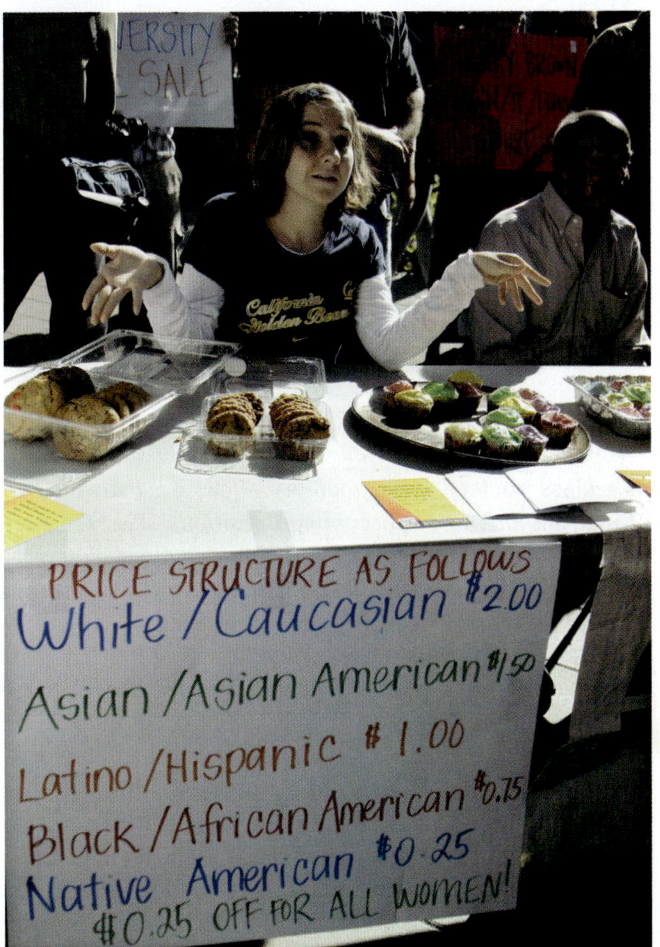

AP Photo/Ben Margot

In a protest against affirmative action in college admissions, a "diversity bake sale" held at a California college by the College Republicans set pastry prices by racial and gender group. The action provoked anger among those who argue that affirmative action is a means of ensuring equal access to educational opportunities. Interest has grown recently in focusing affirmative action policies on class rather than on race or gender. Is this likely to provoke controversy as well?

Caste systems are far less common in countries and communities today than they were in centuries past. For example, India is now home to a rising middle class (see Chapter 8 for a fuller discussion of caste and class in India), but it has long been described as a caste-based society because of its historical categorization of the population into four basic castes (or *varnas*): priests, warriors, traders, and workmen. These

Social inequality: A high degree of disparity in income, wealth, power, prestige, and other resources.

Social stratification: The systematic ranking of different groups of people in a hierarchy of inequality.

Caste society: A system in which the social levels are closed, so that all individuals remain at the social level of their birth throughout life.

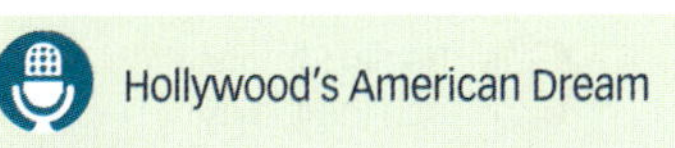
Hollywood's American Dream

categories, which can be further divided, are based on the country's majority religion, Hinduism. At the bottom of this caste hierarchy one finds the *Dalits* or "untouchables," the lowest caste.

Since the 1950s, India has passed laws to integrate the lowest caste members into positions of greater economic and political power. Some norms have also changed, permitting members of different castes to intermarry. While members of the lowest castes still lag in educational attainment compared to higher-caste groups, India today is moving closer to a class system.

CLASS SOCIETIES

In a **class society** *social mobility allows an individual to change his or her socioeconomic position.* Class societies exist in modern economic systems and are defined by several characteristics. First, they are *economically based,* at least in theory—that is, class position is determined largely by economic status (whether earned or inherited) rather than by religion or tradition. Second, class systems are *relatively fluid*: Boundaries between classes are violable and can be crossed. In fact, in contrast to caste systems, in class systems social mobility is looked at favorably. Finally, class status is understood to be *achieved rather than ascribed*: Status is, ideally, not related to a person's position at birth or religion or race or other inherited categories, but to the individual's merit or achievement in areas like education and occupation.

As we will see in this chapter, these ideal-typical characteristics of class societies do not necessarily describe historical or contemporary reality, and class status can be profoundly affected by factors like race, gender, and class of birth.

SOCIOLOGICAL BUILDING BLOCKS OF STRATIFICATION AND SOCIAL CLASS

Nearly all socially stratified systems share three characteristics. First, rankings apply to **social categories** of people—that is, to *people who share common characteristics without necessarily interacting or identifying with one another.* In many societies, women may be ranked differently than men, wealthy people differently than the poor, and highly educated people differently than those with little schooling. Individuals may be able to change their rank (through education, for instance), but the categories themselves continue to exist as part of the social hierarchy.

Second, people's life experiences and opportunities are powerfully influenced by how their social categories are ranked. Ranking may be linked to **achieved status**, which is *social position linked to a person's acquisition of socially valued credentials or skills,* or **ascribed status**, which is *social position linked to characteristics that are socially significant but cannot generally be altered (such as race or gender).* While anyone can exercise individual agency, membership in a social category may influence whether an individual's path forward (and upward) is characterized by obstacles or opportunities.

© Bettmann/CORBIS

In *Loving v. Virginia* (1967), the U.S. Supreme Court ruled unanimously that a law forbidding interracial marriage was unconstitutional. Richard and Mildred Loving, shown here, were married in the District of Columbia in 1958. Their arrest in Virginia, where they resided, prompted the case.

The third characteristic of a socially stratified system is that the hierarchical positions of social categories tend to change slowly over time. Members of those groups that enjoy prestigious and preferential rankings in the social order tend to remain at the top, though the expansion of opportunities may change the composition of groups over time.

Societal stratification has evolved through different stages. The earliest human societies, based on hunting and gathering, had little social stratification; there were few resources to divide, so differences within communities were not very pronounced, at least materially. The development of agriculture produced considerably more wealth and a consequent rise in social stratification. The hierarchy in agricultural societies increasingly came to resemble a pyramid, with a large number of poor people at the bottom and successively smaller numbers in the upper tiers of more economically advantaged members.

Class society: A system in which social mobility allows an individual to change his or her socioeconomic position.

Social categories: Categories of people sharing common characteristics without necessarily interacting or identifying with one another.

Achieved status: Social position linked to an individual's acquisition of socially valued credentials or skills.

Ascribed status: Social position linked to characteristics that are socially significant but cannot generally be altered (such as race or gender).

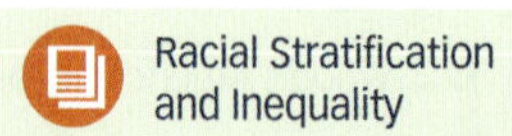

Racial Stratification and Inequality

■ **FIGURE 7.1** **Class in the United States (Gilbert-Kahl Model)**

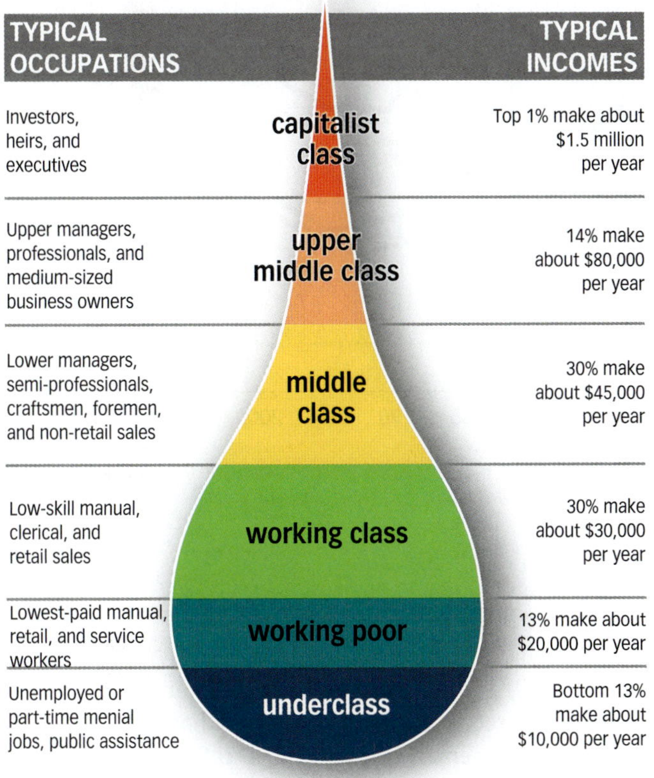

SOURCE: Gilbert, D. L. (2011). *The American class structure in an age of growing inequality.* Thousand Oaks, CA: Pine Forge.

Modern capitalist societies are, predictably, even more complex: Some sociologists suggest that the shape of class stratification resembles a teardrop (Figure 7.1), with a large number of people in the middle ranks, a slightly smaller number of people at the bottom, and very few people at the top.

Before we continue, let's look at what sociologists mean when they use the term *class.* **Class** refers to *a person's economic position in society, which is associated with income, wealth, and occupation.* Class position at birth strongly influences a person's **life chances**, *the opportunities and obstacles the person encounters in education, social life, work, and other areas critical to social mobility.* **Social mobility** is *the upward or downward status movement of individuals or groups over time.* Many middle-class Americans have experienced downward mobility in recent decades. Upward social mobility may be experienced by those who earn educational credentials or have social networks they can tap. A college degree is one important step toward upward mobility for many people.

Class: A person's economic position in society, usually associated with income, wealth, and occupation, and sometimes associated with political voice.

Life chances: The opportunities and obstacles a person encounters in education, social life, work, and other areas critical to social mobility.

Social mobility: The upward or downward status movement of individuals or groups over time.

The class system in the United States is complex, as class is composed of multiple variables. We may, however, identify some general descriptive categories. Our descriptions follow the class categories used by Gilbert and Kahl, as shown in Figure 7.1 (Gilbert, 2011). At the bottom of the economic ladder, one finds what economist Gunnar Myrdal (1963), writing in the 1960s, called the *underclass*: "a class of unemployed, unemployables, and underemployed who are more and more hopelessly set apart from the nation at large" (p. 10). The term has also been used by sociologists like Erik Olin Wright (1994) and William Julius Wilson (1978), whose work on the "black underclass" described that group as "a massive population at the very bottom of the social ladder plagued by poor education and low-paying, unstable jobs" (p. 1).

People who perform manual labor or work in low-wage sectors like food service and retail jobs are generally understood to be working class, though some sociologists distinguish those in the *working class* from the *working poor.* Households in both categories cluster below the median household income in the United States and are characterized by breadwinners whose education beyond high school is limited or nonexistent. People in both categories depend largely on hourly wages, though the working poor have lower incomes and little or no wealth; while they are employed,

© Bob Rowan/Progressive Image/Corbis

How would you define the U.S. middle class? Is the definition used by the White House Task Force on the Middle Class too broad or not broad enough? Should aspirations or achievements be the foundation of a definition of a socioeconomic class? ■

their wages fail to lift them above the poverty line, and many struggle to meet even basic needs. Author David Shipler (2005) suggests that they are "invisible," as U.S. mainstream culture does not equate work with poverty.

Those who provide skilled services of some kind (whether legal advice, electrical wiring, nursing, or accounting services) and work for someone else are considered—and usually consider themselves—middle-class. Lawyers, teachers, social workers, plumbers, auto sales representatives, and store managers are all widely considered to be middle class, though there may be significant income, wealth, and educational differences among them, leading some observers to distinguish between the (middle) *middle class* and the *upper-middle class*. As most Americans describe themselves in surveys as "middle class," establishing quantitative categories is challenging. In fact, in 2010, the White House Task Force on the Middle Class, led by Vice President Joe Biden, opted for a descriptive rather than statistical definition of the middle class, suggesting that its members are "defined by their aspirations more than their income. [It is assumed that] middle class families aspire to homeownership, a car, college education for their children, health and retirement security and occasional family vacations" (U.S. Department of Commerce, Economics and Statistics Administration, 2010).

FIGURE 7.2 U.S. Real Median Household Income by Racial and Ethnic Group, 1967–2013

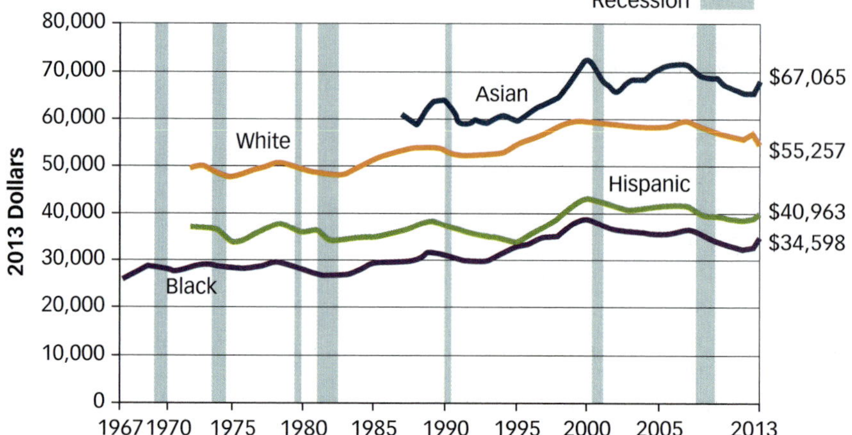

SOURCE: U.S. DeNavas-Walt, C., & Proctor, B. D. (2014). *Income and poverty in the United States: 2013* (Current Population Reports P60-249). Washington, DC: U.S. Census Bureau.

Those who own or exercise substantial financial control over large businesses, financial institutions, or factories are generally considered to be part of the upper class, a category Gilbert and Kahl term the *capitalist class* (Gilbert, 2011). This is the smallest of the categories and consists of those whose wealth and income, whether gained through work, investment, or inheritance, are dramatically greater than those of the rest of the population.

Below we look more closely at some key components of social class position: *income, wealth, occupation,* and *political voice.*

INCOME

Income is *the amount of money a person or household earns in a given period of time.* Income is earned most commonly at a job and less commonly through investments. Household income also includes government transfers such as Social Security payments or disability checks. Income typically goes to pay for food, clothing, shelter, health care, and other costs of daily living. It has a fluid quality in that it flows into a household in the form of pay-period checks and then flows out again as the mortgage or rent is paid, groceries are purchased, and other daily expenses are met.

U.S. household incomes have largely stagnated over the past decades, a topic we cover in detail later in the chapter. Effects of the recent economic crisis have not been felt evenly, but they have been experienced by all U.S. ethnic and racial groups (Figure 7.2). Income gains in the United States, however, have been disproportionately concentrated among top earners. In May 2014, the Associated Press reported that the median pay of chief executive officers (CEOs) in the United States had passed the $10 million mark the previous year, noting, "A chief executive now makes about 257 times the average worker's salary, up sharply from 181 times in 2009" (Sweet, 2014).

WEALTH

Wealth (or net worth) differs from income in that it is *the value of everything a person owns minus the value of everything he or she owes.* Wealth becomes a more important source of status as people rise on the income ladder.

For most people in the United States who possess any measurable wealth, the key source of wealth is home equity, which is essentially the difference between the market value of a home and what is owed on the mortgage. This form of wealth is *illiquid* (as opposed to *liquid*); illiquid assets are those

Income: The amount of money a person or household earns in a given period of time.

Wealth (or net worth): The value of everything a person owns minus the value of everything he or she owes.

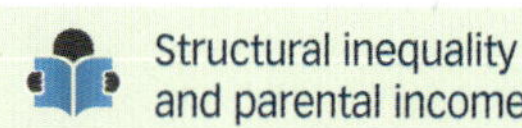

that are logistically difficult to transform into cash because the process is lengthy and complicated. So a family needing money to finance car repairs, meet educational expenses, or even ride out a period of unemployment cannot readily transform its illiquid wealth into cash.

Economists and sociologists treat **net financial assets** as *a measure of wealth that excludes illiquid personal assets such as home and car.* Examples of net financial assets are stocks, bonds, cash, and other forms of investment assets. These are the principal sources of wealth used by the rich to secure their position in the economic hierarchy and, through reinvestment and other financial vehicles, to accumulate still more wealth.

Wealth, unlike income, is built up over a lifetime and passed down to the next generation. It is used to create new opportunities rather than merely to cover routine expenditures. Income buys shoes, coffee, and car repairs; wealth buys a high-quality education, business ventures, and access to travel and leisure that are out of reach of most, as well as financial security and the creation of new wealth. Those who possess wealth have a decided edge at getting ahead in the stratification system. In the United States, wealth is largely concentrated at the very top of the economic ladder.

OCCUPATION

An **occupation** is *a person's main vocation.* In the modern world, this generally refers to *paid employment.* Occupation is an important determinant of social class because it is the main source of income in modern societies. The U.S. Bureau of Labor Statistics tracks 840 detailed occupational categories in the United States. Sociologists have used various classifications to reduce these to a far smaller number of categories. For example, jobs are described as *blue-collar* if they are based primarily on manual labor (factory workers, agricultural laborers, truck drivers, and miners) and *white-collar* if they require mainly analytical skills or formal education (doctors, lawyers, and business managers). The term *pink-collar* is sometimes used to describe semiskilled, low-paid service jobs that are primarily held by women (waitresses, salesclerks, and receptionists).

In the 1990s, some writers adopted the term *gold-collar* to categorize the jobs of young professionals who commanded huge salaries and high occupational positions very early in their professional careers thanks to the technology bubble and economic boom of the 1990s (Wonacott, 2002). After the bubble burst, gold-collar workers were more often found in the financial sector, earning very substantial salaries and benefits. The economic recession that commenced in 2007 put a damper on growth in salaries and benefits of gold-collar workers, but they have risen again in recent years.

Net financial assets: A measure of wealth that excludes illiquid personal assets such as home and car.

Occupation: A person's main vocation or paid employment.

Status: The prestige associated with a social position.

Political power: The ability to exercise influence on political institutions and/or actors in order to realize personal or group interests.

STATUS

Status refers to *the prestige associated with social position.* It varies based on factors such as family background and occupation. A considerable amount of social science research has gone into classifying occupations according to the degrees of status or prestige they hold in public opinion.

We might expect white-collar jobs to rank more highly in prestige than blue-collar jobs, but do they? Doctors and scientists are indeed at the top of the prestige scale—but so are less highly paid professionals such as nurses and firefighters (who top the poll results discussed in this section, with 62% of respondents indicating that firefighters have "very great prestige"). Also in the top ranks are teachers and military officers (both with 51% conferring "very great prestige" on them). At the bottom are actors, stockbrokers, accountants, and real estate agents (just 5% of respondents indicated "very great prestige" for real estate agents). It seems occupations that require working with ideas (scientist, engineer) or providing professional services that contribute to the public welfare (teacher, doctor, firefighter) have the highest prestige, and, perhaps surprisingly, the U.S. public does not always relate prestige to income (Harris Interactive, 2009).

Prestige rankings of specific occupations have been relatively stable over time, though changes do occur. For instance, since 1977 both scientists and lawyers have lost ground, falling 9 points to 57% and 10 points to 26%, respectively. What factors might explain these drops? Have societal changes taken place that might contribute to our understanding of why occupations like these rise and fall on the prestige scale?

POLITICAL VOICE

Political power is *the ability to exercise influence on political institutions and/or actors in order to realize personal or group interests.* It involves the mobilization of resources (such as money or technology or political support of a desired constituency) and the successful achievement of political goals (such as the passage of legislation favorable to a particular group).

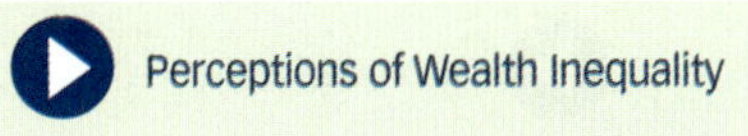

Sociological analyses of power have revealed a pyramid-shaped stratification system in the United States—as well as in most advanced industrial societies, including those of Western Europe. At the top are a handful of political figures, businesspeople, and other leaders with substantial power over political decision making and the national economy. Moving down the pyramid, we encounter more people—and less power (Domhoff, 2009).

Sociologist C. Wright Mills began to write as early as the 1950s about the existence of a "power elite," which he defined as a group comprising elites from the executive branch of government, the military, and the corporate community who share social ties, a common "worldview" born of socialization in prestigious schools and clubs, and professional links that create revolving doors between positions in these three areas (Mills, 1956/2000a).

In contrast to the *pluralist perspective* on U.S. democracy, which suggests that political power is fluid and passes, over time, among a spectrum of groups and interests who compete in the political arena, Mills offered a critical perspective. He described a concentration of political power in the hands of a small elite. According to Mills, while some power over local issues remains in the hands of elected legislatures and interest groups, decision-making power over issues of war and peace, global economic interests, and other matters of international and national consequence remain with the power elite. The power of the masses is little more than an illusion in Mills's view; the masses are composed of "entirely private" individuals wrapped up in personal concerns and largely disconnected from the political process. (We discuss the power elite and pluralism more fully in Chapter 14.)

Today, the middle class is at the center of electoral discourse, but are decision makers addressing the fundamental economic concerns, including stagnating wages, of the middle class? Or do the interests of the wealthy guide policy making? Are the voices of the poor present in politics? What do you think? In the following we look more closely at trends in inequality in the United States.

CLASS AND INEQUALITY IN THE UNITED STATES: DIMENSIONS AND TRENDS

The United States prides itself on being a nation of equals. Indeed, except for the period of the Great Depression of the 1930s, inequality declined throughout much of the 20th century, reaching its lowest levels during the 1960s and early 1970s. But during the past three decades, inequality has been on the rise again. The rich have gotten much richer, middle-class incomes have stagnated, and a growing number of poor are struggling to make ends meet.

INCOME INEQUALITY

Sociologist Richard Sennett (1998) writes that "Europeans from [Alexis de] Tocqueville on have tended to take the face value for reality; some have deduced we Americans are indeed a classless society, at least in our manners and beliefs—a democracy of consumers; others, like Simone de Beauvoir, have maintained we are hopelessly confused about our real differences" (p. 64). Was Tocqueville right, or Beauvoir? Are we classless or confused? What are the dimensions of our differences? Let us look at what statistics tell us.

Every year the U.S. Census Bureau calculates how income is distributed across the population of earners. All households are ranked by annual income and then categorized into *quintiles,* or fifths. The Census Bureau calculates how much of the *aggregate income,* or total income, generated in the United States each quintile gets. In other words, imagine all legally earned and reported income thrown into a big pot—that is the aggregate income. The Census Bureau wants to know (and we do too!) how much of this income goes to each quintile of earners. In a society with equal distribution across quintiles, each fifth of earners would get about one-fifth of the income in the pot. Conversely, in a society with complete inequality across quintiles, the top would get everything, and the bottom quintiles would be left empty-handed. The United States, like all other countries, falls between these two hypothetical extremes.

In Figure 7.3, we see how aggregate income in the United States is divided among quintiles of earners. When we look at

FIGURE 7.3 Shares of Aggregate U.S. Income by Quintile, 2013

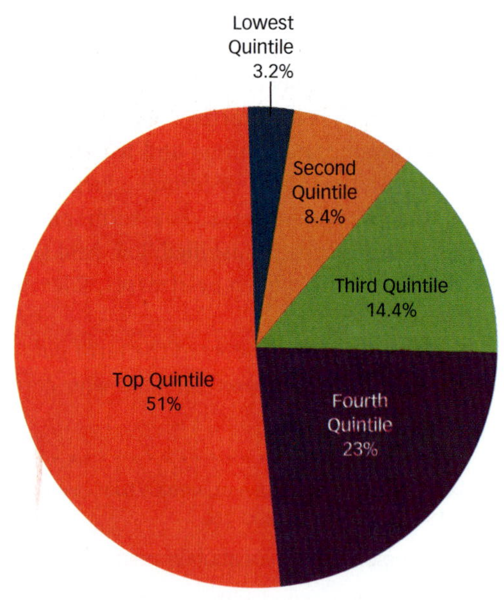

SOURCE: U.S. Census Bureau. (2013). *Income, poverty, and health insurance coverage in the United States: 2012. Current Population Reports.* Washington, DC: C. DeNavas-Walt, B. D. Proctor, & J. C. Smith.

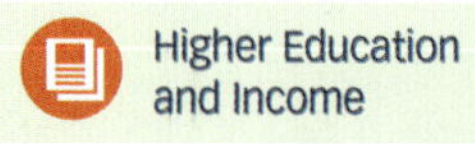

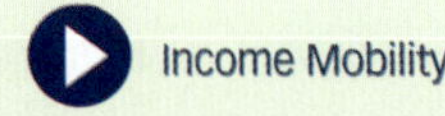

the pie, we see that income earners at different levels take in disparate proportions of the income total. Those in the bottom quintile take in just over 3% of the aggregate income, while those in the top quintile get more than half; that means the top 20% of earners bring in as much as all in the bottom 80% combined. No less significant is the fact that the top 5% take in more than 22% of the total income—more than the bottom 40% combined (DeNavas-Walt & Proctor, 2014).

Data compiled by economists Emmanuel Saez and Thomas Piketty, with a formula that uses pretax income (as do the census figures) but includes capital gains, suggest an even more stratified picture. According to Saez and Piketty's calculations, about 50% of pretax income goes to the top 10% of earners. Within this well-off decile (or tenth) of earners, there is a still more dramatic division of income, because the top *1%* of earners takes about a fifth of the aggregate income (Saez, 2010). Clearly, gains have been concentrated at the top of the income ladder. As economist Joseph Stiglitz (2012) points out, the fraction of the aggregate income taken by the upper 1% has doubled since 1980, while the fraction that goes to the upper 0.1% has nearly tripled over that period.

When we study issues like income inequality, we benefit from understanding the data we gather in their historical context. Figure 7.3 presents a snapshot of one moment in time, but what about decades past? The economic prosperity of the middle to late 1990s brought some benefit to most American workers: The median U.S. income rose faster at the end of the 1990s than it had since the period from the late 1940s to the middle 1950s. Saez (2010) calculates that the real annual growth of income among the bottom 99% of earners grew 2.7% in the period he terms the "Clinton Expansion" (1993–2000), but it dropped during the 2000–2002 recession (by 3.3%) and again during the 2007–2008 period (by 6.9%). On the whole, the period from 1993 to 2008 saw a real annual growth of just 0.75% for the incomes of the bottom 99%. Over the same period, the top 1% of earners experienced a real annual growth of almost 4% (though this group too experienced significant losses in the recessionary periods).

From about World War II until the middle 1970s, the top 10% earned less than a third of the national income pool (Pearlstein, 2010). In the years since, however, the incomes of people at or near the top have risen far faster than those of earners at the bottom or middle of the income scale (Figure 7.4). The stagnation of wages is illustrated by the poor growth (and even decline) of average wages of new college graduates. As we see in Figure 7.5, in the period between 2000 and 2012 the wages of new college graduates fell by 8.5% (Shierholz, 2013).

FIGURE 7.4 **Changes in Income Inequality in the United States, 1967–2013**

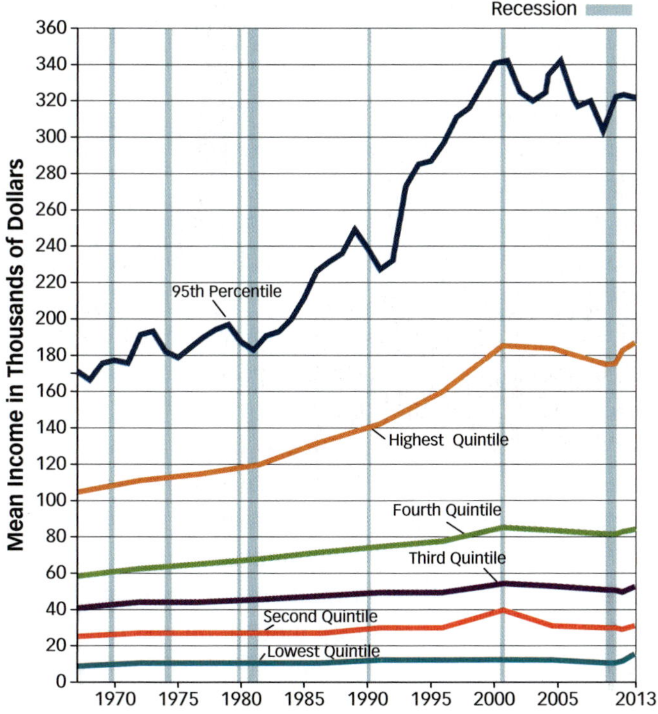

SOURCE: U.S. Census Bureau. (2012). *Income, poverty, and health insurance coverage in the United States: 2011. Current Population Reports*. Washington, DC: C. DeNavas-Walt, B. D. Proctor, & J. C. Smith.

FIGURE 7.5 **Average Hourly Wages of U.S. College Graduates Ages 21–24, 1989–2012**

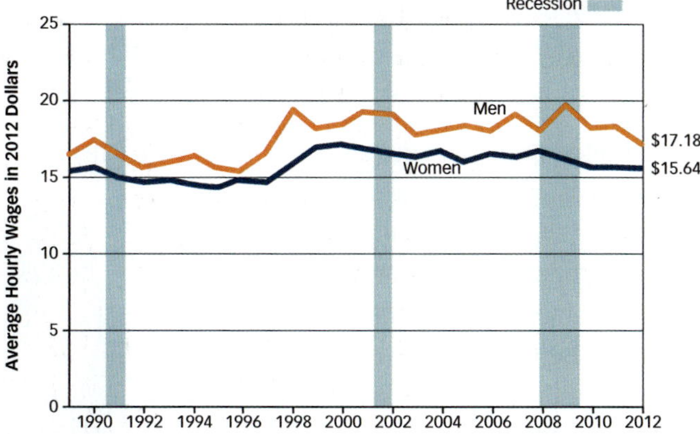

SOURCE: Shierholz, H. (2013). *Wages of young college graduates have failed to grow over the last decade*. Washington, DC: Economic Policy Institute.

WEALTH INEQUALITY

We see the growth of inequality in the distribution of income, but what about the wealth gap? What are its dimensions? Is it growing or shrinking? Recall that while income has a fluid quality—flowing into the household with a weekly or monthly

CQR Income Inequality

POVERTY AND WORK IN THE UNITED STATES: THE MINIMUM WAGE DEBATE

In the United States, we do not normally associate work with poverty. Work, after all, is widely understood to be a foundation of prosperity. At the same time, in 2012, according to the U.S. Bureau of Labor Statistics (2014c), the incomes of 10.6 million American workers fell below the poverty line. Among these are more than 4% of workers who are employed full-time and more than 15% of those who work part-time. A key factor explaining their poverty, according to the Bureau of Labor Statistics, is "low earnings." Poverty, our sociological imagination may suggest, can be linked to structural factors, including a minimum wage that leaves even many full-time workers struggling. Below we examine some key arguments in the national debate over the minimum wage.

FIGURE 7.6 **Minimum Wage Rates in the United States, 2014**

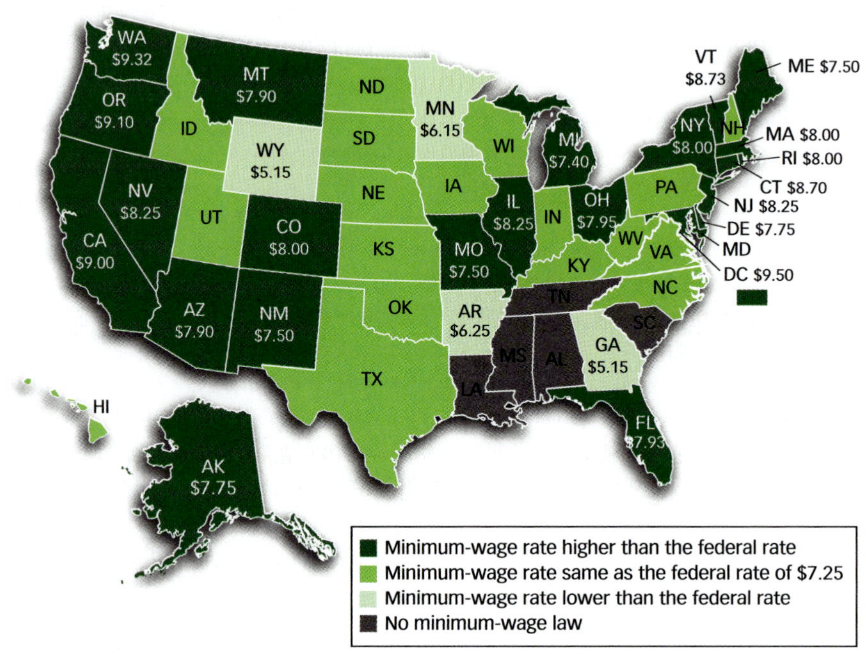

SOURCE: Minimum Wage Laws in the United States, January 1, 2014. United States Department of Labor.

In July 2009, the federal minimum wage rose to $7.25 an hour, the third and final increase mandated by the amended Fair Labor Standards Act. A full-time employee earning the federal minimum wage today makes a yearly pretax income of about $15,000. An effort by Democrats in Congress in early 2014 to mandate an increase in the minimum wage to $10.10 was blocked by Republican opponents.

Clearly, no one gets rich on the minimum wage—it is a *minimum* wage level legally mandated for U.S. workers (though exceptions exist in the law, such as one that applies to full-time students under the age of 20). But is it enough to ensure a minimum standard of living? Should the minimum wage be raised? Or should it be lowered or even abolished altogether?

Proponents of minimum wage laws and increases argue that the current minimum wage does not support the idea that "work pays." Many minimum wage workers earn below or just barely above the U.S. official poverty line. A single parent with one child working full-time at a minimum wage job is below the 2013 poverty threshold of $16,057 for one adult under age 65 supporting one child (U.S. Census Bureau, 2013c). An increased minimum wage, proponents argue, would have the potential to increase the standard of living of the neediest U.S. workers and their children.

From a macroeconomic perspective, higher wages also push up consumption because the poor spend all or most of their wages. This is beneficial for the economy, which is highly dependent on consumption; the government may also collect increased tax revenue as workers earn more income. Other benefits that proponents cite include greater employee motivation and retention, which lower the cost of training new employees, and less need for government support of poor workers in the form of food stamps and housing subsidies.

Opponents of minimum wage laws suggest that a federally mandated minimum wage hurts both low-wage workers and private businesses. They argue that mandated increases may reduce hiring as businesses seek to cut labor costs—the result is fewer jobs for those in the low-wage sector. Further, a rising minimum wage, say opponents, can discourage high school students from completing their education by enticing them to join the job market prematurely. Consumers may also be harmed as higher labor costs are passed on in the form of higher prices for goods and services. Finally, profit margins for small businesses, already slim, may be further reduced by mandated wage increases. Opponents of minimum wage laws assert that if such laws were abolished, markets would set the minimum wage by balancing what employers will pay with what employees will accept.

THINK IT THROUGH

▶ What is the answer to the minimum wage conundrum? Should the minimum wage be raised at the federal level? (Currently, 22 states and the District of Columbia have higher minimum wages than federal law requires.) How strong are the competing arguments on the two sides of the debate? Can you locate credible research supporting or challenging these arguments?

check and flowing out again as bills are paid and other goods of daily life are purchased—wealth has a more solid quality. Wealth represents possessions that do not flow into and out of the household regularly but instead provide a set of assets that can buy security, educational opportunity, and comfortable retirement years. The distribution of wealth gives us another important gauge of how U.S. families are doing relative to one another in terms of security, opportunity, and prospects.

Today more Americans than ever have money invested in the stock market—many through 401(k) and other retirement accounts. Does that mean wealth is more evenly spread across the population than before? No, it does not—in fact, the distribution of wealth is even more unequal than the income gap and, like that gap, is growing. If we exclude the ownership of cars and homes—which, as we noted, are not normally sources of wealth that people can use to pay regular bills or get richer—the difference in wealth between high-income families and everyone else is particularly pronounced. Figure 7.7 shows the expanding ratio of the average wealth of the top 1% and the national median wealth.

Minority groups hold far fewer net financial assets than Whites. The wealth held by minority households has historically lagged dramatically; for instance, in 1990, Black households held about 1% of total U.S. wealth (Conley, 1999). This percentage rose markedly in the economic boom years of the 1990s and continued to expand into the 2000s. Black household wealth reached an average of just over $12,000 in 2005. This climb, however, has been reversed by the housing crisis and the Great Recession, which saw a 53% fall in household wealth among Blacks to just $5,677. Among Hispanics, the fall was even more stark, with household wealth dropping 66% from a high of $18,359 in 2005. In the aftermath of the economic crisis, the median household wealth of Whites is fully 20 times that of Black households and 18 times that of Hispanic households (Kochhar, Fry, & Taylor, 2011).

Many U.S. families have zero or negative net worth, a condition worsened by the recent recession. Consider a Pew Research Center finding that while the median wealth of Latino households in 2009 was just over $6,000, nearly one third had zero or negative net worth, a figure that put them between White households (15% had zero or negative net worth) and Black households (35% had zero or negative net worth; Kochhar et al., 2011).

FIGURE 7.7 Wealth of Top 1%, 1962–2010

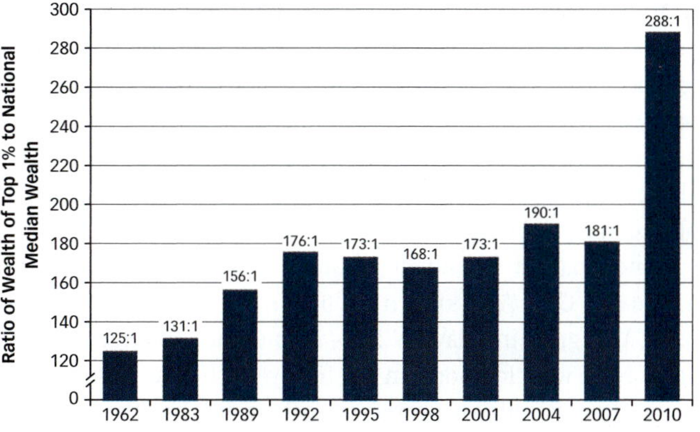

SOURCE: Wolff. (2012). "Ratio of average top 1% household wealth to median wealth, 1962–2010." *The State of Working America*. Washington, DC: Economic Policy Institute. Reprinted with permission.

© Jeremy Horner/Corbis

Many city neighborhoods lack access to large, well-stocked supermarkets with competitive prices. Residents must often choose between overpriced and often poor-quality goods, and a long trip to a suburban market. The low rates of private vehicle ownership among the urban poor can make shopping for healthy food a burden.

OTHER GAPS: INEQUALITIES IN HEALTH CARE, HEALTH, AND ACCESS TO CONSUMER GOODS

Along with the gap in income and wealth, there is a critical gap in employer benefits, including health insurance. From the 1980s to the 1990s, health care coverage for workers in the bottom quintile of earners fell more dramatically than for any other segment of workers: From a rate of 41% coverage it dropped to just 32% in the late 1990s (Reich, 2001). In 2011, about 25% of those living in households earning less than $25,000 a year were uninsured, along with more than 21% of those in households earning $25,000–$49,999 (U.S. Census Bureau, 2012c). Altogether, more than 15% (48.6 million) of the U.S. population was without health insurance, including 7 million children under age 18 (U.S. Census Bureau, 2012c).

Many of the jobs created in the 1980s and 1990s were positions in the service sector, which includes retail sales and food service. While the *quantity* of jobs created in this period helped push down the unemployment rate, the *quality* of jobs created for those with less education was not on par with the quality of many of the jobs lost as U.S. manufacturing became automated or moved overseas. Many service sector jobs pay wages at or just above minimum wage and have been increasingly unlikely to offer employer benefits.

One goal of President Obama's Patient Protection and Affordable Care Act (known simply as the Affordable Care Act or ACA), signed into law in 2010, is to expand insurance coverage for the working poor. In the first year the law was in effect, more than 8 million people signed up for health insurance plans under the Affordable Care Act, and 57% of those people had been uninsured before enrolling in ACA-compliant plans. Moreover, those who enrolled in ACA-compliant plans reported slightly worse health than nonenrollers, and most said that they would not have sought insurance if the law had not taken effect (Hamel et al., 2014).

Perhaps predictably, data show a powerful relationship between health and class status. Empirical data show that those with greater income and education are less likely than their less well-off peers to have and die of heart disease, diabetes, and many types of cancer. Just as income is distributed unevenly in the population, so is good health. Notably, modern medical advances have disproportionately provided benefits for those at the top of the income spectrum (Scott, 2005).

Children in disadvantaged families are more likely than their better-off peers to have poor physical and mental health. According to the Kaiser Family Foundation (2008), the rate of hospitalization for asthma for Black children is four to five times higher than that for White children. The problem is not only the lack of health insurance in families—though this factor is important—but also the lack of physical activity that may result when children don't have safe places to play and exercise, and when their families are unable to provide healthy foods because both money and access to such foods are limited.

The problem of poor health related to a lack of good food is linked to another disadvantage experienced by those on the lower economic rungs: lack of access to high-quality goods at competitive prices. Most middle-class shoppers purchase food at large chain grocery stores that stock items like fresh fruit and vegetables and meat at competitive prices. In contrast, inhabitants of poor neighborhoods are likely to shop at small stores that have less stock and higher prices, because large grocery chains choose not to locate in poor areas. If they want to shop at big grocery stores, poor residents may need to travel great distances, a substantial challenge for those who do not own cars.

Some writers have referred to *areas that lack sources of competitively priced healthy and fresh food* as **food deserts**. A *USA Today* article quotes Louisville retiree Jessie Caldwell, who regularly makes an hour-long bus trip to get fresh vegetables or meat: "For her and many others, it's often tempting to go to a more convenient mini-market or grab some fast food. 'The corner stores just sell a lot of potato chips, pop and ice cream,' she said. 'But people are going to eat what's available'" (Kenning & Halladay, 2008).

While we do not always think of access to stores with competitive prices and fresh goods as an issue of class inequality, lack of such access affects people's quality of life, conferring advantage on the already advantaged and disadvantage on those who struggle to make ends meet. Writer Barbara Ehrenreich (2001) highlights this point:

> There are no secret economies that nourish the poor; on the contrary, there are a host of special costs. If you

Food deserts: Areas that lack sources of competitively priced healthy and fresh food.

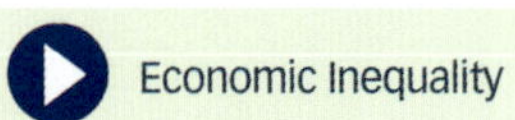

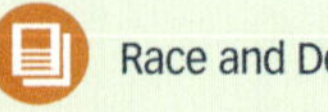

Economic Inequality

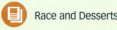

Race and Desserts

can't put up the two months' rent you need to secure an apartment, you end up paying through the nose for a room by the week. If you have only a room, with a hot plate at best, you can't save by cooking up huge lentil stews that can be frozen for the week ahead. You eat fast food and hot dogs and Styrofoam cups of soup that can be microwaved in a convenience store. (p. 27)

WHY HAS INEQUALITY GROWN?

There is a significant split between the fortunes of those who are well educated and those who do not or cannot attend college. The demand for labor over the past several decades has been differentiated on the basis of education and skills—workers with more education are more highly valued, while those with little education are becoming less valuable. These effects are among the results of the transition to a postindustrial economy in the United States.

The nation's earlier industrial economy was founded heavily on manufacturing. U.S. factories produced a substantial proportion of the goods Americans used—cars, washing machines, textiles, and the like—and a big part of the economy depended on this production for its prosperity. This is no longer the case. In the postindustrial economy of today, the United States manufactures a smaller proportion of the goods Americans consume and fewer goods overall. Many manufacturing jobs have either been mechanized or gone abroad, drawn to the low-cost labor in developing countries. New manufacturing jobs created in the United States offer lower wages overall than did their predecessors in the unionized factories of the industrial Midwest (we discuss this issue in greater detail in Chapter 15). The modern U.S. economy has produced larger numbers of jobs in the production of knowledge and information and the provision of services.

One group that has grown is made up of professionals who engage in what former secretary of labor Robert Reich (1991) has called "symbolic analysis," or "problem-solving, problem-identifying, and strategic-brokering activities" (p. 111). These occupational categories—law, engineering, business, technology, and the like—typically pay well and offer some job security, but they also require a high level of skill and at least a college education. Even well-educated middle-class workers, however, have been touched by automation and outsourcing. As well, a rising proportion of middle-level jobs have converted from relatively stable and secure long-term positions to contractual work. We examine these issues in greater detail in Chapter 15.

The fastest-growing sector of the postindustrial economy beginning in the 1980s was the service sector, which includes jobs in food service, retail sales, health care (for instance, home health aides and nurse's aides), janitorial and housecleaning services, and security. These jobs do not require advanced education or technical skills, but they typically pay poorly and offer weak job security and few benefits.

FIGURE 7.8 Job Losses and Gains in the U.S. Economy, 2008–2012

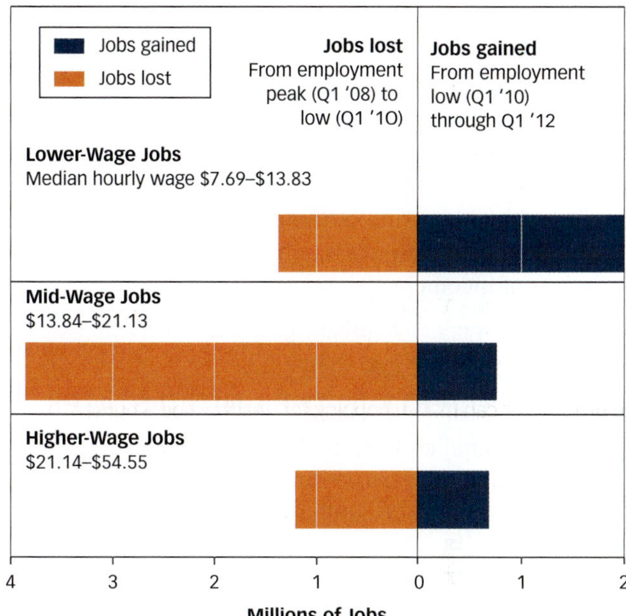

SOURCE: Adapted from National Employment Law Project, "The Low-Wage Recovery and Growing Inequality." Data Brief, August, 2012, p.2.

In the period following the official end of the Great Recession, the bulk of new jobs were low-wage positions, many of them service sector positions in areas like hospitality, tourism, and retail. While middle-wage, middle-skill jobs have failed to recover in the years after the economic crisis, jobs on the low end of the pay scale have multiplied (Figure 7.8). According to one estimate, fully 43% of jobs created since 2010 can be categorized as "low wage," paying $16 or less per hour. This may help explain the fact that while the unemployment rate has dipped in recent years, there have been meager gains in household income: In the period 2011–2012, the median U.S. household income grew by just 1.1% (Foroohar, 2014).

By providing jobs to those with less education, the service sector has, in a sense, moved into the void left by the manufacturing sector of the industrial economy over the past few decades. The service sector, which offers lower pay scales and fewer benefits, does not typically provide the kinds of jobs that offer a solid road to the middle class. Another difference is that manufacturing, especially in the automaking and steel industries, was overwhelmingly a male bastion, while service jobs favor women. The "advantage" enjoyed by less educated women over their male counterparts does not, however, translate into substantial economic gains for women or their families. Wage gains for women overall have been more fully driven by gains made by college-educated women.

The stratification of the U.S. labor force into a low-wage service sector and a better-paid knowledge and technology sector appears to be continuing unabated. The narrative of a "disappearing middle class" has become a common theme in both social science and mainstream political discourse. Do you see such a trend in your own community? How does this narrative coexist with Americans' long-existing tendency to self-identify as middle-class, almost regardless of income?

FIGURE 7.9 Poverty Levels in the United States, 1959–2013

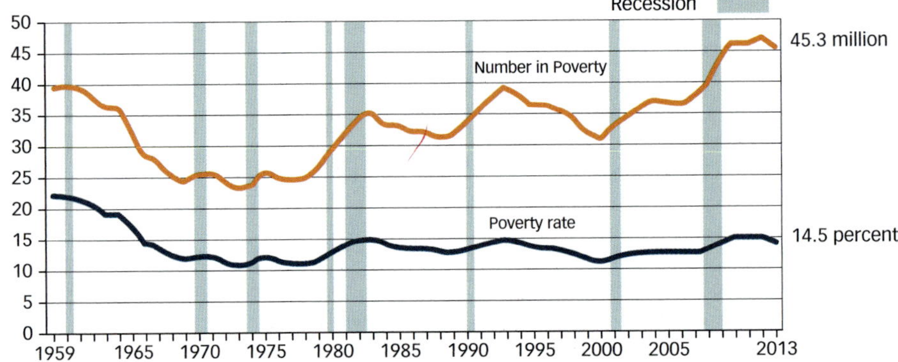

SOURCE: U.S. Census Bureau. (2012). Historical Poverty Tables—People. Poverty; Bishaw, A. (2013). Poverty: 2000 to 2012. American Community Survey Briefs. Washington, D.C.: U.S. Census Bureau

AT THE BOTTOM OF THE LADDER: POVERTY IN THE UNITED STATES

> There is a familiar America. It is celebrated in speeches and advertised on television and in the magazines. It has the highest mass standard of living the world has ever known.
>
> In the 1950s this America worried about itself, yet even its anxieties were products of abundance. . . . There was introspection about Madison Avenue and tail fins; there was discussion of the emotional suffering taking place in the suburbs. In all this, there was an implicit assumption that the basic grinding economic problems had been solved in the United States. . . .
>
> While this discussion was being carried on, there existed another America. In it dwelt between 40,000,000 and 50,000,000 citizens of this land. They were poor. They still are.
>
> To be sure, the other America is not impoverished in the same sense as those poor nations where millions cling to hunger as a defense against starvation. This country has escaped such extremes. That does not change the fact that tens of millions of Americans are, at this very moment, maimed in body and spirit, existing at levels beneath those necessary for human decency. If these people are not starving, they are hungry, and sometimes fat with hunger, for that is what cheap foods do. They are without adequate housing and education and medical care. (Harrington, 1963, pp. 1–2)

These words, first published in 1963, helped to open the eyes of many to the plight of the U.S. poor, who were virtually invisible to a postwar middle class comfortably ensconced in suburbia. Michael Harrington's classic book *The Other America: Poverty in the United States* also caught the interest of President John F. Kennedy's administration and later the Johnson administration, which inaugurated the War on Poverty in 1964.

When President Lyndon B. Johnson began his War on Poverty, around 36 million U.S. citizens lived in poverty. Within a decade, the number had dropped sharply, to around 23 million. But then, beginning in the early 1970s, poverty again began to climb, reaching a high of 39 million people in 1993 before receding. It has climbed once more, and since 2008 poverty has surpassed the peak set in 1993 (Figure 7.9). In 2013, the number of officially poor stood at nearly 45.3 million people—or about 14.5% of the population, a small drop from the prior year (DeNavas-Walt & Proctor, 2014).

We pause on the topic of "official poverty" because it is important for us to be critical consumers of information. We are surrounded by statistics, subject to a barrage of information about the proportion of the population who support the president or reject the health care initiatives of a political party, about the numbers of teen pregnancies and births, about the percentages who are unemployed or in poverty. These statistics illuminate the social world around us and offer us a sense of what we as a nation are thinking or earning or debating. On the other hand, statistics—including social indicators like the poverty numbers (Table 7.1)—may also obscure some important issues. To use indicators such as the poverty numbers wisely, we should know where they come from and what their limitations are.

What is poverty from the perspective of the U.S. government? How were these numbers generated? The **official poverty line** is *the dollar amount set by the government as the minimum necessary to meet the basic needs of a family.* In 2013, the U.S. government used the following thresholds:

- One person, under age 65: $12,119
- One person, 65 or older: $11,173

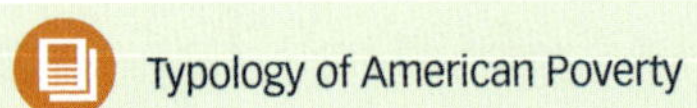

TABLE 7.1 Poverty Rates of Selected U.S. Subgroups, 2013

Category	Percentage
All people	**14.5**
Whites	12.3
Blacks	27.2
Hispanics	23.5
Asians	10.5
Married couples	5.8
Female heads of household, no husband present	30.6

SOURCE: U.S. Census Bureau. (2013). Income, poverty, and health insurance coverage in the United States: 2012. *Current Population Reports*. Washington, DC: C. DeNavas-Walt, B. D. Proctor, & J. C. Smith.

- Three persons (one adult, two children): $18,769
- Four persons (two adults, two children): $23,624
- Five persons (two adults, three children): $27,801

From the federal government's perspective, those whose pretax income falls beneath the threshold are officially poor; those whose pretax income is above the line (whether by $10 or $10 million) are "nonpoor." How are these thresholds generated? The *Behind the Numbers* box on page 170 explains.

Notably, official poverty numbers and the data we see in Table 7.1 offer us a picture of what the Census Bureau calls the "annual poverty rate." This figure captures the number of households whose total income over the 12 months of the year fell below the poverty threshold, but it does not illuminate how many families may have dropped into or climbed out of poverty and how many dwell there over a longer period. A recent Census Bureau report points out that while the official poverty figure is around 14.5%, in the period 2009 to 2011 about one third of U.S. households fell below the poverty threshold for at least 2 months. At the same time, just 3.5% remained poor for the full 3-year period under study (Edwards, 2014). While few households languish at the very bottom of the economic ladder for years, it is significant that nearly 10 times more households experienced periods of poverty.

Inequality and poverty in the United States are serious issues that demand both analysis and attention. While inequality is part of any modern capitalist state, the steep rise of inequality in recent decades presents a challenge to societal mobility and perhaps, ultimately, stability.

Official poverty line: The dollar amount set by the government as the minimum necessary to meet the basic needs of a family.

THE PROBLEM OF NEIGHBORHOOD POVERTY

In this section, we discuss the issue of concentrated poverty, looking specifically at measures, causes, and consequences of high levels of neighborhood (or area) poverty. We thus distinguish between household poverty, which an individual or family may experience while living in a mixed-income neighborhood, and neighborhood-level poverty. Notably, research suggests that being poor in a poor neighborhood has more negative social, economic, and educational effects than household poverty in a more economically heterogeneous context (Wilson, 2010). Neighborhood poverty affects those households that are poor, but it also affects those in the neighborhood who are not officially poor.

A recent Census Bureau report shows that a growing proportion of Americans reside in "poverty areas," defined in the report as census tracts featuring 20% or more households in poverty (Bishaw, 2014). (Census tracts are areas with between 1,200 and 8,000 residents; most tracts fall in the 4,000 range.) In 2000, just over 18% of U.S. inhabitants lived in poverty areas; by 2010, nearly a quarter did. Poverty areas can be rural, suburban, or urban: Just over half are in central cities, another 28% are in the suburbs, and about 20% are outside metropolitan areas (see Figure 7.10). Female-headed households are more likely than other family types to live in poverty areas: In 2010, more than 38% of female-headed households resided in areas with more than 20% poverty.

© Nathan Benn/CORBIS

Living in an impoverished neighborhood has significant consequences for both poor and non poor households. Diminished opportunities for work, education, consumption, and recreation affect entire neighborhoods.

BEHIND THE NUMBERS

CALCULATING U.S. POVERTY

How does the U.S. government measure poverty? In the early 1960s, an economist at the Social Security Administration, Mollie Orshansky, used a 1955 U.S. Department of Agriculture study to establish a poverty line. She learned from the study that about one third of household income went to food, so she calculated the cost of a "thrifty food basket" and tripled it to take into account other family needs such as transportation and housing. Then she adjusted the figure again to take into account the size and composition of the family and the age of the head of household. The result was the poverty threshold, which is illustrated in Figure 7.10.

Orshansky's formula represented the first systematic federal attempt to count the poor, and it has been in use for more than half a century. But its age makes it a problematic indicator for the 21st century. Some critics argue that it may underestimate the number of those struggling with material deprivation. Consider the following points:

- The multiplier of three was used because food was estimated to constitute one third of a family budget in the 1960s. Food is a smaller part of budgets today (about one fifth), and housing and transport are much bigger ones. Using a higher multiplier would raise the official poverty line and, consequently, increase the number of households classified as poor.
- The formula makes no adjustment for where people live, though costs of living vary tremendously by region. While a family of four may be able to make basic ends meet on a pretax income of $15,000 in South Dakota or Nebraska, it is doubtful that the housing costs of such areas as Boston, San Francisco, New York City and Washington, D.C., would permit our hypothetical family to survive in basic decency.

On the other hand, some critics have suggested that the poverty rate overestimates the problem, because it does not account for noncash benefits that some poor families receive, including food stamps and public housing vouchers. Adding the value of those (though they cannot be converted into cash) would increase the income of some families, possibly raising them above the poverty line.

FIGURE 7.10 The Poverty Threshold Calculation

SOURCE: U.S. Census Bureau. (2010). *Poverty: 2008 and 2009. American community survey briefs*. Washington, DC: A. Bishaw & S. Macartney.

We might thus conclude that while the official poverty statistics give us some sense of the problem of poverty and poverty trends over time, they must be read with a critical eye.

THINK IT THROUGH

▶ Taking into consideration forms of inequality and issues of poverty discussed in this chapter, how would you create an instrument to measure poverty in the United States? The current measurement focuses on a "crisis food basket." What variables would you include?

Sociologists study the development of poverty areas, particularly in urban neighborhoods (Wilson, 1996, 2010). The rise of the suburbs in the post–World War II period fostered the out-migration of many city residents, particularly members of the white middle class, and was accompanied by a shift of public resources to new neighborhoods outside cities. Public housing built in U.S. cities around the same period was intended to offer affordable domiciles for the poor, but it also contributed to the development of concentrated poverty, as policies foresaw income limitations that foreclosed the possibility of maintaining mixed-income neighborhoods. Racially discriminatory policies and practices, including limitations on Black access to mortgages or to homes in White neighborhoods, made Blacks far more vulnerable than their White counterparts to becoming trapped in poor neighborhoods. Even today, Black and Hispanic households are more likely to reside in poverty areas (Bishaw, 2014).

FIGURE 7.11 Percentages of Americans Living in Poor Neighborhoods, 2010

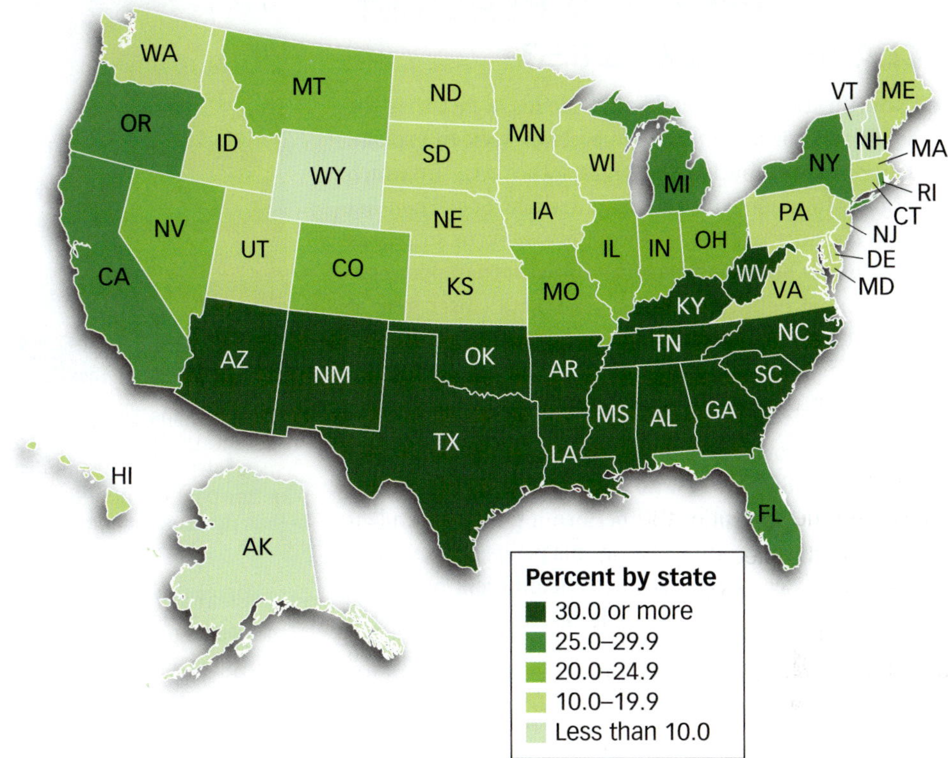

SOURCE: U.S. Census Bureau, 2008–2012 5-year American Community Survey.

As many families moved to the suburbs in the 1950s and 1960s, jobs eventually followed, contributing to a "spatial mismatch" between jobs in the suburbs and potential workers in urban areas (Wilson, 2010). The decline of manufacturing in the 1970s and the decades following also had a profound effect on some urban areas, such as Chicago and Detroit, which were deeply reliant on heavy industry for employment.

As noted earlier, area poverty compounds the negative effects of household poverty and presents challenges to all residents of economically disadvantaged neighborhoods. Research has shown, for instance, that nonpoor Black children are more likely than their White counterparts to reside in poor neighborhoods and to experience limitations to social mobility; even those in the top three income quintiles are vulnerable to downward economic mobility (Sharkey, 2009). Poor areas are more likely than better-off or even mixed-income neighborhoods to experience high levels of crime, to have low-quality housing and education, and to offer few job opportunities to residents (Federal Reserve System & Brookings Institution, 2008). Among the challenges to poor neighborhoods is that individual households that have enough resources to leave may choose to do so, contributing to even less circulating capital and an increasing withdrawal of businesses, fewer employed residents, weaker social and economic networks, and more empty buildings (Wilson, 1996). Cities like Detroit and Cleveland have, in fact, lost thousands of residents in recent decades.

The revival of economically devastated neighborhoods is an important public policy challenge. How can the fortunes of poor—particularly very poor—neighborhoods be reversed? How does such a process begin and what does it entail? What do you think?

In the following section we examine the issues of stratification and poverty from the functionalist and conflict perspectives. As you read, consider how these perspectives can be used as lenses for understanding phenomena like income and wealth inequality, household and neighborhood poverty, and other issues discussed above.

WHY DO STRATIFICATION AND POVERTY EXIST AND PERSIST IN CLASS SOCIETIES?

We find stratification in virtually all societies, a fact that the functionalist and social conflict perspectives seek to explain. The functionalist perspective highlights the ways in which stratification is functional for society as a whole. Social conflict theorists, in contrast, argue that inequality weakens society as a whole and exists because it benefits those in the upper economic, social, and political spheres. We take a closer look at each of these theoretical perspectives next.

THE FUNCTIONALIST EXPLANATION

Functionalism is rooted in part in the writings of sociologist Émile Durkheim (1893/1997), who suggested that we can best understand economic positions as performing interdependent functions for society as a whole. Using this perspective, we can think of social classes as equivalent to the different organs in the human body: Just as the heart, lungs, and kidneys serve different yet indispensable functions for human survival, so do the different positions in the class hierarchy.

In the middle of the 20th century, Kingsley Davis and Wilbert Moore (1945) built on these foundations to offer a detailed functionalist analysis of social stratification. They argued that in all societies some positions—the most "functionally important" positions—require more skill, talent, and training than others. These positions are thus difficult to fill—that is, they may suffer a "scarcity of personnel." To ensure they get filled, societies may offer valued rewards like money, prestige, and leisure to induce the best and brightest to make "sacrifices," such as getting a higher education, and to do these important jobs conscientiously and competently. According to Davis and Moore, social inequality is an "unconsciously evolved device by which societies ensure that the most important positions are conscientiously filled by the most qualified persons" (p. 243).

An implication of this perspective is that U.S. society is a **meritocracy**, *a society in which personal success is based on talent and individual effort.* That means your position in the system of stratification depends primarily on your talents and efforts: Each person gets more or less what he or she deserves or has earned, and society benefits because the most functionally important positions are occupied by the most qualified individuals. Stratification is then ultimately functional for society, because the differential distribution of rewards ensures that highly valued positions are filled by well-prepared and motivated people. After all, Davis and Moore might say, we all benefit when we get economic information from good economists, drive across bridges designed by well-trained engineers, and cure our ills with pharmaceuticals developed by capable medical scientists.

SARAH LEEN/National Geographic Creative

Herbert Gans suggests that poverty ensures a pool of workers "unable to be unwilling" to do difficult and dirty jobs for low pay. Such jobs could also be filled in the absence of poverty—through better pay and benefits. But, says Gans, this would be costly, and thus dysfunctional, to the nonpoor.

Clearly the idea that the promise of higher pay and prestige motivates people to work hard has some truth. Yet it is difficult to argue that the actual differences in rewards across positions are necessarily suitable ways of measuring the positions' relative worth to society (Tumin, 1953, 1963, 1985; Wrong, 1959). Is an NBA point guard really worth more than a teacher or a nurse, for instance? Is a hedge fund manager that much more important than a scientist (particularly given that both positions require extensive education)?

Moreover, when people acquire socially important, higher-status positions by virtue of their skills and efforts, they are then often able to pass along their economic privilege, and the educational opportunities and social connections that go with it, to their children, even if their children are not particularly bright, motivated, or qualified. As Melvin Tumin (1953) points out in his critique of Davis and Moore, stratification may *limit* the discovery of talent in society rather than *ensuring* it, by creating a situation in which those who are born to privilege are given fuller opportunities and avenues to realize occupational success while others are limited by poor schooling, little money, and lack of networks upon which to call. Such a result would surely be dysfunctional for society rather than positively functional.

How would functionalism account for the fact that people are often discriminated against because of their skin color, sex, and other characteristics determined at birth that have nothing to do with their talents or motivations, resulting in an enormous waste of society's human skills and talents? Can you see other strengths or weaknesses to Davis and Moore's perspective on stratification?

Meritocracy: A society in which personal success is based on talent and individual effort.

In a twist on the functionalist perspective, sociologist Herbert Gans (1972) poses this provocative question: How is poverty positively functional in U.S. society? Gans begins with a bit of functionalist logic, namely, that if a social phenomenon exists and persists, it must serve a function or else it would evolve out of existence. But he does not assume that poverty is functional for everyone. So *for whom* is it functional? Gans suggests that eliminating poverty would be costly to the better-off. Thus, poverty is functional for the nonpoor, but not functional for the poor—or even for society as a whole.

Among the "benefits" to the nonpoor of the existence of a stratum of poor people, Gans includes the following:

- Poverty ensures there will be low-wage laborers prepared—or driven by circumstances—to do society's "dirty work." These are the jobs no one else wants because they are demeaning, dirty, and sometimes dangerous. A large pool of laborers desperate for jobs also pushes down wages, a benefit to employers.
- Poverty creates a spectrum of jobs for people who help the poor (social welfare workers), protect society from those poor people who transgress the boundaries of the law (prison guards), or profit from the poor (owners of welfare motels and cheap grocery shops). Even esteemed sociologist Herbert Gans has built an academic career on analyzing poverty.
- Poverty provides a market for goods and services that would otherwise go unused. Day-old bread, wilting fruits and vegetables, and old automobiles are not generally purchased by the better-off. The services of second-rate doctors and lawyers, among others, are also peddled to the poor when no one else wants them.
- Beyond economics, the poor also serve cultural functions. They provide scapegoats for society's problems and help guarantee some status for those who are not poor. They also give the upper crust of society a socially valued reason for holding and attending lavish charity events.

Gans's (1972) point is stark. He notes that the "functions" served by the poor have *functional alternatives*—that is, they could be fulfilled by means other than poverty. However, he suggests, those who are better-off in society are not motivated to fight poverty comprehensively because its existence is demonstrably functional for them. While he is not arguing that anyone is in favor of poverty (which is difficult to imagine), he is suggesting that "phenomena like poverty can be eliminated only when they become dysfunctional for the affluent or powerful, or when the powerless can obtain enough power to change society" (p. 288). Do you agree with his argument? Why or why not?

THE SOCIAL CONFLICT EXPLANATION

Social conflict theory draws heavily from the work of Karl Marx. As we saw in the opening chapter, Marx divided society into two broad classes: workers and capitalists, or *proletarians* and *bourgeoisie*. The workers do not own the factories and machinery needed to produce wealth in capitalist societies—they possess nothing of real value except their labor power. The capitalists own the necessary equipment—the *means of production*—but require the labor power of the workers to run it.

Dimas Ardian / Stringer/Getty Images

The poor often face limited choices in terms of housing, employment, and transportation due to financial constraints. Their options are restricted by affordability with little room for personal preference. They may find themselves forced to purchase low-quality products, such as the decrepit vehicles pictured above.

These economic classes are unequal in their access to resources and power, and their interests are opposed. Capitalists seek to keep labor costs as low as possible in order to produce goods cheaply and make a profit. Workers seek to be paid adequate wages and to secure safe, decent working conditions and hours. At the same time, the two groups are interdependent: The capitalists need the labor of the workers, and the workers depend on the wages they earn (regardless of how meager) to survive.

Although more than a century has passed since Marx formulated his theory, a struggle between workers and owners (or, in our time, between workers and owners, managers, and even stockholders, who all depend on a company's profits) still exists. Conflict is often based on the irreconcilability of these competing interests. A recent study found that collective action lawsuits alleging wage and hour violations have skyrocketed, increasing 400% in the past 11 years. Among companies such as Bank of America, Walmart, and Starbucks, Taco Bell has been one of the latest to be sued for allegedly forcing employees to work overtime without pay (Eichler, 2012).

The source of inequality, from this perspective, lies in the fact that the bourgeoisie own the means of production and can use their assets to make more money and secure their position in society. Most workers do not own substantial economic assets aside from their own labor power, which they use to earn a living. While successful lawsuits for lost wages show that workers have avenues for asserting their

INEQUALITY MATTERS

CHILD LABOR IN THE 21ST CENTURY

In early industrial America, some poor families sent children to work to support their households. Many employers welcomed young laborers, who were perceived to be more passive and less expensive than adult workers. Children worked in a variety of settings, including in canneries and the meatpacking industry, in the manufacture of textiles, and in agriculture; some peddled goods or shined shoes. Early in the 20th century, Congress passed two separate laws (in 1918 and 1922) seeking to regulate child labor, but the U.S. Supreme Court declared both unconstitutional. With the support of unions and other activists, however, the Fair Labor Standards Act of 1938 set minimum ages and maximum hours for young workers. These standards remain in effect today: 16 is the minimum age for work during school hours, and 14 is the minimum for certain jobs that can be done after school hours. For designated "dangerous" jobs, 18 is the minimum age.

A report released by the nonprofit advocacy group Human Rights Watch in 2014, however, raises the question of whether child labor in the United States is only a thing of the past. The introduction to the report, which focuses on child labor in the farming of tobacco, states:

> Ninety percent of tobacco grown in the US is cultivated in four states: North Carolina, Kentucky, Tennessee, and Virginia. Between May and October 2013, Human Rights Watch interviewed 141 child tobacco workers, ages 7 to 17, who worked in these states in 2012 or 2013. Nearly three-quarters of the children interviewed by Human Rights Watch reported the sudden onset of serious symptoms—including nausea, vomiting, loss of appetite, headaches, dizziness, skin rashes, difficulty breathing, and irritation to their eyes and mouths—while working in fields of tobacco plants and in barns with dried tobacco leaves and tobacco dust. Many of these symptoms are consistent with acute nicotine poisoning. (pp. 3–4)

The report also notes that "child tobacco workers often labor 50 or 60 hours a week in extreme heat, use dangerous tools and machinery, lift heavy loads, and climb into the rafters of barns several stories tall, risking serious injuries and falls" (p. 3), and describes their exposure to the agricultural pesticides used in tobacco farming.

Why is it the case that more than 70 years after the passage of the Fair Labor Standards Act young workers are toiling in American tobacco fields? One important reason is that the laws

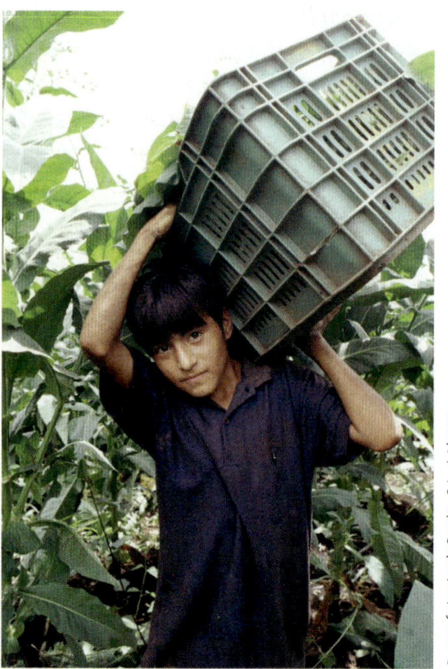
© age fotostock Spain, S.L. / Alamy

pertaining to child labor are far more lax regarding agricultural labor than they are concerning other forms of work. For example, from age 12, children can be hired for unlimited hours outside school hours with parental permission; on small farms, there is no minimum age. Of course, children have worked on family farms for centuries, helping to sow and reap crops and tend farm animals. Government interference in rural traditions surrounding the family farm has not been welcomed. According to Human Rights Watch, however, most of the child workers interviewed in its study are not supporting their own family farms; most are, according to a *Washington Post* editorial on the subject, "day laborers, migrants or the children of migrants; some have U.S. citizenship, others don't" ("Obama Administration," 2014).

The editorial also points to a second reason that child agricultural labor is lightly regulated in spite of its consequences for young people and potential for exploitation: Rural agricultural interests have lobbied the U.S. Department of Labor in an effort to prevent passage of more restrictive laws. In 2012, for instance, they succeeded in derailing a department proposal to tighten rules on child labor. Notably, prior to the passage of child labor laws in the early 20th century, industrial and agricultural interests did not support the prohibition or regulation of child labor, which was cheap and beneficial to their production. In the early 21st century, the effort to protect children from dangerous labor is being waged—as it was a hundred years ago—by outside advocacy organizations, including Human Rights Watch and some immigrants' rights groups.

THINK IT THROUGH

▶ If parents permit their children to work in order to supplement household income, should child labor in the tobacco fields (or other agricultural or even industrial settings) be permitted? What is the government's appropriate role in regulating child labor? Who benefits from permissive laws on child labor? Who loses?

rights against employers, the conflict perspective contrasts these small victories with the far more significant power and control exercised by large economic actors in modern society.

In short, the conflict perspective suggests that significant and persistent stratification exists because those who have power use it to create economic, political, and social conditions that favor them and their children, even if these conditions are detrimental to the lower classes. Inequality thus is not functional, as Davis and Moore argued. Rather, it is dysfunctional, because it keeps power concentrated in the hands of the few rather than creating conditions of meritocracy that would give equal opportunity to all.

Like the functionalist perspective, the conflict perspective has analytical weaknesses. It overlooks cooperative aspects of modern capitalist businesses, some of which have begun to take a more democratic approach to management, offering workers the opportunity to participate in decision-making processes in the workplace. Modern workplaces in the technology sector, for instance, thrive when decision making and the production of ideas come from various levels rather than just from the top down.

WHY STUDY INEQUALITY?

Many people today struggle to make ends meet on wages that have stagnated in recent decades. As we saw in this chapter's opening story, the downward mobility of many in the U.S. middle class is spawning new investor interest in market sectors like low-cost trailer parks. We have looked at the dimensions of both class and inequality in the United States and asked why inequality exists and persists.

The questions raised by the theoretical perspectives we have studied are not just academic: They are critical to our understanding of the world in which we live and in which (if we so choose) we will raise our children. Is it the case, as functionalists Davis and Moore asserted, that inequality is positively functional for society, and that we collectively benefit from it because it ensures that the best and brightest take the most important jobs? Or, as Tumin argues, does inequality ensure just the opposite, limiting the discovery of the full range of talent in society? How much should we worry about inequality and its growth? The answer may depend on whether we subscribe to the functionalist or the conflict view of socioeconomic stratification.

What about poverty? Poverty in individual cases may be the result of bad luck or poor choices, but the sheer magnitude of the problem of poverty suggests that it has structural roots as well, and a full explanation cannot be found at the individual level. Neighborhood poverty, as we have seen, is also a key public issue, though it is certainly experienced as a personal trouble, even by residents of poor neighborhoods who are not poor. Why does poverty exist and persist in a country that is arguably the wealthiest in the world? This is a question that asks us to fire up our sociological imaginations.

The topics of class and inequality are among sociology's most fundamental concerns. Recall that some of sociology's important theoretical roots are in analyses of early industrial capitalism and its effects on society and the economy. Today, challenges include understanding the roots of growing income inequality, the effects of postindustrialism on different social groups, and the causes and consequences of contemporary household and neighborhood poverty. What are the questions about class and inequality that you find most compelling, and how would you go about studying them?

WHAT CAN I DO WITH A SOCIOLOGY DEGREE?

SKILLS AND CAREERS: QUANTITATIVE RESEARCH SKILLS

Sociologists use quantitative research skills to conduct systematic empirical investigations of social phenomena using statistical methods. *Quantitative research comprises those studies in which data are expressed in terms of numbers.* The objective of quantitative research in sociology is to gather rigorous data and to use those numerical data to characterize the dimensions of an issue or the extent of a problem (this could include, for instance, the collection of statistical data on rates of obesity and poverty in neighborhoods or states and the calculation of the correlation of the two phenomena) and, often, to use those data to develop or test hypotheses about the roots of the problem at hand.

In Chapter 7, we saw a broad spectrum of quantitative data; such a spectrum is key to both academic studies and policy making on issues such as poverty, wealth and income inequality, and postindustrial changes in the labor market. We cited data collected by the U.S. government to measure household incomes and to establish the dimensions of the division of aggregate income across quintiles of earners. We also looked at data collected by the Pew Research Center on the gaps in net worth between Whites, Blacks, and Latinos. As you advance in your sociological studies, you will have the opportunity to become familiar with quantitative data on important sociological issues and to see how these data are used in analyses—and you will have the opportunity to learn how to do quantitative sociology. For example, you might learn to measure and compare trends in income differences by race, ethnicity, and gender or to assess the significance of variables such as neighborhood unemployment, educational attainment, and median income as predictors of neighborhood street crime.

Knowledge of quantitative methods is a valuable skill in today's job market. Learning quantitative methods of research, which is an important part of a sociological education, prepares you to do a wide variety of *job tasks,* including survey development, questionnaire design, market research, brand health tracking, and financial quantitative modeling and analysis. These kinds of tasks are commonly part of the *job descriptions* of, among others, market research analysts, marketing specialists, social science research assistants, clinical research coordinators, criminal justice and law enforcement teachers, financial quantitative analysts, markets quantitative analysts, and statistical research analysts. These are jobs that can be found in a variety of *occupational fields,* including education, marketing, criminal justice, health and medicine, business and management, finance, and social science research.

THINK ABOUT CAREERS

▶ Social statistics are used in a broad variety of analyses of the social world, and researchers often use quantitative methods to study relationships between different sociological variables. How do you think the job tasks of people who use quantitative data in occupational fields such as marketing, health, criminal justice, and business might be similar to and different from what quantitative sociologists do?

SUMMARY

- Class societies are more open than caste societies. In a **caste society**, a person's position in the hierarchy is determined by ascribed characteristics such as race or birth status. In a **class society**, a person's position is determined by what he or she achieves, and mobility is looked upon favorably. However, barriers to mobility similar to those in caste societies still exist in class societies.

- **Class** refers to a person's economic role in society, associated with income, wealth, and the type of work he or she does. Class position strongly influences an individual's **life chances**—the opportunities and obstacles he or she encounters in areas such as education, social life, and work. Important components of class position are occupation, income, and wealth.

- We can measure inequality in the United States by looking at disparities in **income**, **wealth**, health, and access to credit and goods. All these indicators show that inequality in the United States is substantial and growing.

- Since the early 1970s, the gap between the rich and the poor has grown, as has the gap between the rich and everyone else. Some of this growth is attributable to the transformation of the U.S. economy from industrial to postindustrial, which has helped the best educated and hurt the least educated.

- Poverty is a significant problem in the United States: In 2013, 14.5% of the population was officially poor. The formula used to measure poverty gives us a sense of the problem, but it has limitations of which we should be aware.

- Researchers distinguish between household (or individual) poverty and neighborhood poverty. Studies suggest that living in a poor neighborhood amplifies the effects of poverty and also poses challenges, including limited mobility, for nonpoor residents.

- Functionalist theorists argue that inequality exists and persists because it is positively functional for society. According to this perspective, inequality is necessary to motivate the best people to assume the most important occupational positions.

- Conflict theorists argue that the privileged classes benefit from inequality and that inequality inhibits the discovery of talented people rather than fostering it. This perspective suggests that classes with differential access to power and resources are in conflict and that the interests of the well-off are most likely to be realized.

KEY TERMS

social inequality, 157
social stratification, 157
caste society, 157
class society, 158
social categories, 158
achieved status, 158
ascribed status, 158
class, 159
life chances, 159
social mobility, 159
income, 160
wealth (or net worth), 160
net financial assets, 161
occupation, 161
status, 161
political power, 161
food deserts, 166
official poverty line, 169
meritocracy, 172

DISCUSSION QUESTIONS

1. What is the difference between wealth and income? Why is it sociologically important to make a distinction between the two? Which is greater in the United States today, the income gap or the wealth gap?
2. What are the key dimensions and trends related to income inequality in the United States today? What about wealth inequality? How would you expect these trends to evolve or change in the coming decade? Explain your reasoning.
3. Herbert Gans talks about the "uses of poverty" for the nonpoor. Recall some of his points presented in the chapter and then add some of your own. Would you agree with the argument Gans makes about the existence and persistence of poverty? Why or why not?
4. How is the poverty rate determined in the United States? What is the origin of this formula, and what are its strengths and weaknesses?
5. What is the difference between individual or household poverty and neighborhood poverty? Why is the distinction important? How does being poor in a poor neighborhood amplify the effects of economic disadvantage?

Sharpen your skills with SAGE edge at **edge.sagepub.com/chambliss2e**

A personalized approach to help you accomplish your coursework goals in an easy-to-use learning environment.

© Lisa Wiltse/Corbis

GLOBAL INEQUALITY AND POVERTY

IN THIS CHAPTER

Reuters/Carlos Jasso

WHAT DO YOU THINK?

1. What is global inequality? What indicators can be used to measure it?
2. Why are some countries tremendously prosperous while others are desperately poor?
3. How might the spread of modern technologies like mobile phones have an impact on inequality?

Reuters/Finbarr O'Reilly (CHAD)

WEALTH AND POVERTY ON THE ROAD

How did you get to your sociology class today? Perhaps you walked from your dormitory, or maybe you took a bus or the subway to the campus. You may have driven a car or ridden your bicycle from home or work. How did you reach your last vacation destination? Did you fly, drive, or maybe take the train? Did you go by ship? There are many ways in which we reach the places we need or want to go—school, a job, the doctor's office, the mall, an amusement park, a friend's home. The means people choose—or are compelled by circumstances to use—to get where they are going can tell us something about their economic conditions as well. Consider the following two stories.

According to a recent article in the *New York Times*: "If you wish and are a person of means, you can fly first-class round trip in luxury between Los Angeles and Dubai on an Emirates Airline A380 superjumbo jet. You will enjoy superb food and drink and be cosseted in a private compartment with a sliding door, a lie-flat seat with mattress, a vanity, a personal minibar and flat-screen television set, and a luxury bathroom down the aisle where you can take a shower. The fare: $32,840" (Sharkey, 2014). The article points out that in the middle of the 20th century, flying was often luxurious, but it was largely limited to the very few passengers who could afford air travel in its early days. By the 1970s, more Americans had economic access to air travel as fares fell, but the level of airborne comfort became increasingly stratified in the decades that followed. The article notes that "technology, including elaborate premium cabin and in-flight entertainment innovations, began more sharply delineating first and business class from coach when British Airways and Virgin Atlantic introduced lie-flat beds in luxurious new international business-class cabins in the mid-'90s." Today, "premium passengers" account for just over 8% of the share of fliers; the rest share the increasingly cramped quarters of economy class high in the sky.

On the ground, 30,000 feet below the jets crisscrossing the world's oceans and continents, many communities are unable to meet even the most basic transportation needs. According to a report by

World Bank researchers, women in particular struggle across much of the developing world with finding safe, reliable, and affordable transportation: "Women in most developing countries have very limited access to transport services and technology. This imposes severe constraints on their access to health, education and other social facilities and services, making them and their children more vulnerable to serious injury or death as a result of childbirth or another medical emergency" (Riverson, Kunieda, Roberts, Lewi, & Walker, 2006, p. 2). Among the problems encountered by women are lack of access even to donkeys, mules, or wheelbarrows to carry water or firewood: "Consequently the women experienced not only the physical burden of transportation by back loading and head loading but also the time burden as a result of the lack of transport" (p. 4). Amnesty International (2010) has focused a campaign on rural South African women whose lack of access to transportation puts them at greater risk of illness or injury, as it limits their ability to reach health providers or shelter from gender-based violence. ■

Across the globe, countries, communities, and households are stratified: While some struggle to meet the most basic needs, others enjoy comfortable lives, broad opportunities, and modern amenities. We begin this chapter with a look at the some of the dimensions of global inequality, examining such factors as per capita income, literacy, education, sanitation, and health in order to understand more about the hierarchy of countries that exists in our global system. We consider one area—mobile technology—where the gap is closing. This is followed by a look at theoretical perspectives that seek to understand why these deep global disparities exist and persist. We then consider the question of whether there exists a global elite that crosses national boundaries and what its characteristics may be. We end with a brief consideration of the question of why sociologists take an interest in global inequality.

DIMENSIONS OF GLOBAL INEQUALITY AND POVERTY

Much of the world is poor. According to the Population Reference Bureau (2011), about 48% of the earth's inhabitants live on the equivalent of less than $2 a day. Almost all of these deeply impoverished people live in the developing world. Just a small fraction of the world's population consumes much of its valued resources: The United States is home to less than 5% of the globe's population but uses about a fifth of the oil, coal, and natural gas produced globally (U.S. Energy Information Administration, 2011).

Global inequality: The systematic disparities in income, wealth, health, education, access to technology, opportunity, and power among countries, communities, and households around the world.

We can identify a global class system with some very wealthy states (although, of course, as we saw in Chapter 7, not all their inhabitants share the good fortune), some very poor states, and a wide swath of countries in between (Figure 8.1). In this chapter, we look at some of the dimensions of this **global inequality**, which can be defined as the *systematic disparities in income, wealth, health, education, access to technology, opportunity, and power among countries, communities, and households around the world.* While the focus is largely on differences among countries, we will see that these are only one part of a broader picture of global inequality.

We follow the World Bank in categorizing countries using four economic categories: high income, upper-middle income, lower-middle income, and low income (Figure 8.1). Beginning in July 2014, the World Bank defined these classifications quantitatively using the following gross national income (GNI) per capita limits:

- Low-income economies: $1,045 or less
- Lower-middle-income economies: $1,046 to $4,125
- Upper-middle-income economies: $4,126 to $12,745
- High-income economies: $12,746 or more

Qualitatively, we can describe the *high-income countries* as those that are highly industrialized, characterized by the presence of mass education, and both urbanized and technologically advanced. Among the high-income countries we find nations such as the United States, Canada, Japan, Germany, Norway, Estonia, and Australia. High-income countries are home to about 15% of the global population.

More than 70% of the world's population lives in *middle-income countries* (the lower- and upper-middle categories combined), which include a wide variety of nations, among them former Soviet states like Armenia and Belarus; South and Central American states like Brazil and Belize; Middle Eastern countries like Lebanon and Iran; Asian states such as Indonesia, India, and China; and African countries like Morocco and Senegal. Many of these countries are on a path to economic diversification and development, though most also started down the road to urbanization and industrialization much later than the high-income countries and still lag in instituting mass education. Some middle-income countries, like those in the Middle East and Africa, are home to vast natural resources, though the conversion of those resources to shared prosperity has, for reasons that theorists and observers debate, not been widespread.

CQR Global Wealth Disparities

World Poverty and Education

FIGURE 8.1 High-Income, Upper-Middle-Income, Lower-Middle-Income, and Low-Income Countries

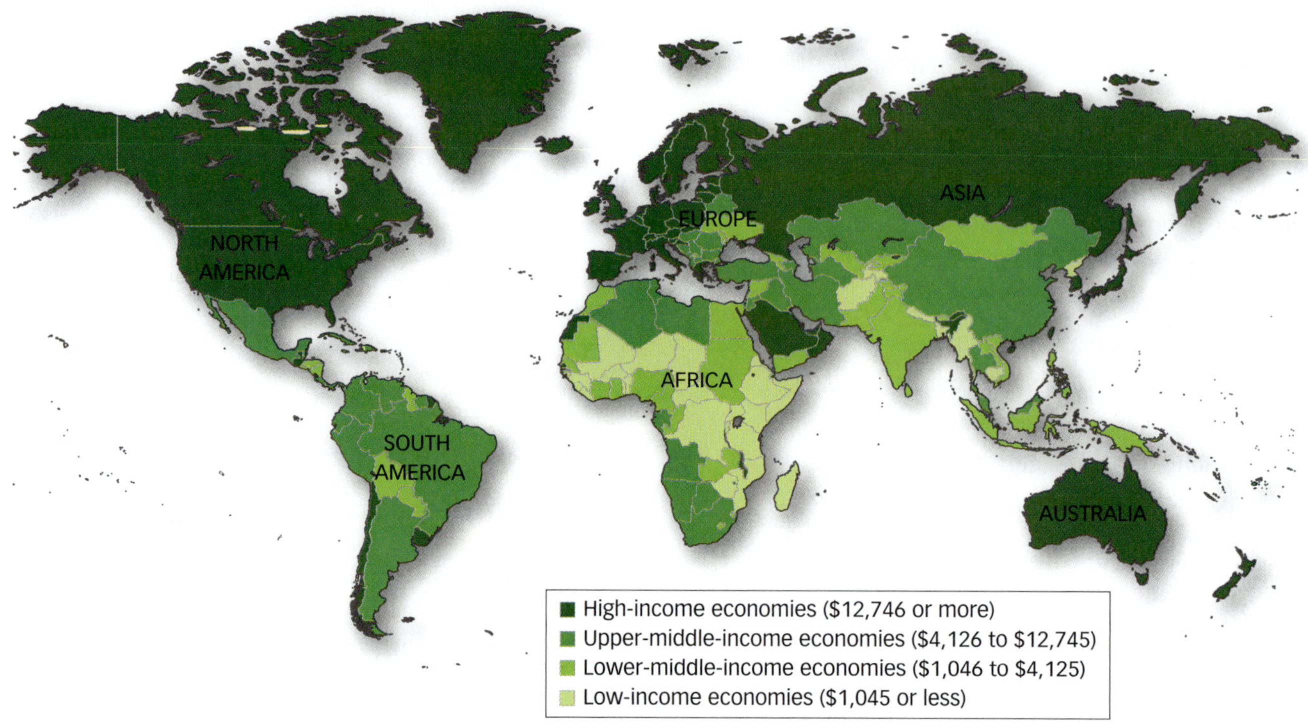

SOURCE: Country and Lending Groups. The World Bank.

Like high-income countries, *low-income countries* constitute a relatively small proportion of the global total. Many are agricultural states with rapidly growing populations. While urbanization is a growing phenomenon, cities in these countries often lack the jobs and services that rural migrants seek, and both rural and urban dwellers struggle with hunger and malnutrition, economic and educational deprivatioon, and preventable diseases. Low-income countries may have small and wealthy groups of elites, but they lack stable middle-class populations. Low-income countries include South Asian states like Bangladesh and Cambodia, as well as Africa's poorest countries, like Somalia and the Central African Republic.

In the remainder of this section, we describe some of ways in which inequalities are manifested around the globe. Later in the chapter, we consider the key question of *why* this inequality exists and persists and examine various theoretical perspectives on the issue.

We begin with a look at **gross national income–purchasing power parity per capita (GNI-PPP)**, *a comparative economic measure that uses international dollars to indicate the amount of goods and services someone could buy in the United States with a given amount of money.* At one end of the class spectrum, we find countries with very high GNI-PPP, such as the United States ($50,610), Canada ($42,690), Norway ($64,030), Switzerland ($54,870), and Japan ($36,320). In the middle are countries ranging from South Korea ($30,890) and Estonia ($21,990) to Turkey ($17,500) and Brazil ($11,720). At the bottom are countries whose GNI-PPP can be as low as that of Nicaragua ($3,960) or Kenya ($1,760; Population Reference Bureau, 2013). While GNI-PPP cannot tell us a great deal about the resources of individual families in the given countries, it gives us some insight into the economic resources available to the state and society from a macro perspective, and it offers a comparative measure for looking at stratification in the global system.

HUNGER, MORTALITY, AND FERTILITY IN POOR COUNTRIES

As we saw in our discussion of social stratification in the United States, one important indicator of inequality is health. One key aspect of good health is adequate food, in terms of both sufficient calories and good nutrition. While the world has the capacity to produce enough food for all its inhabitants, the Food and Agriculture Organization of the United Nations (2012) estimates that 870,000 million people are chronically undernourished, including about 15% of the population of developing states. At the turn of the millennium,

Gross national income–purchasing power parity per capita (GNI-PPP): A comparative economic measure that uses international dollars to indicate the amount of goods and services someone could buy in the United States with a given amount of money.

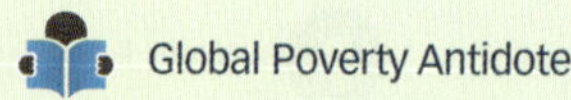

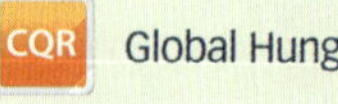

BEHIND THE NUMBERS

THE CHALLENGE OF MEASURING GLOBAL POVERTY

The United Nations estimates that in 2013, about 1.2 billion people around the world were living in "extreme poverty." The U.N. *Millennium Development Goals Report 2013* offers both encouraging and discouraging figures in its review of the organization's goals on poverty reduction in the world's most economically disadvantaged communities and countries. On one hand, the report points out that "poverty rates have been halved, and about 700 million fewer people lived in conditions of extreme poverty in 2010 than in 1990" (United Nations, 2013b, p. 6). On the other hand, improvements have not reached every region: "Sub-Saharan Africa is the only region that saw the number of people living in extreme poverty rise steadily, from 290 million in 1990 to 414 million in 2010" (p. 7).

When the United Nations offers these figures to show both progress and stagnation in the pursuit of development goals, what do the numbers illuminate about the condition of countries, communities, and households—and what do they obscure?

The measure used to obtain the figures—including 1.2 billion living in extreme poverty worldwide and 48% in sub-Saharan Africa and 30% in Southern Asia living in extreme poverty—is the absolute poverty threshold of "living on less than $1.25 a day." The measure, then, is based on income, largely as reported by countries themselves using national household surveys (United Nations, 2013b, pp. 6–7).

In a historical perspective on poverty, economist Peter Townsend (2006) points out that "poverty concepts have evolved, based on ideas of subsistence, basic needs and relative deprivation" (p. 5). *Subsistence* implies that those below the poverty line lack the resources to sustain their basic physical needs. An income threshold such as that used by the United Nations is one way of using "subsistence" to define poverty.

The idea of *basic needs* represents recognition of poverty as a condition of multiple deprivations. Consistent with the declaration adopted at the World Summit on Social Development in 1995, absolute poverty can be understood qualitatively as "a condition characterized by severe deprivation of human needs, including food, safe drinking water, sanitation facilities, health, shelter, education, and information. It depends not only on income but also on access to services" (quoted in Gordon, 2005). In this conception, poverty is recognized as a condition in which one is deprived of economic and social needs. The United Nations Development Programme does, in fact, use as a measure the multidimensional Human Poverty Index (HPI), which draws together phenomena like early mortality risk, adult illiteracy, and access to safe drinking water. Interestingly, income poverty and "human poverty" are not always correlated as one might expect: Some countries with low income poverty have high "human

FIGURE 8.2 **Percentages of People Living on Less Than $1.25 a Day, 1990, 2005, and 2010**

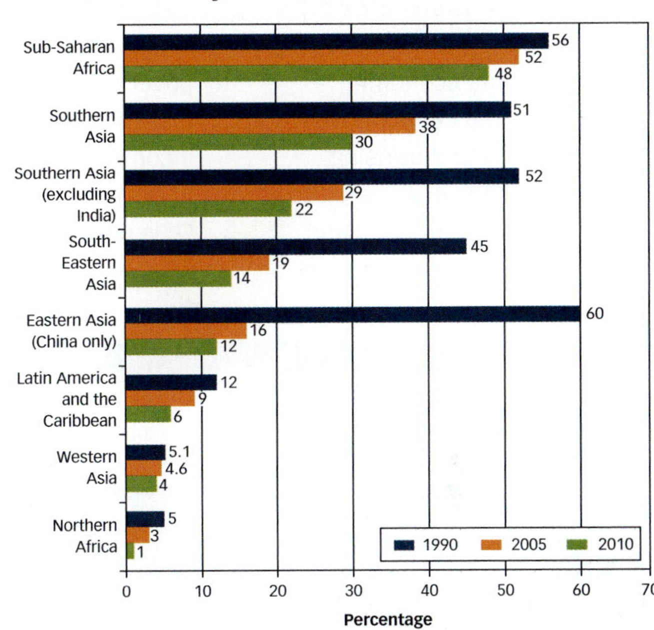

SOURCE: *The Millennium Development Goals Report 2013*. Copyright © United Nations, 2013. Reprinted with permission from the United Nations.

NOTE: No sufficient country data are available to calculate the aggregate values for Oceania.

poverty" because investment in public resources like education and health is low; other countries with higher income poverty have better measures on the HPI because they offer more expansive services to poor populations (Fukuda-Parr, 2006).

Relative deprivation is a newer formulation of the concept of poverty that puts economic disadvantage in a comparative frame, recognizing that rising standards of living in some places render more acute the real and perceived deprivations in others. Townsend (2006) writes that, in this perspective, "poor people are not just the victims of a maldistribution of resources but . . . they lack, or are denied, the resources to fulfill social demands and observe the customs, as well as the unfolding laws, of society" (p. 6).

What, then, is poverty? Absolute poverty on a global scale is widely measured as living below the income threshold of $1.25 per day. But is poverty only about income? Or is poverty a more broadly experienced marginality that is social, educational, and political, as well as economic? Should poverty be measured relative to a societal or community-defined standard of living? What do you think?

THINK IT THROUGH

▶ How useful are measures like the $1.25 per day income measure of poverty used by the United Nations or the widely cited World Bank income measure of $2.00 per day in illuminating global deprivation? What do these measures tell us? What do they fail to show?

TABLE 8.1 Global Inequality Indicators

Country	GNI-PPP (2012 data)	Percentage of Population Living on Less Than $2/Day (2011 data)	Infant Mortality Rate per 1,000 Live Births (2013 data)
World	**$11,690**	**53**	**40**
United States	$50,610	n/a	5.9
Germany	$41,370	n/a	3.3
Hungary	$20,200	2	4.9
Mexico	$16,630	26	15
China	$9,210	47	16
India	$3,840	81	44
Nigeria	$2,420	91	97
Bangladesh	$2,070	83	35

SOURCES: Population Reference Bureau. (2011). *2011 World Population Data Sheet;* Population Reference Bureau. (2013). *2013 World Population Data Sheet.*

the United Nations set as a goal the substantial reduction of hunger around the globe. In fact, data suggest that there have been marked improvements in access to adequate food supplies in many of the world's regions, most notably in those that have experienced rapid economic growth, including parts of Southeast Asia and Central and South America. At the same time, hunger has increased in other areas, including sub-Saharan Africa (Figure 8.3).

An important cause of hunger at the household level is poverty; many of those who lack sufficient food do not have the economic resources to acquire it. Subsistence farmers in developing countries, many of whom survive from season to season on their own small-scale crop yields, are vulnerable to weather events and natural disasters that can push their families into destitution and starvation. Hunger at a community level is more complex. While entire communities may suffer poverty and malnutrition, large-scale hunger is often the outcome of political decisions or armed conflicts. In early 2014, for example, Amnesty International reported that the government of Bashar al-Assad in Syria was preventing the delivery of food supplies to civilians in areas held by his opponents in the Syrian civil war that has raged since 2011. Regardless of the causes of hunger, the costs of undernourishment are serious and often lasting: By one estimate, fully 25% of all children under age 5 are stunted—that is, their growth progression is impaired—by lack of access to adequate nutrition (United Nations Educational, Scientific, and Cultural Organization [UNESCO], 2014b).

In evaluating global health, we can also compare across countries the **infant mortality rate**—that is, *the number of deaths of infants under age 1 per 1,000 live births per year.* This figure gives some insight into the health status of populations, and

Infant mortality rate: The number of deaths of infants under age 1 per 1,000 live births per year.

FIGURE 8.3 Number of Undernourished by Region, 1990–1992 and 2011–2013 (in millions)

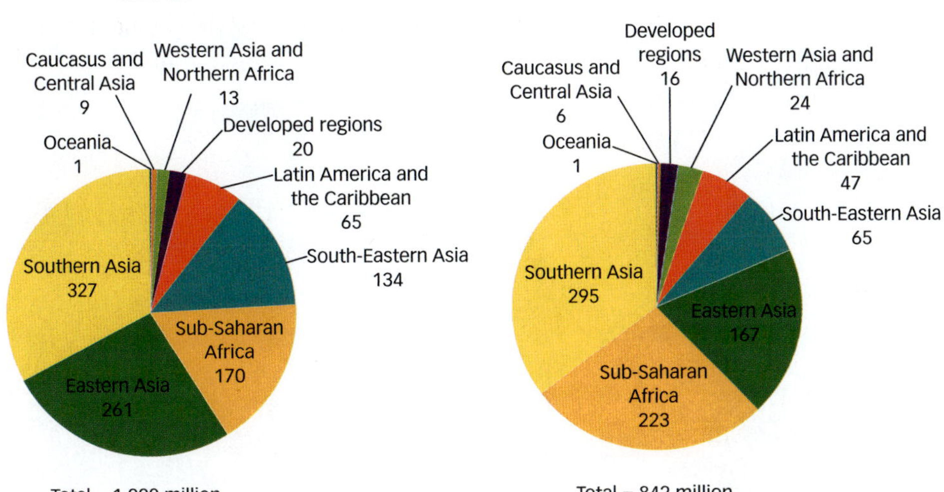

SOURCE: *The State of Food Insecurity in the World 2013. Economic growth is necessary but not sufficient to accelerate reduction of hunger and malnutrition.* Food and Agriculture Organization of the United Nations. Reproduced with permission.

NOTE: The areas of the pie charts are proportional to the total number of undernourished in each period. All figures are rounded.

of women and children in particular, because infant mortality rates are lowest in states that offer access to safe pre- and antenatal care and sanitary childbirth facilities, as well as good nutrition during pregnancy. Consider the vast differences in the infant mortality rates among categories of countries: In 2013, the most developed countries had an infant mortality rate of just 5 per 1,000 live births. By contrast, the less developed countries had a rate of 44 per 1,000 live births and the least developed countries posted a rate of 66 per 1,000 live births. Across specific countries, rates vary from lows in countries such as Norway (2.4) and Austria (3.1) to highs such as those in Haiti (59), Pakistan (74), and Sierra Leone (128; Population Reference Bureau, 2013).

Global health indicators like infant and child mortality rates are linked not only to income differences *between countries* but also to income stratification *within countries.* Data suggest that those countries with highly unequal distribution of income also experience highly variable health outcomes. For instance, in Cambodia, which is deeply stratified by income, among the top fifth of income earners the infant mortality rate is 23 per 1,000 live births, while for those in the bottom fifth the rate is 77 per 1,000 live births (Population Reference Bureau, 2013).

Our discussion of health may also be linked to the issue of fertility. Demographers measure **total fertility rate (TFR)**, which is *the average number of children a woman in a given country will have in her lifetime if age-specific fertility rates hold throughout her childbearing years* (ages 15–49). We can use this measure to look at childbearing over space and time. It is notable that many of the world's poorest countries have the highest fertility rates. For example, while the TFR is 1.8 in Norway, 1.4 in Germany, and 2.1 in the United States, rates in the least developed countries remain high. In 2013, some of the world's highest TFRs were found in Somalia (6.8), the Central African Republic (6.3), Nigeria (6.0), and Afghanistan (5.4). Rates of fertility within many countries also vary by economic status; for instance, in the African country of Uganda, women in the top fifth of the income hierarchy have a TFR of 4.0, while their sisters in the lowest fifth have a TFR that is nearly double (7.9; Population Reference Bureau, 2013).

What sociological factors help explain differences in fertility? One factor is the link between infant and child mortality and fertility: In regions or countries where early child survival is threatened by disease, poverty, or other risks, families may choose to have more children in order to ensure that some survive into adulthood to contribute to the household and care for elderly parents, particularly in countries without social welfare supports for retirees. Second, it has been said that children are a poor man's riches—indeed, in many agricultural economies, many hands are needed to do work, and

Total fertility rate (TFR): The average number of children a woman in a given country will have in her lifetime if age-specific fertility rates hold throughout her childbearing years.

Marc Jourdier/Afp/Getty Images

Total fertility rates have fallen across the developing world as more families gain access to information on family planning and to safe, effective contraception. In sub-Saharan Africa, however, at least a quarter of couples who would like to postpone their next birth by 2 years do not use contraception (Guengant & May, 2013).

AP Photo/UNRWA

The Syrian civil war has led to massive displacement of residents, many of whom have lost homes, work, and family members in the conflict. In this 2014 photo, refugees in the capital city of Damascus queue up to receive desperately needed food supplies.

children are active contributors to a family's economic well-being. Economic modernization correlates historically with drops in fertility (see Chapter 17 for a fuller discussion of this topic). As well, where a lack of access to maternal and child health care is common, there may also be little access to safe, effective contraceptives that would enable women to control their fertility. In Nigeria, for instance, which has a TFR of 6.0, less than 10% of women use modern contraceptive methods (Population Reference Bureau, 2013).

SAFE SANITATION

Access to safe, hygienic sanitation facilities has emerged as an issue of public health concern for many poor communities, but also as an issue of dignity and security for girls and women. Specifically, female inhabitants of communities that lack accessible, safe toilet facilities face serious vulnerabilities when they need to meet normal bodily needs. Consider the following story from June 2014: In a small Indian village in the northern state of Uttar Pradesh, two girls, ages 12 and 14, went together one evening to relieve themselves in the wild bamboo fields several minutes from their home, which has no bathroom facilities. In the darkness, the girls were brutally attacked, raped, and hanged from a mango tree, allegedly by three brothers (Banerjee, 2014).

The majority of India's 1.2 billion inhabitants do not have access to private toilets or latrines. According to the Population Reference Bureau (2013), just 60% of urban Indians and 24% of rural Indians were using "improved sanitation facilities" in 2011; while this measure focuses on the "hygienic separation of sewage from human contact" rather than safety or privacy, it points to a presence or lack of access to basic toilet facilities. In Uttar Pradesh, which is the country's largest state, about 64% of Indians have no indoor plumbing (McCarthy, 2014). Although some villages have public bathrooms, one press account notes that "many women avoid using them because they are usually in a state of disrepair and because men often hang around and harass the women." The same report quotes a local Indian

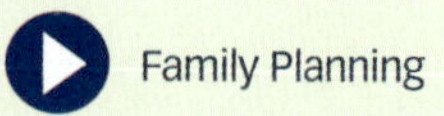

Reuters/Muhammad Hamed

In 2014, an outbreak of Ebola in West Africa killed thousands of victims. Poor health-care infrastructure in countries like Liberia, Sierra Leone, and Guinea contributed to the spread of the devastating disease. In this photo, a Liberian health-care worker sprays a suspected victim with disinfectant to reduce the risk that his remains would infect others.

police official's estimate that more than 60% of rapes occur in similar circumstances (Banerjee, 2014). A 2012 study reported that "approximately 30% of women from the underprivileged sections of Indian society experience violent sexual assaults every year because lack of sanitation facilities forces them to go long distances to find secluded spots or public facilities to meet their bodily needs" (Bhatia, 2013).

The problem is not limited to India. Similar stories of violation and violence have been documented from Nepal to South Africa, where private toilet facilities are the exception rather than the rule (Bhatia, 2013). In Nepal, for instance, just 50% of urban residents and 32% of rural Nepalese were using "improved sanitation facilities" in 2011. Figures on access to safe and sanitary facilities vary from a full 100% in most developed countries to just 4% for rural residents of Niger (Population Reference Bureau, 2013). According to the United Nations, about 2.5 billion people still lack access to basic, safe sanitation facilities, a figure linked not only, as noted above, to violence and degradation of women but also to high rates of diarrheal diseases among children. Reduction of that number is one of the Millennium Development Goals set by the United Nations for the improvement of global economic, environmental, and social progress and security in the 21st century.

EDUCATION MATTERS

In most developed countries, nearly all young people complete primary school, and most move on to high school. In less developed states, access to education is more limited, and the opportunity to go to school may be affected by a spectrum of factors. In some countries and communities, girls are discouraged or even prevented from attending school by economic or cultural factors. In others, school fees present obstacles to poor families who cannot afford to enroll their children. Sometimes schools and teachers are themselves not available because of the presence of armed conflict or the absence of communities that could sustain them.

A study by the United Nations Educational, Scientific, and Cultural Organization found that in 2011, about 57 million children worldwide were out of school. While many children do not attend school because of armed conflicts in their countries or regions, about half of those not in school are, according to UNESCO (2014b), "expected never to make it to school" (p. 8). In the poorest countries, many children are without access to basic education: In sub-Saharan Africa, for instance, less than a quarter of girls have completed primary education. Even where schools are available in poor countries, the quality of education is lacking: UNESCO reports that about 250 million children are without basic literacy and numeracy skills, although about half of them have completed at least 4 years of school. Inadequate teacher preparation may combine with overcrowding—the African state of Malawi reported an average of 130 children in a grade 1 classroom—and lack of textbooks to render efforts to educate children ineffective. Issues discussed earlier, including the lack of safe transportation and toilet facilities, may also discourage children, and particularly girls, from attending school regularly.

Uneducated or poorly educated children pass into adulthood without basic skills. Literacy and numeracy skills not achieved in the years of primary school are rarely achievable in adulthood in developing countries, which have not established a tradition of adult education. UNESCO (2014b) estimates that in 2011 there were 774 million fully illiterate adults worldwide, about two-thirds of whom were women. Interestingly, about 72% of illiterate adults are concentrated in just 10 countries (Figure 8.4).

Reuters/Muhammad Hamed

In 2012, Pakistani schoolgirl Malala Yousafzai was shot three times by a gunman after she publicly advocated for education in a region controlled by Taliban fighters whose interpretation of Islam forbids the education of girls. Malala recovered and has continued her passionate fight for female education around the world.

CQR Global Security

Women's Education

■ **FIGURE 8.4 Countries With the Highest Rates of Illiteracy, 1985–1994 and 2005–2011**

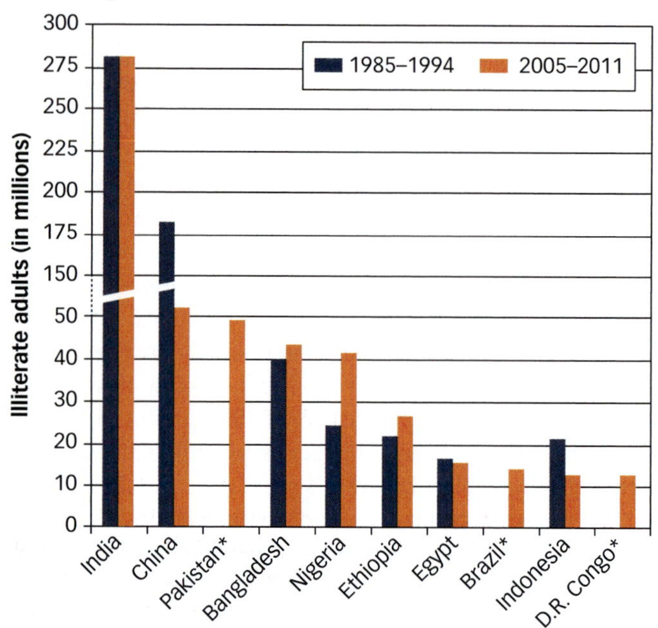

SOURCE: *Teaching and Learning: Achieving Quality for All.* Copyright © UNESCO 2014. Reprinted by permission of the UNESCO Institute for Statistics.

*Data for 1985–1994 not available.

Education improves the lives of communities and families in a multitude of ways. UNESCO (2014b) estimates that, on the global level, a year of school can equal a 10% boost in income. Education benefits both those who work for wages, by improving skills, and those who farm, by increasing access to knowledge about effective, efficient farming methods. Education also helps workers to avoid exploitation and better advocate for their interests. Apart from opening up broader avenues for economic advancement, better education is also linked to positive health outcomes. This relationship is particularly strong for women's education and child health outcomes. Research has documented a positive correlation between maternal education (even at the primary level) and decreased risk of child mortality (Glewwe, 1999; LeVine, LeVine, Schnell-Anzola, Rowe, & Dexter, 2012). For instance, a recent study on Nigeria found that better reading skills among mothers were linked to lower rates of child mortality (Smith-Greenaway, 2013). Other work suggests that greater maternal education translates into a greater probability that a woman's children will be educated (UNESCO, 2014b).

Significant strides have been made in many countries and regions in recent decades in educating young people, and women in particular, but much remains to be done. Currently, about a quarter of young people in the low-income and lower-middle-income countries are unable to read a sentence (UNESCO, 2014b).

TECHNOLOGY: THE GREAT EQUALIZER?

As we have seen, global inequality is manifested today in a broad spectrum of ways, ranging from a lack of income and food to little access to good education and sanitation. At the same time, new technologies have emerged whose adoption has not been limited to the well-off. Consider the mobile phone, a technology that is bringing opportunities and change to many of the world's developing countries and their populations.

A finding of India's most recent decennial census (conducted in 2011) is that about 53% of India's estimated 1.2 billion people have mobile phones, even though only a little over 36% have toilets in their homes and an even smaller percentage have indoor sources of drinking water (Hannon, 2012; see Figure 8.5). In China, one finds a similar contrast between the absence of basic household amenities and the adoption of new technologies: According to a report by the United Nations (2013b), in China 14 million people have no access to toilets in their homes, but 980 million of China's 1.3 billion inhabitants have cell phones. Across the globe, mobile phone use has surged; according to a summary of the report, "of the world's seven billion people, six billion have mobile phones" (United Nations, 2013a).

While, as noted earlier in the chapter, the absence of safe and sanitary toilet facilities is a burden and danger to communities,

■ **FIGURE 8.5 Ownership of Select Assets and Household Amenities in India 2011**

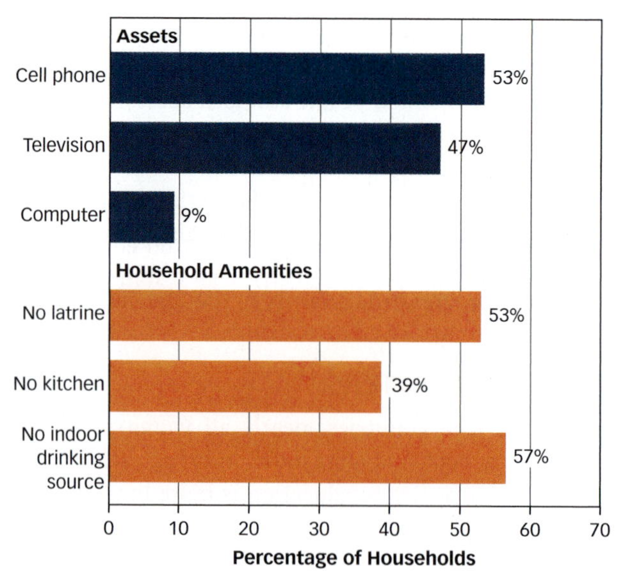

SOURCE: "India's Census: Lots of Cellphones, Too Few Toilets," by Elliot Hannon. NRP. April 08, 2012. Indian Census 2011. Melanie Taube/NPR

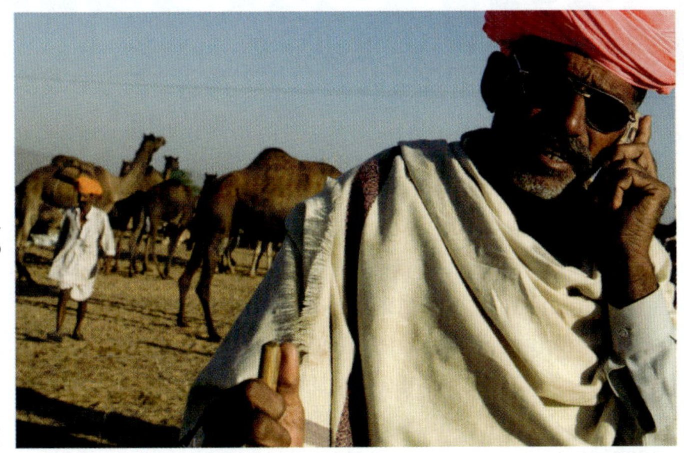

Mobile phone technology has begun to reach even the remotest parts of the globe, bringing new opportunities for contact and commerce, as well as activism, education, and health care.

the mass global adoption of the mobile phone is, data suggest, an important change with the potential to affect health, education, agriculture, and social activism, among other facets of life. A recent online article posted by the *MIT Technology Review* notes out that in just over a decade, Africa has transformed from a continent with little telecommunications infrastructure to a continent where about one in six inhabitants has a mobile phone; for example, "Nigeria alone has gone from a nation of just 30,000 cell subscriptions in 2000 to more than 140 million today, or roughly 87 percent penetration" (Berkley, 2013). It has been estimated that Africa will have a billion mobile phones by 2016 (Ogunlesi & Busari, 2012). This change has important implications for health care on the continent: For instance, birth registrations that parents can easily complete on their mobile phones can make government databases on live births and infant mortality more accurate. Also, mobile phone technology can improve the operation of the vaccine supply chain by allowing real-time data on vaccine availability or deficits in clinics to reach suppliers (Berkley, 2013). Scientists hope that this technology will eventually be used for diagnostic purposes, enabling even residents of remote areas to access medical advice.

Mobile phones are also having an effect on education and literacy across the globe. In South Africa, for instance, the country's most popular social media platform has partnered with a global telecommunications firm to offer an accessible math-teaching tool to users, and it is hoped that such technology can eventually be used to offer a wide variety of lessons to students (Ogunlesi & Busari, 2012). No less important, access to mobile phones is providing access to books for both new and advanced readers. As a UNESCO (2014a) report notes, "Many people from Lagos to La Paz to Lahore . . . do not read for one reason: they don't have books" (p. 13). The report goes on to observe that "a well-respected study of 16 sub-Saharan African countries found that most primary schools have few or no books, and in many countries these low levels are not improving" (Ross, 2010, cited in UNESCO, 2014a, pp. 13–14). This lack of books may compromise reading acquisition and have longer-term academic consequences. As well, mobile phone technology offers opportunities to read—whether for pleasure, formal education, reading to children, or news—to those who may lack the resources to obtain text for reading in other ways. If 6 billion of the world's 7 billion people can now access working mobile phones, a new world of literacy may be at their fingertips.

Even agriculture in the developing world, much of which is still concentrated in small family farms, is being affected by mobile technology. In countries where agriculture is still a primary sector of the economy, technology has the potential to affect both micro- and macro-level economic indicators. According to a CNN report on mobile phones in Africa, "By serving as platforms for sharing weather information, market prices, and micro-insurance schemes, mobile phones are allowing Africa's farmers to make better decisions, translating into higher-earning potentials." Farmers with cattle, for instance, can use the mobile app iCow to track cows' gestation periods and to learn additional information about breeding and nutrition (Ogunlesi & Busari, 2012).

Finally, technology has brought to the developing world a new platform for social activism. Citizen mobilization against crime, corruption, violence, and other social ills has been fostered by mobile technology that rapidly passes information across communities. Mobile phones have played important roles in many events, from Kenya in 2008, where citizens used phones to report violent incidents ion the country's disputed elections, to the citizen uprisings against authoritarian regimes in North African countries like Tunisia in 2011, to Nigeria in 2014, where the viral Twitter campaign #BringBackOurGirls brought global attention to the plight of more than 300 girls kidnapped by the radical Islamist organization Boko Haram.

Can mobile phone technology contribute to bringing greater prosperity—and equality—to the planet? How might mass adoption of mobile phones contribute to addressing some of the inequalities described in this chapter?

FIGURE 8.6 Number of Libraries per Population Ratio in the United Kingdom and Nigeria

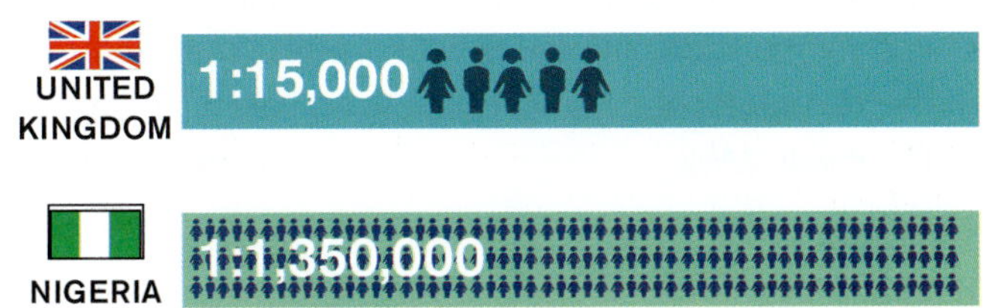

SOURCE: United Nations Educational, Scientific and Cultural Organization. (2014). *Reading in the mobile era: A study of mobile reading in developing countries.* Paris: Author. Retrieved from http://www.unesco.org/new/en/unesco/themes/icts/m4ed/mobile-reading/reading-in-the-mobile-era.

TECHNOLOGY & SOCIETY

#FIRSTWORLDPROBLEMS

If you are a user or follower of Twitter, you may be familiar with the popular hashtag #FirstWorldProblems. The site attracts a broad audience of both readers and contributors who engage in self-mocking about the relative insignificance of the daily tribulations of life in the prosperous modern world. The online *Urban Dictionary* defines "first world problems" as "problems from living in a wealthy, industrialized nation that third worlders would probably roll their eyes at" (www.urbandictionary.com). The following are some samples of such "problems" gathered from the site in June 2014:

- It's nice enough outside today to wear shorts, but the office is too cold so you need to wear pants.
- I hate being home while my cleaning ladies are here.
- When your phone charger doesn't reach your bed.
- Uh oh. The part of the commute where there's no 4G coverage for nine whole minutes is coming up.
- My phone isn't charged enough yet for me to have a bath.
- I only got one dipping sauce with my 20 nuggets and had to ration it like it was WWII.

The site attracts posters from around the globe. June's sample featured posts in German, Spanish, Dutch, and Arabic, among others.

Interestingly, some posters take advantage of the hashtag's popularity to attract interest in real problems that exist in the developing world. For example, the charitable organization WATERisLIFE, which raises funds to assist communities that lack clean drinking water, posted a YouTube video featuring impoverished Haitian children and adults reading some of the #FirstWorldProblems posts (such as "I hate it when I go to the bathroom and forget my phone"). The video, arguably, both critiques and takes advantage of the hashtag to draw attention to the organization's cause. While the video drew a lot of attention to the charity, the advertising agency that made it said that WATERisLIFE hoped to eliminate a hashtag on Twitter that "showcases concerns that seem important to those living in wealthy, industrialized countries, yet are, fact, trivial compared to the issues faced by those struggling to survive in many parts of the world." This drew an angry response from some posters who suggested that the agency failed to grasp the irony in the posts (Edwards, 2012).

The Twitter hashtag has attracted other criticism as well. While the tone of the hashtag #FirstWorldProblems is self-mocking, and posters presumably "get" that the problems they are lamenting are trivial in comparison to those faced by many communities in poorer states, some writers suggest that the hashtag's purpose is not to bring recognition to the problems of the developing world but rather to act as a platform for wit and irony shared among the privileged (Madrigal, 2011). As well, as Teju Cole, a Nigerian American writer, has pointed out, people in developing countries are not beings so easily labeled as different from their "first world" counterparts: "Here's a First World problem: the inability to see that others are as fully complex and as keen on technology and pleasure as you are" (quoted in Madrigal, 2011).

THINK IT THROUGH

▶ How would you characterize the sociological significance of #FirstWorldProblems? What are its functions in the "first world"? Would you agree more fully with its critics or with its defenders?

THEORETICAL PERSPECTIVES ON GLOBAL INEQUALITY

In this section we analyze global inequality from several theoretical perspectives, raising the questions of what explains global inequality and why it exists and persists. Later, we take a critical look at the theories.

Modernization theory is *a market-oriented development theory* associated with the work of Walt Rostow (1961) and others. In contrast to many perspectives on stratification, the modernization perspective asks not why some countries are poor but why some countries are rich. In asking this question, it makes the assumption that the historical norm in states has been poverty; that is, the populations of most countries at most times have subsisted rather than prospered. The answer it proposes is that affluent states have "modern" institutions, markets, and worldviews; by "modern," Rostow meant those that emulate the democratic and capitalist states of the West. He argued that economically underdeveloped states can progress if they adopt Western institutions, markets, and worldviews. Rostow used the analogy of an airplane taking flight to illustrate his key ideas about the stages of development:

- **The traditional stage:** In this "pre-Newtonian" (that is, prescientific) stage, societies are present and past time oriented, looking back into history for models of economic and political behavior rather than looking forward and seeking new models. They embrace tradition over innovation. Economic development is limited by low rates of savings and investment, and by a work orientation that elevates subsistence over ambition and prosperity. The airplane is grounded and has not yet begun its journey to affluence. Today, few such countries exist. One might look at individual communities within developing countries to find these traditional orientations.

  In some developing countries, however, traditional beliefs about women's roles hinder their educational attainment and access to the labor market. Arguably, this is a cultural norm that also stifles national development, as it keeps a segment of the population that could potentially constitute half the workforce (women) from contributing its talents and skills.

- **The takeoff stage:** In this stage, societies are moving away from traditional cultural norms, practices, and institutions and are embracing economic development with a sense of purpose and increasing practices of savings and investment. The plane rises as the weight of tradition is cast overboard in favor of modernity.

  Rostow, an originator of modernization theory, was an adviser to President Kennedy, whose administration was responsible for the development of the Peace Corps. The Peace Corps, which has for decades sent young U.S. workers abroad to spread innovations in agriculture and technology, to teach English, and to train leaders in developing countries in methods of modern governance, could be seen as a vehicle for moving countries from the traditional to the takeoff stage. Today, some African countries with modernity-oriented leadership, such as Liberia, might be categorized as members of the "takeoff" group.

- **In flight with technological progress and cultural modernity:** In this next stage, as the plane moves forward, technology is spreading to areas like agriculture and industry, innovation is increasing, and resistance to change is declining. Many people are adopting "modern" cultural values, and governance increasingly reflects the rule of law. Advanced countries facilitate these processes by offering advice and money.

  Progress may take the form of industrialization, which drives greater urbanization as rural dwellers leave poor agricultural areas to seek their fortunes in cities. It may also be accompanied by lower fertility, driven by the increased use of contraception as opportunities for women grow in education and the labor market. India might be considered a modern example of this stage, as it has a growing educated middle class, rising urbanization and industrialization, and (for better or worse) soaring consumer ambitions.

- **The stage of high mass consumption and high living standards:** In this stage, there is a greater emphasis on the satisfaction of consumer desires, as new affluence expands the ranks of those with disposable income. This is the stage that advanced countries like those of Western and Northern Europe, the United States, Israel, and Japan have reached.

As these stages suggest, modernization theory assumes we can understand a given state's level of development by looking at its political, economic, and social institutions and its cultural orientation. That is, the theory uses a country's *internal variables* as key measuring sticks. In contrast, two later theories take a conflict perspective, focusing on countries' conflicting interests, unequal resources, and exploitative relationships, though they emphasize different aspects of inequality.

Just as Marx posited a fundamentally exploitative relationship between the bourgeoisie and the proletariat, so too does **dependency theory** (Emmanuel, 1972; Frank, 1966, 1979; Ghosh, 2001), which argues that *the poverty of some countries is a consequence of their exploitation by wealthy states, which control the global capitalist system.* While exploitation originated

Modernization theory: A market-oriented development theory that envisions development as evolutionary and guided by "modern" institutions, practices, and cultures.

Dependency theory: The theory that the poverty of some countries is a consequence of their exploitation by wealthy states, which control the global capitalist system.

in colonial relationships, when powerful Western states such as Britain, the Netherlands, and Belgium dominated countries such as the Congo, South Africa, and India, it continues through the modern vehicle of multinational corporations that reap great profits from the cheap labor and raw materials of poor countries while local populations draw only bare subsistence from their human and natural resources.

Dependency theory draws its name from the idea that prices on the global market for human and natural resources held by poor states are intentionally kept low to benefit high-income states, so low-income states cannot fully develop industrially, technologically, or economically. Thus, these states remain in a *dependency relationship* with the well-off states that buy and exploit their labor and raw materials. Whereas modernization theory implies that high-income states want to encourage the full development of low-income countries, dependency theory suggests there is a direct relationship between the affluence of one and the poverty of the other.

World systems theory shares some of these basic ideas. Immanuel Wallerstein (1974, 1974/2011a, 1980/2011b, 1989/2011c, 2011d), one of the pioneers of the theory, argues that *the global capitalist economic system has long been shaped by a few powerful economic actors, who have constructed it in a way that favors their class interests.* He suggests that the world economy is populated by three key categories of countries:

- **Core countries:** The core countries are economically advanced, technologically sophisticated, and home to well-educated, skilled populations. They control the vast majority of the world's wealth and reap the greatest benefits from the world economic order, including trade and production practices. They include the United States, Canada, the states of Western and Northern Europe, and Japan, among others.
- **Peripheral countries:** The peripheral states have low national incomes and low levels of technological and industrial development; many still depend on agriculture. They have been exploited by the core states for their cheap labor (and, historically, slave labor) and for cheap raw materials that are exported to advanced countries and made into finished goods that bring far greater profit to core companies and consumers. Peripheral countries include parts of Central and Latin America, Asia, and many of sub-Saharan Africa's states. Some of those in Africa provide the critical mineral components of modern electronics for which consumers pay top dollar, such as smartphones and iPads, but they still suffer dire poverty.
- **Semiperipheral states:** The semiperiphery shares some characteristics with both the core and peripheral states, occupying an intermediate and sometimes stabilizing position between them. Semiperipheral states such as China, India, and Brazil may be exploited by core states, but they may in turn have the capacity to exploit the resources of peripheral states. For example, China, which has advanced industrial capacity and a growing middle class of consumers, has begun to foster economic relationships with African countries that can offer oil resources for the populous and economically growing state.

World systems theory sees the world as dynamic rather than static, with peripheral and semiperipheral states seeking to rise in the ranks and core countries attempting to hold fast to global power. The key unit of analysis in world systems theory is less individual countries (as it is in modernization theory) than it is relationships between countries and regions of the world. Like dependency theory, world systems theory sees relationships between states, such as those between core and periphery states, as fundamentally exploitative; that is, some countries benefit to the detriment of others.

Below we use these perspectives to examine the case of Nigeria, a developing African country. Application of the perspectives will help us to assess their utility as analytical tools for understanding development and global inequality.

APPLYING THE THEORIES: THE CASE OF NIGERIAN OIL WEALTH

A *National Geographic* story on the Niger Delta begins like this:

> Oil fouls everything in southern Nigeria. It spills from the pipelines, poisoning soil and water. It stains the hands of politicians and generals, who siphon off its profits. It taints the ambitions of the young, who will try anything to scoop up a share of the liquid riches—fire a gun, sabotage a pipeline, kidnap a foreigner.
>
> Nigeria had all the makings of an uplifting tale: poor African nation blessed with enormous sudden wealth. . . . By the mid-1970s, Nigeria had joined OPEC (Organization of Petroleum Exporting Countries), and the government's budget bulged with petrodollars. (O'Neill, 2007)

Using the case of Nigeria and its vast oil reserves in the southern Niger Delta, we can evaluate the theories we have just described and compare how well they illuminate the case of this devastatingly poor state, where about 84% of the population lives on less than $2 a day and, in spite of the wealth of natural resources, GNI-PPP is just $2,240 (Population Reference Bureau, 2012).

World systems theory: The theory that the global capitalist economic system has long been shaped by a few powerful economic actors, who have ordered it in a way that favors their interests.

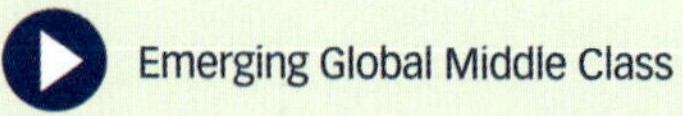

Recall that the modernization perspective highlights internal variables such as the lack of modern state, economic, and legal institutions and inadequately modern cultures to explain why some countries have lagged in development. A modernization theorist would thus point to the rampant culture of corruption and lack of rule of law that have characterized countries like Somalia and North Korea, which Transparency International (2011), a corruption watchdog agency, has ranked as the most corrupt countries in the world. Nigeria is also near the top of the agency's list. Clearly, there are links between state corruption, the lack of an effective legal and civic structure, and the dire poverty in and around Port Harcourt. Though it is the capital of Nigeria's oil-rich Rivers state, Port Harcourt has "no electricity, no clean water, no medicine, no schools" (O'Neill, 2007). But does the modernization perspective miss some key aspects of the problem of global poverty?

Critics argue that in attending almost exclusively to internal variables, the modernization perspective fails to recognize external obstacles to development and the ways in which well-off states benefit from the inferior economic position of poor states. According to *National Geographic,* in the wake of independence from colonial Britain, few observers expected that Nigeria would become a global oil source. In the decades that followed, however, five multinational oil companies—Royal Dutch Shell, Total, Italy's Agip, ExxonMobil, and Chevron—transformed the Rivers state. "The imprint: 4,500 miles . . . of pipelines, 159 oil fields, and 275 flow stations" (O'Neill, 2007). The United Nations Development Programme and the International Crisis Group point to decades of problematic economic strategies employed by oil companies, which have taken advantage of weak environmental controls, offered little compensation for land and few employment opportunities to local communities, engaged in corrupt deals for oil, and used private security forces to commit violence against those who resisted their efforts to control the oil fields of the Niger Delta (Brock & Cocks, 2012; O'Neill, 2007).

From the dependency and world systems perspectives, a relationship of fundamental exploitation exists between Nigeria and high-income countries, including the United States and Britain, for which Nigeria provides a critically important resource. If the United States is a core state, Nigeria appears from this perspective a peripheral state supplying oil, the basic raw building block of modern economies, without seeing the benefit of its own natural wealth. Semiperipheral states aggressively seeking to develop their own economies and wealth are also part of the picture: "China, India, and South Korea, all energy-hungry, have begun buying stakes in Nigeria's offshore [oil] blocks" (O'Neill, 2007). The dependency theory perspective suggests that developed and rapidly developing states benefit from lax government oversight of environmental pollution, low-wage pools of local labor, and corruptible officials willing to bend rules to accommodate corporate wishes.

Like modernization theory, the dependency and world systems theoretical perspectives illuminate some aspects of the case while obscuring others. Variables like the exploitative power of Western oil companies are a key part of understanding the failure of Nigeria to develop in a way that benefits the

FIGURE 8.7 Where the Oil Is in Africa

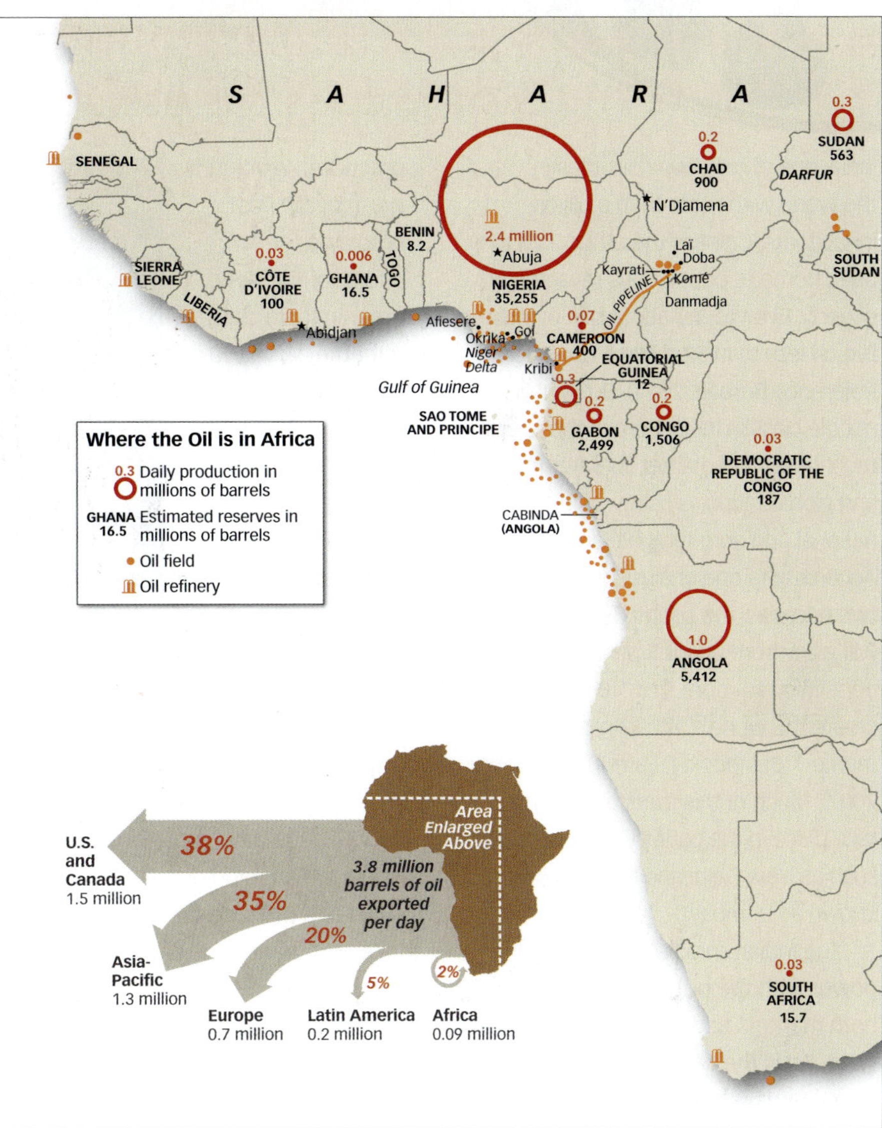

INEQUALITY MATTERS

CASTE TO CLASS: THE RISING MIDDLE CLASS IN INDIA

India, one of only two countries in the world with more than a billion inhabitants (China is the other), has long been home to populations ravaged by poverty. Even today, about half of Indians live on less than $2 a day (Population Reference Bureau, 2011). But a new middle class in India, born in the age of technology and market liberalization and globalization, is rising rapidly to national and demographic prominence. According to one analysis, "Over the next two decades, the country's middle class will grow from about 5 percent of the population to more than 40 percent and create the world's fifth-largest consumer market" (Beinhocker, Farrell, & Zainulbhai, 2007). Much of this transformation will take place in the country's massive cities, such as New Delhi and Mumbai (formerly known as Bombay).

The Indian middle class is a rising power with the potential to change both markets and politics in significant ways. As is the case around the globe, a hallmark of the middle class in India is consumption. Having achieved some disposable income, members of the middle class aspire to new automobiles, bigger dwellings, and more educational and cultural opportunities. The U.S. Department of State (2012a) estimates that at least 50 million Indians have disposable incomes in a middle-class range (between about $4,100 and $20,800 annually), and the next 15 years will see a tenfold rise in those who have the means to join the new class of consumers.

While middle-class Indians promise to drive growth in the consumer market, they are also putting their stamp on government institutions and practices. A recent *Washington Post* article on the efforts of the new urban middle class to battle pervasive corruption in state structures points out that "in the past, cynical lawmakers figured that they could get away with almost anything as long as they threw a few sops to the rural poor at election time every five years. But two decades of economic liberalization have brought into being a new Indian middle class . . . whose votes and opinions can no longer be taken for granted" (Denyer & Lakshmi, 2011).

Steve Raymer/National Geographic Creative

A rising Indian middle class has begun to enjoy the benefits of comfort and consumption that in the past were limited to a smaller group of wealthy inhabitants.

"The consumer revolution that we have experienced in the past two decades has told the citizen that he can expect a higher quality of governance," social anthropologist Shiv Viswanathan has suggested. "The information revolution has created a revolution of rising expectation" (quoted in Denyer & Lakshmi, 2011).

As India's middle class grows in number and economic resources, it is attracting more political attention. While the group is still of modest size in comparison to the number of Indian poor, middle-class politics is of growing significance in this rapidly developing country.

So how do states become "modern"—that is, economically and technologically developed and responsively governed? In its pursuit of entrepreneurial opportunities and cleaner governance, the Indian middle class has embraced what Walt Rostow would have described as components of modernity. India has also changed from a British colony growing cotton for the profit of British mills to an independent, increasingly well-educated and entrepreneurial regional powerhouse with the potential to exercise global power in markets and politics. Although neither modernization theory nor dependency theory looks at the middle class as an agent of change, in India, the new middle class is challenging both internal and external obstacles and transforming the country domestically and globally.

THINK IT THROUGH

▶ Why do growing middle-class populations in many developing states have an interest in addressing governmental corruption? How does corruption undermine the interests of the middle class?

Reuters/Eric Gay/Pool

Port Harcourt, located in Nigeria's River State, is a key exporter of crude oil. Despite its economic strength, many citizens in the region still face extreme hardship, including poverty, and environmental threats.

broader population, but conflict-oriented perspectives pay little attention to the agency of poor states and, in particular, their governing bodies in setting a solid foundation for development.

IS THERE A GLOBAL ELITE?

Sociological perspectives on global inequality often focus on *countries* as objects of analysis. While it is recognized that countries are also stratified internally, discussions of global inequality like those we presented earlier in this chapter compare, contrast, and analyze countries and their regions. Sociology also, however, takes an interest in the idea that there exists a **global elite**, a *transglobal class of professionals who exercise considerable economic and political power that is not limited by national borders.* Some writers suggest that an identifiable global power elite, while not an entirely new phenomenon, is a product of modernity, brought into growing significance by technological innovation and globalization. In this section we look at the descriptive dimensions of this phenomenon. We then turn to a consideration of some key sociological ideas about the characteristics and functions of a global elite.

One important measure of membership in the global elite is wealth. In 2014, *Forbes* magazine identified 1,226 people around the world who are billionaires. Financial writer Chrystia Freeland (2012) suggests that today's global power elite, members of which she calls "the plutocrats," is composed largely of working professionals who have made their fortunes rather than inherited them: 840 of the 1,226 are described as "self-made" (p. 45). Most have made their fortunes in business, media, or technology. According to *Forbes,* in 2014 the aggregate wealth of the world's billionaires topped $6.7 trillion ("The World's Billionaires," 2014) While many of today's multimillionaires and billionaires live in developed countries like the United States, quite a few also live in developing countries like China, Russia, and India, where rapid economic growth, including the privatization of previously government-held industries like oil, has opened up unprecedented opportunities for establishment and expansion of personal wealth. The world's richest man in 2014 was Carlos Slim, a Mexican national.

In the context of a growing global list of billionaires, being a millionaire looks more commonplace than extraordinary, though millionaires are certainly few in number in the context of the global population of 7 billion. According to one recent calculation, there are just under 30 million millionaires (defined as those whose net assets exceed $1 million) in the world, though the fact that many of these millionaires hail from developing countries is notable. North America and Europe each account for about 37% of the world's millionaires. Excluding China and India, about 19% of millionaires are from Asia, just over 3% are from China, and the remainder (just under 3%) are from India, Africa, and Latin America. While the ranks of millionaires and billionaires have expanded globally, there is a substantial gap between those who are rich and those who are superrich—or "ultra high net worth individuals" (UHNWI), defined by Credit Suisse bank as those with assets that top $50 million. By the bank's estimate, in 2011 there were about 84,700 UHNWIs in the world; about 29,000 of these had

Global elite: A transglobal class of professionals who exercise considerable economic and political power that is not limited by national borders.

assets greater than $100 million and 2,700 had assets greater than $500 million (Freeland, 2012).

While there is unprecedented national diversity on the current roster of the rich and the superrich, there has also been a marked rise in the gap between the world's economic elites and everyone else. According to a 2014 report by the development organization Oxfam, nearly half of the world's wealth is owned by 1% of the globe's population; further, the world's richest 85 people have as much wealth as all the bottom half of the planet's population combined (Fuentes-Nieva & Galasso, 2014).

Seeking to outline a definition of the global elite, writer David Rothkopf (2008) suggests that

> the distribution of power has clearly shifted, not just away from the United States and Europe, but away from nations. . . . had [sociologist C. Wright] Mills been writing today, he would have turned his attention from the national elite in America to a new and more important phenomenon: the rise of a global power elite, a superclass that plays a similar role in the hierarchy of the global era to the role that the U.S. power elite played in that country's first decade as a superpower. (p. 9)

Rothkopf emphasizes the idea that the global elite is powerful not only because it is rich, but because it is *influential* in political decision making, global markets and industries, technological innovation, the production of cultural or intellectual ideas, and even world religions. The global elite and its decisions have impacts on the lives of thousands or even millions of citizens, consumers, workers, and worshippers. The global power elite, Rothkopf argues, includes corporate executives, presidents and prime ministers of powerful states, technological innovators, those who control flows of global resources like oil, media moguls, some military elites, and a handful of well-known and active cultural and religious figures. Their power is multiplied by the fact that they are deeply networked, sharing links to other members of the elite through both personal and professional ties. Their exercise of power is not always direct, but their influence is palpable in politics, economics, and media, among other areas.

Sociologist Leslie Sklair (2002) conceptualizes the notion of a modern global elite in his writings on "transnational capitalism." His work highlights the position that nations and borders are of declining significance in capitalist globalization. He argues that important objects of analysis in a globalizing world are what he terms "transnational practices"—that is, "practices that cross state borders but do not originate with state actors, agencies, or institutions" (p. 10). He suggests that understanding the modern economic order requires recognizing how power has become transnational rather than limited by national borders. As part of his examination of transnational practices, Sklair theorizes the rise of a *transnational capitalist class* that is composed not of capitalists (that is, the bourgeoisie) in the classical Marxian sense but of four categories of members: (1) a *corporate fraction* drawn from transnational corporations, (2) a *state fraction* composed of global political elites, (3) a *technical fraction* representing globalizing professionals, and (4) a *consumerist fraction* made up of executives of marketing and media.

While Sklair's theorized class would appear to encompass a broader swath of members than Rothkopf's (2008) global elite, his characterization of the transnational capitalist class reflects an idea shared with Rothkopf that global economic integration and the mobility of capital have fostered the birth of a transglobal class. The members of this class have the following characteristics:

- They share global (not only local) interests and perspectives, as well as consumer lifestyle choices.
- They seek to exercise control or influence over key political, economic, and cultural-ideological processes on a global level.
- They hail from different national backgrounds, but they see themselves as citizens of the world rather than just citizens of particular states.

Freeland (2012) echoes the last point in her journalistic account of the global elite, noting that members often feel they have more in common with their fellow elites than with their countrymen. She points out that this, however, may not be a new development: She quotes an early theorist of capitalism, Adam Smith, who wrote in 1776, "The proprietor of land is necessarily a citizen of the particular country in which his estate lies. The proprietor of stock is properly a citizen of the world, and is not necessarily attached to a particular country" (p. 67).

The transnational capitalist class is a global elite that exercises political, economic, and cultural-ideological power and acts to organize "conditions under which its interests and the interests of the global system . . . can be furthered" (Sklair, 2002, p. 99). Sklair also theorizes a particular function for the transnational capitalist class: It is a vehicle by which *transnational corporations,* modern and powerful economic entities, expand and legitimate the consumerist culture and ideology that is needed to sustain the global system of capitalist production.

In an interesting variation on the conceptualization of globalized classes, Zygmunt Bauman (1998) has written on what he describes as a "space war." Bauman's analysis points not toward the cosmos but toward modern citizens' relationship to physical spaces and places, including countries. Bauman posits that the "winners" of globalization (and the "space war") are those who are mobile, who can move through space to create value and meaning—he calls them *tourists* (though he does not mean that in the strictly conventional sense). They can move across the globe, enabled by transportation and communication technologies and their economic and professional

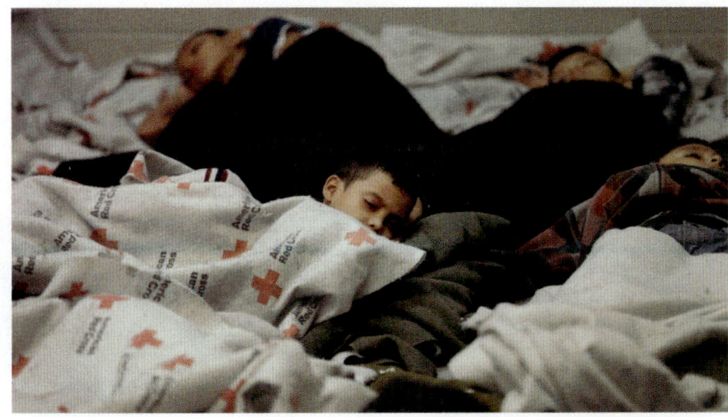

Reuters/Eric Gay/Pool

In 2014, tens of thousands of unaccompanied children streamed across the U.S. border from their homelands of Guatemala, El Salvador, and Honduras, in search of safety, family, and opportunities. Their arrival from these impoverished and violent states was met with vigorous political debate about what to do with a massive group of young people who appeared to have no haven at home or in the U.S.

resources. They exist, suggests Bauman, in time rather than in space because space is not constraining to them. What Bauman is describing is a globalized category of the world population whose mobility is enabled by education, economic resources, and social networks. For example, business professionals, high-level government bureaucrats and representatives, and cultural elites and celebrities have the means to seek out both personal pleasures and professional opportunities globally.

By contrast, the "losers" of modernity are those who are tied to places and spaces that have been devastated by globalization. Lacking resources, they are rooted in place and denied geographic and economic mobility. In thinking about this category, one might consider diverse groups, ranging from former automobile plant workers stripped of their livelihood by globalization and stuck in economically devastated cities to poor urban dwellers in the developing world whose lives revolve around difficult and dangerous low-wage jobs that they cannot afford to lose. Among the losers of a globalizing world are also, Bauman points out, those who are on the move, but they differ from the mobile global elite; rather, they are what he terms *vagabonds,* moving across the globe as refugees or poor economic migrants, unable to live in their own countries and unwanted elsewhere.

Bauman does not specify the precise qualities of his loosely defined global classes, but his work points to the idea that globalization has created different experiences for different groups that are not easily characterized through reference to national boundaries. This perspective may lead us to consider global inequality as a modern phenomenon that crosses borders and shapes new opportunities as well as obstacles.

WHY STUDY GLOBAL INEQUALITY FROM A SOCIOLOGICAL PERSPECTIVE?

Global inequality is manifested in the systematic disparities in income, wealth, health, education, and opportunities that exist between households, communities, and countries. Understanding inequality—both its dimensions and its roots—is, as you have seen in earlier chapters, one of sociology's key goals. As we have learned in this chapter, global poverty exists across different areas; it is rarely only a disparity of income that characterizes poverty. Economic disadvantage is a product but also a root of other disadvantages in areas like health, education, and even access to safe sanitary facilities.

At the global level, we find countries arranged in a stratified hierarchy of positions, with some exercising economic, political, and cultural dominance and others lagging behind, unable to convert valued human and natural resources into national prosperity. What accounts for these differences? Sociology offers us some insights—it's up to us to study different cases and to test a variety of explanations.

Global inequality can also be studied in terms of transglobal forms of stratification, including the development of a global elite whose composition and influence transcend borders. Globalization has wrought a world system that is deeply interconnected, and both capital and people are mobile, traversing borders in pursuit of profit, power, and pleasure. Sociology considers the question of globalization's diverse effects on populations across the planet, asking about the roots, benefits, and consequences of the rapid changes of the globalizing social world.

Global inequality matters because in an ever more densely populated, interconnected, and interdependent world, the misfortunes and good fortunes of different countries and classes will not remain isolated in their effects.

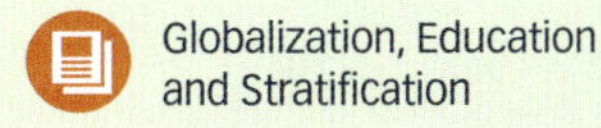

WHAT CAN I DO WITH A SOCIOLOGY DEGREE?

SKILLS AND CAREERS: CONFLICT DYNAMICS AND RESOLUTION SKILLS

Conflict resolution skills are of value when two or more entities—individuals, employees and employers, social groups, businesses, or countries, among others—engage in a process to resolve a disagreement that may be related to values or perceptions, or to social, economic, environmental, or political interests. Sociological study offers students the opportunity to develop competencies in the *analysis of conflict dynamics.* Understanding the dynamics of conflict involves the ability to research and recognize the fundamental issues at the root of conflicts, to take the perspectives of different parties in a conflict, and to communicate effectively with groups in conflict. Understanding conflict dynamics and using this knowledge to resolve conflicts are related to sociology's general orientation toward problem analysis and problem solving.

In Chapter 8, we looked at the most acute manifestations of global inequality. Many poor states are home to large economically marginal populations whose members also seek better lives—lives like those of people in richer states, of which they are quite aware given the spread of mobile phones and mass media across the globe. As the population grows, particularly in developing states, conflicts over resources will likely increase at both international and community levels. But violent conflict need not be inevitable. It is in our interest as sociologists and citizens of the world to think in informed and creative ways about averting and addressing conflicts over resources, as well as other sources of tension between states, societies, and groups. As a sociology student, you will have the opportunity to study different theoretical perspectives on conflict and its sources and to become familiar with research studies that delve into the roots of conflicts from the community to the global level.

Understanding conflict dynamics and utilizing that knowledge to address and prevent or resolve conflicts are skills of great value in a heterogeneous and complex social and global environment. These kinds of tasks are often part of the *job descriptions* of, among others, civil and family mediators, foreign service officers, lawyers, parenting trainers, negotiators, ombudsmen, prison project officers, human rights advocates, and religious leaders such as ministers and rabbis. These jobs may be found in *occupational sectors* such as community organizing, politics, nonprofit management, criminal justice, and international development, among others.

THINK ABOUT CAREERS

- Using what you have learned in sociology to this point, identify some particular conflicts that exist and persist between groups in society. Are people in any of the occupational fields or jobs listed above involved in managing, mediating, or resolving these conflicts?
- Think about possible career paths of interest to you. How might knowledge concerning conflict dynamics and conflict resolution skills be of value to you in a future job?

SUMMARY

- **Global inequality** can be described in terms of disparities in income, wealth, health, education, and access to safe, hygienic sanitation, among other things. Global gaps in equality between high-income, middle-income, and low-income countries remain substantial even as some countries are effectively addressing problems like malnutrition.
- While global inequalities remain substantial, access to mobile technology is improving, as nearly 6 billion of the world's 7 billion people now have access to working mobile phones.
- **Modernization theory** posits that global underdevelopment exists in states that cling to traditional cultures and fail to build modern state and market institutions. **Dependency theory** and **world systems theory** highlight external variables that point out how high-income states benefit from the economic marginality of low-income states.
- Sociologists describe and analyze the phenomenon of a **global elite,** a transglobal class of professionals who exercise considerable economic and political power that is not limited by national borders. The global power elite, while not an entirely new phenomenon, is a product of modernity, brought into growing significance by technological innovation and globalization.
- Sklair theorizes a transnational capitalist class that is composed of elites with economic, political, and cultural ideological influence; he asserts that the members of this class organize the global order in a manner that realizes their own interests and contributes to the expansion and legitimation of a global consumerist ideology. Bauman looks at the development of population categories as defined by their relationships to space, in particular their mobility or lack of mobility.

KEY TERMS

global inequality, 183

gross national income–purchasing power parity per capita (GNI-PPP), 184

infant mortality rate, 186

total fertility rate (TFR), 187

modernization theory, 193

dependency theory, 193

world systems theory, 194

global elite, 197

DISCUSSION QUESTIONS

1. What is global inequality and what are key ways in which it is manifested? Aside from the aspects of inequality discussed in the chapter, what other aspects might sociologists want to look at?
2. Why do many of the world's poorest countries also have the highest fertility rates? What sociological factors can be used to explain the correlation?
3. Can the mass adoption of modern technologies like mobile phones have an impact on poverty in developing countries? What does the chapter suggest? What other effects can you envision?
4. How do modernization theory, dependency theory, and world systems theory explain the existence and persistence of inequality between countries and regions? What are the strengths of these perspectives as analytical tools? What are their weaknesses?
5. What is meant by the term *global elite*? Who are the members of the global elite, and how do they differ from the upper-class elites described in an earlier chapter?

SAGE edge™

Sharpen your skills with SAGE edge at **edge.sagepub.com/chambliss2e**

A personalized approach to help you accomplish your coursework goals in an easy-to-use learning environment.

RACE AND ETHNICITY

IN THIS CHAPTER

Aaron Huey/National Geographic Creative

WHAT DO YOU THINK?

1. What makes a group a "minority"? Does this term have both qualitative and quantitative dimensions?
2. Why does racial residential segregation exist and persist in major U.S. cities? What are the consequences of racial residential segregation?
3. How is the ethnic and racial composition of the United States changing? What factors are driving this change?

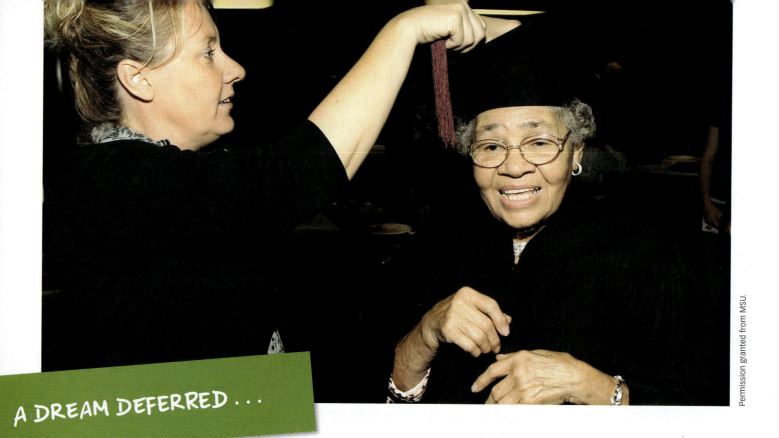

Permission granted from MSU.

A DREAM DEFERRED . . .

African American poet Langston Hughes (1902–1967) is known for, among other writings, the poem “A Dream Deferred” *(sometimes called “Harlem”):

> What happens to a dream deferred
>
> Does it dry up
> like a raisin in the sun?
> Or fester like a sore—
> And then run?
> Does it stink like rotten meat?
> Or crust and sugar over—
> like a syrupy sweet?
>
> Maybe it just sags
> like a heavy load.
>
> *Or does it explode?*

In the 1920s and 1930s, Hughes was one of the writers of the Harlem Renaissance, highlighting issues of race relations and inequality. In his most famous poem, Hughes contemplated the consequences of a “dream deferred.” Indeed, the dreams of many African Americans had been deferred—or denied. Mary Jean Price Walls was among them.

*SOURCE: “Dream Deferred” from *The Collected Poems of Langston Hughes* by Langston Hughes, edited by Arnold Rampersad with David Roessel, Associate Editor. Copyright © 1994 by The Estate of Langston Hughes. Used by permission of Alfred A. Knopf, an imprint of Knopf Doubleday Publishing Group, a division of Random House LLC, and Harold Ober Associates. All rights reserved.

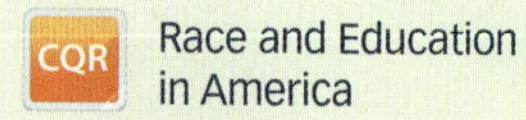

Mary Jean Price Walls, the child of a Black mother and a White father, dreamed of being a teacher. In 1950, Mary Jean was the salutatorian of her graduating class at Lincoln High School, an all-Black school. She applied for admission to Missouri State University (MSU), the only institution of higher education near her home and, thus, the only one she could afford to attend. She never received an answer and never went to college, instead becoming mother to eight children and, later, cleaning homes and working as a janitor (Moore, 2012).

At age 52, one of Walls's sons, Terry Walls, went back to college, enrolling at MSU. As a student, he sought to find out why his mother had been denied admission to the school. Using the university archives, he tracked down the thin, onionskin paper on which his mother's application for admission was written. He also learned that MSU's regents had held a special meeting: "Formal minutes reveal that her application was denied because those same classes were available at the all-black college four hours away" (Moore, 2012). Without funds to attend a college away from home, Mary Jean could not realize her dream of being a teacher. Desegregation of U.S. education would begin slowly with the Supreme Court ruling in *Brown v. Board of Education* in 1954, too late for Mary Jean to achieve her ambition.

In 2010, MSU granted Mary Jean an honorary degree, recognizing the opportunity that had been closed to her by racism. In 2012, MSU awarded a diploma to Terry Walls, her son, for completion of his college work.

What are we to conclude from Mary Jean's story? Clearly, her dream was denied. Today, African Americans like Mary Jean's children have legally protected opportunities for education and professional success. But race is still a powerful social force, influencing interpersonal interactions and institutional arrangements in the United States. And racism, though often more subtle than that experienced by Mary Jean, remains a potent obstacle for many who seek to fulfill dreams of education, housing, and professional achievement. ■

Race: A group of people who share a set of characteristics (usually physical characteristics) deemed by society to be socially significant.

CQR Post Racial Society: Fact or Fiction?

Race and ethnicity are key issues in sociology. We begin this chapter with a discussion of the social construction of race and ethnicity. We then consider some of forms that minority-majority group relations may take. We also look at theoretical perspectives on ethnicity, racism, and minority group status. This leads to a discussion of prejudice and discrimination and the consequences of these social phenomena. We then examine the experiences of different racial and ethnic groups in the United States and how group membership may shape people's political, economic, and social status. Finally, we consider the historical and contemporary significance of race in a global perspective, focusing in particular on racial labeling and the crime of genocide in recent history.

THE SOCIAL CONSTRUCTION OF RACE AND ETHNICITY

Sociologists W. I. Thomas and Dorothy Thomas (1928) observed that "if [people] define situations as real, they are real in their consequences" (pp. 571–572). The wisdom of the Thomases' observation is powerfully demonstrated by the way societies construct definitions of racial and ethnic groups and then respond as though the definitions represent objective realities.

RACE

One of the most dynamic areas of scientific research in recent years has been the Human Genome Project. Among its compelling findings is the discovery that genetically all human beings are nearly identical. Less than 0.01% of the total gene pool contributes to racial differences (as manifested in physical characteristics), whereas thousands of genes contribute to traits that include intelligence, artistic talent, athletic talent, and social skills (Angier, 2000; Cavalli-Sforza, Menozzi, & Piazza, 1994). Based on this research, many scientists agree that "race is a *social concept*, not a *scientific* one. . . . we all evolved in the last 100,000 years from the same small number of tribes that migrated out of Africa and colonized the world" (Angier, 2000).

Sociologists define a **race** as *a group of people who share a set of characteristics (usually physical characteristics) deemed by society to be socially significant.* Notice that this definition suggests that physical characteristics are not the only—or even necessarily the most important—way of defining "races." For many years, Catholics and Protestants in Ireland defined one another as separate races, and the United States long considered Jews a separate racial category from Europeans, even though distinctive physical characteristics between these groups are in the eye of the beholder rather than objectively verifiable (Schaefer, 2009).

While sociologists do not treat race as scientifically significant, it is, as we will see in this chapter, *socially significant.* Following the observation of the Thomases, we can conclude that because race is defined as real, it is real in its consequences. Racial differentiation has historically been linked to power: Racial categories have facilitated the treatment (or maltreatment) of others based on membership in given racial groups.

Notably, race is also social scientifically significant. Statistical data on phenomena ranging from obesity and poverty to crime and educational attainment are gathered and sorted by race. This book features such data throughout its pages. While sociologists generally agree that races cannot be objectively, biologically differentiated, it is a fact that they also use race to sort statistics and establish social facts about groups in society. This implicitly acknowledges that this "social concept" is profoundly real as a differentiating mechanism with historical and contemporary consequences.

ETHNICITY

Although race may be a particularly significant social category in terms of consequences for people's lives, other socially defined categorizations are also important. Among these, ethnicity ranks next to race in significance. **Ethnicity** refers to *characteristics of groups associated with national origins, languages, and cultural and religious practices.* While ethnicity can be based on cultural self-identification (that is, one may choose to embrace one's Irish or Brazilian roots and traditions), an acknowledgment or degree of acceptance by a larger group is often necessary. For example, a third-generation Italian American may choose to self-identify as Italian. If he cannot speak Italian, however, others who identify as Italian may not see him as "authentically" Italian. The sociological significance of belonging to a particular racial or ethnic group is that society may treat group members differently, judging them or giving them favorable or unfavorable treatment based on membership and perceived affiliation.

MINORITIES

Any racial, ethnic, religious, or other group can constitute a "minority" in a society. **Minorities** are *less powerful groups who are dominated politically and economically by a more powerful group and, often, who experience discrimination on the basis of characteristics deemed by the majority to be socially significant.* Minorities are usually distinguished by gender or physical and cultural attributes that make them recognizable to the dominant group. Minorities often are fewer in number than the dominant population. In the United States, African Americans, Latinos, and Asians are less numerous than the White majority, though the higher number of births among non-Whites, combined with immigration, will begin to change this fact in coming decades.

Although one usually thinks of minorities as being fewer in number (the term implies a numerical difference), the important aspect of being a minority group is that the group has relatively *less access to power and resources valued by society.* Thus, sociologically, women in the United States, and in most cultures worldwide, may be considered a minority despite the fact that they outnumber men. In South Africa before the end of apartheid rule in the early 1990s, a small number of Whites dominated the much larger minority of what were termed Black, colored, and mixed races.

MINORITY AND DOMINANT GROUP RELATIONS

Modern societies are characterized by racial and ethnic heterogeneity, as well as by divisions between dominant and minority groups. The coexistence of racial and ethnic groups can be a source of social conflict. Among minorities' most frequently used methods of resolving such conflict are social movements designed to challenge and change existing social relations. In extreme cases, resolution may be sought through revolution or rebellion. Dominant populations respond to such social movements with a variety of social and political policies, ranging from expulsion and segregation to assimilation of minorities and the acceptance of cultural pluralism. We discuss this spectrum of relationships below.

EXPULSION

Conflicts between White settlers and Native Americans over land and resources in the United States in the 1800s often ended with the removal of Native Americans to isolated reservations. Sociologically, *the process of forcibly removing people from one part of the country* is referred to as **expulsion**. Native Americans populated broad swaths of North America when the first European settlers arrived. As U.S. settlement expanded westward, Native Americans were driven under military arms to march, sometimes thousands of miles, to areas designated by the government as Native American reservations. These reservations continue to be socially and economically marginal areas (Figure 9.1).

Today, across the globe, people are being forced from their homes due to civil wars, ethnic and sectarian conflicts, and rebellions. It is estimated that in 2013 the number of displaced persons and refugees reached more than 39 million: 29 million internally

Ethnicity: Characteristics of groups associated with national origins, languages, and cultural and religious practices.

Minorities: Less powerful groups who are dominated by a more powerful group and, often, discriminated against on the basis of characteristics deemed by the majority to be socially significant.

Expulsion: The process of forcibly removing a population from a particular area.

FIGURE 9.1 American Indian Reservations in the United States

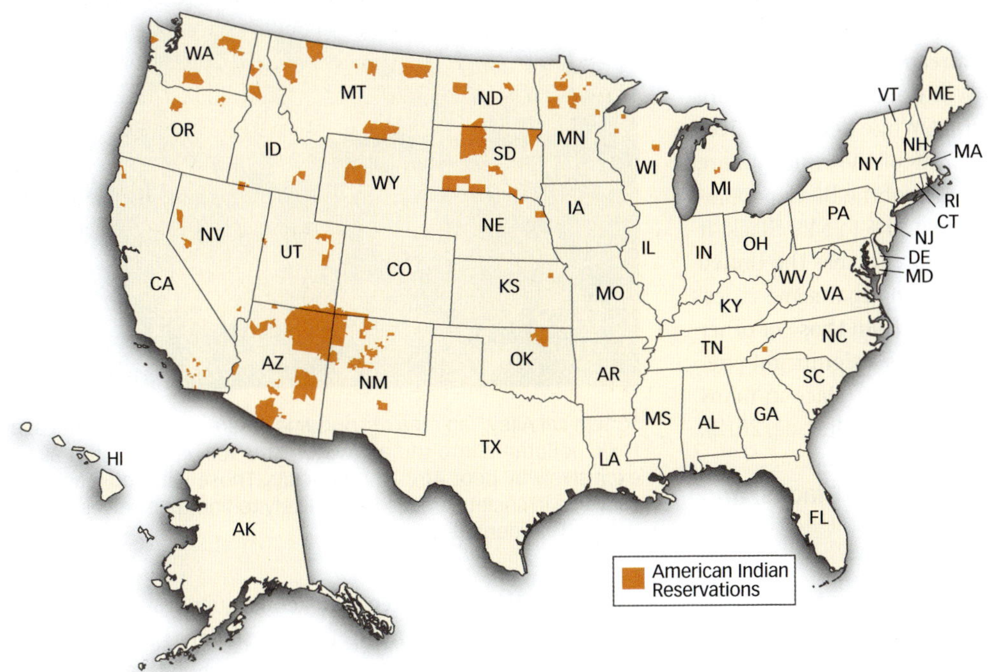

SOURCE: U.S. Parks Service.

displaced and more than 10 million refugees. While not all are victims of official policies of expulsion, many suffer the dire consequences of ethnic clashes between dominant and minority groups (United Nations High Commissioner for Refugees, 2012, 2013).

SEGREGATION

Conflict and tensions involving race and ethnicity can also be linked to institutionalized and enforced **segregation**, *the practice of separating people spatially or socially on the basis of race or ethnicity.* In South Africa, apartheid was state policy until the beginning of the 1990s. The release from prison of antiapartheid activist Nelson Mandela in 1990 and the end of a ban on previously forbidden groups began the process of desegregation in that country, which has slowly evolved in the wake of the establishment of democracy in 1994. Apartheid was an extreme form of segregation that included not only prohibitions on where members of different racial and ethnic groups could live, but where they could travel and at what hours of the day they could be in different parts of particular cities. While apartheid is no longer policy, the legacy of segregation lives on in many South African communities, where the White, Black, and colored populations still live separately and unequally.

Before the 1960s, segregation on the basis of race was common practice and legally upheld in many parts of the United States. In some places it was a crime for Whites to rent apartments or sell homes to non-Whites (Molotch, 1972). In the South, Blacks could not sit in the same restaurants as Whites. When they rode the same buses, Blacks were required by law to sit at the back. In other parts of the country, restaurants and hotels could refuse to serve dark-skinned customers.

The civil rights movement of the 1960s succeeded in securing the passage of federal laws that outlawed segregation. Despite this success, high levels of racial segregation remain a reality in U.S. cities. Why is this the case in the post–civil rights era? First, it is legal and commonplace for housing markets to be segregated by income. Since minorities tend to be poorer then Whites, many cannot afford to live in predominantly White neighborhoods, where residents may be wealthier and housing costs higher. Second, laws outlawing the consideration of race in home rental and sale practices are not always followed by real estate agents, landlords, and lenders, who may steer minorities away from predominantly White neighborhoods (Squires, 2003; Squires, Friedman, & Saidat, 2002). Third, White residents sometimes move out of neighborhoods when increasing numbers of minority residents move in (Woldoff, 2011).

Segregation: The practice of separating people spatially or socially on the basis of race or ethnicity.

South Africa's apartheid was a system of privilege based on race. With racial identity determining social status and access to resources in society, Whites sat atop a hierarchy of power, while Black South Africans were at the bottom.

Low-income African Americans and Latinos are especially likely to live in highly segregated communities in the largest U.S. cities, such as Los Angeles, Chicago, and Milwaukee (Figure 9.2). According to the U.S. Census Bureau (2010), some urban neighborhoods are more than 90% White and others are more than 90% Black or Hispanic. The average White household lives in a neighborhood where more than 75% of the residents are White. On the other hand, more than 50% of the Black population lives in neighborhoods that vary from 34% to 54% Black. It is important to note that metropolitan areas across the United States vary greatly in racial composition and that some cities' neighborhoods are less racially segregated than those of other cities. Racial residential segregation remains a significant phenomenon, though positive changes have taken place in many metropolitan areas in recent decades (Turner & McDade, 2012).

FIGURE 9.2 Concentration of Whites, Blacks, and Hispanics in Milwaukee, 2010

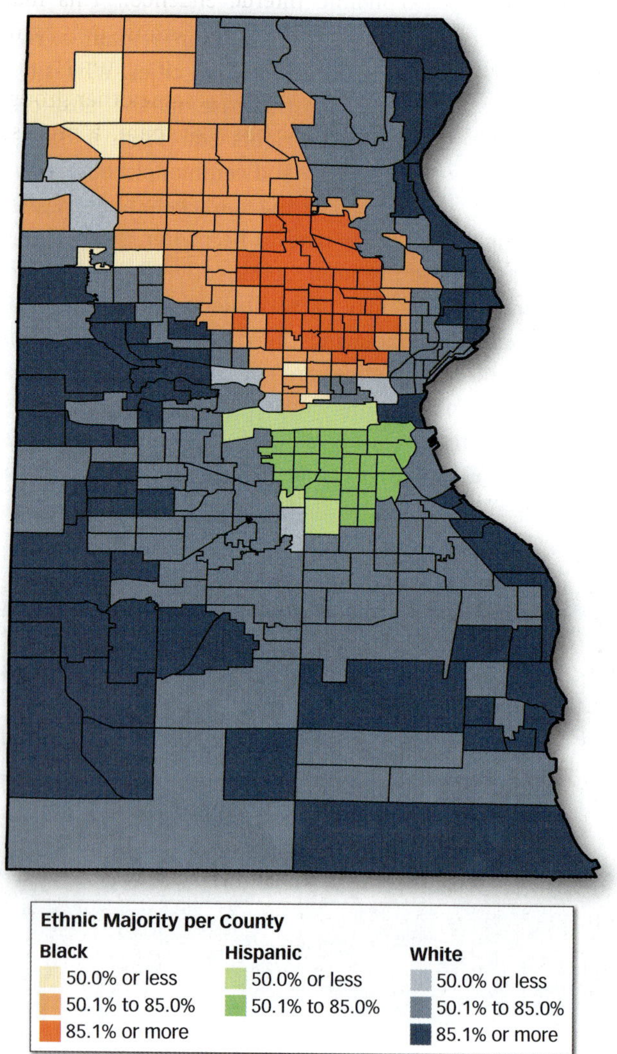

SOURCE: Sharp, G. (2011, March 30). 2010 census data on residential segregation. Sociological Images. Retrieved from http://thesocietypages.org/socimages/2011/03/30/2010-census-data-on-residential-segregation.

"Chemical Alley," an area of Louisiana where chemical plants spew toxic pollutants into the air, water, and soil, is populated almost exclusively by poor African Americans. Those with the least political voice in society are also most likely to find themselves in highly polluted residential areas.

Segregation has negative consequences for minority groups. Apart from denying them residential choice, it often compels them to live in poorer neighborhoods that offer less access to high-quality schools, jobs, and medical facilities (Kozol, 1995; Massey & Denton, 1993). The significant racial wealth gap (Figure 9.3) reflects in part the effects of segregated neighborhoods. As we noted in Chapter 7, the primary source of wealth for most working- and middle-class Americans is home equity. Lower average property values in minority neighborhoods, then, translate to lower wealth in the community. Poor and segregated neighborhoods and regions are also more likely to be the locations of hazardous waste facilities and other sources of pollution, a problem that plagues minority communities from urban Los Angeles to rural Louisiana.

In sum, racial residential segregation contributes to the concentration of economic disadvantage. Pursuing greater opportunities, members of minority groups may seek to move to more diverse neighborhoods. Unfortunately, historically and today, powerful social forces of poverty and discrimination have kept and continue to keep many from achieving this goal.

ASSIMILATION AND CULTURAL PLURALISM

Throughout much of the 20th century, sociologists who studied minorities, race, and ethnicity assumed that the ultimate destiny of most minority groups was **assimilation**, or *absorption into the dominant culture.* U.S. citizens have long prided themselves on being part of a vast "melting pot" in which fundamental ethnic differences gradually disappear and the population is boiled into a single cultural soup. This view was strengthened by the experience of many immigrant groups,

Assimilation: The absorption of a minority group into the dominant culture.

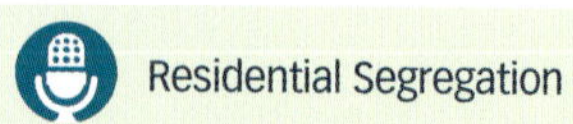

FIGURE 9.3 Average and Median Net Worth of Households by Race, 2009

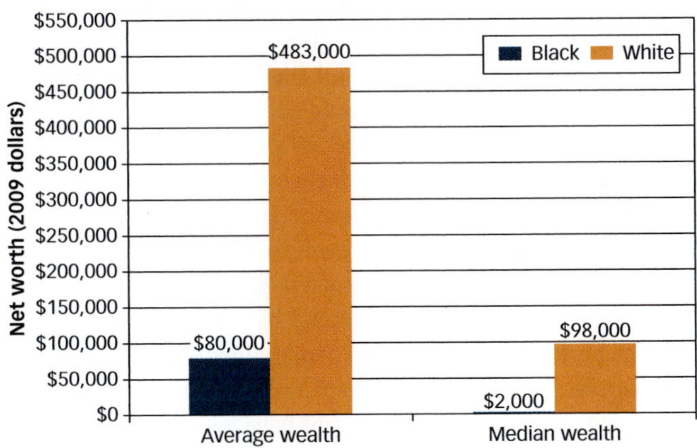

SOURCE: Adapted from "Trends in median wealth by race," Lawrence Mishel, September 21, 2011. Economic Policy Institute.

particularly from Northern European countries, who adopted the norms, values, and folkways of the dominant culture to increase their social acceptance as well as their economic success.

While migrant groups have historically sought to assimilate into the dominant majority group, many also want to retain their unique identities. Some American Indian nations, for example, have long sought to keep alive their own traditions and beliefs. In **cultural pluralism**, *the coexistence of different racial and ethnic groups is characterized by acceptance of one another's differences.* Such a society resembles a *salad bowl* rather than a *melting pot.* Cultural differences are respected for their contribution to the richness of society as a whole. While cultural pluralists criticize the forced segregation that results from prejudice and discrimination, they argue that people's continuing connections to their own ethnic communities help them to preserve their cultural heritages and, at the same time, provide networks of mutual social and economic support.

The relative merits of assimilation and cultural pluralism remain controversial, but sociologists generally agree that the debates over these issues will continue to be a fundamental part of changing racial and ethnic relations in the modern world.

THEORETICAL APPROACHES TO ETHNICITY, RACISM, AND MINORITY STATUS

Throughout this text, we seek to highlight the ways in which key theoretical perspectives in sociology can illuminate social phenomena, including socioeconomic stratification, poverty, and deviance. In this section, we look at ethnicity, racism, and minority group status using the functionalist, conflict, and symbolic interactionist lenses.

Cultural pluralism: The coexistence of different racial and ethnic groups, characterized by acceptance of one another's differences.

THE FUNCTIONALIST PERSPECTIVE

One of functionalism's key assumptions is that a social phenomenon exists and persists because it serves a positive function in a community or society, contributing to order and harmony. Beginning with classical sociologists Auguste Comte and Émile Durkheim and extending to contemporary functionalist theorizing, the basic functionalist assumption is that solidarity characterizes social groupings. Durkheim believed that social groups held together by *mechanical solidarity* and based on homogeneity in, among other things, language and culture are more culturally durable than are those based on *organic solidarity,* which involves interdependence (for instance, economic interdependence). This may help us understand the cohesion of many ethnic groups in the United States. Whether they are Armenian Americans, Egyptian Americans, Cuban Americans, or some other group, people gravitate toward those who are like them, a process rooted in shared pasts and practices.

It is far more challenging to apply the functionalist perspective to *racism* as a phenomenon. Racism cannot be positively functional for a community or society because, by definition, it marginalizes some members of the group. It can, however, be positively functional for some groups while being detrimental for others. Asking "How is this functional for some groups?" takes us close to the key conflict question: "Who benefits from this phenomenon or institution—and who loses?" In the next section, we examine *who benefits* from racism.

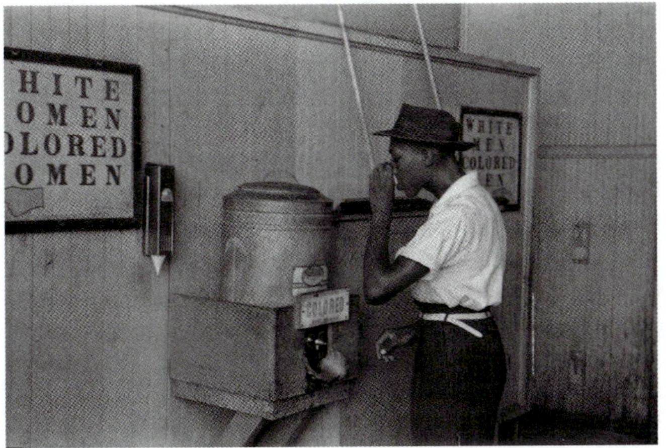

Prior to the passage of civil rights legislation in the 1960s, many U.S. societal institutions and places—from public transportation and education to public restrooms and access to housing—were legally separated along racial lines. Signs like the one in the photo were commonplace.

The cognitive dissonance of espousing values of freedom, equality, and justice for all, while simultaneously maintaining an inhumane system of slave labor, required some kind of rationalization. The cruel treatment of Blacks in the era of slavery suggests that many White Americans at the time did not view them as fully human.

THE CONFLICT PERSPECTIVE

Consider that **racism**, *the idea that one racial or ethnic group is inherently superior to another,* offers a justification for racial inequality and associated forms of stratification such as socioeconomic inequality. If a powerful group defines itself as "better" than another group, then the unequal treatment and distribution of resources can be rationalized as acceptable—or even "natural."

Slavery in the United States was a fundamentally racist phenomenon. It was possible for Whites in the South (and many in the North) to justify the maltreatment of Blacks because they did not see Blacks as fully human. Senator John Calhoun, who represented South Carolina and died just over a decade before the Civil War, wrote in a letter that "the African is incapable of self-care and sinks into lunacy under the burden of freedom. It is a mercy to him to give him the guardianship and protection from mental death" (quoted in Silva, 2001, p. 71).

In legal terms, racism was clear in the Three-Fifths Compromise, which emerged at the Constitutional Convention in Philadelphia in 1787. Delegates from the North and South agreed that for purposes of taxation and political representation, each slave would be counted as three fifths of a person. The compromise was needed because abolitionists wanted to count only free people. Slaveholders and their supporters wanted to count slaves, whose presence would add to their states' population counts and thus their representation in Congress. Those who held slaves but did not permit them to be free or to vote still gained politically from their presence. In economic terms, slavery was of benefit to plantation owners and their families, who could reap the financial benefits of a population of workers who could be bought and sold, who could be exploited and abused, and who performed difficult and demanding work without pay.

It can be argued that capitalism and economic development in the early United States would not have been so robust without the country's reliance on an enslaved labor force, which contributed most fully to the development of a growing agricultural economy in the South. The North, too, was home to numerous beneficiaries and proponents of slavery.

After the end of slavery, racism continued to manifest in new forms, including Jim Crow laws, which followed in the decade after slavery and lasted until the middle of the 20th century. These laws legally mandated segregation of public facilities in the South and fundamentally limited Blacks' ability to exercise their rights. The schools, accommodations, and opportunities afforded to Blacks were invariably inferior to those offered to Whites. Local and state governments could therefore expend fewer funds on their Black populations, and White populations benefited from reduced competition in higher education and the labor market. Racism made Jim Crow laws both possible and widely acceptable, because it offered a basic justification for their existence and persistence.

While racism is clearly of no benefit to its victims and has negative effects on society as a whole, the conflict perspective entreats us to recognize the ways in which it has provided benefits for some more powerful groups in society. These benefits help to explain the existence and persistence of racism over time.

THE SYMBOLIC INTERACTIONIST PERSPECTIVE

Sociologist Louis Wirth (1945) has noted that minority groups share particular traits. First, membership in a minority group is essentially involuntary—that is, someone is socially classified as a member of a group that is discriminated against and is not, in most instances, free to opt out. Second, as we discussed above, minority status is a question not of numbers ("minorities" may outnumber the dominant group) but rather of control of valued

Racism: The idea that one racial group is inherently superior to another; often results in institutionalized relationships between dominant and minority groups that create a structure of economic, social, and political inequality based on socially constructed racial or ethnic categories.

resources. Third, minorities do not share the full privileges of mobility or opportunity enjoyed by the dominant group. Finally, membership in the minority group conditions the treatment of group members by others in society. Specifically, Wirth states, societal minorities are "treated as members of a category, irrespective of their individual merits" (p. 349).

Wirth's definition recalls symbolic interactionist Erving Goffman's concept of a **stigma**, an *attribute that is deeply discrediting to an individual or a group because it overshadows other attributes and merits the individual or group may possess.* Goffman (1963b) presented the unlikely scenario of a young woman born without a nose: While the young woman has a spectrum of interesting and engaging characteristics—she is a bright student and a good dancer—she is defined by her stigma, and her treatment by others is ever defined and determined by her "difference."

Goffman examined what he called **mixed contacts**—that is, *interactions between those who are stigmatized and those who are "normal"* (by *normal,* he meant only those who are members of the dominant, nonstigmatized group—the term was not intended to denote normality as contrasting with deviance). Goffman concluded that mixed contacts are shaped by the presence of the stigma, which influences the way each social interaction unfolds. While the stigmatized identity may not be the point of the interaction, it is inevitably a part of it. Think about your own social interactions: Have you experienced what Goffman describes? How would you expand or modify his sociological description based on those experiences?

In the next section, we turn to issues of prejudice and discrimination, considering how our judgments about someone's race or ethnicity—or about the racial or ethnic identity of an entire group—are manifested in practice.

PREJUDICE, STEREOTYPING, AND DISCRIMINATION

Prejudice is *a belief about an individual or a group that is not subject to change on the basis of evidence.* Prejudices are thus inflexible attitudes toward others. Sociologist Zygmunt Bauman (2001), writing about the Holocaust, eloquently captures this idea: "Man *is* before he *acts*; nothing he does may change what he is. That is, roughly, the philosophical essence of racism" (p. 60). Recall Wirth's point about the characteristics of a social minority: Membership in the disadvantaged group matters more than individual merit.

When prejudices are strongly held, no amount of evidence is likely to change the belief. Among neo-Nazis, for example, prejudice against Jews runs deep. Some neo-Nazis even deny the occurrence of the Holocaust, despite clearly authentic firsthand accounts, films, and photographs of Nazi Germany's concentration camps, where millions of Jews were killed during World War II. Why do prejudicial beliefs trump evidence in cases such as Holocaust denial? Why is prejudice difficult to overcome, even with facts? We may gain some insight into these issues by looking at another social phenomenon linked to prejudice—stereotyping.

Stereotyping is *the generalization of a set of characteristics to all members of a group.* Ethnic and racial stereotypes are often produced and reproduced in popular films: Think about images in U.S. action movies of scheming Italian mafiosi, tough African American street gangs, and violent Asian gangsters or martial artists. Or consider the ways that we may attribute characteristics—intelligence, entrepreneurship, sloth, or slyness—to entire groups based on experiences with or information from others about just a few members of that group. Stereotyping offers a way for human beings to organize and categorize the social world—but the attributions we make may be deeply flawed.

From a sociological perspective, we may argue that while stereotypes are often flawed, they are also functional for some groups—though dysfunctional for others. Consider that one of the social forces contributing to racism is the desire of one

Prejudice: A belief about an individual or a group that is not subject to change on the basis of evidence.

Stigma: An attribute that is deeply discrediting to an individual or a group because it overshadows other attributes and merits the individual or group may possess.

Mixed contacts: Interactions between those who are stigmatized and those who are "normal." **Stereotyping:** The generalization of a set of characteristics to all members of a group.

Discrimination: The unequal treatment of individuals on the basis of their membership in a group.

© AP Photo/David Longstreath

Many popular sports teams proudly utilize Native Americans as their mascots, a practice that has generated an increasing amount of controversy. The *Washington Post*'s editorial page recently announced that it would no longer use the name "Redskins" in its writings on the team (though the news and sports sections may still do so). Where do you stand on the use of Native Americans as sports mascots?

White Privilege

group to exploit another. Research on early contacts between Europeans and Africans suggests that negative stereotypes of Africans developed *after* Europeans discovered the economic value of exploiting African labor and the natural resources of the African continent. That is, White Europeans stereotyped Black Africans as, for instance, unintelligent or less than human when such images suited the Europeans' need to justify enslavement and economic exploitation of this population.

Discrimination is *the unequal treatment of individuals on the basis of their membership in a group.* Discrimination is often targeted and intentional, but it may also be unintentional—in either case, it denies groups and individuals equal opportunities and blocks access to valued resources.

Sociologists distinguish between individual and institutional discrimination. **Individual discrimination** is *overt and intentional unequal treatment, often based on prejudicial beliefs.* If the manager of an apartment complex refuses to rent a place to someone on the basis of his or her skin color or an employer chooses not to hire someone, even if qualified, because he or she is foreign-born, that is individual discrimination. **Institutionalized discrimination** is *discrimination enshrined in law, public policy, or common practice—it is unequal treatment that has become part of the routine operation of major social institutions like businesses, schools, hospitals, and the government.* Institutionalized discrimination is particularly pernicious because, while it may be clearly targeted and intentional (as in the 1831 law prohibiting teaching slaves to read), it may also be the outcome of customary practices and bureaucratic decisions that result in discriminatory outcomes.

Discrimination against African Americans and women was initially institutionalized in the Constitution of the United States, which excluded members of both groups from voting and holding public office. In 1866, Congress passed the first civil rights act, giving Black men the right to vote, hold public office, use public accommodations, and serve on juries. In 1883, however, the U.S. Supreme Court declared the 1866 law unconstitutional, and states then passed laws restricting where minorities could live, go to school, receive accommodations, and such. These laws were upheld by the U.S. Supreme Court in the case of *Plessy v. Ferguson* in 1896. It took more than 75 years for the court to reverse itself.

In the 1960s, the Supreme Court held that laws institutionalizing discrimination were unconstitutional. Open forms of discrimination, such as signs and advertisements that said "Whites only" or "Jews need not apply," were deemed illegal. Research and experience suggest, however, that discrimination often continues in more subtle and complex forms. Consider, once again, the case of housing and discrimination. Institutionalized discrimination affects opportunities for housing and, by extension, opportunities for building individual and

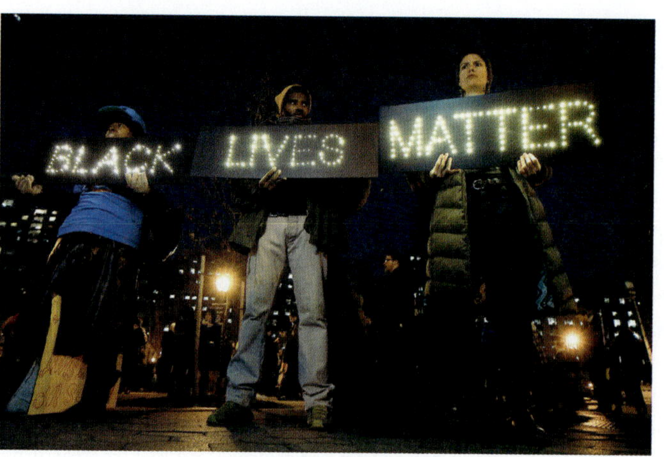

©John Moore/Getty Images

In the fall of 2014, thousands of demonstrators marched in cities including New York, Washington, and Ferguson, Missouri, to protest police brutality and to draw attention to several cases in which unarmed Black men were killed by officers.

community wealth through home ownership. We noted earlier in the chapter that African Americans often still live in segregated neighborhoods. Discrimination is part of the reason; for example, Blacks have been historically less likely to secure mortgages. Paired testing studies in which researchers have sent Black and White applicants with nearly identical financial profiles to apply for mortgages have determined that Whites as a group continue to be advantaged in their treatment by lending institutions (Silverman, 2005). Among other benefits, Whites enjoy higher rates of approval and better loan conditions (Turner, Popkin, & Rawlings, 2009).

These practices, as we saw earlier, have had a powerful effect on the wealth gap between Whites and African Americans. Because most wealth held by the U.S. middle class exists in the form of home equity, the opportunity to own a home in a neighborhood with good property values is a key way to accrue wealth.

The turn of the millennium, however, ushered in a shift in mortgage lending. Banks had plenty of money to lend for home purchases, and among those targeted by banks eager to make mortgage loans were minorities, even those with low incomes and poor credit. The lending bonanza was no boon for these groups, however, because many of the loans made were subprime (subprime loans carry a higher risk that the borrower will default, and the terms are more stringent to compensate for this risk). Subprime loans were five times more common in predominantly Black neighborhoods than in White ones (Pettit & Reuben, 2010), and many borrowers did not fully understand the terms of their loans, such as "balloon" interest rates that rose dramatically over the life of a loan. One consequence was a massive wave of foreclosures beginning in 2008.

Individual discrimination: Overt and intentional unequal treatment, often based on prejudicial beliefs.

Institutionalized discrimination: Unequal treatment that has become a part of the routine operation of such major social institutions as businesses, schools, hospitals, and the government.

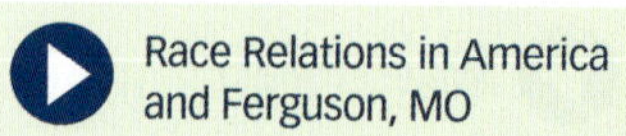

While minority and poor communities were not the only ones affected by the subprime loan fiasco, they were disproportionately harmed. The Center for Responsible Lending (2011) estimates that "property depreciation related to foreclosures between 2009 and 2012 [will] end up costing black communities $194 billion and Latino communities $177 billion." Foreclosures have hit these communities hard: In 2011, the Latino foreclosure rate was nearly 12%, and for Blacks it was just under 10%. By comparison, the foreclosure rate for Asians was just over 6%; for Whites it was 5% (Weller, Ajinkya, & Farrell, 2012).

In the three sections that follow, we discuss contemporary manifestations and consequences of individual and institutionalized discrimination, highlighting housing, the justice system, and women's health.

TECHNOLOGIES OF DISCRIMINATION

Have you recently rented or purchased an apartment or a home? Did you consult the classified ads in your local newspaper, or drive around desirable neighborhoods looking for rental or sale signs? In all likelihood, you went to the Internet and headed for a site such as Craigslist, which offers, among many other things, advertisements for rental units of all sizes and price points. Between 50% and 70% of all renters utilize the Internet in searching for a home, up from just 2% in 1995 (National Association of Realtors, 2006). Among those seeking a home to buy, the figure is even higher. Enforcement of the Fair Housing Act, the primary purpose of which is to keep discriminatory practices in check, has not kept pace with the explosive growth of the online housing market. From blatant "Whites only" statements to more veiled implications that people of color will not be accepted, the Internet is rife with the potential for housing discrimination.

Recent research shows that some housing providers and sellers are selecting interested parties who have "White"-sounding names over those whose names sound "ethnic." For example, a recent study used Craigslist to analyze responses of potential housing providers to home seekers giving their names as Neil, Tyrone, and Jorge (Friedman, Squires, & Galvan, 2010). The researchers found that respondents with "White-sounding" names (for example, Neil) were most likely to get multiple responses, be put in touch with the housing provider, be offered the opportunity to look at the house, and be told the property is available. While racial and ethnic discrimination are not legal in modern America, new forms of digitally enabled discrimination are challenging integration efforts and reinforcing long-existing patterns of segregation in U.S. communities. The Internet can also be a source of other forms of prejudice and discrimination, as we discuss in the *Technology and Society* box on page 214.

PRISON, POLITICS, AND POWER

One of the key rights of U.S. citizenship is the right to vote—that is, the right to have a voice in the country's political process. Some citizens, however, are denied this right. Many of those who cannot vote have been legally disenfranchised because of state laws that prohibit ex-felons who have served their prison sentences from voting. Statistically speaking, this translates into about 5.3 million disenfranchised individuals, including roughly 1.4 million Black men. A staggering 13% of the Black population cannot legally vote as a direct result of these laws (Sentencing Project, 2011).

In the mid-20th century, more than 70% of those incarcerated in the United States were White; by the end of the 20th century those numbers had reversed, and most prisoners were non-White (Wacquant, 2002; Western & Pettit, 2010). This shift has had a profound effect on African Americans: 48 states prohibit inmates from voting while they are incarcerated, 35 prohibit parolees from voting, and 30 prohibit people on probation from voting. In addition, Virginia, Kentucky, Iowa, and Florida all have lifetime voting bans on anyone who has been convicted of a felony (Sentencing Project, 2011).

Among those disenfranchised African Americans is Jarvious Cotton. Law professor Michelle Alexander writes about Cotton in her book *The New Jim Crow: Mass Incarceration in the Age of Colorblindness* (2010):

> Like his father, grandfather, great-grandfather, and great-great-grandfather, [Jarvious Cotton] has been denied the right to participate in our electoral democracy. . . . Cotton's great-great-grandfather could not vote as a slave. His great-grandfather was beaten to death by the Ku Klux Klan for attempting to vote. His grandfather was prevented from voting by Klan intimidation. His father was barred from voting by poll taxes and literacy tests. Today, Jarvious Cotton cannot vote because he, like many black men in the United States, has been labeled a felon and is currently on parole. . . .
>
> . . . Once you're labeled a felon, the old forms of discrimination—employment discrimination, housing discrimination, denial of the right to vote, denial of educational opportunity, denial of food stamps and other public benefits, and exclusion from jury service—are suddenly legal. . . . We have not ended racial caste in America; we have merely redesigned it. (pp. 1–2)

Alexander (2010) argues that the U.S. criminal justice system effectively functions as a modern incarnation of the Jim Crow laws. Today, she suggests, the expansion of the prison population to include nonviolent offenders, particularly people of color, has contributed to the development of a population denied opportunities to have a political voice as well as education, work, and housing. Prison populations also include women of color (though they are fewer in number). The *Behind the Numbers* box on page 215 points to another aspect of discrimination in the criminal justice system—*colorism.*

Racial Disparities in incarceration

TECHNOLOGY & SOCIETY

HATE GOES DIGITAL

Sociologists use the term **scapegoating** to refer to *one group blaming another for problems that members of the first group face.* As early as the 14th century, social theorist Ibn Khaldun observed that the perception of an outside threat serves to increase solidarity within a society. Scapegoating also aids the bonding of social groups that share a fear or hatred of other populations.

In the United States, scapegoating is commonly used by "hate groups," whose numbers have spiraled upward in recent years. Organized White separatist and supremacist groups target their appeals primarily to lower-income Whites, blaming their poor economic position on other groups, in particular immigrants and Blacks, though Jews have also historically been a target. According to the Southern Poverty Law Center (2013), which tracks hate groups, there were 939 known active hate groups across the United States in 2013, including neo-Nazis, Ku Klux Klan groups, racist skinhead groups, neo-Confederate groups, Black separatists, border vigilantes, and a growing number of antigovernment militias. Hate group activities range from criminal acts to marches, rallies, speeches, pamphlet and book publication, video production, and meetings, both public and secret.

Since 2000, there has been an estimated 54% increase in the number of hate groups (or at least groups known to researchers). Why has the number risen? Key reasons include Latino immigration and an associated perception of threat as the demographic composition shifts away from White dominance in some states, including Texas and California, and among the youngest generations; the election of the first Black president; and the economic crisis, which, even before its official beginning in 2008, hit many communities hard (Southern Poverty Law Center, 2011).

Another potential factor in the growth of hate groups is the Internet. The ease of interaction with like-minded individuals on popular social networking sites has provided fertile soil for hate groups to form, recruit, and spread their messages. The ease of forming or joining a group on the Internet (and the anonymity it offers), the changes in U.S. demographics, and economic uncertainty are a powerful mix: A recent study of online hate group activity identified more than 20,000 "problematic" sites, which included blogs, Twitter accounts, Facebook groups, and other forums associated with the spread of hate. The study also suggested that "digital hate" is on the rise: The number of sites identified as problematic rose by 30% from 2012 to 2013 (Simon Wiesenthal Center, 2013).

"Digital hate" can be manifested as "trolling," taking over a targeted web user's identity and damaging his or her reputation. Antihate activists and groups, including the Southern Poverty Law Center, are among those targeted by hackers representing hate groups or working alone to discredit them. Another digital aspect of the subculture of hate is the popularity of "hate games" that transform violence against gays, immigrants, people of color, or Jews into "entertainment" (Simon Wiesenthal Center, 2011).

The Internet is a powerful method of exercising one's freedom of speech. Some racist groups, like this White pride organization, have taken advantage of the Internet to spread messages of hate. ■

Hate groups have a long history in the United States, but the Internet has transformed the social landscape by offering new forums for communication and recruitment, as well as new and anonymous means of expressing hate and prejudice. While the Internet is also home to groups and organizations actively engaged in combating these trends, the broad proliferation of digital hate remains a problem to be addressed and solved.

THINK IT THROUGH

▶ Can hate speech—or hateful speech—be controlled on the Internet? Should communities or states try to control it through legislation? What are other means of addressing it?

BEHIND THE NUMBERS

BLACK WOMEN, "COLORISM," AND PRISON SENTENCING

In 2011, 26,000 African American women were serving time in U.S. prisons for federal and state crimes (Carson & Sabol, 2012). What characterizes these female prisoners? Most were convicted of nonviolent crimes, including drug crimes. Many are parents from poor communities. According to researchers at Villanova University, another characteristic of imprisoned women is darker skin tone. Related to racism, but useful to distinguish from it, is the phenomenon of *colorism*—that is, discrimination based on skin tone. What does colorism look like in practice?

Researchers examined more than 12,000 cases of Black women sentenced to prison in North Carolina. In order to ensure comparability of cases, they took into account the types of crimes for which the women were sentenced as well as the women's criminal histories. They concluded that women with lighter skin tone were given more lenient sentences and served shorter prison terms than their darker-skinned peers. Specifically, lighter-skinned women were sentenced to about 12% less time and served about 11% less time (Viglione, Hannon, & DeFina, 2011).

Does colorism explain the difference in sentencing? Researchers believe the perception of how "White" someone is does matter—to both Whites and Blacks. William Darity, a professor of African American studies and economics at Duke University and director of the Research Network on Racial and Ethnic Inequality, has conducted research on the impact of skin tone on marriage rates for women and employment for men. Darity points out that "all blacks don't face the same type or degree of discrimination." Furthermore, the preference for lighter-skinned women is expressed by both Black and White men (quoted in Sanders, 2011).

While understanding and combating racism remain key issues on the agenda of researchers and policy makers, *colorism,* reacting to others on the basis of skin color, is also a topic of consequence. A 2008 initiative by the U.S. Equal Employment Opportunity Commission explicitly includes colorism as a form of discrimination (Sanders, 2011).

© Scott Houston/Corbis

THINK IT THROUGH

▶ How might a sociologist explain the more acute discrimination faced by African Americans with darker skin in comparison with their lighter-skinned peers?

CONSEQUENCES OF PREJUDICE AND DISCRIMINATION: RACE AND HEALTH

Sociologists studying discrimination are also interested in the health of populations. Some researchers argue that racism and other disadvantages suffered by Black women in the United States contribute to the much higher level of negative birth outcomes in this population, including low birth weight and infant mortality (Colen, Geronimus, Bound, & James, 2006). Consider the following statistics: Black women are 60% more likely than White women to experience premature births, and Black babies are about 230% more likely than White babies to die before the age of 1 (Norris, 2011). Black women are also more than twice as likely to give birth to very low-weight infants than their White or Latina sisters (Ventura Curtin, Abma, & Henshaw, 2012).

These data suggest that race trumps other identified predictors of health, including age, income, and educational attainment (Norris, 2011). While health outcomes are predictably favorable among White women as they gain economic status and give birth in

Scapegoating: A process in which one group blames another for the problems that members of the first group face.

Racialization of Crime and Punishment in America

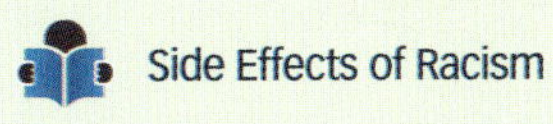

Side Effects of Racism

their 20s and early 30s (rather than their teens), Black women's birth outcomes do not appear to follow this pattern (Colen et al., 2006).

Why is race such a powerful predictor of birth outcomes? Answers to this question are varied and complex. Public health researcher Arline Geronimus (1992) argues that the racial disparity in birth outcomes—and its stubborn resistance to improvement even as Black women make educational and economic gains—can be attributed to a phenomenon she terms *weathering.* Geronimus describes weathering as an amalgamation of racism and stressors ranging from environmental pollutants to crime to poor health care. These lead, she argues, to a demonstrable deterioration of health, including poor birth outcomes, advanced aging, and even early death.

Geronimus's argument was met with skepticism when she proposed it two decades ago, but it has increasingly gained acceptance. Even in their 20s and 30s, Geronimus says, African American women are "suffering from hypertension at two or three times the rate of whites their own age. African-Americans at age 35 have the rates of disability of white Americans who are 55, and we haven't seen much traction over 20 to 30 years of trying to reduce and eliminate these disparities" (quoted in Norris, 2011). To see such medical statistics through the prism of social science is a goal of **social epidemiology**, which is *the study of communities and their social statuses, practices, and problems with the aim of understanding patterns of health and disease.*

It is challenging to draw a direct connection between race-related social stressors and negative health outcomes; critics have questioned the link, and more work remains to be done. However, the work of Geronimus demonstrates how sociology can highlight connections between private troubles—such as the birth of a low-weight or preterm infant—and public issues (Figure 9.4). As Geronimus points out, we are just beginning to see the impact of public policy choices in areas such as housing and economics on women's health (Norris, 2011).

FIGURE 9.4 Racial Disparities in Birth Outcomes in the United States, 1990–2007

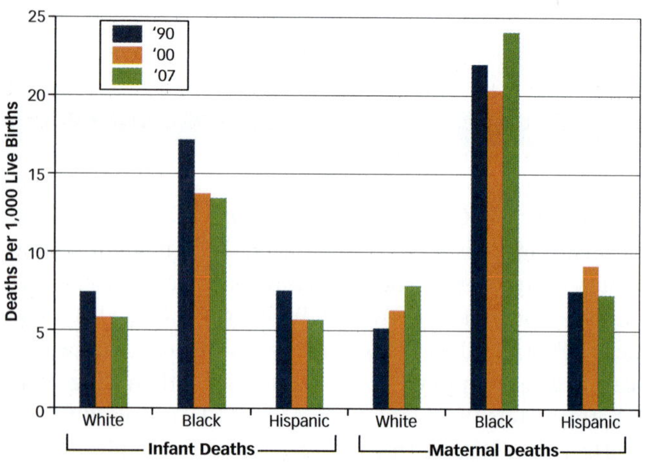

SOURCE: Ventura, S. J., Curtin, S. C., Abma, J. C., & Henshaw, S. K. (2012). Estimated pregnancy rates and rates of pregnancy outcomes for the United States, 1990–2008. *National Vital Statistics Reports, 60*(7).

FIGURE 9.5 U.S. Population by Race and Hispanic Origin, 2012 and 2060 (projected)

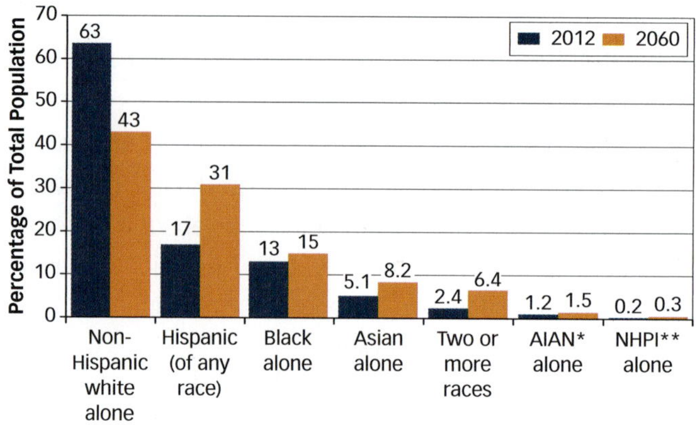

*AIAN: American Indian and Alaska Native

**NHPI: Native Hawaiian and Other Pacific Islander

SOURCE: U.S. Census Bureau. (2012). USA QuickFacts.

Prejudice and discrimination have a long history and take a multitude of forms, some overt, many quite subtle. Will the United States see a decline in prejudice and discrimination as ethnic and racial diversity grows, or will the changing demographic picture make conflicts more acute? Next we look at some of the major groups that make up the U.S. population and see how their numbers are changing.

RACIAL AND ETHNIC GROUPS IN THE UNITED STATES

The area now called the United States was once occupied by hundreds of Native American nations. Later came Europeans, most of whom were English, though early settlers also included the French, Dutch, and Spanish, among others. Beginning in 1619, Africans were brought as slaves and added a substantial minority to the European population. Hundreds of thousands of Europeans continued to arrive from Norway, Sweden, Germany, and Russia to start farms and work in the factories of early industrial America. In the mid-1800s, Chinese immigrants were brought in to provide the heavy labor for building railroads and mining gold and silver. Between 1890 and 1930, nearly 28 million people immigrated to the United States. After the 1950s, immigrants came mostly from Latin America and Asia (Figure 9.6).

Social epidemiology: The study of communities and their social statuses, practices, and problems with the aim of understanding patterns of health and disease.

FIGURE 9.6 Number of Persons Obtaining Legal Permanent U.S. Resident Status, 1820–2010

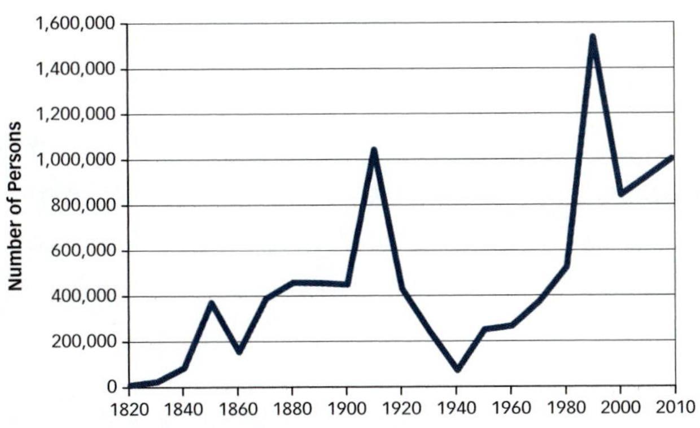

SOURCE: Department of Homeland Security, Office of Immigration Statistics, *Yearbook of Immigration Statistics*, 2010.

Today, non-Whites make up just under 30% of the U.S. population. If current trends hold, non-Whites will constitute a numeric majority nationwide by about 2040. Non-Whites already constitute a majority in Texas, which has a growing Latino population. Between 2000 and 2012, the U.S. Latino population nearly doubled, to more than 16% percent of the U.S. population, surpassing African Americans (about 13%). Asians also experienced double-digit growth from 2000 to 2010 and now constitute about 5% of the U.S. population (Humes, Jones, & Ramirez, 2011).

The rapid growth of minority populations reflects growth from both new births and migration. Migration is the primary engine of population growth in the United States. In fact, demographers estimate that by the middle of the 21st century, fully one fifth of the U.S. population will be immigrants. In a population estimated to reach more than 438 million by 2050, 67 million will be immigrants, and about 50 million will be the children and grandchildren of immigrants (Pew Research Center, 2008). Overall, the trend toward a more racially and ethnically diverse country is clear: At the time of the 2010 census, the majority of children under 2 years old were non-White.

In the following sections we look in more depth at the racial and ethnic groups that have come together to constitute U.S. culture and society today.

AMERICAN INDIANS

There is no agreement on how many people were living in North America when the Europeans arrived around the beginning of the 16th century, but anthropologists' best guess is about 20 million. Thousands of thriving societies existed throughout North and South America in this period. Encounter between European explorers and Native Americans soon became conquest, and despite major resistance, the indigenous populations were eventually defeated and their lands confiscated by European settlers. It is believed that between 1500 and 1800 the North American Indian population was reduced from more than 20 million to fewer than 600,000 (Haggerty, 1991). American Indians, like conquered and oppressed peoples everywhere, did not passively accept the European invasion. The "Indian Wars" are among the bloodiest in U.S. history, but resistance was not enough. First, White settlers had access to superior weaponry that Native Americans could not effectively counter. Second, Whites' control of political, economic, and environmental policies gave them a powerful advantage. Consider, for instance, the U.S. government's decision to permit the unregulated slaughter of bison (buffalo) in the post–Civil War era. From about 1866, when millions of bison roamed the American West and the Great Plains, to the 1890s, this key Native American resource was decimated until just a few thousand remained (Moloney, 2012; Smits, 1994).

Since the 1960s, some Native Americans have focused on efforts to force the U.S. government to honor treaties and improve their living conditions, particularly on reservations. In 1969, the group Indians of All Tribes (IAT), citing the Treaty of Fort Laramie (1868), which states that all unused or abandoned federal land must be returned to the Indians, seized the abandoned island of Alcatraz, a former prison island in the San Francisco Bay, and issued a proclamation that contained the following (deliberately ironic) declarations: "We, the native Americans, re-claim the land known as Alcatraz Island in the name of all American Indians by right of discovery. . . . We feel that this so-called Alcatraz Island is more than suitable for an Indian Reservation, as determined by the white man's own standards." The IAT went on to note the island's "suitability" by pointing out that, among other things, it had no fresh running water, no industries to provide employment, no health care facilities, and no oil or mineral rights for inhabitants. This comparison was intended to point to the devastating conditions on most reservations.

The IAT occupied Alcatraz for more than 18 months. The occupation ended when some IAT members left due to poor living conditions, as the federal government shut off all power and water to the island, and others were removed when the government took control of the island in June 1971.

Despite centuries of struggle, more than 60% of the 4.9 million American Indians in the United States today live in urban areas and are among the poorest people in the nation: More than half of all Native American children are born into poverty, three times the rate for White children. About 1.9 million Native Americans live on reservations, where unemployment rates run as high as 50%. With limited economic opportunities, Native Americans also have relatively low educational attainment: Just 13% have earned bachelor's degrees (Ogunwole, Drewery, & Rios-Vargas, 2012).

Native American Struggles

©AARON HUEY/National Geographic Creative

American Indians lived in the territorial United States long before the political state was established. They suffered the loss of territory and population as a result of U.S. government policies. Even today, American Indian communities face unique challenges.

The *Inequality Matters* box on page 220 raises another issue pertinent to the status of Native Americans in the United States: Who has the power to name this population?

AFRICAN AMERICANS

In 1903, W. E. B. Du Bois penned the following words: "The problem of the Twentieth Century is the problem of the color line" (1903/2008, p. 9). By that he meant that grappling with the legacy of 250 years of slavery would be one of the great problems of the 20th century. Indeed, as this chapter shows, Du Bois was right, although he did not foresee that the "color line" would incorporate not just African Americans but Hispanics, Asians, American Indians, and other minorities as well.

Slavery forcibly brought more than 9 million people, mostly from West Africa, to North and South America. Although the stereotype of slaves gratefully serving their White masters dominated U.S. culture for many years, the fact is that slave revolts were frequent throughout the South. More than 250 Black uprisings against slavery were recorded from 1700 to 1865, and many others were not recorded (Greenberg, 1996; Williams-Meyers, 1996).

Immediately following the end of slavery, during the Reconstruction period, African Americans sought to establish political and economic equality. Former slaves gained the right to vote, and in some jurisdictions they constituted the majority of registered voters. Black legislators were elected in every southern state. Between 1870 and 1901, 22 Blacks served in the U.S. Congress, while hundreds of others served in state legislatures, on city councils, and as elected and appointed officials throughout the South (Holt, 1977). Their success was short-lived. White southern legislators, still a majority, passed Jim Crow laws excluding Blacks from voting and using public transportation. In time, every aspect of life was constrained for Blacks, including access to hospitals, schools, restaurants, churches, jobs, recreation sites, and cemeteries. By 1901, because literacy was required to vote and most Blacks had been effectively denied even a basic education, the registration of Black voters had dwindled to a mere handful (Morrison, 1987).

The North's higher degree of industrialization offered a promise of economic opportunity, even though social and political discrimination existed there as well. Between 1940 and 1970, more than 5 million African Americans left the rural South for what they hoped would be a better life in the North (Lemann, 1991). Whether they stayed in the South or moved to the North, however, many Blacks were still being denied fundamental rights nearly 100 years after slavery was abolished.

By the 1950s, the social landscape was changing—consider the fact that having fought against a racist regime in Nazi Germany in the 1940s, the United States found it far more difficult to justify continued discrimination against its own minority populations. Legal mandates for equality, however, did not easily translate to actual practices, and the 1960s saw a wave of protest from African Americans eager to claim greater rights and opportunities. The civil rights movement was committed to nonviolent forms of protest. Participants in the movement used strikes, boycotts, voter registration drives, sit-ins, and freedom rides in their efforts to achieve racial equality. In 1964, following what was at the time the largest civil rights demonstration in the nation's history, a march on Washington, D.C., the federal government passed the first in a series of civil rights laws that made it illegal to discriminate on the basis of race, sex, religion, physical disability, or ethnic origin.

All African Americans have not benefited from legislation aimed at abolishing discrimination (Wilson, 2010). In particular, the poorest Blacks—those living in disadvantaged urban and rural areas—lack the opportunities that could make a difference in their lives. Many poor Black Americans suffer from having very little social capital, including uneducated parents, inadequate schools, lack of skills and training, and poor local job opportunities. As a result, nearly half of all African American workers are today employed in unskilled or semi-skilled service jobs—as health care aides, janitors, and food service workers, for example—compared with only a quarter of all Whites. Few of these occupations offer the opportunity to earn a living wage.

Over time, African Americans have been broadly successful in improving their economic circumstances. The economic gains of African Americans, however, have been more tenuous than those of most other groups, and the Great Recession that began in 2007 substantially eroded Black wealth and income in America. Consider that from 2007 to 2010 the median income of Black Americans fell by about 10%, while that of White Americans dropped by 5% (Mishel, Bivens, Gould, & Shierholz, 2012).

Although African Americans have had mixed success in gaining economic power, as a group they have seen important gains in political power. In the early 1960s, there were only 103 African Americans holding public office in the United States. By 1970, about 715 Blacks held elected office at the city and county levels. By the 1990s, however, the figure had surpassed 5,000, and in recent decades major cities—including New York, Los Angeles, Chicago, and Washington—have elected Black mayors, and Black representation on city and town councils and state bodies has grown dramatically. At the federal level there have been fewer gains, although, clearly, President Obama's election in November 2008 and reelection in 2012 represented a profound political breakthrough for Blacks. Following the congressional elections of November 2012, the House of Representatives had 42 Black members, but only a single African American was serving in the Senate.

LATINOS/LATINAS

The category of Latino (or Hispanic, the term used by the U.S. Census Bureau) includes people whose heritages lie in the many different cultures of Latin America. Latinos largely share the Spanish language as part of their ethnic heritage. According to official estimates, there are 32 million Latinos living in the United States, making them the largest minority group. It is probable that official data actually underestimate the total Latino population, given that they likely miss a sizable number of undocumented immigrants. Latinos are increasing in numbers more rapidly than any other minority group, because of both high immigration rates and high birthrates. By 2025, they are expected to number nearly 59 million and make up about a fifth of the U.S. population.

Many Latinos trace their ancestry to a time when the southwestern states were part of Mexico. During the mid-19th century, the United States sought to purchase from Mexico what are now Texas and California. Mexico refused to sell, leading to the 1846–1848 U.S.–Mexican War. Following its victory, the U.S. government forced Mexico to sell two fifths of its territory, enabling the United States to acquire all the land that now makes up the southwestern states, including California, Texas, New Mexico, and Arizona. Along with this vast territory came the people who inhabited it, including tens of thousands of Mexicans who were forced by White settlers to forfeit their property and who suffered discrimination at the hands of the Whites (Valenzuela, 1992).

Latinos have experienced some of the same obstacles of prejudice and discrimination in the United States as have African Americans. They continue to be discriminated against and live below the standards of the dominant population. At the same time, the very category of *Latino* is problematic for sociologists because it encompasses several different ethnic groups with very different experiences of immigration. Latinos are often referred to in a way that implies uniformity across members of this group, when in reality Latinos constitute a diverse ethnic population with roots in a range of countries in Central America, South America, and the Caribbean (Figure 9.7). To add to the complexity, Latinos who are born in the United States, or who have the majority of their families anchored in the United States, are increasingly different from the people who permanently reside in their families' countries of origin. We discuss two of the most prominent Latino groups below.

INEQUALITY MATTERS

WHO HAS THE POWER TO NAME?

"A language is a dialect that has an army and a navy," said sociolinguist Max Weinreich. Before White Europeans came to North America, one of the largest Indian nations was the Dineh, a name that means "the People of the Earth." No one knows exactly why, but the Spaniards renamed them "Navajo," the designation by which Europeans have referred to them ever since. While Native Americans were being outgunned and oppressed by the wave of White European settlers, their language was also subject to marginalization, as was their power to name themselves.

Sociologist Pierre Bourdieu (1991) has pointed out that language is a medium of power, a vehicle that may confer either status or function as a means of devaluation and exclusion. Historically, minority groups have been denied opportunities to name themselves. What is the appropriate name for the people who lived for thousands of years in what today is known as North and South America? They are commonly referred to as *Indians, Native Americans, indigenous peoples,* or simply *Natives.* Two prominent organizations—the National Congress of American Indians and the American Indian Movement—use *American Indian* to describe themselves. Yet others object to the term because, like the word *Navajo,* it was given to them by European settlers and their descendants.

Those who object to *American Indian* feel the alternative, *Native American,* captures the fact that they alone among ethnic groups are truly native to this continent, but this name also was given by European settlers. Others argue that nothing short of the correct name for each nation (such as Sioux, Pawnee, Cheyenne, Dineh, or Cherokee) is acceptable. However, referring to each separate nation is problematic when we speak of the collective of Native Americans. After years of controversy among the members of the various nations, their leaders agreed to accept *American Indian* to refer to themselves collectively (Scott, Tehranian, & Mathias, 2002).

The name for a particular racial or ethnic group may be highly contested, since it carries with it information about the group's social history. The effort by many groups to "name themselves" reflects their belief that to passively accept the name given by society's dominant group is to potentially accept being silenced. American Indian activists Laura Waterman Wittstock and Elaine J. Salinas (1998) suggest in their history of the American Indian Movement that "in the 30 years of its formal history, the American Indian Movement (AIM) has given witness to a great many changes. We say formal history, because the movement existed for 500 years without a name. The leaders and members of today's AIM never fail to remember all of those who have traveled on before, having given their talent and their lives for the survival of the people."

THINK IT THROUGH

▶ Bourdieu highlights the "power to name" as one that is more likely to be held and exercised by dominant groups in society. Can you name another situation in which the power to name gives an advantage to one group and disadvantage to another?

MEXICAN AMERICANS Mexicans are the largest group of Latinos in the United States. A large proportion of the Mexican American population lives in California, New Mexico, Texas, and Arizona, though migration to the American South has grown substantially. The immigration of Mexican Americans has long reflected the immediate labor needs of the U.S. economy (Barrera, 1979; Muller & Espenshade, 1985). During the 1930s, state and local governments forcibly sent hundreds of thousands of Mexican immigrants back to Mexico, but when the United States experienced a labor shortage during World War II, immigration was again encouraged. After the war the *bracero* (manual laborer) program enabled 4 million Mexicans to work as temporary farm laborers in the United States, often under exploitative conditions. The program was ended in 1964,

■ **FIGURE 9.7 Countries of Origin of the Hispanic Population in the United States, 2010**

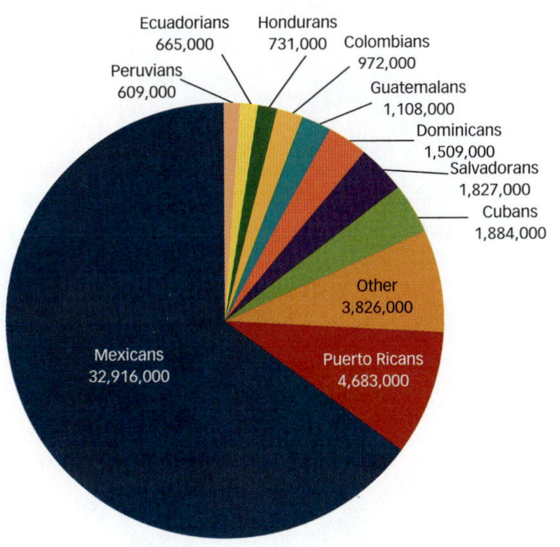

SOURCE: Data from Pew Research Center. 2012. *Hispanic origins profiles, 2010* by Seth Motel and Eileen Patten. Pew Hispanic Center.

but by the 1980s, immigration was on the upsurge, with millions of people fleeing poverty and political turmoil in Latin America by illegally entering the United States.

Political rhetoric about the threat of illegal immigrants seeking U.S. jobs has become increasingly heated in the recession that began in 2008, although the numbers of such immigrants have likely been falling. In fact, recent data suggest that a host of factors—including the dangers of crossing the U.S.–Mexico border due to drug violence on the Mexican side, harsher immigration laws in states from Georgia to Arizona, and the dearth of employment in the wake of the recession—have pushed illegal immigration down, perhaps to the point that more undocumented migrants are leaving the United States than entering it (Massey, 2011).

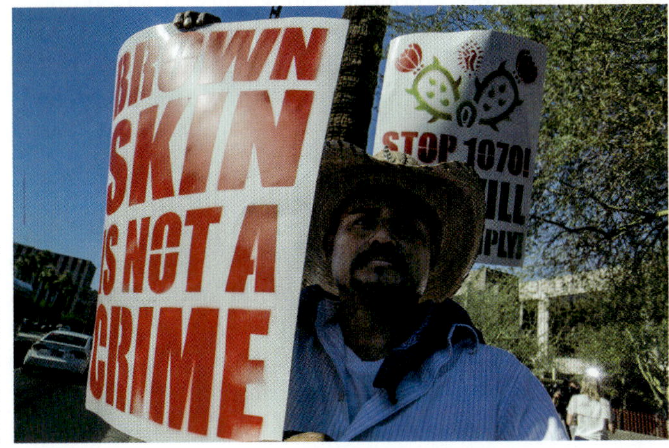

© ZUMA Press, Inc. / Alamy

Arizona's SB 1070 legislation gives law enforcement officers the right to ask for proof of legal residency within the United States. This controversial law allows officers to exercise discretion in determining who "looks" like a legal or illegal resident. ■

Most ethnic Mexicans in the United States are legal residents, and the number of those rising into the middle class has grown considerably, though the number living in poverty has also risen, particularly in the wake of the economic crisis.

CUBAN AMERICANS When Fidel Castro came to power in Cuba in 1959, Cubans who opposed his communist regime sought to emigrate to the United States. These included some of Castro's political opponents, but most were middle-class Cubans whose standard of living was declining under Castro's economic policies and the U.S. economic embargo of Cuba. About half a million entered the United States, mostly through Florida, which is just 90 miles away from Cuba.

The Cuban community has enjoyed both economic and, perhaps as a result, political success in Florida (Ferment, 1989; Stepick & Grenier, 1993). In contrast to many immigrants, who tend to come from the poorer strata of their native countries, Cuban immigrants were often highly educated professionals and businesspeople before they fled to the United States. They brought with them a considerable reserve of training, skill, and sometimes wealth.

The anticommunist stance of the new migrants was also a good fit with U.S. foreign policy and the effort to crush communist politics in the Western Hemisphere. The U.S. government provided financial assistance such as small business loans to Cuban immigrants. It also offered a spectrum of language classes, job training programs, and recertification classes for physicians, architects, nurses, teachers, and lawyers who sought to reestablish their professional credentials in the United States. About three-quarters of all Cubans arriving before 1974 received some form of government benefits, the highest rate of any minority community.

While Cuban migrants have tended to have higher levels of education than Mexican immigrants do, their status in the United States has also been strongly influenced by the political and economic (that is, the structural) needs of the U.S. government. U.S. economic needs have determined whether the government encouraged or discouraged the migration of manual labor power from Mexico, while political considerations have fostered a support network for migrants endorsing the U.S. government's effort to end the communist Castro regime in Cuba.

ASIAN AMERICANS

Asian immigrants were instrumental in the development of industrialization in the United States. In the mid-1900s, construction began on the transcontinental railroad that would link California with the industrializing East. At the same time, gold and silver were discovered in the American West. Labor was desperately needed to mine these natural resources and to work on building the railroad. At the time, China was suffering a severe drought. U.S. entrepreneurs seeking labor quickly saw the potential fit of supply and demand, and hundreds of thousands of Chinese were brought to the United States as inexpensive manual labor. Most came voluntarily, but some were kidnapped by U.S. ship captains and brought to the West Coast.

About 4% of Americans today trace their origins to Asian countries such as India, China, Japan, Korea, and Vietnam. The number of Asian Americans is growing, primarily because of immigration (Asian American birthrates, following the pattern in Asian countries, are low). Like Latinos, Asian Americans constitute a population of great ethnic diversity; the wide-ranging characteristics of this population cannot be fully captured by the term *Asian American* (Figure 9.8).

Asian Americans, like members of other minority groups, have experienced prejudice and discrimination. For example, during World War II, many Japanese Americans were forcibly placed in internment camps, and their property was confiscated (Daniels, 2004; Harth, 2001). The U.S. government feared their allegiances were with Japan—an enemy in World War II—rather than the United States. While the teaching of German was banned in some schools, drastic measures were not taken against German or Italian Americans, although Germany and Italy were allied with Japan during the war.

In spite of obstacles, the Asian American population has been successful in making economic gains. Asian Americans as a whole have the highest median household income of any minority group, as well as the lowest rates of divorce, teenage pregnancy, and unemployment. Their economic success reflects the fact that, like Cuban Americans, recent Asian immigrants have come from higher socioeconomic backgrounds, bringing greater financial resources and more human capital (Zhou, 2009). Family networks and kinship obligations

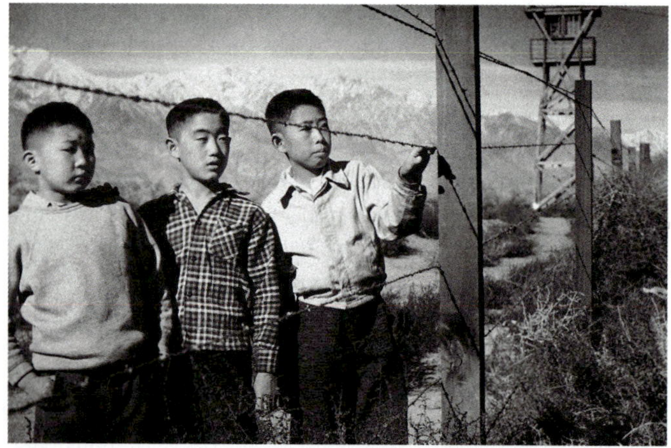

© AP Photo/anonymous

Beginning in 1942, the U.S. government relocated an estimated 110,000 Japanese Americans living on the West Coast to internment camps. The government feared disloyalty after the Japanese attack on Pearl Harbor, in spite of the fact that more than 60% of those interned were U.S. citizens.

FIGURE 9.8 Countries of Origin of the Asian Population in the United States, 2010

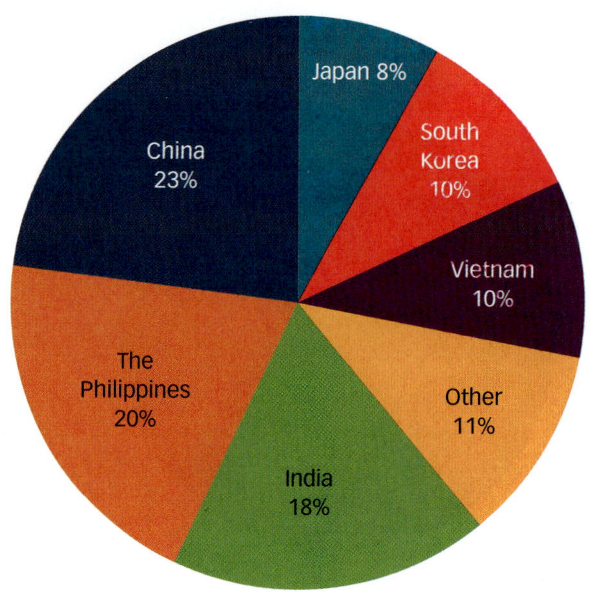

SOURCE: Data from Pew Research Center. 2012. *The rise of Asian Americans*. Pew Social & Demographic Trends.

also play an important role. In many Asian American communities, informal community-based lending organizations provide capital for businesses, families and friends support one another as customers and employees, and profits are reinvested in the community (Ferment, 1989; Gilbertson & Gurak, 1993; Kasarda, 1993).

At the same time, there are substantial differences within the Asian American population. Nearly half of all Asian Indian Americans, for example, are professionals, compared with less than a quarter of Korean Americans, who are much more likely to run small businesses and factories. Poverty and hardship are more prevalent among those from Southeast Asia, particularly immigrants from Cambodia and Laos, which are deeply impoverished countries with less educated populations.

ARAB AMERICANS

Immigrants from Arab countries began coming to the United States in the 1880s. The last major wave of Arab migration occurred in the decade following World War II (PBS, 2011). Contrary to popular perceptions, most members of today's Arab American population were born in the United States. The majority trace their roots back to Lebanon, Syria, Palestine, Egypt, and Iraq (Arab American Institute, 2012).

Arab Americans face a unique set of challenges and obstacles. Immediately following the September 11, 2001, terrorist attacks, Arab Americans as a group suffered stigma, and acts of discrimination against them increased sharply. The terror

Arab Americans Post 9/11

FIGURE 9.9 Legal Migration to the United States by Region of Origin, 1820–2009

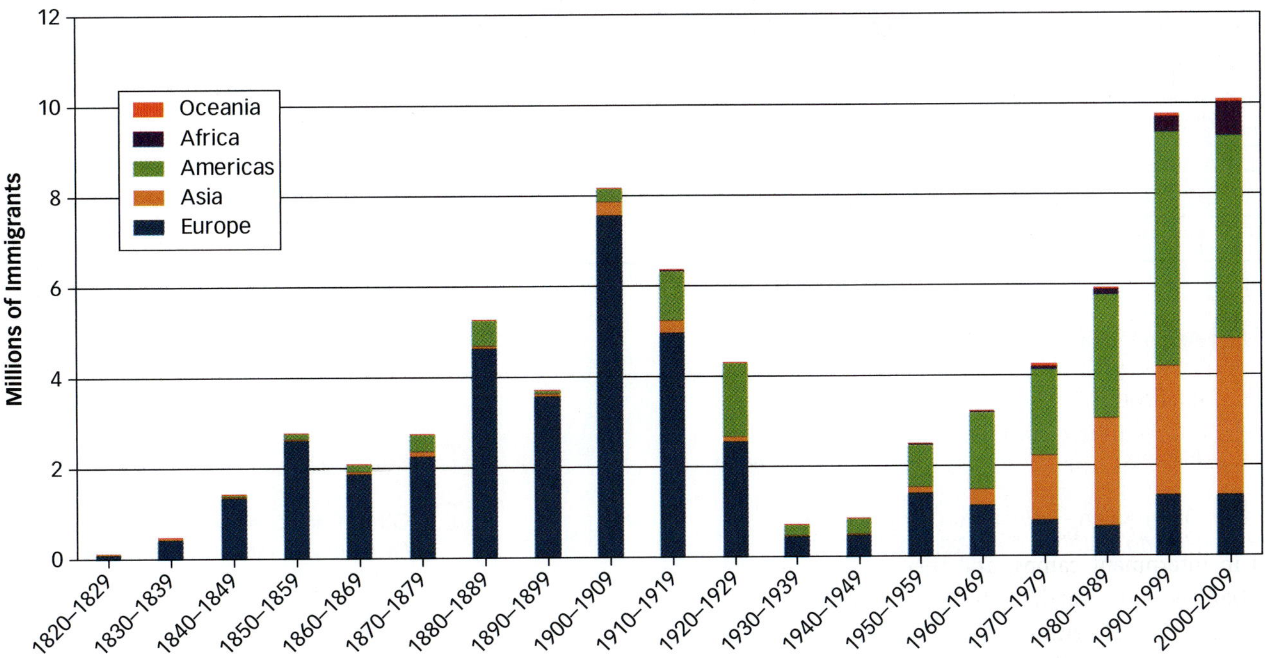

SOURCE: Data from Table 2, Persons Obtaining Legal Permanent Resident Status by Region and Selected Country of Last Residence: Fiscal Years 1820 to 2012. *Yearbook of Immigration Statistics: 2012 Legal Permanent Residents*. U.S. Department of Homeland Security.

attacks provided an avenue for legitimating the views of racists and xenophobes (Salaita, 2005), but institutionalized prejudice was also obvious in the increase in "random" screenings and searches that targeted Arab Americans.

At the same time, Arab Americans represent a "model minority"—a racial or ethnic group with higher levels of achievement than the general population in areas such as education and income. Like Asian Americans, Arab Americans as a demographic group have been notably successful in these two fields; 45% have at least a bachelor's degree or higher (compared to 28% for the general population), and in 2008 their mean individual income was 27% higher than the national average (Arab American Institute Foundation, 2011).

WHITE ETHNIC AMERICANS

White people have always made up a high percentage of the foreign-born population in the United States. The stereotype of minorities as people of color leaves out significant pockets of White ethnic minorities. In the early days of mass migration to the United States, the dominant group was White Protestants from Europe. Whites from Europe who were not Protestant—particularly Catholics and Jews—were defined as ethnic minorities, and their status was clearly marginal in U.S. society.

In mid-19th-century Boston, for example, Irish Catholics made up a large portion of the city's poor and were stereotyped as drunken, criminal, and generally immoral (Handlin, 1991). The term *paddy wagon,* used to describe a police van that picks up the drunk and disorderly, came from the notion that the Irish were such vans' most common occupants. (*Paddy* was a derogatory term for an Irishman.) Over time, however, White ethnic groups assimilated with relative ease because, for the most part, they looked much like the dominant population (Prell, 1999). To further their assimilation, some families changed their names and encouraged their children to speak English only. Today, most of these White ethnic groups—Irish, Italians, Russians, and others—have integrated fully into U.S. society (Figure 9.9). They are, on the whole, born wealthier, have more social capital, and encounter fewer barriers to mobility than other racial and ethnic groups.

If dark skin has historically been an obstacle in U.S. society, light skin has been an advantage. That advantage, however, may go unrecognized. As Peggy McIntosh writes in her thought-provoking article "White Privilege: Unpacking the Invisible Knapsack" (1990), "as a white person, I realized I had been taught about racism as something that puts others at a disadvantage, but had been taught not to see one of its corollary aspects, white privilege, which puts me at an advantage. . . . I have come to see white privilege as an invisible package of unearned assets that I can count on cashing in each day, but about which I was 'meant' to remain oblivious" (p. 31).

McIntosh goes on to outline these "assets," including the following: When Whites are told about their national heritage, or the origins of "civilization," they are shown that White

FIGURE 9.10 **Race, Ethnicity, and Hispanic Origin Questions, U.S. Bureau of the Census Form, 2010**

6. **What is this person's race?** *Mark* [X] *one or more boxes.*

☐ White

☐ Black, African Am., or Negro

☐ American Indian or Alaska Native — *Print name of enrolled or principal tribe.*

☐ Asian Indian ☐ Japanese ☐ Native Hawaiian

☐ Chinese ☐ Korean ☐ Guamanian or Chamorro

☐ Filipino ☐ Vietnamese ☐ Samoan

☐ Other Asian — *Print race, for example, Hmong, Laotian, Thai, Pakistani, Cambodian, and so on.*

☐ Other Pacific Islander — *Print race, for example, Fijian, Tongan, and so on.*

☐ Some other race – *Print race.*

SOURCE: U.S. Bureau of the Census.

people shaped it. Posters, picture books, greeting cards, toys, and dolls all overwhelmingly feature White images. As a White person, she need not worry that her coworkers at an affirmative action employer will suspect she got her job only because of her race. If she needed any medical or legal help, her race alone would not be considered a risk factor or hindrance in obtaining such services. These are just a few among the 50 unearned privileges of White skin that McIntosh identifies. Her argument is essentially that obliviousness to the advantages of White skin "maintain[s] the myth of meritocracy, the myth that democratic choice is equally available to all" (1999, p. 36). Recognition of skin privilege, in contrast, would be a challenge to the structure of power, which prefers to ignore whatever does not support the story of achievement as an outcome of merit.

Is the recognition of racial or ethnic *advantages* as important as recognition of racial or ethnic *disadvantages*? Can this help to level the field of opportunity for all Americans? What do you think?

MULTIRACIAL AMERICANS

As we note in the *Inequality Matters* box on page 220, naming is an important sociological action. It may be an exercise of power or an act of recognition. In 2000, the U.S. Census Bureau's questionnaire for the first time permitted respondents to select more than one race in describing themselves. In 2000, about 2.4% of Americans, or 6.8 million people, identified themselves as multiracial. In the 2010 census that figure grew to 9 million people (2.9% of Americans). Interestingly, the self-reported multiracial population grew much more dramatically than than the single-race population: The former rose by 32%, while the latter rose by just over 9% (Jones & Bullock, 2012).

The rise in the numbers of U.S. residents describing themselves as belonging to more than one race should perhaps not come as any surprise. On one hand, more children are being born into interracial partnerships: In 2010, 10% of heterosexual married couples (5.4 million) were interracial, and the figure is even higher among unmarried couples (Lofquist, Lugaila, O'Connell, & Feliz, 2012). On the other hand, because this is a self-reported status, more people may be choosing to identify themselves as multiracial as the availability of the category becomes more widely known and as multiracial status becomes more broadly accepted.

Notably, being biracial or multiracial is not a new phenomenon. It is, in some respects, a newly named phenomenon that is also of growing interest to researchers. The politics of multiracialism can be complicated, with competing interests at play. For example, leading up to the 2000 census, many mixed-race individuals and advocacy groups favored the addition of an entirely separate "multiple race" option on the census questionnaire, as opposed to allowing respondents to check multiple boxes from among the established racial categories. They argued that the addition of such an option would allow for fluidity in the way that individuals identify themselves, freeing them from the constraints of categories imposed on them by the state. Others, including some prominent civil rights leaders, countered that identification according to the established racial categories is necessary to ensure that civil rights legislation is enforced and that inequalities in housing, income, education, and so on are documented accurately (Roquemore & Brunsma, 2008). On one hand, the lived experience of multiracial Americans and their right to self-identify must be respected; on the other hand, the Census Bureau must fulfill its obligation to provide legislators with accurate information on inequality. Social science research tells us that individuals' racial identification plays an important role in how others interact with them, their social networks, and even their life chances (Khanna, 2011). Thus, the question of how a person self-identifies, and how others perceive him or her, has real consequences in that individual's everyday life.

RACE AND ETHNICITY IN A GLOBAL PERSPECTIVE

While our focus to this point has been on the United States, issues of racial and ethnic identities and inequalities are global in scope. Around the world, unstable minority and majority relationships, fears of rising migration from developing countries, and even ethnic and racial hatreds that explode into brutal violence highlight again how important it is for us to understand the causes and dynamics of categories that, while socially constructed, are powerfully real in their consequences.

European countries such as France, Germany, and Denmark have struggled in recent years to deal with challenges of immigration, discrimination, and prejudice. Migration to Northern and Western Europe from developing states, particularly those in North Africa and the Middle East, has risen, driven by a combination of *push factors* (social forces such as dire economic conditions and inadequate educational opportunities that encourage migrants to leave their home countries) and *pull factors* (forces that draw migrants to a given country, such as labor shortages that can be filled by low- or high-skilled migrants or an existing ethnic network that can offer new migrants support). In a short period of time, the large numbers of job seekers from developing countries in search of better lives have transformed the populations of many European countries from largely ethnically homogeneous to multicultural—a change that has caused some political and social tensions.

Genocide: The mass, systematic destruction of a people or a nation.

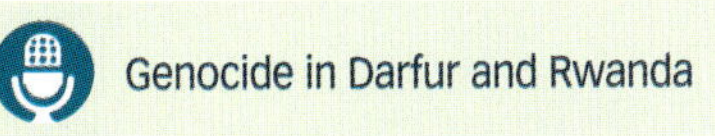

Tensions in Europe revolve at least in part around the fact that a substantial proportion of migrants from developing states are Muslim, and some have brought with them religious practices, such as veiling, that are not perceived to be a good fit with largely secular European societies. By some estimates, Muslims will account for about a fifth of the population of the European Union by 2050 (Mudde, 2011). In 2011, France, in which about 10% of the population is Muslim, became the first country in Europe to ban the full face veil, also known as the burqa, which is the customary dress for some Muslim women. Similar legislation has been introduced, but not passed, in Belgium and the Netherlands. Earlier, when France banned all overt religious symbols from schools in 2004, civil defiance and violence followed. The Parisian suburbs burned as young French Muslims rioted, demanding opportunity and acceptance in a society that has traditionally narrowly defined who is "French."

In some cases, ethnic and racial tensions have had even more explosive effects. Earlier in this chapter, we talked about four forms that majority–minority relations can take: expulsion, segregation, assimilation, and cultural pluralism. Here we add a fifth form: genocide.

GENOCIDE: THE MASS DESTRUCTION OF SOCIETIES

Genocide can be defined as *the mass, systematic destruction of a people or a nation.* According to the Convention on the Prevention and Punishment of the Crime of Genocide, adopted by the United Nations General Assembly in 1948, when genocide was declared a crime under international law, it includes "any of the following acts committed with intent to destroy, in whole or in part, a national, ethnical, racial or religious group, as such:

a. Killing members of the group;

b. Causing serious bodily or mental harm to members of the group;

c. Deliberately inflicting on the group conditions of life calculated to bring about its physical destruction in whole or in part;

d. Imposing measures intended to prevent births within the group;

e. Forcibly transferring children of the group to another group."

The mass killing of people because of their membership in a particular group is ages old. Hans Van Wees (2010) notes that ancient Christian and Hebrew religious texts contain evidence of early religiously motivated mass killings. Roger W. Smith (2002) points out that the Assyrians, Greeks, Romans, and Mongols, among others, engaged in genocide, but their perspective on mass killing was shaped by their time. He notes that rulers boasted about the thousands they killed and the peoples they eliminated. Genocide as both a term and a defined crime is much more recent.

FIGURE 9.11 Select Genocides Around the World, 1914–Present

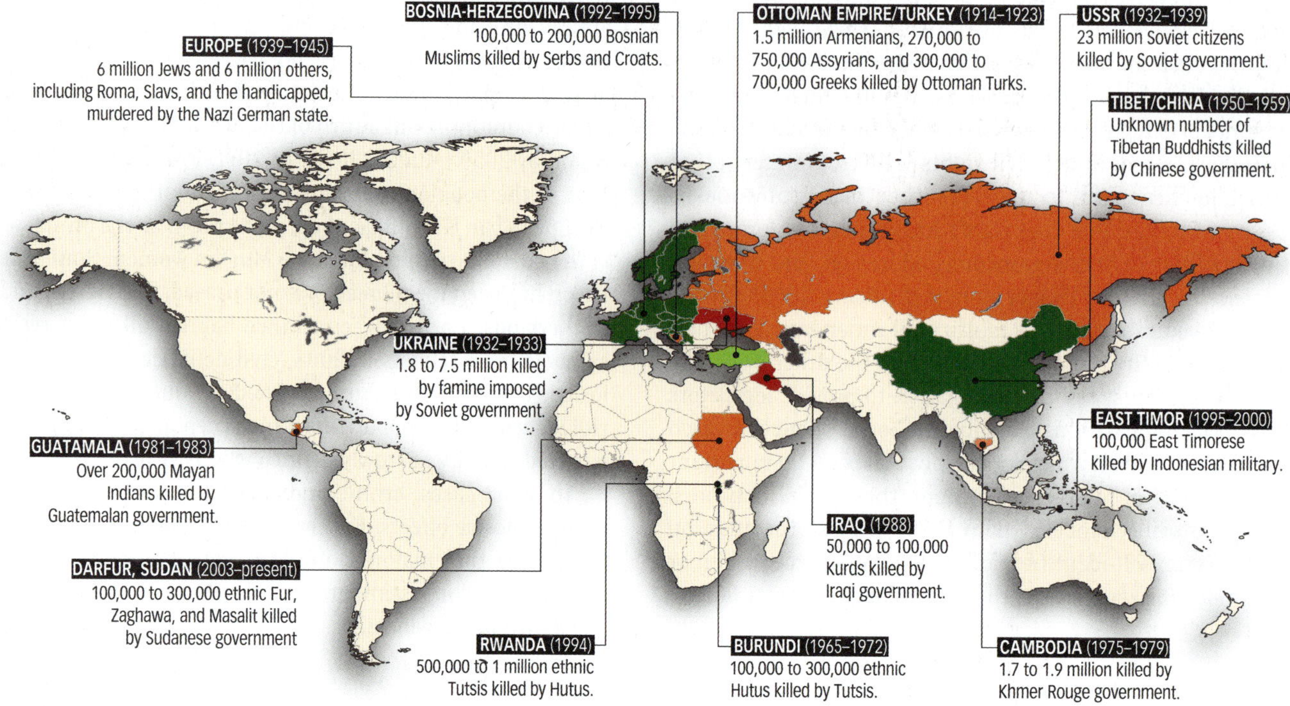

EUROPE (1939–1945)
6 million Jews and 6 million others, including Roma, Slavs, and the handicapped, murdered by the Nazi German state.
BOSNIA-HERZEGOVINA (1992–1995)
100,000 to 200,000 Bosnian Muslims killed by Serbs and Croats.
OTTOMAN EMPIRE/TURKEY (1914–1923)
1.5 million Armenians, 270,000 to 750,000 Assyrians, and 300,000 to 700,000 Greeks killed by Ottoman Turks.
USSR (1932–1939)
23 million Soviet citizens killed by Soviet government.
TIBET/CHINA (1950–1959)
Unknown number of Tibetan Buddhists killed by Chinese government.
UKRAINE (1932–1933)
1.8 to 7.5 million killed by famine imposed by Soviet government.
GUATAMALA (1981–1983)
Over 200,000 Mayan Indians killed by Guatemalan government.
EAST TIMOR (1995–2000)
100,000 East Timorese killed by Indonesian military.
IRAQ (1988)
50,000 to 100,000 Kurds killed by Iraqi government.
DARFUR, SUDAN (2003–present)
100,000 to 300,000 ethnic Fur, Zaghawa, and Masalit killed by Sudanese government
RWANDA (1994)
500,000 to 1 million ethnic Tutsis killed by Hutus.
BURUNDI (1965–1972)
100,000 to 300,000 ethnic Hutus killed by Tutsis.
CAMBODIA (1975–1979)
1.7 to 1.9 million killed by Khmer Rouge government.

The word *genocide* was coined in the 1940s by Polish émigré Raphael Lemkin, who left his native country in the late 1930s, several years before Adolf Hitler's Nazi army overran it. A lawyer and an academic, Lemkin was also a crusader for human rights, and, aware of Nazi atrocities in Europe, he sought to inspire U.S. decision makers to act against the mass killing of Jews and other targeted groups. In a 1941 radio broadcast, British prime minister Winston Churchill decried the "barbaric fury" of the Nazis and declared, "We are in the presence of a crime without a name." Lemkin, who heard the broadcast, undertook to name the crime and, through this naming, to bring an end to it (Power, 2002).

Sociologist Pierre Bourdieu (1991) points to the significance of language in structuring the perception that social agents (such as governments or populations) have of the world around them. The very act of naming a phenomenon confers on it a social reality. Lemkin sought to use the act of naming as a vehicle for action against Nazi atrocities and against future threats to the physical, political, cultural, and economic existence of collectivities (Shaw, 2010). Lemkin settled on *genocide,* a hybrid of the Greek *geno,* meaning "tribe" or "race," and the Latin *cide* (from *caedere*), or "killing."

The 1948 U.N. Convention on the Prevention and Punishment of the Crime of Genocide created a potentially powerful new political reality, though it narrowed the definition from the broad articulation championed by Lemkin (Shaw, 2010). Theoretically, state sovereignty could no longer shield a country from the consequences of committing genocide, because the nations that signed the U.N. convention were bound by it to prevent, suppress, and punish such crimes. At the same time, the notion of an obligation to intervene is loose and open to interpretation, as history has shown. Humanitarian organizations such as Genocide Watch and institutions such as the U.S. Holocaust Memorial Museum have sounded the alarm on recent atrocities, often labeling them genocide even while many governments have resisted using the term.

Genocides in the second half of the 20th century include slaughters carried out by the Khmer Rouge in Cambodia in the 1970s, Saddam Hussein's 1987–1988 campaign against ethnic Kurds in Iraq, and Serb atrocities in the former Yugoslav states of Bosnia-Herzegovina and Kosovo in the late 1990s (Figure 9.11). The 21st century has already seen the genocidal destruction of Black Africans, including the Darfuris, Abyei, and Nuba, by Arab militias linked to the government in Sudan.

One of the most discussed cases of genocide in the late 20th century took place in Rwanda, where in 1994 no fewer than 800,000 ethnic Tutsis were killed by ethnic Hutus in the space of just 100 days. Many killings were done by machete, and women and girls were targeted for sexual violence. By most accounts, Tutsis and Hutus are not so different from one another; they are members of the same ethnic group, live in the same areas, and share a common language. One cultural difference of considerable importance, however, is that for the Tutsis the cow is sacred and cannot be killed or used for food. The Hutus, who have a long tradition of farming, were forced to leave large areas of land open for cattle grazing, thus limiting the fertile ground available for farming. As the cattle herds multiplied, so did tensions and conflict. Notably, for many years the Tutsis, while fewer in number (representing approximately 14% of the population), dominated the Hutus politically and economically (Kapuscinski, 2001).

Rwanda was long a colony of Belgium, but in the 1950s, Tutsis began to demand independence, as did many other colonized peoples in Africa. The Belgians incited the Hutus to rebel against the Tutsi ruling class. The rebellion was unsuccessful, but the seeds for genocide were planted in fertile soil, and sporadic ethnic violence erupted in the decades that followed. Belgium finally relinquished power and granted Rwanda independence in 1962. From the early 1970s, the government was headed by a moderate Hutu leader, Major General Juvénal Habyarimana (BBC, 2008). In the early 1990s, General Habyarimana agreed to a power-sharing arrangement with Tutsis in Rwanda, angering some nationalist Hutus, who did not want to see a division of power. In 1994, the general was assassinated (his private jet was shot down), and radical Hutus took the opportunity to turn on both Tutsi countrymen and moderate Hutus, murdering at least 800,000 people in just a few short months.

In the section below, we consider the question of how genocide—such as the mass killing of Rwanda's Tutsi population in 1994—looks through a sociological lens.

The award-winning film *Hotel Rwanda* captured just a fragment of the 1994 genocide in Rwanda. Nearly a million ethnic Tutsis were systematically killed by ethnic Hutus in less than 100 days

WHAT EXPLAINS GENOCIDE?

Taking a sociological perspective, we might ask, "Who benefits from genocide?" Why do countries or leaders make a choice to pursue or allow genocidal actions? Genocide is the product of conscious decisions made by those who stand to benefit from it and who anticipate minimal costs for their actions.

Chalk and Jonassohn (1990) suggest that those who pursue genocide do so to eliminate a real or perceived threat, to spread fear among enemies, to eliminate a real or potential threat to another group, to gain wealth or power for a dominant group, and/or to realize an ideological goal. Shaw (2010) has noted that "genocide is a crime of social classification, in which power-holders target particular populations for social and often physical destruction" (p. 142).

Anton Weiss-Wendt (2010) points out that to the degree that genocide "requires premeditation" (p. 81), governments are generally implicated in the crime. Among the necessary parts is also the creation of a "genocidal mentality," not only among the leadership but also among a sufficient number of individuals to ensure the participation, or at least the support or indifference, of a large proportion of the population (Goldhagen, 1997; Markusen, 2002). Part of creating a genocidal mentality is dehumanizing the victims. By emphasizing their "otherness," or the idea that the group to be victimized is less than fully human, agents of genocide stamp out sympathy for their targets, replacing it with a sense of threat or disgust. Modern media have made the process of disseminating the propaganda of dehumanization increasingly easy. Radio broadcasts to a Hutu audience in Rwanda in the time leading up to the genocide implored Hutus to "kill [Tutsi] cockroaches" (Gourevitch, 1999).

Another mechanism is the "establishment of genocidal institutions and organizations," which construct propaganda to justify and institutions or other means to carry out the genocide. Finally, the recruitment and training of perpetrators is important, as is the establishment of methods of group destruction (Markusen, 2002). In Rwanda, it is notable that some Hutu Power groups had already in the early 1990s begun to arm civilians with hand weapons like machetes, ostensibly as self-defense against Tutsi rebels. Many of these were later used in the genocide. As Hutus and Tutsis lived side by side in many cities and rural areas, identification of victims was rapid and easy.

Choosing genocide as a policy incurs costs as well as benefits. Clearly, outside forces can impose costs on a genocidal regime; we have seen that signatories to the 1948 U.N. convention are theoretically obligated to intervene. But historically, intervention has often been too little and too late. Why, in the face of overwhelming evidence of genocide (as in Rwanda or Bosnia-Herzegovina or Sudan), does the international community not step in? One answer is that these states also make choices based on perceived costs and benefits. Intervention in the affairs of another state can be costly, and many leaders avoid it. In a historical overview of U.S. responses to genocide, for instance, Samantha Power (2002) argues: that "American leaders did not act because they did not want to. They believed that genocide was wrong, but they were not prepared to invest the military, financial, diplomatic, or domestic political capital needed to stop it" (p. 508).

Genocide is an extreme and brutal manifestation of majority–minority relations. It is the effort to destroy indiscriminately an entire racial or ethnic group. Does genocide continue to be a viable option for states or regimes wishing to destroy groups labeled by powerful leaders as inferior or dangerous? How should outside states—and concerned individuals—respond when conflict and intolerance evolve into genocide? What do you think?

WHY STUDY RACE AND ETHNICITY FROM A SOCIOLOGICAL PERSPECTIVE?

Living in the United States, we are surrounded by serious and casual discussions and comments about race, ethnic jokes, and anecdotes, stories, and studies about race and ethnicity. Rarely do we stop to ask ourselves what racial and ethnic categories really mean and why they are significant. Who decided they should be significant, and why? What institutions in society reinforce this belief? What institutions challenge it? As a society we have simply accepted such categories as "Black" and "White" as real. Sociologists, however, argue that they are "socially constructed"—what is real is not race but rather the consequences of racism, with its accompanying prejudice and discrimination.

Sociologically defined concepts such as "race"—as well as prejudice, discrimination, assimilation, and the like—help us see domestic and international conflicts in a different light. We may begin to understand that socially constructed categories marginalize and even dehumanize certain groups, and that we must recognize these symbolic acts, as well as the violent acts—from hate crimes to genocides—that may accompany them.

We benefit in our personal lives too from recognizing the socially constructed nature of categories such as race. We ought to pause and ask ourselves: Why is treatment of individuals often conditioned on skin color? Why has our society opted to define this marker as significant? What must we do culturally, socially, politically, educationally, and economically to pull down the artificial barriers imposed by socially constructed categories?

WHAT CAN I DO WITH A SOCIOLOGY DEGREE?

SKILLS AND CAREERS: CRITICAL THINKING SKILLS

Critical thinking is the ability to evaluate claims about society, politics, the economy, culture, the environment, or any other area of knowledge by using reason and evidence. Critical thinking skills are very broad, but they encompass the ability to evaluate and interpret data logically and rigorously to form ideas and understandings, determine actions, and identify solutions to problems. They also include the inclination and knowledge required to be a critical consumer of information, thoughtfully questioning rather than simply accepting arguments or solutions at face value. Critical thinking is not about *criticizing* but about deeply understanding.

Every chapter in this book seeks to help you sharpen your critical thinking by helping you to see more deeply into the social processes and structures that affect our lives and society and to raise questions about social phenomena we may take for granted. In this chapter we saw, for instance, that racial residential segregation is still widespread in the United States—that is, people of different racial groups often live in different neighborhoods. As well, neighborhoods dominated by Whites tend to have the greatest access to desired resources such as good public schools, safe places to play, and a variety of shopping options. Applying critical thinking to this issue means *asking questions about the existence and persistence of racial residential segregation in the contemporary United States, assessing and addressing our own assumptions about the issue, and working to reason out answers by seeking reliable information and evidence that can be applied to analysis of the issue.* As a sociologist in training you will develop a more comprehensive understanding of your social world and will learn both to ask critical questions about why things are as they are and to seek out and find evidence-based answers to those questions.

The ability to exercise critical thinking skills is of great value in both graduate education and the world of work. Critical thinking skills are a key part of *job tasks* that include analysis, argumentation, research, and investigation. These kinds of tasks are commonly part of the *job descriptions* of, among others, lawyers and judges, government investigators, reporters and correspondents, intelligence analysts, professors and researchers, and management consultants. These jobs are to be found in a diverse array of *occupational fields* that include business/management, government, criminal justice, media, education, health care, and the law.

THINK ABOUT CAREERS

▶ How is critical thinking different from criticizing? How does it differ from other kinds of "thinking" we might apply to issues or problems?

▶ Notice that critical thinking is a skill often associated with occupations and jobs that demand investigation and analysis. What is the connection between these kinds of tasks and critical thinking?

SUMMARY

- **Race** is not a biological category but a social construct. Its societal significance derives from the fact that people in a particular culture believe, falsely, that there are biologically distinguishable races and then act on the basis of this belief. The perceived differences among "races" are often distorted and lead to **prejudice** and **discrimination**.
- Many societies include different ethnic groups with varied histories, cultures, and practices.
- **Minorities**, typically because of their race or **ethnicity**, may experience prejudice and discrimination. Different types of minority–dominant group relations include **expulsion**, **assimilation**, **segregation**, and **cultural pluralism**.
- Prejudice usually relies on **stereotyping** and **scapegoating**. During difficult economic times prejudice may increase, as people seek someone to blame for their predicament.
- The civil rights struggles that began in the United States more than 60 years ago led to passage of civil rights and affirmative action legislation that has reduced, but not eliminated, the effects of prejudice and discrimination against minorities.
- Although discrimination is against the law in the United States, it is still widely practiced. **Institutionalized discrimination** in particular results in the unequal treatment of minorities in employment, housing, education, and other areas.
- The United States is a multiethnic, multiracial society. Minority groups—including American Indians, African Americans, Latinos, and Asian Americans—make up more than 30% of the population. The U.S. Census Bureau has projected that this figure will rise to nearly 50% in the next 40 years.
- Historically, the vast majority of immigrants to the United States have come from Europe, but in recent years the pattern has changed, and currently most come from Latin America and Asia.
- With a few exceptions, minority groups are disadvantaged in the United States relative to the majority White population in terms of income, numbers living in poverty, and the quality of education and health care, as well as political voice. Though the disadvantages of dark skin are recognized, the privileges of light skin have not been widely acknowledged.
- **Genocide** is the mass and systematic destruction of a people or a nation. The 1948 United Nations Convention on the Prevention and Punishment of the Crime of Genocide obligates signatories to act against genocide.

KEY TERMS

race, 205
ethnicity, 206
minorities, 206
expulsion, 206
segregation, 207
assimilation, 208
cultural pluralism, 209
racism, 210
stigma, 211
mixed contacts, 211
prejudice, 211
stereotyping, 211
discrimination, 211
individual discrimination, 212
institutionalized discrimination, 212
scapegoating, 215
social epidemiology, 216
genocide, 225

DISCUSSION QUESTIONS

1. If genetic differences between people who have different physical characteristics (like skin color) are minor, why do we as a society continue to use race as a socially significant category?
2. As noted in the chapter, racial residential segregation remains a key problem in the United States. What sociological factors explain its persistence in an era when housing discrimination is illegal?
3. What links have researchers identified between race and health outcomes in the United States? What sociological factors explain relatively poorer health among minorities than among Whites? How might public policy be used to address this problem?
4. Do you think immigration will continue to grow in coming decades in the United States? What kinds of factors might influence immigration trends?
5. What factors make communities vulnerable to genocide? How should other countries respond when genocide seems imminent or is already under way?

Sharpen your skills with SAGE edge at **edge.sagepub.com/chambliss2e**

A personalized approach to help you accomplish your course-work goals in an easy-to-use learning environment.

GENDER AND SOCIETY

Reuters/Mark Blinch

WHAT DO YOU THINK?

1. Why do boys as a group outscore girls as a group on the SAT, even though girls on average do better in school?
2. Why are women today more likely to enroll in and complete college than their male peers?
3. Why do men as a group continue to outearn women as a group?

Reuters/Larry Downing

WHERE THE BOYS ARE (NOT)

If you attend college on a coed campus and suspect that there are fewer men than women in many of your courses, it is not your imagination. A 2010 article about campus life at a U.S. college begins as follows:

> Another ladies' night, not by choice.
>
> After midnight on a rainy night last week in Chapel Hill, N.C., a large group of sorority women at the University of North Carolina squeezed into the corner booth of a gritty basement bar. Bathed in a neon glow, they splashed beer from pitchers, traded jokes and belted out lyrics to a Taylor Swift heartache anthem thundering overhead. As a night out, it had everything—except guys.
>
> "This is so typical, like all nights, 10 out of 10," said Kate Andrew, a senior from Albemarle, N.C. The experience has grown tiresome: they slip on tight-fitting tops, hair sculpted, makeup just so, all for the benefit of one another, Ms. Andrew said, "because there are no guys."
>
> North Carolina, with a student body that is nearly 60 percent female, is just one of many large universities that at times feels eerily like a women's college. Women have represented about 57 percent of enrollments at American colleges since at least 2000, according to a recent report by the American Council on Education. Researchers there cite several reasons: women tend to have higher grades; men tend to drop out in disproportionate numbers; and female enrollment skews higher among older students, low-income students, and Black and Hispanic students. (Williams, 2010)

This story suggests that women are moving ahead in academic achievement—and men are falling behind. This is a significant social phenomenon that we explore in this chapter.

Women's advancements in higher education represent a powerful social transformation. This change, however, is only part of a story that still finds women earning less than their male counterparts in the workforce and reaching fewer positions at the top of the corporate ladder and in politics. Women across the globe remain deeply vulnerable to violence and exploitation. Deep-seated prejudices hamper both men and women who do not behave as their societies expect: Gays, lesbians, transgendered individuals, and others who "do gender" differently may be subject to ostracism, discrimination, and abuse. In this chapter, we look at the social category of gender and its continuing significance in modern society, examining its effects on individuals, groups, and societies.

Football remains a male-dominated sport at all levels of play, but some young women have taken advantage of new opportunities to join teams. Most current female players are kickers, but a few also populate the ranks of other field positions like linebacker.

We begin with a discussion of key concepts of sex and gender and how those are used in sociological study. We then address the construction of gendered selves, looking at agents of socialization—including the family, media, and schools—and examining the idea that gender is as much an action and a process as an identity. This leads us to a wide-ranging discussion of gender and society. We focus on gender and family life, higher education, the wage gap, and sexual harassment to understand how gender norms, roles, and expectations shape the experiences of men and women in key societal institutions. Next we turn to both the classical canon and contemporary feminist thinking about gender, ending with a section on women's global concerns, including maternal mortality, sex trafficking, and rape in war. We examine the marginality of women and the steps being taken to empower them to change their own lives and communities.

SOCIOLOGICAL CONCEPTS OF SEX AND GENDER

Sociologists acknowledge that complex interactions between biology and culture shape behavioral differences associated with gender. They seek to take both forces into account, though most believe culture and society play more important roles in structuring gender and **gender roles**, *the attitudes and behaviors considered appropriately "masculine" or "feminine" in a particular culture.* Sociologists thus argue that gender-specific behaviors are not reducible to biological differences; rather, biology, culture, and social learning all interact to shape human behaviors.

To highlight the distinction between biological and social factors, sociologists use the term *sex* to refer to biological identity and the term *gender* to refer to the "masculine" or "feminine" roles associated with sex. **Sex** encompasses the *anatomical and other biological differences between males and females that originate in human genes.* Many of these biologically based sex differences, such as differences in genitalia, are usually present at birth. Others, triggered by male or female hormones, develop later—for example, female menstruation and differences in muscle mass, facial hair, height, and vocal characteristics.

Gender encompasses *the norms, roles, and behavioral characteristics associated in a given society with being male or female.* Gender is less about being biologically male or female than about conforming to mainstream notions of *masculinity* and *femininity,* though the characteristics we associate with gender vary across time and space. Biologically based sex differences are not unimportant in shaping social norms of gender. The fact that only biological women can bear and nurse children, for example, has enormous implications for women's roles in all societies (Huber, 2006), but this does not mean that, as Sigmund Freud asserted, biology is destiny.

Before we move on, it is worth noting that many sociologists consider both sex and gender to be dynamic concepts. While it is clear that *gender,* which is associated with norms, roles, and behaviors that shift over time, is socially constructed, a growing number of researchers have suggested that *sex* is also socially

Gender roles: The attitudes and behaviors that are considered appropriately "masculine" or "feminine" in a particular culture.

Sex: The anatomical and other biological characteristics that differ between males and females and that originate in genetic differences.

Gender: Behavioral characteristics that differ between males and females based on culturally enforced and socially learned norms and roles.

Gender Stereotyping

Gender Norms

Kristian Dowling/TB / Contributor/Getty Images/ AP Photo/Aaron Vincent Elkaim

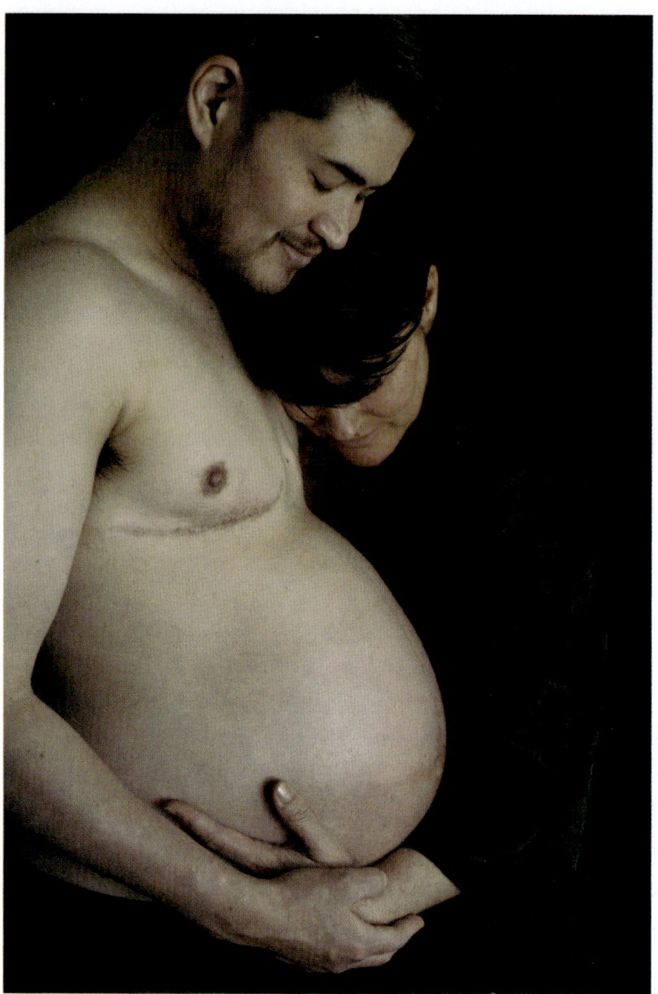

Thomas Beatie (left) attracted attention in 2007 as the first "pregnant man." Beatie is a transgender male who preserved his female reproductive organs after transitioning. Jenna Talackova (right) attracted the public's attention in 2012 as the first male-to-female transgender contestant in the Miss Universe Canada pageant. Both individuals transgress traditional sex and gender boundaries, inviting both positive and negative reactions in society

constructed rather than solely biological (Preves, 2003). They cite cases of infants born with ambiguous sex characteristics and/or an abnormal chromosomal makeup. Such uncertainties in sex categorization are rarely tolerated by doctors, parents of these infants, or society. As a result, such children are usually subjected to surgeries and medications intended to render them "categorizable" in societally normative terms.

Transgender is an umbrella term used to describe *those whose gender identity, expression, or behavior differs from their assigned sex at birth or is outside the two gender categories.* A person who was female assigned at birth (FAAB) but identifies as a man (FTM) may be described as transgender, as may a person who was male assigned at birth (MAAB) but identifies as a woman (MTF). Transgender also includes, but is not limited to, other categories and identities, such as transsexual, cross-dresser, androgynous, genderqueer, bigender, third gender, and gender nonconforming. **Transsexual** usually refers to *people who use surgery and hormones to change their sex to match their preferred gender.* It is important to note that being trans is a *gender orientation,* not a **sexuality**. Transgendered people may have heterosexual, lesbian, gay, or bisexual sexual orientation.

Clearly, both sex and gender can be complicated. In early 2012, officials of the Miss Universe Canada competition disqualified would-be contestant Jenna Talackova, who was born a male; they claimed that being born a female was a requirement to compete. Within days, however, the judges decided

Transgender: An umbrella term used to describe those whose gender identity, expression, or behavior differs from their assigned sex or is outside the gender binary.

Transsexual: A term used to refer to people who use surgery and hormones to change their sex to match their preferred gender.

Sexuality: The ways in which people construct their sexual desires and relationships, including the norms governing sexual behavior.

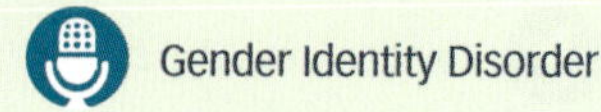
Gender Identity Disorder

Talackova could compete (Schabner, 2012). In a YouTube video for Miss International Queen, a transgender/transsexual pageant in which she had previously competed, Talackova said she began hormone therapy at age 14 and had sexual reassignment surgery at 19. She defines herself as a woman, and her gender display is clearly feminine. Is sex at birth an immutable category? Or should individuals have the freedom to define themselves, pushing boundaries of both gender and sex?

In spite of the controversy that surrounded her entry in the May 2012 Miss Universe Canada pageant, Talackova placed among the top 12 finalists and earned one of four "Miss Congeniality" ribbons.

© Robin Utrecht Fotografie/HillCreek Pictures/Corbis

The Surma people of the Omo Valley in Ethiopia use body adornments as part of members' gender display. Ear labrets are worn by women as well as men, though lip plates, which stretch the lower lip away from the mouth, are only worn by women.

CONSTRUCTING GENDERED SELVES

Across the diverse cultures of our planet, males are generally expected to behave in culturally defined "masculine" ways and females in "feminine" ways. Few people fully conform to these stereotypes—most exhibit a blend of characteristics. Still, in many cultures people believe male and female stereotypes represent fundamental and real sex differences, and while some "blending" is acceptable, there are social consequences for diverging too far from the social scripts of gender.

What is considered "masculine" and "feminine" differs across cultures, and gender displays can vary dramatically. Among the Canela of Brazil, for example, large, colorful disks called *kui* are inserted into holes pierced into a boy's ears. Repeated piercings and insertions stretch the holes to a large size in order to enable the ears to eventually accommodate disks that are several inches across. This painful process is performed to enable the boy to better hear the wisdom of his elders, as well as to make him attractive to women (Crocker, 1986, 1990, 1994). This practice would not be considered masculine in U.S. culture, although earrings, once considered a mark of femininity, are now commonplace symbols of masculinity in some U.S. subcultures.

Pressures to conform to conventional gender roles exist in all cultures. At the same time, norms and characteristics are dynamic, meaning men and women both shape and are shaped by these expectations. We can think of gender roles as being continuously learned and relearned through social interaction (Fenstermaker & West, 2002). That is, they are neither biologically determined nor passively acquired from others. Rather, each of us plays a dynamic role in learning what it means to be a boy or a girl and a man or a woman in a particular culture. In becoming accomplished actors of these roles, we often forget we are playing parts and become closely identified with the roles themselves. Yet, because we are constantly renegotiating our gender roles in social interaction, we can change and challenge those "rules" regarding gender that we find to be limiting.

Crucial early influences on gender roles include family, peer groups, the mass media, and schools. These are among the important *agents of gender socialization* that contribute to the creation of our gendered selves.

THE ROOTS OF GENDER: THE FAMILY

Children learn a great deal about socially normative gender roles from their families, particularly their parents. The power of the family in the production and reproduction of gender has led some sociologists to call the home a "factory of gendered personalities" (Fenstermaker Berk, 1985; Goldscheider & Waite, 1991).

Often parents have particular beliefs about how their infant daughters and sons are supposed to behave, and they communicate these attitudes in countless subtle and not-so-subtle ways. A girl may play with a toy truck with few social consequences, while a boy may face acute teasing for enjoying a baby doll. This distinction may seem to favor girls, but we can also argue that it highlights the stigmatization and marginalization of practices and objects associated with femininity.

A number of studies have shown that many parents have senses of gender differences that affect their behaviors toward children, often from birth (Eliot, 2009; Marini, 1990). One study found that mothers spoke differently to their babies in utero depending on if they knew the babies were boys or girls (K. Smith, 2005).

Hilary Lips (2008) has written that parents give their daughters "roots" and their sons "wings"—that is, they nurture closer and more dependent ties with girls than they do with boys. Some studies have also shown that boys are more likely to be taught to complete tasks on their own, while girls are instructed to ask for help or have tasks completed for them (Lindsey & Mize, 2001), a difference that has been documented in the early-education classroom (Sadker & Zittleman, 2009).

Echoing these findings, Denny (2011) found marked differences in the types of activities required of Boy Scouts and Girl Scouts. Girl Scouts' activities are more likely to be group oriented and artistic in nature than are Boy Scouts' activities, which are more likely to be solo and scientific.

Toys and books also function as staples of early childhood socialization in the family. Consider a recent study that examined 300 children's picture books published from 1902 to 2000 (DeWitt, Cready, & Seward, 2013). The researchers studied portrayals in the books of mothers and fathers as, variously, companions, disciplinarians, caregivers, nurturers, and providers. Perhaps surprisingly, they found that, in spite of dramatic societal changes over the period examined, the traditional model of the nurturing, homemaking mother and the breadwinning father still prevailed in books published late in the 20th century. Underscoring the significance of the finding, the authors note that books do not just "entertain"; they also "socialize."

While parental practices may reinforce gender stereotypes, parents can play an equally important part in countering gender stereotyping by being role models and socializing their children into norms and values reflecting greater gender equality. For example, daughters encouraged to excel in traditionally "male" areas like science and mathematics are more likely to grow up to pursue science- or math-related careers (Bhanot & Jovanovic, 2005; Tenenbaum & Leaper, 2003). Just a few decades ago, women were a clear minority in most institutions of higher education. Legal measures such as Title IX legislation, which was enacted in 1972, prohibited discrimination in educational institutions receiving federal funding and opened more educational opportunities to women. By the 1960s and 1970s, young women had greater social and economic support at home as well. Both society and families have been part of the revolution in women's higher education, though women still lag in the well-paid but historically male-dominated fields of science, math, and engineering.

GENDER AMONG FRIENDS: PEER INFLUENCES

The actions and judgments of our peers affect the ways we enact our gender roles. Beginning at an early age, girls and boys learn stereotypical gender roles in peer groups (Martin & Fabes, 2001). Aina and Cameron (2011) suggest that friendship patterns and peer pressure reflect and affirm stereotypes. This is particularly acute among boys, who "police" peers, stigmatizing perceived feminine traits. Playing in same-sex peer groups, interestingly enough, may have a different effect from playing more often in mixed groups. Martin and Fabes (2001) point to a "social dosage effect," such that play among young girls who stay with all-girl groups tend to reflect norms of encouragement and support, while young boys in same-gender groups develop a tendency toward more aggressive and competitive play.

Are gender differences between little girls and little boys more natural or learned? Think about evidence you would use to support both arguments. Which seems more persuasive? Why?

Research on elementary school playgroups has found that girls often gather in smaller groups, playing games that include imitation and the taking of turns. Boys, on the other hand, play in larger groups at rule-governed games that occur over larger physical distances than girls occupy (Richards, 2012; Thorne, 1993). Long before they become teenagers, young people learn that gender matters and that the roles, norms, and expectations of boys and girls are often different.

During late childhood and adolescence, children are especially concerned about what their friends think of them—far more than about what their parents think. In her ethnography of a racially diverse working-class high school, C. J. Pascoe (2007) uncovered how teenage boys reinforced norms of masculinity and heterosexuality by disciplining behavior deemed inappropriate, feminine, or otherwise "unmanly," using slurs like "fag" and "faggot."

Pressures for peer conformity remain strong into college, where sororities, fraternities, athletic teams, and other social groups may reproduce stereotypical gender behavior (Edwards, 2007). Homophobia can be acute during this period and, as we will see later in the chapter, may result in sexual harassment (D'Augelli, Pilkington, & Hershberger, 2002; Wyss, 2007). As young people move into adulthood, the pressures for gender conformity decline somewhat—or perhaps more models for gender roles become available to those who opt not to conform to dominant expectations.

MEDIA POWER: REFLECTING AND REINFORCING GENDER

Scholars have written extensively on the role television plays in reinforcing gender identities in society (Barner, 1999; Condry, 1989; Gauntlett, 2008). According to the American Academy of Child and Adolescent Psychiatry (2011), the average child in the United States spends 3 to 4 hours per day in front of the

© Sandy Huffaker/Corbis

A recent report in the *New York Times* documents the harassment of females in online gaming communities, a phenomenon that is now pervasive, particularly in competitive games with strangers. Some women seek safer playing environments in smaller online "clans" of identified gamers (O'Leary, 2012).

TV, more if the child has a television in his or her bedroom. We might therefore predict that the often highly gendered messages conveyed by everything from characters to themes to advertisements will have powerful impacts on images, norms, and identities. While much has changed in U.S. society in terms of gender roles, media images often appear frozen in time, persistently peddling domestic or highly sexualized images of women—or cattiness, a trait for women that appears frequently on "reality" TV programs like the various *Real Housewives* shows and *Dance Moms*—and images of men as aggressive if also analytic and often financially successful (as in television's *Mad Men*).

Cartoons also convey gendered images. One study found that male cartoon characters outnumber female characters four to one—the same ratio as 25 years before. Moreover, male cartoon characters tend to be powerful, dominant, smart, and aggressive; female characters generally lack personalities altogether (Spicher & Hudak, 1997; Thompson & Scantlin, 2007). Other research has found that male cartoon characters use more physical aggression, while females are more likely to display behaviors that are fearful, polite and supportive, or romantic (Gokcearslan, 2010; Leaper, Breed, Hoffman, & Perlman, 2002). An analysis of prime-time TV sitcoms in Canada concluded that the body types of female characters are often a factor in the humor; the heavier the character, the more likely she is to be the target of negative comments by male characters, as a means of getting a laugh (Fouts & Burggraf, 2000; Himes & Thompson, 2007).

The music industry, too, traffics in gender stereotypes. Wallis (2011) and Turner (2011) found that popular music videos tend to portray women as sex objects who are submissive in relation to men. Indeed, as Aubrey and Frisby (2011) state, "although sexual objectification is commonplace in media culture, music videos provide the most potent examples of it" (p. 475). Caputi (2014) notes the sexism inherent in the way that young female pop stars are "branded," with the media hypersexualizing them and subjecting their romantic relationships to intense scrutiny. While research finds the objectification of women in the music industry to be strongest in hip-hop and pop music, it can be observed across genres (Aubrey & Frisby, 2011). Moreover, because music videos today are often viewed online and on mobile devices in addition to the more traditional outlets of television channels such as MTV, these gendered images reach a wider audience than they might have even a decade ago.

Video games offer an area for expanding research on media and socialization. By some estimates, fully 92% of children ages 2 to 17 play video games. The majority of gamers are male, though the proportion of girls has been growing (NPD Group, 2006). This is significant because content studies suggest that popular video games consistently convey stereotypical gender images. Downs and Smith (2010), in an analysis of 60 video games with a total of 489 characters, determined that women were likely to be presented in hypersexualized ways that included being partially nude or wearing revealing attire. Reflecting common findings that men are "action" figures while women are largely passive, Haninger and Thompson (2004) discovered that in the 81 teen-rated games they sampled, fully 72 had playable male characters, while just 42 had playable female characters. The consequences of these gender messages are significant, as female gamers report sexual threats and harassment from their male counterparts in the interactive online gaming community (O'Leary, 2012).

In an age of growing media influence, when stories and images and ideas reach us not only through television, films, and games but also through computers, phones, and other devices, it is important to consider what kinds of gender images are being "sold" to us. Do new media sources offer more diverse images? Are old stereotypes still pervasive? What do you think?

GENDER IN THE CLASSROOM: SCHOOLS AND SOCIALIZATION

According to some researchers, in addition to providing instruction in basic subjects, schools are an important site of a "hidden curriculum," or the unspoken socialization to norms, values, and roles—including gender roles (Basow, 2004; Margolis, 2001). For example, there is evidence that from an early age shyness is discouraged in boys at school because it is viewed as violating the masculine norm of assertiveness (Doey, Coplan, & Kingsbury, 2013). The roles of teachers, administrators, and other adults in the school provide some early lessons to students about their future career prospects. Pre-K and elementary teaching is still largely female dominated, and in many elementary schools the only men are administrators, physical education teachers or coaches, and janitors (Figure 10.1).

Gender Segregation at School

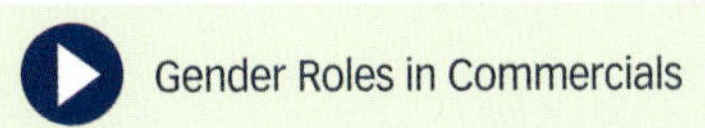

Gender Roles in Commercials

FIGURE 10.1 Percentage of Female Teachers in Educational Occupations

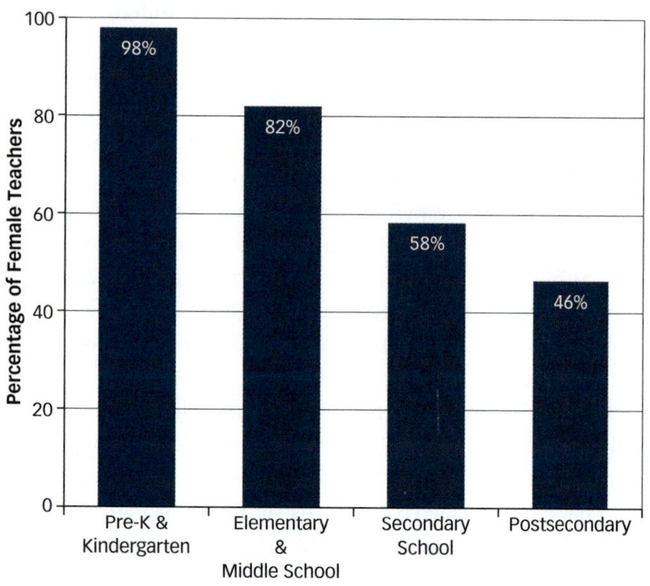

SOURCE: Bureau of Labor Statistics. (2012c). 11. Employed persons by detailed occupation, sex, race, and Hispanic or Latino ethnicity. *Household Data Annual Averages*. Washington, DC: U.S. Government Printing Office.

Classroom materials reflect gender power and position too. Books on history, for instance, are still heavily populated by male characters, the great heroes and villains of the global and local past. Until very recently, when books began to present a more diverse cast of historical characters,

> women were not viewed as an integral part of the historical record. The vast majority remained silent and invisible, their history subsumed under general descriptions of men's lives. . . . Extraordinary figures like the queens of sixteenth-century Europe or the nineteenth-century reformers in the United States, active agents in their own right, fared no better. Though [they were] sometimes praised for having successfully assumed male roles, traditional, patronizing phrases and denigrating stereotypes abstracted and diminished even their exceptional personalities and experiences. (Zinsser, 1993, p. 3)

Even today, where women (and, often, minorities) appear in history textbooks, they may still be shown in special features (such as essay boxes) outside the main text that are more likely to be overlooked. In their book *Failing at Fairness* (1997), David Sadker and Myra Sadker argue that in most history texts students see few women. Their study of one 819-page text yielded less than a full page of references devoted to women. Another book contained four pictures of men for every one of women, and just about 3% of the text was allotted to telling about women.

The authors write about challenging high school seniors to name 20 famous U.S. women, past or present (not including sports or entertainment figures). In the allotted 5 minutes, most students were able to come up with just a handful, but they had little trouble naming famous men (Sadker & Sadker, 1997). Clearly, changes have been made in the teaching of history since Sadker and Sadker's work. Have those altered the gender balance in history teaching? How would you perform on such a quiz, and what sociological factors would you cite to explain your performance?

DOING GENDER

Sociologists commonly define gender as a product of agents of socialization, the combined influences of which create gendered selves. The implication is that gender is an internalized identity, not natural, but still a fundamental aspect of the social self. Another sociological perspective, described below, suggests that gender is less an identity than an activity.

As we saw in Chapter 4, sociologist Erving Goffman (1959) argued that the social self is the *product* of a social interaction. Thus, the individual engages in "impression management" to tailor his or her presentation of self in a way most favorable to the given situation. Goffman argued that the individual (or a group) is concerned with defining the situation and ensuring a believable performance.

Goffman's work does not have gender at its center, though some of his examples of impression management are telling. For instance, he illustrated *idealization,* in which we present ourselves in ways that exemplify the values and norms of society, with a young woman choosing not to appear smarter than her male date. While her decision to "play dumb" may have gone the way of the 1950s (when Goffman's book was written), it demonstrates how individuals seek to perform gender in accordance with societal expectations.

Building on some of Goffman's ideas, Candace West and Don Zimmerman's (1987) article "Doing Gender" suggests that gender is an activity we *do* rather than a fixed identity. West and Zimmerman posit that *sex* is a set of biological categories for classifying people as male or female; a person's **sex category** is the *socially required identification display that confirms his or her membership in a given category,* including displaying and enacting gender as social norms and expectations determine. Thus, *gender* is an activity that creates differences between men and women that, while not biological, appear natural because they are so consistently enacted. Membership in a sex category also brings differential access to power and resources, affecting interpersonal relationships and social status.

Recall Jenna Talackova, the transsexual Miss Universe Canada contestant. Since she was raised as a male, she had to

Sex category: The socially required identification display that confirms someone's membership in a given category.

Doing Gender: Women on the Force

learn to "do gender" in a way consistent with the sex she aspired to be—female. While most men and women "do gender" largely without effort, thanks to socialization, for a trans individual the process may be more conscious, deliberate, and apparent—and no less important for acceptance as a member of his or her new sex category.

GENDER AND SOCIETY

Anthropological studies have found that inequalities in almost all known societies, past and present, favor men over women (Huber, 2006). Women are occasionally equal to men economically, politically, or socially, but in no known society do they have greater control over economic and political resources, exercise greater power and authority, or enjoy more prestige than men (Chafetz, 1984). Many sociologists explain this inequality by noting that women alone can give birth to and (particularly important before modern bottle-feeding) nurse infants, two activities essential to a society's continuation but usually lacking in social status. Given that a major source of power, wealth, and status is the ability to earn money or acquire other goods of value, any limitations on women's ability to pursue these rewards affects their social position.

In hunting and gathering and early horticultural societies, women produced nearly as much food as men and were more equal in power and prestige, though wealth differences were minimal in such subsistence economies (Huber, 1990, 1993; Mukhopadhyay & Higgins, 1988). With the emergence of agricultural societies and the development of metallurgy, trade and warfare became much more central features of social organization. Because women spent large portions of their active years pregnant or nursing infants, they were less likely to become merchants or warriors. Strong states emerged to manage warfare and trade, and these were controlled by men. Research suggests that women's status suffered accordingly (Friedl, 1975; Grant, 1991).

In modern industrial societies, the requirements of physical survival, reproduction, and economic organization no longer exert the same sorts of constraints. The ability to have fewer children, along with the invention of bottle-feeding around 1910, freed women from long periods of pregnancy and nursing. Mass education, established in most industrial nations by the end of the 19th century, encouraged women to seek knowledge and eventually careers outside the home.

Today, gender stratification persists, but in a rapidly changing and dynamic social environment. Families, the educational system, and the labor force are all in flux. Below we examine these areas and the ways women's and men's status and roles are changing.

Second shift: The unpaid housework that women typically do after they come home from their paid employment.

AP Photo/Rui Vieira

How do you see the future division of labor in your family? If you are already a spouse or parent, think about your level of satisfaction with how household work is divided in your family. What might you want to change and why? ■

GENDER AND FAMILY LIFE

Domestic tasks—child care, cooking, cleaning, and shopping for necessities of living—can entail long hours of work. In the United States, women still do the disproportionate share of housework and child care. Men are more likely to engage in nonroutine domestic tasks, such as making home repairs or taking the children on outings.

Attitudes and practices change, though slowly. Just over a generation ago, a study found that fewer than 5% of husbands did as much housework as their wives (Coltrane & Ishii-Kuntz, 1992). In a 15-year study that tracked thousands of men and women born after World War II, Goldscheider and Waite (1991) found that, in two-parent families with teenage boys and girls, girls were assigned five times as many household chores as their brothers.

More recently, a 2007 *Time* magazine survey found that 84% of respondents (men and women) agreed that husbands and wives "negotiate the rules, relationships and responsibilities more than those earlier generations did" (Gibbs, 2009). A study by the University of Michigan found that the total amount of housework done by women has fallen since 1976 from an average of 26 hours per week to about 17, while the amount done by men has grown from 6 hours to 13 hours (Achen & Stafford, 2005; Reaney & Goldsmith, 2008). Clearly, there has been some convergence. Labor-saving devices (like the microwave oven) have contributed to changes, as has the ability of more dual-earner households to pass the burden of domestic work to housekeepers, gardeners, and the like. At the same time, women are still primarily responsible for domestic work in most two-parent households (Davis, Greenstein, & Marks, 2007). Arlie Hochschild (2012) calls this responsibility the **second shift**—*the unpaid housework women typically do after they come home from their paid employment.*

Some data show that unmarried women who live with men spend less time on housework than do married women—even when numbers of children and hours of paid work are taken into account (Davis et al., 2007). The division of household labor is more likely to be equal among lesbian and gay couples (Kurdek, 2007). What might explain these differences? One recent study with about 17,000 respondents in 28 countries suggests that marriage has a "traditionalizing" effect on couples, even those who describe themselves and their practices in egalitarian terms (Davis et al., 2007).

GENDER IN HIGH SCHOOL: WHY DO BOYS OUTSCORE GIRLS ON THE SAT?

Girls outperform boys on many academic measures: earning high grades, enrolling in Advanced Placement (AP) courses, achieving academic honors, finishing in the top 10% of their class, and graduating, to name a few. One measure where boys have consistently outpaced their female peers, however, is the SAT (originally the Scholastic Aptitude Test, later renamed the Scholastic Assessment Test, and now officially known by the initials SAT). In 2013, the average score for males on the mathematics section of the SAT was 531 out of 800; females scored an average of 499. While both boys' and girls' scores have risen over time, the gap has remained largely steady (Figure 10.2). While boys' advantage on the verbal section of the SAT is smaller, it too has persisted, though girls tend to earn markedly better average grades in courses such as English.

What explains the difference? Some researchers suggest the gap points to a gender bias in the test (Sadker & Sadker, 1997; Sadker & Zittleman, 2009). Why, they ask, do boys continue to outscore girls if girls do better in school and continue doing better in college? After all, the SAT is intended

The Washington Post / Contributor/Getty Images

Think back to our discussion of agents of gender socialization. Are there any clues in these materials about why boys outscore girls on standardized math tests such as the SAT?

FIGURE 10.2 Average SAT Mathematics Scores for Males and Females, 1972–2013

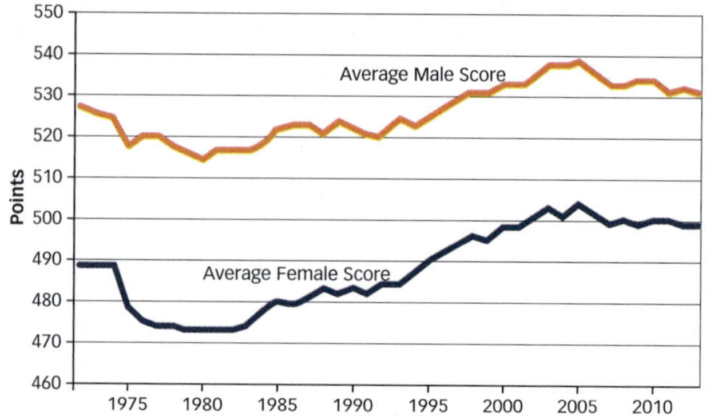

SOURCE: CollegeBoard. (2010). 2010 College-bound seniors: Total group profile report; CollegeBoard. (2013). SAT® Percentile Ranks for Males, Females, and Total Group, 2013 College-Bound Seniors—Mathematics; CollegeBoard. (2012). SAT® Percentile Ranks for 2012 College-Bound Seniors, Critical Reading, Mathematics and Writing Percentile Ranks by Gender and Ethnic Groups; CollegeBoard. (2011). 2011 College-bound seniors: Total group profile report.

to measure college readiness. In a study published in 1989, Rosser argued that girls did better than boys on questions focused on relationships, aesthetics, and the humanities, while boys performed better when questions involved sports, the natural sciences, or business. Rosser's study followed an earlier report by Carol Dwyer of the Educational Testing Service (ETS). Dwyer (1976) concluded that gender differences could be altered through selective use of test items. In an effort to "balance" the test, she reported, ETS added more test items highlighting politics, sports, and business, areas on which boys did better. Questions about whether the test favors boys continue to be raised 40 years later (Sadker & Zittleman, 2009).

Some researchers argue that girls may underperform on math tests because they have been socialized to believe that boys are better at math. This is an example of what researchers call **stereotype threat**, *a situation in which an individual is at risk of confirming a negative stereotype about his or her social group* (Steele & Aronson, 1995). This concept highlights the assertion that a person's performance on a task may be negatively affected by anxiety related to perceived low expectations of the individual's group—such as the expectation that "girls are not good at math." One experimental study showed that informing female test takers of stereotype threat before a test improved their performance (Johns, Schmader, & Martens, 2005).

On the other hand, some observers suggest that boys' higher scores on the math section of the SAT are a result of a different phenomenon. Christina Hoff Sommers (2000) argues

Stereotype threat: A situation in which an individual is at risk of confirming a negative stereotype about his or her social group.

that more girls—and girls representing more varying levels of achievement and ability—take the test, explaining their lower average score. Boys' higher average score, suggests Hoff, is the product of a limited pool of test takers representing the best-prepared young men.

Is the SAT gender biased because it shows boys outperforming girls, even though girls end up earning better grades and dropping out of college less frequently? Or is it evidence of girls' advantages, because girls are more likely to take college entrance exams and go to college? What other factors may be at play here?

GENDER AND HIGHER EDUCATION

We began this chapter by noting that more women than men are studying in U.S. institutions of higher education. Consider that by age 24, nearly 28% of women today have earned a bachelor's degree, while just 19% of men have done so (U.S. Bureau of Labor Statistics, 2012a). The gap is smaller for Whites and larger in Black and Hispanic populations

Today women make up the larger share of college students; in the past they were actively discouraged from pursuing higher education. In the late 19th century, powerful social barriers stood in the way, such as beliefs about women's capacity to succeed at *both* education and reproduction. Some believed that the "ovaries—not the brain—were the most important organ in a woman's body" (Brumberg, 1997, p. 8). Author Joan Brumberg (1997) writes,

> The most persuasive spokesperson for this point of view was Dr. Edward Clarke, a highly regarded professor at Harvard Medical School, whose popular book *Sex in Education; Or, A Fair Chance for the Girls* (1873) was a powerful statement of the ideology of "ovarian determinism." In a series of case studies drawn from his clinical practice, Clarke described adolescent women whose menstrual cycles, reproductive capacity, and general health were all ruined, in his opinion, by inattention to their special monthly demands [menstruation]. . . . Clarke argued against higher education because he believed women's bodies were more complicated than men's; this difference meant that young girls needed time and ease to develop, free from the drain of intellectual activity. (p. 8)

While the idea of a "brain–womb conflict" faded as the United States entered the 20th century, other beliefs persisted. Ordinary families with resources to support college study were more likely to invest them in their sons, who were expected to be their future families' primary breadwinners. Families that did seek education for their daughters ran into structural barriers. For example, until the passage of Title IX in 1972, some U.S. colleges and universities, particularly at the graduate and professional school level, limited or prohibited female enrollment.

Although Title IX is often associated with increasing equity in women's access to collegiate athletic opportunities, in fact it requires gender equity for men and women in every educational program receiving federal funding. In 1972, women were earning just 7% of law degrees and 9% of medical degrees in the United States (National Organization for Women, n.d.). By contrast, the U.S. Census Bureau reported in 2010 that 11% of men and 10% of women 25 and older had attained an education higher than a bachelor's degree. As well, women make up 60% of advanced degree holders ages 25 to 29. In addition, according to data from the U.S. Census Bureau (2011a), more women than men now hold degrees overall, with 37% having earned at least a bachelor's degree compared to 35% of men.

The *proportion* of women enrolled in college has been greater than the proportion of men since 1991, though the actual *numbers* of women have been greater since the early 1980s, since women make up a larger share of the population (Figure 10.3). Women's climb to equality in educational opportunity has been long and slow, but their gains in higher education since Title IX have been dramatic and rapid (National Center for Education Statistics, 2011b).

Researchers suggest several reasons for women's growing presence in higher education. First, a high school degree is a prerequisite to college, and more men than women leave high school without diplomas. Among ethnic groups in the United States, only in the Asian/Pacific Islander category are men and women essentially equal in the proportion of those who finish high school (Figure 10.4).

Second, young women as a group have higher grades than young men: In 2009, the mean high school grade point average for female students was 3.10 of a possible 4.0, while for male

FIGURE 10.3 Percentage of Male and Female High School Graduates Enrolling in College, 1970–2012

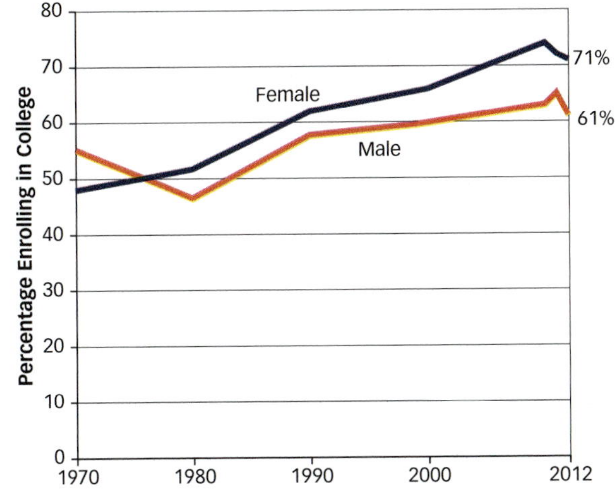

SOURCE: National Center for Education Statistics. (2011). Recent high school completers and their enrollment in college, by sex: 1960 through 2010. *Digest of Education Statistics*.

students it was 2.90 (National Center for Education Statistics, 2009). This makes women more likely candidates for college matriculation. Third, the numbers are affected by substantially higher female enrollment among some demographic groups, including Black and Hispanic, low-income, and older students. Black women substantially outpace their male peers in completing college: Fully 63% of college-educated young Black adults are female, while just 37% are male (Wang & Parker, 2011). Among older ("nontraditional") students, women outnumber men by about two to one (U.S. Department of State, 2008).

Finally, men are more likely than women to leave college without finishing a degree. (See Figure 10.5.) A recent study points to the pivotal role of student debt in this process. For most American college students, the ability to secure loans has become a prerequisite to entering college. For some, mounting debt during their undergraduate years leads to a rethinking of the benefit of the degree versus dropping out to enter the workforce. Data suggest that men may be more averse than women to accruing debt: Men drop out with lower levels of debt than women do, but they are also more likely to leave before graduating (Dwyer, Hodson, & McCloud, 2013).

FIGURE 10.4 Status Completion Rates of 18- Through 24-Year-Olds Not Currently Enrolled in High School, by Race/Ethnicity and Sex, 2009

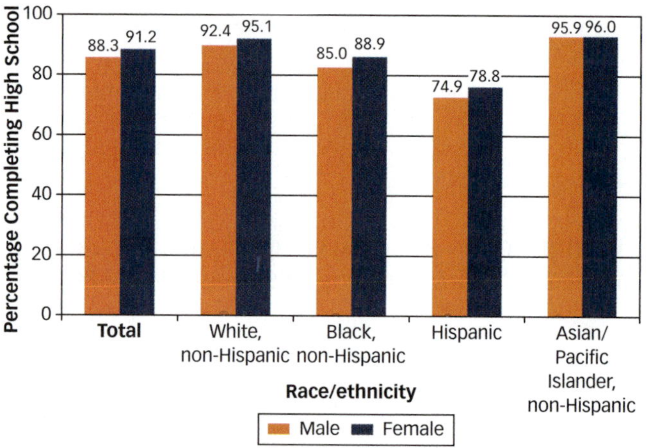

NOTE: Status completion rates measure the percentage of 18- through 24-year-olds who are not enrolled in high school and who also hold a high school diploma or alternative credential, such as a Gereral Educational Development (GED) certificate. Those still enrolled in high-school are excluded from the analysis. Respondents were able to identify themselves as being two or more races. The white, non-Hispanic; Black, non-Hispanic; Asian/Pacific Islander, non-Hispanic; and American Indian/Alaska Native, non-Hispanic categories consist of individuals who considered themselves to be one race and who did not identify as Hispanic. Non-Hispanics who identified themselves as multiracial are included in the "two or more races, non-Hispanic" category. The Hispanic category consists of Hispanics of all and racial combinations.

SOURCE: U.S. Department of Education. (2012). *Trends in high school dropout and completion rates in the United States: 1972–2009.*

FIGURE 10.5 Cumulative U.S. College Degree Gap in Favor of Women, 1982–2013

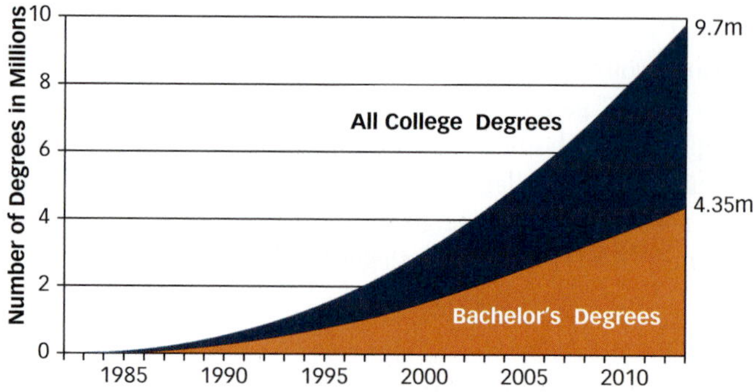

*Includes associate, bachelor's, master's, and doctoral degrees.

SOURCE: U.S. Department of Education.

Interestingly, a 2011 Pew Research Center survey found that women are more likely than men to say college was "very useful" in increasing their knowledge and helping them grow intellectually (81% compared to 67%), as well as helping them grow and mature as a person (73% compared to 64%). Public perceptions about the necessity of a college education for "getting ahead in life" were also split by gender: 77% of respondents indicated this was true for women, while 68% felt it was true for men (Wang & Parker, 2011).

In 2009, the U.S. Commission on Civil Rights began an investigation into whether some college admissions offices discriminate against qualified female applicants in order to support a desired "gender balance" in student population (Jaschik, 2009). Ironically, Title IX does give admissions departments in private liberal arts colleges the legal right to consider gender as a factor in admission. As of March 2011, the investigation was shelved due to disagreements over the data collected from 19 schools (Lederman, 2011). What does the general public believe about women's gains (and men's proportional losses) in the attainment of higher education? The *Behind the Numbers* box on page 245 suggests some answers.

GENDER AND ECONOMICS: MEN, WOMEN, AND THE GENDER WAGE GAP

Given their rising achievements in education, are women enjoying earnings that equal or surpass those of men? Women have made tremendous gains in the workplace, but in the United

BEHIND THE NUMBERS

GENDER AND HIGHER EDUCATION: QUESTIONS AND PERCEPTIONS

Experienced social researchers will tell you that myriad variables can affect the findings of a survey, including the wording and the order of the questions. Consider the questions asked by the Pew Research Center on the shifting proportion of men and women in higher education.

When asked whether the fact that "*more women than men* are graduating from college is a good thing, rather than a bad thing," 52% of respondents evaluated the trend positively, 7% said it was a "bad thing," and 39% said it "made no difference" (Wang & Parker, 2011; Figure 10.6). In contrast, when asked whether the fact that "*fewer men than women* are graduating from college" is a good or bad thing for society, only 46% said it was a "bad thing"; 12% said it was good, and 38% that it "made no difference" (Figure 10.7).

While the percentage of people who thought the phenomenon was not important did not change significantly, the difference in the number who thought it was good was quite dramatic. When a positive trend (more women graduating) was emphasized, survey respondents reacted positively. When a negative trend (fewer men graduating) was emphasized, survey respondents reacted negatively. In evaluating social research, we need to be critical and informed consumers of information and pay attention not only to survey responses but to the questions the researchers posed as well.

THINK IT THROUGH

▶ What does the Pew study tell us about public attitudes toward the phenomenon of changing demographics in higher education? What does it tell us about the significance of question wording in public surveys? Would your responses have differed depending on the question wording?

FIGURE 10.6 Attitudes Toward Female Graduation Rates

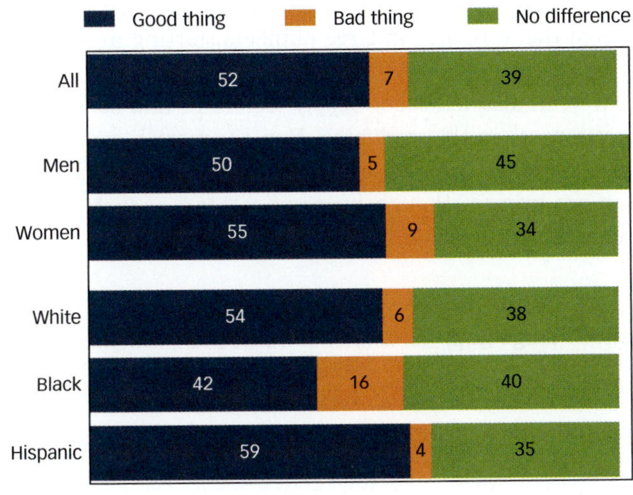

FIGURE 10.7 Attitudes Toward Male Graduation Rates

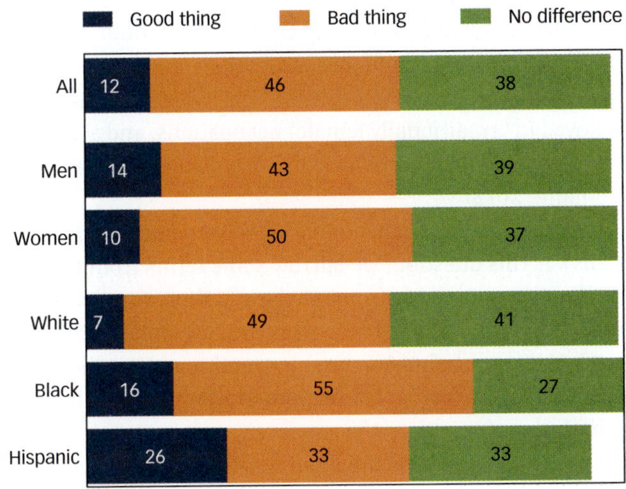

SOURCE: Based on Pew Research Center. (August 17, 2011). *Women see value and benefits of college; Men lag on both fronts, survey finds*, Wendy Wang and Kim Parker. Washington, DC: W. Wang & K. Parker. Reprinted with permission.

States and across the globe, as a group they continue to lag behind men in earnings in most occupational categories. The **gender wage gap** is *the difference between the earnings of women who work full-time year-round as a group and those of men who work full-time year-round as a group.* Why does it persist?

At the end of the 19th century, only one in five women age 16 or older was paid for her work; most paid workers were young, unmarried, or poor (often all three) and held very low-wage jobs. By 1950, five years after the end of World War II, the proportion of American women working outside the home for pay rose to one-third. The enormous economic expansion that continued through the 1970s drew even more women into the paid workforce, attracted by higher pay and supported by the passage of laws such as the Equal Pay Act of 1963, which made unequal pay for equal work illegal. Women's educational gains also opened up more professional and well-paid positions to them. By 1980, more than half of U.S. women were in the paid workforce.

At the beginning of the 20th century, median earnings for women working in full-time, year-round jobs were only half as much as those for men. In 1963 they were still only about three fifths as much, but by 1999 the gap had narrowed, and women earned just over 72% of the median male wage. These gains were partly the result of postwar "baby boom" women, many of them educated and skilled, entering the workforce and moving into higher-paying jobs as they gained experience.

Figures from early 2014 show that women working full-time and year-round earned about 80% of what their male counterparts earned, with variations by race and ethnicity (see Figure 10.8). This translates to average weekly earnings of $722 for women and $872 for men. This continuing difference has two key components, which we look at next.

One important aspect of the gender wage gap is the fact that *men and women are still,* and more than we might think, *concentrated in different occupations.* Researchers label this phenomenon **occupational segregation by gender**. When we identify the 20 most common occupations for women and for men, only 4 appear on both lists. Nearly 40% of women are employed in "traditionally female" occupations, and about 44% of men work in "traditionally male" occupations (Hegewisch & Liepmann, 2012).

Why does gender occupational segregation exist and persist? To answer this question, we borrow some terms from economics. For the purposes of our analysis, **labor supply factors** *highlight reasons that women or men may "prefer" particular occupations,* preparing for, pursuing, and accepting these positions in the labor force. **Labor demand factors** highlight *the needs and preferences of the employer.*

Labor supply factors draw our attention to the agency we exercise in choosing a career path and the decisions we make about how and when to be a part of the paid labor force. A generation ago many high school– or college-educated working women were likely to work in one of three occupational

FIGURE 10.8 The Gender Wage Gap by Race and Ethnicity for Full-Time U.S. Workers 16 and Older, 2014

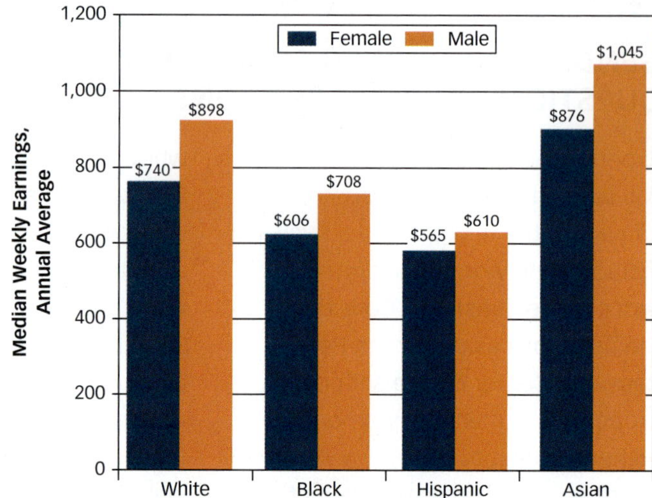

SOURCE: U.S. Bureau of Labor Statistics 2012, *Median usual weekly earnings of full-time wage and salary workers by selected characteristics, annual averages;* U.S. Bureau of Labor Statistics. (2014). Median usual weekly earnings of full-time wage and salary workers by selected characteristics, annual averages. *Economic News Release*. Washington, DC: U.S. Government Printing Office.

categories: secretarial work, nursing, and teaching (below the college level). Why did they opt for these occupations? One key factor was socialization; women were encouraged to choose "feminine" occupations, and many did. Another factor may be choices women made based on their families' needs; a teacher's daytime hours and summers off better fit her children's schedules than a full year of full-time work.

Today, women are far less limited by either imagination or structural obstacles, as we have seen in the educational and occupational statistics. At the same time, the top 10 jobs most commonly occupied by women today still include several heavily and traditionally "feminine" jobs done by women since they entered the workforce in large numbers starting in the 1960s and 1970s (see Table 10.1).

We can also use labor supply factors to talk about men's "preferences" in the workforce. Men are more broadly spread throughout the U.S. Census Bureau's occupational categories than are women, though in many categories, such as engineer and pilot, they make up a substantial share of all workers.

Gender wage gap: The difference between the earnings of women who work full-time year-round as a group and those of men who work full-time year-round as a group.

Occupational segregation by gender: The concentration of men and women in different occupations.

Labor supply factors: Factors that highlight reasons that women or men may "prefer" particular occupations.

Labor demand factors: Factors that highlight the needs and preferences of the employer.

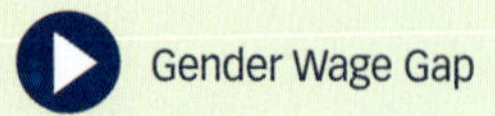
Gender Wage Gap

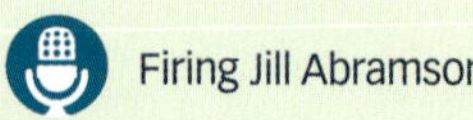
Firing Jill Abramson

TABLE 10.1 Most Common Occupations for U.S. Women and Men (Full-Time), 2012

Rank	Most Common Occupations for Women	Most Common Occupations for Men
1	Secretaries and administrative assistants	Drivers/sales workers and truck drivers
2	Elementary and middle school teachers	Managers, all others
3	Registered nurses	First-line supervisors/managers of retail sales workers
4	Nursing, psychiatric, and home health aides	Retail sales workers
5	Customer service representatives	Janitors or building cleaners
6	First-line supervisors/managers of retail sales workers	Laborers and movers
7	Cashiers	Construction workers
8	Managers, all others	Cooks
9	Accountants and auditors	Software developers
10	First-line supervisors/managers of office and administrative support workers	Sales representatives, wholesale and manufacturing

SOURCE: Hegewisch, A. and Matite, M. (2013). Gender wage gap by occupation. *IWPR #C350a,* Tables 1 and 2. Institute for Women's Policy Research, Washington, DC. Reprinted with permission.

Imagine a young man interested in health and medicine. Would he be encouraged to pursue a career as a nurse? There is still a powerful sense in our society that nursing is a "female" occupation. The popular film *Meet the Parents* (2000) centers on a daughter's young male suitor, a nurse, whose occupation is the object of both jokes and concern that he is not smart enough to be doctor. We even use the term *male nurse* when referring to men in the nursing profession because our default understanding of "nurse" is a woman. Perhaps it is not surprising, then, that men still make up just a small fraction of nurses.

Labor demand factors highlight what employers need and prefer—employees with **human capital**, or *the skills valuable in the particular workplace.* A landscaper seeking a partner will want to hire someone with skills in landscaping; an office manager will seek an administrative assistant who is tech savvy and organized; an accounting firm will want a competent accountant. These preferences are not gendered but instead focus on skills and credentials.

However, other labor supply factors may introduce gender into employer preferences. For example, some employers believe they will incur higher *indirect labor costs* by hiring females. **Indirect labor costs** include *the time, training, or money spent when an employee takes time off to care for sick family members, opts for parental leave, arrives at work late, or leaves after receiving employer-provided training.* Because women are still associated with the roles of wife and mother, employers often assume they are more likely than men to be costly employees.

Stereotypes may also condition employers' views, especially when jobs are strongly perceived as "feminine" or "masculine." Just as a preschool or child-care center might be wary of hiring a man to work with small children or infants (because women are perceived to be more nurturing), a construction firm might hesitate to hire a woman to head a team of workers (because men are widely perceived to be more comfortable under male leadership).

Human capital: The skills and knowledge a person possesses that make him or her valuable in a particular workplace.

Indirect labor costs: Costs in time, training, or money incurred when an employee takes time off to care for sick family members, opts for parental leave, arrives at work late, or leaves a position after receiving employer-provided training.

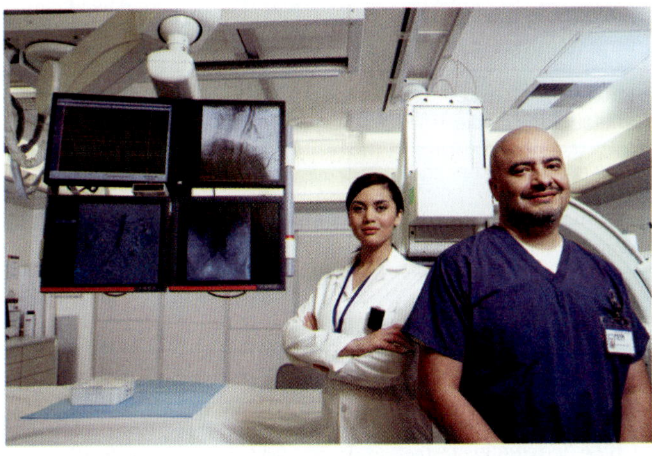

Corbis Flirt / Alamy

The proportion of female physicians and surgeons is rising: between 2003 and 2011, their share rose from about 30 percent to nearly 34 percent. The proportion of male registered nurses has also grown, to about 9 percent in 2011 from 8 percent in 2003. What factors might account for these shifts?

CQR Gender and Work Debate

Looking at labor supply and labor demand factors can help us to sort out how men and women have become concentrated in different occupations. Gender occupational segregation is significant because jobs dominated by men have historically paid more than jobs dominated by women. That is, those jobs have higher pay scales, which means that men's earnings tend to start higher and end higher than women's earnings.

Even *within* occupational categories, men tend to earn more than their female counterparts. Data from the U.S. Bureau of Labor Statistics (2012c) show that, for example, among retail salespersons (an occupation that is 41% female), women earn about 75% of men's median weekly earnings. For waiters and waitresses, the gap is larger: Women earn just 64% of the median weekly earnings of their male counterparts. In other occupations, such as bookkeeping/accounting, there is no gap, but this is an exception. Table 10.2 offers some additional comparisons.

What explains these differences within occupations? First, while the Equal Pay Act of 1963 made it illegal to pay men and women different wages for the same work, numerous violations have been documented in fields from journalism to construction to academia. Second, in some occupations, men and women concentrate in different specialties, with men tending to occupy the most lucrative sectors. For instance, male physicians are more likely than females to specialize in cardiology, which pays better than areas where women tend to concentrate, such as pediatrics. Similarly, women real estate agents are more likely to sell residential properties, while men are more likely to sell commercial properties, which bring in higher profits and commissions. Even among restaurant servers, men tend to concentrate in high-end restaurants, while women dominate in diners and chain restaurants.

TABLE 10.2 The Pay Gap in Selected Occupations, 2011

Occupation	Median Weekly Pay	
	Men	Women
Chief executive officers	$2,266	$1,811
Physicians and surgeons	$2,087	$1,497
Bookkeeping, accounting, and auditing clerks	$751	$670
Real estate brokers and sales agents	$928	$756
Waiters and waitresses	$449	$400
Elementary and middle school teachers	$1,025	$937
First-line supervisors of retail sales workers	$778	$612
Office and administrative support occupations	$673	$628

SOURCE: Bureau of Labor Statistics. (2012d). 39. Median weekly earnings of full-time wage and salary workers by detailed occupation and sex. *Household Data Annual Averages*. Washington, DC: U.S. Government Printing Office.

MEN, WOMEN, AND WORKPLACE PROMOTION: GLASS CEILINGS AND GLASS ESCALATORS

When it comes to the positions with the highest status and pay, qualified women still encounter a **glass ceiling**, *an artificial boundary that allows them to see the next occupational level even as structural obstacles keep them from reaching it.* A 2006 study of 1,200 executives in eight countries, including the United States, Austria, and Australia, found that a substantial proportion of women (70%) and a majority of men (57%) agreed that a glass ceiling prevents women from moving ahead in the business hierarchy (Clark, 2006). They may be correct; women occupied just 18 chief executive officer positions in the *Fortune* 500 companies in 2012 (Hoare, 2012).

An earlier study of women of color in corporate management found that female managers in general earned significantly less than White male managers, and that Black, Latina, and Asian American female managers earned less than their male counterparts. Non-White female managers also tended to be concentrated in the lowest-paying management positions. Those who did reach the senior management level often complained about lacking influential mentors and not having "a style men are comfortable with" as barriers to their advancement (Catalyst, 1997, 1999).

Recent data show that just under 6% of women are working in traditionally male occupations and just 4.6% of men work in traditionally female occupations (Hegewisch & Liepmann, 2012). While these figures are small, sociologist Christine Williams's (1995) work suggests that when men work in traditional "women's" jobs, such as librarianship, social work, nursing, and elementary school teaching, they benefit from a **glass escalator**, a *nearly invisible promotional boost that men gain in female-dominated occupations.* Williams found that bosses often presumed that the men in her study wanted to move up—for example, a teacher was assumed to want an

Glass ceiling: An artificial boundary that allows women to see the next occupational or salary level even as structural obstacles keep them from reaching it.

Glass escalator: The nearly invisible promotional boost that men gain in female-dominated occupations.

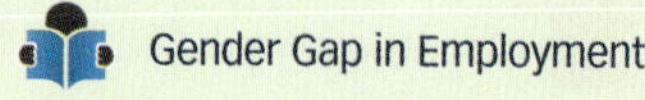
Gender Gap in Employment

administrative position, or a nurse was assumed to want to be a head nurse. Many of the men were put on promotional tracks even when they were ambivalent about leaving positions in which they felt satisfied. However, it should be noted that men experience the glass escalator effect differently based on their race. Wingfield (2008), for example, found that African American male nurses did not benefit from their gender in the same way that White male nurses did, despite their dedication to the field.

SEXUAL HARASSMENT

According to federal Equal Employment Opportunity Commission guidelines, **sexual harassment** *consists of unwelcome sexual advances, requests for sexual favors, or physical conduct of a sexual nature when such conduct is used as a condition of employment, instruction, evaluation, benefits, or other opportunities; or when such conduct interferes with an individual's performance or contributes to an intimidating, hostile, or offensive environment.* This definition describes two key types of sexual harassment. **Quid pro quo sexual harassment** is *"something for something," or the demand or implication that a sexual favor will buy a promotion or just an opportunity to keep one's job.* **Hostile environment harassment** *is defined by conditions someone perceives as intimidating, uncomfortable, or otherwise distressing.*

Quid pro quo sexual harassment typically occurs in a situation of unequal power—for example, between supervisor and employee or between professor and student. It ranges from crude and explicit efforts to coerce someone into a clearly unwanted sexual relationship to subtle innuendoes that carry the same meaning.

Sexual harassment is found between peers in school as well. In a 1990s study of 1,600 students from 79 high schools across the country, 4 of 5 young people reported being sexually harassed at least once, mainly by other students. Harassment ranged from unwanted sexual comments to forced sexual activity. Only a moderately higher percentage of girls than boys reported being harassed. Girls were harassed more frequently, however, and about a quarter reported that the experience was so distressing it forced them to stay home or cut class, interfering with their studies (American Association of University Women, 1993).

Has growing awareness of the problem changed the situation? A survey conducted in 2011 found that, in fact, "sexual harassment is part of everyday life in middle and high schools. About 48 percent of the students surveyed experienced some form of sexual harassment in the 2010–2011 school year, and the majority of those students (87 percent) said it had a negative effect on them" (Hill & Kearl, 2011, p. 2). New means of harassment have grown, too, including texting, e-mail, and Facebook, and nearly one third of the students reported experiencing harassment through electronic media. The report's authors point out that even witnessing sexual harassment, as a third to a quarter of students do, can negatively affect perceptions of safety and appear to "normalize" the offense.

The most likely victims of sexual harassment in schools continue to be girls and students of both sexes who are or are perceived to be gay or lesbian. Girls are more likely to report physical or sexual harassment. They also report more acutely negative effects, from emotional to academic consequences (Hill & Kearl, 2011). Many harassers have themselves been victims, and, paradoxically, many also characterize their behavior toward others as "no big deal" or funny. Yet a recent study found sexual harassment at school had a more negative effect on teens' health than bullying, even though bullying was more common (Gruber & Fineran, 2008).

What, then, is the relationship between sexual harassment and gender? It may be indirect. If, for instance, the popular media frequently portray women as hypersexualized, sexually available, and passive, these images may influence the ways boys see girls and girls see themselves (Jhally, 2007). Or consider that heterosexuality is elevated as the norm; nearly all media portrayals of relationships highlight heterosexual couples, and adolescents still commonly use the word *gay* as an insult. What other connections between sexual harassment and societal messages about gender can we as sociologists make to more fully understand the persistence of this problem?

CLASSICAL THEORIES AND FEMINIST THINKING

Until the middle of the 20th century, most sociological theories assumed that existing sex roles and norms were positively functional for society—and natural. Contemporary scholarship, particularly by feminist sociologists, challenges this perspective.

CLASSICAL SOCIOLOGICAL APPROACHES TO GENDER

For the "founding fathers" of sociology, whom we met in Chapter 1, gender stratification was all but invisible. While Friedrich Engels did address women's experience of inequalities,

Sexual harassment: Unwelcome sexual advances, requests for sexual favors, or physical conduct of a sexual nature when such conduct is used as a condition of employment, instruction, evaluation, benefits, or other opportunities; or when such conduct interferes with an individual's performance or contributes to an intimidating, hostile, or offensive environment.

Quid pro quo sexual harassment: The demand or implication that a sexual favor will buy a promotion or an opportunity to keep one's job.

Hostile environment harassment: Conditions in the workplace that someone perceives as intimidating, uncomfortable, or otherwise distressing.

Gender Theory

INEQUALITY MATTERS

LEGAL GENDER DISCRIMINATION IN THE UNITED STATES

Alex Wong / Staff/Getty Images

Is employment discrimination on the basis of gender, race, ethnicity, religion, or sexual orientation ever acceptable?

Until 1963, it was legal for employers to pay male and female workers different wages for doing the same job. The Equal Pay Act (EPA) of 1963 prohibits employers from discriminating on the basis of sex for jobs that entail "equal skill, effort, and responsibility, and which are performed under similar working conditions." While some objected that the EPA would increase unemployment among women, it was broadly supported and has been credited with narrowing the gender wage gap.

The EPA was followed by Title VII of the Civil Rights Act of 1964, which forbade discrimination on the basis of sex in hiring, promotion, and other basic conditions of employment. While conditions of work for women have yet to achieve full equality, legal protections have significantly improved women's opportunities to achieve economic independence, to support their families, and to contribute to the economic growth of the country.

Advocacy organizations, including the Human Rights Campaign (HRC; www.hrc.org), argue that these opportunities are not fully afforded to U.S. workers who are gay, lesbian, bisexual, or transgender. According to the HRC (2014), it is legal in 29 states for employers to discriminate based on sexual orientation, and in 33 states to do so based on gender identity or expression. As a result, LGBT people may face legal discrimination in employment, including in hiring, firing, or promotion. As of early 2014, however, 17 states and the District of Columbia prohibited discrimination based on either sexual orientation or gender identity, while 4 others forbade discrimination based on sexual orientation. Similar federal legislation has not been enacted; the Employment Non-Discrimination Act (ENDA) has been proposed to prohibit public and private employers, employment agencies, and labor unions from "using an individual's sexual orientation or gender identity as the basis for employment decisions, such as hiring, firing, promotion or compensation," but it has not passed Congress.

THINK IT THROUGH

▶ Why would it be in the interest of an employer to discriminate on the basis of race, gender, sexual orientation, sexual identity, or other group membership? What sociological factors might be used to explain discrimination in the workplace?

a common theme was that men and women were organically and naturally suited to the unequal gender roles in European society. Auguste Comte and Émile Durkheim drew on earlier philosophers, including Jean-Jacques Rousseau, to argue that women were best suited to "private" family roles such as nurturance, childbearing, and child rearing and were in many ways "naturally" subordinate to men. Men were seen as possessing inherent advantages in such "public" spheres as science, industry, and government (Comte, 1975; Durkheim, 1895/1964).

The roots of this perspective were sought in human physiology. In one popular theory, women were reported to have smaller brain capacity than men based on their relative skull sizes. (By this standard, elephants should be more intelligent than humans, because their skulls are larger.) Because of ostensible differences in brain size, men were assumed to be biologically more rational, with an advantage in pursuits that required skills of reasoning and logic, such as business and governance. Women were seen as inherently more emotional and better at pursuits requiring emotional skills, such as nurturing.

Few women's voices were present or prominent in early sociology. Charlotte Perkins Gilman (1898) was one of the first female and feminist sociologists. Gilman viewed heterosexual marriage between males and females as a *sexuoeconomic relation*. Women were expected to be financially dependent on men, and in turn serve as caregivers for their husbands and children. Women's gender socialization included significant pressure to find husbands, who in turn felt obligated to support their wives. Thus, the sexual relationship between men and women also became an economic one, with negative effects for the relationship as well as for women's autonomy.

Until relatively recently, some sociologists (predominantly men) argued that sex-role differences—whether biological or social in origin—were positively functional for social harmony, order, and stability. For example, functionalist sociologist Talcott Parsons, one of the most influential midcentury U.S. sociologists, offered a theory of sex roles in the U.S. kinship system that sought to explain them in terms of their functionality (Parsons, 1954; Parsons & Bales, 1955).

Parsons argued that in an industrial society women make their societal contribution by raising children and maintaining the family unit; men do so by earning the family income through outside labor. Parsons did not attribute this role specialization to biology; rather, he argued, women were socialized in the family to acquire the "expressive" qualities, such as sympathy and emotionality, needed in the private sphere of the home. Men were socialized into such "instrumental" qualities as rationality and competitiveness, which were needed for the capitalist workplace. Competition for standing in the family was thus avoided, and the family's status in society was clear because it derived from the man's position. Hence, sex roles functioned on both the micro (family) and macro (society) levels.

Feminist theorists rejected Parsons's theory. While he did recognize sex roles as the product of socialization rather than nature, his perspective appeared to justify what many feminists saw as a sex–role division rooted in, and reproducing, fundamental inequalities. In a capitalist society, power derives from the ability to earn independently, and the role Parsons foresaw for women was one of economic and social dependence.

CONTEMPORARY U.S. FEMINIST THINKING ON GENDER

> If you were a woman . . . 40 years ago, the odds were good that your husband provided the money to buy [this magazine]. That you voted the same way he did. That if you got breast cancer, he might be asked to sign the form authorizing a mastectomy. That your son was heading to college but not your daughter. That your boss, if you had a job, could explain that he was paying you less because, after all, you were probably working just for pocket money. (Gibbs, 2009)

The fact that the world looks fundamentally different today is to a large degree thanks to the feminist movements of both the distant and the recent past.

Feminism is *the belief that social equality should exist between the sexes*; the term also refers to *social movements aimed at achieving that goal*. Feminism is directly tied to both analysis and action. It seeks to explain, expose, and eliminate **sexism**, *the belief that one sex is innately superior to the other and is therefore justified in having a dominant social position*. In the United States and most other societies, sexism takes the form of men's dominance over women. Feminists seek to analyze why it exists and how it can be eliminated.

Feminism emerged in the United States in connection with abolitionism, the attempts to end slavery during the 1830s; this movement gave birth to the struggle by women to achieve basic rights, such as the rights to vote and to own land. The first wave of feminism began in 1848, when Elizabeth Cady Stanton and Lucretia Mott organized a convention in Seneca Falls, New York, to pursue women's expanded rights. While their efforts were a landmark in women's history, the results they sought were achieved only much later (women did not gain the vote in the United States until 1920). Feminist activism was also limited to a small group of women and their male supporters in an environment that saw sex differences as natural.

The 1963 publication of Betty Friedan's *The Feminine Mystique*, which argued that stereotypes of femininity distorted women's actual experiences and contributed to their

Feminism: The belief that social equality should exist between the sexes; also, the social movements aimed at achieving that goal.

Sexism: The belief that one sex is innately superior to the other and is therefore justified in having a dominant social position.

Emma Watson's Gender Equality Speech

Feminism

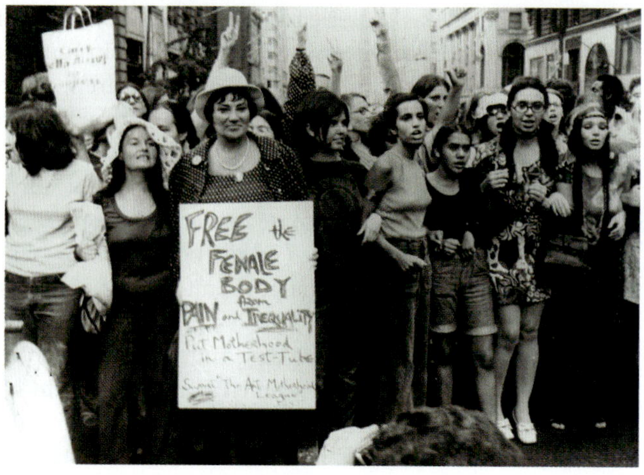

Activists have long sought to bring attention to conditions of female oppression and male dominance. While mid-20th-century activists including Bella Abzug highlighted problems such as limited roles for women outside of motherhood, 21st-century activists have come out against societal practices such as the shaming of women who violate conventional norms of dress or sexuality.

unhappiness, helped initiate the second wave of the women's movement, with social theorizing and activism that was much broader in scope (Bernard, 1981, 1982; Epstein, 1988; Friedan, 1963, 1981). Women's experiences in the civil rights and anti–Vietnam War social movements also helped shape a growing feminist consciousness.

The second wave, like the first, called for the equal treatment of women. Women and men were to be viewed not as fundamentally different but as similar; given equal opportunity, women would show themselves the equals of men in all respects. This revival of feminist thinking strongly appealed to the growing number of well-educated, professional women drawn to work and public life during the 1960s (Buechler, 1990), and an explosion of feminist thinking and activism followed.

Women in their 20s, 30s, and 40s today came of age after the feminist social movement had already made great strides and are less likely to have experienced the same degree of discrimination as their predecessors. At the same time, although only about a quarter of all U.S. women describe themselves as "feminist," more than two thirds believe the women's movement has made their lives better—including 75% of all women under age 35. Further, 82% of U.S. women believe that the status of women has improved over the past 25 years, and about half of all younger women believe there is still a need for a strong women's movement (Alfano, 2009).

Several broad streams of feminist thinking agree on the importance of basic economic, social, and political equality for women—equal pay for equal work and the sharing of housework. They differ in their analyses of the causes of inequality, however, and in the solutions they propose. Below we provide a brief overview of feminism's varied manifestations.

Liberal feminism, reflected in the work of Betty Friedan and those who followed her lead, holds that *women's inequality is primarily the result of imperfect institutions, which can be corrected by reforms that do not fundamentally alter society itself.* To eliminate this inequality, liberal feminists have fought to elect women to the U.S. House and Senate, to enact an Equal Rights Amendment (ERA) to the U.S. Constitution, and to protect women's rights to make choices about their fertility and their family lives.

As its name implies, **socialist feminism** is rooted in the socialist tradition. It is deeply critical of capitalist institutions and practices and regards *women's inequality as the result of the combination of capitalistic economic relations and male domination (patriarchy), arguing that both must be fundamentally transformed before women can achieve equality* (Chafetz, 1997). This viewpoint originated in the writings of Marx and Engels, who argued that inequality, including that of women, is an inevitable feature of capitalism. Engels (1884/1942), for example, sought to demonstrate that the family unit was historically based on the exploitation and male "ownership" of women (the practice of a father "giving away" his daughter in marriage is rooted in the symbolic "giving" of a young woman from one "keeper" to a new one). Socialist feminism in the United States emerged in the 1960s, when liberal feminists became frustrated by the pace of social reform and began to address more fundamental sources of women's oppression (Hartmann, 1984; Jaggar, 1983; MacKinnon, 1982; Rowbotham, 1973).

Some feminists grew frustrated with the civil rights and antiwar organizations of the 1960s and 1970s, which were headed by male leaders who often treated women as second-class citizens. Mindful that true equality for women has yet

Liberal feminism: The belief that women's inequality is primarily the result of imperfect institutions, which can be corrected by reforms that do not fundamentally alter society itself.

Socialist feminism: The belief that women's inequality results from the combination of capitalistic economic relations and male domination; argues that both must be transformed fundamentally before women can achieve equality.

to be achieved under any existing political economic system, **radical feminism** argues that *women's inequality underlies all other forms of inequality.* Radical feminists point to gender inequality in the economy, religion, and other institutions to argue that relations between the sexes must be radically transformed before women can hope to achieve true equality. Radical feminists thus focus their attention on the nature of **patriarchy**, *any set of social relationships in which men dominate women,* pointing to male dominance in economics and politics as chief examples.

Radical feminists argue that if patriarchal norms and values go unchallenged, many women will accept them as normal, even natural. Thus, while men should also work to end male domination, it is only by joining with other women that women can hope to truly empower themselves and confront male domination in whatever form. Radical feminists advocate all-women efforts to provide shelters for battered women, rape crisis intervention, and other issues that affect women directly (Barry, 1979; Dworkin, 1981, 1987, 1989; Faludi, 1991; Firestone, 1971; Griffin, 1978, 1979, 1981; Millett, 1970).

Multicultural feminism aims to *understand and end inequality for all women, regardless of race, class, nationality, age, sexual orientation, physical ability, or other characteristics* (B. Smith, 1990). Multicultural feminists seek to build coalitions among women, creating international and global organizations, networks, and programs to achieve women's equality. They acknowledge that much of the contemporary women's movement originated among heterosexual, White, and middle- or upper-class women in Europe and North America and that as a result its central ideas reflect these women's perspectives. These perspectives are being challenged and changed by feminists of color from Africa, Asia, and Latin America, as well as homosexual, bisexual, and trans women, contributing to an enriched multicultural feminist understanding (Andersen & Collins, 1992; Anzaldúa, 1990; Chafetz, 1997; Narayan & Harding, 2000; Zinn, Weber, Higginbotham, & Dill, 1990).

Third-wave feminism emerged in the early 1990s as a response to some of the perceived shortcomings of second-wave feminism. While third-wave feminists have paid significant attention to issues such as gender violence and rape, reproductive rights, and "reclamation of femininity," they also argue that any issue a feminist finds important can and should be talked about. Choice is a central tenet; whether a woman wants to wear makeup, dress in feminine clothing, and be a stay-at-home mother or whether she wants to cut her hair short, wear gender-ambiguous clothing, and work in a male-dominated field—any choice is valid.

There is also an emphasis on *intersectional feminism,* which recognizes the intersecting oppressions of race, class, gender, sexuality, and so on. Intersectional feminism is a response to the critique of second-wave feminism that has suggested it caters mainly to the needs of middle-class, White, heterosexual women. Third-wave feminists also use the Internet and social media as vehicles of activism. Although the current movement is not often recognized as a "wave" by academics, perhaps because of its broad focus and lack of definition, many young people identify as third-wave feminists (Baumgardner & Richards, 2010).

Do you identify with any of the types of feminism mentioned above? What would you identify as important feminist issues today?

Radical feminism: The belief that women's inequality underlies all other forms of inequality, including economic inequality.

Patriarchy: Any set of social relationships in which men dominate women.

Multicultural feminism: The belief that inequality must be understood—and ended—for all women, regardless of race, class, nationality, age, sexual orientation, physical ability, or other characteristics.

Standpoint theory: A perspective that says the knowledge we create is conditioned by where we stand, or our subjective social position.

Standpoint epistemology: A philosophical perspective that argues that what we can know is affected by the position we occupy in society.

FEMINIST PERSPECTIVES ON DOING SOCIOLOGY

Sociologists Dorothy Smith and Patricia Hill Collins offer valuable perspectives on what it means to do sociology from a feminist perspective, explicitly recognizing women as both subjects and creators of new knowledge. Smith (1987, 1990, 2005) is a key originator of **standpoint theory**, which says *the knowledge we create is conditioned by where we stand—that is, by our subjective social position.* Our sociological picture of the world has emerged from a variety of standpoints, but until recently they were largely the perspectives of educated and often economically privileged White males. Smith thus suggests that our world of knowledge is incomplete.

Standpoint theory offers a challenge to the sociological (and general scientific) idea that researchers can be, in Max Weber's words, "value-free." Smith argues that standpoint does matter, since we do not so much *discover* knowledge as we *create* it from data we gather and interpret from our own standpoint. Recall Victorian doctor Edward Clarke's influential book about the "brain–womb" conflict, positing that higher education could damage young women's reproductive capacity. Could such "knowledge" have emerged from the research of a female physician of that time? Would the theorizing of Karl Marx or Talcott Parsons look the same from a woman's perspective? What do you think?

Patricia Hill Collins (1990) has integrated elements of these ideas into her articulation of "Black feminist thought." She offers **standpoint epistemology**, *a philosophical perspective*

In the film *The Fault in Our Stars* (2014), actress Shailene Woodley portrays Hazel, a young woman facing cancer who falls in love with a fellow patient, Augustus. The two bond over their shared battle and develop a tender and loving relationship. In *Divergent* (2014), Woodley plays Beatrice, a 16-year-old living in a dystopian future society in which teens face dangerous choices in a deeply divided society. "Tris" is compelled by circumstances to heroically seek a critical secret of her society. How might young women relate differently to these two characters? What makes each character relatable to the audience?

that what we can know is affected by the position we occupy in society. Epistemology is the study of how we know what we know and how we discern what we believe to be valid knowledge. Collins argues that Black women have long been denied status as "agents of knowledge"—that is, creators of knowledge about their own lives and experiences. Other groups have used their power to define Black women, creating a picture that is incomplete and disempowering. Collins calls for recognition of Black women as agents of knowledge and the use of Black feminist thought as a tool for resisting oppression.

Collins points to factors that fundamentally affect status and standpoint, including gender, race, class, and sexual orientation. The concept of a **matrix of domination**, *a system of social positions in which any individual may concurrently occupy a status (for example, gender, race, class, or sexual orientation) as a member of a dominated group and a status as a member of a dominating group,* highlights this point. Collins (1990) writes that "all groups possess varying amounts of penalty and privilege in one historically created system. . . . Depending on the context, an individual may be an oppressor, a member of an oppressed group, or simultaneously oppressor and oppressed" (p. 225).

Black women's experience of multiple oppressions makes them wary of dominant frames of knowledge, few of which have emerged from their own experience. Thus, Collins argues, comprehensive knowledge is born of a multitude of standpoints, and creation of knowledge is a form of power that should extend across social groups.

TOWARD A SOCIOLOGY OF MASCULINITY

Integrating women's voices into contemporary sociology is an important goal. At the same time, as sociologist Michael Kimmel (1986) argues, because men still dominate sociology it is also necessary to develop a *sociology of masculinity.* Sociologist Raewyn Connell (2010) notes that "masculinities" are not the same as men, adding that masculinities concern in particular the position of men in the gender order.

Kimmel (1996) follows David and Brannon's (1976) idea that in U.S. culture there are four "basic rules of manhood":

- No "sissy stuff"—avoid any hint of femininity.
- Be a "big deal"—acquire wealth, power, and status.
- Be a "sturdy oak"—never show your emotions.
- "Give 'em hell"—exude a sense of daring and aggressiveness.

These "rules" reflect the concept of *hegemonic masculinity,* or the culturally normative idea of male behavior, which often emphasizes strength, domination, and aggression (Connell & Messerschmidt, 2005). Kimmel argues that such notions of masculinity are so deeply ingrained in culture that when we discuss social problems, ranging from "teen violence" in U.S. schools to "ethnic cleansing" in Bosnia-Herzegovina, we forget that we are really talking almost entirely about the behavior of men. Masculinity as a factor in violence remains obscured.

Before sociologists can understand these social problems, says Kimmel, they must understand how masculine socialization contributes to them. This means "men's studies"—the study of masculinity—should become as much a part of the college curriculum as "women's studies." Of course, Kimmel acknowledges that men are already well integrated into college curricula. In fact,

> if you look at the college curriculum, every course that doesn't have the word "women" in the title is about men.

Matrix of domination: A system of social positions in which any individual may concurrently occupy a status (for example, gender, race, class, or sexual orientation) as a member of a dominated group and a status as a member of a dominating group.

Every course that isn't in "women's studies" is de facto a course in men's studies. Except we call it history, political science, literature, chemistry. But it's always about men as political leaders, military heroes, scientists, writers, artists. Men, themselves, are invisible *as men.* Rarely, if ever, do we see a course that examines the lives of men as men. What is the impact of gender on the lives of these famous men? How does masculinity play a part in the lives of great artists, writers, presidents, etc.? (Kimmel, 2000, pp. 5–6)

Notably then, the role played by gender in shaping power relations is largely overlooked. Kimmel's research reminds us how unstated notions of masculinity run through the ideas and pronouncements of men who "shaped history." For example, Louis Stack Sullivan, the inventor of the skyscraper, once said his ambition was to create "masculine forms," and President Lyndon Johnson, during the Vietnam War, said of North Vietnam's communist leader, "I didn't just screw Ho Chi Minh, I cut his pecker off" (Kimmel, 1996, p. 268).

Only by studying the social construction of masculinity can we hope to understand that "men" are made and not born. And that, Kimmel believes, is an important step toward achieving gender equality in both attitudes and practices.

GENDER IN A GLOBAL PERSPECTIVE

Being born a woman is a risk. If you are reading these words in the United States, you might feel that statement is an exaggeration. Certainly, women in the United States are at greater risk than their male counterparts of falling victim to crimes such as sexual assault or rape, of experiencing discrimination in the workplace, or of being subjected to sexual harassment on the street, at work, or in school. American women are also much more likely to be poor or uninsured than their female counterparts in many European states, including Sweden, Denmark, and Germany.

At the same time, as we have seen in this chapter, women have made dramatic gains in areas such as education, which have brought them independence, earning power, and greater workplace opportunities. Women are in positions of power in politics, the economy, culture, and education. Being born a woman carries risks—and opportunities.

In many places across the globe where you might be reading these words you are likely a male, because millions of women are denied education and cannot read. They are also more likely than men to be denied medical care, trafficked into the sex trade, and denied the right to own or inherit property. They are less likely to go to school, to earn wages equivalent to their work, and to eat when the family's food is scarce. In this section, we highlight issues of gender and equality from a global perspective.

Gender and Social Change

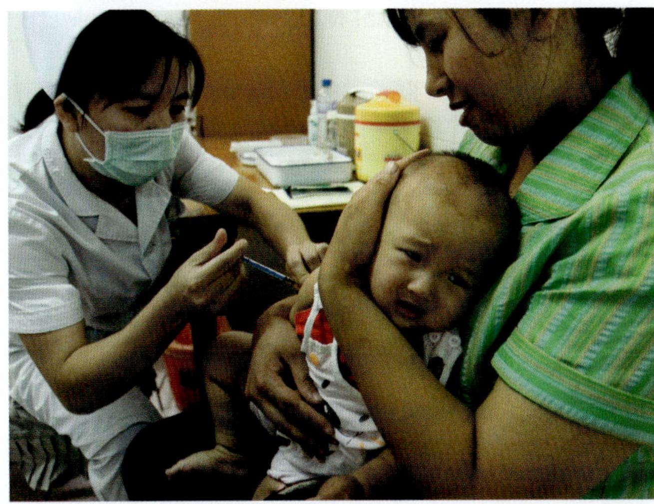

AP Photo/Andy Wong

Hospitals in many industrialized countries have tried to cope with nursing shortages by enticing trained nurses from developing countries to migrate. Because modern hospitals offer good pay and clean, well-supplied working conditions, many nurses, by choice or necessity, leave their home countries behind to work abroad.

MOTHERS AND CHILDREN: THE THREAT OF MATERNAL MORTALITY

In a small hospital in Yokadouma, Cameroon, 24-year-old Prudence died in childbirth. Here is a small piece of her story:

Prudence had been living with her family in a village seventy-five miles away [from the hospital], and she had received no prenatal care. She went into labor at full term, assisted by a traditional birth attendant who had no training. But Prudence's cervix was blocked, and the baby couldn't come out. After three days of labor, the birth attendant sat on Prudence's stomach and jumped up and down. That ruptured Prudence's uterus. The family paid a man with a motorcycle to take Prudence to the hospital. The hospital's doctor . . . realized that she needed an emergency cesarean. But he wanted $100 for the surgery, and Prudence's husband and parents said that they could raise only $20. . . . If she had been a man, the family probably would have sold enough possessions to raise $100. (Kristof & WuDunn, 2009, pp. 109–110)

The dangers of childbirth have been nearly alleviated in industrialized countries, and maternal mortality is a rarity. In many developing countries, however, the dangers are just as much social, cultural, and economic as physical (Table 10.3). Kristof and WuDunn (2009) write that Prudence died due to a massive infection, but apart from physical and biological factors, her history also included lack of schooling, lack of rural health care capacity, and cultural disregard for women.

WOMEN AND EDUCATION Educated, literate women are healthier women; there is a powerful correlation between education and health. A 2010 global study also found a conclusive

TABLE 10.3 Maternal Mortality Rate for Selected Countries, 2010

Country	Maternal Deaths per 100,000 Live Births
Cameroon	690
Afghanistan	460
Bangladesh	240
India	200
Brazil	56
China	37
United States	21
Turkey	20
Canada	12
Denmark	12

SOURCE: World Health Organization. (2012). Maternal mortality country profiles. *Global Health Observatory (GHO).*

TABLE 10.4 Physicians Density Rate in Selected Countries

Country	Physicians per 1,000 Population
Germany	3.50 (2008)
Denmark	3.40 (2007)
Austria	2.99 (2009)
Egypt	2.80 (2009)
United States	2.60 (2004)
Brazil	1.70 (2007)
India	0.59 (2005)
Cameroon	0.19 (2004)
Mali	0.04 (2008)
Afghanistan	0.02 (2009)

SOURCE: World Health Organization. (2011). Health workforce—Aggregated data, density per 1,000. *Data Repository: World Health Statistics.*

link between greater education of mothers and lower child mortality, as more educated mothers are more likely to understand and practice good hygiene and health practices (Brown, 2010). Lower child mortality also correlates with fewer pregnancies and smaller families, because if women feel confident their children will survive, they are less inclined to feel the need for "extra" children who can reach adulthood and support the family.

A better-educated birth attendant can treat her patient more effectively; she is clearly less likely to sit on a patient's stomach and risk rupturing her uterus. By raising income potential, education can also offer families like Prudence's the opportunity to pay for needed medical services without delay.

LACK OF RURAL HEALTH SYSTEMS Kristof and WuDunn (2009) write that "if Cameroon had a better health care structure, the hospital would have operated on Prudence as soon as she arrived. It would have had powerful antibiotics to treat her infection. It would have trained rural birth attendants in the area, equipped with cell phones to summon an ambulance. Any one of these factors might have saved Prudence" (p. 114). The global ratio of physicians to population is dramatically skewed, with wealthy countries far more likely to have more doctors per 1,000 population than poor states (see Table 10.4). Global "brain drain" is also an obstacle to the development of rural health care systems.

DISREGARD FOR WOMEN Countries where women are marginalized have high rates of maternal mortality. Indeed, where women have little social, cultural, economic, or political voice, their lives seem to carry little significance, and scarce resources may be directed elsewhere (Hausmann, Tyson, & Zahidi, 2011). In 21st-century China, "39,000 girls die annually . . . because parents don't give them the same medical care and attention that boys receive—and that is just in the first year of life" (Kristof & WuDunn, 2009, p. xiv).

In spite of the power of some women on the global stage (recent U.S. secretaries of state Condoleezza Rice, Madeleine Albright, and Hillary Clinton come to mind, as well as German chancellor Angela Merkel and influential International Monetary Fund head Christine Lagarde of France), women's global voice is still limited. Inadequate funding of "women's concerns," including maternal health initiatives—and perhaps even their definition as "women's concerns" rather than family or national concerns—speak to the priority they hold.

THE PRICE OF (BEING) A GIRL

On the illicit global market, available goods include weapons, drugs, pirated software and films, and women and girls. Impoverished girls from the developing world are particularly vulnerable to sexual exploitation and trafficking. According to the annual *Trafficking in Persons Report* published by the U.S. Department of State (2012c), it is difficult to pin down the extent of this "modern-day slavery." The International Labour Organization estimates that more than 12 million adults and children experience forced or bonded labor or sexual servitude, with 55% of forced labor and 98% of sex trafficking victims being women and girls. Of these, just under a million and a half may be victims of commercial sexual exploitation (U.S. Department of State, 2012c).

In India, the sex trade and sex trafficking are pervasive (Kara, 2009). According to Kristof and WuDunn (2009),

GLOBAL ISSUES

SON PREFERENCE IN MODERNIZING SOCIETIES

In the natural order of things, 104 to 106 boys are born for every 100 girls. We don't know the precise reasons for this difference, though as far as we do know, it has always existed.

In the societal order of things, from the ancient Greeks to the modern world, many families have pursued the goal of bringing forth a male heir. Aristotle counseled that "men should tie off their left testicle during intercourse if they wanted a son" (Hvistendahl, 2011, p. xv) because the Greeks believed it was the right testicle that produced boys. Far more sophisticated techniques for sex selection are available today, including prenatal identification of sex through ultrasound.

Intuitively, we might associate son preference and the determined pursuit of a male child with traditional societies. After all, greater opportunity and equality for women are among the hallmarks of modern societies. Some researchers suggest, however, that rising sex ratio gaps in regions including East Asia (China, Vietnam), South Asia (India, Pakistan), and Asia Minor (Armenia, Azerbaijan, Georgia) are associated with societal modernization (Guilmoto, 2007; Hvistendahl, 2011). That is, while son preference is rooted in traditional cultural norms, the means to ensure the birth of a son are decidedly modern.

How skewed are sex ratios in these regions? In some parts of China, Hvistendahl (2011) reports, there is a dramatic divergence from the natural ratio: "In Yichun, Jiangxi, there are 137 boys for every 100 girls under age four. In Fangchenggang, Guangxi, the number jumps to 153. And in Tianmen, Hubei, 176" (p. 23). While these figures are statistical outliers, the country figures are also striking: In 2010, China's male-to-female birth ratio was estimated at 121:100, and India's was 112:100 (Hvistendahl, 2011).

Son preference has led to substantially skewed gender ratios in some regions of China. How might the overrepresentation of boys in a school classroom affect the dynamics of teaching, learning, and socializing?

Tim Graham / Contributor/Getty Images

Demographer Christophe Guilmoto (2007) points to three commonalities among the regions where sex ratios have become acutely skewed. First, advances in health care brought by rapid development have made prenatal screening widely available. Second, fertility rates have often shown steep declines. Third, abortion is pervasive. The first two factors are clearly correlated with modernization, though their relationship to skewing sex ratios is unexpected. Guilmoto notes, however, that low fertility translates into a lowered natural probability of having a son. (Vietnam has a total fertility rate—that is, average births per wom an—of just 1.9; the rate in China is 1.5.) This fact, together with the technological means to select for sex, is one of the drivers of the higher number of boys. Hvistendahl (2011) observes that "Guilmoto found sex selection typically starts with the urban, well educated stratum of society. Elites are the first to gain access to a new technology. . . . But like any new technology, sex selection does not remain the domain of the elite" (pp. 10–11).

Modernization has brought women new opportunities, gains in education and pay, and a more prominent voice in society. It has also brought new and perhaps unexpected threats to the female sex, particularly where it meets the currents of traditional cultural norms such as son preference.

THINK IT THROUGH

▶ How should states and societies respond to the manifestation of son preference in sex-selective abortions? Is a solution to the problem more likely to be a product of changes in attitudes or a result of changes in policies?

Reuters/Pool New

In 1997, Madeleine Albright became the first female U.S. Secretary of State in history. She served until 2001. Condoleezza Rice served from 2005 to 2009, when she was replaced by Hillary Clinton (pictured), who occupied the position until early 2013.

> India almost certainly has more modern [sex] slaves . . . than any other country. There are 2 to 3 million prostitutes in India. . . . One 2008 study of Indian brothels found that of Indian and Nepali prostitutes who started as teenagers, a significant number have said that they had been coerced into the brothels; women who began working in their twenties were more likely to have made the choice themselves, often to feed their children. (p. 5)

Among the reasons for this situation are, first, in conservative societies such as India, Pakistan, and other neighboring states, societal norms dictate that young couples wait until marriage to consummate a relationship. "Respectable" middle-class girls are expected to save their virginity for their husbands. For young men, then, access to prostitutes offers a penalty-free way to gain sexual pleasure and experience before marriage. Second, the girls and young women in the brothels are usually poor, illiterate villagers with no power or voice and few advocates or protectors (Kara, 2009). Police are not only unlikely to help them but may participate in their exploitation as well.

The diminished status conferred by deep poverty and being female imposes a profound double burden on girls and women. It is no coincidence that in a global environment that so often marginalizes women and girls, the trade in their bodies and lives is vast, widespread, and often ignored by authorities.

WOMEN AND CONFLICT: RAPE IN WAR

The existence of rape in war has a long and grim history across the globe. Women, who are often perceived in society as property rather than autonomous individuals, have been taken by soldiers and officers as "spoils of war" for many centuries. During World War I, when Germany invaded Belgium and France, German soldiers terrorized villages by burning houses, raping women, and killing villagers. During World War II, rape was practiced by all sides, with Nazi German forces assaulting girls and women as they beat a path into the Soviet Union. When the war shifted in favor of the Allies, Soviet soldiers took revenge, in part through brutal assaults on German women. In the Asian theater of conflict in World War II, it is estimated that between 100,000 and 200,000 Korean women were kidnapped by Japanese soldiers and transported to the front lines, where they were pressed into sexual slavery as "comfort women."

In the late 20th and early 21st centuries, wars in Rwanda, the Democratic Republic of Congo (DRC), and the former Yugoslavia have been scenes of mass sexual violence against women. In the DRC, for example, tens of thousands of women have been raped by armed combatants in the country's civil war. In recent years, scholars have begun to draw attention to the proposition that rape is not just a *product* of war but also a *policy* of war. That is, rape is a conscious instrument of war for combatants (Niarchos, 1995).

As in any rape, the victim in war is likely to see the assault and its consequences as a serious personal trouble, which it clearly is. However, the scale of the phenomenon of rape in war suggests that it is not just a private trouble but also a public issue. We might begin with the question, "What is the role of rape in war?" To ask the question is not to justify rape in war (such a thing is morally impossible) but to analyze how it functions as a practice and policy in conflict. We propose several responses to this question.

First, rape has historically been a "normal" component of war and a "right" of the victors. Those who have conquered their enemies may make a claim on the spoils of war, which include female bodies perceived as another form of property to be appropriated or conferred as "rewards." Amnesty International, a nonprofit organization that lobbies for awareness and change in the area of human rights, reported that in Northern Uganda, the Lord's Resistance Army (LRA) was abducting young girls and women and handing them over as "wives" to LRA fighters as prizes for "good behavior," which included following orders to kill villagers and prisoners of war (Amnesty International, 2004; Lough & Denholm, 2005).

Second, rape targets women for political and strategic reasons, including territorial gain. In the former Yugoslavia, for instance, rape and its threat were used to drive women from their homes so that the territory could be occupied by the aggressors (Thomas & Ralph, 1999). Rape may also be a way of physically destroying a community or group, as the brutality of war rapes can leave women unable to bear children (Frederick & AWARE Committee on Rape, 2001). In some areas, raped women are also considered dishonorable and may be shunned by their families and the community, as has sometimes been the case in the DRC (Moore, 2010).

Third, it has been suggested that rape is a means of communication between male combatants on opposing sides. Where women are considered the "property" of their fathers, husbands, brothers, or the patriarchal social order itself, rape is a symbolic assault on the men who have failed to protect them. This "function" has powerful historical roots: "Even as a system of law [on war] developed, rape was defined as a property crime against the man who owned the raped woman" (Frederick & AWARE Committee on Rape, 2001, p. 12).

Rape in war is thus not just an incidental phenomenon but a strategic one as well. Women are targeted as representatives of a community and a gender. They are victimized by their rapists and often again by families and communities that feel shamed by the rapes. This private trouble has, as we see, many links to public issues.

CHANGE HAPPENS: WOMEN'S EMPOWERMENT

It is possible to empower women across the globe. The nonprofit organization Oxfam America (www.oxfamamerica.org), for example, features a program called Saving for Change, which emphasizes "savings-led microfinance." Participating groups of women save and pool their money, agree on guidelines for investing or lending in their communities, and organize their resources to serve local needs. The groups enhance not only the women's economic capital but also their social capital, building ties that support them in times of economic or other crises. While Oxfam funds coaches who help the women get started, Saving for Change groups are not financed or managed from the outside; they are fully autonomous and run by the women themselves.

According to Hausmann et al. (2011), Mali has a female literacy rate of just 18% (men's literacy rate is also low at 35%), high rates of early marriage, and few legal protections for women. But Mali, a site of where the Saving for Change program is in operation, also has a growing practice of savings-led microfinance empowering women to save, earn, lend, and invest. With coaching, women can gain financial literacy and empowerment despite their lack of schooling. More mature savings groups are serving the global market for local commodities such as shea butter, a popular cosmetic ingredient. Other countries where women are participating in savings-led microfinance programs are Senegal, with a female literacy rate of 39% (compared to men's rate of 62%), and Cambodia, where female literacy is somewhat higher at 71% (to men's 85%). Expansion continues around the world.

Some fear that women's empowerment can foster backlash, manifested as violence or social repercussions. Some patriarchal, conservative societies may not be ready to see women take the initiative to address sexual exploitation, bring attention to crimes against women, or grow economically independent of men, and the victimization of women who step out of traditionally subjugated roles is a risk.

On the other hand, greater independence—social or economic—may allow women to leave violent relationships or challenge norms that marginalize them. The effects of women's economic empowerment can also go beyond their own lives, improving prospects for their children and communities. Studies suggest that when women earn and control economic resources, family money is more likely to go toward needs such as food, medicine, and housing (Kristof & WuDunn, 2009). Maternal and child mortality are reduced with women's empowerment, as are the poverty, marginality, and illiteracy that may lead desperate girls and women to the global sex trade. Mobilization of human and intellectual capital is a critical part of domestic development for a country. It is not a coincidence that countries offering opportunity and mobility to women prosper economically; where fully half the population is deprived of rights, education, and access to the labor market, the consequences are ultimately borne by the whole society and state.

Rebecca Blackwell / Oxfam America

According to the British nonprofit organization Oxfam, by 2012 more than 7,000 Saving for Change groups existed in 2,625 villages in Mali. The women make small weekly deposits into a common fund and lend to one another from the fund at a 10% monthly interest rate.

WHY STUDY GENDER FROM A SOCIOLOGICAL PERSPECTIVE?

Gender matters. Whether we are talking about the toys a child may receive on a birthday, encouragement to study different academic subjects, or pay and promotions on the job, gender can make a difference in someone's experience. It can determine whether someone has the opportunity to visit a health clinic, attend school, or work in a paid job. Historically and often today it still gives men the power to choose whom women will marry, what they can own, and whether they can assert control over their own lives, fertility, economic independence, and physical safety.

When we study gender roles, we have the opportunity to recognize the power of sex and gender as categories that offer opportunities and construct obstacles. Girls and women have made tremendous strides in schools, families, and workplaces, and for many, equality seems achievable. For many others, marginality is still the hallmark of societal experiences. But women have agency, and even women in deprived circumstances can develop economic and political and social voice. Public interest and political will can open doors to better lives for millions of girls and women.

Boys and men are part of this picture too. Women's growing roles challenge men to reconsider long-held ideas about sex and gender and to imagine, along with women, a world in which gender equality improves not only individual lives but also families, communities, and countries.

CQR Women and Human Rights

WHAT CAN I DO WITH A SOCIOLOGY DEGREE?

SKILLS AND CAREERS: ACTIVE UNDERSTANDING OF DIVERSITY

The development of an *understanding of diversity* is central to sociological study. As a sociology student, you will gain knowledge related to the histories, practices, and perspectives of diverse groups and will develop intercultural competence. You will also study and apply theories that lend themselves to the analysis of diversity and ways in which it can underpin societal harmony as well as conflict. The close understanding of diversity can inform important research about societal challenges and potential solutions. Active reflection on this knowledge supports the development of skills to effectively work through and with differences that may divide communities and individuals by race, gender, sexuality, culture, religion, and class, among others.

A key part of developing an active understanding of diversity is learning to see the world from the perspectives of others. In this chapter, we learned about the feminist sociological perspectives of Dorothy Smith and Patricia Hill Collins. Recall Smith's *standpoint theory,* which suggests that the knowledge we construct is conditioned by where we stand—that is, by our subjective social position. Collins points to the idea that some groups have historically had the power to create knowledge about and mainstream images of themselves, while other groups, including African American women, have been denied this power. These theorists advocate for the integration of more "standpoints" and a more diverse discipline that recognizes that creation of knowledge and even "facts" is not just an objective process but can also reflect one's social position and power. As a major in the social scientific discipline of sociology, you will be exposed to a breadth of theoretical and empirical work that illuminates the social world from a variety of perspectives and helps you to see how the positions of different groups in the social structure may affect perceptions, practices, and opportunities. You will be well prepared for the diverse and dynamic workplace of the future—and the present.

An understanding of diversity and possession of the skills to work effectively with diverse groups of colleagues, clients, students, and leaders are important assets in today's job market. Among the many *job titles* for which diversity knowledge and skills are essential are diversity workshop trainer, equal employment officer, cultural diversity liaison, manager of diversity initiatives, organizational development and leadership consultant, director of college/university diversity services, and case manager. These jobs are to be found in a broad range of *occupational fields,* including higher education, human resources, business and management, media, medicine, law, government, the nonprofit sector, and human services.

THINK ABOUT CAREERS

- How would you describe to an employer the skill of understanding diversity (or intercultural competence)?
- How would you explain to a colleague or friend the importance of this skill?

SUMMARY

- **Gender roles** are the attitudes and behaviors considered appropriately "masculine" or "feminine" in a particular culture. In understanding such roles, sociologists use the term **sex** to refer to biological differences between males and females, and **gender** to refer to differences between males and females that are socially learned.

- Children begin to learn culturally appropriate masculine and feminine gender identities as soon as they are born, and these roles are reinforced and renegotiated throughout life.

- Gender roles are learned through social interaction with others. Early family influences, peer pressure, the mass media, and the hidden curriculum in schools are especially important sources of gender socialization.

- Gender stratification is found in virtually all known societies, largely because, until the advent of modern industrial production, the requirements of childbearing and nursing constrained women to roles less likely to provide major sources of food. In modern societies, technological changes have removed such barriers to full equality, although stratification continues to persist.

- Women do more housework than men in all industrial societies, even when they engage in full-time paid employment outside the home.

- Women typically work in lower-paying occupations than men and are paid less than men are for similar jobs. They have made gains but are still less likely to be promoted in most positions than are their male peers.

- **Sexual harassment** continues to be a problem. Schools are sites of harassment that can target young people based on gender or sexual orientation.

- **Liberal feminism** argues that women's inequality is primarily the result of imperfect institutions. **Socialist feminism** argues that women's inequality results from the combination of capitalistic economic relations and male domination. **Radical feminism** focuses on **patriarchy** as the source of domination. Finally, **multicultural feminism** emphasizes ending inequality for all women, regardless of race, class, nationality, age, sexual orientation, or other characteristics. Third-wave feminism is a nascent movement highlighting women's agency.

- Globally, being born female is still a risk. Women are disadvantaged in access to power, health care, and safety. At the same time, women are taking the initiative in many developing areas to improve their own lives and those of their communities and families.

KEY TERMS

gender roles, 235

sex, 235

gender, 236

transgender, 236

transsexual, 236

sexuality, 236

sex category, 240

second shift, 241

stereotype threat, 242

gender wage gap, 246

occupational segregation by gender, 246

labor supply factors, 246

labor demand factors, 246

human capital, 247

indirect labor costs, 247

glass ceiling, 248

glass escalator, 248

sexual harassment, 249

quid pro quo sexual harassment, 249

hostile environment harassment, 249

feminism, 251

sexism, 251

liberal feminism, 252

socialist feminism, 252

radical feminism, 253

patriarchy, 253

multicultural feminism, 253

standpoint theory, 253

standpoint epistemology, 253

matrix of domination, 254

DISCUSSION QUESTIONS

1. How does one "become" a man or a woman? Explain how the individual is socialized into a gender at the following life stages: early childhood, preteen years, adolescence, young adulthood, parenthood. Now consider the other gender. How is this socialization different?

2. Data show that more women than men enroll in and complete college. What are the key reasons for this? Be sure to distinguish between the issues of enrollment and completion and to consider how gender may (or may not) play a role.

3. Throughout the chapter, we learned about gender inequalities in institutions including the family, education, and the workplace. Think about another institution, such as religion, politics, or criminal justice. What kinds of research questions could we create to study gender inequality there?

4. There have been several waves of feminism, and women have gained a spectrum of legal rights and new opportunities. Is feminism as an ideology still needed in our society? Explain your answer.

5. Why is maternal mortality much higher in some developing countries than in more economically advanced countries? How might countries with high rates of maternal mortality address this problem effectively? How can the international community contribute to reducing the incidence of maternal mortality?

SAGE edge™

Sharpen your skills with SAGE edge at **edge.sagepub.com/chambliss2e**

A personalized approach to help you accomplish your course-work goals in an easy-to-use learning environment.

REUTERS/Mark Blinch

FAMILIES AND SOCIETY

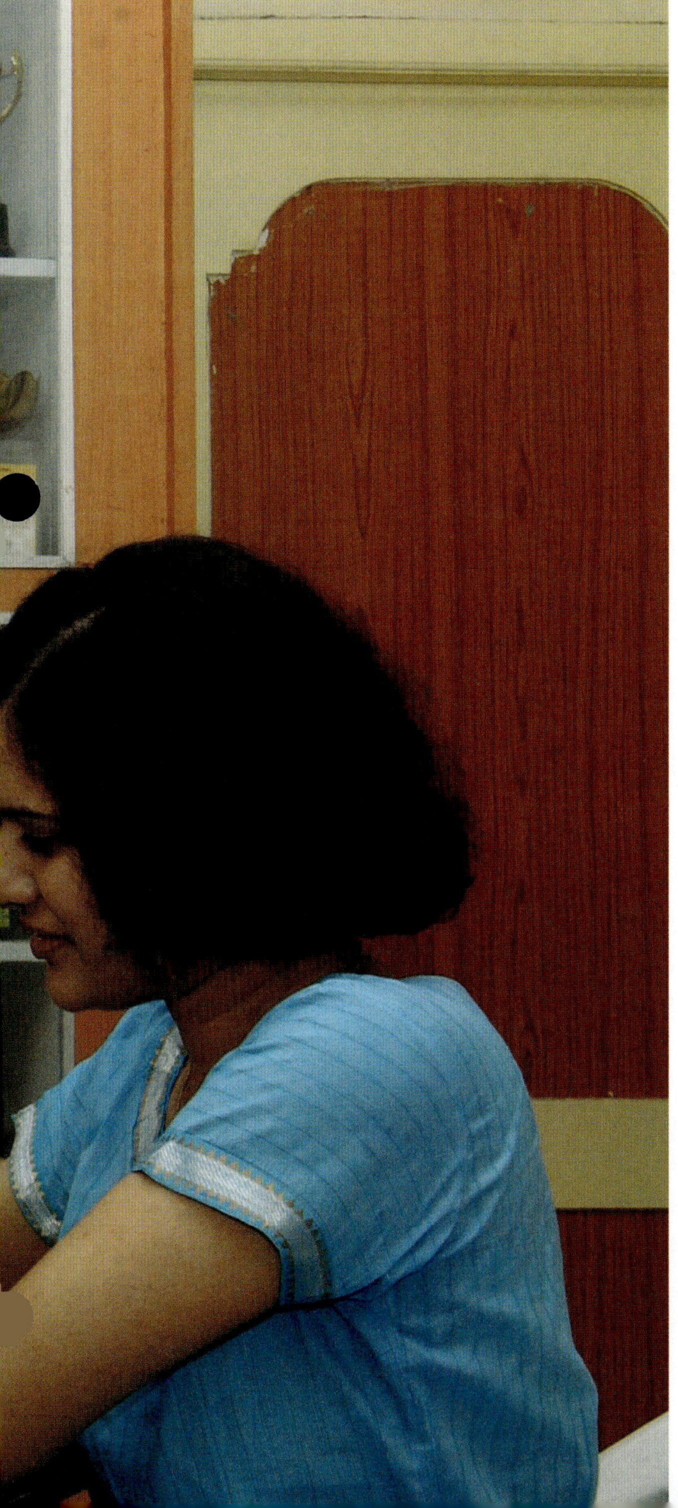

The India Today Group / Contributor/Getty Images

WHAT DO YOU THINK?

1. Is the burden of student debt preventing some young people from marrying and starting families?
2. Why are poor and working-class women in the United States less likely than their middle-class counterparts to marry—and more likely to divorce?
3. What is a family? Who should have the power to decide what constitutes a family?

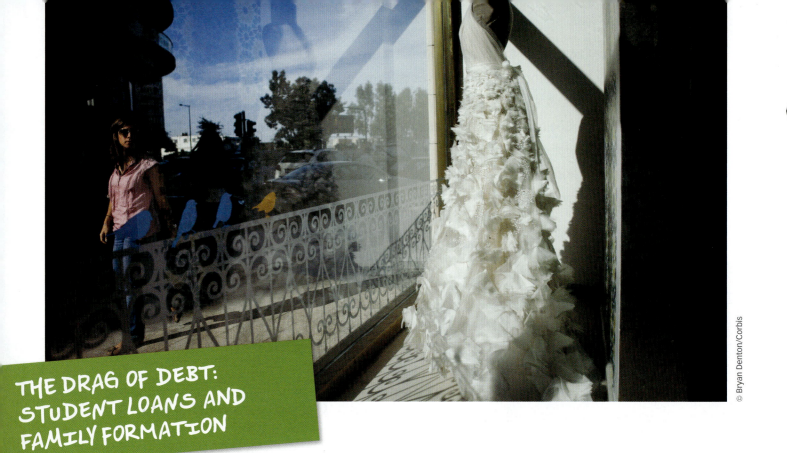

© Bryan Denton/Corbis

THE DRAG OF DEBT: STUDENT LOANS AND FAMILY FORMATION

According to an article on the CNN website's *CNNMoney* page, students today are graduating from college with unprecedented levels of debt:

> College seniors who took out loans to fund their college education owed an average of $25,250, [or] 5% more than the class of 2009 owed, according to a report from the Institute for College Access & Success Project on Student Debt. . . .
>
> "Most students in the Class of 2010 started college before the recent economic downturn, but the economy soured while they were still in school, widening the gap between rising college costs and what students and their parents could afford," the report stated. (Ellis, 2011)

Student loan debt now exceeds consumer credit card debt: The Consumer Financial Protection Bureau estimates that student loan debt is more than $1 trillion, and an estimated 14% of student loans are past due (Brown, Haughwout, Lee, Mabutas, & van der Klaauw, 2012; Chopra, 2012).

Why is this topic of interest to us in a chapter on families in the United States? Here is why: Research has begun to show a correlation between the student debt burden and the ability or willingness of young adults to start families—that is, to marry and have children (Smock, Manning, & Porter, 2005). Whereas in the past young people in their early to middle 20s were marrying and perhaps purchasing first homes, today's substantial and widespread student debt may be delaying entry into both family life and the associated consumption of "big-ticket items" such as houses and cars. Indeed, students graduating from higher education in the past decade are the first U.S. generation to finance so much of their education with interest-bearing loans. The relationship between rising student debt and social trends like the

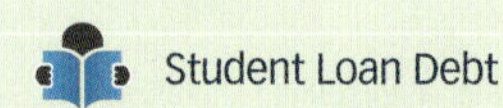

declining rate of marriage among young adults is relevant to sociologists, students, and society.

So what does research show? A 2002 survey from Nellie Mae, a nonprofit corporation and until recently the largest private source of student loans, offers some early insights into the relationship between debt and delayed family formation. In the survey, 14% of borrowers indicated that "loans delayed marriage," a rise from 9% in 1987, when the debt burden was smaller. More than one fifth responded that they had "delayed having children because of student loan debt," an increase from 12% in 1987. Among low-income recipients of Pell Grants, the figures were still higher: 19% indicated they delayed marriage, and 24% delayed childbearing due to debt (Baum & O'Malley, 2003).

The findings of a study concerning debt and life choices further reinforce this point: About half the young single adults in the study "indicate that their current debts will probably delay their plans to start a family" (Manning, 2005, p. 56). More recently, an IHS Global Insight report highlighted the fact that while other types of debt have declined, student loan debt continues to rise—and it correlates with a discernible trend among young adults of delaying marriage and childbearing (Dwoskin, 2012).

As we will see later in this chapter, marriage rates among today's young adults have declined compared to those of earlier generations. Some suggest that marriage is an outdated institution, or that more economically independent women are choosing singlehood over marriage, while others cite a shortage in some communities of "marriageable" men. There are a host of possible explanations. Might debt be one that sociologists should further explore? Is it an obstacle to family formation, and is this a generational and "public issue" rather than just a "personal trouble"? What do you think?

Family: Two or more individuals who identify themselves as being related to one another, usually by blood, marriage, or adoption, and who share intimate relationships and dependency.

Marriage: A culturally approved relationship, usually between two individuals, that provides a degree of economic cooperation, emotional intimacy, and sexual activity.

Monogamy: A form of marriage in which a person may have only one spouse at a time.

Polygamy: A form of marriage in which a person may have more than one spouse at a time.

Polygyny: A form of marriage in which a man may have multiple wives.

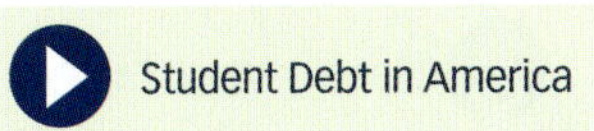

In this chapter, we focus on the U.S. family, its demographics, trends, variations, and challenges. We begin by introducing the key concepts used in the sociological study of families and discuss the idea of the family as an institution. Then we review the functionalist and feminist perspectives on families and, in particular, on the character of sex roles in marital relationships. We devote a broad section of the chapter to an overview of U.S. families today, looking at trends in marriage and divorce, as well as family life in a sampling of subcultures—immigrant, Native American, and deaf families. Sociologists take a strong interest in issues of social class and its roots and effects, so next we explore practices of child rearing and differences across class, the decline of marriage in the poor and working classes, and work and family life in the middle class. Finally, we explore the relationship between globalization and family in the United States and beyond.

SOME CONCEPTS SOCIOLOGISTS USE TO STUDY FAMILIES

Families come in a broad spectrum of forms, but they share basic qualities. A **family**, at the most basic level, is *two or more individuals who live together and have a legally or normatively recognized relationship* based on, among other things, marriage, birth, or adoption. The family is a key social institution. Though families and their structures vary, the family as an institution is an organized system of social relationships that both reflects societal norms and expectations and meets important societal needs. It plays a role in society as a site for the reproduction of community and citizenry, socialization and transmission of culture, and the care of the young and old. Families, as micro units in the social order, also serve as sites for the allocation of social roles, like "breadwinner" and "caregiver," and contribute to the economy as consumers.

Many families are formed through marriage. Sociologists define **marriage** as a *culturally normative relationship, usually between two individuals, that provides a framework for economic cooperation, emotional intimacy, and sexual relations.* Marriages may be legitimated by legal or religious authorities or, in some instances, by the norms of the prevailing culture. Although marriage has historically united partners of different sexes, same-sex marriages have become increasingly common in the United States and other modern countries, though their legal recognition is still incomplete.

Most societies have clear and widely accepted norms regarding the institution and practice of marriage that have varied across time and space. Two common patterns are **monogamy**, in which *a person may have only one spouse at a time,* and **polygamy**, in which *a person may have more than one marital partner at a time.* Within the latter category are **polygyny**, in which a

Stephan Gladieu / Contributor/Getty Images

The polygynist practice of a man taking multiple wives is unusual (and not legally recognized) in the United States, but according to researchers at Brigham Young University, an estimated 30,000 to 50,000 U.S. residents practice polygamy. Many are members of breakaway sects of the Mormon church.

man may have multiple wives, and **polyandry**, in which *a woman is permitted to have multiple husbands.* In feudal Europe and Asia monogamy prevailed, though in some parts of Asia wealthy men supported concubines (similar to mistresses; Goody, 1983). George Peter Murdock's (1949) classic anthropological study of 862 preindustrial societies found that 16% had norms supportive of monogamy, 80% had norms that underpinned the practice of polygyny, and just 4% permitted polyandry.

The polygynist practice of a man taking multiple wives is unusual (and not legally recognized) in the United States, but according to researchers at Brigham Young University, an estimated 30,000 to 50,000 U.S. residents practice polygamy. Many are members of breakaway sects of the Mormon church

Some sociologists have suggested that, because divorce and remarriage are so common in postindustrial countries such as the United States, our marriage pattern might be labeled **serial monogamy**, the *practice of having more than one wife or husband, but only one at a time.* Most modern societies are strongly committed to monogamy, and to the selection of a lifelong mate—in principle, if not always in actual practice. Later in this chapter, we will explore another key trend in families: More women and men in modern countries are forgoing marriage altogether, turning the tables on an institution that has long been considered normative and necessary in the life course—and the social order.

In many societies, marriages tend to be **endogamous**—that is, *limited to partners who are members of the same social group or caste.* Sexual or marital partnerships outside the group may be cause for a range of sanctions, from family disapproval to social ostracism to legal consequences. Consider that in the United States, **antimiscegenation laws**—that is, *laws prohibiting interracial sexual relations and marriage*—were ruled unconstitutional only in 1967. Until then, some states defined miscegenation as a felony, prohibiting residents from marrying outside their racial groups. Today such laws are history. In fact, the Pew Research Center reported in 2010 that nearly 15% of new marriages were between spouses of different races or ethnicities. The data show that among newlyweds in 2008, about 9% of Whites, 16% of Blacks, 26% of Hispanics, and 31% of Asians married outside their own race or ethnicity (Passel, Wang, & Taylor, 2010).

While intermarriage has increased, more than doubling between 1980 and today, most people who marry still do so within their own racial or ethnic group. Think about married couples you know: Would you say that most "match up" on the basis of characteristics such as race, ethnicity, religion, and class? How much of this matching might be attributable to chance or personal preferences? To exposure in the "marriage markets" such as college or places of worship? To normative pressures?

Clearly, marriage in modern societies is most often the outcome of choices made by two people in a relationship. At the same time, as sociologists, we need to attend to the social context in which "choice" is exercised. Later in this chapter we examine U.S. patterns of partnership and family dissolution in greater detail.

FAMILIES AND THE WORK OF RAISING CHILDREN

The role of *parent* or primary caregiver in the United States and much of Europe has traditionally been assumed by biological parents (occasionally stepparents), but this is one of many possible family formations in which adults have raised children in different times and places. Consider the Baganda tribe of Central Africa, in which the biological father's brother was traditionally responsible for raising the children (Queen, Habenstein, & Adams, 1961). The Nayars of southern India offer another variation, assigning responsibility to the mother's eldest brother (Renjini, 2000; Schneider & Gough, 1974). In Trinidad and other Caribbean communities, extended family members have often assumed the care of children whose parents have migrated north (to the United States in most instances) to seek work (Ho, 1993).

A substantial minority of children in the United States also live in **extended families**, *social groups consisting of one or*

Polyandry: A form of marriage in which a woman may have multiple husbands.

Serial monogamy: The practice of having more than one wife or husband, but only one at a time.

Endogamous: A characteristic of marriages in which partners are limited to members of the same social group or caste.

Antimiscegenation laws: Laws prohibiting interracial sexual relations and marriage.

Extended families: Social groups consisting of one or more parents, children, and other kin, often spanning several generations, living in the same household.

In the film *We Bought A Zoo* (2011), actor Matt Damon portrays a widowed father of two children who buys and revives a failing animal park. His new endeavor, grief over the loss of his wife, and a troubled young teenager are the key challenges that underpin the film. Even today, only a small percentage of children live exclusively with their father and few films offer stories of such families. ■

more parents, children, and other kin, often spanning several generations, living in the same household. An extended family may include grandparents, aunts and uncles, cousins, and other close relatives. In Northern and Western Europe, Canada, the United States, and Australia, most children live in **nuclear families**—that is, *families characterized by parents living with their biological children and apart from other kin*—while extended families are more common in Eastern and Southern Europe, Africa, Asia, and Central and Latin America. In the United States, the extended family form is most common among those with lower income, in rural areas, and among recent migrants and minorities.

For close and extended family members to function as caregivers is neither new nor unusual. In fact, a growing number of children in the United States live with one or a pair of grandparents, though the proportion who live with neither parent is still just 4%. In 2013, 69% of children lived with two parents, and just under 24% lived with only their mothers, while 4% resided with just their father (U.S. Census Bureau, 2013b).

THEORETICAL PERSPECTIVES ON FAMILIES

When sociologists study families, their perspectives are shaped by their overall theoretical orientations toward society. Thus, as in the study of other institutions, it is helpful to distinguish between the functionalist and conflict perspectives, though, as we will see, there are some important variations and additions to these classic categories.

Nuclear families: Social groups consisting of one or two parents and their biological, dependent children, living in a household with no other kin.

THE FUNCTIONALIST PERSPECTIVE

Recall a key functionalist question: What positive functions does a given institution or phenomenon serve in society? Based on this question and the foundational assumption that if something exists and persists, it must serve a function, functionalist theory has tended to highlight in particular the economic, social, and cultural functions of the family. Arguably, the shift from agricultural to industrial to postindustrial economies has made the family's economic purpose less central than its reproductive and socializing functions, though the family's micro-level consumption decisions continue to drive a macro-level economy that is deeply dependent on consumer activity and acquisition.

In his work on sex roles in the U.S. kinship system, functionalist sociologist Talcott Parsons (1954) theorized that men and women play different but complementary roles in families. In the "factory of personalities"—in other words, the family—socialization produces males and females prepared for different roles in the family and society. Parsons posited that women were socially prepared for the *expressive* role of mothers and wives, while men were prepared for *instrumental* roles in the public sphere, working and earning money to support the family. As well, socialization prepares men and women to *want* to enact the roles that society needed them to do. These complementary roles, Parsons suggested, were positively functional, as they ensured harmony rather than the conflict that might emerge from husbands and wives competing for status or position. Distinct sex roles also clarified the social status of the family, which was derived from the male's social position.

Aside from his belief that the family served the function of primary socialization—that is, the process of learning and internalizing social roles and norms (such as those relating to gender)—Parsons suggested that the nuclear family of his time functioned to support adult family members emotionally, a phenomenon he called *personality stabilization* (Parsons & Bales, 1955). In industrial societies, in which the nuclear family unit was often disconnected from the extended kin networks that characterized earlier eras, this stabilization function was of particular value.

Writing in the 1950s, Parsons worried that disruption of the roles he observed in families could have dysfunctions for the family and society. Indeed, though he did not live to see it, there has been some correlation between women's assumption of autonomous roles outside the home and the rise of divorce. Correlation is, of course, not causation. Possible explanations for the link include the advent of no-fault divorce laws, decline in the normative stigma related to divorce, and women's greater economic independence,

Lambert / Contributor/Getty Images; FOX / Contributor/Getty Images

According to the Census Bureau, about one fifth of U.S. households today consist of married couples with children. In 1950, about 43% of households fit this description. Some contemporary television shows including *Family Guy* both parody and reproduce traditional family images and gender roles

which has enabled them to leave unhappy marriages that might earlier have been sustained by their dependence on spouses' wages.

Critics see Parsons's work as reinforcing and legitimating traditional roles that have both positive functions and problematic dysfunctions. The functionalist perspective—and Parsons's expression of it—has been criticized for neglecting the power differentials inherent in a relationship where one party (the wife) is economically dependent on the other (the husband). In a capitalist system, power tends to accrue to those who hold economic resources. Functionalists also neglect family dysfunctions, including ways in which the nuclear family, central to modern society yet in many respects isolated from support systems such as kin networks, may perpetuate gender inequality and even violence.

THE FEMINIST APPROACH: A CONFLICT PERSPECTIVE . . . AND BEYOND

You can probably anticipate that in looking at the family, the conflict perspective will ask how it might produce and reproduce inequality. Feminist theorizing about the family has reflected a conflict orientation in its efforts to unpack and understand the family as a potential site of both positive support and unequal power. From the 1970s, a period following intense activity in the women's movement and an increase in the number of women taking jobs outside the home, feminist perspectives became central to sociological debates on the family.

While early theorizing about the family highlighted its structure and roles, as well as its evolution from the agricultural to the industrial era, feminist theorizing in the late 20th century turned its attention to women's experiences of domestic life and their status in the family and social world. Feminists endeavored to critique the **sexual division of labor in modern societies**, *the phenomenon of dividing production functions by gender (men produce, women reproduce) and designating different spheres of activity, the "private" to women and the "public" to men.* While theorists including Parsons saw this division as fundamentally functional, feminists challenged a social order that gave males privileged access to the sphere offering capitalism's prized rewards, including status, independence, opportunities for advancement, and, of course, money.

HIS AND HER MARRIAGE An important sociological analysis that captures some of liberal feminism's key concerns is Jessie Bernard's *The Future of Marriage* (1982). (See Chapter 10 for a fuller discussion of varieties of modern feminism, including liberal feminism.) Bernard confronts the issue of equality in marriage, positing that husband and wife experience different marriages. In her analysis of marriage as a cultural system comprising beliefs and ideals, an institutional arrangement of norms and roles, and a complicated individual-level interactional and intimate experience, Bernard identifies *his and her marriage experiences*:

- *His* marriage is one in which he may define himself as burdened and constrained (following societal norms that indicate this is what he *should* be experiencing) while at the same time experiencing authority, independence, and a right to the sexual, domestic, and emotional "services" of his wife.
- *Her* marriage is one in which she may seek to define herself as fulfilled through her achievement of marriage (following societal norms that indicate this is what she *should* be experiencing) while at the same time experiencing associated female dependence and subjugation.

Sexual division of labor in modern societies: The phenomenon of dividing production functions by gender and designating different spheres of activity, the "private" to women and the "public" to men.

Bernard understood these gender-differentiated experiences as rooted in the cultural and institutional foundations of marriage in the era she studied. Marriage functioned, from this perspective, to allocate social roles and expectations—but not to women's advantage. In a good example of the sociological imagination, Bernard saw a connection between the personal experiences of individual men and women and the norms, roles, and expectations that create the context in which their relationship is lived.

Bernard's analysis pointed to data showing that married women, ostensibly "fulfilled" by marriage and family life, and unmarried men, ostensibly privileged by "freedom," scored highest on stress indicators, while their unmarried female and married male counterparts scored lowest. Although this was true when Bernard was writing several decades ago, recent social indicators show a mix of patterns. Some are similar to those she identified. For instance, a 2010 article in the *Harvard Men's Health Watch Newsletter* reported:

> A major survey of 127,545 American adults found that married men are healthier than men who were never married or whose marriages ended in divorce or widowhood. Men who have marital partners also live longer than men without spouses; men who marry after age 25 get more protection than those who tie the knot at a younger age, and the longer a man stays married, the greater his survival advantage over his unmarried peers. (Harvard Medical School, 2010)

Other studies paint a different picture. For instance, a 2007 examination of a spectrum of marriage studies determined that married women were less likely to experience depression than their unmarried counterparts. Researchers controlled for such factors as the possibility that less depressed people were more likely to get married (which would confound results) and found that self-selection was not an issue. That is, marriage did seem to have positive health effects for women (Wood, Goesling, & Avellar, 2007).

In fact, however, the issue is more complex than either Bernard's work or recent scientific studies can embrace in a single narrative. Consider some other variables at play here. For example, men do seem to have *more* health benefits than women from marriage, even if women have some. Yet marriage as an institution does not appear to confer health benefits; rather, it is the *quality* of marriage that matters. Solid and low-conflict marriages are healthy, and unstable, high-conflict marriages are not. The never married are better off than those in high-conflict marriages (Parker-Pope, 2010).

Bernard's work gives us an opportunity to look at marriage as a *gendered institution*—that is, one in which gender fundamentally affects the experience on a large scale. While her 30-year-old analysis cannot fully capture the reality of today's U.S. marriages, her recognition that men and women can experience marriage in quite different ways remains an important insight.

The feminist perspective and other conflict-oriented perspectives offer a valuable addition to functionalist theorizing. However, their focus on the divisive and unequal aspects of family forms and norms may overlook the valuable functions of caring, socializing, and organizing that families have long performed and continue to perform in society. Indeed, both these macro-level approaches may have difficulty capturing the complexities of any family's lived experiences, particularly as they evolve and change over years through interpersonal negotiations and decisions. Nonetheless, they offer us a useful way of thinking about families and family members, their place in the larger social world, and the way they influence and are influenced by societal institutions and cultures.

THE PSYCHODYNAMIC FEMINIST PERSPECTIVE Sociologist Nancy Chodorow (1999) asks, "Why do women mother?" She suggests that to explain women's choice to "mother," a verb that describes a commitment to the care and nurturing of children, and men's choice to "not mother" (that is, to assume a more distant role from child rearing), we must look at personality development and relational psychology. While mothering is rooted in biology, Chodorow argues that biology cannot fully explain mothering, because fathers or other kin can perform key mothering functions as well.

Drawing from Sigmund Freud's object relations perspective, Chodorow argues that an infant of either sex forms his or her initial bond with the mother, who satisfies all the infant's basic needs. Later, the mother pushes a son away emotionally, whereas she maintains the bond with a daughter. Through such early socialization, daughters come to identify more fully with their mothers than with their fathers; boys, on the other hand, develop "masculine" personalities, but those draw from societal models of masculinity (or, sometimes, hypermasculinity) rather than predominantly from their fathers, who take a far less prominent role in child rearing than do mothers. Chodorow suggests that "masculinity" in boys may thus develop in part as a negation and marginalization of qualities associated with femininity, which is rejected for both social and psychological reasons.

Women, reared by mothers who nurture close and critical bonds, are rendered "relational" through this process, seeking close bonds and defining themselves through relationships (Anna's mom, Joe's wife, and the like). Men, by contrast, define themselves more autonomously and have a harder time forming close bonds. Again, the roots of this difficulty are social (society defines men as autonomous and independent) and psychological (the pain of an early break in the mother–son bond results in fear or avoidance of these deep bonds). So why do women "mother" then? Because men in heterosexual relationships are not socially or psychologically well prepared for close relational bonding, women choose to mother in order to reproduce this connection with someone else.

"White flight" to residential suburbs in the post-World War II period left many minority families behind in economically struggling neighborhoods. Suburban advantages in access to good education, housing, and recreation were in many cases a stark contrast to the disadvantages of poor urban areas.

While these processes play out primarily on the micro level of the family and relationships, Chodorow also recognizes macro-level effects. For instance, if, for lack of available male role models at home, the masculine personality develops in part as a negation of the feminine personality, when the boy makes his psychological break from the mother, this devaluation of the feminine and its associated traits may be reflected in the societal institutions that men still dominate. That is, the higher valuation of traits associated with masculinity in areas such as politics, business, and the labor market is, at least in part, linked to the *devaluation* of the feminine that men carry with them from their early childhood experiences.

Chodorow's work on sex roles and socialization in the family offers a merger of Freud and feminism that is both challenging and compelling, asking us to consider the effects that psychological processes in early childhood have on social institutions from the family to politics and the economy.

U.S. FAMILIES YESTERDAY AND TODAY

The traditional nuclear family often appears in popular media and political debates as a nostalgic pinnacle of values and practices to which U.S. families should return. Historian Stephanie Coontz (2000, 2005), who has written about the history of U.S. families, points out that this highly venerated traditional nuclear family model is, in fact, a fairly recent development.

Consider that in the preindustrial era, when the U.S. economy was primarily agricultural, families were both social and economic units. Households often included multiple generations, and sometimes boarders or farmworkers too. The family was large, and children were valued for their contributions to its economic viability, participating along with the other members in the family's productive activities. Marriages tended to endure; divorce was neither normative nor especially easy to secure. At the same time, average life expectancy was about 45 years (Rubin, 1996). As life spans increased, divorce also became more common, replacing death as the factor most likely to end a marriage.

The period of early industrialization shifted these patterns somewhat, not least because it was accompanied by urbanization, which brought workers and their families to cities for work. The family's economic function declined; some children worked in factories, but the passage of child labor laws and the rise of mass public schooling made this increasingly uncommon (though, according to one source, at the end of the 19th century a quarter of textile workers in the American South were children, whose cheap labor was a boon to employers; Wertheimer, 1977). Over time, children became more of an economic cost than a wage-earning benefit; in a related development, families became smaller and began to evolve toward the nuclear family model.

The basic nuclear family model, with a mother working in the private sphere of the home while focused on child rearing and a father working in the public sphere for pay, evolved among middle-class families in the late 19th century. It was far less common among the working class at this time; working-class women, in fact, often toiled in the homes of the burgeoning middle class, as housekeepers and nursemaids.

Coontz (2000) points out that, just as the popular imagination suggests, the mother-as-homemaker and father-as-breadwinner model of the nuclear family is most characteristic of the widely idealized era of the 1950s. The post–World War II era witnessed a range of interconnected social phenomena, including suburbanization, supported by federal government

FIGURE 11.1 Living Situations of Children Under 18, 2013

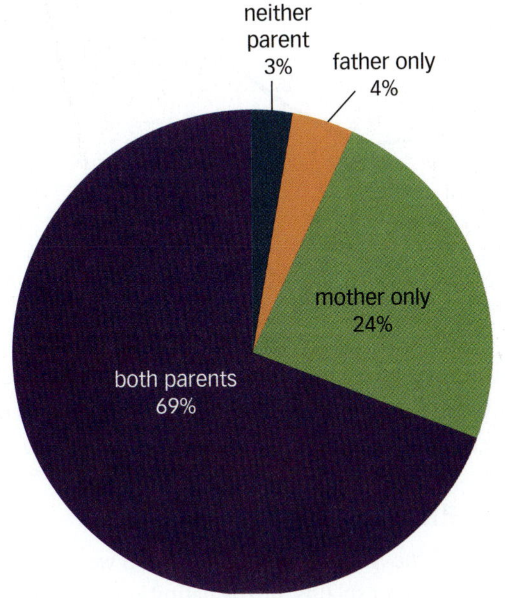

SOURCE: U.S. Census Bureau. (2013a). *America's families and living arrangements: 2013: Children (C table series).*

initiatives to build a network of highways and encourage home ownership; a boom in both economic growth (and wages) that brought greater consumption power, along with technologies that made the home more comfortable and convenient; and a "baby boom," as a wave of pregnancies delayed by the years of war came to term.

While prosperity and technology brought new opportunities to many, mass suburbanization largely left behind minorities, including Black Americans, who were not given access to the government's subsidized mortgages and were left in segregated, devalued neighborhoods. As the jobs followed White workers to the suburbs, the economic condition of many Black families was further diminished.

Further, it is not clear that all was well in the prosperous suburbs either. As we noted in the section on feminist theoretical perspectives, some sociological observers detected a streak of discontent that ran through the nuclear family so idealized today. Betty Friedan's book *The Feminine Mystique* (1963) highlighted "the problem that has no name," a broad discontent born of women's exclusion from or marginalization in the workplace and the disconnect between their low status and opportunities and society's expectation that marriage and children were the ultimate feminine fulfillment. Coontz (2000) points out that tranquilizers, one of many medical innovations of the era, were largely consumed by women, and in considerable quantities—at least 1.15 million pounds in 1959 alone.

MARRIAGE AND DIVORCE IN THE MODERN UNITED STATES

The traditional nuclear family with the man as breadwinner and the woman as caregiver is still in existence, though it has changed in many respects since the 1950s and today represents only about 7% of U.S. households (see the *Behind the Numbers* box on page 275). At the same time, while commentators often lament the "decline of the family," most children in the United States (69% in 2013) still live in two-parent households, and, as we saw above, all but 3% live with at least one parent (U.S. Census Bureau, 2013b; see Figure 11.1). More children are living with single parents than in the past, but more adults are also living in nonfamily households, consisting of either a single householder or unrelated individuals. The trend toward living alone—which about 27% of people in the United States do (Figure 11.2)—is one we will discuss more below.

One reason for the growth of single-person households is the rising age at first marriage, now about 29 for men and 27 for women (Taylor et al., 2011), which means many people are not marrying until their 30s or even later. Most U.S. adults indicate a wish to marry, and most will at some point in their lives; more than 2.1 million married in 2011, and the U.S. marriage rate exceeds that of most other modern societies (Centers for Disease Control and Prevention, 2013). By contrast, Western and Northern Europe are home to very high rates of **cohabitation** and **common-law marriage**, *in which partners live as if married but without marriage's formal legal framework.*

Cohabitation: Living together as a couple without being legally married.

Common-law marriage: A type of relationship in which partners live as if married but without marriage's formal legal framework.

FIGURE 11.2 Changes in U.S. Household Composition, 1940–2010

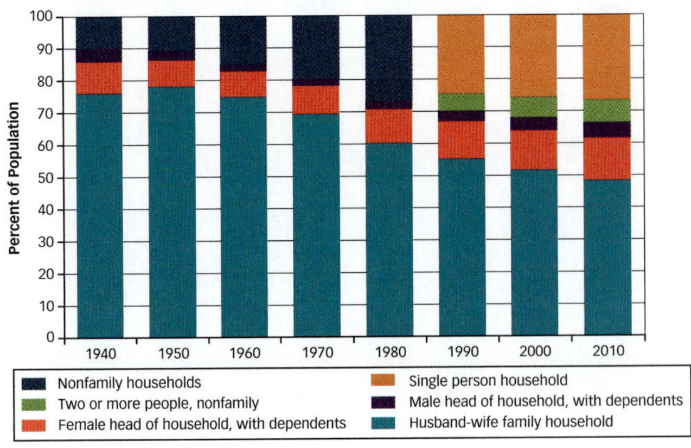

SOURCE: U.S. Census Bureau. (2003). *Statistical Abstract of the United States, No. HS-12. Households by Type and Size: 1900 to 2002*. Washington, DC: U.S. Government Printing Office; U.S. Census Bureau. (2012). *Households and Families: 2010*. Washington, DC: U.S. Government Printing Office.

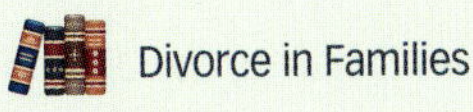
Divorce in Families

While marriage remains socially normative in most U.S. communities, rates of marriage have declined (Figure 11.3). Between 1960 and 2010, the rate per 1,000 women declined by about 20 percentage points, and today only about half of U.S. adults over age 18 are married, compared to about 72% in 1960 (Taylor et al., 2011). These declines have been far more pronounced among the less educated than among those who have a college education, though the latter also marry later. In the section below on class and marriage, we will look at some of the factors driving this decline, particularly among poor women.

With the decline of marriage, the United States has also experienced a decline in divorce. After rising through the 1960s and 1970s, the rate of divorce has leveled off. There is a logic to these two phenomena, since a smaller number of marriages reduces the pool of people who can divorce. The rate overall is still high, however, and the United States has one of the highest divorce rates in the world, with the rate for second and later marriages exceeding that for first marriages (Figure 11.4).

Why is the U.S. divorce rate, while declining, persistently high? Historian Stephanie Coontz (2005) argues that divorce is in part driven by our powerful attachment to the belief that marriage is the outcome of romantic love. While historically many societies accepted marriage primarily as part of an economic or social contract, and some still do, modern U.S. adults are smitten with love. Yet the powerful early feelings and passion that characterize many relationships are destined to wane over time. In a social context that elevates romantic love and passion in films, music, and books, we may have less tolerance for the more measured emotions inherent in most long-term marriages. Could our strong focus on romantic love be a driver of both marriage *and* divorce? What do you think?

FIGURE 11.3 Marital Status in the United States, 1960–2012

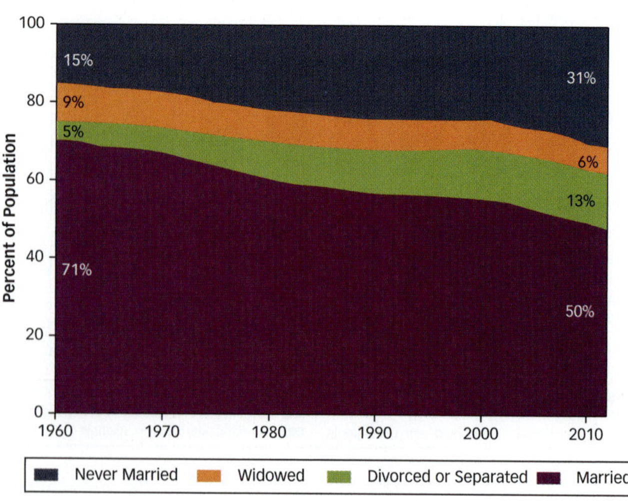

SOURCE: U.S. Census Bureau. (2013). America's families and living arrangements: 2013: Adults (A table series): Table A1.

FIGURE 11.4 U.S. Divorce Rate, 1950–2010

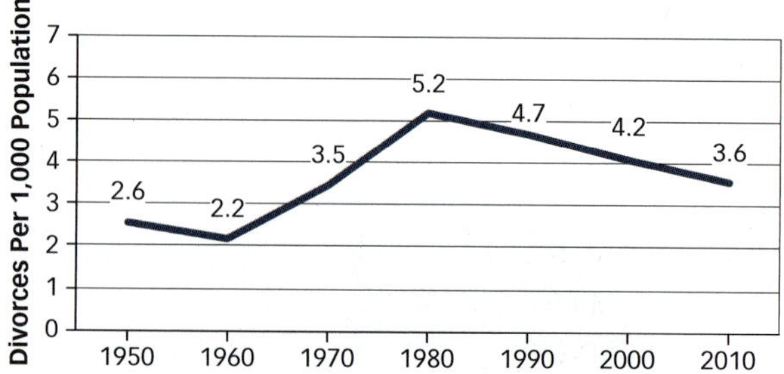

SOURCE: National Center for Health Statistics. (2012). *Aggregate data 1950–2010.* Atlanta, GA: Centers for Disease Control and Prevention.

Families are surely in the process of changing—and not only in the United States. See the *Global Issues* box on page 279 for a look at family issues in Japan.

GAY MARRIAGE . . . AND DIVORCE

In the *Behind the Numbers* box on page 275 we ask, "What is a family?" As the box explains, by the definition of the federal government many U.S. household configurations are *not* counted as "families," including same-sex partners. At the same time, in 2012 there were more than 180,000 married same-sex households and more than 630,000 nonmarried same-sex partner households in the United States. More than 115,000 of the same-sex households were raising children (U.S. Census Bureau, 2012a).

Many U.S. states follow the federal government in their rejection of same-sex marriage; in mid-2014, 33 states prohibited it while just 17 states and the District of Columbia permitted it (Ahuja, Barnes, Chow, & Rivero, 2014). States that reject same-sex marriage often use the same language as the federal law, the Defense of Marriage Act (DOMA): "The word 'marriage' means only a legal union between one man and one woman as husband and wife." DOMA was signed into law by President Bill Clinton in 1996. It also includes the provision that states are not obligated to recognize same-sex marriages conducted in states or cities that permit them.

Some states that do not permit same-sex marriage do recognize **civil unions**, which are *legal unions that fall short of marriage but provide some state-level legal rights and benefits,* or **domestic partnerships**, which are *legal unions that provide a circumscribed spectrum of rights and benefits to same-sex couples.* The more expansive set of social and economic opportunities available to couples recognized as legally married by the federal government, including Social Security and survivor benefits and joint filing of income taxes, is not available to those in civil unions or domestic partnerships.

Civil unions: Legal unions that fall short of marriage but provide some state-level legal rights and benefits.

Domestic partnerships: Legal unions that provide a circumscribed spectrum of rights and benefits to same-sex couples.

Female Perceptions of Strength and Divorce

BEHIND THE NUMBERS

WHAT IS A FAMILY?

The U.S. Census Bureau uses the household as a key unit in calculating a spectrum of national statistics, from income to poverty. A *household* is composed of all the people who occupy a given housing unit. The Census Bureau further distinguishes between *family households*—consisting of immediate relatives such as a husband, wife, and children or a mother and her children—and *nonfamily households,* which include just about everyone else, such as those who live alone and those who live with "nonrelative" household members. Implicit in these bureaucratic categories is a definition of what a family is from the government's perspective.

Reuters/Lucas Jackson

For same-sex couples, the struggles and joys of family life do not differ significantly from those of heterosexual couples.

In 2011, of more than 114 million households in the United States, more than a third were nonfamily households (Vespa, Lewis, & Kreider, 2013). But aside from those living alone, are these households necessarily "nonfamilies" from a sociological perspective? Sociologist Brian Powell sought to answer this question in a study that surveyed more than 2,300 U.S. adults about their definitions of family. Powell and his team identified three categories of respondents in the study: "exclusionists," who embrace a narrow and largely traditional definition of family; "moderates," who expand beyond the traditional to include, for instance, same-sex couples if there are children; and "inclusionists," who hold an expansive view of what can constitute a family, ranging from opposite- or same-sex cohabiters to people with pets. Children seemed to be a decisive factor in whether a household was seen as a family: For instance, while only 33% of respondents agreed that a gay male couple was a family, the addition of children to this unit raised the figure to 64% (Powell, Bolzendahl, Geist, & Steelman, 2010).

The public's definition of what constitutes a family is rapidly changing. Powell noted a significant change even in a short period of time; for instance, the proportion of respondents favoring a narrowly traditional view of a family as married parents and children dropped by 11% between 2003 and 2010. More people are accepting cohabiting and gay or lesbian couples as families as well.

The definitions used by the Census Bureau and other institutions, including those that govern estates and inheritance, adoption, and hospitalization and medical consent, lag behind those embraced by a growing number of U.S. adults. Perhaps within the third of the population living in "nonfamily" households, we would find quite a few families too.

THINK IT THROUGH

▶ How would you define the term *family*? What experiences or influences led you to that particular definition?

FIGURE 11.5 Same-Sex Marriage Laws as of October, 2014

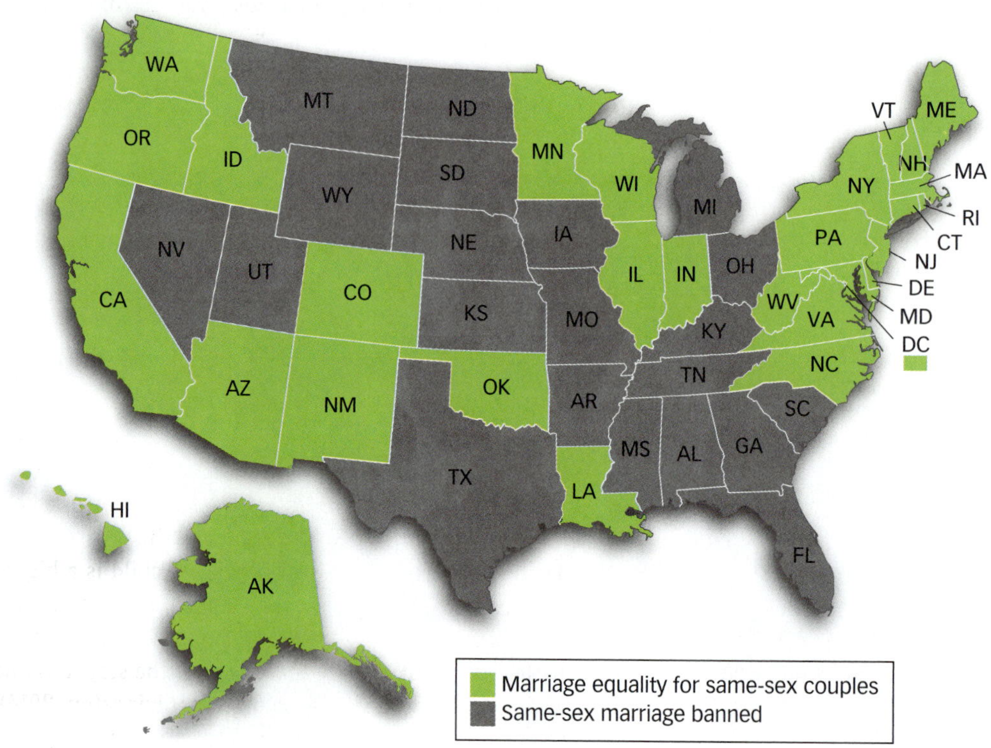

SOURCE: National Public Radio. (2012). "State by State: The Legal Battle Over Gay Marriage." Associated Press; "The Changing Landscape of Same-Sex Marriage," by Masuma Ahuja, Robert Barnes, Emily Chow and Cristina Rivero. *Washington Post*, July 28, 2014.

While state legislatures and Congress have not been as quick to adopt broad definitions of marriage and family as many individuals have, the picture of legal prohibition and recognition around the country makes for a rapidly changing map. Figure 11.5 shows the laws in effect at the time this book went to press.

Same-sex couples who seek to marry—and their advocates—often argue that they face mass denial of a basic civil right on the grounds of sexual orientation. Why should those in a committed relationship be denied the right to sanctify and legalize it regardless of sexual orientation? Those who object to same-sex marriage respond that this broad definition of marriage constitutes a threat to traditional marriage and families, not least because same-sex marriage cannot produce shared biological children. As well, say some opponents, the legitimation of same-sex marriage could lead to its spread, threatening heterosexual marriage. While more people are beginning to favor the legalization of same-sex marriage, a substantial minority of Americans remain vehemently opposed (Figure 11.6).

With about half of all U.S. marriages ending in divorce, it is not surprising that the battle for same-sex partners to secure marriage rights has recently evolved into a fight for their right to divorce, particularly in cases where couples share children or own property in common. U.S. divorce rates may be driven by many factors, including frustration with waning passion, economic stress, and poor compatibility of partners. One factor sometimes noted by observers, however—the ease of divorce in the United States, partly a product of no-fault divorce laws—does not apply to same-sex partners.

A problem arises when a same-sex couple married in a state permitting their legal union seek a divorce in a state that does not recognize gay and lesbian marriages. In a 2012 case in the state of Maryland, a lesbian couple married in 2008 in California sought a divorce. The women were, according to the *Washington Post*, expecting a smooth and simple legal procedure; their property had been divided, the divorce was uncontested, and they had no children. They were stunned when the judge denied them. As the *Post*'s story points out, the "case represents just one of the many blind spots in the legal infrastructure of same-sex marriage in America. Couples often have different rights when they cross jurisdictional lines and may not have the same status in the eyes of the federal government as they do in their home states. The laws are constantly evolving" (McCarthy, 2012). A Maryland court ruled in May 2012, however, that the couple could proceed with their divorce—though, ironically, same-sex couples were denied the right to marry in Maryland until 2013.

Cases like these present a conundrum in a country where states may make their own laws governing the prohibition or recognition of unions the federal government has not legally

FIGURE 11.6 Changing Attitudes of U.S. Adults: Approval of Same-Sex Marriage, 2001–2012

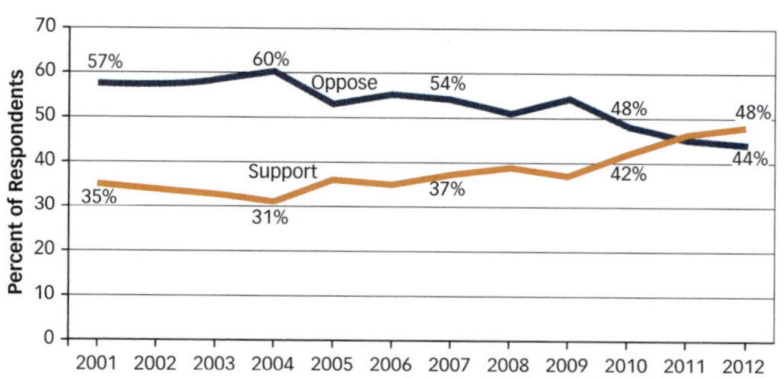

SOURCE: Adapted from Newport, F. (2012, May 8). Half of Americans support legal gay marriage. Gallup Politics.

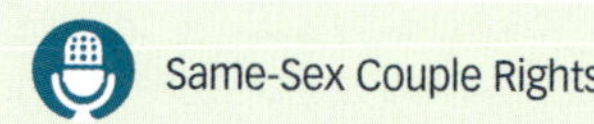

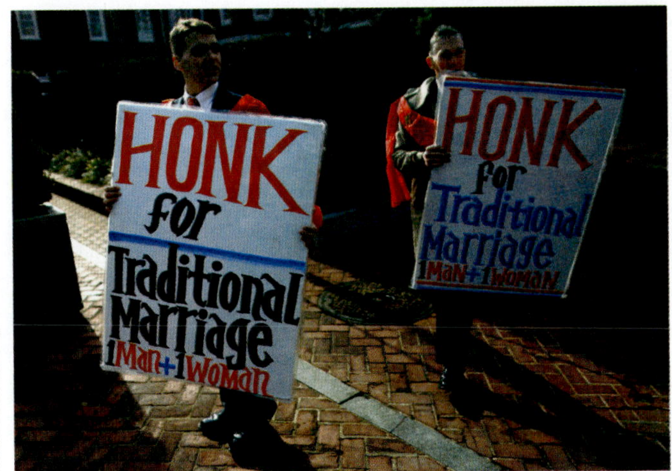

In U.S. political discourse, we encounter discussions of "family values," which are often linked to traditional heterosexual marriage. How would you define family values? Do you think most people could agree on a common definition?

recognized. While Maryland had no law in place expressly banning the recognition of same-sex marriages performed in other states, it also had no law allowing such recognition. Is the manifest function of divorce law to permit a couple to legally end a union that is no longer viable, or is it to act as a symbol of a state's position on marriage and family? How can a conflict between these two functions of divorce law be resolved?

WHO'S MINDING THE CHILDREN? CHILD CARE IN THE UNITED STATES TODAY

In a reversal of a longtime (nearly four-decade) trend in the United States, increasing numbers of mothers are staying home to care for children: In 2012, 29% of mothers reported that they did not work outside the home. About two thirds of today's stay-at-home mothers are part of "traditional" families; that is, they care for children in the home while their husbands work for pay. The rest include single and cohabiting women, as well as women whose husbands are unemployed. The shift toward fewer mothers working outside the home is driven by a variety of social, cultural, and economic factors. Among these are the growing percentage of immigrant women who are mothers and stagnating wages that have led some women to conclude that the costs of outside child care outweigh the benefits of working for pay (Cohn, Livingston, & Wang, 2014).

At the same time, in the slow growth of another trend, more fathers are assuming the primary child-care role in the home. According to a recent study, about 16% of stay-at-home parents today are fathers, up from 10% in 1989. Interestingly, this trend appears to be driven by labor market and health issues more than by changes in social or cultural norms that support more active fathering. Data show that while about three quarters of mothers are motivated by a desire to care for the family, only one fifth of men offer the same explanation: Almost 60% of stay-at-home fathers indicate that they are at home because they are either ill or disabled or because they are unemployed (Livingston, 2014). Notably, public attitudes about men as primary caregivers are, in spite of myriad changes in family life, still only nominally supportive. Livingston (2014) reports on a Pew Research Center poll in which about 76% of respondents said that they believed children are "just as well off" if their father works, but only 34% said that children are "just as well off" if their mother works, and 51% said that children are "better off" if the mother stays home; just 8% responded that the children are "better off" with the father at home (Figure 11.7).

Most mothers and fathers of young children are, in fact, in the labor force, though child care has remained largely in the domain of the family. Data show that about half of children age 4 and younger whose mothers work for pay are cared for by relatives. A quarter get their primary care in child-care centers or preschools, and around 13% are looked after in home-care arrangements or by a nanny or other nonrelative (ChildStats, 2013).

While choosing who will care for a young child is a highly personal decision for a family, there are some discernible patterns in child-care arrangements by socioeconomic status. For example, poorer fathers are more likely to be stay-at-home parents than are their better-off male peers (Livingston, 2014). As well, working mothers who hold college degrees are most likely to use center-based child care, which is often very costly (ChildStats, 2013). How would you explain these patterns? What other patterns of child care could you hypothesize?

IMMIGRATION AND FAMILY PATTERNS

The United States has more foreign-born residents than any other country in the world. Given its low fertility rate, a

FIGURE 11.7 Public Opinion of the Importance of Stay-at-Home Moms and Stay-at-Home Dads 2014

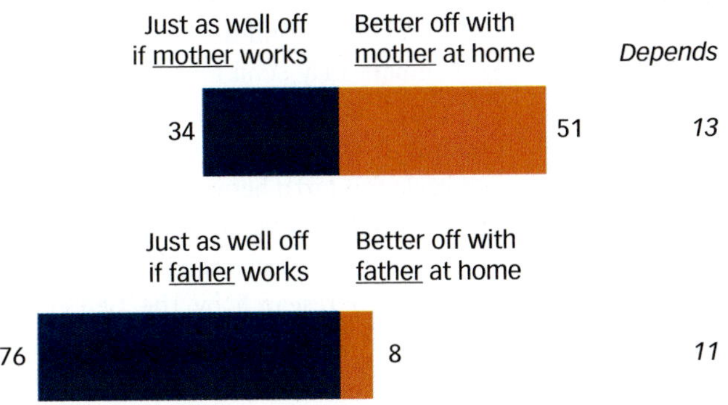

Note: The questions were asked separately for mothers and fathers. "Don't know/Refused" now shown.

SOURCE: Growing Number of Dads Home With the Kids: Biggest Increase Among Those Caring for Family, by Gretchen Livingston, Kim Parker, and Caroline Klibanoff. June 5, 2014. Pew Research, Social & Demographic Trends. Reprinted with permission.

Consequences of Parental Divorce

CQR The Fatherhood Movement

TABLE 11.1 Top 10 Feeder Countries for Migration to the United States, 2010

Country of Birth	Population	Percentage of U.S. Migrants by Country of Origin
Mexico	11,711,103	29
China	1,608,095	5
India	1,780,322	4
Philippines	1,777,588	4
Vietnam	1,240,542	3
El Salvador	1,214,049	3
Cuba	1,104,679	3
Korea	1,100,422	3
Dominican Republic	879,187	2
Guatemala	830,824	2

SOURCE: U.S. Census Bureau. (2010). *Place of birth for the foreign-born population*. Washington, DC: U.S. Government Printing Office.

substantial proportion—about a third—of the country's population growth is the result of immigration (Table 11.1 and Figure 11.8). With the proportion of foreign-born residents at about 13%, it is not surprising that immigrants and the cultures they carry with them have important effects on family patterns in the United States.

Predictably, more recent immigration correlates with a group's stronger ties to its homeland culture (Moore & Pinderhughes, 2001). Many scholars are now focusing on the *transnational* nature of immigrant families. Embodying transnationalism may mean living, working, worshipping, and being politically active in one nation while still maintaining strong political, social, religious, and/or cultural ties to other nations (Levitt, 2004). Family members may send money to relatives in their countries of origin, keep in nearly constant contact with those they left behind through modern communication technologies, and travel back and forth between countries frequently in order to maintain close emotional ties.

Many immigrant parents also prefer their children to marry within the group. According to research by the Center for Immigration Studies, in some devout Muslim communities parents' traditional values exist in a tense relationship with new norms embraced by their children:

> Just when Muslim girls traditionally would be separated from boys, taken out of school, and perhaps start wearing a head covering, their American counterparts begin to discover and experiment with their sexuality. To prevent such experimentation, Muslim parents seek to enforce the traditional rules . . . sometimes even cloistering their daughters. [However,] . . . by law, girls must go to school until 16 or so; and at 18, they acquire additional rights. . . .
>
> To encourage the young to marry within the faith, American Muslims are developing a number of novel solutions, including summer camps, socials for singles, and marriage advertisements. But even these Muslim institutions have a difficult time keeping boys and girls apart. (Pipes & Durán, 2002, pp. 5–6)

Interestingly, reflecting the influence of home cultures on migrants that we discussed in the opening of this section, first-generation migrants often have birthrates above those of the native-born U.S. population. One study found that among some groups, immigrant women in the United States were having more children on average (2.9) than women in their home countries (2.3; Camarota, 2005). In the second generation, however, the rate typically declines to the average U.S. rate—that is, approximately 2.1 children per woman (Hill & Johnson, 2002). However, some studies have found that the trend toward decreasing fertility in first- and second-generation immigrant women may actually be reversed in the third generation for some groups (Parrado & Morgan, 2008). Historically, fertility rates have decreased for immigrant families the longer they reside in the United States. However, it is important to note that factors such as country of origin, education, religion, and cultural attitudes add to the complexity of understanding these trends.

FIGURE 11.8 Region of Birth as Percentage of Total Migrant Population, 2010

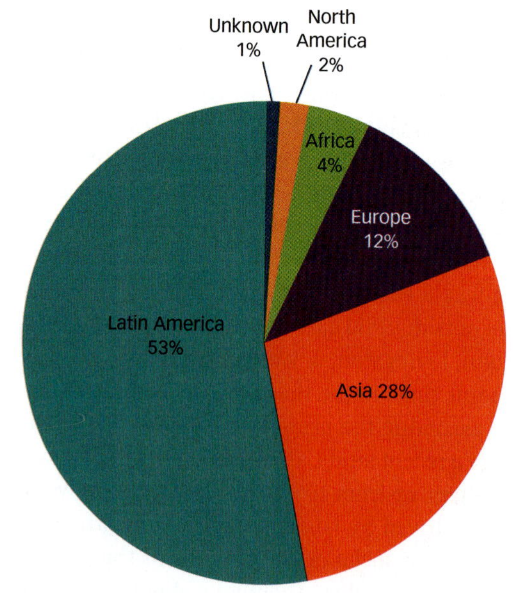

SOURCE: U.S. Census Bureau. (2010). *Place of birth for the foreign-born population*. Washington, DC: U.S. Government Printing Office.

GLOBAL ISSUES

FUNCTIONAL ALTERNATIVES TO THE FAMILY IN MODERN JAPAN

People need and want families for a wide variety of reasons. Some are emotional: Families can provide warmth, comfort, and pleasurable interactions. Others are social and cultural: Families are expected to be in attendance at key cultural rituals in our lives, such as holidays, weddings, and religious ceremonies. Some needs are practical, as families also fulfill important caregiving functions. But what if family members are estranged or far away? Or if someone has no living relatives? In Japan, modernity has brought what Robert Merton termed "functional alternatives" to the family. Below we describe two of them.

Yoshikazu Tsuno/AFP/Getty Images

The high-tech robot "Pepper" greets some young and curious visitors. Pepper's creators say that the robot can understand between 70% and 80% of spontaneous conversations, though it must choose from a set of programmed responses.

Japan is the first country to develop a nascent market in "rental families." In the early 1990s, Japan Efficiency Corporation was "doing a booming business renting families to the lonely," especially the elderly. Asked to comment on the small but significant phenomenon, a Japanese sociologist stated, "It's extremely strange to me that people would want to rent families, and even more surprising that they seem to be satisfied. . . . I suppose people nowadays really find the need for kinship. Compared to 50 years ago, the family system in Japan has really changed, and family-like relationships are gradually disappearing" (quoted in Watanabe, 1992).

Today the market for rental families has expanded further. Office Agents, a Tokyo firm, offers "friends" and "family members" for rent as event guests. "Many in Japan see weddings as a formal event that must be attended by as many family members, friends, and co-workers as possible. . . . But what if you've got no one to do that for you?" Office Agents has about 1,000 "fakes" available for occasions that may vary from weddings to funerals to training seminars. The company's head notes that sometimes even a marriage partner is unaware there are fake guests at his or her wedding (Kubota, 2009).

In 2014, global media reported on a technological breakthrough with implications for society—and the family in particular. In June, the Japanese company Softbank introduced Pepper, a robot with the capability of sensing and responding to emotions. According to a press report on Pepper, "with a rapidly ageing population, coupled with a falling birth rate, the demand for robots is expected to increase. . . . The growth is expected to come not only from businesses looking to offset labour shortages and rising wage costs, but also from households seeking an alternative to paying for care workers for elderly relatives" (BBC, 2014c). Pepper may soon be a resident in some Japanese homes—and perhaps homes across the aging Western world.

THINK IT THROUGH

▶ What do the phenomena described above say about family and its functions? Are rented "relatives" a viable functional alternative for people who lack families? Are robots a viable alternative? Could you see these phenomena taking root in the United States? Why or why not?

Lawrence Migdale / Photo Researchers, Inc.

The 2010 U.S. Census counted just over half a million (557,185) American Indian and Alaska Native families in the United States. About 57% were reported to be married-couple families.

Below we narrow our focus to a pair of specific examples of family subcultures in the United States—those of Native Americans and deaf families.

AMERICA'S FIRST NATIONS: NATIVE AMERICAN FAMILIES

Family patterns among Native Americans are highly diverse. There are nearly 500 different nations, although more than half of all American Indians identify as coming from just 6 of these (U.S. Census Bureau, 2011b). American Indians often live in extended family households that include uncles, aunts, cousins, and grandparents. According to Harriett Light and Ruth Martin (1996), writing in the *Journal of American Indian Education,* "the central unit of Indian society is the family. . . . Indian families do not have the rigid structure of relationships found in Western white culture. Instead, Indians relate to people outside the immediate family in supportive and caring ways (Levine & Laurie, 1974)."

An example of family involvement in child rearing outside the immediate parents is found in Sioux families. This involvement begins early in a child's life, when a second set of parents are selected for the newborn (Sandoz, 1961). Therefore, the "total" family involved in child rearing and support includes unrelated members of the Indian community (Ryan, 1981). This community support and protection can be viewed as responsibility for others' actions (Light & Martin, 1996).

More recent studies have shown that Native American family ties extend across generations. Native American grandparents have shown high levels of involvement in the care of their grandchildren (Mutchler, Baker, & Lee, 2007). Native Americans also report high levels of caregiving to their elderly relatives (McGuire, Okoro, Goins, & Anderson, 2008). Indeed, Native American culture and families traditionally emphasize sensitivity toward kin, tribe, and land and value the collective over the individual, in contrast to the mainstream U.S. emphasis on individual fulfillment and achievement (Light & Martin, 1996; Newcomb, 2008). Research on Native Americans of the Southwest suggests that many members of these groups see their children as belonging to the entire American Indian nation: to the land, the sky, the tribe, and its history, customs, and traditions (Nicholas, 2009).

Some controversies over family life taking place within Native American communities mirror those taking place in U.S. society more generally. For instance, beginning in 2008, some tribes began to permit same-sex marriage; in that year, the Coquille tribe of Oregon was the first to pass a law defining marriage or domestic partnership as a "formal and express civil contract entered into by two persons, regardless of their sex." Today, eight tribes offer similar marriage rights. The sovereign Navajo Nation, however, has resisted this step, defining marriage exclusively as a relationship between one man and one woman (Hamedy, 2014). Interestingly, some research shows that gay partnerships were historically accepted in many tribal cultures, where the term *two spirits* was used to categorize gay, lesbian, bisexual, and transgender members (Kronk, 2013).

DEAF CULTURE AND FAMILY LIFE

Census Bureau data show that about one-fifth of the U.S. population has some kind of disability. How does disability affect family life? In this subsection, we examine the case of deaf people and the choices and challenges that family life brings for them. According to the Gallaudet Research Institute (2005), approximately 2 to 4 of every 1,000 people in the United States are "functionally deaf," or unable to hear normal conversation even with the use of a hearing aid. Fewer than 1 in 1,000 were deaf before the age of 18; more than half became deaf at some point after childhood. Family life poses unique challenges for many deaf people, and, as a consequence, some prefer to practice endogamy, marrying others who are deaf and therefore share a common experience.

There has been a movement within the deaf community to redefine the meaning of deafness to denote not a form of disability but a positive culture. Some deaf people see themselves as similar to an ethnic group: sharing a common language (American Sign Language, or ASL), possessing a strong sense of cultural identity, and taking pride in their heritage. Identifying as an ethnic group rather than as a disability group, some deaf people believe that cochlear implant surgery, a procedure through which some deaf people can become hearing, is problematic, especially when it is performed on children who cannot consent. Often, deaf people who undergo this surgery are still unable to attain mastery of any oral language (Lane, 2005). The National Association of the Deaf (2000) takes a cautionary stance on cochlear implants, advising hearing parents of deaf children to conduct thorough research, create a support system, and, most important, communicate with their children

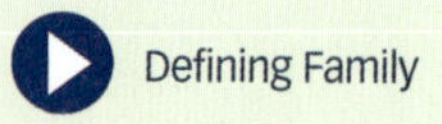

Andy Nelson / Contributor/Getty Images

Gallaudet University in Washington, D.C., is unique in serving specifically the deaf and hearing-impaired, offering bilingual instruction in English and ASL. The rising proportion of students who are hearing or come from mainstream schools and do not know ASL has led to debates over the centrality of deaf culture at the school.

before undertaking the transition. Julie Mitchiner takes pride in being deaf. She writes,

> Growing up with deaf parents and attending deaf schools, I have a strong sense of pride of being deaf and being part of the Deaf community. I do not look at myself as disabled. I often say if I were given a choice to hear or stay deaf, I'd choose to stay deaf. It is who I am. My family, my friends, and my community have taught me that being deaf is part of our culture and is a way of life. (Mitchiner & Sass-Lehrer, 2011, p. 3)

Many deaf people succeed in the hearing world, but they may confront daunting problems (Heppner, 1992). Often they are not able to speak in a way that hearing people fully understand, and most hearing people do not know ASL. It is not surprising that an estimated 85% of deaf people choose to marry others who share their own language and culture (Cichowski & Nance, 2004), or that many deaf parents are wary when their deaf children form relationships with hearing people. When a deaf couple has a hearing child, the family must make difficult choices as they negotiate not only the ordinary challenges of child rearing but also the raising of a child who may be "functionally hearing" but "culturally deaf" (Bishop & Hicks, 2009; Preston, 1994).

Families ordinarily confer their own cultural status on their children, but this may not be true for 9 of 10 deaf children born to hearing parents. On one hand, hearing parents want the same sorts of things for their deaf children as any parents want for their children: happiness, fulfillment, and successful lives as adults. Many would like their children to mainstream into the hearing world as well as possible, in spite of challenges. On the other hand, some in the deaf community argue that the deaf children of hearing parents can never fully belong to the hearing world. Many in the deaf community believe hearing parents should send their deaf children to residential schools for the deaf, where they will be fully accepted, learn deaf culture, and be with people who share their experience of deafness (Dolnick, 1993; Lane, 1992; Sparrow, 2005).

The situations of deaf parents raising a hearing child and hearing parents raising a deaf child raise interesting and fundamental questions about what happens when family members are also members of different cultures and how the obstacles of difference within a micro unit such as the family are negotiated.

SOCIOECONOMIC CLASS AND FAMILY IN THE UNITED STATES

An array of family differences are linked to social class differences. In this section we consider research showing that social class may have an effect on child-rearing practices, as well as on family formation through marriage.

SOCIAL CLASS AND CHILD REARING

Parents are often caught in a dilemma: They must instill some degree of conformity in their children as they attempt to socialize them into the norms and values that will be socially appropriate for adult behavior, but at the same time they must foster a degree of independence—after all, children must eventually leave the nest and survive in the adult world. Given the tension between protecting children and instilling independence, it should not be surprising that in most families neither is fully achieved. Parents may understand that they need to help build their children's independence yet still be unwilling to trust their children's judgment, especially during adolescence. They may hang on to their children, prolonging dependence past the point where the children are ready to make decisions on their own. Growing up includes some degree of conflict no matter what approach parents use.

Some studies suggest that parental attitudes toward children's independence differ markedly by social class. In U.S. culture, middle- and upper-class families tend to value self-direction and individual initiative in their children. Working-class parents, by contrast, have been observed by some researchers to value respect for authority, obedience, and a higher degree of conformity, and to rely on punishment when these norms are violated. Sociologist Melvin Kohn (1989), who spent many years studying class differences in child rearing, attributes these differences to the parents' work experiences: Middle- and upper-class jobs often require individual initiative and innovation, while working-class jobs tend to emphasize conformity.

Annette Lareau (2002) goes beyond Kohn's focus on work experiences to argue that social class, which we experience in a

Immigrant Family Issues

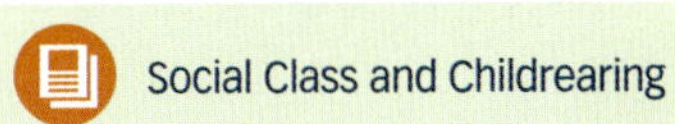

Social Class and Childrearing

© Gene J. Puskar/ /AP/Corbis

Are middle-class parents "overparenting," raising risk-averse young people characterized by a sense of entitlement? Popular magazines have run articles with provocative titles such as "How to Land Your Kid in Therapy" (Gottlieb, 2011), expounding the virtues of less-involved parenting. How might this debate fit into Lareau's characterization of middle-class parenting styles?

multitude of ways, has an impact on family life, in particular on the styles of child rearing in which parents engage. In reporting her study, in which 88 White and Black American families were interviewed and 12 were closely observed at home, Lareau writes,

> It is the interweaving of life experiences and resources, including parents' economic resources, occupational conditions, and educational backgrounds, that appears to be most important in leading middle-class parents to engage in concerted cultivation and working-class and poor parents to engage in the accomplishment of natural growth. (pp. 771–772)

These two concepts, concerted cultivation and accomplishment of natural growth, form a key foundation for Lareau's argument. She defines *concerted cultivation* as a style of parenting associated most fully with the middle class and characterized by an emphasis on negotiation, discussion, questioning of authority, and cultivation of talents and skills through, among other things, participation in organized activities. Lareau explains the *accomplishment of natural growth* as the parenting style associated with working-class and poor families. Directives rather than negotiation and explanation, a focus on obedience, and an inclination to care for children's basic needs characterize this style, in which parents leave children to play and grow in a largely unstructured environment. Notably, Lareau identifies a tension between obedience and trust in this style, suggesting it is characterized by something close to distrustful consent born of frustration with authority and dominant institutions but a sense of powerlessness in their presence. From this, she suggests, children take away an emerging sense of constraint. Consider the following observation by Kathryn Edin and Maria Kefalas (2005):

> While poor mothers see keeping a child housed, fed, clothed, and safe as noteworthy accomplishments, their middle-class counterparts often feel they must earn their parenting stripes by faithfully cheering at soccer league games, chaperoning boy scout camping trips and attending ballet recitals or martial arts competitions. (p. 141)

What are the outcomes of these differing styles of child rearing, which Lareau argues are associated with class status? Examining the outcomes for children of parents she studied in the years of young adulthood, Lareau (2002) concludes that the accomplishment of natural growth style not only tends to cultivate early independence but also leads young people toward jobs that require respect for authority and obedience to directives, like those associated with the working class. In contrast, the concerted cultivation approach to child raising leads young people both to hold a sense of entitlement and to pursue careers that require a broad vocabulary and ease in negotiating with people in authority. Following up with the families she studied, Lareau found that all the middle-class children had completed high school and that most were attending college. Many of the children of low-income families had left high school and few were in college. "In sum," she writes, "differences in family life lie not only in the advantages parents obtain for their children, but also in the skills they transmit to children for negotiating their own life paths" (p. 749).

The studies discussed above strongly suggest that family life, and practices of child rearing in particular, contributes to the reproduction of class status. While structural factors, including obstacles related to education and other important resources for mobility, are an important part of the picture, Lareau suggests that the orientations and skills developed in childhood, which become part of a young adult's human capital as he or she negotiates the path through school and toward a job, are also relevant to understanding socioeconomic outcomes and the reproduction of class status.

ECONOMY, CULTURE, AND FAMILY FORMATION

Class status is linked with changing patterns of family life in another important way. Some sociologists believe that macro-level economic changes, in particular the rise of a postindustrial economy and associated labor market, have had a powerful effect on micro-level practices of family formation (Edin & Kefalas, 2005; Wilson, 1996, 2010). In this section we examine the sociological roots of the decline of marriage and the rise of nonmarital births in poor and working-class Black, White, and Latino communities.

In 1965, Daniel Patrick Moynihan, a former professor of sociology who was then assistant U.S. secretary of labor and would later become a U.S. senator from New York, published a controversial study of the African American family titled

The Negro Family: The Case for National Action, which later came to be called the Moynihan Report. In it, Moynihan argued that lower-class Black family life was often dysfunctional, as reflected in high rates of family dissolution, single parenting, and the dominance of female-headed families.

Moynihan saw the breakdown of Black families, together with continued racial inequality, as leading to "a new crisis in race relations." He identified the legacy of slavery, which intentionally broke up Black families, as one of the roots of the problem. He also argued that many rural Blacks had failed to adapt adequately to urban environments. Moynihan concluded that these patterns in family life were at least in part responsible for the failure of many low-income Black Americans to make it into the economic mainstream in the United States. He saw Black poverty and inner-city violence, which exploded in the urban riots of the 1960s, as partly the result of Black family breakdown.

The Moynihan Report was widely criticized as racist and sexist, and Moynihan was accused of blaming the victims of racism and poverty (primarily Black female heads of household) for their disadvantages. Many critics ignored Moynihan's attention to *structural* as well as *cultural* factors in his analysis, however. While he wrote that "at the center of the tangle of pathology is the weakness of the family structure," he also implicated social phenomena such as unemployment, poverty, and racial segregation in the decline of families and the rise of dysfunctions. Still, critics focused largely on his cultural analysis, and Moynihan's findings were disregarded while sociologists avoided examining the connections among race, family characteristics, and poverty for at least two decades.

In 1987, sociologist William Julius Wilson published *The Truly Disadvantaged: The Inner City, the Underclass, and Public Policy,* in which he revisited the issues Moynihan had raised in the 1965 report. In the two intervening decades, much had changed—and much had stayed the same. The family patterns that Moynihan had identified as problematic, including nonmarital births and high levels of family dissolution, had become more pronounced among poor and working-class Black Americans. At the same time, social problems such as joblessness in the inner city had grown more acute, as deindustrialization and the movement of jobs to the suburbs dramatically reduced the number of positions available for less educated and low-skilled workers. These changes, Wilson noted, had important consequences for family formation.

Almost 10 years later, Wilson (1996) argued that falling rates of marriage and rising numbers of nonmarital births were, at least in part, rooted in the declining numbers of "marriageable men" in inner-city neighborhoods. He posited that the ratio of unmarried Black women to single and "marriageable" Black men of similar age was skewed by male joblessness, high rates of incarceration, and high death rates for young Black men. The loss of jobs in the inner city had a powerfully negative effect on male employment opportunities. The consequences were felt not only in the economic fortunes of communities but also, and no less importantly, in families, where women were choosing motherhood but options for marriage were diminished by the uneven ratio of single women to marriageable men. While rates of nonmarital births had previously been high in Black communities, where extended families have traditionally been available to support mothers and children (Gerstel & Gallagher, 1994), Wilson saw new urban circumstances as central to the rise of nonmarital births among Black Americans from one-quarter in 1965 (when Moynihan published his report) to about 70% by the middle 1990s, where it remains today (Figure 11.9). By then about half of Black American families were headed by a woman (Wilson, 2010).

When Wilson revisited this issue in 2010, he found that research on the relationship between male employment and rates of marriage and single parenthood offered mixed findings:

> Joblessness among black men is a significant factor in their delayed entry into marriage and in the decreasing rates of marriage after a child has been born, and this relationship has been exacerbated by sharp increases in incarceration that in turn lead to continued joblessness. Nevertheless, much of the decline in marriages in the inner city, including marriages that occur after a child has been born, remains unexplained when only structural factors are examined. (p. 108)

Wilson (2010) also cited cultural factors in the fragmentation of the poor Black family. While sociologists have been reluctant to use culture as an explanation, not least due to fear of the backlash generated by the Moynihan Report, Wilson writes that structure and culture interact to create normative contexts for behavior. He points out, for instance, that "both

FIGURE 11.9 Nonmarital Birthrate by Race/Ethnicity in the United States, 2013

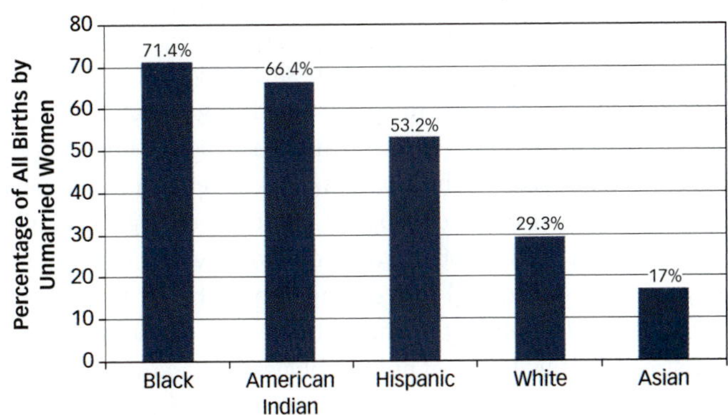

SOURCE: Based on "Appendix 1—Percentage of All Births that Were to Unmarried Women, by Race and Hispanic Origin, and Age: Selected Years, 1960–2013." Child Trends DataBank.

inner-city black males and females believe that since most marriages will eventually break up and no longer represent meaningful relationships, it is better to avoid the entanglements of wedlock altogether. . . . Single mothers who perceive the fathers of their children as unreliable or as having limited financial means will often—rationally—choose single parenthood" (p. 125). In this social context, the stigma of unmarried parenthood is minimal, and behaviors rooted in structure become culturally normative.

Examining the phenomenon of low marriage rates and high nonmarital births in some communities, sociologists Kathryn Edin and Maria Kefalas (2005) looked at data on low-income White, Black, and Puerto Rican single mothers in Camden, New Jersey, and Philadelphia, Pennsylvania. Black communities have historically had higher nonmarital birthrates and lower rates of marriage than White and Latino communities, but in low-income White and Latino communities comparable trends have taken root.

Edin and Kefalas found that the women in their study placed a high value on both motherhood and marriage. They saw motherhood as a key role and central achievement in their lives, and few made serious efforts to delay motherhood. If anything, they saw early motherhood as something that had forced them to mature and kept them from getting into trouble. At the same time, they held a utopian view of marriage that may, ironically, have put it out of their reach. Many dreamed of achieving financial security and owning a home before marrying—but their poverty made this a challenge. More problematic, perhaps, was that they did not consider the men in their lives—often the fathers of their children—to be good partners, their marriageability undermined by low education, joblessness, poor economic prospects, criminal records, violence, drug and alcohol abuse, and infidelity.

Notably, then, while they highly valued marriage, the women had few realistic opportunities to achieve stability and independence first, and little hope of finding stable partners. Motherhood, however, was an achievable dream, an opportunity to occupy an important social role and to achieve success as a parent, where other paths of opportunity were often blocked by poor structural circumstances.

Statistics show that children in single-mother homes are among those most likely to be born and to grow up impoverished. They are also more likely than their better-off peers to repeat the patterns of their parents and to remain in poverty. Here some interesting sociological questions emerge: Is single parenthood a cause (not the only one) of poverty, or is living in poverty a sociological root of single parenthood? Or perhaps both are true? What are the implications of the answers to these questions for the design of public policies that address poverty?

The relationships among class, poverty, and family patterns are complex, but Wilson and Edin and Kefalas offer sociological lenses for understanding some of the structural and cultural roots of low marriage rates and high nonmarital birthrates in many poor U.S. communities. As Wilson notes in his 2010 book *More Than Just Race: Being Black and Poor in the Inner City,* "How families are formed among America's poorest citizens is an area that cries out for further research" (p. 129). What other factors should sociologists examine? How would you conduct such a study? What kinds of questions would you ask?

FAMILY LIFE IN THE MIDDLE CLASS

Today, parents in the U.S. middle class, particularly its upper fraction, devote an unprecedented amount of resources to child rearing. While some of the rising financial outlays are for basic needs and child care, parents are also committing time and money to "enrichment" activities intended to give their offspring advantages in competition, education, and the future labor market. According to a 2013 study, the growing U.S. income gap is reflected in a gap in spending on children that opened up in the period from the 1990s to the 2000s, with families in the top half of the income distribution spending more on their progeny while the bottom spend less (Kornrich & Furstenberg, 2013). More economically advantaged parents are actively engaged in building what Hilary Levey Friedman (2013) calls "competitive kid capital." Friedman's study of 95 families with elementary school–age children who were involved in competitive after-school activities such as chess, dance, and soccer found that many parents "saw their kids' participation in competitive afterschool activities as a way to develop certain values and skills: the importance of winning; the ability to bounce back from a loss to win in the future; to succeed in stressful situations; and to perform under the gaze of others" (p. 31). Interestingly, Friedman points out that parents of upper-middle-class girls are more likely to enroll their girls in soccer or chess than in dance, pursuing an "aggressive femininity" that they perceive to offer their daughters a future labor market advantage.

Middle-class family life is often characterized by a strong commitment to constructive and active child rearing (as we saw in Lareau's study and the research described above) and to the parents' pursuit of careers. These competing commitments often leave parents without the time to do everything, to do it well, and to feel satisfied instead of rushed and stressed.

Sociologist Arlie Russell Hochschild (2001b) has come to some interesting and perhaps surprising conclusions about this modern dilemma. Hochschild conducted a series of interviews with employees at a well-known *Fortune* 500 firm that had gone to some lengths to be family-friendly, offering flextime, the option of part-time work, parental leave, job sharing, and even a course titled "Work-Life Balance for Two-Career Couples." But she noticed that the family-friendly measures didn't make much of a difference. Most employees said they put "family first," but they also felt strained to the limit, and almost none cut back on work time. Few took advantage of parental leave or the option of part-time employment.

Why do people say they want to strike a better balance between work and the rest of their lives yet do nothing about it when they have the opportunity? Some reasons are practical; a number of employees in Hochschild's study feared that taking advantage of liberal work policies would count against them in their careers, while others simply needed the money—they couldn't afford to work less. Yet Hochschild identified a more surprising reason many people worked long hours: They liked being at work better than being at home. Previous research had shown that many men regard work as a haven, and Hochschild found that a notable number of working women now feel the same way. Despite the stress of long hours and guilt about being away from their families, they are reluctant to cut back on their commitment to paid work.

Hochschild found that both men and women often derive support, companionship, security, pride, and a sense of being valued when they are working. In the absence of family time and kin and community support at home, some parents sought and found—and sometimes preferred—a sense of competence and achievement in the workplace. In about a fifth of the families Hochschild studied, work rather than home was the site at which the parents derived the most satisfaction.

Many studies since have found that workplaces with more "family-friendly" policies have higher levels of workplace satisfaction and productivity, as well as lower levels of stress (Bilal, Zia-ur-Rehman, & Raza, 2010; Frye & Breaugh, 2004). Still, Hochschild's (2001b) research suggests that many people derive satisfaction from being workaholics. As she concludes, "Working families are both prisoners and architects of the time bind in which they find themselves" (p. 249).

Family stresses reach across the socioeconomic spectrum and create a variety of challenges. Sometimes problems manifest as violence, an issue we tackle below.

VIOLENCE AND THE FAMILY

Domestic (or family) violence is *physical or sexual abuse committed by one family member against another.* It may be perpetrated by adults toward their children, by one spouse against another, by one sibling toward another, or by adult children against their elderly parents. As little as three to four decades ago, domestic violence was rarely studied. Many people regarded violence in the home as a private matter, an attitude that was reflected in lawmaking as well, which provided few sanctions for violence that did not reach the level of severe injury or death. Today domestic violence is understood to be a serious public issue, as researchers have come to realize that it is sadly commonplace (Catalano, 2012).

Domestic (or family) violence: Physical or sexual abuse committed by one family member against another.

Family Violence and Police

CQR Domestic Abuse in Families

Accurate data on family violence are difficult to obtain for a variety of reasons. Abused partners or children are reluctant to call attention to the fact that they are abused. Police do not want to mediate or make arrests in family conflicts, and even today the courts are hesitant to intervene in what are often perceived as family matters (Tolan, Gorman-Smith, & Henry, 2005). Some good estimates of the prevalence of this crime are available, however. According to the U.S. Bureau of Justice Statistics, family violence accounted for about 11% of both reported and unreported violence between 1998 and 2002. Of the 3.5 million violent crimes committed against family members, 49% were crimes against spouses, 11% involved victimized sons or daughters, and 41% were crimes against other family members (Durose et al., 2005).

The National Intimate Partner and Sexual Violence Survey, an ongoing survey developed and administered by the Centers for Disease Control and Prevention, found in 2010 that one in three women and one in four men surveyed had been victims of *intimate partner violence* (IPV) in their lifetimes. As defined by the CDC, IPV includes physical violence, rape, and stalking by a former or current partner or spouse. About one in four women and one in seven men surveyed had experienced severe physical violence at the hands of their partners. While these data are for experiences over the life course, even the data from a single year reveal a serious epidemic of intimate partner violence. According to the survey, more than 12 million people experienced IPV in 2010 (Centers for Disease Control and Prevention, 2010b).

Child abuse—sexual and/or physical assaults on children by adult members of their families—is also common in our society. According to the U.S. Department of Health and Human Services (2010), approximately 3.3 million child abuse reports and allegations were made in 2009 involving about 6 million children. On any given day, no fewer than 5 children die as the result of abuse (U.S. Government Accountability Office, 2011), though the main form of abuse is neglect (U.S. Department of Health and Human Services, 2010). Boys and girls are equally likely to be physically abused, but girls are more likely to be sexually abused as well. According to Childhelp (2010), an organization dedicated to the prevention of child abuse, the cycle of abuse is difficult to break; one study suggests that about 30% of abused and neglected children will later abuse their own children.

Elder abuse is the victimization of elderly persons by family members or other caregivers. In a 2009 National Institute of Justice study, 11% of elderly U.S. adults (those 65 or older) surveyed reported experiencing either emotional, physical, or sexual abuse or potential neglect (Acierno, Hernandez-Tejada, Muzzy, & Steve, 2009). Like child abuse, elder abuse is likely underreported, because victims are often in a subordinate position in the family and unable to access help outside the home. Elder abuse also shares with child abuse some of its forms, including neglect—the failure of caregivers to provide for basic needs like nutritious food and hygienic conditions—and

INEQUALITY MATTERS

DOMESTIC VIOLENCE AND HOMELESSNESS

How are women's experiences of poverty and homelessness linked to the societal phenomenon of domestic violence? In addition to consequences such as physical and psychological injury, violence is both a cause and a consequence of homelessness among women.

According to the National Law Center on Homelessness and Poverty (n.d.), "Domestic and sexual violence are leading causes of homelessness nationally, especially for women" (p. 1). By one 2008 estimate, 28% of homeless families were homeless as a result of domestic violence (National Coalition for the Homeless, 2009a). A 2011 study conducted by a Los Angeles women's center noted that nearly half of the homeless women surveyed had experienced domestic violence in their lifetimes, and a third of the women had experienced domestic violence in the past year. Nearly a third of the women surveyed had gone to the women's shelter directly after experiencing domestic violence and/or assault (Downtown Women's Action Coalition, 2011).

Other violence-linked causes of homelessness include a failure to secure alternative housing, which may be the result of unemployment or denial of resources by a controlling abuser. In a 2003 study, 44% of homeless women in Fargo, North Dakota, reported they had previously stayed in abusive relationships for lack of alternative places to live; in Minnesota, the figure was 46% (National Coalition for the Homeless, 2007). In 2012, the city of Chicago reported that 33% of its homeless residents were victims of domestic violence (Chicago Coalition for the Homeless, 2014). Notably, 39% of U.S. cities name domestic violence as the single largest cause of family homelessness (National Coalition for the Homeless, 2009a). While women may face violence upon returning home to abusers, they are also at risk on the streets, since homelessness makes them vulnerable to assault, robbery, rape, and other threats.

Domestic violence is a key precipitator of homelessness, particularly among poor and minority women, who may already face considerable obstacles to finding safe and adequate housing and solid employment opportunities. One societal response is to support safe housing for survivors of domestic violence. A more important one for the long term is to address the causes of abuse and to end both the acceptance and practice of domestic violence.

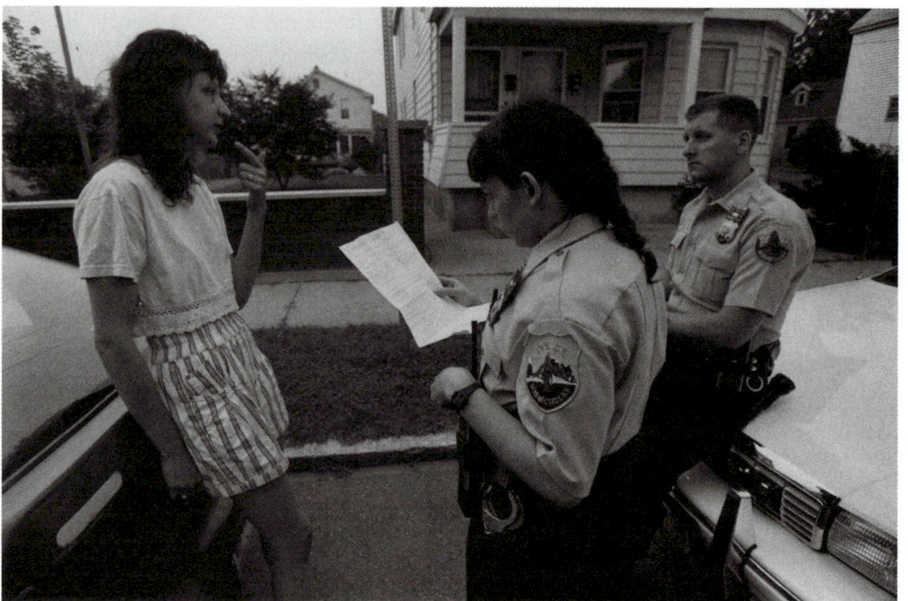

© Viviane Moos/Corbis

Domestic violence is an underreported crime, and many official reports fail to capture the extent of the problem. Why are many people reluctant to report incidents of domestic violence to the police?

THINK IT THROUGH

▶ How might communities effectively address the problem of domestic violence, as well as associated troubles such as homelessness? Consider issues of both attitudes and policies in answering this question.

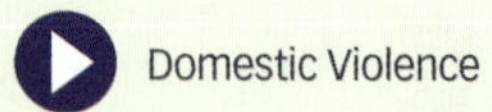

Domestic Violence

physical abuse. Some aspects of elder abuse differ from abuse of other kinds of victims, however. For example, elder abuse may take the form of financial exploitation or outright theft of property. Those who care for elderly relatives may feel entitled to the resources the seniors possess—or they may just take advantage of the older persons' vulnerabilities.

As sociologists examining a problem that is both a private trouble and a public issue, we need to ask, "Why does domestic violence exist and persist as a widespread phenomenon?" The acceptance of a husband's "right" to subject his wife to physical discipline has roots in Anglo-American culture. British common law permitted a man to strike his wife and children with a stick as a form of punishment, provided the stick was no thicker than his thumb; the phrase "rule of thumb" originates in this practice. Through the end of the 19th century in the United States, men could legally beat their wives (Renzetti & Curran, 1992). Research has found that domestic violence is most likely to be prevalent in societies in which family relationships are characterized by high emotional intensity and attachment, there is a pattern of male dominance and sexual inequality, a high value is placed on the privacy of family life, and violence is permitted or occurs in other institutional spheres, such as entertainment or popular culture (Straus & Gelles, 1990; Straus, Gelles, & Steinmetz, 1988).

People have become far more aware of child and spouse abuse and its spectrum of consequences in recent years, largely because of efforts by the women's movement to bring them into the open (see the *Inequality Matters* box on page 286). Shelters for battered women and children enable victims to be protected from violence. While still limited in number, such refuges have enabled women to get counseling while terminating abusive relationships in relative safety (Haj-yahia & Cohen, 2009). Family violence is clearly a dysfunctional social phenomenon. It is both a personal trouble and a public issue. A fuller understanding of its roots and consequences can contribute to both a better-informed national conversation about the problem and more robust efforts to address it.

GLOBALIZATION AND FAMILIES

The impact of globalization on families depends to a substantial degree on social class and country or region of residence. In this section, we look at the experience of globalization among families, its costs and benefits, and the uneven way in which those costs and benefits are distributed.

Consider the economic and labor market impact of globalization on U.S. families. Among upper-class and upper-middle-class families, globalization has increased employers' demands for men and women with high degrees of skill and formal training as professionals, managers, administrators, and engineers. While low-skilled U.S. workers have been priced out of many sectors of the global job market by their replaceability (lower-wage labor is readily available elsewhere), high-skilled labor in fields that are not easily "offshored" or replaced by technology may still benefit, because globalization can produce national economic gains even as it diminishes the prospects of some categories of workers.

The effects of economic globalization on families have been uneven, with negative consequences borne disproportionately by those with less education. Can you identify any current trends that suggest the circumstances of households headed by adults with a high school education or less will improve or worsen in coming decades?

About 70% of the individuals who make up the U.S. labor force do not hold 4-year college degrees. As we see elsewhere in this text, these are the workers who have been hit hardest by global economic change. Writing about domestic manufacturing industries, journalist Louis Uchitelle (2007) observes: "As customers defected, sales plummeted and failed to bounce back. Nowhere was that more apparent than in the auto industry's struggle with [lower-cost] Japanese imports. But nearly every manufacturer was hit, and the steep recession in 1981 and 1982 compounded the damage. The old world has never returned" (p. 8).

Many working-class families have found themselves confronting flat or declining incomes as a result of competition with a global workforce. Household incomes at the bottom of the economic spectrum have declined most dramatically since the 1970s, when globalization began to transform the domestic economy. This decline has had a multitude of effects on U.S. families. Recall our earlier discussion of the diminished pool of "marriageable" males. Here we see some of the effects of declining job opportunities and wages in manufacturing, which used to offer gainful employment to less educated men.

The need for a family to have two incomes to make ends meet is one of the reasons for the dramatic increase in the number of women working outside the home. The movement of women into the paid workforce has, in turn, provided some women with a degree of economic independence and an opportunity to rethink the meaning of marriage. As women join the paid workforce, some postpone marriage until they are older. Couples choose cohabiting as an alternative to marriage, and when they do decide to have children, their families are likely to be smaller. Some may never marry; as we learned earlier, marriage has declined most among those with the least education.

Globalization means greater mobility for families and more fluid ways of organizing work and life. The benefits of globalization enjoyed by some U.S. families are accompanied by the losses suffered by others. Globalization may be having the effect of further stratifying U.S. families economically.

INTERNATIONAL FAMILIES AND THE GLOBAL WOMAN

We have seen that macro processes of globalization have affected U.S. families at different socioeconomic status levels. In this section, we examine the dual phenomena of *international families* and the *global woman* to emphasize some of the micro-level effects of globalization, and to consider the ways that women, particularly women from the developing world, are experiencing globalization in their own lives.

Anthropologist Christine Ho (1993) has examined what she terms **international families**—that is, *families that result from globalization.* Focusing on mothers who emigrate from the Caribbean to the United States, Ho documents how they often rely on child minding, an arrangement in which extended family members and even friends cooperate in raising the women's children while they pursue work elsewhere, often thousands of miles away. This practice adds a global dimension to cooperative child-rearing practices that are a long-standing feature of Caribbean culture.

Ho suggests in her profiles of these female global citizens, most of whom work in lower-wage sectors of the economy, including clerical work and child care, that such global family arrangements enable Caribbean immigrants to avoid becoming fully Americanized: International families and child minding provide a strong sense of continuity with their Caribbean homeland culture. Ho predicts that Caribbean immigrants will retain their native culture by regularly receiving what she characterizes as "bicultural booster shots" through the shuttling of family members between the United States and the Caribbean. At the same time, Ho notes, this process contributes to the Americanization of the Caribbean region, which may eventually give rise to an ever more global culture.

Barbara Ehrenreich and Arlie Russell Hochschild (2002) have turned their attention to what they call the "global woman." Like Ho, they examine the female migrant leaving home and family to seek work in the wealthy "first world." Unlike Ho, however, they take a pointedly critical view of this phenomenon, suggesting that these female workers, most of them engaged in "care work" as nannies or housekeepers (or even prostitutes), are filling a "care deficit" in the wealthier countries, where many female professionals have pursued opportunities outside the home. In doing so the migrants create a new deficit at home, leaving their own children and communities behind: "Third World migrant women achieve their success only by assuming the cast-off domestic roles of middle- and high-income women in the First World—roles that have been previously rejected, of course, by men. And their 'commute' entails a cost we have yet to fully comprehend" (Ehrenreich & Hochschild, 2002, p. 3).

Ehrenreich and Hochschild (2002) argue that Western global power, previously manifested in the extraction of natural resources and agricultural goods, has evolved to embrace an "extraction" of women's labor and love, which is transferred to the well-off at a cost to poorer countries, communities, and—most acutely perhaps—families:

> The lifestyles of the First World are made possible by a global transfer of the services associated with a wife's traditional role—child care, homemaking, and sex—from poor countries to rich ones. To generalize and perhaps oversimplify: in an earlier phase of imperialism, northern countries extracted natural resources and agricultural products . . . from lands they conquered and colonized. Today, while still relying on Third World countries for agricultural and industrial labor, the wealthy countries also seek to extract something harder to measure and quantify, something that can look very much like love. (p. 4)

While the women from the developing world are, for the most part, agents in their own choice to migrate to countries of the developed world in search of work (unless they are trafficked or tricked into migration), Ehrenreich and Hochschild point to powerful social forces that figure into this "choice." On one hand, many women encounter the "push" factor of poverty, the choice of facing destitution at home or leaving families behind to earn what are, for them, substantial wages abroad. On the other hand, there is the "pull" factor of opportunities abroad: Their services are welcomed and needed. While these women make choices, their decisions are often driven by desperation and carry substantial noneconomic costs.

WHY STUDY FAMILY THROUGH A SOCIOLOGICAL LENS?

In the United States today, there are many possible ways of understanding what constitutes a family. They range from the narrower definitions embraced by the U.S. government

International families: Families that result from globalization.

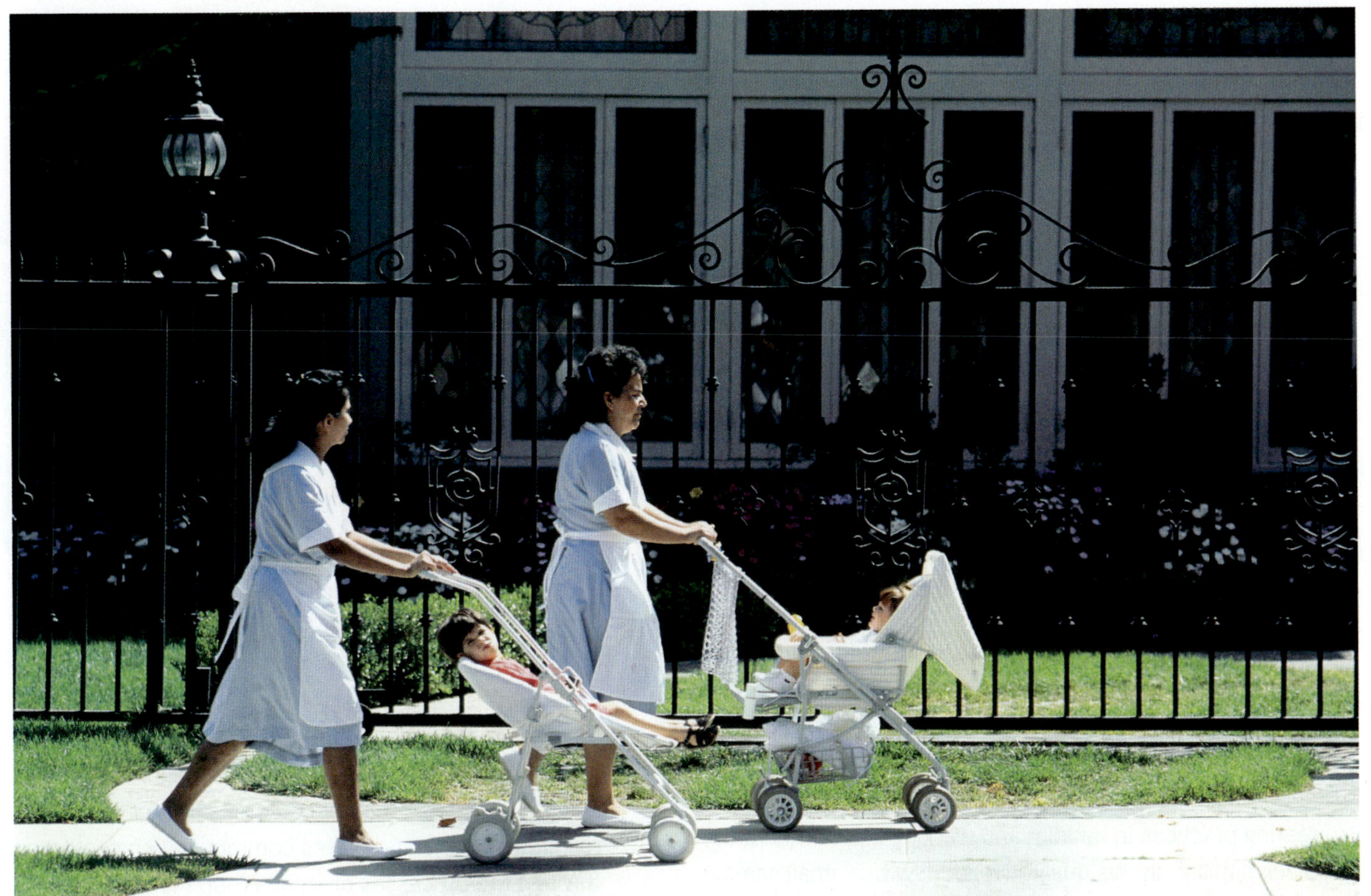
© Catherine Karnow/Corbis

Arlie Hochschild defines the nanny chain thus: "An older daughter from a poor family in a third world country cares for her siblings, while her mother works as a nanny caring for the children of a nanny migrating to a first world country, who, in turn, cares for the child of a family in a rich country" (Hochschild, 2001a).

and socially conservative communities to the broader options a growing number of groups are recognizing. A sociological perspective helps us to understand the roots of both stasis and change in family life and family formation. The decline of marriage, the rise of divorce beginning in the latter part of the 20th century, and the dramatic increase in nonmarital births are, as Émile Durkheim might have suggested, "social facts," and *social facts can be explained only by other social facts*. These are not changes that appear randomly; rather, they are the results of complex sociological phenomena with identifiable and interesting social, cultural, and economic antecedents.

Theoretical perspectives on the family and associated sex roles add another layer of analysis to the picture. Functionalist theory looks at the family's functions for societal stability, emphasizing reproduction, the nurturance and socialization of children, and the allocation of family members into complementary roles that ensure harmony and order. The more conflict-oriented feminist theory looks at the way the family reproduces gender inequality, ignoring the differential experiences and resources of men and women in relationships. The psychodynamic feminist perspective blends psychology and sociology to draw together the experiences of early childhood with relationship choices of adulthood and structural obstacles and opportunities. While all these perspectives have strengths and weaknesses, they offer us a range of possible lenses through which we can consider why families and roles are constituted as they are. The field remains open for new theoretical perspectives, and the family remains a fruitful area of research for sociologists.

Sociologists are concerned with commonalities and differences across families and explanations for these. Class, race, immigration status, health status—all of these may influence the ways that family formation, roles, cultures, and practices are manifested. Macro-level societal changes also have powerful impacts on families; globalization, deindustrialization, and the massive growth of student debt in an era of rapidly rising college costs are all seemingly "nonfamily" phenomena that may, in fact, have important impacts on families across the globe. Sociology helps us to make these connections.

WHAT CAN I DO WITH A SOCIOLOGY DEGREE?

SKILLS AND CAREERS: QUALITATIVE RESEARCH SKILLS

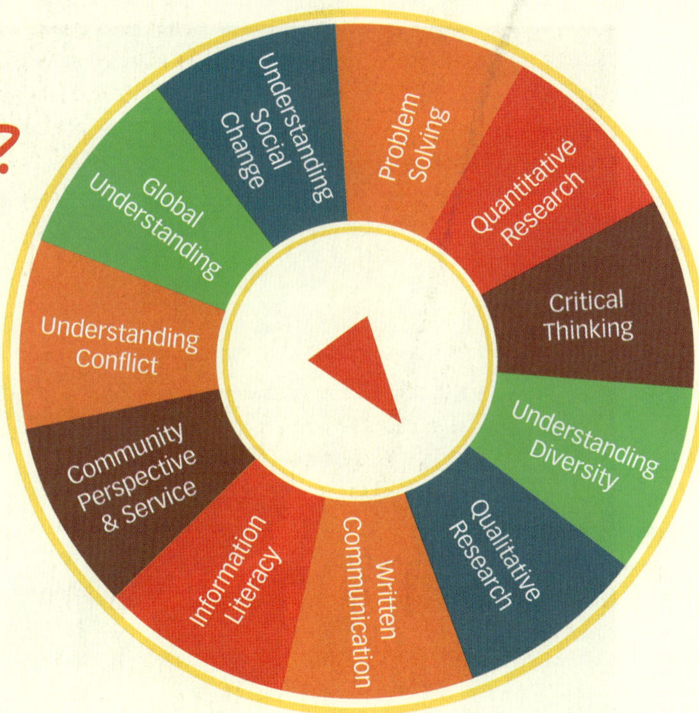

Sociologists use *qualitative research skills* to gather rigorous, in-depth information on social behaviors, phenomena, and institutions. Qualitative research highlights data that cannot be quantified (that is, cannot be converted into numbers). It relies on the gathering of data through methods such as focus groups, participant and nonparticipant observation, interviews, and archival research. Generally, population samples are small in qualitative research because the aim of the research is to gain deep understanding.

In this chapter, we reviewed research that used qualitative data to examine issues as broad as the decline of marriage in the U.S. working class and the struggle for a work–life balance among middle-class families. Annette Lareau (2002) used nonparticipant observation and interviews to look at child-rearing practices in middle- and working-class White and Black families. In this qualitative work with a small sample (88 families were interviewed, and 12 were closely observed at home), Lareau sought to develop a detailed and in-depth understanding of how class-associated styles of parenting contribute to the reproduction of class status. Throughout this book you will encounter numerous qualitative research studies, and you will see how they contribute to our knowledge of the social world. As you advance in your sociological studies, you will have the opportunity to learn how to do qualitative sociology. For example, you may learn to prepare interview questions that will allow you to accurately assess respondents' attitudes toward a particular social trend, or you may learn to take detailed field notes on observations you make of a practice or population you seek to study.

Knowledge of qualitative research methods is a beneficial skill in today's job market. Learning to collect data through observation, interviews, and focus groups, for instance, prepares you to do a wide variety of *job tasks,* including survey development, questionnaire design, data collection and reporting, and market research. Further, qualitative research experience fosters communication competencies through the processes of small-group management and rapport building, as well as negotiation with study participants. These kinds of tasks are associated with *job titles* such as market research analyst or manager, social science research assistant, program analyst, community engagement analyst, and survey designer, and with *occupational fields* as broad as sociology, psychology, marketing, politics, public relations, community relations, and business and management, among others.

THINK ABOUT CAREERS

▶ Think about a topic you have read about in your sociology class that was of particular interest to you. What kind of qualitative research method might offer an effective and rigorous way of studying that issue?

▶ How might you imagine using your knowledge of qualitative research methods in a career field like public relations, community relations, politics, management, or marketing?

SUMMARY

- The meaning of **family** is socially constructed within a particular culture, and in the United States, as in other modern societies, the meaning and practices of family life have been changing.
- **Marriage**, found in some form in all societies, can take several different forms, from the most common, **monogamy**, to many variations including **polygamy**, in which a person has multiple spouses simultaneously.
- The functionalist perspective highlights the family's functionality in terms of social stability and order, emphasizing such activities as sex-role allocation and child socialization.
- Feminist perspectives on the family are more conflict oriented, highlighting the **sexual division of labor** in society and its stratifying effects. Feminist perspectives also examine the different experiences of men and women in marriage and the way social expectations and roles affect those experiences. The psychodynamic feminist perspective takes a sociopsychological approach, emphasizing the impact of early mothering on the later assumption of gender roles.
- In U.S. society today the composition of families and the roles within families are shifting. The age at first marriage has risen across the board, and rates of marriage have declined, particularly among the less educated; currently, nonmarital births account for more than 40% of all births. Divorce has leveled off but remains at a high level. Same-sex marriage has growing public support, though legislation at the state and federal levels legalizing it—and addressing same-sex divorce—lags behind changes in public attitudes.
- Socioeconomic class status affects child-rearing practices and family formation patterns. Lower rates of marriage and high rates of nonmarital births are present in the working class and among the poor. Middle-class family life is often structured around the needs of children.
- In addition to being a site of nurturing and caring, the family may be a site of violence such as spousal abuse and child abuse (both of which occur at high rates), as well as elder abuse.
- In the United States, the effects of globalization include changes in household income and employment opportunities. Women from developing countries often leave their homes and children to work for families in the developing world.

KEY TERMS

family, 267

marriage, 267

monogamy, 267

polygamy, 267

polygyny, 267

polyandry, 268

serial monogamy, 268

endogamous, 268

antimiscegenation laws, 268

extended families, 268

nuclear families, 269

sexual division of labor in modern societies, 270

cohabitation, 273

common-law marriage, 273

civil unions, 276

domestic partnerships, 276

domestic (or family) violence, 285

international families, 288

DISCUSSION QUESTIONS

1. Why do people get married? Why do people *not* marry? Think about individual and sociological reasons. Link your answers to the discussion of marriage trends and the experience of marriage discussed in this chapter.

2. Recent data show some changes in the child-care practices of U.S. families. What do trends show? How do sociological factors help to explain the changes?

3. How does the case of deaf families with hearing children show the opportunities and challenges of family life characterized by different cultures? Can this case be compared to immigrant families with children? What similarities and differences can you identify?

4. Lareau's research suggests that middle- and working-class families have different child-rearing styles. How does she describe these styles? Why might the differences be sociologically significant?

5. Who is the "global woman"? What are the costs and benefits to women and families of a global labor market for care work?

Sharpen your skills with SAGE edge at **edge.sagepub.com/chambliss2e**

A personalized approach to help you accomplish your course-work goals in an easy-to-use learning environment.

EDUCATION AND SOCIETY

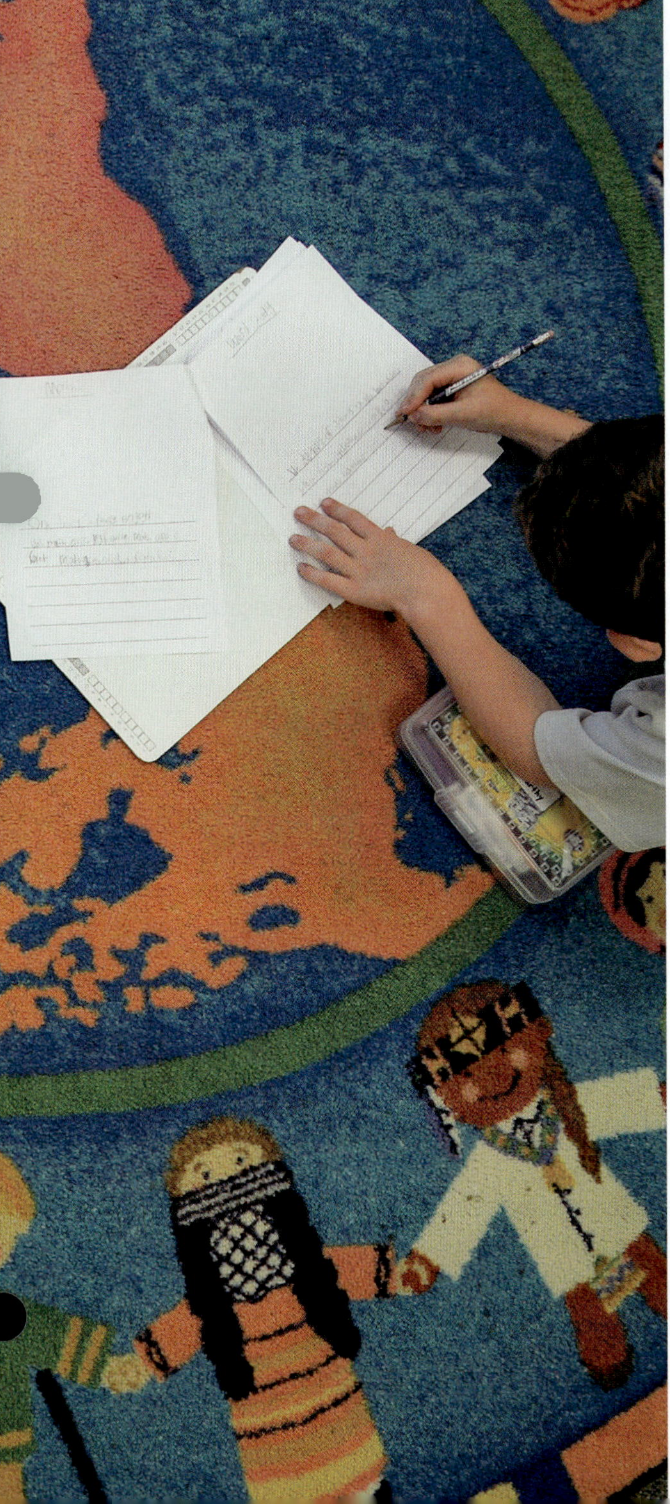

The Washington Post / Contributor/Getty Images

WHAT DO YOU THINK?

1. Why do significant numbers of students drop out of college before completing their degrees?
2. Why does racial segregation exist and persist in many U.S. public schools?
3. Why do schoolchildren in the United States have long summer holidays? What are the benefits and consequences of a long holiday from school?

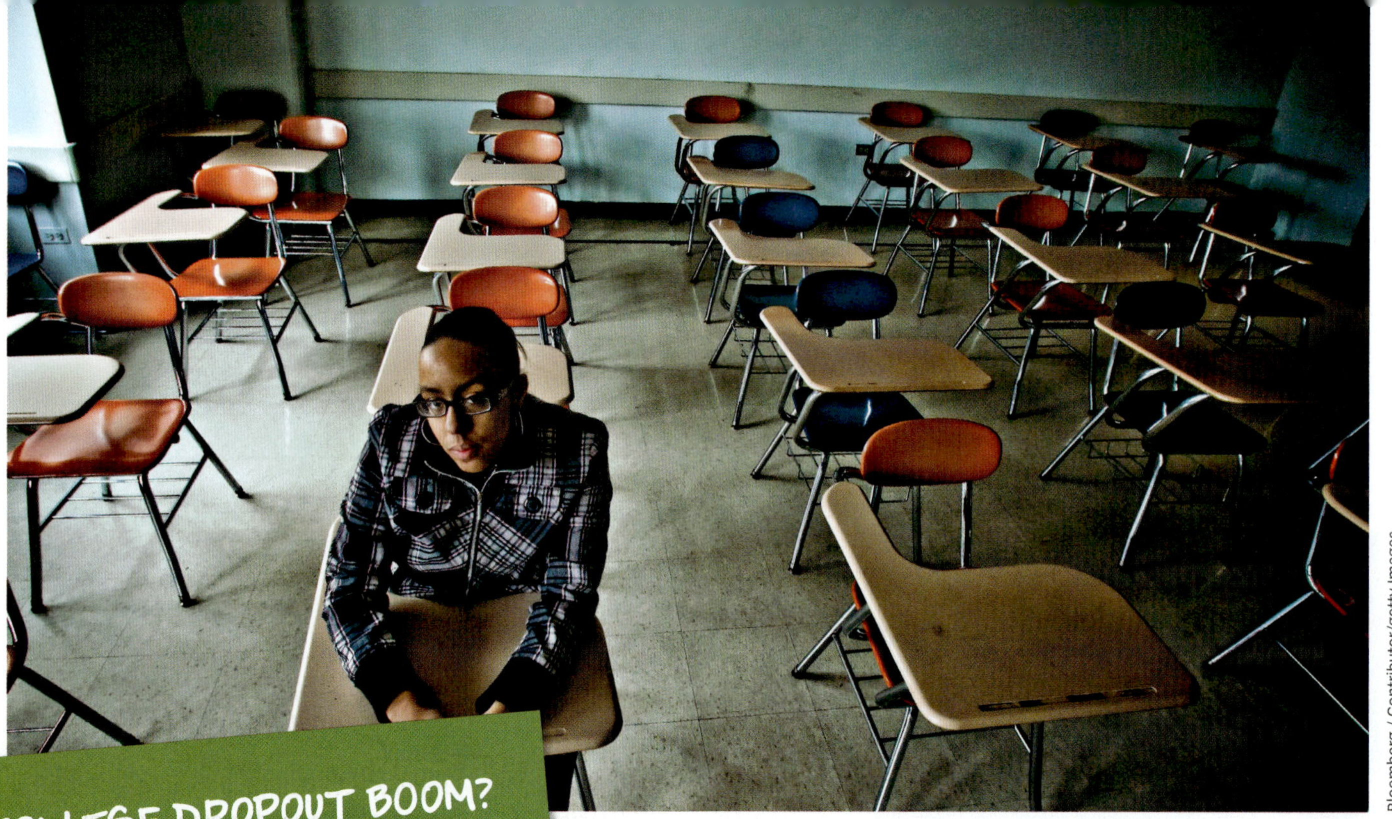

Bloomberg / Contributor/getty Images

A COLLEGE DROPOUT BOOM?

Most high school graduates in the United States today go to college. According to data from the National Center for Education Statistics (2013b), in 2012, 66% of high school completers enrolled in college. This figure has grown over time: In 1960, it was just 45%. Data suggest that education is more critical than ever for raising earning potential and ensuring competitiveness in the job market. In light of this, it is not surprising that more students are seeking to continue their education beyond high school.

Some critical observers, however, point out that all is not well in the hallowed halls of U.S. higher education. In fact, they suggest, the high rate of enrollment obscures a more troubling reality: Many students leave college with debt—and no degree. Journalist David Leonhardt (2009) writes that "in terms of its core mission—turning teenagers into educated college graduates—much of the system is simply failing."

Leonhardt observes that while the United States does an excellent job getting high school graduates to enroll in higher education, colleges on the whole have been far less successful in retaining students and fostering their timely graduation. A study done by the Harvard Graduate School of Education in 2011 notes that in the United States as a whole, just over half of college students (56%) complete 4-year degrees in a period of 6 years—and only 29% of those who enroll in 2-year college programs complete them in 3 years (Symonds, Schwartz, & Ferguson, 2011). The low graduation figures put the United States at the bottom of an 18-country Organisation for Economic Co-operation and Development (OECD) list for completion rates, with 46% of students completing college once they begin higher education—far behind countries such as Japan (89%) and Poland (61%).

What happens to the students who don't complete college? Why do they leave? Where do they go? These questions are of critical importance. On one hand, at the macro level, the U.S. economy needs an educated workforce. Dropouts diminish the potential for productivity and are costly in other ways as well:

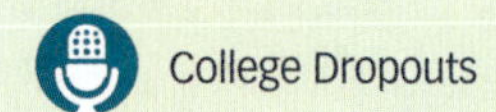

College Dropouts

States paid out about $6.2 billion to 4-year colleges and universities between 2003 and 2008 to support the education of students who never returned for a second year of studies (American Institutes for Research, 2010). On the other hand, at the micro level, most workers are better off for having completed college: Median weekly earnings for those who have a bachelor's degree are nearly 50% higher than the earnings for those who have some college, but no degree (U.S. Bureau of Labor Statistics, 2013a). The differences are even greater when those without a college degree are compared with those who have graduate, professional, and doctoral degrees. In this chapter, we examine the issue of college dropouts in more detail, looking into the sociological antecedents of this widespread phenomenon.

We begin the chapter with a discussion of the roots of mass public education in the United States and the development of the "credential society" that is driving rising enrollments in higher education today. We continue with a critical look at education, using the functionalist, conflict, and symbolic interactionist perspectives to think about its functions and outcomes in modern society. We then turn to the fundamentally important issue of education and inequality, examining education as a key to understanding how inequality is both reproduced and reduced. We next return to the theme introduced in the opener—that is, higher education in the United States. We consider the relationship between higher education and income, the growing internship phenomenon, and the problem of college dropouts. Finally, we look at education in a global perspective, comparing the United States to other countries in terms of the relationship between education and employment and discussing the growing interest of U.S. students in studying abroad.

EDUCATION, INDUSTRIALIZATION, AND THE "CREDENTIAL SOCIETY"

As societies change, so too does the role of **education**, *the transmission of society's norms, values, and knowledge base by means of direct instruction.* For much of human history, education occurred informally, within the family or the immediate community. Children often learned by doing—by working alongside their parents, siblings, and other relatives in the home, in the field, or on the hunt.

With the emergence of industrial society, **formal education**, *education that occurs within academic institutions such as schools,* became increasingly common. As schooling became increasingly important in industrial societies, it came to be seen as the birthright of all society members. **Mass education**, or *the extension of formal schooling to wide segments of the population,* is the norm today. Not only is mass education consistent with the democratic ideals held in most modern and economically advanced or advancing societies, but it is also the principal means by which people acquire the skills they need to participate effectively as workers and citizens in the midst of technological, cultural, and economic change of dramatic proportions.

Modern society requires its members to master a large number of complex skills. People must know how to read and write, but that is rarely enough. Societies need people to organize production, invent new products, and program computers—others engage in creating art or literature, curing diseases, resolving human conflicts, and addressing scientific challenges like climate change. Building an educated population requires more than the on-the-job training of apprentices or helpers. It requires the transmission of more knowledge than most families are willing or able to pass on from one generation to the next.

The first educational institutions in the United States were created in the 17th century by the religious leaders of the New England Puritan communities. Their original intent was to provide religious education; children were taught to read so that they could study Scripture (Monroe, 1940; Vinovskis, 1995). In 1647, the Massachusetts Bay Colony passed a law requiring every community of 50 or more people to establish a town school. The law, named Ye Old Deluder Satan Act, was intended to protect New England's youth from acquiescing to the temptations of the devil.

By the 18th century, the goal of education had shifted from religious training to cultivating practical and productive skills (Vinovskis, 1995). The emergence of industrial societies not only increased the need for people to be literate—**literacy** is defined as *the ability to read and write at a basic level*—but it also required that they learn skills, work habits, and discipline that would prepare them for jobs as industrial laborers, accountants, inventors, designers, merchandisers, lawyers, operators of complex machinery, and more (Bergen, 1996).

From the outset, schools in the United States were divided along social class lines. The sons of the middle and upper classes went to private schools that trained them for business and the professions. There were initially few public schools, and

Education: The transmission of society's norms, values, and knowledge base by means of direct instruction.

Formal education: Education that occurs within academic institutions such as schools.

Mass education: The extension of formal schooling to wide segments of the population.

Literacy: The ability to read and write at a basic level.

Changing Education Paradigms   CQR College and Social Mobility

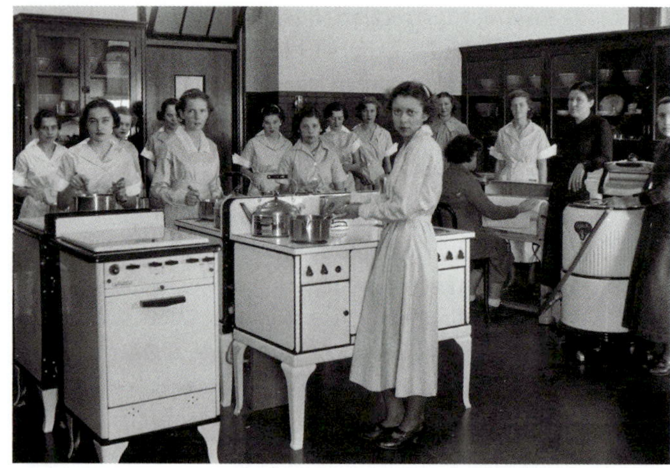

In the United States, girls and boys used to be educated separately and unequally in many public schools. Far fewer young women than today had the opportunity to go on to college and their high school education was more likely to emphasize skills in cooking and homemaking.

those that existed provided working- and lower-class children with the minimal education necessary for them to acquire the skills and obedience for factory work or farming (Bowles & Gintis, 1976; Wyman, 1997).

When workers began forming labor unions in the 19th century, one of their demands was for free **public education** for their children, *a universal education system provided by the government and funded by tax revenues rather than student fees* (fees served to exclude economically disadvantaged students from the classroom; Horan & Hargis, 1991). Political activists, philanthropic organizations, and newspapers joined the unions in their demand. By the late 19th century, public elementary schools had been established in most of the industrial centers of the United States, and mass public schooling soon spread throughout the country, though segregated by gender and race. In some places, no schooling was provided for girls or African Americans. In other places, girls and boys were educated separately and unequally, with girls receiving training in cooking and homemaking skills and boys being educated to be literate (Riordan, 1990; Tyack & Hansot, 1982). Schools for African Americans were segregated by law in the southern states until the U.S. Supreme Court ruled the practice unconstitutional in 1954; elsewhere in the country, Blacks and Whites attended different schools that offered unequal opportunities in education because they lived in different neighborhoods and schools were locally funded (Aviel, 1997; Bergen, 1996).

In some states, school attendance was compulsory for at least the first 6 years. The concept of public education was soon expanded to include high schools, and by the end of the 19th century, the average U.S. student achieved 8 years of schooling, while 10% completed high school and 2% completed college or university (Bettelheim, 1982; Vinovskis, 1992; Walters & James, 1992).

With the creation of mass public education, the United States increasingly became a **credential society**, *one in which access to desirable jobs and social status depends on the possession of a certificate or diploma certifying the completion of formal education* (Collins, 1979; Vinovskis, 1995). A socially validated credential such as a bachelor's degree or professional degree thus serves as a filter, determining the kinds of jobs and promotions for which a person is eligible. People with only high school diplomas have a difficult time competing in the job market with those who have college degrees, even if they possess keen intellect and good skills. If a position announcement indicates that a college degree is required, the candidate with only a high school diploma is unlikely to be considered at all. Since a person's job is a major determinant of income and social class, educational credentials play a major role in shaping opportunities for social and economic mobility.

Next we look at some key theoretical perspectives on education and its functions in modern society.

THEORETICAL PERSPECTIVES ON EDUCATION

What is the role of the educational system in society? While functionalist theorists highlight the ways in which the educational system is positively functional for society, conflict theorists point to its role in reinforcing and reproducing social stratification. Symbolic interactionist theories help to illuminate how relational processes in the classroom may contribute to educational success—or failure.

Public education: A universal education system provided by the government and funded by tax revenues rather than student fees.

Credential society: A society in which access to desirable work and social status depends on the possession of a certificate or diploma certifying the completion of formal education.

© Gideon Mendel/Corbis

School is an important agent of socialization. Among the lessons young children learn in school are obedience to authority and conformity to schedules, imperatives that some sociologists say are rooted in early capitalism's need for compliant workers.

THE FUNCTIONALIST PERSPECTIVE

Émile Durkheim (1922/1956, 1922/1973b), whose work forms a foundation for functionalist theorizing in sociology, wrote about the importance of education in modern societies. According to Durkheim, modern societies are complex, with specialized yet interdependent institutions. This complexity creates a special problem for *social solidarity*—that is, the bonds that unite the members of a social group. Modern society is no longer characterized by communities with high degrees of cultural, religious, or social homogeneity, so social ties have weakened. One function of mass education is to address this problem by socializing members of a society into the norms and values necessary to produce and maintain social solidarity. Durkheim talked about this function in terms of *moral education,* meaning that educational institutions not only provide the knowledge and training necessary for members to fulfill their economic roles in modern society but also function to socialize individuals, building solidarity in the group.

Contemporary functionalist theories echo Durkheim's concerns about social solidarity, emphasizing the function of formal education in socializing people into the norms, values, and skills necessary for society to survive and thrive (Parsons & Mayhew, 1982). Functionalist theory also proposes that education has both manifest and latent functions (Bourdieu & Coleman, 1991; Merton, 1968). What are these functions?

The manifest, or intended, functions of education include the transmission of general knowledge and specific skills needed in society and the economy, such as literacy and numeracy. The latent, or unintended, functions include the propagation of societal norms and values that Durkheim argued should be explicit concerns of *moral education.* For example, beginning with kindergarten, children learn to organize their lives according to schedules, to sit at desks, to follow rules, and to show respect for authority. Sociologist Harry Gracey (1991) has argued that "the unique job of the kindergarten seems . . . to be teaching children the student role. The student role is the repertoire of behavior and attitudes regarded by educators as appropriate to children in school" (p. 448). Having "mastered" the student role, children internalize the external social norms and rules that govern the school day and their academic lives.

Consider other latent functions of the system of mass public education in the United States. For example, in keeping children occupied from about 8:00 a.m. until 3:00 p.m., schools serve as supervisors for a large population of children whose parents work in order to contribute to both the micro-level economies of their homes and the productivity of the macro-level economy. Schools are also sources of peer socialization, offering an environment in which conventional gender roles are enacted and enforced. While some young people challenge expected roles through dress, for example, many conform in order to avoid conflict or ostracism. Can you think of other latent functions of mass education that are social, cultural, economic, or political?

What are the weaknesses of the functionalist perspective in furthering our understanding of the system of education? Critics suggest that it ignores schools' contribution to reproducing social inequality. Functionalist theory assumes, for instance, that the educational system educates people in accordance with their abilities and potential, giving credentials to those who deserve them and who can contribute most to society while withholding credentials from those incapable of doing the most demanding work. Critics, however, say schools function to reproduce the existing class system, favoring those who are already the most advantaged and putting obstacles in the paths of those who are disadvantaged. They point to substantial differences in educational attainment across socioeconomic groups (a topic we take up later in this chapter) as evidence that socioeconomic class status is just as important as intellectual capability in influencing educational attainment within the institution of education (Bowles & Gintis, 1976).

Notably as well, although education may socialize students into society's norms and values, it also undermines societal authority by promoting a critical approach to dominant ideas. Education contributes substantially to the development of a capacity for "self-direction" (Miller, Kohn, & Schooler, 1986), and students often develop inquiring, critical spirits because they are exposed to views and ways of thinking that challenge their previously held ideas. For example, Phelan and McLaughlin (1995) found that people with higher levels of education are more sympathetic to and less likely to blame homeless people for their condition than are people with lower levels of education.

THE CONFLICT PERSPECTIVE

Conflict theorists agree that education trains people in the dominant norms and values of society and the work skills and habits demanded by the economic system. However, they reject the functionalist notion that the system of education channels individuals into the positions for which they are best suited in terms of ambition, skills, and talents. Instead, they believe, it reproduces rather than reduces social stratification and, rather than ensuring that the best people train for and conscientiously perform the most socially important jobs (Davis & Moore, 1945), ensures that the discovery of talent will be limited (Tumin, 1953).

According to conflict theory, poor and working-class children have fewer opportunities to demonstrate their talents and abilities because they lack equal access to educational opportunities. Moreover, part of the "hidden curriculum" of the classroom is to socialize members of the working class to accept their class position (Bowles & Gintis, 1976). Children are taught at an early age to define their academic ambitions and abilities in keeping with the social class of their parents. These lowered educational ambitions are reinforced through inferior educational opportunities and labeling and discrimination in the classroom (Bowles & Gintis, 1976; Glazer, 1992; Kozol, 1991; Oakes, 1985; Willis, 1990).

Consider the experience of Malcolm X, a prominent champion of the rights of African Americans who was assassinated in 1965. In his autobiography, Malcolm X recounts how, despite being a top student, he was discouraged by his high school English teacher from becoming a lawyer:

> Mr. Ostrowski looked surprised, I remember. . . . He kind of half-smiled and said, "Malcolm, one of life's first needs is for us to be realistic. Don't misunderstand me, now. We all like you, you know that. . . . A lawyer—that's no realistic goal for a [Black man]. You need to think about something you can be. You're good with your hands—making things. . . . Why don't you plan on carpentry? People like you as a person—you'd get all kinds of work." (Haley & Malcolm X, 1964, p. 41)

Poor and minority children still experience lowered expectations and educational opportunities. Author Jonathan Kozol (2000) writes,

> Many people in Mott Haven [an impoverished neighborhood in the South Bronx] do a lot of work to make sure they are well-informed about the conditions in their children's public schools. Some also know a great deal more about the schools that serve the children of the privileged than many of the privileged themselves may recognize. They know that "business math" is not the same as calculus and that "job-readiness instruction" is not European history or English literature. They know that children of rich people do not often spend semesters of their teenage years in classes where they learn to type an application for an entry-level clerical position; they know that these wealthy children are too busy learning composition skills and polishing their French pronunciation and receiving preparation for the SATs. They come to understand the process by which a texture of enlightenment is stitched together for some children while it is denied to others. They also understand that, as the years go by, some of these children will appear to have deserved one kind of role in life, and some another. (pp. 100–101)

Among the most prominent conflict theorists in the sociology of education are Samuel Bowles and Herbert Gintis, whose 1976 book *Schooling in Capitalist America* posited three key arguments. First, the authors argued that schools not only impart cognitive skills but also "prepare people to function well and without complaint in the hierarchical structure of the modern corporation" (p. ix). Second, Bowles and Gintis used statistical data to support the argument that parental economic status is passed on to children, at least in part, through unequal educational opportunity, though the advantages conferred on children of higher-social-status families are not limited to their educational preparation. Finally, the authors suggested that the modern school system was not the product of the evolutionary perfection of democratic pedagogy, but rather primarily a reflection of the interests of expanding capitalist enterprises such as factories.

Frequently cited results of Bowles and Gintis's early work include a graph showing the powerful correlation between socioeconomic status (as measured by income) and educational attainment. The data, from a sample of men with similar childhood IQ scores, demonstrate an unmistakable relationship between the socioeconomic backgrounds of the subjects and the average number of years of education they completed (Figure 12.1).

FIGURE 12.1 Relationship Between U.S. Family Income and Years of Schooling for White Males Ages 35–44, 1962

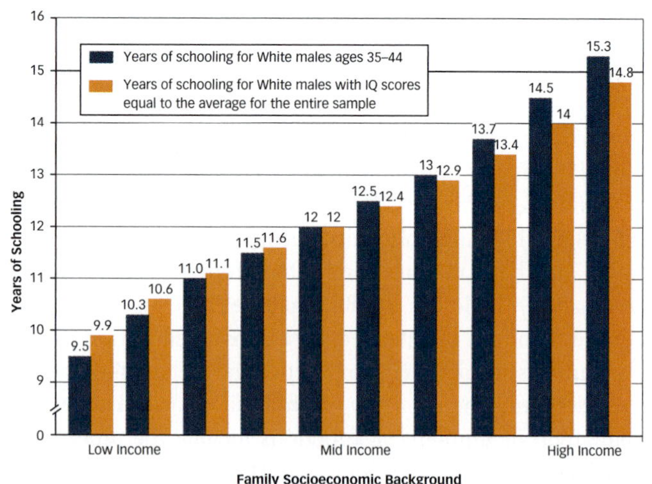

SOURCE: Bowles, Samuel, and Herbert Gintis. *Schooling in Capitalist America: Educational Reform and the Contradictions of Economic Life.* Copyright © 1976 Bowles, Samuel; Gintis, Herbert M. Reprinted by permission of Basic Books, a member of the Perseus Books Group.

FIGURE 12.2 Bachelor's Degree Completion Rates by Family Income Quartile and SAT-Equivalent Score

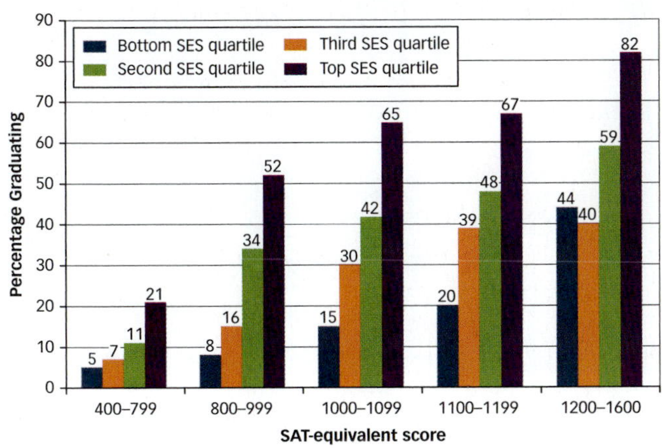

SOURCE: Fox, M. A., Connolly, B. A., & Snyder, T. D. (2005). *Youth indicators 2005: Trends in the well-being of American youth* (NCES 2005-050). U.S. Department of Education, National Center for Education Statistics. Washington, DC: U.S. Government Printing Office

While a precise update of Bowles and Gintis's data is not available, other data on the correlations among family income category, demonstrated academic potential, and educational attainment show that the same relationship identified by the theorists is still relevant decades later. For example, Figure 12.2 shows bachelor's degree completion rates by both family income quartile (fourth) and SAT-equivalent score. Note that among the highest scoring students, fully 82% of high-income students graduated, whereas just 44% of low-income students graduated. The graduation gap appears to be consistent across score categories: In every category, students in the top two income groups were far more likely to graduate than are their lower-income counterparts.

Critics of conflict theories of education point out that education, even in highly stratified societies, offers an important way for poor and working-class people to improve their circumstances, and it remains the primary means of upward mobility. Education has been a crucial path by which generations of U.S. immigrants have escaped poverty. Thus, although it may contribute to the reproduction of an unequal socioeconomic structure, the educational system also provides meaningful opportunities for mobility and change.

THE SYMBOLIC INTERACTIONIST PERSPECTIVE

The functionalist and conflict perspectives highlight the role of education in society. Symbolic interactionists, in contrast, study what occurs in the classroom, alerting us to subtle and not-so-subtle ways in which schools affect students' self-images. By looking at how students are labeled, for instance, symbolic interactionists shed light on the way schools help to reinforce and perpetuate differences among students.

In a classic study, Rosenthal and Jacobson (1968) conducted an intriguing experiment in which elementary school teachers were intentionally misinformed about the intelligence test scores of selected students. The teachers were told, in confidence, that certain students had scored unusually high on standardized tests the previous year. In fact, these students had been randomly selected and were no different in known intelligence from their peers. Rosenthal and Jacobson then observed the interactions between these students and their teachers and monitored the students' academic performance. The students labeled "exceptional" soon outperformed their peers, a difference that persisted for several years.

The teachers described the labeled students as "more curious" or "more interested" and communicated their heightened expectations of these learners through their voices, facial expressions, and use of praise. Enacting a *self-fulfilling prophecy,* the students came to see themselves through their teachers' eyes and began performing as if they were, in fact, more intelligent than their peers, earning still more positive attention from teachers. Younger students, whose self-images were more flexible, exhibited the greatest improvements in performance. Rosenthal and Jacobson concluded that the teachers behaved differently toward some students because the students had been labeled "exceptional."

The findings of other studies suggest similar conclusions. A study of student–teacher interaction in a largely African American kindergarten found that such labels as "fast" and "slow," which the teacher assigned by the eighth day of class, tended to stay with the labeled students throughout the year (Rist, 1970). More recent research has confirmed the harmful effects of teachers' stereotyped beliefs about minority students' competence on those students' performance (Garcia & Guerra, 2004). Another study found that female and Asian American

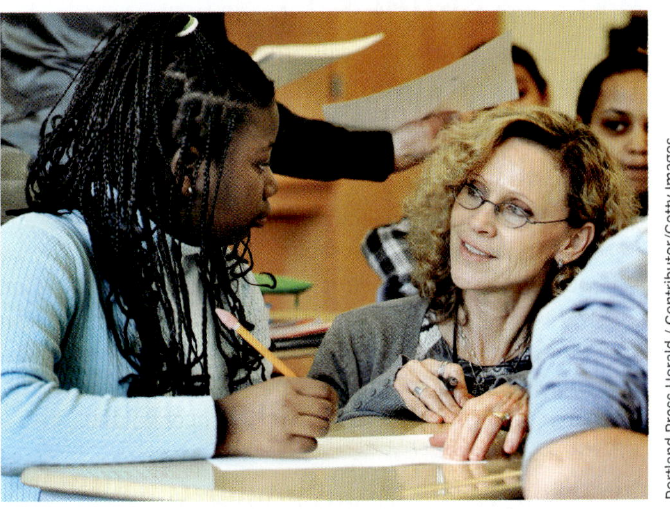

Portland Press Herald / Contributor/Getty Images

Rosenthal and Jacobson's experiment raises interesting questions: Is intentionally deceptive labeling ethical, as it both misinforms the teacher and may confer advantage on some students to the detriment of others? Can it be justified as a social scientific endeavor?

students frequently received classroom grades higher than their actual test scores, while Latino, Black, and White males received lower grades (Farkas, Grobe, Sheehan, & Shuan, 1990; Farkas, Sheehan, & Grobe, 1990). The differences had to do with the teachers' perceptions of their students' "attitudes." Those who appeared to be attentive and cooperative were judged to be hard workers and good students, and were graded up; those who appeared to be indifferent or hostile were graded down. Again, more recent research has reached similar findings regarding teacher bias (Rosenbloom & Way, 2004).

Classroom labeling has been studied in other countries as well. In one influential study, Paul Willis (1990) found that British boys from working-class families were systematically labeled as low academic achievers and socialized to think of themselves as capable of doing only working-class jobs. The boys understood quite well that this labeling process worked against them, and they resisted it by the use of humor and other challenges to authority. These behaviors reinforced their teachers' perception that the boys would never make it and would eventually drop out of school and assume their "rightful position" in the working class. The boys thus accepted their teachers' labeling, creating a self-fulfilling prophecy in which they wound up in working-class jobs.

Symbolic interactionism is well suited to studying the ways in which teachers consciously or unintentionally affect their students, but a critic might note that because it focuses on social interaction, it cannot give us a picture of the role of the educational system in society as a whole or help us recognize and analyze structural problems such as unequal funding of schools across poor, middle-class, and wealthy areas.

EDUCATION, OPPORTUNITY, AND INEQUALITY

Functionalists argue that education provides a means for mobility and for filling the positions necessary for society to survive and thrive. Conflict theorists posit that the educational system reinforces existing inequalities by unequally according opportunities based on class, race, or gender. In fact, the U.S. educational system may operate to open avenues to mobility *and* create obstacles to achievement among the less privileged—that is, it may both reduce and reproduce inequality. In the following sections we look at issues of education and inequality, focusing in particular on questions about early childhood literacy and later educational achievement, income and poverty, school segregation by race and income, and public school funding.

ILLITERACY AND WORD POVERTY: THE CHILDHOOD CHALLENGE

Researcher Louisa Cook Moats uses the term *word poverty* to characterize the impoverished language environments in which some children grow up. Word poverty is a particular problem in economically disadvantaged homes: Research on a community in California found that by age 5, children in impoverished language environments had heard 32 million fewer words spoken to them than the average middle-class child. Perhaps not surprisingly, the fewer words that were spoken to children, the fewer they could actively use themselves: In a study of how many words children could produce at age 3, "children from impoverished environments used less than half the number of words already spoken by their more advantaged peers" (Wolf, 2008, pp. 102–103).

© Sebastien Desarmaux/Corbis

Early literacy has been linked by researchers to later academic achievement. Children who do not learn to read by early elementary school often struggle to catch up later and are at higher risk than their peers of dropping out of high school.

Word poverty is also linked to a deficit of books in the homes of many children. Research conducted in three Los Angeles communities found that in the most economically impoverished community in the study, it was common to find no children's books in the home. In low- to middle-income homes, an average of 3 books could be found. By contrast, in the most affluent families, there was an average of 200 books in each home (Wolf, 2008). According to a global study, the deficit or wealth of books in a home is of significance in children's later schooling: Being raised in a home without books is as likely to affect children's educational attainment as having parents with very low educational attainment. The researchers conclude that "growing up in a home with 500 books would propel a child 3.2 years further in education, on average" (Evans, Kelley, Sikora, & Treiman, 2010, p. 179). In the United States, the advantage to having an expansive library is an average of more than 2 years of education. Commenting on the study, an article on the website ScienceDaily noted, "the researchers were struck by the strong effect having books in the home had on children's educational attainment even above and beyond such factors as education level of the parents, the country's GDP [gross domestic product], the father's occupation or the political system of the country" (University of Nevada, Reno, 2010).

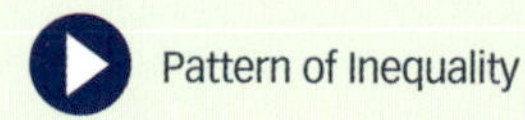

FIGURE 12.3 Literacy Rates of U.S. Adults, 2003

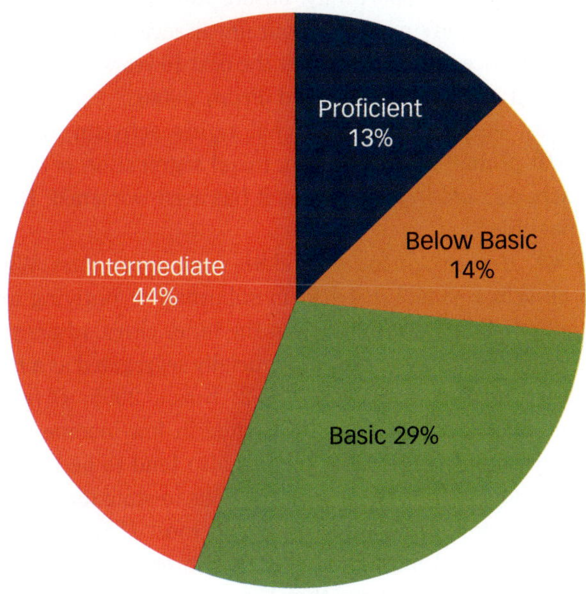

SOURCE: National Center for Education Statistics. 2011. "Literacy skills of adults, by type of literacy, proficiency levels, and selected characteristics: 1992 and 2003." *Digest of Education Statistics, 2010.*

Why is word poverty significant? The answer is that it is linked to low literacy. A fundamental necessity for any country in the modern world is a population that is functionally literate. No less important, literacy is necessary for individual success in education and the job market. The National Assessment of Adult Literacy (NAAL, 2011) defines basic literacy as "using printed and written information to function in society, to achieve one's goals, and to develop one's knowledge and potential." NAAL identifies four categories of literacy: below basic, basic, intermediate, and proficient (Figure 12.3). A large-scale NAAL study using a population of 19,000 representative respondents found the following:

- About 14% of U.S. adults (or 30 million people) fell *below basic* on the literacy test. That is, they could successfully complete "no more than the most *simple* and *concrete* literacy skills," such as locating the intersection of two streets on a clearly labeled map and circling the date of a medical appointment on a hospital appointment slip.
- About 29% of the population (63 million) scored in the *basic* category, meaning they could "perform simple and everyday literacy activities," including finding a table on a specified topic in an almanac and summarizing what articles in a given section of a magazine were about by using information from the table of contents.
- Another 44% (95 million) fell into the *intermediate* category. They could "perform moderately challenging literacy activities" such as following directions on a clearly labeled map and finding the age range during which children should receive a given vaccine using a chart on recommended childhood immunizations.
- Finally, about 13% of the population (28 million) were categorized as *proficient,* which indicated they could "perform complex and challenging literacy activities." They could interpret survey data presented in a nested table and contrast financial information presented in a table about the differences between different types of credit cards.

Wolf (2008) suggests that a strong foundation in literacy is a key to later educational success. That is, students who enter high school with shaky foundations in literacy as a result of early childhood experiences such as word poverty or a deficit of books in the home have a higher probability of school failure than do their peers who grew up in homes with books and parents who read to them at an early age. At the same time, failure to complete high school is likely to affect someone's ability to complete literacy activities successfully (45% of adults in the lowest literacy category had completed high school). If you were to research the correlation between prose literacy and high school completion, how might you proceed? What variables would you choose to study and why? What kind of relationship would you hypothesize?

SCHOOL SEGREGATION

School segregation, *the education of racial minorities in schools that are geographically, economically, and/or socially separated from those attended by the racial majority (Whites),* is a long-standing pattern that is worsening today, despite more than four decades of civil rights legislation intended to alleviate it and reduce its devastating effects. School segregation has long been linked to educational inequality in the United States.

Before slavery was abolished in the United States, it was a crime to teach slaves to read and write; formal education was reserved solely for Whites. Immediately following the abolition of slavery and the end of the Civil War, schools were integrated, but Jim Crow laws soon initiated a century of discrimination against Black Americans in the South. These laws determined, among other things, where Black Americans could live, where they could eat and shop, and where they would be educated. In the North, there were no laws segregating schools by race, but segregated schooling occurred nonetheless as a consequence of racial residential segregation.

Both law and custom created schools segregated by race in the United States until the 1950s (Jordan, 1992). Black activists

School segregation: The education of racial minorities in schools that are geographically, economically, and/or socially separated from those attended by Whites.

CQR Desegregation in School

Gender-segregated classrooms are uncommon in public schools today. Racially segregated classrooms, however, continue to be common.

challenged the constitutionality of segregation, but U.S. courts repeatedly found it did not violate the U.S. Constitution. For example, in its 1896 *Plessy v. Ferguson* decision, the U.S. Supreme Court upheld the states' rights to segregate public accommodations as long as they followed the principle of "separate but equal." In 1954, however, the Supreme Court reversed itself. Relying in part on social science research showing that segregated schools were not in fact equal, the Court ruled in *Brown v. Board of Education of Topeka* that laws segregating public schools were unconstitutional (Miller, 1995).

This decision met with considerable resistance, especially in the South, where schools were segregated by law. Governor George Wallace of Alabama personally blocked the entrance to the University of Alabama in an effort to stop Black students from enrolling, and a Black college student named James Meredith went to prison for trying to enroll and attend classes at the University of Mississippi. Black and White students who tried to integrate schools were beaten by police and fellow citizens (Branch, 1988; Chong, 1991; McCartney, 1992).

Court challenges, civil protests, and mass civil disobedience ultimately broke down barriers, and some racial integration of schools took place across the country. Although the Supreme Court decision in *Brown v. Board of Education* had prohibited purposeful discrimination on the basis of race, it did not provide for specific methods to achieve school integration. The fact that racial and ethnic groups were residentially segregated meant that, in fact, most Blacks would continue to attend schools that were predominantly Black, while Whites would continue to attend mostly White schools.

Subsequent court decisions provided one method of achieving integration: *school busing,* a court-ordered program of transporting public school students to schools outside their neighborhoods. Mandated busing proved highly controversial, provoking criticism among some academics and hostility among many parents and policy makers. Controversy erupted in 1974 when Black students were bused into poor Irish neighborhoods in South Boston, whose schools were among the worst in the state. Instead of providing equal educational opportunity, busing worsened racial conflict in some of Boston's most economically disadvantaged neighborhoods. Violence resulted, and over the next 10 years public school enrollment in the city plummeted (Frum, 2000).

Today, despite decades of civil rights activism and laws aimed at promoting integration, racial segregation persists in U.S. schools, and in some places it has even worsened. How is this possible?

First, the movement of middle- and upper-class Whites into all-White school districts in suburban or outlying areas has left mostly poor minorities in the inner cities, where some schools have become almost fully racially segregated as a result (Coleman, Hoffer, & Kilgore, 1982; Kozol, 2005; Orfield & Eaton, 1996). Because they are located in low-income neighborhoods, highly segregated schools also tend to be the most poorly funded. While there are variations in state formulas for funding schools, the source on which most U.S. school districts still depend most heavily is local property tax revenue. While this system ensures that those who live in areas with high property values will generally accrue adequate—or even excellent—funds for the physical plant and academic programs of their schools, it also puts those who live in poor rural and urban areas at a distinct disadvantage, since even high property tax rates cannot bring in the level of resources that schools in middle- to upper-class areas enjoy. Further, White families that remain in urban areas often choose to send their children to private schools. As a consequence, most students still attend schools with a high degree of racial segregation (Ball, Bowe, & Gewirtz, 1995; Kozol, 2005).

Second, U.S. Supreme Court decisions such as *Board of Education of Oklahoma City v. Dowell, Freeman v. Pitts,* and *Missouri v. Jenkins* have limited the scope of previous laws aimed at promoting racial integration of schools. The Court has ruled that segregated schools resulting from "residential preferences" are a result of people making choices about where to reside and are therefore beyond the scope of the law. The Court declared in these cases that school districts that previously had made an effort to integrate schools could send students back to neighborhood schools even if those schools were segregated and inferior (Orfield & Eaton, 1996).

Latino and Black students are more likely to be in segregated schools today than in earlier decades (Figure 12.4). In Chicago in 2011, for instance, 43% of students enrolled in public school were either Black or Hispanic; 9% were White. In Washington, D.C., public school enrollment is 91% African American and Latino—in Detroit the figure is 92% (Federal Education Budget Project, 2012). Schools that operate under **de facto segregation** face many daunting problems, including

De facto segregation: School segregation based on residential patterns or student choice, which persists even though legal segregation is now outlawed in the United States.

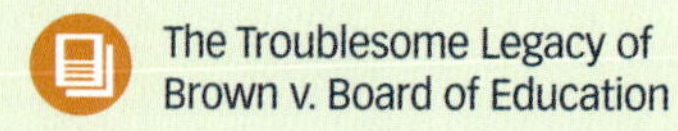
The Troublesome Legacy of Brown v. Board of Education

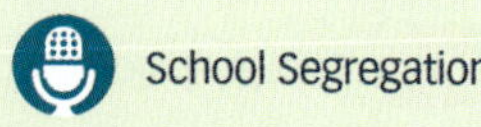
School Segregation

Which classroom would you rather be in? Across the country, unequal funding of public schools and the resulting inequalities in resources are problems that perpetuate disparities in education and upward mobility.

low levels of competition and expectation, less qualified teachers who leave as soon as they get seniority, more limited curricula, peer pressure against academic achievement and supportive of crime and substance abuse, high levels of teen pregnancy, few connections with colleges and employers who can assist students, less serious academic counseling and preparation for college, and powerless parents who themselves failed in school and do not know how to evaluate or change schools. (Orfield & Eaton, 1996, p. 54)

FIGURE 12.4 Racial Composition of U.S. Public Schools in Selected Cities, 2011

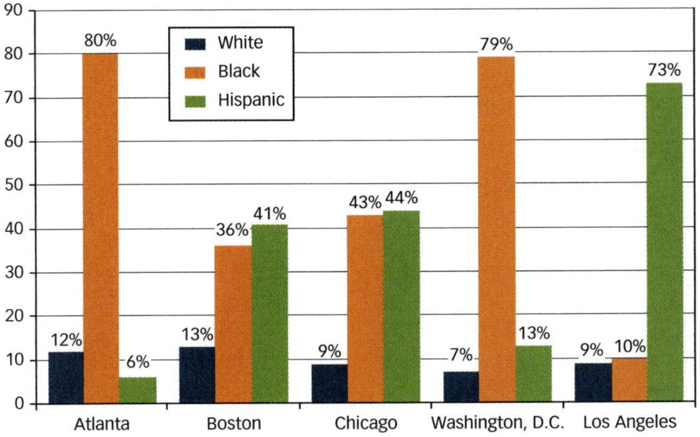

SOURCE: Federal Education Budget Project. 2012. "Comparative analysis of funding, student demographics and achievement data." New America Foundation.

By contrast, middle-class Asian American students are almost entirely integrated into schools with Whites. Asian American communities such as "Chinatowns" and "Little Saigons" are exceptions to this rule, however, especially among recent immigrants from China, Vietnam, Korea, and other Asian countries (Chen, 1992; Loo, 1991; Zhou, 2009).

American Indians on reservations are the most segregated of all minorities. The various tribes are recognized by treaty as separate nations whose rights are governed by agreements between them and the U.S. government. Their schools are run by the Bureau of Indian Affairs, which employs teachers and sets the curriculum. Treaties between the U.S. government and Indian nations have sought to ensure education that recognizes the value of American Indian culture and tradition. Yet the teachers employed by the Bureau of Indian Affairs are ordinarily expected to cover the standard subjects of U.S. school curricula, and in English. Problems within the tribal communities have resulted, since Indians often see such instruction as failing to respect their linguistic and cultural differences.

LIVING IN THE PAST? THE U.S. SCHOOL CALENDAR IN MODERN SOCIETY

Some people believe that students in the United States are falling behind their international peers because they spend less time in the classroom (Table 12.1). Two popular proposals to expand classroom time are lengthening the school day and lengthening the school year. Below we explore these two ideas, look at the roots of the current calendar, and consider some of its consequences.

TABLE 12.1 Mandated School Days in Selected Countries, 2009

Country	Average Number of School Days per Year
United States	180
France	180
England	190
Germany	198
Italy	200
Netherlands	200
Spain	200
Korea	220

SOURCE: International Review of Curriculum and Assessment Frameworks Internet Archive. 2009. "Table 15.1: Organisation of School Year."

As economist Peter Orszag (2012) notes, "School hours in the United States were developed during the 19th century, in part to allow students to help their families with farm work in the afternoon." Thus, around the time mass schooling began, the school day was designed to accommodate the needs of families sustained by agriculture, needs that are no longer so widespread. Should the school day now be lengthened?

On one hand, consider that many students participate in after-school sports, clubs, and other activities. No small number of full-time high school students also work; about 16% worked in 2010, although that is about a 50% decline from the 34% employed in 2000 (U.S. Bureau of Labor Statistics, 2011c). Homework loads, particularly at the high school level, may be substantial; a longer school day, unless it included more study time, might impede students' completion of homework. Also, a longer school day would cost taxpayers more: "In 2008, the Center for American Progress estimated that expanding learning time by 30 percent—or adding between 90 minutes and two hours to the school day—would add 6 to 20 percent to school budgets" (Orszag, 2012).

On the other hand, a longer school day has been shown to correlate with academic gains (Dobbie & Fryer, 2011), suggesting one avenue for raising achievement levels as the United States works to build a competitive workforce for the future. As well, about 15 million children, including some as young as 5 years old, are currently unsupervised by an adult after school (Orszag, 2012). The opportunity to stay longer in a safe learning environment may benefit children who might otherwise have little to do. It might even reduce crime. According to the Office of Juvenile Justice and Delinquency Prevention (2010), most violent juvenile crimes occur in the hours after the school day ends. As sociologists we are always aware that correlation is not causation, but this relationship bears close examination. While some of the young people getting into trouble in these hours are dropouts who would not be affected by a longer school day, some offenders and victims are also full-time students.

What about lengthening the school year? In the early part of the 19th century, schoolchildren attended school mostly in the winter and summer, so they could participate in spring and fall planting and harvest seasons (Gold, 2002). By the mid- to late 19th century, the average school calendar stretched across those seasons, but summer classes had largely been eliminated—not to accommodate agriculture as is commonly believed but rather to respond to the desires of a socioeconomic elite for holidays and a break from mental work. In the early 20th century, a time of high immigration from Europe, some "vacation schools" arose in cities to "decongest and decriminalize crowded neighborhoods, assimilate immigrant children, and provide practical skills" (Gold, 2002, p. 5). Later these were replaced by summer schools, the purpose of which was largely to serve those who had fallen behind during the regular school year.

Is it time to return to summertime education? Some contend that doing so would be costly in a time of shrinking budgets. And, as in the mid- to late 19th century, the now much larger middle and upper classes might object to a school year that impinges on their holiday calendar.

On the other hand, some research suggests that children may lose up to 2 months of acquired grade-level skills in math computation skills over the course of the summer. The same study found that low-income children, who are about 2.5 years behind their better-off peers by grade 5, also lose the equivalent of 2 months of reading achievement (Cooper, Nye, Charlton, Lindsay, & Greathouse, 1996). A study conducted in Baltimore suggests that about two-thirds of the reading achievement gap between ninth graders in lower- and higher-income groups is traceable to differences in summer experiences. Compounding this effect, differences in summer learning activities during elementary school may have an impact on whether a child graduates from high school and matriculates in college (Alexander, Entwisle, & Olson, 2007). While many middle- and upper-income students have the opportunity for enriching camp, holiday, and educational experiences in the summer—and middle-class children make small gains in reading achievement during these months—low-income children whose parents may not have the time or resources to offer these advantages are particularly susceptible to what educators term *summer slide,* the loss of knowledge and skills gained during the school year.

Should the school day or year be lengthened to serve the new economy, young people, poor families, or other groups? Or should the United States continue to use the model that has been in place for more than a century?

BEHIND THE NUMBERS

HOW MANY PEOPLE DROP OUT OF HIGH SCHOOL?

According to the National Center for Education Statistics (NCES; 2013a), in 2009, 8% of U.S. students dropped out of high school. This statistic includes White students with a dropout rate of 5%, Black students with a dropout rate of 9%, Hispanic students with a dropout rate of over 17%, and Asian or Pacific Islander students with a dropout rate of more than 3%. These figures represent the *status dropout rate,* the percentage of 16- through 24-year-olds in the civilian, noninstitutionalized population who are not enrolled in school and have not earned a high school credential, whether a high school diploma or a general equivalency degree (GED).

Here is another view of the picture. Data from the U.S. Census Bureau (2012d) show that 3.1% of U.S. students dropped out of high school in 2009. Within this category, 3% of Whites dropped out, as well as more than 4% of Black and 5% of Hispanic students. These data represent *event dropout rates,* or the percentage of 10th to 12th graders who dropped out in a single year without completing high school.

High school dropout can also be measured with the *cohort dropout rate,* which focuses on the outcomes for a single group (cohort) of students over a period of time—for example, the percentage of ninth graders in New York City who are reported as dropouts 4 years later (having left high school without completing a degree). This measure yields, predictably, the largest dropout rate of the three, because it is stretched across a longer time span. The cohort dropout rate, unlike the status dropout rate, generally does not count GED credentials as high school completion.

When we read press articles or hear public discussions of the dropout phenomenon in the United States, we are rarely given information on the sources of the statistics or instruments used to measure them. For example, a *New York Times* article on the cost of dropouts to the U.S. economy notes that "only 7 of 10 ninth graders today will get high school diplomas . . . about 80 percent of white and Asian students graduate from high school, compared with only 55 percent of blacks and Hispanics" (Levin & Rouse, 2012). It is unclear from these figures which of the dropout measures is being used or how "dropouts" are defined.

FIGURE 12.5 Percentages of Incarcerated U.S. Males Ages 16–24 by Educational Attainment, 2006–2007

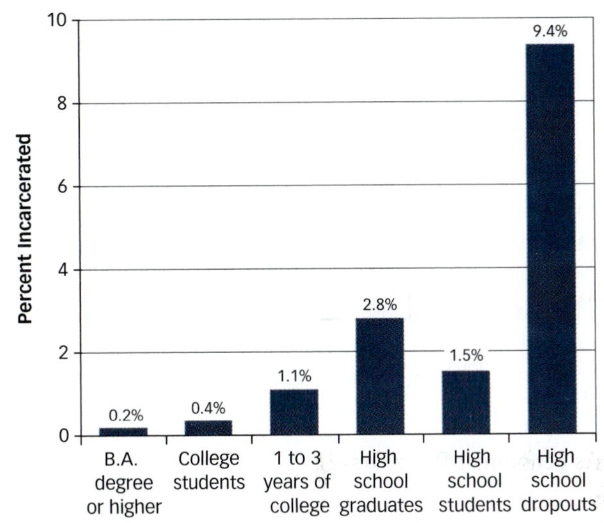

SOURCE: Sum, Andrew; Khatiwada, Ishwar; and McLaughlin, Joseph, "The consequences of dropping out of high school: joblessness and jailing for high school dropouts and the high cost for taxpayers" (2009). *Center for Labor Market Studies Publications.* Paper 23.

Further, as with poverty and unemployment figures, the institutionalized (imprisoned) population is excluded from most calculations of dropouts. In 1980, the status dropout rate for African Americans in the NCES measure was 19.1%. In 2009, it was 9.3%, a significant decline. On one hand, this represents more robust efforts on the part of schools to reduce rates of early school leaving and greater educational gains for African Americans overall. On the other hand, it also represents a measurement issue. Because the proportion of African American men who are in prison *and* are high school dropouts is high (see Figure 12.5), the failure to include them gives us a potentially incomplete picture.

It is important for us to be critical consumers of information and to pay attention not only to what is being measured but also to *how* it is measured, what a statistic illuminates and obscures, and how figures are used in the press and public discourse.

THINK IT THROUGH

▶ Use the search engine of a major national newspaper or other news source to search for the term *high school dropout rates*. You may want to include the name of a state or city in your search as well. Examine what you find. Do the sources of data you find include information on how the data were collected? Why is it important to know this?

EDUCATION, INCOME, AND POVERTY

What is the relationship between education and income? There is a powerful correlation, with greater education generally leading to a higher level of income. For example, in 2012, the mean earnings of a high school graduate were just over $33,000, while for a bachelor's degree holder they were over $55,000. For those who did not complete high school, mean earnings were just $24,492 (U.S. Bureau of Labor Statistics, 2013a).

The relationship between education and income opportunities and prospects has grown in significance as the labor market in the United States has shifted from industrial to postindustrial. In the former, positions with solid incomes and security were available in manufacturing for those with a high school education (or less). In particular, men with less education had opportunities to earn a living wage and advance their economic position over time. In contrast, the postindustrial economy has increased the number of jobs for those with high levels of skill and training, and the number of jobs in the service sector for those with less education. However, service jobs—including retail sales, child and elder care, and restaurant jobs—fail to provide the standard of living that many manufacturing jobs, particularly those in unionized sectors, once offered. As a result, the income advantage of those with higher education and the relative and absolute disadvantages of those with less education have grown markedly.

The correlation between education and income, and that between education and wealth, can be further linked to labor force participation. That is, those with higher incomes are more likely to participate in the paid labor force. U.S. Bureau of Labor Statistics (2014d) data show that in 2013, the labor force participation rate for those without a high school diploma was 40%, while for high school graduates it was over 54% and for college graduates over 72%.

Clearly, low income and poverty are powerfully linked to the lack of human capital among those who have not completed a high school or college education. Are they thus the products of an individual's failure to invest in him- or herself by ambitiously pursuing an education? The sociological imagination suggests a more complex relationship: To paraphrase C. Wright Mills, if, in a country of 300 million, only a handful of men or women are poor or undereducated, we properly look to the character of the individual, his or her skills, and his or her immediate opportunities. But when, in a nation of 300 million inhabitants, more than 15%—over 46 million people—are poor and millions have not achieved a high school education (see the *Behind the Numbers* box on page 307), we may not hope to find the explanation or solution in the choices, character, or behavior of any given individual. "Both the correct statement of the problem and the range of possible solutions require us to consider the economic and political institutions of the society, and not merely the personal situation and character of a scatter of individuals" (Mills, 1959/2000b, p. 9).

To appreciate the sociological linkages between education and low income or poverty, we need to look not only at the well-established relationship between education and income but also at factors that affect educational attainment. We should understand educational attainment as the product of both *agency* and *structure*. Individuals have agency. That is, they make choices about pursuing schooling, sacrificing immediate income for deferred income, and investing time and money in an education. On the other hand, the choices they make are based on the opportunities available to them, and those from more privileged backgrounds typically have more opportunities for good-quality schooling, from preschool through college. A higher family income raises the likelihood of a person's finishing high school and, as we will see later in the chapter, college.

The sociological imagination would lead us to conclude that in order to understand the linkage between income and education, we need to look beyond the simple relationship between educational attainment and income level and examine the way socioeconomic status itself influences the level of education an individual achieves, which then further influences income in a cycle that can be challenging to break.

ISSUES IN U.S. HIGHER EDUCATION

In the United States today, nearly three quarters of high school graduates continue on to higher education. The value and even the necessity of higher education in the modern world and economy are common themes in both educational and political discourse. The good jobs of the future, we have been told, will require higher education. Below we look at the general issue of college and income, examining the relationship of education to income today. We continue with an examination of the college internship, a growing phenomenon that has invited both praise and critique. We end with a closer discussion of the topic raised in the opening vignette—that is, the college dropout phenomenon, its dimensions, and its probable causes and possible cures.

COLLEGE AND INCOME

In Figure 12.6, we see a clear and unequivocal correlation between educational attainment and income, and between educational attainment and vulnerability to unemployment. We have seen in other chapters that educational attainment has grown in importance in the postindustrial era, as the living wage jobs of the industrial era in sectors such as automobile manufacturing, steel, and textiles have fallen victim to outsourcing and automation. What remains as the foundation of the U.S. economy are advanced professional occupations, which require higher education and often even graduate degrees, and service jobs, which are often part-time, low-pay, and low-benefit positions in sectors such as child and elder care, retail, and hospitality. While some manufacturing has continued to be sited in the United States, new manufacturing jobs are far less likely to be unionized, more likely to involve short-term contracts, and characterized by a lower pay scale than similar jobs in the past (see Chapter 15). A substantial number of new manufacturing jobs demand proficiency with high-technology equipment, which may require either college education or other advanced training beyond high school. In this economic environment, education does, indeed, appear to pay—handsomely so.

FIGURE 12.6 Earnings and Employment by Educational Attainment in the United States, 2013

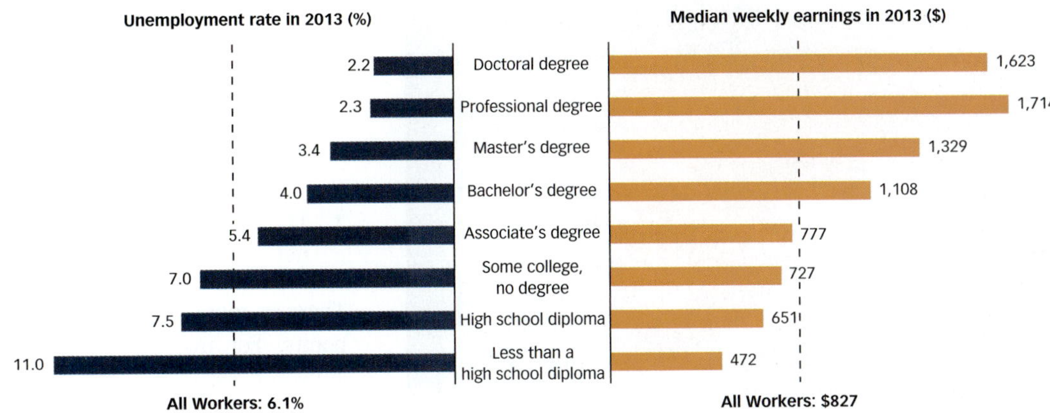

SOURCE: Bureau of Labor Statistics. 2012. "Employment Projections: Education Pays." United States Department of Labor.

Yet while college graduates today are still, as a group, outearning their peers with less education, their own income prospects have diminished somewhat in comparison to those of earlier graduates. As Figure 12.7 shows, entry-level wages of graduates have dropped from the peak reached at the turn of the millennium, reflecting a larger labor market trend in stagnating or slow wage growth. In spite of their higher graduation rates, women continue to lag behind their male counterparts. As we will see in the next section, some entry-level jobs have evolved into unpaid internships, rendering the first step on the career ladder more tenuous for new graduates.

Though graduates' entry-level wages increased slightly in 2011, only 24% of new graduates had an employment offer at the time of graduation (Goudreau, 2011). Low levels of employment, particularly in positions requiring a college degree, continue to plague new graduates, though entry-level wages appear to be climbing very slowly: From 2012 to 2013, the average entry-level wage rose from $44,482 per year to $45,633 (National Association of Colleges and Employers, 2014).

FIGURE 12.7 U.S. Entry-Level Real Hourly Wages for New Graduates Ages 23–29, 1973–2009

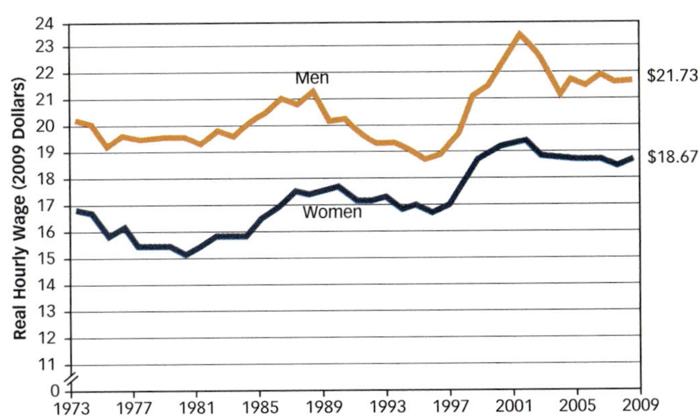

SOURCE: Shierholz, Heidi. (2011). "New College Grads Losing Ground on Wages." *Economic Snapshot—Education*. Washington, DC: Economic Policy Institute. Reprinted with permission.

While wages have stagnated and many new graduates are struggling with unemployment or underemployment, the student debt burden has grown. Student loan debt is particularly likely to be carried by minority students, more of whom come from homes with lower incomes. For instance, data from the 2007–2008 academic year (prior to the economic recession, when debts continued to balloon) show that a substantial proportion of minority students carry heavy educational debt, defined here as $30,500 or more at graduation. Among bachelor's degree graduates, 27% of Black students, 16% of White students, 14% of Hispanic students, and 9% of Asian students had heavy educational debt (Austin, 2010). Debt presents a substantial challenge to students as they begin their careers.

At the same time, the assertion that "education pays," which headlined the Bureau of Labor Statistics data noted in Figure 12.6, remains essentially correct, particularly in light of the U.S. Department of Labor's projections about the direction of the U.S. economy. A report published in 2005 on growth sectors in the labor market notes that "professional and related occupations and service occupations . . . which are on opposite ends of the educational attainment and earnings spectrum, are expected to provide about 60 percent of the total job growth from 2004 to 2014" (Hecker, 2005, p. 71). While both income and debt are critical concerns for students, their families, and the economy as a whole, educational attainment will continue to grow in importance as a pathway to professional careers and higher earning potential.

INTERNSHIPS AND HIGHER EDUCATION

Thousands of U.S. college students build their résumés and job experience with unpaid internships, which have become a

Boston Globe / Contributor/Getty Images

As an undergraduate student, you may have the opportunity to do an unpaid internship. Interns provide public and private organizations with important yet unpaid labor, while students benefit from getting work experience.

staple of summer or a part of the regular academic year for students living in cities such as Washington, D.C., and New York, where opportunities are abundant to work in politics, the fashion industry, public relations, and other fields. Many universities require each student to complete an internship to earn credit toward a major or graduation. More students than ever are also working in unpaid internships *after* graduation, having been unable to secure paid entry-level positions even with their degrees. Critics, however, are raising questions about the legality and morality of employing young people, sometimes full-time, without paying them wages or salaries. While some internships offer stipends or pay, most do not.

What are some of the benefits to students of participating in unpaid internships? Both students and their universities often believe internships are a vital component of building human capital in preparation for the world of paid and professional work. Universities have an interest in helping students work outside campus on activities that can build their knowledge base, and students have an interest in developing skills and social networks that will help them find good jobs after graduation. Many look forward with excitement to the possibility of working with a representative in Congress, a lawyer, a public relations specialist, a fashion designer, or an executive with a favorite nonprofit. For many students, the internship experience is a positive one.

The U.S. Department of Labor's Wage and Hour Division (2010) recognizes legal internships as a means for preparing interns for work and has established a set of six criteria that most public and private institutions must meet:

- The internship, even though it includes actual operation of the facilities of the employer, is similar to training that would be given in an educational environment.
- The internship experience is for the benefit of the intern.
- The intern does not displace regular employees, but works under close supervision of existing staff.
- The employer that provides the training derives no immediate advantage from the activities of the intern, and on occasion its operations may actually be impeded.
- The intern is not necessarily entitled to a job at the conclusion of the internship.
- The employer and the intern understand that the intern is not entitled to wages for the time spent in the internship.

There is room for interpretation of these criteria on multiple points. For instance, can we clearly determine whether an employer "derives no immediate advantage from the activities of the intern"? Or that no "regular employees" have been "displaced"?

Another way of looking at internships is to ask how an arrangement intended by law to benefit students and other prospective workers may benefit other entities—perhaps even to the detriment of the intern, as writer Ross Perlin (2011) points out. Among the points Perlin raises are the following: Universities benefit from mandating student internships for credit, because students are thereby required to pay tuition dollars for an experience that—unlike the classroom experience—costs the university comparably little. And employers are effectively provided with the services of often well-educated and enthusiastic workers—for no pay. Perlin argues that a range of institutions and employers thus exploit the services of young workers for their own economic advantage in the fashion and finance industries, in politics, and in the nonprofit world.

Who loses in this equation? Perlin (2012) and Eisenbrey (2012) suggest that lower-income students are losers in the internship game. That is, while students from better-off families can afford (at least for a while) to work for nothing in order to secure human and social capital, poor and working-class students need to work for pay, even if it's in a field unrelated to their area of career interest. Perlin (2012) argues that "lucrative and influential professions—politics, media and entertainment, to name a few—now virtually require a period of unpaid work, effectively barring young people from less privileged backgrounds." All students, however, are potentially disadvantaged where jobs that once were or might otherwise have been entry-level jobs are reinvented as unpaid internships, a shift that removes an economically and professionally important stepping-stone for students leaving school with degrees.

Perlin (2011, 2012) asserts that the internship boom also has other, even broader, effects: It constricts social and professional mobility, contributes to growing inequality, and supports an economy in which those in the top tier are becoming less and less diverse. Even more seriously, a fundamental ethic in American life is under threat: the idea that a hard day's work demands a fair wage.

What, then, are we to conclude about internships, a growing and pervasive phenomenon that will be part of the experience of thousands of students this year and in years to come? It is clear that students benefit from spending time in a professional market that values both formal educational credentials and hands-on work experience. Universities benefit from giving their students opportunities to link classroom learning to experiential learning. And employers benefit from the creativity, skills, and enthusiasm of young workers. On the other hand, it remains important that benefits should not accrue disproportionately to the parties with the most power—universities and employers—to the detriment of students. How can students, their schools, and the law ensure opportunity and contribute to making internships meaningful work experiences that provide foundations for careers? What do you think?

DROPPING IN, DROPPING OUT: WHY ARE COLLEGE DROPOUT RATES SO HIGH?

We began this chapter by looking at the phenomenon of college dropouts, noting that the United States has been tremendously successful in ensuring that a high proportion of high school completers—fully 70%—enroll in higher education. Statistics suggest, however, that many who enroll in college never finish with degrees, though many end their college careers with substantial debt.

College attainment levels have remained flat for generations (Lewin, 2011a). A little more than half of those enrolled in 4-year institutions go on to graduate, while less than half of those enrolled in 2-year institutions graduate (Figure 12.8). Recent data show that the average graduation rate for 1,575 4-year colleges nationwide was just over 57% (for completion in 6 years), with public colleges at 56% and private colleges at 65%. Figures for 2-year institutions are even lower (CollegeMeasures, 2013). Dropouts can be costly, both to the nation as a whole, which loses potentially educated and productive workers, and to individuals, whose earning potential is diminished by their failure to obtain degrees.

FIGURE 12.8 U.S. Graduation Rates by Race and Ethnicity, Selected Cohort Entry Years, 1996–2007

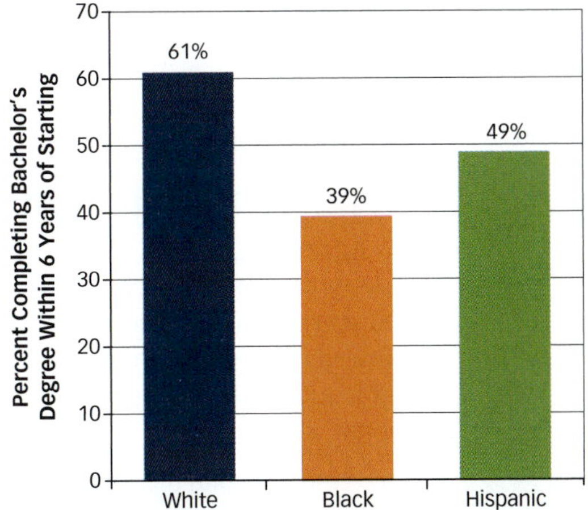

SOURCE: National Center for Education Statistics. 2011. "Table 345: graduation rates of first-time postsecondary students who started as full-time degree/certificate-seeking students, by sex, race/ethnicity, time to completion, and level and control of institution where student started: Selected cohort entry years, 1996 through 2007." *Digest of Education Statistics.*

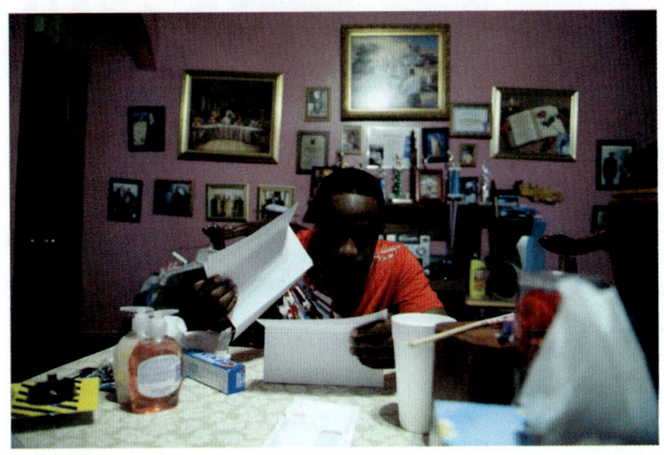

Many students seeking to go to college face conflicting emotions: joy when they are admitted, but anxiety over how to pay for their education.

The Washington Post / Contributor/Getty Images

So what is behind the college dropout phenomenon? Several factors contribute. First, high college costs drive many students out of higher education. The cost of a 4-year private college education tripled from 1980 to 2010—student loan debt for new bachelor's degree graduates now averages about $23,000 (Carlozo, 2012). Costs are a particularly acute issue for low-income students, who are more likely to drop out than their better-off peers. The financial burden of a college education falls more heavily on those with fewer resources, often even when some grant money is available. As well, low-income students are more likely to attend colleges that "excel in producing dropouts" (Leonhardt, 2009).

Second, the rigors of college work lead some students to drop out. This factor is complex. Some students who enroll in college may indeed be unready for the workload or the level of work. Half of students in associate degree programs and about a fifth of those in bachelor's programs are required by their institutions to enroll in remedial classes to address academic shortcomings. Some of these courses do not confer college credit, lengthening the time needed to earn a degree and increasing the likelihood that a student will leave without completing college. Advocates for students suggest that colleges can do more to help students stay and succeed with coaching, scheduling that meets the needs of working students, and accelerated programs that speed the time to degree with rigorous work offered in concentrated time periods (Lewin, 2011a). At the same time, budget cuts, particularly at state institutions, have reduced rather than expanded opportunities to provide targeted services to struggling students.

Many students find it challenging to balance the rigors of school and work. According to Complete College America, the majority of community college students work more than 20 hours per week, and a substantial proportion also take care of families. While attending college part-time seems like a viable solution, in fact it substantially lowers the chance that a student will ever earn a degree. Only about a quarter of students

Cost of a Degree

TECHNOLOGY & SOCIETY

MCDONALDIZATION AND EDUCATION

Sociologist George Ritzer (2010) writes that the life experiences of U.S. adults (and a growing number of others across the globe) are influenced from cradle to grave by *McDonaldized institutions.* These institutions have absorbed and put into practice the key characteristics of the fast-food restaurant: efficiency, calculability (a focus on the quantifiable aspects of what is sold), predictability, and the control of humans by nonhuman technologies. Ritzer follows classical sociologist Max Weber's argument on formal rationality in suggesting that society, including education, is becoming more "formally rationalized" but that while this rationalization serves the profit motive of capitalism well, it does not necessarily serve the individuals who are dehumanized by processes that quantify, control, and "cage" them in a web of rationalized structures.

From preschool to the university level, say Ritzer and others (Hayes & Wynyard, 2002), the experience of education is permeated by the principles of the fast-food restaurant. At the preschool level, Ritzer argues, early education is dominated by child-care chains such as KinderCare, which tends to hire short-term employees whose work in the classroom is governed by an "instruction book" that lays out detailed activities for each day, creating an environment that, for better or worse, is predictable from center to center. Individual interpretation and innovation are not encouraged.

Can we also say that higher education is McDonaldized? Ritzer (2010) writes that "most courses run for a standard number of weeks and hours per week . . . little attention is devoted to determining whether a given subject is best taught in a given number of weeks or hours per week. The focus seems to be on how many students ('products') can be herded through the system and what grades they earn rather than the quality of what they have learned and of the educational experience" (p. 84). Both before and after college, students take standardized examinations with quantifiable results, such as the PSAT, the SAT, and the GRE. An entire high school or college experience can be summed up in a single number, the grade point average (GPA). Think about your experience at college or university. What aspects of it would you say are McDonaldized?

The growth of online education is another avenue of interest for those who are concerned about the McDonaldization of higher education. According to the National Center for Education Statistics (2011a), in 2007–2008 about a fifth of U.S. students took some kind of distance learning course. The proportion taking a full program online was smaller—just 3.7%—but rising. As of 2011, the rate of enrollment growth of online programs (10%) was far exceeding the growth rate of enrollment in all higher education (2%; Allen & Seaman, 2011).

A key benefit of online programs is that students who work or are not able to attend classroom lectures can now be part of an active learning community and earn credits toward the completion of a degree. On the other hand, online learning may reduce the "inefficient" human contact that many students and instructors value in education, including debates and discussions, in-class activities such as role-playing, and personal mentoring and encouragement. The collective aspects and pleasures of learning in a course are replaced in some cases by dozens or hundreds of students alone with their computers. Technology has clearly brought both new opportunities and new costs to those seeking higher education.

THINK IT THROUGH

▶ Ritzer argues that we are seeing a "dehumanization of education" today. Do you agree with this assertion? How is technology changing education in both positive and negative ways?

today fit the stereotypical model of full-time, on-campus students supported largely by their parents.

According to the Organisation for Economic Co-operation and Development (2011), the United States ranks 16th among OECD countries in the percentage of young adults with a college degree (Table 12.2). At one time, it topped the list. While everyone may not desire or even need a college degree, the competitive global economic environment has put a premium value on higher education, which offers greater security from unemployment and greater earning potential than a high school credential alone. Understanding why students drop out is the first step to addressing this problem effectively.

TABLE 12.2 Percentage of Young Adults Ages 25–34 With a College Degree for Selected Countries, 2009

Rank	Country	Percentage
1	Korea	63
2	Canada	56
3	Japan	56
4	Russia	55
5	Ireland	48
6	Norway	47
7	New Zealand	47
8	Luxembourg	44
9	United Kingdom	45
10	Australia	45
16	United States	41

SOURCE: OECD. 2011. "Percentage of population that has attained tertiary education, by age group (2009)." The Organisation for Economic Cooperation and Development.

Are there other factors you see as important in explaining the high number of U.S. students who leave college without degrees? What should students do to address the problem? What should schools do?

EDUCATION IN A GLOBAL PERSPECTIVE

Education brings gains to individuals, communities, and countries. Today, more people than ever are literate, attending institutions of higher education and completing degrees, and sharing knowledge globally across new communication platforms. It is not unusual for a U.S. classroom to have a partner in another country so students can "meet" other students through the Internet to share interests and ideas. Nor is it unusual to meet U.S. students abroad who are studying for credit and seeing places they might only have read about in books. Education has the potential to bring people and cultures together to foster greater understanding, innovation, and prosperity. Next, we take a look at how the United States lines up with its global peers in areas related to education, and at what some American students are doing in their studies across the planet.

HIGHER EDUCATION AND JOB OPPORTUNITIES

When the Organisation for Economic Co-operation and Development was formed in 1960, its members were 18 European nations, the United States, and Canada. Today, the OECD has 34 member states across the globe, including countries as geographically, culturally, and economically diverse as Mexico and Turkey. Its goal is to both foster and track economic and policy development and changes in member states. Among the important data the OECD collects on a regular basis are those on the relationship between higher education and employment. From these data we can get a basic picture of where the United States falls in relation to other member states in the achievement of educational credentials and the fortunes of college graduates.

In the 34 OECD states, though they include both highly developed states such as the United States and Germany and developing countries such as Mexico and Chile, the correlations we have observed among educational attainment, income, and labor market prospects hold true. The global economic crisis that began in 2008 hit many member countries hard, and unemployment grew in every one. The most heavily affected workers were adults without post–high school education, whose unemployment rates rose overall from nearly 9% to more than 11%. For those with higher education, however, unemployment rates grew only one percentage point between 2008 and 2009 and stayed below 5% in most countries through 2009 (Spain and Turkey were the most notable exceptions). No less important, those with higher education continued to enjoy substantially higher wages than their peers with less education. Clearly, then, education matters across the globe (OECD, 2011).

U.S. STUDENTS MEET THE WORLD

For many U.S. students, the world beckons. Seized by curiosity to see and experience the world outside home, campus, and work, they are taking advantage of a small but growing number of college study-abroad programs (Table 12.3). In the academic year 2009–2010, more than 260,000 U.S. students studied abroad for credit, a small increase from the previous year and part of a rising trend. The top destinations, which have remained largely steady over time, include the United Kingdom, France, Spain, and Italy. In the 2009–2010 academic year, however, almost 14,000 students went to China, compared to just 3,000 a decade earlier. Other destinations that are growing in popularity are India, Israel, Brazil, and New Zealand (Institute of International Education, 2010).

Any study-abroad experience holds the potential for culture shock, especially when it involves venturing to a new destination with a culture quite divergent from that of the mainstream United States. Clearly, however, many students are excited to embrace this possibility. More U.S. students are spending their junior years abroad in places about which they knew little before they entered college, such as the American University in Cairo and Ibadan University in Nigeria: "These students visit places most Americans know only through news reports—the West Bank, Ethiopia and even northern Iraq" (Conlin, 2010).

Global Achievement Gap

GLOBAL ISSUES

MAKING A LINK BETWEEN EDUCATION AND HIV/AIDS IN SUB-SAHARAN AFRICA

What is the connection between HIV/AIDS and education in sub-Saharan Africa? The state of education in many countries, including Zimbabwe, Zambia, Kenya, Malawi, and Uganda, has been significantly affected by the dramatic pandemic of HIV/AIDS in the region. According to data from the United Nations, the proportion of teachers infected with HIV/AIDS surpasses 20% in parts of Malawi and South Africa and 13% in Zambia (UNAIDS, 2010b). In 2006, there was a shortage of more than 45,000 teachers in Tanzania because so many had either died or left the profession because of HIV/AIDS. A study in South Africa found that 21% of teachers ages 24–34 were living with HIV/AIDS (UNAIDS, 2006).

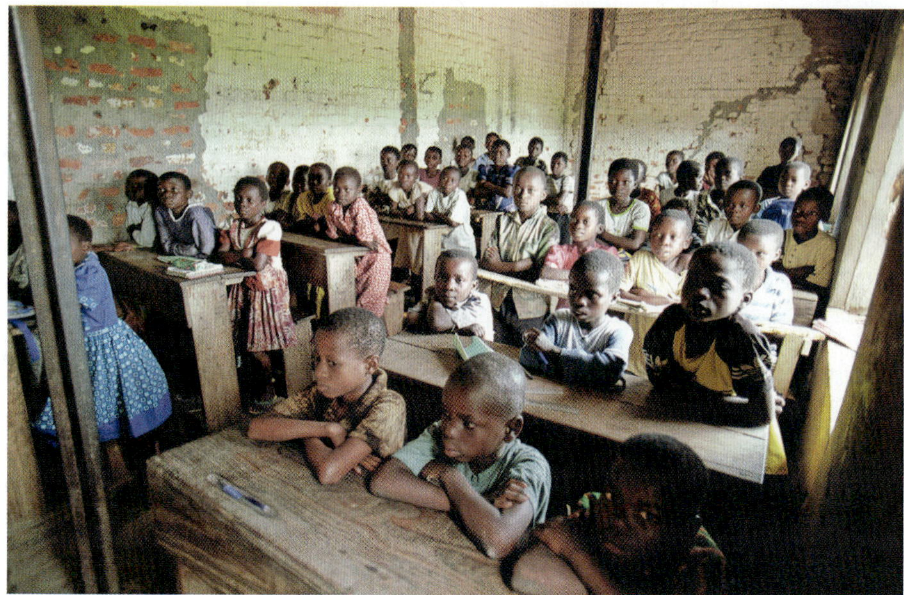

National Film Board of Canada / Contributor/Getty Images

The loss of educators to HIV/AIDS in large numbers results in overcrowded classrooms and a lack of personnel and talent that could be used to educate the next generation of workers and leaders.

In the country of Botswana, more than one quarter of the population is infected. According to AVERT (2010), one of the world's leading HIV/AIDS prevention organizations, an estimated 22.5 million people there have HIV/AIDS. In South Africa alone, more than 5.6 million people are living with the disease. A substantial share of those infected are adults in their working and child-rearing years, and, significantly for communities, families, and schools, the majority are women. Their incapacitating illnesses and deaths leave behind motherless children and, because most teachers are female, schoolchildren without instruction.

Clearly, the loss of educators has a powerful impact on developing economies with a need for more educated workforces, and the loss of teachers is only part of the larger tragedy of HIV/AIDS in sub-Saharan Africa. Not only is the blow to schooling part of the general devastation wrought by the widespread deaths of individuals in their productive years, but each death also diminishes the opportunities for members of the next generation to achieve the education they will need to replace the depleted workforce and push forward toward greater prosperity. While the link between the HIV/AIDS pandemic and educational opportunities and institutions in developing countries may not be immediately visible, the discipline of sociology trains us to look beneath the surface to see the myriad ways in which changes or problems in one part of the social system lead to sometimes unexpected changes and problems in other parts.

THINK IT THROUGH

▶ What kinds of creative solutions might both the international and local communities design to address the shortage of educators in sub-Saharan Africa? Can technology be part of a solution that both addresses HIV/AIDS prevention needs and the need to educate a new generation?

Yamil Lage / Stringer/Getty Images

More U.S. students than ever are studying abroad. While many still choose traditional destinations like London and Paris, others are seeking education and cultural experiences in places like Latin America, Africa, and Asia.

Part of the growth of academic interest in the Middle East in particular is driven by the availability of new Critical Language Scholarships, created in 2006 by the U.S. Department of State to facilitate the study of languages such as Arabic, Pashto, Dari, Azerbaijani, and Punjabi—languages not typically offered for study in U.S. high schools or colleges. Some students desire to be part of the political discourse, study public diplomacy, and witness the potential for change in a tumultuous region of the world. Others want to work in nongovernmental organizations or with the American Foreign Service (Conlin, 2010).

TABLE 12.3 Top Destinations for U.S. Students Studying Abroad

Rank	Country
1	United Kingdom
2	Italy
3	Spain
4	France
5	China
6	Australia
7	Germany
8	Mexico
9	Ireland
10	Costa Rica
11	Japan
12	Argentina
13	South Africa
14	India
15	Greece

SOURCE: Data from Institute of International Education. 2012. "Study Abroad by U.S. Students Slowed in 2008/09 with More Students Going to Less Traditional Destinations." *Press Release*.

Whether the study-abroad experience takes them to London, Beijing, Beirut, Rio de Janeiro, or Cairo, many students say their worldviews are forever transformed by the opportunity to live in places they might otherwise know only from books or television. As one student said, "I will never again look at a story about the Middle East with such a one-sided perspective." Another added, "I genuinely enjoyed watching the bottom fall out of every one of my preconceived ideas about the Muslim world" (quoted in Conlin, 2010).

WHY STUDY EDUCATION FROM A SOCIOLOGICAL PERSPECTIVE?

Education opens up the world to us. Through education, we have the opportunity to gain new perspectives, to develop a critical approach to problems and the skills to imagine solutions, and to understand other people, cultures, and communities more fully. In an increasingly interdependent and interconnected world, this is a powerful advantage. Opportunities for education are not equally distributed, however, and, as we have seen in this chapter, factors such as socioeconomic status and race are among those that can fundamentally affect access to a good education. This matters because talent that remains unnurtured cannot better individual lives or the life of the community and country.

Sociology helps us look critically at an issue such as educational inequality and understand the roots of the problem. It is common in the United States to say that "education is the great equalizer," and, while that goal is certainly an achievable one, it cannot be realized when ZIP codes determine the quality of schooling, or when low expectations and inadequate resources in poor communities lead to poor educational outcomes. Education may then reproduce rather than reduce inequalities.

Sociology also entreats us to use our sociological imaginations to ask questions about the intersection between personal troubles and public issues. If, for instance, a student is experiencing difficulties balancing work and school, or having trouble financing his or her education, we can easily see this as a *personal trouble*. Recognizing it as part of the larger problem of a substantial proportion of U.S. college enrollees not graduating, however, we begin to see the outlines of a *public issue*, one that cannot be explained by the circumstances of a single case or a dozen cases. In both its causes and its consequences, failure to graduate is an authentic public issue, and addressing it requires a critical ability to root out its sociological antecedents. A sociological education in particular helps us gain perspective on the factors that make education increasingly vital today, as well as those that create obstacles to or opportunities for educational attainment.

The Rise and Fall of Education Inequality

WHAT CAN I DO WITH A SOCIOLOGY DEGREE?

CAREER DEVELOPMENT: CONSIDERING GRADUATE AND PROFESSIONAL EDUCATION, PART I

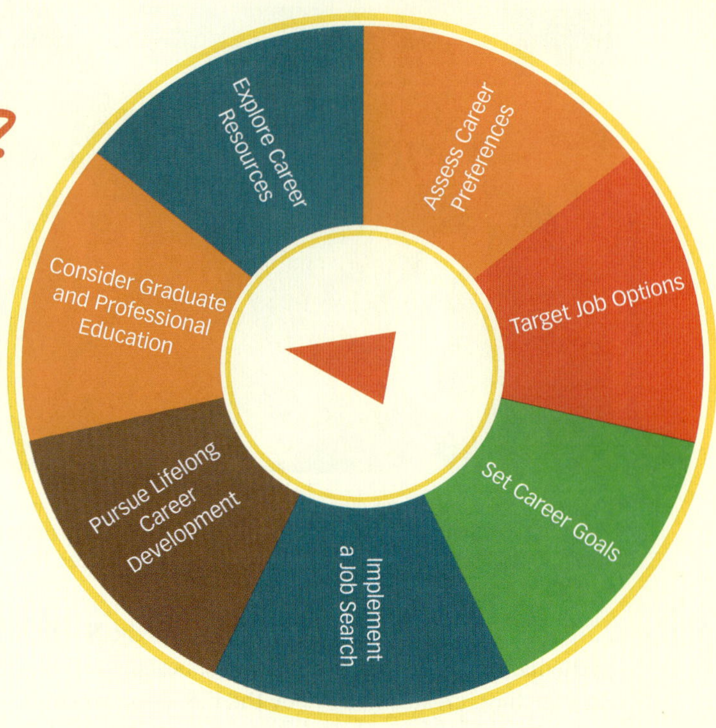

The American Sociological Association has reported that 18 months after graduation, about 35% of students who participated in a postgraduation survey were enrolled in graduate or professional schools. The decision to pursue a graduate or professional degree is a significant commitment of time, resources, and energy and will affect your career options and opportunities. In this chapter, we looked broadly at education through a sociological lens. One of the terms with which you became familiar is *credential society.* We do, in fact, live in a credential society, and in the contemporary world of work, your credentials—specifically, the higher education degree or degrees you earn—will have a big impact on your path to a career. For some students, that path may lead through graduate or professional school.

As you consider whether to pursue graduate or professional education, you should *examine your motivations, assess your career choices, research graduate schools and degree options,* and *reflect on practical challenges and how you will meet them.* In this chapter feature, we focus on the examination of motivations and assessment of career choices. In the next chapter feature, we turn our attention to researching graduate and professional schools and reflecting on opportunities and challenges.

Examine Your Motivations

Some students know from an early age that academic study at the advanced level is their goal—aspiring physicians, lawyers, and college professors, for instance, need to plan to continue their studies after they earn an undergraduate degree. Other students develop a new interest in an academic or professional area as undergraduates and then decide to stay in school for a second or third degree. Still others know that graduate or professional school may be in their future but prefer to explore occupational opportunities rather than attending immediately. All options have advantages and disadvantages, but *the best is the one that is best for you.* Take time to reflect on your motivations for pursuing graduate or professional study.

Students have various reasons for continuing their education immediately following completion of a bachelor's degree:

- The effective study skills they have mastered as undergraduates will apply to the rigors of graduate or professional school.
- They are motivated now and think they may not return to school later.
- They have few or no family and financial commitments that might prevent them from attending.
- The economy and labor market are currently challenging but may improve in a few years.
- They enjoy and succeed in academic settings.
- They lack clarity about pursuing professional opportunities immediately or are anxious about career interests and goals.
- Their desired occupational field or job requires a graduate degree or professional degree for entry-level positions.

Students also consider reasons to postpone graduate school upon completing a bachelor's degree:

- They want to gain work experience to better determine their career options.
- Their desired study program requires some employment experience in a professional setting.

- They plan to explore nonacademic options and gain work experience.
- They hope to find positions with employers who will contribute to paying graduate or professional school expenses.
- They need to reduce their undergraduate debt before embarking on new commitments.
- They would like to enhance their application for an advanced degree program with additional accomplishments.

Assess Your Career Choices

In considering graduate or professional school, examine your skills, interests, and values to identify likely career options and explore opportunities to determine a career path. *Develop your career goals before you consider or commit to graduate or professional school so that further education enhances your future and career plans.* One way to do this is to research careers and occupations to determine educational requirements, labor market trends, possible employers, regional employment information, and expected compensation. Another step is to participate in internships as an undergraduate or, following graduation, to gather firsthand knowledge about an organization or profession. You might also test career information by visiting potential employers, speaking to professionals, and networking with alumni to determine which career best fits your aspirations and life goals.

The core knowledge and diverse skills that you acquire as a sociology major prepare you for the rigors of graduate or professional school by helping you develop competencies in research, writing, communication, and critical thinking, among others. If you think that graduate or professional school might be in your future, look at the next chapter's feature to learn about types of degree programs that may fit your aspirations and to explore opportunities and challenges in advanced study.

THINK ABOUT CAREERS

- Have you considered graduate or professional studies?
- Are you interested in testing out professional opportunities before going on to graduate or professional school, or does your desired career choice require further credentials for an entry-level position?
- What would be the advantages and disadvantages for you of choosing to further your studies after earning a bachelor's degree?

SUMMARY

- **Education** is the transmission of society's norms, values, and knowledge base by means of direct instruction.
- **Mass education** spread with industrialization and the need for widespread **literacy**. Today the need is not just for literacy but for specialized training as well. All industrial societies today, including the United States, have systems of **public education** that continue through the high school level, and frequently the university level as well. Such societies are sometimes termed **credential societies**, in that access to desirable jobs and social status depends on the possession of a certificate or diploma.
- Functionalist theories of education emphasize the role of the school in serving the needs of society by socializing students and filling positions in the social order, while conflict theories emphasize education's role in reproducing rather than reducing social inequality.
- Symbolic interactionist theory, by focusing on the classroom itself, reveals how teachers' perceptions of students—as well as students' self-perceptions—are important in shaping students' performance.
- Early literacy and later educational attainment are powerfully correlated. Access to books and early reading experiences are among the strongest predictors of basic literacy at an early age. Researchers measure multiple levels of literacy.
- U.S. public schools are highly segregated by race and ethnicity. Before the 1954 U.S. Supreme Court decision in *Brown v. Board of Education,* segregation was legal. Since that time, schools have continued to show **de facto segregation**, because segregated residential patterns still exist, because many White parents decide to send their children to private schools, and because the courts have recently limited the scope of previous laws aimed at promoting full integration.
- The issues of extending the school day and extending the school year have long been subjects of debate in the United States. The roots of today's school calendar help us to understand its evolution and to consider its differential effects on children from different socioeconomic classes.
- Differences in school funding by race, ethnicity, and class reinforce existing patterns of social inequality. In general, the higher someone's social class, the more likely he or she is to complete high school and college. Low-income people, in contrast, are often trapped in a cycle of low educational attainment and poverty.
- There are strong demonstrable relationships between educational attainment and employment prospects and between educational attainment and income. There is also a correlation between the socioeconomic status of a family and the probability of its members' further educational attainment.
- Both the utility and the legality of college internships have become hotly debated. Internships may offer students substantial value in terms of experience, but critics say they also exploit students' labor and skills.
- U.S. college dropout rates are high, exceeding those of many other industrialized countries. Key reasons for dropping out include financial strain, lack of academic preparation, and difficulty balancing competing demands of school, work, and family.
- The correlation between educational attainment and income and employment opportunities holds around the globe.
- U.S. students are studying abroad more often and in more places than in the past. Interest in new destinations, including the Middle East, is opening the world to more young people.

KEY TERMS

education, 297
formal education, 297
mass education,297
literacy, 297
public education, 298
credential society, 298
school segregation, 303
de facto segregation, 304

DISCUSSION QUESTIONS

1. What are some of the key reasons students drop out of college? How can identifying the sociological roots of the problem help us to develop effective policies to address it?

2. What do contemporary data show us about the relationship between family income and academic achievement, as measured by variables like educational attainment or SAT scores? How do sociologists explain the relationship? What are strengths and weaknesses of their arguments?

3. What is the current state of racial segregation in U.S. public schools? How has it changed since the civil rights era of the 1960s? What sociological factors help explain high levels of racial segregation in schools?

4. What historical factors help explain the organization of the modern school day in the United States? Should the school day be reorganized to meet new societal needs? What might a new school day look like?

5. What is the role of internships in higher education today? Who benefits from the growth in students' participation in internships? How can internships be structured to maximize student knowledge and employability?

Sharpen your skills with SAGE edge at **edge.sagepub.com/chambliss2e**

A personalized approach to help you accomplish your course-work goals in an easy-to-use learning environment.

RELIGION AND SOCIETY

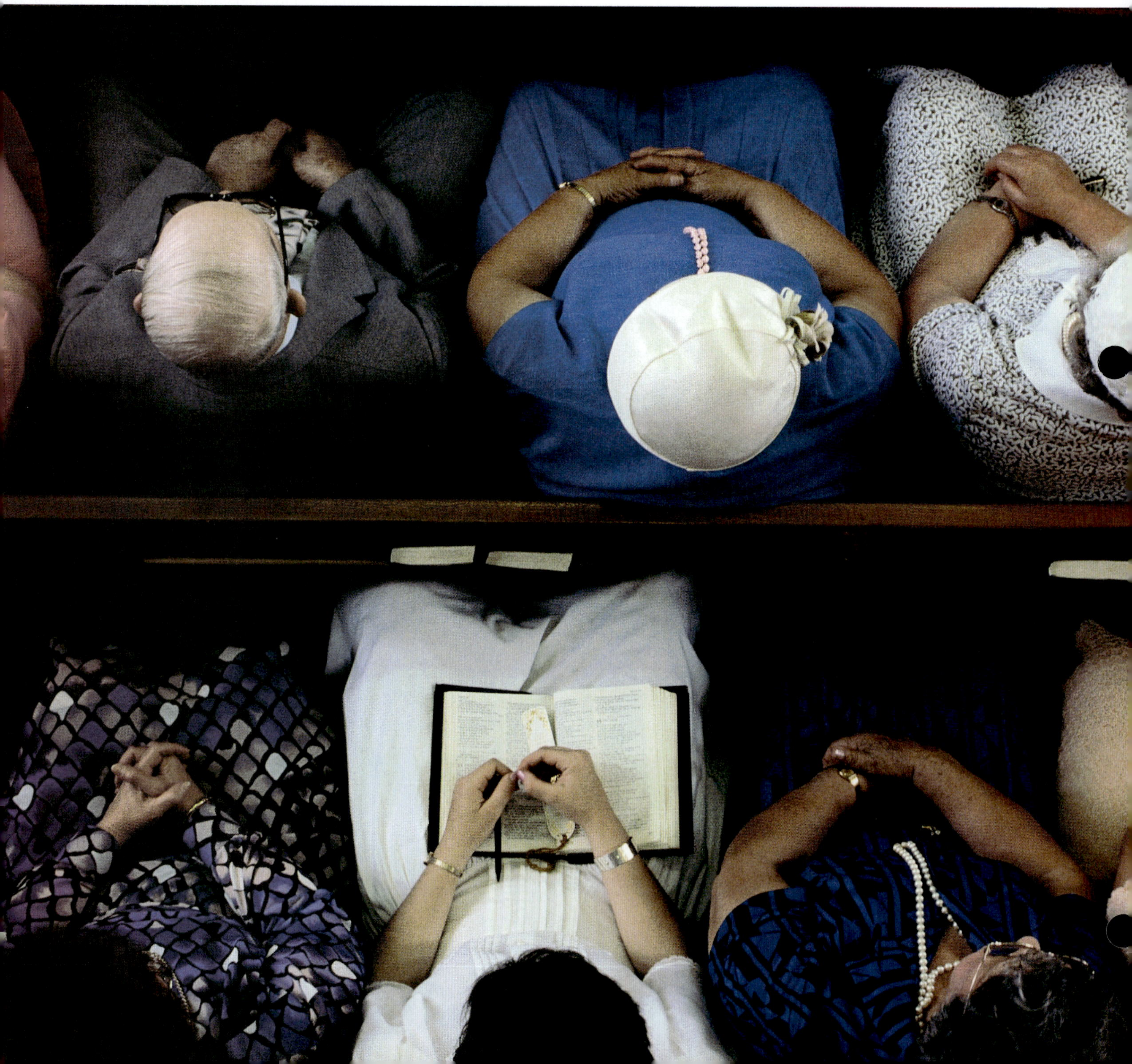

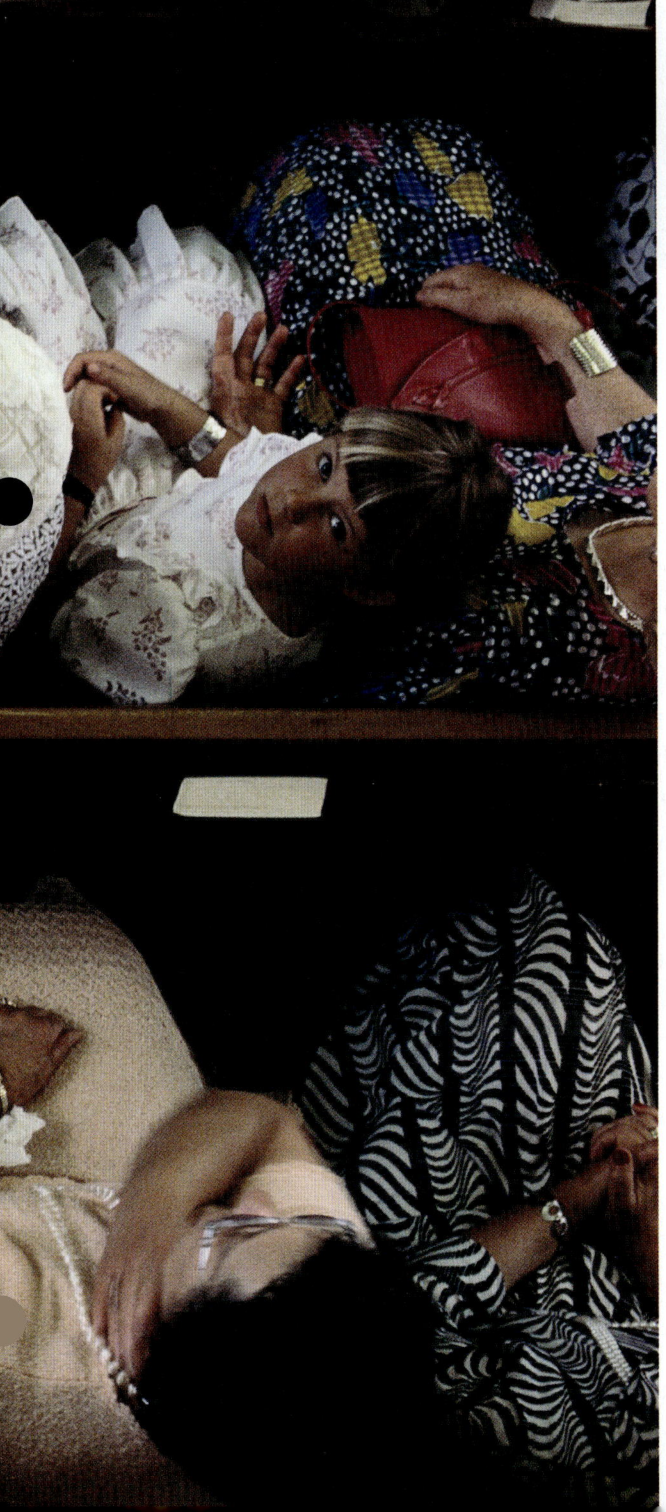

© Gideon Mendel/Corbis

WHAT DO YOU THINK?

1. What is the societal function of religion in a multicultural country such as the United States?
2. Do most people in the United States choose their religion? How do people "get" religion?
3. Is religion a source of stability or a source of conflict on a global scale? Might it be both?

AP Photo/Paul Sakuma

I PLEDGE ALLEGIANCE...

I pledge allegiance to the flag of the United States of America, and to the Republic for which it stands, one nation, under God, indivisible, with liberty and justice for all.

In 2004, the U.S. Supreme Court reversed an appeals court ruling that requiring students in classrooms to recite the Pledge of Allegiance, with the words "under God," was unconstitutional because it violated the separation of church and state enshrined in the Constitution. The First Amendment to the U.S. Constitution contains what is known as the **Establishment Clause**: "Congress shall make no law respecting an establishment of religion, or prohibiting the free exercise thereof." The basis of the Supreme Court's ruling, however, was specifically related to the case at hand: The court argued that the petitioner, a California atheist, did not have standing to sue on behalf of his school-age daughter. The implication was that his daughter could have sued, but he could not sue for her (Pew Forum on Religion and Public Life, 2004).

In 2013, an anonymous family in the state of Massachusetts brought the issue back to the courts, claiming that the phrase "under God" is in violation of that state's equal rights laws. Rather than challenging the constitutionality of the words, the petitioners argued that the phrase discriminates against atheists. Attorney David Niose, representing the plaintiffs, argued in his opening statement that the repeated use of the Pledge of Allegiance in public schools is "indoctrinating and alienating" to atheists (Rosenbaum, 2013). As of this writing, a decision in the case has not been issued.

The Pledge of Allegiance has been used in American public life for more than a century, but the phrase "under God" was added by Congress only in 1954. At that time the solicitor general of the United States argued before the Supreme Court that "under God" is "descriptive" and "ceremonial" rather than a prayer or "religious invocation" (Pew Forum on Religion and Public Life, 2004), suggesting that it embodies a civic rather than an overtly religious value.

How should we interpret the inclusion of the words "under God" in the Pledge of Allegiance? What is the function of this brief but provocative phrase? Should we interpret it as *civic* or *religious*? Is it inclusive or exclusive? And more generally, what is the role of religion in a multicultural United States?

In this chapter we examine the relationship between religion and society, beginning with a consideration of what religion is and what roles it plays in societies. We explore classical and contemporary theoretical perspectives on religion and society and examine the place of religion in people's private and public lives. We look at different types of religious organizations, as well as the great world religions. We then explore issues of religion in the United States, including the rise of evangelicalism and the decline of religious affiliation among the young. We conclude by looking at global concerns of the sociology of religion.

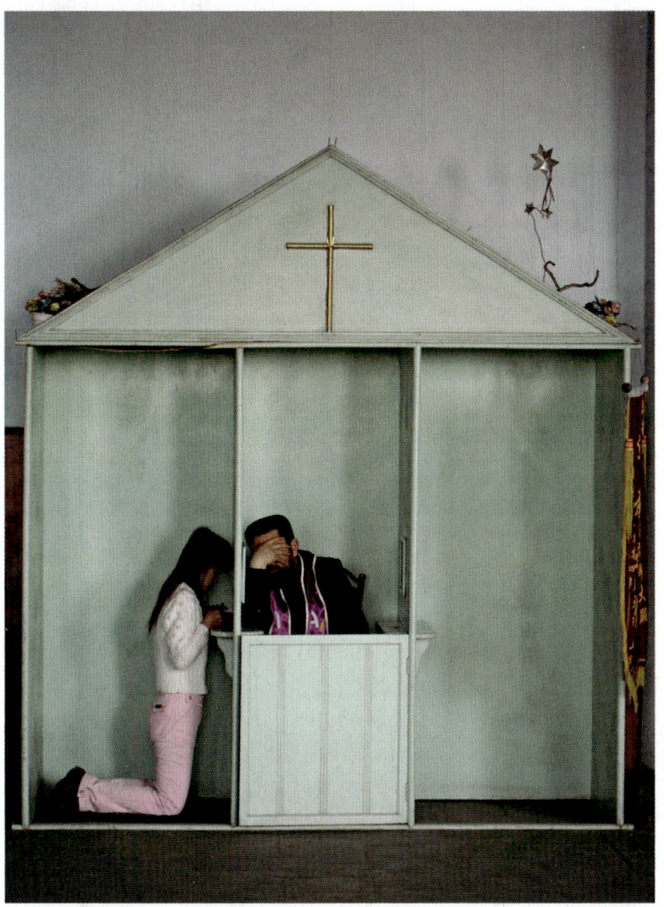

Reuters/Reinhard Krause

The practice of sacred rites is a characteristic of religions. Among the sacred rites of Catholicism (also called sacraments) is confession. The church entreats members to cleanse themselves of sin by being contrite, confessing their sins to a member of the clergy, and not repeating their transgression.

HOW DO SOCIOLOGISTS STUDY RELIGION?

From a sociological perspective, we define a **religion** as a system of common beliefs and rituals centered on "sacred things" that unites believers and provides a sense of meaning and purpose (Durkheim, 1912/2008). We often think of **theism**, a belief in one or more supernatural deities, as basic to religion (the term originates from the Greek word for god, theos), but there is no clear conceptual distinction between worship of a spiritual being and worship of an entity such as a nation. Indeed, we could see nationalism as a form of civic religion.

Sociologists look at religion in the context of society, asking about its role and function and identifying its basic social elements. First, religion is a form of culture. Recall from Chapter 3 that culture consists of *the shared beliefs, values, norms, ideas, institutions, and organizations that create a common identity among a group of people.* Religion embodies these characteristics, as it is constituted by a common worldview that draws together those who identify with it.

Second, religion includes the ritualization and routinization of beliefs. All religions have a behavioral aspect: Adherents engage in practices that identify them as members of the group and create or affirm group bonds. Sociologist Émile Durkheim (1912/2008) argued that religious rituals create and reinforce social cohesion. Robert Merton (1968) added to this idea, suggesting that while rituals have a manifest, or obvious, function, they also have the latent—secondary or unintentional—function of reinforcing group solidarity. The manifest function of the Hopi rain dance was to bring rain; its latent function was to strengthen community ties.

Third, religion provides a sense of purpose and meaning. Religions commonly tell coherent and compelling stories about the forces that transcend everyday life, in ways that other aspects of culture such as a belief in democracy typically cannot (Geertz, 1973; Wuthnow, 1988). Where we may not find

Establishment Clause: The passage in the First Amendment to the U.S. Constitution, that states, "Congress shall make no law respecting an establishment of religion, or prohibiting the free exercise thereof."

Religion: A system of common beliefs and rituals centered on "sacred things" that unites believers and provides a sense of meaning and purpose.

Theism: A belief in one or more supernatural deities.

© Andrew Holbrooke/Corbis

A cow occupies a corner of a fabric shop in India. A statue of the god Krishna riding a cow can be seen in the background. In Hinduism, cows symbolize wealth, strength, abundance, and a full earthly life. They roam freely in many Indian villages and cities.

empirical answers to fundamental questions about life, death, and fate, faith may stand in.

When sociologists study religion, they do so as sociologists, not as believers or atheists. From the sociological perspective, religion is an important social institution. How, then, do sociologists approach the study of religion in society?

First, they do not study whether religious beliefs are true or false. They regard religious beliefs not as truths decreed by deities but as the social constructions of human beings. Throughout history humans have told stories about the world in which they live. Before the coming of Christianity to Northern Europe, for instance, people told stories about gods of nature or divinities who brought good fortune or ill fate to explain the tension between good and evil in human existence. Communities have always sought to construct logical frameworks to explain the world around them, and organized religion is only one way they engage in the quest for understanding and control.

Second, sociologists are interested in the social organization of religion. Within Christianity and Judaism, for example, religious practice often occurs in formal organizations, such as churches or synagogues. Yet this is not necessarily true of Hinduism and Buddhism, whose rituals may be practiced in the home or in natural settings. In Islamic societies such as Saudi Arabia and Iran, religious beliefs and practices are incorporated into daily life and guide political, cultural, and even economic practices.

Third, sociologists examine the function of religion as a source of solidarity within a group or society. Émile Durkheim (1912/2008) described religion as a "unified system of beliefs and practices related to sacred things" that are held in awe and elevated above the "profane" elements of daily existence, and that unite believers in a moral community (p. 47). According to Durkheim, the "god of the clan," the object of worship, is "nothing else than the clan itself, personified and represented to the imagination" (p. 206). This view highlights the importance of the group in constructing and worshipping, through the objects of devotion, an image of itself.

If a single religion dominates a society, it may function as a key source of social stability. If one religion is not dominant, differences between religions or sects may lead to sectarian conflicts. Recent examples of destabilizing religious conflicts include struggles among Sikhs, Hindus, and Muslims in India; between Muslims and Christians in Bosnia and Kosovo; and between Sunni and Shiite Muslims in Iraq and Pakistan.

Today we experience constant contact between countries that embrace different religious practices, making it relevant to ask whether religion is a stabilizing or destabilizing force on a global level. For instance, some observers have asserted that an evolving "clash of civilizations" between the Muslim and Christian worlds will shape the future of international relations (Huntington, 1993, 1997; Lewis, 2010).

Finally, sociologists study the ways in which social forces, rather than individual spiritual experiences, affect people's commitment to religion. Religious beliefs are deeply personal for many, creating a profound sense of connection with forces that transcend everyday reality. Sociologists do not question the depth of such feelings, but they do not limit themselves to spiritual explanations of religious devotion. They examine ways that "getting religion" coincides with community or individual experiences of loss, grief, poverty, or disaster. This perspective has deep historical roots: As far back as the first century B.C., the Latin poet Lucretius saw religion as originating in human fears and needs. He believed "men had dreamed of gods, to whom they attributed omnipotence and immortality. Unable to account for natural phenomena, especially in its more terrifying aspects, men had gone on to ascribe all such things to the gods, whom they consequently feared and sought to propitiate" (Brandon, 1973, p. 93).

THEORETICAL PERSPECTIVES ON RELIGION AND SOCIETY

In this section, we examine classical sociological perspectives on the role of religion in society, but we begin by considering the birth of religion and early human society through the lens of a sister discipline, anthropology. **Anthropology** is *the study of human cultures and societies and their development.* Like sociology, it offers different perspectives on questions, including the relationships among religion, human civilization, and agriculture, or different theoretical "glasses" we can use to see the development of our common human past.

Anthropology: The study of human cultures and societies and their development.

© Vincent J. Musi/National Geographic Society/Corbis

Göbekli Tepe is an ancient sanctuary erected at the top of a mountain ridge in the Southeastern Anatolia region of Turkey. It is the oldest known human-made religious structure. Archeologists estimate that the temple was built by hunter-gatherers in the 10th millennium B.C.E.

Our story begins in what is now southern Turkey, near the border with Syria. As long as 11,600 years ago, pillars measuring 18 feet and weighing up to 16 tons were raised at Göbekli Tepe, the home of what archaeologists believe to be the world's oldest temple (Mann, 2011). Carved into the temple are animal totems, figures that may represent guardian spirits. Still under excavation by archaeologists, Göbekli Tepe has challenged a long-held anthropological belief that organized religion arose as a way for humans to establish social bonds when hunter-gatherers evolved from living in nomadic bands into forming village communities. Instead, says archaeologist Klaus Schmidt, the massive temple shows that organized religion may predate the rise of agriculture and other key aspects of civilization. Lacking evidence of human settlement, Göbekli Tepe may have been a gathering place for foragers living within a hundred-mile radius. Settled agricultural activity may have arisen from a need to ensure adequate food for those drawn to the temple. We may then understand religion—in this instance, "the human impulse to gather for sacred rituals [that] arose as humans shifted from seeing themselves as part of the natural world to seeking mastery over it" (Mann, 2011)—as a critical precursor to agriculture and village settlements.

Did organized religion arise in response to a need for cohesion in early human societies, or did religion come first, fostering a shift from nomadic hunting and gathering to settled agricultural communities? These questions shed light on the concerns of both anthropologists and sociologists of religion.

Profane: A sphere of routine, everyday life.

Sacred: That which is set apart from the ordinary, the sphere endowed with spiritual meaning.

Totems: Within the sacred sphere, ordinary objects believed to have acquired transcendent or magical qualities connecting humans with the divine.

THE CLASSICAL VIEW: RELIGION, SOCIETY, AND SECULARIZATION

Classical sociological theorizing on religion focuses on the relationship between religion and society and includes the work of Karl Marx, Max Weber, and Émile Durkheim. Next we discuss each of these key perspectives.

DURKHEIM: THE FUNCTIONS OF RELIGION Émile Durkheim's *The Elementary Forms of the Religious Life* (1912/2008) sets forth one of the most influential and enduring theories in the sociology of religion. Durkheim based his theories on studies of Australian Aborigines, small hunting and gathering tribes who had lived in much the same way for thousands of years. Aborigines divided their world into two parts: the **profane**, *a sphere of routine, everyday life,* and the **sacred**, *that which is set apart from the ordinary, the sphere endowed with spiritual meaning.* The sacred sphere included many ordinary objects, which Durkheim called **totems**, *items believed to have acquired transcendent or magical qualities connecting humans with the divine.* Durkheim posited that "totemism" was the most primitive form of religion. Like the ancient worshippers at Göbekli Tepe, early Native Americans elevated elements of the natural world to sacred status, giving particular pride of place to the bison. Contemporary examples of totems include the wafer and wine used in a Catholic Mass, which the devout believe are ritually transformed into the body and blood of Christ.

Sacred activities for the Australian Aborigines included rituals and ceremonies that provided a heightened emotional awareness and a spiritual connection with divine forces and other members

Aaron Huey/National Geographic Creative

The U.S. Flag Code, adopted by Congress in 1942, says the flag "represents a living country and is itself considered a living thing." National flags, in this respect, can be understood as totems of civil religion by which a country elevates a symbol of worship that embodies its own self.

PRIVATE LIVES, PUBLIC ISSUES

ÉMILE DURKHEIM AND THE FUNCTION OF RELIGION IN SUICIDE

As a sociologist interested in what makes society cohesive and leads to social order, Émile Durkheim wanted to understand why suicide rates varied among different groups in society. He argued that because there are many different personal causes of suicide—mental illness, depression, pride, and even imitation—a general theory of why individuals commit suicide is impossible. A more scientific approach, he argued, is to search for social structural characteristics of different groups and societies that could explain suicide rates, rather than the motivation of individuals to commit suicide.

Durkheim's theory suggests that it is the degree of social solidarity in a society or group that explains the suicide rate: The greater the solidarity, the lower the suicide rate. Durkheim identified a number of different groups within European society to test his theory: He posited that single men compared to married men, widowed men, and women, as well as Catholics compared to Protestants, experienced higher levels of social cohesion and therefore should have lower suicide rates. The data he relied on, although primitive by contemporary standards of statistical sophistication, confirmed his theory.

Durkheim's empirical work led him to label four different types of suicide: egoistic, altruistic, anomic, and fatalistic. Here we focus on the first—*egoistic suicide,* which he understood as stemming from "excessive individuation," or a lack of integration into a community and weakness of community ties. Lack of integration, Durkheim argued, contributes to a sense of purposelessness, whereas integration offers the protection of a "collective conscience" that endows life with a purpose greater than the individual. Of the role of religion in promoting such a collective conscience, Durkheim (1897/1951) suggested:

Reuters/Pool News

Sociologist Émile Durkheim identified Catholicism as a religion with strong social bonds. Durkheim's research on suicide suggests that strong bonds make suicide less likely. In this photo, Pope Francis, the spiritual head of the Catholic Church, greets well-wishers.

> Religion protects man against the desire for self-destruction. . . . What constitutes religion is the existence of a certain number of beliefs and practices common to all the faithful, traditional and thus obligatory. The more numerous and strong these collective states of mind are, the stronger the integration of the religious community, also the greater its preservative value. (p. 170)

From Durkheim's perspective, the collective conscience that emerged from being integrated into a religious community was protective. It shielded the individual from the egoism of living only for the fulfillment of his or her own needs, which could not all be met. His sociological perspective places suicide at the intersection of the personal and the social, helping us to examine and empirically test the societal context in which suicide becomes more or less likely. Were we to test Durkheim's theory today we would first identify different groups across which the degree of social solidarity varies; we would then compare the suicide rates of the different groups. If, for example, Durkheim was correct in saying that Catholics experience a higher level of social solidarity than Protestants (we would have to develop some method of measuring social solidarity in the two groups), then by comparing the suicide rates of Catholics and Protestants we would be able to test Durkheim's theory.

THINK IT THROUGH

▶ Does membership in a religious organization provide a protective social barrier to suicide? What about membership in a civic organization? How would you design a research study to test and compare the protective effects of religious and civic group membership?

of the community. During such rituals, Durkheim suggested, people lost their sense of individuality and merged with the larger group. His key theoretical conclusion was that the realm of the sacred serves an important social function—it brings the community together, reaffirms its norms and values, and strengthens its social bonds. According to Durkheim, the realm of the sacred is society's projection of itself onto divine objects or beings, a view with roots in early history. Xenophanes, a philosopher who lived around 570 B.C., wrote that humans have created gods in their own image. The sacred *is* the group, endowed with divine powers and purpose. By worshipping the sacred, society worships itself, becoming stronger and more cohesive as a result.

Durkheim believed the sacred was disappearing from modern industrial society, with the realm of the profane extending over wider areas of life. However, while societies were likely to eventually reject the religiosity of earlier communities, Durkheim believed they could create *secular* forms of religion with the same function but a different form. In the United States, for instance, we can identify rituals, both religious and civic, that function to create or reinforce a "collective conscience" or group solidarity, such as rooting for American athletes in the Olympic Games, reciting the Pledge of Allegiance, and singing the national anthem. The U.S. flag carries a symbolic meaning because it stands for the collective nation; in "worshipping" the flag by, for instance, affording it pride of place in venues from classrooms to ballparks, the community venerates itself and its values, beliefs, and practices.

Durkheim's work suggests that one of religion's key functions in society is to create and reinforce the collective bond. Sociologist Herbert Blumer (1969) notes that the meaning of a thing for a person grows out of the ways in which others respond to the object and the person's actions toward it. A flag, as a physical object, is just a piece of colored fabric, but citizens of a country endow it with a meaning that elevates it to a sacred symbol. A wafer is just a wafer unless it is blessed in a Christian religious ceremony, when it becomes a representation of the body of Christ and its consumption an act of worship.

MARX: RELIGION AND INEQUALITY Karl Marx's writings about religion examine its role in society and the capitalist class hierarchy. In Marx's view, religion serves the interests of the ruling class by providing an outlet for human misery that obscures the true source of suffering among the subordinate classes—their exploitation by the ruling class.

Marx (1844/2000) wrote that "religion is the sigh of the oppressed creature, the feeling of a heartless world, and the soul of soulless circumstances. It is the opium of the people" (p. 72). In other words, by promising spiritual solutions—such as a better afterlife—as the answer to human suffering, religion discourages oppressed people from understanding the nature of their oppression in the present life and serves the interests of the powerful, who then have an easier time maintaining passivity among the economically deprived masses. After all, if there are rewards in the afterlife, then striving for betterment in the present life is not only unnecessary but also possibly counterproductive.

Secularization: The rise in worldly thinking, particularly as seen in the rise of science, technology, and rational thought, and a simultaneous decline in the influence of religion.

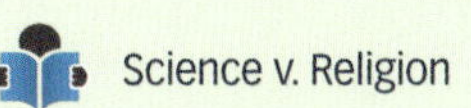
Science v. Religion

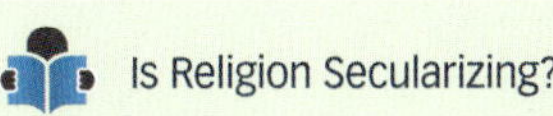
Is Religion Secularizing?

The Soviet Union was an atheistic communist state in which religious life was discouraged and sometimes actively persecuted. This Soviet poster from the 1930s makes a link between imperialism, capitalism, and the "poison drug of religion."

Marx also believed that once capitalism was overthrown, religion would no longer be necessary, since the stratification and dire economic disadvantage he saw as inevitable in the capitalist system would no longer exist. Like Durkheim, Marx believed secularization was inevitable. **Secularization** is the *rise in worldly thinking, particularly as seen in the rise of science, technology, and rational thought, and a simultaneous decline in the influence of religion.* While Durkheim was concerned about the fraying of social bonds that he believed would accompany secularization, Marx viewed secularization as a progressive trend, since the social solidarity and harmony promoted by religion were contrary to the interests of the masses and prevented their recognition of their own exploitation.

WEBER: RELIGIOUS VALUES AS SOURCES OF SOCIAL CHANGE Religion was a key subject for sociologist Max Weber, who wanted to explain, in particular, why the culture of modern capitalism had emerged first in England, France, and Germany rather than in India or China—which had once been more advanced than Northern and Western Europe in science, culture, and commerce. Weber concluded that capitalism first appeared where the Protestant Reformation had taken hold, and that the driving force behind its development was Protestantism's religious tenets and the economic behaviors they fostered.

Weber (1904–1905/2002) found that the beliefs of early Protestantism provided fertile ground for capitalism's development. First was the idea that God places each person on earth to fulfill a particular "calling." Whether someone would be saved was predestined by God, but people could find evidence of God's plan in a life dedicated to hard work because economic success was an indicator of salvation. Second, since Protestantism held that consumption-centered lifestyles were sinful, believers were expected to live simple lives, work hard, and save and reinvest their earnings rather than enjoy the immediate gratifications of idleness or acquisition. A hardworking, frugal, sober population reinvesting its earnings in new economic activities was, suggested Weber, a fundamental foundation for economic growth and, significantly, for early capitalism.

Yet Weber also wrote that once capitalism took hold, it became institutionalized and shed the religious ethic that fueled its development. Capitalism, scientific ways of thinking, and bureaucratic forms of organization, he said, would marginalize religion in the drive for productivity and profit. Weber was concerned about the disenchantment he believed would result from secularization and bureaucratization. Modern society, in his well-known metaphor, would become an "iron cage," imprisoning people in "rationalized" but irrational bureaucratic structures, rote work, and lives bereft of spirituality or creativity.

SYNTHESIZING THE CLASSICAL THEORIES Durkheim's observations that sacred rituals and objects function to strengthen community solidarity and embody the community itself were among his most important contributions to the sociology of religion. However, his perspective seems most applicable to highly homogeneous and cohesive societies such as the small Australian tribes that provided inspiration for his ideas. In modern, complex societies, which are racially, socially, and ethnically diverse, religion no longer serves such a clear purpose. Durkheim recognized a relationship between modernization and secularization and wrote of the potential for alienation in secular societies, but he also saw that "religion," perhaps in another form, might foster social solidarity.

Marx's insight that religion may divert people from the immediate problems of daily life is illuminating, particularly where the same elite circles hold both religious and political power. Yet his central idea that religion is purely a mystification enabling the ruling class to deceive the masses is problematic for at least two reasons. First, while religions have supported ruling groups in many historical instances, they have also challenged such groups. Catholicism, along with the labor movement, was a powerful driving force in the social movements that overthrew the Polish communist state through nonviolent mass mobilization, replacing it with a democratic government in 1989.

Second, for many people religious beliefs fill a need that has little to do with political or economic power—a function Marx ignored. When communist countries such as Cuba and the former Soviet Union sought to follow Marx's ideas and marginalize religion, they were remarkably unsuccessful. Religious beliefs flourished underground, and in countries such as Poland, Ukraine, and Uzbekistan they experienced a resurgence after the fall of communism.

Finally, while Weber's idea that a *religious* ethic of hard work and thrift contributes to economic growth has been used to explain examples of economic success around the world (Berger, 1986; Berger & Hsiao, 1988; Morishima, 1982), it has also been criticized on a number of grounds. First, his conclusions were based on the writings of Protestant theologians rather than on the actual practices of Protestants. During the colonial period he cited as the birthplace of the U.S. capitalist ethic, "Boston's taverns were probably fuller on Saturday night than were its churches on Sunday morning" (Finke & Stark, 1992, p. 23). Second, some scholars argue that capitalism developed among Jews and Catholics—and, for that matter, among Hindus, Muslims, and Confucians—as well as among Protestants (Collins, 1980; Hunter, 1987).

No single theoretical perspective can capture the full sociological picture of religion. Together, however, these perspectives may help us understand why religion exists and persists and how it functions in human societies. Next we look at contemporary theorizing on religion, which draws from modern perspectives on economic exchange.

CONTEMPORARY SOCIOLOGICAL THEORY AND THE "RELIGIOUS ECONOMY" PERSPECTIVE

One recent and influential approach to the sociology of religion is tailored to modern societies, including the United States, which are home to a wide variety of religious faiths. Taking their cue from economic theory, sociologists developed the **religious economy** approach, which suggests that *religions can be fruitfully understood as organizations in competition with one another for followers* (Finke & Stark, 1988, 1992, 2005; Hammond, 1992; Moore, 1994; Stark & Bainbridge, 1987/1996; Warner, 1993). In this view competition is preferable to monopoly for ensuring religious vitality. Compare this view to that of the classical theorists Durkheim, Marx, and Weber, who assumed religion weakens when challenged by competing religious or secular viewpoints.

The religious economy perspective suggests that competition leads to increased engagement in religious organizations for two reasons. First, competition compels each religious group to exert more effort to win followers, reaching out to the masses in a variety of ways in order to capture their attention. Second, the presence of a multitude of religions means there is likely to be something for just about everyone. In a culturally diverse society such as the United States, a single religion will probably appeal to only a limited range of followers, but the presence of Indian gurus, fundamentalist preachers, and mainline churches may encourage broad religious participation.

Religious economy: An approach to the sociology of religion that suggests that religions can be fruitfully understood as organizations in competition with one another for followers.

The religious economy analysis is adapted from the business world, in which competition (in theory) encourages the emergence of specialized products that appeal to specific markets. Sociologists who embrace this perspective even borrow the language of business. According to Finke and Stark (1992), a successful religious group must be well organized for competition, have eloquent preachers who are engaging "sales reps" in spreading the word, offer beliefs and rituals packaged as an appealing product, and develop effective marketing techniques. Religion, in this view, is a business much like any other. Television evangelists, for example, have been effective purveyors of religious "products."

While people's motivations are not easy to pinpoint, a study conducted by the Pew Forum on Religion and Public Life (2010) found that about 28% of U.S. adults change their religious affiliations over the course of their lives. If we count those who change their affiliations *within* religious traditions (for instance, from Baptist to Lutheran, both Protestant religions), the figure rises to 44% (Figure 13.1).

The religious economy approach is, of course, also subject to critique. It likely overestimates the extent to which people rationally pick and choose among different religions, as if they were shopping for a new car or a pair of shoes. Among deeply committed believers, particularly in societies or communities that lack religious pluralism, it is not obvious that religion is a matter of rational choice. Even when people are allowed to choose among different religions, most are likely to practice their childhood religions without ever considering alternatives (Roof, 1993). Further, if we consider that the most common shift in affiliation is from a religious group to the "nonaffiliated" group—7.3% of adults were "unaffiliated" as children, but today more than 16% indicate they are not affiliated with a religious group—then it is not clear that U.S. believers are trading one set of beliefs for another set that is better marketed or more enticing. They would, in fact, seem to be leaving organized religion behind. Can the religious economy perspective account for this large and growing shift? What about the classical perspectives? What do you think?

FIGURE 13.1 Changing Religious Affiliations of U.S. Adults, 2007

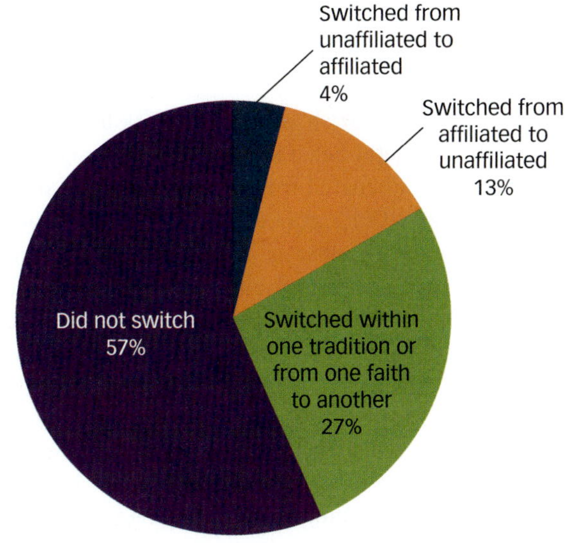

SOURCE: Data from 2007 U.S. Religious Landscape Survey. Reprinted in Pew Forum on Religion & Public Life 2010. *Religion among the millennials*. Washington, DC: Pew Research Center. Retrieved from http://www.pewforum.org/files/2010/02/millennials-report.pdf.

Church: A well-established religious organization that exists in a fairly harmonious relationship with the larger society.

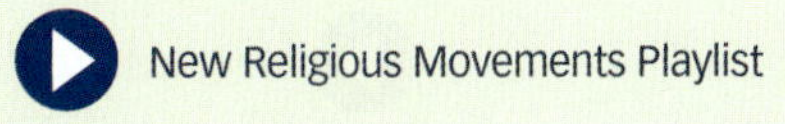
New Religious Movements Playlist

TYPES OF RELIGIOUS ORGANIZATIONS

Sociologist Thomas O'Dea (1966) captures an important distinction when he writes that in traditional societies "the same social groups provide satisfaction for both expressive and adaptive needs; in modern societies, organizations which meet adaptive needs tend to be separated out from those which provide an outlet for expressive needs" (p. 36). That is, in modern societies, religion may soothe people's fears about death or the future, inject meaning into the routine of daily life, and comfort the sick or grieving, but rarely is it an exclusive channel for education and medical services (though certainly students may attend religious schools from prekindergarten to college, and many private hospitals are affiliated with religious groups).

In modern societies, religion is typically "institutionalized." Max Weber (1921/1963) wrote that after the loss of the charismatic figure from whose life a religion was born, there is a crisis among followers, but there can also be a subsequent "routinization of charisma," which institutionalizes the religion and beliefs into an organizational structure. Early theorists such as Weber, Ernst Troeltsch (1931), and Richard Niebuhr (1929) described religious organizations as falling along a continuum based on the degree to which they are well established and conventional: Churches, for instance, lie at one end (they are conventional and well established), *cults* lie at the other (they are neither), and *sects* fall somewhere between. These distinctions were based on the study of European and U.S. religions, and there is some debate over how well they apply to the non-Christian world. Also, because the terms *sect* and *cult* have negative connotations today, sociologists sometimes use the phrase *new religious movements* to characterize novel religious organizations that lack mainstream credibility (Hadden, 1993; Hexham & Poewe, 1997). Next we look at the different forms religious organizations take.

CHURCH

A **church** is *a well-established religious organization that exists in a fairly harmonious relationship with the larger society*

(Finke & Stark, 1992). In everyday terms, churches are respectable, mainstream organizations that reflect their religious communities' prevailing values and beliefs. They are likely to be formally and bureaucratically organized, with fairly conventional practices. In the United States, examples include the Presbyterian, United Methodist, Greek Orthodox, and Roman Catholic churches.

A church can take one of two forms. An **ecclesia** is *formally allied with the state and is the official religion of the society.* As such, it is likely to enjoy special rights and privileges that other churches lack. In Greece, for instance, while the practice of other religions is not prohibited or punished, the constitution holds that the Greek Orthodox Church is the "prevailing" religion of the country. A **denomination**, in contrast, is *a church that is not formally allied with the state.* Since there is no established church (or ecclesia) in the United States, all U.S. churches are by definition denominations. The existence of denominations allows for freedom of religious choice, so different denominations may compete with one another for membership, and none enjoys the special favor of the state.

SECT

Unlike a church, which exists in relative harmony with the larger society, a **sect** is a religious organization that has splintered off from an established church in an effort to restore perceived "true" beliefs and practices believed to have been lost by the established religious organization. Protestant fundamentalist and evangelical religious groups are typically sects.

Sects often tend to hold religious beliefs consistent with the dominant ones in society. Yet, because they are splinter groups, they also may exist in tension with more established religious organizations. While churches tend to intellectualize religious practice, sects may emotionalize it, emphasizing heightened personal experience and religious conversion (Finke & Stark, 1992; Stark & Bainbridge, 1987/1996). Sects often appeal more to marginalized individuals than to people in the mainstream, drawing followers from among lower-income households, racial and ethnic minorities, and the rural poor.

Yet sects provide new sources of religious ideas and vitality outside mainstream faiths. When they are successful they may grow in size and evolve into churches, becoming bureaucratized and losing their emotional appeal (Niebuhr, 1929). A new sect may then break off, seeking to return to its religious roots. This occurred within both U.S. Protestantism and Japanese Buddhism in the late 20th century. Disturbed by the increasingly intellectualized and liberal direction taken by mainstream Protestant churches, numerous sects broke off, seeking to return to what they viewed as the biblical roots of the Protestant faith (Finke & Stark, 1992). Similarly, Buddhist sects in Japan sought a return to original Buddhist beliefs in response to what they regarded as the social isolation and irrelevance of mainstream Buddhist groups (Davis, 1991).

CULT

A **cult** is *a religious organization that is thoroughly unconventional with regard to the larger society* (Finke & Stark, 1992; Richardson, 2009). While sects often originate as offshoots of well-established religious organizations, cults tend to be new, with unique beliefs and practices that typically originate outside the religious mainstream. They may be led by charismatic figures who draw on a wide range of teachings to develop their novel ideas (Stark & Bainbridge, 1987/1996). The presence of a powerful personality can thus define a cult, and the loss of the leader can spell its end.

Cults may have relationships with the larger society that are characterized by strife and distrust. In recent years, "doomsday cults" that prophesy the end of the world have proliferated. The Church Universal and Triumphant (CUT), led by the charismatic leader Elizabeth Clare Prophet, is an example. The CUT's doctrine amalgamated bits of major religions such as Christianity and Buddhism along with mysticism, astrology, Western philosophy (Melton, 1996), and a belief in reincarnation (rebirth). Prophet herself, who led the cult after the death of her husband, Mark Prophet, claimed to have lived past lives as Marie Antoinette, Queen Guinevere of King Arthur's court, and the biblical figure Martha.

In 1990, Prophet predicted that the world would end, and hundreds of her followers fled to bomb shelters near Yellowstone National Park where the CUT had created a self-reliant community. Apparently, the group was also stockpiling weapons in its underground bunkers, and several members were later prosecuted on weapons charges. While the CUT lost members after the failed doomsday prediction, it continued to operate and grew in later years, though Elizabeth Clare Prophet passed away in 2009.

Like sects, cults flourish when there is a breakdown in well-established societal belief systems or when segments of the population feel alienated from the mainstream and seek meaning elsewhere. Cults may originate within or outside a society. Interestingly, what is perceived as a cult in one country may be accepted as established religious practice in another. Christianity began as an indigenous cult in ancient Jerusalem, and in many Asian countries today, evangelical Protestantism is regarded as a cult imported from the United States.

Ecclesia: A church that is formally allied with the state and is the "official" religion of the society.

Denomination: A church that is not formally allied with the state.

Sect: A religious organization that has splintered off from an established church in an effort to restore perceived "true" beliefs and practices believed to have been lost by the established religious organization.

Cult: A religious organization that is thoroughly unconventional with regard to the larger society.

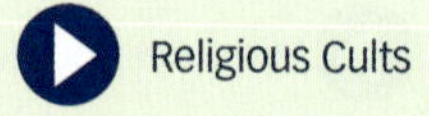

TECHNOLOGY & SOCIETY

ESCHATOLOGY ON THE INTERNET

Eschatology is the study of practices and beliefs related to the "end times"—that is, the end of the world as we know it. Religious scholars from many traditions have been drawn to this subject throughout history, and today interest appears to have blossomed among evangelical Christians, who make up a growing proportion of the churchgoing population in the United States.

The best-selling Left Behind book series chronicles the fictional adventures of a group of evangelical Christians living through the trials of the end times, including the rise of the Antichrist, plagues of illness and locusts, the battle of Armageddon, and Jesus's Second Coming. The Internet plays a dual role in relation to this series: First, it is an important part of the story line, as the unfolding tale includes a prophet addressing millions of new converts on his website about the biblical meaning of contemporary events. Second, the Left Behind site itself (http://leftbehind.com) purports to serve a similar role, offering to explain "how current events may actually relate to End Times prophecy" and providing a forum for both author and reader testimonials, as well as audio and video resources (including a recently added Russian-language site for its growing audience).

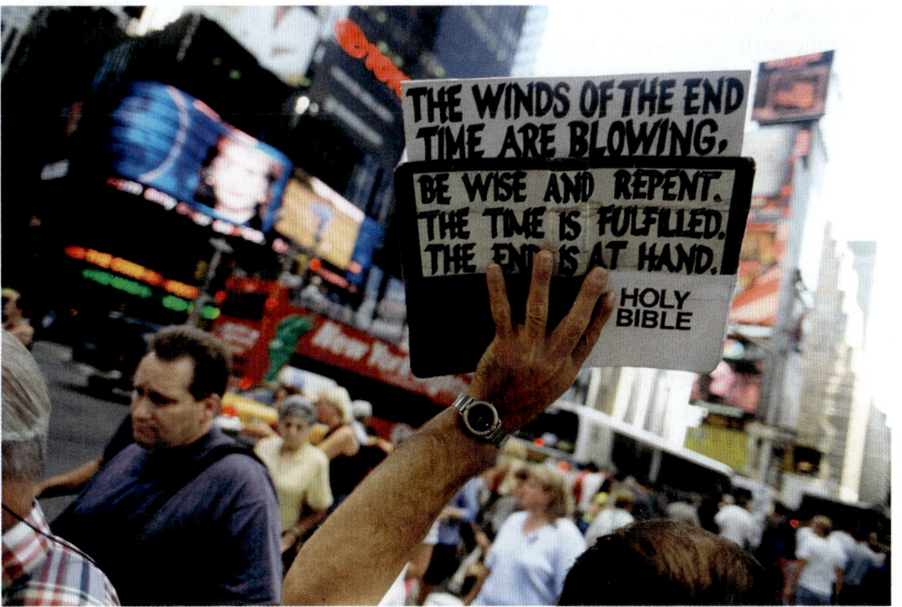

People have long been fascinated by stories about the end of the world. What makes these stories so powerful and compelling?

In light of this burgeoning interest in eschatology, dialogue and debate about the end of the world have become a widespread Internet phenomenon. Websites such as Rapture Ready (http://raptureready.com) cover a wide range of related topics, including the top 10 signs of the imminence of the end of the world as we know it, message boards, and long lists of frequently asked questions such as "What is hell like?" "How will the Antichrist take over the world?" and "When is the world going to end?"

While religious communities have long been home to self-styled prophets who claim to know when the world will end, the Internet has proved a powerful tool for the marketing of the ideas and products of evangelical Christianity and the dissemination of beliefs about how the end will occur (Clarke, 2011).

THINK IT THROUGH

▶ Do social media capture and reflect public interest in end-times stories, or do they actively create and expand that interest?

The youth culture of the 1960s and 1970s was fertile ground for the flowering of religious cults, leading sociologists of religion to adopt a more neutral term to describe them: **new religious movements (NRMs)**, or *new spiritual groups or communities that occupy a peripheral place in a country's dominant religious landscape.* Such movements may be small and based on the charisma of a single leader, evolving out of existence with the leader's death or departure. The growth of NRMs presented an ideal situation for sociological research into the development of new religions, helping to shed light on how the world's great religions came into being. There are many NRMs—by one estimate, between 1,500 and 2,000 in North America and in Africa perhaps 10,000—but few are enduring and most exist outside their countries' religious mainstreams (Hadden, 2006). NRMs may, however, evolve into sustained religious movements.

One such well-known religious movement is Scientology. The Church of Scientology began in the 1950s largely as a self-help movement. Today, it is a religious movement with members across the globe, and it benefits from the endorsement of a number of Hollywood figures such as Tom Cruise and John Travolta. As it has grown, Scientology has also courted its fair share of controversy. Its founder, L. Ron Hubbard, was a charismatic leader revered by adherents and reviled by detractors. Scientologists believe that Hubbard's ideology provides a path to greater self-awareness and spiritual enlightenment, while critics counter that the secretive religion is a cult that brainwashes its members and convinces them to pay exorbitant sums of money to access the esoteric knowledge central to their faith. While the controversy shows no signs of abating, Scientology's high-profile followers and considerable financial resources make it likely that this religious movement is here to stay (Urban, 2011).

FIGURE 13.2 The World's Dominant Religions by Percentage of Believers

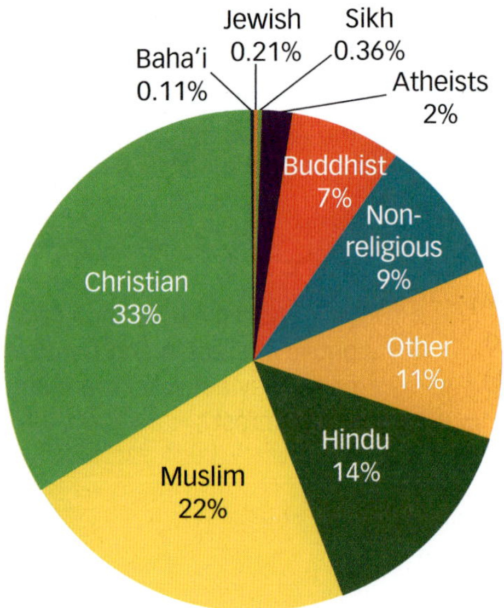

SOURCE: Central Intelligence Agency. (2013). The world factbook: World. Retrieved from https://www.cia.gov/library/publications/the-world-factbook/geos/xx.html.

THE GREAT WORLD RELIGIONS

From humankind's beginnings, the spiritual search for meaning and the need for religion as an organizing principle in communities have brought us to a point where thousands of different religions are followed throughout the world. However, just three—Christianity, Islam, and Hinduism—are practiced by nearly three-quarters of the people on earth. We look at these below, as well as at Judaism, Buddhism, and Confucianism, all of which have had powerful influence on global religious and social practices.

CHRISTIANITY

With more than 2.1 billion followers—nearly a third of the world's population—Christianity encompasses a broad spectrum of denominations, sects, and even new religious movements (Barrett, 2001). Common to all these is the belief that Jesus of Nazareth was the Messiah or savior foretold in the Hebrew Bible. While doctrinal differences separate the Christian faiths, almost all teach that, at the beginning of time, humans fell from God's grace through their sinful acts, and that acceptance of Christ and his teachings provides the key to salvation. Most Christians also believe in the New Testament account of the Resurrection, according to which Jesus rose from the dead on the third day after his crucifixion and then ascended to heaven. Christianity is a form of **monotheism**—*belief in a single all-knowing, all-powerful God*—although in most Christian faiths God is also regarded as a trinity made up of a Heavenly Father, His Son the Savior, and His sustaining Holy Spirit.

When Christianity emerged in Palestine some 2,000 years ago, it was a persecuted sect outside the mainstream of Jewish and Roman religious practices. Within four centuries it had become an ecclesia, or official religion, of the Roman Empire. In the 11th century, it divided into the Eastern Orthodox Church (based in Turkey) and the Catholic Church (based in Rome). A second great split occurred within the Catholic branch when the 16th-century Protestant Reformation gave rise to numerous Protestant denominations, sects, and cults. Protestants tend to emphasize a direct relationship between the individual and God. Catholics, by contrast, emphasize the importance of the church hierarchy as intermediary between the individual and God, with the pope in Rome being the final earthly authority.

New religious movements (NRMs): New spiritual groups or communities that occupy a peripheral place in a country's dominant religious landscape.

Monotheism: Belief in a single all-knowing, all-powerful God.

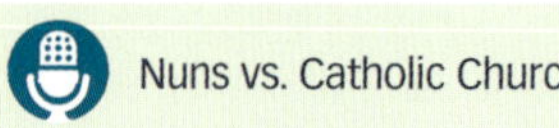

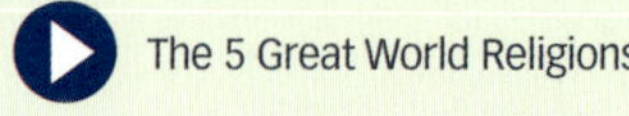

FIGURE 13.3 Muslims as Percentage of Country Population

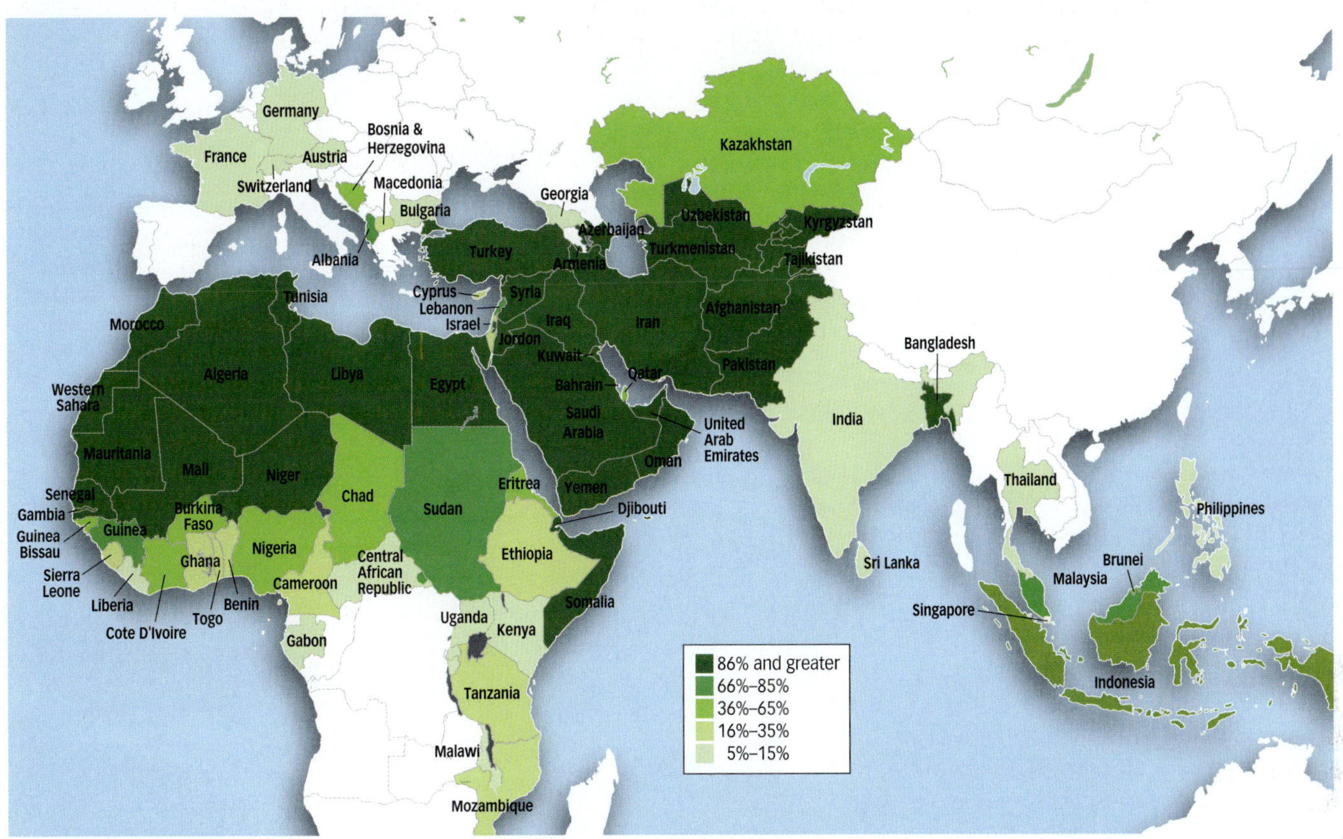

ISLAM

With 1.6 billion believers, Islam is the second-largest and the fastest-growing religion in the world today. *Muslim* is the term for those who practice *al-Islam,* an Arabic word meaning submission without reservation to God's will. About 60% of Muslims live in the Asia Pacific region, and about 20% in the Middle East and North Africa. Sub-Saharan Africa, Europe, and the Americas have growing Muslim populations as well (Pew Forum on Religion and Public Life, 2011a).

Although modern Islam dates to the seventh-century Arab prophet Muhammad, Muslims trace their religion to the ancient Hebrew prophet Abraham, also the founder of Judaism. The precepts of Islam as revealed to Muhammad are contained in a sacred book dictated to his followers and called the Koran (or Qur'an), which means "recitation." Muhammad's ideas were not initially accepted in his birthplace of Mecca, so in 622 he and his followers moved to Medina (both cities are in today's Saudi Arabia). This migration, called the *hijra,* marks the beginning of Islam, which later spread throughout Arabia. Muhammad is not worshipped by Muslims, who believe in positive devotion to Allah (God). Nor is Mohammad a messiah; he is rather a teacher and prophet, the last in a line that includes Abraham, Noah, Moses, and Jesus.

Islam's sacred *sharia* (or way) includes prescriptions for worship, daily life, ethics, and even government. Muslim life is governed by the Five Pillars of Islam, which are (1) accepting Allah as God and Muhammad as Allah's messenger; (2) worshipping according to rituals, including facing toward Mecca and bowing in prayer at five set times each day; (3) observing Ramadan, a month of prayer and fasting during the daylight hours; (4) giving *alms,* or donations, to those who are poor or in need; and (5) making a holy pilgrimage to Mecca at least once in a lifetime (Weeks, 1988). While all Muslims share these basic tenets, they are broadly divided into Sunnis and Shiites, between whom there may be tension, as in Iraq, which is Shiite dominated but has a strong Sunni minority. Globally, there are more Sunnis than Shiites.

The Koran also invokes *jihad* as a spiritual, personal struggle for enlightenment. Most Islamic terrorist groups, including al-Qaeda, however, translate *jihad* as armed struggle against the West and Western values. While some scholars argue that the shift from the struggle for personal enlightenment to armed struggle against Western values reflects "the growing confidence of the community as it developed from being a persecuted sect in Mecca to the triumphant 'super-tribe' of Muhammad's final years" (Ruthven, 2011, p. 83), others argue that it represents diverging attitudes of believers who are

© Kazuyoshi Nomachi/Corbis

In the last month of the Muslim year, thousands of Muslims make an annual pilgrimage (a hajj) to a holy shrine called the Ka'aba in Mecca. This site is believed to be the original location of a place of worship that God commanded Abraham and Ishmael to build over 4,000 years ago.

divided on the notion of struggle and the legitimate use of violence (Donner, 2012).

JUDAISM

With about 13 million followers worldwide, Judaism is the smallest of the world's major religions. Most Jews live in just two countries, Israel (home to about 42% of the global Jewish population) and the United States (39%), with small populations in many other countries (DellaPergola, 2010). Judaism has exerted a strong influence on the world, first as a key foundation of Islam and Christianity. Second, in European and U.S. culture, Jews have played a role disproportionate to their numbers in such diverse fields as music, literature, science, education, and business. Third, the existence of Israel as a Jewish state since 1948 has given the Jewish people and faith international prominence.

Judaism was one of the first religions to teach monotheism. Like many other religions, it teaches that its followers are God's chosen people, but unlike other religions, it does not teach that followers have a duty to convert others to their faith. The primary religious writing for the Jews is the Torah (or "law"), a scroll on which are inscribed the first five books of the Bible. Biblical tradition holds that Jewish law was given by God to Moses when he led the Jews out of slavery in Egypt about 3,500 years ago, and since then it has been elaborated upon by rabbis, or teachers. Today it is codified in books called the Mishnah and the Talmud.

Three principal divisions in Judaism reflect differing perspectives on the nature of biblical law. Orthodox Judaism believes that the Bible derives from God and that its teachings are absolutely binding, while Reform Judaism views the Bible as a historical document containing important ethical precepts,

© Kevin Frayer/AP/Corbis

The Bar Mitzvah (for boys) and Bat Mitzvah (for girls) rituals are an important rite of passage for Jewish youth.

but not literally the word of God. Conservative Judaism occupies a middle ground, maintaining many traditional practices while adapting others to modern society.

Jews have often suffered persecution, and anti-Semitism has a long global history. From the 12th century on, European and Russian Jews were often forced to live in special districts termed *ghettos,* where they lacked full rights as citizens and were sometimes targets of harassment and violence. Partly in reaction to these conditions, and partly because the Torah identifies Jerusalem as the center of the Jewish homeland, some Jews embraced **Zionism**, *a movement calling for the return of Jews to Palestine and the creation of a Jewish state.* (Zion is a biblical name for the ancient city of Jerusalem.)

Zionists established settlements in Palestine early in the 20th century, living for the most part peacefully with their Arab and Palestinian neighbors. Following World War II and the Nazi extermination of 6 million Jews, the state of Israel was created as a homeland for the survivors, an action that both gave refuge to Jews and ignited territorial tensions in the region that continue to this day.

HINDUISM

Hinduism, about 2,000 years older than Christianity, is one of the oldest religions in the world and the source of Buddhism and Sikhism. It is not based on the teachings of any single individual, and its followers do not trace their origins to a single deity. It is a broadly defined religion that calls for an ideal way of life. According to a report on international religious freedom by the U.S. Department of State (2010), there are between 950 million and 1 billion Hindus throughout the world, primarily in India, where they make up the large majority of the population.

Indian social structure is characterized by a caste system, officially abolished in 1949 but still powerful, in which people are believed to be born to a certain status that they must occupy for life. This system has its origins in the Hindu belief that one achieves an ideal life in part by performing the duties appropriate to one's caste. Hindus, like Buddhists, believe in *samsara,* the reincarnation of the soul according to a person's *karma,* or actions on earth. Whether someone is reborn into a higher or lower caste depends on the degree to which the person is committed to *dharma,* or the ideal way of life. Although orthodox Hinduism requires observance of caste duties, for the past 500 years religious societies have organized around gurus who break with caste conventions, emphasizing devotional love as the central spiritual act. This tradition influenced Mahatma Gandhi, the leader of India's independence movement, and others who have viewed Hinduism as a vehicle for social reform (Juergensmeyer, 1995).

Perhaps because Hinduism does not have a central organization or leader, its philosophy and practice are particularly diverse. Religious teachings touch all aspects of life, from the enjoyment of sensual pleasures to stark renunciation of earthly pursuits. Hindus believe in the God-like unity of all things, yet their religion also has aspects of **polytheism**, the belief that *different gods represent various categories of natural forces.* For example, Hindus worship different gods representing aspects of the whole, such as the divine dimension of a spiritual teacher (Basham, 1989).

BUDDHISM

Buddhism was founded in India by Siddhartha Gautama five centuries before Christ. According to legend, the young Siddhartha renounced an upper-caste life of material splendor in search of a more meaningful existence. A lifetime of wandering, occasional poverty, and different spiritual practices eventually taught him the way to achieve enlightenment, and he became the *Buddha,* the awakened or enlightened one. Buddhism is an example of a **nontheistic religion**, in that it involves *belief in the existence of divine spiritual forces rather than a god or gods.* It is more a set of rules for righteous living than a doctrine of belief in a particular god.

Gautama Buddha's philosophy is contained in the Four Noble Truths. First, all beings—gods, humans, and animals—are caught up in an endless round of suffering and rebirth, the result of their karma or actions. Second, suffering results from desire or attachment. To the extent that we depend on wealth or friends or family or even religious beliefs for satisfaction, we are condemned to suffer unending frustration and loss. Third, suffering can be overcome if we break the endless cycle of karma

Zionism: A movement calling for the return of Jews to Palestine and the creation of a Jewish state.

Polytheism: The belief that there are different gods representing various categories of natural forces.

Nontheistic religion: Belief in the existence of divine spiritual forces rather than a god or gods.

FIGURE 13.4 The World's Dominant Religions by Region

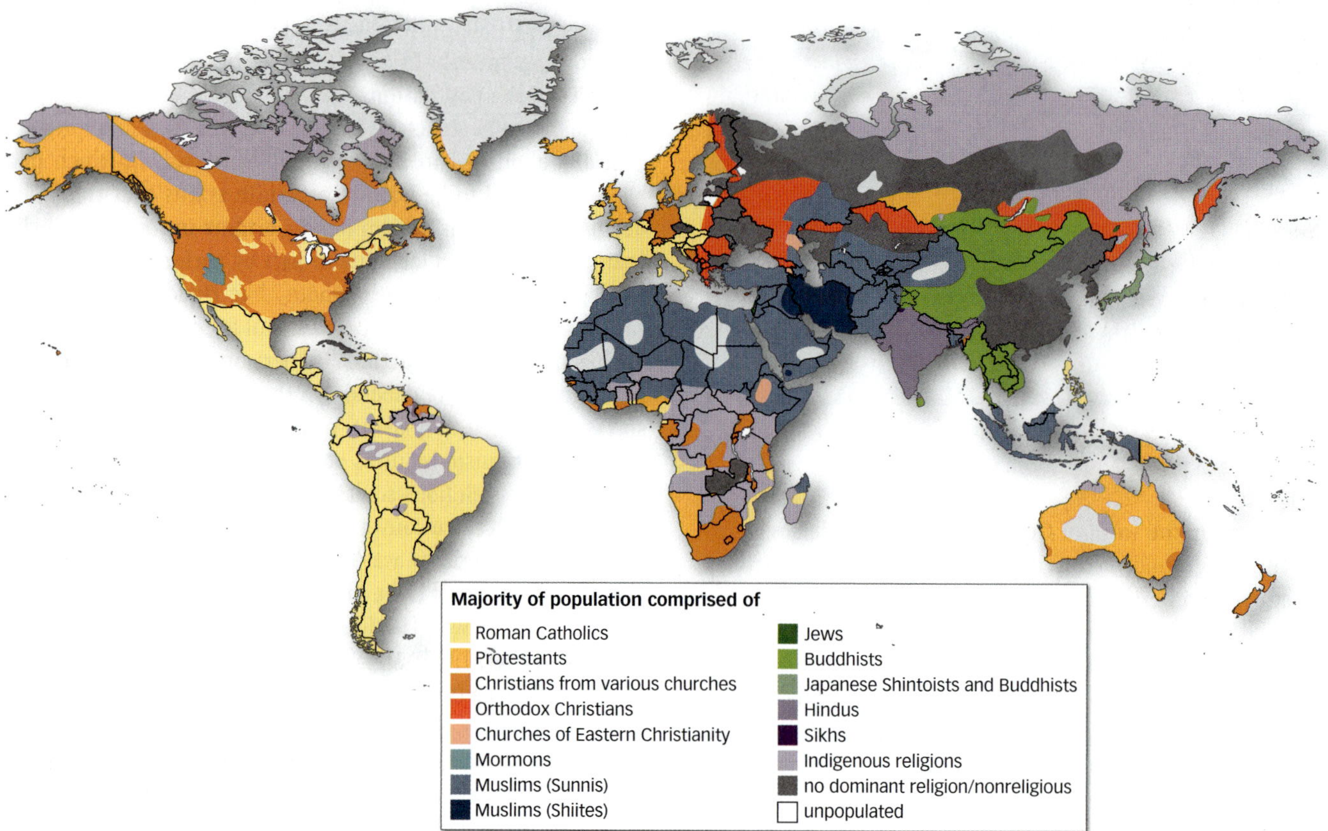

and rebirth and achieve nirvana—a blissful state of emptiness. Fourth, the means of achieving nirvana are contained in the Eightfold Path, which advocates ethical behavior, a simple lifestyle, renunciation of material pleasures, meditation, and eventually enlightenment.

Many people practice certain precepts of Buddhism without calling themselves Buddhists, so it is difficult to estimate accurately the number of Buddhists in the world today. Estimates put the figure at about 350 million (Central Intelligence Agency, 2013). Theravada Buddhism, the "Way of the Elders" or the "Lesser Vehicle," predominates in Myanmar, Thailand, Laos, Cambodia, and Sri Lanka. It is strongly identified with local cultures, and traditional rulers in Thailand and Sri Lanka are religious figures as well. Mahayana Buddhism, the "Greater Vehicle," is practiced in China, Korea, and Japan, where it is not the official religion but mixes with other cultural strands. In China, Buddhism is intertwined with Taoist folk religion and Confucian codes of ethical practice. In Japan, Shinto Buddhism combines emperor worship with elements of **animism**, the belief, common to many religions, *that naturally occurring phenomena, such as mountains and animals, are possessed of indwelling spirits with supernatural powers.*

Buddhism's meditative lifestyle may strike some people as incompatible with life in a modern industrial society, which emphasizes work, consumption, achievement, and all forms of karma that Buddhists regard as barriers to enlightenment and happiness. On the other hand, it is primarily Buddhist monks rather than ordinary practicing Buddhists who devote extended periods to meditation. Perhaps because of its emphasis on contemplation and meditation, Buddhism continues to attract followers in Western countries, including celebrities such as actor Orlando Bloom, singer Tina Turner, and the late Steve Jobs of Apple (Lampman, 2006; MacLeod, 2011).

CONFUCIANISM

Confucianism, the name of which comes from the English pronunciation of the name of its founder, K'ung-Fu-tzu (551–479 B.C.), is more of a philosophical system for ethical living on earth than a religion honoring a transcendental god (Fingarette, 1972). K'ung-Fu-tzu never wrote down his teachings, but his followers compiled many in a book called *The Analects* that became the foundation of official ethics and

Animism: The belief that naturally occurring phenomena, such as mountains and animals, are possessed of indwelling spirits with supernatural powers.

politics for some 2,000 years in China, until Confucianism was banned after the communist revolution in 1949. Though there are only about 6 million practitioners of Confucianism—almost all in Asia—this religion has had enormous influence in China, neighboring countries such as Korea and Vietnam, and Japan (Barrett, 2001).

Confucianism emphasizes harmony in social relations; respect for authority, hierarchy, and tradition; and the honoring of elders. Rulers are expected to be morally virtuous, setting an example for others to imitate. The group is more important than the individual. The key element in Confucian ethics is *jen,* meaning "love" or "goodness" and calling for faithfulness and altruism; we should never do anything to another person we would not want done to ourselves. Contemporary Confucianism, sometimes called "neo-Confucianism," has mystical elements as well as moral ones, including belief in the Tao (pronounced *dow*), or "way of being," determined by the natural harmony of the universe.

Confucianism teaches that opposites are not necessarily antagonistic; together they make up a harmonious whole that is constantly in a creative state of tension or change. The two major principles in the universe, *yin* (the female principle) and *yang* (the male principle), are found in all things, and their dynamic interaction accounts for both harmony and change. The *I Ching* (Book of Changes) contains philosophical teachings based on this view and a technique for determining a wise course of action.

Today many scholars argue that Confucian values such as respect for authority and a highly disciplined work ethic partly explain the current rapid economic growth in Singapore, Taiwan, China, and other Asian countries (Berger, 1986; Berger & Hsiao, 1988; MacFarquhar, 1980). On one hand, this perspective supports Weber's argument that actions rooted in religious beliefs are linked to economic development. On the other hand, it challenges Weber's exclusive emphasis on Western religion, and Protestantism in particular, as the source of this development.

WOMEN AND RELIGION

Although both men and women embrace the major religions of the world, the principal deities, prophets, and leaders of religions are often male. God is depicted as male, beliefs typically emphasize male religious and political superiority, and women are often excluded from positions of theological power. The sociological explanation is straightforward: These religions were initially developed by men within patriarchal societies and therefore reflect patriarchal norms and values. As we noted earlier, sociologists see religions as social creations reflecting the norms, roles, and values embraced by communities and societies.

According to the Jewish and Christian Bible, Eve, the first woman, violated God's command and tempted Adam to eat fruit from the Tree of Knowledge, leading to the pair's loss of innocence and expulsion from the Garden of Eden, or Paradise. Consequently, all human suffering can be traced to Eve's deception (Genesis 3). The book of Proverbs instructs the good wife to oversee the servants, to care for her family, and to be kind, fertile, obedient, and submissive to her husband. Even today, Orthodox Jewish males recite a daily prayer thanking God "that thou hast not created me a Gentile [non-Jew], a Slave, or a Woman." For Christians, Saint Paul's teachings instructed wives "to submit yourselves to your husbands as to the Lord. For the husband is the head of the wife, even as Christ is the head of the church. . . . So also wives should submit to their husbands in everything" (Ephesians 5:23–24).

Women have long played an important but unheralded role in religion. For example, Ann Lee (1736–1784), the leader of the "Shaking Quakers" in England, led a group to the United States and founded the first Shaker settlement in 1776. Alma White (1862–1946) was not only the first female evangelist ordained a bishop in the United States but also a pioneer in the use of an electronic medium, the radio, to spread beliefs (Stanley, 1993). Aimee Semple McPherson (1890–1944) founded the International Church of the Foursquare Gospel, which today claims some 26,000 churches in 74 countries (Epstein, 1993). Mary Baker Eddy (1821–1910) founded Christian Science, along with the newspaper the *Christian Science Monitor.* Her influence was felt not only in religion but also in the early women's movement. Eddy was a strong feminist who argued passionately for women's equality: "In natural law and in religion, the right of women to fill the highest measure of enlightened understanding and the highest places in government is inalienable. . . . This is women's hour, with all its sweet amenities and its moral and religious reforms" (Eddy, 1887/1999, p. 45).

In recent years there has been an upsurge of feminist spirituality, especially within the United States. Some women have turned to religious traditions that predate Judaism and Christianity, including the celebration of Goddess-based religions. The Goddess acts not only as a literal divine entity but also as a symbol of the historical significance and celebration of the feminine ideal.

Some feminist activists have sought reform within mainstream religions, fighting for the reimagination of God as ungendered, calling for nonsexist language in Scripture and services, and redesigning traditions and rituals along nonsexist lines (Eller, 2000; Wallace, 1992; Weidman, 1984). Almost all Protestant denominations now have female clergy, and even some Catholic churches offer women the opportunity to act as lay clergy, although the mainstream Catholic Church continues to oppose the practice (Wallace, 1992).

INEQUALITY MATTERS

WOMEN, HUNGER, AND RELIGIOUS EMPOWERMENT

Women have historically lacked a prominent role in the theologies and hierarchies of mainstream religions. We find an interesting historical counterexample, however, in the fasting women of medieval Europe. In *Fasting Girls* (2000), Joan Jacobs Brumberg writes that among 13th- to 16th-century Catholics, particularly women, food was a symbolic language: "Control of appetite was linked to piety and belief; through fasting, the medieval ascetic strove for perfection in the eyes of her God" (p. 48). According to Brumberg, fasting women of the medieval period spoke of their "hunger" for God and their "inebriation" with the holy wine. Their fasts, lasting from weeks to years, elevated them within their communities as objects of spiritual awe; through this act they claimed religious power, or at least widespread reverence from the religious community. Though their behavior had a label, "anorexia mirabilis," it was not seen as a psychological, biological, or cultural affliction (as anorexia nervosa is today). Rather, it was a demonstration of piety and celebrated as such.

Though the link between fasting behavior and spiritual elevation was somewhat weaker by the end of the 16th century, Brumberg suggests there were still ample instances of female holiness being associated with the ascetic denial of food and drink, continuing into the Victorian era in both Western Europe and the United States. In this period, there was both skepticism and celebration of "fasting girls," women who seemed to have transcended the worldly body and its physical needs. According to Brumberg, "Many who were pietists or pious Catholics embraced the cause of a particular fasting girl, either because her story reinvigorated the tradition of anorexia mirabilis and Christian miracles or because her existence demonstrated the independence of the spirit from the flesh, a central tenet of Victorian Spiritualism" (p. 64). Spiritualists were those who embraced the idea of transcendence over the material body, and fasting girls offered a focal point for challenging the belief that the body needed food to live.

By the 19th century, food refusal was labeled a disease. No longer did women whose fasts lasted for weeks or months attract celebration and elevation. Rather, they became objects of medical attention, parental concern, and societal curiosity. Anorexia mirabilis, however, whether piety or affliction, remains an interesting premodern manifestation of women's use of food as a symbolic language, and of food refusal as a means to garner attention and, arguably, empowerment. In their emaciation and asceticism, some women found an avenue to affirmation and adoration in early religious communities, though achieved in part through their physical enervation and even death from starvation.

Fasting is a cultural staple of some religions. Catherine of Siena, a Roman Catholic, practiced extended fasts, even putting her life in jeopardy for her faith.

THINK IT THROUGH

▶ From a contemporary perspective, was the historical phenomenon of anorexia mirabilis a manifestation of women's religious marginalization or of their empowerment?

 Women and Religious Self-Identity

RELIGION IN THE UNITED STATES

Compared to citizens of other modern industrial nations, Americans are unusually religious. While secularization has weakened the power of religious institutions, religious adherence and beliefs remain strong in the United States, where most adults profess an affiliation with a religious group (Figure 13.5): About 78% self-identify as Christian, with smaller numbers identifying as Jewish (1.8%), Muslim (0.9%), and Buddhist (1.2%). About 16% of U.S. adults are unaffiliated with a religion; 6% say they are religious but unaffiliated, while the rest are secular unaffiliated, agnostic, or atheist. About 39% attend religious services at least weekly, 35% read Scripture weekly, and 58% pray on a daily basis (Pew Forum on Religion and Public Life, 2010).

TRENDS IN RELIGIOUS AFFILIATION

The United States is more religious than other economically developed countries. One reason for the continuing high levels of religious group membership among Americans is that churches, synagogues, and mosques are important sources of social ties and friendship networks, connecting people with others who share the same beliefs and values. Another reason is simply that there are an enormous number of such organizations to belong to—supporting the religious economy perspective we examined earlier. The United States is the most religiously diverse country in the world, with more than 1,500 distinct religions (Melton, 1996; T. W. Smith, 2002). In the remainder of this section we look at two seemingly contrasting trends in U.S. religious life: the rise of conservative Protestantism, specifically evangelicalism, and the declining level of religious affiliation among young U.S. adults.

FIGURE 13.5 **Religious Affiliation in the United States, 2010**

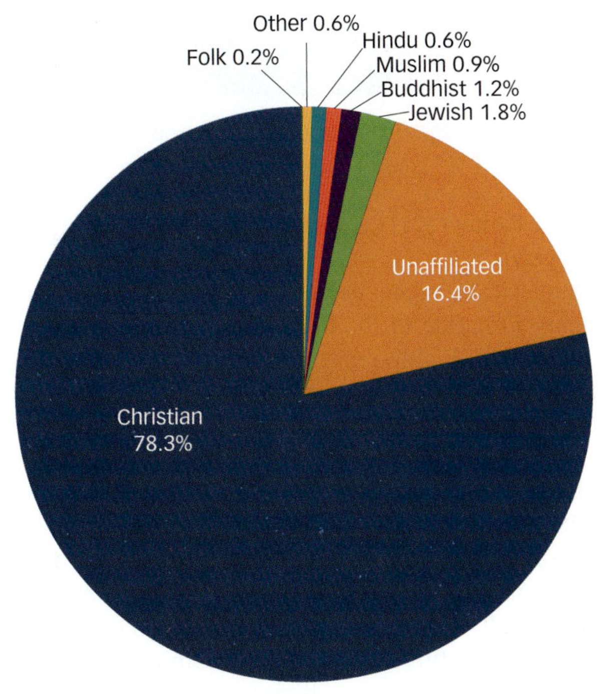

SOURCE: Pew Forum on Religion and Public Life. (2012a). *The global religious landscape: A report on the size and distribution of the world's major religious groups as of 2010*. Washington, DC: Pew Research Center. Retrieved from http://www.pewforum.org/files/2014/01/global-religion-full.pdf.

The conservative strand of U.S. Protestantism has been growing in both membership and influence in recent years. Conservative Protestants emphasize a literal interpretation of the Bible, Christian morality in daily life as well as public politics, and conversion of others through evangelizing. Liberal Protestants generally adopt a more flexible, humanistic approach to their religious practices, and moderate Protestants are somewhere in between. While all groups grew from the 1920s through the 1960s, both liberal and moderate churches have since experienced a decline in membership, while the number of conservative Protestants has expanded considerably (Pew Forum on Religion and Public Life, 2008).

A key aspect of this growth is the rise of **evangelicalism**, *a belief in spiritual rebirth (being "born again")*. This often includes the admission of personal sin and salvation through acceptance of Christ, a literal interpretation of the Bible, an emphasis on highly emotional and personal spiritual piety, and a commitment to spreading "the Word" to others (Balmer, 1989). (The word *evangel* comes from the Greek for "bringing good news.") We can interpret the rise of evangelicalism as a response to growing secularism, religious diversity, and, in general, the decline of once-core Protestant values in U.S. life (Wuthnow, 1988).

Conservative Protestants have been an active force in U.S. politics, and their growing numbers may be linked to a recent rise in their political influence, particularly within the Republican Party. They have, in fact, become a key constituency for Republicans. Data from the past decade confirm the emergence of a "worship attendance gap" in presidential politics; specifically, "the more observant members of religious communities tend to vote Republican while their less observant co-religionists tend to vote Democratic. This attendance gap has been largest among the white Christian traditions, but has appeared in a more modest form within nearly all religious affiliations" (Dionne & Green, 2008, p. 5). Not only are strongly religious voters more likely to vote Republican, but they also seem increasingly more likely to vote at all. That is, they are active in politics to a degree that many other groups are not.

Consider, for instance, the political influence of the Tea Party movement, whose members affiliate with the Republican

Evangelicalism: A belief in spiritual rebirth (conventionally denoted as being "born again").

CQR Religion in Politics   CQR Megachurches

© Geoffrey Clements/Corbis

Some evangelical Christian groups have access to extensive resources for recruitment and worship. The facility here used to be home to the Houston Rockets, and was converted to an evangelical church that took about $75 million to renovate.

Party and draw a substantial degree of support from White evangelical Protestants. Those who identify as Tea Party members are far more likely than registered voters as a whole to say that "religion is the most important factor in determining their opinion on . . . social issues [in politics, such as abortion and same-sex marriage]" (Pew Forum on Religion and Public Life, 2011b). Surveys conducted by the Pew Forum on Religion and Public Life also show that White evangelical Protestants are about five times as likely to agree with the ideas of the Tea Party as to disagree (44% versus 8%), though substantial numbers also have no opinion or have not heard of the movement (48%). When we consider that members of the Tea Party, still a nascent political movement in 2010, made up fully 41% of the voters in the November elections that year, we can see the strong potential for religious communities and beliefs to shape political life in the United States (Pew Forum on Religion and Public Life, 2011b).

Many U.S. voters' political beliefs and actions are shaped by religious faith. Not surprisingly, then, many also expect their political leaders to share their faith: A 2011 survey showed that fully 61% of respondents would be less likely to support a presidential candidate who "does not believe in God" (Pew Research Center, 2011), a figure that has held steady across recent years.

Paradoxically, recent decades have also seen the decline of religious affiliation in the United States. That is, while U.S. adults are still highly religious compared to their counterparts in other modern states (European states in particular), recent research suggests that a generational shift is taking place with the potential to transform the U.S. religious landscape. While just 16% of U.S. adults report being "unaffiliated" with a religion, fully a quarter of those between 18 and 29 are not affiliated. This is in stark contrast to older generations: Just 14% of Americans ages 50 to 59, 10% of those 60 to 69, and 8% of those 70 and older do not profess an affiliation. (The shift may also help explain why more women than men claim religious affiliation—just 13% of women are unaffiliated compared to nearly 20% of men: Due to differences in life expectancy, there are more women than men in the oldest age groups.) Further, today's young adults are more likely than young adults of earlier generations to indicate no religious affiliation; in studies done in the 1970s and 1980s, about half as many young adults identified themselves as unaffiliated with a religion. The Pew Forum on Religion

FIGURE 13.6 Composition of Religiously Unaffiliated Americans, 2012

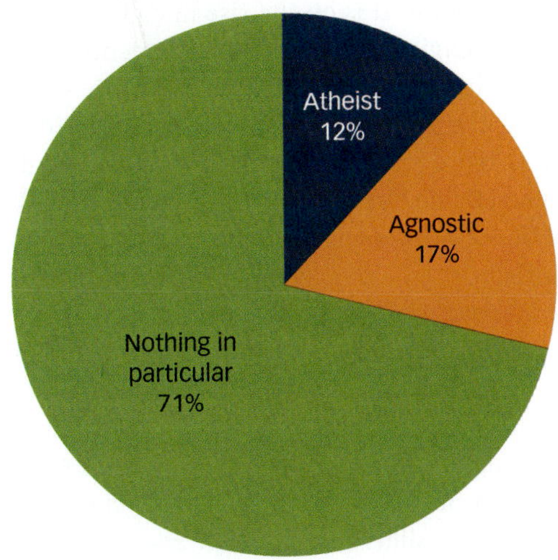

SOURCE: Pew Research Center. (2012). *Nones on the rise: One-in-five adults have no religious affiliation*. Washington, DC: Pew Research Center. Retrieved from http://www.pewforum.org/2012/10/09/nones-on-the-rise/. Reprinted with permission.

and Public Life (2010) suggests that this change is "a result, in part, of the decision by many young people to leave the religion of their upbringing without becoming involved with a new faith" (p. 4).

Recall the religious economy perspective discussed earlier. Can it help us understand the growing numbers of young people who do not affiliate with a religion? Does it suggest that religious organizations are failing to "market" themselves effectively? Or does it mean that other sources of spiritual or personal fulfillment are available to young adults and act as what Robert Merton called "functional equivalents," fulfilling the functions of religion but assuming a different form?

RELIGION AND DISESTABLISHMENT

According to Phillip Hammond (1992), religion in the United States has three times undergone **disestablishment**, *a period during which the political influence of established religions is successfully challenged.* One occurred with the 1791 ratification of the first 10 amendments to the U.S. Constitution (the Bill of Rights), the first of which calls for a firm separation of church and state. Some sociologists see this separation as part of a larger trend in industrial societies, in which different institutions specialize in different functions—from economics to medicine, from education to politics. Religion is no exception (Alexander & Thompson, 2008; Chaves, 1993, 1994; Parsons, 1951, 1960, 1966). Recall Thomas O'Dea's (1966) suggestion, noted earlier, that in traditional societies "the same social groups provide satisfaction for both expressive and adaptive needs," whereas modern societies separate these two functions (p. 36).

The second period of disestablishment occurred between the 1890s and the 1920s, fed by an influx of about 17 million immigrants, mainly European and many Catholic. For the first time, the notion of a predominantly Protestant United States was challenged, and the mainstream Protestant churches never regained their influence in politics or in defining national values. The third period occurred during the 1960s and the 1970s, when core religious beliefs and values were further eroded by the anti–Vietnam War movement, the fight for racial equality, and experimentation with alternative lifestyles. Fundamental challenges came in the form of increased openness about sexuality and lifestyle preferences, the women's movement, and changes in attitudes and laws about birth control (Glock & Bellah, 1976; Hammond, 1992; Roof & McKinney, 1990; Wuthnow, 1976, 1978).

Disestablishment of religion reduces its political influence but does not make it less important to individuals. In fact, if religious groups compete with one another for followers, religious practices are more likely to be tailored to public tastes (Moore, 1994); this result fits the perspective of religious economy we discussed earlier. We have also seen, however, that conservative Protestant religious organizations have increasingly made their voices heard in U.S. politics. President George W. Bush's period in office was marked by close ties between Bush and conservative religious organizations, and some political analysts suggest that his aspirations to democratize the Middle East, for instance, reflected not only pragmatic political considerations but also a spiritual sense that the United States is called to be a "beacon of freedom and democracy." More recently, as we noted earlier, the Tea Party movement has raised the profile and power of U.S. conservative religious groups.

"CIVIL RELIGION" IN THE UNITED STATES

Some sociologists have argued that the United States has a **civil religion**, *a set of sacred beliefs and practices that become part of how a society sees itself* (Alexander & Thompson, 2008; Bellah, 1968, 1975; Mathisen, 1989). Civil religion usually involves the use of "god language" in reference to the nation, including historical myths about the society's divine origins, beliefs about its sacred historical purpose, and, occasionally, religious restrictions on societal membership (Wuthnow, 1988).

The infusion of divine meaning into historical events is visible in President Abraham Lincoln's (1809–1865) oratory on the Civil War. In the Gettysburg Address, Lincoln, who was not

Disestablishment: A period during which the political influence of established religions is successfully challenged.

Civil religion: A set of sacred beliefs and practices that become part of how a society sees itself.

Contextualizing Civil Religion

highly religious himself, drew on religious imagery to attach meaning to the brutal destruction and enormous human cost of the war. He labeled his fellow citizens the "almost chosen people" and called the United States "the last, best hope on earth." You might have noticed that even today, the president and other politicians often end their speeches with the words "God bless America."

As we noted in this chapter's opening vignette, the phrase "under God" was added to the Pledge of Allegiance by Congress in 1954, amid fears of the Cold War and "godless communism." The words are consistent with the construction of a civil religion and a nation worshipping itself and envisioning itself as fulfilling a divine destiny. Even though the First Amendment to the U.S. Constitution clearly calls for a separation of church and state, this profession of allegiance to "one nation, under God" came to be seen as central to U.S. citizenship. What do you think about the content of the Pledge of Allegiance? Does it endorse religion, or is it a civil rather than a religious declaration? Why do you think different people read this legal question differently?

RELIGION AND GLOBAL SOCIETIES

Thanks in part to the Internet, globalization has transformed religion into a more fluid form that easily crosses boundaries and mixes traditions from different areas. While religions have always evolved, today's sustained and regular contact among people of varying religious traditions is unprecedented. The embrace of new ideas may create harmony, tension, or even violence.

The global emergence of a scientific-technological culture that colors people's views and behaviors presents a powerful challenge to the world's traditional religions. It means that fewer people may employ religious explanations for natural or social phenomena as increasing numbers probe beyond explanations that refer to a divine plan. Religion may still enrich personal lives, but its role in public life, at least in the most economically advanced countries, has declined.

A second challenge of globalization is the growing contact between large religions with mass followings that claim to possess exclusive accounts of history and the nature of reality. This contact is both a potential and an actual source of tension and conflict, which can fuel "culture wars" as well as real wars that leaders cast as battles between religions and values or even between "good and evil." In fact, rather than leading to a merging of religions (in the manner of a global "culture" of consumption or popular music), globalization may be fostering a backlash against blending that reveals itself as fundamentalism. Fundamentalism is also associated with the rise of religious nationalism.

Religious nationalism is *the linkage of religious convictions with beliefs about a nation's or ethnic group's social and political destiny.* It is on the rise in countries around the world where religious nationalist movements have revived traditional religious beliefs and rejected the separation of religion and the state (Beyer, 1994; Kinnvall, 2004). While the trend is more pronounced among Islamic fundamentalists in some Middle Eastern countries, the United States has also experienced the rising political influence of evangelical Protestantism.

The conservative Christian lobby in the United States has been particularly vocal—and often influential—on domestic issues such as abortion and gay marriage, both of which it opposes. It has also had some impact on global policy making. For example, Christian evangelicals have lobbied for U.S. intervention in Sudan, the site of a bloody civil war between Christians and Muslims in the north and a genocide perpetrated by Arab militias (supported by the Sudanese government) against Black Africans in Darfur.

Christian and Islamic religious nationalist movements accept modern technology, politics, and economics; many use the Internet and social media to disseminate information and ideas. At the same time, they interpret religious values strictly and reject secularization, drawing selectively on traditions and past events that serve their current beliefs and interests. Benedict Anderson (1991) writes about "imagined communities," suggesting that nations are real but not "natural"—that is, they are unified by both real and invented traditions and heroes that legitimate their claims about territories, the past, and the present. Part of the Israeli and Palestinian conflict over land is rooted in different narratives of history that tell diverging stories about who has "true" dominion over the territory.

Religious affiliations can bring communities together or tear them apart. India is the world's largest democracy, one of the world's largest countries in terms of population (more than 1 billion), and home to Hindus, Muslims, Christians, and believers in dozens of other religions. Diversity and democracy sometimes appear to be on shaky ground there, however, particularly when the extreme nationalist ideology of *Hindutva* (or "Hinduness") comes into contact with Muslim extremism. In the northern Indian town of Ayodhya, a mosque was built in the early 16th century on the site where Hindus believe Lord Ram, a sacred deity in Hinduism, was born. Since the 19th century, clashes between Hindus and Muslims have taken place on the site. In 1992, Hindu nationalists attacked the mosque, sparking riots across the country that killed more than 2,000 people. The site continues to be the object of contention, though the conflict appears to have shifted to the Indian courts: In 2010, a

Religious nationalism: The linkage of religious convictions with beliefs about a nation's or ethnic group's social and political destiny.

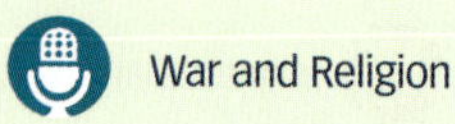
War and Religion

Reuters/Nayef Hashlamoun

The Israeli–Palestinian conflict is a deeply entrenched battle between two political-religious groups and their supporters. This conflict has demanded the attention and resources of the United States and other countries as they try to find a diplomatic solution to the conflict. ■

high court ruled that the site should be split among Muslims, Hindus, and a local sect (BBC, 2012).

Most of the world's religions actively embrace the values of peace, humanity, and charity. Many believe religion is the basis of morality. On the other hand, religion in various forms, including religious nationalism, has been and remains associated with intolerance, discrimination, and violence. How are we to reconcile these two sides of religion as a local, national, and global institution? Is religion as an institution a force for positive change or a rationale for conflict? Might it be both? What do you think?

WHY STUDY THE SOCIOLOGY OF RELIGION?

Studying religion from a sociological perspective does not mean embracing or rejecting religious values; it means examining and analyzing an institution that is central to humans on an individual, societal, and global level. In the United States today, the sociology of religion may be especially relevant. First, the question of whether disestablishment is proceeding or receding is an important one. Though the country's political foundations call for the separation of church and state, religious organizations seek to influence politics and public policy. Can religious devotion mix comfortably with domestic and foreign policy, or are the two a volatile brew to be avoided? These are questions of both intellectual and political significance.

Second, on a global level, the "war on terror" initiated by President George W. Bush in 2001 in the wake of the terrorist attacks of 9/11 brought questions about religion and politics to the forefront across the globe. For instance, the United States was faulted for failing to recognize why calling the "war on terror" a "crusade" would offend Muslim sensibilities. Tensions between the West and the Muslim world provoked questions about whether there is a "clash of civilizations" that makes conflict difficult to avoid. Some in the United States worry about the "Islamization" of the Middle East and other regions, while others question the power and political influence of religion in their own U.S. government. Debates about religion and its place in communities, societies, and the world will continue to challenge sociologists in the decades to come.

WHAT CAN I DO WITH A SOCIOLOGY DEGREE?

CAREER DEVELOPMENT: CONSIDERING GRADUATE AND PROFESSIONAL EDUCATION, PART II

In the previous chapter's feature essay, we looked at how you might go about assessing your motivations to pursue graduate or professional education and ways you can begin to explore potential career fields associated with graduate or professional study. Below you will learn about degree options available to those who have completed a bachelor's degree and the challenges and opportunities associated with advanced study.

Research Degree Options and Graduate Schools

There are several types of graduate degrees. The most traditional are the master's and doctoral degrees. Master's degrees are academic or professional. The academic master's degrees, master of arts (MA) and master of science (MS), focus on intellectual development and the mastery of a core of knowledge in a particular discipline. One may, for instance, earn a master's degree in sociology, anthropology, biology, or English. Professional master's degrees include the master of business administration (MBA) and the master of social work (MSW), which are designed to advance careers or professions in their respective fields.

The doctor of medicine (MD) and juris doctor (JD) degrees focus on the acquisition of advanced skills and knowledge in the areas of medical practice and law, respectively. The typical amount of time required to earn these professional degrees is generally lengthier than that for a master's-level professional degree such as the MBA or MSW.

The doctor of philosophy degree (PhD), or doctorate, focuses on advancing intellectual knowledge through original research. The focus of doctoral studies is on the broad mastery of disciplinary knowledge, the development of areas of specialization in the discipline, and rigorous, original research that contributes to the discipline and, perhaps, to policy and general societal knowledge of important topics. Consider this chapter's key focus, religion. As we saw, the sociological study of religion highlights the understanding of societal functions of religion. A student interested in the sociology of religion who is studying to earn a PhD might build a doctoral dissertation project around a question such as "How do religious beliefs affect political behavior?" or "Why are young Americans today less likely than those in previous generations to profess a religious affiliation?" Doctoral study opens many avenues for students to pursue original research on topics about which they are intellectually curious, though doctoral study is a lengthy commitment, often requiring a minimum of 4 years.

Once you have considered different degree options, learn about graduate schools by conducting research and speaking to professors in your field of interest. If you are interested in academic master's or doctoral programs, you may also wish to do the following:

- Get a fuller sense of your interest in and aptitude for research through a research position while an undergraduate student.
- Meet with professors to seek recommendations regarding advanced study programs in particular fields.
- Build relationships with professors and seek information about their research.
- Volunteer to assist with research projects in the community, local hospitals, or think tanks.
- Identify requirements of graduate programs, such as credit hours, comprehensive exams, and research and thesis requirements.

Reflect on the Practical Challenges Related to Graduate and Professional School

Advanced study presents both opportunities and challenges. It expands your knowledge horizon, builds your skills, and broadens your career options. Getting there and succeeding, however, also means recognizing in advance some of the challenges inherent in the process of applying and attending. Consider the following questions as you think about graduate or professional study:

- Do you meet the admission requirements? Do you have the undergraduate GPA you need to be competitive? (It is never too soon to do the work needed to achieve a competitive GPA.)
- Are there entrance exams to complete? Can you take a preparatory course? If so, how soon should you take it?
- How will you finance your education? Will you have the option to attend graduate school full-time, or will you want or need to attend part-time?
- How will your attending graduate school affect you and your family?
- How have you managed your workload as an undergraduate? Will you be able to meet the challenges of a graduate or professional school workload?
- What is the right time for graduate or professional school in your personal and career path?

Graduate or professional training beyond the bachelor's degree is an option that many students will eventually choose. The American Sociological Association found in a survey that a little over a third of sociology majors were studying in graduate or professional school 18 months after graduation. Of these, just under a quarter were pursuing sociology at the graduate level, but others were studying social work (17%), law (11%), education (11%), psychology/counseling (9%), business/management (5%), or other fields. Choosing whether to pursue advanced study, as well as when to do so, is a very individual decision. Assess your situation—academic, personal, professional, and financial—before you decide. And seek the guidance of professors, career counselors at your school, and your family as you prepare your study and career plan.

THINK ABOUT CAREERS

▶ If you are interested in graduate or professional studies, with whom might you speak to get advice on selecting schools to apply to or programs that could be suitable for you? Make a list of people you know through your family, school, or work who could be of help to you in choosing a program or school.

SUMMARY

- **Religion** is a system of common beliefs and rituals centered on "sacred things" that unites believers and provides a sense of meaning and purpose. Religion may serve many functions in society, lending groups a common worldview, helping to ritualize or routinize behaviors or beliefs, and providing people with a sense of purpose.
- Sociologists who study religion are interested in how religion helps to organize and structure societies and group behavior, along with the functions religion serves for producing and maintaining group solidarity (or, conversely, creates instability in certain circumstances), and how religion becomes a force in society and within the lives of individuals.
- Classical theorists have differing interpretations of religion's sociological function. Marx emphasized the role of religion in pacifying the oppressed masses; Weber highlighted the role of Protestantism in the development of capitalism; Durkheim looked at the role of religion in reinforcing social solidarity.
- The modern **religious economy** perspective emphasizes the role of competition between groups as religions seek followers and potential adherents seek affiliations.
- Religions manifest themselves in more than just shared beliefs. They take the form of institutions. Types of religious organizations can be conceptually placed on a spectrum of conventionality in larger society. A **church** would be on the far end of conventionality, and a **cult** would fit on the opposite end of the spectrum.
- **New religious movements (NRMs)** represent a break from existing religious organizations and a push toward new religious practices.
- Christianity, Islam, and Hinduism are the three largest and most practiced religions on earth, but Judaism, Buddhism, and Confucianism are also influential.
- Women have been historically marginalized in major world religions. Today some activists seek to introduce nonsexist language into Scripture and services and to expand women's roles and representation in religious beliefs and practices.
- Youth and young adults in the United States today are less likely than older adults to claim a religious affiliation. At the same time, religious faith continues to exercise influence in U.S. life, including in politics.
- **Disestablishment** refers to periods in which the political influence of religion is significantly challenged.
- **Civil religion** involves the elevation of a nation as an object of worship.
- Globalization has provided both challenges and opportunities to religions of the world. Religions may function to bring both peace and conflict at the global level.

KEY TERMS

DISCUSSION QUESTIONS

1. How do classical sociologists theorize the role of religion in society? Compare and contrast the views of Durkheim and Marx.
2. If religion serves as a source of stability, as functionalists claim, does that mean that a nation of atheists would be less stable than a nation of religious believers? Make a sociological case to support your position.
3. Consider the issues related to women and religion raised in this chapter. Where societal norms are increasingly progressive but dominant religious doctrines are traditional, which one might be reasonably expected to change? Explain your reasoning.
4. What are the key characteristics of the current generational shift in religious affiliation in the United States? How might sociologists explain this shift? Do you believe it will continue? Explain your reasoning.
5. Describe the role of religion in U.S. politics today. Has the role of religion in politics changed in recent years or decades? Considering trends in religious affiliation, might we expect it to change in the near future?

SAGE edge™

Sharpen your skills with SAGE edge at **edge.sagepub.com/chambliss2e**

A personalized approach to help you accomplish your course-work goals in an easy-to-use learning environment.

THE STATE, WAR, AND TERROR

IN THIS CHAPTER

Reuters/Nayer Haslamoun

WHAT DO YOU THINK?

1. What means do states have to maintain control over their populations? What means do citizens have to maintain control over their own governance?
2. Why do states go to war? What are the functions and dysfunctions of war? Is war inevitable?
3. It is sometimes said that "one person's terrorist is another person's freedom fighter." What does this statement mean? Do you agree with this statement?

© Eddie Gerald / Demotix/Corbis

THE BIRTH AND DEATH OF COUNTRIES

How is a country born? Countries come into being in a variety of ways. They may be established through armed conflict or diplomatic negotiation. They may be the products of indigenous ethnic groups striving for their own states or the results of colonial powers drawing borders that suit their political and economic interests. The 195 recognized countries in the world today are the products of a spectrum of historical times and events.

The world's newest recognized country is South Sudan, which came into being in 2011 after a decades-long civil war with the state from which it separated, Sudan. Other countries have much longer histories: Both Japan and China claim origins that date back more than 2,000 years. China marks 221 B.C. as its founding year. European states such as France, Austria, Denmark, and Hungary are more than five centuries old. The United States as a political entity came into being only in the 18th century after separating from its colonial parent, Great Britain, putting it in the large category of fairly young states.

Just as countries are born out of the circumstances and interests of their times, they may also die, torn apart by political turmoil, economic collapse, or armed conflict. In 1991, the Soviet Union, a country that officially came into being in 1922 as the successor state to a fallen Russian Empire, split into 15 different countries. While there was some violence in the last months of the Soviet Union's existence as those with a stake in its future fought for the continuation of the communist state, the split was largely peaceful, and the enormous country (it covered 11 time zones) was dissolved with signatures on paper rather than lethal weapons.

In 2014, the country of Iraq appeared to be on the verge of dissolution. Iraq as a recognized state came into existence in 1920, after the collapse of the Ottoman Empire. It was, like many states of its time, created by a colonial power, Britain, which drew Iraq's boundaries based on political expediency rather than along ethnic, religious, or tribal community lines. Britain continued to administer the country until it gained independence in 1932.

From 1979, Iraq was under the rule of Saddam Hussein, a brutal dictatorial leader whose Baath Party favored the interests of Sunni Muslims over the more numerous Shiite Muslims and minority Kurds in the country. In 1990, Saddam's Iraqi forces invaded the neighboring country of Kuwait, a U.S. ally. A large-scale U.S.-led effort, now known as the First Gulf War, commenced to liberate Kuwait, and Iraqi forces were compelled to withdraw in February 1991. Relations between the United States and Iraq continued to be tense, and U.S. forces invaded Iraq in 2003 after President George W. Bush accused the country of possessing weapons of mass destruction (which were not subsequently found and the existence of which has not been definitively shown). The U.S. occupation of Iraq followed shortly after U.S. forces invaded Afghanistan and deposed the Taliban rulers who were believed to harbor international terrorist Osama bin Laden. The military action against Iraq was commonly understood to be part of the "global war on terror" that the United States began after the terrorist attacks of September 11, 2001, on the World Trade Center and the Pentagon.

The large-scale U.S. military presence in Iraq ended in 2011. Iraq, already politically fragile, remained unstable, wracked by tension between Sunni and Shiite communities that was exacerbated by an Iraqi government dominated by Shiite leaders who were reluctant to share power with Iraq's Sunni and Kurdish populations. In 2014, the addition of a new source of strife, the aggressive presence of a radical Sunni terror organization called ISIS (Islamic State of Iraq and Syria; also known as ISIL, for Islamic State of Iraq and the Levant, or simply as the Islamic State), threatened to fragment the country into Shiite-dominated, Sunni-dominated, and Kurdish regions and, potentially, to end the existence of a governable political entity called Iraq.

The world has seen the births and deaths of hundreds of states. Some have endured for centuries or even millennia—others have lasted just a few decades. Countries are core parts of the modern world, and they represent key vehicles for the exercise of power domestically and globally. They are also human-created entities and are subject to dramatic and dynamic change, which makes them a topic of interest to sociologists. ■

Nation-state: A single people (a "nation") governed by a political authority (a "state"); similar to the modern notion of "country."

We begin this chapter with a discussion of power and the modern nation-state and an examination of citizenship rights and their provision. We then look at theoretical perspectives on state power, its exercise, and its beneficiaries. A consideration of types of authority and forms of governance in the modern world provides the background for an examination of the U.S. political system. We then turn to a discussion of war and society and an analysis of war from the functionalist and conflict perspectives. This is followed by a critical look at the issue of terrorism, as well as the question of defining who is a terrorist. We conclude with a consideration of the question of why we study state power and its manifestations in phenomena that range from elections to making war.

THE MODERN STATE

For most of human history, people lived in small and homogeneous communities within which they shared languages, cultures, and customs. Today, however, the world's more than 7 billion people are distributed across 195 countries (the number of countries recognized by the United States, though other entities exist that claim statehood, including Palestine and Kurdistan). On the world stage, countries are key actors: They are responsible for war and peace, the economic and social welfare of their citizens, and the quality of our shared global environment and security, among others.

Social scientists commonly characterize the modern country as a **nation-state**—that is, *a single people (a nation) governed by a political authority (a state)* (Gellner, 1983). Very few countries neatly fit this model, however. Most are made up of many different peoples brought together through warfare, conquest, immigration, or boundaries drawn by colonial authorities without respect to ethnic or religious differences of the time. For instance, many Native Americans think of themselves as belonging to the Navajo, Lakota, Pawnee, or Iroquois nation rather than only to the United States. In Nigeria, most people identify primarily with others who are Yoruba, Ibo, or Hausa rather than with a country called Nigeria. In Iraq, a shared Iraqi identity is less common than allegiance to the Sunni or Shia Muslim or the Kurdish community. Because most political entities are not characterized by the homogeneity implied by the definition of nation-state, we will use the more familiar terms *country* and *state* rather than *nation-state.*

While not all countries possess them in equal measure, the characteristics we list below represent what Max Weber would term an *ideal-typical model,* a picture that approximates but

Obtaining citizenship is a dream for many immigrants to the United States. Every year, thousands take the Naturalization Oath of Allegiance to the United States.

does not perfectly represent reality. Modern countries emerged along with contemporary capitalism, which benefited from strong central governments and legal systems that regulated commerce and trade both within and across borders (Mann, 1986; Wallerstein, 1974; Weber, 1921/1979). This history accounts for several unique features of modern countries that distinguish them from earlier forms of political organization:

- Underlying the social organization of the modern country is a system of **law**, *the codified rules of behavior established by a government and backed by the threat of force* (Chambliss & Seidman, 1982). The rule of law is a critical aspect of democratic governance.
- The governments of modern countries claim complete and final authority over the people who reside within the countries' borders (Hinsley, 1986).
- People living within a country's borders are divided between **citizens**, *individuals who are part of a political community in which they are granted certain rights and privileges and, at the same time, have specified obligations and duties,* and **noncitizens**, *people who are temporary or permanent residents and who do not have the same rights and privileges as citizens* (Held, 1989).

Citizenship rights may take several forms. *Civil rights,* which protect citizens from injury by individuals and institutions, include the right to equal treatment in places such as the school or workplace regardless of race, gender, sexual orientation, or disabilities. *Political rights* ensure that citizens can participate in governance, whether by voting, running for office, or openly expressing political opinions. *Social rights,* which call for the governmental provision of various forms of economic and social security, include such things as retirement pensions and guaranteed income after losing a job or becoming disabled. Citizens are afforded legal protections from arbitrary rule and in turn are expected to pay taxes, to engage in their own governance through voting or other activities, and to perform military service (with specific expectations of such service varying by country). In reality, the extent to which all people enjoy the full rights of citizenship in any given country varies. Below we discuss two specific aspects of citizenship rights—the first relates to the evolution of state provisions for ensuring social rights, the second to the degree to which citizens enjoy freedom in the form of political rights and civil liberties.

THE WELFARE STATE

In most modern countries, political and civil rights evolved and were institutionalized before social rights were realized. The category of social rights is broad and encompasses entitlements that include health care insurance, old-age pensions, unemployment benefits, a minimum wage floor for workers, and a spectrum of other benefits intended to ensure social and economic security for the citizenry. Social rights have largely been won by groups of citizens mobilizing (on the basis of the civil and political rights they enjoy) to realize their interests.

Social rights are often embodied in what is termed the **welfare state**, *a political order characterized by the broad provision of social and economic welfare benefits for the citizenry.* The welfare state has been a part of Western systems of governance in the post–World War II period. In the United States, Social Security, a key social welfare program that ensures an income for retired workers, and Medicare, which provides for at least basic health care for the elderly, are examples of the U.S. welfare state. Social Security was created through the Social Security Act of 1935, signed by President Franklin D. Roosevelt, which established a social insurance program to provide continuing income for retired workers at age 65 or older (Social Security Administration, 2013). Although the provision of basic health care coverage was the vision of President Harry S. Truman, Medicare and Medicaid did not get signed into law until a few decades later, when they

Law: A system of binding and recognized codified rules of behavior that regulate the actions of people pertaining to a given jurisdiction.

Citizens: Legally recognized inhabitants of a country who bear the rights and responsibilities of citizenship as defined by the state.

Noncitizens: Individuals who reside in a given jurisdiction but do not possess the same rights and privileges as the citizens who are recognized inhabitants; sometimes referred to as *residents, temporary workers,* or *aliens.*

Welfare state: A government or country's system of providing for the financial and social well-being of its citizens, typically through government programs that provide funding or other resources to individuals who meet certain criteria.

Welfare State Debate

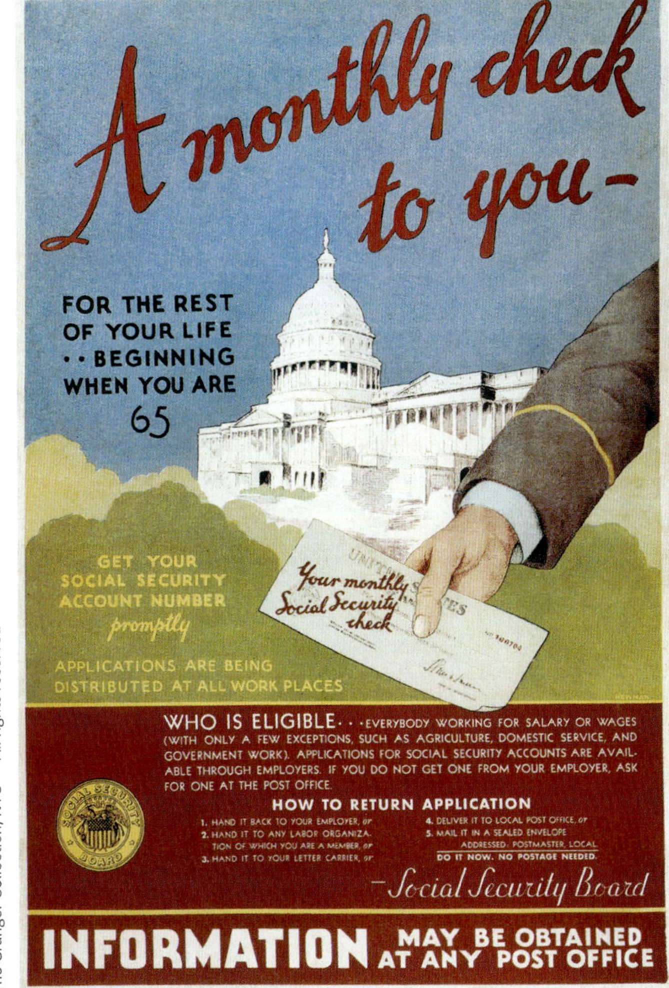

The idea for Social Security was first championed by President Truman, but it took a few presidential administrations before President Roosevelt signed it into law in 1935. Social Security benefits have contributed to the reduction of poverty among seniors in the United States. ■

were endorsed by President Lyndon B. Johnson. The welfare state has long been a hallmark of advanced and wealthy countries; most developing states have much thinner social safety nets, and few have had the resources to provide for retirees or even, often, for the unemployed or ill.

While it has come to represent a culmination of the three key rights of citizenship in modern countries, the welfare state is shrinking rather than expanding today. Factors such as global wage competition and growing debt loads borne by countries from the United States to Sweden to France and beyond have hampered the expansion of social rights. While it is difficult to reduce benefits to already existing constituencies—for example, in the United States, discussion of reducing Social Security payments or even raising the age of eligibility evokes vehement protest from retirees—the economic crises of recent years have led to attempts by lawmakers to curb benefits to less powerful constituencies, including the poor and immigrants.

POLITICAL RIGHTS AND CIVIL LIBERTIES

Every year, Freedom House, an organization dedicated to monitoring and promoting democratic change and human rights, publishes an evaluation of "freedom" in 195 countries, as well as 14 related and disputed territories (Figure 14.1). The report includes ratings that measure *political rights* (based on the electoral process, political pluralism, and participation) and *civil liberties* (based on freedom of expression and belief, rights of association and organization, rule of law, and individual rights).

Even in the United States, which earns top scores in Freedom House's survey, problems with voting procedures have raised the question of whether some voters, especially minorities, have been denied a political voice in elections. Nationwide, more than 5 million U.S. citizens, including more than 4 million who are not in prison, are barred from voting due to felony convictions. In Alabama and Florida, for instance, nearly one third of African American men are permanently disenfranchised (Froomkin, 2010).

Recently, some U.S. state legislatures have sought to implement voter identification laws, which require voters to show identification when they vote in person. In 2014, 11 states had such laws, and 8 of those required the ID to include a photograph (Figure 14.2).

Critics point out that members of minority groups, in particular those who are elderly or poor, are among those least likely to have photo identification in the form of a driver's license or passport. The practical effect of voter ID laws, they say, is not to combat voter fraud (which has been infrequently documented in the United States), but rather to disenfranchise minorities and the poor (Cohen, 2012). What do you think about voter ID laws? Do they bring greater benefits or costs?

Later in this chapter, we discuss more fully the issue of political voice, or the representation of a group's interests in bodies such as state and national legislatures, and ways in which political voice may vary. In the next section we turn to

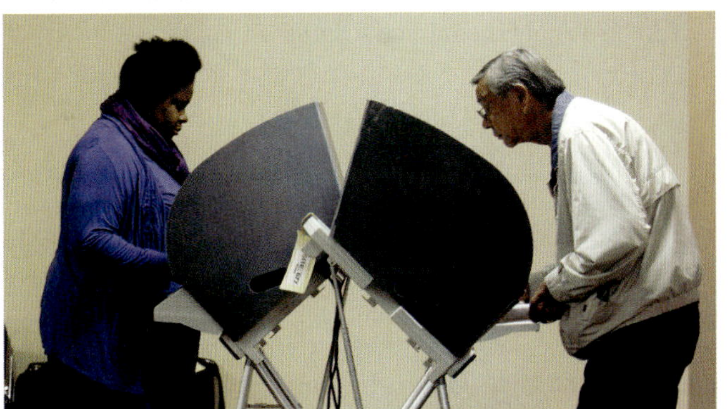

Voter ID laws created controversy in the 2012 federal election campaign. While about three quarters of the population expressed support for the laws, critics pointed out that their implementation risked disenfranchising the populations least likely to have government-issued ID, including the elderly, minorities, and the poor. ■

FIGURE 14.1 **Freedom Status Worldwide, 2014**

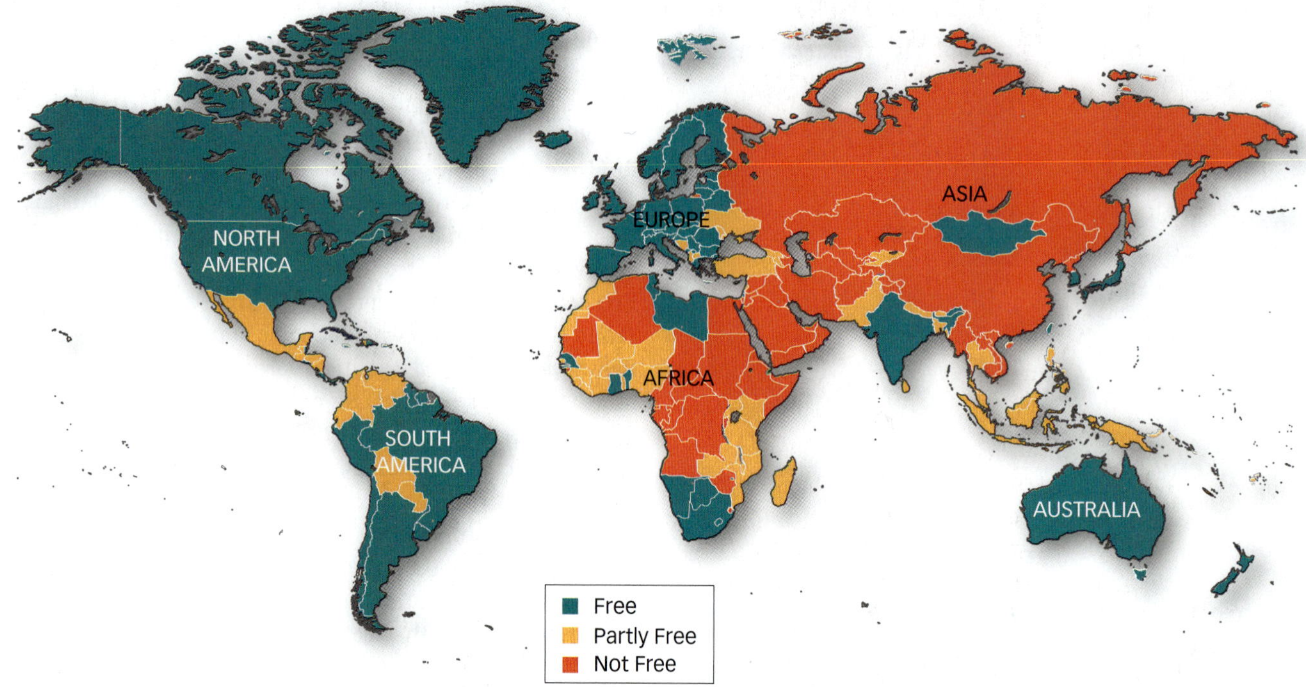

SOURCE: Freedom House. (2014). 2014 Freedom in the World.

broader sociological perspectives on state power, which can give us a fuller context for analyzing contemporary debates on power and politics.

THEORIES OF STATE POWER

Sociologists have developed different approaches to explaining how authority is exercised in modern states. Below we highlight two theoretical approaches, which disagree about how expansively power is shared. These theories are based largely on governance in the United States today, although we can also apply them to other modern societies.

THE FUNCTIONALIST PERSPECTIVE AND PLURALIST THEORY

Classical sociologist Émile Durkheim (1922/1956, 1922/1973b) saw government as an institution that translates broadly shared values and interests into fair-minded laws and effective policies. Contemporary functionalist theorists recognize that modern societies are socially and culturally heterogeneous and likely to have a greater diversity of needs and perspectives. The government, they suggest, is a neutral umpire, balancing the conflicting values, norms, and interests of a variety of competing groups in its laws and actions.

In the United States, most people agree on such general values as liberty, democratic governance, and equality of opportunity, but debate occurs on many more specific issues, such as abortion, the death penalty, the waging of war, funding for medical care when people are old or ill, and the size of government. Recognizing the pluralistic—that is, diverse—nature of contemporary societies, sociologists and political scientists have developed theories of government that highlight this aspect of state power.

Pluralist theory tries to answer the question "Given that modern societies are pluralistic, how do they resolve the inevitable conflicts?" To answer this question Robert Dahl (1961, 1982, 1989) studied decision making in New Haven, Connecticut. Dahl (1961) concludes that power is exercised through the political process, which is dominated by different groups of leaders, each having access to a different amalgamation of political resources. Dahl argues that, in their efforts to exert political influence, individuals come together in **interest groups**—*groups made up of people who share the same concerns on particular issues who use their organizational and social resources to influence legislation and the functioning of social institutions.* An interest group may be short-lived, such as a local citizens' group that bands together to have a road repaved or a school built, or long-lasting, such as a labor union or a manufacturers' association.

Interest groups: Advocacy or lobby groups that utilize their organizational and social resources to influence legislation and the functioning of social institutions.

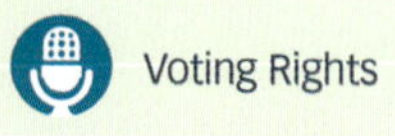

Affirmative Action

FIGURE 14.2 Voter Identification Laws, 2014

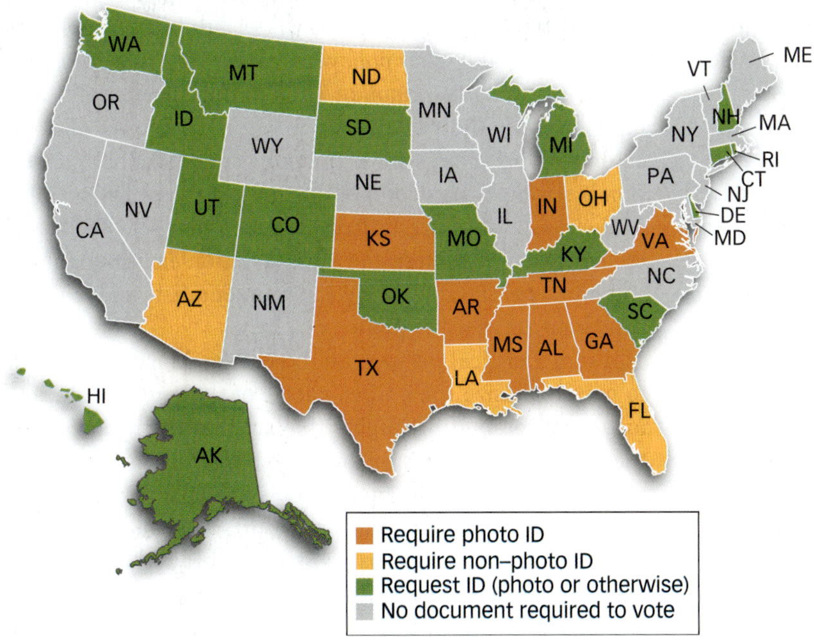

SOURCE: Voter identification requirements. *Legislature & Elections*. Copyright © 2012 National Conference of State Legislatures; National Conference of State Legislatures. (2014). Voter identification requirements: Photo ID laws. Reprinted with permission.

Dahl's theory asserts that interest groups serve the function of seeing that everyone's perspectives (values, norms, interests) are represented in the government. The influence of one group is offset by the power of another. For instance, if a group of investors bands together to seek government approval to clear-cut a forest to build homes, a group of citizens concerned about the environment may coalesce into an interest group to oppose the investors' plan. The ideal result, according to Dahl, would be a compromise: Perhaps cutting would be limited, or some particularly sensitive areas would be preserved. Similarly, big businesses and organized labor routinely face off, so neither exercises disproportionate influence on the political process.

When powerful interests oppose one another, pluralists see compromise as the likely outcome, and the role of the government is therefore to broker solutions that benefit as many interests as possible. In this view, power is dynamic, passing from one stakeholder to another over time rather than being concentrated in the hands of a powerful few. This competition and fluidity of power contribute to democratic governance and society.

A critical view of the pluralist characterization of political power points out that government is unlikely to represent or recognize all interests (Chambliss & Seidman, 1982; Domhoff, 2006). Critics also dispute the assumption that government is a neutral mediator between competing interests. They argue that laws may favor some groups over others: For example, when the U.S. Constitution was framed by White male property owners, only White male property owners could vote: People without property, women, Blacks, and American Indians were excluded from the political process.

As well, some interest groups are more powerful than others. Governments do not apply the rules neutrally, as the theory claims; rather, they interpret (or even bend) the rules to favor the most powerful groups in society, including big business and other moneyed interests that finance increasingly costly political campaigns for those who favor them (Domhoff, 2006, 2009; Friedman, 1975, 1990).

As a consequence of all these factors, critics contend, even if laws are passed to protect the values and interests of people who are not economically powerful, the laws may not be actively and forcefully implemented or their reach may be limited. For example, de facto racial segregation and discrimination continue to exist even though school segregation has been outlawed in the United States since 1954 and most other forms of racial discrimination became illegal in the decade that followed.

THE CONFLICT PERSPECTIVE AND CLASS DOMINANCE THEORY

Social conflict theory highlights power differences between social groups. This perspective recognizes that modern societies are pluralistic, but it argues that the interests of social groups are often incompatible with one another. Further, conflict theory posits that some groups are more powerful than others and are therefore more likely to see their interests, values, and norms reflected in government policies and laws. Groups with greater resources use their power to create systems of law, economy, politics, and education that favor them, their children, and other group members.

Unlike pluralistic theory, which views competing interests as having relatively equal and shifting opportunities and access to power, conflict theory sees power as being concentrated in the hands of a privileged few groups and individuals. The gains of the elite, conflict theorists suggest, come at the expense of those who have fewer resources, including economic, cultural, and social capital.

The roots of conflict theory are found in the ideas of Karl Marx. You may recall from previous chapters that Marx believed the most important sources of social conflict are economic, and that, as a consequence, class conflict is fundamental to all other forms of conflict. Within a capitalist society, in Marx's view, government represents and serves the interests of the capitalist class or bourgeoisie, the ruling class that exerts disproportionate influence on the government. Still, a well-organized working class can effectively press government for

Interest Group Politics

such economic reforms as a shorter working day or the end of child labor.

Contemporary conflict theory extends Marx's concept of the ruling class to include contemporary groups that wield considerable power. **Class dominance theory**, for instance, argues that *power is concentrated in the hands of a relatively small number of individuals who compose a power elite* (Domhoff, 1983, 1990, 2002; Mills, 1956/2000a). These individuals have often attended the same elite schools, belong to the same social organizations, and cycle in and out of top positions in government, business, and the military (the so-called revolving door). Class dominance theory complements Marx's original ideas with a focus on the elite social networks themselves, rather than only on capitalism as a political economic system.

G. William Domhoff (2002, 2006, 2009) posits that we can show the existence of a dominant class by examining the answers to several basic questions, which he terms "power indicators": *Who benefits? Who governs? Who wins?*

- In terms of "Who benefits?" Domhoff asks us to consider who gets the most of what is valued in society. Who gets money and material goods? What about leisure and travel or status and prestige? Domhoff (2006) asserts that "those who have the most of what people want are, by inference, the powerful" (p. 13).
- In terms of "Who governs?" he asks who is positioned to make the important political and economic and legal decisions in the country or community. Are all demographic groups relatively well represented? Are some disproportionately powerful? Domhoff (2006) suggests, "If a group or class is highly overrepresented or underrepresented in relation to its proportion of the population, it can be inferred that the group or class is relatively powerful or powerless, as the case may be" (p. 14).
- Asking "Who wins?" entails inquiring about which group or groups have their interests realized most often. Domhoff concedes that movements with fewer resources, including, for instance, environmental groups, may "win" desired legislation sometimes. However, we need to look at who has their desires realized most consistently and often. Is it small interest groups representing civil rights, environmental activists, or same-sex marriage advocates? Is it large corporate interests with friends in high places and the ability to write big campaign donation checks?

After examining the power indicators in his book *Who Rules America?* Domhoff concludes that it is the upper class, particularly the owners and managers of large for-profit enterprises, that benefits, governs, and wins. This, he suggests, challenges the premise of pluralist theories that power is not concentrated but dynamic, moving among a variety of interests and groups. Domhoff argues that there exists a small but significant **power elite**, which is made up of *individuals who are linked to the social upper class, the corporate community, and the policy-formation organizations that influence government policy.* Though the corporations, organizations, and individuals who make up the power elite may be divided on some issues, Domhoff contends that cooperation is stronger than competition among them: The members of the power elite are united by a common set of interests, including a probusiness and antiregulation environment, and common enemies, including environmentalists and labor and consumer activists.

From a critical perspective, class dominance theory tends to overemphasize the unified nature of the "ruling class." For instance, Domhoff highlights the fact that many members of the power elite share similar social backgrounds. Often, they attend the same private high schools and colleges, spend their vacations in the same exclusive resorts, and marry into one another's families. They share a strong belief in the importance and value of capitalism and, as Domhoff argues, are steeped in a similar set of worldviews. However, it is difficult to show that they necessarily share the same political beliefs or even economic orientations (Chambliss & Seidman, 1982; Chambliss & Zatz, 1994).

Further, government decisions sometimes appear to be in direct opposition to the expressed interests of powerful capitalist groups. For example, when faced with major conflicts between labor and management during the Depression years of the 1930s, the U.S. government passed laws legalizing trade unions and giving workers the right to bargain collectively with their corporate employers, even though both laws were strongly opposed by corporation executives and owners (Chambliss & Zatz, 1994; Skocpol, 1979; Tilly, 1975). Mark Smith (2000) found that when businesses act to influence public policy to support or oppose a given issue, they may experience backlash as labor and public interest groups organize in opposition to the perceived power seizure.

Does a power elite exercise disproportionate influence in the political sphere of the United States? Domhoff and other conflict theorists would answer in the affirmative. A pluralist perspective might see corporations, the upper class, and policy organizations as some among many players who compete in the political power game, balanced by other groups such as unions and environmentalists, and answer in the negative. What do you think?

Class dominance theory: The theory that a small and concentrated group of elite or upper-class people dominate and influence societal institutions; compatible with conflict theory.

Power elite: A group of people with a disproportionately high level of influence and resources who utilize their status to influence the functioning of societal institutions.

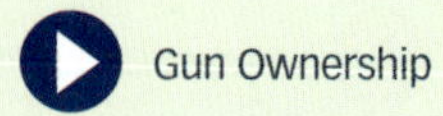

POWER AND AUTHORITY

In the section above we looked at different perspectives on how state power functions and who it serves. We now turn to the question of how states exercise their power in practice, asking, "How do governments maintain control over their populations?"

One way that states exercise power is through outright **coercion**—*the threat or use of physical force to ensure compliance.* Relying solely on coercion, however, is costly and difficult because it requires surveillance and sometimes suppression of the population, particularly those segments that might be inclined to dissent. Governments that ground their authority in coercion are vulnerable to instability, as they generally fail to earn the allegiance of their people. It is more efficient, and in the long run more enduring, if a government can establish legitimate authority, which, as you recall from Chapter 5, is *power that is recognized as rightful by those over whom it is exercised.*

One of sociology's founders, Max Weber (1864–1920), was also one of the first social scientists to analyze the nature of legitimate authority, and his ideas have influenced our understanding of power and authority in the modern world. Weber sought to answer the question, "Why do people consent to give up power, allowing others to dominate them?" His examination of this question, which was based on detailed studies of societies throughout history, identified three key forms of legitimate authority: traditional, rational-legal, and charismatic.

TRADITIONAL AUTHORITY

For most of human history, state power relied on **traditional authority**, *power based on a belief in the sanctity of long-standing traditions and the legitimate right of rulers to exercise authority in accordance with these traditions* (Weber, 1921/1979). Traditional rulers claim power on the basis of age-old norms, beliefs, and practices. When the people being governed accept the legitimacy of traditional authority, it tends to be relatively stable over time. The monarchies of Europe, for example, ruled for hundreds of years based on traditional authority. Their people were considered the king's or queen's "subjects," whose loyalty derived from their recognition of the fundamental legitimacy of monarchical rule, with its long-standing hierarchy and distribution of power on the basis of blood and birth. In modern Europe, however, monarchies such as those in Denmark and Sweden have little more than symbolic power—they have been largely stripped of political power. Traditional authority, in these instances, coexists with the rational-legal authority exercised by modern elected bodies, which we discuss below.

Coercion: The threat or use of physical force to ensure compliance.

Traditional authority: Power based on a belief in the sanctity of long-standing traditions and the legitimate right of rulers to exercise authority in accordance with those traditions.

Rational-legal authority: Power based on a belief in the lawfulness of enacted rules (laws) and the legitimate right of leaders to exercise authority under such rules.

In Great Britain, traditional authority peacefully and functionally coexists with rational-legal authority. In this photo, British Prime Minister David Cameron, who is the head of government, shakes hands with Queen Elizabeth II, who is the constitutional monarch.

Traditional authority supports the exercise of power at both the macro and micro levels: Just as reverence for traditional norms and practices may give legitimacy to a state, a religion, or other government, so too may it drive the decisions and actions of families. If a family marks a particular holiday or date with an obligatory ritual, then even if an individual questions the need for that ritual, the reasoning "We've *always* done that" is a micro-level exercise of traditional authority that ensures compliance and discourages challenges by any member of the group.

RATIONAL-LEGAL AUTHORITY

Traditional authority, in Weber's view, was incompatible with the rise of modern capitalist states. Capitalism is based on forms of social organization that favor rational, rule-governed calculation rather than practices grounded in tradition. As capitalism evolved, traditional authority gave way to **rational-legal authority**, *power based on a belief in the lawfulness of enacted rules (laws) and the legitimate right of leaders to exercise authority under such rules* (Weber, 1921/1979). The legitimacy of rational-legal authority derives from a belief in the rule of law. We do something not simply because it has always been done that way but because it conforms to established rules and procedures.

In a system based on rational-legal authority, leaders are regarded as legitimate as long as they act according to law. Laws, in turn, are enacted and enforced through formal, bureaucratic procedures, rather than reflecting custom and tradition or the whims of a ruler. Weber argued that rational-legal authority is compatible with modern economies, which are based on rational calculation of costs and benefits, profits, and other economic decisions. Rational-legal authority is commonly exercised in the ideal-typical modern state described at the start of this chapter. In practice, we could take the United States, Canada, Japan, or the countries of the European Union as specific examples of states governed by rational-legal authority.

CHARISMATIC AUTHORITY

Weber's third form of authority can threaten both traditional and rational-legal authority. **Charismatic authority** is *power based on devotion inspired in followers by the personal qualities of a leader* (Weber, 1921/1979). It derives from widespread belief in a given community that an individual has a "gift" of great—even divine—powers, so it rests most significantly on an individual personality, rather than on that individual's claim to authority on the basis of tradition or legal election or appointment. Charismatic authority may also be the product of a "cult of personality," an image of a leader that is carefully manipulated by the leader and other elites. In North Korea's long-standing dictatorship, power has passed through several generations of the same family, as has the government's careful construction of a cult of personality around each leader that elevates him as supremely intelligent, patriotic, and worthy of unquestioning loyalty.

Prominent charismatic leaders in religious history include Moses, Jesus Christ, the Prophet Muhammad, and Buddha. Some military and political rulers whose power was based in large part on charisma are Julius Caesar, Napoleon Bonaparte, Vladimir Lenin, and Adolf Hitler (clearly, not all charismatic leaders are charitable, ethical, or good).

More recently, charismatic leaders have emerged to lead communities and countries toward democratic development. Václav Havel, a dissident playwright in what was then communist Czechoslovakia, challenged the authority of a government that was not elected and that citizens despised; he spent years in prison and doing menial jobs because he was not permitted to work in his artistic field. Later, he helped lead the 1989 opposition movement against the government and, with its fall, was elected president of the newly democratic state. (Czechoslovakia no longer exists; its Czech and Slovak populations wanted to establish their own nation-states, and in 1993 they peacefully formed two separate republics.) Similarly, Nelson Mandela, despite spending 27 years in prison, was a key figure in the opposition movement against the racist policies of apartheid in South Africa. Mandela became South Africa's first democratically elected president in 1994, 4 years after his release from prison. His death in 2013 marked the passing of a significant era in South African politics.

Notably, Weber also pointed to a phenomenon he termed the *routinization of charisma*. That is, with the decline, departure, or death of a charismatic leader, his or her authority may be transformed into legal-rational or even traditional authority. While those who follow may govern in the charismatic leader's name, the authority of successive leaders rests either on emulation (traditionalized authority) or on power that has been routinized and institutionalized (rationalized authority).

Authority exists in a larger context, and political authority is often sited in a government. Governance takes place in a variety of forms, which we discuss below.

FORMS OF GOVERNANCE IN THE MODERN WORLD

In the modern world, the three principal forms of governance are authoritarianism, totalitarianism, and democracy. Below we discuss each type, offering ideal-typical definitions as well as illustrative examples. Two modern global trends in governance are the growth of rational-legal authority and the spread of representative democracy.

AUTHORITARIANISM

Under **authoritarianism**, *ordinary members of society are denied the right to participate in government, and political power is exercised by and for the benefit of a small political elite.* At the same time, authoritarianism is distinguished from totalitarianism (which we will discuss shortly) by the fact that at least some social, cultural, and economic institutions exist that are not under the control of the state. Two prominent types of authoritarianism are monarchies and dictatorships.

Monarchy is *a form of governance in which power resides in an individual or a family and is passed from one generation to the next through hereditary lines.* Monarchies, which derive their legitimacy from traditional authority, were historically the primary form of governance in many parts of the world, and in Europe until the 18th century. Today, the formerly powerful royal families of Europe have been either dethroned or relegated to peripheral and ceremonial roles. For example, the queens of England, Denmark, and the Netherlands and the kings of Sweden and Spain do not have any significant

Monarchy: A form of governance in which power resides in an individual or a family and is passed from one generation to the next through hereditary lines.

Charismatic authority: Power based on devotion inspired in followers by the personal qualities of a leader.

Authoritarianism: A form of governance in which ordinary members of society are denied the right to participate in government, and political power is exercised by and for the benefit of a small political elite.

political power or formal authority to govern. A few countries in the modern world are still ruled by monarchies, including Saudi Arabia, Jordan, Qatar, and Kuwait. Even the monarchs of these nations, however, govern with the consent of powerful religious and social or economic groups.

In the territory of Saudi Arabia, for instance, the royal family, also known as the House of Saud, has ruled for centuries, though the country of Saudi Arabia itself was established only in 1932. The Basic Law of 1992 declared Saudi Arabia to be a monarchy ruled by the sons and grandsons of King Abdul Aziz al-Saud, making the country the only one in the world named after a family. The constitution of the country is the Koran, and, consequently, sharia law, which is based on Islamic traditions and beliefs, is in effect. The country does not hold national elections, nor is the formation of independent political parties permitted. However, the royal rulers govern within the bounds of the constitution, tradition, and the consent of religious leaders, the *ulema*.

A more modern form of authoritarianism is **dictatorship**, *a form of governance in which power rests in a single individual.* An example of an authoritarian dictatorship is the government of Iraqi president Saddam Hussein, who ruled his country from 1979 to 2003, when he was deposed. As this case shows, the individual in power in a dictatorship is actually closely intertwined with an inner circle of governing elites. In Iraq, Saddam was linked to the inner circle of the Báath Party. Further, because of the complexity of modern society, even the most heavy-handed authoritarian dictator requires some degree of support from military leaders and an intelligence apparatus. No less important to the dictator's power is the compliance of the masses, whether it is gained through coercion or consent.

We might argue that today it would be difficult for a single individual or even a handful of individuals to run a modern country effectively for any length of time. In recent years, many dictators have been deposed by foes or ousted in popular revolutions. Some have even allowed themselves to be turned out of office by relatively peaceful democratic movements, as happened in the former Soviet Union and the formerly communist states of Eastern Europe, such as Czechoslovakia and Hungary. China, which has become progressively more capitalistic while retaining an authoritarian communist government, remains an exception to this pattern.

TOTALITARIANISM

When authoritarian dictatorships persist and become entrenched, the end result may be a totalitarian form of government.

Dictatorship: A form of governance in which power rests in a single individual.

Totalitarianism: A form of governance that denies popular political participation in government and also seeks to regulate and control all aspects of the public and private lives of citizens.

According to a BBC report, "Every night, North Korea's news bulletin begins with a song about the mythical qualities of the country's leader Kim Jong-il" (Williamson, 2011). Political and military leaders in this isolated totalitarian state nurture the image of the late "Dear Leader" and the son who succeeded him.

Totalitarianism *denies popular political participation in government and goes one step further by seeking to regulate and control all aspects of the public and private lives of citizens.* In totalitarianism, there are no limits to the exercise of state power. All opposition is outlawed, access to information not provided by the state is stringently controlled, and citizens are required to demonstrate a high level of commitment and loyalty to the system. A totalitarian government depends more on coercion than on legitimacy in exercising power. It thus requires a large intelligence apparatus to monitor the citizenry for antigovernment activities and to punish those who fail to conform. Members of the society are urged to inform on any of their fellow members who break the rules or criticize the leadership.

One characteristic shared by totalitarian regimes of the 20th century was a ruthless commitment to power and coercion over the rule of law. Soviet leader Vladimir Lenin has been quoted as stating that "the dictatorship—and take this into account once and for all—means unrestricted power based on force, not on law" (Amis, 2002 p. 33). Another characteristic of these regimes was a willingness to destroy the opposition by any means necessary. Joseph Stalin's regime in the Soviet Union, which lasted from 1922 to 1953, purged millions of perceived, potential, or imagined enemies; Stalin's Great Terror tore apart the ranks of even the Soviet military apparatus. Martin Amis (2002) cites the following statistics in characterizing Stalin's "war" on his own military: From the late 1930s to about 1941, Stalin purged 3 of 5 marshals, 13 of 15 army commanders, 154 of 186 divisional commanders, and at least 43,000 officers lower down the chain of command (p. 175). An often-told story about Stalin cites him telling his political inner circle that each should find two replacements for himself.

Perhaps more than any other political system, totalitarianism is built on terror and the threat of terror—including genocide, imposed famine, purges, deportation, imprisonment,

Nazi Germany, the Soviet Union under the leadership of Lenin and later Stalin, Chile under August Pinochet, and the Spain of Francisco Franco were examples of totalitarian regimes. This image of "Big Brother," a symbol of totalitarianism's penetration of private as well as public life, comes from the film version of George Orwell's classic book, *1984*.

torture, and murder. Fear keeps the masses docile and the dictator in power. Torture has a long, brutal history in the dictatorships of the world, and, in trying to uncover its function, Amis (2002) makes the compelling observation that "torture, among its other applications, was part of Stalin's war against truth. He tortured, not to force you to reveal a fact, but to force you to collude in a fiction" (p. 61).

Today, few totalitarian states exist. Certainly, in the age of the Internet, control of information is an enormous challenge to states that seek full control of their populations. North Korea remains one of the last remaining totalitarian states, where the citizenry is nearly fully isolated from the rest of the world and few North Koreans outside the elite have electricity or enough nutritious food, not to speak of Internet connections or computers.

DEMOCRACY

Democracy, *a form of governance in which citizens are able to participate directly or indirectly in their own governance*, literally means "the rule of the people." (The word comes from the Greek *demos*, "the people," and *kratos*, "rule.") The concept of democracy originated in the Greek city-state of Athens during the fifth century B.C., where it took the form of **direct democracy**, in which *all citizens fully participate in their own governance*. This full participation was possible because Athens was a small community by today's standards and because the vast majority of its residents (including women and slaves, on whose labor the economy relied) were excluded from citizenship (Sagan, 1992).

Direct democracy is rarely possible today because of the sheer size of most countries and the complexity of their political affairs. One exception is the referendum process that exists in some U.S. states, including California and Oregon. In Oregon, for instance, the signatures of a specified percentage of registered voters can bring a referendum to the ballot. In 2012, Oregonians voted on Ballot Measure 80, which sought to decriminalize personal marijuana usage. Although backers of the measure met the signature requirement to have the initiative placed on the ballot, the measure was ultimately defeated by state voters (CNN, 2012).

Democracy in the modern world more typically takes the form of **representative democracy**, *a political system in which citizens elect representatives to govern them*. In a representative democracy, elected officials are expected to make decisions that reflect the interests of their constituents. Representative democracy first took hold in the industrial capitalist countries of Europe. It is now the principal form of governance throughout the world, although some parts of the populations in democratic states may be disenfranchised. For instance, only in recent years have women been legally granted the right to vote in many countries (Figure 14.3). Some countries, such as China, the largest remaining authoritarian society, claim to have free elections for many government positions, but eligibility is limited to members of the Communist Party. Thus, even though voting is the hallmark of representative democracy, the mere fact of voting does not ensure the existence of a true democracy.

THE U.S. POLITICAL SYSTEM

Politics in democratic societies is *structured around competing political parties whose purpose is to gain control of the government by winning elections*. Political parties serve this

Democracy: A form of governance in which citizens are able to participate directly or indirectly in their own governance.

Direct democracy: A political system in which all citizens fully participate in their own governance.

Representative democracy: A political system in which citizens elect representatives to govern them.

Politics: The art or science of influencing public policy.

FIGURE 14.3 When Women Won the Right to Vote in Selected Countries, 20th Century

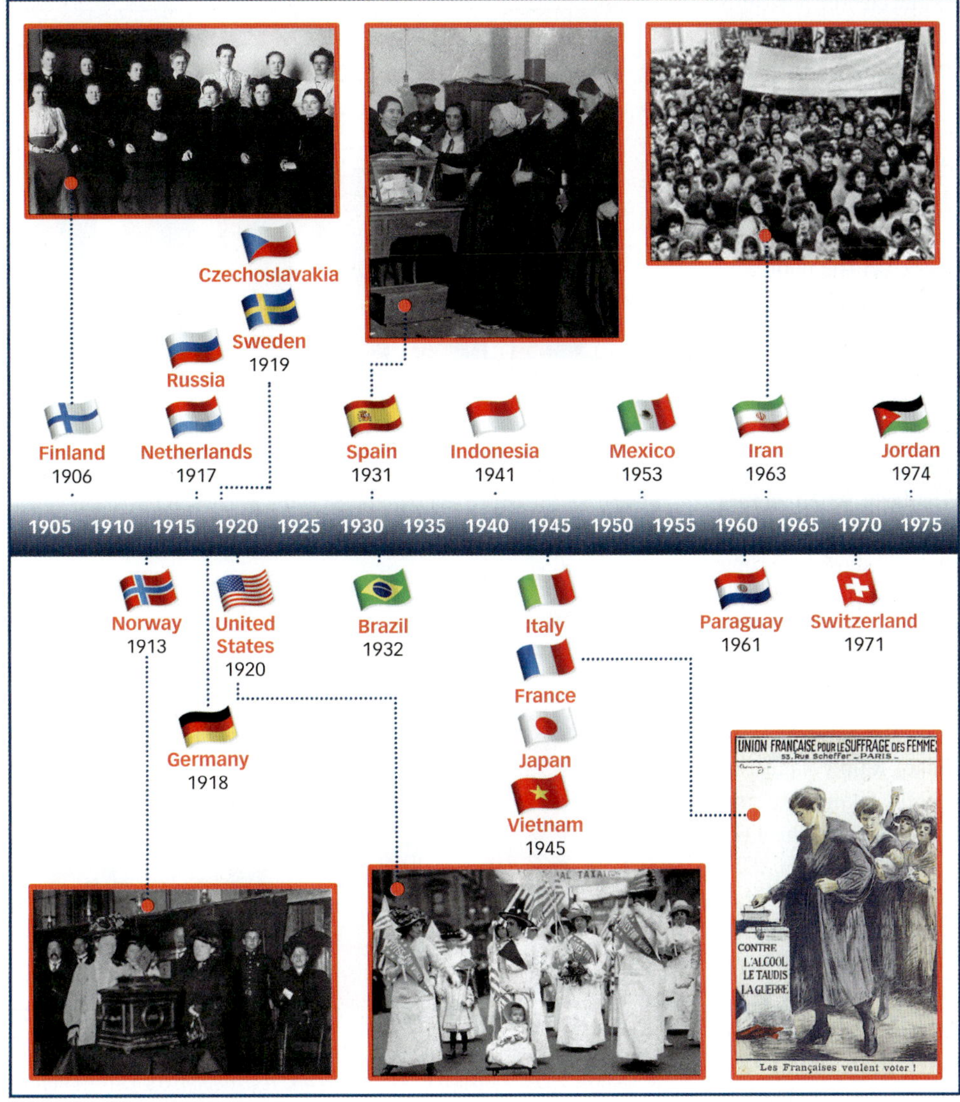

SOURCE: Data from "Women's Suffrage: When Did Women Vote?" Interactive Map. Scholastic.com.

purpose by defining alternative policies and programs, building their membership, raising funds for their candidates, and helping to organize political campaigns. Not only must candidates win elections and retain their offices, but also, once in office, they must make decisions with far-reaching financial and social effects. These decisions ideally reflect the needs and desires of their constituents as well as the interests of their parties and the entities that contribute to their campaigns. Some politicians argue that their constituents' issues take priority; other observers suggest that politicians are beholden to party or donor interests.

In the section below we discuss electoral politics in the United States. Sociologists take an interest in electoral politics because it is an important site at which power in modern countries is exercised. Thus, key questions that sociologists ask—*How is this functional for society? Who benefits from the existing social order? How do perceptions structure behaviors in the electoral process?*—can be applied to electoral politics.

ELECTORAL POLITICS AND THE TWO-PARTY SYSTEM

Most modern democracies are based on a parliamentary system, in which the chief of state (called a *prime minister*) is the head of the party that has the largest number of seats in the national legislature (typically called a *parliament*). Britain, for example, has a parliamentary system. This arrangement can give a significant degree of influence to minority parties (those that have relatively few representatives in parliament), since the majority party often requires minority party support to pass legislation, or even to elect a prime minister.

In the United States, the president is chosen by popular vote—although, as happened in the 2000 presidential election, a candidate who wins the popular vote (in this case, Al Gore) cannot become president without also winning the requisite number of Electoral College votes. Voters in the United States have often chosen a president from one party and a Congress dominated by the other.

The separate election of the president and Congress is intended to help ensure a separation of powers between the executive and legislative branches of the government. At the same time, it weakens the power of minority or third parties, since—unlike the case in parliamentary systems—they are unlikely to have much impact on who will be selected chief of state. In Britain or Germany, by contrast, if a minority party stops voting with the majority party in parliament, its members can force a national election, which might result in a new prime minister. This gives minority parties potential power in parliament to broker deals that serve their interests. No such system exists in the United States, and, as a consequence, third parties play only a minor role in national politics. No third-party candidate

Electoral College

has won a presidential election since Abraham Lincoln was elected in 1860.

The domination of of national elections and elected positions by the Republican and Democratic Parties is virtually ensured by the current political order. Parties representing well-defined interests are ordinarily eliminated from the national political process, since there are few avenues by which they can exert significant political power. Unlike in many other democracies, there are no political parties in the United States that effectively represent the exclusive interests of labor, environmentalists, or other constituencies at the national level. On the contrary, there is a strong incentive for political groups to support one of the two major political parties rather than to "waste" their votes on third parties that have no chance at all of winning the presidency; at most, such votes are generally offered as "protest" votes.

Third parties can occasionally play an important, even a decisive, role in national politics, particularly when voters are unhappy with the two dominating parties. The presidential campaign of H. Ross Perot, of the Reform Party, in 1992 was probably significant in taking votes away from Republican George Bush and helping Democrat Bill Clinton to win the presidential election. Perot, running at the head of his own party organization, won nearly 19% of the popular vote. In 2000, the situation favored Republicans, as Democrat Al Gore probably lost votes to Green Party candidate Ralph Nader; in some states, George W. Bush had fewer votes than Gore and Nader combined, but more than Gore alone. Bush won the electoral votes of those states.

VOTER ACTIVISM AND APATHY IN U.S. POLITICS

One consequence of the lack of political choices in the entrenched two-party system in the United States may be a degree of political apathy, reflected in voter turnouts that are among the lowest in the industrialized world. Among democracies, the United States scores in the bottom fifth when it comes to voter participation.

Whereas many European countries typically have voter turnouts between 70% and 90% of the eligible voters, in 2000, about 54% of the "voting eligible" U.S. population participated in the presidential election. The percentage has risen in subsequent presidential election years: Estimates put turnouts for 2004 at about 60% and 2008 at more than 61%. In 2012, about the same proportion of voting-eligible citizens participated, though differences exist by state: About 70% of New Hampshire voters turned out, while only about half of Arkansans opted to vote (U.S. Elections Project, 2013).

Historically, the proportion of eligible voters turning out for elections in the United States has varied by education (Figure 14.4), race and ethnicity (Figure 14.5), and age (Figure 14.6). Voters who are White, older, and more educated

FIGURE 14.4 U.S. Voter Participation by Education Level, 2008–2012

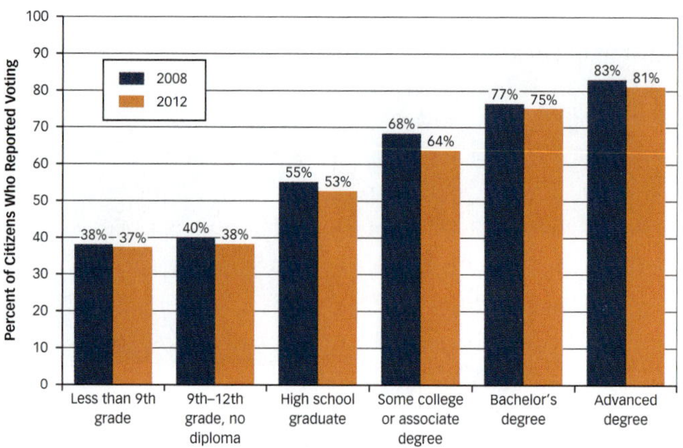

SOURCE: U.S. Census Bureau. (2010). Voting and registration in the election of November 2008—Detailed tables. *Voting and registration*; U.S. Census Bureau. (2011). Voting and registration in the election of November 2010—Detailed tables. *Voting and registration*.

FIGURE 14.5 U.S. Voter Participation by Race and Ethnicity, 2008–2012

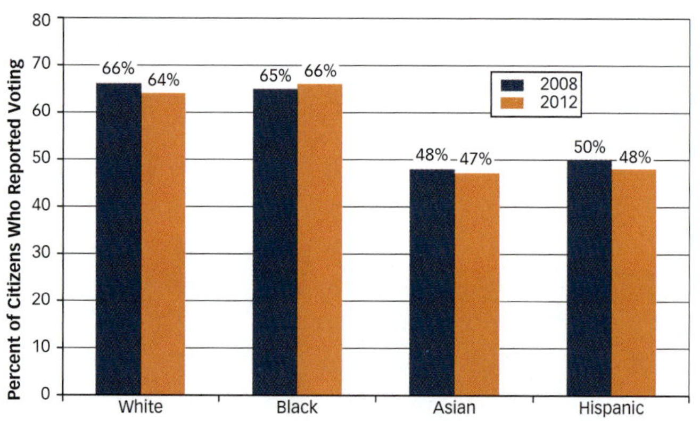

SOURCE: U.S. Census Bureau. (2010). Voting and registration in the election of November 2008—Detailed tables. *Voting and registration*; U.S. Census Bureau. (2011). Voting and registration in the election of November 2010—Detailed tables. *Voting and registration*.

FIGURE 14.6 U.S. Voter Participation by Age, 2008–2012

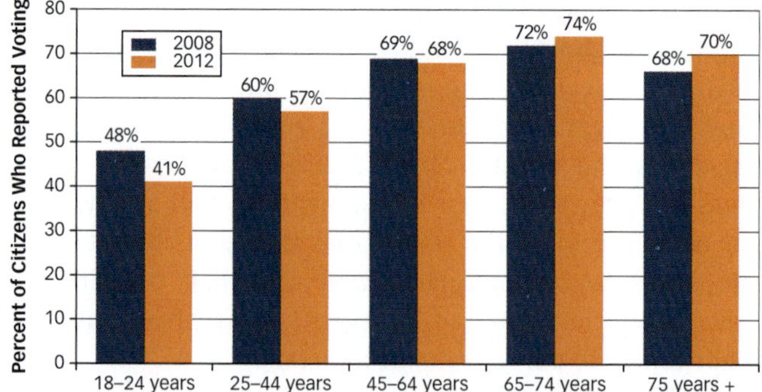

SOURCE: U.S. Census Bureau. (2010). Voting and registration in the election of November 2008 - Detailed tables. *Voting and registration*; U.S. Census Bureau. (2011). Voting and registration in the election of November 2010—Detailed tables. *Voting and registration*.

CQR Tea Party Politics

have historically had greater influence than other demographic groups on the election of officials and, consequently, on government policies. Interestingly, however, data suggest that President Obama's 2012 reelection was driven in part by the votes of young people (60% of voters 18–29 cast a vote for Obama) and minorities (for example, about 70% of ethnic Latino voters cast a ballot for Obama; Pew Research Center for the People and the Press, 2012).

Though the votes of young people and minorities had a notable effect on the outcome of the 2012 presidential election, the lower proportions of these groups among voters prompt us to ask why people who are poor or working class, minority, and/or young are less likely to be active voters. One thesis is that voters do not turn out if they do not perceive that the political parties represent their interests (Delli Carpini & Keeter, 1996). Some of Europe's political parties represent relatively narrow and specific interests. If lower- to middle-class workers can choose a workers' party (for instance, the Labour Party in Britain or the Social Democratic Party in Germany), or environmentalists a Green Party (several European states, including Germany, have active Green Parties), or minority ethnic groups a party of their ethnic kin (in the non-Russian former Soviet states that are now democracies, Russians often have their own political parties), they may be more likely to participate in the process of voting. This is particularly likely if membership in the legislative body—say, a parliament—is proportionally allocated, in contrast to a "winner-takes-all" contest such as that in the United States.

In the United States, the legislative candidate with the greater number of votes wins the seat; the loser gets nothing. In several European countries, including Germany, parties offer lists of candidates, and the total proportion of votes received by each party determines how many members of the list are awarded seats in parliament. In *proportional voting,* small parties that can break a minimum barrier (in Germany, it is 5% of the total vote) are able to garner at least a small number of seats and enjoy a political voice through coalition building, or by positioning themselves in the opposition.

Consider the winner-takes-all system and the proportional division of electoral votes. Is one more representative of the "will of the people" than the other? What do you think?

Some other reasons for low voter turnout among some demographic groups might be practical; low-wage workers may work two or more jobs and may not be able to visit polling places on the designated day of voting (for federal elections in the United States, the first Tuesday following the first Monday of November, usually between about 6:00–8:00 a.m. and 6:00–8:00 p.m.). In many European states, Election Day is a national holiday, and workers are given the day off to participate in the voting process. Recently, a growing number of U.S. states have offered early voting, extending the opportunity to vote by several days or even weeks at designated polling places. Oregon has allowed voting by mail since 1998, and other states have also begun to offer this alternative. Data suggest that these initiatives increase voter participation. However, in advance of the 2012 election, five states either passed or attempted to pass legislation that would shorten the time for early voting. Most of the laws involved curbing the number of days in which early voting could take place; for example, Florida reduced the early voting period from 14 days to 8 days.

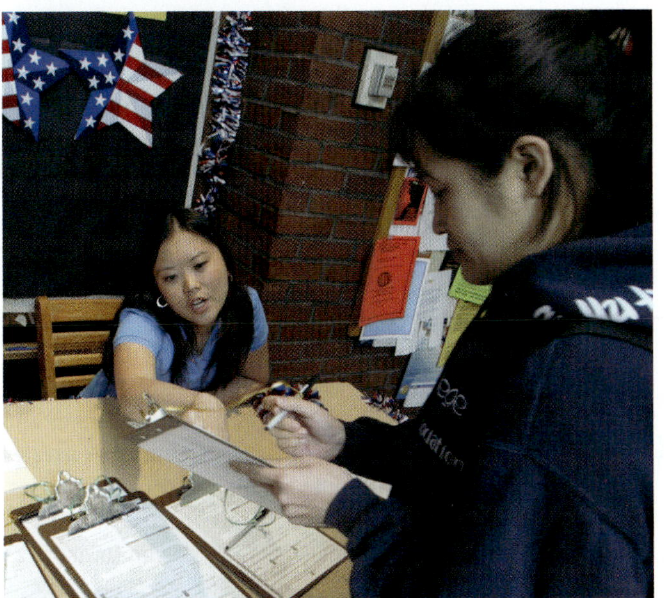

Boston Globe / Contributor/Getty Images

The participation of young adults (18–29) has been higher in the last two presidential elections than in most that preceded them. The volunteer in this picture is helping a college student register to vote so the student can vote via absentee ballot. Do you think increases in youth voting are a trend that will continue to grow?

What about young people? In 1971, the Twenty-Sixth Amendment to the U.S. Constitution lowered the voting age from 21 to 18, giving 18- to 20-year-olds the right to vote. This age group has taken advantage of suffrage in relatively small numbers, however: 18- to 24-year-olds are less than half as likely as older citizens to cast ballots. The 2008 presidential election, in which about 52% of those under 20 voted, was a historical exception driven largely by the enthusiasm of the young for Barack Obama's candidacy.

A 2010 survey found that young people are generally not apathetic about civic involvement; in fact, many responded that they volunteer and are eager to "give back" to their communities (cited in Center for Information & Research on Civic Learning and Engagement, 2010). Voting, however, does not appear to inspire the same commitment. The young are less likely to be courted by the parties and candidates, who tailor messages to attract the interests of groups such as the elderly, who vote in larger numbers, and other groups who are historically more likely to turn out at the polls or make campaign donations. Perhaps because of a perception that the candidates and parties do not seem to speak to or for them, younger voters reciprocate with limited participation in the voting process.

Other factors have also been identified as relevant in influencing the youth vote, including the accessibility of information about where and when to vote and the level of civic education on issues and candidates. Notably, data show that states offering same-day registration on election day have higher youth voting rates: In 2008, youth turnout in same-day registration states was about 59%, whereas it was about 50% in states not permitting same-day registration (Center for Information & Research on Civic Learning and Engagement, 2010).

Before we move on to the next section, which discusses the issue of political influence, we might pause to consider the following questions: How might our elected government and its policies be altered if people turned out to vote in greater numbers? Would higher turnouts among the poor, minorities, and young people make issues particularly pertinent to them higher priorities for decision makers? What do you think?

POWER AND POLITICS

While parts of the general public may show apathy about elections and politics, wealthy and powerful individuals, corporations, labor unions, and interest groups have a great deal at stake. Legislators have the power to make decisions about government contracts and regulations, taxes, federal labor and environmental and health standards, national security budgets and practices, and a spectrum of other important policies that affect profits, influence, and the division of power among those competing to have a voice in legislation.

The shortest route to political influence is through campaign contributions. The cost of campaigning has gone up dramatically in recent years, and candidates for public office must spend vast sums of money on getting elected. The 2012 presidential campaign was by far the most expensive in history, with more than $2 billion spent altogether. President Barack Obama's campaign, along with the Democratic National Committee and Priorities USA Action, a special kind of political action committee (PAC) known as a super PAC, spent more than $1.1 billion, while Mitt Romney's campaign, the Republican National Committee, and the super PAC Restore Our Future spent between $1 billion and $1.1 billion. Spending reflected money raised from a range of sources, from very small donors to very large donors (Blake, 2012).

A substantial proportion of the money candidates and parties raise comes from corporate donors and well-funded interest groups. In many instances, companies and well-resourced interest groups donate money to candidates of both parties in order to ensure that they will have a voice and a hand in decision making regardless of the electoral outcome. Clearly, while most politicians would deny that there is an explicit *quid pro quo* (a term that means "something for something") with big donors, most would also admit that money can buy the time and interest of a successful candidate and determine which issues are most likely to be heard. Small interest groups and grassroots organizations lacking financial means may not be able to purchase passes into the halls of power.

The 2008 presidential election offers a rather different story, however. Democratic nominee Barack Obama raised an unprecedented amount of campaign money, both from big donors and from a massive number of small donations successfully solicited via social media, demonstrating the power of the Internet in political fund-raising. Fund-raising and advertising online first became popular during the 2004 election, particularly after their successful use by Democratic contender Howard Dean and later by the Democratic National Committee. They returned as key strategies in 2012 as well.

The 2012 election also ushered a new player, the *super PAC,* into electoral politics (as noted above in our description of spending in the 2012 election). **Political action committees (PACs)** are *organizations created by groups such as corporations, unions, environmentalists, and other interest groups for the purpose of gathering money and contributing to political candidates that favor the groups' interests.* In 2010, the U.S. Supreme Court ruled in *Citizens United v. Federal Election Commission* that the government cannot restrict the monetary expenditures of such organizations in political campaigns, citing the First Amendment. This effectively means that these entities can contribute unlimited amounts of money to PACs. The term *super PAC* is used to describe the numerous well-funded PACs that have sprung up since the *Citizens United* decision.

While super PACs cannot contribute directly to specific campaigns or parties, they can demonstrate support for particular candidates through, for instance, television advertising. Many critics of the *Citizens United* decision have been disturbed by the implications of unlimited corporate spending in politics. The primary drivers of this new political spending have been extremely wealthy individuals and often anonymous donors. According to the Center for Responsive Politics, the top 100 individual donors to super PACs make up less than 4% of contributors but have been responsible for more than 80% of donations made (Riley, 2012).

Efforts to influence legislation are not limited to direct or indirect campaign contributions. Special interest groups often hire **lobbyists**, *paid professionals whose job it is to influence legislation.* Lobbyists commonly maintain offices in Washington, D.C., or in state capitals, and the most

Political action committees (PACs): Organizations created by groups such as corporations, unions, environmentalists, and other interest groups for the purpose of gathering money and contributing to political candidates who favor the groups' interests.

Lobbyists: Paid professionals whose job it is to influence legislation.

powerful lobbies are staffed by full-time employees. Many of the best-funded lobbies represent foreign governments. Lobbying is especially intense when an industry or other interest group stands to gain or lose a great deal if proposed legislation is enacted. Oil companies, for instance, take special interest in legislation that would allow or limit drilling on U.S. territories, as do environmental groups. In an instance like this, lobbyists from green groups and the oil and gas industry generally stand opposed to one another and seek to influence political decision makers to side with them.

Many lobbyists are former politicians or high-level government officials. Since lobbyists are often experts on matters that affect their organizations' interests, they may help in writing the laws that elected officials will introduce as legislation. Consider the example described below.

In an article titled "A Stealth Way a Bill Becomes a Law," the magazine *Bloomberg Businessweek* pointed out that that several state-level bills rejecting cap-and-trade legislation (which is intended to reduce carbon dioxide emissions, believed by most scientists to contribute to climate change) used identical wording: "There has been no credible economic analysis of the costs associated with carbon mandates" (Fitzgerald, 2011). What was the source of this wording? It was supplied by the American Legislative Exchange Council, an organization supported by companies such as Walmart, Visa, Bayer, ExxonMobil, and Pfizer. In exchange for a large "membership" fee, a corporation can buy itself a seat on the bill-writing "task force," which prepares model legislation, primarily for Republican political decision makers. The group boasts that it gets about 200 state laws passed each year.

Is the interaction of private sector corporations and public sector legislators an example of fruitful and appropriate cooperation on matters of mutual interest? When, if ever, is the writing of laws by corporate sponsors appropriate? When is it inappropriate?

SOCIAL MOVEMENTS, CITIZENS, AND POLITICS

Well-organized, popularly based social movements can also be important in shaping public policy. Among the most important social movements of the 19th and 20th centuries was the drive for women's suffrage, which invested half a century of activism to win U.S. women the right to vote. The movement's leaders fought to overcome the ideas that women ought not vote because their votes were represented by their husbands, because the muddy world of politics would besmirch feminine purity, and because women, like adolescents and lunatics, were not fit to vote.

The women's suffrage movement was born in the United States in 1869, when Susan B. Anthony and Elizabeth Cady Stanton founded the American Woman Suffrage Association. It worked for decades to realize its goal: In 1920, the Nineteenth Amendment to the Constitution was ratified and women were granted the right to vote on a national level (some states had granted this right earlier).

The second wave of the women's movements, which began in the 1960s, boasted other important achievements, including the passage of laws prohibiting gender-based job discrimination and rules easing women's ability to obtain credit independent of their husbands.

The temperance movement, symbolized by Carry Nation's pickax attacks on saloons in the early 1900s, sought to outlaw the use and sale of alcoholic beverages. This movement eventually resulted in the 1919 ratification of the Eighteenth Amendment to the Constitution, which made it a crime to sell or distribute alcoholic beverages. The Twenty-First Amendment eventually repealed Prohibition in 1933.

The labor movement grew throughout the first half of the 20th century, providing a powerful counterweight to the influence of business in U.S. politics. Labor unions were critical in getting federal and state laws passed to protect the rights of workers, including minimum wage guarantees, unemployment compensation, the right to strike, and the right to engage in collective bargaining. By midcentury, at the height of the unions' power, roughly 25% of all U.S. workers belonged to labor unions. Today globalization and the flight of U.S. factories to low-wage areas have contributed to a decline in union membership, and just under 12% of workers belong to unions (U.S. Bureau of Labor Statistics, 2013e). At the same time, large unions, including the AFL-CIO, have retained a good deal of political power, and candidates, particularly Democrats, vie for the unions' endorsements, which bring with them the virtual guarantee of large blocs of votes.

On one hand, social movements provide a counterbalance to the power and influence in politics of large corporate donors, which we discussed above. These movements offer a political voice to grassroots groups representing interests contrary to those of big business, such as labor rights and environmental protection. On the other hand, if we return to Domhoff's (2002) question, "Who wins?" we see that these groups rarely have more influence than large corporations and donors.

CONSTITUENTS Wealthy individuals, interest groups, PACs, and lobbyists exert considerable political influence through their campaign contributions. Still, these factors alone are not sufficient to explain political decisions. If they hope to be reelected, elected representatives must also serve their constituents. That is why politicians and their aides poll constituents, read their mail and e-mail, and look closely at the last election results.

One way politicians seek to win their constituents' support is by securing government spending on projects that provide jobs for or otherwise help their communities and constituents.

Citizens United Ruling

INEQUALITY MATTERS

MONEY MATTERS: ENVIRONMENTALISTS VERSUS CORPORATIONS

Sociologists understand *interest groups* as groups organized with the goal of pursuing particular interests and agendas. Environmental interest groups have historically pushed for more aggressive measures to ensure clean air and water, reduce emissions of pollutants, protect fragile ecosystems and endangered species, and the like. Since their efforts sometimes have the effect of regulating industrial activities or imposing antipollution measures that bring new business costs, the interests of environmental groups and those of corporations, whose key interest is the pursuit of profit, are often in conflict.

Sociologist William J. Domhoff (2002) suggests that one way to measure power is to ask the question, "Who wins?" We might add, "And how much does victory cost?"

The Center for Responsive Politics reports that in 2009, pro-environmental groups spent about $22.4 million on federal lobbying efforts, an unprecedented sum for these groups. At the same time, the oil and gas industry initiated an even more costly effort to block new environmental regulations: In 2009, it spent about $175 million on lobbying—fully eight times what the pro-environmental lobby had invested in its efforts. By July of that year, according to the report, "congressional debate on global warming stopped cold" (Mackinder, 2010).

Lobbying efforts against climate change–related legislation have emboldened a bloc of climate change deniers and skeptics within Congress. Some representatives and senators maintain either that the scientific evidence of climate change is manufactured by big-government liberals who want the power to regulate businesses or that environmental activists have dramatically overstated the seriousness of the situation. Initially, funds backing this viewpoint could be traced to a number of conservative foundations. More recently, however, this money has been disbursed through third-party, pass-through organizations that conceal the identities of their donors. It is difficult to know exactly who is financially supporting the agenda of climate change denial and skepticism (Fischer, 2013).

Reuters/David W Cerny

Despite its financial edge, this interest lobby has not necessarily won the battle for hearts and minds among the American people. Two-thirds of Americans believe that the evidence for climate change is solid and that there ought to be stricter carbon emissions limits on power plants. Even so, few Americans feel that climate change should be a top priority for Congress and the president, and overall opinion about the issue is sharply divided along partisan lines (Pew Research Center, 2014a). Thus, "Who wins?" is not always fully clear.

Many pro-environmental groups lauded the passage in 2009 of the American Clean Energy and Security Act, which pushed forward with caps on carbon emissions that could help limit climate change. On the other hand, they lamented the loopholes that exempted large parts of the energy and coal industries from the caps, even as those industries argued vehemently that further regulations would result in job cuts and higher energy costs for Americans.

After the 2010 congressional elections, in which Republicans regained a majority in the House of Representatives and gained seats in the Democratic-majority Senate, the debate over climate change moved lower on the national agenda. In the wake of the 2012 election, President Obama expressed a willingness to push for greater efforts to reduce greenhouse gas emissions linked to climate change. For the moment, at least, the "winner" is unclear, though the lobbying expenditures on both sides of the issue continue to be substantial.

THINK IT THROUGH

▶ Well-funded interest groups expend vast sums of money lobbying for their causes. What are available avenues for expressing political opinions and influence for individuals and less well-funded interest groups? Should there be limits on how much interest groups can spend on lobbying U.S. legislative representatives?

If a new prison is to be built, for instance, legislators vie to have it placed in their district. Although a prison may seem like an undesirable neighbor, it can represent an economic windfall for a state or region. Among other things, prisons provide jobs to individuals who may not have the education or training to work in professional sectors of the economy and would otherwise be unemployed or working in the poorly paid service sector.

Projects that legislators push to bring to their home districts are sometimes labeled "pork." Pork may be superfluous or unnecessary for the macro-level economy but good for the legislator's home district. On the other hand, when a government commission proposes closing military bases, cost-conscious members of Congress will support the recommendation—*unless* any of the bases marked for closure are in their districts.

Politicians spend substantial amounts of time in their home districts. Over the course of the calendar year, the U.S. Congress is in session for an average of 103 days (Library of Congress, 2012). Congressional representatives spend much of their off-session time in their home districts because they are interested in hearing the views of their constituents—as well as in raising money and getting reelected.

CONTRADICTIONS IN MODERN POLITICS: DEMOCRACY AND CAPITALISM

Leaders in modern democratic capitalist societies like the United States are caught between potentially contradictory demands. They seek widespread popular support, yet they must satisfy the demands of the elites whose financial backing is essential for electoral success. On one hand, voters are likely to look to their political leaders to back benefits such as retirement income (in the form of Social Security, for instance), housing supports (affordable housing for low-income families or mortgage tax breaks for wealthier ones), and environmental protection. On the other hand, such programs are costly to implement and entail economic costs to corporations, developers, and other members of the elite. Some theorists argue that modern governments thus are caught in a conflict between their need to realize the interests of the capitalist class and their desire to win the support and loyalty of other classes (Held, 1989; Offe, 1984; Wolfe, 1977).

Jürgen Habermas (1976), a contemporary theorist with a conflict orientation, argues that modern countries have integrated their economic and political systems, reducing the likelihood of economic crisis while increasing the chances of a political crisis. He terms this the *legitimation crisis.* Governments have intervened in the market and, to some degree, solved the most acute contradictions of capitalism—including extreme income inequalities and tumultuous economic cycles—that Marx argued could be addressed only in a proletarian revolution. Governments often act to keep inflation and deflation in check, to regulate interest rates, and to provide social assistance to those who have lost jobs. Thus, economics is politicized, and the citizenry may come to expect that economic troubles will be solved through state structures and social welfare.

To understand Habermas's argument more fully, imagine a postindustrial U.S. city. The loss of jobs and industries manifests itself as a crisis—thousands of jobs in auto and other manufacturing industries move abroad, local businesses suffer as the amount of disposable income held by local people plummets, and economic pain is acute. How, in modern society, does our hypothetical city (which has hundreds of authentic counterparts in the United States) respond? Does it erupt in revolutionary fervor, with displaced laborers calling for class struggle? Or do people look to their local, state, and federal governments to provide relief in the form of tax cuts or credits, unemployment benefits, and plans for attracting new industries?

The citizenry of modern capitalism, says Habermas, does not widely question the legitimacy of capitalism. If there is a "crisis," it is political, and it is "solved" with policies that may smooth capitalism's bumpy ride. In a sense, the state becomes the focus of discontent—in a democracy, political decision makers can be changed and a crisis averted. The economic system that brings many of these crises into being, however, remains in shadow, its legitimacy rarely questioned.

In the next part of the chapter, we look into some of the other challenges confronted by states and their populations, including war and terrorism. States are key players in modern warfare, and military conflict is an important domestic political issue and global concern. Terrorism has also become increasingly entwined with war today, as recent wars undertaken by the United States, for instance, have been part of an effort to combat the threat of terrorism.

WAR, STATE, AND SOCIETY

Conflict between ethnic or religious groups, states, and other social entities has a long history. War has been part of human societies, cultures, and practices in some form for millennia. In the 5th century B.C., the ancient Greeks created a game called *petteia,* the first board game known to have been modeled on war. In the 6th century A.D., chess, another game of strategic battle, was born in northern India; it developed into its modern form by the 15th century. Military training in ancient Greece also gave birth to the first Olympic Games. In the 20th century, war games took on far more advanced forms, ranging from battlefield exercises used to prepare for defensive or offensive war to sophisticated computer simulations used for both popular entertainment and military readiness training (Homans, 2011).

Today, the countries of the world spend trillions of dollars preparing for war or fighting in wars. At the same time, armed conflict and associated casualties have declined. Goldstein (2011) suggests that the nature of armed conflict has changed, shifting from larger wars in which powerful

FIGURE 14.7 Combined Military and Civilian Casualties of Some 20th- and 21st-Century Wars

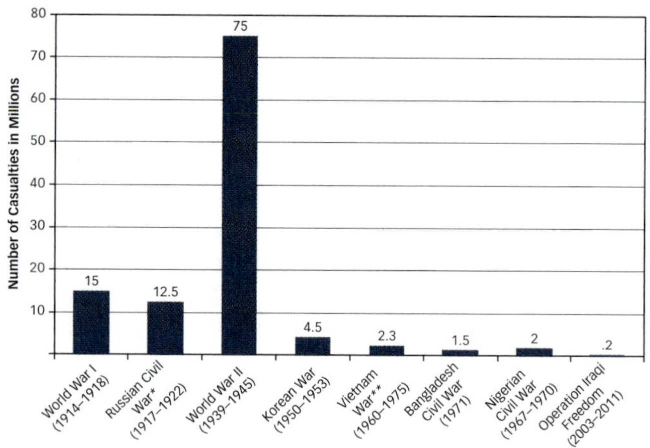

*Including Soviet–Polish conflict.

**Including North Vietnam versus South Vietnam.

Leitenberg, Milton. 2006. "Deaths in Wars and Conflicts in the 20th Century." Cornell University Peace Studies Program, Occasional Paper #29, 3rd edition; Fischer, Hannah. 2010. "Iraq Casualties: U.S. Military Forces and Iraqi Civilians, Police, and Security Forces." Congressional Research Service.

state actors confronted one another directly (such as World War II or the Korean War of the 1950s) to asymmetrical guerrilla wars, such as those the United States fought in Iraq and Afghanistan in the past decade. He notes, "Worldwide, deaths caused directly by war-related violence in the new century have averaged about 55,000 per year, just over half of what they were in the 1990s (100,000 a year), a third of what they were during the Cold War (180,000 a year from 1950 to 1989), and a hundredth of what they were in World War II" (p. 53) (Figure 14.7).

Whatever the forms war has taken, it has been a key part of the human experience throughout history. What explains its existence and persistence? Recall from earlier chapters that *manifest functions* are intended and obvious, while *latent functions* are hidden, unexpected, or "nonpurposive" (in Robert Merton's words). Functionalists look at a phenomenon or an institution that exists in society, assert that its existence presupposes a function, and ask what that function is. If something did not serve a function, it would cease to exist. Does war have a function? We begin with a functionalist perspective on war, considering its role and consequences at the macro and micro societal levels.

A FUNCTIONALIST PERSPECTIVE ON WAR

What are the manifest functions of war? Historically, one function has been to gain territory. The Roman Empire (27 B.C.–476 A.D.) waged war on surrounding territories, acquiring a substantial swath of the Middle East, including Cleopatra's Egypt, and then holding it with its massive armies. Another manifest function of war is to gain control of the natural resources of another state, while a third is to prevent the disintegration of a territorial unit. The American Civil War (1861–1865) sought to avert the secession of the South, which still favored slavery, from the North, which sought to abolish slavery.

What about the latent functions of war? First, war has historically operated as a stimulus to the economy: The term **war economy** refers to *the phenomenon of war boosting economic productivity and employment, particularly in capital- and labor-intensive sectors such as industrial production.* Notably, however, the wars in which the United States took part in the 20th century were fought outside its borders, and the benefits to the U.S. economy, especially in the World War II era, were not necessarily repeated elsewhere. The Soviet Union, France, Belgium, Poland, and many other European countries on whose territory World War II was waged emerged with shattered economies.

As well, the first wars in which the United States has engaged in the 21st century—the conflict in Afghanistan that began in October 2001 and the military occupation of Iraq, which began in March 2003—have arguably had negative effects on the U.S. economy and have failed to benefit all but a few large corporations in the defense and energy sectors (Table 14.1).

A second latent function of war is the fostering of patriotism and national pride. In times of war, governments implore their citizens to rally around the national cause, and citizens may display their patriotism with flags or demonstrations. Even those who oppose military action may shy away from open opposition in a climate of war-inspired patriotism: During the early years of the conflict in Iraq, officials of President George W. Bush's administration several times chastised those who expressed criticism of the president and his actions "in a time of war," raising the question of whether dissent was unpatriotic.

A third latent function of war is its effect on family life and demographics. In the post–World War II years, the United States (and a number of other countries that had participated in the conflict) experienced a "baby boom," partially the product of the return of men who had been away at war and of childbearing postponed in the war years.

Of course, family life and individual lives are also prone to the deep dysfunctional consequences of war. With the long absence or loss of a father, husband, or son (or mother, wife, or

War economy: The phenomenon of war boosting economic productivity and employment, particularly in capital- and labor-intensive sectors such as industrial production.

TABLE 14.1 Armed Civil and Interstate Conflicts of Recent Decades

Year(s)	Countries Involved	Type
1964–present	Colombia	Civil
1967–present	Israel, Palestinian Nation	Interstate
1991–present	Somalia	Civil
1998–present	Democratic Republic of Congo; Former Zaire	Interstate
2001–present	USA (with allies); Afghanistan	Interstate
2002	Algeria, Chad, Mali, Mauritania, Morocco, Niger, Tunisia	Interstate
2002	Ivory Coast	Civil
2004	Yemen, Saudi Arabia	Civil
2008	Cambodia, Thailand	Interstate
2009	Yemen	Civil
2009–present	Sudan and South Sudan	Interstate
2011–present	Syria	Civil
2011	Libya	Civil
2011–present	Yemen	Civil

SOURCE: Pike, J. (2013). The world at war: Current conflicts. GlobalSecurity .org.

daughter), families may be drawn closer together, or they may break apart. They may experience economic deprivation with the loss of an income. A spouse who has not previously worked outside the home may be compelled by circumstances to join the labor force. War may also have disproportionate effects on different socioeconomic classes, as history shows that it has often been members of the working class who bear the greatest burden in war fighting. Clearly, war has a spectrum of manifest and latent functions as well as dysfunctions.

A CONFLICT PERSPECTIVE ON WAR

The conflict perspective suggests that some groups benefit from a given social order or phenomenon at the expense of others. We can turn a conflict-oriented lens on war to ask, "Who benefits from war? Who loses?"

While we might be inclined to answer that the war's victor wins and the defeated state or social group loses, the conflict perspective offers us the opportunity to construct a more nuanced picture. Consider the conflict in Iraq that spanned from the U.S. occupation of that country in March 2003 to the final withdrawal of troops at the end of 2011. Who benefited from this war in Iraq?

Beneficiaries of any conflict include those who are freed from oppressive state policies or structures or from ongoing persecution by the defeat of a regime. Among the beneficiaries in Iraq we might count the minority Kurdish population, who were victims of Saddam Hussein's genocidal attacks in 1987 and 1988 and were threatened by the Iraqi dictator's presence. Were the rest of the people of Iraq beneficiaries? To the degree that Saddam was an oppressive political tyrant, the answer may be yes; Saddam's ruling Báath Party, composed primarily of Sunni Muslims, persecuted the majority Shiite Muslim population of the country, particularly after some Shiites sought to foment an uprising at the end of the First Gulf War (1990–1991). Ordinary Sunni Muslims as well had no voice in the single-party state that Saddam ruled with a strong hand. At the same time, the long war led to thousands of civilian and military casualties, fundamentally destabilized the country, and left it with a badly damaged economy and infrastructure. Today, Iraq continues to be plagued by *sectarian violence*—that is, violence between religious groups—that threatens to spiral into an existential threat to the country itself. Notably, by mid-2014, a debate had arisen about the possibility of U.S. reengagement in Iraq, though few were calling for active participation in combat.

Other beneficiaries of the nearly decadelong Iraq War were corporations (mostly U.S.-based) that profited from lucrative government contracts to supply weapons and other military supplies. War generates casualties and destruction—it also generates profits. In assessing who benefits from war, we cannot overlook capitalist enterprises for which war is a business and investment opportunity.

Among those who benefit directly from war and conflict are private military corporations (PMCs), which provide military services such as training, transportation, and the protection of human resources and infrastructure. The use of private contractors in war has a long history. The new U.S. government, fighting against the British in the American Revolution, paid private merchant ships to sink enemy ships and steal their cargo. The modern military term *company,* which refers to an organized formation of 200 soldiers, comes from the private "companies" of mercenaries who were hired to fight in conflicts during the Middle Ages in Europe.

At the same time, until recently, wars in the modern world were largely fought by the citizens of the nation-states involved. Sociologist Katherine McCoy (2009) writes, "Scholars have long thought of fighting wars as something nation-states did through their citizens. Max Weber famously defined the modern state as holding a monopoly over the legitimate use of violence, meaning that only state agents—usually soldiers or police—were allowed to wield force" (p. 15).

Abu Ghraib and Imprisonment

In today's conflicts, governments, including the U.S. government, increasingly rely on PMCs to provide a vast array of services that used to be functions of the governments or their militaries. This situation raises critical questions about the accountability and control of these private armies, which are motivated by profit rather than patriotism (McCoy, 2009). The rise of PMCs has been driven by reductions in the size of armies since the end of the Cold War, the availability of smaller advanced weaponry, and a political-ideological trend toward the privatization and outsourcing of activities previously conducted by governments (Singer, 2003).

The conflict perspective on war also asks, "Who loses?" Losers, of course, include those on both sides of a conflict who lose their lives, limbs, or livelihoods in war. Increasingly, according to some reports, they have been civilians, not soldiers. By one estimate, in World War I, about 5% of casualties were civilians (Swiss & Giller, 1993). In World War II, the figure has been estimated at 50% (Gutman & Rieff, 1999). While some researchers argue that the figure is much higher (Swiss & Giller, 1993), Goldstein (2011) suggests that the ratio of civilian to military casualties has remained at about 50:50 into the 21st century. Specific casualty figures also vary widely, often depending on the methodologies and motivations of the organizations or governments doing the counting (Table 14.2). This topic is examined in more detail in the *Behind the Numbers* box on page 371.

What about the less apparent "losers"? Who else pays the costs of war? Modern military action has substantial financial costs, which are largely borne by taxpayers. In the decade between 2001, when the United States was the victim of terrorist attacks, and 2011, when the Iraq War ended and the war in Afghanistan began to wind down, the country spent an estimated $7.6 trillion on defense and homeland security. Even since the end of active U.S. engagement in Iraq and Afghanistan, the United States has continued to devote a substantial part of its federal budget to the Departments of Defense and Homeland Security. At the same time, many U.S. domestic programs in areas such as education, job training, and environmental conservation have lost funding as budgets have shrunk. Growth in the defense and security allocations of the federal budget has not been without costs.

In the next section we consider the phenomena of terrorists and terrorism, which have been drivers—and consequences—of some of the world's most recent armed conflicts.

TABLE 14.2 Casualty Estimates for Darfur and Congo Conflicts

Conflict	Estimated Number of Casualties
Congo conflict, 1998–2008	
International Rescue Committee	5.4 million
Human Security Report Project, Simon Fraser University	900,000
Darfur conflict, 2003–2005	
Coalition for International Justice	400,000
U.S. Deputy Secretary of State Robert Zoellick	60,000–160,000
United Nations	300,000
Sudanese President Omar al-Bashir	9,000

SOURCE: Rieff, D. (2011, September/October). Millions may die . . . or not. *Foreign Policy,* pp. 22–25.

TERRORISTS AND TERRORISM

The "global war on terror," or GWOT, was initiated in 2001 after the September 11 attacks on the World Trade Center and the Pentagon. This term has been used to refer to the international (though U.S.-led) overt and covert military campaign against the Islamic group al-Qaeda and similar groups believed to threaten the United States and its allies. The term was first used by President George W. Bush and other officials of his administration. President Barack Obama has not adopted the term, and in March 2009, the U.S. Department of Defense dropped it officially. Though it continues to be used in some political commentary, the designation "overseas contingency operation" (OCO) has largely replaced GWOT. The focus of U.S. military, diplomatic, and economic efforts on combating terrorism has, however, continued unabated.

The unprecedented events of September 2001 brought terrorism and terrorists more fully than ever into the U.S. experience and consciousness. The political response was to refocus domestic priorities on the GWOT and homeland security, drawing resources and attention from other areas such as education and immigration reform. Terrorism became a key theme of U.S. politics, policies, and spending priorities and a subject of concern and discussion from the U.S. Congress to ordinary citizens. The concepts of *terrorist* and *terrorism,* however, are broad and may not be defined or understood in the same ways across groups or countries. Acts of violence labeled by one group as terrorism may be embraced as heroic by another. The label of terrorist may be inconsistently applied depending on the ethnicity, religion, actions, and motivations of an individual or a group. Below we examine these concepts and consider their usage with a critical eye.

WHO IS A TERRORIST?

Close your eyes and picture a terrorist. What does your imagined terrorist look like? Why do you think that particular image appeared to you? The images we generate are

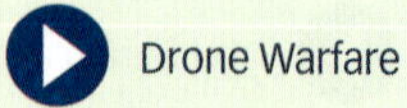

BEHIND THE NUMBERS

COUNTING THE CIVILIAN CASUALTIES OF WAR

In the U.S.-led occupation of Iraq that began in 2003, civilian casualties resulted from the actions of multiple actors, including U.S., coalition, and Iraqi forces and armed insurgents, and many resulted from the sectarian violence between Iraq's Sunni and Shiite Muslim populations that followed. An accurate count of civilian casualties remains difficult to pinpoint. For example, the Associated Press places the civilian casualties from 2005 through 2008 at 34,832 killed and 40,174 wounded. By contrast, an article published in the medical journal *The Lancet* estimated the total number of deaths to be between 426,000 and 793,600 (Fischer, 2008). Clearly, the difference between 35,000 and 790,000 deaths is vast. What accounts for this disparity?

Reuters/Thaier al-Sudani

Although the deaths of U.S. and allied military personnel were carefully counted while troops were serving in Iraq, there are no official estimates of the number of Iraqi civilians killed in the long-running conflict in that country. Estimates range widely.

One factor is the way civilian deaths are initially reported. Some may go unreported, some may be reported multiple times, and still others may only be estimated when identifying victims is difficult. Local hospital records are often not maintained accurately in conflict-ridden areas. Finally, some bodies never make it to hospitals if they are taken away by family or are rendered unidentifiable, a tragic but common problem.

The Associated Press tallied the number of individuals listed as killed in news reports and identified as "civilians" (Fischer, 2008). Relying only on reports of deaths in news accounts likely led to underestimation of the total number. The *Lancet* estimate relied on two cluster sample surveys of Iraqi households, but the journal was criticized for, among other problems, failing to gather demographic information that might have shed light on the reliability of counts.

A third casualty count, also based on cluster sample surveys, sampled 20 times as many households as the *Lancet* study. Sponsored by the World Health Organization and the Iraq Family Health Survey, it was nationally representative and had an 89% response rate. The result was an estimate that placed the number of civilian casualties at just over 115,000 (Fischer, 2008).

These widely varying counts highlight the fact that casualty statistics can be influenced by how the data are collected and analyzed. Because states, relief agencies, and international organizations use casualty figures to make their cases for intervention, cessation of operations, and budgetary increases, it is important to recognize that different methodologies may render dramatically different figures.

THINK IT THROUGH

▶ Why is it more difficult to count civilian casualties than military casualties? Why do different entities often produce differing casualty figures?

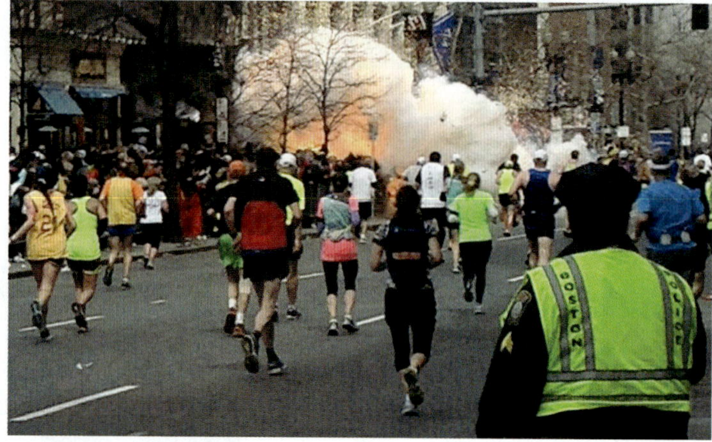

Terrorist acts are often intentionally dramatic and calculated to inflict harm, instill fear, and attract media attention. The attacks on the World Trade Center and Pentagon on September 11, 2001 (left), and the Boston Marathon bombing on April 15, 2013 (right), fit this model of terrorism.

culturally conditioned by the political environment, the mass media, and the experiences we have, and they differ across communities, countries, and cultures. The idea of a terrorist is not the same across communities because, as we will see below, violent acts condemned by one community may be embraced by another as necessary sacrifices in the pursuit of political ends.

It has been said that one person's terrorist is another person's freedom fighter. Michael Collins was born in West Cork, Ireland, in 1890. Before he turned 20, he had sworn allegiance to the Irish Republican Brotherhood, a group of revolutionaries struggling for Irish independence from three centuries of British rule, and he worked and fought with them throughout the first decades of the 20th century. In Ireland and Northern Ireland today, Collins is widely regarded as a hero (Coogan, 2002). The 1996 film *Michael Collins,* starring Liam Neeson and Julia Roberts, cast him in a generally positive light: The film's tagline declared, "Ireland, 1916. His dreams inspired hope. His words inspired passion. His courage forged a nation's destiny."

In Britain, however, many consider Collins to be a terrorist. In 1920, while he was director of intelligence for the Irish Republican Army (IRA), his secret service squad assassinated 14 British officers (Coogan, 2002). The British responded to the IRA with violence as well. Notably, the Continuity Irish Republican Army (CIRA) continues to be on the U.S. Department of State's (2012b) global list of terrorist groups.

Was Michael Collins a terrorist or a hero? How do we judge Britain's violent military response? The label of terrorist is a subjective one, conditioned by whether one rejects or sympathizes with the motives and actions under discussion. As an expert on terrorism notes, "If one party can successfully attach the label *terrorist* to its opponent, then it has indirectly persuaded others to adopt its moral viewpoint" (Hoffman, 2006, p. 23).

The issue is, arguably, more complex when it involves acts of mass violence perpetrated by domestic terrorists, for example, incidents in the U.S. committed by U.S. citizens or residents. On April 20, 1995, 168 people perished in the bombing of a federal building in Oklahoma City, Oklahoma. While initial media suspicion pointed to foreign perpetrators, further investigation determined that Timothy McVeigh, an American, with the cooperation of a small group of antigovernment compatriots, was responsible for the crime. In the wake of the incident, the U.S. government planned closer scrutiny of domestic threats. The terrorist incidents of September 11, 2001, which were perpetrated by Islamic radicals, shifted attention to the Middle East, including Afghanistan and, later, Iraq and Pakistan, among others.

Recent domestic incidents of violence, including shootings at two Jewish centers in Kansas in 2014 that killed 3 people, the Boston Marathon bombing of 2013 that resulted in 3 deaths and injuries to more than 260 people, and the killing of 6 people at a Sikh temple in Wisconsin in 2012, have refocused attention on internal incidents. In 2014, the U.S. Department of Justice relaunched the work of a group focused on domestic threats. As a Council on Foreign Relations publication points out, however, there is inconsistency in understandings and legal approaches to what "terrorism" is and whether domestic and international incidents of violence both fall under that term (Masters, 2011). Consider that the alleged killer in the Kansas Jewish center shootings, who is affiliated with White supremacist groups, has been charged with first-degree murder, while one of the Boston bombers (the other was killed by police) has been charged with, among other crimes, use of a weapon of mass destruction to kill. Are individuals or small groups in the United States who target government buildings, public events, or other groups for violence *terrorists*? What is the significance of using that term rather than using terms like *criminal* or even *extremist*?

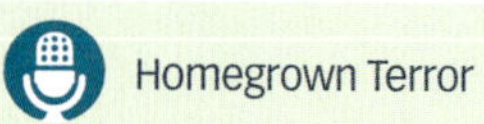

Homegrown Terror

Terrorism and Depression

THE TERROR SHOW

The Internet, and in particular social media platforms like Facebook and Twitter, has become a fundamental part of contemporary terrorism. If, as Timothy Furnish (2005) writes, "the purpose of terrorism is to strike fear into the hearts of opponents in order to win political concession," then social media have multiplied the effects of acts of terror, expanding the audience for horrific violence and transforming single incidents of violence into media shows that can be played over and over again. But social media appear to have a second key function for terrorism as well—to win over new followers and entice recruits.

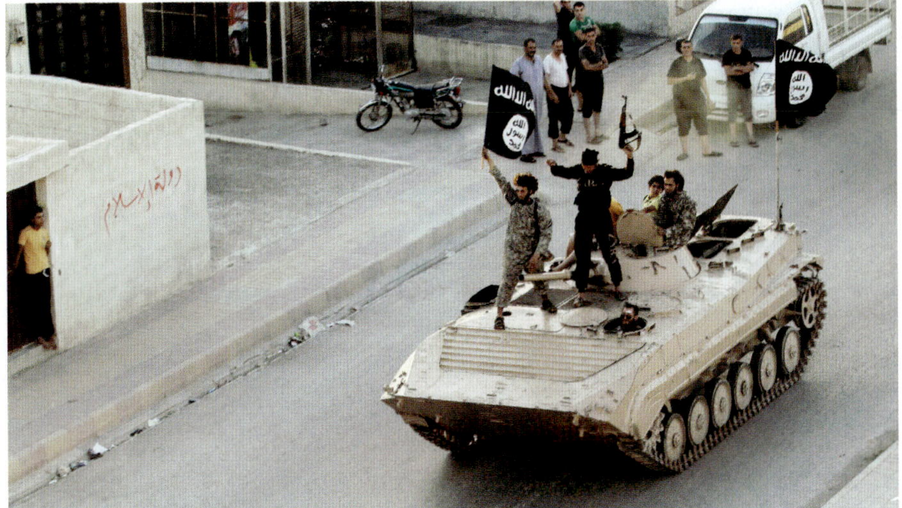

Reuters/Stringer

In 2014, Islamic State (IS or ISIS) fighters occupied substantial swaths of territory in Syria and Iraq. While small, the radical Islamist group has successfully recruited thousands of fighters from Western countries like England and the United States.

In the summer of 2014, the Middle Eastern terror group ISIS (Islamic State of Iraq and Syria; also known as ISIL, for Islamic State of Iraq and the Levant, or simply as the Islamic State) took to Twitter to disseminate images of the killing of Iraqi soldiers loyal to the state ISIS was seeking to destroy. ISIS has been a presence in the Syrian civil war and, according to reports, is an offshoot of the better-known terror group al-Qaeda. While both al-Qaeda and ISIS are adherents of an extreme brand of Sunni Islam, the two groups apparently broke over ISIS's unfettered willingness to slaughter Muslim civilians. A writer on the Vox Media news website has pointed out that the multitude of graphic images circulated by ISIS on Twitter in June was not just "ISIS bragging about their murderousness. ISIS has a well-developed social media presence, which they're using deliberately in this campaign to do two things: intimidate Iraqis who might oppose them and win supporters in their battle with al-Qaeda for influence over the international Islamist extremist movement" (Beauchamp, 2014).

Indeed, ISIS's use of social media appears carefully managed; it involves tweeting at regular intervals and choosing hashtags that will reach the audiences they seek (Beauchamp, 2014). Notably, Twitter responded within a day by suspending the account used by ISIS to post the photos of the slaughter, following Facebook, which earlier had suspended an ISIS fan page. By this time, however, the images had already been reproduced across the Internet, appearing on many mainstream media sites. ISIS continued to post on Twitter, presumably using an alternative account.

Clearly, it is highly problematic when social media platforms, most of which have codes of conduct, are used to disseminate images of violence and horror. At the same time, it has been pointed out in the press that shocking images can impel the international community toward action in some cases (Chandler, 2014). They may also offer the documentation that countries and the international community need to prosecute killers for the crimes they have chosen to glorify.

While fundamentalist terror groups like ISIS embrace an archaic and deeply conservative interpretation of Islam, their means of sharing their brutal battles are thoroughly modern.

THINK IT THROUGH

▶ What functions do social media serve for contemporary terror groups? How should social media platforms like Facebook and Twitter respond to users who represent or are affiliated with terror groups?

WHAT IS TERRORISM?

There is no single definition of **terrorism**. The U.S. Department of Defense (2011) defines it as "the unlawful use of violence or threat of violence to instill fear and coerce governments or societies. Terrorism is often motivated by religious, political, or other ideological beliefs and committed in the pursuit of goals that are usually political." This definition highlights the idea that terrorism is intended to provoke both fear and change. Does it then also include the bombings of war, such as the brutal Nazi air attacks on London or the U.S. nuclear bombing of Nagasaki and Hiroshima during World War II? What about genocidal acts against populations? What factors make terrorism difficult to define clearly?

The U.S. Department of State offers another definition in which terrorism is "premeditated, politically motivated violence perpetrated against noncombatant targets by subnational groups or clandestine agents" (quoted in National Institute of Justice, 2011). This definition implies that terrorism is committed not by states but by groups, and that its targets are noncombatants. While this is often true, it is not invariably true: States have also been complicit in supporting acts of terror. For example, it is alleged that Libya's former leader Colonel Muammar Gaddafi ordered the bombing of an international civilian airliner, Pan Am Flight 103, that crashed on December 21, 1988, killing all 259 people on board. While Gaddafi rejected the allegation, in 2003 the Libyan government accepted responsibility for the act and paid compensation to families of the victims.

We can also understand terrorism as *performative*—that is, it is violence that is intentionally dramatic, enacted for the purpose of attracting attention and publicity and spreading fear. This definition points more deliberately to terrorism as an instrument of horrific political theater whose direct victims are props on the stage of a larger political or ideological play. While such "media-oriented terrorism" does not, by one analysis, make up the majority of the terror acts of the past half century, it is widespread and has historical roots in the acts of 19th-century anarchists, who pioneered the concept of "propaganda of the deed" (Surette, Hansen, & Noble, 2009).

In some sense the media do offer a "stage" for acts of atrocity, not only functioning as reporters of terror events but also conditioning terrorist groups' selection of targets and actions (see the *Technology and Society* box on page 373). Media-oriented terrorism is thus particularly likely to be perpetrated in democratic rather than authoritarian states, because democracies allow the wide dissemination of information about events such as terror attacks. Media attention, which has expanded from the print media and television to include the Internet, the "Twitterverse," and other new media, has a powerful multiplier effect on modern terrorism, offering a broad platform of publicity even for small and relatively weak groups whose combat and political capabilities are otherwise very limited (Surette et al., 2009).

Notably, the success of some nations in building strong, centralized militaries may also have contributed to terrorism's spread. As an effective form of asymmetric conflict, terrorism is one of the few avenues open to those who want power, attention, or change yet lack the military means to challenge dominant global powers directly. Robert Pape (2005) has pointed to terrorism as a weapon of the weak. Based on his analysis of 315 incidences of suicide terrorism between 1980 and 2003, he concluded that a consistent causal logic of these events was the attempt to exercise coercive power against a stronger democratic state perceived as a homeland occupier.

Currently, the United Nations Comprehensive Convention on International Terrorism remains in draft form, subject to debate and negotiation, particularly over language that highlights terrorism's roots in the motive to "intimidate a population, or to compel a Government or an international organization to do or abstain from doing any act." At issue here, among other things, is what constitutes the line between an act of terrorism and an act of war. Is an act of war by a state an act of "politically motivated violence" subject to the convention's regulation? Leaders also debate whether to include in the definition of terrorist groups national "liberation movements," examples of which could be the Irish Republican Army, Palestinian movements such as Hamas, and Kurdish militants in Turkey. Those who support the aims of such groups say no. In light of the fact that perceptions of a given act may differ widely across groups and countries, is a global definition of terrorism even possible? Is it necessary in order to reduce the threat of violence to states and civilian populations? What do you think?

WHY STUDY THE STATE AND WARFARE THROUGH A SOCIOLOGICAL LENS?

In the modern world, politics and the state directly affect the lives of everyone. Understanding how politics and the state work is essential to our lives as informed, active local and global citizens. In this chapter we have inquired into the processes that directly affect the functioning of the state and politics and into state decision making, including the decision to go to war. In the face of the apparently overwhelming power of the state and the seeming distance of political decision making from the

Terrorism: "The calculated use of violence or the threat of violence to inculcate fear; intended to coerce or to intimidate governments or societies in the pursuit of goals that are generally political, religious, or ideological" (U.S. Department of Defense, 2011).

lives of most people, it is easy for us to shrug our shoulders and feel powerless. Yet one of the lessons we learn from the sociological analysis of the state and politics is that both are subject to influence by ordinary citizens, especially when people are mobilized into social movements and interest groups, politically aware, and able to evaluate politics and policies critically. Public ignorance and apathy benefit those who use politics to ensure their own or their social groups' well-being; active citizenship is an authentic instrument of power, even where it faces significant obstacles.

Understanding issues of state and politics also helps us understand the roots and consequences of armed conflict. Wars are the products of choices made by leaders—usually the civilian or military leaders of countries or empires. Wars do not just happen. In understanding war, we benefit from recognizing the ways in which it confers benefits and incurs costs. Those with power make calculations and choices. Those without power—women and children and sometimes citizens and soldiers—do not make such choices, though they may pay the cost. While war is a reality in our world, we need to move beyond a simple understanding of war as an inevitable part of the human experience to recognize its more complex and less obvious sociological elements. Perhaps with a better understanding of war and its motivations and consequences we can help to clear a path to greater civility and peace in the world.

Robert Merton (1968) posited the idea of functional alternatives. If we recognize that war has functions (as we have seen in this chapter), we might also begin to imagine *functional alternatives*—that is, other means of realizing those functions. For instance, if war has a manifest function of acquiring access to needed or desired natural resources such as oil or water, perhaps greater conservation of the resources would diminish the need for aggressive action to secure access. If war acts as a way of resolving territorial disputes, perhaps creative diplomatic thinking can begin to carry us toward more nonmilitary alternatives. If war is also functional in fostering patriotism, perhaps a country could construct national pride and patriotism on a foundation other than the battlefield of glory and sacrifice, as so many countries do.

Social change demands imagination—a changed world must be imagined before it can be realized. While a future without war seems unimaginable, our expanded understanding of this phenomenon may give us some of the tools we need to make it less probable and less costly to civilians and soldiers alike.

WHAT CAN I DO WITH A SOCIOLOGY DEGREE?

SKILLS AND CAREERS: WRITTEN COMMUNICATION SKILLS

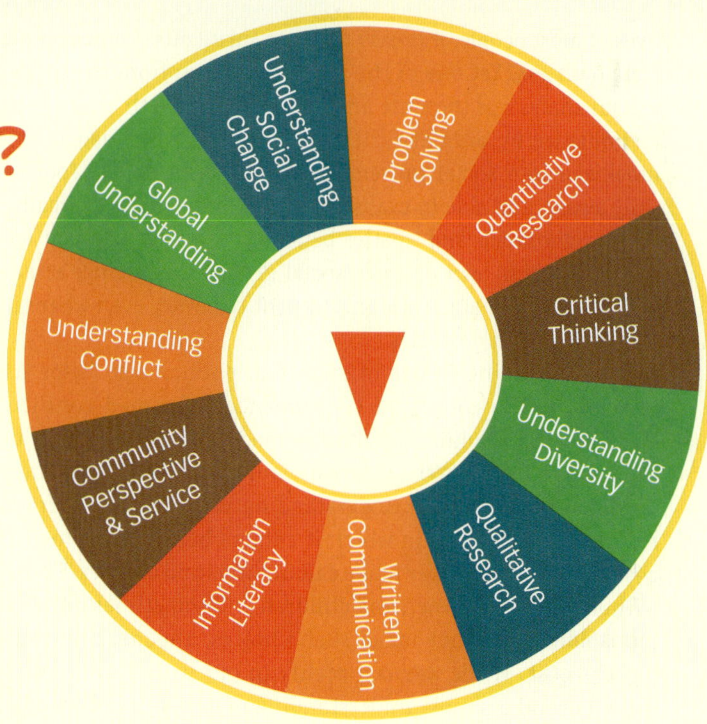

Written communication is an essential skill for a broad spectrum of 21st-century careers. Sociology students have many opportunities to practice and sharpen written communication skills. Among others, sociologists learn to write *theoretically,* applying classical and contemporary theories to the understanding of social issues or phenomena, and to write *empirically,* preparing and communicating evidence-based arguments about the social world. Sociology majors write papers in a variety of forms and for a variety of audiences; these may include reaction papers, book reviews, theoretical analyses, research papers, quantitative analysis reports, field note write-ups, letters to decision makers or newspaper editors, and reflections on sociological activities or experiences. Strong written communication skills are absolutely essential in a variety of fields.

In every chapter of this book, we explore the research findings of social scientists. This chapter, for instance, discussed the work of classical theorist Max Weber and contemporary sociologist G. William Domhoff. Sociologists need to be able to communicate effectively in writing in order to organize their research projects and to convey their findings to a wider audience (like you!). The success of other professionals is also dependent on writing skills. Consider the broad field of politics, which comprises politicians and their staffs, journalists, lobbyists, public interest advocacy groups, business coalitions, and many more actors. In politics, getting and keeping the attention of valuable constituencies or allies is often done through informed public policy ideas and the astute presentation of arguments. In politics, writing skills are a key foundation of an individual's ability to draft public policy, to persuade voters or donors, to explain political issues, or to report on current events.

Excellent written communication is fundamental in many *occupational fields,* including politics, business and entrepreneurship, communications and marketing, law and criminal justice, community organizing and advocacy, journalism, higher education, law, and public relations. Effective writing is critical for employees holding *job titles* such as social media writer or webmaster, grant writer, researcher, professor or instructor, public relations writer, journalist or reporter, English as a second language teacher, lawyer or judge, speech writer, editor, or copywriter. You may notice that quite a few of these fields and jobs require graduate or professional education; sharp and organized writing is also a key to success in postbachelor's educational pursuits.

THINK ABOUT CAREERS

- What are your strengths as a writer? What are your weaknesses? What are your goals for improvement?
- Consider possible career paths that might be of interest to you. What kinds of writing do you think people in those fields do? How can you gain experience in those types of writing?

SUMMARY

- The world today is politically divided into 195 **nation-states**. Most countries are made up of many different peoples, brought together through warfare, conquest, or boundaries drawn by colonial authorities without respect to preexisting ethnic or religious differences.
- Modern countries are characterized by governments that claim complete and final authority over their **citizens**, systems of **law**, and notions of citizenship that contain obligations as well as civil, social, and political rights.
- State power is typically based on one of three kinds of legitimate authority: **traditional authority**, based on custom and habit; **rational-legal authority**, based on a belief in the law; or **charismatic authority**, based on the perceived inspirational qualities of a leader.
- Functionalist theories of power argue that the role of the government is to mediate neutrally between competing interests; they assert that the influence of one group is usually offset by that of another group with an opposing view. Conflict theories of state power draw the opposite conclusion: that the state serves the interests of the most powerful economic and political groups in society. Different versions of social conflict theories emphasize the importance of a **power elite**, structural contradictions, and the relative autonomy of state power from the economic elites.
- Governance in the modern world takes a number of forms, including **authoritarianism** (including monarchies and dictatorships), **totalitarianism**, and **democracy**.
- Democracy is one of the primary forms of governance in the world today, and most countries claim to be democratic in theory if not in practice. Most democratic countries practice **representative democracy** rather than **direct democracy**.
- The U.S. political system is characterized by low voter turnouts. Voter participation varies, however, on the basis of demographic variables like age and education.
- In the United States, elected officials depend heavily on financial support to get elected and to remain in office. Fund-raising is a major part of **politics**, and individuals and organizations that contribute heavily do so in hopes of influencing politicians. Special interests use **lobbyists** to exercise influence in U.S. politics. Politicians still depend on their constituents' votes to get elected, and so they must satisfy voters as well as special interests.
- We can examine war from various sociological perspectives. The functionalist perspective asks about the manifest (obvious) and latent (hidden) functions of war and conflict in society. The conflict perspective asks who benefits from war and conflict, and who loses.
- The global war on terror was initiated in 2001 after the September 11 terrorist attacks on U.S. soil. The GWOT encompassed the diplomatic, military, and economic actions taken by the United States and its allies to fight terrorism. The term *global war on terror* was officially dropped by the U.S. Defense Department in 2009.
- No single image of a terrorist threat is shared across communities and countries and cultures. Irishman Michael Collins is an example of someone regarded as a hero by some and a terrorist by others.
- **Terrorism** is a calculated use of violence to coerce or to inspire fear. It is also "theater"—intended to send a powerful message to a distinct or a global audience.

KEY TERMS

nation-state, 351

law, 352

citizens, 352

noncitizens, 352

welfare state, 352

interest groups, 354

class dominance theory, 356

power elite, 356

coercion, 357

traditional authority, 357

rational-legal authority, 357

charismatic authority, 358

authoritarianism, 358

monarchy, 358

dictatorship, 359

totalitarianism, 359

democracy, 360

direct democracy, 360

representative democracy, 360

politics, 360

political action committees (PACs), 364

lobbyists, 364

war economy, 368

terrorism, 374

DISCUSSION QUESTIONS

1. In this chapter, you learned about theories of state power. Would you say that U.S. governance today is characterized more by pluralism or by the concentration of power in the hands of an elite? Cite evidence supporting your belief.
2. What is authoritarianism? What potential roles do modern technology and social media play in either supporting or challenging authoritarian governments around the world?
3. The chapter raised the issue of low voting rates for young people. Recall the reasons given in the chapter and then think about whether you can add others. Do most of the young people you know participate in elections? What kinds of factors might explain their participation or nonparticipation?
4. What are the manifest and latent functions and dysfunctions of war? Review the points made in the chapter. Can you add some of your own?
5. What is terrorism? How should this term be defined and by whom? Should domestic incidents of mass violence be labeled terrorism, or should the term be reserved for international incidents?

SAGE edge™

Sharpen your skills with SAGE edge at **edge.sagepub.com/chambliss2e**

A personalized approach to help you accomplish your coursework goals in an easy-to-use learning environment.

REUTERS/Nayer Haslamoun

WORK, CONSUMPTION, AND THE ECONOMY

IN THIS CHAPTER

Reuters/Vivek Prakash

WHAT DO YOU THINK?

1. How have job market conditions changed in your lifetime? Should you expect to experience a job market similar to that your parents or grandparents experienced?
2. Do you agree with the societal attitude that parents who are not in the paid labor force and who stay home to care for children or aging parents "don't work"? How should "work" be defined?
3. Why has average household debt grown in recent decades?

Reuters/Chris Keane

THE LOW-WAGE U.S. LABOR FORCE

In October 2010, the *Washington Post* reported that a BMW automotive plant, owned by a German parent company, had created 1,000 new jobs for workers in South Carolina (Whoriskey, 2010). In early 2014, BMW announced its intention to invest another billion dollars in its Spartanburg factory, expanding the facility to become its largest manufacturing plant and creating positions for another 800 workers (Levin, 2014). We hear much today about deindustrialization—that is, the decline of U.S. manufacturing, much of which has been automated or moved to lower-wage locations overseas. There has, however, been a small but growing movement of manufacturing operations *into* the United States in recent decades, including, very recently, from China. In March 2012, Xinxiang, which produces copper tubing used for air-conditioning, refrigeration, and cars, began construction on a new Chinese-owned and -operated plant in Thomasville, Alabama. The plant, which began partial operations in May 2014, is expected eventually to create 300 jobs (Kavilanz, 2012; Made in Alabama, 2014).

Why, after decades of industrial job loss to countries with low labor costs, are some manufacturers moving their operations to the United States? In the case of BMW, the automobile company wants to have a manufacturing presence in the United States, its largest foreign market. As well, as a representative of the Labor and Industry Group at the Center for Automotive Research has pointed out, "We are a low-wage country compared to Germany." Skilled, productive U.S. workers cost BMW about half the hourly wages of their unionized German counterparts, who earn the equivalent of about $33 per hour (Whoriskey, 2010).

Another important characteristic of the new BMW jobs is that many workers at the plant do not work for BMW. They are employed through a contractor, which means the positions are less secure and less well paid than those offered directly by BMW. According to a recent *Forbes* magazine article on the decline of the United Auto Workers union's influence, between 20% and 40% of autoworkers at foreign-owned factories today are temporary hires (Muller, 2014). The phenomenon of contracted work—that is, temporary work that minimizes the commitment of both employer or employee to a long-term economic relationship—has become a key characteristic of the modern U.S. economy as businesses seek to maximize efficiency, flexibility, and profitability by reducing (or "downsizing") the numbers of their workers who have regular "permanent" positions (Figure 15.1). Computer giant Microsoft's use of "permatemps," initiated in the 1990s, is a striking example. During this time, 1,500 permatemps worked with the 17,000 regular domestic employees of the company. While they performed comparable tasks, the permatemps, some of whom had been in their jobs for 5 years or more, not only were denied the same vacation, health, and retirement benefits as other workers but also were denied discounts at the Microsoft store, opportunities for further job training, and even use of the company basketball court. A class-action suit was filed against Microsoft, and the company agreed to an out-of-court settlement of $97 million (FACE Intel.com, 2000).

In the past 30 to 40 years, many businesses in the United States have used mass layoffs to "downsize" every aspect of their operations, from factories and production workers to managerial and professional staffs (Uchitelle, 2007). A growing proportion of American workers, even in the professional sector, find themselves engaged in short-lived jobs with little security (Greenhouse, 2008). Many more in the service sector are laboring part-time, sometimes in several jobs that lack benefits, mobility, and living wages. Wages at the bottom and in the middle tier have stagnated for a generation, despite a growing U.S. economy.

In recent decades the clear majority of economic gains have streamed upward to earners already at the top of the ladder. According to the U.S. Census Bureau (2012b), today fully half of U.S. aggregate income goes to the top 20% of earners, continuing a long-term trend toward a concentration of gains at the top. This is the culmination of a longer-term trend. According to economist Emmanuel Saez (2013), from 1993 to 2011, real annual income growth for the bottom 99% of earners was just over 6%, while it was nearly 58% for those in the top 1%.

Economy: The social institution that organizes the ways in which a society produces, distributes, and consumes goods and services.

Goods: Objects that have an economic value to others, whether they are the basic necessities for survival or things that people simply want.

Services: Economically productive activities that do not result directly in physical products; may be relatively simple or quite complex.

Low Wage Labor

Predatory Pending and Payday Loans

FIGURE 15.1 Temporary Workers in Selected U.S. Industries, 2005

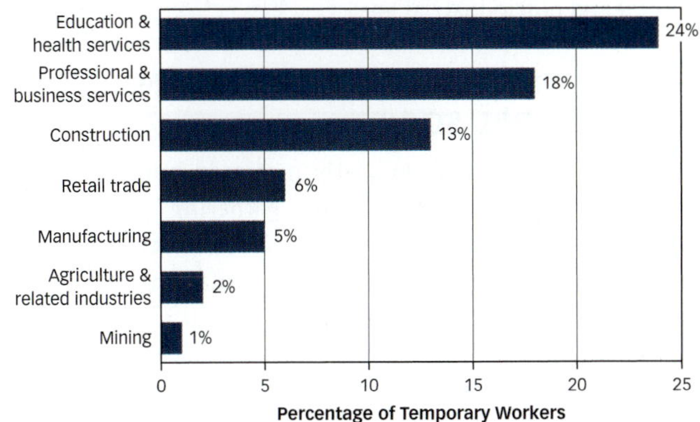

SOURCE: Table 4 "Employed Contingent and noncontingent workers by occupation and industry, February 2005." U.S. Bureau of Labor Statistics. "Contingent and Alternative Employment Arrangements, February 2005." U.S. Department of Labor (USDL 05-1433). 2005.

In this chapter, we discuss key issues of economic sociology and examine the implications of a new globalized economy—postindustrial, technologically sophisticated, and consumption oriented—for the world and for U.S. society in particular. We begin with a brief historical overview of the three great economic revolutions that have transformed human society. We then look at capitalism and communism, the two principal types of economic systems that dominated the 20th century and continue to influence the 21st century. Next we turn to a discussion of work in the formal and informal economies. In this context, we also discuss social and economic issues of consumption, hyperconsumption, and debt. The chapter concludes with a discussion of the changes and challenges globalization has brought to our economic system and prospects.

THE ECONOMY IN HISTORICAL PERSPECTIVE

The **economy** is *the social institution that organizes the ways in which a society produces, distributes, and consumes goods and services.* By **goods** we mean *objects that have an economic value to others,* whether they are the basic necessities for survival (a safe place to live, nutritious food to eat, weather-appropriate clothing) or things that people simply want (designer clothing, an iPad or iPhone, popcorn at the movies). **Services** are *economically productive activities that do not result directly in physical products*; they can be relatively simple (shining shoes, working a cash register, serving cocktails) or quite complex (repairing an airplane engine or computer, conducting a medical procedure).

In human history three technological revolutions have brought radically new forms of economic organization. The first led to the growth of agriculture several millennia ago, and the second to modern industry some 250 years ago. We are now in the throes of the third revolution, which has carried us into a digital and postindustrial age.

THE AGRICULTURAL REVOLUTION AND AGRICULTURAL SOCIETY

The agricultural revolution vastly increased human productivity over that of earlier hunting, gathering, and pastoral societies. This achievement was spurred by the development of innovations such as irrigation and crop rotation methods, as well as by expanding knowledge about animal husbandry and the use of animals in agriculture. A simple development such as the plow, which came into use about 5,000 years ago, had a transformational effect on agriculture when it was harnessed to a working animal. Greater productivity led to economic surplus. While the majority of people in agricultural societies still engaged in subsistence farming, an increasing number could produce surplus crops, which they could then barter or sell.

Eventually, specialized economic roles evolved. Some people were farmers; others were landowners who profited from farmers' labor. A number of families specialized in the making of handicrafts, working independently on items of their own design. This work gave rise to cottage industries—so called because the work was usually done at home.

The production of agricultural surpluses, as well as handicrafts, created an opportunity for yet another economic role to emerge—that of merchants, who specialized in trading surplus crops and crafted goods. Trading routes developed and permanent cities grew up along them, and the number and complexity of economic activities increased. By about the 15th century, early markets arose to serve as sites for the exchange of goods and services. Prices in markets were set (as they are in free markets today) at the point where *supply* (available goods and services) was balanced by *demand* (the degree to which those goods and services are wanted).

THE INDUSTRIAL REVOLUTION AND INDUSTRIAL SOCIETY

The Industrial Revolution, which began in England with the harnessing of water and steam power to run machines such as looms, increased productivity still further. Cottage industries were replaced by factories, the hallmark of industrial society, and urban areas became centers of economic activity, attracting rural laborers seeking work and creating growing momentum for urbanization. Industrialization spread through Europe and the United States, and then to the rest of the world. The change was massive. In 1810, about 84% of the U.S. workforce worked in agriculture and only 3% in manufacturing; by 1960, just 8% of all U.S. workers labored in agriculture, and fully a quarter of the total workforce was engaged in manufacturing (Blinder, 2006).

Industrial society is characterized by the increased use of machinery and mass production, the centrality of the modern

Public Domain -Library of Congress

Karl Marx saw industrial workers as "instruments of labor" tethered to an exploitive system. One 19th British mother described her 7-year-old to a government commission: "He used to work 16 hours a day . . . I have often knelt down to feed him, as he stood by the machine, for he could not leave it or stop" (quoted in Hochschild, 2003, p. 3). ■

industrial laborer, and the development of a class society rooted in the modern division of labor.

INCREASED USE OF MACHINERY AND MASS PRODUCTION

Machines increase the productive capacity of individual laborers by enabling them to produce more goods efficiently at lower cost. New machines have historically required new sources of energy as well: Waterwheels gave way to steam engines, then the internal combustion engine, and eventually electricity and other modern forms of power.

In 1913, automobile mogul Henry Ford introduced a new system of manufacturing in his factories. **Mass production** is *the large-scale, highly standardized manufacturing of identical commodities on a mechanical assembly line.* Under Ford's new system, a continuous conveyor belt moved unfinished automobiles past individual workers, each of whom performed a specific operation on each automobile: One worker would attach the door, another the windshield, another the wheels. (The term *Fordism* is sometimes used to describe this system.) Mass production resulted in the development of large numbers of identical components and products that could be produced efficiently at lower cost. This linked system of production became a foundation for the evolution and expansion of productive industries that went far beyond auto manufacturing.

THE BIRTH OF THE INDUSTRIAL LABORER With the birth of industry came the rise of the industrial labor force,

Mass production: The large-scale, highly standardized manufacturing of identical commodities on a mechanical assembly line.

comprising mostly migrants from poorer rural areas or abroad seeking their fortunes in growing cities. Often the number of would-be workers competing for available jobs created a surplus of labor. Karl Marx described this as a **reserve army of labor**, *a pool of job seekers whose numbers outpace the available positions and thus contribute to keeping wages low and conditions of work tenuous* (those who do not like the conditions of work are easy to replace with those seeking work).

If it is possible to create an assembly line on which each worker performs a single, repetitive task, why not design those tasks to be as efficient as possible? This was the goal of **scientific management**, *a practice that sought to use principles of engineering to reduce the physical movements of workers.* Frederick Winslow Taylor's *Principles of Scientific Management,* published in 1911, gave factory managers the information they needed to greatly increase their control over the labor process by giving explicit instructions to workers regarding how they would perform their well-defined tasks. While Taylor was focused on the goal of efficiency, "Taylorism" also had the consequence of further deskilling work. Deskilling rendered workers more vulnerable to layoffs, since they—like the components they were making—were standardized and therefore easily replaced (Braverman, 1974/1988).

CLASSES IN INDUSTRIAL CAPITALISM New economic classes developed along with the rise of industrial capitalist society. One important new class was composed of industrialists who owned what Marx called the *means of production*—for example, factories. Another was made up of wage laborers—workers who did not own land, property, or tools. They had only their labor power to sell at the factory gate. Work in early industrial capitalism was demanding, highly regimented, and even hazardous. Workers labored at tedious tasks for 14 to 16 hours a day, 6 or 7 days a week, and were at risk of losing their jobs if economic conditions turned unfavorable or if they raised too many objections (recall the concept of the reserve army of labor). The pool of exploitable labor was expanded by migrant workers from rural areas and abroad, and even children of poor families were sometimes forced to labor for wages.

Influenced by the poor conditions they saw in 19th-century English factories, Karl Marx and Friedrich Engels posited that these two classes, which they termed the *bourgeoisie,* or capitalists, and the *proletariat,* or working class, would come into conflict. They argued in the *Manifesto of the Communist Party* (1848) that the bourgeoisie exploited the proletariat by appropriating the surplus value of their labor.

Reserve army of labor: A pool of job seekers whose numbers outpace the available positions and thus contribute to keeping wages low and conditions of work tenuous.

Scientific management: A practice that sought to use principles of engineering to reduce the physical movements of workers.

That is, capitalists paid workers the minimum they could get away with and kept the remainder of the value generated by the finished products for themselves as profit, or as a means to gather more productive capital in their own hands. The exploitation of wage labor by capitalists would, they believed, end in revolution and the end of private ownership of the means of production.

While some observers of early capitalism, including Marx and Engels, offered scathing critiques of the social and economic conditions of factory laborers, the early and middle decades of the 20th century (with the exception of the period of the Great Depression) witnessed improved conditions and opportunities for the blue-collar workforce in the United States. In the early 20th century, Henry Ford, the patriarch of Fordist production, took the audacious step of paying workers on his Model T assembly line in Michigan fully $5 for an 8-hour day, nearly three times the wage of a factory employee in 1914. Ford reasoned that workers who earned a solid wage would become consumers of products such as his Model T. Indeed, his workers bought, his profits grew, and industrial laborers (and, eventually, the workers of the unionized U.S. car industry) set off on a slow but steady path to the middle class (Reich, 2010).

The class structure that emerged from advanced industrial capitalism in the United States, Europe, Japan, Canada, and other modern states boasted substantial middle classes composed of workers who ranged from well-educated teachers and managers to industrial workers and mechanics with a high school or technical education. The fortunes of blue-collar and semiprofessional workers were boosted by a number of factors. Among these were extended periods of low unemployment in which workers had greater leverage in negotiating job conditions (Uchitelle, 2007). Unions supported autoworkers, railroad workers, and workers in many other industries in the negotiation of contracts that ensured living wages, as well as job security and benefits. Unionization surged following the Great Depression and the 1935 passage of the Wagner Act, which "guaranteed the rights of workers to join unions and bargain collectively" (VanGiezen & Schwenk, 2001), growing to more than 27% of the labor force by 1940. At their peak in 1979, U.S. unions claimed 21 million members (Mayer, 2004).

Changes in the U.S. economy, including those we saw illustrated in this chapter's opening story, have shaken the relatively stable middle class that emerged around the middle of the 20th century. Since the 1970s, mass layoffs have grown across industries, though manufacturing has been hit hardest (Uchitelle, 2007). As a result, today the industrial laborer—and his or her counterpart in the lower and middle levels of the white-collar workforce—is less likely to belong to a union, less likely to have appreciable job security, and more likely to have experienced a decline in wages and benefits. Income gains have slipped, and, for many, membership in the U.S. middle class has become tenuous (Table 15.1).

TABLE 15.1 Selected Characteristics of Industrial and Postindustrial Societies

Characteristic	Industrial Society	Postindustrial Society
Principal technology	Industrial machinery	Advanced technologies, including computers, automation of tasks
Key types of labor categories	Industrial workers and professionals	"Knowledge workers" and service workers
Type of production	Mass production	Flexible production
Labor control	"Scientific management"	Outsourcing, threatened and real; technological control of work
Selected social stratification characteristics	Development of a modern class society with a dominant economic class, an expanding middle class that may integrate workers, and an economic underclass	Segmentation of the middle class by educational attainment, concentration of wealth and income at the top, and an expanding stratum of working poor

THE INFORMATION REVOLUTION AND POSTINDUSTRIAL SOCIETY

During the past quarter century the "information revolution," which began with Intel's invention of the microchip in 1971, has altered economic life, accelerating changes in the organization of work that were already under way. Pressured by global competition that intensified by the end of the 1970s, U.S. firms began to move away from the inflexible Fordist system of mass production, seeking ways to accommodate rapid changes in products and production processes and to reduce high labor costs that were making U.S. products less competitive. Postindustrial economic organization is complex, so the sections below focus on just some of the key aspects, including the growth of automation and flexible production, reliance on "outsourcing" and "offshoring," and the growth of the service economy.

AUTOMATION AND FLEXIBLE PRODUCTION Postindustrial production relies on ever-expanding **automation**, *the replacement of human labor by machines in the production process.* Today, robots can perform tedious and dangerous work that once required the labor of hundreds of workers. While automation increases efficiency, it has also eliminated jobs.

Computer-driven assembly lines can be quickly reprogrammed, allowing manufacturers to shift to new products and designs rapidly and to shorten the time from factory to buyer. "Just-in-time" delivery systems also minimize the need for businesses to maintain warehouses full of parts and supplies; instead, parts suppliers ship components to factories on an as-needed basis so they move right to the production floor and into the products. Such reliance on more flexible, less standardized forms of production is sometimes termed *post-Fordism.*

Notably, while to this point automation has had its most visible impact on manufacturing jobs, it is becoming significant in the large U.S. service industry as well. Consider, for instance, the recent introduction of electronic tabletop ordering devices at some popular restaurants like Chili's and California Pizza Kitchen. According to a recent article in the *Wall Street Journal,* airports in New York City and Minneapolis now have some eating establishments that are "wait-staff free," and "in 2011, McDonald's announced that it was replacing human cashiers with touch-screen alternatives at more than 7,000 European locations" (Saltsman, 2014). While offering lower labor costs to employers and some convenience to consumers, self-ordering and self-checkout technologies are also reducing the numbers of jobs available at dining and retail establishments.

RELIANCE ON OUTSOURCING AND OFFSHORING Businesses can perform activities associated with producing and marketing a product "in house," or they can contract some of the work to outside firms, which in turn can do their own subcontracting to other firms. The term *outsourcing* often describes the use of low-cost foreign labor, but it can also mean contracting U.S. workers to do needed tasks, typically for less pay than a company employee would earn. Outsourcing has long been part of industrial production; striking today is the emergence of outsourcing across a wide spectrum of industries. For example, United Airlines used to rely on its own mechanics to service the company's planes. The mechanics were well paid and enjoyed benefits negotiated by their union. By the late 1990s, however, United increasingly turned to nonunionized mechanics operating from lower-cost, lower-wage hangars in the South. The terrorist attacks of September 11, 2001, which temporarily halted air travel, exacerbated the financial difficulties of airlines. In spite of billions in government aid and loans, airlines have continued to struggle. Major carriers have become even more reliant on outsourcing to cut costs (Uchitelle, 2007).

Offshoring refers more specifically to the practice among U.S. companies of contracting with businesses outside the

Automation: The replacement of human labor by machines in the production process.

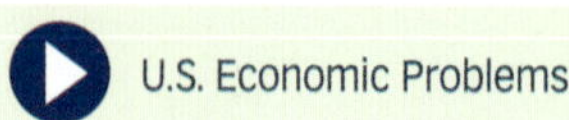

country to perform services that would otherwise be done by U.S. workers. The movement of manufacturing jobs overseas to lower-wage countries, as noted earlier in the chapter, has been taking place since the 1970s and 1980s. More recently, however, workers and policy makers have expressed concern about the offshoring of professional jobs, such as those in information technology. According to a recent Congressional Research Service paper on the topic, this trend has been fostered by the widespread adoption of technologies enabling rapid transmission of voice and data across the globe, economic crises in the United States that have created greater pressure to achieve economic "efficiencies" (such as lower labor costs), and the availability of a growing pool of well-educated and often English-speaking labor abroad (Levine, 2012).

TRANSFORMATION OF THE OCCUPATIONAL AND CLASS STRUCTURE Among the most highly compensated workers in the modern economy are those who invent or design new products, engineer new technologies, and solve problems. They are creative people who "make things happen," organizers who bring people together, administrators who make firms run efficiently, and legal and financial experts who help firms to be profitable (Bell, 1973; Reich, 2010). Workers in this category are sometimes called "symbolic analysts" (Reich, 1991) or "knowledge workers." Most symbolic analysts are highly educated professionals who engage in mental labor and, in some way, the manipulation of symbols (numbers, computer codes, words). They include engineers, university professors, scientists, lawyers, and financiers and bankers, among others.

While the ranks of symbolic analysts have grown overall in recent decades and the ranks of "routine production workers" in manufacturing have been falling, most job growth has been concentrated in the service sector. Services constitute a diverse sector of the labor market. As of 2012, the service sector employed more than 116 million U.S. workers and accounted for almost 80% of the U.S. workforce (U.S. Bureau of Labor Statistics, 2013d). Service occupations include some jobs that require higher education but also include retail sales, home health and nurses' aides, food service, and security services. Overall, the service jobs available to workers with a high school education (or less) do not pay as well as the manufacturing positions of the past, making membership in the middle class less likely and less secure for those without higher education.

Many service positions do not require extensive education or training, and a growing fraction are part-time rather than full-time, are nonunionized, and have few or no benefits. Quite a few of these jobs require "people skills" stereotypically associated with females and are often viewed as "women's jobs" (but by no means invariably, since private security guards, a growing occupation, tend to be men). By contrast, many routine production jobs in the past were manufacturing jobs that commonly employed men. The decline in manufacturing

Ap Photo/Paul Sakuma

Many of today's highly compensated workers have specialized skills in inventing, designing, or producing innovative technological products. Facebook founder and CEO Mark Zuckerberg represents a generation of young entrepreneurs, many of whom are based in Silicon Valley, who have both led and profited from the dramatic growth of social media use across the globe. ■

employment opportunities, along with declines in educational attainment among men (a topic we examined in Chapter 12), has made unemployment and underemployment particularly acute for some demographic groups, including minority males (Autor, 2010).

Together, these diverse labor market trends point to significant shifts in the U.S. class structure. Economist David Autor (2010) argues that a polarization of job opportunities has taken place, particularly in the past two decades. Autor sees a modern economy characterized by "expanding opportunities in both high-skill, high-wage occupations and low-skill, low-wage occupations, coupled with contracting opportunities in middle-wage, middle-skill, white-collar and blue-collar jobs." He views this as the basis of a split in the middle class, with those whose membership in that group was bolstered by, for instance, good manufacturing jobs now losing ground, and those who occupy the upper, professional rungs of the middle class maintaining their status amid growing opportunities (Figure 15.4).

However, not all economists agree with this assessment. Economist Alan Blinder (2006) argues that "many people blithely assume that the critical labor-market distinction is, and will remain, between highly educated (or highly skilled) people and less-educated (or less-skilled) people—doctors versus call-center operators, for example. The supposed remedy for the rich countries, accordingly, is more education and a general 'upskilling' of the work force. But this view may be mistaken" (p. 118). Blinder suggests that the more critical social division in the future may not be between jobs that require high levels of education and those that do not, but rather between work that can be wirelessly outsourced and work that cannot. Consider the growth of online university education. Whereas a college professor may be able to accommodate 100 or even 500 students in a massive lecture hall, an online instructor can have thousands of students and teach them at a considerable cost

BEHIND THE NUMBERS

COUNTING THE EMPLOYED AND THE UNEMPLOYED IN THE UNITED STATES

According to the U.S. Bureau of Labor Statistics (BLS; 2014b), in June 2014 the U.S. labor force participation rate (that is, the labor force as a percentage of the civilian noninstitutional population) was almost 63%, and more than 146.2 million U.S. residents were *employed.* At the same time, about 6.1% of U.S. workers, or 9.5 million individuals, were counted by the BLS as *unemployed* (Figure 15.2).

What do these numbers tell us? What do they illuminate, and what do they obscure? Consider how the BLS defines the condition of being *employed.* In BLS statistics, employed persons are those who are 16 years of age or older in the civilian, noninstitutional population (that is, not in the military or in mental or penal institutions) who did any paid work—even as little as one hour—in the reference week or worked in their own businesses or farms. The employment figure, however, fails to capture the significant problem of *underemployment,* including workers forced to work part-time when they would like to work full-time or workers employed in jobs that are well below their skill level. According to the BLS, in mid-2014, there were at least 7.5 million involuntary part-time workers.

The **unemployed** are *people who are jobless, have actively looked for work in the prior 4 weeks, and are available for work.* The BLS figures are based on the monthly Current Population Survey, which uses a representative sample of 60,000 households and has been conducted every month since 1940. While the BLS cannot count every U.S. household, the size of the sample and its configuration are believed to ensure a statistically accurate representation of the U.S. labor force. Official unemployment figures, however, do not include those who, after a brief or extended period of joblessness, have given up looking for work, or whose job seeking is "passive"—for instance, limited to scanning newspaper or online classified ads. Those persons are categorized as **not in the labor force**, because they are *neither officially employed nor officially unemployed.* Persons who would like to work and have searched actively for a job in the past 12 months are categorized as **marginally attached to the labor force**—according to the Bureau of Labor Statistics, there are about 2 million such individuals. Widely cited official unemployment statistics omit these categories and may thus underestimate the numbers of those who need and want to work.

FIGURE 15.2 Unemployment in the United States, 2002–2013

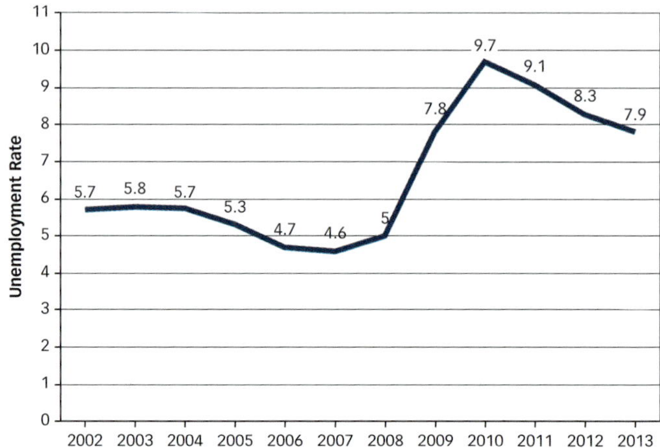

SOURCE: U.S. Bureau of Labor Statistics. (2013). Labor Force Statistics from the *Current Population Survey.*

Notably as well, some researchers point out that indicators intended to measure the social and economic well-being of the population are distorted because they omit the large U.S. prison population (Western & Pettit, 2010). Prisoners are disproportionately from low socioeconomic backgrounds, yet they do not figure into important social indicators like the poverty rate or the unemployment rate. Jails and prisons are not households and therefore are not counted, though they house more than 2 million people (U.S. Bureau of Justice Statistics, 2010).

Consider the effect of this exclusion on employment figures. In 2008, the incarceration rate of African American men who dropped out of high school was about 37% (Western & Pettit, 2010). The distorting effect is considerable if we seek, for instance, to determine how African American men without a high school education are faring in the labor market (Figure 15.3). Western and Pettit (2010) write that "[conventional] estimates of the employment rate show that by 2008, around 40 percent of African American male dropouts were employed"; however, when "prison and jail inmates are included

FIGURE 15.3 Unemployment Rate by Educational Attainment for Blacks and Whites 25 and Older in the United States, 2012

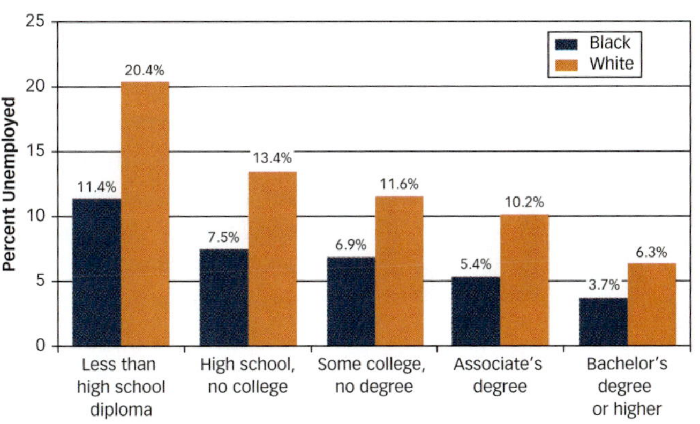

SOURCE: U.S. Bureau of Labor Statistics. (2011). The African-American Labor Force in the Recovery, Chart 3.

in the population count (and among the jobless), we see that employment among young African American men with little schooling fell to around 25 percent by 2008" (p. 12).

Clearly, the exclusion of the incarcerated population from social indicators such as poverty, employment, and unemployment may render an incomplete picture of the economic fortunes (and misfortunes) of some demographic groups in the United States, as we learn when we look behind the numbers.

THINK IT THROUGH

▶ Should the institutionalized population of the United States be included in socioeconomic indicators like poverty, employment, and unemployment figures? Can you make a persuasive case to support your position on this question?

savings to the institution—and, in some instances, to the students. Some universities, such as the Massachusetts Institute of Technology (MIT), are offering free college course lectures online (though these are not yet available for credit). While this is not "outsourcing" as we typically imagine it, trends suggest that even many highly educated workers will be vulnerable to technological changes in the decades ahead.

Outsourcing and offshoring, automation, and the shift to more flexible workplaces characterized by temporary workers are among the factors that have reduced opportunities in the middle-level jobs that built and sustained the once-stable U.S. middle class (discussed in more detail in Chapter 7). As noted in the preceding section, while the effects of these processes have been most apparent in manufacturing, the effect on employment opportunities has also been felt in professional and service jobs. It is quite likely that the shape of the labor market in the coming decades will continue to shift as technology and economic factors drive many changes that are already under way.

THE SERVICE ECONOMY AND EMOTIONAL LABOR

Many service sector jobs today require a substantial amount of "emotional labor." According to sociologist Arlie Hochschild (2003), **emotional labor** is the *commodification of emotions, including "the management of feeling to create a publicly observable facial and bodily display"* (p. 7). Like physical labor, the symbol of the industrial economy, emotional labor is also "sold for a wage and . . . has exchange value" (p. 7).

Hochschild (2003) uses the example of flight attendants, who do emotional labor in the management of airline passengers' comfort, good feelings, and sense of safety, but we could also use as examples customer service workers, retail sales associates, and restaurant servers. While these workers may enjoy their jobs, they are also forced to feign positive feelings even when such feelings are absent and to labor to evoke positive feelings in their customers. The emotional laborer is, in a sense, compelled to "sell" his or her smile in exchange for a wage, just as the industrial laborer sells his or her physical labor. The emotional laborer's actions are programmed for profit and efficiency, as he or she is asked to perform emotions that maximize both. The strain between real and performed feelings, notes Hochschild, leads to an emotive dissonance—that is, a "disconnect"—between what the worker really feels and the emotions to be shown or suppressed. Hochschild posits that just as Marx's proletarian laboring in a mill was alienated from the work and from him- or herself, so too is the emotional laborer alienated from work and his or her emotional life.

Unemployed: Persons who are jobless, actively looked for work in the prior 4 weeks, and are available for work.

Not in the labor force: Persons who are neither officially employed nor officially unemployed.

Marginally attached to the labor force: Persons who would like to work and have searched actively for a job in the past 12 months.

Emotional labor: The management of feelings or emotions to create a publicly observable facial and bodily display in return for a wage.

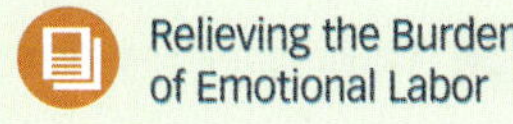
Relieving the Burden of Emotional Labor

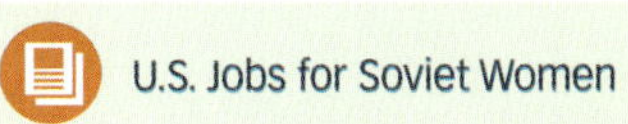
U.S. Jobs for Soviet Women

TYPES OF ECONOMIC SYSTEMS

Two principal types of economic systems have dominated the 20th century: capitalism and socialism. Industrialization

FIGURE 15.4 Employment Change by Occupational Sector in the United States, 1979–2009

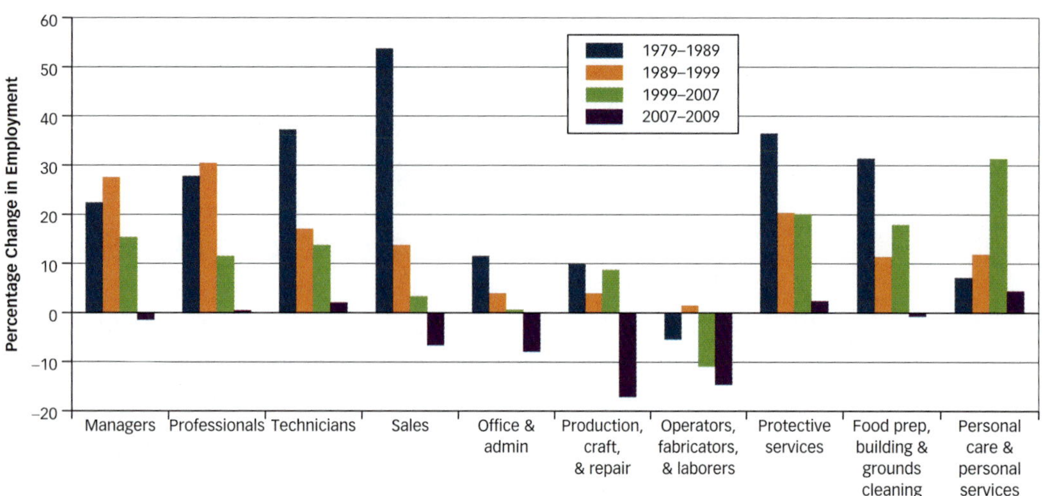

SOURCE: Autor, David. 2010. "The Polarization of Job Opportunities in the U.S. Labor Market: Implications for Employment and Earnings." Center for American Progress and the Hamilton Project. Figure 3, p. 9. This material was created by the Center for American Progress (www.americanprogress.org).

occurred in capitalist economic systems in North America and most of Western Europe, and under socialism in the Soviet Union, Eastern Europe, China, Vietnam, Cuba, and parts of Africa. After 1989, the collapse of socialism in Eastern Europe and the (former) Soviet Union fostered the expansion of capitalist market systems. Orthodox socialism appears to be in decline elsewhere as well, notably in economically growing China. Even Cuba, which remains steadfast in its socialist rhetoric, recently introduced some capitalist-style reforms.

Even though capitalism and socialism share a common focus on economic growth and increased living standards, they differ profoundly in their ideas about how the economy should be organized to achieve these goals. The following descriptions are of "ideal-typical" (that is, model) capitalist and socialist systems. Real economies often include some elements of both.

CAPITALISM

Capitalism is *an economic order characterized by the market allocation of goods and services, production for private profit, and private ownership of the means of producing wealth.* Workers sell their labor to the owners of capital in exchange for a wage, and capitalists are then free to make a profit on the goods their workers produce. Capitalism emphasizes free, unregulated markets and private, rather than government, economic decision making. At the same time, governments in capitalist economies often play a key role in shaping economic life, even in countries such as the United States that have historically tended to keep the government's role to a minimum (which is sometimes referred to as *laissez-faire* capitalism—literally, hands-off capitalism). In a capitalist country, the labor market is composed of both public sector jobs and private sector jobs. The **public sector** is *linked to the government (whether national, state, or local) and encompasses production or allocation of goods and services for the benefit of the government and its citizens.* The **private sector** also *provides goods and services to the economy and consumers, but its primary motive is profit.*

Because capitalists compete with one another, they experience persistent pressure from consumers to keep costs and therefore prices down. They can gain a competitive edge by adopting innovative processes such as mass production (think of early Fordism), reducing expensive inventories, and developing new products that either meet existing demands or create new demands (which sociologists call *manufactured needs*). One important process innovation is minimizing the cost of labor, which capitalists often do by adopting technologies that increase productivity and keep wages low.

On one hand, capitalism can create uneven development, inequality, and conflict between workers and employers, whose interests may be at odds. On the other hand, it has been successful in producing diverse and desirable products and services, encouraging invention and creativity by entrepreneurs who are willing to take risks in return for potential profit, and raising living standards in many countries across the globe.

Capitalist systems are based on an individualistic work ethic, which posits that, ideally, if people work hard and diligently pursue their personal goals, both society and the individuals will prosper. The roles of government vary widely among different capitalist economies. In the United States and England, for example, there is greater skepticism about government's role in the private

Capitalism: An economic order characterized by the market allocation of goods and services, production for private profit, and private ownership of the means of producing wealth.

Public sector: The sector of the labor market in which jobs are linked to the government (whether national, state, or local) and encompass production or allocation of goods and services for the benefit of the government and its citizens.

Private sector: The sector of the labor market that provides goods and services to the economy and consumers with the primary motive of gaining profit.

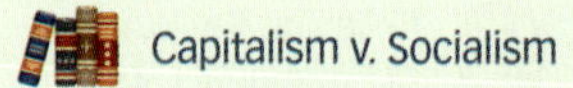

sector and greater emphasis on the private sector as the means for allocating goods and services (though Britain, unlike the United States, has nationalized health care). In contrast, in many European economies, government takes a strong role in individual lives. Sweden and France offer "cradle to grave" social supports, with paid parental leave, child allowances, national health insurance, and generous unemployment benefits. Japan, on the other hand, does not expect government to take such a major role but does expect businesses to assume almost family-like responsibility for the welfare of their employees.

A CASE OF CAPITALISM IN PRACTICE: A CRITICAL PERSPECTIVE

Profit is the driving motive of capitalist systems. While the desire for profit spawns creativity and productivity, it may also give rise to greed, corruption, and exploitation. Industries cut costs in order to increase profits; there is economic logic in such a decision. Cutting costs, however, can also compromise the health and safety of workers and consumers.

What do such compromises look like? A case study of profit over people in the meat industry in the United States offers one example. In the first decade of the 20th century, Upton Sinclair's novel *The Jungle* offered a powerful and frightening fictionalized account of the real-life problems of the meat industry. The novel chronicles the struggles of a Lithuanian immigrant family working and struggling in "Packingtown," Chicago's meat district. An excerpt follows:

> It was only when the whole ham was spoiled that it came into the department of Elzbieta. Cut up by the two-thousand-revolutions-a-minute flyers, and mixed with half a ton of other meat, no odor that ever was in a ham could make any difference. There was never the least attention paid to what was cut up for sausage. . . . There would be meat stored in great piles in rooms, and the water from leaky roofs would drip over it, and thousands of rats would race about on it. . . .
>
> Such were the new surroundings in which Elzbieta was placed, and such was the work she was compelled to do. It was stupefying, brutalizing work; it left her no time to think, no strength for anything. She was part of the machine she tended, and every faculty that was not needed for the machine was doomed to be crushed out of existence. (Sinclair, 1906/1995, pp. 143–145)

Sinclair was critical of capitalism and the profit motive, which he felt explained the suffering of the workers and the stomach-turning products churned out in the filthy packinghouses. His work was a stirring piece of social criticism dressed as fiction, and it spurred change. President Theodore Roosevelt's inquiry into the conditions described by Sinclair brought about legislation requiring federal inspection of meat sold through interstate commerce and the accurate labeling of meat products and ingredients (Schlosser, 2002). The novel had little effect, however, on the conditions experienced by industrial laborers, to which Sinclair had endeavored to draw attention. As he later wryly remarked, "I aimed for the public's heart . . . and by accident I hit it in the stomach."

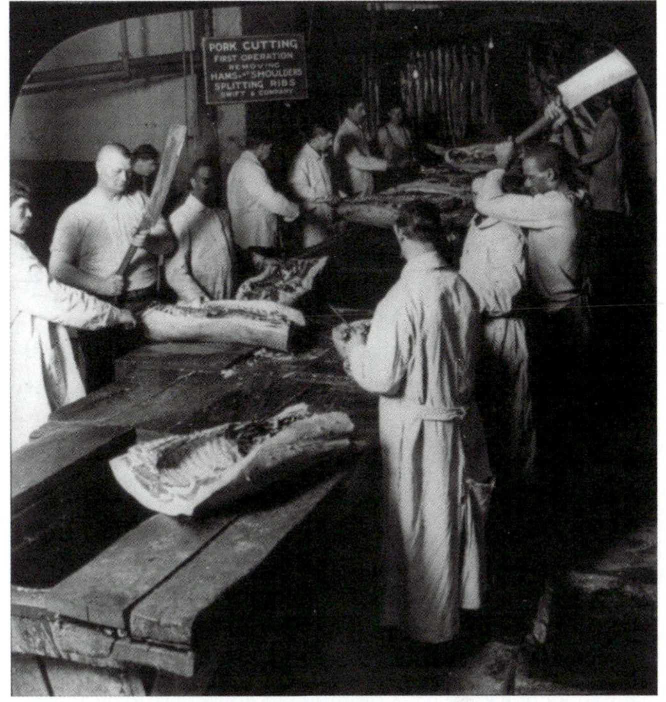

Public Domain -Library of Congress

Upton Sinclair's *The Jungle,* chronicling immigrants' suffering in the unregulated meatpacking industry of the early 20th century, emerged from his investigations of Chicago's Packingtown. In 1904, Sinclair worked in the plants to gather material for a book that eventually spurred disgust and outrage, as well as the 1906 Pure Food and Drug Act.

In the years since Sinclair's novel was published, capitalism has evolved (as has regulation), though profit and the need to cut costs have remained basic characteristics. What does cost cutting look like in today's more closely regulated meat industry? In *Fast Food Nation* (2002), writer Eric Schlosser describes his experience in a modern meat plant:

> A man turns and smiles at me. He wears safety goggles and a hardhat. His face is splattered with gray matter and blood. He is the "knocker," the man who welcomes cattle to the building. Cattle walk down a narrow chute and pause in front of him, blocked by a gate, and then he shoots them in the head with a captive bolt stunner. . . . For eight and a half hours, he just shoots. . . .
>
> When a sanitation crew arrives at a meatpacking plant, usually around midnight, it faces a mess of monumental proportions. . . . Workers climb ladders with hoses and spray the catwalks. They get under tables and

conveyor belts, climbing right into the bloody muck, cleaning out grease, fat, manure, leftover scraps of meat. (pp. 170–171, 177)

The work is not only brutal; it is also dangerous. Profit still drives the meat industry to endanger its workers' safety, and Schlosser notes the words of a local nurse, who says she always "[knew] the line speed . . . by the number of people with lacerations coming into my office" (pp. 173–174).

Critics of capitalism would suggest that conditions in the meat industry past and present illuminate a fundamental problem of capitalism: Capital accumulation and profit are based on driving down the costs of production. The case of the meat industry shows that capitalists sometimes drive down the costs by compromising worker and consumer safety. The potentially high human cost is a central point of the critique of capitalism.

SOCIALISM AND COMMUNISM

Modern ideas about communism and socialism originated in the theories of 19th-century philosophers and social scientists, especially those of Karl Marx. **Communism**, in its ideal-typical form, is *a type of economic system without private ownership of the means of production and, theoretically, without economic classes or economic inequality.* In an ideal-typical communist society, the capitalist class has been eliminated, leaving only workers, who manage their economic affairs cooperatively and distribute the fruits of their labor "to each according to his needs, from each according to his abilities." Since Marx believed that governments exist primarily to protect the interests of capitalists, he concluded that once the capitalist class was eliminated, there would be no need for the state, which would, in his words, "wither away."

Marx recognized that there would most likely have to be a transitional form of economic organization between capitalism and communism, which he termed **socialism**. In a socialist system, theoretically, *the government manages the economy in the interests of the workers; it owns the businesses, factories, farms, hospitals, housing, and other means of producing wealth and redistributes that wealth to the population through wages and services.* The laborer works for a state-run industrial enterprise, the farmer works for a state-run farm, and the bureaucrat works in a state agency. Profit is not a driving economic imperative.

Before the collapse of the Soviet Union and its socialist allies in Eastern Europe, nearly a third of the world's population lived in socialist countries. Far from withering away as Marx predicted, these socialist governments remained firmly in place until 1989 (1991 in the Soviet Union), when popular revolutions ushered in transformations—not to the classless communist economies Marx envisioned, but to new capitalist states. The largest remaining socialist country in the world—China—has transitioned over the past 20 years into a market economy of a size and scale to nearly rival that of the United States, though the state still exercises control over large industries.

UniversalImagesGroup / Contributor/Getty Images

In the socialist period in the Soviet Union and allied countries of Eastern Europe, the state controlled all production, essentially eliminating competition in the marketplace for goods and services. Instead of advertisements in public spaces, political posters and propaganda elevated the achievements and builders of socialism and denigrated the capitalist way of life. ■

These transformations occurred in part because socialism proved too inflexible to manage a modern economy. Having the central government operate tens of thousands of factories, farms, and other enterprises was a deterrent to economic growth. Further, though the capitalist class was eliminated, a new class emerged—the government bureaucrats and communist officials who managed the economy and who were often inefficient, corrupt, and

Communism: A type of economic system without private ownership of the means of production and, theoretically, without economic classes or economic inequality.

Socialism: A type of economic system in which, theoretically, the government manages the economy in the interests of the workers; it owns the businesses, factories, farms, hospitals, housing, and other means of producing wealth and redistributes that wealth to the population through wages and services.

more interested in self-enrichment than in public service (Djilas, 1957). Moreover, most socialist governments were intolerant of dissent, often persecuting, imprisoning, and exiling those who disagreed with their policies. At the same time, socialist regimes were often successful in eliminating extreme poverty and providing their populations with housing, universal education, health care, and basic social services. Inequality was typically much lower in socialist states than in capitalist economies—although the overall standard of living was lower as well.

The dramatic rise in economic inequality and poverty in the newly capitalist states of the former Soviet Union and Eastern Europe has created some nostalgia for the socialist past, particularly among the elderly, who have a threadbare social safety net in many states. While few miss the authoritarian political regimes, there is some longing for the basic economic and social security that socialism offered.

A CASE OF SOCIALISM IN PRACTICE: A CRITICAL PERSPECTIVE

In theory, a driving motive of socialist systems is achievement of a high degree of economic equality. This is realized in part through the creation of full-employment economies. In the Soviet Union, full employment gave all citizens the opportunity to earn a basic living, but it also brought about some socially undesirable results. For instance, inefficiency and waste flourished in enterprises that were rewarded for how much raw material they consumed rather than how much output they produced (Hanson, 2003). Human productivity was only partially utilized when work sites had to fill required numbers of positions but did not have meaningful work for all who occupied them. Disaffection and anger grew in workplaces where promotions were as likely to be based on political reliability, connections, and Communist Party membership as on merit. A system that theoretically ensured the use of resources for the good and equality of all workers was undermined by the realities of Soviet-style communism.

In practice, socialist systems such as that of postwar Hungary were characterized by both low wages and low productivity: A popular saying among workers was that "we pretend to work and the state pretends to pay us." Lacking a competitive labor market, workers may not have felt compelled to work particularly hard; unemployment was rare. At the same time, public sector (government) jobs, which made up the bulk of the labor market, were poorly paid; many workers sought supplementary pay in the informal economy (Ledeneva, 1998).

Socialism in practice, according to sociologists Michael Burawoy and Janos Lukács (1992), was in part a performance:

> Painting over the sordid realities of socialism is simultaneously the painting of an appearance of brightness, efficiency, and justice. Socialism becomes an elaborate game of pretense which everyone sees through but which everyone is compelled to play. . . . The pretense becomes a basis against which to assess reality. If we have to paint a world of efficiency and equality—as we do in our [factory] production meetings, our brigade competitions, our elections—we become more sensitive to and outraged by inefficiency and inequality. (p. 129)

In the book he coauthored with Lukács, *The Radiant Past: Ideology and Reality in Hungary's Road to Capitalism* (1992), Burawoy, a U.S. sociologist who spent time working in socialist enterprises in Poland and Hungary as part of his study of socialist economies, recounts an instance of such a "painting ritual" when the Hungarian prime minister makes a visit to the Lenin Steel Works. Areas of the factory to be visited are literally painted over in bright hues, debris is swept up, and workers halt their productive tasks to create an "appearance" of productivity, for the prime minister "had to be convinced that the Lenin Steel Works was at the forefront of building socialism" (p. 127). For critics of socialism the case of Hungarian steel in the socialist period highlights a fundamental problem of the system as it was practiced: Its weaknesses were made more rather than less apparent by the "painting" rituals that asked workers to pretend socialism was fundamentally efficient and equal when their own experience showed it was not. This was among the flaws that led to the collapse of socialism in Eastern Europe and the Soviet Union.

WORKING ON AND OFF THE BOOKS

Work consists of *any human effort that adds something of value to the goods and services that are available to others.* By this definition, work includes paid labor in the factory or office, unpaid labor at home, and volunteer work in the community. Workers include rock stars and street musicians, corporate executives and prostitutes, nurses and babysitters. Almost the only activities excluded from this definition of work are those that individuals conduct purely for their own pleasure or benefit, such as pursing a hobby or playing a musical instrument for fun.

The concept of work as consisting exclusively of labor that is sold for a wage is a relatively recent development of modern industrial society. Throughout most of human history, work was not ordinarily paid, at least in monetary terms. In agricultural societies, subsistence farming was common: Families often worked their own plots of land and participated with others in the community in a **barter economy**, *based on the exchange of goods and services rather than money.* With

Work: Any human effort that adds something of value to the goods and services that are available to others.

Barter economy: An economy based on the exchange of goods and services rather than money.

 Socialism

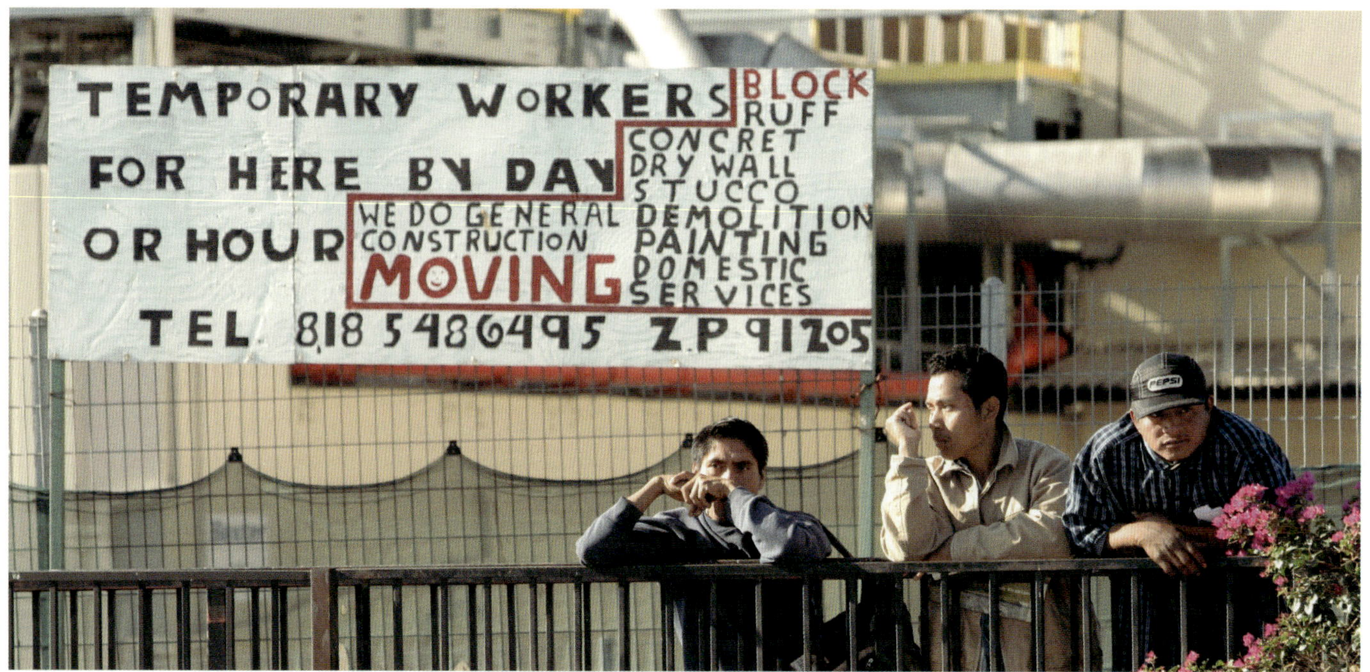

Spencer Grant / Photo Researchers, Inc

Day laborers often work for low pay in unregulated conditions. Some of them are illegal migrants. Their status and language barriers make it challenging for them to report dangerous or abusive conditions of work.

the advent of industrial society, however, work shifted largely to the economic setting of a formal, paid, and regulated job. Today, work for pay occurs in two markets: the formal economy and the informal (or underground) economy. We look at each of these next.

THE FORMAL ECONOMY

The **formal economy** consists of *all work-related activities that provide income and are regulated by government agencies.* It includes work for wages and salaries, as well as self-employment; it is what people ordinarily have in mind when they refer to work. It has grown in importance since the Industrial Revolution. Indeed, one of the chief functions of government in industrial society is regulation of the formal economy, which contributes to the shape and character of the labor market (Sassen, 1991; Tilly & Tilly, 1994).

In the United States, as in most countries of the world, private businesses are supposed to register with governmental entities ranging from tax bureaus (the Internal Revenue Service) to state and local licensing agencies. Whether they work in the private or the public sector, U.S. workers must pay income, Medicare, and Social Security taxes on their earnings, and employers are expected to withhold such taxes on their behalf and report employee earnings to the government. Numerous agencies regulate wages and working conditions, occupational health and safety, the environmental effects of business activities, product quality, and relationships among firms.

As of mid-2014, about two thirds (63%) of all people in the United States over 16 years of age who were not in the armed forces (which is also, of course, an employment sector), prisons, or mental hospitals, were in the labor force—about 6% were unemployed (U.S. Bureau of Labor Statistics, 2014b). When statistical indicators such as employment and unemployment are tabulated by government entities such as the Bureau of Labor Statistics, they rely on data from the formal economy. Work also is done in the informal economy, which is not included in BLS numbers.

THE INFORMAL OR UNDERGROUND ECONOMY

A notable amount of income-generating work avoids formal regulation and is not organized around officially recognized jobs. This part of the economy is termed the **informal (or underground) economy**; it includes *all income-generating activities that are not reported to the government as required by law.* Some of these sources of income are illegal, such as selling guns or pirated DVDs, drug dealing, and sex trafficking. Other work activities are not illegal but still operate under the government radar. These include selling goods at garage sales and on Internet auction sites such as eBay; housecleaning, gardening, and babysitting for employers who pay without

Formal economy: All work-related activities that provide income and are regulated by government agencies.

Informal (or underground) economy: Those income-generating economic activities that escape regulation by the governmental institutions that ordinarily regulate similar activities.

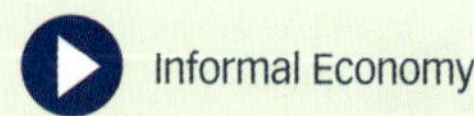
Informal Economy

AP Photo/Rene Macur

The term *underground economy* may bring up images of drugs, weapons, and stolen passports, but this type of economy involves much needed products, like food. Los Angeles and other major cities have unlicensed and unregistered vendors providing food and services for residents who demand them, which has a mixture of positive and negative consequences.

reporting the transactions to the government; and informal catering of neighborhood events for unreported pay. In one way or another, most of us participate in the informal economy at some point in our lives.

Workers' reasons for participating in the informal economy are varied. A worker with a regular job may take up a second job "off the books" to make up a deficit in his or her budget, or someone may be compelled to work outside the legal economy because of his or her undocumented immigration status. Others may find the shadow economy more profitable (Schneider & Enste, 2002). Many of the underground economy's workers occupy the lowest economic rungs of society and are likely to be pursuing basic survival rather than untold riches. They are disproportionately low income, female, and immigrant, and the jobs they do lack the protections that come with many jobs in the formal economy, such as health care benefits, unemployment insurance, and job security.

Among the employers in the illegal U.S. underground economy are unlicensed "sweatshop" factories that make clothing, furniture, and other consumer goods (Castells & Portes, 1989; Sassen, 1991). Factories in the United States are competing with factories around the world where workers are paid a fraction of U.S. wages. To remain competitive (or to raise profits), U.S. firms sometimes subcontract their labor to low-cost sweatshop firms in the informal sector. Requirements to comply with environmental laws, meet health and safety standards, make contributions to Social Security and other social benefit programs, and pay taxes lead some businesses to seek to establish themselves off the books. Small businesses may operate without licenses, and large firms may illegally subcontract out some of their labor to smaller, unlicensed ones.

CQR Immigration Conflict

While the United States has a broad informal sector, researchers estimate that the underground economy is substantially larger in developing counties than in advanced economies such as those of Western Europe and the United States. For example, a report commissioned by the International Monetary Fund estimates that in developing nations (Nigeria, Singapore, Bolivia, and others) the informal economy accounts for 35% to 44% of gross domestic product (Schneider & Enste, 2002).

CONSUMERS, CONSUMPTION, AND THE U.S. ECONOMY

As we have seen in this chapter, production has been an important part of the rise of modern capitalist economies. In modern industrial countries, including the United States, however, production has receded in importance. The economies of advanced capitalist states today rely heavily on consumption to fuel their continued growth. Today, an estimated 70% of the U.S. economy is linked to consumption. In this section we examine consumption and its relationship to the economy, as well as to our lives as consumers.

THEORIZING THE MEANS OF CONSUMPTION

Karl Marx is well known for his concept of the *means of production* (defined in Chapter 1), which forms a basis for his theorizing on capitalism, exploitation, and class. While the early industrial era in which Marx wrote influenced his focus on production, he also sought to understand consumption in 19th-century capitalism. Marx defined the term *means of consumption* as "commodities that possess a form in which they enter individual consumption of the capitalist and working class" (quoted in Ritzer, 1999, p. 56). Marx distinguished between the levels of consumption of different classes,

© Ringo Chiu/Zuma Press/Corbis

"Cathedrals of Consumption" like the casinos and hotels of Las Vegas, entice consumers to spend with bright, fun, and fantastical venues.

PRIVATE LIVES, PUBLIC ISSUES

MUST WORK BE PAID TO BE ECONOMICALLY IMPORTANT?

Being a parent means taking on a spectrum of tasks that are time-consuming and important for the economic, educational, and social care of the family: Housekeeping, child care, cooking, budget management, driving, and teaching are among the key jobs of modern parents. Much of this work is done by women. Today there are fewer than 215,000 stay-at-home fathers in the United States, while more than 5 million mothers with children under age 15 are outside the paid labor force as the primary caregivers of their children (Livingston, 2014). Their work is often treated as marginal. Historian of the family Stephanie Coontz (2012) points out that while men are increasingly sharing the burdens of housework, the "real gender inequality in marriage stems from the tendency to regard women as the default parent, the one who, in the absence of family-friendly work policies, is expected to adjust her paid work to shoulder the brunt of domestic responsibilities. Women who quit their jobs or cut their hours suffer a wage penalty that widens over the years, even if they return to the job market and work continuously for two more decades."

The sociological imagination enables us to understand how ignoring unpaid labor systematically discounts many of women's contributions to society and fails to recognize the consequences and real economic value of work that is not done for pay. The website Salary.com offers an annual calculation of the value of the "mom job," basing its figures on the 10 "typical" job functions of mothers (and including 40 full-time hours plus 56.5 hours of overtime). Using a survey of more than 15,000 mothers, the site's researchers determined that in 2014 the time spent in these tasks, if compensated, was worth $118,905 for a stay-at-home mother and $70,107 for a mother who worked outside the home (Salary.com, 2014). Unpaid work in the home or community (such as volunteering at schools) can be critical to the well-being of families and society. It also contributes, if indirectly, to the macro-level economy: Consider that a stay-at-home parent frees up the other parent to work in the formal economy.

Richard Nowitz/National Geographic Creative

Might the societal devaluation of the unpaid work parents (most often women) do in the home contribute to lower pay scales for "women's work" in the paid labor market?

THINK IT THROUGH

▶ Why is it conventional in our society to say that stay-at-home parents (mothers or fathers) "don't work"? What explains this devaluation of domestic tasks? Is there another phrase that could be used that recognizes the value of their labor?

suggesting that subsistence consumption ("necessary means of consumption") characterizes the working class, whereas luxury consumption is the privilege of the exploiting capitalist class. In sum, Marx's definition focused on the consumption of the end products of the exploitative production process.

Sociologist George Ritzer has expanded Marx's concept. He distinguishes between the end product (that is, a consumer good such as a pair of stylish dress shoes, a new car, or a gambling opportunity) and the means of consumption that allow us to obtain the good (for instance, the shopping mall, the cruise ship, or the Las Vegas casino). For Ritzer (1999), the **means of consumption** are *"those things that make it possible for people to acquire goods and services and for the same people to be controlled and exploited as consumers"* (p. 57). For example, a venue such as a mall offers the consumer buying options and opportunities, but it is also part of a system of consumer control through which consumers are seduced into buying what they do not need, thinking they need what they merely want, and spending beyond their means.

Means of consumption: Things that make it possible for consumers to acquire goods and services and, at the same time, foster their control and exploitation as consumers.

 The Poor or the Working Class?  Oil industry Jobs

Ritzer's concept of the means of consumption also integrates German sociologist Max Weber's ideas about rationalization, enchantment, and disenchantment. Briefly, the Weberian perspective holds that premodern societies were more "enchanted" than modern societies. That is, societies or communities, which were often small and homogeneous, were grounded in ideas that he characterized as magical and mystical. Individuals and groups defined and pursued goals based on abstract teachings such as the ideals and ideas of a religion rather than on detailed, specific rules and regulations. Even early capitalism was linked to an enchanted world. Weber theorized that early Protestantism (and Calvinism in particular) embraced values of thrift, efficiency, and hard work, and viewed economic success as an indicator of divine salvation. This so-called *Protestant ethic,* which he identified as characteristic in Northern Europe, laid foundations for the rise of capitalism, though capitalism eventually shed its religious aspects (Weber, 1904–1905/2002).

Modern capitalism lacks authentic enchantment: It is a highly rationalized system characterized by efficiency, predictability, and the pursuit of profit (rather than divine salvation!). This heavily bureaucratized and regulation-reliant environment is virtually devoid of spontaneity, spirituality, or surprise. Ritzer argues, however, that enchantment is important for controlling consumers, because consumption is, at least in part, a response to a fantasy about the item or service being consumed. Consequently, disenchanted structures must be "reenchanted" through spectacle and simulation (Baudrillard, 1981), which draw in consumers. For instance, Disney simulates a kind of childhood dreamworld (think of the Magic Kingdom), Niketown is a sports fantasy, and Las Vegas aims to bring to a single city the dazzle of Egyptian pyramids, New York's towering urban structures, and Paris's Eiffel Tower. In such a context, the consumer is not just buying sneakers (say, at Niketown) but embracing a broader fantasy about athletic achievement. In sum, from Ritzer's perspective, the means of consumption are a modern instrument of control not of the *worker* but of the *consumer,* who is enchanted, led to believe that he or she "needs" certain goods, and given optimal—sometimes nearly inescapable—avenues for acquisition, such as malls with long hallways and few exits to maximize the number of shops a consumer must pass before exiting.

© Jennifer Wright / Alamy

One of Disney World's long-standing attractions is the Jungle Cruise, described on the website of the park as an adventure cruise of the most "exotic and 'dangerous' rivers in Asia, Africa, and South America," although it is a virtually danger-free boat trip on a man-made waterway populated by plastic figures. Modern consumers, George Ritzer suggests, are buying the fantasy rather than the reality of such experiences.

A HISTORICAL PERSPECTIVE ON CONSUMPTION

Consumer society is a political, social, and economic creation. Consider, for instance, that during World War II, the U.S. government asked its citizen-consumers to serve the greater good by reducing consumption. In contrast, in the wake of the terror attacks on the United States in 2001 and the wars that followed, citizen-consumers were encouraged to spend more money to stimulate the economy. Former secretary of labor Robert Reich termed this appeal for consumption "market patriotism."

Taking a broader perspective, economist Juliet Schor (1998) argues that consumption patterns and the dramatic growth of consumption in the United States are heavily driven by Americans' reliance on reference groups. That is, consumers compare themselves and their consumption to the reference groups in their social environments. Significantly, says Schor, those reference groups have changed. In the 1950s, suburban middle-class consumers knew and emulated their neighbors. The substantial number of women outside the paid workforce meant that neighbors were more aware of what others were doing, wearing, and driving. By the 1970s, more women were moving into the workforce; consequently, fewer people knew their neighbors, and the workplace became an important source of reference groups. In contrast to the economically homogeneous neighborhood, however, the workplace is heterogeneous. Low five-figure wages coexist in the same space as

Underground Pro-Soccer Economy

Worldwide Informal Economy

high six-figure salaries, and coworkers may aspire upward and far beyond their means.

The 1980s, 1990s, and 2000s brought further upscaling of ambitions and spending, as television sold a powerful picture of consumer decadence masked as "normal life." In the 1990s, young consumers embraced media referents such as the television sitcom *Friends,* about a group of young professionals living in lavish New York City apartments, wearing ever-changing stylish wardrobes, and casually consuming the pleasures around them. Lavish consumption came to seem normal rather than unreachable for people of average incomes (Schor, 1998). A new generation is now exposed to "reality" TV shows including *The Real Housewives of New Jersey* (and other locales), *Keeping Up With the Kardashians, Million Dollar Decorators,* and *Say Yes to the Dress,* which emphasize the benefits of conspicuous consumption among celebrities and "ordinary" people alike.

A somewhat different perspective on how the U.S. consumer economy has been built and sustained is offered by Robert Reich (2010), who believes the consumption-driven economy originated in a "basic bargain" between workers and employers that offered good pay in sectors such as manufacturing, creating a consumer class that could afford to spend (recall Henry Ford's decision to pay above-average wages so his autoworkers could buy cars). Reich notes that, until about 1970, pay rose more quickly in the middle- and lower-income segments of the U.S. labor pool than it did at the top. Consumption grew with the standard of living. The real value of workers' pay stagnated in the 1970s, however, profoundly affected by forces that included globalization and automation. While income rose at the very top of the economic ladder, in the middle and lower strata it stalled. Consumption continued to rise, however, driven not by gains in income but by the growing credit markets, which offered new ways to spend with or without cash on hand. Next we review the consequences of that shift to credit-driven spending.

CREDIT: DEBT AND MORE DEBT

Do you have a credit card? Do you carry debt? If you answered yes to either or both these questions, you are not alone. In 2013, U.S. consumers held almost 392 million credit cards, and their combined credit card debt was about $870 billion (Ray & Ghahremani, 2014). Each credit card holder had an average of 3.7 cards and owed about $8,222, a huge increase from the 1990 average of roughly $2,966 (Hoffman, Brinker, & Roberts, 2010; Ray & Ghahremani, 2014). By one estimate, the debt payments of nearly 15% of U.S. households exceed 40% of the households' income (Bricker, Kennickell, Moore, & Sabelbaus, 2012).

Bankruptcies have also become more common. In the early years of the 21st century, "Americans were more likely to go bankrupt than to get divorced" (Quiggin, 2010, p. 26). Consumption (or overconsumption) was not the direct cause of bankruptcies, most of which were precipitated by the loss of a job or unexpected health care costs, but the "culture of indebtedness," the widespread tendency to owe a great deal of money, left people less able to bear any added financial stress. While financial reforms passed into law in 2005 made the declaration of bankruptcy more onerous and less common, the financial crisis that began in 2007 saw another rise in bankruptcies: More than 1.5 million bankruptcy filings were made in 2010 (Administrative Office of the United States Courts, 2011).

Humorist Will Rogers commented during the Great Depression that the United States was the first country to drive to the poorhouse in an automobile (cited in Sullivan, Warren, & Westbrook, 2000, p. 3). Car debt was a particularly notable burden during the late 1990s and early 2000s, when many U.S. drivers opted to purchase high-end cars, especially aggressively advertised sport utility vehicles. The massive Hummer SUV, manufactured in three different styles by General Motors, became, for many, a symbol of the trend toward bigger and more ostentatious vehicles. Rising gasoline prices through the 2000s, coupled with the economic recession that struck in 2007, reversed the trend, and consumers began opting for more fuel-efficient sedans, hybrid vehicles, and smaller crossover vehicles that combine features of cars and SUVs.

As more people joined the ranks of the long-term unemployed and financial insecurities grew, many households cut back on spending. Overall, the average U.S. consumer spent nearly 3% less in 2009 than in 2008; spending was down on consumer items such as meals away from home, apparel, housing, and transportation (U.S. Bureau of Labor Statistics, 2011b). These numbers may seem insignificant, but they represent millions of dollars that would normally have flowed into small and large businesses alike. By the middle of 2013, the picture had changed only slightly, with overall consumer spending moderately greater than the year before, but spending on groceries, apparel, and some other services decreasing (U.S. Bureau of Labor Statistics, 2014a).

GLOBALIZATION AND THE NEW ECONOMIC ORDER

The U.S. economic order today has been powerfully affected by the emergence of a unified global economic system. In fact, some writers have argued that it no longer makes sense to think of the United States—or any other country—as an isolated economic society at all: In many respects, we can regard the world as a single economic unit (Friedman, 2005). We conclude this chapter by examining how global economic interdependence and the global labor market have affected work and economic life in the United States and by considering the possible shape of a future green global economy.

GLOBAL ECONOMIC INTERDEPENDENCE

The U.S. economy is interwoven with the economies of other countries. Many goods made in the United States are sold in foreign markets, while many goods bought by U.S. consumers

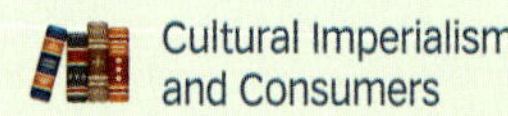

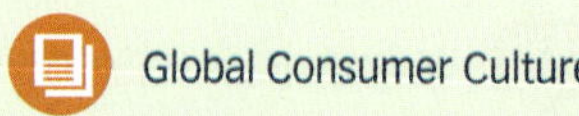

are made by foreign workers. Economic integration is multidimensional and can be "shallow" or "deep" (Dicken, 1998). Shallow integration is more characteristic of the globalization of several decades past, when a single product (say, a German automobile) was made in a single country and that country's government would regulate its export, as well as the import of other goods into the country. Countries did business with one another, but their ties were looser and less interdependent.

Deep integration is characteristic of the modern global economy, in which corporations are often multinational rather than just national, products are made of raw materials or parts from a spectrum of countries, and a corporation's management or engineering may be headquartered in one country while the sales force or customer service contingent may reside anywhere from Denver to Delhi (Figure 15.5). Familiar companies such as Nike, Apple, and Ford are among the many with globalized labor forces.

A GLOBAL MARKET FOR LABOR

As a result of economic globalization, a growing number of U.S. workers are competing with workers all over the world. This trend may affect the job prospects of all workers, whether they hold only high school diplomas or advanced degrees. There are substantial wage differences between countries. While the United States is intermediate among industrial countries, its wages are considerably higher than those in developing countries (Figure 15.6).

Jobs will increasingly go wherever on the planet suitable workers can be found. Low labor costs, the decline or absence of labor unions, and governments that enforce worker compliance through repressive measures are all factors influencing the globalization of labor. Some sociologists call this trend a "race to the bottom" (Bonacich & Appelbaum, 2000), in which companies seeking to maximize profits chase opportunities to locate wherever conditions are most likely to result in the lowest costs. This has been the case in, for example, apparel manufacturing; much of the clothing we buy and wear today, including brands sold at popular shops such as H&M and Zara, is made by young workers abroad who labor for very low wages under poor working conditions. A 2010 *New York Times* article pointed out that Bangladesh was challenging China as a low-wage destination for manufacturers and was at that time the world's third-largest garment manufacturer (Bajaj, 2010). In 2013, a government-appointed panel in Bangladesh voted to raise the minimum wage for garment workers; under the plan, it would rise from a monthly minimum of about $38 to $66. While this represents a state response to worker protests against unsafe and exploitative conditions of work, Bangladeshi garment manufacturing wages remain the lowest in the world. Few workers in Bangladesh would have the means to purchase the products that they labor to produce.

We have seen above that the emergence of an increasingly global labor market has resulted in job losses and declining wages in many U.S. industries, including auto and apparel manufacturing. We may be witnessing the emergence of a *global wage,* equivalent to the lowest worldwide cost of obtaining comparable labor for a particular task once the costs of operating at a distance are taken into account. For virtually any job, this wage is far lower than U.S. workers are accustomed to receiving.

The global labor market is not limited to manufacturing. A global market is emerging for a wide range of professional and technical occupations as well. In fact, some of the "knowledge worker" jobs touted as the jobs of the future may be among the most vulnerable to globalization. Unlike cars or clothing, engineering designs and computer programs can move around the globe electronically at no cost, and transportation time is, for all practical purposes, nonexistent. Electronic engineering, computer programming, data entry, accounting, insurance claims processing, and other specialized services, such as medical image reading, can now be inexpensively purchased in such low-wage countries as India, Malaysia, South Korea, China, and the Philippines, where workers communicate digitally with employers in the United States.

Also among those selling their labor on the new global market are highly educated professionals from postsocialist

FIGURE 15.6 Hourly Compensation Among Production Workers in Select Countries, 2010

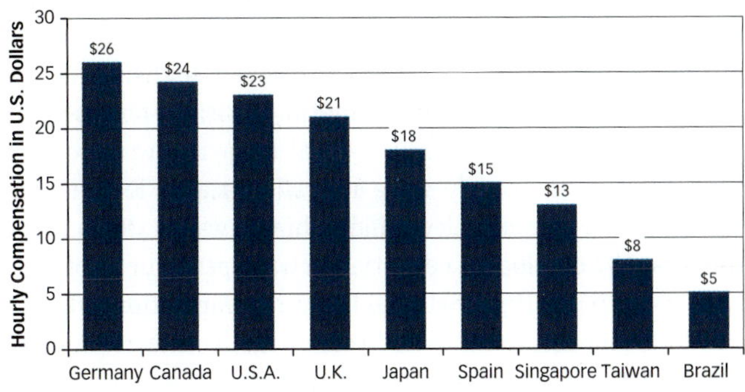

SOURCE: International Labour Organization. (2012, December 7). A snapshot of comparative pay levels around the world.

FIGURE 15.5 Global Origins of Boeing 787 Parts

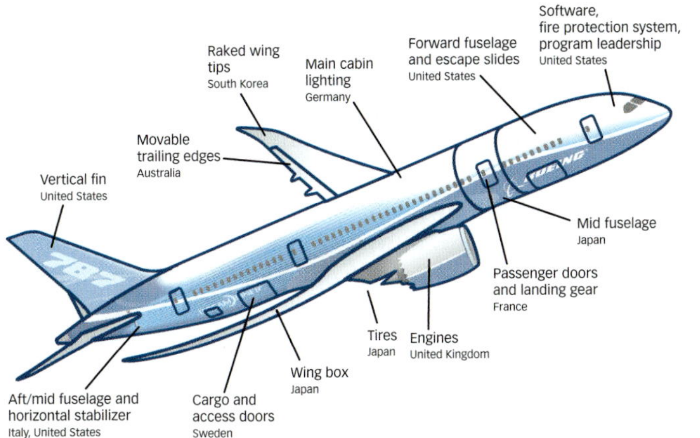

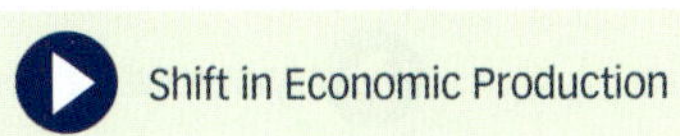
Shift in Economic Production

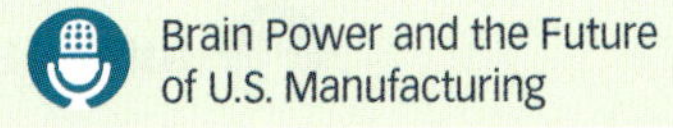
Brain Power and the Future of U.S. Manufacturing

countries such as Estonia and Hungary, both of which have full literacy, educated populations, and many individuals fluent in English and other world languages. While we often associate cheap labor with the low-wage factories of developing countries, these post-Soviet European states also advertise their educated workers (on their investment-promoting websites, for instance) as "cheap labor." Indeed, much global labor is low in cost. In 2010, the normal hourly wage in well-educated Estonia was $6.10; in 2008 in rapidly developing China it was $1.36; in India, also a rapidly developing country, the wage per hour as of 2007 was a paltry $1.17 (International Labour Organization, 2012).

While globalization has had some negative effects on earnings for American workers in the lower- to middle-income ranges, corporate executive salaries have skyrocketed. Even in the midst of a plummeting economy (2007–2009), as the federal government was distributing billions of bailout dollars to corporations, banks, and investment firms to prevent them from failing, chief executive officers (CEOs) in the United States were bringing home multiple millions of dollars in compensation (Table 15.2). While median CEO pay declined somewhat during the recession period, it has rebounded in the postcrisis period, reaching an average of more than $12 million in 2012 (Liberto, 2012). Figure 15.7 compares average CEO compensation to the compensation of average workers in a variety of industries. Notably, in 1980 CEOs made about 42 times what the average worker earned; in 2012, average CEO pay was more than 350 times greater than that of the average worker (who was estimated to be earning just over $34,600 that year; Liberto, 2012).

IS THE FUTURE OF THE GLOBAL ECONOMY GREEN?

Businesses, consumers, and federal officials alike, eager to promote job growth and greater energy independence, are increasingly interested in developing a new "green" economic sector in the United States. In his first State of the Union

TABLE 15.2 Annual Compensation of Selected CEOs, 2012

Corporation	CEO	Compensation
Oracle	Larry Ellison	$99.2 million
Walt Disney	Bob Iger	$37.1 million
Nike	Mark G. Parker	$35.3 million
Starbucks	Howard Schultz	$28.9 million
American Express	Ken Chenault	$28 million
Ford Motor Company	Alan Mulally	$21 million

NOTE: Annual compensation includes the value of executives' base salary, value of stock and option awards, and other financial compensation vehicles.

SOURCE: Data from "20 Top-Paid CEOs," CNN Money.

FIGURE 15.7 Ratio of Average CEO Pay to Average Worker Pay in Selected Industries, 1965–2012

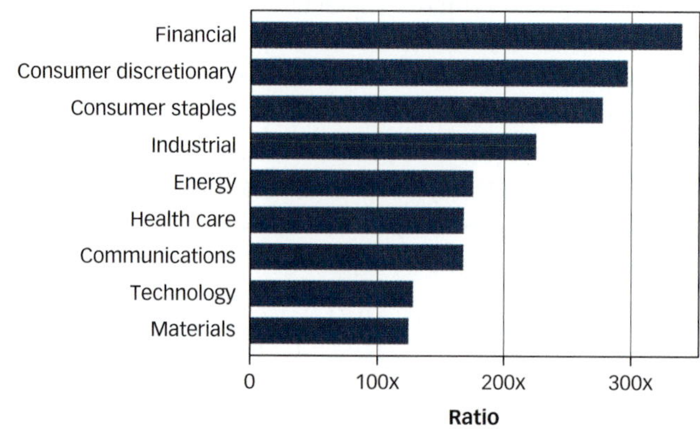

SOURCE: Adapted from "Pay Gap by Industry Sector" in Disclosed: The Pay Gap Between CEOs and Employees, by Elliot Blair Smith and Phil Kuntz, *Bloomberg Business Week,* May 2, 2013.

address, President Barack Obama suggested that "the country that harnesses the power of clean, renewable energy will lead the 21st century." In his second State of the Union address, he urged the creation of clean-energy facilities, rebates for those who make their homes more energy efficient, and tax breaks to encourage businesses to keep the majority of their labor forces within the United States (Peters, 2013).

The drive to develop, manufacture, and implement new energy-efficient and eco-friendly products and services has been swift and encompasses everything from hybrid, electric, and fuel cell automobiles to solar panels, wind turbines, and alternative fuels (such as ethanol, biodiesel, methanol, hydrogen, and liquefied natural gas), as well as environmentally friendly versions of consumer products such as dishwashers, stoves, washing machines and clothes dryers, cleaning products, toothpaste, paper goods, clothing, and food. The pursuit of a "greener" economy is, arguably, driven by both a desire on the part of companies to cash in on a global trend and a recognition of the need to curb the effects of pollution and climate change on the planet.

The green economy also holds the potential to generate jobs. According to a 2008 report by the United Nations Environment Programme, 2.3 million new jobs in renewable energy were created in a span of several years; 406,000 of those were in the United States. The solar power system developer and installer groSolar saw its labor force increase from 2 when it was founded in 1998 to 155 in 2010; likewise, in just 3 years (2006–2009) its revenues increased 389%, from $11.5 million in 2006 to just over $56 million in 2009 (groSolar, 2010; Inc., 2010). In 2011, the U.S. Bureau of Labor Statistics found green jobs to be growing at a rate four times faster than all other industries combined (Lee, 2013).

Relative to other nations, especially China, Brazil, the United Kingdom, Germany, and Spain, the United States has awakened slowly to the potential of the green economy. China currently

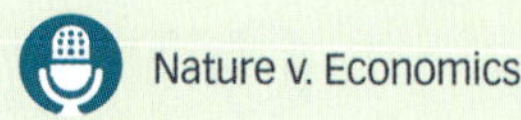

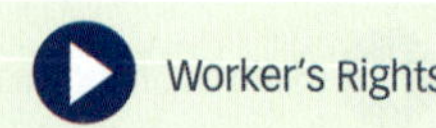

TECHNOLOGY & SOCIETY

THE DIGITAL SWEATSHOP

The exploitation of labor is a fundamental characteristic of industrial capitalism, according to Karl Marx. While in Western countries today few industrial sites like those he and Upton Sinclair described exist, factories with strikingly poor conditions and large pools of low-wage labor flourish in other countries, including China and Thailand. Workers in developing countries bear many of the costs of the high technology we enjoy in the form of advanced computers, phones, and other necessities and amenities.

In January 2012, the *New York Times* published an investigative article about Foxconn, one of Apple's key suppliers in China. The article points out that while "Apple and its high-technology peers—as well as dozens of other American industries—have achieved a pace of innovation nearly unmatched in modern history. . . . the workers assembling iPhones, iPads and other devices often labor in harsh conditions, according to employees inside those plants, worker advocates and documents published by companies themselves" (Duhigg & Barboza, 2012). Among documented issues noted by workers and their advocates are excessive employee overtime, difficult work conditions that include long hours standing, and work injuries resulting from poisonous chemicals used in the manufacture and cleaning of products such as iPads. The article adds that "under-age workers have helped build Apple's products, and the company's suppliers have improperly disposed of hazardous waste and falsified records."

AFP / Stringer/Getty Images

Apple and other global companies have been under scrutiny for the hazardous working conditions in some offshore factories. Some workers have responded with strikes. A small number have committed suicide on factory grounds.

Apple representatives argue that the company has conducted investigations into these conditions and has standards to which its manufacturers must conform (Duhigg & Greenhouse, 2012). Like any modern capitalist enterprise, however, Apple exists in a deeply competitive economic environment, and holding costs down is a path to greater profit. Tightly controlled and rapid manufacturing is also key to maintaining the innovations that drive the technology marketplace.

The *New York Times* article points out that Apple is one of the most admired U.S. brands. A survey the newspaper conducted in 2011 found that fully 56% of respondents could not think of anything negative about the company. Negative opinions were far more likely to be linked to the cost of Apple products (14%) than to its overseas labor practices (2%). Without pressure for change from consumers or companies themselves, the voices of laborers are least likely to be heard and their interests least likely to be realized.

As an Apple executive interviewed for the story noted, "You can either manufacture in comfortable, worker-friendly factories, or you can reinvent the product every year, and make it better and faster and cheaper, which requires factories that seem harsh by American standards. . . . And right now, customers care more about a new iPhone than working conditions in China" (quoted in Duhigg & Barboza, 2012).

THINK IT THROUGH

▶ Consider the interests that come into play in this environment: Apple and its manufacturers are interested in low labor costs, efficient and effective production, and high profits. Consumers are interested in new gadgets and technologies to increase their productivity and pleasure. Workers are interested in safe working conditions and good pay. Can all these interests be realized? What do you think?

© Ryan Pyle/Corbis

The green revolution is here, and you are living in the middle of it. Today's economy will demand that companies and countries alike invest in renewable, cleaner energy that will help reduce their carbon footprint and slow the negative effects of climate change and depletion of earth's natural resources.

leads the world in green (or "clean") industry investments, with an annual commitment of more than $100 billion. China is the world leader in the production of solar cells (the main component of solar panels), harnesses more hydropower than any other nation, and in the very near future is poised to surpass other countries in wind power production (Boudreau, 2010). Paradoxically perhaps, it is also a flagrant polluter—the dramatic levels of air pollution in Beijing led some athletes competing in the 2008 Summer Olympic Games, hosted by the city, to consider dropping out. In recent years, some major urban centers in China have experienced "smog emergencies" severe enough to shut down schools and airports.

In fact, China has assumed such a dominant position in the new green industrial revolution, thanks to strong policies and production benchmarks set by the nation's powerful centralized government, that some U.S. energy experts have expressed fears that if the United States does not soon assume a more dominant position in green technologies, industries, jobs, and research and development, it will lose the opportunity to do so and become dependent on green energy imported from foreign countries, much as it now relies on the importation of oil and fossil fuels. Already 25 of the top 30 green industries are located outside the United States, in countries where "green" has become a requirement, not an option (Boudreau, 2010).

WHY STUDY ECONOMIC SYSTEMS AND TRENDS?

Whether you were born in the 1960s, the 1970s, the 1980s, the 1990s, or earlier, the U.S. economy has experienced some dramatic changes in your lifetime. In 1953, for instance, manufacturing accounted for 30% of the U.S. gross domestic product (Blinder, 2006), and about a third of the workforce was unionized (Reich, 2010). By the mid-2000s, that share of jobs in manufacturing had declined to about 13%, and the proportion of unionized workers had fallen to 12.3%, or 15.3 million people, down from 20% or 17 million people in 1980, the first year for which comparable data are available (U.S. Bureau of Labor Statistics, 2013c).

In the 1960s, more than one third of the U.S. nonagricultural workforce was engaged in manufacturing, and about two thirds of American workers were in the service sector. Since that time, the service sector's share of jobs has grown by nearly 20%, a massive change that has brought both new opportunities and new challenges, particularly to those workers without higher education.

In the latter years of the 1970s, the United States experienced a steep rise in imports—U.S.-made goods and U.S. workers were increasingly forced to compete with lower-priced goods and lower-priced labor. From this period forward, the share of goods made in the United States and the number of workers making them fell (Uchitelle, 2007).

Starting in the early 1980s, U.S. wages, which had increased for decades, stagnated. Former secretary of labor Robert Reich (2010) writes that "contrary to popular mythology, trade and technology have not really reduced the number of jobs available to Americans. . . . The real problem [is] that the new [jobs] they got often didn't pay as well as the ones they lost" (pp. 53–54). Today, wages in the middle and lower segments of the economic hierarchy remain flat.

By the 1990s, advances in computer technologies brought a new wave of outsourcing, not of manufacturing jobs, many of which had already moved offshore, but of information technology and, increasingly, customer service jobs (Erber & Sayed-Ahmed, 2005). Countries such as India, with large populations of educated and English-speaking workers, benefited from American firms' pursuit of lower-cost labor not only in manufacturing but in service as well. This movement of technology jobs and other jobs that, as economist David Autor (2010) points out, can be done "over the wires" continues unabated today.

The shape of our economy and our economic fortunes has changed in myriad ways and continues to do so. Is the growth of "green" industries the next important shift in the world economy? How will globalization affect today's high-skill, high-wage jobs in the United States and elsewhere? Can the fortunes of the declining middle class be reversed? Understanding economic patterns and trends of the past and present is critical to gaining a perspective on how we as individuals and as a country can both prepare for and shape our economic future.

Green Jobs in the United States

WHAT CAN I DO WITH A SOCIOLOGY DEGREE?

SKILLS AND CAREERS: DATA AND INFORMATION LITERACY

Paradoxically, in the modern world we are surrounded by information, but we are not always truly well informed. The abilities to distinguish between credible and questionable data, to seek out solid and reliable sources of information, and to use those sources wisely are critical skills in our "information society"—and in today's job market. *Data and information literacy* encompasses the skills to identify the information needed to understand an issue or problem, to seek out credible and accurate sources of information, to recognize what a body of data illuminates and what it obscures, and to apply the information to a description and analysis of the issue at hand.

Consider a key topic covered in this chapter—unemployment. If you were charged with gathering data on unemployment in the United States or unemployment among particular demographic groups in the United States, where would you begin? Many of us turn to Google or other popular search engines to guide our research. While there is value in using these large search engines, experienced researchers seeking to gather unemployment data are more likely to turn to credible and frequently updated sources of information such as the U.S. Bureau of Labor Statistics (BLS; www.bls.gov). The BLS provides solid data that can be broken out by demographic categories, states, and other variables. It also provides researchers with information on *how the data are gathered,* giving critical insight into what the data illuminate and what they obscure. For example, in this chapter's *Behind the Numbers* box on page 388 we learned that the BLS unemployment figures do not take into account the institutionalized population in the United States. With more than 2 million people—many of them men of color—incarcerated, this exclusion actually results in an incomplete picture of the dire economic position of this demographic group. This does not mean that the data generated by the BLS are not useful. What it means is that we have collected good data—and recognized its limitations. This recognition can help us to use the data more effectively and perhaps to fill in the gaps with information gathered from other sources, such as the U.S. Bureau of Justice Statistics (www.bjs.gov), which provides information on issues related to criminal justice. As a sociology major you will be asked to do research on social issues and problems, and you will learn to use information sources to gather good data. You will have the opportunity to develop key skills that enable you to be a solid researcher and a critical consumer of information.

As a student, you need the skills of data and information literacy to complete tasks such as writing research papers and preparing class presentations. As a consumer, you employ these skills to guide your decisions about the purchase of a home or a vehicle. As a citizen, you need the tools of data and information literacy to make informed political choices about which candidates or causes to support. Data and information literacy is no less significant in the world of work. It is a critical part of jobs that involve *tasks* such as research, the assessment of problems and identification of solutions, and the rigorous gathering and organization of bodies of data that inform policy, marketing, or training, among others. This is a skill of significant value in *occupational fields* such as business and management, marketing and advertising, health care administration, information technology, government, education, research, politics and campaign management, polling, insurance, and management consulting. Among the *job titles* one finds in these fields are management/data/information analyst, market researcher, consumer survey adviser, demographic analyst, mass communications analyst, job analyst/labor force and human resources analyst, life quality researcher, policy analyst, program director, research librarian, survey research technician/specialist, and social survey director.

THINK ABOUT CAREERS

▶ How would you characterize your information literacy skills at this point? What would you like to learn in order to sharpen your skills?

▶ How would you explain the skills of data and information literacy to a potential employer in a field of interest to you?

SUMMARY

- The **economy**—the social institution that organizes the ways in which a society produces, distributes, and consumes **goods** and **services**—is one of the most important institutions in society.
- Three major technological revolutions in human history have brought radically new forms of economic organization. The first led to agriculture, the second to modern industry, and the third to the postindustrial society that characterizes the modern United States.
- Industrial society is characterized by **automation**, the modern factory, **mass production**, **scientific management**, and modern social classes. Postindustrial society is characterized by the use of computers, the increased importance of higher education for well-paying jobs, flexible forms of production, increased reliance on outsourcing, and the growth of the service economy.
- Although postindustrial society holds the promise of prosperity for people who work with ideas and information, automation and globalization have also allowed for new forms of exploitation of the global workforce and job loss and declining wages for some workers in manufacturing and other sectors.
- **Capitalism** and **socialism** are the two principal types of political economic systems that emerged with industrial society. While both are committed to higher standards of living through economic growth, they differ on the desirability of private property ownership and the appropriate role of government. Both systems have theoretical and practical strengths and weaknesses.
- **Work** consists of any human effort that adds something of value to goods and services that are available to others. Economists consider three broad categories of work: the **formal economy**, the **informal (or underground) economy**, and unpaid labor.
- The informal economy is an important part of the U.S. economy even though it does not appear in official labor statistics. Although in industrial societies the informal economy tends to diminish in importance, in recent years this process has reversed itself.
- In the modern economy, consumption replaces production as the most important economic process. The **means of consumption**, as defined by sociologist George Ritzer (1999), are "those things that make it possible for people to acquire goods and services and for the same people to be controlled and exploited as consumers" p. 57). A mall offers consumers buying options, but it also is part of a system of consumer control, as consumers are seduced into buying what they do not need.
- We acquire goods in part based on our consideration of reference groups. As consumption reference groups have changed in the past decades, U.S. consumers have increased spending and taken on a much larger debt load.
- Economic globalization is the result of many factors: technological advances that greatly increased the speed of communication and transportation while lowering their costs, increased educational attainment in low- and middle-income countries, and the opening of many national economies to the world capitalist market. Globalization has had profound effects on the U.S. economy.

KEY TERMS

economy, 383
goods, 383
services, 383
mass production, 384
reserve army of labor, 385
scientific management, 385
automation, 386
unemployed, 389
not in the labor force, 389
marginally attached to the labor force, 389
emotional labor, 389
capitalism, 390
public sector, 390
private sector, 390
communism, 392
socialism, 392
work, 393
barter economy, 394
formal economy, 394
informal (or underground) economy, 394
means of consumption, 396

DISCUSSION QUESTIONS

1. How is unemployment in the United States measured? What aspects of this phenomenon does the unemployment rate measure and what aspects does it fail to capture?

2. How have U.S. manufacturing jobs changed since the 1970s? What were key characteristics of those jobs in the middle of the 20th century and what are key characteristics today? How is the change socially significant?

3. What are the main differences between the formal economy and the informal economy? What are the similarities? What sociological factors explain the existence of the informal economy in the United States?

4. What are the main characteristics of a socialist economic system? Where have such systems been found in recent history? What are their strengths and weaknesses?

5. What sociological factors explain the dramatic rise of consumer debt in the United States over the past three to four decades? Why should this be of concern to society and to policy makers?

Sharpen your skills with SAGE edge at **edge.sagepub.com/chambliss2e**

A personalized approach to help you accomplish your course work goals in an easy-to-use learning environment.

HEALTH AND MEDICINE

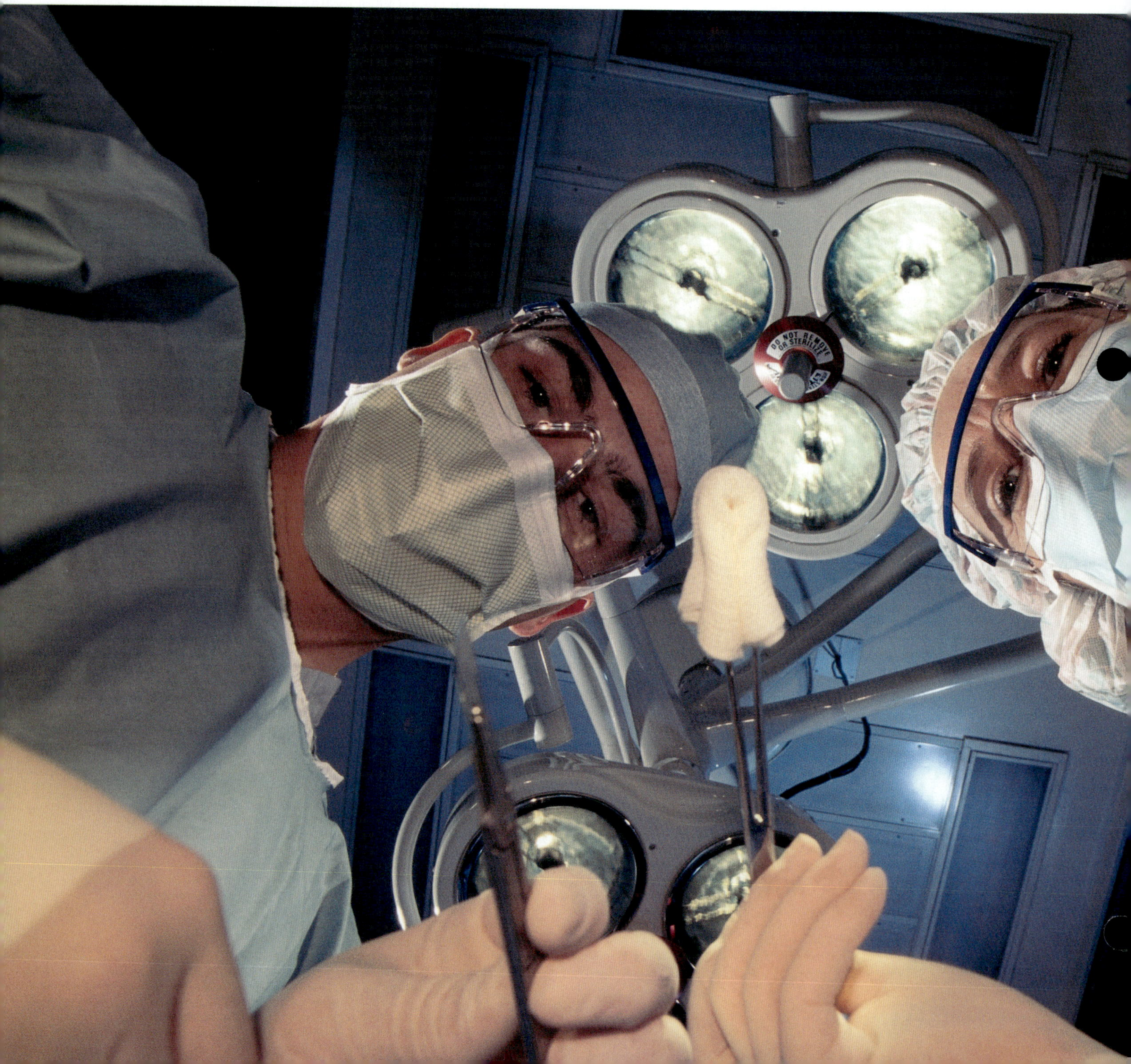

IN THIS CHAPTER

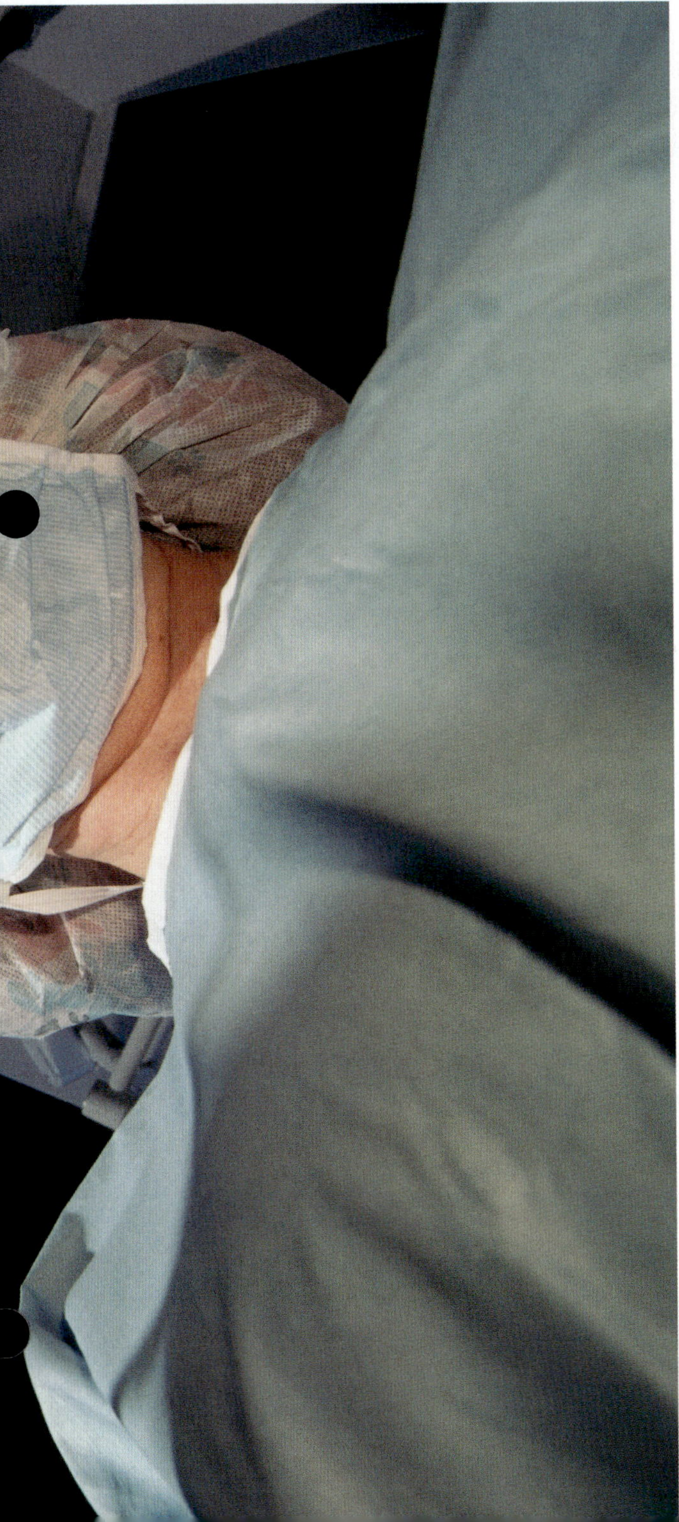

WHAT DO YOU THINK?

1. Should universities and colleges regulate and punish the use of "study drugs"?
2. Do you think that use of the Internet, like the use of drugs or tobacco or alcohol, can become an addiction? If so, how should society respond?
3. Why are the poor more likely than their middle-class counterparts to be obese? What sociological factors might researchers look at to understand this correlation?

THE RISE OF "STUDY DRUG" USE AMONG U.S. STUDENTS

In the fall of 2011, Duke University in North Carolina added a new bullet point to its list of behaviors that constitute academic dishonesty: "the unauthorized use of prescription medication to enhance academic performance." This policy, which so far has not been adopted at most other universities, represents Duke's attempt to address student use and abuse of so-called study drugs, prescription medications intended to alleviate conditions such as attention-deficit/hyperactivity disorder (ADHD). Sales of prescription stimulants such as Ritalin and Adderall have surged in recent years: From 2006 to 2010, they increased from $4 billion to more than $7 billion. According to the Higher Education Research Institute, about 5% of incoming freshmen in 2011 had diagnosed ADHD (Johnson, 2011). But the proportion of students using the drugs prescribed to treat ADHD is larger. By one estimate, as many as a quarter of students on some college campuses have used the drugs in the past year (Trudeau, 2009). According to a recent study, 62% of college students will be offered such stimulants by their fourth year (Wild, 2013).

Interestingly, a report on the problem argues that those using "study drugs" are more likely to perform below average academically and exhibit poor study habits. At the same time, the use of such substances—sometimes called "Ivy League crack"—is found among students at all levels of achievement. Students take the drugs to enhance their concentration and increase the time they can spend on tasks, though such use also carries the risk of irregular heartbeat, panic attacks, addiction, and even death (Johnson, 2011). With more students using them, concerns about the drugs' legality and safety have been accompanied, as at Duke, by questions about how institutions of higher education should respond.

Duke administrators believe that use of the drugs by students to whom they have not been prescribed constitutes cheating, a position supported by the university's newspaper. A recent study suggests that many college students do not agree. In a survey of 1,200 male college freshmen, more respondents labeled the use of performance-enhancing drugs for sports (such as anabolic steroids) as "unethical" than condemned the use of stimulants for the purpose of improving grades (George Washington University, 2012).

Why would the use of drugs to enhance performance be judged more harshly in one context than in another? In an interview, Tonya Dodge, one of the authors of the study, suggested that "in sports there can be only one winner so misuse of a substance is less acceptable for achieving success than in academics. In academics, one's success does not necessarily come at the expense of someone else, but in sports it does."

Do you agree with Duke University that the use of "study drugs" is a form of academic dishonesty? Or do you believe, as many students in the study suggested, that it is okay because one student's improvements do not come at the expense of his or her peers? Should the drugs be more fully regulated because of their medical dangers—or because they constitute cheating? Or should their use be permitted for those willing to take the health risks? What kinds of policies, if any, should your university or college enact in response to this phenomenon?

At one time, sociology and medicine went their separate ways. In the past half century, however, this situation has changed significantly (Cockerham & Glasser, 2000; Weitz, 2012). Today it is widely accepted that sociology can contribute to our understanding of mental and physical health and illness, social group disparities in health, and public health issues such as smoking and obesity—and the growing use and abuse of "study drugs" by young people. ■

In this chapter, we look at health and medicine from a sociological perspective. We focus on the important role that social forces play in health and health care in the United States, and we address issues at the crossroads of medicine, health, public policy, and sociology. We begin by distinguishing health from medicine. We then turn to an examination of the ways in which ideas about health and illness are socially constructed in culture. We look at health and safety, as well as the relationship between class status and health care and outcomes in the United States, delving into the important issue of health care access and reform in the United States. Further, we highlight sociological issues related to public health, including tobacco use, obesity, and teen pregnancy. We offer ideas about the development of a sociology

© Per-Anders Pettersson/Corbis

Research has shown that people in every age group benefit physically and mentally from regular exercise. In this photo, an 84-year-old South African woman exercises outside her Soweto home. City authorities in Soweto have invested in parks and outdoor gyms to encourage residents to be active. ■

of HIV/AIDS, a problem that continues to threaten lives, livelihoods, and entire communities and countries. We finish with a consideration of global issues of health and their sociological roots.

CULTURAL DEFINITIONS OF HEALTH AND ILLNESS

Although health and medicine are closely related, sociologists find it useful to distinguish between them. **Health** is *the extent to which a person experiences a state of mental, physical, and social well-being.* It encompasses not merely the absence of illness but a positive sense of soundness as well. This definition, put forth by the World Health Organization (WHO, 2005), draws attention to the interplay of psychological, physiological, and sociological factors in a person's sense of well-being. It makes clear that excellent health cannot be achieved in purely physical terms. Health cannot be realized if the body is disease-free but the mind is troubled or the social environment is harmful.

Medicine is *an institutionalized system for the scientific diagnosis, treatment, and prevention of illness.* It focuses on identifying and treating physiological and psychological conditions that prevent a person from achieving a state of normal health. In this effort medicine typically applies scientific knowledge derived from physical sciences such as chemistry, biology, and physics, as well as psychology. In the United States, we usually view medicine in terms of the failure of health: When people become ill, they seek medical advice to address the problem. Yet, as the above definition suggests, medicine and health can go hand in hand. The field of **preventive medicine**—*medicine emphasizing a healthy lifestyle that will prevent poor health before it occurs*—is of key interest to health professionals, patients, and policy makers.

Health: The extent to which a person experiences a state of mental, physical, and social well-being.

Medicine: An institutionalized system for the scientific diagnosis, treatment, and prevention of illness.

Preventive medicine: Medicine that emphasizes a healthy lifestyle that will prevent poor health before it occurs.

Culture and Health Care

THE SICK ROLE

Cultural definitions of sickness and health and their causes vary widely (Sagan, 1987). There are sick roles in every society. **Sick roles** are rooted in *cultural definitions of the appropriate behavior of and response to people labeled as sick* and are thus sociologically determined (Cockerham & Glasser, 2000; Parsons, 1951, 1975). The sick role of being mentally ill, for instance, varies enormously across time and space (Foucault, 1988). In some societies, mentally ill people have been seen as having unique spiritual qualities, while in others they have been labeled as victims of demonic possession. In modern societies, mental illness is characterized sometimes as a disease with physiological antecedents and at other times as a sign of character weakness.

One of the pioneers in the sociology of medicine, Talcott Parsons (1975), observed that, in the United States, the role of "sick person" includes the right to be excused from social responsibilities and other "normal" social roles. Parsons, whose theories reflect a functionalist perspective on social life, suggested that illness is both biologically and socially defined, because a "normal" state of functioning includes both physiological equilibrium and the ability to enact expected social roles and behaviors.

Even if illness results from a lifestyle that puts a person at risk, society does not usually hold him or her accountable. On the other hand, the sick person has a societal obligation to try to get well and to seek competent medical help in order to do so. Failure to seek help can lead others to refuse to confer on the suffering individual the "benefits" of the sick role.

The notion that a sick person is enacting a social role may remind us of Erving Goffman's (1959) ideas about humans as actors on a social stage. Goffman suggested that life is like a dramatic play, with front and back stages, scripts for certain settings, costumes, and props. In order to define situations in ways that are favorable to ourselves, he argued, we all play roles on the "front stage" that conform to what is expected and that will show us in the best light.

Imagine a doctor's office as a stage: The doctor arrives wearing a "costume" (often a white lab coat and stethoscope). The patient also wears a "costume" (a cloth or paper gown rather than street clothing). The doctor is expected to greet the patient, ask questions about the illness, examine the patient, and offer advice. The patient is expected to assume a more passive role, submitting to an examination, accepting the diagnosis, and taking advice rather than dispensing it. Now imagine a scenario in which the doctor arrives dressed in evening attire, and the patient gives the doctor medical counsel or refuses to lie on the examining table, choosing instead to sit in the rotating "doctor's chair." The result would be failed expectations about the encounter, as well as an unsuccessful social and medical interaction. As Parsons pointed out, the sick person has an expected "role," but so too do doctors, nurses, and others who are part of the "sick play."

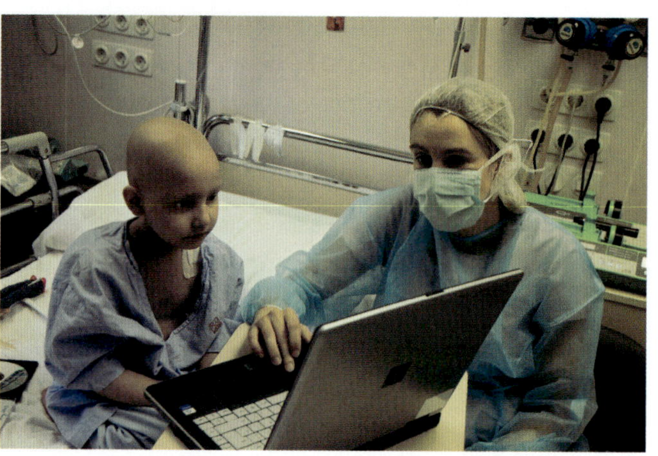

Sociologist Talcott Parsons introduced the concept of the "sick role," which offers sociologists the opportunity to think about the condition of being ill as not only a physical condition, but also a social status with particular characteristics and expectations.

THE SOCIAL CONSTRUCTION OF ILLNESS

Parsons's model underscores the fact that the sick role is culturally determined. Illnesses that are culturally defined as legitimate, such as cancer and heart disease, entitle those diagnosed with them to adopt the role of sick person. The afflicted are forgiven for missing time at work, spending days in bed, and asking others for consideration and assistance. A seriously ill person who persists in leading a "normal" life is given credit for an extraordinary exertion of effort.

Changes in U.S. society's response to alcoholism highlight the importance of cultural definitions of illness. In the middle of the 20th century, people addicted to alcohol were widely seen as weak and of questionable character. In 1956, however, the American Medical Association (2013) declared alcoholism an illness. With the broad acceptance of this medical model of alcoholism, alcoholics often expect and receive sympathy from family members for their illness, employers may offer programs to help them fight the disease, and the government funds research in an effort to combat the problem.

While there also exists a disease model of drug addiction (Le Moal & Koob, 2007), someone addicted to illegal drugs is more likely than an alcoholic to be denied the sick role. Cocaine, heroin, and methamphetamine addicts, for example, face the possibility of being sent to prison if they are found in possession of the drugs, and they may or may not be referred for treatment of their addiction. In at least 19 U.S. states, women who use illicit drugs during pregnancy are subject to civil or even criminal charges. In 2014, Tennessee passed a law that permits prosecutors to charge a woman with criminal assault if she uses narcotics while she is pregnant. The first new mother was arrested and charged under this law in April 2014 (McDonough,

Sick roles: Social roles rooted in cultural definitions of the appropriate behavior of and response to people labeled as sick.

Sociology and the Sick Role Concept

College Student Drug Use

INEQUALITY MATTERS

FEMINIST STANDPOINT THEORY AND THE CONSTRUCTION OF "FEMALE" ILLS

Joan Jacobs Brumberg writes in *The Body Project: An Intimate History of American Girls* (1997):

> According to Victorian medicine, the ovaries—not the brain—were the most important organ in a woman's body.
>
> The most persuasive spokesperson for this point of view was Dr. Edward Clarke, a highly regarded professor at Harvard Medical School, whose popular book *Sex in Education; Or, A Fair Chance for the Girls* (1873) was a powerful statement of the ideology of "ovarian determinism." In a series of case studies drawn from his clinical practice, Clarke described adolescent women whose menstrual cycles, reproductive capacity, and general health were all ruined, in his opinion, by inattention to their special monthly demands. . . . Clarke argued against higher education because he believed women's bodies were more complicated than men's; this difference meant that young girls needed time and ease to develop, free from the drain of intellectual activity. (pp. 7–8)

Medical facts and information are powerful and, because they are cloaked in the credibility of hard science, come to be seen in society as neutral, universal, and true. Feminist standpoint theorists such as Dorothy Smith (1987, 2005) suggest, however, that because "facts," including medical knowledge, have, until quite recently, been produced almost exclusively by men, they reflect a "male standpoint" on the world. Standpoint theorists argue that women's standpoints may well be different from men's, and that "facts" produced from just one standpoint cannot be seen as neutral or universal.

A key part of standpoint theory is the analysis of the power that lies in the production of knowledge, and it asks, "Who has the power to produce 'facts'"?

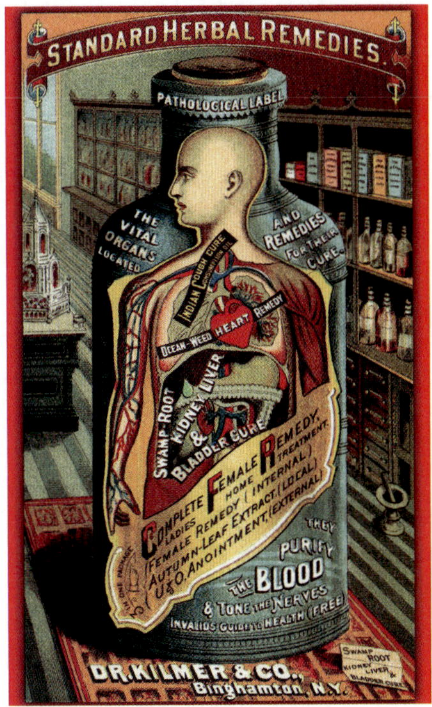

In the 19th century, female hysteria was a commonly diagnosed "ailment" among women. Today is it not recognized as a medical category at all. In the 19th century, women's ills were almost exclusively labeled by male physicians. Can you see a connection between these facts?

THINK IT THROUGH

▶ Does the creation of the medical "knowledge" described above about female education and ovulation suggest that men's and women's research and conclusions may be conditioned by the researchers' positions in society? How likely is it that a female physician or researcher would have come to the scientific conclusion that education interferes with women's menses or reproductive capacity?

2014). While there are clear reasons to be concerned about the welfare of infants born to addicted mothers, it is less clear that there are greater benefits to criminally charging new mothers and separating them from their children than to supporting their recovery in treatment programs.

Some drug addiction is widely understood as "illness" while some is labeled as "deviance," transforming the status of the individual who carries the label (Goffman, 1963b). What explains the difference? Do you think these differing definitions are justified?

HEALTH CARE IN THE UNITED STATES

Health care can be defined as *all those activities intended to sustain, promote, and enhance health.* An adequate health care system includes more than the provision of medical services for those who need them—it also encompasses policies that minimize violence and the chance of accidents, whether on the highways, at work, or at home; policies that promote a clean, nontoxic environment; ecological protection; and the availability of clean water, fresh air, and sanitary living conditions.

TABLE 16.1 Rate of Gun Deaths for Selected Countries, 2011

Country	Gun Homicides per 100,000 Population	Unintentional Gun Deaths per 100,000 Population	Gun Suicides per 100,000 Population
United States	3.6	0.3	6.3
Canada	0.5 (2009)	.08 (2001)	1.79 (2006)
Germany	0.7	0.01 (2010)	0.92
Sweden	0.19 (2010)	0.01	1.2 (2010)
Australia	0.11	0.05	0.62
United Kingdom	0.06	0.0	0.15

SOURCE: Alpers, P., & Wilson, M. (2012). *Guns in the United States: Facts, Figures and Firearm Law.* Sydney School of Public Health, The University of Sydney.

HEALTH AND PUBLIC SAFETY ISSUES

By the standards noted above, few societies come close to providing excellent health care for their citizens. Some, however, do much better than others. The record of the United States in this regard is mixed.

On one hand, the U.S. government spends vast sums of money in its efforts to construct safe highways, provide clean drinking water, and eliminate or reduce air and ground pollution. Laws are in place to regulate working conditions with the aim of promoting healthy and safe workplace environments: The federal Occupational Safety and Health Administration is responsible for enforcing stringent regulations intended to guard the lives and health of U.S. workers. Local health inspectors visit the premises of restaurants and grocery stores to check that food is handled in a sanitary manner, and agricultural inspectors check the quality of U.S. and imported food products. States require drivers to use seat belts, motorcyclists to wear helmets, and children to be strapped into car seats, all of which have been shown to reduce injuries and fatalities in road accidents. While these efforts do not guarantee the safety of life, work, food, or transport, they contribute to public safety in important ways.

On the other hand, compared to most other modern countries, the United States is more violent, a factor that compromises safety, in particular for some high-risk groups. Gun violence and firearm accidents leading to death are serious problems in the United States (Table 16.1). Children ages 5 to 14 are killed by guns in the United States at a rate 11 times higher than the rates of 22 comparable large, high-income countries. A recent analysis of WHO statistics on gun deaths found that fully 80% of the gun deaths in 23 industrialized countries happened in the United States (Richardson & Hemenway, 2011). Homicide is a leading cause of death among young African American males, and the majority of this violence is perpetrated using guns (Kaiser Family Foundation, 2006; Violence Policy Center, 2010). Studies have also noted that rates of homicide victimization are higher in U.S. states with high rates of gun ownership, as are rates of gun suicides (Miller, Azrael, & Hemenway, 2007).

Domestic violence puts thousands of women at risk: At least 85% of victims of domestic violence are women, and an average of three women are murdered by a husband or boyfriend every day in the United States. In 2010, 38% of all female murder victims in the United States were killed by a husband or boyfriend (National Center for Victims of Crime, 2012). The abuse may start young: In one study, one in three adolescent females reported being physically and/or sexually abused by a dating partner (Davis, 2008). Additionally, 9% of high school students report purposeful physical abuse by a partner within the past 12 months (National Center for Injury Prevention and Control, 2014). This occurs in spite of the fact that there are myriad laws against abuse, mechanisms for securing restraining orders against would-be attackers, and shelters for battered women. Efforts to protect victims and potential victims of domestic violence may fall short because batterers are often given a pass by those hesitant to interfere and because victims lack resources to leave their abusers or fear reprisals.

Different social groups experience different degrees of violence and safety. Black Americans are far more likely than Whites to be victims of homicide, and women are more likely than men to be killed by intimate partners. Why are some groups in society more vulnerable to violence? Is there a link between physical safety and the power a group has (or does not have) in society? What do you think?

Health care: All those activities intended to sustain, promote, and enhance health.

TECHNOLOGY & SOCIETY

ADDICTION AND THE INTERNET

A recent advertisement for a leading telecommunications company opens with an earnest spokesman meandering through a family's home and declaring, "Today we live online." He adds that in a just a few years, the number of gadgets in our homes will double. Around him, four family members are engaged in their own individual electronic worlds, each interacting with someone or something other than those in his or her immediate environment. The scenario is presented as pleasant, progressive, and unproblematic. Might something be missing from this picture?

Richard Lewisohn / Contributor/Getty Images

How many hours each day do members of your family spend on line? What about your friends and you? What are the costs and benefits of our increasing dependence on electronic gadgets and social media? ■

Scientific studies point to a growing epidemic of technological dependency, even addiction. A recent *Newsweek* article on the issue notes, "In less than the span of a single childhood, Americans have merged with their machines, staring at a screen for at least eight hours a day, more time than we spend on any other activity including sleeping" (Dokoupil, 2012a). Some Internet users neglect sleep, family, and health in favor of the virtual world: In one extreme case, a South Korean couple allowed their infant daughter to starve while they were nurturing an online "baby" for hours at a time (BBC, 2010). At least 10 cases have been documented of Internet surfers getting fatal blood clots from prolonged sitting at the computer. While most cases are not so acute in their consequences, the American Psychiatric Association considered including "Internet addiction disorder" in the fifth edition of the *Diagnostic and Statistical Manual of Mental Disorders* (*DSM-5*), the foundation of modern mental health practice, as a diagnosis "for further study" (Dokoupil, 2012a). However, when *DSM-5* was published in 2013, the disorder was not included.

A recent publication by psychiatric researchers in Asia, which has very high rates of heavy Internet use, particularly by gamers, points out, "A functional magnetic resonance imaging (MRI) study found that a cue-induced online gaming urge among individuals with Internet gaming abuse activated brain areas similar to those involved in craving in people with drug addiction" (Yen, Yen, & Ko, 2010). Observers suggest that while questions remain about whether brain changes lead to addictive behavior or heavy Internet use fosters brain changes, it is becoming increasingly clear that technology is linked in some way to problems that include addictive behavior, declining attention spans, increasing impulsiveness, anxiety, and depression.

THINK IT THROUGH

▶ Is "living online" stigmatized in our society, or is it celebrated? If Internet or other technology use is addictive and vast swaths of people, particularly the young, are becoming addicted, how should society respond?

The Creation of "Madness"

Internet Addiction

SOCIAL INEQUALITIES IN HEALTH AND MEDICINE

By nearly every measure, health follows the social class curve: Poor people are more likely than their better-off counterparts to suffer chronic illnesses and die earlier. Among children, poverty affects health, food security, housing stability, and maltreatment, with the former two factors playing a significant role in the likelihood of developing chronic illnesses and other negative outcomes such as malnutrition, stunted growth, and suppressed immunity (Henry, 2010). Recessions and economic slumps also hurt families, straining their ability to afford quality food and health care.

Lower-income people are more likely to live in areas that have high levels of air pollution, which raises their risks of asthma, heart disease, and cancer (Calderón-Garcidueñas & Torres-Jardón, 2012). Many have a greater probability of exposure to violence and the mental and physical health problems that entails. Their work is also more likely to involve physical and health risks than is the work of middle- and upper-class people (Commission to Build a Healthier America, 2009). Figure 16.1 highlights class differences in self-perceptions of health and well-being.

The poor often have less healthy diets than do their higher-income counterparts: Inexpensive foods may be highly processed, fatty, and high in sugar. Fresh fruits and vegetables and lean meats may be out of financial reach for those who struggle to make ends meet, and time pressures can limit a workingman's or -woman's opportunities to shop for and prepare healthy foods. Children in poor communities may also lack access to safe places for active outdoor play and exercise. Another factor that affects the health of the poorer classes is the fact that they are less likely to perceive the symptoms of illness as requiring attention from a physician (Keeley, Wright, & Condit, 2009).

FIGURE 16.1 Self-Reported Health Status by Income, 2011

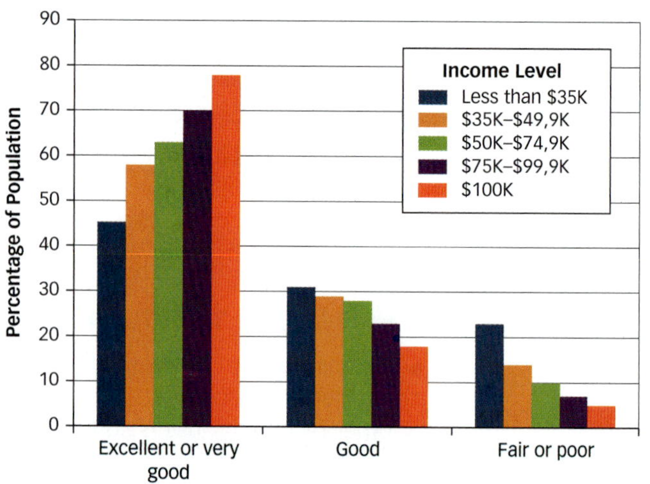

SOURCE: Centers for Disease Control and Prevention. (2012). Table XIII. Crude percent distributions of health status among persons aged 18 years and over, by selected characteristics: United States, 2010. *Summary health statistics for U.S. Adults: National Health Interview Survey, 2010.*

FIGURE 16.2 Life Expectancy in the United States, 2011

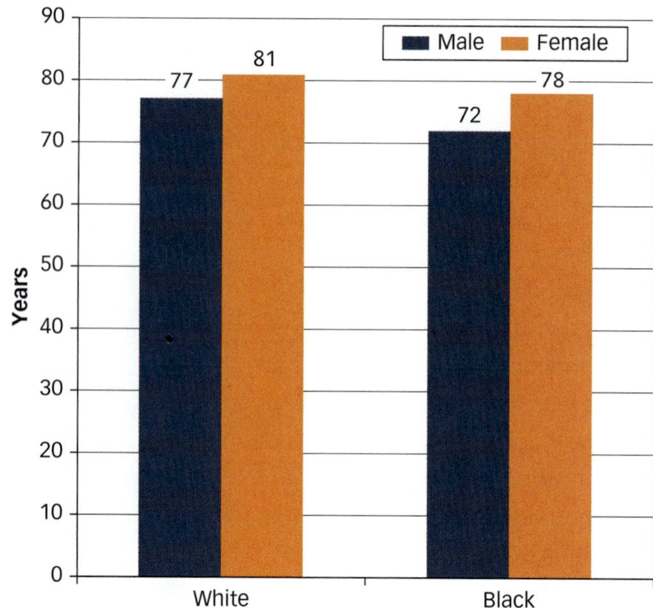

SOURCE: Hoyert, D. L., & Xu, J. (2012). Deaths: Preliminary data for 2011. *National Vital Statistics Reports, 61*(6). Washington, DC: Centers for Disease Control and Prevention.

Because race and class closely intersect in the United States, racial minorities, on average, suffer from poorer health than Whites, which is reflected in the discrepancies in life expectancy between the two groups (see Figure 16.2 above). In 2010, the overall life expectancy at birth in the United States was 78.7 years. White women's life expectancy was higher at 81.3, while Black women's was lower at 78.2. White men had a life expectancy of 76.6 years, but their Black counterparts had a life expectancy of just 72.1 years (Centers for Disease Control and Prevention [CDC], 2011a). The differences are linked to, among other factors, higher rates of death among Blacks due to heart disease, cancer, diabetes, and homicide. Inequalities, however, start even before birth, since poor mothers are less likely to have access to prenatal care. A report prepared for the Annie E. Casey Foundation suggests that "at any age, and at any income, education or socioeconomic level, an African American mother is more than twice as likely to lose her infant as a white woman" (Shore & Shore, 2009, p. 6). These findings are supported by 2008 data (Table 16.2) showing a mortality rate of 5.52 per 1,000 for White babies and a far higher rate of 12.67 deaths per 1,000 live births for babies of Black mothers (Hoyert & Xu, 2012).

The medical establishment in the United States has also used poor minorities to advance the frontiers of science. In the infamous Tuskegee study, which ran from the 1930s to the

Race, Pollution, and Health

Income Inequality and Health

GLOBAL ISSUES

RICH COUNTRIES AND POOR PATIENTS

Who benefits from disease and poverty in developing countries? Your initial response is likely to be a decisive "nobody!" But considered from a conflict-oriented perspective, the question may elicit a different response. As noted in this chapter, U.S. medical science "benefited" from the diseased bodies of Black men in the Tuskegee study, as well as from the subjects' relative powerlessness and lack of knowledge about what was happening to them in the study (Washington, 2007).

Recall that sociologist Herbert Gans (1972) asserted that the nonpoor benefit from having a class of poor people (see Chapter 7). He was not arguing in favor of poverty—he meant that because poverty is *positively functional for the nonpoor,* its elimination could be costly for more economically well-off and powerful groups. Gans's work offers us a way of understanding why poverty exists and persists, even in a wealthy country like the United States.

We can construct a similar conflict-oriented argument around global poverty and disease. Who benefits from global inequality and poverty—for instance, from the poor health that often accompanies economic marginality?

In terms of health and medicine, the existence of poor, undereducated populations in developing states benefits the West by offering pharmaceutical companies "guinea pigs" on whom to test new medicines where fewer restrictions on testing with human subjects are in force. Examples were cited by a *Washington Post* investigation in 2000: "An unapproved antibiotic was tested by a major pharmaceutical company on sick children during a meningitis epidemic in Nigeria. The country's lax regulatory oversight, the sense among some doctors that they could not object to experiment conditions for political or economic reasons, the dearth of alternative health care options, combined with the desire of the company to rapidly prepare for market a potential 'blockbuster' drug underpinned a situation in which disease victims were treated as test subjects rather than patients" (quoted in Eglitis, 2010, p. 203).

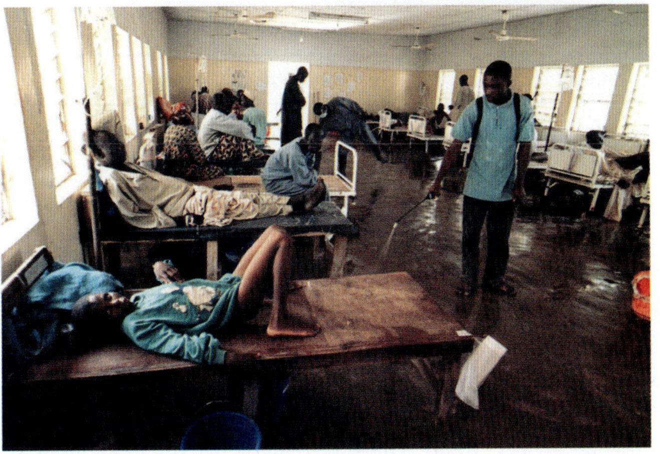

The Washington Post / Contributor/Getty Images

Controls on drug testing in many countries of the developing world are less stringent than in countries such as the United States and Canada. Clinical drug trials run in countries such as Nigeria (shown here) have led to criticism of pharmaceutical company practices.

A 2012 report on India noted that in one hospital that serves India's lowest societal caste, the *Dalits,* pharmaceutical trials conducted by British and German companies had resulted in injuries and deaths. Some of the hospital patients or their families were illiterate and signed consent forms they could not understand. Others claimed they were never asked for consent. "Over the past seven years, some 73 clinical trials on 3,300 patients—1,833 of whom were children—have taken place at Indore's Maharaja Yeshwantrao Hospital. Dozens of patients have died during the trials, however no compensation has been paid to the families left behind" (Lloyd-Roberts, 2012). The poor patients in the trials were, according to the report, hesitant to question what was happening to them. Many felt grateful that they were getting access to drugs they would not be able to afford themselves. Few understood that some of those drugs were untested. According to the report, in the 7 years leading up to 2012, almost 2,000 drug trials had taken place across the country.

THINK IT THROUGH

▶ Who benefits from global poverty—and who loses? Is it possible for Western companies to conduct drug safety trials in poor developing countries in a way that benefits the companies, the patient participants, and Western consumers?

TABLE 16.2 Infant Mortality and Birth Weight per 1,000 Live Births Among Black and White Infants in the United States, 2008

	Infant Mortality	Low Birth Weight	Very Low Birth Weight
Black	12.6	69.6	262.7
White	5.5	47.7	216.7

SOURCE: Centers for Disease Control and Prevention. (2012). Infant Mortality Statistics from the 2008 Period Linked Birth/Infant Death Data Set. *National Vital Statistics Reports*, *60*(5).

1970s, Black males who had contracted syphilis were intentionally left untreated so researchers could study the progress of the disease (Brandt, 1983; Washington, 2007). During the Cold War, U.S. government agencies funded and conducted hundreds of research tests on unwitting citizens to assess the effects of radiation and other by-products of war (Budiansky, Goode, & Gest, 1994). These tests were usually conducted on the poor and disproportionately on minorities (Washington, 2007). This chapter's *Global Issues* essay further explores the issue of medical testing on human beings and the questions that inevitably arise about who benefits from such activities and who loses.

ACCESS TO HEALTH CARE

One important reason the poor—as well as some families in the working and middle classes—in the United States are less likely to experience good health is that a notable proportion are unable to access regular care for prevention and treatment of disease. In the fall of 2010, 3 years after the start of the Great Recession and shortly before the Patient Protection and Affordable Care Act (which we discuss below) was signed into law, the U.S. Census Bureau reported that more than 16% of people in the United States were without health insurance, the highest figure in 23 years (Kaiser Family Foundation, 2010a). Key sources of this decline were the economic crisis and the associated rise in unemployment; most U.S. adults get health insurance coverage from their employers. Workplace coverage is variable, however, and ranges from full benefits requiring little or no financial contribution from the employee to partial benefits paid for through shared employer and employee contributions. Cost-saving measures in U.S. workplaces in recent decades have shifted a greater share of the cost of these benefits from employers to employees.

As the economic picture has improved since 2010, many people have gone back to work, but millions of employees are still uninsured or underinsured. This problem has been worsened by a changing labor market and economic structure that favors part-time or contractual employment, with fewer benefits such as the employer-based health insurance coverage that has traditionally applied to full-time employees.

A substantial number of Americans have access to health care through government-funded programs such as Medicare, an elder insurance program that covers most of those ages 65 and over (about 41.5 million in 2012) and some younger residents with disabilities (about 9.4 million in 2012) (Centers for Medicare and Medicaid Services, 2012). Medicaid, a shared federal and state insurance program that provides coverage for many poor adults and children, reached an enrollment of 54.1 million in June 2012 (Kaiser Family Foundation, 2013b). Medicare was created in 1965 to serve as a federal health insurance program for people age 65 and older, regardless of income or medical history. It covers very diverse populations, since most people over the age of 65 and those with permanent disabilities are entitled to coverage (Kaiser Family Foundation, 2014). Medicaid, on the other hand, is the country's major health insurance program designed to assist low-income people of all ages with their health care needs, but it is not available to everyone who needs long-term services; to be eligible for Medicaid, individuals must meet stringent financial qualifications (Kaiser Family Foundation, 2012a).

A contemporary issue related to Medicare is the fact that members of the post–World War II baby-boom generation (those born between about 1946 and 1964) are now entering the 65+-year-old cohort. As the "boomers" reach eligibility age, their massive numbers will have an effect on the nation's need for health care dollars and resources. The U.S. Census Bureau reports that between 2000 and 2010, the 65+ age cohort grew at a faster rate than the total population; the total population of the United States increased by less than 10%, while the population of those 65 and older grew by more than 15% (Werner, 2011). The increase in eligible Medicare recipients, medical advancements that extend the lives of the elderly, and a relatively smaller tax base are the ingredients of a debate over care and government spending that will grow more acute in the years to come (Antos, 2011). The effect of the Obama administration's health care legislation on Medicare is not yet fully clear.

At the opposite end of the age spectrum, the State Children's Health Insurance Program (SCHIP) was created in the late 1990s in an aggressive effort to cover more uninsured children. Because individual states administer SCHIP in partnership with the federal government, state governments largely dictate its implementation, so the comprehensiveness of coverage and eligibility standards vary from state to state.

While the care that the poorest U.S. adults can access through Medicaid is limited, it is often the working poor and other low-income employees who are shut out of insurance coverage altogether. They are most likely to be working in economic sectors such as the service industry (fast-food restaurants, retail establishments, and the like) that provide few or no insurance benefits to employees, while earning too little to afford self-coverage but too much to qualify for government health coverage. The fact, as noted above, that low-income people are more likely to have health problems has also affected their ability to get

Ebola and the Making of Pariahs

insurance coverage in the past, because insurers were allowed to exclude those with "preexisting conditions" such as diabetes, high blood pressure, and other illnesses and disabilities.

The Patient Protection and Affordable Care Act (known simply as the Affordable Care Act, or ACA), signed into law by President Barack Obama in 2010, endeavors to expand insurance coverage to most people in the United States at a time when the numbers of the uninsured had been rising. The goal of this health care overhaul is to bring more people into the insurance fold by making coverage more broadly accessible and affordable, in part by requiring that everyone buy insurance and that private insurance companies offer coverage under new terms that extend benefits to those who may have had difficulty purchasing insurance in the past, such as those with preexisting conditions. While the purchasing mandate (or "individual mandate") went into effect in 2014, other parts of the ACA were already in place when the U.S. Supreme Court ruled on the constitutionality of the mandate in June 2012. Among these provisions were the requirement that insurance companies permit young people up to age 26 to remain on their parents' health insurance policies if they do not have other coverage.

Since its passage, the ACA has been the source of heated political debate. President Obama and other supporters of the act argue that the new law is expanding insurance coverage to a broader swath of people, many of whom had been locked out of the insurance market due to preexisting conditions or unaffordability of individual insurance policies. They suggest that the law supports this expansion of coverage through the operation of new state-level insurance markets (or exchanges) that keep prices down by enabling purchasers to buy insurance as part of a group. Those with low incomes are eligible for federal subsidies to support their insurance purchases. Supporters also note that as the population of uninsured people declines, so will taxpayer-borne costs, including those incurred when the uninsured seek medical care at emergency rooms, which are obligated by law to treat everyone regardless of their ability to pay.

Opponents argue that the U.S. government is overstepping the limits of its powers in requiring that people purchase health insurance or pay a penalty tax for failing to do so. Many see the individual mandate as an infringement on their freedom to choose whether or not to purchase insurance. There have also been attempts to portray the ACA as a path to "socialized medicine," though most people will still receive their insurance through private insurance companies rather than through the government.

Both supporters and opponents of the ACA have expressed concerns about the costs of the U.S. health care system. Indeed, the United States spends more per capita on health care than most economically developed states (Figure 16.3), though many of its health indicators compare poorly to those of its peers. Opponents of health care reform argue that the ACA will drive up costs by, for instance, requiring insurers to cover those who have costly health conditions. Supporters of the law point out that having a large pool of uninsured contributes to higher costs when they fail to get preventive care and must resort to far more costly emergency room care. The cost trajectory of health care is not yet clear. Certainly, an aging U.S. population will likely need more, not fewer, health care services in the future. The effect of the ACA on both U.S. health indicators and access to care will become clearer with the passage of time.

CAN TECHNOLOGY EXPAND HEALTH CARE ACCESS?

Would you like to have a "doctor on demand"? Some technological innovations are bringing health care into people's homes, opening the door for greater access to medical care as well as a potential reduction in unneeded doctor's office visits. As a recent *Time* magazine article on the technological expansion of access to medical care points out, such technology was "previously reserved mostly for luxe private practices or rural communities that lack access to health care" (Sifferlin, 2014). Today, it may be coming to an app near you.

New technological innovations like Doctor on Demand, Health Tap, and AskMD offer a range of services, from the opportunity to ask

FIGURE 16.3 Per Capita Health Care Spending for Selected Developed Countries, 2010

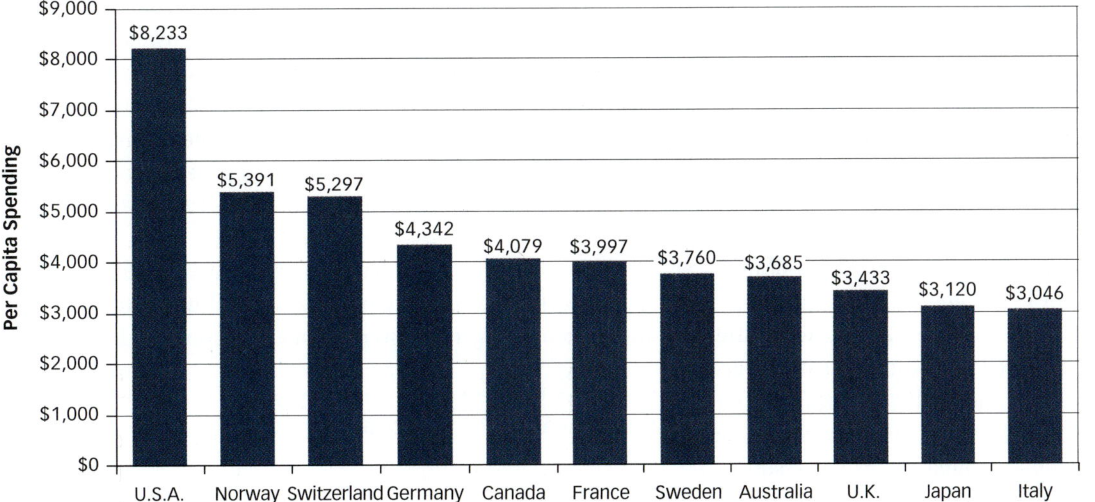

SOURCE: Kaiser Family Foundation (2013) Health Expenditure Per Capita.

physicians medical questions by text and receive free responses to online appointments that require payment for consultations. Beneficiaries of these technologies include both patients, who have new avenues to reach medical professionals, and doctors, as online consultations can help them build their public profiles and earn some extra income.

Are there potential pitfalls to the use of these technologies as well? Are there potential losers? Those patients who have acute or urgent needs are still best served by personal visits to physicians. As well, those who do not own computers or smartphones or cannot pay the fees for online consultations may still be locked out of these opportunities. "Doctor on demand" technology may, however, offer a potential vehicle for bringing medical advice to both advantaged and underserved communities. Can you think of ways that technological innovations like these could be used to address medical needs across the income spectrum?

SOCIOLOGY AND ISSUES OF PUBLIC HEALTH IN THE UNITED STATES

Public health is *the science and practice of health protection and maintenance at a community level.* Public health officials try to control hazards and habits that may harm the health and well-being of the population. They have long sought to educate the public about the hazards of tobacco use, for example, and to prevent young people from taking up smoking. More recently, they have warned that obesity is becoming an ever more serious problem for young and old alike. The issue of teen pregnancy has also garnered attention, though rates of pregnancy among teenagers have fluctuated.

SMOKING

One of the largest and most profitable industries in the United States is the manufacture and sale of tobacco products, estimated to be a $47.1 billion industry. At the same time, tobacco is the number one cause of premature death in the United States, claiming more than 443,000 lives each year and surpassing the toll from alcohol, homicide, suicide, drugs, auto accidents, and AIDS combined (CDC, 2011c). Even nonsmokers are at risk. The CDC (2011c) estimates that secondhand smoke exposes 88 million nonsmokers to measurable levels of toxic chemicals associated with cigarette smoke. About 90% of men and 80% of women who die of lung cancer are smokers (U.S. Department of Health and Human Services, 2004). According to the CDC (2014b), smoking-related lung cancer deaths averaged 74,300 per year among men and 53,400 per year among women from 2005 to 2009. While the smoking rate in the United States fell between 2000 and 2005, it has since stalled at about 21%, a figure that translates to more than 45 million smokers (CDC, 2011c).

© Bettmann/Corbis

Communications researcher Jean Kilbourne (1999) says female-targeted cigarette ads often contain subtexts about female thinness, using "thin," "slim," or "light" in the product name. Ads also imply that smoking can help women lose weight; in the past Lucky cigarettes urged, "Reach for a Lucky instead of a sweet."

While statistics on **morbidity**, meaning *the rate of illness,* and **mortality**, *the rate of death,* highlight important *medical* aspects of cigarette smoking, we can also use sociological analysis to illuminate this public health issue. Why do so many people continue to smoke and so many young people take up smoking despite the evidence of its ill effects? Why do more men than women smoke? Why are young women the fastest-growing population of new smokers? (See Figure 16.4.) Why does the government not regulate the production and sale of such an addictive and dangerous product more stringently?

Sociology offers us some insight into these questions. Among other things, cigarette advertising both constructs and reinforces gender stereotypes (Kilbourne, 1999). Male

Public health: The science and practice of health protection and maintenance at a community level.

Morbidity: The rate of illness in a particular population.

Mortality: The rate of death in a particular population.

■ FIGURE 16.4 **Cigarette Smoking in the United States, 2012**

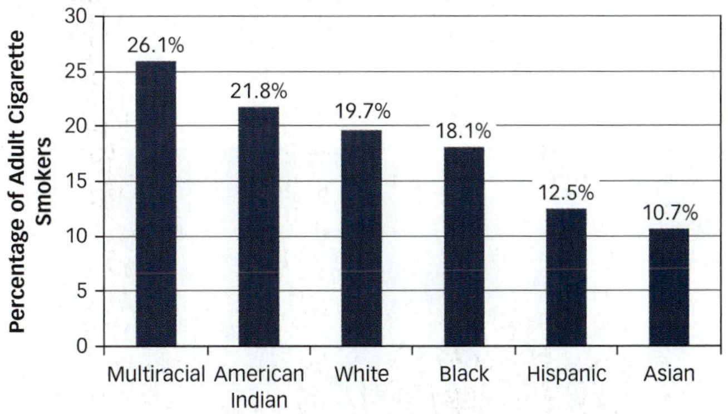

SOURCE: Centers for Disease Control and Prevention. (2012). Adult Cigarette Smoking in the United States: Current Estimate. *Smoking & Tobacco Use*.

smoking has been associated with independence, ruggedness, and machismo (think of the Marlboro Man, an iconic figure in U.S. advertising). On the other hand, female smoking has been associated with images that are elegant, chic, and playful or carefree. A symbolic interactionist might highlight the way in which a cigarette is more than just tobacco rolled in paper. To a young teen, it might be a symbol of maturity; to an older teen, it might represent being cool or rebellious. In what other ways do cigarettes function as symbols of self in our society?

TWO THEORETICAL PERSPECTIVES ON PUBLIC HEALTH: THE CASE OF CIGARETTES The conflict perspective offers some insight into why cigarettes are not regulated more stringently despite their addictive properties: Who benefits from the existence of a large population of smokers? Who loses?

Smoking may give pleasure to smokers, but its benefits are largely outweighed by its consequences, which include poorer health and a thinner wallet. Smoking does, however, bring profit to the tobacco companies, which have tenaciously defended their product for decades. Tobacco companies are generous contributors to candidates for political office. They are advantaged by wealth and access to the halls of government, where their voices are heard. While the smoker gets a mixed bag of benefits (pleasure) and consequences (addiction, disease, financial cost) from smoking, cigarette companies clearly benefit from purchases of their goods and the recruitment of new smokers—men and boys, women and girls—to replace those who die or quit.

Is the easy availability of cigarettes also functional? A functionalist might suggest that, in fact, it is positively functional in its creation of jobs, which range from tobacco farming to marketing and lobbying for the tobacco cause, and in its contribution to rural economies that depend on income from farming tobacco. The highly coveted plant has been subject to human cultivation and use for hundreds of years. Consider its historical functions: Tobacco became a major influence in the development of the economy of early America. During the Revolutionary War, profits from the tobacco trade helped to the Revolution by serving as collateral for loans provided to Americans by France (Randall, 1999). In contemporary times, according to the Center for Responsive Politics (2013), the tobacco lobby employed about 133 lobbyists and spent more than $17 million on behalf of 25 clients in 2011 alone. The modern tobacco industry is a multimillion-dollar enterprise with a strong political influence despite increased awareness of the deleterious effects that tobacco products have on the human body.

Viewing cigarette smoking through a theoretical lens lets us see it as more than just an individual choice or action. Rather, cigarettes and smoking are social symbols and phenomena with profound effects on public heath, as well as sources of profit for some and pain for others.

OBESITY

The CDC identifies obesity in the United States as a national health problem: It is a major cause of mortality, second only to smoking. According to the CDC (2012d) and the Kaiser Family Foundation (2011), more than 34% of adults in the United States between the ages of 20 and 74 are obese, and more than 63% are overweight (this statistic includes those who are classified as obese). The rates of being overweight/obese vary by gender and ethnicity, as we see in Figure 16.5.

The rate of obesity in American children has risen even faster and is twice what it was in the late 1970s. Children who are much bigger than their peers sometimes experience social ostracism. Further, they may suffer serious health effects.

■ FIGURE 16.5 **Rates of Obesity and Overweight in the United States by Race and Ethnicity, 2012**

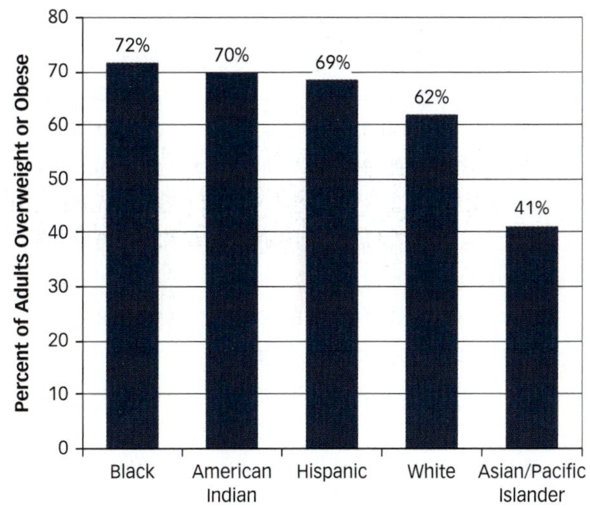

SOURCE: The Kaiser Family Foundation. (2011). Overweight and Obesity Rates for Adults by Race/Ethnicity, 2011. Statehealthfacts.org

CQR Obesity in America

POVERTY, MALNUTRITION, AND OBESITY

Obesity and being overweight are, in important ways, what many of us would see as "private troubles," reflecting choices individuals make about nutrition, exercise, and health. Clearly, however, these public health problems affect millions in the United States. No less important to sociologists is the fact that the risk of falling into the categories of obese or overweight is not evenly distributed across social groups in this country.

Think for a moment about the problems of hunger and malnutrition. What kinds of images enter your mind? Are you picturing the heartrending scenes of starvation in the world's least developed countries that are brought to us by the media? Yet hunger and malnutrition are also present in our own country, though their manifestation is often quite different. Poor access to nutritious food in the United States is more likely to be manifested in obesity than in emaciation. Consider, for example, that some of the country's poorest states have the highest obesity rates. In Kentucky 30.4% of adults are obese; in Louisiana, 33.4%; and in Mississippi, 34.9% (CDC, 2012d).

Among the demographic groups most likely to be poor are also those most at risk of obesity; fully half of African American women are obese, as are 45% of Hispanic women (CDC, 2012d). Those without a high school education are more likely to be obese (32.9%) than those who complete high school (over 29%) or college (nearly 21%; Ogden, Lamb, Carroll, & Flegal, 2010). According to the *Handbook on Obesity,* "In heterogeneous and affluent societies like the United States, there is a strong inverse correlation of social class and obesity" (quoted in Critser, 2003, p. 117).

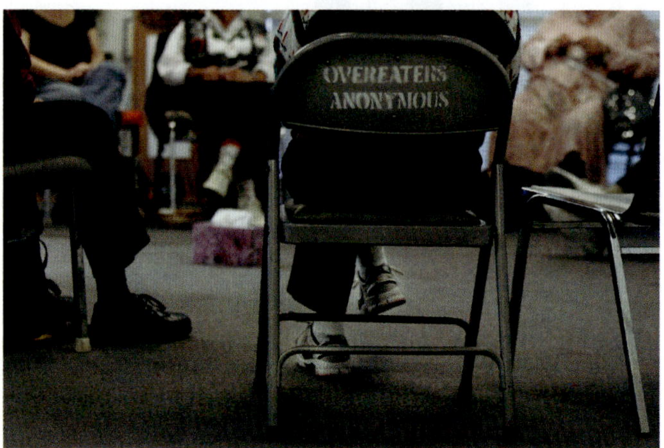

© ZUMA Press, Inc. / Alamy

Obesity is not exclusively about overconsumption of food. Factors including the higher cost of healthy meals and the lack of access to recreational spaces also play a key role in understanding why many Americans, particularly the poor, struggle with obesity. ■

Can we use the sociological imagination to examine the relationship between poverty and obesity? What sociological factors are pertinent for understanding this phenomenon? Though individual factors such as bone structure, genes, appetite, and personal choices have an important influence, obesity is also a product of social environment and socioeconomic conditions. Those who are poor are more likely to consume less nutritious food for a host of reasons. Nutritionally poor food is generally less expensive than high-quality goods, and large grocery stores with wide selections and competitive pricing are disproportionately located in suburbs, while convenience stores plying overpriced, processed foods serve inner-city communities (Critser, 2003), though some cities, including Washington, D.C., have increased the incentives they offer for big grocery stores to locate in poor neighborhoods.

The poor are also more likely than those in other socioeconomic groups to have limited access to recreational facilities such as safe playgrounds and sports fields that offer opportunities for exercise. Facing budgetary pressures, some schools in poor neighborhoods have cut important physical education programs. Good nutrition, healthy lifestyles, and healthy weight are privileges of class in ways we may not have imagined.

THINK IT THROUGH

▶ What kinds of social programs or policies might a sociologist design to address the prevalence of overweight and obesity in poor communities?

Very obese children have been observed to suffer health problems once believed to affect only older adults, including heart attacks and type 2 diabetes (CDC, 2012e). With the popularity of sedentary activities such as video games, participation in social media, and television viewing, society will likely see this problem increase.

Among the factors to which the rise in size has been attributed is that families in the United States eat more meals outside the home than in the past, and many of these meals are consumed at fast-food establishments. As well, the portions diners are offered in restaurants are growing because many ingredients have become very inexpensive. In *Fast Food Nation,* Eric Schlosser (2001) notes that "commodity prices have fallen so low that the fast food industry has greatly increased its portion sizes, without reducing profits, in order to attract customers" (p. 243), a point supported by mathematician and physicist Carson C. Chow, who argues that the obesity epidemic in the United States is an outcome of the overproduction of food since the 1970s (cited in Dreifus, 2012). Federal subsidies for food production favor meat and dairy, which soak up almost three-quarters of these funds. Just over 10% support the production of sugar, oils, starches, and alcohol, and less than a third of 1% support the growing of vegetables and fruits. These data show that the U.S. Congress has opted to subsidize the production of foods that contribute to obesity rather than those, including fruits and vegetables, recommended in the government's own nutrition guidelines (Rampell, 2010).

Physician and scientist Deborah A. Cohen (2014) argues in her book *A Big Fat Crisis* that "obesity is primarily the result of exposure to an obesogenic environment" (p. 191), and she points to three key components of that environment. First, she notes (consistent with Chow) that factors like agricultural advances have led to an abundance of cheap food. Second, she suggests that the availability of food, particularly junk food, has grown: More than 41% of retail stores, including hardware stores, furniture stores, and drugstores, offer food. Third, food advertising has vastly expanded. Cohen notes that grocery stores today earn more from companies paying for prime display locations than from consumers buying groceries.

Damage to health is not the only harmful effect of obesity. In 2010, a study found that, on average, the annual individual cost of being obese in the United States was $4,879 for women and $2,646 for men. Obese women were also more financially disadvantaged than were obese men and suffered 38% more job-related costs, such as absenteeism (Dor, Ferguson, Langwith, & Tan, 2010).

Clearly, obesity is a complex phenomenon driven by a variety of factors—biological, genetic, environmental, social, and economic. As you will see below, poverty is also an important factor in the prevalence of obesity. From a sociological perspective, we consider the connection between the *personal trouble* and the *public issue* of obesity and overweight. That is, if one individual or a handful in a community are obese, that may be a personal trouble, attributable to genetics, illness, eating habits, or any other set of factors. However, when more than one-third of the U.S. population is obese (Ogden, Carroll, Kit, & Flegal, 2012), including majorities in some communities, this is a public issue and one that, to paraphrase C. Wright Mills, we may not hope to explain by focusing just on individual cases. Rather, we need to seek out its sociological roots.

Consider how this issue might look through the conflict lens. Who benefits, and who loses? While "losers" in this instance are surely those whose health is compromised by excessive weight, there are also macro-level effects such as lost productivity when employees miss work due to obesity-linked illnesses such as diabetes. In fact, the CDC has estimated that the medical care costs associated with obesity in the United States total about $147 billion annually (Finkelstein, Trogdon, Cohen, & Dietz, 2009).

Who benefits? The food industry, particularly fast-food companies, arguably benefit when consumers prioritize quantity over quality. By offering bigger portions (which cost only a bit more to provide), restaurants draw bigger crowds and bigger profits The $60 billion weight-loss industry (Clark, 2011; Marketdata Enterprises, 2011) also benefits, since the rise in obesity exists in the presence of widespread societal obsession with thinness. Often, the same companies that market high-fat, unhealthy foods also peddle "lite" versions (Lemonnier, 2008).

TEEN PREGNANCY

About 750,000 teenage girls become pregnant in the United States each year, and an estimated 444,690 give birth (Kost & Henshaw, 2012). Most of the young mothers (about 81%) are unmarried when they give birth (Henshaw, 2002; Turner, 2003). Figure 16.6 shows changes in the birthrate among teens across recent decades.

FIGURE 16.6 Birthrates for Teens of Different Races Ages 15–19 in the United States, 1993–2012

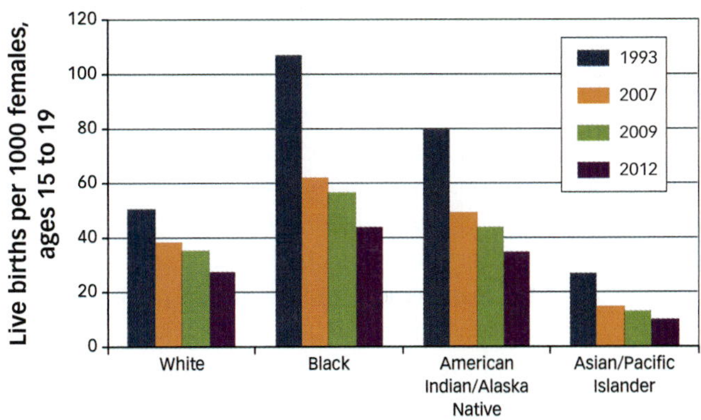

SOURCE: Data from Martin, J.A., Hamilton, B.E., Osterman, M.J.K., Curtin, S.C., & Mathews, T.J. (2013). "Births: Final Data for 2012." *National Vital Statistics Reports,* Vol. 62, No.

CQR Teen Sex and Pregnancy

Pregnancy and births among teenagers are public health issues because young women who conceive or give birth before their bodies are fully developed put themselves and their babies at risk. Compared to older mothers, teen mothers have worse health, more pregnancy complications, and more stillborn, low-weight, or medically fragile infants. But teen pregnancy and birth are of more than medical concern. They are also associated with another public health problem: poverty.

Giving birth early and outside marriage compounds the risk that young women and their children will become or remain poor; about 34% of all female-headed households in the United States live below the poverty line, compared with about 7% of married-couple families (DeNavas-Walt, Proctor, & Smith, 2012). Parenthood is a leading cause of dropping out of school among teenage women; teen mothers are at greater risk than their peers of not completing high school—only about 40% of women who become mothers before the age of 18 earn a high school diploma, and fewer than 2% earn a college degree by age 30 (National Campaign to Prevent Teen Pregnancy, 2010).

The relationship between teen pregnancy and birth and poverty is complicated. On one hand, as noted, early and unwed motherhood compounds the risk of poverty. On the other hand, poverty is itself a risk factor for teenage motherhood: An estimated 80% of teen mothers grew up in low-income households (Shore & Shore, 2009), and poor teens have a higher incidence of early sexual activity, pregnancy, and birth than their better-off peers (National Campaign to Prevent Teen Pregnancy, 2010).

In her book *Dubious Conceptions: The Politics of Teenage Pregnancy* (1996), sociologist Kristin Luker suggests that poverty is a *cause* as well as a *consequence* of teen pregnancy and birth. She argues that poor young women's probability of early motherhood is powerfully affected by "disadvantage and discouragement" (p. 111). By *disadvantage* she means the social effects of poverty, which reduce opportunities for a solid education and the realization of professional aspirations. Consider, for instance, a high school senior from an affluent household: She may spend her 18th year contemplating whether to begin college immediately or take a year off for travel abroad. A young woman who hails from a poor household in rural Louisiana or the Bronx's depressed Mott Haven neighborhood may have received an inferior education in her underfunded school, and, having little money, has no hope for college. Travel beyond her own state or even city is unthinkable. Local jobs in the service industry are an option, as is motherhood. *Discouragement,* according to Luker, is the effect of poverty that may prevent poor young women from exercising agency in confronting obstacles. In an impoverished situation, the opportunity costs of early motherhood—that is, the educational or other opportunities lost—may seem relatively low.

Notably, a study by Kathryn Edin and Maria Kefalas (2005) found that many poor young women embrace early motherhood

Tina Stallard / Contributor/Getty Images

Early parenthood is a leading reason that teen women drop out of school. About a third cite this reason for leaving high school. Staying in school, however, is key to job prospects that enable families to stay out of poverty. What might schools do to encourage young mothers to graduate?

as an honorable and even desirable choice. Some of the women the researchers interviewed also saw it as something that "saved" them from trouble with drugs or the law and "matured" them. Most of the women Edin and Kefalas interviewed expressed a desire to marry and embark on a career in the future. At the same time, discouraged by what they perceived as a limited pool of stable partners, whose marriageability was compromised by poor employment prospects and problems such as alcohol and drug use, the women did not put marriage ahead of motherhood, though many retained hopes for marriage at a point when they felt financially independent. In neighborhoods where early motherhood was the norm, many expressed a preference to have their children while young, a preference shared by the young men with whom they had relationships. While few of these young women's pregnancies were planned, many couples took no steps to avoid pregnancy.

Though rates of teen motherhood remain higher in the United States than in many other economically advanced countries, they have declined in some groups. Among other factors, the use of condoms has increased markedly (U.S. Department of Health and Human Services, 2013), perhaps due to a desire to protect against both pregnancy and sexually transmitted infections. There have also been small drops in the numbers of teenagers approving of and engaging in premarital sexual activity, and the rate of births among teenage women has dropped compared to the rate in earlier decades (Ventura & Hamilton, 2011).

Teen pregnancies and births are *social facts,* or phenomena that, as Émile Durkheim put it, we can explain only by using other social facts. That is, to understand sociologically both the rise and the fall of the rates of teen pregnancies and births, we must recognize that these are not just "personal troubles" or individual issues, but that they are fundamentally tied to other economic, social, and cultural issues in society.

DEVELOPING A SOCIOLOGY OF HIV/AIDS

The case of acquired immunodeficiency syndrome (AIDS) and the virus that causes it, human immunodeficiency virus (HIV), is another example of the importance of understanding the social construction of illness. Perceptions of HIV/AIDS and those who contract HIV have varied across time, depending on who the most visible victims have been. As well, the infection—which is a global pandemic—demands a sociological approach because it is closely intertwined with a host of sociological issues, including gender inequality, poverty, violence and conflict, and the pursuit of both medical breakthroughs and profits in a globalizing world.

It is estimated that more than 1 million persons in the United States have HIV/AIDS. Of these, about 236,000, or 1 in 5 (about 20%), have not been diagnosed and likely do not know they are infected (CDC, 2011b).

GENDER AND HIV/AIDS

We can better understand the spread of sexually transmitted diseases, including HIV/AIDS, if we examine how these diseases are related to gender and inequality. Globally, the number of women with HIV/AIDS has risen: Fully half of new infections are now diagnosed among women. In some regions, women's infection rates outpace men's: In sub-Saharan Africa, of the 22.5 million people living with AIDS, 60% are women (UNAIDS, 2010b).

Norms and traditions in many regions reinforce women's lower status in society. In some traditional communities in Africa, for example, it is socially acceptable—or even desirable—for men to have multiple sexual partners both before and after marriage. In this case, marriage itself becomes a risk factor for women. Many women also still lack accurate knowledge regarding sexually transmitted diseases, a problem made more acute by widespread female illiteracy in poor regions. Women who are uninfected may not know how to protect themselves, and women who are infected may not know how to protect their partners.

Gender stereotypes and vulnerability to HIV/AIDS are also pertinent. In a *New York Times Magazine* article examining the phenomenon of Black men who present themselves to the outside world as heterosexual but engage in homosexual activity "on the down low," Benoit Denizet-Lewis (2003) writes about a culture of Black masculinity in which Black male bisexuality and homosexuality are little discussed and little accepted. Hence, Black males who want to have sexual relationships with males are often compelled to put on a facade for their families and society. In the words of one man on the down low, "If you're white, you can come out as an openly gay skier or actor or whatever. It might hurt you some, but it's not like if you're black and gay, because it's like you've let down the whole black community, black women, black history, black pride" (quoted in Denizet-Lewis, 2003). An important consequence is that some men who are having sex with other men are also having sex with women—wives and girlfriends. Notably, CDC (2010a) data show that Blacks made up about half of those found to have HIV in 2008, but only about three in five had ever been tested for HIV. This suggests that many men who are HIV-positive are likely unaware of their status, which puts them, as well as their partners, whether male or female, at risk.

FIGURE 16.7 Estimated New HIV Infections in the United States by Subpopulation, 2010

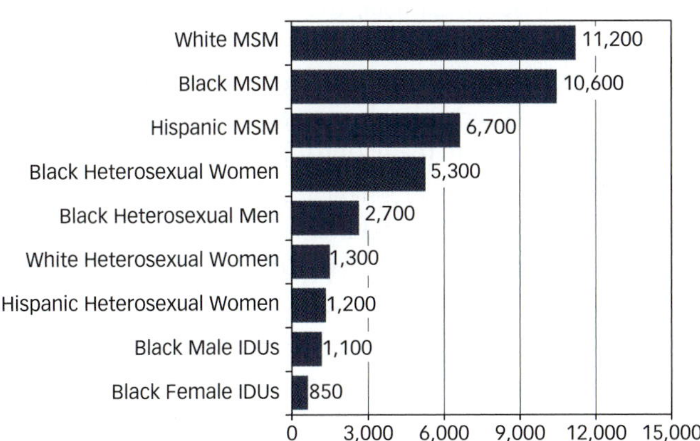

NOTE: MSM stands for "Men who have sex with men." IDU stands for "Injecting drug use."

SOURCE: The Kaiser Family Foundation. (2009). Estimated Numbers of Persons Living with an AIDS Diagnoses, All Ages, by Race/Ethnicity, 2009. *Statehealthfacts.org*

FIGURE 16.8 HIV/AIDS Prevalence by Race and Ethnicity in the United States, 2009

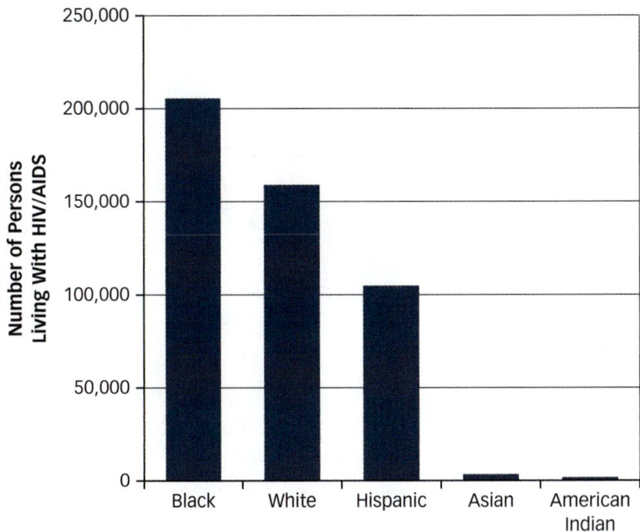

SOURCE: Centers for Disease Control and Prevention.

FIGURE 16.9 HIV/AIDS Prevalence Worldwide, 2010

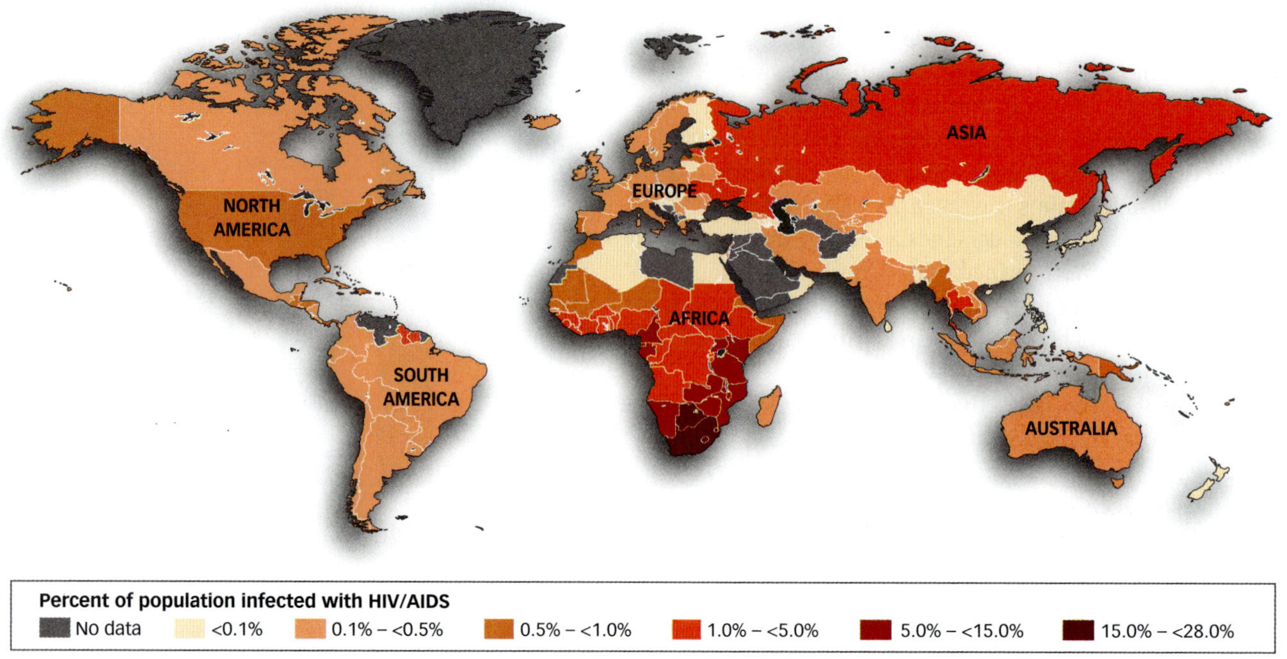

SOURCE: Data from UNAIDS. (2010). HIV Prevalence Map. *United Nations Programme on HIV/AIDS Global Report 2010*.

POVERTY AND HIV/AIDS

Across the globe, there is a powerful relationship between the risk of HIV/AIDS and poverty. China, for instance, has experienced a rise in new cases in the past decade. A serious epidemic was detected in central China's Henan Province, where tens of thousands of rural villagers have been infected in the past decade through selling their blood for money under unsafe and unsterile conditions. In China as a whole, it is estimated that at the end of 2005 there were 55,000 commercial blood and plasma donors infected with HIV ("AIDS in China," 2007). In developing countries, economic insecurity and the lack of gainful employment sometimes drive workers (particularly men) to seek work far from home. For example, migrant workers from surrounding countries toil in the mines of South Africa. Away from their families and communities, some of these men seek out the services of prostitutes, who may be infected (UNAIDS, 2010b).

The sex workers themselves are often victims of dire and desperate economic circumstances. Women in the sex trade, some of whom have been trafficked and enslaved, are highly vulnerable to HIV/AIDS. They have little protection from robbery or rape and limited power to negotiate safe sex with paying customers, though some countries, such as Thailand, have sought to empower sex workers to demand condom use (UNAIDS, UNFPA, & UNIFEM, 2004).

Poor states, as well as poor individuals, are vulnerable to the ravages of disease. Consider the cases of many southern African states: HIV prevalence among adults ages 15–49 is about 25% in Botswana, 23% in Lesotho, and 13% in Zimbabwe (Lesotho, 2012; Republic of Botswana, 2012; Zimbabwe, 2012). The high rates of infection and death among young and middle-aged adults also mean that countries are left with diminished workforces. Without productive citizens, the state of a country's economy declines, further reducing the resources that might be put into HIV/AIDS prevention or treatment. Even those who are training the next generation of workers have been hard-hit by the disease: In Zambia, the number of teachers dying of AIDS outpaces the number graduating as teachers (Oyoo, 2003). While HIV/AIDS is far from limited to poor victims or poor countries, poverty clearly increases the risk of disease at both the individual and the national level.

VIOLENCE AND HIV/AIDS

Women's risk of contracting HIV/AIDS is increased by situations of domestic violence. Data gathered by the United Nations suggest that up to half the women in the world may experience violence from a domestic partner at some point; this includes forced sex, which is not likely to take place with a condom (UNAIDS et al., 2004).

The rape of men by other males, not uncommon in prison settings, can also be implicated in the spread of the infection. In many countries, the incidence of HIV/AIDS in prisons is significantly higher than the incidence of the disease in the noninstitutionalized population. Part of this phenomenon is

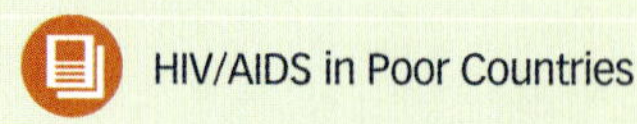
HIV/AIDS in Poor Countries

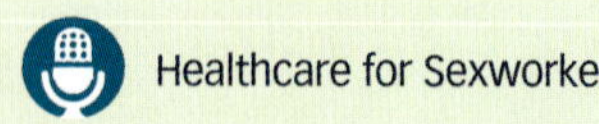
Healthcare for Sexworkers

© Marco Baroncini/Corbis

Much progress has been made in developing medicine that helps keep HIV/AIDS under control and maintains one's quality of life, and even better advancements have been made in prevention, awareness, and education on how to avoid contracting HIV. Nevertheless, it continues to be a global epidemic that claims millions of lives. In this photo, a woman infected with HIV who has been ostracized from her village sits outside her small hut.

linked to the sharing of needles among drug-injecting prisoners or to consensual male sexual activity, but part is also linked to the underreported sexual violence behind bars.

HIV/AIDS is a medical issue. It is also a sociological issue. Vulnerability to infection is compounded by factors such as gender stereotypes and poverty. At a time when hope of new treatments and prevention strategies has materialized but the pandemic continues to ravage communities and countries, a sociological perspective can help us to identify the social roots of HIV/AIDS and to seek the most fruitful paths for combating its spread.

GLOBAL ISSUES IN HEALTH AND MEDICINE

Ever since human beings first began to migrate from their African origins, taking their illnesses with them, the spread of disease has known no global boundaries. Plagues and epidemics have traveled from populations that have developed some degree of biological immunity to others that have not. During the 14th century, the bubonic plague, known as the Black Death, arrived in Europe by way of Asia and eliminated a third of the European population in only 20 years. The European conquerors of the Americas brought syphilis and other diseases with them that virtually eliminated the indigenous population in many areas (Thornton, 1987).

U.S. soldiers returning from Europe at the end of World War I carried previously unknown influenza strains that killed an estimated 20 million people worldwide. Today, tuberculosis, once all but eliminated from the industrialized nations, is making a comeback, with new treatment-resistant strains brought by immigrants from poor nations.

Global Disparities in Heart Health

In 2010, the United States publicly apologized to the nation of Guatemala when it was discovered that in the 1940s, U.S. government researchers deliberately infected hundreds of Guatemalan mental patients with gonorrhea and syphilis for observational purposes and encouraged them to transfer their infections to others (Bazell, 2010). Such unethical experiments endanger larger populations by introducing diseases that can erupt in outbreaks.

Overall, however, the 20th century witnessed a striking global triumph over many diseases, as sanitation, clean water, sewage systems, knowledge about the importance of diet, and other public health and medical practices and treatments spread throughout the world. For example, in only a few years, the WHO's plan for "Health for All by the Year 2000" succeeded in immunizing half the world's children against measles, polio, and four other diseases (Steinbrook, 1988). Successes have continued into the 21st century. In 2004, the Bill and Melinda Gates Foundation, working with the Global Alliance for Vaccines and Immunization, was able to vaccinate an estimated 78% of children in the world against diphtheria, tetanus, and whooping cough (Bill and Melinda Gates Foundation, 2006). Today, the Bill and Melinda Gates Foundation (2013) reports that it is 99% of the way toward eradicating polio and that a new vaccine will save the lives of an additional 400,000 children per year on a global scale. Successes such as these have produced a sharp decline in death rates in most of the world's countries (Andre et al., 2008).

The AIDS epidemic is the most recent example of the global spread of a fatal disease. What makes it unique is the rapidity with which it spread around the world, to industrialized and less developed nations alike. HIV/AIDS is also a global issue in terms of treatment and prevention. Globalization is both functional and dysfunctional for real and potential victims of the infection. On one hand, HIV/AIDS was global in its path of spread, and it appears likely that its defeat will also be global, as it was for other once-deadly and widespread diseases such as smallpox, polio, and malaria (Steinbrook, 1988). There is a concerted global effort to combat the disease. Doctors across the globe work together to share information and knowledge on HIV/AIDS and their efforts to stop it. International organizations including the United Nations are also instrumental in leading information and empowerment campaigns.

On the other hand, globalization has thrown obstacles in the path of those who seek to expand the reach of therapeutic drugs that lengthen health and life for those with the infection. The global market in HIV/AIDS treatment has been dominated by Western pharmaceutical companies, most of which have jealously guarded their patent rights on the drug therapies shown to be most effective for treatment. Their fierce desire to protect patents and profits has made it more difficult for drug makers in developing states to manufacture less expensive generic versions that could save more lives in poor countries.

Together with HIV/AIDS, one of the most threatening diseases in developing countries is malaria: According to some estimates, malaria is a threat to no less than half the global population. It kills more than 800,000 people every year. The most vulnerable populations are children and pregnant women in Africa, which has the most malaria deaths (CDC, 2012b).

The toll taken by malaria is felt at the individual, community, and national levels. For individual families, malaria is costly in terms of drugs, travel to clinics, lost time at work or school, and burial, among other expenses. For governments, malaria means the potential loss of tourism and productive members of society and the cost of public health interventions, including treatments and mosquito nets, which many individuals are unable to pay for themselves (CDC, 2012b). Malaria, together with HIV/AIDS and tuberculosis, has attracted a substantial proportion of available funding from international and national donors and governments seeking to improve the health of populations in the developing world.

Critics of international health spending priorities point to a growing threat in the developing world that has not received substantial funding or attention: chronic disease. Heart disease, stroke, and cancer have long been chronic maladies associated with the habits of the populations of developed countries, such as overeating, lack of exercise, and smoking. One scientist notes that while 80% of global deaths from chronic diseases take place in low- and middle-income countries, those illnesses receive the smallest fraction of donor assistance for health. Of the nearly $26 billion allocated for health in 2009, just 1% targeted chronic disease (Lomborg, 2012).

Chronic disease, however, is a growing threat in the developing world, driven by a dramatic rise in both obesity and smoking. According to the World Health Organization, global obesity rates doubled between 1980 and 2008. The WHO estimates that about half the adult populations of Brazil, Russia, and South Africa are overweight. In Africa, around 8% of adults are obese. While these figures are low compared to those in the United States, where two thirds of adults are estimated to be overweight and one third are obese, the numbers are rising. A variety of factors contribute to this phenomenon, including growing incomes in many parts of the developing world, which enable more consumption, economic changes that shift work from physical labor to indoor and sedentary labor, and the movement of fast-food restaurants into new regions where people can now afford to splurge on burgers and soda (Kenny, 2012).

While smoking has decreased in many developed countries in recent decades, it has grown dramatically in some parts of the developing world. Today, about 80% of smokers live in the developing world (Qian et al., 2010). By some estimates, China has 350 million smokers (which is more people than live in the United States), and about 60% of Chinese men smoke. Tobacco use has grown fourfold in China since the 1970s and has become a key component of the nation's growing prosperity. Cigarettes, and particularly expensive brands of cigarettes, are given as gifts to friends and family; red cigarettes are special presents for weddings, bringing "double happiness." China also has its own tobacco manufacturing industry, which is run by the government. This creates a conflict of interest, since the same entity that regulates tobacco and might be interested in promoting better public health is profiting from the large number of tobacco users (PBS, 2010). Since 2001, when China joined the World Trade Organization and its markets opened to new goods, Western cigarette makers have also been aggressively marketing their products there, targeting relatively untapped consumer categories such as women, who are otherwise less likely than men to smoke (Qian et al., 2010).

Growing income and improvements in the standards of living in developing countries represent important changes. For the most part, these changes are positive and include growing opportunities for education, health care, and access to technology, among others. At the same time, the chronic diseases long associated with the developed world threaten populations in new ways. Whether and how the international community, national governments, and local institutions react to these problems today will have an enormous impact on the health of populations in the decades to come.

WHY SHOULD SOCIOLOGISTS STUDY HEALTH?

Even as our medical and technological knowledge grows, threats to the goal of a healthy society and world continue to expand. In a globalizing world, no one is isolated from diseases spawned in distant places; we are all part of the same community, linked by communications, travel, and commerce. Neither are we isolated from the far-reaching consequences of health dangers that threaten to destabilize regions far from our own. In a world where the very poor exist together with the very wealthy and billions are seeking to scramble up the ladder of prosperity, the acute illnesses of poverty can be found alongside the chronic maladies of affluence. Sociology offers us the tools to examine the sociological antecedents of a spectrum of public health problems.

By using a sociological perspective, we can recognize the ways that medical issues such as HIV/AIDS intersect with social phenomena such as gender inequality, gender stereotypes, violence, and poverty. We can examine the global obesity epidemic through new eyes when we see that individuals' choices about food and fitness are made in social and economic environments that profoundly affect those choices. While medicine and technology clearly have an enormous amount to contribute to reducing the consequences of serious health issues, including HIV/AIDS, obesity, and tobacco-related illnesses, sociology too has a role to play in discovering the social roots of and imagining creative, constructive responses to health problems that threaten many lives and livelihoods.

The Most Dangerous Idea in Mental Health

WHAT CAN I DO WITH A SOCIOLOGY DEGREE?

SKILLS AND CAREERS: COMMUNITY RESOURCE AND SERVICE SKILLS

Community resource competencies link knowledge of nonprofit, government, and private community resources with the skills to access appropriate services and funding to best serve clients, organizations, and communities. Resources in communities take multiple forms, including individual donors, volunteers, politicians, business owners, religious leaders, schools, libraries and community centers, and public and private service agencies. *Service skills* may be developed through the study of and active participation in community organizations that engage with local populations and issues.

In this chapter, we discussed problems of public health, including the local and global challenge of HIV/AIDS. While public health and medical workers worldwide are doing a commendable job getting effective treatments to more people than ever, much remains to be done. In many communities, HIV/AIDS is stigmatized, and its carriers are regarded with suspicion. Reaching out to individuals and groups who may fear seeking help, or even being tested, for HIV/AIDS requires the services not only of medical personnel but also of those who have a deep cultural understanding of an affected community and the knowledge to link populations in need with resources that can help prevent and treat HIV/AIDS. As a sociology major you will develop important intercultural competencies and understandings of diversity. You will also learn important occupational skills such as the ability to gather and summarize data in order to characterize community needs effectively and develop the habits of mind to be resourceful in addressing problems in ways that take account of different perspectives. Many educational institutions offer opportunities for service learning or volunteering that enable students to become familiar with the particular needs and resources of their own communities.

Knowledge of community resources and practice in community service are assets in a variety of *occupational fields,* ranging from social work and counseling to organizational development, nonprofit management, and criminal justice. *Job titles* in these and related fields include family, school, and health care social worker; volunteer coordinator; psychologist; counselor; social or human service assistant; community resources specialist; city or regional planning aide; and vocational counselor in mental health or rehabilitation.

THINK ABOUT CAREERS

▶ What kinds of opportunities for community service are offered at your college or university? Take some time to research available options for volunteering or service learning, and consider how sharpening your skills and knowledge in this area might be of value to your career plan.

SUMMARY

- **Health** is to the degree to which a person experiences a generalized state of wellness, while **medicine** is an institutionalized approach to the prevention of illness. Although the two are clearly related, they are not the same thing.
- Notions of illness are socially constructed, as are the social roles that correspond to them. The sociological concept of the **sick role** is important to an understanding of societal expectations and perceptions of the ill individual.
- Not all forms of addiction are treated the same in society. Some, including alcoholism, are medicalized, while others, including drug use, are criminalized.
- The U.S. health care system does not serve all segments of the population equally. Good health and good **health care** are still often privileges of class and race.
- **Public health** issues such as smoking, obesity, and teen pregnancy can be examined through a sociological lens. The sociological imagination gives us the opportunity to see the relationship between private troubles (such as being addicted to tobacco, being obese, or becoming a teen mother) and public issues ranging from the relentless drive for profits in a capitalist country to the persistent poverty of generations.
- The global pandemic of HIV/AIDS demands a sociological approach as well as a medical approach. The mass spread of the infection is closely intertwined with sociological issues. Gender inequality makes women vulnerable to infection. Poverty renders both individuals and countries more vulnerable to the disease. Violence and war are pathways for the spread of HIV/AIDS.
- Rising standards of living in many parts of the developing world have had many positive effects, but the accompanying sedentary lifestyles and access to fast food and tobacco have also contributed to an increase in chronic diseases associated with obesity and smoking.

KEY TERMS

health, 409
medicine, 409
preventive medicine, 409
sick roles, 410
health care, 412
public health, 418
morbidity, 418
mortality, 418

DISCUSSION QUESTIONS

1. What is the sick role as defined by sociologist Erving Goffman? What are our expectations of the ill in contemporary U.S. society? Do the responsibilities of the sick role vary by community or culture?
2. The chapter discussed the argument that some addictions are "medicalized" while others are "criminalized." What is the difference? How might we explain why different addictions are labeled and approached in varying ways?
3. African Americans and Latinos in the United States experience worse health and higher mortality rates than their White and Asian American counterparts. What sociological factors help to explain this health gap?
4. The chapter looked at cigarettes and smoking through a sociological lens. Recall how we applied the functionalist and conflict perspectives to this topic, and try applying those perspectives to junk food, such as soda, candy, and fast food.
5. How is HIV/AIDS a sociological issue as well as a medical one? What are key sociological roots of the spread of this disease in communities and countries?

Sharpen your skills with SAGE edge at **edge.sagepub.com/chambliss2e**

A personalized approach to help you accomplish your coursework goals in an easy-to-use learning environment.

POPULATION, URBANIZATION, AND THE ENVIRONMENT

IN THIS CHAPTER

WHAT DO YOU THINK?

1. Should we be concerned about global population growth? What are the costs and benefits of a growing global population?
2. Who should bear the costs of the safe and environmentally sound disposal of the electronic waste generated by the manufacture and use of the gadgets that pervade our lives today?
3. Are the goals of a sustainable environment and a growing economy irreconcilable? Can we have both?

Narinder Nanu/Stringer/Getty Images

DEMOGRAPHIC DILEMMA: WHERE ARE THE GIRLS?

Millions of women are missing from our planet. According to the United Nations Population Fund (UNFPA; 2007), "One of the most alarming changes in Asia's population dynamics in recent decades has been a dramatic increase in the proportion of males within its local populations. . . . if the continent's overall sex ratio was the same as elsewhere in the world, in 2005 Asia's population would have included almost 163 million more women and girls." Where did they go? How could so many girls and women go missing? What are the sociological roots of this dramatic loss?

The missing girls are the result of systematic gender discrimination manifested as a preference for sons. Globally, the natural ratio of male births to female births varies from 104:100 to 106:100. In some Asian countries, however, male births dramatically outpace female births. In China there were 118 male births for every 100 female births in 2011; in Anhui Province the ratio of boys to girls was a dramatic 129:100 in 2010. In Vietnam the ratio is about 111:100, and in India the national ratio is 110:100, though individual states, such as Punjab, record higher figures—in 2008 to 2010, the male-to-female birth ratio in Punjab was 120:100 (UNFPA, 2012, pp. 19–20).

In all three countries—China, Vietnam, and India—there has been widespread use of prenatal sex selection: That is, parents learn the sex of their fetus prior to birth and are more likely to opt for an abortion if it is female, particularly if the family already has a girl child (UNFPA, 2012). While sex-selective abortion is illegal in all three countries, enforcement of the prohibition has been difficult and often lax. Since the skewed sex ratio was first documented beginning around the early 1980s, the numbers have balanced out in several of India's states, thanks in part to central and state government intervention, including implementation of policies to enforce the ban on sex-selective abortions, and initiatives that raise awareness and educate Indian families about problems related to the sex ratio imbalance (UNFPA, 2007).

Reasons for son preference are complex. In India, the preference is driven by a widespread belief that boys have greater economic, social, and religious value for the family. Where a bride's parents are required to pay dowry to the groom's family, the costs to a poor (or even middle-class) family can be great; consequently, girls are often seen as economic liabilities (Mutharayappa, Choe, Arnold, & Roy, 1997; Seager, 2003). Even among families who can afford dowries for their daughters (and, paradoxically, dowry sizes have decreased as brides have become more scarce), boys are more highly valued because they pass on the family line, provide old-age security to parents, and are responsible for fulfilling religious traditions such as lighting the pyres at parents' funerals (International Development Research Centre, n.d.; Mutharayappa et al., 1997).

Interestingly, sex selection is more prevalent among affluent urban dwellers in India than among their rural counterparts, though traditional norms are more likely to be associated with the latter. It is significant that members of the urban population are likely to have greater access to medical technologies such as prenatal sex screening. As well, they are likely to want and have fewer children than do rural dwellers, so the perceived urgency of having a son in the first two or three births is more acute (Hvistendahl, 2011).

Son preference has important sociological causes and effects on both micro and macro levels. Personal decisions based on economic factors as well as societal and cultural norms are made in individual families, but they have macro-level consequences. Guilmoto (2011) hypothesizes a coming "marriage squeeze" in China and India. He estimates that between 2020 and 2055, unmarried men will outnumber unmarried women in China by as much as 60%, and in India unmarried men will outnumber unmarried women by a similar proportion between 2040 and 2060. The men most likely to be pushed out of the marriage market are the poorest and least educated. An analysis of the Chinese case by Edlund, Hongbin, Junjian, and Junsen (2007) identifies a correlation between the rising imbalance in the sex ratio and the incidence of crimes, including, but not limited to, rape, bride abduction, sex trafficking, and prostitution; the researchers conclude that about one seventh of the rise in crime over 20 years of the increasingly skewed sex ratio could be explained by the phenomenon.

To understand phenomena such as rapid or slow population growth, sex ratios that favor males over females, and rising or falling fertility among women, we must take a sociological perspective that melds private lives and public issues. ■

Demography: The science of population size, distribution, and composition.

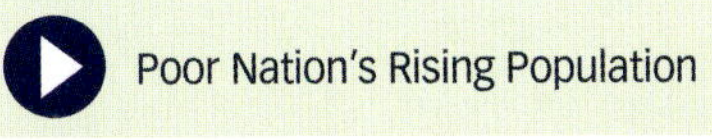
Poor Nation's Rising Population

In this chapter we explore demography, a subfield of sociology. **Demography** is the *science of population size, distribution, and composition* (Keyfitz, 1993). First, we discuss issues of global population growth and look at the debate on rising population. We also examine issues of urbanization and the growth of megacities around the world. Finally, we turn to the global environment and address some of the ways in which the dual pressures of population growth and urbanization are affecting our planet.

While the three key topics addressed in this chapter are diverse, they share an important common thread: As we noted in the introductory discussion of son preference, *individual choices add up to phenomena that can have powerful wider impacts.* Any individual family may exercise a preference for a son or for seven children rather than one, just as any individual family may opt to move to a city to seek better economic fortune or may decide to buy a large sport utility vehicle rather than a fuel-efficient automobile. What appears at the micro level as an individual decision with direct effects only on a particular family can add up to macro-level phenomena with national or global effects and consequences.

GLOBAL POPULATION GROWTH

The world's population is growing at a rapid rate, expanding as much since 1950 as it did in the preceding 4 million years.

Reuters/Rafiquar Rahman

Dhaka, the capital of Bangladesh, is one of Asia's rapidly growing cities. While urbanization is a key characteristic of modernity, it also brings new health, cultural, political, and economic challenges. ■

FIGURE 17.1 Estimated World Population Growth, 1950–2100

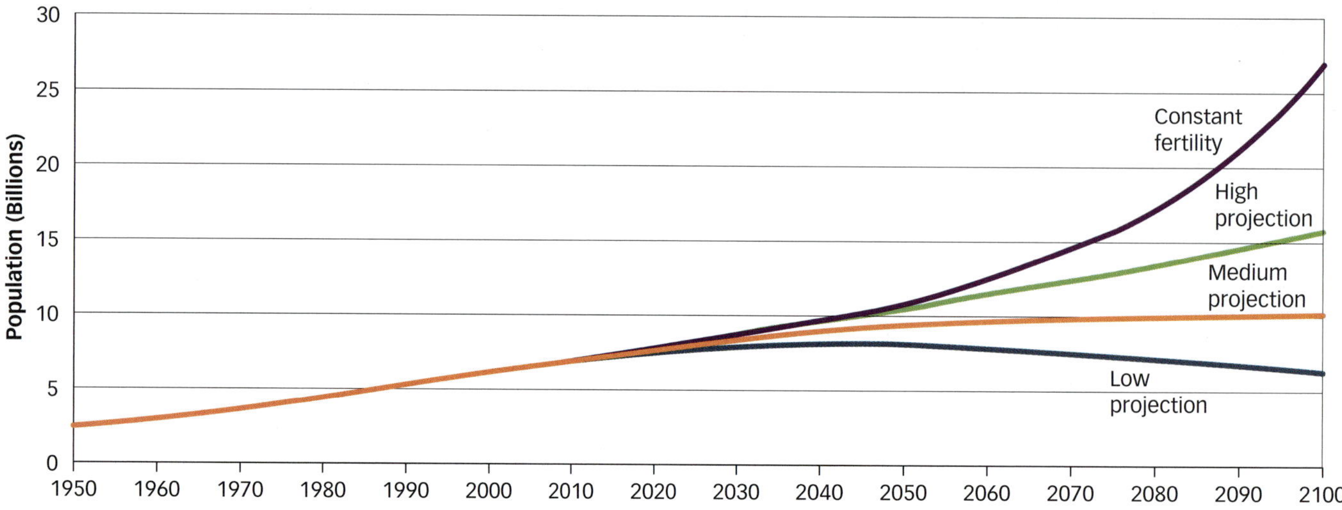

SOURCE: United Nations, Department of Economic and Social Affairs, Population Division. (2011). *World population prospects: The 2010 revision, highlights and advance tables* (Working Paper ESA/P/WP.220). New York: Author.

By 1850, global population reached 1 billion; by 1950, it was 2.3 billion. As of 2012, it had reached more than 7 billion (Figure 17.1).

Population growth is highly uneven around the world, with the greatest expansion taking place in developing countries. Consider that about half of the increase in global population between 2010 and 2050 is projected to take place in just nine countries, all but one of which are in the developing world: India, Pakistan, Nigeria, Ethiopia, the United States, the Democratic Republic of Congo, Tanzania, China, and Bangladesh. In the United States, most population growth will take place as a result of immigration; elsewhere, it will be the product of *natural population increase*—that is, it will result from births outpacing deaths.

While the global total fertility rate (TFR)—the *average number of births per woman,* as noted in Chapter 8—was 2.4 in 2012, TFR differed substantially across countries and regions. In reporting TFR, the Population Reference Bureau distinguishes among "more developed countries," "less developed countries," and "least developed countries." In the more developed countries in 2013, the TFR was 1.6, in less developed countries it was 2.6 (3.0 when China is excluded), and in the least developed countries it was 4.4 (Population Reference Bureau, 2013, p. 7; Table 17.1). *Replacement rate fertility*—that is, the rate at which two parents are just replacing themselves—is represented by a TFR of 2.1 (with an allowance of risk for mortality in the fraction above 2.0). Below this rate, populations decline; above it, they grow.

Central Africa, which comprises mainly less developed and least developed countries, is the fastest-growing region in the world. Its population is expected to grow 129% between 2010 and 2050, whereas South America's population is estimated to rise 23% in the same period, and Western Europe's will grow by only 0.5%. Other regions will lose population, including Eastern Europe, where the population is expected to decrease 14% by 2050, due in large part to below-replacement-level fertility rates (Population Reference Bureau, 2010; Table 17.2).

China and India, the world's most populous countries, present interesting cases for a discussion of population

TABLE 17.1 Total Fertility Rates for Selected Countries, 2013

Country	Total Fertility Rate
Germany	1.4
South Korea	1.3
China	1.5
Russia	1.6
United States	1.9
Iran	1.9
Brazil	1.8
Mexico	2.2
South Africa	2.4
India	2.4
Pakistan	3.8
Niger	7.6

SOURCE: Population Reference Bureau (2013). *2013 world population data sheet.* Washington, DC: Author. Retrieved from http://www.prb.org/pdf13/2013-population-data-sheet_eng.pdf.

■ **TABLE 17.2** **Projected Population Growth for Global Regions, 2025 and 2050**

Region	Current Population (millions)	2025 Projected Population (millions)	2050 Projected Population (millions)	Rate of Natural Increase (%)
World	**7,058**	**8,082**	**9,624**	**1.2**
Sub-Saharan Africa	902	1,245	2,092	2.6
Northern Africa	213	263	346	2.0
Western Africa	324	450	774	2.7
Eastern Africa	342	477	799	2.7
Middle Africa	134	193	352	2.6
Southern Africa	59	63	68	1.0
Northern America	349	391	471	0.5
Central America	160	185	212	1.6
Caribbean	42	46	49	1.1
South America	397	441	479	1.2
Western Asia	244	303	403	1.9
South Central Asia	1,823	2,145	2,565	1.6
Southeast Asia	608	696	801	1.2
East Asia	1,585	1,635	1,516	0.4
Northern Europe	101	111	122	0.3
Western Europe	190	194	194	0.1
Eastern Europe	295	287	259	–0.2
Southern Europe	154	158	157	0.0
Oceania	37	44	57	1.1

SOURCE: Population Reference Bureau. (2012). *2012 world population data sheet.* Washington, DC: Author. Retrieved from http://www.prb.org/pdf12/2012-population-data-sheet_eng.pdf.

growth. China and India both have more than 1 billion inhabitants and high **population momentum**, which is *the tendency of population growth to continue beyond the point when replacement rate fertility has been achieved because of the high concentration of people of childbearing age.* China has sought to check its population growth with a one-child policy, which has slowed its rate of growth and put its total fertility rate below replacement rate (1.5). India's population growth has also declined markedly over time (today the TFR is 2.4), but the nation's population momentum remains high (Population Reference Bureau, 2013).

Population momentum: The tendency of population growth to continue beyond the point when replacement rate fertility has been achieved because of the high concentration of people of childbearing age.

CQR One Child Per Family Policies

To the east of China is Japan, which, like its close neighbor Russia and distant neighbors in Eastern and Western Europe, is also experiencing population decline: It has a TFR of 1.6 and is expected to see a 25% population drop (unless, of course, the difference is made up by increased immigration). Russia, currently one of the world's most populous countries, has a TFR of 1.6 and is also expected to lose population by midcentury (Central Intelligence Agency, 2012).

While some developing countries struggle with rapid population growth because it puts a strain on basic services like sanitation and education, as well as on the conservation of natural resources, many modern industrialized countries are lamenting a "birth dearth" that leaves aging populations dependent for their social welfare (in the form of public retirement benefits, for instance) on the financial contributions of fewer young workers.

Reuters/Sebastien Pirlet

Imagine a pond with a single waterlily that doubles in size each day and covers the entire pond in 30 days. On what day does it cover just half the pond? The answer gives us a way of thinking about how population momentum drives rising population sizes, even given a constant growth rate. The answer can be found at the end of the chapter on page 459. (Edward O. Wilson, "Is Humanity Suicidal? *New York Times Magazine*, May 30, 1993.)

DEMOGRAPHY AND DEMOGRAPHIC ANALYSIS

Demographers have developed statistical techniques for predicting future population levels on the basis of current characteristics. Annual population growth or decline in a country is the result of four factors: (1) the number of people born in the country during the year, (2) the number who die, (3) the number who immigrate into the country, and (4) the number who emigrate out. In the language of demographers, population changes are based on **fertility**, or *live births*; mortality, or *deaths*; and **net migration**, which is *in-migration minus out-migration.*

Let's look at fertility first. Demographers estimate future fertility on the basis of past fertility patterns of women of childbearing age. Although it is possible to make a rough estimate of population growth on the basis of **crude birthrate**—*the number of births each year per 1,000 women*—a far more accurate measure is **age-specific fertility rate**, or *the number of births typical for women of a specific age in a particular population.* Demographers divide women into 5-year cohorts—for example, women ages 15 to 19, 20 to 24, 25 to 29, and so on. If the current average number of live births per 1,000 women is known for each of these age groups, it is relatively easy to project future fertility. Five years from now, for example, today's 15- to 19-year-old women will be 20 to 24, which means that the fertility rates of today's 20- to 24-year-old women can be applied to them. In this way, each successive cohort of women can be "aged" at 5-year intervals, and the result is an estimate of total live births. Since fertility rates in most cultures peak during women's late teens and 20s, the largest number of babies will be born to women in these age groups; thereafter, as the cohort ages into the 30s and 40s, the total number of babies born to the group will decline, dropping to zero as the cohort ages out of childbearing altogether.

The second source of population change is mortality. Again, although **crude death rate**—the *number of deaths each year per 1,000 people*—yields a rough measure, demographers prefer to rely on **age-specific mortality rate**, or *an estimate of the number of deaths typical in men and women of specific ages in a particular population.* Like age-specific fertility rates, these rates are then applied to successive cohorts of men and women as they age. As you might guess, female mortality rates also affect the number of babies born, since as a cohort of females ages, some of its members will die, leaving fewer women of childbearing age. While in industrialized regions such as Western Europe most women live well beyond their childbearing years, female mortality rates in younger cohorts may have notable effects on birthrates in regions such as sub-Saharan Africa, where AIDS kills many such women.

One measure of the overall mortality of a society is its **life expectancy**, the *average number of years a newborn is expected to live based on existing health conditions in the country.* In almost all societies, the life expectancy at birth is higher for females than for males. In the United States, for example, in 2010 the average life expectancy for females was 80 years, while for males it was 75. In some countries of Eastern Europe, the gap between male and female life expectancy is as much as 12 years (Population Reference Bureau, 2010). Some of this gap is attributable to the fact that males are more likely than females to die in early childhood, to die from accidents or violence in young adulthood, and to experience early death from poor health in middle to later life.

Life expectancy in general varies enormously among countries of the world (Table 17.3). Japan ranks highest among all countries in terms of life expectancy (83 years), while the African country of Swaziland ranks very low, with a life expectancy at birth of just 48 years (Swaziland has an HIV/AIDS prevalence rate [among adults aged 15–49] of 26%; Population Reference Bureau, 2011, 2012).

Fertility: The number of live births in a given population.

Net migration: In-migration minus out-migration.

Crude birthrate: The number of births each year per 1,000 women.

Age-specific fertility rate: The number of births typical for women of a specific age in a particular population.

Crude death rate: The number of deaths each year per 1,000 people.

Age-specific mortality rate: The number of deaths typical in men and women of specific ages in a particular population.

Life expectancy: The average number of years a newborn is expected to live based on existing health conditions in the country.

TABLE 17.3 Life Expectancy at Birth for Selected Countries, 2013

Country	Life Expectancy at Birth
South Africa	58
Niger	57
India	66
Pakistan	66
Russia	70
Iran	73
Brazil	74
China	75
Mexico	77
United States	79
Germany	80
South Korea	81

SOURCE: Population Reference Bureau. (2013). *2013 world population data sheet*. Washington, DC: Author. Retrieved from http://www.prb.org/pdf13/2013-population-data-sheet_eng.pdf.

It is difficult to make predictions about population growth with precision because such predictions depend on assumptions about human behavior. If a government is effective in implementing family planning programs, for example, the fertility of the population may differ substantially after a decade or two. An unforeseen epidemic (on a scale such as that of AIDS) may greatly increase mortality; conversely, the development of new drugs (such as new antibiotics or a cure for AIDS) could greatly reduce it. For this reason, demographers typically offer a range of estimates of future populations: a low estimate that assumes high mortality and low fertility; a high estimate that assumes low mortality and high fertility; and an intermediate estimate that represents an informed figure somewhere in between.

Population forecasting also depends on fertility, but, again, momentum is critical. In 1979, China decided to limit fertility by rewarding one-child families with additional income and preferential treatment in terms of jobs, housing, health care, and education, while threatening punishment for those who refused to keep their families small. This policy reduced China's TFR to 1.5. Yet this reduction does not mean China's population will decline markedly from the 1.35 billion people it reached in 2012. With about 18% of its population under the age of 15—nearing childbearing years—China has a substantial amount of population momentum. According to the Population Reference Bureau (2012), its population will grow to about 1.4 billion in 2025 before likely falling to 1.31 billion by 2050.

Demography of Poverty and Migration

THEORY OF THE FIRST DEMOGRAPHIC TRANSITION

Extrapolating from the Western model of population change, demographers have argued that many societies go through roughly the same stages of population transition. They suggest that societies begin with an extended stage of low or no growth resulting from high fertility and equally high mortality, pass through a transitional stage of explosive growth resulting from high fertility and low mortality, and end up in a final stage of slow or no growth resulting from low fertility and low mortality (Figure 17.2). This perspective on population change is called the *theory of the first demographic transition*. We outline this transition in more detail below.

Early agricultural societies had high fertility and mortality rates that generally counterbalanced one another. Consequently, the population was either stable or grew very slowly. Crude death rates as high as 50 per 1,000 were caused by harsh living conditions, unstable food supplies, poor medical care, and lack of disease control. Epidemics, famines, and wars produced high rates of death, periodically reducing the population even more dramatically. Such societies had to develop strong norms and institutions in support of high fertility to prevent a decline in population. Children were valued for a variety of cultural and economic reasons, particularly where they made contributions to hunting, farming, herding, weaving, and the other work necessary in a household-based economy (Simon, 1981).

As societies modernized (that is, became more urban and industrial), their birthrates initially remained high. At the same time, mortality rates plummeted due to improved food supplies brought about by growing trade links, sanitation control that accompanied greater public health knowledge and prosperity, and, eventually, modern medicine. Consider, for

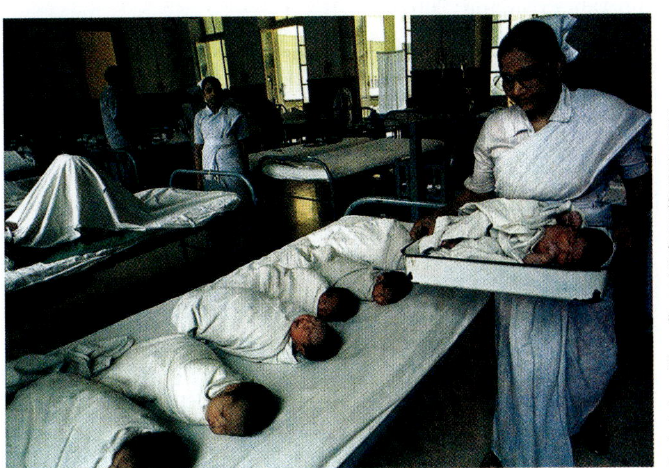

Deshakalyan Chowdhury / Stringer/Getty Images

About a third of India's 1.27 billion people are under 15, representing momentum for future population growth, even if family planning leads to smaller cohorts in the future. But son preference skews sex ratios at birth in some regions, which may affect the number of future mothers.

FIGURE 17.2 The First Demographic Transition Model in Four Stages

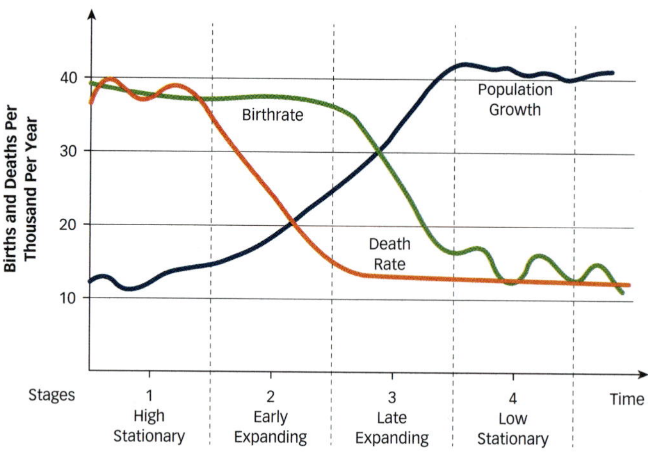

instance, the discovery that hand washing is important for doctors attending women giving birth. While this does not sound revolutionary today, it had a critical impact on maternal and child survival. In the 19th century, women in Europe and the United States had stunning rates of maternal mortality: Up to 25% of women delivering babies at hospitals died from puerperal sepsis, also known as childbed fever. Dr. Ignaz Semmelweis, a Viennese physician practicing in the 1840s, observed this phenomenon and recommended that attending physicians wash their hands with a chlorinated solution before assisting in childbirth. Semmelweis and his findings were harshly criticized, and he was ostracized for speaking out; his medical colleagues, nearly all of whom hailed from the upper classes, did not believe that gentlemen (even those attending a birth after dissecting a cadaver) could have dirty hands. As support for germ theory spread, however, Semmelweis's discovery proved to be critically important for the reduction of maternal mortality (Nuland, 2003).

Because people did not initially change their fertility behavior—specifically, they did not stop having many children—as death rates dropped, the result was rapid population growth. Eventually, however, expanding industrialization and urbanization brought about a fall in fertility. Although during the early stages of industrialization children often worked in factories and contributed to family income, the hardships of child labor eventually led to its legal prohibition. Rather than being an economic necessity, then, children became an expense. Urban living was also less amenable to large families than rural life had been. Population growth stabilized as low mortality came to be matched by falling fertility. At this point, the first demographic transition in the industrialized societies of the West was complete.

The theory of the first demographic transition offers a useful perspective based on a pattern observed in Western countries. We can critique it, however, for the same reason; that is, it describes the historical experience of today's modern Western societies. It does not describe nearly as well the experience of the developing world, which accounts for most global population growth today. In newly industrializing low-income countries, families do not always drastically reduce their fertility. And many low-income nations have not industrialized, yet their mortality rates have declined because populations have access to food, medicine (particularly antibiotics), agricultural and sanitation technologies, and pesticides, which contribute to better health and longer lives. Drops in mortality, however, have not been accompanied by drops in fertility as in modern industrialized states, where decreased fertility stemmed from economic growth, urbanization, industrialization, and expanded educational opportunities.

High fertility combined with low (or relatively low) mortality underlies much of the population explosion in the developing world. Fertility remains high in poor countries for a number of reasons, including health and culture. For instance, families in regions that still experience high child mortality are more likely to have "extra" children to ensure that some survive, and notions about the "ideal" size of families are culturally variable.

Economic factors also shape fertility decisions. Consider the relationship between economic rationality and childbearing. The saying "Children are a poor man's riches" highlights the fact that in agricultural societies in particular, children (specifically male children) are a value more than a cost. In rich and industrialized countries, children, while emotionally valued, are economically costly and contribute little or nothing to the household in terms of economic value. Economic rationality, then, is present in both the decision of a poor household in the developing world to have many children and

Dr. Ignaz Semmelweis observed higher maternal mortality in Clinic 1 of his hospital, staffed by male obstetricians who performed autopsies, than in Clinic 2, staffed by female midwives who did not. Chlorine washing of male birth attendants' hands reduced maternal mortality until 1850, when Semmelweis left the hospital and old practices resumed.

the decision of a rich household in the developed world to have few.

One of the most important factors contributing to both reduced fertility and improved child survival is the education of women (Figure 17.3). According to a recent study, for every 1-year increase in the average education of women in their childbearing years, a country experienced a 9.5% fall in child mortality (Gakidou, Cowling, Lozano, & Murray, 2010). Women who are more educated are more likely to be familiar with family planning methods and more likely to use them. Better-educated women are also more likely to have jobs in the formal labor force and, consequently, to limit their fertility in order to bring in economic resources. Finally, women with some economic resources also tend to have more decision-making power in the family, allowing them to participate in making choices about birth control and family size (United Nations, 1995).

Better health services for children and declining infant and child mortality also have important effects on fertility decisions. When women have reason to believe that all or most of their offspring will survive into adulthood, they are less likely to have "extra" children to ensure that a few survive (Kibirige, 1997).

Developed countries and the governments of some high-fertility countries have helped finance family planning programs in order to educate people about birth control. In addition, they have provided residents with condoms, birth control pills, and other means of reducing fertility. While such programs have met with some success, they often run up against deep-seated religious and other cultural values, some of which are found in the developed states as well. For instance, during Ronald Reagan's presidency and the presidencies of both George H. W. Bush and George W. Bush, U.S. governmental funding of family planning programs abroad was cut significantly because birth control (and especially abortion) violated the beliefs of conservative supporters of those administrations. It is clear that global efforts in family planning are fraught with problems. It remains to be seen whether they will ultimately succeed in reducing fertility (and hence global population growth).

FIGURE 17.3 Relationship Between Fertility and Female Education (Scattergram of Countries)

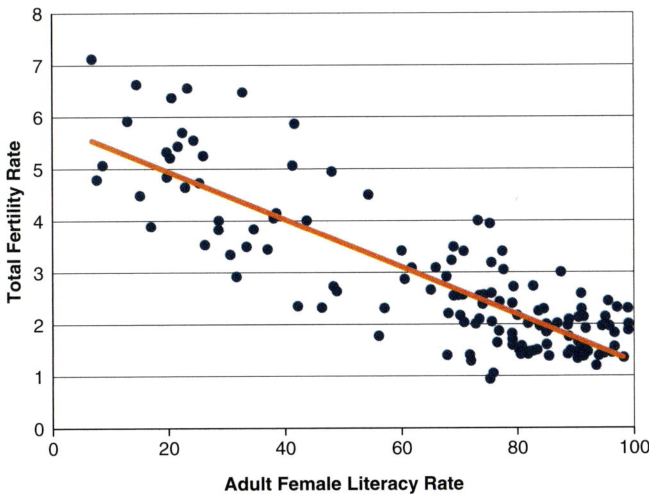

SOURCE: European Environment Agency. (2012). Correlation between fertility and female education. Retrieved from http://www.eea.europa.eu/data-and-maps/figures/correlation-between-fertility-and-female-education.

With the assistance of international organizations, Afghanistan has sought to increase the number of girls with access to schooling, but poverty and the cultural priority given to boys' education have kept female literacy low, and few women work in the paid labor force. At 5.4 children per woman, Afghanistan's total fertility rate remains among the world's highest.

IS A SECOND DEMOGRAPHIC TRANSITION OCCURRING IN THE WEST?

In the theory of the first demographic transition, population reaches a point of stabilization in Stage 4. What happens after that? Some demographers argue that at least in the most developed countries, stabilization has been followed by a *second demographic transition* (Lesthaeghe, 1995; McNicoll, 2001) characterized by broad changes in family patterns. Countries experiencing a second demographic transition may be characterized by increased rates of divorce and cohabitation, for

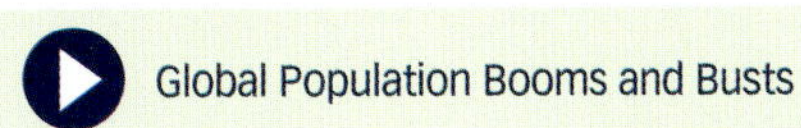

Declining Fertility Rates

Global Population Booms and Busts

instance, as well as decreased rates of marriage and fertility and a rise of nonmarital births as a proportion of all births. According to some demographers, Germany, France, and Sweden are among the countries experiencing a second demographic transition. Because changes in family patterns are associated with smaller families, the second demographic transition often includes a decline in the population's **rate of natural increase (RNI)**—that is, *the crude birthrate minus the crude death rate.*

If a country has a negative RNI, this can lead to population declines. Russia, for example, is experiencing relatively rapid loss of population: People are dying at a faster rate than they are being born, and Russia can expect to see a population loss of about 10% through the middle of the century (Population Reference Bureau, 2010). The result is an inverted age pyramid, wider at the top and narrower at the bottom (Figure 17.4). Some countries with a negative RNI, however, still experience growing populations as a result of immigration. By contrast, countries with above-replacement-level fertility rates and growing populations have "normal" pyramids, such as that for Mexico shown in Figure 17.4.

FIGURE 17.4 Population Pyramids for Russia and Mexico, 2012

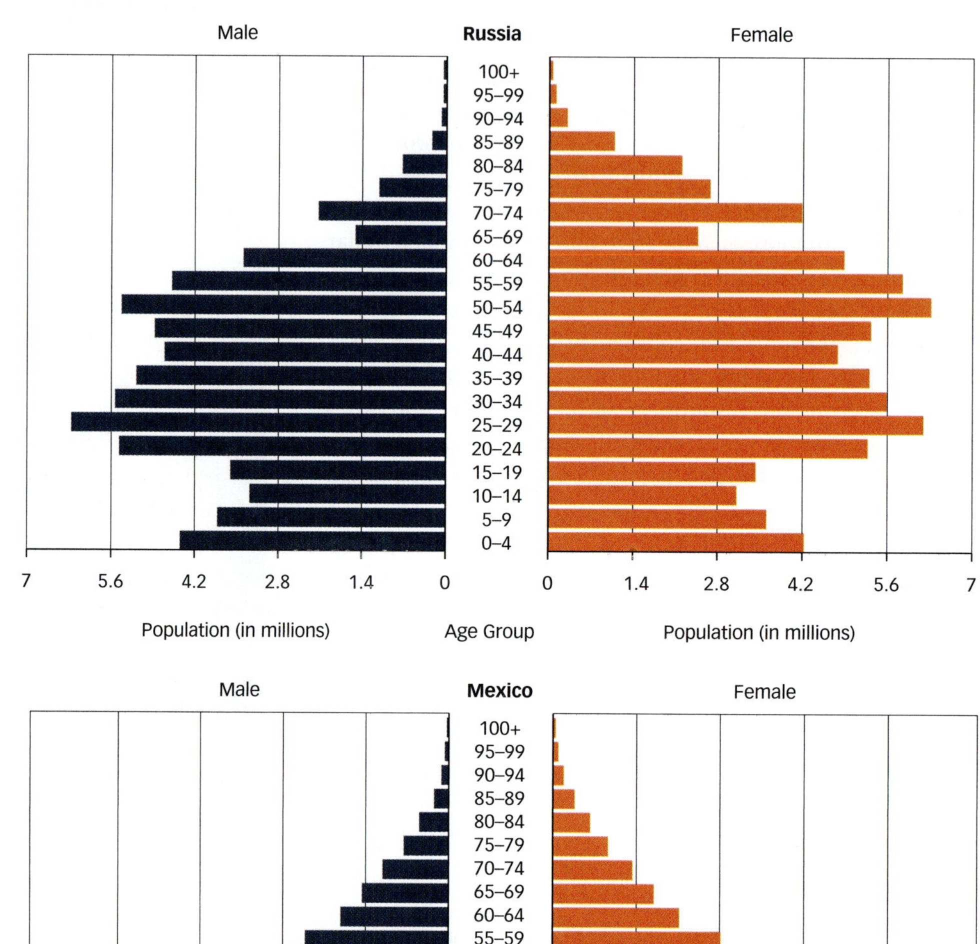

SOURCE: U.S. Census Bureau International Database.

What accounts for the second demographic transition? Demographer Ron Lesthaeghe (1995) argues that "the motivations underlying the 'second transition' are clearly different from those supporting the 'first transition,' with individual autonomy and female emancipation more central to the second than to the first" (p. 18). According to this perspective, more people associate personal satisfaction with consumption and personal fulfillment and are not as likely to seek fulfillment through family relationships. Female emancipation has also been broadened by the medical evolution of the "perfectly contracepting society" (Westoff & Ryder, 1977), such that women have unprecedented control over their fertility, and many have chosen smaller families or have opted not to have children.

Critics suggest that the second transition describes only a fraction of the world's population. However, the number of countries experiencing below-replacement birthrates is rising, and a sociological and demographic perspective such as the theory of the second transition offers sociologists analytical tools for understanding these key trends in advanced industrial states.

Rate of natural increase (RNI): The crude birthrate minus the crude death rate.

MALTHUS AND MARX: HOW MANY PEOPLE ARE TOO MANY?

High rates of population growth in some parts of the world may seem daunting, even alarming to some, but numbers alone do not tell the entire story. There is still a great deal of sparsely settled land in the world, and if the planet's 7 billion people were all somehow transplanted to the territory of the United States, the resulting crowding would be no greater than currently exists in the country of Taiwan.

Is the world overpopulated? This question is the subject of debate. On one side are those who predict catastrophe if population growth is not slowed or stopped altogether. Activists who fear that a population doomsday is just around the corner often conclude that drastic measures are required, including stringent public policies that promote small families. On the other side are those who argue that while population growth should be slowed, extreme measures are unwarranted. They tend to favor expanded female education, voluntary family planning programs (though some groups object to contraception as well as abortion), and economic policies that raise living standards, making smaller families a more rational economic choice.

MALTHUS: OVERPOPULATION AND NATURAL LIMITS

The argument that the world is overpopulated was first made two centuries ago by British social philosopher Thomas Malthus (1766–1834). Malthus (1798/1926) developed the theory of exponential population growth: the belief that, like compound interest, a constant rate of population growth produces a population that grows by an increasing amount with each passing year. **Exponential population growth**, thus, refers to *a constant growth rate that is applied to a base that is continuously growing in size.* Malthus also posited that although population grows exponentially, the food supply does not; the earth's resources are finite. Consequently, though the population may continue to double, the amount of food is more likely to grow at a constant rate. The result, according to Malthus's dire warning, is a growing mismatch between population and food resources. Unless we take steps to control our population growth, Malthus predicted, nature will do it for us: Wars fought over scarce resources, epidemics, and famine will keep population in check. Back when only a billion people occupied the entire planet, Malthus believed doomsday was already on the horizon.

How accurate was Malthus's prediction? Although war, epidemic, and famine have in fact been sadly evident throughout human history, and population has continued to grow exponentially, the food supply has grown along with it. Malthus failed to recognize that modern technology can also be applied to agriculture, yielding an exponential growth in food supplies—at least for a time. A report by the Food and Agriculture Organization of the United Nations (2009) concludes that although the world's population may reach 9.1 billion by 2050, "the required increase in food production can be achieved if the necessary investment is undertaken and policies conducive to agricultural production are put in place," along with "policies to enhance access by fighting poverty, especially in rural areas, as well as effective safety net programmes" (p. 2).

Although Malthus's predictions of global catastrophe have not been borne out, there may be a limit to the carrying capacity of the planet. World population cannot continue rapid growth indefinitely without consequences. Yet to point out that population growth presents serious challenges is not the same as concluding that the limits have been reached. Despite Malthus's pessimistic prophecies and Paul Ehrlich's dire warnings in *The Population Bomb* (1968), the long-predicted population doomsday has yet to arrive. In fact, the connection between population growth and human misery appears to be more complicated than many analyses have suggested. The issue is not simply how much additional food will be required to feed more mouths, but also whether the food that is produced will reach those who need it. Mass hunger in many countries is as much a product of politics as of true lack of food; in civil conflicts, for instance, hunger may be used as a weapon, with opposing forces blocking food shipments to enemy areas.

Exponential population growth: A constant rate of population growth applied to a base that is continuously growing in size, producing a population that grows by an increasing amount with each passing year.

SIMON: A MODERN CRITIC TAKES ON MALTHUS

Economist Julian Simon (1977, 2000) became well-known for his pointedly anti-Malthusian perspective on population. Simon not only rejected the notion that unchecked population growth would lead humanity down a path to hunger, deprivation, and poverty but also posited precisely the opposite. He argued that population growth has positive economic effects. In his most recent work, published posthumously, Simon (2000) suggested that *sudden modern progress* (SMP)—the rapid rise in living standards and technology—is the result of population growth and density. Put another way, the great population growth of the modern period was a causal factor of "the great breakthrough" (which is also the title of his book)—that is, population growth brings about technological progress. More people means more minds and more innovation, so human-generated resources, Simon argued, can overcome limitations on natural resources. Unlike Malthus, Simon was encouraged rather than daunted by the prospect of rising populations.

Indeed, the question of whether more minds can balance the pressure caused by more bodies is an engaging and imperative one. Can population growth be both problematic and powerful? What do you think?

DESIGN PICS INC/National Geographic Creativ

Only India and China have reached the 1 billion population mark. While its large population strains the country's resources, India has also experienced steady economic growth and gains in education and innovation. One of the results is a growing middle class with rising incomes (Ablett et al., 2007).

MARX: OVERPOPULATION OR MALDISTRIBUTION OF WEALTH?

Malthus forecast misery and inevitable overpopulation under conditions of growth. Simon saw population growth and density as necessary conditions for economic progress. Karl Marx focused on the unequal distribution of resources across populations.

Marx was concerned about the dominance of an economic system that enables the wealthy few to consume the world's resources at the expense of the impoverished masses. He was critical of Malthus for claiming that overpopulation is the central cause of human starvation and misery. In Marx's (1867/1992a) view, the central problem is not a mismatch between population size and resource availability, but rather the unequal distribution of resources; in most societies, as well as in the world as a whole, he argued, the members of a small elite enjoy the lion's share of the wealth and resources while the majority are left to take up the crumbs that fall from the richly endowed tables of the few.

Parente (2008) notes that even after adjustments are made for differences in relative prices and gross domestic product per capita, the living standards in the wealthiest industrial countries are about 50 to 60 times greater than those in the world's poorest countries. Most of the world's resources and goods are consumed by the West: Western Europe and North America, with 12% of the world's population, account for 60% of private consumption expenditures. In contrast, sub-Saharan Africa and South Asia, which together are home to more than one-third of humanity, account for just over 3% of private consumer expenditures. At the beginning of the new millennium, about two fifths of the earth's inhabitants lived on less than $2 per day (Worldwatch Institute, 2011). Marx argued that such maldistribution is the result of a capitalist economic system that divides people into unequal social classes.

Both Malthus and Marx were writing when the world's population was only around 1 billion people. Marx's criticism of Malthus has stood the test of time, since world population has doubled and more than doubled again since Malthus's predictions were made, but global resources have not run dry. Looking critically at Marx's ideas, we might note that although the maldistribution of wealth is an important factor in understanding poverty and human misery, Marx underestimated the importance of population growth itself as a variable.

MALTHUS, MARX, AND MODERNITY

Consider this question: What is the greater threat to the health and survival of our global environment—the rapid growth of the populations of the developing world or the overconsumption of resources by the small stratum of the wealthy? While some policy makers in the West express concern about the threats posed by unchecked population growth or the use of "dirty" technologies in developing states or the decimation of rain forests in the Amazon and elsewhere, there is little vigorous mainstream debate over the global threat presented by the recklessly wasteful consumption of resources by Western consumers. To cite just one example of the way Western consumption is masked by a focus on the global poor: Broad media attention has been given to the millions of acres of rain forest lost to clear-cutting in poor states, not least because of the immense biodiversity that has been sacrificed. Many in the United States have donated money to campaigns aimed at saving these precious resources. At the same time, heedless U.S. consumers of steaks, burgers, and other beef products may not recognize that some of the clear-cutting is done by ranchers seeking land on which to farm cattle, the meat from which will be sent to our supermarkets, restaurants, and dinner tables.

The question of whether overpopulation or overconsumption is the greater threat is a provocative one. Neither phenomenon is without consequences. Malthus feared that population would outpace food production; Marx posited that elites would consume far more than their share. A modern take on this debate points us to the conflict between underdevelopment in some states and "overdevelopment" in others.

As we shall see later in this chapter, environmental stresses have grown substantially since Malthus's and Marx's time, and some scientists believe we are approaching a point of no return in inflicting environmental damage on the planet. While overconsumption presents threats to our future, the consequences of the population explosion must also be faced. Since much of the world's population increase is currently concentrated in urban areas, we will next examine the impact of urbanization on modern life before turning to the environmental effects of urbanization and population growth combined.

Leemage / Contributor/Getty Images/ © Burstein Collection/CORBIS

Like all global cities, Paris has long been a city of contrasts. In a single city, one finds extremes of wealth and poverty, as well as leisure and struggle.

URBANIZATION

What is a city? Do you find it easy or difficult to come up with a definition? Early urban sociologist Louis Wirth (1938) wrote that "a sociologically significant definition of the city seeks to select those elements of urbanism which mark it as a distinctive mode of human group life" (p. 4). For sociological purposes, and thus for ours too, Wirth's definition is useful: A **city** *is "a relatively large, dense, and permanent settlement of socially heterogeneous individuals"* (p. 8).

In the eyes of some literary writers, cities are grim places of human degradation and misery. In the 19th-century poem "The City of Dreadful Night," James Thomson (1874) describes such a place:

> That city's atmosphere is dark and dense,
>
> Although not many exiles wander there,
>
> With many a potent evil influence,
>
> Each adding poison to the poisoned air;
>
> Infections of unalterable sadness,
>
> Infections of incalculable madness,
>
> Infections of incurable despair.

Other writers have praised the modernity, power, and culture of the city, while still others have recognized the contradictions of cities, their beautiful madness, their inhabitants' paradoxical excitement and indifference, and their ability to both attract and repel. Honoré de Balzac wrote of the inhabitants of Paris in 1833:

> By dint of taking in everything, the Parisian ends by being interested in nothing. No emotion dominating his face, which friction has rubbed away, it turns gray like the faces of those houses upon which all kinds of dust and smoke have blown. . . . [The Parisian] grumbles at everything, consoles himself for everything, jests at everything, forgets, desires, and tastes everything, seizes all with passion, quits all with indifference—his kings, his conquests, his glory, his idols of bronze or glass—as he throws away his stockings, his hats, and his fortune. In Paris, no sentiment can withstand the drift of things.

The city is a place of kings and presidents, as it is a place of thugs and beggars. It is lovely and disgusting, wealthy and poor, rewarding and despairing. Cities have become part of our lives and lore, but they were not always so. Cities have a long history, but until the Industrial Revolution, most people were rural dwellers. Today, most of the world's people live in cities and embody the beauties, miseries, and contradictions of those places. Below we turn a sociological lens on the cities of the United States and the world.

City: A relatively large, dense, and permanent settlement of socially heterogeneous individuals.

Urbanization and Environment

THE RISE OF INDUSTRY AND EARLY CITIES

Preindustrial cities, based on both agriculture and trade, first appeared 10,000 to 12,000 years ago. The development of settled agricultural areas enabled farmers to produce an **agricultural surplus**, *food beyond the amount required for immediate survival.* This surplus in turn made it possible for cities to sustain populations in which residents were not engaged primarily in farming. The first known cities were small, their populations seldom exceeding a few thousand, since the surplus production of 10 or more farmers was required to support a single nonfarming city dweller. The need for access to transportation routes and rich soil for farming figured prominently in the siting of the earliest cities along major river systems (Hosken, 1993). Early city residents included government officials, priests, handicraft workers, and others specializing in nonagricultural occupations, although many city dwellers engaged in some farming as well. Until modern times, very few cities in the world surpassed 100,000 people. More than 2,000 years ago, Rome was considered an enormous metropolis with 800,000 people; today it would be comparable in population to a U.S. city such as San Francisco (Mumford, 1961).

The Industrial Revolution of the 18th century radically changed the nature of cities. While cities of the past had served primarily as centers of trade, industrial cities now emerged as centers of manufacturing. Although some of the earliest English factories were in smaller cities, by the 19th century industrialization was moving hand in hand with **urbanization**, *the concentration of people in urban areas.* At the beginning of the 19th century there were barely 100 places in England with more than 5,000 inhabitants; by the end of the century there were more than 600, together containing more than 20 million people. The city of London grew from 1.1 million to 7.3 million people between 1800 and 1910 (Hosken, 1993), becoming a center of industry as well as an ever more important hub of commerce and culture. In the United States as well, the explosion of cities coincided with the onset of industrialization at the end of the 19th century. By the early 20th century, most U.S. citizens could be classified as urban, and today, as in Britain and other Western European industrial states, the vast majority live in metropolitan areas.

SOCIOLOGISTS AND THE CITY

The early industrial cities were grimy places in which people lived in shanties and shacks, often in the shadows of the factories where they spent more than a dozen working hours each day. In the absence of proper sanitation and sewage systems, illness and epidemics were common, and many people died of typhoid, cholera, dysentery, and tuberculosis. Writers such as Charles Dickens captured the miseries of early urban industrial life, where men, women, and children toiled in dank, squalid conditions and lived lives of deprivation and degradation. Early sociologists too turned their lenses on the city, some viewing urban life as bordering on the pathological. At the same time, most recognized that cities provided opportunities for individuality and creativity.

During the rapid urbanization of the 19th century, some of the earliest sociologists worried about the differences between a presumably serene country life and the "death and decay" of city life (Toennies, 1887/1963). The rural community (*Gemeinschaft* in the original German) was contrasted with urban society (*Gesellschaft*), much to the disadvantage of the latter. Rural community life was said to be characterized by intimate relationships, a strong sense of family, powerful folkways and mores, and stabilizing religious foundations. Urban life, by contrast, was believed to be characterized by impersonal and materially based relationships, family breakdown, and the erosion of traditional beliefs and religious values. The behavior of city dwellers was viewed as governed no longer by long-standing folkways and mores, but by cold cost-benefit calculations, individual preferences rather than group norms, and ever-changing public opinion.

While alienation was assumed to be a product of this chilly urban world, Émile Durkheim put forth the notion that the *mechanical solidarity* of traditional community life (based on homogeneity) could be replaced by the *organic solidarity* of modern societies, with complex divisions of labor in which people were heterogeneous but interdependent for survival and prosperity.

During the 1920s and 1930s, researchers at the University of Chicago turned their city into a vast laboratory for urban studies, pioneering urban sociology as a field. Early 20th-century U.S. sociology centered on the study of "social problems" such as hoboes, the mentally ill, juvenile delinquents, criminals, prostitutes, and others who were seen as casualties of urban living. Urbanism was believed to be a specific way of life that resulted from the geographic concentration of large numbers of socially diverse people (see the *Inequality Matters* box on page 445). Sociologists believed one feature of this life was a good deal of mutual mistrust, leading city residents to segregate themselves on the basis of race, ethnicity, class, and even lifestyle into neighborhoods of like-minded people (Wirth, 1938). Of course, as we saw in our discussion of race in Chapter 9, self-segregation should be distinguished from imposed segregation that is the result of individual or institutional racism.

Although early sociologists often linked city life with pathology, even in supposedly impersonal cities people maintain intense social networks and close personal ties. Numerous sociological studies have found that significant community relationships persist within even the largest cities (Duneier, 1992; Fischer, 1982, 1984; Gans, 1962a, 1962b; Liebow, 1967; Whyte, 1943; Wirth, 1928). Physical characteristics such as size and density do not by themselves account for urban problems. What is important is the way a particular society organizes itself in cities. Below we look at the case of cities in the United States.

Agricultural surplus: Food beyond the amount required for immediate survival.

Urbanization: The concentration of people in urban areas.

INEQUALITY MATTERS

THE GEOMETRY OF THE CITY

Among the important early urban sociologists at the University of Chicago was Ernest Burgess (1886–1966). Burgess (1925) developed the *concentric zone hypothesis* in part to explain how different social groups come to be distributed across urban spaces. It suggests that sociological factors, including socioeconomic class, are relevant to understanding the competition for favorable locations in an urban area.

Burgess believed a key city pattern could be represented by five concentric circles (Figure 17.5). The small inner circle represents the *central business district,* a relatively affluent zone characterized by government buildings, financial institutions, and major retailers. The next ring is a *zone in transition,* with low-rent areas occupied by poor and minority residents and some manufacturing. The third ring from the center is the *workingman's zone,* with housing typified by small individual units and apartments. The fourth ring is the *middle-class residential district,* with more upscale housing options. The outer ring is the *commuters' zone or suburban zone,* with larger housing units and upper-income residences.

FIGURE 17.5 Burgess's Concentric Zone Hypothesis

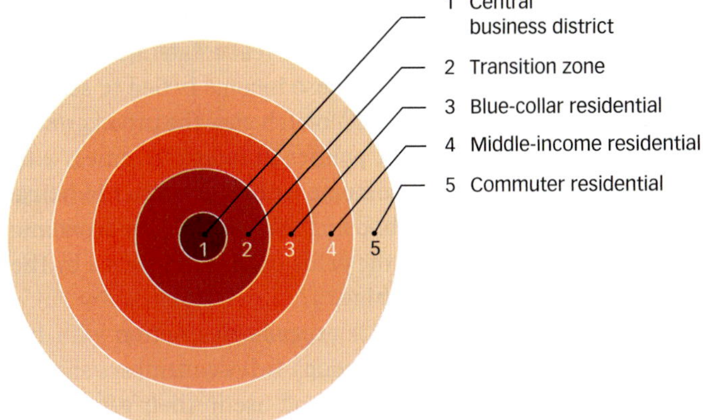

Burgess noted that as we move from the inner zone to the outer circle, we find decreased population density and increased class status, higher rates of home ownership, lower rates of crime, and smaller families. The patterns could be explained, he argued, by the amount people and businesses were willing to pay for land, with valued commercial space in the center (which has the greatest access to customers) and valued residential space in outer areas.

Burgess's model has been criticized for, among other flaws, hypothesizing a cityscape that has characterized many U.S. cities but cannot capture the patterns of global cities, many of which exhibit the opposite pattern of class composition, with the wealthiest in the center and suburban districts of poverty at the city's edges. Contemporary gentrification in some U.S. cities has also brought high-rent residences and pricey condominiums to previously poor and neglected urban neighborhoods.

At the same time, Burgess's work is important because it seeks to cast a sociological eye on the U.S. city and to recognize sociological factors that help explain social group distribution across the urban landscape.

THINK IT THROUGH

▶ Can you create a sociological map of your own city or town? What kinds of patterns of commercial activity or residence can you detect, and how would you explain them sociologically?

CITIES IN THE UNITED STATES

Transportation and communication technologies have played important roles in helping to shape U.S. cities. The automobile and urban rail and subway systems enabled cities to expand outward by allowing people to travel greater distances between home and work. Similarly, modern construction technologies permitted cities to expand skyward, with massive skyscrapers that take up little land space but create living or working space for thousands.

THE SOCIAL DYNAMICS OF U.S. CITIES AND SUBURBS

Political and economic forces are also key to shaping modern cities. Sociologists John Logan and Harvey Molotch (1987;

Molotch, 1976; Warner, Molotch, & Lategola, 1992) have argued that cities are shaped by what they call the **urban growth machine**, consisting of *those persons and institutions that have a stake in an increase in the value of urban land and that constitute a power elite in most cities.* These people and institutions are said to include downtown businesses, real estate owners (particularly those who own commercial and rental property), land developers and builders, newspapers (whose advertising revenues are often tied to the size of the local population), and the lawyers, accountants, architects, real estate agents, construction workers, and others whose income is tied to serving those who own land. Logan and Molotch view the urban growth machine as dominating local politics in most U.S. cities, with the result that cities often compete with one another to house factories, office buildings, shopping malls, and other economic activities that will increase the value of the land owned by the members of the growth machine.

G. William Domhoff (2002) expands this notion with his concept of *growth coalitions,* groups "whose members share a common interest in intensifying land use in their geographic locale" (p. 39). Growth coalitions are a powerful force in local politics, though they encounter conflicts in their pursuit of growth and profit. Domhoff notes that "neighborhoods are something to be used and enjoyed in the eyes of those who live in them, but they are often seen as sites for further development by growth coalitions, who justify new developments with a doctrine claiming the highest and best use for land" (p. 40).

Consider Domhoff's conflict-oriented analysis of U.S. politics and decision making, which we examined in Chapter 14. Recall that Domhoff asks us to ponder the questions *Who benefits? Who governs? Who wins?* Looking at growth politics—the increasing development of already crowded suburbs or the gentrification of urban neighborhoods at the expense of older neighborhoods—we may ask who has the power and the resources to realize their interests. Are those who favor *use value* (the enjoyment of the neighborhood) or those who favor *exchange value* (the economic development of an area) more powerful? Is the shape of modern cities and suburbs a product primarily of those who inhabit them or those who profit from them?

The post–World War II development of U.S. cities and suburbs illustrates how the growth machine operates at the national level. The rapid growth of suburbs during the 1950s and the 1960s is often attributed to people's preference for suburban living, but it was also a product of economic forces and government policies designed to stimulate the postwar economy (Jackson, 1985; Mollenkopf, 1977). The government influence is illustrated by the 1956 National Interstate and Defense Highways Act, which established a highway trust fund paid for by a federal tax on gasoline. This legislation ensured a self-renewing source of funding to construct high-speed freeways connecting cities and suburbs across the country. The legislation eventually financed nearly 100,000 miles of highway,

© SuperStock/Corbis

The great highway building projects of the post-war period literally paved the roads to America's suburbanized future. Robert Fishman suggests that "every true suburb is the outcome of two opposing forces, an attraction toward the opportunities of the great city and a simultaneous repulsion against urban life" (quoted in Gainsborough, 2001, p. 33). Is this an accurate characterization? Why or why not?

characterized by President Dwight Eisenhower at the time as "the greatest public works program in history" and enough to build a "Great Wall" around the world 50 feet wide and 9 feet high. The law originated in the planning efforts of a powerful consortium of bankers, corporations, and unions connected with the automobile, petroleum, and construction industries (Mollenkopf, 1977).

The Highways Act, in combination with other government programs, spurred the growth of the U.S. economy, both by improving transportation and by promoting the automobile and construction industries. The existence of freeways encouraged people to buy more cars and to drive additional miles, generating still more gasoline tax revenues for additional highway construction. Large numbers of people bought houses in the suburbs with federally insured and subsidized loans, commuted on federally financed highways to work in federally subsidized downtown office buildings, and even shopped in

Urban growth machine: Those persons and institutions that have a stake in an increase in the value of urban land and that constitute a power elite in cities.

suburban shopping centers built in part with federal dollars. All this development ushered in a quarter century of growth and relative prosperity for working- and middle-class residents of the suburbs.

In fact, the rapid growth of suburbs in this period represents one of the most dramatic population shifts in U.S. history. In 1950, cities contained 33% of the U.S. population, considerably more than their surrounding suburbs (23%). During the 1960s the suburbs overtook the cities, and by 1990 the suburban population had reached 46% of the U.S. total, while the city population had declined slightly to 31% (Frey & Speare, 1991). In 2000, 46% lived in the suburbs, while the proportion in central cities dropped slightly to 30% (Hobbs & Stoops, 2002). In 2010, more than 80% of the U.S. population inhabited metropolitan areas, but the 2010 census also showed a shift back toward urban growth (Mackun & Wilson, 2011).

The emergence of postindustrial society has encouraged further development beyond the economic activity of the urban core. Modern information technology has made it easier for corporations to locate high-tech factories and office parks in once-remote suburban or even rural locations, where they take advantage of relatively inexpensive land, wooded landscapes, and other amenities. Since 1980, more than two-thirds of employment growth in the United States has taken place outside central cities, and even manufacturing, while in decline nationally, has found a home in the suburbs; today, about 70% of manufacturing is suburban (Wilson, 2010).

While those who benefit from such relocations tend to be well-educated managerial, technical, and professional specialists, the suburbs are also home to a substantial proportion of entry-level positions. This is significant because it contributes to the loss of employment opportunities in central cities. Sociologist William Julius Wilson (2010) writes of the *spatial mismatch* between urban job seekers and suburban jobs, noting that "opportunities for employment are geographically disconnected from the people who need the jobs" (p. 41). He offers the example of Cleveland, where, "although entry-level workers are concentrated in inner-city neighborhoods, 80 percent of the entry-level jobs are located in the suburbs" (p. 41).

The migration of middle- and upper-income families from the cities begun in the post–World War II era evolved into a critical socioeconomic disparity between the suburbs and central cities. Analyzing the concentrated poverty of urban core areas such as South Chicago, Wilson (2010) points out that political forces created a "new urban poverty" that plagues inner-city neighborhoods deeply segregated by both race and class. These forces included government support for highway building, a postwar mortgage lending boom that benefited predominantly White veterans and their families, and the decline of the industrial base that long provided economic sustenance to U.S. cities and less educated workers.

The decline of U.S. cities, most visible in the economically distressed urban cores of cities including Chicago; Washington, D.C.; and Baltimore, has fostered efforts toward **urban renewal**, or *the transformation of old neighborhoods with new buildings, businesses, and residences.* Urban renewal is linked to **gentrification**, a process characterized by *the attempt to change the socioeconomic composition of old and poor neighborhoods with the remodeling of old structures and building of new residences and shops to attract new middle- and high-income residents.* On one hand, gentrification may be successful in transforming dilapidated neighborhoods into flourishing (and more economically valuable) urban spaces that offer cultural and business opportunities to residents and visitors. Cities may benefit from gentrification as the process rebuilds a middle-class base of residents and pushes up the value of taxable property and, consequently, revenues for city governments. On the other hand, rising property values also tend to herald a rise in rents and other costs of living, which may push out longtime low-income residents who cannot afford to be part of the boom in condominiums or the luxury amenities intended to make gentrified spaces inviting to upwardly mobile new residents.

In the fall of 2010, the city of Washington, D.C., announced the closing one of its few bilingual shelters for the homeless. The shelter was located in Columbia Heights, a "rapidly developing" neighborhood described as "a focus of city redevelopment efforts" (Rott, 2010). City officials tried to move the shelter's residents to apartments before the shelter was to be destroyed to make way for condominiums and a new shopping complex. As an advocate for the homeless noted, however, "the remaining men's shelters are in the poorest parts of the city" (quoted in Rott, 2010).

What, then, are we to conclude about gentrification? How can urban renewal and efforts to bring upwardly mobile residents back to U.S. city centers be balanced with the needs and aspirations of low-income residents, whether in apartments, houses, or shelters, who may be displaced?

THE EMERGENCE OF GLOBAL CITIES

We live in the first age of decisive urban dominance. Today, more than half the world's population resides in cities, many of which are massive global centers such as London (population 10.2 million), New York (20.7 million), and Tokyo (37.6 million) (Demographia, 2014). **Global cities** are *metropolitan areas that*

Urban renewal: The transformation of old neighborhoods with new buildings, businesses, and residences.

Gentrification: The attempt to change the socioeconomic composition of old and poor neighborhoods with the remodeling of old structures and building of new residences and shops to attract new middle- and high-income residents.

Global cities: Metropolitan areas that are highly interconnected with one another in their role as centers of global political and economic decision making, finance, and culture.

Gentrification 'Without the Negative'

FIGURE 17.6 The World's Megacities, 2013

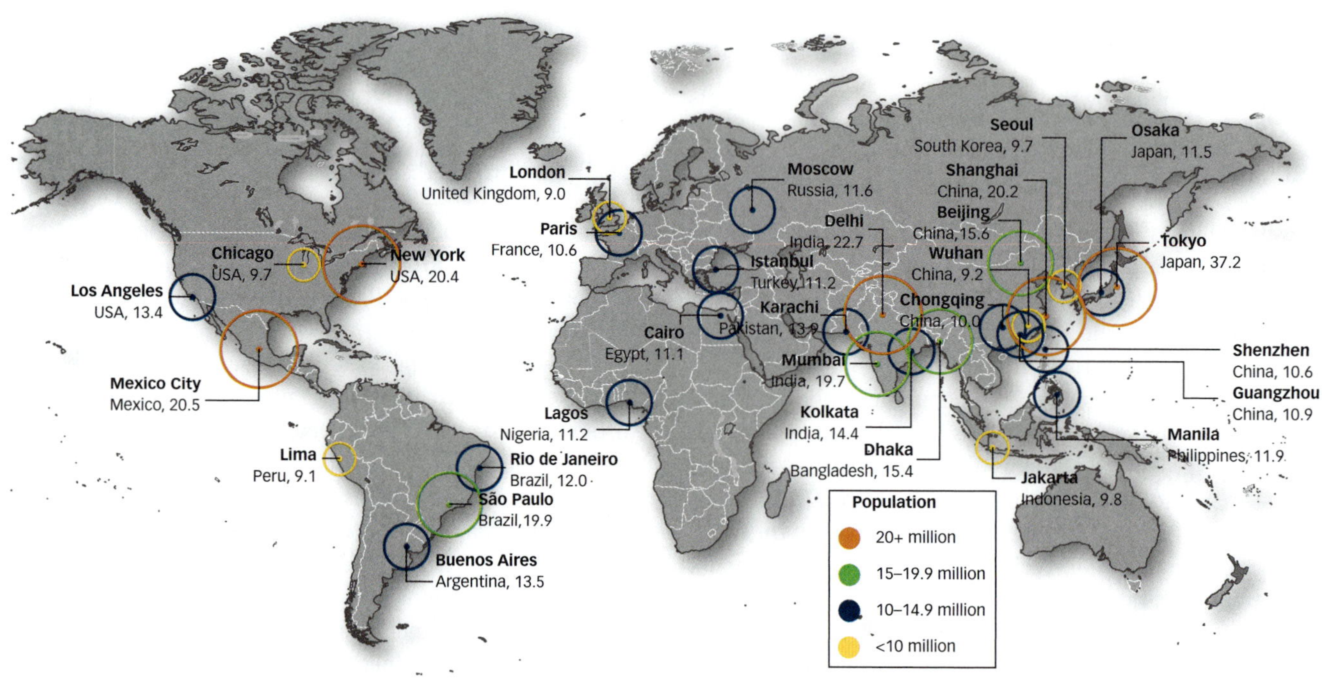

SOURCE: Population Reference Bureau. (2013). *2013 world population data sheet.* Washington, DC: Author. Retrieved from http://www.prb.org/pdf13/2013-population-data-sheet_eng.pdf.

are highly interconnected with one another in their role as centers of global political and economic decision making, finance, and culture (Sassen, 1991). Their economic role is defined as much by the large role they play in the global economy as by their influence in their immediate geographic regions.

Saskia Sassen (1991) identifies four principal functions of global cities. First, they are "command posts" in the organization of the world economy. Second, they serve as key locations for businesses related to finance, accounting, marketing, design, and other highly specialized (and profitable) services that are replacing manufacturing as the leading economic sectors. Third, they are the most important sites of innovation and new product development. Finally, they serve as the principal markets for global businesses. Sassen (2000) also notes that "whether at the global or regional level, these cities must inevitably engage each other in fulfilling their functions. . . . There is no such entity as a single global city" (p. 4).

In global cities, multinational corporations and international bankers maintain their headquarters and oversee the operation of diverse production and management operations that are spread across the globe. Global cities are sites for the creation and concentration of enormous economic wealth: By one recent estimate, just 100 cities account for 30% of the world's economy. It is notable that "New York City's economy alone is larger than 46 of sub-Saharan Africa's economies combined" (Khanna, 2010).

At the same time, cities have long been magnets for those who cannot make an adequate living elsewhere, whether in other countries or in the impoverished rural areas or small towns of the cities' own countries. Low-wage services, low-skill factory production, and sweatshops coexist with the most profitable activities of international businesses in global cities; we find dire poverty and spectacular wealth side by side. In Los Angeles, for example, hundreds of thousands of immigrants from Mexico and Central America work in the shadows of the downtown skyscrapers that house the world's largest banks and corporations. These immigrants labor as janitors, domestics, or workers in small clothing factories that sew apparel for global garment manufacturers (Milkman, 2006; Singer, 2012). Cities are places of intense contrasts and contradictions: The inequalities that permeate relationships, institutions, and countries are on vivid display in the global cities of the world. The box *Global Issues* on page 449 highlights the particular problem of urbanization and HIV/AIDS.

WORLD URBANIZATION TODAY

Some of the most highly urbanized countries in the world today are those that only a century ago were almost entirely rural. As recently as 1950, only 18% of the inhabitants of developing countries lived in urban areas. In 2012, 51% did. For the first time in history, there are more people living in urban

GLOBAL ISSUES

URBANIZATION AND THE SPREAD OF HIV/AIDS: THE CASE OF SOUTH AFRICA

One of the critical problems faced by many large cities in developed and developing countries is the spread of HIV/AIDS, primarily through sexual contact and intravenous drug use. Consider urban South Africa, which has experienced rapid urbanization since the end of the racist apartheid regime in 1994. With the lifting of apartheid-era regulations that kept many Black South Africans out of White-dominated cities, urban populations have expanded dramatically. High levels of migration to cities are among a host of sociological factors intertwined with the spread of HIV/AIDS, the prevalence of which was as high as 26% in the city of Johannesburg at the turn of the millennium (van Donk, 2002). In the province of KwaZulu-Natal, which includes the city of Durban, the prevalence today stands at almost 40% (South African Department of Health, 2012).

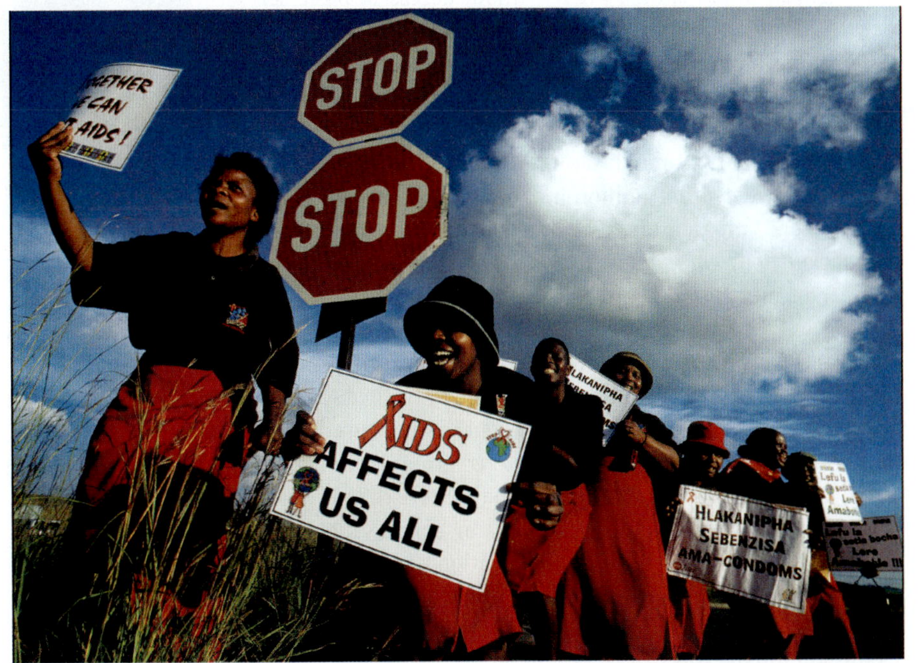

Brent Stirton / Staff/Getty Images

Women in a South African mining town distribute condoms and leaflets on safe sex practices. Some of the women are sex workers, but concern about safe sex is widespread, as HIV/AIDS is a serious threat in mining communities where many male workers are migrants who leave their families for long periods of time and may seek out the services of sex workers. ■

Urban areas are vulnerable to HIV/AIDS epidemics for a number of reasons. First, the promise of jobs draws migrant laborers from impoverished small towns and rural areas, many of them young males who are unmarried or have left families behind. Some are drawn to the urban sex markets that arise to cater to unattached men, where sexually transmitted infections are rampant and easily passed from person to person. Further, men returning to their villages from cities may carry with them infections they pass to their wives, who do not have the power to ask their men to use prophylactics. Other newcomers to the cities, unable to secure legal work, may be drawn into criminal activities such as drugs or prostitution, which also foster an environment conducive to the spread of disease (van Donk, 2002).

The Joint United Nations Programme on HIV/AIDS (known as UNAIDS) estimates that 6.1 million people in South Africa are infected with HIV/AIDS. Many reside in South Africa's cities. Among South Africans between 15 and 49 years of age—who are in both their productive and their reproductive years—there was a prevalence rate of HIV/AIDS of 17.9% in 2012 (UNAIDS, 2012). Increasing levels of ill health and death in this demographic group have the potential to seriously compromise the economic activity and prosperity of the country and its communities and families.

In 2009, South Africa's government announced a new, more vigorous campaign to combat HIV/AIDS and increase access to treatment (Sidibé, 2009). According to South Africa's most recent progress report to the United Nations, its national HIV counseling and testing program has reached 13 million people, the prevalence of HIV has stabilized, and mortality rates are declining, particularly among women (Republic of South Africa, 2012).

THINK IT THROUGH

▶ How might sociologists go about studying the relationship between rapid urbanization and the spread of disease? How would you measure these variables? How would you design research questions to test whether correlation equals causation?

Urbanization Across 10,000 Years

areas than in rural areas throughout the world (Population Reference Bureau, 2012). Today, more than 30% of the world's poor inhabit cities—some in the developed countries, most in developing countries. A 2012 UNICEF report identifies urban poverty as a critical and growing problem, particularly for children, noting that "in fact, hundreds of millions of children today live in urban slums, many without access to basic services. They are vulnerable to dangers ranging from violence and exploitation to the injuries, illnesses and death that result from living in crowded settlements atop hazardous rubbish dumps or alongside railroad tracks" (p. v).

According to the United Nations, as of 2011 there were 456 cities worldwide with 1 million inhabitants or more. Globally, there were 29 **megacities**, usually defined as *cities with total population of 10 million or more* (Demographia, 2014). The number of megacities is projected to increase to 37 by 2025. About 1 in 20 people worldwide currently reside in a megacity, and projections indicate that about 1 in 13 people will reside in a city of more than 10 million people by 2025 (United Nations, 2011). Khanna (2010) suggests that "we need to get used to the idea of nearly 100 million people clustered around Mumbai [in India] or Shanghai [in China]. Across India, more than 275 million people are projected to move into the country's teeming cities over the next two decades, a population nearly equivalent to that of the United States" (p. 123). It is estimated that by 2025 China will be home to fully 15 cities with an average of 25 million inhabitants.

Cities are dynamic places and the centerpiece of modern life in many countries, sites of innovation, creativity, education, and positive social change. They are also often wasteful producers of garbage, pollution, and greenhouse gases. In the next section, we explore the environmental challenges that cities and modern society present for our planet.

THE LOCAL AND GLOBAL ENVIRONMENT

The year 2012 went down as the hottest on record. Across the globe, a spectrum of devastating weather events took place. The U.S. government's National Climatic Data Center, part of the National Oceanic and Atmospheric Administration (NOAA), has reported the following:

- In late October 2012, Hurricane Sandy became the largest Atlantic hurricane ever recorded, causing $20 billion worth of damage. The hurricane traveled through the Caribbean, leaving wreckage in Jamaica, Haiti, the Dominican Republic, Puerto Rico, and Cuba before carving a destructive path up the East Coast of the United States. A total of 24 U.S. states were affected, with the worst damage occurring in New York and New Jersey, where heavy winds and flooding left millions without power. At least 185 people were killed by the storm.

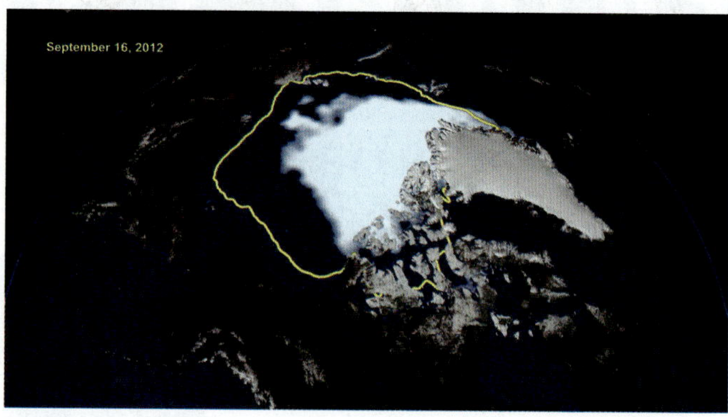

NASA

Satellite photos from the National Aeronautics and Space Administration show that arctic sea ice cover dropped to a record low on September 16, 2012. NASA scientists say the melt has taken place more rapidly than they predicted.

- The period of January–August 2012 was the warmest 8 months on record, with 33 U.S. states record warm in addition to 12 states that were top 10 warm. The contiguous U.S. temperature average for January–August was 58.7 °F, a startling 4.0 °F above average.
- The farmland states of the U.S. Midwest, which produce much of the nation's food crops, have been experiencing the worst drought in the past 56 years. The resulting arid conditions led to the destruction of 3.6 million acres by wildfires in August 2012 alone.
- Thaws have brought ice levels in the Arctic to record lows. As average global temperatures rise, Arctic ice is melting with increasing rapidity. Warming has reduced the thickness of the ice, which also fosters faster melting.
- Increasingly intense weather events have continued across the globe, and scientists link them to climate change. In November 2013, for example, Typhoon Haiyan slammed the Philippines and other parts of Southeast Asia, killing more than 6,000 people.
- In the spring of 2014, evidence showed that the melting of the West Antarctica ice sheet is now irreversible. This melting could lead to dramatic rises in sea level.

The events of recent years follow on the heels of other occurrences of extreme weather, including the U.S. tornado outbreak of 2011; the 2009 heat waves in Argentina; numerous tropical storms and cyclones throughout South Asia in 2008; the 2005 hurricanes Katrina and Rita, which devastated the Gulf Coast; and the 2004 Indian Ocean tsunami that laid waste to parts of Thailand, Myanmar (Burma), Bangladesh, and Southern India.

Megacities: Metropolitan areas or cities with total population of 10 million or more.

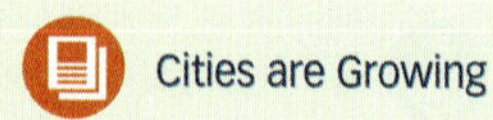

■ **FIGURE 17.7** Natural Catastrophes Worldwide, 2012

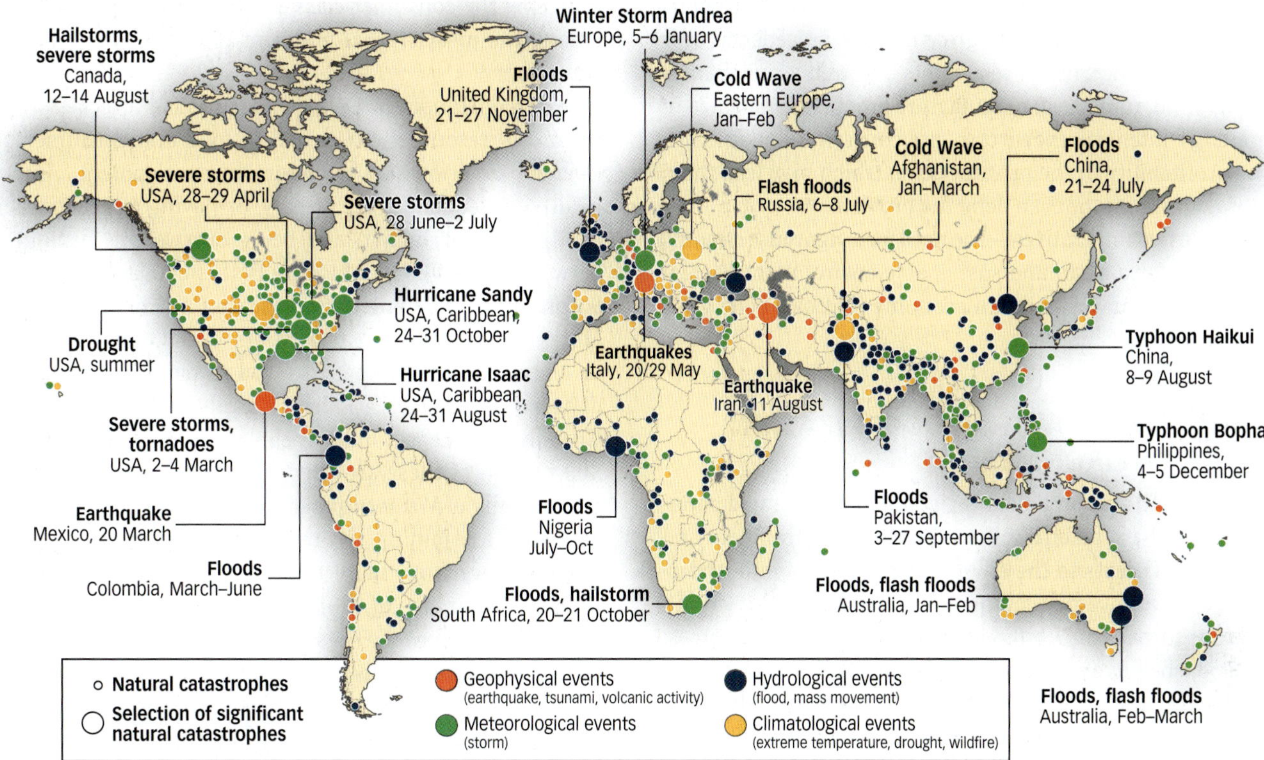

What is behind the increase in extreme weather events across the globe? Many scientists suspect it is global warming, also referred to as climate change, since not all its effects are manifested in the form of rising temperatures. Global warming is widely understood to occur because so-called greenhouse gases, by-products of industrialization such as carbon dioxide (CO_2) and methane gas, become trapped in the earth's atmosphere and hold heat at the surface. While part of this process is naturally occurring and is related to a climate cycle that keeps the earth at a habitable temperature, the industrial era has seen a growing concentration of greenhouse gases in the atmosphere. The resulting "greenhouse effect" is believed to be causing an unprecedented rise in air temperatures, melting the world's ice caps and glaciers and raising ocean temperatures and sea levels. Warm air also retains more water vapor than cold air, a condition that scientists warn will be linked to greater downpours and a higher probability of floods (McKibben, 2011).

The escalation of climate change and the growing reach of its effects are on the research agendas of climate scientists, biologists, and other physical scientists. Sociologists have also taken an interest. Among their concerns is the way in which this phenomenon, which most climate scientists accept as a credible threat to our planet and its inhabitants, has been framed in the mainstream social and political discourse as a societal problem. Some sociologists have argued that public attention to problems such as climate change depends in part on the presence of a "social scare" (Ungar, 1992)—that is, an event (such as extreme weather) that draws attention to a phenomenon by allowing it to "piggyback on dramatic real-world events" (Ungar, 1992, p. 483).

Recent extreme weather events, however, do not seem to have had an appreciable effect on public concern. Interestingly, while there has been an increase in the availability of information on the science and manifestations of climate change, particularly in the age of the Internet, the proportion of the U.S. population expressing concern about the issue has remained fairly steady over the past two decades and has even dropped in recent years. In a 2012 Gallup survey, 42% of respondents indicated they felt "the seriousness of global warming" was "generally exaggerated," about one third believed it to be "generally correct," and about a quarter suggested that it was "generally underestimated" (Saad, 2012).

Why is there little apparent sense of urgency or mobilization of action in the face of an environmental threat such as climate change? There is a spectrum of possible explanations. For example, research suggests that the "creeping nature" of climate change—that is, the fact that effects are not constantly apparent and are perceived to be far in the future—leads some people to discount it as a potential problem (Moser & Dilling,

2004). Some sociologists also point to the **treadmill of production**, *the constant and aggressive growth needed to sustain the modern economy* (Schnaiberg & Gould, 1994). On the political and economic agenda this growth takes precedence over environmental concerns. Governments—as well as companies that drill for oil, mine coal, manufacture products, or engage in other energy-intensive endeavors—are concerned about maintaining profitability in the private sector, which may lead them to ignore, minimize, or even deny the problem.

Are these two imperatives—the need for a vigorous economy and the need for a clean and sustainable environment—irreconcilable? How can we build an economy that can both grow and be green?

POPULATION GROWTH, MODERNIZATION, AND THE ENVIRONMENT

Industrialization and urbanization, combined with rapid population growth, have taken a toll on the global environment and its resources. Threats to the environment exist in both underdevelopment and overdevelopment. On one hand, the world's population, surpassing 7 billion people, needs basic resources: water, food, shelter, and energy. As humans seek to meet these needs, they tax the earth by impinging on the natural habitats of unique animal and plant species to make room for human habitation. More important, perhaps, the rise of the **global consumer class**—*those who actively use technology, purchase consumer goods, and embrace the culture of consumption*—has meant that more individuals are using more resources per person than ever before.

By some estimates, a quarter of the world's population falls within the global consumer class. A large percentage of the members of this class live in developed countries; according to the Worldwatch Institute, the United States and Canada, home to just over 5% of the world's population, account for about 31% of private consumption expenditures, and Western Europe, with around 6% of the globe's people, accounts for more than 28% of expenditures. However, the consumer class is expanding. More than half its members now live in areas of advancing prosperity in the developing world, such as China and India. In 2009, China passed the United States to become the biggest market for automobiles on the planet (Langfitt, 2013), and half of the world's new shopping malls are being built in China, where luxury consumption is growing particularly rapidly ("Chinese Consumers," 2014). The future consumer markets of the world are in developing countries rather than developed countries, which are characterized by sagging population growth and already high consumption rates.

In many respects, urbanization and industrialization are important achievements in the developing world, where more people have the opportunity to meet their needs and realize their dreams, leaving behind the travails of deprivation. Though the gulf between rich and poor remains wide, prosperity has advanced around the globe. Development's darker underbelly, however, becomes visible when we look at the problems presented by the consumer class and its growing ranks. Arguably, among the most critical problems of development is overconsumption.

Overconsumption may be understood as a recklessly wasteful use of resources, from fuel to food and consumer goods. Overconsumption is a symptom of development. Among its health consequences are obesity, or having a body mass index (BMI) of 30 or higher, and being overweight, having a BMI between 25 and 29.9 (a healthy BMI is between 18.5 and 24.9, according to the Centers for Disease Control and Prevention). More than two-thirds of U.S. adults (78 million) are overweight or obese, conditions that can lead to heart disease and other dangerous maladies (Ogden, Carroll, Kit, & Flegal, 2012). Globally more than 1 billion people are overweight, and at least 300 million of these are obese. While these problems used to be problems of Western prosperity, more people in developing countries are joining the ranks of the overweight and obese as they move from more traditional diets to "modern" foods (Popkin, Adair, & Ng, 2012). High-fat and high-sugar foods are widely consumed: These foods are aggressively advertised, cheap, and popular, especially among young people.

Rising consumption also threatens the environment, as more people buy, use, and toss away ever more "stuff." The global fleet of passenger cars is more than 531 million and growing; in the United States there are more cars than licensed drivers. Many modern consumers also value size as a sign of material success: The size of SUVs has expanded more rapidly than their fuel efficiency, and new houses in the United States were nearly 38% bigger in 2002 than in 1975, though households on average were smaller (Worldwatch Institute, 2004, 2010). As a comparison, at 2,265 square feet, the average U.S. home today is twice as big as the average European or Japanese dwelling and 26 times bigger than the typical living space in Africa (Worldwatch Institute, 2010).

As more people across the globe strive, understandably, for prosperity and modernity, it may be wise for us to ask: Can such consumption be sustained? Those who live in the prosperous countries might also ask: Is it hypocritical to raise concerns about the global destruction wrought by overconsumption when the West has been the primary consumer of the world's resources for the past century? (See the *Technology and Society* box on page 453 for more on this.) To give you the opportunity to consider these important questions, we discuss below the environmental impacts of population growth

Treadmill of production: The constant and aggressive growth needed to sustain the modern economy.

Global consumer class: Those who actively use technology, purchase consumer goods, and embrace the culture of consumption.

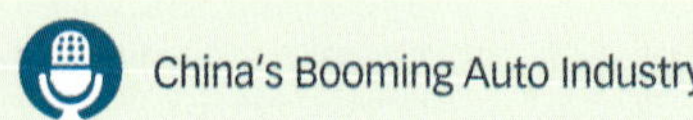

TECHNOLOGY & SOCIETY

YOUR COMPUTER AND THE ENVIRONMENT

One of the fastest-growing industries on the planet is the manufacture of electronics, including personal computers and mobile phones. On one hand, this is positive: More people than ever before can connect with one another and gain access to the educational, professional, and recreational power of personal computers. On the other hand, discarded computers, mobile phones, and other electronic devices are creating a growing toxic waste problem in all countries. A report by the United Nations Environment Programme (2009) suggests that the volume of "e-waste" generated by computers alone could rise by 200% to 400% of 2007 levels in China and South Africa over the coming decade. In India, the report predicts, the increase in computer e-waste could reach 500% of the 2007 level.

REUTERS/Stringer Indonesia

Nearly all work in Indonesia's tin mines is done by hand with pickaxes and hoes. Global demand by electronics manufacturers has pushed tin mining into the seabed, disrupting the fishing industry which has been a traditional economic staple. One journalist found tin pits dug around Bangka airport's only runway (Simpson, 2012).

Computers and mobile devices have demonstrable detrimental environmental and health effects, particularly at the start and end of their useful lives. A recent *Bloomberg Businessweek* article documents the disturbing origin of tin, which is used in every modern smartphone and electronic tablet. About one third of all tin used in these consumer devices originates in Bangka, an island that is part of Indonesia. About half the mined tin is turned into solder for the electronics industry. The miners—who number between 15,000 and 50,000—work in difficult and dangerous conditions, and, "if they're lucky, the members of a crew find enough 'tin sand' to each earn about $5 a day" (Simpson, 2012, p. 52). Tin mines, particularly those dug deep to retrieve the valuable mineral, are vulnerable to collapse and mudslides, among other hazards. Desperate for money, residents of the island endanger their safety and degrade the environment with deep pits dug legally and illegally to get to tin that can be sold.

At the other end of their productive lives, electronics once again present a serious hazard to human health and the environment. According to some estimates, for every new computer that enters the marketplace each year, another one is discarded into the solid-waste stream, carrying toxic ingredients such as lead, phosphor, barium, and cadmium with it (Worldwatch Institute, 2004). Although e-waste makes up only 1% to 2% of total waste in the United States, it accounts for 70% of toxic waste (Environmental Protection Agency, 2011).

Advanced economies such as the United States use many of the electronics produced around the world and may feel some of the effects of their disposal, but they are able to export many of the toxic effects to developing countries. Despite a global ban on trade in hazardous waste, between 50% and 80% of "recycled" computers are believed to end their lives in developing countries such as India, Pakistan, and China, where workers disassembling the machines are exposed to chemicals that can cause organ, nervous system, and brain damage (United Nations Environment Programme, 2009; Worldwatch Institute, 2004).

THINK IT THROUGH

▶ How should we as consumers of computers and other electronic devices respond to the environmental and health problems associated with the production and disposal of these devices? Whose problem is it, and who should pay for the safe disposal of e-waste?

PRIVATE LIVES, PUBLIC ISSUES

WHAT'S ON THE MENU?

Among Americans' favorite dinner treats are dishes made with shrimp. Italian restaurants serve shrimp scampi; Chinese and Thai restaurants offer a wide variety of spicy, saucy shrimp dishes; and shrimp cocktail has long been a popular appetizer. More than 1 billion pounds of shrimp are consumed in the United States each year, 90% of which are imported from overseas (Natural Resources Defense Council, 2011). Where exactly does all that shrimp come from?

A great deal comes from shrimp farms in developing countries. Some governments and wealthy donor nations have encouraged shrimp farming, arguing that it contributes to economic development in poor states and promotes a so-called blue revolution to increase the production of seafood without depleting natural marine stocks.

© XPACIFICA/National Geographic Creative

If people know that a particular food is sourced unsustainably, or even unethically, will that alter their choice to purchase the product? What would you predict, and why?

Community activists, farmers, and environmentalists, however, have questioned the benefits of shrimp farms (Gatsiounis, 2008; Trent, Williams, Thornton, & Shanahan, 2004; Worldwatch Institute, 2004). From a conflict perspective, we might ask who benefits, and who loses, from the expansion of shrimp farming in developing states.

Major beneficiaries include consumers in the United States, Europe, and Japan, who purchase and eat most of the shrimp produced. Thailand, for instance, exports up to 90% of its farmed shrimp (Fish Site, 2009). Other beneficiaries are the governments of exporting countries, since shrimp exports can bring in substantial revenue, and the private owners of shrimp farms, who are often foreign nationals.

According to some researchers and activists, losers in the blue revolution of shrimp farming are local communities and the marine environment. Common problems include the loss of agricultural land, which is flooded with saline water to create shrimp ponds, and the reduced availability of crabs and fish for consumption and exchange in the local economy (Gatsiounis, 2008; Trent et al., 2004). The salinization process can also pollute supplies of drinking and washing water. In Thailand, "as local fishermen have pulled back from shrimp farming, large-scale conglomerates have filled the void. Behind the small concrete houses . . . backhoes are digging out shrimp ponds as far as the eye can see. Villagers say there will be 100 ponds in total, owned by industrial conglomerates based in Bangkok, and operated mainly by imported labor" (Gatsiounis, 2008). Shrimp peelers working in Thai factories also absorb the costs, laboring for exploitative wages and under the threat of violence or job loss for taking time off. Many are underage or migrant workers forced into debt slavery to pay off loans to smugglers (Motlagh, 2012).

THINK IT THROUGH

▶ Where did the shrimp in your supermarket or favorite restaurant originate? Should you care? Should other consumers of shrimp care? How can we balance our culinary desires with social justice?

 Population Growth in Oil Boomtowns

Massive ships used by developed countries for the transportation of goods and oil end their useful lives on the shores of developing states such as India and Pakistan. Workers at shipbreaking yards deconstruct the giant and complex vessels, a process that releases dangerous toxins into the environment and into their bodies.

in developing states and of consumption growth in developed states and newly prosperous areas.

UNDERDEVELOPMENT AND OVERDEVELOPMENT IN THE MODERN WORLD

Environmental problems that appear in one part of the globe often result from actions taken elsewhere and may have far-reaching effects for all of the planet's inhabitants. They are indeed global. However, many immediate environmental effects are local.

The most degraded local environments tend to be those inhabited by the poorest people. Air pollution is far worse in Bangkok, Mexico City, and Beijing than in the most polluted U.S. cities such as Los Angeles. China's rapid development has brought new prosperity to many Chinese, but the rising number of factories, power stations, and cars has also brought serious pollution. A 2007 World Health Organization study suggests that more than 650,000 people die each year in China from causes associated with air pollution; another 95,000 are killed by polluted drinking water (Platt, 2007).

Disease runs rampant in the large cities of India, where the infrastructure, including sewage systems, which should carry away waste and ensure the flow of potable water, cannot meet the needs of growing populations. In some coastal areas of India, toxic pollution streams flow from ship-breaking yards, where laborers take apart ships no longer fit to sail the seas. Local environmental problems have also arisen from deforestation in the tropical rain forests of Central America and the destruction of mangrove ponds and wetlands in Asia, as these areas are transformed into agricultural production sites for growing numbers of farmers.

Population pressures in developing countries are important contributors to these problems. However, the world's developed states are also implicated. Consider, for instance, deforestation and wetlands destruction. Some of the rain-forest land in the Amazon has been cleared to make room for cattle ranching that produces beef to be consumed not locally but in the United States and other developed nations. Similarly, the wetlands of some coastal areas of Asia are being transformed into shrimp farms to grow the delicacy enjoyed in wealthy countries. The ships in India's coastal ship-breaking yards are largely the

How Population Growth and Urbanization Relate to Global Climate Change.

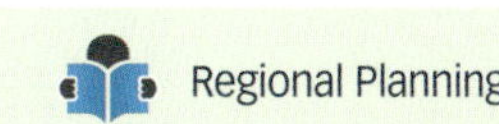

Regional Planning

In Wuhan City in China, young people walk with masks to protect their lungs from a thick haze that settled on the city in June of 2012. Authorities attributed the hazardous air to straw burning, a practice undertaken by some farmers to dispose of surplus crops in the fields. Industrial and automobile pollution are also frequent threats to air quality in Chinese towns and cities—and significant contributors to greenhouse gases. .

corpses of Western fleets. The consequences of the developed world's consumption are, indeed, felt in the furthest corners of the developing world, highlighting the fact that we cannot understand threats to the earth exclusively in terms of population explosion. We should also recognize environmental dangers as the products of choices made by a small wealthy elite of countries and consumers (Eglitis, 2010).

Industrialization in both the developed and developing worlds is also a critical aspect of the environmental equation. On one hand, some developing countries, such as China, are aggressively pursuing industrialization and multisector economic growth. Because of its enormous size and rapid move toward industrialization, China is fast becoming the world's major contributor to greenhouse gases. Coal, a highly polluting source of energy, provides the country with three-quarters of its energy, creating so much pollution in some urban areas that residents must wear surgical masks for protection. In the southern and eastern parts of the country, where urbnization and industrialization are proceeding at historically unprecedented rates, the environmental damage has been considerable. On the other hand, just as it did in the West, industrialization is bringing greater prosperity and prospects to many Chinese. This raises the question of whether we must choose between a "good life" and a "good earth." What would it mean to achieve a balance between the needs and desires of people around the world and the needs of the planet? The *Private Lives, Public Issues* box on page 454 looks at the problem of the desires of humans and needs of the planet through the prism of what we choose to eat.

WHY STUDY POPULATION AND ENVIRONMENT FROM A SOCIOLOGICAL PERSPECTIVE?

We opened this chapter by describing the effects of son preference in China, India, and South Korea. The global effect of an individual choice is not apparent to us, but populations are the products of millions or billions of such choices, some made by families, some made by states. Demographics are both statistics and lived realities. Whether we live in fast-growth states whose resources may be increasingly taxed by rapidly rising populations or in no-growth states that may experience economic troubles as workers age without being replaced, our lives will be affected in some way by demographic forces.

Similarly, we make individual choices about consumption and disposal, a topic we look at in the *Technology and Society* box in this chapter. When we purchase a new car or truck, order a meal in a restaurant, toss out bags of old clothes at spring cleaning, or decide to replace an outdated computer, we are part of a mass of other global consumers making similar choices, and our choices—like theirs—affect the economies and environments of countries around the world. Just as there is no "single global city" (in Saskia Sassen's words), there are no single choices about fertility or consumption or disposal that do not cumulatively have global effects. By understanding the social forces that affect personal choices, as well as the way personal choices affect phenomena such as population growth or decline, rising urban prosperity and poverty, and environmental health or degradation, we become better equipped to recognize and confront some of the paramount global challenges of this century.

CQR Global Biodiversity

WHAT CAN I DO WITH A SOCIOLOGY DEGREE?

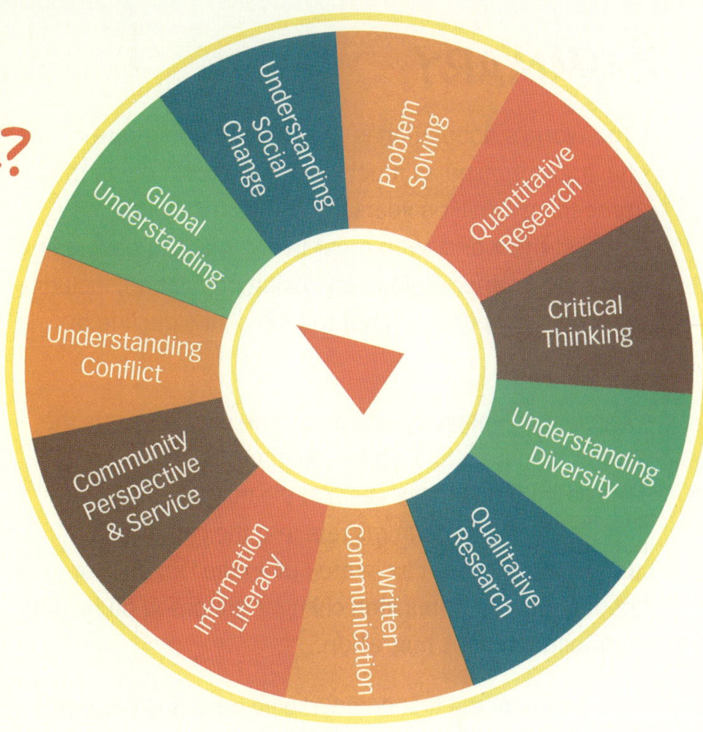

SKILLS AND CAREERS: THE GLOBAL PERSPECTIVE

The study of sociology helps you develop a broad understanding of the social world, which includes relationships between cultures and countries over time and space and the ability to see the world from a variety of perspectives. A *global perspective* encompasses knowledge and skills. A global perspective evolves through study and experiences that lead to a strong understanding and appreciation of the significance and effects of global cultural, economic, political, and social connections on individuals, communities, and countries. It also encompasses the development of skills for working effectively in intercultural environments.

In this chapter we looked at issues related to population trends, urbanization, and the environment. For example, we examined some urgent problems of the global environment. You know that nearly 200 diverse countries with sometimes competing and even conflicting domestic agendas share a single planet. Borders do not necessarily limit the effects of economic, political, or ecological decisions made by these states. Understanding different cultures, recognizing a diverse spectrum of legitimate political and economic interests, and having the ability to see issues from multiple perspectives are key to global efforts to deal cooperatively with environmental threats to the planet. As a sociology student, you will have the opportunity to develop the kind of thoughtful global perspective that will enable to you make critical connections between decisions about, for instance, economic consumption or production, which are made at the individual or community or country level, and effects that are experienced globally.

Having a global perspective is of tremendous value in today's globalized labor market and in occupations that demand proficiency in intercultural relationships and communication. *Occupational fields* such as government service, international business, health and medicine, travel and tourism, international development, and diplomacy are just a few of the areas where a global perspective is needed. *Job titles* in these sectors include foreign service officer, intelligence analyst, health worker, global social entrepreneur, cross-culture specialist, translator, and human rights organizer. Below you will find a partial list of global industries, companies, and organizations that you can research to learn about opportunities in these exciting areas of employment:

- **Global culture industries:** music, film, and sports, including MTV, Disney, and the NBA
- **Global environment:** World Wide Fund for Nature, Greenpeace, and Sierra Club
- **Global health:** World Health Organization and Centers for Disease Control and Prevention
- **Global marketing agencies:** BBDO, J. Walter Thompson, and Leo Burnett
- **Human justice organizations:** Amnesty International and Human Rights Watch
- **International governing agencies:** United Nations, World Bank, and International Monetary Fund
- **International service agencies:** Red Cross, CARE, UNICEF, and Peace Corps
- **International development agencies:** USAID and relief funds
- **International businesses:** Sony, Microsoft, Apple, and GlaxoSmithKline
- **Mass communication:** CNN, ESPN, and foreign correspondence
- **Travel and tourism:** travel agencies, global tour companies, and cruise lines
- **U.S. government offices and agencies:** Foreign Service and Department of State

THINK ABOUT CAREERS

▶ How is intercultural knowledge developed through sociological study? How can you expand your global perspective outside the classroom? Why is a global perspective of particular importance in the modern world?

▶ How might a global perspective be of value in some of the career fields of interest to you? Might changes taking place in these fields as a result of globalization or other labor market trends increase the importance of the global perspective?

SUMMARY

- The world's population is growing at a rapid rate, having increased as much since 1950 as it did in the preceding 4 million years. Growth is highly uneven around the world, with most taking place in developing countries. Other regions are losing population, including Eastern Europe (projected to face a 14% decline by 2050).
- Annual population growth or decline in a country is the result of four factors: (1) the number of people born in the country during the year, (2) the number who die, (3) the number who immigrate into the country, and (4) the number who emigrate out. In the language of demographers, population changes are based on **fertility**, mortality, and **net migration**.
- The theory of the first demographic transition proposes that many societies go through roughly the same stages of population growth: low growth resulting from high fertility and equally high mortality, a transitional stage of explosive growth resulting from high fertility and low mortality, and a final stage of slow or no growth resulting from low fertility and low mortality.
- Advanced industrial states may be undergoing a second demographic transition, seen as changes in family patterns that affect population. For instance, in the world's industrialized states divorce has increased, cohabitation has increased, marriage has declined, fertility has fallen, and nonmarital births as a proportion of all births have increased.
- Thomas Malthus developed the theory of **exponential population growth**: the belief that, like compound interest, a constant rate of population growth produces a population that grows by an increasing amount with each passing year. Malthus claimed that while population grows exponentially, the food supply does not; the earth's resources are finite. Others, such as economist Julian Simon, have suggested that population growth increases humanity's potential for uncovering talent and innovation.
- Karl Marx was critical of Malthus and felt the central problem was not a mismatch between population size and resource availability, but rather inequitable distribution of resources between the wealthy and the disadvantaged.
- Sociologist Louis Wirth (1938) defined the city as a large, densely populated, and permanent settlement that brought together heterogeneous populations. While cities of the past served primarily as centers of trade, in the 18th century industrial cities emerged as centers of manufacturing. By the 19th century industrialization was advancing hand in hand with **urbanization**.
- Some of the most highly urbanized countries in the world today are those that only a century ago were almost entirely rural. As recently as 1950, only 18% of the inhabitants of developing countries lived in urban areas. In 2010, fully 44% did. By 2015, the proportion of the world's people living in **cities** across the world approached 50%.
- With the emergence of postindustrial society, **global cities** have appeared. These metropolitan areas are highly interconnected with one another and serve as centers of global political and economic decision making, finance, and culture. Examples include New York, London, Tokyo, Hong Kong, Los Angeles, Mexico City, and Singapore.
- The combination of rapid population growth and modernization, in the form of industrialization and urbanization, takes a toll on the global environment and its resources. Both under- and overdevelopment threaten the environment.
- The study of **demography** and population growth helps us gain a fuller understanding of the ways that micro-level events, such as childbearing decisions in a family, are linked to macro-level issues, such as population growth or decline, threats of mortality, and challenges to the sustainability of resources and development.

KEY TERMS

demography, 433

population momentum, 435

fertility, 436

net migration, 436

crude birthrate, 436

age-specific fertility rate, 436

crude death rate, 436

age-specific mortality rate, 436

life expectancy, 436

rate of natural increase (RNI), 440

exponential population growth, 441

city, 443

agricultural surplus, 444

urbanization, 445

urban growth machine, 446

urban renewal, 447

gentrification, 447

global cities, 447

megacities, 450

treadmill of production, 452

global consumer class, 452

DISCUSSION QUESTIONS

1. What key factors have contributed to the decline of population growth in many modern countries? What are the benefits and consequences of fertility declines?
2. Do populations stop growing when fertility declines to replacement rate fertility (a total fertility rate of 2.1)? Explain your answer.
3. As you saw in the chapter, urbanization continues to increase across the globe. What draws populations to cities? What sociological factors point to this trend continuing?
4. What is the global consumer class? What are the global costs and benefits to the expansion of this group?
5. Are economic growth and environmental protection irreconcilable values? Consider what you have read both in earlier chapters about economic growth and employment and in this chapter about environmental challenges such as climate change, and respond thoughtfully to the question.

Answer to question on page 436: on the 29th day.

SOCIAL MOVEMENTS AND SOCIAL CHANGE

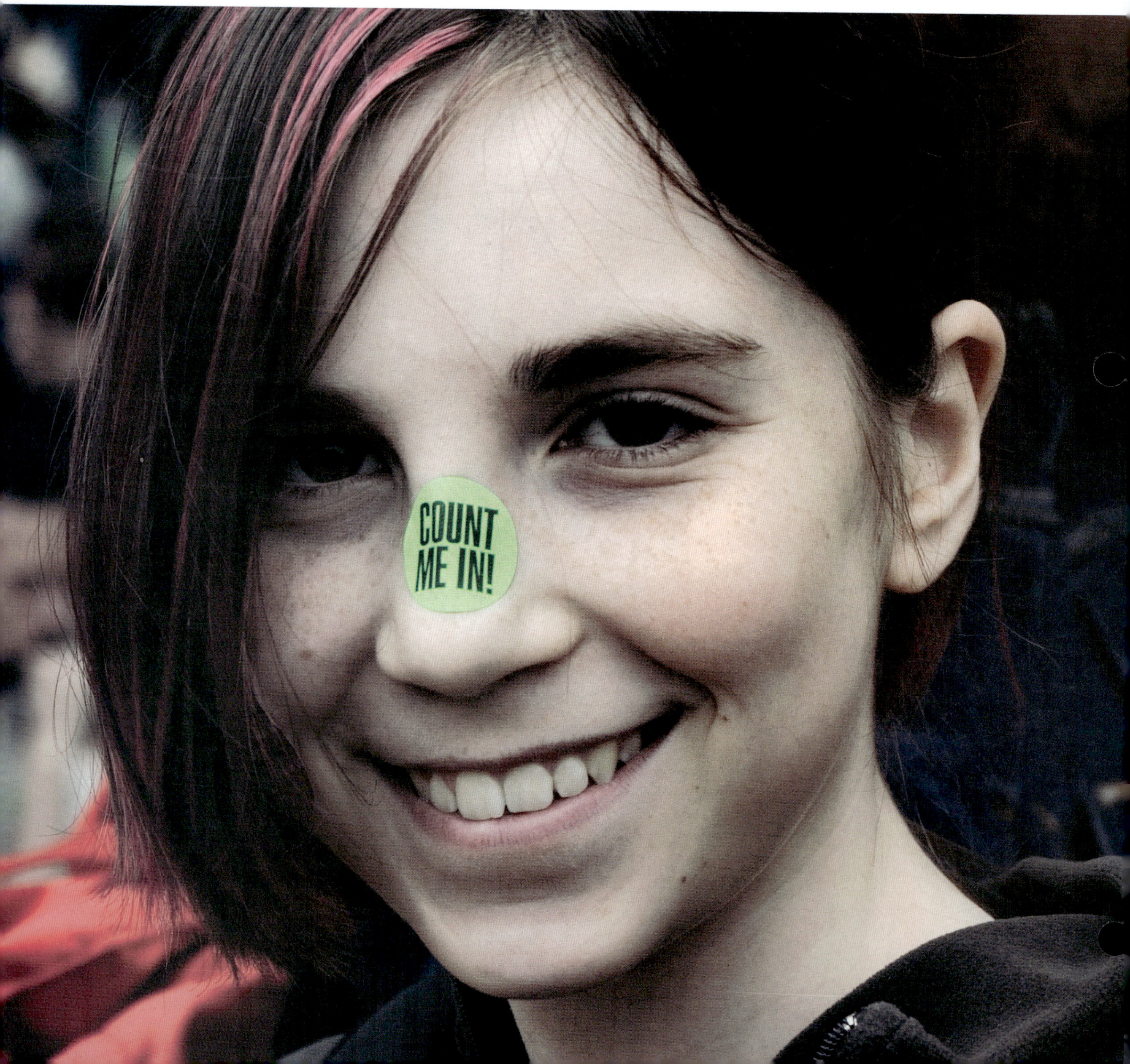

© Carl & Ann Purcell/Corbis

WHAT DO YOU THINK?

1. What social, political, or economic conditions make revolutionary changes in societies more likely?
2. Do people behave differently in crowds than they would individually or in small groups? What sociological factors explain crowd behavior?
3. How has social activism changed in the age of the internet?

AP Photo/Paul Sancya

A LOW-WAGE REVOLUTION?

In 2014, across the United States, low-wage workers in the retail and food service sectors participated in strikes intended to draw attention to their economic plight and to push large employers like McDonald's, Wendy's, and Walmart to raise wages. On May 15, 2014, thousands of fast-food workers, organized by the advocacy group Fast Food Forward, participated in labor strikes in U.S. cities from Boston and New York to Miami and Seattle. The 15th day of the month was chosen for the protest to highlight the demonstrators' demand that the federal minimum wage be raised to $15 an hour from the current $7.25. Similar strikes by fast-food workers took place in other countries as well, including Japan, England, and South Korea. Less than a month later, Walmart workers took to the streets in about 20 U.S. cities to advocate for higher wages.

What is behind these strikes? The protests, which have been organized largely by coalitions of unions and workers, are the outcome of a confluence of factors. First, many part-time and full-time workers in these sectors earn wages that put them below or just barely above the poverty line. Consider that, according to Walmart, about half of the company's full-time hourly workers earn more than $25,000 per year—that leaves the other half of full-time store employees of the country's biggest private employer taking in under $25,000 annually (Reich, 2014). In fact, recent research by some public policy organizations found that employees at the country's major low-wage employers, including McDonald's and Walmart, are among the biggest consumers of public assistance. Rather than pay their employees a living wage, employers like McDonald's are offering employees information (through such tools as McDonald's McResource phone line) on applying for housing, health, and food aid from the government (Allegretto et al., 2013).

Second, the rise of worker movements may be driven by the growth of the "low-wage economy" in the United States (Reich, 2014). Data show that while about a fifth of the jobs lost in the most

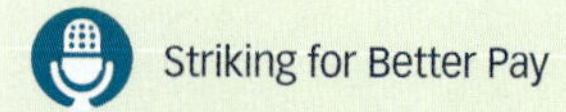
Striking for Better Pay

recent economic crisis (early 2008 to early 2010) were in low-wage sectors like retail and food service, about 44% of the jobs added in the 4 years following have been in those sectors (National Employment Law Project, 2014). Although jobs in areas like fast food are often associated in the public mind with teenagers earning pocket money, a recent report suggests that more workers in these areas are older workers, many with families: Today, about 68% of fast-food workers are single or married adults who are not in school, and about a quarter are raising children (Berfield, 2013).

Among the key demands of workers in recent protests has been an increase in the minimum wage. While most workers earn above the federal minimum wage of $7.25 an hour, the median wage in the fast-food industry is below $9.00, and many employees are offered only part-time hours (Allegretto et al., 2013). Notably, this industry features the most skewed CEO-to-worker pay ratio, which is estimated to be about 1,000:1 (Reich, 2014). Raising the minimum wage is a controversial issue that has drawn a spectrum of political and economic interests into the debate (which we examined in some detail in Chapter 7). Despite the ongoing controversy, some change is taking place, perhaps in response to the workers' movement. In 2014, the U.S. Congress considered, but failed to pass, a bill that would have raised the federal minimum wage to $10.10. At the same time, by mid-2014, seven states and several cities had raised the minimum wage on their own. In a landmark decision, the city of Seattle, Washington, passed a bill to raise the minimum wage gradually to $15.00 per hour. ■

We begin this chapter with an overview of the foundations of sociological theorizing on social change. We continue with an examination of key sources of social change, focusing in particular on collective behavior and resources from which strikers such as those described above draw. Next we provide an overview of forms that social movements take, and we conclude with some reflections on the nature of social change going forward in a rapidly changing and globalized world.

Differentiation: The development of increasing societal complexity through the creation of specialized social roles and institutions.

Media and Social Movements

SOCIOLOGICAL PERSPECTIVES ON SOCIAL CHANGE

The concept of social change is all-encompassing. It refers to small-group changes, such as a social club changing a long-standing policy against admitting women or minorities, and to global-level and national-level transformations, such as the outsourcing of jobs to low-wage countries and the rise of social movements that seek to address the threat of climate change.

When sociologists speak of social change, they are generally referring to changes that occur throughout the social structure of an entire society. *Societies* are understood sociologically as entities comprising those people who share a common culture and common institutions. *Social change* may refer to changes within small, relatively isolated communities such as those of the Amish or the small, culturally homogeneous tribes that dot the Amazon basin; changes across complex and modern societies such as the United States, Japan, or Germany; or changes common across similar societies, such as the economically advanced states of the West or the Arab countries of North Africa and the Middle East.

Three key types of social change theories in sociology are functionalist theories, conflict theories, and cyclical theories. Sociological perspectives on social change begin with particular assumptions about both the social world and basic processes of change. Below we briefly consider each theoretical perspective and discuss its utility for helping us understand the nature of social change in the world today.

THE FUNCTIONALIST PERSPECTIVE

Functionalist theories of social change assume that as societies develop, they become more complex and interdependent. Herbert Spencer (1892) argued that what distinguishes modern societies is **differentiation**—that is, *the development of increasing societal complexity through the creation of specialized social roles and institutions.* Spencer was referring to what Émile Durkheim conceptualized as the division of labor, which is characterized by the sorting of people into interdependent occupational and task categories (and, by extension, class categories). Think of medieval England, when craftsmen working at home made tools and shoes that they exchanged for food or clothing, using a broad range of skills to act relatively independently of one another. Compare this to modern society, where factory workers each produce parts of an automobile, managers sell completed cars to dealerships, and salespeople sell them to customers. Today people master a narrow range of tasks within a large number of highly specialized (differentiated) institutional roles and thus are highly interdependent. (Note the similarity here to Durkheim's notion that societies evolve over time from *mechanical* to *organic solidarity*—the former being characteristic of

By today's standards, Quakers were a highly homogenous society, where consensus of opinion allowed for a type of religiously rooted social organization and structure that would likely not be possible in modern societies.

traditional, homogeneous societies and the latter characteristic of diverse, modern societies.)

The earliest functionalist theories of social change were *evolutionary theories,* which assumed that all societies begin as "simple" or "primitive" and eventually develop into more "complicated" and "civilized" forms along a single, unidirectional evolutionary path (Morgan, 1877/1964). During the 20th century, however, this notion of unilinear development became increasingly shaky, as anthropologists came to believe that societies evolve in many different ways. More recent evolutionary theories (sometimes termed *multilinear*) argue that multiple paths to social change exist, depending on the particular circumstances of the society (Moore, 2004; Sahlins & Service, 1960). Technology, environment, population size, and social organization are among the factors that play roles in determining the path a society takes.

Some evolutionary theorists viewed societies as eventually reaching an equilibrium state in which no further change would occur unless an external force set it in motion. For example, Durkheim believed that "primitive," or less developed, societies were largely unchanging unless population growth resulted in such a differentiation of social relationships that organic solidarity replaced mechanical solidarity. Talcott Parsons (1951) viewed societies as equilibrium systems that constantly seek to maintain balance, or the status quo, unless something external disrupts equilibrium, such as changes in technology or economic relationships with other societies. Parsons later came to argue, however, that societies do change by becoming more complicated systems that are better adapted to their external environments (Parsons & Shils, 2001).

Although no one can deny that modern societies contain many more specialized roles and institutions than earlier ones, evolutionary theories also assume that social changes are progressive and that "modern" (European) societies are more evolved than earlier "primitive" ones. Such beliefs appealed to countries whose soldiers, missionaries, and merchants were conquering or colonizing much of the rest of the world, since they helped justify those imperialist actions as part of the "civilizing" mission of a more advanced people. Anthropologists and sociologists eventually rejected these ideas (Nolan & Lenski, 2009).

On a more micro level, consider de-differentiation in the mainstream marital relationship. Traditionally, the man was the "head of the household" and often ruled his wife and children with an iron fist. Both the norm and the reality of marriage today are characterized by a de-differentiation of roles in which men take on domestic responsibilities and, increasingly, the wife is a major income producer for the family.

Since different parts of society undergo the processes of differentiation and de-differentiation to varying degrees and at different times, considerable conflict may arise between them (Alexander, 1998; Alexander & Colomy, 1990; Colomy, 1986, 1990). It is, however, the conflict perspective that assumes conflict as the foundation for social change. We look at that perspective below.

THE CONFLICT PERSPECTIVE

Conflict theories suggest that conflict is the product of divergent and perhaps irreconcilable social group interests and contradictory goals of social relationships. Even if a population or technology is in a state of stasis rather than change, conflict theorists see social change as inevitable, as people create ways of dealing with the conflicts and contradictions inherent in social life. Responding to the conflicts and contradictions can potentially bring a society to the brink of sharp and sometimes violent breaks with the past.

Unlike their functionalist peers in sociology, conflict theorists do not see social stability as the ultimate goal of social organization. They recognize conflict as a vital, transformative part of social life.

Karl Marx focused his research on the contradictions and conflicts built into capitalist societies, where the world is divided between owners of the means of production and workers, who own only their own labor power and must sell it under conditions not of their own making. In Marx's view, the revolutionary transformation of a society into a new type—from feudalism to capitalism, or from capitalism to socialism, for example—would occur when the consciousness of the people or the concentration of power in one social class was sufficient to create a social movement able to transform the political and economic institutions into new sets of social relationships. As we have seen throughout this text, Marx's conflict theory

What We can Learn from Occupy Wallstreet

adhered to its own evolutionary view of social change, in which all societies would advance to the same final destination: a classless, stateless society. We have earlier noted a number of weaknesses in this theory. Of particular importance is Marx's tendency to overemphasize economic conflict while underestimating cultural conflict and other noneconomic factors, such as gender, ethnicity, race, and nationalism, which have become increasingly important in the world today.

Later conflict theorists have also addressed key questions about processes of social change, such as how groups come to want and pursue social change. Italian Marxist Antonio Gramsci (1971), for instance, highlighted the importance of ideas in maintaining order and oppression in society. He observed that the ruling class is often able to create *ideological hegemony,* a generally accepted view of what is of value and how people should relate to their economic and social status in society. Ideological hegemony may lead people to consent to their own domination by, for instance, socializing them to believe that the existing hierarchy of power is the best or only way to organize society. Consider as well that in the past women were socialized by agents such as schools, families, and religious institutions to believe they should not have jobs outside the home or vote. The idea that women should not hold positions outside the home could be considered a *hegemonic idea* of this period.

Gramsci also spoke of *organic intellectuals*—those who emerge from oppressed groups to create counterhegemonies that challenge dominant (and dominating) ideas. In the mid-19th century, women's suffrage activists including Lucretia Mott and Elizabeth Cady Stanton were organic intellectuals, challenging powerful beliefs that women should be excluded from politics. Over time and through the efforts of activists, the counterhegemonic idea that women should have a voice in politics became, in fact, the hegemonic, or dominant, belief in Western society.

In the 1950s, in response to the dominant functionalist paradigm, sociologist Ralf Dahrendorf published an influential article titled "Out of Utopia" (1958). Dahrendorf argued that functionalist theory, with its emphasis on how social institutions exist to maintain the status quo, overlooks critically important characteristics of society that lead to social conflict, such as the role of power, social change, and the unequal distribution of resources. The distribution of authority in society, said Dahrendorf, is a means of determining the probability of conflict. Where hierarchical structures such as states, private economic entities such as manufacturing firms, and even religious organizations are all dominated by the same elite, the potential for conflict is higher than in societies where authority is more dispersed. Put another way, if Group A dominates all or most key hierarchical authority structures and Group B is nearly always subordinate, conflict will be likely because Group B has little stake in the existing social order. However, if Group B has authority in some hierarchical structures and Group A has authority in others, neither group has great incentive to challenge the status quo.

Marx emphasized control of the means of production as a source of power and conflict; Gramsci highlighted control of dominant ideas in society as an important source of power and change; and Dahrendorf put authority and its concentration or distribution at the center of his work. Conflict theorists differ in their beliefs about what sources are most likely to underlie social conflict and social change, but all agree that social conflict and social change are both inevitable and desirable components of society and progress.

Rise-and-fall theories of social change: Theories that see social change as characterized by a cycle of growth and decline.

RISE-AND-FALL THEORIES OF SOCIAL CHANGE

Rise-and-fall theories of social change deny that there is any particular forward direction to social change; rather,

© H.M. HERGET/National Geographic Creative

Global military and political dominance, sophisticated technology, specialization and division of labor, political institutions, and the social class structure are all strikingly similar between the United States and the fallen Roman Empire. Is there a cautionary tale here about a possible future of the United States?

Conflict within Social Movements

INEQUALITY MATTERS

SPORTS AND SOCIAL CHANGE

For many of us, sports play an important role in our lives: From watching the Olympics to rooting for our college teams to playing weekend games with friends, we take pleasure in the competition, the action, and the company. At some pivotal points in U.S. history, sports have also played an important role in driving social change. Consider the 1972 passage of Title IX, a federal law that prohibits discrimination on the basis of sex in any federally funded education program or activity. Title IX is credited with, among other things, opening up unprecedented opportunities for girls and young women to participate in organized sports, because it requires every school receiving federal funding to offer team sports to both male and female athletes and prohibits the denial of equal participation opportunities for women in organized sports. In the year prior to the implementation of Title IX, just a little more than 300,000 girls and women were playing high school and college sports across the United States. By 2012, the figure was well over 3 million ("Before and After Title IX," 2012).

Before Title IX, however, a young athlete with big dreams was an important driver of social change in racial integration in the United States. Some sports sociologists suggest that Jackie Robinson, the first African American player to integrate Major League Baseball, drove the first significant change in Black and White relations in the 20th century. In the words of sociologist Richard Zamoff, "A year before President [Harry] Truman's executive order desegregating the military, seven years before *Brown v. Board of Education,* and more than ten years before most people in America had ever heard about Rosa Parks or Martin Luther King, Jr." (personal communication, 2014), Jackie Robinson and his Brooklyn Dodgers team initiated a sometimes fraught but entirely necessary dialogue in U.S. society about race relations and integration. In the words of Gerald Early (2011), we can divide Black–White relations in the 20th century into two periods: "before Robinson and after Robinson."

Photo Researchers, Inc.

Baseball player Jackie Robinson was the first African-American to play in on a Major League Baseball team. He was recruited by the Brooklyn Dodgers and played for the team for the first time in 1947. In 1997, his uniform number, 42, was retired across major league baseball.

Before Robinson's integration of the minor leagues in 1946 and then the Major League in 1947, professional baseball had been segregated for more than half a century. Robinson's debut with the Dodgers was not welcomed in all quarters, and he suffered threats and abuse from fans, the press, and even other players. Notably, Robinson had agreed to the condition imposed by Dodgers general manager Branch Rickey that he not fight back in response to the racist taunts. By the end of the season, Robinson had not only endured the intense challenges of integrating the league but had also won the admiration of scores of fans with his grace under fire and his athletic achievements, which included helping to lead his team to the National League pennant and an appearance in the World Series in his first year with the Dodgers.

Jackie Robinson has been widely recognized for both his individual accomplishments and the contributions he made to the game of baseball and a society still struggling with racism in the middle of the 20th century. Interestingly, 25 years after his initial integration of baseball, he nearly refused to participate in a commemorative event because of his disappointment in the fact that Major League Baseball had yet to appoint a Black team manager. The first Black manager of a Major League Baseball team was hired by the Cleveland Indians in 1975, 3 years after Robinson's death.

Sports has been a driver of social change in the United States and across the globe. The progress it has wrought is, as Robinson saw, incomplete and imperfect but nonetheless of great significance.

THINK IT THROUGH

▶ What makes sports a potential vehicle for social change rather than "just a game"? Can you think of other instances in which sports or particular athletes have had a powerful social impact?

they *argue that change reflects a cycle of growth and decline.* Rise-and-fall or cyclical theories are common in the religious myths of many cultures, which view social life as a reflection of the life cycle of living creatures, or the seasons of the year, with the end representing some form of return to the beginning. Sociology, emerging in an era that equated scientific and technological advancement with progress, at first tended to reject such cyclical metaphors in favor of more evolutionary or revolutionary ones that emphasized the forward motion of progress.

There have been a number of significant exceptions, however, among historically oriented social theorists. Pitirim Sorokin (1957/1970, 1962), a historical sociologist of the mid-20th century, argued that societies alternate among three different kinds of mentalities: those that give primacy to the senses, those that emphasize religiosity, and those that celebrate logic and reason. Societies that value hedonism and the satisfaction of immediate pleasures more highly than the achievement of long-term goals give primacy to the senses; religiosity occurs in societies that value following the tenets of a religion over enjoying the senses or solving problems through logic and reason. We tend to think of modern societies as defined largely by the emphasis on logic and reason.

Societies everywhere have contained a mixture of religiosity, an emphasis on the senses, and the celebration of logic and reason. Sorokin's "ideal types" may nonetheless be useful for describing the *relative* emphasis of each of these modes of adaptation in different societies. For example, we might say that the modern Western world puts greater emphasis on logic and reason than on religion or giving primacy to the senses; it would be a mistake, however, to say that there is no emphasis on the senses or religion, because these traits too play important roles in shaping the modern Western world.

In *The Rise and Fall of the Great Powers* (1987), historian Paul Kennedy traces the conditions associated with national power and decline during the past five centuries. As nations grow in economic power, he argues, they often seek to become world military powers as well, a goal that in the long run proves to be their undoing. Wielding global military power eventually weakens a nation's domestic economy, undermining the prosperity that once fueled it. Kennedy forecasts that this might well be the fate of the United States. More recently, writer Cullen Murphy (2007) has pointed to parallels between the Roman Empire and the United States, noting that Rome too was characterized by an overburdened and costly military, a deep sense of exceptionalism, and a tendency to denigrate and misunderstand other cultures. He notes as well the Roman pattern of shifting the onus for providing services to citizens away from the public sector to the private sector, seeing this as a form of enrichment for the few but a disadvantage for the many. A key point in rise-and-fall narratives is that social change can be both progressive and regressive—power does not invariably beget more power; it may also beget decline.

The most renowned sociologist considered by some to be a cyclical theorist is Max Weber. Although he took an evolutionary view of society as increasingly moving toward a politically and economically legal-rational society governed by rules and regulations, Weber (1919/1946) also emphasized the role of irrational elements in shaping human behavior. For example, while he wrote about the growing formal rationality of the modern world, he also recognized the possibility that a society's path could be altered by the appearance of a charismatic figure whose singular personal authority transcended institutionalized authority structures. Leaders who drastically changed a nation's trajectory include Haile Selassie, who governed Ethiopia for half a century, Adolf Hitler in Germany, Mao Zedong in China, and Fidel Castro in Cuba. In the United States, Martin Luther King Jr. led

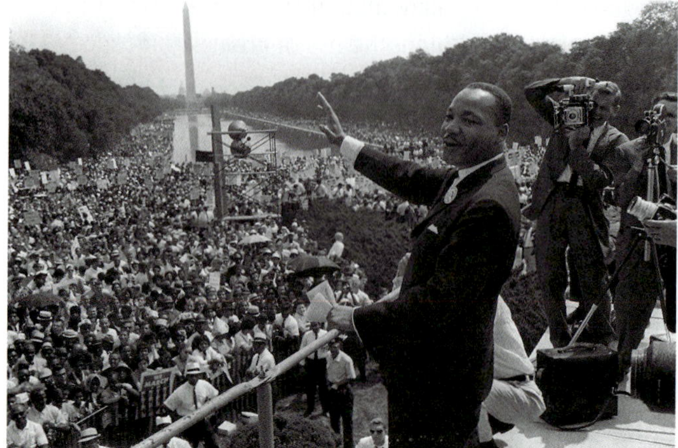

AFP / Stringer/Getty Images

Dr. Martin Luther King Jr. had a transformational dream. His words and deeds inspired and continue to inspire social change. The actions of a single person can be truly significant.

the civil rights movement in the 1960s and fundamentally changed race relations.

Cyclical theories have not enjoyed great popularity among sociologists. Even Weber's theory is not truly cyclical; his idea of *charismatic authority* is a sort of wild card, providing an unpredictable twist in an otherwise predictable march of social change from one form of authority to another. The more far-reaching versions of cyclical theory, such as Sorokin's theory that society swings among three different worldviews, are framed in such broad terms that it is challenging to prove them right or wrong.

SOURCES OF SOCIAL CHANGE

Social change ultimately results from human action. Sociologists studying how change occurs often analyze the mass action of large numbers of people and the institutionalized behaviors of organizations. In this section we examine social change within the context of mass action by groups of people, focusing on theories of collective behavior and the role played by social movements.

COLLECTIVE BEHAVIOR

Collective behavior is *voluntary, goal-oriented action that occurs in relatively disorganized situations in which society's predominant social norms and values cease to govern individual behavior* (Oberschall, 1973; Turner & Killian, 1987). Although collective behavior is usually associated with disorganized aggregates of people, it may also occur in highly regimented social contexts when order and discipline break down.

Beginning with the writings of the 19th-century French sociologist Gustave Le Bon (1896/1960), the sociological study of collective behavior has been particularly concerned with the behavior of people in **crowds**—that is, *temporary gatherings of closely interacting people with a common focus.* People in crowds were traditionally seen as prone to being swept up in group emotions, losing their ability to make rational decisions as individuals. The "group mind" of the crowd has long been viewed as an irrational and dangerous aspect of modern societies, with crowds believed to consist of rootless, isolated individuals prone to herdlike behavior (Arendt, 1951; Fromm, 1941; Gaskell & Smith, 1981; Kornhauser, 1959).

More recently, however, it has become clear that there can be a fair degree of social organization in crowds. For example, the Occupy Wall Street movement of 2011–2012 and the Arab Spring revolutions, which began in late 2010, although representing spontaneous beginnings, quickly developed a degree of predictability and organization, and in turn became social movements. It is important to note that crowds alone do not constitute social movements, but they are a critical ingredient in most cases. We must rethink the very notion of "spontaneity" in a global context, given that the use of social media has been a precipitating factor in collective behaviors ranging from flash mobs to street protests to revolutions.

Sociologists seek to explain the conditions that may lead a group of people to engage in collective behavior, whether violent or peaceful. Below we examine three principal sociological approaches: contagion theories, which emphasize nonsocial factors such as instincts; emergent norm theories, which seek out some kind of underlying social organization that leads a group to generate norms governing collective action; and value-added theories, which combine elements of personal, organizational, and social conditions in order to explain collective behavior.

CONTAGION THEORIES Contagion theories assume that human beings can revert to herdlike behavior when they come together in large crowds. Herbert Blumer (1951), drawing on symbolic interactionism, emphasized the role of raw imitation, which leads people in crowds to "mill about" much like a group of animals, stimulating and goading one another into movement actions, whether peaceful or violent. Individual acts, therefore, become contagious; they are unconsciously copied until they eventually explode into collective action. A skilled

Collective behavior: Voluntary, goal-oriented action that occurs in relatively disorganized situations in which society's predominant social norms and values cease to govern individual behavior.

Crowds: Temporary gatherings of closely interacting people with a common focus.

Moral Panic

On September 17, 2011, protesters filled the streets around Wall Street in New York City. Many carried signs protesting growing economic inequality in the United States. Occupy Wall Street demonstrators also spoke out for greater environmental protection, union power, campaign finance reform, an end to the war in Iraq, and myriad other social issues. The OWS movement has declined, but the issues it raised continue to spark activism like that described in the opening story. ■

leader can effectively manipulate such behavior, "working the crowd" until it reaches a fever pitch.

Sociologists have used the contagion theory perspective to study the panic flights of crowds, "epidemics" of bizarre collective behaviors such as uncontrollable dancing or fainting, and reports of satanic child abuse. In 1983, a local "panic" erupted in a small California city after a parent of a preschool child accused teachers at her child's school of raping and sodomizing dozens of students. The trial in the case stretched on for years, but no wrongdoing was ever proven and no defendant convicted. Accusations in the case, which drew on allegations from children and parents, included stories about teachers chopping up animals at the school, clubbing to death a horse, and sacrificing a baby. Public accounts of the trial unleashed a national panic about abuse and satanism in child-care facilities, though there was no serious documentation of such activities (Haberman, 2014). Some sociologists believe that a few well-publicized cases of deviant behavior—including wild accusations like those described above—can trigger imitative behavior until a virtual "epidemic" emerges that then feeds on itself (Goode, 2009).

How does the contagion actually spread? What are the mechanisms that affect whether people imitate one another's behavior in the interest of grabbing attention or promoting social change? In the case of the Occupy Wall Street movement, we might conclude that as increasing numbers of people realized there was an avenue they could use to protest the political and economic conditions in the United States, they began establishing Occupy camps all over the country. The decline of the movement over time was more gradual. The movement to bring a living wage to the fast-food sector has, arguably, taken on momentum in a similar fashion.

While copycat behavior may build momentum rapidly, an explanation limited to this factor is unlikely to account fully for collective behavior. Furthermore, such explanations are sometimes used to discredit particular instances of collective behavior as resulting from an irrational (and therefore dangerous) tendency of people to jump on the bandwagon. Critics of the Occupy movement often depicted participants as little more than copycats engaging in occupying city space, rather than as members of a movement with serious concerns about the state of contemporary society. In the 1960s, some people dismissed antiwar and civil rights protesters as misled "flower children" rather than recognizing them as people concerned about injustice and war. Sociologists, however, seek ways to determine *why* collective behavior occurs and to understand the rational and organizational basis for its emergence (Chafetz & Dworkin, 1983; Wright, 1993). We look next at what some other theories suggest.

EMERGENT NORM THEORIES Most sociologists prefer to look for norms and values that shape conscious human behavior rather than rely on the idea that instincts govern unconscious processes. Some have suggested that emergent norms offer an explanation for collective behavior. We can define **emergent norms** as *norms that are situationally created to support a collective action*. For example, Ralph H. Turner and Lewis M. Killian (1987) argue that even when crowd behavior appears chaotic and disorganized, norms emerge that explain the crowd's actions. Crowd members take stock of what is going on around them, are mindful of their personal motivations, and, in general, collectively define the situation in which they find themselves. In this respect, crowd behavior is not very different from ordinary behavior; there is no need to fall back on "instincts" or "contagion" to explain it.

The Tea Party political movement in the United States (which we discussed briefly in Chapter 13) began as a collective protest against "big government." It soon developed a package of emergent norms that morphed into a political movement emphasizing the importance of getting like-minded politicians elected to office, as well as norms that emphasized the importance of adherence to the central ideas of the U.S. Constitution, lower taxes, more limited government, and reduced government spending.

The emergent norm approach offers only a partial explanation of collective behavior. First, all crowds do not develop norms that govern their actions; crowds often emerge out of shared sets of norms among the participants. Second, purely spontaneous emotional outbursts may also occur as people act on their immediate impulses. Furthermore, when norms governing crowd behavior do emerge, they are unlikely by themselves to account fully for collective behavior. When an

Emergent norms: Norms that are situationally created to support a collective action.

Social Change and Non-Violence

CQR Tea Party Movement

amateurish video appeared on the Internet in the fall of 2012 depicting the Prophet Muhammad in an unfavorable and even absurd light, crowds spontaneously gathered in some Middle Eastern countries to protest against the United States, where the video was made. These crowds were responding to religious leaders who informed their members of the existence of the video and encouraged protests. Emergent norms played little part in these actions; the norms (and grievances) being expressed had long historical standing in the communities where the protests took place.

VALUE-ADDED THEORY Both contagion and emergent norm theories focus primarily on the micro level of individual action and thought, largely ignoring macro-level factors—poverty, unemployment, governmental abuses of authority, and so on—that may explain the emergence of collective behavior. More than 50 years ago, Neil Smelser (1962) sought to develop what he termed a "value-added" approach to understanding collective behavior. He identified a number of both micro- and macro-level factors that each contribute something of value to the outcome and that form a foundation for collective behavior. Think about a revolution or social movement discussed in this chapter or that you have learned about elsewhere—can you identify the factors below in that context?

1. *Structural conduciveness* exists when the existing social structure favors the emergence of collective behavior.
2. *Structural strain* occurs when the social system breaks down.
3. *Generalized beliefs* are shared explanations of the conditions that are troubling people. People must define the problem, identify its causes, and—to use C. Wright Mills's phrase—come to see their personal problems as public issues.
4. *Precipitating factors* are dramatic events that confirm the generalized beliefs of the group, thereby triggering action.
5. *Mobilization for action* occurs when leaders arise who encourage action.
6. *The failure of social control* leaves those charged with maintaining law and order unable to do so in the face of mounting pressures for collective action.

Smelser's approach has been used to analyze collective behavior in a variety of settings, including self-help groups (Smith & Pillemer, 1983), social welfare organizations (Smith & Moses, 1980), and nuclear-weapons-freeze activism (Tygart, 1987). The theory's strength is that it combines societal-, organizational-, and individual-level factors into one comprehensive theory. Yet it has also been criticized for emphasizing the part that people's reactions play in collective behavior more than the fact that people themselves are conscious agents creating the conditions required for social change.

HOW DO CROWDS ACT?

We have all participated in some form of collective behavior in our social lives. Collective behavior comes in a spectrum of different forms, including riots, fads, fashions, panics, crazes, and rumors. We discuss each of these forms of collective behavior in turn below.

RIOTS A **riot** is *an illegal, prolonged outbreak of violent behavior by a large group of people directed against individuals or property.* Riots represent a form of crowd behavior; often they are spontaneous, although sometimes they are motivated by a conscious set of concerns. Prison and urban riots are common examples. During a riot, conventional norms, including respect for the private property of others, are suspended and replaced with other norms developed within the group. For example, inmates may destroy property to force prison officials to adopt more humane practices, and the theft of property during an urban riot may reflect the participants' desire for a more equitable distribution of resources.

The very use of the term *riot* to characterize a particular action is often highly political. In 1773, a crowd of Bostonians protesting British taxation of the American colonies seized a shipment of tea from a British vessel and dumped it into Boston Harbor. While the British Crown roundly condemned this action as the illegal act of a rioting mob, U.S. history books celebrate the "Boston Tea Party" as the noble act of inspired patriots and an opening salvo in the Revolutionary War.

© Lee Jin-man/ /AP/Corb

The mass demonstrations against police brutality that took place in late 2014 were precipitated by a series of deaths of unarmed Black men at the hands of police and decisions of several grand juries not to indict officers involved in the deaths. In this photo, students at American University in Washington, DC, participate in a protest action.

Riot: An illegal, prolonged outbreak of violent behavior by a sizable group of people directed against people or property.

Fads: Temporary, highly imitated outbreaks of mildly unconventional behavior.

CQR 'Occupy' Movement

FADS AND FASHIONS The desire to join others in being different (itself perhaps something of an irony) continually feeds the rise of new looks and sounds. **Fads**, or *temporary, highly imitated outbreaks of mildly unconventional behavior,* are particularly common responses to popular entertainment such as music, movies, and books and require social networks (electronic or otherwise) in order to spread (Iribarren & Moro, 2007). The fads of piercing body parts to wear ornaments and extensive body tattooing have captured several generations and seem to be continuing today. Other fads have included wearing blue jeans with holes in the knees, staging "panty raids" on sorority houses, and adopting the "hipster" style popularized by young people united by a common interest in alternative music and Pabst Blue Ribbon beer.

As fads become popular, they sometimes cease being fads and instead become **fashions**, that is, *somewhat long-lasting styles of imitative behavior or appearance.* Georg Simmel (1904/1971) first examined the sociological implications of fashions more than a century ago. He pointed out that fashions reflect a tension between people's desire to be different and their desire to conform. By adopting a fashion, a person initially appears to stand out from the group, yet the fashion itself reflects group norms. As the fashion catches on, more and more people adopt it, and it eventually ceases to express any degree of individuality. Its very success undermines its attractiveness, so the eventual fate of all fashions is to become unfashionable.

Simmel's observations offer another insight into fashions: Unlike fads, they often grow out of the continuous and well-organized efforts of those who work in design, manufacturing technology, marketing, and media to define what is in style. As "grunge" music became popular, it spawned a profitable clothing industry, and highly paid fashion designers created clothing that was grungy in everything but price. Today there are several fashion trends that resonate with different audiences and subcultures. Whether it is the hipster look of skinny jeans, oversized glasses, and ironic sweatshirts or the EDM (electronic dance music) scene of neon colors, high-waist shorts, and playful accessories, manufacturers will spend millions of dollars attempting to convince youthful consumers that they must buy particular products in order to be fashionable and popular.

PANICS AND CRAZES A **panic** is *a massive flight from something feared.* The most celebrated example was created by an infamous radio broadcast on the night before Halloween in 1938: Orson Welles's Mercury Theatre rendition of H. G. Wells's science fiction novel *War of the Worlds.* The broadcast managed to convince thousands that Martians had landed in Grover's Mill, New Jersey, and were wreaking havoc with deadly laser beams. People panicked, flooded the telephone lines with calls, and fled to "safer" ground.

A historically notable panic actually happened unintentionally. A 1938 Halloween radio broadcast narrated H. G. Wells's science fiction novel. Many listeners did not realize that the radio was broadcasting a work of fiction, causing them to panic.

Panics are often ignited by the belief that something is awry in the corporate world or in consumer technology. As the year 2000 approached, panic over the Y2K problem, also known as the "millennium bug," gripped many people who believed reports that computer systems worldwide would crash when the year 2000 began (supposedly computers would be unable to distinguish the year 2000 from 1900, because they used only two digits to designate the year). A recent example of a panic involved the Mayan calendar, which was projected to "end" during our calendar equivalent of December 2012. The fact that the structure of the Mayan calendar and the Mayan system of counting and noting dates did not pass December 2012 led many to believe that the Mayans had predicted the end of the world.

Some panics, like that around Y2K, reflect the fear that, in modern industrial society, we are highly dependent on products and technological processes about which we have little knowledge and over which we have no control.

A **craze** is *an intense attraction to an object, a person, or an activity.* Crazes are like fads but more intense. Body disfigurement has been a periodic craze, ranging from nose piercing to putting rings through nipples, belly buttons, lips, and tongues. The fact that these practices instill horror in some people probably accounts in part for the attraction they hold for others. In many cultures, body disfigurement is considered a necessary condition of beauty or attractiveness. While such practices would be regarded as crazes in the West, they are normal enhancements of beauty in other cultures (Brown, Edwards, & Moore, 1988).

Fashions: Styles of imitative behavior or appearance that are of longer duration than fads.

Panic: A massive flight from something that is feared.

Craze: An intense attraction to an object, a person, or an activity.

50 Years Before Ferguson, MO

Rumors are *unverified forms of information that are transmitted informally, usually originating in unknown sources.* The classic study on rumors was conducted more than 65 years ago by Gordon W. Allport and Leo Postman (1947). In one version of this research, a White student was asked to study a photograph depicting an urban scene: two men on a subway car, one menacing the other. The student was then asked to describe the picture to a second White student, who in turn was asked to pass the information along to a third, and so on. Eventually, after numerous retellings, the information changed completely to reflect the students' previously held beliefs. For example, as the "rumor" in the study took shape, the person engaging in the menacing act was described as Black and the victim as White—even though in the actual photograph the reverse was true.

Allport and Postman's research revealed a number of features unique to rumors. The information they contain is continually reorganized according to the belief systems of those who are passing them along. Some information is forgotten, and some is altered to fit into more familiar frameworks, such as racist preconceptions in the example above. Furthermore, the degree of alteration varies according to the nature of the rumor; it is greatest for rumors that trigger strong emotions or that pass through large numbers of people.

For a rumor to have an effect, it must tap into collectively held beliefs, fears, or hopes. For some the rumor that the world will be ending imminently is a hopeful message; for others it is a source of great fear. Rumors often reinforce subcultural beliefs. The rumor that the Central Intelligence Agency and the National Security Agency are planting listening devices in everyone's homes feeds into the belief that the government is out to control us. Political campaigns are infamous for starting and perpetuating rumors: For example, the rumors that President Barack Obama is not a U.S. citizen, is a Muslim, and is trying to create European-style socialism in the United States have been spread by political opponents. Despite the fact that an abundance of evidence contradicts these rumors, some groups have embraced them.

SOCIAL MOVEMENTS

Theories of collective behavior generally emphasize the passive, reactive side of human behavior. Social movement theory, in contrast, regards human beings as the active makers of their own history—agents who have visions and goals, analyze existing conditions, weigh alternative courses of action, and organize themselves as best they can to achieve success.

A **social movement** is *a large number of people who come together in a continuing and organized effort to bring about (or resist) social change, and who rely at least partially on noninstitutionalized forms of political action.* Social movements thus have one foot outside the political establishment, and this is what distinguishes them from other efforts aimed at bringing about social change. Their political activities are not limited to such routine efforts as lobbying or campaigning; they include noninstitutionalized political actions such as boycotts, marches and other demonstrations, and civil disobedience.

Social movements often include some degree of formal organization oriented toward achieving longer-term goals, along with supporting sets of beliefs and opinions, but their strength often derives from their ability to disrupt the status quo by means of spontaneous, relatively unorganized political actions. As part of its support for the civil rights movement in the 1960s, the National Association for the Advancement of Colored People (NAACP) advocated the disruption of normal business activities, such as boycotting buses and restaurants, in order to force integration. The people who participate in social movements typically are outside the existing set of power relationships in society; such movements provide one of the few forms of political voice available to the relatively powerless (McAdam, McCarthy, & Zald, 1988; Tarrow, 1994). A recent example is the Dreamer movement, which supports passage of the Dream Act. This immigration reform legislation would allow undocumented young people who migrated to the United States with their families when they were children to have access to higher education and, over time, permanent residency or citizenship. An executive order signed by President Obama in 2012 allows the Dreamers to apply for deferred action permits and avoid deportation under certain conditions. The Dreamer movement is active at the time of this writing.

The body of research on social movements in the United States is partially the result of movements that began in the late 1950s and gained attention and support in the 1960s and early 1970s. Theories of collective behavior, with their emphasis on the seemingly irrational actions of unorganized crowds, were ill equipped to explain the rise of well-organized efforts by hundreds of thousands of people to change government policies toward the Vietnam War and civil rights for African Americans. As these two social movements spawned others, including the second-wave feminist movement, which saw women demanding greater rights and opportunities in the workplace, sociologists had to rethink their basic assumptions and develop new theoretical perspectives. Below we examine different types of social movements, looking especially at sociological theories about why they arise.

TYPES OF SOCIAL MOVEMENTS

Social movements are typically classified according to the direction and degree of change they seek. For purposes of our discussion, we will distinguish five different kinds: reformist,

Rumors: Unverified forms of information that are transmitted informally, usually originating in unknown sources.

Social movement: A large number of people who come together in a continuing and organized effort to bring about (or resist) social change, and who rely at least partially on noninstitutionalized forms of political action.

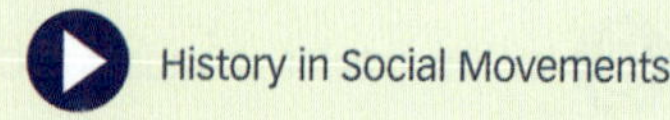
History in Social Movements

© Parker Haeg/Demotix/Corb

Political activism swept the country in the 1960s and 1970s with widespread demonstrations focused on civil rights, women's rights, and the Vietnam War. The dramatic protests and social transformations of this period helped fuel the reformulation of theories on social change.

revolutionary, rebellious, reactionary, and utopian (Table 18.1). In fact, these distinctions are not clear-cut, and the categories are not mutually exclusive. Rather, they represent ideal types. In the final section of the chapter, we will also consider some examples of a new sixth category: social movements that aim to change values and beliefs.

REFORMIST MOVEMENTS **Reformist social movements** seek to *bring about social change within the existing economic and political system* and usually address institutions such as the courts and lawmaking bodies and/or public officials. They are most often found in societies where democratic institutions make it possible to achieve social change within the established political processes. Yet even reformist social movements can include factions that advocate more sweeping, revolutionary social changes. Sometimes the government fails to respond, or it responds very slowly, raising frustrations. At other times, the government may actively repress a movement, arresting its leaders, breaking up its demonstrations, and even outlawing its activities.

Reformist social movements: Movements seeking to bring about social change within the existing economic and political system.

The American Woman Suffrage Association, formed in 1869 by Susan B. Anthony and Elizabeth Cady Stanton, was a reformist organization that resulted in significant social changes. During the latter part of the 19th century, it became one of the most powerful political forces in the United States, seeking to liberate women from oppression and ensure them the right to vote (Vellacott, 1993), precipitating the first wave of the women's movement. In 1872, Victoria Woodhull helped to organize the Equal Rights Party, which nominated her for the U.S. presidency (even though, by law, no woman could vote for her); she campaigned on the issues of voting rights for women, the right of women to earn and control their own money, and free love (Underhill, 1995). After a half century of struggle by numerous social movement activists, women finally won the right to vote with the ratification of the Nineteenth Amendment to the U.S. Constitution in 1920.

The civil rights movement of the late 1950s and the 1960s called for social changes that would enforce the constitutionally mandated civil rights of African Americans; it often included nonviolent civil disobedience directed at breaking unjust laws. The ultimate aim of the civil rights movement was to change those laws, rather than to change society as a whole. Thus, for example, when Rosa Parks violated the laws of Montgomery, Alabama, by refusing to give up her seat on a city bus to a White person, she was challenging the city ordinance, but not the government itself.

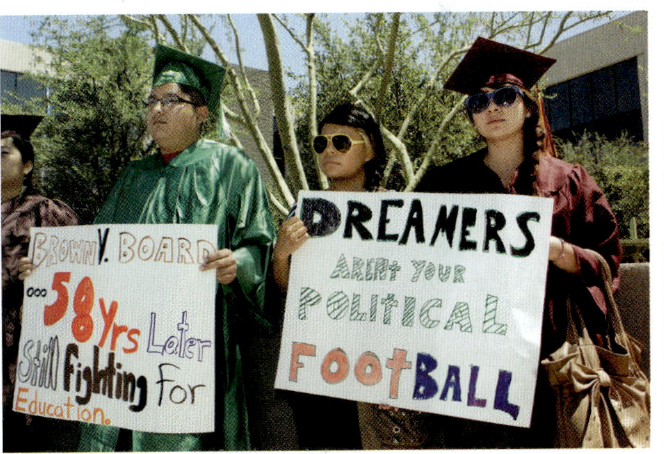

© ISHARA S.KODIKARA / Stringer/Getty Images

The Dreamer movement consists of people who support immigration reform, including access to opportunities and a legitimate route to residency or citizenship for young people brought to the United States by undocumented parents. Many have been barred from educational institutions or job opportunities due to their immigration status.

TECHNOLOGY & SOCIETY

#SOCIALCHANGE

A preeminent form of social activism today is what has been termed "hashtag activism" (Dewey, 2014), essentially the movement to spread awareness online regarding social issues embraced and defined as important by well-known public figures and ordinary people alike. Hashtag activism is conducted on Twitter, an Internet platform actively used by 255 million account holders across the world and passively followed by millions more (Twitter, 2014). According to a study conducted for the Pew Research Center's Internet Project, in 2013, 18% of online adults had Twitter accounts (a 2% increase from the year before) (Duggan & Smith, 2014). Twitter is not the only online platform used for social activism, but it has played a part in a number of broad public campaigns, such as the effort to capture alleged war criminal Joseph Kony, wanted for crimes of mass murder and rape in Uganda (#Kony2012), and the effort to draw attention to injustice in the killing of Trayvon Martin and the subsequent acquittal of the man who shot him, George Zimmerman (#JusticeforTrayvon).

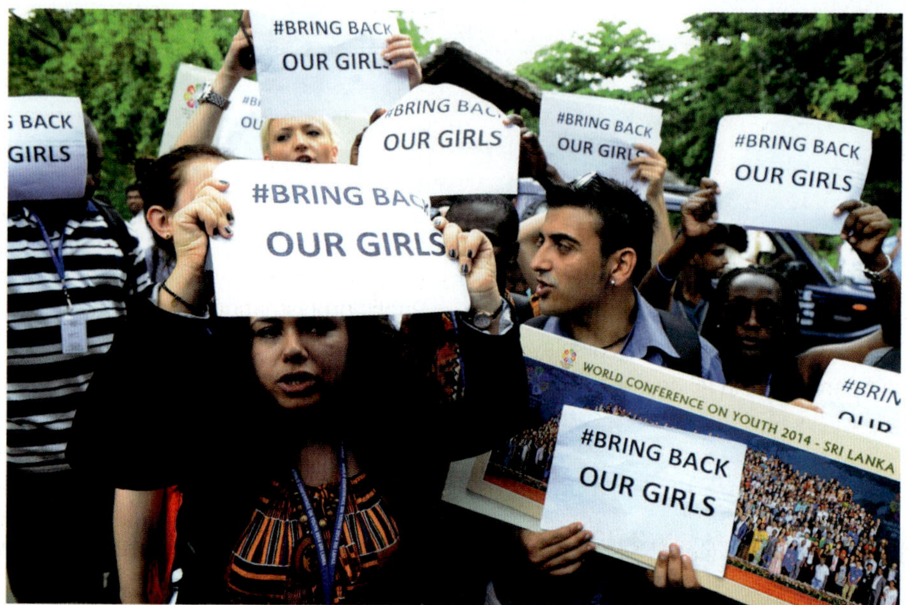

© Parker Haeg/Demotix/Corbis

In the spring of 2014, a major campaign of hashtag activism was undertaken in response to the kidnapping of more than 200 schoolgirls from a provincial Nigerian boarding school. Outrage over the girls' abduction by a self-proclaimed radical Islamic group called Boko Haram (which means "Western education is a sin" in the local Hausa language) spread quickly in April and May of that year from domestic Nigerian activists and the young women's aggrieved parents to become a global movement functioning primarily online through #BringBackOurGirls. Among the political and cultural luminaries tweeting their support of the kidnapped girls and demanding their safe return were First Lady Michelle Obama, British prime minister David Cameron, media personalities Ellen DeGeneres and Piers Morgan, young Pakistani activist for women's and girls' rights Malala Yousafzai, and even celebrities like Chris Rock and Amy Poehler. By the beginning of May, #BringBackOurGirls had accrued well over 2 million tweets (McGann, 2014). Online appeals also spurred public protests outside Nigeria, including demonstrations in Los Angeles and Washington, D.C., calling for the safe return of the kidnapped girls.

Hashtag activism is, arguably, a potentially powerful technological instrument of social activism. First, it is a means for raising awareness of issues that might otherwise go unnoticed in our information-saturated modern world, particularly if well-known figures involve themselves in campaigns (as was the case in the #BringBackOurGirls campaign). Supporters of social media activism point out that heightened public awareness can put pressure on officials who are in a position to make or change policies or foster action on actionable issues (Seay, 2014). Second, hashtag activism has the potential to draw together concerned individuals and groups across the globe who might not otherwise have a means for uniting around a common cause.

Such activism is not without its critics, however. It has been termed "slacktivism" and "armchair activism." According to a *Washington Post* article on this modern phenomenon, "Users are urged to 'like' posts and pages on Facebook, share Twitter and blog posts with everyone they know, and to create videos or take a picture for Instagram relating to their cause" (Seay, 2014). "Slacktivism" has been the subject of recent social scientific research in which it was defined as the "willingness to perform a relatively costless, token display of support for a social cause, with an accompanying lack of willingness to devote significant effort to meaningful change" (Kristofferson, White, & Peloza, 2014, p. 1149). The researchers examined the question of whether "slacktivism" is likely to translate into more substantial (more costly or time-consuming or long-term) engagement with a cause. Interestingly, they found that those whose initial "activism" was private rather than public (for instance, writing a letter to a member of Congress versus "liking" or posting on Facebook) were more likely to engage deeply in the cause of interest. Public proclamations of interest were less likely to translate into meaningful engagement.

Online social activism is likely to be a part of our lives for the foreseeable future, and we are likely to see hashtag and similar campaigns that seek our attention to a range of social, political, economic, and environmental issues. Sociological engagement with this phenomenon is still in its infancy. What would you like to know about it? How would you go about researching online social activism?

THINK IT THROUGH

▶ What are the strengths of online activism? What are its weaknesses? In what cases might it be more or less effective in fostering social change?

TABLE 18.1 Principal Types of Social Movements

Type	Principal Aims	Examples
Reformist	To bring about change within the existing economic and political system	• U.S. civil rights movement • Same-sex marriage rights movement • Climate change activism • Labor movements, including the low-wage worker movements • International human rights activism
Revolutionary	To fundamentally change the existing social, political, and/or economic system in light of a detailed alternative vision	• 1776 U.S. Revolutionary War • 1905 and 1917 Russian Revolutions • 1991 South African antiapartheid movement • 2010 Arab Spring
Rebellious	To fundamentally alter the existing political and/or economic system without a detailed alternative vision	• Nat Turner slave rebellion • Urban riots following the assassination of Martin Luther King Jr. • Rebellions against austerity measures in Greece, Spain, and Portugal
Reactionary	To restore an earlier social system—often based on a mythical past	• White supremacist organizations in the United States and Europe • German skinheads • Serbian nationalists
Utopian	To withdraw from society and create a utopian community	• Religious communities such as the Quakers, Mennonites, and Mormons • 1960s communes in the United States
New social movements	To make fundamental changes in values, culture, and private life	• Gay, lesbian, bisexual, and transgender rights movements • Environmental movements

Much early civil rights activism was oriented toward registering southern Blacks to vote, so that by exercising their legal franchise, they could achieve a measure of political power. Within the civil rights movement, however, there were activists who concluded that the rights of Black Americans would never be achieved through reformist activities alone. Like many social movements, the civil rights movement was marked by internal struggles and debates regarding the degree to which purely reformist activities were adequate to the movement's objectives (Branch, 1988). The Black Panther Party, for example, argued for far more radical changes in U.S. society, advocating "Black power" instead of merely fighting for an end to racial segregation. The Black Panthers often engaged in reformist activities, such as establishing community centers and calling for the establishment and support of more Black-owned businesses. At the same time, they also engaged in revolutionary activities, such as arming themselves against what they viewed to be a hostile police presence within Black neighborhoods.

The experience of U.S. labor unions, another example of a reformist social movement, shows the limits of the reformist approach to social change. Organized labor's principal demands have been for fewer hours, higher wages and benefits, job security, and safer working conditions. (In Europe, similar demands have been made, although workers there have sought political power as well.) Labor unions within the United States seldom appeal to a broad constituency beyond the workers themselves, and as a result, their success has depended largely on workers' economic power. U.S. workers have lost much of that power since the early 1970s, as economic globalization has meant the loss of many jobs to low-wage areas. Threats of strikes are no longer quite as menacing, as corporations can close factories down and reopen them elsewhere in the world.

REVOLUTIONARY MOVEMENTS **Revolutionary social movements** seek to *fundamentally alter the existing social, political, and economic system in keeping with a vision of a new social order.* They frequently result from the belief that reformist approaches are unlikely to succeed because the political or economic system is too resistant. In fact, whether a social movement becomes predominantly reformist or revolutionary may well hinge on the degree to which its objectives can be achieved within the system.

Revolutionary movements call for basic changes in economics, politics, norms, and values, offering a blueprint for a new social order that can be achieved only through mass action, usually by fostering conflict between those who favor change and those who favor the status quo. They are directed at clearly identifiable targets, such as a system of government believed to be unjust or an economy believed to be based on exploitation. Yet even the most revolutionary of social movements is likely to have reformist elements, members or factions who believe some change is possible within the established institutions. In most social movements, members debate the relative importance of reformist and revolutionary activities. While the rhetoric may favor revolution, most day-to-day activities are likely to support reform. Only when a social movement is suppressed and avenues to reform are closed off will its methods call for outright revolution.

© David Turnley/Corbis

Revolutionary social movements are not always violent. In Czechoslovakia (now the two countries of the Czech Republic and Slovakia), the Communist regime led by General Secretary Miloš Jakeš ceded power in 1989 and allowed for a peaceful democratic transition to take place.

Revolutionary social movements sometimes, although by no means always, include violence. In South Africa, for example, the movements that were most successful in bringing about an end to apartheid were largely nonviolent. Those that defeated socialism in the former Soviet Union and Eastern Europe did so with a minimal amount of bloodshed. However, revolutionary movements associated with the Arab Spring, which began in 2010 in countries like Egypt, Tunisia, and Libya, have resulted in considerable violence, most often perpetrated against the protesters by those already in power or their allies. It has yet to be determined whether the Arab Spring movements have been truly revolutionary; some new governments are not radically more democratic than their predecessors. It takes time for political and economic conditions to change within any given country, and while some dictators have been removed from power, it remains to be seen whether these changes in political office will result in the changes desired by constituents.

REBELLIONS **Rebellions** seek to *overthrow the existing social, political, and economic systems but lack detailed plans for a new social order.* They are particularly common in societies

Revolutionary social movements: Movements seeking to fundamentally alter the existing social, political, and economic system in keeping with a vision of a new social order.

Rebellions: Movements seeking to overthrow the existing social, political, and economic systems but lacking detailed plans for a new social order.

BEHIND THE NUMBERS

MILLIONS OF DEMONSTRATORS . . . OR NOT

How many demonstrators attended a protest action on a given day in a particular place? This can be a surprisingly contentious issue. For example, how many people attended the Million Man March, a huge 1995 grassroots gathering intended to highlight issues of concern to urban and minority men and their families? As Ira Flatow noted on the National Public Radio program *Science Friday* in 2010: "It depends on whom you ask. According to the U.S. Park Police, about 400,000. But the organizers of the march took issue with that number and asked for a recount. And using different images . . . a crowd counting expert at Boston University estimated the crowd to be closer to 800,000—almost twice the number that the Park Service had."

REUTERS/Lucas Jackson

What kind of collective action or issue would bring you out into the street?

Once you become familiar with the importance of research methods, you find that the *method* of obtaining information can be at least as important as the information itself. When a statistic, fact, or figure is produced, it is always important to consider the process behind its production. We often hear media accounts that report numbers of demonstrators in given units of space or time (for instance, there are 200 protesters in New York City, or there are 200,000 demonstrators on the National Mall). During the peak months of the Occupy movement, it was common for news organizations to report figures ostensibly representing the numbers of participants attending various actions. Where do these numbers come from? Who is keeping count?

In taking a critical look behind the numbers in the U.S. case, we find that the National Park Service does not conduct official head counts of the demonstrators in given public spaces. McPherson Square, a park in Washington, D.C., was one of two nuclei for the Occupy movement in that city. The National Park Service conducted periodic estimates of the crowds there to ensure they did not surpass the regulated limit of 500 protesters (Farhi, 2011). Nevertheless, these estimates were not methodologically rigorous. Journalists often rely on best-guess estimates for crowds. Satellite pictures have become sources of information on crowds, though each such photo captures just a few moments in time (National Public Radio, 2010).

So how does one get a good count of the number of participants at any given event? Stephen K. Doig, a professor at the Cronkite School of Journalism at Arizona State University, has a formula. He asserts that we can get closer to the "objective and scientifically accurate" end of the estimating spectrum if we know the following three variables: the human density of the demonstration, the carrying capacity of the space, and how much of the available space is occupied (National Public Radio, 2010). A perfect count, however, will likely remain elusive.

THINK IT THROUGH

▶ Why are counts of participants at public demonstrations potentially controversial and contested? What makes them significant?

where effective mobilization against existing structures is difficult or impossible because of the structures' repressive nature. The histories of European feudalism and U.S. slavery are punctuated by examples of rebellions. Nat Turner, a Black American slave, led other slaves in an 1831 uprising against their White owners in the state of Virginia. Before the uprising was suppressed, 55 Whites were killed, and subsequently Turner and 16 of his followers were hanged (Greenberg, 2003).

REACTIONARY MOVEMENTS **Reactionary social movements** seek to *restore an earlier social system—often based on a mythical past—along with the traditional norms and values that once presumably accompanied it.* These movements are termed *reactionary* because they arise in reaction to recent social changes that threaten or have replaced the old order. They are also sometimes referred to as *countermovements* or *resistance movements* for the same reason.

For these groups, a mythical past is often the starting point for pursuing goals aimed at transforming the present. The Ku Klux Klan, the White Aryan Resistance, and other White supremacist organizations have long sought to return to a United States where Whites held exclusive political and economic power. Their methods have ranged from spreading discredited social and biological theories that expound the superiority of the "White race" to acts of violence against Black Americans, Asians, Latinos, Jews, gays and lesbians, and others deemed to be inferior or otherwise a threat to the "American way of life" (Gerhardt, 1989; Moore, 1991).

Whether a social movement is viewed as reactionary or revolutionary depends to some extent on the observer's perspective. In Iran, for example, a social movement led by the Ayatollah Khomeini overthrew the nation's pro-U.S. leader in 1979 and created an Islamic republic that quickly reestablished traditional Muslim laws. In the pronouncements of U.S. policy makers and the mass media, the new Iranian regime was reactionary: It required women to be veiled, turned its back on democratic institutions, and levied death sentences on those who violated key Islamic values or otherwise threatened the Islamic state. Yet from the point of view of the clerics who led the upheaval, the movement overthrew a corrupt and brutal dictator who had enriched his family at the expense of the Iranian people and had fostered an alien way of life offensive to traditional Iranian values. From this standpoint, the movement claimed to be revolutionary, promising to provide a better life for Iranians.

As globalization threatens traditional ways of life around the world, we might expect to see an increase in reactionary social movements. This is especially likely to be the case if threats to long-standing traditional values are accompanied by declines in standards of living. In Germany, for example, a decline in living standards for many working-class people has spawned a small but significant resurgence of Nazi ideology, and racial supremacist groups blame foreign immigrants for their economic woes. The result has been a vocal campaign

After the Civil War, the Ku Klux Klan instituted vigilante justice and lynched over 4,000 African Americans for alleged crimes, including looking "the wrong way" at a White woman. White supremacist groups exemplify a resistance or countermovement that rejects racial integration and expansion of civil rights.

by skinhead groups against immigrants, particularly in the states that made up the former East Germany, which have seen greater economic upheavals than other parts of the country.

Social movement participants frequently stage public demonstrations to spread their messages. Sometimes the sizes of protesting groups—which may be small but very vocal or may be awe-inspiring—are unclear, as we see in the *Behind the Numbers* box on page 477.

UTOPIAN MOVEMENTS **Utopian social movements** seek to *withdraw from the dominant society by creating their own ideal communities.* The youth movements of the 1960s had a strong utopian impulse; many young (and a few older) people "dropped out" and formed their own communities, starting alternative newspapers, health clinics, and schools and in general seeking to live according to their own value systems outside the established social institutions. Some sought to live communally as well, pooling their resources and sharing tasks and responsibilities. They saw these efforts to create "intentional" communities, based on cooperation rather than competition, as the seeds of a revolutionary new society.

Although religious utopian movements have proved to be somewhat enduring, those based on social philosophy have not. Some "utopian socialist" communities were founded in the United States during the 19th century; some provided models for the socialist collectives of the 1960s. Few lasted for any length

Reactionary social movements: Movements seeking to restore an earlier social system—often based on a mythical past—along with the traditional norms and values that once presumably accompanied it.

Utopian social movements: Movements seeking to withdraw from the dominant society by creating their own ideal communities.

of time. The old ways of thinking and acting proved remarkably tenacious, and the presence of the larger society—which remained basically unchanged by the experimentation—was a constant temptation. "Alternative" institutions such as communally run newspapers and health clinics found they had to contend with well-funded mainstream competitors. Most folded or reverted to mainstream forms (Fairfield, 1972; Nordhoff, 1875/1975; Rothschild & Whitt, 1987).

WHY DO SOCIAL MOVEMENTS ARISE?

Although social movements have existed throughout history, modern society has created conditions in which they thrive and multiply. The rise of the modern democratic nation-state, along with the development of capitalism, has fueled their growth. Democratic forms of governance, which emphasize social equality and the right of political participation, legitimate the belief that people should organize themselves politically to achieve their goals. Democratic nation-states give rise to social movements—and often protect them as well. Capitalism, which raises universal economic expectations while producing some inequality, further spurs the formation of such movements.

Given these general historical circumstances, sociologists have advanced a number of theories to explain why people sometimes come together to create or resist social change. Some focus on the micro level, looking at the characteristics and motivations of the people who join social movements. Some focus on the organizational level, looking at the characteristics that result in successful social movement organizations. Some focus on the macro level, examining the societal conditions that give rise to social movements. More recently, theories have emphasized cultural dimensions of social movements, stressing the extent to which social movements reflect—as well as shape—larger cultural understandings. An ideal theory would bridge all these levels, and some efforts have been made to develop one.

MICRO-LEVEL APPROACHES Much research has focused on what motivates individuals to become active members of social movements. Psychological factors turn out to be poor predictors. Neither personality nor personal alienation adequately accounts for activist leanings. Rather, participation seems motivated more by psychological identification with others who are similarly afflicted (Marwell & Oliver, 1993; McAdam, 1982).

Sociology generally explains activism in such terms as having had prior contact with movement members, belonging to social networks that support movement activity, and having a history of activism (McAdam, 1986; Snow, Zurcher, & Ekland-Olson, 1980). Coming from a family background of social activism may also be important. One study, for example, found that many White male activists during the early 1960s social movements had parents who themselves had been activists 30 years earlier (Flacks, 1971). A lack of personal constraints may also be a partial explanation; it is obviously easier for individuals to engage in political activity if work or family circumstances afford them the necessary time and resources (McCarthy & Zald, 1973). Finally, a sense of moral rightness may provide a powerful motivation to become active, even when the work is difficult and the monetary rewards are small or nonexistent (Jenkins, 1983).

Social movements always suffer from the **free rider problem**, however—that is, *many people avoid the costs of social movement activism* (such as time, energy, and other personal resources) *and still benefit from its success* (Marwell & Oliver, 1993). Why not let others join the social movement and do the hard work, since if the movement succeeds everyone will benefit, regardless of degree of participation? Clearly it takes a great deal of motivation and commitment, as well as a conviction that their efforts may make a difference, for people to devote their time to mailing leaflets or organizing marches; building such motivation and commitment is a major challenge faced by all social movements.

ORGANIZATIONAL-LEVEL APPROACHES Some recent research has been devoted to understanding how social movements are consciously and deliberately organized to create social change. This research focuses on **social movement organizations (SMOs)**, *formal organizations that seek to achieve social change through noninstitutionalized forms of political action.* The study of SMOs represents a major sociological step away from regarding social change as resulting from unorganized individuals and crowds. Instead, it places the study of social change within the framework of the sociology of organizations.

Because social movement organizations constitute a type of formal organization, sociologists use the same concepts and tools to study civil rights organizations and revolutionary groups as they do to study business firms and government bureaucracies. Researchers conceptualize SMOs' actions as rational, their goals as more or less clearly defined, and their organizational structures as bureaucratically oriented toward specific measurable goals (Jenkins, 1983; McCarthy & Zald, 1977).

Social movement organizations range from informal volunteer groups to professional organizations with full-time leadership and staff. A single social movement may sustain numerous such organizations: A partial list associated with the 1960s civil rights movement includes the NAACP, the Student Nonviolent Coordinating Committee (SNCC), the Congress of Racial Equality (CORE), the Southern Christian Leadership Conference (SCLC), Students for a Democratic Society (SDS),

Free rider problem: The problem that many people avoid the costs of social movement activism (such as time, energy, and other personal resources) and still benefit from its success.

Social movement organizations (SMOs): Formal organizations that seek to achieve social change through noninstitutionalized forms of political action.

and the Black Panther Party. As social movements grow, so too do the number of SMOs associated with them, each vying for members, financial support, and media attention.

One influential approach to the study of social movement organizations is **resource mobilization theory**, *a theory that focuses on the ability of social movement organizations to generate money, membership, and political support to achieve their objectives.* This approach argues that since discontent and social strain are always present among some members of any society, these factors cannot explain the rise or the relative success of social movements. Rather, what matters are differences in the resources available to different groups and how effectively they use them. The task for sociologists, then, is to explain why some SMOs are better able to deploy scarce resources than others (Jenkins, 1983; McAdam, 1988). Among the most important resources are tangible assets such as money, facilities, and means of communication, as well as such intangibles such as a central core of dedicated, skilled, hard-working members (Jenkins, 1983).

Much like businesses, then, social movement organizations rise or fall on their ability to be competitive in a resource-scarce environment. Some scholars have even written of "social movement industries," with competing organizations engaging in "social marketing" to promote their particular "brands" of social change (Jenkins, 1983; Zald & McCarthy, 1980).

Governmental policies are important determinants of the success or failure of social movement organizations. The government may repress an organization, driving it underground so that it has difficulty in operating. Or the government may favor more moderate organizations (for example, Martin Luther King Jr.'s Southern Christian Leadership Conference) over other, more radical ones (such as the Black Panther Party). Other ways in which the government affects SMOs are through regulating them, providing favorable tax treatment for those that qualify, and refraining from excessive surveillance or harassment (McAdam et al., 1988).

The success or failure of social movement organizations also depends on their ability to influence the mass media. During the 1960s, the anti–Vietnam War organizations became very effective in commanding the television spotlight, although this effectiveness proved a mixed blessing: Media coverage frequently sensationalized demonstrations rather than presenting the underlying issues, thus contributing to rivalries and tensions within the antiwar movement (Gitlin, 1980). Today, arguably, social media exercise even greater influence on movement success.

Although some scholars have argued that larger, more bureaucratic social movement organizations are likely to be successful in the long run (Gamson, 1975), others have claimed that mass defiance, rather than formal organization, is the key to success (Piven & Cloward, 1977). Paradoxically, too much success may undermine social movements, since their strength derives partly from their being outside society's power structures as they make highly visible demands for social change. Once a group's demands are met, the participants are often drawn inside the very power structures they once sought to change. Movement leaders become bureaucrats, their fights are conducted by lawyers and government officials, and rank-and-file members disappear; the militant thrust of the organization is then blunted (Piven & Cloward, 1977).

A related problem is goal displacement, which occurs when a social movement organization's original goals become redirected toward enhancing the organization and its leadership (McCarthy & Zald, 1973). The U.S. labor movement is an example: Once labor unions became successful, many of them became large and prosperous bureaucracies that were perceived as distanced from the needs of their rank-and-file members.

In the end, social movement organizations have to motivate people to support their causes, often with dollars as well as votes. Many groups engage in **grassroots organizing**, *attempts to mobilize support among the ordinary members of a community.* This organizing may range from door-to-door canvassing to leafleting to get people to attend massive demonstrations. Most social movements emerge from a group that has some grievance, and their active members consist largely of people who will directly benefit from any social change that occurs.

Some social movement organizations also depend on **conscience constituents**, *people who provide resources for a social movement organization but who are not themselves members of the aggrieved group that the organization champions* (McCarthy & Zald, 1973). Such supporters are motivated by strong ethical convictions rather than by direct self-interest in achieving the social movement's goals. The National Coalition for the Homeless, for example, consists primarily of public interest lawyers, shelter operators, and others who advocate on behalf of homeless people; only a relatively small number of homeless people are directly involved in the organization. Homeless advocacy groups raise money from numerous sources, including media celebrities and direct mailings to ordinary citizens (Blau, 1992).

MACRO-LEVEL APPROACHES Regardless of the efforts particular social movement organizations make, large-scale economic, political, and cultural conditions ultimately determine a movement's success or failure. For a social movement to arise and succeed, conditions must be such that people feel it is

Resource mobilization theory: A theory about social movement organizations that focuses on their ability to generate money, membership, and political support in order to achieve their objectives.

Grassroots organizing: Attempts to mobilize support among the ordinary members of a community.

Conscience constituents: People who provide resources for a social movement organization but who are not themselves members of the aggrieved group that the organization champions.

AP Photo/JEFF WIDENER

This iconic image shows one man standing in opposition to four tanks in Tiananmen Square, China, on June 5, 1989. Thousands of pro-democracy demonstrators sought political and economic changes in a weeks long occupation of the square. Many were injured or killed in a government crackdown. ■

necessary and are willing to support it. Therefore, social movements emerge and flourish in times of other social change, particularly if people experience that change as disruptive of their daily lives (McAdam et al., 1988; Tilly, 1978). For example, the labor movement arose with the emergence of industrial capitalism, which brought harsh conditions to the lives of many people, and the women's movement reemerged in the 1960s, when expanded educational opportunities for women left many female college graduates feeling marginalized and alienated as full-time homemakers and workplace discrimination threw obstacles in the way of their workplace aspirations.

Some political systems encourage social movements, while others repress them (Gale, 1986). When a government is in crisis, it may respond by becoming more repressive, or it may create a space for social movements to flourish. The former action occurred in China in 1989, when thousands of students and workers, frustrated by deteriorating economic conditions and rigid government controls, took to the streets to demand greater economic and political freedom. The brutal crackdown at Beijing's Tiananmen Square, televised live to a global audience, ended the nascent social movement for democracy. Likewise, government crackdowns on demonstrators and social movement participants have been widespread throughout the Middle East and North Africa as the Arab Spring movements have progressed—Syria's protest movement has, as of this writing, deteriorated into a civil war between the authoritarian government and those who seek its replacement.

Just as economic and political collapse may facilitate the rise of social movements, so too may prosperity. Resources for social activism are more abundant, mass media and other means of communication are more likely to be readily available, and activists are more likely to have independent means of supporting themselves. Prosperous societies are also more likely to have large classes of well-educated people, a group that has historically provided the leadership in many social movements (McAdam et al., 1988; McCarthy & Zald, 1973; Zald & McCarthy, 1980).

Finally, even the spatial organization of society has been seen as having an impact on social movements. Dense, concentrated neighborhoods or workplaces facilitate social interaction and spur the growth of social movements. A century and a half ago, Karl Marx recognized that cities and factories were powerful breeding grounds for revolutionary insurgency against capitalism, since they brought previously isolated workers together in single locations. Subsequent research has sustained his conclusion (Marx & Engels, 1848/1998; Tilly, 1975). The concentration of students on college campuses contributed to the rise of student activism in the 1960s (Lofland, 1985).

CULTURAL-LEVEL STUDIES AND "FRAME ALIGNMENT" Much of the research we have discussed emphasizes the political, economic, and organizational conditions that either help or hinder the rise of social movements. Sociologists have often regarded social movements as by-products of favorable social circumstances rather than as the active accomplishments of their members. Today, however, instead of stressing how important it is for conditions to be ripe for social movements to thrive, many sociologists are thinking about how social movement organizations themselves are continually interpreting events so as to align themselves better with the cultural understanding of the wider society. The Tea Party movement is a good example. While it has a long list of political goals it wants to achieve, it has succeeded in rallying people around the idea that "big government" and taxation are a threat to freedom and liberty. These are ideas that resonate with those who have some suspicion of intrusive government. The movement seeks to create a "good fit" between itself and the people who are its likely constituents.

Sociologists think of that fit in terms of **frame alignment**, *the process by which the interests, understandings, and values of a social movement organization are shaped to match those in the wider society.* If their members' understandings align with the understandings of others in a community or society, social movements are likely to be successful; otherwise they are likely to fail. Social movement organizations achieve frame alignment in a variety of ways, ranging from modifying the beliefs of members to attempting to change the beliefs of the entire society (Snow, Rochford, Worden, & Benford, 1986).

In one common situation, people already share the social movement's concerns and understandings but lack the means to bring about the desired changes. In this case, there is no need for the social movement organization to get people to change their thinking about the problem; rather, the task is to

Frame alignment: The process by which the interests, understandings, and values of a social movement organization are rendered congruent with those of the wider society.

get people to support the movement's efforts to do something about it. The SMO must "get the word out," whether through informal networks, social media, or direct-mail campaigns.

Sometimes the social movement's concerns are only weakly shared by others. In this case, the challenge for the social movement organization is to get people engaged and concerned enough to take action, perhaps by amplifying their concern that something they strongly believe in requires political action. The environmental movement is a case in point. Many scientists and a large number of other people are convinced that the earth is warming at a rapid rate due to the emission of industrial gases into the atmosphere. The movement has grown rapidly, but it has also produced a large number of skeptics, including politicians, who deny that climate change is taking place. Groups such as the Sierra Club and Greenpeace and the owners of retail chains such as Patagonia and REI actively provide information on climate change to the public in the hope of spurring individuals to action.

Finally, a social movement organization may seek to build support by attempting to change the way people think entirely. Revolutionary SMOs, for example, urge people to stop thinking of themselves as victims of bad luck, focusing attention instead on the faults of the political or economic system, which presumably requires a drastic overhaul.

To sum up, social movement organizations are competing for the hearts and minds of their constituents, with whom they must somehow bring their own beliefs and analyses into alignment if they are to succeed.

MICROMOBILIZATION CONTEXTS FOR BUILDING SOCIAL MOVEMENTS

Some conditions are ideal for social movement organizations to spring up. Sociologists call these *micromobilization contexts,* small-group settings in which people are able to generate a shared set of beliefs to explain some social problem, along with the necessary social organization to do something about it (McAdam et al., 1988). Both formal and informal social networks usually exist in these settings, making it easier for members to understand why a micro-level problem, such as a personal experience of racism, is in fact the result of macro-level social forces, such as institutional racism. The civil rights movement, for example, emerged at a time when the Black community was developing strong local organizations, including schools, churches, and political groups. These highly interconnected institutions provided fertile ground for the seeds of social activism (McAdam, 1982). Other examples are unions, student support groups, and even friendship networks, which are more elaborate in the age of Facebook, Twitter, and other social media (Bekkers, Edwards, & Moody, 2010).

Micromobilization contexts also create the basic organizational framework required to address a problem—including leadership, mass media, and other communications technologies—as well as specific roles for movement activists and motivation to get involved. These incentives range from the emotional rewards that come from belonging to a group dedicated to a common cause to paid salaries. Micromobilization contexts thus serve as the bridge that connects the personal concerns of individuals to collectives hoping to create large-scale social change (Abrahams, 1992; Scott, 1990).

REUTERS/Gerardo Garcia

While environmental activism has a long history in the United States, in the past 10 to 15 years it has been reignited and challenged in a debate over climate change. Scientists, academics, and activists are concerned by scientific evidence that global warming is being accelerated by human activity. Today there is a global environmental movement fighting for greater attention and resources.

Finally, micromobilization contexts provide the starting point for cycles of protest that begin in one place and then spread—to new locations as well as to new social movements (Tarrow, 1983). Members of social movement organizations learn from one another and copy one another's techniques, acquiring large repertoires of protest activities in the process (Bekkers et al., 2010; Tilly, 1978).

NEW SOCIAL MOVEMENTS

Social movements have often served as a means to an end: People come together to achieve specific objectives, such as improving the conditions of workers, gaining equality for the disadvantaged, or protesting a war. In the past, participation in such social movements was often separate from members' personal lives. Since the 1960s, however, many social movements have sought to break the boundary between politics and personal life. In addition to being a means for changing the world, the social movement organization has come to be seen as a vehicle for personal change and growth (Giugni & Passy, 1998).

New social movements: Movements that have arisen since the 1960s and are fundamentally concerned with the quality of private life, often advocating large-scale cultural changes in how people think and act.

In a sense, this progression reflects the *sociological imagination*, which calls for us to understand the relationship between our personal experiences and larger social forces. Social movements that have embraced this perspective have been labeled **new social movements**. While they often address political and economic issues, they *are fundamentally concerned with the quality of private life, often advocating large-scale changes in the way people think and act.*

New social movements may be formally organized, with clearly defined roles (leadership, recruiting, and so on), or they may be informal and loosely organized, preferring spontaneous and confrontational methods to more bureaucratic approaches. Part of the purpose of new social movements in protesting, in fact, is not to force a distinction between "them" and "us" but to draw attention to the movement' own right to exist as equals with other groups in society (Gamson, 1989; Omvedt, 1992; Tucker, 1991).

The new social movements aim to improve life in a wide range of areas subject to governmental, business, or other large-scale institutional control, from the workplace to sexuality, health, education, and interpersonal relationships. Four characteristics set these movements apart from earlier ones (Melucci, 1989):

1. The new social movements focus not just on the distribution of material goods but also on the control of symbols and information—an appropriate goal for an "information society" in which the production and ownership of knowledge are increasingly valuable.
2. People join new social movement organizations not purely to achieve specific goals but also because they value participation for its own sake. For instance, LGBT (lesbian, gay, bisexual, and transgender) movements have provided safe havens for members in addition to pursuing social change.
3. Rather than large, bureaucratically run, top-down organizations, the new social movements are often networks of people engaged in routine daily activities. For example, a small online movement was begun by a woman who objected to an unannounced $5 charge on her credit card bill; her protest was joined by thousands of others, and the bank rescinded the charge. Groups trying to raise awareness of climate change and threats to the environment often are loosely organized and register their concerns online and through other media such as newspapers and television talk shows.
4. The new social movements strongly emphasize the interconnectedness of planetary life and may see their actions as tied to a vision of the planet as a whole, rather than centering on narrow self-interest. "Think globally, act locally" is the watchword and includes but is not limited to an acute awareness of environmental issues.

WHY STUDY SOCIAL CHANGE?

Human beings make their own history, but they do not make it out of thin air. Every generation inherits certain *constraints*, characteristics of the society that limit their vision and their choices, and *resources*, characteristics of the society that they can mobilize in new and creative ways. People are constrained by existing institutions and social relationships. Social structures provide the resources for human action, even as the actions themselves are oriented toward changing those structures (Giddens, 1985).

The sociologically significant processes of globalization and technological change provide both resources and constraints for people everywhere. Social movements themselves may become increasingly internationalized (Marx & McAdam, 1994). Economic globalization, like most social processes, has both positive and negative effects. On one hand, it opens up the possibility of a vast increase in global productive capacity, technological advances, global cooperation, and an increase in the standard of living for people around the world. On the other hand, globalization may also lead to lowered wages and to job losses in high-wage industrial countries, as well as to exploitative labor conditions in the low-wage countries of the world. Concerns about such problems have given rise to labor and environmental groups that operate across national borders (Barry & Sims, 1994).

We live at a moment in history that contains enormous possibilities as well as daunting problems. Without an understanding of these social forces, we will be unable to act intelligently to bring about the kind of world we most desire. Your understanding of the forces shaping social change today will enable you and tomorrow's citizens to act more effectively to shape your social world.

Violence Against Women Social Movement

WHAT CAN I DO WITH A SOCIOLOGY DEGREE?

CAREER DEVELOPMENT: SELECTED SOCIOLOGY CAREER RESOURCES

> Sociology is the study of social life, social change, and the social causes and consequences of human behavior. Sociologists investigate the structure of groups, organizations, and societies, and how people interact within these contexts. The subject matter of sociology ranges from the intimate family to the hostile mob; from organized crime to religious cults; from the divisions of race, gender, and social class to the shared beliefs of a common culture; and from the sociology of work to the sociology of sports. In fact, few fields have such broad scope and relevance for research, theory, and application of knowledge.
>
> —*American Sociological Association, 2005*

The study of sociology offers a broad spectrum of knowledge and skills. Sociology majors can also benefit from knowledge of academic, professional, and career resources. This feature offers an overview of resources that you can use for further research. Additional resources are available at the book's website.

Professional Associations for Sociologists

- American Society of Criminology: www.asc41.com
- American Sociological Association: www.asanet.org
- Archaeological Institute of America: www .archaeological.org
- Association for Applied and Clinical Sociology: www .aacsnet.net
- Association for Humanist Sociology: web.ccsu.edu/ahs
- Eastern Sociological Society: www.essnet.org
- Good Works Foundation: www.goodworks.org
- International Sociological Association: www.isa-sociology.org
- Midwest Sociological Society: www.themss.org
- National Association for the Practice of Anthropology: www.practicinganthropology.org
- National Organization for Human Services: www. nationalhumanservices.org
- North Central Sociological Association: www.ncsanet.org
- Pacific Sociological Association: www.pacificsoc.org
- Social Science Research Council: www.ssrc.org
- Society for American Archaeology: www.saa.org
- Society for Applied Anthropology: www.sfaa.net
- Society for the Study of Social Problems: www.sssp1.org
- Sociologists for Women in Society: www.socwomen.org
- Southern Sociological Society: www .southernsociologicalsociety.org
- Southwestern Social Science Association: www .sssaonline.org
- Urban Affairs Association: www .urbanaffairsassociation.org

Selected Occupational Fields for Sociology Majors

- Business and management
- Community organizing/advocacy/affairs
- Criminal justice
- Education
- Human services
- Journalism/writing
- Law
- Management consulting
- Marketing and advertising
- Nonprofit management/administration
- Policy research, planning, and development
- Politics
- Program analysis/management
- Public relations

- Social work
- Sociology
- Youth services

Sample Work Settings

- Business/management
- City management
- Community outreach organizations
- Courts/law enforcement agencies
- Departments of human services/children's services/education/justice/veterans' affairs
- Elementary, secondary, and higher education
- Federal, state, and local government
- Law firms
- Marketing/market research/sales
- Nonprofits/nongovernmental organizations
- Political campaigns and offices
- Public relations/advertising
- Research institutes
- Social service agencies
- Think tanks
- Universities and colleges

sources of Information on Employment Trends and Employment Sectors

- American Enterprise Institute
- American Institutes for Research
- American Sociological Association
- Brookings Institution
- Economic Policy Institute
- Gallup
- National Association of Colleges and Employers
- National Opinion Research Center
- O*NET (U.S. Department of Labor Occupational Network)
- Partnership for Public Service
- RAND Corporation
- Westat
- Urban Institute
- U.S. Bureau of Labor Statistics
- U.S. Census Bureau
- Your university or college career center

Online Job Search Tools

- www.bridgespan.org (nonprofit jobs)
- www.careerbuilder.com (social work jobs)
- www.change.org
- www.geron.org
- www.idealist.org
- www.linkedin.com
- www.nonprofitjobseeker.com
- www.opportunityknocksnow.org
- www.ourpublicservice.org
- www.USAjobs.gov

OTHER Resources

National Association of Colleges and Employers: www.naceweb.org

Occupational Outlook Handbook: www.bls.gov/ooh

O*NET OnLine: www.onetonline.org

Weigers Vitullo, M. (2009). Searching for a job with an undergraduate degree in sociology. *ASA Footnotes, 37*(7). Retrieved from http://www.asanet.org/footnotes/septoct09/job_0909.html

SUMMARY

- Sociologists disagree about whether social change is gradual or abrupt, and about whether all societies are changing in roughly the same direction. The evolutionary, revolutionary, and **rise-and-fall theories of social change** are three approaches to these questions.
- Some early sociologists viewed **collective behavior** as a form of group contagion in which the veneer of civilization gave way to more instinctive, herdlike forms of behavior.
- A more sociological approach, **emergent norm** theory, examines the ways in which **crowds** and other forms of collective behavior develop their own rules and shared understandings.
- The most comprehensive theory of collective behavior, value-added theory, attempts to take into account the necessary conditions for collective behavior at the individual, organizational, and even societal levels.
- Social movements have been important historical vehicles for bringing about social change. They are usually achieved through **social movement organizations (SMOs)**, which we study using the tools and understandings of organizational sociology.
- We can classify social movements as **reformist**, **revolutionary**, **rebellious**, **reactionary**, **utopian**, or "**new**," depending on their vision of social change.
- **Resource mobilization theory** argues that we can explain the success or failure of SMOs not by the degree of social strain that may explain their origins but by their organizational ability to marshal the financial and personal resources they need.
- In recent years sociologists have sought to explain how **social movements** align their own beliefs and values with those of their potential constituents in the wider society. **Frame alignment** activities range from modifying the beliefs of the SMO to attempting to change the beliefs of the entire society.
- Many social movements depend heavily on **conscience constituents** for their support. Micromobilization contexts are also important incubators of social movements.
- Globalization has created an opportunity for the formation of global social movements, since many of the problems in the world today are global and require global solutions.
- **New social movements**, organized around issues of personal identity and values, differ from earlier social movements in that they focus on symbols and information as well as material issues, participation is frequently seen as an end in itself, the movements are organized as networks rather than bureaucratically, and they emphasize the interconnectedness of social groups and larger social entities.

KEY TERMS

differentiation, 463

rise-and-fall theories of social change, 465

collective behavior, 468

crowds, 468

emergent norms, 469

riot, 470

fads, 470

fashions, 471

panic, 471

craze, 471

rumors, 472

social movement, 472

reformist social movements, 473

revolutionary social movements, 476

rebellions, 476

reactionary social movements, 478

utopian social movements, 478

free rider problem, 479

social movement organizations (SMOs), 479

resource mobilization theory, 480

grassroots organizing, 480

conscience constituents, 480

frame alignment, 481

new social movements, 482

DISCUSSION QUESTIONS

1. Consider what you have learned about social movements and social change in this chapter. How is the global expansion of social media likely to change how people pursue social change? How has it done so already?
2. Under what kinds of societal conditions do movements for social change seem to emerge? Describe a societal context that has brought about or could bring about the development of such a movement.
3. How do fads differ from fashions? Offer some examples of each, and consider whether and how setting phenomena in these different categories can shed light on their roots and functions.
4. What are the different types of social movements identified by sociologists? What characteristics are used to differentiate these types?
5. Design a social movement. What problem or issue would you want to address? How would you overcome the problems of social movements that were identified in this chapter?

Sharpen your skills with SAGE edge at **edge.sagepub.com/chambliss2e**

A personalized approach to help you accomplish your coursework goals in an easy-to-use learning environment.

GLOSSARY

Achieved status: Social position linked to an individual's acquisition of socially valued credentials or skills.

Agency: The ability of individuals and groups to exercise free will and to make social changes on a small or large scale.

Age-specific fertility rate: The number of births typical for women of a specific age in a particular population.

Age-specific mortality rate: The number of deaths typical in men and women of specific ages in a particular population.

Agricultural surplus: Food beyond the amount required for immediate survival.

Alliance (or coalition): A subgroup that forms between group members, enabling them to dominate the group in their own interest.

Animism: The belief that naturally occurring phenomena, such as mountains and animals, are possessed of indwelling spirits with supernatural powers.

Anomie: A social condition of normlessness; a state of normative uncertainty that occurs when people lose touch with the shared rules and values that give order and meaning to their lives.

Anthropology: The study of human cultures and societies and their development.

Anticipatory socialization: Adoption of the behaviors or standards of a group one emulates or hopes to join.

Antimiscegenation laws: Laws prohibiting interracial sexual relations and marriage.

Ascribed status: Social position linked to characteristics that are socially significant but cannot generally be altered (such as race or gender).

Assimilation: The absorption of a minority group into the dominant culture.

Atavisms: Throwbacks to primitive early humans.

Authoritarianism: A form of governance in which ordinary members of society are denied the right to participate in government, and political power is exercised by and for the benefit of a small political elite.

Automation: The replacement of human labor by machines in the production process.

Barter economy: An economy based on the exchange of goods and services rather than money.

Behaviorism: A psychological perspective that emphasizes the effect of rewards and punishments on human behavior.

Beliefs: Particular ideas that people accept as true.

Bias: A characteristic of results that systematically misrepresent the true nature of what is being studied.

Bourgeoisie: The capitalist (or property-owning) class.

Bureaucracies: Formal organizations characterized by written rules, hierarchical authority, and paid staff, intended to promote organizational efficiency.

Capitalism: An economic order characterized by the market allocation of goods and services, production for private profit, and private ownership of the means of producing wealth.

Capital offenses: Crimes considered so heinous they are punishable by death.

Caste society: A system in which the social levels are closed, so that all individuals remain at the social level of their birth throughout life.

Causal relationship: A relationship between two variables in which one variable is the cause of the other.

Charismatic authority: Power based on devotion inspired in followers by the personal qualities of a leader.

Church: A well-established religious organization that exists in a fairly harmonious relationship with the larger society.

Citizens: Legally recognized inhabitants of a country who bear the rights and responsibilities of citizenship as defined by the state.

City: A relatively large, dense, and permanent settlement of socially heterogeneous individuals.

Civil religion: A set of sacred beliefs and practices that become part of how a society sees itself.

Civil unions: Legal unions that fall short of marriage but provide some state-level legal rights and benefits.

Class: A person's economic position in society, usually associated with income, wealth, and occupation, and sometimes associated with political voice.

Class conflict: Competition between social classes over the distribution of wealth, power, and other valued resources in society.

Class dominance theory: The theory that a small and concentrated group of elite or upper-class people dominate and influence societal institutions; compatible with conflict theory.

Class-dominant theories: Theories that propose that what is labeled deviant or criminal—and therefore who gets punished—is determined by the interests of the dominant class in a particular culture or society.

Class society: A system in which social mobility allows an individual to change his or her socioeconomic position.

Coercion: The threat or use of physical force to ensure compliance.

Coercive organizations: Organizations in which people are forced to give unquestioned obedience to authority.

Cognitive development: The theory, developed by Jean Piaget, that an individual's ability to make logical decisions increases as the person grows older.

Cohabitation: Living together as a couple without being legally married.

Collective behavior: Voluntary, goal-oriented action that occurs in relatively disorganized situations in which society's predominant social norms and values cease to govern individual behavior.

Collective conscience: The common beliefs and values that bind a society together.

Common-law marriage: A type of relationship in which partners live as if married but without marriage's formal legal framework.

Communism: A type of economic system without private ownership of the means of production and, theoretically, without economic classes or economic inequality.

Concepts: Ideas that describe a number of things that have something in common.

Conscience constituents: People who provide resources for a social movement organization but who are not themselves members of the aggrieved group that the organization champions.

Control theory: The theory that the cause of deviance lies in the arena of social control and, specifically, the life experiences and relationships that people form.

Conversation analysis: The study of how participants in social interaction recognize and produce coherent conversation.

Correlation: The degree to which two or more variables are associated with one another.

Craze: An intense attraction to an object, a person, or an activity.

Credential society: A society in which access to desirable work and social status depends on the possession of a certificate or diploma certifying the completion of formal education.

Crime: Any act defined in the law as punishable by fines, imprisonment, or both.

Critical thinking: The ability to evaluate claims about truth by using reason and evidence.

Crowds: Temporary gatherings of closely interacting people with a common focus.

Crude birthrate: The number of births each year per 1,000 women.

Crude death rate: The number of deaths each year per 1,000 people.

Cult: A religious organization that is thoroughly unconventional with regard to the larger society.

Cultural capital: Wealth in the form of knowledge, ideas, verbal skills, and ways of thinking and acting.

Cultural inconsistency: A contradiction between the goals of ideal culture and the practices of real culture.

Cultural pluralism: The coexistence of different racial and ethnic groups, characterized by acceptance of one another's differences.

Cultural relativism: A worldview whereby the practices of a society are understood sociologically in terms of that society's norms and values, and not the norms and values of another society.

Culture: The beliefs, norms, behaviors, and products common to the members of a particular group.

Deductive reasoning: The process of taking an existing theory and logically deducing that if the theory is accurate, we should discover other patterns of behavior consistent with it.

De facto segregation: School segregation based on residential patterns or student choice, which persists even though legal segregation is now outlawed in the United States.

Democracy: A form of governance in which citizens are able to participate directly or indirectly in their own governance.

Demography: The science of population size, distribution, and composition.

Denomination: A church that is not formally allied with the state.

Dependency theory: The theory that the poverty of some countries is a consequence of their exploitation by wealthy states, which control the global capitalist system.

Dependent variables: Variables that change as a result of changes in other variables.

Deviance: Any attitude, behavior, or condition that violates cultural norms or societal laws and results in disapproval, hostility, or sanction if it becomes known.

Dictatorship: A form of governance in which power rests in a single individual.

Differential association theory: The theory that deviant and criminal behavior results from regular exposure to attitudes favorable to acting in ways that are deviant or criminal.

Differentiation: The development of increasing societal complexity through the creation of specialized social roles and institutions.

Direct democracy: A political system in which all citizens fully participate in their own governance.

Discrimination: The unequal treatment of individuals on the basis of their membership in a group.

Disestablishment: A period during which the political influence of established religions is successfully challenged.

Document analysis: The examination of written materials or cultural products: previous studies, newspaper reports, court records, campaign posters, digital reports, films, pamphlets, and other forms of text or images produced by individuals, government agencies, or private organizations.

Domestic (or family) violence: Physical or sexual abuse committed by one family member against another.

Domestic partnerships: Legal unions that provide a circumscribed spectrum of rights and benefits to same-sex couples.

Double consciousness: Among African Americans, an awareness of being both American and Black, never free of racial stigma.

Doxic: Taken for granted as "natural" or "normal" in society.

Dramaturgical approach: Developed by Erving Goffman, the study of social interaction as if it were governed by the norms of theatrical performance.

Dyad: A group consisting of two persons.

Ecclesia: A church that is formally allied with the state and is the "official" religion of the society.

Economic capital: Money and material that can be used to access valued goods and services.

Economy: The social institution that organizes the ways in which a society produces, distributes, and consumes goods and services.

Education: The transmission of society's norms, values, and knowledge base by means of direct instruction.

Ego: According to Sigmund Freud, the part of the mind that is the "self," the core of what is regarded as a person's unique personality.

Egocentric: Experiencing the world as if it were centered entirely on oneself.

Emergent norms: Norms that are situationally created to support a collective action.

Emic perspective: The perspective of the insider, the one belonging to the cultural group in question.

Emotional labor: The management of feelings or emotions to create a publicly observable facial and bodily display in return for a wage.

Endogamous: A characteristic of marriages in which partners are limited to members of the same social group or caste.

Establishment Clause: The passage in the First Amendment to the U.S. Constitution, that states, "Congress shall make no law respecting an establishment of religion, or prohibiting the free exercise thereof."

Ethnicity: Characteristics of groups associated with national origins, languages, and cultural and religious practices.

Ethnocentrism: A worldview whereby one judges other cultures by the standards of one's own culture and regards one's own way of life as "normal" and better than others.

Ethnomethodology: A sociological method used to study the body of commonsense knowledge and procedures by which ordinary members of a society make sense of their social circumstances and interaction.

Etic perspective: The perspective of the outside observer.

Evangelicalism: A belief in spiritual rebirth (conventionally denoted as being "born again").

Experiments: Research techniques for investigating cause and effect under controlled conditions.

Exponential population growth: A constant rate of population growth applied to a base that is continuously growing in size, producing a population that grows by an increasing amount with each passing year.

Expulsion: The process of forcibly removing a population from a particular area.

Extended families: Social groups consisting of one or more parents, children, and other kin, often spanning several generations, living in the same household.

Fads: Temporary, highly imitated outbreaks of mildly unconventional behavior.

Falsifiability: The ability for a theory to be disproven; the logical possibility for a theory to be tested and proven false.

Family: Two or more individuals who identify themselves as being related to one another, usually by blood, marriage, or adoption, and who share intimate relationships and dependency.

Fashions: Styles of imitative behavior or appearance that are of longer duration than fads.

Feminism: The belief that social equality should exist between the sexes; also, the social movements aimed at achieving that goal.

Feminist perspective on deviance: A perspective that suggests that studies of deviance have been subject to gender bias and that both gender-specific cultural norms and the particular ways in which women are victimized by virtue of their gender help to account for deviance among women.

Fertility: The number of live births in a given population.

Fieldwork: A research method that relies on in-depth and often extended study of a group or community.

Folkways: Fairly weak norms that are passed down from the past, the violation of which is generally not considered serious within a particular culture.

Food deserts: Areas that lack sources of competitively priced healthy and fresh food.

Formal economy: All work-related activities that provide income and are regulated by government agencies.

Formal education: Education that occurs within academic institutions such as schools.

Formal organization: An organization that is rationally designed to achieve its objectives, often by means of explicit rules, regulations, and procedures.

Formal rationality: A context in which people's pursuit of goals is shaped by rules, regulations, and larger social structures.

Formal social control: Official attempts to discourage certain behaviors and visibly punish others; most often exercised by the state.

Frame alignment: The process by which the interests, understandings, and values of a social movement organization are rendered congruent with those of the wider society.

Free rider problem: The problem that many people avoid the costs of social movement activism (such as time, energy, and other personal resources) and still benefit from its success.

Gender: Behavioral characteristics that differ between males and females based on culturally enforced and socially learned norms and roles.

Gender roles: The attitudes and behaviors that are considered appropriately "masculine" or "feminine" in a particular culture.

Gender wage gap: The difference between the earnings of women who work full-time year-round as a group and those of men who work full-time year-round as a group.

Generalized other: The abstract sense of society's norms and values by which people evaluate themselves.

Genocide: The mass, systematic destruction of a people or a nation.

Gentrification: The attempt to change the socioeconomic composition of old and poor neighborhoods with the remodeling of old structures and building of new residences and shops to attract new middle- and high-income residents.

Glass ceiling: An artificial boundary that allows women to see the next occupational or salary level even as structural obstacles keep them from reaching it.

Glass escalator: The nearly invisible promotional boost that men gain in female-dominated occupations.

Global cities: Metropolitan areas that are highly interconnected with one another in their role as centers of global political and economic decision making, finance, and culture.

Global consumer class: Those who actively use technology, purchase consumer goods, and embrace the culture of consumption.

Global culture: A type of culture—some would say U.S. culture—that has spread across the world in the form of Hollywood films, fast-food restaurants, and popular music heard in virtually every country.

Global elite: A transglobal class of professionals who exercise considerable economic and political power that is not limited by national borders.

Global inequality: The systematic disparities in income, wealth, health, education, access to technology, opportunity, and power among countries, communities, and households around the world.

Globalization: The process by which people all over the planet become increasingly interconnected economically, politically, culturally, and environmentally.

Goods: Objects that have an economic value to others, whether they are the basic necessities for survival or things that people simply want.

Grassroots organizing: Attempts to mobilize support among the ordinary members of a community.

Gross national income–purchasing power parity per capita (GNI-PPP): A comparative economic measure that uses international dollars to indicate the amount of goods and services someone could buy in the United States with a given amount of money.

Groupthink: A process by which the members of a group ignore ways of thinking and plans of action that go against the group consensus.

Habitus: The internalization of objective probabilities and subsequent expression of those probabilities as choice.

Health: The extent to which a person experiences a state of mental, physical, and social well-being.

Health care: All those activities intended to sustain, promote, and enhance health.

Hidden curriculum: The unspoken classroom socialization into the norms, values, and roles of a society that schools provide along with the "official" curriculum.

High culture: The music, theater, literature, and other cultural products that are held in particularly high esteem in society.

Hostile environment harassment: Conditions in the workplace that someone perceives as intimidating, uncomfortable, or otherwise distressing.

Human capital: The skills and knowledge a person possesses that make him or her valuable in a particular workplace.

Hypotheses: Ideas about the world, derived from theories, that can be disproved when tested against observations.

I: According to George Herbert Mead, the part of the self that is the impulse to act; it is creative, innovative, unthinking, and largely unpredictable.

Id: According to Sigmund Freud, the part of the mind that is the repository of basic biological drives and needs.

Ideal culture: The values, norms, and behaviors that people in a given society profess to embrace.

Income: The amount of money a person or household earns in a given period of time.

Independent or experimental variables: Variables that cause changes in other variables.

Indirect labor costs: Costs in time, training, or money incurred when an employee takes time off to care for sick family members, opts for parental leave, arrives at work late, or leaves a position after receiving employer-provided training.

Individual discrimination: Overt and intentional unequal treatment, often based on prejudicial beliefs.

Inductive reasoning: The process of generalizing to an entire category of phenomena from a particular set of observations.

Inequality: Differences in wealth, power, and other valued resources.

Infant mortality rate: The number of deaths of infants under age 1 per 1,000 live births per year.

Informal (or underground) economy: Those income-generating economic activities that escape regulation by the governmental institutions that ordinarily regulate similar activities.

Informal social control: The unofficial mechanism through which deviance and deviant behaviors are discouraged in society; most often occurs among ordinary people during the course of their interactions.

Institutionalized discrimination: Unequal treatment that has become a part of the routine operation of such major social institutions as businesses, schools, hospitals, and the government.

Interest groups: Advocacy or lobby groups that utilize their organizational and social resources to influence legislation and the functioning of social institutions.

International families: Families that result from globalization.

International governmental organization (IGO): An international organization established by treaties between governments for purposes of commerce, security, promotion of social welfare and human rights, or environmental protection.

International nongovernmental organization (INGO): An international organization established by agreements between the individuals or private organizations making up its membership and existing to fulfill an explicit mission.

Interview: A detailed conversation designed to obtain in-depth information about a person and his or her activities.

Iron law of oligarchy: Robert Michels's theory that there is an inevitable tendency for a large-scale bureaucratic organization to become ruled undemocratically by a handful of people.

Labeling theory: A symbolic interactionist approach holding that deviance is a product of the labels people attach to certain types of behavior.

Labor demand factors: Factors that highlight the needs and preferences of the employer.

Labor supply factors: Factors that highlight reasons that women or men may prefer particular occupations.

Language: A system of symbolic verbal, nonverbal, and written representations rooted within a particular culture.

Latent functions: Functions of an object, an institution, or a phenomenon that are not recognized or expected.

Law: A system of binding and recognized codified rules of behavior that regulate the actions of people pertaining to a given jurisdiction.

Laws: Codified norms or rules of behavior.

Leading questions: Questions that tend to elicit particular responses.

Legitimate authority: A type of power that is recognized as rightful by those over whom it is exercised.

Liberal feminism: The belief that women's inequality is primarily the result of imperfect institutions, which can be corrected by reforms that do not fundamentally alter society itself.

Life chances: The opportunities and obstacles a person encounters in education, social life, work, and other areas critical to social mobility.

Life expectancy: The average number of years a newborn is expected to live based on existing health conditions in the country.

Literacy: The ability to read and write at a basic level.

Lobbyists: Paid professionals whose job it is to influence legislation.

Looking-glass self: The concept developed by Charles Horton Cooley that our self-image results from how we interpret other people's views of us.

Macro-level paradigms: Theories of the social world that are concerned with large-scale patterns and institutions.

Mandatory minimum sentences: Legal requirements that persons found guilty of particular crimes must be sentenced to set minimum numbers of years in prison.

Manifest functions: Functions of an object, an institution, or a phenomenon that are obvious and intended.

Marginally attached to the labor force: Persons who would like to work and have searched actively for a job in the past 12 months.

Marriage: A culturally approved relationship, usually between two individuals, that provides a degree of economic cooperation, emotional intimacy, and sexual activity.

Mass education: The extension of formal schooling to wide segments of the population.

Mass media: Media of public communication intended to reach and influence a mass audience.

Mass production: The large-scale, highly standardized manufacturing of identical commodities on a mechanical assembly line.

Material culture: The physical objects that are created, embraced, or consumed by society that help shape people's lives.

Matrix of domination: A system of social positions in which any individual may concurrently occupy a status (for example, gender, race, class, or sexual orientation) as a member of a dominated group and a status as a member of a dominating group.

Me: According to George Herbert Mead, the part of the self through which we see ourselves as others see us.

Means of consumption: Things that make it possible for consumers to acquire goods and services and, at the same time, foster their control and exploitation as consumers.

Means of production: The sites and technology that produce the goods we need and use.

Medicine: An institutionalized system for the scientific diagnosis, treatment, and prevention of illness.

Megacities: Metropolitan areas or cities with total population of 10 million or more.

Meritocracy: A society in which personal success is based on talent and individual effort.

Micro-level paradigm: A theory of the social world that is concerned with small-group social relations and interactions.

Minorities: Less powerful groups who are dominated by a more powerful group and, often, discriminated against on the basis of characteristics deemed by the majority to be socially significant.

Mixed contacts: Interactions between those who are stigmatized and those who are "normal."

Modernization theory: A market-oriented development theory that envisions development as evolutionary and guided by "modern" institutions, practices, and cultures.

Monarchy: A form of governance in which power resides in an individual or a family and is passed from one generation to the next through hereditary lines.

Monogamy: A form of marriage in which a person may have only one spouse at a time.

Monotheism: Belief in a single all-knowing, all-powerful God.

Morbidity: The rate of illness in a particular population.

Mores: Strongly held norms, the violation of which seriously offends the standards of acceptable conduct of most people within a particular culture.

Mortality: The rate of death in a particular population.

Multicultural feminism: The belief that inequality must be understood—and ended—for all women, regardless of race, class, nationality, age, sexual orientation, physical ability, or other characteristics.

Multiculturalism: A commitment to respecting cultural differences rather than trying to submerge them into a larger, dominant culture.

Nation-state: A single people (a "nation") governed by a political authority (a "state"); similar to the modern notion of "country."

Negative correlation: A relation between two variables in which one increases as the other decreases.

Net financial assets: A measure of wealth that excludes illiquid personal assets such as home and car.

Net migration: In-migration minus out-migration.

New religious movements (NRMs): New spiritual groups or communities that occupy a peripheral place in a country's dominant religious landscape.

New social movements: Movements that have arisen since the 1960s and are fundamentally concerned with the quality of private life, often advocating large-scale cultural changes in how people think and act.

Noncitizens: Individuals who reside in a given jurisdiction but do not possess the same rights and privileges as the citizens who are recognized inhabitants; sometimes referred to as *residents, temporary workers,* or *aliens.*

Nonmaterial culture: The abstract creations of human cultures, including language and social practices.

Nontheistic religion: Belief in the existence of divine spiritual forces rather than a god or gods.

Normative organizations: Organizations that people join of their own will to pursue morally worthwhile goals without expectation of material reward; sometimes called *voluntary associations.*

Norms: Accepted social behaviors and beliefs.

Not in the labor force: Persons who are neither officially employed nor officially unemployed.

Nuclear families: Social groups consisting of one or two parents and their biological, dependent children, living in a household with no other kin.

Objectivity: The ability to represent the object of study accurately.

Occupation: A person's main vocation or paid employment.

Occupational segregation by gender: The concentration of men and women in different occupations.

Official poverty line: The dollar amount set by the government as the minimum necessary to meet the basic needs of a family.

Operational definition: A definition of a concept that allows the concept to be observed and measured.

Opportunity theory: The theory that people differ not only in their motivations to engage in deviant acts but also in their *opportunities* to do so.

Organization: A group with an identifiable membership that engages in concerted collective actions to achieve a common purpose.

Organized crime: Crime committed by criminal groups that provide illegal goods and services.

Panic: A massive flight from something that is feared.

Patriarchy: Any set of social relationships in which men dominate women.

Personal power: Power that derives from a leader's personality.

Phrenology: A theory that the skull shapes of deviant individuals differ from those of nondeviants.

Pluralistic societies: Societies made up of many diverse groups with different norms and values.

Political action committees (PACs): Organizations created by groups such as corporations, unions, environmentalists, and other interest groups for the purpose of gathering money and contributing to political candidates who favor the groups' interests.

Political power: The ability to exercise influence on political institutions and/or actors in order to realize personal or group interests.

Politics: The art or science of influencing public policy.

Polyandry: A form of marriage in which a woman may have multiple husbands.

Polygamy: A form of marriage in which a person may have more than one spouse at a time.

Polygyny: A form of marriage in which a man may have multiple wives.

Polytheism: The belief that there are different gods representing various categories of natural forces.

Popular culture: The entertainment, culinary, and athletic tastes shared by the masses.

Population: The whole group of people studied in sociological research.

Population momentum: The tendency of population growth to continue beyond the point when replacement rate fertility has been achieved because of the high concentration of people of childbearing age.

Positional power: Power that stems officially from the leadership position itself.

Positivist: Science that is based on facts alone.

Power: The ability to mobilize resources and achieve goals despite the resistance of others.

Power elite: A group of people with a disproportionately high level of influence and resources who utilize their status to influence the functioning of societal institutions.

Prejudice: A belief about an individual or a group that is not subject to change on the basis of evidence.

Presentation of self: The creation of impressions in the minds of others in order to define and control social situations.

Preventive medicine: Medicine that emphasizes a healthy lifestyle that will prevent poor health before it occurs.

Primary deviance: A term developed by Edwin Lemert; the first step in the labeling of deviance, it occurs at the moment an activity is labeled deviant (see also *secondary deviance*).

Primary groups: Small groups characterized by intense emotional ties, face-to-face interaction, intimacy, and a strong, enduring sense of commitment.

Principle of falsification: The principle, advanced by philosopher Karl Popper, that a scientific theory must lead to testable hypotheses that can be disproved if they are wrong.

Private sector: The sector of the labor market that provides goods and services to the economy and consumers with the primary motive of gaining profit.

Profane: A sphere of routine, everyday life.

Proletariat: The working class; wage workers.

Property crimes: Crimes that involve the violation of individuals' ownership rights, including burglary, larceny/theft, arson, and motor vehicle theft.

Psychoanalysis: A psychological perspective that emphasizes the complex reasoning processes of the conscious and unconscious mind.

Public education: A universal education system provided by the government and funded by tax revenues rather than student fees.

Public health: The science and practice of health protection and maintenance at a community level.

Public sector: The sector of the labor market in which jobs are linked to the government (whether national, state, or local) and encompass production or allocation of goods and services for the benefit of the government and its citizens.

Qualitative research: Research that is characterized by data that cannot be quantified (or converted into numbers), focusing instead on generating in-depth knowledge of social life, institutions, and processes.

Qualitative variables: Variables that express qualities and do not have numerical values.

Quantitative research: Research that gathers data that can be quantified and offers insight into broad patterns of social behavior and social attitudes.

Quantitative variables: Factors that can be counted.

Quid pro quo sexual harassment: The demand or implication that a sexual favor will buy a promotion or an opportunity to keep one's job.

Race: A group of people who share a set of characteristics (usually physical characteristics) deemed by society to be socially significant.

Racism: The idea that one racial group is inherently superior to another; often results in institutionalized relationships between dominant and minority groups that create a structure of economic, social, and political inequality based on socially constructed racial or ethnic categories.

Radical feminism: The belief that women's inequality underlies all other forms of inequality, including economic inequality.

Random sampling: Sampling in which everyone in the population of interest has an equal chance of being chosen for the study.

Rape culture: A social culture that provides an environment conducive to rape.

Rate of natural increase (RNI): The crude birthrate minus the crude death rate.

Rational-legal authority: Power based on a belief in the lawfulness of enacted rules (laws) and the legitimate right of leaders to exercise authority under such rules.

Reactionary social movements: Movements seeking to restore an earlier social system—often based on a mythical past—along with the traditional norms and values that once presumably accompanied it.

Real culture: The values, norms, and behaviors that people in a given society actually embrace and exhibit.

Rebellions: Movements seeking to overthrow the existing social, political, and economic systems but lacking detailed plans for a new social order.

Reference groups: Groups that provide standards for judging our attitudes or behaviors.

Reformist social movements: Movements seeking to bring about social change within the existing economic and political system.

Reliability: The extent to which researchers' findings are consistent with the findings of different studies of the same thing, or with the findings of the same study over time.

Religion: A system of common beliefs and rituals centered on "sacred things" that unites believers and provides a sense of meaning and purpose.

Religious economy: An approach to the sociology of religion that suggests that religions can be fruitfully understood as organizations in competition with one another for followers.

Religious nationalism: The linkage of religious convictions with beliefs about a nation's or ethnic group's social and political destiny.

Replication: The repetition of a previous study using a different sample or population to verify or refute the original findings.

Representative democracy: A political system in which citizens elect representatives to govern them.

Research methods: Specific techniques for systematically gathering data.

Reserve army of labor: A pool of job seekers whose numbers outpace the available positions and thus contribute to keeping wages low and conditions of work tenuous.

Resocialization: The process of altering an individual's behavior through control of his or her environment, for example, within a total institution.

Resource mobilization theory: A theory about social movement organizations that focuses on their ability to generate money, membership, and political support in order to achieve their objectives.

Revolutionary social movements: Movements seeking to fundamentally alter the existing social, political, and economic system in keeping with a vision of a new social order.

Riot: An illegal, prolonged outbreak of violent behavior by a sizable group of people directed against people or property.

Rise-and-fall theories of social change: Theories that see social change as characterized by a cycle of growth and decline.

Role-taking: The ability to take the roles of others in interaction.

Rumors: Unverified forms of information that are transmitted informally, usually originating in unknown sources.

Sacred: That which is set apart from the ordinary, the sphere endowed with spiritual meaning.

Sample: A portion of the larger population selected to represent the whole.

Scapegoating: A process in which one group blames another for the problems that members of the first group face.

School segregation: The education of racial minorities in schools that are geographically, economically, and/or socially separated from those attended by Whites.

Scientific: A way of learning about the world that combines logically constructed theory and systematic observation.

Scientific management: A practice that sought to use principles of engineering to reduce the physical movements of workers.

Scientific method: A way of learning about the world that combines logically constructed theory and systematic observation to provide explanations of how things work.

Scientific theories: Explanations of how and why scientific observations are as they are.

Secondary deviance: A term developed by Edwin Lemert; the second step in the labeling of deviance, it occurs when a person labeled deviant accepts the label as part of his or her identity and, as a result, begins to act in conformity with the label (see also *primary deviance*).

Secondary groups: Groups that are large and impersonal and characterized by fleeting relationships.

Second shift: The unpaid housework that women typically do after they come home from their paid employment.

Sect: A religious organization that has splintered off from an established church in an effort to restore perceived "true" beliefs and practices believed to have been lost by the established religious organization.

Secularization: The rise in worldly thinking, particularly as seen in the rise of science, technology, and rational thought, and a simultaneous decline in the influence of religion.

Segregation: The practice of separating people spatially or socially on the basis of race or ethnicity.

Serial monogamy: The practice of having more than one wife or husband, but only one at a time.

Services: Economically productive activities that do not result directly in physical products; may be relatively simple or quite complex.

Sex: The anatomical and other biological characteristics that differ between males and females and that originate in genetic differences.

Sex category: The socially required identification display that confirms someone's membership in a given category.

Sexism: The belief that one sex is innately superior to the other and is therefore justified in having a dominant social position.

Sexual division of labor in modern societies: The phenomenon of dividing production functions by gender and designating different spheres of activity, the "private" to women and the "public" to men.

Sexual harassment: Unwelcome sexual advances, requests for sexual favors, or physical conduct of a sexual nature when such conduct is used as a condition of employment, instruction, evaluation, benefits, or other opportunities; or when such conduct interferes with an individual's performance or contributes to an intimidating, hostile, or offensive environment.

Sexuality: The ways in which people construct their sexual desires and relationships, including the norms governing sexual behavior.

Sick roles: Social roles rooted in cultural definitions of the appropriate behavior of and response to people labeled as sick.

Significant others: According to George Herbert Mead, the specific people who are important in children's lives and whose views have the greatest impact on the children's self-evaluations.

Social bonds: Individuals' connections to others (see also *control theory*).

Social capital: The social knowledge and connections that enable people to accomplish their goals and extend their influence.

Social categories: Categories of people sharing common characteristics without necessarily interacting or identifying with one another.

Social class reproduction: The way in which class status is reproduced from generation to generation, with parents "passing on" a class position to their offspring.

Social closure: The ability of a group to strategically and consciously exclude outsiders or those deemed "undesirable" from participating in the group or enjoying the group's resources.

Social conflict paradigm: A theory that seeks to explain social organization and change in terms of the conflict that is built into social relations; also known as *conflict theory.*

Social control: The attempts by certain people or groups in society to control the behaviors of other individuals and groups in order to increase the likelihood that they will conform to established norms or laws.

Social diversity: The social and cultural mixture of different groups in society and the societal recognition of difference as significant.

Social dynamics: The laws that govern social change.

Social embeddedness: The idea that economic, political, and other forms of human behavior are fundamentally shaped by social relations.

Social epidemiology: The study of communities and their social statuses, practices, and problems with the aim of understanding patterns of health and disease.

Social facts: Qualities of groups that are external to individual members yet constrain their thinking and behavior.

Social inequality: A high degree of disparity in income, wealth, power, prestige, and other resources.

Socialism: A type of economic system in which, theoretically, the government manages the economy in the interests of the workers; it owns the businesses, factories, farms, hospitals, housing, and other means of producing wealth and redistributes that wealth to the population through wages and services.

Socialist feminism: The belief that women's inequality results from the combination of capitalistic economic relations and male domination; argues that both must be transformed fundamentally before women can achieve equality.

Socialization: The process by which people learn the culture of their society.

Social learning: The way people adapt their behavior in response to social rewards and punishments.

Social mobility: The upward or downward status movement of individuals or groups over time.

Social movement: A large number of people who come together in a continuing and organized effort to bring about (or resist) social change, and who rely at least partially on noninstitutionalized forms of political action.

Social movement organizations (SMOs): Formal organizations that seek to achieve social change through noninstitutionalized forms of political action.

Social power: The ability to exercise social control.

Social solidarity: The bonds that unite the members of a social group.

Social statics: The way society is held together.

Social stratification: The systematic ranking of different groups of people in a hierarchy of inequality.

Sociological imagination: The ability to grasp the relationship between individual lives and the larger social forces that help to shape them.

Sociological theories: Logical, rigorous frameworks for the interpretation of social life that make particular assumptions and ask particular questions about the social world.

Sociology: The scientific study of human social relations, groups, and societies.

Spurious relationship: A correlation between two or more variables that is actually the result of something else that is not being measured, rather than a causal link between the variables themselves.

Standpoint epistemology: A philosophical perspective that argues that what we can know is affected by the position we occupy in society.

Standpoint theory: A perspective that says the knowledge we create is conditioned by where we stand, or our subjective social position.

State crimes: Criminal or other harmful acts committed by state officials in the pursuit of their jobs as representatives of the government.

Statistical data: Quantitative information obtained from government agencies, businesses, research studies, and other entities that collect data for their own or others' use.

Status: The prestige associated with a social position.

Stereotype threat: A situation in which an individual is at risk of confirming a negative stereotype about his or her social group.

Stereotyping: The generalization of a set of characteristics to all members of a group.

Stigma: An attribute that is deeply discrediting to an individual or a group because it overshadows other attributes and merits the individual or group may possess.

Stigmatization: The branding of behavior as highly disgraceful (see also *labeling theory*).

Strain theory: The theory that when there is a discrepancy between the cultural goals for success and the means available to achieve those goals, rates of deviance will be high.

Structural contradiction theory: The theory that conflicts generated by fundamental contradictions in the structure of society produce laws defining certain acts as deviant or criminal.

Structural functionalism: A theory that seeks to explain social organization and change in terms of the roles performed by different social structures, phenomena, and institutions; also known as *functionalism*.

Structuralism: The idea that an overarching structure exists within which culture and other aspects of society must be understood.

Structural strain: In Merton's reformulation of Durkheim's functionalist theory, a form of anomie that occurs when a gap exists between society's culturally defined goals and the means society makes available to achieve those goals.

Structure: Patterned social arrangements that have effects on agency.

Subcultural theories: Theories that explain deviance in terms of the conflicting interests of more and less powerful segments of a population.

Subcultures: Cultures that exist together with a dominant culture but differ in some important respects from that dominant culture.

Superego: According to Sigmund Freud, the part of the mind that consists of the values and norms of society, insofar as they are internalized, or taken in, by the individual.

Survey: A research method that uses a questionnaire or interviews administered to a group of people in person or by telephone or e-mail to determine their characteristics, opinions, and behaviors.

Symbolic interactionism: A microsociological perspective that posits that both the individual self and society as a whole are the products of social interactions based on language and other symbols.

Symbols: Representations of things that are not immediately present to our senses.

Taboos: Powerful mores, the violation of which is considered serious and even unthinkable within a particular culture.

Technology: The practical application of knowledge to transform natural resources for human use.

Terrorism: "The calculated use of violence or the threat of violence to inculcate fear; intended to coerce or to intimidate governments or societies in the pursuit of goals that are generally political, religious, or ideological" (U.S. Department of Defense, 2011).

Theism: A belief in one or more supernatural deities.

"Three strikes" laws: Laws that require sentences of life in prison for those who are found guilty of committing three felonies, or serious crimes.

Total fertility rate (TFR): The average number of children a woman in a given country will have in her lifetime if age-specific fertility rates hold throughout her childbearing years.

Total institutions: Institutions that isolate individuals from the rest of society in order to achieve administrative control over most aspects of their lives.

Totalitarianism: A form of governance that denies popular political participation in government and also seeks to regulate and control all aspects of the public and private lives of citizens.

Totems: Within the sacred sphere, ordinary objects believed to have acquired transcendent or magical qualities connecting humans with the divine.

Traditional authority: Power based on a belief in the sanctity of long-standing traditions and the legitimate right of rulers to exercise authority in accordance with those traditions.

Transactional leader: A leader who is concerned with accomplishing the group's tasks, getting group members to do their jobs, and making certain that the group achieves its goals.

Transformational leader: A leader who is able to instill in the members of a group a sense of mission or higher purpose, thereby changing the nature of the group itself.

Transgender: An umbrella term used to describe those whose gender identity, expression, or behavior differs from their assigned sex or is outside the gender binary.

Transsexual: A term used to refer to people who use surgery and hormones to change their sex to match their preferred gender.

Treadmill of production: The constant and aggressive growth needed to sustain the modern economy.

Triad: A group consisting of three persons.

Unemployed: Persons who are jobless, actively looked for work in the prior 4 weeks, and are available for work.

Urban growth machine: Those persons and institutions that have a stake in an increase in the value of urban land and that constitute a power elite in cities.

Urbanization: The concentration of people in urban areas.

Urban renewal: The transformation of old neighborhoods with new buildings, businesses, and residences.

Utilitarian organizations: Organizations that people join primarily because of some material benefit they expect to receive in return for membership.

Utopian social movements: Movements seeking to withdraw from the dominant society by creating their own ideal communities.

Validity: The degree to which concepts and their measurements accurately represent what they claim to represent.

Value neutrality: The characteristic of being free of personal beliefs and opinions that would influence the course of research.

Values: The general standards in society that define ideal principles, like those governing notions of right and wrong.

Variable: A concept or its empirical measure that can take on multiple values.

Verstehen: The German word for interpretive understanding; Weber's proposed methodology for explaining social relationships by having the sociologist imagine how subjects might perceive a situation.

Violent crimes: Crimes that involve force or threat of force, including robbery, murder, assault, and rape.

War economy: The phenomenon of war boosting economic productivity and employment, particularly in capital- and labor-intensive sectors such as industrial production.

"War on drugs": Actions taken by U.S. state and federal governments that are intended to curb the illegal drug trade and reduce drug use.

Wealth (or net worth): The value of everything a person owns minus the value of everything he or she owes.

Welfare state: A government or country's system of providing for the financial and social well-being of its citizens, typically through government programs that provide funding or other resources to individuals who meet certain criteria.

White-collar crime: Crime committed by people of high social status in connection with their work.

Work: Any human effort that adds something of value to the goods and services that are available to others.

World systems theory: The theory that the global capitalist economic system has long been shaped by a few powerful economic actors, who have ordered it in a way that favors their interests.

Zionism: A movement calling for the return of Jews to Palestine and the creation of a Jewish state.

REFERENCES

Abrahams, N. (1992). Towards reconceptualizing political action. *Sociological Inquiry, 62,* 327–347.

Achen, A. C., & Stafford, F. P. (2005). *Data quality of housework hours in the Panel Study of Income Dynamics: Who really does the dishes?* (PSID Technical Series Paper 05-04). Ann Arbor: Institute for Social Research, University of Michigan. Retrieved from http://psidonline.isr.umich.edu/Publications/Papers/tsp/2005-04_Data_Qual_of_Household_Hours-_Dishes.pdf

Acierno, R., Hernandez-Tejada, M., Muzzy, W., & Steve, K. (2009). *Final report: The National Elder Mistreatment Study.* Report submitted to the U.S. Department of Justice, National Institute of Justice. Retrieved from https://www.ncjrs.gov/pdffiles1/nij/grants/226456.pdf

Ackbar, S. (2011). *Constructions and socialization of gender and sexuality in lesbian-/gay-headed families* (Doctoral dissertation, University of Windsor). Retrieved from ProQuest (NR77959).

Adachi, P. J. C., & Willoughby, T. (2011). The effect of video game competition and violence on aggressive behavior: Which characteristic has the greatest influence? *Psychology of Violence, 1*(4), 259–274.

Adams, J., Parkinson, L., Sanson-Fisher, R. W., & Walsh, R. A. (2008). Enhancing self-report of adolescent smoking: The effects of bogus pipeline and anonymity. *Addictive Behaviors, 33*(10), 1291–1296.

Adler, F. (1975). *Sisters in crime: The rise of the new female criminal.* New York: McGraw-Hill.

Administrative Office of the United States Courts. (2011). *Report of statistics required by the Bankruptcy Abuse Prevention and Consumer Protection Act of 2005.* Washington, DC: Government Printing Office. Retrieved from http://www.uscourts.gov/uscourts/Statistics/BankruptcyStatistics/BAPCPA/2010/2010BAPCPA.pdf

Adorno, T. (1975). The culture industry reconsidered. *New German Critique, 6*(Fall), 12–19.

Ahola, A. S., Christianson, S., & Hellstrom, A. (2009). Justice needs a blindfold: Effects of gender and attractiveness on prison sentences and attributions of personal characteristics in a judicial process. *Psychiatry, Psychology, and Law, 16*(S1), S90–S100.

Ahuja, M., Barnes, R., Chow, E., & Rivero, C. (2014, September 4). The changing landscape on same-sex marriage. *Washington Post.* Retrieved from http://www.washingtonpost.com/wp-srv/special/politics/same-sex-marriage

AIDS in China: Blood debts. (2007, January 18). *The Economist.* Retrieved from http://www.economist.com/node/8554778

Aina, O. E., & Cameron, P. A. (2011). Why does gender matter? Counteracting stereotypes with young children. *Dimensions of Early Childhood, 39*(1), 11–19.

Albanese, J. S. (1989). *Organized crime in America.* New York: Anderson.

Aldrich, H. E., & Marsden, P. V. (1988). Environments and organizations. In N. J. Smelser (Ed.), *Handbook of sociology* (pp. 361–392). Newbury Park, CA: Sage.

Alexander, J. C. (1998). *Neofunctionalism and after.* Malden, MA: Blackwell.

Alexander, J. C., & Colomy, P. (1990). *Differentiation theory and social change.* New York: Columbia University Press.

Alexander, J. C., & Thompson, K. (2008). *A contemporary introduction to sociology: Culture and society in transition.* Boulder, CO: Paradigm.

Alexander, K. L., Entwisle, D. R., & Olson, L. S. (2007). Lasting consequences of the summer learning gap. *American Sociological Review, 72,* 167–180.

Alexander, M. (2010). *The new Jim Crow: Mass incarceration in the age of colorblindness.* New York: New Press.

Alfano, S. (2009, February 11). Poll: Women's movement worthwhile. CBS News. Retrieved from http://www.cbsnews.com/2100-500160_162-965224.html

Allegretto, S. A., Doussard, M., Graham-Squire, D., Jacobs, K., Thompson, D., & Thompson, J. (2013, October). *Fast food, poverty wages: The public cost of low-wage jobs in the fast-food industry.* Berkeley: University of California, Berkeley, Center for Labor Research and Education. Retrieved from http://laborcenter.berkeley.edu/publiccosts/fast_food_poverty_wages.pdf

Allen, I. E., & Seaman, J. (2011). *Going the distance: Online education in the United States, 2011.* Wellesley, MA: Babson Survey Research Group. Retrieved from http://www.onlinelearningsurvey.com/reports/goingthedistance.pdf

Allport, G. W., & Postman, L. (1947). *The psychology of rumor.* New York: Holt.

Alpers, P., & Wilson, M. (2013). Guns in the United States: Facts, figures and firearm law. Sydney School of Public Health, University of Sydney. Retrieved from http://www.gunpolicy.org/firearms/compare/194/rate_of_gun_homicide/31,66,69,172,192,91

American Academy of Child and Adolescent Psychiatry. (2011). Children and watching TV. *Facts for Families, 54*(4). Retrieved from http://www.aacap.org/cs/root/facts_for_families/children_and_watching_tv

American Association of University Women. (1993). *Hostile hallways: Bullying, teasing, and sexual harassment in school.* Washington, DC: Author.

American Institutes for Research. (2010, October 11). College dropouts cost cash-strapped states billions. Retrieved from http://www.air.org/news/index.cfm?fa=viewContent&content_id=988

American Medical Association. (2013). AMA history timeline 1941–1960. Retrieved from http://www.ama-assn.org/ama/pub/about-ama/our-history/ama-history-timeline.page

American Sociological Association. (2005, January 8). Society and social life. Retrieved from http://www2.asanet.org/student/career/careers.html

Amis, M. (2002). *Koba the dread.* New York: Miramax.

Amnesty International. (2004, October 26). *Democratic Republic of Congo: Mass rape—Time for remedies.* Retrieved from http://www.amnesty.org/es/library/asset/AFR62/022/2004/es/97ac3942-d571-11dd-bb24-1fb85fe8fa05/afr620222004en.pdf

Amnesty International. (2010, April 30). Address the barriers of transport costs undermining rural women's right to health in South Africa. Retrieved from http://www.amnesty.org/en/appeals-for-action/address-barriers-transport-costs-undermining-rural-womens-right-health

Amnesty International. (2012). Jalila al-Salman and Mahdi 'Issa Mahdi Abu Dheeb: Prisoners of conscience. Retrieved from http://www.amnestyusa.org/our-work/cases/bahrain-jalila-al-salman-mahdi-issa-mahdi-abu-dheeb

Amnesty International. (2014, March 10). Syria: Squeezing the life out of Yarmouk: War crimes against besieged civilians. Retrieved from http://www.amnestyusa.org/research/reports/syria-squeezing-the-life-out-of-yarmouk-war-crimes-against-besieged-civilians

Andersen, M. L., & Collins, P. H. (Eds.). (1992). *Race, class, and gender: An anthology.* Stamford, CT: Wadsworth.

Anderson, B. (1991). *Imagined communities: Reflections on the origin and spread of nationalism.* London: Verso.

Anderson, C., Berkowitz, L., Donnerstein, E., Huesmann, L. R., Johnson, J., Linz, D., . . . Wartella, E. (2003). The influence of media violence on youth. *Psychological Science in the Public Interest, 4*(3), 81–110.

Anderson, E. (1999). *Code of the street: Decency, violence and the moral life of the inner city.* New York: Norton.

Anderson, N. (1940). *Men on the move.* Chicago: University of Chicago Press.

Anderson, T. D. (2000). Sex-role orientation and care-oriented moral reasoning: An online test of Carol Gilligan's theory. *Dissertation Abstracts International, 61*(4), 1618-A. Retrieved from http://search.proquest.com.proxygw.wrlc.org/socabs/docview/60390650/13C8E238511536831E/1?accountid=11243

Andre, F. E., Boy, R., Bock, H. L., Clemens, J., Datta, S. K., John, T. J., . . . Schmitt, H. J. (2008). Vaccination greatly reduces disease, disability, death and inequity worldwide. *Bulletin of the World Health Organization, 86*(2). Retrieved from http://www.who.int/bulletin/volumes/86/2/07-040089/en

Angier, N. (2000, August 22). Do races differ? Not really, genes show. *New York Times.* Retrieved from http://www.nytimes.com/2000/08/22/science/do-races-differ-not-really-genes-show.html?pagewanted=all&src=pm

Antos, J. (2011). Medicare reform and fiscal reality. *Journal of Policy Analysis and Management, 30*(4), 934–942.

Anzaldúa, G. (Ed.). (1990). *Making face, making soul: Haciendo caras.* San Francisco: Aunt Lute Foundation.

Appelbaum, R. P. (1986). Testimony on "A report to the secretary on the homeless and emergency shelters." In J. Erickson & C. Wilhelm (Eds.), *Housing the homeless.* New Brunswick, NJ: Rutgers University Center for Urban Policy Research.

Appelbaum, R. P., Dolny, M., Dreier, P., & Gilderbloom, J. (1991). Scapegoating rent control: Masking the cause of homelessness. *Journal of the American Planning Association, 57,* 153–164.

Arab American Institute. (2012). Arab Americans. Retrieved from http://www.aaiusa.org/pages/arab-americans

Arab American Institute Foundation. (2011). Quick facts about Arab Americans. Retrieved from http://b.3cdn.net/aai/fcc68db3efdd45f613_vim6ii3a7.pdf

Archer, D., & Gartner, R. (1984). *Violence and crime in cross-national perspective.* New Haven, CT: Yale University Press.

Arendt, H. (1951). *The origins of totalitarianism.* New York: Harcourt, Brace.

Armstrong, L., Phillips, J. G., & Saling, L. L. (2000). Potential determinants of heavier Internet use. *International Journal of Human-Computer Studies, 53*(4), 537–550.

Asch, S. (1952). *Social psychology.* Englewood Cliffs, NJ: Prentice-Hall.

Asencio, E. K., & Burke, P. J. (2011). Does incarceration change the criminal identity? A synthesis of labeling and identity theory perspectives on identity change. *Sociological Perspectives, 54*(20), 163–182.

Aubrey, J. S., & Frisby, C. M. (2011). Sexual objectification in music videos: A content analysis comparing gender and genre. *Mass Communication and Society, 14*(4), 475–501.

Aubrey, J. S., & Harrison, K. (2004). The gender-role content of children's favorite television programs and its links to their gender-related perceptions. *Media Psychology, 6,* 111–146.

Austin, A. (2010). *Graduate employment gap: Students of color losing ground* (Briefing Paper 282). Washington, DC: Economic Policy Institute. Retrieved from http://www.epi.org/publication/graduate_employment_gap_students_of_color_losing_ground

Austin, J., Dimas, J., & Steinhart, D. (1992). *Over-representation of minority youth in the California juvenile justice system* (Report prepared for the California State Advisory Group on Juvenile Justice and the California Office of Criminal Justice Planning). Washington, DC: National Council on Crime and Delinquency.

Autor, D. (2010, April). *The polarization of job opportunities in the U.S. labor market: Implications for employment and earnings.* Washington, DC: Center for American Progress and the Hamilton Project. Retrieved from http://www.scribd.com/doc/52779456/The-Polarization-of-Job-Opportunities-in-the-U-S-Labor-Market

AVERT. (2010). Sub-Saharan Africa HIV and AIDS statistics. Retrieved from http://www.avert.org/africa-hiv-aids-statistics.htm

Aviel, D. (1997). Issues in education: A closer examination of American education. *Childhood Education, 73*(3), 130–132.

Azuz, C. (2012, August 22). Survey: 17% of high schoolers drink, smoke, use drugs during school day. CNN. Retrieved from http://schoolsofthought.blogs.cnn.com/2012/08/22/survey-17-of-high-schoolers-drink-smoke-use-drugs-during-school-day

Babbie, E. R. (1998). *The practice of social research.* Belmont, CA: Wadsworth.

Babcock, P., & Marks, M. (2010, August). *Leisure college, USA: The decline in student study time* (Research Education Outlook No. 7). Washington, DC: American Enterprise Institute for Public Policy. Retrieved from http://www.aei.org/files/2010/08/05/07-EduO-Aug-2010-g-new.pdf

Bachar, E., Canetti, L., Bonne, O., DeNour, A., & Shalev, A. (1997). Physical punishment and signs of mental distress in normal adolescents. *Adolescence, 38*(128), 945–952.

Bajaj, V. (2010, July 16). Bangladesh, with low wages, moves in on China. *New York Times.* Retrieved from http://www.nytimes.com/2010/07/17/business/global/17textile.html?pagewanted=all

Baldwin, J. D., & Baldwin, J. I. (1986). *Behavior principles in everyday life.* Englewood Cliffs, NJ: Prentice Hall.

Baldwin, J. D., & Baldwin, J. I. (1988). Factors affecting AIDS-related sexual risk-taking behavior among college students. *Journal of Sex Research, 25*(2), 181–196.

Ball, S. J., Bowe, R., & Gewirtz, S. (1995). Circuits of schooling: A sociological exploration of parental choice of school in social class contexts. *Sociological Review, 43*(1), 52–77.

Balmer, Z. (1989). *Mine eyes have seen the glory: A journey into the evangelical subculture in America.* New York: Oxford University Press.

Balzac, H. de. (1833). *The girl with the golden eyes.* Philadelphia: George Barrie & Son.

Balzac, H. de. (1985). *Les employés.* Paris: French & European Publications. (Original work published 1841)

Bandura, A. (1977). *Social learning theory.* Englewood Cliffs, NJ: Prentice Hall.

Bandura, A., & Walters, R. H. (1963). *Social learning and personality development.* New York: Holt, Rinehart & Winston.

Banerjee, B. (2014, June 3). Indian gang rape case highlights lack of toilets. Associated Press. Retrieved from http://bigstory.ap.org/article/india-gang-rape-case-highlights-lack-toilets

Barber, B. K. (1992). Family, personality, and adolescent problem behaviors. *Journal of Marriage and the Family, 54*(2), 69–79.

Barner, M. (1999). Sex-role stereotyping in FCC-mandated children's educational television. *Journal of Broadcasting & Electronic Media, 43*(4), 551–564.

Barnes, R. (2012, November 26). Justices decline to consider whether Constitution requires insanity defense. *Washington Post.* Retrieved from http://articles.washingtonpost.com/2012-11-26/politics/35510546_1_insanity-defense-justices-decline-jeffrey-1-fisher

Barratt, M. J., Ferris, J. A., & Winstock, A. R. (2014). Use of Silk Road, the online drug marketplace, in the United Kingdom, Australia and the United States. *Addiction, 9*(5), 774–783.

Barrera, M. (1979). *Race and class in the Southwest.* Notre Dame, IN: University of Notre Dame Press.

Barrett, D. B. (2001). *World Christian encyclopedia.* New York: Oxford University Press.

Barry, K. (1979). *Female sexual slavery.* Englewood Cliffs, NJ: Prentice Hall.

Barry, T., & Sims, B. (1994). *The challenge of cross-border environmentalism: The U.S.–Mexico case.* Albuquerque, NM: Resource Center Press.

Basham, A. L. (1989). *The origins and development of classical Hinduism.* New York: Oxford University Press.

Basow, S. (2004). The hidden curriculum: Gender in the classroom. In M. Paludi (Ed.), *Praeger guide to the psychology of gender* (pp. 117–132). Westport, CT: Praeger.

Baudrillard, J. (1981). *Simulacra and simulation* (S. F. Glaser, Trans.). Ann Arbor: University of Michigan Press.

Baum, S., & O'Malley, M. (2003). College on credit: How borrowers perceive their education debt. *NASFAA Journal of Student Financial Aid, 33*(3), 7–19.

Bauman, Z. (1998). *Globalization: The human consequences.* New York: Columbia University Press.

Bauman, Z. (2001). *Modernity and the Holocaust.* Ithaca, NY: Cornell University Press.

Baumgardner, J., & Richards, A. (2010). *Manifesta: Young women, feminism, and the future.* New York: Farrar, Straus and Giroux.

Bazell, R. (2010, October 1). U.S. apologizes for Guatemala STD experiments. NBC News. Retrieved from http://www.msnbc.msn.com/id/39456324/ns/health-sexual_health/t/us-apologizes-guatemala-std-experiments/#.ULbLqe-igkI

BBC. (2008, December 18). Rwanda: How the genocide happened. Retrieved from http://news.bbc.co.uk/2/hi/1288230.stm

BBC. (2010, March 5). S Korea child "starves as parents raise virtual baby." Retrieved from http://news.bbc.co.uk/2/hi/asia-pacific/8551122.stm

BBC. (2012, December 6). Timeline: Ayodhya holy site crisis. Retrieved from http://www.bbc.com/news/world-south-asia-11436552

BBC. (2014a, February 17). Former Barclays employees named in Libor criminal case. Retrieved from http://www.bbc.co.uk/news/business-26228635

BBC. (2014b). History: The troubles, 1968–1998. Retrieved from http://www.bbc.co.uk/history/troubles

BBC. (2014c, June 5). Softbank unveils "human-like" robot Pepper. Retrieved from http://www.bbc.com/news/technology-27709828

Beauchamp, Z. (2014, June 16). What ISIS has to gain from tweeting these photos of a massacre. Vox Media. Retrieved from http://www.vox.com/2014/6/16/5814900/isis-photos-horrifying-iraq

Beaver, K. M., Wright, J. P., DeLisi, M., & Vaughn, M. G. (2008). Genetic influences on the stability of low self-control: Results from a longitudinal sample of twins. *Journal of Criminal Justice, 36,* 478–485.

Before and after Title IX: Women in sports. (2012, June 16). *New York Times.* Retrieved from http://www.nytimes.com/interactive/2012/06/17/opinion/sunday/sundayreview-titleix-timeline.html?_r=0#/#time12_264

Beiner, T. M. (2007). Sexy dressing revisited: Does target dress play a part in sexual harassment cases? *Duke Journal of Gender Law & Policy, 14,* 125–152.

Beinhocker, E. D., Farrell, D., & Zainulbhai, A. S. (2007, August). Tracking the growth of India's middle class. *McKinsey Quarterly.* Retrieved from http://www.mckinseyquarterly.com/Tracking_the_growth_of_Indias_middle_class_2032

Bekkers, V., Edwards, A., & Moody, R. (2010, September 16–17). *Micro-mobilization, social media and coping strategies: Some Dutch experiences.* Paper presented at the Internet and Public Policy Conference, St. Anne's College, Oxford University, Oxford, England.

Bell, D. (1973). *The coming of post-industrial society: A venture in social forecasting.* New York: Basic Books.

Bellah, R. N. (1968). Meaning and modernization. *Religious Studies, 4*(1), 37–45.

Bellah, R. N. (1975). *The broken covenant: American civil religion in time of trial.* New York: Seabury Press.

Berfield, S. (2013, October 15). McDonald's low wages come with a 7 billion side of welfare. *Bloomberg Businessweek.* Retrieved from http://www.businessweek.com/articles/2013-10-15/mcdonalds-low-wages-come-with-a-7-billion-side-of-welfare

Bergen, T. J., Jr. (1996). The social philosophy of public education. *School Business Affairs, 62*(6), 22–27.

Berger, P. L. (1986). *The capitalist revolutions: Fifty propositions about prosperity, equality, and liberty.* New York: Basic Books.

Berger, P. L., & Hsiao, H.-H. M. (Eds.). (1988). *In search of an East Asian development model.* Piscataway, NJ: Transaction Books.

Berkley, S. (2013, September 12). How cell phones are transforming health care in Africa. *MIT Technology Review,* guest blog . Retrieved from http://www.technologyreview.com/view/519041/how-cell-phones-are-transforming-health-care-in-africa

Berlin, L. J., Ispa, J. M., Fine, M. A., Malone, P. S., Brooks-Gunn, J., Brady-Smith, C., . . . Bai, Y. (2009). Correlates and consequences of spanking and verbal punishment for low-income White, African American, and Mexican American toddlers. *Child Development, 80*(5), 1403–1420.

Bernard, J. (1981). *The female world.* New York: Free Press.

Bernard, J. (1982). *The future of marriage.* New Haven, CT: Yale University Press.

Bernhardt, A. (2012). *The low-wage recovery and growing inequality.* New York: National Employment Law Project. Retrieved from http://www.nelp.org/page/-/Job_Creation/LowWageRecovery2012.pdf?nocdn=1

Berns, R. (1989). *Child, family, community: Socialization and support.* New York: Holt, Rinehart & Winston.

Bettelheim, B. (1979). *Surviving, and other essays.* New York: Knopf.

Bettelheim. B. (1982). Difficulties between parents and children: Their causes and how to prevent them. In N. Stinnett et al. (Eds.), *Family strengths 4: Positive support systems* (pp. 5–14). Lincoln: University of Nebraska Press.

Beyer, P. (1994). *Religion and globalization.* London: Sage.

Bhanot, R. T., & Jovanovic, J. (2005). Do parents' academic gender stereotypes influence whether they intrude on their children's homework? *Sex Roles, 52*(9–10), 597–607.

Bhatia, S. (2013, February 3). Women, rape, and lack of toilets. Feminist Wire. Retrieved from http://thefeministwire.com/2013/02/op-ed-women-rape-and-lack-of-toilets

Bilal, M., Zia-ur-Rehman, M., & Raza, I. (2010). Impact of family friendly policies on employees' job satisfaction and turnover intention (A study on work–life balance at workplace). *Interdisciplinary Journal of Contemporary Research in Business, 2*(7), 378–395.

Bill and Melinda Gates Foundation. (2006). Ensuring the world's poorest children benefit from lifesaving vaccines. Retrieved from http://www.gatesfoundation.org/learning/Documents/GAVI.pdf

Bill and Melinda Gates Foundation. (2013). What we do: Vaccine delivery strategy. Retrieved from http://www.gatesfoundation.org/vaccines/Documents/vaccines-fact-sheet.pdf

Bishaw, A. (2013). *Poverty: 2000 to 2012* (American Community Survey Brief 12-01). Washington, DC: U.S. Census Bureau. Retrieved from http://www.census.gov/prod/2013pubs/acsbr12-01.pdf

Bishaw, A. (2014). *Changes in areas with concentrated poverty: 2000 to 2010* (American Community Survey Report 27). Washington, DC: U.S. Census Bureau. Retrieved from http://www.census.gov/content/dam/Census/library/publications/2014/acs/acs-27.pdf

Bishaw, A., & Macartney, S. (2010). *Poverty: 2008 and 2009* (American Community Survey Brief 09-1). Washington, DC: U.S. Census Bureau. Retrieved from http://www.census.gov/prod/2010pubs/acsbr09-1.pdf

Bishop, C. J., Kiss, M., Morrison, T. G., Rushe, D. M., & Specht, J. (2014). The association between gay men's stereotypic beliefs about drag queens and their endorsement of hypermasculinity. *Journal of Homosexuality, 62*(4), 554–567.

Bishop, K. (2009). Dead man still walking: Explaining the zombie renaissance. *Journal of Popular Film and Television, 33*(4), 196–205.

Bishop, K. (2010). *American zombie gothic: The rise and fall (and rise) of the walking dead in popular culture.* Jefferson, NC: McFarland.

Bishop, M., & Hicks, S. L. (Eds.). (2009). *Hearing, mother father deaf.* Washington, DC: Gallaudet University Press.

Blake, A. (2012, December 7). Both Romney and Obama ran $1 billion campaigns. *Washington Post.* Retrieved from http://www.washingtonpost.com/blogs/the-fix/wp/2012/12/07/both-romney-and-obama-ran-1-billion-campaigns

Blalock, H. (1967). *Toward a theory of minority group relations.* New York: Wiley.

Blau, J. (1992). *The visible poor: Homelessness in the United States.* New York: Oxford University Press.

Blau, P. M. (1964). *Exchange and power in social life.* New York: Wiley.

Blau, P. M. (1977). *Inequality and heterogeneity: A primitive theory of social structure.* New York: Free Press.

Blau, P. M., & Meyer, M. (1987). *Bureaucracy in modern society* (3rd ed.). New York: Random House.

Blinder, A. S. (2006). Offshoring: The next industrial revolution? *Foreign Affairs, 85*(2), 113–128.

Block, A., & Chambliss, W. J. (1981). *Organizing crime.* New York: Elsevier.

Block, A., & Weaver, A. (2004). *All is clouded by desire: Global banking, money laundering, and international organized crime.* Westport, CT: Praeger.

Block, J. J. (2008). Issues for *DSM-V:* Internet addiction. *American Journal of Psychiatry, 165*(3), 306–307.

Blumberg, J. (2007, October 23). A brief history of the Salem witch trials. *Smithsonian.* Retrieved from http://www.smithsonianmag.com/history-archaeology/brief-salem.html

Blumer, H. (1951). Collective behavior. In A. M. Lee (Ed.), *Principles of sociology* (pp. 166–222). New York: Barnes & Noble.

Blumer, H. (1969). *Symbolic interactionism: Perspective and method.* Englewood Cliffs, NJ: Prentice Hall.

Blumer, H. (1970). *Movies and conduct.* New York: Arno Press.

Boeing. (2013). International team facts: 787 Dream Liner. Retrieved from http://www.boeing.com/commercial/787family/dev_team.html

Bohnert, D., & Ross, W. H. (2010). The influence of social networking Web sites on the evaluation of job candidates. *Cyberpsychology, Behavior, and Social Networking, 13,* 341–347.

Bonacich, E., & Appelbaum, R. P. (2000). *Behind the label: Inequality in the Los Angeles apparel industry.* Berkeley: University of California Press.

Boncar, T. P., & Beck, A. J. (1997). *Lifetime likelihood of going to state or federal prison* (Special Report NCJ-160092). Washington, DC: U.S. Department of Justice, Bureau of Justice Statistics.

Booker, M. K. (2001). *Monsters, mushroom clouds, and the Cold War: American science fiction and the roots of postmodernism, 1946–1964.* Westport, CT: Greenwood.

Borgeson, C. A. (2001). *Parenting strategies: Does corporal punishment lead to antisocial behavior?* Blacksburg, VA: Southern Sociological Society.

Bos, H., & Sandfort, T. G. M. (2010). Children's gender identity in lesbian and heterosexual two-parent families. *Sex Roles, 62*(1–2), 114–126.

Boswell, A. A., & Spade, J. Z. (1996). Fraternities and collegiate rape culture: Why are some fraternities more dangerous places for women? *Gender & Society, 10,* 133–147.

Boudreau, J. (2010, May 11). Silicon Valley races fierce global competition in Cleantech. *Mercury News.* Retrieved from http://www.mercurynews.com/green-energy/ci_14233459

Bourdieu, P. (1977). *Outline of a theory of practice.* New York: Cambridge University Press.

Bourdieu, P. (1984). *Distinction: A social critique of the judgment of taste.* Cambridge, MA: Harvard University Press.

Bourdieu, P. (1991). *Language and symbolic power.* New York: Cambridge University Press.

Bourdieu, P., & Coleman, J. S. (1991). *Social theory for a changing society.* Boulder, CO: Westview Press.

Bowles, S., & Gintis, H. (1976). *Schooling in capitalist America: Educational reform and the contradictions of economic life.* New York: Basic Books.

Branch, T. (1988). *Parting the waters: America in the King years, 1954–1963.* New York: Simon & Schuster.

Brandon, S. G. (1973). *Ancient empires.* New York: Newsweek Books.

Brandt, A. M. (1983). Racism and research: The case of the Tuskegee syphilis study. In J. W. Leavitt & R. L. Numbers (Eds.), *Sickness and health in America* (pp. 392–404). Madison: University of Wisconsin Press.

Branson, C., & Cornell, D. (2009). A comparison of self and peer reports in the assessment of middle school bullying. *Journal of Applied School Psychology* 25, 5–27.

Braverman, H. (1988). *Labor and monopoly capital: The degradation of work in the 20th century.* New York: Monthly Review Press. (Original work published 1974)

Bremer, C. (2012, March). Economic commentary (T. Vaughn, managing director). Retrieved from http://www.tom-vaughn.com/Economic-Commentary-March-2012.c3472.htm

Bremer, J., & Rauch, P. K. (1998). Children and computers: Risks and benefits. *Journal of the American Academy of Child and Adolescent Psychiatry, 37,* 559–560.

Bricker, J., Kennickell, A. B., Moore, K. B., & Sabelbaus, J. (2012). Changes in U.S. family finances from 2007 to 2010: Evidence from the survey of consumer finances. *Federal Reserve Bulletin, 98*(2). Retrieved from http://www.federalreserve.gov/pubs/bulletin/2012/PDF/scf12.pdf

Brock, J., & Cocks, T. (2012, March 8). Insight: Nigeria oil corruption highlighted by audits. Reuters. Retrieved from http://www.reuters.com/article/2012/03/08/us-nigeria-corrup tion-oil-idUSBRE8270GF20120308

Brown, D. (2010, September 16). A mother's education has a huge effect on a child's health. *Washington Post.* Retrieved from http://www.washingtonpost.com/wp-dyn/content/article/2010/09/16/AR2010091606384.html

Brown, D. E., Edwards, J. W., & Moore, R. B. (1988). *The penis inserts of Southeast Asia.* Berkeley, CA: Center for South and Southeast Asian Studies.

Brown, M., Haughwout, A., Lee, D., Mabutas, M., & van der Klaauw, W. (2012, March 5). Grading student loans. Federal Reserve Bank of New York. Retrieved from http://libertystreeteconomics.newyorkfed.org/2012/03/grading-student-loans.html

Brumberg, J. J. (1997). *The body project: An intimate history of American girls.* New York: Vintage Books.

Brumberg, J. J. (2000). *Fasting girls: The history of anorexia nervosa.* New York: Vintage Books.

Buchwald, E., Fletcher, P. R., & Roth, M. (2005). *Transforming a rape culture* (rev. ed.). Minneapolis: Milkweed Editions.

Budiansky, S., Goode, E. E., & Gest, T. (1994, January 16). The Cold War experiments. *U.S. News & World Report.* Retrieved from http://www.usnews.com/usnews/news/articles/940124/archive_012286.htm

Buechler, S. M. (1990). *Women's movements in the United States: Women's suffrage, equal rights, and beyond.* New Brunswick, NJ: Rutgers University Press.

Burawoy, M., & Lukács, J. (1992). *The radiant past: Ideology and reality in Hungary's road to capitalism.* Chicago: University of Chicago Press.

Burgess, E. W. (1925). The growth of the city. In R. E. Park, E. W. Burgess, & R. McKenzie (Eds.), *The city.* Chicago: University of Chicago Press.

Burgess, R. L., & Akers, R. L. (1996). A differential association-reinforcement theory of criminal behavior. *Social Problems, 14*(2), 128–147.

Burns, J. M. (1978). *Leadership.* New York: Harper & Row.

Burt, M. R. (1992). *Over the edge: The growth of homelessness in the 1980s.* New York: Russell Sage Foundation.

Cabeza, M. F., Johnson, J. B., & Tyner, L. J. (2011). Glass ceiling and maternity leave as important contributors to the gender wage gap. *Southern Journal of Business and Ethics, 3,* 73–85.

Calderón-Garcidueñas, L., & Torres-Jardón, R. (2012). Air pollution, socioeconomic status and children's cognition in megacities: The Mexico City scenario. *Frontiers in Developmental Psychology, 3.* Retrieved from http://www.frontiersin.org/Developmental_Psychology/10.3389/fpsyg.2012.00217/full

Camarota, S. (2005). *Birth rates among immigrants in America: Comparing fertility in the U.S. and home countries.* Washington, DC: Center for Immigration Studies. Retrieved from http://www.cis.org/articles/2005/back1105.pdf

Campbell, A. (1984). *The girls in the gang.* New Brunswick, NJ: Rutgers University Press.

Campbell, A., & Muncer, S. (Eds.). (1998). *The social child.* East Sussex, England: Psychology Press.

Campbell, K., Klein, D. M., & Olson, K. (1992). Conversation activity and interruptions among men and women. *Journal of Social Psychology, 132,* 419–421.

Caputi, J. (2014). The real "hot mess": The sexist branding of female pop stars [Review of the book *Gender, branding, and the modern music industry: The social construction of female popular music stars,* by K. J. Lieb]. *Sex Roles, 70*(9–10), 439–441.

Carlozo, L. (2012, March 27). Why college students stop short of a degree. Reuters. Retrieved from http://www.reuters.com/article/2012/03/27/us-attn-andrea-education-dropouts-idUSBRE82Q0Y120120327

Carrell, S. E., Sacerdote, B. I., & West, J. E. (2011). *From natural variation to optimal policy? The Lucas critique meets peer effects* (Working Paper 16865). Cambridge, MA: National Bureau of Economic Research.

Carson, E. A., & Golinelli, D. (2013). *Prisoners in 2012: Trends in admissions and releases, 1991–2012* (BJS Bulletin NCJ 243920). Washington, DC: U.S. Department of Justice, Bureau of Justice Statistics. Retrieved from http://www.bjs.gov/content/pub/pdf/p12tar9112.pdf

Carson, E. A., & Sabol, W. J. (2012). *Prisoners in 2011* (BJS Bulletin NCJ 239808). Washington, DC: U.S. Department of Justice, Bureau of Justice Statistics. Retrieved from http://www.bjs.gov/content/pub/pdf/p11.pdf

Castells, M., & Portes, A. (1989). World underneath: The origins, dynamics, and effects of the informal economy. In A. Portes, M. Castells, & L. A. Benton (Eds.), *The informal economy: Studies in advanced and less developed countries* (pp. 11–37). Baltimore: Johns Hopkins University Press.

Catalano, S. (2012). *Intimate partner violence, 1993–2010* (NCJ 239203). Washington, DC: U.S. Department of Justice, Bureau of Justice Statistics. Retrieved from http://bjs.ojp.usdoj.gov/content/pub/pdf/ipv9310.pdf

Catalyst. (1997). *Women of color in corporate management: A statistical portrait.* New York: Author.

Catalyst. (1999). *Women of color in corporate management: Opportunities and barriers.* New York: Author.

Cavalli-Sforza, L. L., Menozzi, P., & Piazza, A. (1994). *The history and geography of human genes.* Princeton, NJ: Princeton University Press

Cawley, J. (2001). The impact of obesity on wages. *Journal of Human Resources, 39,* 451–474.

Center for Information & Research on Civic Learning and Engagement. (2010). Youth voting: Why youth voting matters. Retrieved from http://www.civicyouth.org/quick-facts/youth-voting

Center for Responsible Lending. (2011). Disparities in mortgage lending and foreclosures. Retrieved from http://www.responsiblelending.org/mortgage-lending/researchanalysis/lost-ground-2011.html

Center for Responsive Politics. (2013, March 4). Industry profile, 2011: Annual lobbying on tobacco. OpenSecrets. Retrieved from http://www.opensecrets.org/lobby/indusclient.php?id=A02&year=2011

Centers for Disease Control and Prevention. (2010a, December). HIV testing in the US. *CDC Vital Signs.* Retrieved from http://www.cdc.gov/vitalsigns/pdf/2010-12-vital signs.pdf

Centers for Disease Control and Prevention. (2010b). *National intimate partner and sexual violence survey.* Atlanta, GA: Author. Retrieved from http://www.cdc.gov/ViolencePrevention/pdf/NISVS_FactSheet-a.pdf

Centers for Disease Control and Prevention. (2011a). Deaths: Final data for 2010.

Retrieved from http://www.cdc.gov/nchs/data/dvs/deaths_2010_release.pdf

Centers for Disease Control and Prevention. (2011b). Estimates of new HIV infections in the United States, 2006–2009. Retrieved from http://www.cdc.gov/nchhstp/newsroom/docs/HIV-Infections-2006-2009.pdf

Centers for Disease Control and Prevention. (2011c). Vital signs: Current cigarette smoking among adults aged ≥ 18 years—United States, 2005–2010. *Morbidity and Mortality Weekly Report, 60*(35), 1207–1212. Retrieved from http://www.cdc.gov/mmwr/preview/mmwrhtml/mm6035a5.htm

Centers for Disease Control and Prevention. (2012a). Behavioral Risk Factor Surveillance System: Prevalence of self-reported obesity among U.S. adults. Retrieved from http://www.cdc.gov/obesity/downloads/dnpao-state-obesity-prevalence-map-2012.pdf

Centers for Disease Control and Prevention. (2012b). Impact of malaria. Retrieved from http://www.cdc.gov/malaria/malaria_worldwide/impact.html

Centers for Disease Control and Prevention. (2012c). National Vital Statistics System: Birth data. Retrieved from http://www.cdc.gov/nchs/births.htm

Centers for Disease Control and Prevention. (2012d). Overweight and obesity: Adult obesity facts. Retrieved from http://www.cdc.gov/obesity/data/adult.html

Centers for Disease Control and Prevention. (2012e). Overweight and obesity: Basics about childhood obesity. Retrieved from http://www.cdc.gov/obesity/childhood/basics.html

Centers for Disease Control and Prevention. (2013). Provisional number of marriages and marriage rate: United States, 2000–2011. Retrieved from http://www.cdc.gov/nchs/nvss/marriage_divorce_tables.htm

Centers for Disease Control and Prevention. (2014a). Adult cigarette smoking in the U.S.: Current estimates. Retrieved from http://www.cdc.gov/tobacco/data_statistics/fact_sheets/adult_data/cig_smoking/index.htm#national

Centers for Disease Control and Prevention. (2014b). Smoking and tobacco use. Retrieved from http://www.cdc.gov/tobacco/data_statistics/fact_sheets/health_effects/tobacco_related_mortality

Centers for Medicare and Medicaid Services. (2012). Medicare enrollment reports. Retrieved from http://www.cms.gov/Research-Statistics-Data-and-Systems/Statistics-Trends-and-Reports/MedicareEnrpts/index.html?redirect=/medicareenrpts

Central Intelligence Agency. (2012). The world factbook: Total fertility rate: Country comparison to the world. Retrieved from https://www.cia.gov/library/publications/the-world-fact book/fields/2127.html

Central Intelligence Agency. (2013). The world factbook: World. Retrieved from https://www.cia.gov/library/publications/the-world-factbook/geos/xx.html

Chafetz, J. S. (1984). *Sex and advantage: A comparative, macro-structural theory of sex stratification.* Totowa, NJ: Rowman & Allanheld.

Chafetz, J. S. (1997). Feminist theory and sociology: Underutilized contributions for mainstream theory. *Annual Review of Sociology, 23,* 97–120.

Chafetz, J. S., & Dworkin, A. G. (1983). Macro and micro process in the emergence of feminist movements: Toward a unified theory. *Western Sociological Review, 14*(1), 27–45.

Chalk, F., & Jonassohn, K. (1990). *The history and sociology of genocide: Analyses and case studies.* New Haven, CT: Yale University Press.

Chambliss, W. J. (1973). The Saints and the Roughnecks. *Society 11*(1), 24–31.

Chambliss, W. J. (1988a). *Exploring criminology.* New York: Macmillan.

Chambliss, W. J. (1988b). *On the take: From petty crooks to presidents.* Bloomington: Indiana University Press.

Chambliss, W. J. (2001). *Power, politics, and crime.* Boulder, CO: Westview Press.

Chambliss, W. J., & Hass, A. (2011). *Criminology: Connecting theory, research, and practice.* New York: McGraw-Hill.

Chambliss, W. J., & King, H. (1984). *Boxman: A professional thief's journey.* New York: Macmillan.

Chambliss, W. J., Michalowski, R., & Kramer, R. C. (Eds.). (2010). *State crime in the global age.* London: Willan.

Chambliss, W. J., & Seidman, R. B. (1982). *Law, order, and power.* Reading, MA: Addison-Wesley.

Chambliss, W. J., & Zatz, M. S. (1994). *Making law: The state, the law, and structural contradictions.* Bloomington: Indiana University Press.

Chandler, A. (2014, June 15). Should Twitter have suspended the violent ISIS Twitter account? The Wire. Retrieved from http://www.thewire.com/global/2014/06/should-twitter-have-suspended-the-violent-isis-twitter-account/372805

Chapman, C., Laird, J., Ifill, N., & KewalRamani, A. (2011). *Trends in high school dropout and completion rates in the United States: 1972–2009* (NCES 2012-06). Washington, DC: U.S. Department of Education, National Center for Education Statistics. Retrieved from http://nces.ed.gov/pubs2012/2012006.pdf

Chaves, M. (1993). Denominations as dual structures: An organizational analysis. *Sociology of Religion, 54*(2), 147–169.

Chaves, M. (1994). Secularization as declining religious authority. *Social Forces, 72*(3), 749–774.

Chen, H. S. (1992). *Chinatown no more: Taiwan immigrants in contemporary New York.* Ithaca, NY: Cornell University Press.

Chesney-Lind, M. (1989). Girls' crime and woman's place: Toward a feminist model of female delinquency. *Crime & Delinquency,* 33(1), 5–29.

Chesney-Lind, M. (2004). Beyond bad girls: Feminist perspectives on female offending. In C. Sumner (Ed.), *The Blackwell companion in criminology.* Oxford: Blackwell.

Chia, R. C., Allred, L. J., Grossnickle, W. F., & Lee, G. W. (1998). Effects of attractiveness and gender on the perception of achievement-related variables. *Journal of Social Psychology, 138*(4), 471–477.

Chiang, S. (2009). Personal power and positional power in a power-full "I": A discourse analysis of doctoral dissertation supervision. *Discourse and Communication, 3*(3), 255–271.

Chicago Coalition for the Homeless. (2014). Frequently asked questions about homelessness. Retrieved from http://www.chicagohomeless.org/faq-studies

Childhelp. (2010). National child abuse statistics: Child abuse in America. Retrieved from http://www.childhelp.org/pages/statistics#gen-stats

ChildStats. (2013). America's children: Key national indicators of well-being, 2013. Retrieved from http://www.childstats.gov/americaschildren/famsoc3.asp

Child Trends. (2014, July). Databank: Appendix 1. Percentage of all births that were to unmarried women, by race and Hispanic origin, and age: Selected years, 1960–2013. Retrieved from http://www.childtrends.org/wp-content/uploads/2012/11/75_appendix1.pdf

Chinese consumers: Doing it their way. (2014, January 25). *The Economist.* Retrieved from http://www.economist.com/news/briefing/21595019-market-growing-furiously-getting-tougher-foreign-firms-doing-it-their-way

Chodorow, N. (1999). *The reproduction of mothering: Psychoanalysis and the sociology of gender.* Berkeley: University of California Press.

Chong, D. (1991). *Collective action and the civil rights movement.* Chicago: University of Chicago Press.

Chopra, R. (2012, March 21). Too big to fail: Student debt hits a trillion. Consumer Financial Protection Bureau. Retrieved from http://www.consumerfinance.gov/blog/2012/03

Christiansen, K. O. (1977). Preliminary study of criminality among twins. In S. A. Mednick & K. O. Christiansen (Eds.), *Biosocial bases of criminal behavior.* New York: Gardner Press.

Church, W. T., II, Jaggers, J. W., & Taylor, J. K. (2012). Neighborhood, poverty, and negative behavior: An examination of differential association and social control theory. *Children and Youth Services Review, 34*(5), 1035–1041.

Cichowski, L., & Nance, W. E. (2004). More marriages among the deaf may have led to doubling of common form of genetic deafness in the U.S. Virginia Commonwealth University News Center. Retrieved from http://www.news.vcu.edu/news/More_marriages_among_the_deaf_may_have_led_to_doubling_of_common

Clark, B. (2011, January 18). The weight loss industry (and public health) dilemma. 24K Marketing. Retrieved from http://24kmarketing.com/2011/01/weight-loss-industry-and-public-health.html

Clark, H. (2006, March 8). Are women happy under the glass ceiling? *Forbes.* Retrieved from http://www.forbes.com/2006/03/07/glass-ceiling-opportunities--cx_hc_0308glass.html

Clarke, S. (2011, December 21). 2012 end-of-the-world countdown based on Mayan calendar starts today. ABC News. Retrieved from http://abcnews.go.com/blogs/headlines/2011/12/2012-end-of-the-world-countdown-based-on-mayan-calendar-starts-today

Cloward, R. A., & Ohlin, L. E. (1960). *Delinquency and opportunity: A theory of delinquent gangs.* Glencoe, IL: Free Press.

CNN. (2012, November 14). Oregon Measure 80: Legalize marijuana. Retrieved from http://www.cnn.com/election/2012/results/state/OR/ballot/01

CNNMoney. (2013, April 8). 20 top-paid CEOs. Retrieved from http://money.cnn.com/gallery/news/companies/2013/04/08/executive-pay/index.html

Cockerham, W. C., & Glasser, M. (2000). *Readings in medical sociology* (2nd ed.). Englewood Cliffs, NJ: Prentice Hall.

Cohen, A. (2012, March 16). How voter ID laws are being used to disenfranchise minorities and the poor. *Atlantic.* Retrieved from http://www.theatlantic.com/politics/archive/2012/03/how-voter-id-laws-are-being-used-to-disenfranchise-minorities-and-the-poor/254572

Cohen, A. K. (1955). *Delinquent boys: The culture of the gang.* Glencoe, IL: Free Press.

Cohen, D. A. (2014). *A big fat crisis: The hidden forces behind the obesity crisis—and how we can end it.* New York: Nation Books.

Cohen, L. J., & DeBenedet, A. T. (2012, July 17). Penn State cover-up: Groupthink in action. *Time.* Retrieved from http://ideas.time.com/2012/07/17/penn-state-cover-up-group-think-in-action

Cohn, D., Livingston, G., & Wang, W. (2014). *After decades of decline, a rise in stay-at-home mothers.* Washington, DC: Pew Research Center. Retrieved from http://www.pewsocialtrends.org/2014/04/08/after-decades-of-decline-a-rise-in-stay-at-home-mothers

Coleman, J. M., & Hong, Y.-Y. (2008). Beyond nature and nurture: The influence of lay gender theories on self-stereotyping. *Self and Identity, 7*(1), 34–53.

Coleman, J. S. (1990). *The foundations of social theory.* Cambridge, MA: Harvard University Press.

Coleman, J. S., Hoffer, T., & Kilgore, S. (1982). *High school achievement: Public, Catholic, and private schools compared.* New York: Basic Books.

Colen, C. G., Geronimus, A. T., Bound, J., & James, S. A. (2006). Maternal upward socioeconomic mobility and Black–White disparities in infant birthweight. *American Journal of Public Health, 96*(11), 2032–2039.

College Board. (2010). *SAT trends: Background on the SAT takers in the class of 2010.* New York: Author. Retrieved from http://professionals.collegeboard.com/profdownload/2010-sat-trends.pdf

College Board. (2011). *2011 college-bound seniors: Total group profile report.* New York: Author. Retrieved from http://professionals.collegeboard.com/profdownload/cbs2011_total_group_report.pdf

College Board. (2012). *SAT percentile ranks for 2012 college-bound seniors: Critical reading, mathematics and writing percentile ranks by gender and ethnic groups.* New York: Author. Retrieved from http://media.collegeboard.com/digitalServices/pdf/research/SAT-Percentile-Ranks-by-Gender-Ethnicity-2012.pdf

College Board. (2013). *SAT percentile ranks for males, females, and total group: 2013 college-bound seniors—mathematics.* New York: Author. Retrieved from http://media.collegeboard.com/digitalServices/pdf/research/SAT-Mathematics-Percentile-Ranks-2013.pdf

CollegeMeasures. (2013). Performance of four-year colleges in the United States. Retrieved from http://collegemeasures.org/4-year_colleges/national/scorecard/strategic-measures

Collins, P. H. (1990). *Black feminist thought: Knowledge, consciousness and the politics of empowerment.* New York: Routledge.

Collins, R. (1979). *The credential society: An historical sociology of education and stratification.* New York: Academic Press.

Collins, R. (1980). Weber's last theory of capitalism: A systematization. *American Sociological Review, 45,* 925–942.

Colomy, P. (1986). Recent developments in the functionalist approach to change. *Sociological Focus, 19,* 139–158.

Colomy, P. (Ed.). (1990). *Functionalist sociology.* Brookfield, VT: Elgar.

Coltrane, S., & Ishii-Kuntz, M. (1992). Remarriage, stepparenting, and household labor. *Journal of Family Issues, 13*(2), 215–233.

Commission to Build a Healthier America. (2009, April). *Race and socioeconomic factors affect opportunities for better health* (Issue brief 5). Princeton, NJ: Robert Wood Johnson Foundation. Retrieved from http://www.commissiononhealth.org/PDF/506edea1-f160-4728-9539-aba2357047e3/Issue%20Brief%205%20April%2009%20-%20Race%20and%20Socioeconomic%20Factors.pdf

Comte, A. (1975). *Auguste Comte and positivism: The essential writings* (G. Lenzer, Ed.). New York: Harper Torchbooks.

Condron, D. J. (2009). Social class, school and non-school environments, and Black/White inequalities in children's learning. *American Sociological Review, 74,* 685–708.

Condry, J. C. (1989). *The psychology of television.* Hillsdale, NJ: Erlbaum.

Conley, D. (1999). *Being Black, living in the red: Race, wealth, and social policy in America.* Berkeley: University of California Press.

Conlin, J. (2010, August 6). For American students, life lessons in the Mideast. *New York*

Times. Retrieved from http://www.nytimes.com/2010/08/08/fashion/08Abroad.html?pagewanted=all

Connell, R. W. (2005). Change among the gatekeepers: Men, masculinities, and gender equality in the global arena. *Signs, 30*(3), 1801–1826.

Connell, R. W. (2010). Masculinities. Retrieved from http://www.raewynconnell.net/p/masculinities_20.html

Connell, R. W., & Messerschmidt, J. W. (2005). Hegemonic masculinity: Rethinking the concept. *Gender & Society, 19*(6), 829–859.

Coogan, T. P. (2002). *Michael Collins: The man who made Ireland.* New York: Palgrave Macmillan.

Cooley, C. H. (1909). *Social organization: A study of the larger mind.* New York: Charles Scribner's Sons.

Cooley, C. H. (1964). *Human nature and the social order.* New York: Schocken Books. (Original work published 1902)

Coontz, S. (2000). Historical perspectives on family studies. *Journal of Marriage and the Family, 62*(2), 283–297.

Coontz, S. (2005). *Marriage, a history: From obedience to intimacy, or how love conquered marriage.* New York: Penguin Books.

Coontz, S. (2012, May 25). Five myths about marriage. *Washington Post.* Retrieved from http://www.washington post.com/opinions/five-myths-aboutmarriage/2012/05/25/gJQAofiMqU_story.html

Cooper, H., Nye, B., Charlton, K., Lindsay, J., & Greathouse, S. (1996). The effects of summer vacation on achievement test scores: A narrative and meta-analytic review. *Review of Educational Research, 66,* 227–268.

Critser, G. (2003). *Fatland: How Americans became the fattest people in the world.* New York: Houghton Mifflin.

Crocker, W. H. (1986). Canela body painting. *Review: Latin American Literature and Arts, 36,* 24–26.

Crocker, W. H. (1990). The Canela (Eastern Timbira), I: An ethnographic introduction. *Smithsonian Contributions to Anthropology, 33.* Washington, DC: Smithsonian Institution Press.

Crocker, W. H. (1994). *The Canela: Bonding through kinship, ritual, and sex (Case studies in cultural anthropology).* Fort Worth, TX: Harcourt Brace College.

Curtiss, S. (1977). *Genie: A psycholinguistic study of a modern-day "wild child."* Boston: Academic Press.

Cutright, P., & Fernquist, R. M. (2000). Effects of societal integration, period, region, and culture of suicide on male age-specific suicide rates: 20 developed countries, 1955–1989. *Social Science Research, 29,* 148–172.

Dahl, R. A. (1961). *Who governs?* New Haven, CT: Yale University Press.

Dahl, R. A. (1982). *Dilemmas of a pluralist democracy: Autonomy vs. control.* New Haven, CT: Yale University Press.

Dahl, R. A. (1989). *Democracy and its critics.* New Haven, CT: Yale University Press.

Dahrendorf, R. (1958). *Out of utopia.* New York: Ardent Media.

Daniels, R. (2004). Incarceration of the Japanese Americans: A sixty-year perspective. *History Teacher, 35*(3), 297–310.

D'Augelli, A. R., Pilkington, N. W., & Hershberger, S. L. (2002). Incidence and mental health impact of sexual orientation victimization of lesbian, gay, and bisexual youths in high school. *School Psychology Quarterly, 17*(2), 148–167.

David, D. S., & Brannon, R. (1976). *The forty-nine percent majority: The male sex role.* New York: Random House.

Davis, A. (2008, September). Interpersonal and physical dating violence among teens. *Focus: Views From the National Council on Crime and Delinquency.* Retrieved from http://nccdglobal.org/sites/default/files/publication_pdf/focus-dating-violence.pdf

Davis, K., & Moore, W. (1945). Some principles of stratification. *American Sociological Review, 10,* 242–249.

Davis, S. N., Greenstein, T. N., & Marks, J. P. (2007). Effects of union type on division of household labor: Do cohabitating men really perform more housework? *Journal of Family Issues, 28*(9), 1246–1272.

Davis, W. (1991). *Fundamentalism in Japan: Religious and political.* Chicago: University of Chicago Press.

Death Penalty Information Center. (2010). Executions. Retrieved from http://www.deathpenaltyinfo.org/executions-united-states

DeBeaumont, R. (2009). Occupational differences in the wage penalty for obese women. *Journal of Socio-Economics, 38,* 344–349.

DeFrancisco, V. L. (1991). The sounds of silence: How men silence women in marital relations. *Discourse & Society, 2*(4), 412–423.

DellaPergola, S. (2010). *World Jewish population 2010* (Current Jewish Population Reports 2). New York: Berman Jewish DataBank. Retrieved from http://www.jewishdatabank.org/Reports/World_Jewish_Population_2010.pdf

Delli Carpini, M. X., & Keeter, S. (1996). *What Americans know about politics and why it matters.* New Haven, CT: Yale University Press.

Demographia. (2014). *Demographia world urban areas (built-up urban areas or world agglomerations).* Belleville, IL: Author. Retrieved from http://demographia.com/db-worldua.pdf

DeNavas-Walt, C., & Proctor, B. D. (2014). *Income and poverty in the United States: 2013* (Current Population Reports P60-249). Washington, DC: U.S. Census Bureau . Retrieved from http://www.census.gov/content/dam/Census/library/publications/2014/demo/p60-249.pdf

DeNavas-Walt, C., Proctor, B. D., & Smith, J. C. (2012). *Income, poverty, and health insurance coverage in the United States: 2011* (Current Population Reports P60-243). Washington, DC: U.S. Census Bureau. Retrieved from http://www.census.gov/prod/2012pubs/p60-243.pdf

DeNavas-Walt, C., Proctor, B. D., & Smith, J. C. (2013). *Income, poverty, and health insurance coverage in the United States: 2012* (Current Population Reports P60-245). Washington, DC: U.S. Census Bureau . Retrieved from http://www.census.gov/prod/2013pubs/p60-245.pdf

Denizet-Lewis, B. (2003, August 3). Double lives on the down low. *New York Times Magazine.* Retrieved from http://www.nytimes.com/2003/08/03/magazine/double-lives-on-the-down-low.html?pagewanted=all&src=pm

Denno, B. W. (1990). *Biology and violence from birth to adulthood.* Cambridge: Cambridge University Press.

Denny, K. E. (2011). Gender in context, content, and approach: Comparing gender messages in Girl Scout and Boy Scout handbooks. *Gender & Society, 25*(1), 27–47.

Denyer, S., & Lakshmi, R. (2011, August 19). Anna Hazare inspires young, middle-class awakening in India. *Washington Post.* Retrieved from http://www.washington post.com/world/asia-pacific/anna-hazare-inspires-young-middle-class-awakening-in-india/2011/08/19/gIQA1NaCQJ_story.html

de Paul, J., & Domenech, L. (2000). Childhood history of abuse and child abuse potential in adolescent mothers: A longitudinal study. *Child Abuse and Neglect, 24*(5), 701–713.

DeSantis, A., & Kayson, W. A. (1997). Defendants' characteristics of attractiveness, race, sex and sentencing decisions. *Psychological Reports, 81,* 679–683.

de Vise, D. (2012, May 21). Is college too easy? As study time falls, debate rises. *Washington Post*. Retrieved from http://www.washingtonpost.com/local/education/is-college-too-easy-as-study-time-falls-debate-rises/2012/05/21/gIQAp7uUgU_story.html

Dewey, C. (2014, May 9). Is tweeting a hashtag better than doing nothing? Or about the same? *Washington Post*, pp. C1, C4.

DeWitt, A. L., Cready, C. M., & Seward, R. R. (2013). Parental role portrayal in twentieth century children's picture books: More egalitarian or ongoing stereotyping? *Sex Roles, 69*(1–2), 89–106.

Diaz, J. D. (1999). *Suicide in the Las Vegas homeless population: Applying Durkheim's theory of suicide* (Doctoral dissertation, University of Nevada, Las Vegas).

Dicken, P. (1998). *The global shift: Transforming the world economy* (3rd ed.). New York: Guilford Press.

Dilmac, B. (2009). Psychological needs as a predictor of cyberbullying: A preliminary report on college students. *Educational Sciences: Theory and Practice, 9*(3), 1308–1325.

DiMaggio, P. J., & Powell, W. (1983). The iron cage revisited: Institutional isomorphism and collective rationality in organizational fields. *American Sociological Review, 48*, 147–160.

Dion, K., Berscheid, E., & Walster, E. (1972). What is beautiful is good. *Journal of Personality and Social Psychology, 24*(3), 285–290.

Dionne, E. J., Jr., & Green, J. C. (2008). *Religion and American politics: More secular, more evangelical . . . or both?* Washington, DC: Brookings Institution. Retrieved from http://www.brookings.edu/~/media/research/files/papers/2008/2/religion%20green%20dionne/02_religion_green_dionne.pdf

Dishion, T. J., McCord, J., & Poulin, F. (1999). When interventions harm: Peer groups and problem behavior. *American Psychologist, 54*, 755–764.

Dittmar, H., Halliwell, E., & Ive, S. (2006). Does Barbie make girls want to be thin? The effect of experimental exposure to images of dolls on the body image of 5- to 8-year-old girls. *Developmental Psychology, 42*(2), 283–292.

Djilas, M. (1957). *The new class: An analysis of the communist system*. New York: Harvest Books.

Dobbie, W., & Fryer, R. G. (2011). Getting beneath the veil of effective schools: Evidence from New York City. *American Economic Journal: Applied Economics, 3*(3), 158–187.

Doey, L., Coplan, R. J., & Kingsbury, M. (2013). Bashful boys and coy girls: A review of gender differences in childhood shyness. *Sex Roles, 70*(7–8), 255–266.

Dokoupil, T. (2012a, July 9). Is the Web driving us mad? *Newsweek*. Retrieved from http://www.thedailybeast.com/newsweek/2012/07/08/is-the-internet-making-us-crazy-what-the-new-research-says.html

Dokoupil, T. (2012b, July 16). Tweets, texts, email, posts: Is the onslaught making us crazy? *Newsweek*, pp. 24–30.

Dollard, J. (1957). *Caste and class in a Southern town* (3rd ed.). New York: Anchor Books.

Dolnick, E. (1993, September). Deafness as culture. *Atlantic Monthly*, pp. 37–53.

Domhoff, G. W. (1983). *Who rules America now?* New York: Simon and Schuster.

Domhoff, G. W. (1990). *The power elite and the state: How policy is made in America*. New York: Aldine de Gruyter.

Domhoff, G. W. (2002). *Who rules America? Power and politics* (4th ed.). New York: McGraw-Hill.

Domhoff, G. W. (2006). *Who rules America? Power, politics, and social change* (5th ed.). New York: McGraw-Hill.

Domhoff, G. W. (2009). *Who rules America? Challenges to corporate and class dominance* (6th ed.). New York: McGraw-Hill.

Donner, F. M. (2012). *Muhammad and the believers: At the origins of Islam*. Cambridge, MA: Harvard University Press.

Dor, A., Ferguson, C., Langwith, C., & Tan, E. (2010). *A heavy burden: The individual costs of being overweight and obese in the United States*. Washington, DC: George Washington University. Retrieved from http://sphhs.gwu.edu/departments/healthpolicy/dhp_publications/pub_uploads/dhpPublication_35308C47-5056-9D20-3DB157B39AC53093.pdf

Douglas, D. (2013, March 6). Attorney general says big banks' size may inhibit prosecution. *Washington Post*, p. A12.

Downs, E., & Smith, S. (2010). Keeping abreast of hypersexuality: A video game character content analysis. *Sex Roles, 62*(11), 721–733.

Downtown Women's Action Coalition. (2011). *2010 downtown women's needs assessment*. Los Angeles: Author. Retrieved from dwcweb.org/needs/DWAC_Needs Assessment2010.pdf

Dreifus, C. (2012, May 14). A mathematical challenge to obesity. *New York Times*. Retrieved from http://www.nytimes.com/2012/05/15/science/a-mathematical-challenge-to-obesity.html

Du Bois, W. E. B. (2008). *The souls of Black folk*. Rockville, MD: Arc Manor. (Original work published 1903)

Duggan, M., & Smith, A. (2014, January). *Social media update 2013*. Washington, DC: Pew Research Center. Retrieved from http://www.pewinternet.org/files/2013/12/PIP_Social-Networking-2013.pdf

Duhigg, C., & Barboza, D. (2012, January 25). In China, human costs are built into an iPad. *New York Times*. Retrieved from http://www.nytimes.com/2012/01/26/business/ieconomy-apples-ipad-and-the-human-costs-for-workers-in-china.html?_r=2&pagewanted=print

Duhigg, C., & Greenhouse, S. (2012, March 29). Electronic giant vowing reforms in China plants. *New York Times*. Retrieved from http://www.nytimes.com/2012/03/30/business/apple-supplier-in-china-pledges-changes-in-working-conditions.html?pagewanted=all

Duin, J. (2012, June 1). Death of snake-handling preacher shines light on lethal Appalachian tradition. CNN. Retrieved from http://religion.blogs.cnn.com/2012/06/01/death-of-snake-handling-preacher-shines-light-on-lethal-appalachian-tradition/?iref=allsearch

Duneier, M. (1992). *Slim's table: Race, respectability, and masculinity*. Chicago: University of Chicago Press.

Dunner, D. L., Gershon, E. S., & Barrett, J. S. (1988). *Relatives at risk for mental disorder*. New York: Ravens Press.

Durkheim, É. (1951). *Suicide*. New York: Free Press. (Original work published 1897)

Durkheim, É. (1956). *Education and sociology* (S. L. Fox, Trans.). New York: Free Press. (Original work published 1922)

Durkheim, É. (1964). *The rules of sociological method*. New York: Free Press. (Original work published 1895)

Durkheim, É. (1973a). *Émile Durkheim on morality and society*. Chicago: University of Chicago Press. (Original work published 1922)

Durkheim, É. (1973b). *Moral education: A study in the theory and application of the sociology of education*. New York: Free Press. (Original work published 1922)

Durkheim, É. (1997). *The division of labor in society*. New York: Free Press. (Original work published 1893)

Durkheim, É. (2008). *The elementary forms of the religious life*. New York: Dover. (Original work published 1912)

Durose, M. R., Harlow, C. W., Langan, P. A., Motivans, M., Rantala, R. R., & Smith,

E. L. (2005). *Family violence statistics: Including statistics on strangers and acquaintances* (NCJ 207846). Washington, DC: U.S. Department of Justice, Bureau of Justice Statistics. Retrieved from http://bjs.ojp.usdoj.gov/content/pub/pdf/fvs.pdf

Dworkin, A. (1981). *Pornography: Men possessing women.* New York: Pedigree.

Dworkin, A. (1987). *Intercourse.* New York: Free Press.

Dworkin, A. (1989). *Letters from the war zone: Writings, 1976–1987.* New York: Dutton.

Dwoskin, E. (2012, March 28). Will you marry me (after I pay off my student loans)? *Bloomberg Businessweek.* Retrieved from http://www.businessweek.com/articles/2012-03-28/will-you-marry-me-after-i-pay-off-my-student-loans

Dwyer, C. (1976). *Research report.* Princeton, NJ: Educational Testing Service.

Dwyer, R. E., Hodson, R., & McCloud, L. (2013). Gender, debt, and dropping out of college. *Gender & Society, 27*(1), 30–55.

Early, G. (2011). *A level playing field: African American athletes and the republic of sports.* Cambridge, MA: Harvard University Press.

Eccles, J. S., & Barber, B. L. (1999). Student council, volunteering, basketball, or marching band: What kind of extracurricular involvement matters? *Journal of Adolescent Research, 14*(1), 10–43.

Eddy, M. B. (1999). *Christian science: No and yes.* Boston: Author. (Original work published 1887)

Edin, K., & Kefalas, M. (2005). *Promises I can keep: Why poor women put motherhood before marriage.* Berkeley: University of California Press.

Edlund, L., Hongbin, L., Junjian, Y., & Junsen, Z. (2007). *Sex ratios and crime: Evidence from China's one child policy* (Discussion Paper 3214). Bonn, Germany: Institute for the Study of Labor.

Edwards, A. N. (2014). *Dynamics of economic well-being: Poverty, 2009–2011* (Household Economic Studies P70-137). Washington, DC: U.S. Census Bureau.

Edwards, J. (2012, October 7). This video of Haitians reading "#FirstWorldProblems" from Twitter is making people really angry. BusinessInsider. Retrieved from http://www.businessinsider.com/anger-over-haitians-reading-firstworldproblems-from-twitter-2012-10#ixzz33sB1IhdT

Edwards, K. E. (2007). *"Putting my man face on": A grounded theory of college men's gender identity development* (Doctoral dissertation, University of Maryland-College Park). Retrieved from ProQuest (3260431).

Effinger, A., & Burton, K. (2014, April 9). Trailer parks lure Wall Street investors looking for double-wide returns. Bloomberg. Retrieved from http://www.bloomberg.com/news/2014-04-10/trailer-parks-lure-investors-pursuing-double-wide-returns.html

Eglitis, D. S. (2010). The uses of global poverty: How economic inequality benefits the West. In J. J. Macionis & N. V. Benokraitis (Eds.), *Seeing ourselves: Classic, contemporary, and cross-cultural readings in sociology* (8th ed., pp. 199–206). New York: Pearson.

Ehrenreich, B. (2001). *Nickel and dimed: On (not) getting by in America.* New York: Metropolitan Books.

Ehrenreich, B., & Hochschild, A. R. (2002). Introduction. In B. Ehrenreich & A. R. Hochschild (Eds.), *Global woman: Nannies, maids, and sex workers in the new economy* (pp. 1–14). New York: Metropolitan Books.

Ehrlich, P. R. (1968). *The population bomb.* New York: Ballantine Books.

Eichler, A. (2012, May 30). Unpaid overtime: Wage and hour lawsuits have skyrocketed in the last decade. Huffington Post. Retrieved from http://www.huffingtonpost.com/2012/05/30/wage-hour-lawsuits_n_1556484.html

Eisenbrey, R. (2012, March 2). Pushing back against illegal unpaid internships. Economic Policy Institute Blog. Retrieved from http://www.epi.org/blog/pushing-back-illegal-unpaid-internships

Eliot, L. (2009). *Pink brain, blue brain: How small differences grow into troublesome gaps—and what we can do about it.* New York: Houghton Mifflin Harcourt.

Eller, C. (2000). *The myth of matriarchal prehistory: Why an inventive past won't give women a future.* Boston: Beacon Press.

Ellis, B. (2011, November 3). Average student loan debt tops $25,000. CNNMoney. Retrieved from http://money.cnn.com/2011/11/03/pf/student_loan_debt/index.htm

Emerson, R. M. (1962). Power-dependence relations. *American Sociological Review, 27,* 31–41.

Emmanuel, A. (1972). *Unequal exchange: A study of the imperialism of trade.* New York: Monthly Review Press.

Engels, F. (1942). *The origins of family, private property, and the state.* New York: International. (Original work published 1884)

Environmental Protection Agency. (2011). *Electronics waste management in the United States through 2009.* Washington, DC: Author.

Epstein, C. F. (1988). *Deceptive distinctions: Sex, gender, and the social order.* New Haven, CT: Yale University Press.

Epstein, D. M. (1993). *Sister Aimee: The life of Aimee Semple McPherson.* New York: Harcourt Brace Jovanovich.

Erber, G., & Sayed-Ahmed, A. (2005). Offshore outsourcing: A global shift in the present IT industry. *Intereconomics, 40*(2), 100–112.

Erikson, E. H. (1950). *Childhood and society.* New York: Norton.

Etter, G. (1998). Common characteristics of gangs: Examining the cultures of the new urban tribes. *Journal of Gang Research, 5*(2), 19–33.

Etzioni, A. (1975). *A comparative analysis of complex organizations: On power, involvement, and their correlates.* New York: Free Press.

European Environment Agency. (2012). Correlation between fertility and female education. Retrieved from http://www.eea.europa.eu/data-and-maps/figures/correlation-between-fertility-and-female-education

Evans, M. D. R., Kelley, J., Sikora, J., & Treiman, D. J. (2010). Family scholarly culture and educational success: Books and schooling in 27 nations. *Research in Social Stratification and Mobility, 28*(2), 171–197.

Facebook. (2012). Newsroom: Key facts. Retrieved from http://newsroom.fb.com/content/default.aspx?NewsAreaId=22

FACE Intel (Former and Current Employees of Intel). (2000). Related class action lawsuits: A huge victory for the worker. Retrieved from http://www.faceintel.com/relatedclassactions.htm

Fairfield, R. (1972). *Communes USA.* Baltimore: Penguin Books.

Faith Warrior. (2010). World religions map. Retrieved from http://nubelieverse.wordpress.com/2010/07/27/world-religions-map

Faludi, S. (1991). *Backlash: The undeclared war against American women.* New York: Crown.

Fantz, A. (2014, February 16). Reality show snake-handling preacher dies—of snakebite. CNN. Retrieved from http://www.cnn.com/2014/02/16/us/snake-salvation-pastor-bite

Farhi, P. (2011, October 31). Occupy D.C.: They're occupying, but who's counting? *Washington Post.* Retrieved from http://www.washingtonpost.com/lifestyle/style/occupy-dc-theyre-occupying-but-whos-counting/2011/10/31/gIQAZBecaM_story.html

Farkas, G., Grobe, R. P., Sheehan, D., & Shuan, Y. (1990). Cultural resources and school success: Gender, ethnicity, and poverty groups within an urban school district. *American Sociological Review, 55,* 127–142.

Farkas, G., Sheehan, D., & Grobe, R. P. (1990). Coursework mastery and school success: Gender, ethnicity, and poverty groups within an urban school district. *American Educational Research Journal, 27*(4), 807–827.

Federal Bureau of Investigation. (2012a). Table 1. Crime in the United States by volume and rate. In *Crime in the United States 2012* (Uniform Crime Reports). Washington, DC: Author.

Federal Bureau of Investigation. (2012b). Persons arrested. In *Crime in the United States 2012* (Uniform Crime Reports). Washington, DC: Author.

Federal Education Budget Project. (2012). Comparative analysis of funding, student demographics and achievement data. New America Foundation. Retrieved from http://febp.newamerica.net/k12/GA/1300120

Federal Reserve System & Brookings Institution. (2008). *The enduring challenge of concentrated poverty in America: Case studies from communities across the U.S.* Washington, DC: Authors. Retrieved from http://www.frbsf.org/community-development/files/cp_fullreport.pdf

Feldman, A. (1991). *Formations of violence: The narrative of the body and political terror in Northern Ireland.* Chicago: University of Chicago Press.

Fenstermaker, S., & West, C. (2002). *Doing gender, doing difference: Inequality, power, and institutional change.* New York: Routledge.

Fenstermaker Berk, S. (1985). *The gender factory: The apportionment of work in American households.* New York: Plenum Press.

Ferment, C. A. (1989). Political practice and the rise of an ethnic enclave: The Cuban American case. *Theory and Society, 18*(January), 47–48.

Financial Crimes Enforcement Network. (2014). JPMorgan admits violation of the Bank Secrecy Act (press release). Retrieved from http://www.fincen.gov/news_room/nr/pdf/20140107.pdf

Finckenauer, J. O., & Waring, E. (1996). Russian emigre crime in the U.S.: Organized crime or crime that is organized? *Transnational Organized Crime, 2*(2–3), 139–155.

Fingarette, H. (1972). *Confucius: The secular as sacred.* Long Grove, IL: Waveland Press.

Finke, R., & Stark, R. (1988). Religious economies and sacred canopies: Religious mobilization in American cities, 1906. *American Sociological Review, 53,* 41–49.

Finke, R., & Stark, R. (1992). *The churching of America, 1776–1980: Winners and losers in our religious economy.* New Brunswick, NY: Rutgers University Press.

Finke, R., & Stark, R. (2005). *The churching of America, 1776–2005: Winners and losers in our religious economy.* New Brunswick, NY: Rutgers University Press.

Finkelstein, E. A., Trogdon, J. G., Cohen, J. W., & Dietz, W. (2009). Annual medical spending attributable to obesity: Payer- and service-specific estimates. *Health Affairs, 28*(5), 822–831.

Firestone, S. (1971). *The dialectic of sex.* London: Paladin.

Fischer, C. (1982). *To dwell among friends: Personal networks in town and city.* Chicago: University of Chicago Press.

Fischer, C. (1984). *The urban experience* (2nd ed.). New York: Harcourt Brace Jovanovich.

Fischer, D. (2013, December 23). "Dark money" funds climate change denial effort. *Scientific American.* Retrieved from: http://www.scientificamerican.com/article/dark-money-funds-climate-change-denial-effort

Fischer, H. (2008). *Iraqi civilian deaths estimate.* Washington, DC: Congressional Research Service. Retrieved from http://www.fas.org/sgp/crs/mideast/RS22537.pdf

Fischer, H. (2010). *Iraq casualties: U.S. military forces and Iraqi civilians, police, and security forces.* Washington, DC: Congressional Research Service. Retrieved from http://fpc.state.gov/documents/organization/145113.pdf

Fishman, P. (1978). Women's work in interaction. *Social Problems, 25*(4), 397–406.

Fish Site. (2009, September 24). News: Thai shrimp exporters expect a good year. Retrieved from http://www.thefishsite.com/fishnews/10852/thai-shrimp-exporters-expect-a-good-year

Fitzgerald, A. (2011, July 28). A stealth way a bill becomes a law. *Bloomberg Businessweek.* Retrieved from http://www.businessweek.com/magazine/a-stealth-way-a-bill-becomes-a-law- 07282011.html

Flacks, R. (1971). *Youth and social change.* Chicago: Markham.

Food and Agriculture Organization of the United Nations. (2009). *How to feed the world in 2050.* Rome: Author. Retrieved from http://www.fao.org/fileadmin/templates/wsfs/docs/expert_paper/How_to_Feed_the_World_in_2050.pdf

Food and Agriculture Organization of the United Nations. (2012). *The state of food insecurity in the world 2012.* Rome: Author. Retrieved from http://www.fao.org/docrep/016/i3027e/i3027e02.pdf

Foroohar, R. (2014, January 2). The flat-paycheck recovery. *Time.* Retrieved from http://time.com/82/the-flat-paycheck-recovery

Forsythe-Brown, I. (2007). *An exploratory analysis of gender, kinscripts and the work of transnational kinship among Afro-Caribbean immigrant families* (Doctoral dissertation, University of Maryland). Retrieved from ProQuest (3307758).

Foucault, M. (1988). *Madness and civilization: A history of insanity in the age of reason.* New York: Vintage Books.

Fouts, G., & Burggraf, K. (2000). Television situation comedies: Female weight, male negative comments, and audience reactions. *Sex Roles, 42*(9–10), 925–932.

Fox, M. A., Connolly, B. A., & Snyder, T. D. (2005). *Youth indicators 2005: Trends in the well-being of American youth* (NCES 2005-050). Washington, DC: U.S. Department of Education, National Center for Education Statistics.

Frank, A. G. (1966). The development of underdevelopment. *Monthly Review, 18*(4): 17–31.

Frank, A. G. (1979). *Dependent accumulation and underdevelopment.* London: Macmillan.

Frederick, S., & AWARE (Association of Women for Action and Research) Committee on Rape. (2001). *Rape: Weapon of terror.* River Edge, NJ: Global.

Freedom House. (2014). Freedom in the world. Retrieved from http://www.freedomhouse.org/report-types/freedom-world#.U7xxE41dWLF

Freeland, C. (2012). *Plutocrats: The rise of the new global super-rich and the fall of everyone else.* New York: Penguin Books.

Freire, P. (1972). *Pedagogy of the oppressed.* New York: Herder & Herder.

Freud, S. (1905). Three essays on sexuality. In *Standard Edition* (Vol. 7). London: Hogarth.

Freud, S. (1929). Civilization and its discontents. In *Standard Edition* (Vol. 21). London: Hogarth.

Freud, S. (1933). *New introductory lectures on psychoanalysis.* New York: Norton.

Freund, C. P. (2002). In praise of vulgarity. *Reason, 33*(10), 24–35.

Frey, W. H., & Speare, A. (1991). *U.S. metropolitan area population growth, 1960–1990: Census trends and explanations* (Population Studies Center Research Report No. 91-212). Ann Arbor: Institute for Social Research, University of Michigan.

Friedan, B. (1963). *The feminine mystique.* New York: Norton.

Friedan, B. (1981). *The second stage.* New York: Summit.

Friedl, E. (1975). *Women and men: An anthropologist's view.* New York: Holt, Rinehart & Winston.

Friedman, H. L. (2013). Tiger girls on the soccer field. *Contexts, 12*(4), 30–35.

Friedman, L. M. (1975). *The legal system: A social science perspective.* New York: Russell Sage Foundation.

Friedman, L. M. (1990). *The republic of choice: Law, authority, and culture.* Cambridge, MA: Harvard University Press.

Friedman, S., Squires, G. D., & Galvan, C. (2010). *Cybersegregation in Dallas and Boston: Is Neil a more desirable tenant than Tyrone or Jorge?* Paper presented at the annual meeting of the Population Association of America, Dallas, TX.

Friedman, T. L. (2000). *The Lexus and the olive tree: Understanding globalization.* New York: Anchor Books.

Friedman, T. L. (2005). *The world is flat: A brief history of the twenty-first century.* New York: Farrar, Straus and Giroux.

Fromm, E. (1941). *Escape from freedom.* New York: Farrar & Rinehart.

Froomkin, D. (2010, May 17). How do you disenfranchise 1 in 8 Black men? Huffington Post. Retrieved from http://www.huffingtonpost.com/2010/03/17/how-do-you-disenfranchise_n_502178.html

Frum, D. (2000). *How we got here: The '70s.* New York: Basic Books.

Frye, N. K., & Breaugh, J. A. (2004). Family-friendly policies, supervisor support, work–family conflict, family–work conflict, and satisfaction: A test of a conceptual model. *Journal of Business and Psychology, 19*(2), 197–220.

Fuentes-Nieva, R., & Galasso, N. (2014). *Working for the few: Political capture and economic inequality* (Briefing Paper 178). Oxford: Oxfam. Retrieved from http://www.oxfam.org/en/policy/working-for-the-few-economic-inequality

Fukuda-Parr, S. (2006, December). The Human Poverty Index: A multidimensional measure. *Poverty in Focus* (UNDP International Poverty Centre), pp. 7–9.

Furnish, T. (2005). Beheading in the name of Islam. *Middle East Quarterly, 12*(2), 51–55. Retrieved from http://www.meforum.org/713/beheading-in-the-name-of-islam

Gahran, A. (2012, August 3). Smartphone users report more phone problems, survey says. CNN Tech. Retrieved from http://www.cnn.com/2012/08/03/tech/mobile/pew-smartphone-problems/index.html

Gakidou, E., Cowling, K., Lozano, R., & Murray, C. J. L. (2010). Increased educational attainment and its impact on child mortality in 175 countries between 1970 and 2009: A systematic analysis. *The Lancet, 376*(9745), 959–974.

Gale, R. P. (1986). Social movements and the state: The environmental movement, counter movement, and governmental agencies. *Sociological Perspectives, 29,* 202–240.

Gallaudet Research Institute. (2005). A brief summary of estimates for the size of the deaf population in the USA based on available federal data and published research. Retrieved from http://research.gallaudet.edu/Demographics/deaf-US.php

Gambino, L. (2014, June 4). Lego to launch female scientist series after online campaign. *Guardian.* Retrieved from http://www.theguardian.com/lifeandstyle/2014/jun/04/lego-launch-female-scientists-series

Gamble, J. L., & Hess, J. J. (2012). Temperature and violent crime in Dallas, Texas: Relationships and implications of climate change. *Western Journal of Emergency Medicine, 13*(3), 239–246.

Gamson, J. (1991). Silence, death, and the invisible enemy: AIDS activism and social movement "newness." *Social Problems, 36*(4), 351–367.

Gamson, W. (1975). *The strategy of social protest.* Homewood, IL: Dorsey Press.

Gans, H. J. (1962a). Urbanism and suburbanism as ways of life. In A. Rose (Ed.), *Human behavior and social processes.* Boston: Houghton Mifflin.

Gans, H. J. (1962b). *The urban villagers: Group and class in the life of Italian-Americans.* New York: Free Press.

Gans, H. J. (1972). The positive functions of poverty. *American Journal of Sociology, 78*(2), 275–289.

Garcia, S. B., & Guerra, P. L. (2004). Deconstructing deficit thinking: Working with educators to create more equitable learning environments. *Education and Urban Society, 36*(2), 150–168.

Garfinkel, H. (1963). A conception of, and experiments with, "trust" as a condition of stable concerted actions. In O. J. Harvey (Ed.), *Motivation and social interaction* (pp. 187–238). New York: Ronald Press.

Garfinkel, H. (1985). *Studies in ethnomethodology.* New York: Blackwell.

Gaskell, G., & Smith, P. (1981, August 20). The crowd in history. *New Society,* pp. 303–304.

Gatsiounis, I. (2008, March 20). In Thailand, pollution from shrimp farms threatens a fragile environment. *New York Times.* Retrieved from http://www.nytimes.com/2008/03/20/business/worldbusiness/20iht-rbog-coast.1.11278833.html?_r=0

Gauntlett, D. (2008). *Media, gender, and identity: An introduction* (2nd ed.). New York: Taylor & Francis.

Geertz, C. (1973). *The interpretation of cultures.* New York: Basic Books.

Gellner, E. (1983). *Nations and nationalism.* Ithaca, NY: Cornell University Press.

George Washington University. (2012, June 1). Drug use for better grades deemed more acceptable than for athletics, GW professor finds (press release). Retrieved from http://mediarelations.gwu.edu/drug-use-better-grades-deemed-more-acceptable-athletics-gw-professor-finds

Gerding, A., & Signorielli, N. (2014). Gender roles in tween television programming: A content analysis of two genres. *Sex Roles, 70*(1–2), 43–56.

Gerhardt, K. F. G. (1989). *The silent brotherhood: Inside America's racist underground.* New York: Free Press.

Geronimus, A. (1992). The weathering hypothesis and the health of African-American women and infants: Evidence and speculations. *Ethnicity and Disease, 2*(3), 207–221.

Gerstel, N., & Gallagher, S. (1994). Caring for kith and kin: Gender, employment, and the privatization of care. *Social Problems, 41*(4), 519–539.

Geybullayeva, A. (2012, February 3). Azerbaijani blogs talk about Armenians: Introducing Hate 2.0. *Osservatorio balcani e caucaso.* Retrieved from http://www.balcanicaucaso.org/eng/Regions-and-countries/Azerbaijan/Azerbaijani-blogs-talk-about-Armenians-introducing-Hate-2.0-111320

Ghosh, B. N. (2001). *Dependency theory revisited.* London: Ashgate.

Gibbs, N. (2009, October 14). The state of the American woman: What women want now. *Time.* Retrieved from http://www.time.com/time/specials/packages/article/0,28804,1930277_1930145_1930309,00.html

Giddens, A. (1985). *The constitution of society.* Berkeley: University of California Press.

Giedd, J. N. (2004). Structural magnetic resonance imaging of the adolescent brain. *Annals of the New York Academy of Sciences, 1021,* 77–85.

Gilbert, D. L. (2011). *The American class structure in an age of growing inequality* (8th ed.). Thousand Oaks, CA: Pine Forge.

Gilbertson, G. A., & Gurak, D. T. (1993). Broadening the enclave debate: The labor market experiences of Dominican and Colombian men in New York City. *Sociological Forum, 8*(June), 205–220.

Gilligan, C. (1982). *In a different voice: Psychological theory and women's development.* Cambridge, MA: Harvard University Press.

Gilligan, C., Ward, J. V., & Taylor, J. M. (Eds.). (1989). *Mapping the moral domain: A contribution of women's thinking to psychological theory and education.* Cambridge, MA: Harvard University Press.

Gilman, C. P. (1898). *Women and economics: A study of the economic relation between men and women as a factor in social evolution.* Boston: Small, Maynard.

Gitlin, T. (1980). *The whole world is watching: Mass media in the making and unmaking of the new left.* Berkeley: University of California Press.

Giugni, M., & Passy, F. (1998). Social movements and policy change: Direct, mediated, or joint effect? *American Sociological Association Section on Collective Behavior and Social Movements Working Paper Series, 9*(4).

Glaze, L. E., & Herberman, E. J. (2013). *Correctional populations in the United States, 2012* (BJS Bulletin NCJ 243936). Washington, DC: U.S. Department of Justice, Bureau of Justice Statistics. Retrieved from http://www.bjs.gov/content/pub/pdf/cpus12.pdf

Glazer, N. (1992). The real world of education. *The Public Interest* (Winter), 57–75.

Glazer, N. (1997). *We are all multiculturalists now.* Cambridge, MA: Harvard University Press.

Glenny, M. (2009). *McMafia: A journey through the global criminal underworld.* New York: Knopf.

Glewwe, P. (1999). Why does mother's schooling raise child health in developing countries? Evidence from Morocco. *Journal of Human Resources, 34,* 124–159.

Global Commission on Drug Policy. (2011, June). *War on drugs: Report of the Global Commission on Drug Policy.* Rio de Janeiro: Author. Retrieved from http://www.globalcommissionondrugs.org/wp-content/themes/gcdp_v1/pdf/Global_Commission_Report_English.pdf

Glock, C. Y., & Bellah, R. N. (1976). *The new religious consciousness.* Berkeley: University of California Press.

Goffman, A. (2014). *On the run: Fugitive life in an American city.* Chicago: University of Chicago Press.

Goffman, E. (1959). *The presentation of self in everyday life.* New York: Doubleday.

Goffman, E. (1961). *Asylums: Essays on the social situation of mental patients and other inmates.* Garden City, NY: Anchor Books.

Goffman, E. (1963a). *Behavior in public place.* New York: Free Press.

Goffman, E. (1963b). *Stigma: Notes on the management of spoiled identity.* Englewood Cliffs, NJ: Prentice Hall.

Goffman, E. (1967). *Interaction ritual: Essays on face to face behavior.* Garden City, NY: Anchor.

Goffman, E. (1972). *Relations in public: Microstudies of the public order.* New York: Harper & Row.

Gokcearslan, A. (2010). The effect of cartoon movies on children's gender development. *Procedia: Social and Behavior Sciences, 2*(2), 5202–5207.

Gold, K. M. (2002). *School's in: The history of summer education in American public schools.* New York: Peter Lang.

Goldhagen, D. J. (1997). *Hitler's willing executioners.* New York: Vintage Books.

Goldscheider, F. K., & Waite, L. J. (1991). *New families, no families? The transformation of the American home.* Berkeley: University of California Press.

Goldstein, J. S. (2011, September/October). World peace could be closer than you think. *Foreign Policy,* pp. 53–56.

Goldstone, J. A. (2001). Towards a fourth generation of revolutionary theory. *Annual Review of Political Science, 4,* 139–187.

Goode, E. (2009). *Moral panics: The social construction of deviance.* Chichester, England: Wiley-Blackwell.

Goodwin, P. Y., Mosher, W. D., & Chandra, A. (2010). *Marriage and cohabitation in the United States: A statistical portrait based on Cycle 6 (2002) of the National Survey of Family Growth* (Vital Health Statistics, Series 23, No. 28). Washington, DC: National Center for Health Statistics. Retrieved from http://www.cdc.gov/nchs/data/series/sr_23/sr23_028.pdf

Goody, J. (1983). *The development of the family and marriage in Europe.* Cambridge: Cambridge University Press.

Gordon, D. (2005, December). *Indicators of poverty and hunger.* Presentation delivered at the Expert Group Meeting on Youth Development Indicators, United Nations Headquarters, New York.

Gottfredson, M. R., & Hirschi, T. (2004). *A general theory of crime.* Stanford, CA: Stanford University Press. (Original work published 1990)

Gottlieb, L. (2011). How to land your kid in therapy. *The Atlantic,* July. Retrieved from http://www.theatlantic.com/magazine/archive/2011/07/

Goudreau, J. (2011, January 6). Best entry-level jobs. *Forbes.* Retrieved from http://www.forbes.com/sites/jennagoudreau/2011/06/01/best-entry-level-jobs

Gourevitch, P. (1999). *We wish to inform you that tomorrow we will be killed with our families: Stories from Rwanda.* New York: Farrar, Straus and Giroux.

Gracey, H. L. (1991). Learning the student role: Kindergarten as academic boot camp. In J. M. Henslin (Ed.), *Down to earth sociology: Introductory readings* (6th ed.). New York: Free Press.

Gramsci, A. (1971). *Selections from the prison notebooks* (Q. Hoare & G. N. Smith, Eds. and Trans.). London: Lawrence & Wishart.

Grant, R. (1991). The sources of gender bias in international relations theory. In R. Grant & K. Newland (Eds.), *Gender and international relations* (pp. 8–26). Bloomington: Indiana University Press.

Green, P., & Ward, T. (2004). *State crime: Governments, violence and corruption.* London: Pluto Press.

Greenberg, K. S. (1996). *The confessions of Nat Turner and related documents.* Boston: Bedford Books.

Greenberg, K. S. (2003). *Nat Turner: A slave rebellion in history and memory.* New York. Oxford University Press.

Greene, K., & Krcmar, M. (2005). Predicting exposure to and liking of media violence: A uses and gratification approach. *Communication Studies, 56*(1), 71–93.

Greenhouse, S. (2008). *The big squeeze: Tough times for the American worker.* New York: Anchor Books.

Grey, S. (2006). *Ghost plane: The true story of the CIA torture program.* New York: Macmillan.

Griffin, S. (1978). *Woman and nature: The roaring inside her.* New York: Harper & Row.

Griffin, S. (1979). *Rape, the power of consciousness.* New York: Harper & Row.

Griffin, S. (1981). *Pornography as silence: Culture's revenge against nature.* New York: Harper & Row.

Grogan, S. (2008). *Body image: Understanding body dissatisfaction in men, women, and children.* New York: Routledge.

groSolar. (2010). groSolar history. Retrieved from http://www.grosolar.com/company/our-story

Gruber, J. E., & Fineran, S. (2008). Comparing the impact of bullying and sexual harassment victimization on the mental and physical health of adolescents. *Sex Roles, 59*(1–2), 1–13.

Grusky, O., Bonacich, P., & Webster, C. (1995). The coalition structure of the four person family. *Current Research in Social Psychology, 2,* 16–28.

Guerino, P., & Beck, A. J. (2011). Sexual victimization reported by adult correctional authorities, 2007–2008 (BJS Special Report NCJ 231172). Washington, DC: U.S. Department of Justice, Bureau of Justice Statistics. Retrieved from http://bjs.ojp.usdoj.gov/content/pub/pdf/svraca0708.pdf

Guilmoto, C. Z. (2007). *Characteristics of sex-ratio imbalance in India, and future scenarios.* Paper presented at the Fourth Asia Pacific Conference on Reproductive and Sexual Health and Rights, Hyderabad, India.

Guilmoto, C. Z. (2011). *Skewed sex ratios at birth and future marriage squeeze in China and India, 2005–2100* (Working Paper 15). Paris: Centre Population & Développement.

Gump, L. S., Baker, R. C., & Roll, S. (2000). Cultural and gender differences in moral judgment: A study of Mexican Americans and Anglo-Americans. *Hispanic Journal of Behavioral Sciences, 22*(1), 78–93.

Gunnell, J. J., & Ceci, S. J. (2010). When emotionality trumps reason: A study of individual processing style and juror bias. *Behavioral Sciences & the Law, 28*(6), 850–877.

Gunnoe, M. L. (1997). Toward a developmental contextual model of the effects of parental spanking on children's aggression. *Archives of Pediatrics and Adolescence, 151*(8), 768–775.

Gutman, R., & Rieff, D. (1999). *Crimes of war: What the public should know.* New York: Norton.

Haberman, C. (2014, March 9). The trial that unleashed hysteria over child abuse. *New York Times.* Retrieved from http://www.nytimes.com/2014/03/10/us/the-trial-that-unleashed-hysteria-over-child-abuse.html?_r=0

Habermas, J. (1976). *Legitimation crisis.* London: Heinemann.

Habermas, J. (1989). *The structural transformation of the public sphere: An inquiry into a category of bourgeois society.* Cambridge: MIT Press. (Original work published 1962)

Hadden, J. K. (1993). *Religion and the social order: The handbook on cults and sects in America.* Bingley, England: Emerald Group.

Hadden, J. K. (2006). New religious movements. Hartford Institute for Religion Research. Retrieved from http://hirr.hartsem.edu/denom/new_religious_movements.html

Haggerty, R. A. (Ed.). (1991). *Dominican Republic and Haiti: Country studies* (2nd ed.). Washington, DC: Federal Research Division, Library of Congress.

Haj-yahia, M. M., & Cohen, H. C. (2009). On the lived experience of battered women residing in shelters. *Journal of Family Violence, 24*(2), 95–109.

Haley, A., & Malcolm X. (1964). *The autobiography of Malcolm X.* New York: Ballantine Books.

Hall, E. (1973). *The silent language.* New York: Doubleday.

Hall, P. M. (2003). Interactionism, social organization, and social processes: Looking back there, reflecting now here, and moving ahead then. *Symbolic Interaction, 26,* 33–55.

Hamedy, S. (2014, January12). Navajo battle set on gay marriage. *Washington Post.* Retrieved from http://www.washingtonpost.com/politics/navajo-fight-is-set-over-same-sex-unions/2014/01/01/4514642c-7309-11e3-9389-09ef9944065e_story.html

Hamel, L., Rao, M., Levitt, L., Claxton, G., Cox, C., Pollitz, K., & Brodie, M. (2014). *Survey of non-group health insurance enrollees: A first look at people buying their own health insurance following implementation of the Affordable Care Act.* Menlo Park, CA: Kaiser Family Foundation. Retrieved from http://kaiserfamilyfoundation.files.wordpress.com/2014/06/survey-of-non-group-health-insurance-enrollees-findings-final1.pdf

Hamermesh, D. S. (2011). *Beauty pays: Why attractive people are more successful.* Princeton, NJ: Princeton University Press.

Hamermesh, D. S., & Parker, A. (2005). Beauty in the classroom: Professorial pulchritude and putative pedagogical productivity. *Economics of Education Review, 24,* 369–376.

Hamm, M. S. (2002). Apocalyptic violence: The seduction of terrorist subcultures. *Theoretical Criminology, 8*(3), 323–339.

Hammond, E. M., Berry, M. A., & Rodriguez, D. N. (2011). The influence of rape myth acceptance, sexual attitudes, and belief in a just world on attributions of responsibility in a date rape scenario. *Legal and Criminological Psychology, 16*(2), 242–252.

Hammond, P. E. (1992). *Religion and personal autonomy: The third disestablishment in America.* Columbia: University of South Carolina Press.

Handlin, O. (1991). *Boston's immigrants, 1790–1880: A study in acculturation.* Cambridge, MA: Belknap Press.

Haney, C., Banks, W. C., & Zimbardo, P. G. (1973). Interpersonal dynamics in a simulated prison. *International Journal of Criminology and Penology, 1,* 69–97.

Haninger, K., & Thompson, K. M. (2004). Content and ratings of teen-rated video games. *Journal of the American Medical Association, 291*(7), 856–865.

Hannon, E. (2012, April 8). India's census: Lots of cellphones, too few toilets. *Weekend Edition,* NPR. Retrieved from http://www.npr.org/2012/04/08/150133880/indias-census-lots-of-cellphones-too-few-toilets

Hanson, P. (2003). *An economic history of the USSR, 1945–1991.* New York: Longman.

Harper, B. (2000). Beauty, stature and the labour market: A British cohort study. *Oxford Bulletin of Economics and Statistics, 62,* 771–800.

Harring, H. A., Montgomery, K., & Hardin, J. (2011). Perceptions of body weight, weight, weight management strategies, and depressive symptoms among US college students. *Journal of American College Health, 59*(1), 43–50.

Harrington, M. (1963). *The other America: Poverty in the United States.* New York: Simon & Schuster.

Harris, J. R. (2009). *The nurture assumption: Why children turn out the way they do* (2nd ed.). New York: Free Press.

Harris Interactive. (2009, August 4). Firefighters, scientists and doctors seen as most prestigious occupations (press release on the Harris Poll no. 86). Retrieved from http://www.harrisinteractive.com/vault/Harris-Interactive-Poll-Research-Pres-Occupations-2009-08.pdf

Harth, E. (2001). *Last witnesses: Reflections on the wartime internment of Japanese Americans.* London: Palgrave Macmillan.

Hartmann, H. (1984). The unhappy union of Marxism and feminism: Toward a more progressive union. In A. M. Jaggar & P. S. Rothenberg (Eds.), *Feminist frameworks: Alternative theoretical accounts of the relations between women and men* (2nd ed., pp. 172–188). New York: McGraw-Hill.

Harvard Medical School. (2010, July). Marriage and men's health. *Harvard Men's Health Watch Newsletter.* Retrieved from http://www.health.harvard.edu/newsletters/Harvard_Mens_Health_Watch/2010/July/marriage-and-mens-health

Hattery, A. J. (2001). *Families in crisis: Men and women's perceptions of violence in partner relationships.* Blacksburg, VA: Southern Sociological Society.

Hausmann, R., Tyson, L. D., & Zahidi, S. (2011). *The global gender gap report.* New York: World Economic Forum. Retrieved from http://reports.weforum.org/global-gender-gap-2011/#=

Hayes, D., & Wynyard, D. (2002). *The McDonaldization of higher education.* Westport, CT: Bergin & Garvey.

Hecker, D. E. (2005, November). Occupational employment projections to 2014. *Monthly Labor Review,* pp. 70–101. Retrieved from http://www.bls.gov/opub/mlr/2005/11/art5full.pdf

Hedwig, L. (2011). Inequality as an explanation for obesity in the United States. *Sociology Compass, 5*(3), 215–232.

Hegewisch, A., & Liepmann, H. (2012). *Fact sheet: The gender wage gap by occupation.* Washington, DC: Institute for Women's Policy Research. Retrieved from http://www.iwpr.org/publications/pubs/the-gender-wage-gap-by-occupation

Hegewisch, A., & Matite, M. (2013). *Fact sheet: The gender wage gap by occupation.* Washington, DC: Institute for Women's Policy Research. Retrieved from http://www.iwpr.org/publications/pubs/the-gender-wage-gap-by-occupation-2

Held, D. (1989). *Political theory and the modern state.* Stanford, CA: Stanford University Press.

Henry, T. (2010, November 15). Even short-term poverty can hurt kids' health. CNNHealth. Retrieved from http://thechart.blogs.cnn.com/2010/11/15/even-short-term-poverty-can-hurt-kids-health

Henshaw, S. K. (2002). *Unplanned pregnancy rates in the United States, 1981–2002.* Washington, DC: National Campaign to Prevent Teen and Unplanned Pregnancy. Retrieved from http://www.thenationalcampaign.org

Heppner, C. M. (1992). *Seeds of disquiet: One deaf woman's experience.* Washington, DC: Gallaudet University Press.

Heritage, J., & Greatbatch, D. (1991). On the institutional character of institutional talk: The case of news interviews. In D. H. Zimmerman & D. Boden (Eds.), *Talk and social structure* (pp. 93–137). Cambridge: Polity Press.

Hersey, P., Blanchard, K., & Natemeyer, W. (1987). *Situational leadership, perception, and the use of power.* Escondido, CA: Leadership Studies.

Hess, H. (1973). *Mafia and mafiosi: The structure of power.* Farnborough, England: Saxon House.

Hesse-Biber, S. (1997). *Am I thin enough yet? The cult of thinness and the commercialization of identity.* New York: Oxford University Press.

Hexham, I., & Poewe, K. (1997). *New religions as global cultures: Making the human sacred.* Boulder, CO: Westview Press.

Hill, C., & Kearl, H. (2011). *Crossing the line: Sexual harassment at school.* Washington, DC: American Association of University Women. Retrieved from http://www.aauwmi.org/state/High%20School%20Girls/CrossingTheLine.pdf

Hill, L. E., & Johnson, H. P. (2002). *How fertility changes across immigrant generations.* San Francisco: Public Policy Institute of California. Retrieved from http://www.ppic.org/content/pubs/rb/RB_402LHRB.pdf

Himes, S. M., & Thompson, J. K. (2007). Fat stigmatization in television shows and movies: A content analysis. *Obesity, 15,* 712–718.

Hine, T. (2000). *The rise and fall of the American teenager.* New York: Bard/Avon.

Hinsley, F. H. (1986). *Sovereignty* (2nd ed.). Cambridge: Cambridge University Press.

Hirschi, T. (1969). *Causes of delinquency.* Berkeley: University of California Press.

Hirschi, T. (2004). Self-control and crime. In R. F. Baumeister & K. D. Vohs (Eds.), *Handbook of self-regulation: Research, theory, and applications* (pp. 537–552). New York: Guilford.

Ho, C. (1993). The internationalization of kinship and the feminization of Caribbean migration: The case of Afro-Trinidadian immigrants in Los Angeles. *Human Organization, 52*(1), 32–40.

Hoare, R. (2012, May 9). Meet Fortune 500's female powerbrokers. CNN. Retrieved from http://edition.cnn.com/2012/05/08/business/f500-leading-women/index.html

Hobbs, F., & Stoops, N. (2002). *Demographic trends in the 20th century* (Census 2000 Special Report CENSR-4). Washington, DC: U.S. Census Bureau. Retrieved from http://www.census.gov/prod/2002pubs/censr-4.pdf

Hochschild, A. R. (2001 b). *The time bind: When work becomes home and home becomes work.* New York: Holt.

Hochschild, A. (2001a). The nanny chain. *The American Prospect,* December 19. Retrieved from http://prospect.org/article/nanny-chain

Hochschild, A. R. (2003). *The managed heart: Commercialization of human feeling.* Berkeley: University of California Press.

Hochschild, A. R. (with Machung, A.). (2012). *The second shift: Working families and the revolution at home* (rev. ed.). New York: Penguin Books.

Hoffman, B. (2006). *Inside terrorism.* New York: Columbia University Press.

Hoffman, Brinker & Roberts. (2010). Credit card debt statistics. Retrieved from http://www.hoffmanbrinker.com/credit-card-debt-statistics.html

Holt, T. (1977). *Black over White: Negro political leadership in South Carolina during Reconstruction.* Urbana: University of Illinois Press.

Homans, C. (2011, September/October). Anthropology of an idea: War games. *Foreign Policy,* pp. 30–31.

Hooton, E. A. (1939). *The American criminal: An anthropological study.* Cambridge, MA: Harvard University Press.

Hopper, R. (1991). Hold the phone. In D. H. Zimmerman & D. Boden (Eds.), *Talk and social structure* (pp. 217–231). Cambridge: Polity Press.

Horan, P. M., & Hargis, P. G. (1991). Children's work and schooling in the late nineteenth century family economy. *American Sociological Review, 56,* 583–596.

Horkheimer, M. (1947). *The eclipse of reason.* Oxford: Oxford University Press.

Hosken, F. (1993). City. In *Academic American encyclopedia.* Danbury, CT: Grolier.

Hoyert, D. L., & Xu, J. (2012). Deaths: Preliminary data for 2011. *National Vital Statistics Reports, 61*(6). Retrieved from http://www.cdc.gov/nchs/data/nvsr/nvsr61/nvsr61_06.pdf

Huber, J. (1990). Macro-micro links in gender stratification: 1989 presidential address. *American Sociological Review, 55,* 1–10.

Huber, J. (1993). Gender role change in families: A macrosociological view. In T. Brubaker (Ed.), *Family relations: Challenges for the future.* Newbury Park, CA: Sage.

Huber, J. (2006). Comparative gender stratification. In J. S. Chafetz (Ed.), *Handbook of the sociology of gender* (pp. 65–80). New York: Springer.

Hudson, J. I., Hiripi, E., Pope, H. G., & Kessler, R. C. (2007). The prevalence and correlates of eating disorders in the National Comorbidity Survey Replication. *Biological Psychiatry, 61,* 248–258.

Huffman, M. L., & Torres, L. (2002). It's not only "who you know" that matters: Gender, personal contacts, and job lead quality. *Gender & Society, 16,* 793–813.

Human Rights Campaign. (2014). *Statewide employment laws and policies.* Retrieved from http://s3.amazonaws.com/hrc-assets//files/assets/resources/employment_laws_1-2014.pdf

Human Rights Watch. (2014). *Tobacco's hidden children: Hazardous child labor in United States tobacco farming.* Washington, DC: Author. Retrieved from http://www.hrw

.org/sites/default/files/reports/us0514_UploadNew.pdf

Humes, K. R., Jones, N. A., & Ramirez, R. R. (2011). *Overview of race and Hispanic origin: 2010* (Census Brief C2010BR-02). Washington, DC: U.S. Census Bureau. Retrieved from http://www.census.gov/prod/cen2010/briefs/c2010br-02.pdf

Hunter, J. D. (1987). *Evangelicalism: The coming generation.* Hutchinson, KS: de Wit Books.

Huntington, S. (1993). The clash of civilizations? *Foreign Affairs, 72*(3), 22–49.

Huntington, S. (1997). *The clash of civilizations and the remaking of world order.* New York: Simon & Schuster.

Hutcheon, D. (1999). *Building character and structure.* Westport, CT: Praeger.

Hvistendahl, M. (2011). *Unnatural selection: Choosing boys over girls, and the consequences of a world full of men.* New York: Public Affairs.

Hyman, H. H. (1942). The psychology of status. *Archives of Psychology, 38*(15), 147–165.

Immerwahr, D. (2007). Caste or colony? Indianizing race in the United States. *Modern Intellectual History, 4*(2), 275–301.

Inc. (2010). groSolar 2010 statistics. Retrieved from http://www.inc.com/inc5000/profile/grosolar

Ingraham, C. (1999). *White weddings: Romancing heterosexuality in popular culture.* New York: Routledge.

Institute of International Education. (2010, November). Study abroad by U.S. students slowed in 2008/09 with more students going to less traditional destinations (press release). Retrieved from http://www.iie.org/Who-We-Are/News-and-Events/Press-Center/Press-Releases/2010/2010-11-15-Open-Doors-US-Study-Abroad

International Campaign to Ban Landmines. (2012). Mine ban treaty: States not party. Retrieved from http://www.icbl.org/index.php/icbl/Universal/MBT/States-Not-Party

International Development Research Centre. (n.d.). *The daughter deficit: Exploring declining sex ratios in India.* Ottawa, ON: Women's Rights and Citizenship. Retrieved from http://web.idrc.ca/uploads/user-S/12040457571daughter_deficit.pdf

International Labour Organization. (2012, December 7). A snapshot of comparative pay levels around the world. Retrieved from http://www.ilo.org/global/research/global-reports/global-wage-report/2012/charts/WCMS_193286/lang--en/index.htm

International Telecommunication Union. (2011). *The world in 2011: ICT facts and figures.* Geneva: Author. Retrieved from http://www.itu.int/ITU-D/ict/facts/2011/material/ICTFactsFigures2011.pdf

International Telecommunication Union. (2014). *The world in 2014: ICT facts and figures.* Geneva: Author. Retrieved from http://www.itu.int/en/ITU-D/Statistics/Documents/facts/ICTFactsFigures2014-e.pdf

Internet Systems Consortium. (2012). Internet host count history. ISC Domain Survey. Retrieved from https://www.isc.org/solutions/survey/history

Internet World Stats. (2012). World Internet usage and population statistics, December 31, 2011. Retrieved from http://www.internetworldstats.com/stats.htm

In the trenches of a language war. (2013, December 21). *The Economist,* pp. 86–87.

Iribarren, J. L., & Moro, E. (2007). Information diffusion epidemics in social networks. *Physical Review Letters, 103.*

Isidore, C. (2012, September 6). 3 answers to the auto bailout debate. CNNMoney. Retrieved from http://money.cnn.com/2012/09/06/autos/auto-bailout

Jackson, K. T. (1985). *Crabgrass frontier: The suburbanization of America.* New York: Oxford University Press.

Jaffee, S., & Hyde, J. (2000). Gender differences in moral orientation: A meta analysis. *Psychological Bulletin, 126*(5), 703–726.

Jaggar, A. M. (1983). *Feminist politics and human nature.* Totowa, NJ: Rowman & Allanheld.

Janis, I. L. (1972). *Victims of groupthink.* Boston: Houghton Mifflin.

Janis, I. L. (1989). *Crucial decisions: Leadership in policy making and crisis management.* New York: Free Press.

Janis, I. L., & Mann, L. (1977). *Decision making: A psychological analysis of conflict, choice, and commitment.* New York: Free Press.

Jaschik, S. (2009, November 2). Probe of extra help for men. Inside Higher Ed. Retrieved from http://www.insidehighered.com/news/2009/11/02/admit

Jenkins, C. D. (1983). Social environment and cancer mortality in men. *New England Journal of Medicine, 308,* 395–408.

Jhally, S. (Producer & Director). (2007). *Dreamworlds 3: Desire, sex & power in music video* [Motion picture]. Northampton, MA: Media Education Foundation.

Johns, M., Schmader, T., & Martens, A. (2005). Knowing is half the battle: Teaching stereotype threat as a means of improving women's math performance. *Psychological Science, 16*(3), 175–179.

Johnson, E. (2014, February 16). Snake-handling pastor, reality star dies from snakebite. WBIR. Retrieved from http://www.wbir.com/story/news/local/2014/02/16/pastor-dies-after-snake-he-was-handling-bit-him/5529907

Johnson, J. (2011, November 27). College administrators worry that use of prescription stimulants is increasing. *Washington Post.* Retrieved from http://articles.washingtonpost.com/2011-11-27/local/35281941_1_prescription-drugs-study-drugs-prescription-stimulants

Johnson, J. M., & Ferraro, K. J. (1984). The victimized self: The case of battered women. In J. A. Kotarba & A. Fontana (Eds.), *The existential self in society* (pp. 119–130). Chicago: University of Chicago Press.

Johnson, T. D., Ríos, M., Drewery, M. P., & Ennis, S. R. (2010). *People who spoke a language other than English at home by Hispanic origin and race: 2009* (American Community Survey Brief 09-19). Washington, DC: U.S. Census Bureau. Retrieved from http://www.census.gov/prod/2010pubs/acsbr09-19.pdf

Johnston, L. D., Bachman, J. G., O'Malley, P. M., & Schulenberg, J. E. (2012). *Monitoring the Future: A continuing study of 12th grade youth.* Ann Arbor: Institute for Social Research, University of Michigan.

Johnston, L. D., O'Malley, P. M., Bachman, J. G., Schulenberg, J. E., & Miech, R.A. (2014). *Demographic subgroup trends among adolescents in the use of various licit and illicit drugs, 1975–2013* (Monitoring the Future Occasional Paper 81). Ann Arbor: Institute for Social Research, University of Michigan. Retrieved from http://www.monitoringthefuture.org/pubs.html#papers

Johnston, L. D., O'Malley, P. M., Miech, R. A., Bachman, J. G., & Schulenberg, J. E. (2014). *Monitoring the Future national results on drug use: 1975–2013: Overview, key findings on adolescent drug use.* Ann Arbor: Institute for Social Research, University of Michigan.

Jones, N. A., & Bullock, J. (2012). *The two or more races population: 2010* (Census Brief C2010BR-13). Washington, DC: U.S. Census Bureau. Retrieved from http://www.census.gov/prod/cen2010/briefs/c2010br-13.pdf

Jordan, M. (1992, January 9). Big city schools become more segregated in the 1980s, a study says. *Washington Post,* p. A3.

Josephson Institute Center for Youth Ethics. (2012). Report card on the ethics of American youth. Retrieved from http://charactercounts.org/programs/reportcard/2012/index.html

Josephson Institute of Ethics. (2009). *A study of values and behavior concerning integrity:*

The impact of age, cynicism and high school character. Los Angeles: Author.

Juergensmeyer, M. (1995). The social significance of Radhasoami. In D. Lorenzen (Ed.), *Bhakti religion in North India: Community identity and political action* (pp. 67–89). Albany: State University of New York Press.

Kagay, M. R. (1994, July 8). Poll on doubt of Holocaust is corrected: Roper says 91% are sure it occurred. *New York Times.*

Kahlenberg, S. G., & Hein, M. M. (2010). Progression on Nickelodeon? Gender-role stereotypes in toy commercials. *Sex Roles, 62*(11–12), 830–847.

Kahlor, L. A., & Morrison, D. (2007). Television viewing and rape myth acceptance among college women. *Sex Roles, 56*(11–12), 729–739.

Kaiser Family Foundation. (1998). American values: 1998 national survey of Americans on values. Retrieved from http://www.kff.org/kaiserpolls/1441-index.cfm

Kaiser Family Foundation. (2006, July). *Race, ethnicity, and health care: Fact sheet.* Menlo Park, CA: Author. Retrieved from http://kaiserfamilyfoundation.files.wordpress.com/2013/01/7541.pdf

Kaiser Family Foundation. (2008, October). *Eliminating racial/ethnic disparities in health care: What are the options?* (Health Care and the 2008 Elections). Menlo Park, CA: Author. Retrieved from http://www.kff.org/minorityhealth/upload/7830.pdf

Kaiser Family Foundation. (2009). State health facts: Estimated numbers of persons living with an AIDS diagnosis, all ages, by race/ethnicity, 2009. Retrieved from http://www.statehealthfacts.org/comparetable.jsp?ind=848&cat=11

Kaiser Family Foundation. (2010a, September 17). Census Bureau: Recession fuels record number of uninsured Americans. Kaiser Health News. Retrieved from http://www.kaiserhealthnews.org/daily-reports/2010/september/16/uninsured-census-statistics.aspx

Kaiser Family Foundation. (2010b). *Role of government survey.* Retrieved from http://www.washingtonpost.com/wp-srv/special/politics/Post-Kaiser-Harvard-Role-of-Government-2010.pdf

Kaiser Family Foundation. (2011). State health facts: Percent of adults who are overweight or obese, 2011. Retrieved from http://www.statehealthfacts.org/comparemaptable.jsp?ind=89&cat=2

Kaiser Family Foundation. (2012a). Medicaid and long-term care services and supports. Retrieved from http://www.kff.org/medicaid/upload/2186-09.pdf

Kaiser Family Foundation. (2012b). State health facts: Overweight and obesity rates for adults by race/ethnicity, 2012. Retrieved from http://kff.org/other/state-indicator/adult-overweightobesity-rate-by-re

Kaiser Family Foundation. (2013a). Health expenditure per capita: 2010. Retrieved from http://kff.org/global-indicator/health-expenditure-per-capita

Kaiser Family Foundation. (2013b). Medicaid enrollment: June 2012 data snapshot. Retrieved from http://kaiserfamilyfoundation.files.wordpress.com/2013/08/8050-06-medicaid-enrollment.pdf

Kaiser Family Foundation. (2014, September 2). Medicare at a glance. Retrieved from http://kff.org/medicare/fact-sheet/medicare-at-a-glance-fact-sheet

Kanazawa, S., & Still, M. C. (2000). Parental investment as a game of chicken. *Politics and the Life Sciences, 19,* 17–26.

Kandal, T. R. (1988). *The woman question in classical sociological theory.* Gainesville: University of Florida Press.

Kanter, R. M. (1983). *The change masters: Innovation for productivity in the American corporation.* New York: Simon & Schuster.

Kappeler, V. E., Sluder, R. D., & Alpert, G. P. (1998). *Forces of deviance: Understanding the dark side of policing.* Prospect Heights, IL: Waveland Press.

Kapuscinski, R. (2001). *The shadow of the sun.* New York: Vintage Books.

Kara, S. (2009). *Sex trafficking: Inside the business of modern slavery.* New York: Columbia University Press.

Karpinski, A. C., & Duberstein, A. (2009). *A description of Facebook use and academic performance among undergraduate and graduate students.* Columbus: Ohio State University, College of Education and Human Ecology. Retrieved from http://researchnews.osu.edu/archive/facebook2009.jpg

Kasarda, J. (1993). Urban industrial transition and the underclass. In W. J. Wilson (Ed.), *The ghetto underclass* (pp. 43–64). Newbury Park, CA: Sage.

Katz, J. (2006). *The macho paradox.* Naperville, IL: Sourcebooks.

Katz, J., & Chambliss, W. J. (1995). Biology and crime. In J. F. Sheley (Ed.), *Criminology: A contemporary handbook* (2nd ed.). Belmont, CA: Wadsworth.

Katz, J., & Jhally, S. (2000a, February 13). Manhood on the mat: The problem is not that pro wrestling makes boys violent: The real lesson of the wildly popular pseudo-sport is more insidious. *Boston Globe.* Retrieved from http://www.jacksonkatz.com/pub_manhood.html

Katz, J., & Jhally, S. (2000b, June 25). Put the blame where it belongs: On men. *Los Angeles Times.* Retrieved from http://articles.latimes.com/2000/jun/25/opinion/op-44616

Kaufman, J. M. (2009). Gendered responses to serious strain: The argument for a general strain of deviance. *Justice Quarterly, 26*(3), 410–444.

Kavilanz, P. (2012, April 26). China off-shores manufacturing to U.S. CNNMoney. Retrieved from http://money.cnn.com/2012/04/24/smallbusiness/china-us-manufacturing/index.htm?hpt=hp_t2

Kavner, L. (2012, August 15). Compliance, a low budget indie, might be the most disturbing movie ever made. Huffington Post. Retrieved from http://www.huffingtonpost.com/2012/08/15/compliance-movie-film_n_1779123.html

Keeley, B., Wright, L., & Condit, C. M. (2009). Functions of health fatalism: Fatalistic talk as face saving, uncertainty management, stress relief and sense making. *Sociology of Health and Illness, 31*(5), 734–747.

Kelley, B., & Carchia, C. (2013, July 11). "Hey, data data—swing!": The hidden demographics of youth sports. ESPN The Magazine. Retrieved from http://espn.go.com/espn/story/_/id/9469252/hidden-demographics-youth-sports-espn-magazine

Kellner, D. (1990). *Television and the crisis of democracy.* Boulder, CO: Westview Press.

Kena, G., Aud, S., Johnson, F., Wang, X., Zhang, J., Rathbun, A., . . . Kristapovich, P. (2014). *The condition of education 2014* (NCES 2014-083). Washington, DC: U.S. Department of Education, National Center for Education Statistics. Retrieved from http://nces.ed.gov/pubs2014/2014083.pdf

Kennedy, P. (1987). *The rise and fall of the great powers: Economic change and military conflict from 1500 to 2000.* New York: Random House.

Kennedy-Pipe, C. (1997). *The origins of the present troubles in Northern Ireland.* New York: Longman.

Kenning, C., & Halladay, J. (2008, January 25). Cities study dearth of healthy food. *USA Today.* Retrieved from http://usatoday30.usatoday.com/news/health/2008-01-24-fooddesert_N.htm

Kenny, C. (2012, June 4). The global obesity bomb. *Bloomberg Businessweek.* Retrieved from http://www.businessweek.com/articles/2012-06-04/the-global-obesity-bomb

Kessler, E.-M., Racoczy, K., & Staudinger, U. (2004). The portrayal of older people in prime time television series: The match with gerontological evidence. *Ageing and Society, 24*(4), 531–552.

Keyfitz, N. (1993). Thirty years of demography and *Demography. Demography, 30*(4), 533–549.

Khanna, N. (2011). *Biracial in America: Forming and performing racial identity.* Lanham, MD: Lexington Books.

Khanna, P. (2010, August 16). Beyond city limits: The age of nations is over. The new urban era has begun. *Foreign Policy.* Retrieved from http://www.foreignpolicy.com/articles/2010/08/16/beyond_city_limits?page=full

Kibirige, J. S. (1997). Population growth, poverty, and health. *Social Science & Medicine, 45,* 247–259.

Kilbourne, J. (1999). *Deadly persuasion: Why women and girls must fight the addictive power of advertising.* New York: Free Press.

Kimmel, M. S. (1986). Toward men's studies. *American Behavioral Scientist, 29*(5), 517–529.

Kimmel, M. S. (1996). *Manhood in America: A cultural history.* New York: Free Press.

Kimmel, M. S. (2000). *The gendered society.* New York: Oxford University Press.

King, H., & Chambliss, W. J. (1984). *Harry King: A professional thief's journey.* New York: Macmillan.

Kinnvall, C. (2004). Globalization and religious nationalism: Self, identity, and the search for ontological security. *Political Psychology, 25*(4), 741–767.

Kluckhohn, F. R., & Strodtbeck, F. L. (1961). *Variations in value orientations.* Evanston, IL: Row, Peterson.

Kochhar, R., Fry, R., & Taylor, P. (2011). *Wealth gaps rise to record highs between Whites, Blacks, Hispanics.* Washington, DC: Pew Research Center. Retrieved from http://www.pewsocialtrends.org/files/2011/07/SDT-Wealth-Report_7-26-11_FINAL.pdf

Kohlberg, L. (1969). Stage and sequence: The cognitive-developmental approach to socialization. In A. Goslin (Ed.), *Handbook of socialization theory and research* (pp. 347–480). Chicago: Rand McNally.

Kohlberg, L. (1983). *The philosophy of moral development.* New York: Harper & Row.

Kohlberg, L. (1984). *The psychology of moral development.* New York: Harper & Row.

Kohn, M. L. (1989). *Class and conformity: A study in values* (2nd ed.). Chicago: University of Chicago Press.

Kolowich, S. (2011, August 22). What students don't know. Inside Higher Ed. Retrieved from http://www.insidehighered.com/news/2011/08/22/erial_study_of_student_research_habits_at_illinois_university_libraries_reveals_alarmingly_poor_information_literacy_and_skills

Kornhauser, W. (1959). *The politics of mass society.* Glencoe, IL: Free Press.

Kornrich, S., & Furstenberg, F. (2013). Investing in children: Changes in parental spending on children, 1972–2007. *Demography, 50*(1), 1–23.

Kost, K., & Henshaw, S. (2012). *U.S. teenage pregnancies, births and abortions, 2008: National trends by age, race and ethnicity.* New York: Guttmacher Institute. Retrieved from http://www.guttmacher.org/pubs/USTPtrends08.pdf

Kozol, J. (1991). *Savage inequalities: Children in American schools.* New York: HarperCollins.

Kozol, J. (1995). *Amazing grace: Lives of our children and the conscience of a nation.* New York: Crown.

Kozol, J. (2000). *Ordinary resurrections: Children in the years of hope.* New York: Crown.

Kozol, J. (2005). *The shame of the nation: The restoration of apartheid schooling in America.* New York: Three Rivers Press.

Kramer, R. C., & Michalowski, R. J. (2005). War, aggression and state crime: A criminological analysis of the invasion and occupation of Iraq. *British Journal of Criminology, 45,* 446–469.

Kraut, R., Patterson, M., Lundmark, V., Kiesler, S., Mukopadhayay, T., & Scherlis, W. (1998). Internet paradox: A social technology that reduces social involvement and psychological well-being? *American Psychologist, 53,* 1017–1032.

Kristof, N., & WuDunn, S. (2009). *Half the sky: Turning oppression into opportunity for women worldwide.* New York: Knopf.

Kristofferson, K., White, K., & Peloza, J. (2014). The nature of slacktivism: How the social observability of an initial act of token support affects subsequent prosocial action. *Journal of Consumer Research, 40*(6), 1149–1166.

Kronk, E. A. (2013, April 16). One statute for two spirits: Same-sex marriage in Indian country. Jurist Forum. Retrieved from http://jurist.org/forum/2013/04/elizabeth-kronk-two-spritis.php

Kubota, Y. (2009, June 8). Tokyo firm rents fake family, friends for weddings. Reuters. Retrieved from http://www.reuters.com/article/2009/06/08/us-japan-weddings-idUSTRE5571IY20090608

Kubrin, C. E. (2005). Gangstas, thugs, and hustlas: Identity and the code of the street in rap music. *Social Problems, 52*(3), 360–378.

Kurdek, L. A. (2007). The allocation of household labor by partners in gay and lesbian couples. *Journal of Family Issues, 28,* 132–148.

Kushner, D. (2014, February 13). Dead end on Silk Road. *Rolling Stone,* pp. 52–59.

Lampman, J. (2006, September 14). American Buddhism on the rise. *Christian Science Monitor.* Retrieved from http://www.csmonitor.com/2006/0914/p14s01-lire.html

Lane, H. (1992). *The mask of benevolence: Disabling the deaf.* New York: Random House.

Lane, H. (2005). Ethnicity, ethics, and the deaf world. *Journal of Deaf Studies and Deaf Education, 10*(3), 291–310.

Langfitt, F. (2013, April 29). As the car market moves east, an extravaganza in Shanghai. National Public Radio. Retrieved from http://www.npr.org/blogs/thetwo-way/2013/04/27/179025891/as-the-car-market-moves-east-an-extravaganza-in-shanghai

Lareau, A. (2002). Invisible inequality: Social class and childrearing in Black families and White families. *American Sociological Review, 67,* 747–776.

LaRosa, J. (2011, May 9). U.S. weight loss market worth $60.9 billion. PRWeb. Retrieved from http://www.prweb.com/releases/2011/5/prweb8393658.htm

Laub, J., & Sampson, R. J. (2003). *Shared beginnings, divergent lives.* Cambridge, MA: Harvard University Press.

Lauzen, M., Dozier, D., & Horan, N. (2008). Constructing gender stereotypes through social roles in primetime television. *Journal of Broadcasting & Electronic Media, 52*(2), 200–214.

Leaper, C., Breed, L., Hoffman, L., & Perlman, C. A. (2002). Variations in the gender-stereotyped content of children's television cartoons across genres. *Journal of Applied Social Psychology, 32*(8), 1653–1662.

Leaper, C., & Robnett, R. D. (2011). Women are more likely than men to use tentative language, aren't they? A meta-analysis testing for gender differences and moderators. *Psychology of Women Quarterly, 35*(1), 129–142.

Le Bon, G. (1960). *The crowd: A study of the popular mind.* New York: Viking Press. (Original work published 1896)

Ledeneva, A. V. (1998). *Russia's economy of favours: Blat, networking, and informal exchange.* Cambridge: Cambridge University Press.

Lederman, D. (2011, March 16). An investigation abandoned. Inside Higher Ed. Retrieved from http://www.insidehighered.com/news/2011/03/16/civil_rights_commission_ends_inquiry_into_admissions_preferences_for_men_and_title_ix

Lednicer, L. G. (2014, August 8). Want a tech job? Study this. Advice from Mozilla, Reddit, Tumblr and more. *Washington Post Magazine.* Retrieved from http://www.washingtonpost.com/lifestyle/magazine/want-a-tech-job-study-this-advice-from-the-bosses-at-mozilla-reddit-tumblr/2014/07/30/41443afe-06f0-11e4-bbf1-cc51275e7f8f_story.html

Lee, D. (2013, March 19). Green jobs grow four times faster than others. *Los Angeles Times.* Retrieved from http://articles.latimes.com/2013/mar/19/business/la-fi-mo-green-jobs-20130319

Lee, M. M., Carpenter, B., & Meyers, L. S. (2007). Representations of older adults in television advertisements. *Journal of Aging Studies, 21*(1), 23–30.

Leitenberg, M. (2006). *Deaths in wars and conflicts in the 20th century* (3rd ed.). Ithaca, NY: Cornell University, Peace Studies Program. Retrieved from http://cissm.umd.edu/papers/files/deathswarsconflictsjune52006.pdf

Lemann, N. (1991). *The promised land: The great Black migration and how it changed America.* New York: Vintage Books.

Lemert, E. (1951). *Social pathology.* New York: McGraw-Hill.

Le Moal, M., & Koob, G. F. (2007). Drug addiction: Pathways to the disease and pathophysiological perspectives. *European Neuropsychopharmacology, 17*(6), 377–393.

Lemonnier, J. (2008, February 18). Big players in diet industry shift focus to online presences. Consumer Lab. Retrieved from http://consumerlab.wordpress.com/2008/02/18/big-players-in-diet-industry-shift-focus-to-online-presences

Lempert, D. (2007). *Women's increasing wage penalties from being overweight and obese.* Washington, DC: U.S. Bureau of Labor Statistics. Retrieved from http://www.bls.gov/osmr/abstract/ec/ec070130.htm

Lenning, E. (2007). Execution for body parts: A case of state crime. *Contemporary Justice Review, 10*(2), 173–191.

Leonhardt, D. (2009, September 8). Colleges are failing in graduation rates. *New York Times.* Retrieved from http://www.nytimes.com/2009/09/09/business/economy/09leonhardt.html

Lesotho. (2012). *Global AIDS response country progress report.* Retrieved from http://www.unaids.org/en/dataanalysis/knowyourresponse/countryprogressreports/2012countries/ce_LS_Narrative_Report%5B1%5D.pdf

Lester, D. (Ed.). (2000). *Suicide prevention: Resources for the millennium.* Philadelphia: Brunner-Routledge.

Lesthaeghe, R. (1995). The second demographic transition in Western countries: An interpretation. In K. O. Mason & A. Jensen (Eds.), *Gender and family change in industrialized countries* (pp. 17–62). Oxford: Clarendon Press.

Levin, D. (2014, April 2). BMW bets big on South Carolina. CNNMoney. Retrieved from http://features.blogs.fortune.cnn.com/2014/04/02/bmw-factory-south-carolina

Levin, H. M., & Rouse, C. (2012, January 26). The true cost of high school dropouts. *New York Times.* Retrieved from http://www.nytimes.com/2012/01/26/opinion/the-true-cost-of-high-school-dropouts.html?_r=0

Levine, L. (2012, December 17). *Offshoring (or offshore outsourcing) and job loss among U.S. workers* (CRS 7-5700; RL32292). Washington, DC: Congressional Research Service. Retrieved from http://fas.org/sgp/crs/misc/RL32292.pdf

Levine, M., & Crowther, S. (2008). The responsive bystander: How social group membership and group size can encourage as well as inhibit bystander intervention. *Journal of Interpersonal Psychology, 95*(6), 1429–1439.

LeVine, R. A., LeVine, S., Schnell-Anzola, B., Rowe, M. L., & Dexter, E. 2012. *Literacy and mothering: How women's schooling changes the lives of the world's children.* New York: Oxford University Press.

Levine, S., & Laurie, N. O. (Eds.). (1974). *The American Indian today.* Baltimore: Penguin Books.

Levitt, P. (2004, October 1). Transnational migrants: When "home" means more than one country. Migration Policy Institute. Retrieved from http://www.migrationpolicy.org/article/transnational-migrants-when-home-means-more-one-country

Lewin, T. (2011a, September 27). College graduation rates are stagnant even as enrollment rises, a study finds. *New York Times.* Retrieved from http://www.nytimes.com/2011/09/27/education/27remediation.html

Lewin, T. (2011b, October 25). Screen time higher than ever for children. *New York Times.* Retrieved from http://www.nytimes.com/2011/10/25/us/screen-time-higher-than-ever-for-children-study-finds.html

Lewis, B. (2010). *Faith and power: Religion and politics in the Middle East.* New York: Oxford University Press.

Liberto, J. (2012, April 19). CEO pay is 380 times average worker's—AFL-CIO. CNNMoney. Retrieved from http://money.cnn.com/2012/04/19/news/economy/ceo-pay

Library of Congress. (2012). Days in session calendars: 112th Congress 2nd session. Retrieved from http://thomas.loc.gov/home/ds/h1122.html

Liebow, E. (1967). *Talley's corner: A study of Negro streetcorner men.* Boston: Little, Brown.

Lienert, P., & Thompson, M. (2014, April 2). GM avoided defective switch redesign in 2005 to save a dollar each. Reuters. Retrieved from http://www.reuters.com/article/2014/04/02/us-gm-recall-delphi-idUSBREA3105R20140402

Light, H. K., & Martin, R. E. (1996). American Indian families. *Journal of American Indian Education, 26*(1), 1–5. Retrieved from http://jaie.asu.edu/v26/V26S1ame.htm

Lindsey, E. W., & Mize, J. (2001). Contextual differences in parent–child play: Implications for children's gender role development. *Sex Roles, 44,* 155–176.

LinkedIn. (2012). About us. Retrieved from http://press.linkedin.com/about

Lipka, M. (2014, June 16). 5 facts about the World Cup—and the people who are watching. Pew Research Center, Fact Tank. Retrieved from http://www.pewresearch.org/fact-tank/2014/06/16/5-facts-about-the-world-cup-and-the-people-who-are-watching

Lips, H. (2008). *Sex and gender: An introduction* (6th ed.). Boston: McGraw-Hill.

Livingston, G. (2014). *Growing number of dads home with the kids.* Washington, DC: Pew Research Center. Retrieved from http://www.pewsocialtrends.org/2014/06/05/growing-number-of-dads-home-with-the-kids

Livingstone, S., & Brake, D. R. (2010). On the rapid rise of social networking sites: New findings and policy implications. *Children and Society, 24,* 75–83.

Living Tongues Institute for Endangered Languages. (n.d.). Who we are. Retrieved from http://www.livingtongues.org/aboutus.html

Lloyd-Roberts, S. (2012, October 31). Have India's poor become human guinea pigs? BBC. Retrieved from http://www.bbc.com/news/magazine-20136654

Lofland, J. (1985). *Protest: Studies of collective behavior and social movements.* New Brunswick, NJ: Transaction.

Lofquist, D., Lugaila, T., O'Connell, M., & Feliz, S. (2012). *Households and families: 2010* (Census Brief C2010BR-14). Washington, DC: U.S. Census Bureau. Retrieved from http://www.census.gov/prod/cen2010/briefs/c2010br-14.pdf

Logan, J. R., Minca, E., & Adar, S. (2012). The geography of inequality: Why separate means unequal in American public schools. *Sociology of Education, 85*(3), 287–301.

Logan, J. R., & Molotch, H. L. (1987). *Urban fortunes: The political economy of place.* Berkeley: University of California Press.

Lomborg, B. (2012, April 30). The high cost of heart disease and cancer. Slate. Retrieved from http://www.slate.com/articles/technology/copenhagen_consensus_2012/2012/04/copenhagen_consensus_ideas_for_reducing_cancer_and_heart_disease.html

Lombroso, C. (1896). *L'homme criminel.* Paris: F. Alcan.

Lonsway, K. A., Banyard, V. L., Berkowitz, A. D., Gidycz, C. A., Katz, J. T., Koss, M. P., Schewe, P. A., & Ullman, S. E. (2009). *Rape prevention and risk reduction: Review of the literature for practitioners.* Harrisburg, PA: VAWnet. Retrieved from http://oregonsatf.org/wp-content/uploads/2012/05/AR_RapePrevention.pdf

Loo, C. M. (1991). *Chinatown: Most time, hard time.* New York: Praeger.

Lough, R., & Denholm, E. (2005, July 17). *Violence against women in Northern Uganda.* London: Amnesty International. Retrieved from http://www.amnesty.org/en/library/asset/AFR59/001/2005/en/c0fde617-d4ca-11dd-8a23-d58a49c0d652/afr590012005en.pdf

Lubeck, S. (1985). *Sandbox society: Early education in Black and White America.* London: Falmer.

Lucas, J. W., & Lovaglia, M. J. (1998). Leadership status, group size, and emotion in face-to-face groups. *Sociological Perspectives, 41*(3), 617–637.

Luker, K. (1996). *Dubious conceptions: The politics of teenage pregnancy.* Cambridge, MA: Harvard University Press.

Maas, P. (1997). *Serpico.* New York: HarperTorch.

MacFarquhar, R. (1980, February 9). The post-Confucian challenge. *The Economist,* pp. 67–72.

Mac Ionnrachtaigh, F. (2013). *Language, resistance and revival: Republican prisoners and the Irish language in the North of Ireland.* London: Pluto Press.

Mackinder, E. (2010, August 23). Pro-environment groups outmatched, outspent in battle over climate change legislation. OpenSecrets, Center for Responsive Politics. Retrieved from http://www.opensecrets.org/news/2010/08/pro-environment-groups-were-outmatc.html

MacKinnon, C. A. (1982). Feminism, Marxism, method and the state: An agenda for theory. *Signs, 7*(3), 515–544.

MacKinnon, C. A. (1989). *Toward a feminist theory of the state.* Cambridge, MA: Harvard University Press.

Mackun, P., & Wilson, S. (2011). *Population distribution and change: 2000 to 2010* (Census Brief CS2020BR-01). Washington, DC: U.S. Census Bureau. Retrieved from http://www.census.gov/prod/cen2010/briefs/c2010br-01.pdf

MacLeod, C. (2011, November 2). In China, tensions rising over Buddhism's quiet resurgence. *USA Today.* Retrieved from http://www.usatoday.com/news/religion/story/2011-11-01/tibetan-buddhism-china-communist-tension/51034604/1

Made in Alabama. (2014, May 28). Alabama officials welcome Golden Dragon's first U.S. factory. Alabama Department of Commerce. Retrieved from http://www.madeinalabama.com/2014/05/first-golden-dragon-copper-tube-u-s-factory

Madlock, P. E., & Westerman, D. (2011). Hurtful cyber-teasing and violence: Who's laughing out loud? *Journal of Interpersonal Violence, 26*(17), 3542–3560.

Madrigal, A. (2011, November). What's wrong with #FirstWorldProblems? *Atlantic Monthly.* Retrieved from http://www.theatlantic.com/technology/archive/2011/11/whats-wrong-with-firstworldproblems/248829

Maher, J. K., Herbst, K. C., Childs, N. M., & Finn, S. (2008). Racial stereotypes in children's television commercials. *Journal of Advertising Research, 48*(3), 80–93.

Maher, L. (1997). *Sexed work: Gender, race, and resistance in a Brooklyn drug market.* New York: Oxford University Press.

Malacrida, C. (2005). Discipline and dehumanization in a total institution: Institutional survivors' descriptions of time-out rooms. *Disability & Society, 20*(5), 523–537.

Malinauskas, B. M., Raedeke, T. D., Aeby, V. G., Smith, J. L., & Dallas, M. B. (2006). Dieting practices, weight perceptions, and body composition: A comparison of normal weight, overweight, and obese college females. *Nutrition Journal, 5*(11).

Malthus, T. (1926). *First essay on population.* London: Macmillan. (Original work published 1798)

Mann, C. C. (2011, June). The birth of religion. *National Geographic,* pp. 34–59.

Mann, C. R., & Zatz, M. S. (Eds.). (1998). *Images of color, images of crime.* Los Angeles: Roxbury.

Mann, M. (1986). *The sources of social power: Vol. 1. A history of power from beginning until 1760.* New York: Cambridge University Press.

Manning, R. D. (2005). *Living with debt: A life stage analysis of changing attitudes and behaviors.* Rochester, NY: Lending Tree.

Manning, S. (2009, February 20). Is anything made in the U.S.A. anymore? You'd be surprised. *New York Times.* Retrieved from http://www.nytimes.com/2009/02/20/business/worldbusiness/20iht-wb-make.1.20332814.html

Marcuse, H. (1964). *One-dimensional man.* Boston: Beacon Press.

Margolis, E. (2001). *The hidden curriculum in higher education.* New York: Routledge.

Marini, M. M. (1990). Sex and gender: What do we know? *Sociological Forum, 5*(1), 95–120.

Markert, J. (2010). The changing face of racial discrimination: Hispanics as the dominant minority in the United States—A new application of power-threat theory. *Critical Sociology, 36*(2), 307–327.

Marketdata Enterprises. (2011). *The U.S. weight loss and diet control market* (11th ed.; Report FS22). Tampa, FL: Author. Retrieved from http://www.marketdataenterprises.com

MarketingCharts. (2013). The demographics of Instagram and Snapchat users. Retrieved from http://www.marketingcharts.com/wp/online/the-demographics-of-instagram-and-snapchat-users-37745

Markusen, E. (2002). Mechanisms of genocide. In C. Rittner, J. K. Roth, & J. M. Smith (Eds.), *Will genocide ever end?* (pp. 83–90). St. Paul, MN: Paragon House.

Marlowe, C. M., Schneider, S. L., & Nelson, C. E. (1996). Gender and attractiveness biases in hiring decisions: Are more experienced managers less biased? *Journal of Applied Psychology, 81,* 11–21.

Martin, C. L., & Fabes, R. A. (2001). The stability and consequences of young children's same-sex peer interactions. *Developmental Psychology, 37,* 431–446.

Martin, D. S. (2012, March 1). Vets feel abandoned after secret drug experiments. CNN. Retrieved from http://edition.cnn.com/2012/03/01/health/human-test-subjects

Martin, J. A., Hamilton, B. E., Osterman, M. J. K., Curtin, S. C., & Mathews, T. J. (2013). Births: Final data for 2012. *National Vital Statistics Reports, 62*(9). Retrieved from http://www.cdc.gov/nchs/data/nvsr/nvsr62/nvsr62_09.pdf#table02

Martineau, H. (1837). *Society in America*. New York: Saunders & Otley.

Marwell, G., & Oliver, P. (1993). *The critical mass in collective action: A micro-social theory*. New York: Cambridge University Press.

Marx, G. T., & McAdam, D. (1994). *Collective behavior and social movements: Process and structure*. Englewood Cliffs, NJ: Prentice Hall.

Marx, K. (1992a). *Capital: A critique of political economy* (Vol. 1). New York: Penguin Classics. (Original work published 1867)

Marx, K. (1992b). *Capital: A critique of political economy* (Vol. 2). New York: Penguin Classics. (Original work published 1885)

Marx, K. (1992c). *Capital: A critique of political economy* (Vol. 3). New York: Penguin Classics. (Original work published 1894)

Marx, K. (2000). Towards a critique of Hegel's *Philosophy of right*: Introduction. In D. McLellan (Ed.), *Karl Marx: Selected writings* (rev. ed.). New York: Classic Books International. (Original work published 1844)

Marx, K., & Engels, F. (1998). *The communist manifesto*. New York: Verso. (Original work published 1848)

Massey, D. S. (2011). Epilogue: The past and future of Mexico–U.S. migration. In O.-V. Mark (Ed.), *Beyond la frontera: The history of Mexico–U.S. migration* (pp. 241–265). New York: Oxford University Press.

Massey, D. S., & Denton, N. A. (1993). *American apartheid: Segregation and the making of the underclass*. Boston: Harvard University Press.

Masters, J. (2011, February 7). Militant extremists in the United States. Council on Foreign Relations. Retrieved from http://www.cfr.org/terrorist-organizations-and-networks/militant-extremists-united-states/p9236

Mathews, T. J., & MacDorman, M. F. (2012). Infant mortality statistics from the 2008 period linked birth/infant death data set. *National Vital Statistics Reports, 60*(5). Retrieved from http://www.cdc.gov/nchs/data/nvsr/nvsr60/nvsr60_05.pdf

Mathisen, J. A. (1989). Twenty years after Bellah: Whatever happened to American civil religion? *Sociological Analysis, 50*(2), 129–146.

Mayer, G. (2004). *Union membership trends in the United States*. Washington, DC: Congressional Research Service. Retrieved from http://digitalcommons.ilr.cornell.edu/cgi/viewcontent.cgi?article=1176&context=key_workplace

Mazur, E., & Richards, L. (2011). Adolescents' and emerging adults' social networking online: Homophily or diversity? *Journal of Applied Developmental Psychology, 32*(4), 180–188.

Mazzella, R., & Feingold, A. (1994). The effects of physical attractiveness, race, socioeconomic status, and gender of defendant and victims on judgments of mock jurors: A meta-analysis. *Journal of Applied Social Psychology, 24,* 1315–1344.

McAdam, D. (1982). *Political process and the development of Black insurgency, 1930–1970*. Chicago: University of Chicago Press.

McAdam, D. (1986). Recruitment to high-risk activism: The case of freedom summer. *American Journal of Sociology, 92,* 64–90.

McAdam, D. (1988). *Freedom summer: The idealists revisited*. New York: Oxford University Press.

McAdam, D., McCarthy, J. D., & Zald, M. N. (1988). Social movements. In N. J. Smelser (Ed.), *Handbook of sociology* (pp. 695–737). Newbury Park, CA: Sage.

McCarthy, E. (2012, April 9). A court's conundrum: When same-sex partners want to split. *Washington Post*. Retrieved from http://www.washingtonpost.com/lifestyle/style/a-courts-conundrum-when-same-sex-partners-want-to-split/2012/04/09/gIQA vhep6S_story.html

McCarthy, J. (2014, June 2). Double rape, lynching in India exposes caste fault lines. National Public Radio. Retrieved from http://www.npr.org/blogs/parallels/2014/06/02/318259419/double-rape-lynching-in-india-exposes-caste-fault-lines

McCarthy, J. D., & Zald, M. N. (1973). *The trend of social movements in America: Professionalization and resource mobilization*. Morristown, NJ: General Learning.

McCarthy, J. D., & Zald, M. N. (1977). Resource mobilization and social movements: A partial theory. *American Journal of Sociology, 82,* 1212–1241.

McCartney, J. T. (1992). *Black power ideologies: An essay in African American political thought*. Philadelphia: Temple University Press.

McCoy, A. W. (1991). *The politics of heroin: CIA complicity in the global drug trade*. New York: Lawrence Hill.

McCoy, K. (2009). Uncle Sam wants them. *Contexts, 8*(1), pp. 14–19.

McDonald, S., & Day, J. C. (2010). Race, gender, and the invisible hand of social capital. *Sociology Compass, 4*(7), 532–543.

McDonald, S., Lin, N., & Ao, D. (2009). Networks of opportunity: Gender, race, and job leads. *Social Problems, 56*(3), 385–402.

McDonald, S., & Mair, C. A. (2010). Social capital across the life course: Age and gendered patterns of network resources. *Sociological Forum, 25,* 335–359.

McDonough, K. (2014, July 11). First woman arrested under Tennessee law that criminalizes pregnancy outcomes. Salon. Retrieved from http://www.salon.com/2014/07/11/first_woman_arrested_under_tennessee_law_that_criminalizes_pregnancy_outcomes

McGann, L. (2014, May 11). Conservatives skeptical of power of Twitter. Politico. Retrieved from http://www.politico.com/story/2014/05/nigeria-kidnapping-twitter-hastag-bringbackourgirls-106528.html

McGirk, T. (2009, September 16). Behind the Taliban's resurgence in Afghanistan. *Time*. Retrieved from http://www.time.com/time/world/article/0,8599,1923303,00.html

McGregor, J. (2014, January 3). Zappos says goodbye to bosses. *Washington Post*. Retrieved from http://www.washingtonpost.com/blogs/on-leadership/wp/2014/01/03/zappos-gets-rid-of-all-managers

McGuire, L. C., Okoro, C. A., Goins, R. T., & Anderson, L. A. (2008). Characteristics of American Indian and Alaska native adult caregivers: Behavioral Risk Factor Surveillance System, 2000. *Ethnicity & Disease, 18*(4), 520.

McIntosh, P. (1990). White privilege: Unpacking the invisible knapsack. *Independent School, 49*(2), 31–36.

McKee, L., Roland, E., Coffelt, N., Olson, A. L., Forehand, R., Massari, C., . . . Zens, M. S. (2007). Harsh discipline and child problem behaviors: The roles of positive parenting and gender. *Journal of Family Violence, 22*(4), 187–196.

McKenna, K. Y. A., & Bargh, J. A. (1998). Coming out in the age of the Internet: Identity "demarginalization" through virtual group participation. *Journal of Personality and Social Psychology, 75*(3), 681–694.

McKibben, B. (2011, April 7). Resisting climate reality. *New York Review of Books*.

Retrieved from http://www.nybooks.com/articles/archives/2011/apr/07/resisting-climate-reality/?pagination=false

McLean, B., & Elkind, P. (2003). *The smartest guys in the room: The amazing rise and scandalous fall of Enron.* New York: Penguin/Portfolio.

McLean, B., & Nocera, J. (2010). *All the devils are here: The hidden history of the financial crisis.* New York: Penguin/Portfolio.

McLoyd, V. C., & Smith, J. (2002). Physical discipline and behavior problems in African American, European American, and Hispanic children: Emotional support as a moderator. *Journal of Marriage and Family, 64*(1), 40–53.

McLuhan, M. (1964). *Understanding media: The extensions of man.* New York: McGraw-Hill.

McNeely, C. L. (1995). *Constructing the nation-state: International organization and prescriptive action.* Westport, CT: Greenwood.

McNicoll, G. (2001). Government and fertility in transitional and post-transitional societies. *Population and Development Review, 27,* 129–159.

Mead, G. H. (1934). *Mind, self, and society.* Chicago: University of Chicago Press.

Mead, G. H. (1938). *The philosophy of the act.* Chicago: University of Chicago Press.

Mednick, S. A., Gabrielli, W. F., Jr., & Hutchings, B. (1987). Genetic factors in the etiology of criminal behavior. In S. A. Mednick, T. E. Moffitt, & S. A. Stack (Eds.), *The causes of crime: New biological approaches.* Cambridge: Cambridge University Press.

Mednick, S. A., Moffitt, T. E., & Stack, S. A. (1987). *The causes of crime: New biological approaches.* Cambridge: Cambridge University Press.

Mehra, A., Dixon, A. L., Brass, D. J., & Robertson, B. (2006). The social network ties of group leaders: Implications for group performance and leader reputation. *Organization Science, 17*(1), 64–79.

Melton, J. G. (Ed.). (1996). *Encyclopedia of American religions* (5th ed.). New York: Gale Research.

Melucci, A. (1989). *Nomads of the present: Social movements and individual needs in contemporary society.* Philadelphia: Temple University Press.

Merton, R. K. (1938). Social structure and anomie. *American Sociological Review, 3,* 672–682.

Merton, R. K. (1968). *Social theory and social structure.* New York: Free Press.

Merton, R. K. (1996). *On social structure and science.* Chicago: University of Chicago Press.

Messerschmidt, J. W. (1986). *Capitalism, patriarchy and crime: Towards a socialist feminist criminology.* Totowa, NJ: Rowman & Littlefield.

Messerschmidt, J. W. (1993). *Masculinities and crime: Critique and reconceptualization of theory.* Lanham, MD: Rowman & Littlefield.

Meyrowitz, J. (1985). *No sense of place: The impact of electronic media on social behavior.* New York: Oxford University Press.

Michalowski, R., & Dubisch, J. (2001). *Run for the wall: Remembering Vietnam on a motorcycle pilgrimage.* New Brunswick, NJ: Rutgers University Press.

Migration Policy Institute. (2012). Region of birth as a percentage of the total immigrant population, 1960–2011. Retrieved from http://www.migrationinformation.org/datahub/charts/fb.2.shtml

Milgram, S. (1963). Behavioral studies in obedience. *Journal of Abnormal Psychology, 67,* 371–378.

Milkman, R. (2006). *L.A. story: Immigrant workers and the future of the U.S. labor movement.* New York: Russell Sage Foundation.

Miller, K. A., Kohn, M. A., & Schooler, C. (1986). Educational self-direction and personality. *American Sociological Review, 5,* 372–390.

Miller, K. E., Melnick, M. J., Barnes, G. M., Farrell, M. P., & Sabo, D. F. (2005). Untangling the links among athletic involvement, gender, race, and adolescent academic outcomes. *Sociology of Sport Journal, 22*(2), 178–193.

Miller, L. P. (1995). Tracking the progress of *Brown. Teachers College Record, 96*(4), 609–613.

Miller, M., Azrael, D., & Hemenway, D. (2007). State-level homicide victimization rates in the U.S. in relation to survey measures of household firearm ownership, 2001–2003. *Social Science & Medicine, 64,* 656–664.

Miller, T., Govil, N., McMurria, J., & Maxwell, R. (2002). *Global Hollywood.* London: British Film Institute.

Millett, K. (1970). *Sexual politics.* Garden City, NY: Doubleday.

Mills, C. W. (2000a). *The power elite.* New York: Oxford University Press. (Original work published 1956)

Mills, C. M. (2000b). *The sociological imagination* (40th anniversary ed.). New York: Oxford University Press. (Original work published 1959)

Miner, H. (1956). Body ritual among the Nacirema. *American Anthropologist, 58*(3), 503–507.

Mishel, L., Bivens, J., Gould, E., & Shierholz, H. (2012). *The state of working America* (12th ed.). Ithaca, NY: Cornell University Press, Economic Policy Institute.

Mitchiner, J., & Sass-Lehrer, M. (2011). My child can have more choices: Reflections of deaf mothers on cochlear implants for their children. In R. Paludneviciene & I. W. Leigh (Eds.), *Cochlear implants: Evolving perspectives.* Washington, DC: Gallaudet University Press.

Mizruchi, M. S., & Potts, B. B. (1998). Centrality and power revisited: Actor success in group decision making. *Social Networks, 20*(4), 353–387.

Mollenkopf, J. (1977). The postwar politics of urban development. In J. Walton & D. E. Carns (Eds.), *Cities in change* (2nd ed., pp. 549–579). Boston: Allyn & Bacon.

Moloney, C. J. (2012). *The buffalo slaughter and the conquest of the West* (Master's thesis, George Washington University).

Moloney, C. J., & Chambliss, W. J. (2014). Slaughtering the bison, controlling Native Americans: A state crime and green criminology synthesis. *Critical Criminology, 22,* 319–338.

Molotch, H. L. (1972). *Managed integration: Dilemmas of doing good in the city.* Berkeley: University of California Press.

Molotch, H. L. (1976). The city as a growth machine. *American Journal of Sociology, 82,* 309–333.

Molotch, H. L., & Boden, D. (1985). Talking social structure: Discourse, dominance, and the Watergate hearings. *American Sociological Review, 50,* 273–288.

Monroe, P. (1940). *Founding of the American public school system.* New York: Macmillan.

Moore, J. (2010, June 30). Congo war leaves legacy of sexual violence against women. *Christian Science Monitor.* Retrieved from http://www.csmonitor.com/World/Africa/2010/0630/Congo-war-leaves-legacy-of-sexual-violence-against-women

Moore, J. (2012, May 18). Son fulfills dream that racism denied his mother. National Public Radio. Retrieved from http://www.npr.org/2012/05/18/152935623/son-fulfills-dream-racism-denied-to-his-mother

Moore, J., & Pinderhughes, R. (2001). The Latino population: The importance of economic restructuring. In M. L. Andersen & P. H. Collins (Eds.), *Race, class, and gender: An anthology* (4th ed., pp. 251–258). Belmont, CA: Wadsworth.

Moore, J. D. (2004). *Visions of culture: An introduction to anthropological theories and theorists* (2nd ed.). Walnut Creek, CA: AltaMira Press.

Moore, J. W. (1991). *Going down to the barrio: Homeboys and homegirls in change.* Philadelphia: Temple University Press.

Moore, L. R. (1994). *Selling God: American religion in the marketplace culture.* New York: Oxford University Press.

Morgan, J. (1999). *When chickenheads come home to roost: A hip hop feminist breaks it down.* New York: Touchstone.

Morgan, L. H. (1964). *Ancient society, or researches in the lines of human progress, from savagery through barbarism to civilization.* Cambridge, MA: Harvard University Press. (Original work published 1877)

Morgenstern, J. (2008, November 14). "Slumdog" finds rare riches in poor boy's tale. *Wall Street Journal.* Retrieved from http://online.wsj.com/article/SB122661670370126131.html

Morishima, M. (1982). *Why has Japan "succeeded"? Western technology and the Japanese ethos.* New York: Cambridge University Press.

Morrison, M. K. C. (1987). *Black political mobilization: Leadership, power, and mass behavior.* Albany: State University of New York Press.

Moser, S., & Dilling, L. (2004). Making climate hot: Communicating the urgency and challenge of global climate change. *Environment, 46*(10), 32–46.

Motel, S., & Patten, E. (2012, June 27). Hispanic origin profiles, 2010. Pew Research Center, Hispanic Trends Project. Retrieved from http://www.pewhispanic.org/2012/06/27/country-of-origin-profiles

Motlagh, J. (2012, September 19). In a world hungry for cheap shrimp, migrants labor overtime in Thai sheds. *Washington Post.* Retrieved from http://www.washingtonpost.com/world/asia_pacific/in-a-world-hungry-for-cheap-shrimp-migrants-labor-overtime-in-thai-sheds/2012/09/19/3435a90e-01a4-11e2-b257-e1c2b3548a4a_story.html

Moynihan, D. P. (1965). *The Negro family: The case for national action.* Washington, DC: Government Printing Office.

Mudde, C. (2011). *The relationship between immigration and nativism in Europe and North America.* Washington, DC: Migration Policy Institute. Retrieved from http://www.migrationpolicy.org/pubs/Immigration-Nativism.pdf

Mukhopadhyay, C. C., & Higgins, P. (1988). Anthropological studies of women's status revisited: 1977–87. *Annual Review of Anthropology, 17,* 461–495.

Muller, J. (2014, February 15). UAW's loss and what it means for your paycheck. *Forbes.* Retrieved from http://www.forbes.com/sites/joannmuller/2014/02/15/uaws-loss-and-what-it-means-for-your-paycheck

Muller, T., & Espenshade, T. J. (1985). *The fourth wave: California's newest immigrants.* Washington, DC: Urban Institute Press.

Mumford, L. (1961). *The city in history: Its origins, its transformations, and its prospects.* New York: Harcourt.

Muncer, S. J., & Campbell, A. (2000). Comments on "Sex differences in beliefs about aggression: Opponent's sex and the form of aggression" by J. Archer and A. Haigh. *British Journal of Social Psychology, 39*(2), 309–311.

Murdock, G. P. (1949). *Social structure.* New York: Macmillan.

Murphy, C. (2007). *Are we Rome? The fall of an empire and the fate of America.* New York: Houghton Mifflin Harcourt.

Murphy, R. (1988). *Social closure: The theory of monopolization and exclusion.* Oxford: Clarendon.

Mutchler, J. E., Baker, L. E., & Lee, S. (2007). Grandparents responsible for grandchildren in Native-American families. *Social Science Quarterly, 88*(4), 990–1009.

Mutharayappa, R., Choe, M. K., Arnold, F., & Roy, T. K. (1997, March). *Son preference and its effect on fertility in India* (National Family Survey Subject Reports No. 3). Honolulu: East-West Center Program on Population. Retrieved from http://scholarspace.manoa.hawaii.edu/bitstream/handle/10125/3475/NFHSsubjrpt003.pdf?sequence=1

Myrdal, G. (1963). *Challenge to affluence.* New York: Random House.

Narayan, U., & Harding, S. (2000). *Decentering the center: Philosophy for a multicultural, postcolonial, and feminist world.* Bloomington: Indiana University Press.

National Alliance to End Homelessness. (2012). Executive summary. In *The state of homelessness in America 2012.* Washington, DC: Author. Retrieved from http://www.endhomelessness.org/content/article/detail/4361

National Assessment of Adult Literacy. (2011). Definition of literacy. Retrieved from http://nces.ed.gov/naal/fr_definition.asp

National Association of Colleges and Employers. (2014). *NACE salary survey: Starting salaries for new college graduates.* Bethlehem, PA: Author. Retrieved from http://www.naceweb.org/uploadedFiles/Content/static-assets/downloads/executive-summary/2014-january-salary-survey-executive-summary.pdf

National Association of the Deaf. (2000). NAD position statement on cochlear implants. Retrieved from http://www.nad.org/issues/technology/assistive-listening/cochlear-implants

National Association of Realtors. (2006). *Annual report.* Retrieved from http://archive.realtor.org/article/national-association-realtors®-2006-annual-report

National Campaign to Prevent Teen Pregnancy. (2010). Why it matters: Teen pregnancy, poverty, and income disparity. Retrieved from http://www.thenationalcampaign.org

National Center for Charitable Statistics. (2009). Number of nonprofit organizations in the United States, 1999–2009. Retrieved from http://nccs.urban.org/statistics/profiles.cfm

National Center for Education Statistics. (2009). Gender: Grade point average. Nation's Report Card, National Assessment of Educational Progress. Retrieved from http://www.nationsreportcard.gov/hsts_2009/gender_gpa.asp

National Center for Education Statistics. (2011a). Fast facts: Distance learning. Retrieved from http://nces.ed.gov/fastfacts/display.asp?id=80

National Center for Education Statistics. (2011b). Table 209. Recent high school completers and their enrollment in 2-year and 4-year colleges, by sex: 1960 through 2010. In *Digest of education statistics.* Retrieved from http://nces.ed.gov/programs/digest/d11/tables/dt11_209.asp

National Center for Education Statistics. (2011c). Table 345. Graduation rates of first-time postsecondary students who started as full-time degree/certificate-seeking students, by sex, race/ethnicity, time to completion, and level and control of institution where student started: Selected cohort entry years, 1996 through 2007. In *Digest of education statistics.* Retrieved from http://nces.ed.gov/programs/digest/d11/tables/dt11_345.asp

National Center for Education Statistics. (2011d). Table 393. Literacy skills of adults, by type of literacy, proficiency levels, and selected characteristics: 1992 and 2003. In *Digest of education statistics.* Retrieved from http://nces.ed.gov/programs/digest/d10/tables/dt10_393.asp

National Center for Education Statistics. (2013a). Table 219.70. Percentage of high school dropouts among persons 16 through 24 years old (status dropout rate), by sex and race/ethnicity: Selected years, 1960 through 2012. In *Digest of education statistics.*

Retrieved from http://nces.ed.gov/programs/digest/d13/tables/dt13_219.70.asp

National Center for Education Statistics. (2013b). Table 302.10. Recent high school completers and their enrollment in 2-year and 4-year colleges, by sex: 1960 through 2012. In *Digest of education statistics.* Retrieved from http://nces.ed.gov/programs/digest/d13/tables/dt13_302.10.asp

National Center for Health Statistics. (2012). *Aggregate data 1950–2010.* Atlanta, GA: Centers for Disease Control and Prevention.

National Center for Injury Prevention and Control. (2014). *Understanding teen dating violence: Fact sheet.* Washington, DC: Centers for Disease Control and Prevention. Retrieved from http://www.cdc.gov/violenceprevention/pdf/teen-dating-violence-2014-a.pdf

National Center for Victims of Crime (2012). Intimate partner violence. Retrieved from http://www.victimsofcrime.org/library/crime-information-and-statistics/intimate-partner-violence

National Coalition for the Homeless. (2007). *Domestic violence and homelessness fact sheet.* Washington, DC: Author. Retrieved from http://www.nationalhomeless.org/publications/facts/domestic.pdf

National Coalition for the Homeless. (2009a). Domestic violence and homelessness. Retrieved from http://www.nationalhomeless.org/factsheets/domestic.html

National Coalition for the Homeless. (2009b). Employment and homelessness. Retrieved from http://www.nationalhomeless.org/factsheets/employment.html

National Conference of State Legislatures. (2014). Voter identification requirements: Photo ID laws. Retrieved from http://www.ncsl.org/research/elections-and-campaigns/voter-id.aspx#map

National Employment Law Project. (2014, April). *The low-wage recovery: Industry employment and wages four years into the recovery* (Data Brief). New York: Author. Retrieved from http://www.nelp.org/page/-/reports/low-wage-recovery-industry-employment-wages-2014-report.pdf?nocdn=1

National Foundation for Educational Research in England and Wales. (2009). INCA (International Review of Curriculum and Assessment Frameworks) Internet archive: Table 15.1. Organisation of school year. Retrieved from http://www.inca.org.uk/Table15.pdf

National Institute of Justice. (2011, September 13). Terrorism. Retrieved from http://www.nij.gov/topics/crime/terrorism/welcome.htm

National Institute of Mental Health. (2010). The numbers count: Mental disorders in America. Retrieved from http://www.nimh.nih.gov/health/publications/the-numbers-count-mental-disorders-in-america/index.shtml#Hudson

National Law Center on Homelessness and Poverty. (2010). *Homelessness and poverty in America: Real solutions.* Washington, DC: Author. Retrieved from http://www.nlchp.org/hapia.cfm

National Law Center on Homelessness and Poverty. (n.d.). *Some facts on homelessness, housing, and violence against women.* Washington, DC: Author. Retrieved from http://www.nlchp.org/content/pubs/Some%20Facts%20on%20Homeless%20and%20DV.pdf

National Low Income Housing Coalition. (2009). Out of reach: Persistent problems, new challenges for renters. Retrieved from http://www.nationalhomeless.org/factsheets/employment.html#1

National Organization for Women. (n.d.). Education and Title IX. Retrieved from http://www.now.org/issues/title_ix/index.html

National Public Radio. (2010, November 5). Counting crowds: Results may very. *Science Friday.* Retrieved from http://www.npr.org/templates/story/story.php?storyId=131099075

National Survey of Student Engagement. (2012). *Fostering student engagement campuswide: Annual results 2012.* Bloomington: Indiana University Center for Postsecondary Research. Retrieved from http://nsse.iub.edu/html/annual_results.cfm

Natural Resources Defense Council. (2011, July 8). Meals of mass destruction: Shrimp. Retrieved from http://www.nrdc.org/living/shoppingwise/meals-mass-destruction-shrimp.asp

Naylor, N. T. (2002). *Wages of crime: Black markets, illegal finance, and the underworld economy.* Ithaca, NY: Cornell University Press.

Neal, R. W. (2014, January 16). Facebook gets older: Demographic report shows 3 million teens left social network in 3 years. International Business Times. Retrieved from http://www.ibtimes.com/facebook-gets-older-demographic-report-shows-3-million-teens-left-social-network-3-years-1543092

Netcraft. (2012). News: March 2012 Web server survey. Retrieved from http://news.netcraft.com/archives/2012/03/05/march-2012-web-server-survey.html

Neuman, W. L. (2000). *Social research methods: Qualitative and quantitative approaches.* Toronto: Allyn & Bacon.

Newcomb, T. C. (2008). *Parameters of parenting in Native American families* (Doctoral dissertation, Oklahoma State University). Retrieved from ProQuest (3320882).

Newport, F. (2012, May 8). Half of Americans support legal gay marriage. Gallup Politics. Retrieved from http://www.gallup.com/poll/154529/half-americans-support-legal-gay-marriage.aspx

Neyazi, T. A. (2010). Cultural imperialism or vernacular modernity? Hindi newspapers in a globalizing India. *Media, Culture & Society, 32*(6), 907–924.

Niarchos, C. N. (1995). War and rape: Challenges facing the International Tribunal for the Former Yugoslavia. *Human Rights Quarterly, 17*(4).

Nicholas, S. E. (2009). "I live Hopi, I just don't speak it": The critical intersection of language, culture and identity in the lives of contemporary Hopi youth. *Journal of Language, Identity & Education, 8*(5), 321–334.

Niebuhr, H. R. (1929). *The social sources of denominationalism.* New York: Meridian Books.

Nielsen. (2010). *Social media, games, email dominate Web time.* New York: Author.

Nielsen. (2011). *State of the media: The cross-platform report.* New York: Author.

Nisbet, R. (1970). *The social bond: An introduction to the study of society.* New York: Knopf.

Nolan, P., & Lenski, G. (2009). *Human societies: An introduction to macrosociology.* Boulder, CO: Paradigm.

Nordhoff, C. (1975). *The communistic societies of the United States.* New York: Harper & Row. (Original work published 1875)

Norris, M. (2011, July 8). Why Black women, infants lag in birth outcomes. National Public Radio. Retrieved from http://www.npr.org/2011/07/08/137652226/-the-race-gap

NPD Group. (2006, September 19). Report from the NPD Group shows 45 percent of heavy video gamers are in the six- to 17-year-old age group. BusinessWire. Retrieved from http://www.businesswire.com/news/home/20060919005153/en/Report-NPD-Group-Shows-45-Percent-Heavy

Nuland, S. B. (2003). *The doctors' plague: Germs, childbed fever, and the strange story of Ignac Semmelweis.* New York: Norton.

Oakes, J. (1985). *Keeping track: How schools structure inequality.* New Haven, CT: Yale University Press.

Obama administration must do more to protect children harvesting tobacco. (2014, May 18). *Washington Post.* Retrieved from http://www.washingtonpost.com/opinions/obama-administration-must-do-more-to-protect-children-harvesting-tobacco/2014/05/18/23b8a7c4-dd36-11e3-b745-87d39690c5c0_story.html

Oberschall, A. (1973). *Social conflict and social movements.* Englewood Cliffs, NJ: Prentice Hall.

O'Dea. T. (1966). *The sociology of religion.* Upper Saddle River, NJ: Prentice Hall.

Offe, C. (1984). *Contradictions of the welfare state.* Cambridge: MIT Press.

Office of Juvenile Justice and Delinquency Prevention. (2010). Statistical briefing book: Juveniles as offenders. Retrieved from http://www.ojjdp.gov/ojstatbb/offenders/qa03301.asp

Ogden, C. L., Carroll, M. D., Kit, B. K., & Flegal, K. M. (2012). *Prevalence of obesity in the United States, 2009–2010* (NCHS Data Brief 82). Hyattsville, MD: National Center for Health Statistics. Retrieved from http://www.cdc.gov/nchs/data/databriefs/db82.pdf

Ogden, C. L., Lamb, M. M., Carroll, M. D., & Flegal, K. M. (2010). *Obesity and socioeconomic status in adults, 2005–2008* (NCHS Data Brief 50). Hyattsville, MD: National Center for Health Statistics. Retrieved from http://www.cdc.gov/nchs/data/databriefs/db50.pdf

Ogunlesi, T., & Busari, S. (2012, September 14). Seven ways mobile phones have changed lives in Africa. CNN. Retrieved from http://www.cnn.com/2012/09/13/world/africa/mobile-phones-change-africa

Ogunwole, S. U., Drewery, M. P., Jr., & Rios-Vargas, M. (2012). *The population with a bachelor's degree or higher by race and Hispanic origin: 2006–2010* (American Community Survey Brief 10-19). Washington, DC: U.S. Census Bureau. Retrieved from http://www.census.gov/prod/2012pubs/acsbr10-19.pdf

O'Leary, A. (2012, August 2). In virtual play, sex harassment is all too real. *New York Times.* Retrieved from http://www.nytimes.com/2012/08/02/us/sexual-harass ment-in-online-gaming-stirs-anger.html

Omvedt, G. (1992). "Green earth, women's power, human liberation": Woman in peasant movements in India. *Development Dialogue, 1*(2), 116–130.

O'Neill, T. (2007, February). Curse of the black gold: Hope and betrayal on the Niger Delta. *National Geographic.* Retrieved from http://ngm.nationalgeographic.com/2007/02/nigerian-oil/oneill-text

Orfield, G., & Eaton, S. E. (1996). *Dismantling desegregation: The quiet reversal of* Brown v. Board of Education. New York: Norton.

Organisation for Economic Co-operation and Development. (2011). Chart A1.1. Percentage of population that has attained tertiary education, by age group (2009). In *Education at a glance.* Paris: Author. Retrieved from http://www.oecd.org/education/highereducationandadultlearning/48630299.pdf

Orszag, P. (2012, April 19). Get rid of the 3 p.m. school day. *Washington Post.* Retrieved from http://www.washingtonpost.com/opinions/get-rid-of-the-3-pm-school-day/2012/04/19/gIQAbka3TT_story.html

Osborne, D., & Wagner, W. E. (2007). Exploring the relationship between homophobia and participation in core sports among high school students. *Sociological Perspectives, 50*(4), 597–613.

Oyoo, G. O. (2003, December). Impact of HIV/AIDS on education in the sub-Saharan Africa. *East African Medical Journal,* pp. 609–610. Retrieved from http://ajol.info/index.php/eamj/article/viewFile/8775/1904

Paglen, T., & Thompson, A. C. (2006). *Torture taxi: On the trail of the CIA's rendition flights.* Hoboken, NJ: Melville House.

Paoli, L. (2003). *Mafia brotherhoods: Organized crime Italian style.* Oxford: Oxford University Press.

Pape, R. (2005). *Dying to win: The strategic logic of suicide terrorism.* New York: Random House.

Parente, S. L. (2008). Narrowing the economic gap in the 21st century. In K. R. Holmes, E. J. Feulner, & M. A. O'Grady (Eds.), *2008 index of economic freedom.* Washington, DC: Heritage Foundation.

Park, P. (1993). *Voices of change: Participatory research in the United States and Canada.* Westport, CT: Bergin & Garvey.

Park, R. E., & Burgess, E. (1921). *An introduction to the science of sociology.* Chicago: University of Chicago Press

Parker-Pope, T. (2010, April 14). Is marriage good for your health? *New York Times Magazine.* Retrieved from http://www.nytimes.com/2010/04/18/magazine/18marriage-t.html?pagewanted=all

Parkin, F. (1979). Social closure and class formation. In A. Giddens & D. Held (Eds.), *Classes, power, and conflict* (pp. 175–184). Los Angeles: University of California Press.

Parrado, E. A., & Morgan, S. P. (2008). Intergeneration fertility among Hispanic women: New evidence of immigrant assimilation. *Demography, 45*(3), 651–671.

Parsons, T. (1951). *The social system.* New York: Free Press.

Parsons, T. (1954). The kinship system of the contemporary United States. In *Essays in sociological theory* (pp. 189–194). New York: Free Press.

Parsons, T. (1960). Some principle characteristics of industrial societies. In T. Parson (Ed.), *Structure and process in modern societies* (pp. 132–168). New York: Free Press.

Parsons, T. (1966). *Societies: Evolutionary and comparative perspectives.* Upper Saddle River, NJ: Prentice Hall.

Parsons, T. (1967). *The structure of social action.* New York: Free Press.

Parsons, T. (1970). On building social system theory: A personal history. *Daedalus, 99*(4), 826–881.

Parsons, T. (1975). The sick role and the role of the physician reconsidered. *Milbank Memorial Fund Quarterly, Health and Society, 53*(3), 257–278.

Parsons, T. (2007). *Social structure and personality.* New York: Free Press. (Original work published 1964)

Parsons, T., & Bales, R. F. (1955). *Family, socialization and interaction process.* Glencoe, IL: Free Press.

Parsons, T., & Mayhew, H. D. (1982). *On institutions and social evolution: Selected writings.* Chicago: University of Chicago Press.

Parsons, T., & Shils, E. (2001). *Toward a general theory of action: Theoretical foundations for the social sciences.* New Brunswick, NJ: Transaction.

Parsons, T., & Smelser, N. J. (1956). *Economy and society.* New York: Free Press.

Pascoe, C. J. (2007). *Dude, you're a fag: Masculinity and sexuality in high school.* Berkeley: University of California Press.

Passel, J. S., Wang, W., & Taylor, P. (2010). *Marrying out: One-in-seven new U.S. marriages is interracial or interethnic.* Washington, DC: Pew Research Center. Retrieved from http://www.pewsocialtrends.org/files/2010/10/755-marrying-out.pdf

Patterson, D. (1989). *Power in law enforcement: Subordinate preference and actual use of power base in special weapons teams (SWAT)* (Doctoral dissertation, Fielding Institute, Santa Barbara, CA).

PBS. (2010, May 31). China faces growing health threat from prevalent tobacco use. *NewsHour.* Retrieved from http://www.pbs.org/newshour/bb/health/jan-june10/tobacco_05-31.html

PBS. (2011). Caught in the crossfire: Arab Americans. *9/11 stories.* Retrieved from http://www.pbs.org/itvs/caughtinthecrossfire/arab_americans.html

Pearlstein, S. (2010, October 6). The costs of rising economic inequality. *Washington Post.* Retrieved from http://www.washingtonpost.com/wp-dyn/content/article/2010/10/05/AR2010100505535.html

Peek, K. L. (1999). *The good, the bad, and the "misunderstood": A study of the cognitive moral development theory and ethics in the public sector.* Fort Lauderdale, FL: Nova Southeastern University.

Perlin, R. (2011). *Intern nation: How to earn nothing and learn little in the brave new economy.* New York: Verso.

Perlin, R. (2012, February 6). These are not your father's internships. *New York Times.* Retrieved from http://www.nytimes.com/roomfordebate/2012/02/04/do-unpaid-internships-exploit-college-students/todays-internships-are-a-racket-not-an-opportunity

Perry, M. J. (2013, May 13). Stunning college degree gap: Women have earned almost 10 million more college degrees than men since 1982. American Enterprise Institute, Ideas blog. Retrieved from http://www.aei-ideas.org/2013/05/stunning-college-degree-gap-women-have-earned-almost-10-million-more-college-degrees-than-men-since-1982

Peters, G. (2013). State of the Union addresses and messages: Research notes. American Presidency Project. Retrieved from http://www.presidency.ucsb.edu/sou.php

Pethos, A., Fallis, D. S., & Keating, D. (2013, November 2). ShotSpotter detection system documents 39,000 shooting incidents in the District. *Washington Post.* Retrieved from http://www.washingtonpost.com/investigations/shotspotter-detection-system-documents-39000-shooting-incidents-in-the-district/2013/11/02/055f8e9c-2ab1-11e3-8ade-a1f23cda135e_story.html

Pettit, K. L. S., & Reuben, K. (2010). *Investor-owners in the boom and bust.* Urban Institute. Retrieved from http://metrotrends.org/mortgagelending.html

Pew Forum on Religion and Public Life. (2004, June 14). Supreme Court upholds "under God" in Pledge of Allegiance: Court overturns lower court ruling on legal technicality. Retrieved from http://www.pewforum.org/Press-Room/Press-Releases/Supreme-Court-Upholds-Under-God-in-Pledge-of-Allegiance.aspx

Pew Forum on Religion and Public Life. (2008). *Summary of key findings: U.S. Religious Landscape Survey.* Washington, DC: Pew Research Center.

Pew Forum on Religion and Public Life. (2010). *Religion among the millennials.* Washington, DC: Pew Research Center. Retrieved from http://www.pewforum.org/files/2010/02/millennials-report.pdf

Pew Forum on Religion and Public Life. (2011a). *The future of the global Muslim population: Projections for 2010–2030.* Washington, DC: Pew Research Center. Retrieved from http://www.pewforum.org/files/2011/01/FutureGlobalMuslimPopulation-WebPDF-Feb10.pdf

Pew Forum on Religion and Public Life. (2011b, February 23). The Tea Party and religion. Retrieved from http://pewforum.org/Politics-and-Elections/Tea-Party-and-Religion.aspx

Pew Forum on Religion and Public Life. (2012a). *The global religious landscape: A report on the size and distribution of the world's major religious groups as of 2010.* Washington, DC: Pew Research Center. Retrieved from http://www.pewforum.org/files/2014/01/global-religion-full.pdf

Pew Forum on Religion and Public Life. (2012b). *"Nones" on the rise: One-in-five adults have no religious affiliation.* Washington, DC: Pew Research Center. Retrieved from http://www.pewforum.org/files/2012/10/NonesOnTheRise-full.pdf

Pew Research Center. (2008, July 13). Hispanic Trends Project: 2008 national survey of Latinos. Retrieved from http://www.pewhispanic.org/2008/07/13/2008-national-survey-of-latinos

Pew Research Center. (2011, June 2). *Republican candidates stir little enthusiasm.* Washington, DC: Author. Retrieved from http://www.people-press.org/files/legacy-pdf/06-02-11%202012%20Campaign%20Release.pdf

Pew Research Center. (2012a, April 25). *More support for gun rights, gay marriage than in 2008 or 2004.* Washington, DC: Author. Retrieved from http://www.people-press.org/files/legacy-pdf/4-25-12%20Social%20Issues.pdf

Pew Research Center. (2012b). *The rise of Asian Americans.* Washington, DC: Author. Retrieved from http://www.pewsocialtrends.org/2012/06/19/the-rise-of-asian-americans

Pew Research Center. (2014a, January 27). Climate change: Key data points from Pew Research. Retrieved from http://www.pewresearch.org/key-data-points/climate-change-key-data-points-from-pew-research

Pew Research Center. (2014b). *Older adults and technology use.* Washington, DC: Author. Retrieved from http://www.pewinternet.org/files/2014/04/PIP_Seniors-and-Tech-Use_040314.pdf

Pew Research Center for the People and the Press. (2012, November 26). Young voters supported Obama less, but may have mattered more. Retrieved from http://www.people-press.org/2012/11/26/young-voters-supported-obama-less-but-may-have-mattered-more

Phelan, A. M., & McLaughlin, H. J. (1995). Educational discoveries: The nature of the child and practices of new teachers. *Journal of Teacher Education, 46*(3), 165–174.

Phelps, R. J., et al. (1982). *Wisconsin female juvenile offender study project summary report.* Wisconsin: Youth Policy and Law Center, Wisconsin Council on Juvenile Justice.

Piaget, J. (1926). *The language and thought of the child.* New York: Harcourt, Brace.

Piaget, J. (1928). *Judgment and reasoning in the child.* New York: Harcourt, Brace.

Piaget, J. (1930). *The child's conception of physical causality.* New York: Harcourt, Brace.

Piaget, J. (1932). *The moral judgment of the child.* New York: Harcourt, Brace.

Pike, J. (2013). The world at war: Current conflicts. GlobalSecurity.org. Retrieved from http://www.globalsecurity.org/military/world/war

Pinterest. (2012). What is Pinterest? Retrieved from http://pinterest.com/about

Pipes, D., & Durán, K. (2002, August). *Muslim immigrants in the United States.* Washington, DC: Center for Immigration Studies. Retrieved from http://www.cis.org/sites/cis.org/files/articles/2002/back802.pdf

Piven, F. F., & Cloward, R. A. (1977). *Poor people's movements: Why they succeed, how they fail.* New York: Random House.

Platt, K. H. (2007, July 9). Chinese air pollution deadliest in the world, report says. National Geographic News. Retrieved from http://news.nationalgeographic.com/news/2007/07/070709-china-pollution.html

Podsakoff, P., & Schriesheim, C. (1985). Field studies of French and Raven's bases of power: Critique, reanalysis, and suggestions for future research. *Psychological Bulletin, 97*(3), 387–411.

Polaris Project. (2013). Human trafficking statistics. Retrieved from http://www.polarisproject.org

Polivy, J., & Herman, P. (2007). Is the body the self? Women and body image. *Collegium Anthropologicum, 31,* 63–67.

Pond, L. (2012, May 31). Why I watched a snake-handling pastor die for his faith. *Washington Post.* Retrieved from http://www.washingtonpost.com/lifestyle/style/why-i-watched-a-snake-handling-pastor-die-for-his-faith/2012/05/31/gJQA3fRP5U_story.html

Ponton, L. (2000). *The sex lives of teenagers.* New York: Dutton.

Popkin, B. M., Adair, L. S., & Ng, S. W. (2012). Global nutrition transition and the pandemic of obesity in developing countries. *Nutrition Reviews, 70*(1), 3–21.

Popper, K. (1959). *The logic of scientific discovery.* New York: Basic Books.

Population Reference Bureau. (2010). *2010 world population data sheet.* Washington, DC: Author. Retrieved from http://www.prb.org/pdf10/10wpds_eng.pdf

Population Reference Bureau. (2011). *2011 world population data sheet.* Washington, DC: Author. Retrieved from http://www.prb.org/pdf11/2011population-data-sheet_eng.pdf

Population Reference Bureau. (2012). *2012 world population data sheet.* Washington, DC: Author. Retrieved from http://www.prb.org/pdf12/2012-popu lation-data-sheet_eng.pdf

Population Reference Bureau. (2013). *2013 world population data sheet.* Washington, DC: Author. Retrieved from http://www.prb.org/pdf13/2013-population-data-sheet_eng.pdf

Poteet, G. A. (2007). *Perceptions of pretty people: An experimental study of interpersonal attractiveness* (Master's thesis, Washington State University). Retrieved from http://www.dissertations.wsu.edu/Thesis/Spring2007/a_poteet_050307.pdf

Pough, G. D. (2004). *Check it while I wreck it: Black womanhood, hip hop culture, and the public sphere.* Boston: Northeastern University Press.

Powell, B., Bolzendahl, C., Geist, C., & Steelman, L. C. (2010). *Counted out: Same-sex relations and Americans' definitions of family.* New York: Russell Sage Foundation.

Power, S. (2002). *"A problem from hell": America and the age of genocide.* New York: Basic Books.

Prell, R. (1999). *Fighting to become Americans: Jews, gender, and the anxiety of assimilation.* Boston: Beacon Press.

Preston, P. (1994). *Mother father deaf: Living between sound and silence.* Cambridge, MA: Harvard University Press.

Preves, S. E. (2003). *Intersex and identity: The contested self.* New Brunswick, NJ: Rutgers University Press.

Putnam, R. (2000). *Bowling alone: The collapse and revival of American community.* New York: Simon & Schuster.

Qian, J., Cai, M., Gao, J., Tang, S., Xu, L., & Critchley, J. A. (2010). Trends in smoking and quitting in China from 1993 to 2003: National Health Service survey data. *Bulletin of the World Health Organization, 88*(10). Retrieved from http://www.who.int/bulletin/volumes/88/10/09-064709/en/index.tml

Queen, S. A., Habenstein, R. W., & Adams, J. B. (1961). *The family in various cultures* (2nd ed.). Philadelphia: J. B. Lippincott.

Quiggin, J. (2010). *Zombie economics: How dead ideas still walk among us.* Princeton, NJ: Princeton University Press.

Quinney, R. (1970). *Crime and justice in America.* New York: Little, Brown.

Rabiner, S. (2012, March 12). Facebook friend suggestion gets man charged with bigamy. Reuters News Agency. Retrieved from http://blogs.findlaw.com/legally_weird/2012/03/facebook-friend-suggestion-gets-man-charged-with-bigamy.html

Rampell, C. (2010, March 9). Why a Big Mac costs less than a salad. *New York Times.* Retrieved from http://economix.blogs.nytimes.com/2010/03/09/why-a-big-mac-costs-less-than-a-salad

Randall, V. R. (1999). History of tobacco. Boston University Medical Center. Retrieved from http://academic.udayton.edu/health/syllabi/tobacco/history.htm#industry

Rashid, A. (2000). *Taliban: Militant Islam, oil, and fundamentalism in Central Asia.* New York: I. B. Tauris.

Ratner, M., & Ray, E. (2004). *Guantánamo: What the world should know.* New York: Chelsea Green.

Raven, B., & Kruglianski, W. (1975). Conflict and power. In P. Swingle (Ed.), *Structure of conflict* (pp. 177–219). New York: Academic Press.

Ray, D. P., & Ghahremani, Y. (2014). Credit card statistics, industry facts, debt statistics. CreditCards.com. Retrieved from http://www.creditcards.com/credit-card-news/credit-card-industry-facts-personal-debt-statistics-1276.php

Reaney, P., & Goldsmith, B. (2008, April 4). Husbands create 7 hours of extra housework a week: Study. Reuters. Retrieved from http://www.reuters.com/article/2008/04/04/us-housework-husbands-idUSN0441782220080404

Reich, R. (1991). *The work of nations: Preparing ourselves for 21st century capitalism.* New York: First Vintage Books.

Reich, R. (2001, April 9). The case (once again) for universal health insurance. *American Prospect.* Retrieved from http://prospect.org/article/case-once-again-universal-health-insurance

Reich, R. (2010). *Aftershock: The next economy and America's future.* New York: Knopf.

Reich, R. (2014, June 2). Walmart workers are going on strike to speak out. Why Walmart should listen. *Christian Science Monitor.* Retrieved from: http://www.csmonitor.com/Business/Robert-Reich/2014/0602/Walmart-workers-are-going-on-strike-to-speak-out.-Why-Walmart-should-listen

Reiman, J., & Leighton, P. (2012). *The rich get richer and the poor get prison.* New York: Prentice Hall.

Reinders, G. (2006). *Women's reactions to a realistic rape portrayal and the influence of feminist identity and rape myth acceptance* (Doctoral dissertation, University of Missouri). Retrieved from https://mospace.umsystem.edu/xmlui/bitstream/handle/10355/4482/research.pdf?sequence=3

Renjini, D. (2000). *Nayar women today: Disintegration of matrilineal system and the status of Nayar women in Kerala.* India: India Classical.

Renzetti, C. M., & Curran, D. J. (1992). *Women, men, and society* (2nd ed.). Boston: Allyn & Bacon.

Republic of Botswana. (2012). *Progress report of the national response to the 2011 declaration of commitments on HIV and AIDS.* Retrieved from http://www.unaids.org/en/dataanalysis/knowyourresponse/countryprogressreports/2012countries/ce_BW_Narrative_Report%5B1%5D.pdf

Republic of South Africa. (2012). *Global AIDS response progress report 2012.* Johannesburg: South African National AIDS Council.

Residents of Hull House. (1895). *Hull House maps and papers.* New York: Thomas Y. Crowell.

Reskin, B., & Padavic, I. (2002). *Women and men at work* (2nd ed.). Thousand Oaks, CA: Sage.

Richards, C. (2012). Playing under surveillance: Gender performance and the conduct of the self in a primary school playground. *British Journal of Sociology of Education, 33,* 373–390.

Richardson, E. G., & Hemenway, D. (2011). Homicide, suicide, and unintentional firearm fatality: Comparing the United States with other high-income countries, 2003. *Journal of Trauma, Injury, Infection, and Critical Care, 70*(1), 238–43.

Richardson, J. (2009). Satanism in America: An update. *Social Compass, 56*(4), 552–563.

Ridgeway, C. L., & Correll, S. J. (2004). Unpacking the gender system: A theoretical perspective on gender beliefs and social relations. *Gender & Society, 18*(4), 510–531.

Ridgeway, C. L., & Smith-Lovin, L. (1999). The gender system and interaction. *Annual Review of Sociology, 25,* 191–217.

Ridley, M. (1998). *The origins of virtue: Human instincts and the evolution of cooperation.* New York: Viking Press.

Rieff, D. (2011, September/October). Millions may die . . . or not. *Foreign Policy,* pp. 22–25.

Riley, C. (2012, March 26). Can 46 rich dudes buy an election? CNNMoney. Retrieved from http://money.cnn.com/2012/03/26/news/economy/super-pac-donors/index.htm

Riordan, C. (1990). *Girls and boys in school: Together or separate?* New York: Teachers College Press.

Rist, R. S. (1970). Student, social class, and teacher expectations: The self-fulfilling prophecy in ghetto education. *Harvard Educational Review, 40,* 411–451.

Ritzer, G. (1999). *Enchanting a disenchanted world: Revolutionizing the means of consumption.* Thousand Oaks, CA: Pine Forge.

Ritzer, G. (2007). *The globalization of nothing.* Thousand Oaks, CA: Pine Forge.

Ritzer, G. (2010). *The McDonaldization of society* (5th ed.). Thousand Oaks, CA: Sage.

Riverson, J., Kunieda, M., Roberts, P., Lewi, N., & Walker, W. M. (2006). *The challenges in addressing gender dimensions of transport in developing countries: Lessons from the World Bank's projects.* Paper presented at the annual meeting of the Transportation Research Board. Retrieved from http://siteresources.worldbank.org/INTTSR/Resources/462613-1152683444211/06-0592.pdf

Roof, W. C. (1993). *A generation of seekers: Spiritual journeys of the baby boom generation.* San Francisco: HarperSanFrancisco.

Roof, W. C., & McKinney, W. (1990). *American mainline religion: Its changing shape and future.* New Brunswick, NJ: Rutgers University Press.

Roquemore, K., & Brunsma, D. L. (2008). *Beyond Black: Biracial identity in America.* Lanham, MD: Rowman & Littlefield.

Roschelle, A. R., & Kaufman, P. (2004). Fitting in and fighting back: Stigma management strategies among homeless kids. *Symbolic Interaction, 27*(1), 23–46. Retrieved from http://onlinelibrary.wiley.com/doi/10.1525/si.2004.27.1.23/abstract

Rosellini, L., & Mulrine, A. (1998, April 13). When to spank. *U.S. News & World Report,* pp. 52–53, 55.

Rosenbaum, S. (2013, September 4). Pledge of Allegiance challenged in Massachusetts Supreme Court. NBC News. Retrieved from http://www.nbcnews.com/news/us-news/pledge-allegiance-challenged-massachusetts-supreme-court-v20327848

Rosenbloom, S. R., & Way, N. (2004). Experiences of discrimination among African American, Asian American, and Latino adolescents in an urban high school. *Youth & Society, 35*(4), 420–451.

Rosenthal, R., & Jacobson, L. (1968). *Pygmalion in the classroom.* New York: Holt, Rinehart & Winston.

Rosoff, S., Pontell, H., & Tillman, R. (2010). *Profit without honor: White-collar crime and the looting of America.* Upper Saddle River, NJ: Prentice Hall.

Rosser, P. (1989). *The SAT gender gap: Identifying the causes.* Washington, DC: Center for Women Policy Studies.

Rostow, W. W. (1961). *The stages of economic growth.* Cambridge: Cambridge University Press.

Rothe, D. L. (2009). *State criminality: The crime of all crimes.* Lanham, MD: Lexington Books.

Rothkopf, D. (2008). *Superclass: The global power elite and the world they are making.* New York: Farrar, Straus and Giroux.

Rothschild, J., & Whitt, A. (1987). *The cooperative workplace: Potentials and dilemmas of organizational democracy and participation.* New York: Cambridge University Press.

Rothschild-Whitt, J. (1979). The collectivist organization: An alternative to rational-bureaucratic models. *American Sociological Review, 44,* 509–527.

Rott, N. (2010, October 2). Bilingual D.C. homeless shelter to close. *Washington Post.* Retrieved from http://www.washingtonpost.com/wp-dyn/content/article/2010/10/01/AR2010100107181.html

Rowbotham, S. (1973). *Woman's consciousness, man's world.* Middlesex, England: Pelican.

Rubin, B. (1996). *Shifts in the social contract: Understanding change in American society.* Thousand Oaks, CA: Pine Forge.

Rubin, L. B. (2006). What am I going to do with the rest of my life? *Dissent, 53*(4), 88–94.

Rule, J. B. (1999). Silver bullets or land rushes? Sociologies of cyberspace. *Contemporary Sociology, 28*(6), 661–664.

Ruthven, M. (2011). The birth of Islam: A different view. *New York Review of Books, 58*(6), 80–84.

Ryan, R. A. (1981). Strengths of the American Indian family: State of the art. In F. Hoffman (Ed.), *The American Indian family: Strengths and stresses.* Isleta, NM: American Indian Social Research and Development Associates.

Rymer, R. (1993). *Genie: A scientific tragedy.* New York: HarperCollins.

Rymer, R. (2012, July). Vanishing voices. *National Geographic,* pp. 60–93.

Saad, L. (2012, March 30). In U.S., global warming views steady despite warm weather. Gallup Politics. Retrieved from http://www.gallup.com/poll/153608/Global-Warming-Views-Steady-Despite-Warm-Winter.aspx

Sabo, D. F., Miller, K. E., Farrell, M. P., Melnick, M. J., & Barnes, G. M. (1999). High school athletic participation, sexual behavior, and adolescent pregnancy: A regional study. *Journal of Adolescent Health, 25*(2), 597–613.

Sadker, D. M., & Sadker, M. P. (1997). *Failing at fairness: How our schools cheat girls.* New York: Scribner.

Sadker, D. M., & Zittleman, K. (2009). *Still failing at fairness: How gender bias cheats girls and boys in school and what we can do about it.* New York: Scribner.

Sadker, D. M., Zittleman, K., & Sadker, M. P. (2003). *Teachers, schools, and society.* New York: McGraw-Hill.

Saez, E. (2010). *Striking it richer: The evolution of top incomes in the United States (updated with 2008 estimates).* Retrieved from http://elsa.berkeley.edu/~saez/saez-UStopincomes-2008.pdf

Saez, E. (2013). *Striking it richer: The evolution of top incomes in the United States (updated with 2011 estimates).* Retrieved from http://elsa.berkeley.edu/~saez/saez-UStopincomes-2011.pdf

Sagan, E. (1992). *The honey and the hemlock: Democracy and paranoia in ancient Athens and modern America.* New York: Basic Books.

Sagan, L. L. (1987). *The health of nations: True causes of sickness and well-being.* New York: Basic Book.

Sahlins, M. D., & Service, E. R. (1960). *Evolution and culture.* Ann Arbor, MI: Ann Arbor Paperbacks.

Salaita, S. (2005). Ethnic identity and imperative patriotism: Arab Americans before and after 9/11. *College Literature, 32*(2), 146–168.

Salary.com. (2014). Salary.com's 14th annual Mom Salary Survey. Retrieved from http://www.salary.com/mom-paycheck

Saltsman, M. (2014, January 29). The employee of the month has a battery. *Wall Street Journal.* Retrieved from http://online.wsj.com/news/articles/SB10001424052702303448204579342422527561620

Sampson, R. J., & Laub, J. H. (1990). Crime and deviance over the life course: The salience of adult social bonds. *American Sociological Review, 55,* 609–627.

Sanday, P. R. (1990). *Fraternity gang rape: Sex, brotherhood, and privilege on campus.* New York: New York University Press.

Sanders, T. (2011, July 9). The lighter the skin, the shorter the prison term? The Root. Retrieved from http://newamericamedia.org/2011/07/the-lighter-the-skin-the-shorter-the-prison-term.php

Sandoz, M. (1961). *These were the Sioux.* New York: Dell.

Sassen, S. (1991). *The global city: New York, London, Tokyo.* Princeton, NJ: Princeton University Press.

Sassen, S. (2000). *Cities in a world economy* (2nd ed.). Thousand Oaks, CA: Pine Forge.

Schabner, D. (2012, April 2). Trump won't bar transsexual beauty queen from shot at Miss Universe Canada title. ABC News. Retrieved from http://abcnews.go.com/blogs/entertainment/2012/04/trump-wont-bar-transsexual-beauty-queen-from-shot-at-miss-universe-canada-title

Schaefer, D. R. (2011). Resource characteristics in social exchange networks: Implications for positional advantage. *Social Networks, 33*(2), 143–151.

Schaefer, R. T. (2009). *Race and ethnicity in the United States* (5th ed.). Upper Saddle River, NJ: Pearson Prentice Hall.

Scheff, T. J. (1966). *Being mentally ill: A sociological theory.* Chicago: Aldine.

Scheff, T. J. (1988). Shame and conformity: The deference/emotion system. *American Sociological Review, 53,* 395–406.

Schegloff, E. (1990). On the organization of sequences as a source of "coherence" in talk-in-interaction. In B. Dorval (Ed.), *Conversational organization its development* (pp. 55–77). Norwood, NJ: Ablex.

Schegloff, E. (1991). Reflections on talk and social structure. In D. H. Zimmerman & D. Boden (Eds.), *Talk and social structure* (pp. 44–70). Cambridge: Polity Press.

Schiller, J. S., Lucas J. W., & Peregoy J. A. (2012). Table XIII: Crude percent distribution of respondent-assessed health status among adults aged 18 and over, by selected characteristics: United States, 2011. In *Summary health statistics for U.S. adults: National Health Interview Survey, 2011* (Vital Health Statistics, Series 10, No. 256). Washington, DC: National Center for Health Statistics. Retrieved from http://www.cdc.gov/nchs/data/series/sr_10/sr10_256.pdf

Schlosser, E. (2002). *Fast food nation: The dark side of the all-American meal.* New York: Harper Perennial.

Schnaiberg, A., & Gould, K. A. (1994). *Environment and society: The enduring conflict.* New York: St. Martin's Press.

Schneider, D. M., & Gough, K. (1974). *Matrilineal kinship.* Berkeley: University of California Press.

Schneider, F., & Enste, D. (2002, March). Hiding in the shadows: The growth of the underground economy. *Journal of Economic Issues, 30.* Retrieved from http://www.imf.org/external/pubs/ft/issues/issues30/index.htm

Schofield, J. W. (2010). International evidence on ability grouping with curriculum differentiation and the achievement gap in secondary schools. *Teachers College Record, 112*(5), 1492–1528.

Scholastic. (n.d.). Women's suffrage: When did women vote? Interactive map. Retrieved from http://teacher.scholastic.com/activities/suffrage/world_when.htm

Schor, J. B. (1998). *The overspent American: Why we want what we don't need.* New York: Harper Perennial.

Schulhofer, S. J. (2000). *Unwanted sex: The culture of intimidation and the failure of law.* Cambridge, MA: Harvard University Press.

Scott, A. (1990). *Ideology and the new social movements.* London: Unwin Hyman.

Scott, J. (2005, May 16). Life at the top in America isn't just better, it's longer. *New York Times.* Retrieved from http://www.nytimes.com/2005/05/16/national/class/HEALTH-FINAL.html?pagewanted=all

Scott, J. C., Tehranian, J., & Mathias J. (2002). The production of legal identities proper to states: The case of the permanent family surname. *Comparative Studies in Society and History, 44*(1), 4–44.

Scott, W. R., & Meyer, J. W. (1994). *Institutional environments and organizations: Structural complexity and individualism.* Thousand Oaks, CA: Sage.

Seager, J. (2003). *The Penguin atlas of women in the world.* New York: Penguin Books.

Seay, L. (2014, March 12). Does slacktivism work? *Washington Post.* Retrieved from http://www.washingtonpost.com/blogs/monkey-cage/wp/2014/03/12/does-slacktivism-work

Sebald, H. (2000). *Adolescence: A social psychological approach* (4th ed.). Englewood Cliffs, NJ: Prentice Hall.

Sellin, T. (1938). *Culture, conflict and crime.* New York: Social Science Research Council.

Sennett, R. (1998). *The corrosion of character: The personal consequences of work in the new capitalism.* New York: Norton.

Sentencing Project. (2011). Felony disenfranchisement. Retrieved from http://www.sentencingproject.org/template/page.cfm?id=133

Sentencing Project. (2012). Trends in U.S. corrections: State and federal prison population, 1925–2010. Retrieved from http://sentencingproject.org/doc/publications/inc_Trends_in_Corrections_Fact_sheet.pdf

Sentencing Project. (2014). Incarceration. Retrieved from http://www.sentencingproject.org/template/page.cfm?id=107

Shahani-Denning, C. (2003). *Physical attractiveness bias in hiring: What is beautiful is good.* Hempstead, NY: Hofstra University Office for Research and Sponsored Programs. Retrieved from http://www.hofstra.edu/pdf/orsp_shahani-denning_spring03.pdf

Shamir, R. (2011). Mind the gap: The commodification of corporate social responsibility. *Symbolic Interaction, 28*(2), 229–253. Retrieved from http://onlinelibrary.wiley.com/doi/10.1525/si.2005.28.2.229/abstract

Sharkey, J. (2014, May 7). Forget 1960, the golden age is now. *New York Times.* Retrieved from http://www.nytimes.com/2014/05/08/business/forget-1960-the-golden-age-is-now.html?_r=0

Sharkey, P. (2009). *Neighborhoods and the Black-White mobility gap.* Washington, DC: Pew Charitable Trusts, Economic Mobility Project. Retrieved from http://www.pewtrusts.org/~/media/legacy/uploadedfiles/pcs_assets/2009/PEWNEIGHBORHOODS1pdf.pdf

Sharp, G. (2011, March 30). 2010 census data on residential segregation. Sociological Images. Retrieved from http://thesocietypages.org/socimages/2011/03/30/2010-census-data-on-residential-segregation

Shattuck, R. (1980). *The forbidden experiment.* New York: Farrar, Straus and Giroux.

Shaw, M. (2010). Sociology and genocide. In D. Bloxham & A. D. Moses (Eds.), *The Oxford handbook of genocide studies* (pp. 142–161). New York: Oxford University Press.

Sheldon, W. H. (1949). *Varieties of delinquent youth: An introduction to constitutional psychiatry.* New York: Harper.

Sherman, A. M., & Zurbriggen, E. L. (2014). "Boys can be anything": Effect of Barbie play on girls' career cognitions. *Sex Roles, 70*(5–6): 195–208. doi:10.1007/s11199-014-0347-y

Shierholz, H. (2011, August 31). New college grads losing ground on wages. Economic Policy Institute. Retrieved from http://www.epi.org/publication/new_college_grads_losing_ground_on_wages

Shierholz, H. (2013). *Wages of young college graduates have failed to grow over the last decade.* Washington, DC: Economic Policy Institute.

Shierholz, H., Davis, A., & Kimball, W. (2014). *The class of 2014: The weak economy is still idling too many young graduates.* Washington, DC: Economic Policy Institute.

Shin, H. B., & Kominski, R. A. (2010). *Language use in the United States: 2007* (American Community Survey Report 12). Washington, DC: U.S. Census Bureau. Retrieved from http://www.census.gov/hhes/socdemo/language/data/acs/ACS-12.pdf

Shipler, D. K. (2005). *The working poor: Invisible in America.* New York: Vintage Books.

Shore, R., & Shore B. (2009). *Reducing infant mortality* (KIDS COUNT Indicator Brief). Baltimore: Annie E. Casey Foundation. Retrieved from http://www.aecf.org/m/resourcedoc/AECF-KCReducingInfantMortality-2009.pdf

Shukoor, H. (2010, September 3). Taliban tries to stop the music in Afghanistan—again. McClatchyDC. Retrieved from http://www.mcclatchydc.com/2010/09/03/100136/taliban-tries-to-stop-the-music.html

Sidibé, M. (2009, December 1). *South Africa's reinvigorated AIDS response.* Speech delivered at the commemoration of World AIDS Day, Pretoria, South Africa. Retrieved from http://data.unaids.org/pub/SpeechEXD/2009/20091201_ms_speech_wad09_en.pdf

Sifferlin, A. (2014, January 13). The doctor will Skype you now: Telemedicine apps aim to replace nonemergency visits. *Time,* p. 12.

Silva, E. B. (2001). *White supremacy and racism in the post–civil rights era.* Boulder, CO: Lynne Rienner.

Silverman, R. M. (2005). Community socioeconomic status and disparities in mortgage lending: An analysis of metropolitical Detroit. *Social Science Journal, 42,* 479–486.

Simmel, G. (1955). *Conflict and the web of group affiliations* (K. Wolf, Trans.). Glencoe, IL: Free Press.

Simmel, G. (1971). Fashion. In D. Levine (Ed.), *Georg Simmel* (pp. 324–339). Chicago: University of Chicago Press. (Original work published 1904)

Simon, J. L. (1977). *The economics of population growth.* Princeton, NJ: Princeton University Press.

Simon, J. L. (1981). *The ultimate resource.* Princeton, NJ: Princeton University Press.

Simon, J. L. (2000). *The great breakthrough and its cause.* Ann Arbor: University of Michigan Press.

Simon Wiesenthal Center. (2011). Social media must do more to thwart subculture of hate fueling lone wolf terrorism. Retrieved from http://www.wiesenthal.com/site/apps/nlnet/content2.aspx?c=lsKWLbPJLnF&b=4441467&ct=11675937

Simon Wiesenthal Center. (2013, May 8). U.S. Representatives Royce and Engel speak at release of Simon Wiesenthal Center's 2013 Digital Terrorism and Hate Report. Retrieved from http://www.wiesenthal.com/site/apps/s/content.asp?c=lsKWLbPJLnF&b=4442915&ct=13128625#.U6XZ_41dWLE

Simpson, C. (2012, August 27–September 2). Tech's tragic secret. *Bloomberg Businessweek,* pp. 48–57.

Simpson, M. E., & Conklin, G. H. (1989). Socioeconomic development, suicide, and religion: A test of Durkheim's theory of religion and suicide. *Social Forces, 67,* 945–964.

Sinclair, U. (1995). *The jungle.* New York: Doubleday, Page. (Original work published 1906)

Singer, A. (2012). *Immigrant workers in the U.S. labor force.* Washington, DC: Brookings Institution. Retrieved from http://www.brookings.edu/research/papers/2012/03/15-immigrant-workers-singer#8

Singer, P. W. (2003). *Corporate warriors: The rise of the privatized military industry.* Ithaca, NY: Cornell University Press.

Sipes, L. A., Jr. (2012, February 6). Statistics on women offenders. Corrections.com. Retrieved from http://www.corrections.com/news/article/30166-statistics-on-women-offenders

Skinner, B. F. (1938). *The behavior of organisms.* Cambridge, MA: B. F. Skinner Foundation.

Skinner, B. F. (1953). *Science and human behavior.* Cambridge, MA: B. F. Skinner Foundation.

Sklair, L. (2002). *Globalization: Capitalism and its alternatives.* Oxford: Oxford University Press.

Skocpol, T. (1979). *States and social revolutions.* New York: Cambridge University Press.

Slovak, K., & Singer, J. B. (2011). School social workers' perceptions of cyberbullying. *Children & Schools, 33*(1), 1–16.

Smelser, N. J. (1962). *The theory of collective behavior.* New York: Free Press.

Smith, B. (1990). Racism and women's studies. In G. Anzaldúa (Ed.), *Making face, making soul: Haciendo caras.* San Francisco: Aunt Lute Foundation.

Smith, D. (1987). *The everyday world as problematic: A feminist sociology.* Boston: Northeastern University Press.

Smith, D. (1990). *The conceptual practices of power: A feminist sociology of knowledge.* Boston: Northeastern University Press.

Smith, D. (2005). *Institutional ethnography: A sociology for people.* Walnut Creek, CA: AltaMira Press.

Smith, D. H., & Pillemer, K. (1983). Self-help groups as social movement organizations: Social structure and social change. In L. Kriesberg (Ed.), *Research in social movements, conflicts and change* (Vol. 5, pp. 203–233). Greenwich, CT: JAI Press.

Smith, E. B., & Kuntz, P. (2013, May 2). Disclosed: The pay gap between CEOs and employees. *Bloomberg Businessweek.* Retrieved from http://www.businessweek.com/articles/2013-05-02/disclosed-the-pay-gap-between-ceos-and-employees

Smith, K. (2005). Prebirth gender talk: A case study in prenatal socialization. *Women & Language, 28*(1), 49–53.

Smith, M. (2000). *American business and political power: Public opinions, elections, and democracy.* Chicago: University of Chicago.

Smith, M. J., & Moses, B. (1980). Social welfare agencies and social reform movements: The case of the single-parent family. *Journal of Sociology and Social Welfare, 7,* 125–136.

Smith, P. K. (2009). *Obesity among poor Americans: Is public assistance the problem?* Nashville, TN: Vanderbilt University Press.

Smith, P. K., Mahdavi, J., Carvalho, M., Fisher, S., Russell, S., & Tippett, N. (2008). Cyberbullying: Its nature and its impact in secondary school pupils. *Journal of Child Psychology and Psychiatry, 49*(4), 376–385.

Smith, R. W. (2002). As old as history. In C. Rittner, J. K. Roth, & J. M. Smith (Eds.), *Will genocide ever end?* (pp. 31–34). St. Paul, MN: Paragon House.

Smith, S. (2001). *Allah's mountains: The battle for Chechnya.* London: I. B. Tauris.

Smith, T. W. (2002). Religious diversity in America: The emergence of Muslims, Buddhists, Hindus, and others. *Journal for the Scientific Study of Religion, 41*(3), 577–585.

Smith-Greenaway, E. (2013). Maternal reading skills and child mortality in Nigeria: A reassessment of why education matters. *Demography, 50*(5), 1551–1561.

Smits, D. (1994). The frontier army and the destruction of the buffalo: 1865–1883. *Western Historical Quarterly, 25*(3), 312–338.

Smock, P. J., Manning, W. D., & Porter, M. (2005). "Everything's there except money": How money shapes decisions to marry among cohabitating adults. *Journal of Marriage and Family, 67*(3), 680–696.

Snow, D. A., Rochford, E. B., Jr., Worden, S. K., & Benford, R. D. (1986). Frame alignment processes, micromobilization, and movement participation. *American Sociological Review, 51,* 464–481.

Snow, D. A., Zurcher, L. A., Jr., & Ekland-Olson, S. (1980). Social networks and social movements: A microstructural approach to differential recruitment. *American Sociological Review, 45,* 787–801.

Social Security Administration. (2013). Social Security history. Retrieved from http://www.ssa.gov/history

Society for Human Resource Management. (2008). Mensa membership, Kennedy kinship students. *Journal of American College Health,* 59(1), 43–50.

Sokoloff, N. J., & Raffel, B. (1995). *The criminal justice system and women: Offenders, victims, workers* (2nd ed.). New York: McGraw-Hill.

Sommers, C. H. (2000, May). The war against boys. *Atlantic Monthly.* Retrieved from http://www.theatlantic.com/magazine/archive/2000/05/the-war-against-boys/304659

Sorokin, P. (1962). *Society, culture, and personality: Their structure and dynamics.* New York: Cooper Square.

Sorokin, P. (1970). *Social and cultural dynamics: A study of change in major systems of art, truth, ethics, law and social relationships.* Boston: Extending Horizons Books, Porter Sargent Publishers. (Original work published 1957)

South African Department of Health. (2012). *Global AIDS Response Progress Report, 2012.* Johannesburg: Author. Retrieved from http://www.unaids.org/en/dataanalysis/knowyourresponse/countryprogressreports/2012countries/ce_ZA_Narrative_Report.pdf

Southern Poverty Law Center. (2011). Hate and extremism. Retrieved from http://www.splcenter.org/what-we-do/hate-and-extremism

Southern Poverty Law Center. (2013). Active U.S. hate groups. Retrieved from http://www.splcenter.org/get-informed/hate-map

Sparrow, R. (2005). Defending deaf culture: The case of cochlear implants. *Journal of Political Philosophy, 13*(2), 135–152.

Spencer, H. (1892). *Essays, scientific, political and speculative* (2 vols.). New York: Appleton.

Spicher, C. H., & Hudak, M. A. (1997, August). *Gender role portrayal on Saturday morning cartoons: An update.* Paper presented at the annual meeting of the American Psychological Association, Chicago.

Spitzer, S. (1975). Toward a Marxian theory of deviance. *Social Problems, 22*(5), 641–651.

Squires, G. D. (2003). Racial profiling, insurance style: Insurance redlining and the uneven development of metropolitan America. *Journal of Urban Affairs, 24*(4), 391–410.

Squires, G. D., Friedman S., & Saidat, C. E. (2002). Experiencing residential segregation: A contemporary study of Washington, DC. *Urban Affairs Review, 38*(2), 155–183.

Stanley, S. C. (1993). *Feminist pillar of fire: The life of Alma White.* Cleveland: Pilgrim Press.

Stark, R., & Bainbridge, W. S. (1996). *A theory of religion.* New York: Peter Lang. (Original work published 1987)

Steele, C. M., & Aronson, J. (1995). Stereotype threat and the intellectual test performance of African Americans. *Journal of Personality and Social Psychology, 69*(5), 797–811.

Steffensmeier, D., & Allen, E. (1998). The nature of female offending: Patterns and explanations. In R. T. Zaplin (Ed.), *Female offenders: Critical perspectives and effective intervention.* Gaithersburg, MD: Aspen.

Steinbrook, R. (1988, January 29). AIDS summit delegates adopt a unanimous call for action. *Los Angeles Times.* Retrieved from http://articles.latimes.com/1988-01-29/news/mn-26467_1_aids-control

Stepick, A., III, & Grenier, G. (1993). Cubans in Miami. In J. Moore & R. Pinderhughes (Eds.), *In the barrios: Latinos and the underclass debate* (pp. 79–100). New York: Russell Sage Foundation.

Stevenson, B. (2010). Beyond the classroom: Using Title IX to measure the return to high school sports. *Review of Economics & Statistics, 92*(2), 284–301.

Stiglitz, J. E. (2012). *The price of inequality: How today's divided society endangers our future.* New York: Norton.

Stokes, R., & Chevan, A. (1996). Female-headed families: Social and economic context of racial differences. *Journal of Urban Affairs, 8*(3), 245–268.

Stolle, D. (1998). Why do bowling and singing matter? Group characteristics, membership, and generalized trust. *Political Psychology, 19*(3), 497–525.

Straus, M. A., & Gelles, R. J. (Eds.). (1990). *Physical violence in American families: Risk factors and adaptations to violence in 8,145 families.* New Brunswick, NJ: Transaction.

Straus, M. A., Gelles, R. J., & Steinmetz, S. K. (1988). *Behind closed doors: Violence in the American family.* Newbury Park, CA: Sage.

Straus, M. A., Sugarman, D. B., & Giles-Sims, J. (1997). Spanking by parents and subsequent antisocial behavior of children. *Archives of Pediatrics and Adolescence, 151,* 761–767.

Subrahmanyam, K., & Lin, G. (2007). Adolescents on the net: Internet use and well-being. *Adolescence, 42*(168), 659–677.

Sullivan, T. A., Warren, E., & Westbrook, J. (2000). *The fragile middle class: Americans in debt.* Binghamton, NY: Vail-Ballou Press.

Sum, A., Khatiwada, I., & McLaughlin, J. (2009). *The consequences of dropping out of high school: Joblessness and jailing for high school dropouts and the high cost for taxpayers.* Boston: Northeastern University, Center for Labor Market Studies. Retrieved from http://hdl.handle.net/2047/d20000596

Sumner, W. G. (1959). *Folkways: A study of the sociological importance of usages, manners, customs, mores, and morals.* Boston: Ginn. (Original work published in 1906)

Surette, R., Hansen, K., & Noble, G. (2009). Measuring media oriented terrorism. *Journal of Criminal Justice, 37,* 360–370.

Sutherland, E. H. (1929). The person v. the act in criminology. *Cornell Law Quarterly, 14,* 159–167.

Sutherland, E. H. (1983). *White collar crime: The uncut version.* New Haven, CT: Yale University Press. (Original work published 1949)

Swanson, E. (2014, February 8). Most Americans OK with Coke's Super Bowl ad, but still think we should all speak English. Huffington Post. Retrieved from http://www.huffingtonpost.com/2014/02/08/english-official-language-poll_n_4748094.html

Sweet, K. (2014, May 27). Median CEO pay crosses $10 million in 2013. Associated Press. Retrieved from http://bigstory.ap.org/article/median-ceo-pay-crosses-10-million-2013

Swiss, S., & Giller, J. E. (1993). Rape as a crime of war. *Journal of the American Medical Association, 270*(5), 619–622.

Symonds, W. C., Schwartz, R., & Ferguson, R. F. (2011). *Pathways to prosperity: Meeting the challenge of preparing young Americans for the 21st century.* Cambridge, MA: Pathways to Prosperity Project, Harvard University Graduate School of Education. Retrieved from http://dash.harvard.edu/bitstream/handle/1/4740480/Pathways_to_Prosperity_Feb2011-1.pdf

Taibbi, M. (2013, December 11). Apocalypse, New Jersey: A dispatch from America's most desperate town. *Rolling Stone.* Retrieved from http://www.rollingstone.com/culture/news/apocalypse-new-jersey-a-dispatch-from-americas-most-desperate-town-20131211

Tannen, D. (2001). *You just don't understand: Women and men in conversation.* New York: HarperCollins.

Tannenbaum, F. (1938). *Crime and the community.* New York: Columbia University Press.

Tarrow, S. G. (1983). *Struggling to reform: Social movements and policy changes during cycles of protest.* Ithaca, NY: Cornell University Press.

Tarrow, S. G. (1994). *Power in movement: Social movements, collective action, and politics.* New York: Cambridge University Press.

Taslitz, A. E. (1999). *Rape and the culture of the courtroom.* New York: New York University Press.

Taylor, P., Parker, K., Cohn, D., Passel, J. S., Wang, W., & Pattern, E. (2011). *Barely half of U.S. adults are married—A record low.* Washington, DC: Pew Research Center. Retrieved from http://www.pewsocialtrends.org/2011/12/14/barely-half-of-u-s-adults-are-married-a-record-low

Taylor, S., & Butcher, M. (2007). *Extra-legal defendant characteristics and mock juror ethnicity re-examined.* Paper presented at the annual conference of the British Psychological Society, York Conference Park, York, England.

Tenenbaum, H., & Leaper, C. (2003). Parent–child conversations about science: The socialization of gender inequities? *Developmental Psychology, 39*(1), 34–47.

Tews, M. J., Stafford, K., & Zhu, J. (2009). Beauty revisited: The impact of attractiveness, ability, and personality in the assessment of employment suitability. *International Journal of Selection and Assessment, 17*(1), 92–100.

Thomas, D. Q., & Ralph, R. E. (1999). Rape in war: The case of Bosnia. In S. P. Ramet (Ed.), *Gender politics in the Western Balkans: Women and society in Yugoslavia and the Yugoslav successor states* (pp. 203–218). University Park: Pennsylvania State University Press.

Thomas, G. M., Meyer, J. W., Ramirez, F. O., & Boli, J. (1987). *Institutional structure: Constituting state, society, and the individual.* Newbury Park, CA: Sage.

Thomas, W. I., & Thomas, D. S. (1928). *The child in America: Behavior problems and programs.* New York: Knopf.

Thompson, T. L., & Scantlin, R. M. (2007). Gender representation in cartoons. In J. J. Arnett (Ed.), *Encyclopedia of children, adolescents, and the media* (pp. 141–144). Thousand Oaks, CA: Sage.

Thomson, J. (1874). The city of dreadful night. *National Reformer.*

Thorne, B. (1993). *Gender play: Girls and boys in school.* New Brunswick, NJ: Rutgers University Press.

Thornton, R. (1987). *American Indian holocaust and survival: A population history since 1492.* Norman: University of Oklahoma Press.

Tilly, C. (1975). *The formation of national states in Europe.* Princeton, NJ: Princeton University Press.

Tilly, C. (1978). *From mobilization to revelation.* Reading, MA: Addison-Wesley.

Tilly, C., & Tilly, L. (1994). Capitalist work and labor markets. In N. J. Smelser & R. Swedberg (Eds.), *The handbook of economic sociology.* Princeton, NJ: Princeton University Press.

Toennies, F. (1963). *Gemeinschaft and Gesellschaft.* New York: Harper & Row. (Original work published 1887)

Tolan, P., Gorman-Smith, D., & Henry, D. (2005). Family violence. *Annual Review of Psychology 57,* 557–583.

Townsend, P. (2006, December). What is poverty? An historical perspective. *Poverty in Focus* (UNDP International Poverty Centre), pp. 5–6.

Transparency International. (2011). Corruption perceptions index 2011. Retrieved from http://cpi.transparency.org/cpi2011/results

Trent, S., Williams, J., Thornton, C., & Shanahan, M. (2004). *Farming the sea, costing the earth: Why we must green the blue revolution.* London: Environmental Justice Foundation. Retrieved from http://www.ejfoundation.org/pdf/farming_the_sea_costing_the_earth.pdf

Trimble, L. B., & Kmec, J. A. (2011). The role of social networks in the job attainment process. *Sociology Compass, 5,* 165–178.

Troeltsch, E. (1931). *The social teaching of the Christian churches* (Vol. 1). New York: Macmillan.

Trudeau, M. (2009, February 5). More students turning illegally to "smart" drugs. National Public Radio. Retrieved from http://www.npr.org/templates/story/story.php?storyId=100254163

Truman, J., Langton, L., & Planty, M. (2013). *Criminal victimization, 2012* (BJS Bulletin NCJ 243389). Washington, DC: U.S. Department of Justice, Bureau of Justice Statistics.

Tucker, K. H. (1991). How new are the new social movements? *Theory, Culture and Society, 8*(2), 75–98.

Tumin, M. M. (1953). Some principles of stratification: A critical analysis. *American Sociological Review, 18,* 387–393.

Tumin, M. M. (1963). On inequality. *American Sociological Review, 28,* 19–26.

Tumin, M. M. (1985). *Social stratification: The forms and functions of inequality* (2nd ed.). Englewood Cliffs, NJ: Prentice Hall.

Turner, J. S. (2003). *Dating and sexuality in America: A reference handbook.* Santa Barbara, CA: ABC-CLIO.

Turner, J. S. (2011). Sex and the spectacle of music videos: An examination of the portrayal of race and sexuality in music videos. *Sex Roles, 64*(3–4), 173–191.

Turner, M. A., & McDade, Z. (2012). Immigration brings diversity to neighborhoods where African Americans live. Urban Institute. Retrieved from http://www.metrotrends.org/commentary/diversity2.cfm

Turner, M. A., Popkin, S. J., & Rawlings, L. (2009). *Public housing and the legacy of segregation.* Washington, DC: Urban Institute Press.

Turner, R. H., & Killian, L. M. (1987). *Collective behavior* (3rd ed.). Englewood Cliffs, NJ: Prentice Hall.

Twitter. (2014). About: Twitter usage. Retrieved from https://about.twitter.com/company

Tyack, D., & Hansot, E. (1982). *Managers of virtue: Public school leadership in America, 1820–1980.* New York: Basic Books.

Tygart, C. E. (1987). Social structure linkages among social movement participants: Toward a synthesis of micro and macro paradigms. *Sociological Viewpoints, 3*(1), 71–84.

Tyman, K., Saylor, C., Taylor, L. A., & Comeaux, C. (2010). Comparing children and adolescents engaged in cyberbullying with matched peers. *Cyberpsychology, Behavior, and Social Networking, 13*(2), 195–199.

Uchitelle, L. (2007). *The disposable American: Layoffs and their consequences.* New York: Vintage Books.

UNAIDS. (2006). *2006 Report on the global AIDS epidemic.* Geneva: Author. Retrieved from http://www.unaids.org/en/media/unaids/contentassets/dataimport/pub/report/2006/2006_gr_en.pdf

UNAIDS. (2010a). HIV prevalence map. In *United Nations Programme on HIV/AIDS global report 2010.* Geneva: Author. Retrieved from http://www.unaids.org/documents/20101123_2010_HIV_Prevalence_Map_em.pdf

UNAIDS. (2010b). *Malawi HIV and AIDS monitoring and evaluation report: 2008–2009.* Geneva: Author. Retrieved from http://www.unaids.org/en/dataanalysis/knowyourresponse/countryprogressreports/2010countries/malawi_2010_country_progress_report_en.pdf

UNAIDS. (2012). South Africa HIV and AIDS estimates. Retrieved from http://www.unaids.org/en/regionscountries/countries/southafrica

UNAIDS, UNFPA, & UNIFEM. (2004). *Women and HIV/AIDS: Confronting the crisis.* New York: UNFPA. Retrieved from http://www.unfpa.org/hiv/women/docs/women_aids.pdf

Underhill, B. (1995). *The woman who ran for president: The many lives of Victoria Woodhull.* New York: Bridge Works.

Ungar, S. (1992). The rise and (relative) decline of global warming as a social problem. *Sociological Quarterly, 33*(4), 483–501.

UNICEF. (2012). *The state of the world's children, 2012: Children in an urban world.* New York: Author.

Union of International Associations. (2011). Historical overview of number of international organizations by type, 1909–2011. In *Yearbook of international organizations, 2011/2012 edition.* Herndon, VA: Brill.

United Nations. (1995). *Women's education and fertility behavior: Recent evidence from the demographic and health surveys.* New York: Author.

United Nations. (2011). *World urbanization prospects: The 2011 revision.* New York: Author.

United Nations. (2013a). Deputy UN chief calls for urgent action to tackle global sanitation crisis. Retrieved from http://www.un.org/apps/news/story.asp?NewsID=44452

United Nations. (2013b). *The Millennium Development Goals report 2013.* New York: Author. Retrieved from http://www.undp.org/content/dam/undp/library/MDG/english/mdg-report-2013-english.pdf

United Nations, Department of Economic and Social Affairs, Population Division. (2011). *World population prospects: The 2010 revision, highlights and advance tables* (Working Paper ESA/P/WP.220). New York: Author.

United Nations Educational, Scientific and Cultural Organization. (2014a). *Reading in the mobile era: A study of mobile reading in developing countries.* Paris: Author. Retrieved from http://www.unesco.org/new/en/unesco/themes/icts/m4ed/mobile-reading/reading-in-the-mobile-era

United Nations Educational, Scientific and Cultural Organization. (2014b). *Teaching and learning: Achieving quality for all* (Education for All Global Monitoring Report). Paris: Author. Retrieved from http://unesdoc.unesco.org/images/0022/002256/225654e.pdf

United Nations Environment Programme. (2008). *Green jobs: Towards decent work in a sustainable, low-carbon world.* Washington, DC: Worldwatch Institute. Retrieved from http://www.unep.org/PDF/UNEPGreenJobs_report08.pdf

United Nations Environment Programme. (2009). *Recycling: From e-waste to resources.* Berlin: Author. Retrieved from http://www.unep.org/PDF/PressReleases/E-Waste_publication_screen_FINALVERSION-sml.pdf

United Nations High Commissioner for Refugees. (2012). Internally displaced people figures. Retrieved from http://www.unhcr.org/pages/49c3646c23.html

United Nations High Commissioner for Refugees. (2013). Refugee figures. Retrieved from http://www.unhcr.org/pages/49c3646c1d.html

United Nations Office on Drugs and Crime. (2013, February). *Comprehensive study on cybercrime* (draft). Vienna: Author. Retrieved from http://www.unodc.org/documents/organized-crime/UNODC_CCPCJ_EG.4_2013/CYBERCRIME_STUDY_210213.pdf

United Nations Population Fund. (2007, October 29–31). *Characteristics of sex-ratio imbalance in India and future scenarios: Executive summary, India.* Paper presented at the Fourth Asia Pacific Conference on Reproductive and Sexual Health and Rights, Hyderabad, India. Retrieved from http://www.unfpa.org/gender/docs/studies/summaries/india_summary.pdf

United Nations Population Fund. (2012). *Sex imbalances at birth: Current trends, consequences, and policy implications.* Bangkok: Author. Retrieved from http://www.unfpa.org/webdav/site/global/shared/documents/publications/2012/Sex%20Imbalances%20at%20Birth.%20PDF%20UNFPA%20APRO%20publica tion%202012.pdf

University of Nevada, Reno. (2010, May 21). Books in home as important as parents' education in determining children's education level. ScienceDaily. Retrieved from http://www.sciencedaily.com/releases/2010/05/100520213116.htm

Urban, H. B. (2011). *The Church of Scientology: A history of a new religion.* Princeton, NJ: Princeton University Press.

U.S. Bureau of Justice Statistics. (2010, June 23). Number of state prisoners declined by almost 3,000 during 2009; federal prison population increased by 6,800. Retrieved from http://bjs.ojp.usdoj.gov/content/pub/press/pim09st py09acpr.cfm

U.S. Bureau of Justice Statistics, Office of Justice Programs. (2013a). Key facts at a glance: National Crime Victimization Survey property crime trends. Retrieved http://bjs.ojp.usdoj.gov/content/glance/tables/proptrdtab.cfm

U.S. Bureau of Justice Statistics, Office of Justice Programs. (2013b). Key facts at a glance: National Crime Victimization Survey violent crime trends. Retrieved from http://bjs.ojp.usdoj.gov/content/glance/tables/viortrdtab.cfm

U.S. Bureau of Labor Statistics. (2005, July 27). Table 4. Employed contingent and noncontingent workers by occupation and industry, February 2005. In *Contingent and alternative employment arrangements, February 2005* (USDL 05-1433). Washington, DC: U.S. Department of Labor. Retrieved from http://www.bls.gov/news.release/pdf/conemp.pdf

U.S. Bureau of Labor Statistics. (2011a). Chart 3. Unemployment rate for Blacks and Whites aged 25 and older, by educational attainment, 2011 annual average. In *The African-American labor force in the recovery.* Washington, DC: U.S. Department of Labor. Retrieved from http://www.dol.gov/_sec/media/reports/BlackLaborForce/BlackLaborForce.pdf

U.S. Bureau of Labor Statistics. (2011b). *Consumer expenditures in 2009.*

Washington, DC: U.S. Department of Labor. Retrieved from http://www.bls.gov/cex/csxann09.pdf

U.S. Bureau of Labor Statistics. (2011c). Labor force status of persons 16 to 24 years old by school enrollment, educational attainment, sex, race, and Hispanic or Latino ethnicity. Retrieved from http://www.bls.gov/news.release/hsgec.t02.htm

U.S. Bureau of Labor Statistics. (2012a). America's young adults at 24: School enrollment, training, and employment transitions between ages 23 and 24: Summary. Retrieved from http://www.bls.gov/news.release/nlsyth.nr0.htm

U.S. Bureau of Labor Statistics. (2012b). Table 11. Employed persons by detailed occupation, sex, race, and Hispanic or Latino ethnicity. In *Household data annual averages.* Washington, DC: U.S. Department of Labor. Retrieved from http://www.bls.gov/cps/cpsaat11.pdf

U.S. Bureau of Labor Statistics. (2012c). Table 39. Median weekly earnings of full-time wage and salary workers by detailed occupation and sex. In *Household data annual averages.* Washington, DC: U.S. Department of Labor. Retrieved from http://www.bls.gov/cps/cpsaat39.pdf

U.S. Bureau of Labor Statistics. (2013a). Employment projections: Earnings and unemployment rates by educational attainment. Retrieved from http://www.bls.gov/emp/ep_chart_001.htm

U.S. Bureau of Labor Statistics. (2013b). Labor force statistics from the Current Population Survey. Household data annual averages. Table 3. Employment status of the civilian noninstitutional population by age, sex, and race. Retrieved from http://www.bls.gov/cps/cpsaat03.htm

U.S. Bureau of Labor Statistics. (2013c, March 8). Table A-1. Employment status of the civilian population by sex and age. Retrieved from http://www.bls.gov/news.release/empsit.t01.htm

U.S. Bureau of Labor Statistics. (2013d). Table 3. Employment by major industry sector, 2002, 2012, and projected 2022. Retrieved from http://www.bls.gov/news.release/ecopro.t03.htm

U.S. Bureau of Labor Statistics. (2013e). *Union members—2012* (USDL-13-0105). Washington, DC: U.S. Department of Labor. Retrieved from http://www.bls.gov/news.release/pdf/union2.pdf

U.S. Bureau of Labor Statistics. (2014a, May 23). Consumer expenditures midyear update—July 2012 through June 2013 average. Retrieved from http://www.bls.gov/news.release/pdf/cesmy.pdf

U.S. Bureau of Labor Statistics. (2014b, September 5). Employment situation summary. Retrieved from http://www.bls.gov/news.release/empsit.nr0.htm

U.S. Bureau of Labor Statistics. (2014c, March). *A profile of the working poor, 2012* (BLS Reports 1047). Washington, DC: Author. Retrieved from http://www.bls.gov/cps/cpswp2012.pdf

U.S. Bureau of Labor Statistics. (2014d). Table 7. Employment status of the civilian noninstitutional population 25 years and older by educational attainment, sex, race, and Hispanic or Latino ethnicity. In *Household data annual averages.* Washington, DC: U.S. Department of Labor. Retrieved from http://www.bls.gov/cps/cpsaat07.pdf

U.S. Bureau of Labor Statistics. (2014e). Table 7. Median usual weekly earnings of full-time wage and salary workers by selected characteristics, annual averages. Retrieved from http://www.bls.gov/news.release/wkyeng.t07.htm

U.S. Bureau of Labor Statistics. (2014f). Top picks: Weekly and hourly earnings data from the Current Population Survey. Retrieved from http://data.bls.gov/cgi-bin/surveymost?le

U.S. Census Bureau. (2003). No. HS-12. Households by type and size: 1900 to 2002. In *Statistical abstract of the United States: 2003.* Washington, DC: Government Printing Office. Retrieved from http://www.census.gov/statab/hist/HS-12.pdf

U.S. Census Bureau. (2010). Table 59. Households, families, subfamilies, and married couples: 1980 to 2010. In *Statistical abstract of the United States: 2012.* Washington, DC: Government Printing Office. Retrieved from http://www.census.gov/compendia/statab/2012/tables/12s0059.pdf

U.S. Census Bureau. (2011a, April 26). Newsroom: More working women than men have college degrees, Census Bureau reports. Retrieved from http://www.census.gov/newsroom/releases/archives/education/cb11-72.html

U.S. Census Bureau. (2011b). Profile America facts for features: American Indian and Alaska Native Heritage Month: November 2011. Retrieved from http://www.census.gov/newsroom/releases/archives/facts_for_features_special_editions/cb11-ff22.html

U.S. Census Bureau. (2012a). Characteristics of same-sex couple households: 2012. Retrieved from http://www.census.gov/hhes/samesex

U.S. Census Bureau. (2012b). Historical income tables: Households. Table H-2. Share of aggregate income received by each fifth and top 5 percent of households. Retrieved from https://www.census.gov/hhes/www/income/data/historical/household

U.S. Census Bureau. (2012c). Income, poverty, and health insurance coverage: 2012—Tables and figures. Retrieved from http://www.census.gov/hhes/www/hlthins/data/incpovhlth/2012/tables.html

U.S. Census Bureau. (2012d). Table 271. High school dropouts by race and Hispanic origin: 1980 to 2009. In *Statistical abstract of the United States: 2012.* Washington, DC: Government Printing Office. Retrieved from http://www.census.gov/compendia/statab/2012/tables/12s0271.pdf

U.S. Census Bureau. (2012e). Percent in poverty, 2012, by state. Retrieved from http://www.census.gov/did/www/saipe/data/statecounty/maps/iy2012/Pct_Poor2012_state.pdf

U.S. Census Bureau. (2012f). USA QuickFacts. Retrieved from http://quickfacts.census.gov/qfd/states/00000.html

U.S. Census Bureau. (2012g). Voting and registration in the election of November 2012: Detailed tables. Table 5. Reported voting and registration, by age, sex, and educational attainment: November 2012. Retrieved from http://www.census.gov/hhes/www/socdemo/voting/publications/p20/2012/tables.html

U.S. Census Bureau. (2013a). America's families and living arrangements: 2013: Adults (A table series): Table A1. Retrieved from https://www.census.gov/hhes/families/data/cps2013A.html

U.S. Census Bureau. (2013b). America's families and living arrangements: 2013: Children (C table series). Retrieved from http://www.census.gov/hhes/families/data/cps2013C.html

U.S. Census Bureau. (2013c). Income and poverty in the United States: 2013—Tables and figures. Poverty thresholds. Retrieved from http://www.census.gov/hhes/www/poverty/data/incpovhlth/2013/tables.html

U.S. Census Bureau. (2014). Historical income tables: Income inequality. Table H-3. Mean household income received by each fifth and top 5 percent (all races). Retrieved from http://www.census.gov/hhes/www/income/data/historical/inequality/index.html

U.S. Conference of Mayors. (2011). *Hunger and homelessness survey.* Washington, DC: Author.

U.S. Department of Commerce, Economics and Statistics Administration. (2010, January). *Middle class in America* (prepared for the Office of the Vice President of the United States Middle Class Task Force). Washington, DC: Author. Retrieved from http://www.commerce.gov/sites/default/files/documents/migrated/Middle%20Class%20Report.pdf

U.S. Department of Defense. (2011). Dictionary of military terms. Retrieved from http://www.dtic.mil/doctrine/dod_dictionary

U.S. Department of Health and Human Services. (2004). *The health consequences of smoking: A report of the surgeon general.* Washington, DC: Government Printing Office. Retrieved from http://www.cdc.gov/tobacco/data_statistics/sgr/2004/complete_report/index.htm

U.S. Department of Health and Human Services. (2010). Statistics and research: Child maltreatment 2010. Retrieved from http://www.acf.hhs.gov/programs/cb/research-data-technology/statistics-research/child-maltreatment

U.S. Department of Health and Human Services. (2013). *Healthy people 2020.* Washington, DC: Government Printing Office. Retrieved from http://healthypeople.gov/2020

U.S. Department of Homeland Security, Office of Immigration Statistics. (2011). *Yearbook of immigration statistics: 2010.* Washington, DC: Author. Retrieved from http://www.dhs.gov/xlibrary/assets/statistics/yearbook/2010/ois_yb_2010.pdf

U.S. Department of Homeland Security, Office of Immigration Statistics. (2013). *Yearbook of immigration statistics: 2012.* Washington, DC: Author. Retrieved from https://www.dhs.gov/sites/default/files/publications/ois_yb_2012.pdf

U.S. Department of Labor, Wage and Hour Division. (2010). *Internship programs under the Fair Labor Standards Act.* Washington, DC: Author. Retrieved from http://www.dol.gov/whd/regs/compliance/whdfs71.pdf

U.S. Department of Labor, Wage and Hour Division. (2014). Minimum wage laws in the states, September 1, 2014. Retrieved from http://www.dol.gov/whd/minwage/america.htm

U.S. Department of State. (2008). *Nontraditional students enrich college campuses: Older students value challenging courses with real-world implications.* Washington, DC: Government Printing Office. Retrieved from http://www.america.gov/st/educ-english/2008/April/200804281212291CJsamohT0.3335382.html

U.S. Department of State. (2010). *Annual report on international religious freedom: 2010.* Washington, DC: Government Printing Office. Retrieved from http://www.state.gov/j/drl/rls/irf/2010/index.htm

U.S. Department of State. (2012a). *Background note: India.* Washington, DC: Bureau of South and Central Asian Affairs. Retrieved from http://www.state.gov/r/pa/ei/bgn/3454.htm

U.S. Department of State. (2012b, September 28). Foreign terrorist organizations. Retrieved from http://www.state.gov/j/ct/rls/other/des/123085.htm

U.S. Department of State. (2012c). *2012 trafficking in persons report.* Washington, DC: Government Printing Office. Retrieved from http://www.state.gov/j/tip/rls/tiprpt/2012

U.S. Elections Project. (2013, February 9). 2012 general election turnout rates. Retrieved from http://elections.gmu.edu/Turnout_2012G.html

U.S. Energy Information Administration. (2011). International energy outlook 2011. Retrieved from http://www.eia.gov/forecasts/ieo/ieo_tables.cfm

U.S. Fish and Wildlife Service, Office of Law Enforcement Intelligence Unit. (2003). *U.S. wildlife trade: An overview for 1997–2003.* Washington, DC: U.S. Department of the Interior.

U.S. Government Accountability Office. (2011). *Child maltreatment: Strengthening national data on child fatalities could aid in prevention* (GAO-11-599). Washington, DC: Government Printing Office. Retrieved from http://www.gao.gov/new.items/d11599.pdf

Valentine, G. (2006). Globalizing intimacy: The role of information and communication technologies in maintaining and creating relationships. *Women's Studies Quarterly, 34*(1), 365–393.

Valenzuela, J. M. (1992). Permanencia y cambio en las identidades étnicas: La población de origen mexicano en Estados Unidos. *Estudios Sociológicos, 10*(28), 103–125.

Valette, A. (1893). *Socialism and sexualism.* Paris: Verneuil.

Van DeBosch, H., & Van Cleemput, K. (2008). Defining cyberbullying: A qualitative research into the perceptions of youngsters. *CyberPsychology & Behavior, 11*(4), 499–503.

van Dijke, M., & Poppe, M. (2006). Striving for personal power as a basis for social power dynamics. *European Journal of Social Psychology, 36*(4), 537–566.

van Donk, M. (2002). HIV/AIDS and urban poverty in South Africa. South Africa Cities Network. Retrieved from http://www.sacities.net/knowledge-centre/research/publications/69-themes/strategy/527-the-role-of-cities-in-poverty-alleviation

VanGiezen, R., & Schwenk, A. E. (2001, Fall). Compensation before World War I through the Great Depression. *Compensation and Working Conditions* (U.S. Department of Labor, Bureau of Labor Statistics). Retrieved from http://www.bls.gov/opub/mlr/cwc/compensation-from-before-world-war-i-through-the-great-depression.pdf

Van Wees, H. (2010). Genocide in the ancient world. In D. Bloxham & A. D. Moses (Eds.), *The Oxford handbook of genocide studies* (pp. 239–258). New York: Oxford University Press.

Veblen, T. (1899). *The theory of the leisure class.* New York: Macmillan.

Vellacott, J. (1993). *From Liberal to Labour with women's suffrage: The story of Catherine Marshall.* Montreal: McGill-Queen's University Press.

Ventura, S. J., Curtin, S. C., Abma, J. C., & Henshaw S. K. (2012). Estimated pregnancy rates and rates of pregnancy outcomes for the United States, 1990–2008. *National Vital Statistics Reports, 60*(7). Retrieved from http://www.cdc.gov/nchs/data/nvsr/nvsr60/nvsr60_07.pdf

Ventura, S. J., & Hamilton, B. E. (2011). *U.S. teenage birth rate resumes decline* (NCHS Data Brief 58). Hyattsville, MD: National Center for Health Statistics. Retrieved from http://www.cdc.gov/nchs/data/databriefs/db58.pdf

Vespa, J., Lewis, J. M., & Kreider, R. M. (2013). *America's families and living arrangements: 2012* (Population Characteristics P20-570). Washington, DC: U.S. Census Bureau. Retrieved from https://www.census.gov/prod/2013pubs/p20-570.pdf

Viglione, J., Hannon, L., & DeFina, R. (2011). The impact of light skin on prison time for Black female offenders. *Social Science Journal, 48,* 250–258.

Vinovskis, M. A. (1992). Schooling and poor children in 19th-century America. *American Behavioral Scientist, 35*(3), 313–331.

Vinovskis, M. A. (1995). *Education, society, and economic opportunity: A historical perspective on persistent problems.* New Haven, CT: Yale University Press.

Violence Policy Center. (2010). *Black homicide victimization in the United States: An analysis of 2007 homicide data.* Washington, DC: Author. Retrieved from http://www.vpc.org/studies/blackhomicide10.pdf

Wacquant, L. (2002). From slavery to mass incarceration. *New Left Review, 13*(2), 40–61.

Wade, C., & Tavris, C. (1997). *Psychology.* New York: Longman.

Walberg, M. (2009, June 2). Officer's bar beating trial opens, and video is played: Cop's lawyer says it was self-defense, and female bartender takes the stand. *Chicago Tribune.* Retrieved from http://articles.chicagotribune.com/2009-06-02/news/0906010513_1_female-bartender-anthony-abbate-beating

Wald, M. L. (2014, March 30). U.S. agency knew about G.M. flaw but did not act. *New York Times.* Retrieved from http://www.nytimes.com/2014/03/31/business/us-regulators-declined-full-inquiry-into-gm-ignition-flaws-memo-shows.html?_r=0

Wallace, R. (1992). *They call him pastor: Married men in charge of Catholic parishes.* Mahwah, NJ: Paulist Press.

Wallenstein, A. (2014, February 10). How *The Walking Dead* breaks every rule we know about TV hits. *Variety.* Retrieved from http://variety.com/2014/tv/news/how-the-walking-dead-breaks-every-rule-we-know-about-tv-hits-1201089433

Wallerstein, I. (1974). *The modern world-system.* New York: Academic Press.

Wallerstein, I. (2011a). *The modern world-system I: Capitalist agriculture and the origins of the European world-economy in the sixteenth century.* Berkeley: University of California Press. (Original work published 1974)

Wallerstein, I. (2011b). *The modern world-system II: Mercantilism and the consolidation of the European world-economy, 1600–1750.* Berkeley: University of California Press. (Original work published 1980)

Wallerstein, I. (2011c). *The modern world-system III: The second era of great expansion of the capitalist world-economy, 1730–1840s.* Berkeley: University of California Press. (Original work published 1989)

Wallerstein, I. (2011d). *The modern world system IV: Centrist liberalism triumphant, 1789–1914.* Berkeley: University of California Press.

Wallis, C. (2011). Performing gender: A content analysis of gender display in music videos. *Sex Roles, 64*(3–4), 160–172.

Walters, P. B., & James, R. J. (1992). Schooling for some: Child labor and school enrollment of Black and White children in the early 20th century South. *American Sociological Review, 57,* 635–650.

Wang, W., & Parker, K. (2011). *Women see value and benefits of college: Men lag on both fronts, survey finds.* Washington, DC: Pew Research Center. Retrieved from http://www.pewsocialtrends.org/files/2011/08/Gender-and-higher-ed-FNL-RPT.pdf

Warner, K., Molotch, H. L., & Lategola, A. (1992). *Growth of control: Inner workings and external effects.* Berkeley: University of California Press.

Warner, R. S. (1993). A work in progress toward a new paradigm for the sociological study of religion in the United States. *American Journal of Sociology, 98*(5), 1044–1093.

Washington, H. (2007). *Medical apartheid: The dark history of medical experimentation on Black Americans from colonial times to the present.* New York: Doubleday.

Wasserman, I. M. (1999). *African Americans and the criminal justice system: An explanation for changing patterns of Black male suicide.* Paper presented at the annual conference of the Midwest Sociological Society, Minneapolis.

Watanabe, T. (1992, May 13). Rent-a-family fills emotional need in busy Japan. *Los Angeles Times.* Retrieved from http://community.seattletimes.nwsource.com/archive/?date=19920513&slug=1491524

Watson, J. B. (1924). *Behaviorism.* New York: People's Institute.

Weber, M. (1946). *From Max Weber: Essays in sociology* (H. Gerth & C. W. Mills, Eds. and Trans.). New York: Oxford University Press. (Original work published 1919)

Weber, M. (1963). *The sociology of religion.* Boston: Beacon Press. (Original work published 1921)

Weber, M. (1979). *Economy and society: An outline of interpretive sociology* (2 vols.). Berkeley: University of California Press. (Original work published 1921)

Weber, M. (2002). *The Protestant ethic and the spirit of capitalism, and other writings.* New York: Penguin Books. (Original work published 1904–1905)

Weber, M. (2012). *The theory of social and economic organization.* Eastford, CT: Martino Fine Books. (Original work published 1921)

Wedding Report. (2012). United States complete market report: Wedding statistics summary for United States. Retrieved from http://www.theweddingreport.com/wmdb/index.cfm?action=db.viewdetail&t=s&lc=00&setloc=y

Weeks, J. R. (1988). The demography of Islamic nations. *Population Bulletin, 43*(4), 5–54.

Weidman, J. L. (Ed.). (1984). *Christian feminism: Visions of a new humanity.* New York: Harper & Row.

Weiss-Wendt, A. (2010). The state and genocide. In D. Bloxham & A. D. Moses (Eds.), *The Oxford handbook of genocide studies* (pp. 81–101). New York: Oxford University Press.

Weitz, R. (2012). *The sociology of health, illness, and health care: A critical approach* (6th ed.). Boston: Wadsworth Cengage Learning.

Weitzer, R., & Kubrin, C. E. (2009). Misogyny in rap music: A content analysis of prevalence and meanings. *Men and Masculinities, 12*(1), 3–29.

Weller, C. E., Ajinkya, J., & Farrell, J. (2012). *The state of communities of color in the U.S. economy: Still feeling the pain three years into the recovery.* Washington, DC: Center for American Progress. Retrieved from http://cdn.americanprogress.org/wp-content/uploads/issues/2012/04/pdf/comm_of_color.pdf

Wellman, B., & Hampton, K. (1999). Living networked on and offline. *Contemporary Sociology, 28*(6), 648–654.

Wells, T. V., Jr., Karp, B. S., Birenboim, B., & Brown, D. W. (2014, February). *Report to the National Football League concerning issues of workplace conduct at the Miami Dolphins.* New York: Paul, Weiss, Rifkind, Wharton & Garrison LLP. Retrieved from http://63bba9dfdf9675bf3f10-68be460ce43dd2a60dd64ca5eca4ae1d.r37.cf1.rackcdn.com/PaulWeissReport.pdf

Welsh, R. (1998). Severe parental punishment and aggression: The link between corporal punishment and delinquency. In I. A. Hyman & J. H. Wise (Eds.), *Corporal punishment in American education: Readings in history, practice and alternatives* (pp. 126–142). Philadelphia: Temple University Press.

Werdigier, J. (2010, June 4). J. P. Morgan penalized by regulator in Britain. *New York Times,* p. B3.

Werner, C. A. (2011). *The older population: 2010* (Census Brief C2010BR-09). Washington, DC: U.S. Census Bureau. Retrieved from http://www.census.gov/prod/cen2010/briefs/c2010br-09.pdf

Wertheimer, B. (1977). *We were there: The story of working women in America.* New York: Pantheon.

West, C. (1979). Against our will: Male interruptions of females in cross-sex conversations. *Annals of the New York Academy of Sciences, 327,* 81–97.

West, C., & Zimmerman, D. H. (1977). Woman's place in everyday talk: Reflections on parent–child interactions. *Social Problems, 24,* 521–529.

West, C., & Zimmerman, D. H. (1983). Small insults: A study of interruptions in conversations between unacquainted persons. In B. Thorne, C. Kramarae, & N. Henley (Eds.), *Language, gender, and society* (pp. 102–117). Rowley, MA: Newbury House.

West, C., & Zimmerman, D. H. (1987). Doing gender. *Gender & Society, 1*(2), 125–151.

Western, B., & Pettit, B. (2010). Incarceration and social inequality. *Daedalus, 139*(3), 8–19.

Westoff, C. F., & Ryder, N. B. (1977). *The contraceptive revolution.* Princeton, NJ: Princeton University Press.

Whalen, J., & Zimmerman, D. H. (1987). Sequential and institutional contexts in calls for help. *Social Psychology Quarterly, 50,* 172–185.

Whalen, J., & Zimmerman, D. H. (1990). Describing trouble: Epistemology in citizen calls to the police. *Language in Society, 19,* 465–492.

Whalen, J., Zimmerman, D. H., & Whalen, M. R. (1990). When words fail: A single case analysis. *Social Problems, 35,* 335–362.

Whoriskey, P. (2010, October 27). In its biggest foreign market, BMW gets skilled workers for less. *Washington Post.* Retrieved from http://www.washingtonpost.com/wp-dyn/content/article/2010/10/26/AR2010102607165.html

Whyte, W. F. (1943). *Street corner society: The social structure of an Italian slum.* Chicago: University of Chicago Press.

Whyte, W. F. (1991). *Participatory action research.* Newbury Park, CA: Sage.

Wild, W. (2013, November 22). Adderall use rising among college students. ABC7/WJLA. Retrieved from http://www.wjla.com/articles/2013/11/adderall-use-rising-among-college-students-97245.html

Williams, A. (2010, February 7). The new math on campus. *New York Times.* Retrieved from http://www.nytimes.com/2010/02/07/fashion/07campus.html?pagewanted=all

Williams, C. (1995). *Still a man's world: Men who do women's work.* Berkeley: University of California Press.

Williams, J. P., & Kirschner, D. (2012). Coordinated action in the massively multiplayer online game *World of Warcraft. Symbolic Interaction.* Advance online publication. Retrieved from http://onlinelibrary.wiley.com/doi/10.1002/j.1533-8665.2012.00022.x/abstract

Williams, R. M., Jr. (1970). *American society: A sociological interpretation* (3rd ed.). New York: Knopf.

Williams-Meyers, A. J. (1996). Slavery, rebellion, and revolution in the Americas: A historiographical scenario on the theses of Genovese and others. *Journal of Black Studies, 26*(4), 381–400.

Willis, P. (1990). *Common culture: Symbolic work at play in the everyday cultures of the young.* Boulder, CO: Westview Press.

Willoughby, T., Adachi, P. J. C., & Good, M. (2012). A longitudinal study of the association between violent video game play and aggression among adolescents. *Developmental Psychology, 48*(4), 1044–1057.

Wilson, S., & Duke, A. (2013, December 9). 18 L.A. County deputies charged in civil rights, corruption probe. CNN. Retrieved from http://www.cnn.com/2013/12/09/justice/los-angeles-deputies-arrested

Wilson, T. P. (1991). Social structure and the sequential organization of interaction. In D. H. Zimmerman & D. Boden (Eds.), *Talk and social structure* (pp. 22–43). Cambridge: Polity Press.

Wilson, W. J. (1978). *The declining significance of race: Blacks and changing American institutions.* Chicago: University of Chicago Press.

Wilson, W. J. (1987). *The truly disadvantaged: The inner city, the underclass, and public policy.* Chicago: University of Chicago Press.

Wilson, W. J. (1996). *When work disappears: The world of the new urban poor.* New York: Vintage Books.

Wilson, W. J. (2010). *More than just race: Being Black and poor in the inner city.* New York: Norton.

Wingfield, A. H. (2008). Racializing the glass escalator: Reconsidering men's experiences with women's work. *Gender & Society, 23*(1), 5–26.

Wirth, L. (1928). *The ghetto.* Chicago: University of Chicago Press.

Wirth, L. (1938). Urbanism as a way of life. *American Journal of Sociology, 44*(1), 1–24.

Wirth, L. (1945). The problem of minority groups. In R. Linton (Ed.), *The science of man in the world crisis* (pp. 347–372). New York: Columbia University Press.

Wittstock, L. W., & Salinas, E. J. (1998). A brief history of the American Indian Movement. American Indian Movement Grand Governing Council. Retrieved from http://www.aimovement.org/ggc/history.html

Woldoff, R. A. (2011). *White flight/Black flight: The dynamics of racial change in an American neighborhood.* Ithaca, NY: Cornell University Press.

Wolf, M. (2008). *Proust and the squid: The story and science of the reading brain.* New York: Harper Perennial.

Wolfe, A. (1977). *The limits of legitimacy.* New York: Free Press.

Wolfson, A. (2005, October 9). A hoax most cruel: Caller coaxed McDonald's managers into strip-searching a worker. *Courier Journal.* Retrieved from http://www.courier-journal.com/apps/pbcs.dll/article?AID=/20051009/NEWS01/510090392&loc=interstitialskip&nclick_check=1

Wollstonecraft, M. (1792). *A vindication of the rights of women: With strictures on political and moral subjects.* Boston: Peter Edes.

Wonacott, M. E. (2002). *Gold-collar workers* (Eric Digest EDO-CE-02-234). Retrieved from http://www.calpro-online.org/ERIC/docs/dig234.pdf

Wood, G. S. (1993). *The radicalism of the American Revolution.* New York: Vintage Books.

Wood, R. G., Goesling, B., & Avellar, S. (2007). *The effects of marriage on health: A synthesis of recent research evidence.* Princeton, NJ: Mathematica Policy Research. Retrieved from http://www.mathematicampr.com/publications/PDFs/marriagehealth.pdf

Woodiwiss, M. (2000). Organized crime: The dumbing of discourse. In G. Mair & R. Tarling (Eds.), *British Criminology Conference: Selected proceedings* (Vol. 3). London: British Society of Criminology. Retrieved from http://www.britsoccrim.org/volume1/017.pdf

Woodiwiss, M. (2005). *Gangster capitalism: The United States and the global rise of organized crime.* New York: Carroll & Graf.

Workman, J. E., & Freeburg, E. W. (1999). An examination of date rape, victim dress and perceiver variables within the context of attribution theory. *Sex Roles, 41,* 261–277.

World Bank. (2014). Data: Country and lending groups. Retrieved from http://data.worldbank.org/about/country-and-lending-groups#Upper_middle_income

World Health Organization. (2005). Widespread misunderstandings about chronic disease—and the reality. Retrieved from http://www.who.int/chp/chronic_disease_report/media/Factsheet2.pdf

World Health Organization. (2012). Global Health Observatory data repository: Health workforce—aggregated data, density per 1,000. Retrieved from http://apps.who.int/ghodata/?vid=92100

World Health Organization. (2013). Global Health Observatory (GHO): Maternal mortality country profiles. Retrieved from http://www.who.int/gho/maternal_health/countries/en/index.html#U

The world's billionaires. (2014). *Forbes.* Retrieved from http://www.forbes.com/billionaires/list/#tab:overall

Worldwatch Institute. (2004). *State of the world: Consumption by the numbers.* Washington, DC: Author.

Worldwatch Institute. (2010). *State of the world: Transforming cultures from consumerism to sustainability.* Washington, DC: Author.

Worldwatch Institute. (2011). *State of the world: Innovations that nourish the planet.* Washington, DC: Author.

Wright, E. O. (1994). *Interrogating inequality: Essays on class analysis, socialism and Marxism.* New York: Verso.

Wright, E. O. (1998). *Classes* (2nd ed.). New York: Verso.

Wright, J. P., Tibbetts, S. G., & Daigle, L. E. (2008). *Criminals in the making: Criminality across the life course.* Thousand Oaks, CA: Sage.

Wright, L. (1993, May 24). Remember Satan: Part II. *New Yorker,* pp. 54–76.

Wrong, D. H. (1959). The functional theory of stratification: Some neglected considerations. *American Sociological Review, 24,* 772–782.

Wuthnow, R. (1976). *The consciousness reformation.* Berkeley: University of California Press.

Wuthnow, R. (1978). *Experimentation in American religion: The new mysticisms and their implications for churches.* Berkeley: University of California Press.

Wuthnow, R. (1988). *The restructuring of American religion: Society and faith since World War II,* Princeton, NJ: Princeton University Press.

Wuthnow, R. (1989). *Communities of discourse: Ideology and social structure in the Reformation, the Enlightenment, and European socialism.* Cambridge, MA: Harvard University Press.

Wyman, A. (1997). *Rural women teachers in the United States: A sourcebook.* Lanham, MD: Scarecrow Press.

Wyss, S. (2007). "This was my hell": The violence experienced by gender non-conforming youth in US high schools. *International Journal of Qualitative Studies in Education, 17*(5), 709–730.

Yen, C.-F., Yen, J.-Y., & Ko, C.-H. (2010). Internet addiction: Ongoing research in Asia. *World Psychiatry, 9*(2), 97. Retrieved from http://www.ncbi.nlm.nih.gov/pmc/articles/PMC2911088

Young, S., & Martin, D. S. (2012, March 9). CNN readers share stories about secret army drug testing program. CNN. Retrieved from http://edition.cnn.com/2012/03/09/health/soldier-guinea-pigs/index.html

Zald, M., & McCarthy, J. D. (1980). Social movement industries: Competition and cooperation among movement organizations. In L. Kriesberg (Ed.), *Research in social movements, conflicts and change* (Vol. 3). Greenwich, CT: JAI Press.

Zenker, O. (2010). Language matters: Reflexive notes on representation of the Irish language revival in Catholic West Belfast. In O. Zenker & K. Kumoll (Eds.), *Beyond writing culture: Current intersections of epistemologies and representational practices* (pp. 121–138). New York: Berghahn Books

Zhou, M. (2009). *Contemporary Chinese America: Immigration, ethnicity, and community transformation.* Philadelphia: Temple University Press.

Zimbabwe. (2012). *Global AIDS response progress report 2012.* Retrieved from http://www.unaids.org/en/dataanalysis/knowyourresponse/countryprogressreports/2012countries/ce_ZW_Narrative_Report.pdf

Zimbardo, P. G. (1974). On "obedience to authority." *American Psychologist, 29*(7), 566–567.

Zimmerman, D. H. (1984). Talk and its occasion: The case of calling the police. In D. Schiffrin (Ed.), *Meaning, form, and use in context: Linguistic applications* (pp. 210–228). Washington, DC: Georgetown University Press.

Zimmerman, D. H. (1992). The interactional organization of calls for emergency assistance. In P. Drew & J. Heritage (Eds.), *Talk at work: Interaction in institutional settings* (pp. 418–469). New York: Cambridge University Press.

Zimmerman, D. H., & West, C. (1975). Sex roles, interruptions, and silences in conversations. In B. Thorne & N. Henley (Eds.), *Language and sex: Difference and dominance* (pp. 105–129). Rowley, MA: Newbury House.

Zimmerman, D. H., & West, C. (1980). Language and social interaction. *Sociological Inquiry, 50,* 3–4.

Zinn, M. B., Weber, L., Higginbotham, E., & Dill, B. T. (1986). The costs of exclusionary practices in women's studies. *Signs, 11*(2), 290–303.

Zinsser, J. (1993). *History and feminism: A glass half full (The feminist impact on the arts and sciences).* Woodbridge: CT: Twayne.

INDEX

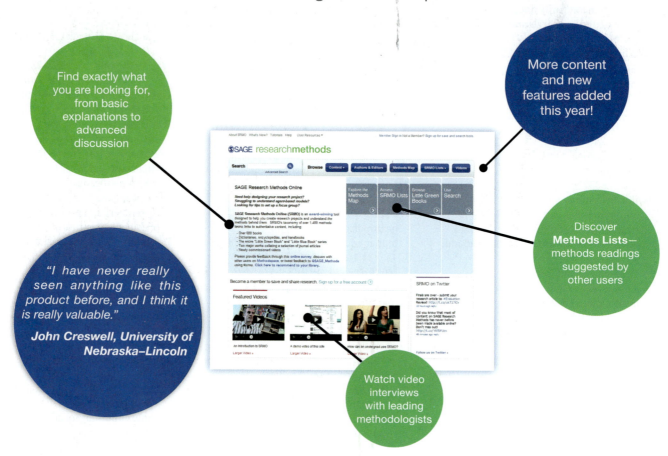

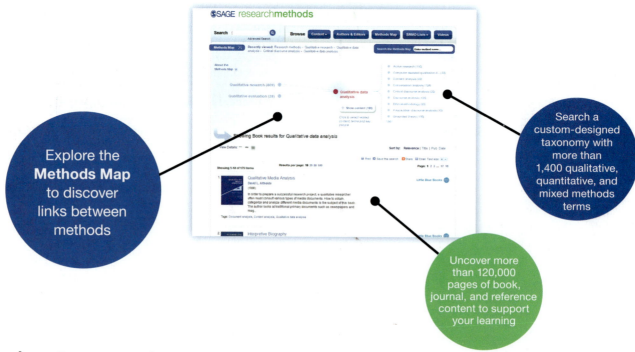